All Cloudless Glory

VOLUME II

THE LIFE OF
GEORGE WASHINGTON

MAKING A NATION

Harrison Clark

REGNERY PUBLISHING, INC.
Washington, D.C.

Library of Congress Cataloging-in-Publication Data

Clark, E. Harrison.
    All cloudless glory : the life of George Washington / E. Harrison Clark.
      p.   cm.
    Includes bibliographical references (p.   ) and index.
    Contents: v. 2. Making a nation
    ISBN 0-89526-445-5 (v. 2)
      1. Washington, George, 1732-1799. 2. Presidents—United States—Biography.
  3. Generals—United States—Biography. 4. United States. Continental Army—Biography.
I. Title.
E312.C56   1996
973.4'1'092—dc20   95-37393
[B]   CIP

Published in the United States by Regnery Publishing, Inc.
An Eagle Publishing Company
422 First Street, SE
Washington, DC 20003

Distributed to the trade by National Book Network
4720-A Boston Way
Lanham, MD 20706

Printed on acid-free paper.
Manufactured in the United States of America

10 9 8 7 6 5 4 3 2 1

Books are available in quantity for promotional or premium use. Write to Director of Special Sales, Regnery Publishing, Inc., 422 First Street, SE, Suite 300, Washington, DC 20003, for information on discounts and terms or call (202) 546-5005.

Designed by Dori Miller
Maps by Chris Capell Computer Graphics

Endpapers: Paintings of Mount Vernon attributed to Edward Savage, 1792. Front: the west front with the circular driveway in the foreground. Back: the east front overlooking the Potomac. (Courtesy of the Mount Vernon Ladies' Association of the Union)

All Cloudless Glory

CONTENTS

LIST OF MAPS

ACKNOWLEDGEMENTS

M Y SPECIAL THANKS go to my editor for this volume, Mrs. Patricia Bozell, to Mr. Alfred S. Regnery, and to Miss Barbara McMillan, the Mount Vernon librarian. I would also like to thank Mr. Richard Vigilante, Mr. David Dortman, Miss Jennifer Reist, and Miss Dori Miller of Regnery Publishing, Mrs. Ellen Miles and Miss Joanna Britto of the National Portrait Gallery, and Mrs. Karen Peters of Mount Vernon.

All Cloudless Glory

ONE

YORKTOWN TO NEWBURGH

1781–1782

T HE YORKTOWN VICTORY brought Washington his greatest acclaim. Many of his countrymen began to speak of him as the Saviour and the Redeemer; the adulation continued till his death and long afterwards. For the next eighteen years he had but to move about the country to find soldiers parading, church bells ringing, cannon firing, choirs singing odes, and officials delivering tiresome addresses to the captive general. He bore it with characteristic grace and habitual modesty and good sense. Abigail Adams after his death expressed it in a precisely right phrase: "He never grew giddy..." Washington's own view of his victory was given in his November 18 letter to Robert Hanson Harrison, his old secretary, who had become Maryland's chief justice:

I thank you for your kind congratulations on the Capitulation of Cornwallis. It is an interesting event and may be productive of much good, if properly improved, but if it should be the means of relaxation and sink us into supineness... it had better not have happened. Great Britain, for sometime past, had been encouraged by the impolicy of our conduct, to continue the War, and should there be an interference of European Politicks in her favour, peace may be further removed from us than we expect, while one thing we are sure of, and that is that the only way to obtain Peace is to be prepared for War. Policy, Interest, Economy, all unite to stimulate the States to fill the Continental Battalions and provide the means of supporting them.

Mr. Custis's death has given much distress in this family...

After arranging with Mrs. Washington's brother, Bartholomew Dandridge, to be guardian of the Custis children and administrator of his estate, Washington left Mount Vernon with his wife for a triumphal procession north. His Alexandria neighbors were the first to greet him. He thanked them on November 19 for their "very kind and affectionate address." He added: "To make a peaceful return to the agreeable society of my fellow Citizens is among the most ardent of my wishes... The late success at York Town is very promising but... a vigorous prosecution of this Success will, in all probability, procure us what we have so long wished to secure, an establishment of Peace, Liberty and Independence." To all addresses from Congress, the states, and the cities, he reiterated the theme—there should be no relaxation of effort, for independence could still be lost.

As Washington moved north, the press reports moved from rapture to adoration. At Annapolis, on November 21, "All business ceased... and... on his appearance, people of every rank and age eagerly pressed forward to feed their eyes with gazing on the man, to whom, under Providence... they owed... their hopes of future liberty and peace..." On the following night "the city was beautifully illuminated, and an assembly prepared for the ladies, to afford them an opportunity of beholding their friend, and thanking their protector with their smiles. His excellency, to gratify the wishes of the fair, crowned the entertainment with his presence, and with graceful dignity and familiar ease, so framed his looks, his gestures, and his words, that every heart o'erflowed with gratitude and love, and every tongue grew wanton in his praise." On November 24: "Our illustrious and beloved commander in chief left the city, attended by innumerable prayers for his health, safety and happiness."

Philadelphia outdid Annapolis. The *Pennsylvania Journal* of November 28 described the arrival, two days previously, of "General WASHINGTON, our victorious and illustrious commander-in-chief, with his Lady. All panegyrick is vain and language too feeble to express our ideas of his greatness. May the crown of glory he has placed on the brow of the genius of America, shine with untarnished radiance and lustre, and in the brightness of its rays be distinctly seen—WASHINGTON, THE SAVIOUR OF HIS COUNTRY!" Charles Wilson Peale, who had painted Washington at various sittings over the years, prepared, for public exhibition, portraits of Washington and Rochambeau, "with rays of glory and interlaced civic crowns over their heads, framed with palm and laurel branches, and the words in transparent letters, SHINE VALIANT CHIEFS; the whole encircled with stars and flowers de luce."

Congress and the council and assembly of Pennsylvania poured verbal libations on Washington. He conveyed his reaction to General Stirling in a letter of November 30: "My Fear is that, from an Over-rating this Success, a Spirit of Relaxation will take place in our Measures, which should it be the Case, will prove very prejudicial to our future Operations or Negotiations, and may serve to protract a War already too long continued."

Under congressional pleading, the general and his wife settled down in the Benjamin Chew house, for a stay in the capital which lasted about four months. This was the first break he had had from the army since the spring of 1775. He wrote his old aide, James McHenry, who had been elected to the Maryland Legislature:

> *My stay in Town is merely to assist in and forward the several arrangements which are upon the Carpet, and I believe you are sufficiently acquainted with me to suppose that I do not fail to urge vigorous measures. I am happy in finding no want of disposition in Congress to adopt the measures required by their Committees and their executive Officers. The requisitions which they have made and which they will shortly make upon the States will evince this. It will afterwards lie with the States to determine whether we are, early in the next campaign, to take advantage of what we have gained in this, or whether we are, as usual, to suffer the enemy to bring their reinforcements from Europe, before we draw ours from the neighborhood of the Army, as it were.*

Congress had appointed General Benjamin Lincoln as war secretary, following the surrender of Cornwallis. This was the first time Washington had a single executive, rather than a congressional committee, to deal with; this relieved him of some of his impossible burdens of detail. Washington knew that his own letters carried more weight with the states than appeals from Congress. He sent circular letters to the states on December 19, January 22, and January 31. The last letter said that the enemy was either going to wage war or to negotiate peace. In either case the United States should be strong. He noted that there had been a great wave of enthusiasm and patriotism "at the commencement of this glorious revolution," but that the "Spirit of Liberty... has sometimes seemed to slumber for awhile."

Washington particularly requested Pennsylvania and Virginia to increase the garrisons at Fort Pitt in order to protect the Ohio River regions. He informed them that he hoped to organize an expedition to proceed as far as Detroit in order to keep the British out of the region. In November, the enemy abandoned Wilmington, North Carolina, drawing its garrison to Charleston. On December 15 Washington wrote Greene:

> *Your private letter of the 22d. Ulto. came to my hands the day before yesterday, and giving fresh assurances of your attachment and regard for me, was received with affection and gratitude; as I feel myself interested in everything that concerns you, it is with unfeigned pleasure I hear the plaudits which are bestowed on your conduct by Men of all descriptions, public and private, and I communicate them to you with heart felt pleasure; there is no man that does not acknowledge your eminent services nor is there any one that does not allow you have done great things with little means...*

> *Mrs. Greene is now in this place on her way to So. Carolina. She is in perfect health, and in good spirits, and thinking no difficulty too great not to be surmounted in the performance of this visit, it shall be my endeavour to strew the way over with flowers. Poor Mrs. Washington, who has met with a most severe stroke in the loss of her amiable Son, Mr. Custis, is here with me, and joins me most cordially in every wish that tends to your happiness and glory.*

The Washingtons dined on Christmas with Robert Morris, Superintendent of Finance. On January 1, 1782, the Friendly Sons of Saint Patrick held a dinner for Washington and his general officers. Next day he and his wife went to an "elegant entertainment [attended by] a brilliant assemblage of ladies and gentlemen." Beaumarchais' *Eugénie,* "an elegant French comedy," was presented, plus a farce and various dances. It closed with a spectacle—thirteen pillars with heads of various generals on top. Biggest of all was Washington's; a cupid held a laurel over the motto: "Washington—the pride of his country and terror of Britain." On March 21 he attended a commencement at the University of Pennsylvania. Next day the Washingtons started north to join the army. They were accompanied out of the city by Joseph Reed and the Philadelphia Light Horse.

Washington's last act before leaving Philadelphia was to place Bushrod Washington, son of his favorite brother, John, as a law student under James Wilson, an authority on constitutional law. Washington had to give Wilson his note for the tuition rather than cash, promising that he would redeem it as soon as possible. Washington was to have the satisfaction, in 1798, of seeing Bushrod Washington take his seat on the United States Supreme Court, as successor to Mr. Justice Wilson.

THE KING IS UNBOWED

On November 3 George III received in audience Lieutenant Colonel Robert Conway, aide to Clinton, who had just arrived from America with the latest news. At six minutes to midnight, the king wrote to Lord North to report what Conway said:

> *His opinion seems to be that Lord Cornwallis will certainly leave the Chesapeake and return to Charles Town after having beat La Fayette, and that both these are likely events... On the whole he supposes we shall in a very few days hear from Lord Cornwallis, and he trusts Sir Henry Clinton will soon have somewhat decisive to communicate: this I own, gives me satisfaction, with such excellent troops if such an event can be effected I think success must ensue; I feel the justness of our cause; I put the greatest confidence in the valour of both Navy and Army and above all in the Assistance of Divine Providence: the moment is certainly anxious... If this Country will persist, I think an honourable termination cannot fail, for truth is ever too strong for such a conduct as France has held, and if we have any material success she will become sick of the part she has acted; duplicity can never withstand any disasters...*

On November 25 the news of Cornwallis' surrender reached Lord George Germain around noon. He got into his carriage, picked up the colonial secretary and the lord chancellor, and they called on Lord North. Lord George reported later that North had taken the news as if he had received a bullet in his breast. He walked up and down, crying out many times, "Oh God! It is all over." Germain then sent a note to the king on the event and went back to his office where the French newspapers had just arrived with confirmation of the defeat. About six that evening Germain had a reply from the king expressing his great concern at the news but assuring him it would not make the slightest difference in the prosecution of the war.

Parliament met two days later. The king's message breathed fire. The following day he asked every member of the cabinet individually to study how best to achieve a united effort. The war, he told North, had to go on, and Parliament should find the necessary means. No one ought to despond, said the king, but he soon found that he was almost alone in the kingdom in wanting to continue.

In Parliament, Charles James Fox opened fire directly on the sovereign: "Those persons who might chance to be ignorant that the speech... was the composition... of a cabinet council... would set it down as containing the sentiments of some arbitrary, despotic, hard-hearted, and unfeeling monarch... We have heard a speech breathing vengeance, blood, misery, and rancour...

What was its purport? 'Much has been lost; much blood, much treasure has been squandered; the burthens of my people are almost intolerable; but my passions are yet ungratified, my object of subjugation and revenge is yet unfilled, and therefore I am determined to persevere.'"

The younger Pitt and others fired steadily at Germain for losing an army, at Sandwich for his naval defeats, and at North for his loans at exorbitant interest. The London Livery told the king he had lost his army, his navy, and his dominions. The cabinet, under hot fire, prayed for some good news from somewhere, but the Spanish took Minorca, and the French, St. Eustatius. A British fleet came back to port after running from a much superior French force. Other posts fell and with them the independent votes which had backed North.

On February 22, 1782, George Washington's fiftieth birthday, General Henry Seymour Conway rose in the House of Commons. Conway was highly respected for his knowledge, integrity, and independence. He had long been a voice of reason. He had moved for the repeal of the stamp tax. He opposed all efforts to coerce America from 1774 to 1776, and he refused to fight the Americans. Now in an eloquent address he pleaded against further hostilities; he concluded by offering a resolution "that the war on the continent of North America might no longer be pursued for the impracticable purpose of reducing the inhabitants of that country to obedience." After stormy debate, the resolve was beaten by one vote, which everyone joked was Lord North's own.

The following day, Conway's cousin, Horace Walpole, wrote: "The power of the crown has increased, is increasing, and ought to be diminished; and it is diminished a good deal indeed. Lord Sandwich escaped on Wednesday but by a plurality of nineteen; and last night the American war survived but by one vote, which will not save its life." On February 28, the friend of liberty, Edmund Burke, wrote Franklin that Conway had succeeded:

> I congratulate you, as the friend of America; I trust, as not the enemy of England; I am sure, as the friend of mankind, and the resolution of the House of Commons, carried by a majority of nineteen, at two o'clock this morning, in a very full house. It was the declaration of two hundred and thirty-four; I think it was the opinion of the whole. I trust it will lead to a speedy peace between the two branches of the English nation, perhaps to a general peace... Mr. Laurens is released from confinement...

The king informed North that he was "hurt" and "mortified" by the vote. On March 4 North reported to the king that a further Conway resolve declaring "all those [to be] enemies of their country who should advise, or in any way attempt to prosecute an offensive war in America, for the purpose of reducing the colonies to obedience by force," had unanimously passed the House of Commons. Next day the house, without a dissenting vote, urged his majesty to conclude peace with America. The king wrote North to complain again that he was "hurt" by all his "trials of late." He said he would not "throw himself into the hands of Opposition." He hinted at other steps, meaning abdication. The king kept on being hurt, but on March 20 it was Lord North who resigned. A week later the Marquess of Rockingham became prime minister. The king drafted his abdication in favor of his oldest son but never handed it in.

On March 27, 1782, the new cabinet took office. Nearly every member— Rockingham, Camden, Grafton, Cavendish, Shelburne, Fox, Richmond, Keppel, and Conway—had been against the American war. The king wrote to Lord North: "At last the fatal day is come which the misfortunes of the times and the sudden change of sentiments of the House of Commons have drove me to, of Changing the Ministry, and a more general removal of the persons than, I believe, was known before... The effusion of my sorrows has made me say more than I had intended... Pray acquaint the Cabinet that they must this day attend at St. James's to resign..." On March 30 the cabinet asked the king to dispatch Sir Guy Carleton to America in place of Sir Henry Clinton.

From Passy, Franklin wrote Washington on April 3: "I have heretofore congratulated your Excellency on your victories over our enemy's generals; I can now do the same on your having overthrown their politicians. Your late successes have so strengthened the hands of opposition in Parliament, that they are become the majority, and have compelled the king to dismiss all his old ministers and their adherents. The unclean spirits he was possessed with are now cast out of him."

WASHINGTON AND KINGSHIP

On March 28 General and Mrs. Washington passed through Morristown where they had spent the grim winter of 1779–1780. There he wrote to Colonel Matthias Ogden, approving his plan to kidnap George III's son, Prince William, as well as Admiral Digby, who were in New York. Ogden was instructed not to offer "insult or indignity" to them and, after their capture, to "treat them with all possible respect." The plan fell through when the British got wind of it and redoubled their guards.

On May 22 Washington received a letter at Newburgh from Colonel Lewis Nicola, breathing veneration and suggesting that he be king. Nicola said that the war had certainly shown how weak the republic was; the army, in consequence, had suffered greatly from every sort of privation. Nonetheless the army had accomplished great things under a single head. Nicola went on to say that "the same abilities which have led us through difficulties, apparently insurmountable by human power, to victory and glory, those qualities that have merited the universal esteem and veneration of an army, would be most likely to conduct and direct us in the smoother paths of peace." Nicola said that some people connected the idea of monarchy with tyranny but he did not think that was necessarily true. There were strong arguments for having the head of state under a new American constitution be king in name as well as in fact. There was no mistaking the man he had in mind for the job.

This was one of Washington's busier days. He was drafting letters to the secretaries of war, finance, and foreign affairs, the governor of South Carolina, and his generals on the Hudson, in the south, and at Pittsburgh. He still found the time to dispatch his famous, blistering reply, the day he received the letter:

> With a mixture of great surprise and astonishment I have read with attention the Sentiments you have submitted to my perusal. Be assured, Sir, no occurrence in the course of the War, has given me more painful sensations than your information of there being such ideas existing in the Army as you have expressed [which] I must view with abhorrence, and reprehend with severity. For the present, the communication of them will rest in my own bosom, unless some further agitation of the matter, shall make a disclosure necessary.

> I am much at a loss to conceive what part of my conduct could have given encouragement to an address which to me seems big with the greatest mischiefs that can befall my Country. If I am not deceived in the knowledge of myself, you could not have found a person to whom your schemes are more disagreeable; at the same time, in justice to my own feelings, I must add that no Man possesses a more sincere wish to see ample justice done to the Army than I do, and as far as my powers and influence, in a constitutional way extend, they shall be employed to the utmost of my abilities to effect it, should there be any occasion. Let me conjure you then, if you have any regard for your Country, concern for yourself or posterity, or respect for me, to banish these thoughts from your Mind, and never communicate, as from yourself or any one else, a sentiment of the like Nature...

Washington often dictated his letters but this one he wrote with his own hand. That he was genuinely upset is indicated by his great number of mistakes in grammar and punctuation. He ordered his file copy endorsed by David Humphreys, his aide, and Jonathan Trumbull, Jr., his secretary, so that if any curious congressman heard of the story, he would have witnesses for the action he took.

Nicola was utterly undone by the roar of thunder and the bolts of lightning from his hero. In great distress next day he wrote Washington that he had experienced many misfortunes in his life but "nothing has ever affected me so much as your reproof." He assured Washington he had meant only good and not evil. On May 24 he wrote him again to say that, since receipt of the letter, he had been "greatly oppressed in mind and distressed" by it. He added that he had a large family to support, he was destitute from having served his country, and he had felt only that the army had to do something to remedy its dreadful situation. On May 28 he followed with a further letter saying "words cannot begin to apologize" for what he had written.

Nicola seems to have advanced only his own personal view on kingship, though Jefferson, the old maid who imagined so many things under the bed, came to believe that a whole cabal of army officers had wanted a Washington monarchy. Nicola did, however, reflect the widespread distrust in the army of the weaknesses of Congress and of the motives and even good sense and patriotism of its members. From this point, with little fighting to do, the rumbles of protest grew to roars and only the hand of Washington kept the army from another revolution. Within five years the forces of protest were constructively channeled into the Constitutional Convention where more than half the attending delegates had served under General Washington.

THE HUDDY AFFAIR

In December 1781 Cornwallis and Arnold sailed for England. Sir Henry Clinton passed a miserable winter in New York which was made more so by the intense cold and by rumors from London of the court's coolness to him. Clinton's final weeks in America were disturbed by an act of a small band of American Tories (or Loyalists, as they were called on the British side) under Captain Richard Lippincott. They had in their charge an American prisoner, Joshua Huddy, whom they accused of having killed a Tory by the name of Philip White. They hanged him in cold blood, attaching a placard to the body: "Up goes Huddy for Philip White." The evidence soon showed that Huddy had been a prisoner when White was killed. The cries of outrage from Congress, the army, and the civilian population were such that Washington had to threaten retaliatory measures unless the British punished Lippincott or delivered him to the Americans for trial. Washington ordered Brigadier Moses Hazen to select an "unconditional" British captain (that is, one not covered by such an agreement as the Yorktown surrender) for reprisal. On May 4 Washington informed the Board of War:

Keenly wounded as my feelings will be at the deplorable destiny of the unhappy
Victim; no gleam of hope can arise to him but from the conduct of the enemy... I
will receive no application nor answer any Letter [from them] on the subject, which
does not inform me that ample satisfaction is made for the death of Capt. Huddy,
on the perpetrators of that horrid deed.

Hazen, in violation of Washington's orders, picked by lot a nineteen-year-old
British captain, Charles Asgill, who was clearly covered by the Yorktown cartel.
British army officers, whether prisoners of the Americans or stationed in New
York, were aroused to fury at the American Loyalists for having committed a
deed for which one of their own might suffer. Sir Henry Clinton was also
highly indignant at this deliberate murder, which he believed the Loyalists
had done to disgrace the British. At the trial it turned out that the Loyalists
had been exceedingly bitter over the surrender of Cornwallis and what
appeared to be their abandonment by the British. It was the head of the
Loyalist board, William Franklin, who had ordered the execution of Huddy.
Because of this, Lippincott was acquitted.

In forwarding the verdict to Washington, the new commander, Sir Guy
Carleton, told Washington that Clinton had regarded the act as "a great barbarity in itself, as well as a daring insult on his own authority." He had
promptly undertaken measures for "punishment and prevention." Carleton
said that he and Clinton agreed that the Loyalist board would have nothing
further to do with prisoners. He added that he thoroughly disapproved of the
execution and that he was ordering a further criminal investigation.
Washington at once wrote Congress to report that this changed the situation,
since his threat of retaliation had been made to prevent a repetition, and he
asked Congress to decide about Asgill. Congress simply ignored his letter.
Several weeks elapsed, and on September 30 Washington appealed to James
Duane, a congressman:

I shall be obliged to you, or some friend in Congress, to inform me what has been,
or is like to be done, with respect to my reference of the case of Captn. Huddy?

I cannot forbear complaining of the cruel situation I now am, and oftentimes, have
been placed in by the silence [to call it by its softest name] * *of Congress in matters*
of high importance, and which the good of the Service, and my official duty, has
obliged me to call upon them (as the Sovereign power of these United States) to
decide. It is only in intricate and perplexing cases I have requested their orders;

---

* Phrase omitted in letter sent.

being always willing to bear my proportion of public embarrassments, and take a full share of responsibility...

When I refer a matter to Congress, every proceeding on it, on my part, is suspended till their pleasure is transmitted; and for this it is well known I have waited with unexampled patience...

In the meantime, the captain's mother, Lady Asgill, appealed to the king and queen of France to save her son. Vergennes wrote Washington that his sovereigns hoped mercy might be extended and that he was sure he would wish to avoid "the disagreeable necessity of this retaliation." Washington forwarded it to Congress with a further request to let him release the prisoner. Congress immediately agreed. In November Washington gave Asgill a passport to New York, with a letter saying that Asgill's relief at the outcome could hardly be greater than Washington's own.

GENERAL CARLETON TALKS PEACE

In April Lord Dunmore reached New York, still claiming to be governor of Virginia, but this was no help to Clinton. On May 15 Sir Guy Carleton arrived to take command. Eight days later, Sir Henry Clinton, who had been in America nearly seven years, sailed for home. Governor Livingston of New Jersey, father-in-law of John Jay, commented: "As fertile as England is in the production of Blockheads, I think they cannot easily send us a greater blunderbuss, unless, peradventure, it should please his Majesty himself to do us the honor of a visit."

Sir Guy Carleton occupied an anomalous role as the new British commander in chief. There is no doubt that the unanimous parliamentary vote to stop the war with America was the will of the British nation. Even the king went along with the idea that all guns should be turned on the French. At the same time, the cabinet could not quite bring itself to believe that Americans did not still want, in their hearts, to be British. In consequence, Carleton was instructed to carry on no offensive operations and to save his army for work elsewhere. If attacked, he was to capitulate on condition that he be allowed to embark his troops. Above all he was instructed to be very kind to "His Majesty's American subjects," which apparently meant all of them, including Washington.

At the same time Britain was fighting France, America's ally. Carleton could not very well inform Washington that he was not permitted to fight by land. Equally, he could not always control his frontier Indians, nor the Royal Navy, so that it was neither peace nor war. As it turned out, he had a logistics problem of formidable magnitude. There were 38,000 British, German, and provincial troops of all ranks in America. With them were immense supplies and equipment. In addition large numbers of Tories wanted to leave, with their furniture, baggage, and slaves. The British did not have the shipping available for this tremendous movement. It took more than eighteen months to complete.

A peculiarity of British politics appeared at this point. Lord Shelburne, who had taken over Lord George Germain's job as colonial secretary, believed that peacemaking with America was in his department. Charles James Fox, the foreign secretary, considered it his province. Both sent delegates to Paris to sound out the Americans. Shelburne also dispatched his private secretary, Maurice Morgann, to New York, with instructions to confer with Congress for a reconciliation, though not on the grounds of independence. Morgann arrived with Carleton, who forwarded to Washington copies of the parliamentary authority, not yet enacted, to restore peace in America. He asked that Morgann be authorized to proceed to Philadelphia. Washington thought this procedure was dangerous and designed to lull Americans into a false security. He so wrote Congress, which refused to receive Morgann. In the meantime the Marquess of Rockingham died, and Lord Shelburne took over in early July as prime minister. By August Digby and Carleton were writing to Washington that "Mr. Grenville" (whose father had authored the stamp tax which began all the trouble) had gone to Paris, with authority to recognize the United States and to begin peace negotiations.

Lord Shelburne had a reputation in his lifetime for duplicity, which was greatly exaggerated. Later, as Marquess of Lansdowne, he became one of Washington's most fervent English admirers. (The "Lansdowne" portrait of Washington by Stuart hung in his house.) Shelburne was a man of broad vision, far in advance of his time. He believed in free trade, liberal and fair dealings with the world, and parliamentary and fiscal reform. When he swung over to independence for America, he decided to go overboard in being fair and generous, in order to rebuild American friendship and avoid all future disputes with the United States. His premiership was brief, but it was to be of inestimable value to America.

WASHINGTON CONFERS WITH ROCHAMBEAU

If the rest of the country tended further to relax into apathy after Yorktown, Washington had no such idea in his mind. Whether there was to be more war, or negotiations for peace, he was determined that the country's military strength be maintained. In May rumors of a great French naval defeat in the

West Indies reached him from his New York intelligence sources; by June its truth was confirmed.

Washington had planned to keep the French army in Virginia, ready to come north, if another allied fleet arrived and New York could be taken, or to move to South Carolina, to join Greene for an attack on Charleston. When Rochambeau heard from Luzerne that a remnant of the French West Indies fleet, under the Marquis de Vaudreuil, was heading to Boston for repairs, he determined, without consulting Washington, to move north. Washington, so informed by Luzerne, wrote Greene that this was not his idea. He informed Rochambeau, very politely, that it would be difficult for him to return south, if Charleston were to be attacked. He asked Rochambeau to meet with him in Philadelphia.

Before leaving for the capital, Washington took a brief holiday trip, his first in seven years, to Schenectady, Albany, and the Saratoga battlefields. The *Pennsylvania Gazette* of July 17 reported that, on his arrival in Albany on June 27, "the bells of all the churches began to ring, and continued their joyful peals until sun-set, when thirteen cannon were discharged from the fort and the city illuminated. Who is more worthy of our love and esteem than the GUARDIAN AND SAVIOUR of his country?" At Schenectady, three days later, "sixty of the principal inhabitants on horseback... attended him into the town amidst the ringing of bells, the firing of cannon and every other public demonstration of felicity." On July 2, at Albany, he went "on board his barge on his way to the army, amidst the benedictions of the multitude, leaving the citizens of this country strongly impressed with the ideas of a *great character*, in which are combined every public and private virtue."

Rochambeau and Washington had a cordial enough meeting in Philadelphia. Washington had to recognize the inevitable when Rochambeau stated that there could be no further French naval aid of any importance; therefore it was not going to be possible to attack Charleston and it would be better if the French joined him on the Hudson. Rochambeau's army moved north very slowly, taking two-and-a-half months to go from Virginia to Westchester.

Entirely by accident the two generals were in Philadelphia when the French minister was giving a ball in celebration of the birth of the dauphin, a young prince who, perhaps fortunately, was to die a natural death in 1789. It was the most exciting spectacle Philadelphia had seen, surpassing even John André's Meschianza. Luzerne, in preparing for it, had a special hall built under the direction of Pierre Charles L'Enfant, the French engineer who later designed the city of Washington. The French army sent up a battalion of chefs. Everyone who was anyone was invited, and those who were nobodies stood outside to watch. The humor of seeing a band of republican revolutionists scrambling for tickets to attend a ball in honor of the birth of the heir to an absolute monarchy was not lost on Dr. Benjamin Rush. He was an inept physician, politician, and military critic, but he was a born writer. He described the affair in a letter of July 16, 1782, to a female friend:

For some weeks past our city has been amused with the expectation of a most splendid entertainment to be given by the Minister of France to celebrate the birth of the Dauphin of France... Hundreds crowded daily to see a large frame building which he had erected for a dancing room... This building... was supported by large pillars and was open all around. The ceiling was decorated with several pieces of neat paintings... The garden... was cut into walks and divided with cedar and pine branches into artificial groves... We were told that the Minister had borrowed thirty cooks from the French army... Eleven hundred tickets were distributed...

For ten days before the entertainment nothing else was talked of in our city. The shops were crowded with customers. Hairdressers were retained; tailors, milliners, and mantua-makers were to be seen covered with sweat and out of breath in every street.

Monday, July 15, was the long expected evening. The morning of this day was ushered in by a corps of hairdressers occupying the place of the city watchmen. Many ladies were obliged to have their heads dressed between four and six o'clock in the morning, so great was the demand and so numerous were the engagements this day of the gentlemen of the comb.

At half-past seven o'clock [P.M.] was the time fixed... The approach of the hour was proclaimed by the rattling of all the carriages in the city... Near the Minister's house there was a collection of all the curious and idle men, women, and children of the city who were not invited... amounting, probably, to ten thousand people.

The scene now almost exceeds description. The numerous lights distributed through the garden, the splendor of the room we were now approaching, the size of the company... the brilliance and variety of their dresses, and the band of music which had just begun to play, formed a scene that resembled enchantment... We entered the room... and here we saw the world in a miniature... here were the president and members of Congress, governors of states and generals of armies, ministers of finance and war and foreign affairs, judges of superior and inferior courts, with all their respective suites of assistants, secretaries and clerks...

It was impossible to partake of the joy of the evening without being struck with the occasion of it. It was to celebrate the birth of a Dauphin of France. How great the revolution in the mind of an American! to rejoice in the birth of a prince whose religion he has been taught to consider as unfriendly to humanity. And above all, how new the phenomenon for republicans and freemen to rejoice in the birth of a prince who must one day be the support of monarchy and slavery!...

Nine days later, Washington left Philadelphia, visiting the Moravian settlements (which had rendered great service in the care of sick and wounded soldiers throughout the war) at Bethlehem, Pennsylvania, and Hope, New Jersey. He reached Newburgh July 27.

WASHINGTON AND CARLETON

Washington had no reason, after his long years of experience, to trust any peaceful British overtures. He kept his intelligence system operating in New York to find out what Carleton was planning. His August 14 instructions to Captain John Pray were clear and succinct:

The first great article of which the General requires to be ascertained is, the state of the British Naval Force at New York; and the arrival or sailing of any Fleet, Transports, Armed Vessels or single Ships of War. This information must, if practicable, be kept up constantly, until further Orders.

In order to obtain this intelligence with certainty and accuracy (without which it will be worth nothing at all) you should have some trusty and intelligent Person or Persons ready in the City to give the earliest notice of any Movement or alteration in the shipping... Money will be furnished for the payment of the actual expenses... but it is expected that the greatest compensation and reward which can be given to well disposed persons within the British Lines, who mean to remain after the enemy have abandoned New York, will be the promise of favour and security to those who shall recommend themselves in this way. It must also be impressed upon all those agents that they should be exceedingly exact and accurate in their accounts, that they should see every thing themselves and make a business of it, at this last hour, that they have intelligence thro' many different Channels and can detect any inaccuracy and falsehood...

The other objects to which you should attend unweariedly, are the number, state and disposition of the Troops... embarkations, arrivals, movements of any kind, indications of remaining in or evacuating the Garrison, European advices, domestic or other intelligence contained in the Newspapers, which might and should be obtained every day; to these should be added the British Orders and everything else that can be interesting in a Political, Military or Naval light...

A typical report of naval movements reached Washington a day or two after they took place: "On Friday evening the 30th of August, the Warwick of 50 guns, with 5 large transport ships, with 1500 or 2000 troops on board, sailed from New York harbour, bound for Halifax; and at 10 o'clock the next day, six ships, supposed to be the same, were seen from the highlands of Middletown, near Sandy Hook, standing to the eastward, with the wind at west."

Sir Guy Carleton's position was a difficult one since his home government had tied his military hands while continuing to encourage its navy to warfare. Dr. Benjamin Rush that summer complained that Philadelphia, in a few months, had lost more than £800,000 through captures by British ships, the proceeds of which were distributed as prizes to the Royal Navy. Washington commented on this policy in a letter of July 10 to Tench Tilghman: "We have nothing New in this Quarter. Sir Guy gives strong assurances of the pacific disposition of his most gracious Majesty, by Land. Sir (that is to be) Digby gives proofs, if he is deficient in assurances, of his Most gracious Majesty's good intention of capturing everything that floats on the face of the Waters... To an American, whose genius is not susceptible of refined Ideas, there would appear some little inconsistency in all this; but to the enlarged and comprehensive Mind of a Briton, these things are perfectly reconcilable."

Washington on his trip north to Albany was informed of renewed Indian raids in the Mohawk Valley under British officers from Canada. On September 8 he wrote Carleton, asking him to explain British policy:

I cannot help remarking that your Excellency has several Times lately, taken occasion to mention that "all hostilities stand suspended on your part." I must confess that, to me, this Expression wants explanation. I can have no Conception of a suspension of Hostilities, but that which arises from a mutual Agreement of the powers at War; and which extends to naval as well as land operations. That your Excellency has thought proper, on your part, to make a partial suspension, may be admitted; but whether this has been owing to political or other motives, is not for me to decide. It is, however, a well-known fact that, at the same Time, the British Cruizers on our Coasts have been more than usually alert, and while Americans are admitted to understand their real Interests, it will be difficult for them, when a Suspension of hostilities is spoken of, to separate the Idea of its extending to Sea, as well as land.

I cannot ascribe the Inroads of the Savages upon our North Western Frontier, to the Causes from whence your Excellency supposes them to originate; neither can I allow that they are committed without the directions from the Commander in Chief in Canada; for by prisoners and Deserters, it is apparent that those ravaging parties are composed of white Troops under the Command of Officers regularly commissioned, as well as Savages; and it would be a Solecism to suppose, that such parties could be out without the knowledge of their Commander in Chief.

Carleton assured Washington that any attacks from Canada were quite contrary to the instructions of the British government, and he would see to it they were stopped. He was as good as his word. On September 26 Washington forwarded to Congress an intelligence report from Quebec: "A number of Indians left a few days ago. They were told… they must not go to War, as the King had compassion on his American Subjects, they having expressed their sorrow for what they had done. The Seneca Sachem replied that the Americans and French had beat the English, that the latter could no longer carry on the War, and that the Indians know it well, and must now be sacrificed or submit to the Americans… The Indians after receiving considerable presents went home little satisfied with their Situation."

PURPLE HEART

In 1782 two awards were introduced into the American army, for enlisted men only. The first was a chevron, for each three years of satisfactory service. The other was a badge of military merit, in the form of a purple heart of cloth or silk, worn on the left breast. Only three men received the latter, by chance all Connecticut sergeants. The first was Daniel Brown, who led the advance on redoubt ten at Yorktown. The second was Elijah Churchill who, "with great gallantry," led the attacks on Forts St. George and Slongo on Long Island, where the watchword was "Washington and glory." The third was Daniel Bissell, selected for the honor by Washington himself for "having performed some important services, within the immediate knowledge of the Commander in chief, in which the fidelity, perseverance, and good sense of the said Sergeant Bissel were conspicuously manifested." At Washington's request, Bissell had deserted, in ostentatious fashion, for New York, where he obtained important assignments at British headquarters. He amassed a full report of the enemy's military strength, escaping with it to the camp of the American commander in chief.

THE IMPECCABLE ARMY

As it was to do for the next 136 years, the United States brought its army to a peak of perfection and then dissolved it.

Throughout the summer the troops went through training and more training. Washington reviewed each brigade individually, giving high praise, when possible, or quietly suggesting that they do more drilling to bring themselves to the standards of other brigades. After concluding his reviews, he expressed his appreciation of the "amazing contrast" between their past and present appearance.

On August 31 Washington conducted the first amphibious training operation in American history, when the whole army moved down the Hudson, "to try in what time a large number of Men could embark, debark, and move a given distance by water." Washington wrote Congress that it had been most successful.

When Rochambeau reached the Hudson on September 14, Washington paraded the army in his honor. According to Dr. Thacher's journal for September 14: "Count Rochambeau was most highly gratified to perceive the very great improvement which our army had made in appearance since he last reviewed them, and expressed his astonishment at their rapid progress in military skill and discipline. He said to General Washington, 'You must have formed an alliance with the King of Prussia. These troops are Prussians.' Several of the principal officers of the French army who have seen troops of different European nations, have... declared that they had seen none superior to the Americans." The Prince de Broglie recorded his "pleasure, astonishment and admiration." Another French officer wrote: "The most exact uniformity, the neat dress of the men, the glittering of their arms, their martial look, and a kind of military luxury gave a most magnificent appearance to this assemblage of citizens... The exactness, order and silence which distinguish veteran armies was here displayed; they changed their front, formed and displayed columns, with admirable regularity..."

THE UNPAID ARMY

Behind the army's brilliant facade was bleak despair which might have been assuaged by modest grants or loans from the French court but France had abruptly cut aid. Washington correctly predicted, in his letter of October 2 to General Lincoln, the war secretary, that the army's distresses would bring a train of evils:

Painful as the task is to describe the dark side of our affairs, it sometimes becomes a matter of indispensable necessity. Without disguize or palliation, I will inform you candidly of the discontents which, at this moment, prevail universally throughout the Army.

The Complaint of Evils, which they suppose almost remediless, are the total want of Money, or the means of existing from One day to another, the heavy debts which they have already incurred, the loss of Credit, the distress of their Families (i.e., such as are married) at home, and the prospect of Poverty and Misery before them. It is in vain, Sir, to suppose that military Men will acquiesce contentedly with bare rations, when those in the Civil walk of life (unacquainted with half the hardships they endure) are regularly paid the emoluments of Office... A Military Man has the same turn to sociability as a person in Civil life, he conceives himself equally called upon to live up to his rank; and his pride is hurt when circumstances restrain him. Only conceive then, the mortification they (even the Genl. Officers) must suffer when they cannot invite a French Officer, a visiting friend, or traveling acquaintance to a better repast than stinking Whiskey (and not always that) and a bit of Beef without vegetables...

The Officers also complain of other hardships which they think might and ought to be remedied without delay, viz., the stopping promotions, where there have been vacancies open for a long time, the withholding Commissions from those who are justly entitled to them...

...No one that I have seen or heard of, appears opposed to the principle of reducing the Army as circumstances may require; Yet I cannot help fearing the Result of the measure in contemplation, under present circumstances, when I see such a Number of Men goaded by a thousand stings of reflection on the past, and of anticipation on the future, about to be turned into the World, soured by penury and what they call the ingratitude of the Public, involved in debts, without one farthing of Money to carry them home, after having spent the flower of their days, and many of them their patrimonies, in establishing the freedom and Independence of their Country, and suffered every thing human Nature is capable of enduring on this side of death; I repeat it, these irritable circumstances, without one thing to soothe their feelings, or frighten the gloomy prospects, I cannot avoid apprehending that a train of Evils will follow, of a very serious and distressing Nature...

I wish not to heighten the shades of the picture, so far as the real life would justify me in doing, or I would give Anecdotes of patriotism and distress which have scarcely ever been parralleled, never surpassed in the history of Mankind; but you may rely upon it, the patience and long sufferance of this Army are almost exhausted, and that there never was so great a spirit of discontent as at this instant. While in the field, I think it may be kept from breaking out into Acts of Outrage, but when we retire into Winter Quarters (unless the Storm is previously dissipated) I cannot be at ease, respecting the consequences...

...You are too well acquainted, from your own service, with the real sufferings of the Army to require a longer detail; I will therefore only add that, exclusive of the common hardships of a Military life, Our Troops have been, and still are obliged to perform more services, foreign to their proper duty, without gratuity or reward, than the Soldiers of any other Army; for example, the immense labours expended in doing the work of Artificers, in erecting Fortifications and Military Works; the fatigue of building themselves Barracks or Huts annually; And of cutting and transporting Wood for the use of all our Posts and Garrison, without any expense whatever to the Public...

LETTERS

Washington's correspondence, except from John Hancock, was enormous that relaxed year of little fighting. Hancock, the general complained, went on ignoring him. Washington's letters could thunder or be gay and even flirtatious. His loudest complaint went to John Price Posey, son of the Thomas Posey who had imposed so much on Washington's good nature. When he heard from his brother-in-law that Posey had cheated the estate of Jacky Custis, Washington wrote him on August 7:

With a mixture of surprise, concern, and even horror have I heard of your treatment of the deceased Mr. Custis; in the abuse and misapplication of the Estate which he had committed, with much confidence I am sure, and I believe personal regard, to your management.

If what I have heard, or the half of it be true, you must not only be lost to the feelings of virtue, honor and common honesty; but you must have suffered an unwarrantable thirst of gain to lead you into errors which are so pregnant with folly and indiscretion, as to render you a mark for every man's arrow to level at. Can you suppose, Sir,...that the Heirs of Mr. Custis will not find friends who will pursue you to the end of the Earth?

Washington, in strong language, suggested that Posey make an immediate and complete accounting and settlement, in order to avoid further trouble, adding that if he did not, the affair "will be probed to the bottom; let the trouble and cost of doing it be what it may." More than four years later, Washington learned that Posey had also robbed him but he was far more restrained in his reaction than he had been to the depredations on his stepson's estate.

He wrote humorously to Gouverneur Morris on August 7: "I asserted pretty roundly to you, but not more confidently than it was asserted to me, that General Dalrymple had sailed for England. Since my return to this place, I have seen a letter from him to General Knox which, at the same time that it contradicts both assertions, announces his speedy departure for the Albion shore. If he should remain in New York after this, charge it to his act, not mine..." To McHenry, a physician who had been sick, Washington wrote that he wished he had medical books around to give him advice, having resolved to quit "the trade of General." By October 17 he, who was wondering as much as anyone else what was happening in Europe with regard to the peace, wrote McHenry: "In a time like this, of general uncertainty with respect to the designs of the British Court, it is not at all wonderful to find men inquiring at every corner for News; the North sends to the South, and the South to the North, to obtain it, but at present, all I believe, are equally ignorant."

PEACE

The small American army at home was now replaced in importance by the brilliant John Jay who, after being treated with calculated contempt at Madrid, had moved to Paris as peace commissioner. Although Jay was but one of four American ministers authorized to make peace, most of the burden fell on him. Henry Laurens was too sick after his release from the Tower of London to go to Paris; Franklin fell seriously ill in August, while John Adams' negotiations in the Netherlands kept him from Paris till October. Jay, whose great-grandfather had been expelled from France as a Protestant, took on, alone, three major powers—France, Great Britain, and Spain.

During the preliminary peace talks, Vergennes was fully candid with Spain but only slightly so with the Americans. The French position in relation to the United States was clear. America's independence was to be recognized by Great Britain, but only as part of a general peace treaty, which met all the demands of France and Spain. The United States was to be restricted as closely as possible to the Allegheny Mountains. Nova Scotia and Quebec were to be British but Quebec was to extend to the Ohio River, as defined by the Quebec Act of 1774. The Mississippi and the territory south of the Ohio were to go to Spain, which did not recognize the United States. Thus France proposed to make permanent two great American grievances against their former British rulers—the proclamation line and the Quebec Act. In addition France wanted to detach Maine from the United States. For generations, New Englanders had participated in the Grand Banks fishing; Vergennes proposed that they be excluded from such operations. Vergennes also wanted all Tories pardoned and their property restored to them.

France had cut off monetary aid to the United States and insisted that all her war loans be repaid by 1788. She also ordered her troops withdrawn from the United States, although the British still held American ports. France and Spain were preparing a siege of Gibraltar, in a final assault on British power; both countries agreed that no peace would be made until Spain regained the rock.

In his plans, Vergennes had taken everything into account, except the intransigence of John Jay, the high-mindedness of the Earl of Shelburne, and the naval abilities (when not fighting Americans) of Admiral Howe. In forcing Congress to surround John Adams with other commissioners, Vergennes, too, had not reckoned that, in the final play, they would all stand together.

When Lord Shelburne took over Lord George Germain's office, he directed Sir Guy Carleton to assure Americans that "the most liberal sentiments" had taken root in England; his treatment of them was to be so "open and generous... as... to captivate their hearts." Shelburne followed with further instructions of June 25 to endeavor to achieve reconciliation "on the noblest terms and by the noblest means." A few days later Shelburne became prime minister and never wavered from his professed ideals.

In July Franklin gave Richard Oswald, Shelburne's emissary, an outline of what he considered to be the necessary points for a peace treaty—recognition of independence, the withdrawal of troops, the restoration of Quebec to its old boundary, and freedom of the fisheries. Franklin also suggested that, for full reconciliation, Canada be given to the United States, war reparations be paid, and British ports be opened to American ships. The necessary points were acceptable to Shelburne and eventually became the basis of the peace treaty. By August, while Franklin was ill, Jay was in daily negotiation with Oswald, and through him, with Shelburne. At the same time, Jay found himself engaged in much more hostile discussions with France and Spain.

Earlier, when Franklin, Jay, and Oswald talked with Vergennes, Jay complained that Oswald's commission authorized him to negotiate with the American colonies. Vergennes waved this aside as unimportant. He assured Jay that American independence would be taken up at the final peace treaty (which, he did not add, could not be signed until Spain got Gibraltar). Vergennes also ordered Jay to negotiate with the Spanish ambassador about the western lands, dismissing Jay's objection that Spain had not recognized the United States. When Rayneval came along to act as interpreter between Jay and the Conde de Aranda, Jay found that the French *chef de cabinet* was arguing the Spanish case for the western lands.

In September, Oswald showed Jay an intercepted dispatch from François Barbé-Marbois, secretary of the French legation at Philadelphia. This outlined a proposal to keep the Americans from the fisheries and suggested that if the British were allowed to hold their western posts, America's dependence on France would increase. At almost the same time, after receiving a lengthy memorandum from Rayneval protesting against American claims to lands beyond the Alleghenies, Jay learned that Rayneval had gone to England for secret negotiations with Shelburne. At this time, although Jay did not know it, the French prime minister was writing about the Americans to Luzerne in Philadelphia: "It behooves us to leave them to their illusions, to do everything we can to make them fancy that we share them, and unostentatiously to defeat any attempts to which these illusions may carry them, if our cooperation is required. The Americans have all the presumption of ignorance, but there is reason to expect that experience will ere long enlighten them." So great was Vergennes' contempt for Americans that he failed even to send his usual spies to find out what they were doing.

In London Lord Shelburne had a difficult role, for he was a statesman of rare vision who had also to be a practical politician in a corrupt country. He was pushed by a powerful king who loathed the word independence; a large group of American Tories in England, who wanted both America and their property back; a divided cabinet; a Parliament split into many factions; and merchants, shippers, and fishermen who all wanted protection of one sort or another. While Shelburne kept to a straight line in dealing with America, his various zigs and zags, which were the despair of Jay and then of Adams and Franklin, arose from the political pressures he encountered from all sides.

Handling the king was the most difficult of all Shelburne's problems; his memoranda to George III were masterpieces of diplomacy. He praised and flattered and said how much he agreed with the king's discerning views but that he ought to point out the many difficulties in doing what he wanted and perhaps they should do things in Shelburne's way. The king had led North around, but Shelburne brought the king to his policies with tact and gentleness. From Shelburne's point of view, a generous peace with America was not only important for the future of both countries but would greatly strengthen his hand in negotiations with France.

When Jay heard that Rayneval, after holding a long conference with the Spanish ambassador, had left hurriedly for England, he rightly suspected the worst. Jay had already told Oswald that he could not negotiate further unless the king would recognize the United States. Jay now dispatched another British negotiator, Benjamin Vaughan, to London with perhaps the most important proposal ever made by an American diplomat: (a) Great Britain should immediately recognize the United States as a touchstone of sincerity; this would be cordially reciprocated by the Americans; and (b) France wanted America's independence postponed until her own terms were met; the United States would adhere to the French treaty, but it was a different thing for Americans to be guided by the French or American interpretation of the Treaty of 1778. Jay worked out with Oswald a formula for recognition, which might be acceptable to Shelburne and to George III, while keeping within the terms of the French treaty. Under it, Oswald would receive a commission empowering him to treat with the commissioners of "the United States of America" but *de jure* recognition could wait for the peace treaty. The United States would abandon any pretentions to Canada, provided the American boundaries extended to the Mississippi. Jay pointed out that neither Congress nor Great Britain could prevent American settlement there. The United States would insist on rights in the fisheries. In return for the backlands and fisheries, America would give Britain generous trading and commercial privileges, as well as freedom of navigation on the Mississippi.

Jay's message offered reciprocal friendship and advantages. Shelburne wrote a little later to Oswald that he was going to trust the Americans and that he hoped he was doing right, or "our heads must answer for it." Jay, too, had placed his own head in jeopardy, for he had violated the instructions of Congress and failed to inform Franklin of his move.

On September 13 Lord Shelburne reported at length to the king on his initial conversations with Rayneval. He described the very extensive demands of the French—for Spain, Gibraltar, and for themselves, various West Indian islands, Senegal for the slave trade, and a return of Dunkirk and her possessions in India. He added that Rayneval seemed "jealous rather than partial to America." The king told Shelburne how shocked he was by French demands and duplicity. Shelburne, on September 15, reported further conversations with Rayneval and then added, as if in afterthought:

> *...I am as clearly of opinion against a Peace as I ever was against American Independence, till in fact the Resolutions of the House of Commons decided the point. I am very clear that Your Majesty has within your Dominions Resources of every kind, if they could be brought forth. But Your Majesty knows, what I am mortyfy'd to allude to... The State of both Army and Navy; The few Subjects capable of supplying what is wanted in regard to both Services; The State of Ireland, and that of the House of Commons... This obliges me... to state as clearly as I am able the other side of the question...*

By September 19, having focused the king's fears on France, Shelburne was ready to hand him full cabinet approval of John Jay's formula for de facto recognition. When the king signed it, he did not realize that, for all practical purposes, he had recognized the independence of the United States. Shelburne's minutes said simply:

It is humbly recommended to Your Majesty that a new Commission be made out under Your Majesty's Great Seal for enabling Mr. Oswald to treat with the Commissions appointed by the Colonys, under the title of Thirteen United States, inasmuch as the Commissioners have offered under that condition to accept the Independence of America as the First Article of the Treaty.

Oswald received his commission in Paris on September 27 and showed it to Jay. With his only objection to negotiations removed, Jay urgently summoned John Adams from The Hague. On September 30 the king received word that the Franco-Spanish siege of Gibraltar had been smashed; soon afterwards Lord Howe's relief forces reached the rock.

Within the broad principles which had been accepted by the British government, the detailed peace negotiations were difficult for the English and Americans. They involved such questions as prewar debts, American demands for reparations, the boundaries of Maine and Florida, the claims of Tories to amnesty and property, fishing rights in British North America, restrictions on American commerce and navigation, and other points between countries which had been once intimately bound politically and economically. Many of the disputed points were slurred over rather than settled, and these became acute problems for Washington as president.

The negotiations were well advanced when John Adams arrived. He had precisely the same opinion of French duplicity as John Jay, and he heartily approved of all Jay had done. Franklin, recovered, protested that their congressional instructions required them to have the approval of the French court, but it soon proved that Franklin's was a rather *pro forma* remark. In the end he agreed to the secret negotiations; from then on the Americans worked as a team.

By November 19 the articles of the preliminary peace treaty between Great Britain and the United States were ready in Whitehall for transmission to Oswald. The secretary of state, Thomas Townshend, sent them to the king, adding that he would also send him the draft of the "Preliminary Articles and the Dispatches as soon as they are ready, without waiting for my seeing the latter: He cannot be surprised at my not having been overly anxious for the perusal of them, as Parliament having to my astonishment come into the idea of granting a Separation to North America, had disabled me from longer defending the just rights of this Kingdom. But I certainly disclaim thinking myself answerable for any evils that may arise from the adoption of this Measure as necessity not conviction had made me subscribe to it."

Next day Rayneval arrived in London to say that the French were unwilling to support the Americans in their "unreasonable demands," which the British prime minister duly reported to the king. On November 23 Vergennes informed his minister in Philadelphia that France had no intention of helping the "pretentious ambitions" of the United States to the Mississippi boundaries.

On November 30 Richard Oswald for Great Britain, and John Adams, John Jay, and Benjamin Franklin signed the preliminary treaty of peace. The United States, at least on paper, was free and independent from the Atlantic to the Mississippi.

On December 7, one of London's darkest and foggiest days, the king went before Parliament. His speech was clearly written by Lord Shelburne, for it called for an "entire and cordial reconciliation with the colonies" but the king read it in a tone which indicated that he, for one, wanted nothing of the sort. He then came to the terrible clause that, to attain reconciliation, "I did not hesitate to declare them free and independent states, by an article to be inserted in the peace treaty." Elkanah Watson, an American who was present, noted that at this point the king "hesitated, choked, and executed the painful duties with an ill grace which does not belong to him." Rayneval also noticed how embarrassed the king was and so reported to Vergennes. The king realized it, for he afterwards asked Lord Oxford: "Did I lower my voice when I came to that part of my speech?" The king then went on: "Religion, language, interest, affection, may and I hope will, yet prove a bond of permanent union between the two countries. To this end, neither attention nor disposition on my part shall be wanting." The old fox had given Lord Shelburne, three weeks before, his real opinion on losing the grapes:

> I cannot conclude without mentioning how sensibly I feel the dismemberment of America from this Empire, and that I should be miserable indeed if I did not feel that no blame on that Account can be laid at my door, and did I not also know that knavery seems to be so much the striking feature of its Inhabitants that it may not in the end be an evil that they become Aliens to this Kingdom.

That night, another American, John Singleton Copley, who had heard the speech, painted an American flag on the ship in the left-hand corner of his portrait of Elkanah Watson. Thus, said Copley, he had raised the first American flag in the port of London.

Vergennes received the details from Franklin after the signing. He was stunned. John Adams described it with more than his usual gracelessness: "No wrestler was ever so completely thrown upon his back as the Comte de Vergennes." The prime minister complained to Rayneval in London, to Franklin and to Fitzherbert, the British negotiator, in Paris, and to Luzerne in Philadelphia, but the deed was irrevocable. Rayneval particularly protested to Shelburne against the grant of the "backlands" which had been a cause of the war between France and Great Britain in 1756.

Vergennes was forced to speed up his own and Spain's treaty with Great Britain which, thanks to Shelburne, came out of the war better than anyone in England could have expected. Even George III agreed on this. Spain did not get Gibraltar. On January 20, 1783, the preliminary treaties and an armistice among Britain, France, Spain, and the United States were signed. Thereafter there were months of tedious negotiations before the final treaty was ready.

In England all the long years of war, followed by anger and frustration at the peace, now exploded onto Lord Shelburne. He had given too much to America, to France, to Spain. He had let down the Tories, the merchants, the businessmen. Lord North and Charles James Fox, bitter enemies, formed an unholy coalition to bring down Shelburne. On February 22, 1783, the first anniversary of General Conway's resolution, Shelburne told the king he would resign. He was never again in power. He knew that he had done the right thing and this was his monument. The day after he quit office, Benjamin Vaughan wrote from London to Franklin: "To you I need not point out any of the absurdities of the public proceedings; but you will now see who has been your friend, and upon what principles... I am much satisfied at having heard him say that he repented of nothing that he had done, that he would do it all over again, and that he sees that he alone had the resolution to go through with it. God be praised that it is done, and that no one asks to have it undone!"

Eight years later, on July 4, 1791, Shelburne, by then Marquess of Lansdowne, wrote to Washington, introducing his son, Lord Wycombe, to the president. He alluded modestly to a role which deserves to rank him among England's great ministers:

I cannot possibly suffer my son to go to America without soliciting your protection of him during his stay within the United States [where] he can meet with no conversation which will not confirm him in those principles of freedom, which have constituted my happiness thro' life. I shall always look upon that as the happiest moment of it, when I had the good fortune to have it in my power to be of some little use in fixing the boundary between the respective dominions in a manner which,

*tho' not desired by the alliance, must, I trust and hope, in the end lay the
foundation of cordial friendship and good understanding.*

Washington replied that the United States had "a grateful recollection" of
Lansdowne's role in the peace treaty and he wished "that the same liberal policy" might again be pursued in England so that the two countries would be
"reciprocally beneficial to each other."

THE FRENCH LEAVE AMERICA

Although the French government had at times acted more as an enemy than
an ally, the French army in America behaved with honor and politeness, and
Washington admired many of its officers as much as they did him. Congress,
however, grumbled that the French army seemed to be leaving in too much of
a hurry, while the British were in occupation of posts in Maine, New York, and
the Northwest Territory. Even the pro-French members of Congress (the
Gallicans, as they were known) thought this rather preposterous.

Most of the French army left the Hudson for Boston near the end of
October. In early December, Rochambeau and Chastellux, who were to sail
from Annapolis, returned to Newburgh to make their farewells in person.
Because Washington's headquarters were so small and crowded, Chastellux
and Rochambeau appeared on separate days. Chastellux wrote of his visit:

*We crossed the North River as night came on, and arrived at six o'clock [December
5] at Newburgh... The headquarters... consists of a single house, neither spacious
nor convenient, which is built in the Dutch fashion. The largest room in it, which
had served as the owner's family parlor and which General Washington has
converted into his dining room, is in truth fairly spacious, but it has seven doors
and only one window... I found the company assembled in a rather small room
which served, and when the hour of bedtime came, I found that the chamber to
which the General conducted me, was this very parlour, in which he had just had a
camp bed set up.*

*We assembled at breakfast the next morning at ten, during which interval my bed was
folded up and my chamber became the sitting room... The smallness of the house and
the difficulty to which I saw that Mr. and Mrs. Washington had put themselves to
receive me, made me apprehensive lest M. de Rochambeau... might arrive... I therefore
took it upon myself to send someone to Fishkill to request him to stay there that night...
He did not join us until the next morning just as I was setting out...*

*On the 7th I took leave of General Washington; it will not be difficult to believe
that this parting was painful for me; but I have too much pleasure in recollecting
the real tenderness with which it affected him, not to mention it...*

Washington may have admired Chastellux more than any other senior French
officer, for a week later he sent Chastellux a letter even more emotional than
his correspondence with Lafayette:

*I felt too much to express anything the day I parted with you; A Sense of your public
Services to this Country, and gratitude for your private friendship quite overcame me
at the moment of our separation. But I should be wanting to the feelings of my heart,
were I to suffer you to leave this Country without the warmest assurances of
affectionate regard for your person and character. Our good friend the Marqs. de la
Fayette prepared me... for those Impressions of Esteem which... your own benevolent
Mind has since improved into a deep and lasting friendship, a friendship which
neither time nor distance can ever eradicate. I can truly say that never in my life did I
part with a Man to whom my Soul clave more sincerely than it did to you... It will be
one of my highest gratifications to keep up a regular intercourse with you by Letter...*

Congress, in gratitude for Yorktown, had ordered that two of the English can-
nons captured there be presented to Rochambeau in the name of the United
States. Washington went to a great deal of trouble to have these orders carried
out. The cannon were hauled from Yorktown to Philadelphia and then on to
West Point when the French army moved north. Washington had to find an
engraver and draw up an inscription. He and Knox decided it should be in
Latin. Washington sent it on to Lincoln, the secretary of war, with instructions
to ask a professor at the college in Philadelphia to put it into "elegant Latin."
The inscription, after translation, was engraved at West Point. The cannon
were eventually trundled back to Philadelphia, for delivery to Rochambeau on
his way to France. Rochambeau thought it too risky to take them home before
the peace and asked Luzerne to send them along after the war. Eventually
they were placed at the Chateau de Rochambeau, on the Loir, where, a few
years later, they were taken by revolutionaries. Washington's letter of farewell
to Rochambeau, though not his final letter sent with the cannon, was forwarded the day he wrote to Chastellux:

*I cannot, my dear Genl., permit you to depart from this Country without repeating
to you the high sense I entertain of the Services you have rendered America, by the
constant attention you have paid to the interests of it.*

By the exact order and discipline of the Corps under your Command, and by your readiness, at all times, to give facility to every measure which the force of the Combined Armies was competent to.

To this testimony of your Public character I should be wanting to the feelings of my heart, were I not to add expressions of the happiness I have enjoyed in your private friendship. The remembrance of which will be one of the most pleasing Circumstances of my life.

My best wishes will accompany you to France, where I have no doubt of your meeting the Smiles and rewards of a generous Prince; and the warmest embraces of affectionate friends.

DISTRESSES

Washington had to turn from affectionate farewells to the growing distress and anger of the army. The day after he wrote his final letters to Rochambeau and Chastellux, he sent a communication to Joseph Jones, a Virginia congressman:

In the course of a few days Congress will, I expect, receive an Address from the Army on the subject of their grievances.

This Address, tho' couched in very respectful terms, is one of those things which tho' unpleasing, is just now unavoidable; for I was very apprehensive once, that matters would have taken a more unfavourable turn, from the variety of discontents which prevailed at this time.

The temper of the Army is much soured, and has become more irritable than at any period since the commencement of the War. This consideration alone, prevented me (for everything else seemed to be in a state of inactivity and almost tranquillity) from requesting leave to spend the winter in Virginia, that I might give some attention to my long neglected private concerns.

The dissatisfactions of the Army had arisen to a great and alarming height, and combinations among the Officers to resign, at given periods, in a body, were beginning to take place, when by some address and management, their resolutions have been converted into the form that will now appear before Congress. What that Honble. Body can, or will do in the matter, does not belong to me to determine; but policy, in my opinion, should dictate soothing measures; as it is an incontrovertible fact, that no part of the community has undergone equal hardships, and borne them with the same patience and fortitude, that the Army has done.

Hitherto the Officers have stood between the lower order of the Soldiery and the public, and in more instances than one, at the hazard of their lives, have quelled very dangerous mutinies. But if their discontents should be suffered to rise equally high, I know not what the consequences may be.

The spirit of enthusiasm which overcame everything at first, is now done away; it is idle therefore to expect more from Military men, than from those discharging the Civil departments of Government. If both were to fare equally alike with respect to the emoluents of Office, I would answer for it that the Military character should not be the first to complain. But it is an invidious distinction, and one that will not stand the test of reason or policy, that one set should receive all, and the other no part... of their pay.

On Christmas day, Washington wrote his quartermaster general that there was such a scarcity of fodder, his horses had not eaten for three days. His general officers could not get to headquarters, even on urgent business, "their horses being too weak to carry them." Even the mail was now coming long distances on the backs of his soldiers. That day, Robert Livingston, the secretary for foreign affairs, informed him of the Oswald commission to negotiate peace. This did not reach him until January 8 but he responded with a note of better cheer: "The Power given to Mr. Oswald... is more than I expected would have happened before the Meeting of Parliament; but as the Gentlemen on the part of America could not treat with Him unless such powers were given, it became an Act of necessity to cede them to effect their other purposes. Thus I account for the indirect acknowledgment of our Independence by the King; who I dare say felt some severe pangs at the time he put his hand to the Letters Patent. It is not however less efficacious or pleasing on that account."

It was only a momentary ray. On January he wrote to General Armstrong and to Tench Tilghman, giving them the news of the Oswald commission. To Armstrong he added: "The Army, as usual, are without Pay; and a great part of the Soldiery without Shirts; and tho' the patience of them is equally threadbear, the States seem perfectly indifferent to their cries... If one were to hazard for them an opinion... it would be that the Army had encountered such a habit of encountering distress and difficulties... that it would be impolitic and injurious to introduce other customs in it." To Tilghman he said: "Upon the whole I am fixed in an opinion that Peace, or, a pretty long continuance of the War will have been determined before the Adjournment [of Parliament] for the Holidays, and as it will be the middle or last of Feby. before we shall know the result, time will pass heavily on in this dreary mansion in which we are fast locked by frost and Snow."

On January 14, a handsome new sleigh, built at General Knox's orders, was driven to his door for his use, thus enabling Washington and his wife to escape and get some air. A pleased Washington wrote Knox that he thought the sleigh "handsome, convenient and well executed. Shall I thank you for giving the Master Workman a couple of Guineas, to be laid out in liquour for those who have been engaged in this business?"

TWO

NEWBURGH TO MOUNT VERNON

1783

T HE WEAKNESSES OF the American confederacy had long been Washington's particular crown of thorns. To John Jay they were an invitation to the wolves of Europe to prey. After describing French and Spanish intrigues to Robert Livingston, November 17, 1782, Jay wrote that Great Britain might well attempt once more to conquer America "if they again thought they could. I think we have no rational dependence except on God and ourselves." On September 24 of the following year, he wrote Gouverneur Morris: "I am perfectly convinced that no time is to be lost in raising and maintaining a national spirit in America. Power to govern the confederacy, as to all general purposes, should be granted and exercised. The government of the different States should be wound up, and become vigorous. America is beheld with jealousy, and jealousy is seldom idle."

As his army service drew to its close, a vigorous and newly politically minded Washington appeared. In brilliant papers to Congress and the states, in his farewell to his soldiers, in individual letters to his officers, confederate executives, state governors, congressmen, and friends, he stressed the danger that a divided country would be "the sport of European politics." His dominant theme, which reached every literate American, was summed up in his last toast as general of the armies: "Competent power to the Congress for general purposes." His countrymen expressed the idea more picturesquely: "Cement to the union... A hoop for the barrel."

BOREDOM

The comte de Vergennes had endeavored to dissuade Franklin and his fellow commissioners from informing Congress of the terms of the November 30 treaty. Franklin asked Vergennes what Congress would think if they heard of it from others. The commissioners seem to have thought the treaty would go quickly to Philadelphia in the *Washington*, Captain Joshua Barney commanding. There is no evidence that the French delayed Barney's departure but he did not sail from France until January 17. His crossing was long and stormy. He did not reach America until March 12 while Washington waited with impatient boredom for news.

From his bleak Newburgh house Washington wrote his old friend Bryan Fairfax on February 5: "At present, we are fast locked in Frost and Snow; without a tittle of news. We look wistfully to the East, and to the South for an arrival; supposing the first European Vessel will bring the Speech of the British King, the Addresses, and debates thereupon; the last of which I expect, will discover the Ultimatum of the national determination respecting the continuance of the War, or acceptance of Peace..." The same day he wrote General William Heath: "Without amusements or avocations, I am spending another Winter (I hope it will be the last that I shall be kept from returning to domestic life) amongst these rugged and dreary Mountains." On February 6, when congratulating Greene on the departure of the last redcoat from the south, Washington made one of his relatively rare reminiscences about the long war:

> *It is with a pleasure which friendship only is susceptible of, I congratulate you on the glorious end you have put to hostilities in the Southern States; the honor and advantage of it, I hope, and trust, you will long live to enjoy. When this hemisphere will be equally free, is yet in the womb of time to discover; a little while, however 'tis presumed, will disclose the determinations of the British Senate with respect to peace or War...*

> *If Historiographers should be hardy enough to fill the page of History with the advantages that have been gained with unequal numbers (on the part of America) in the course of this contest, and attempt to relate the distressing circumstances under which they have been obtained, it is more than probable that Posterity will bestow on their labors the epithet and marks of fiction; for it will not be believed that such a force as Great Britain has employed for eight years in this country*

could be baffled in their plan of Subjugating it by numbers infinitely less, composed of Men oftentimes half starved; always in Rags, without pay, and experiencing, at times, every species of distress which human nature is capable of undergoing...

While waiting for peace, most of the general officers found urgent reasons to request leaves of absence—lawsuits, family troubles, financial problems, and plain ennui. When General St. Clair requested an extension of an already long leave, Washington, irked, wrote that if St. Clair expected to retain his command, he had better come back. "I do not here enter fully into a detail of the reasons which now make it particularly necessary for the Genl. Officers who have been long absent to join without loss of time; it will surely be sufficient to mention that out of nine Generals assigned to the command of the Troops in this Cantonment, seven are actually gone or have made applications to be absent at the same time, so that by gratifying their wishes, the whole weight of the business, and cares and troubles of the Army would devolve upon me, until a sunshine occasion, or a prospect of some brilliant operation would induce them to return and share the pleasures and honors of the service."

The chaplains, also bored, went off in great numbers. On February 15 Washington ordered Divine Service to be held every Sunday, in each brigade, for the "Homage and adoration which are due to the Supreme Being, who has through his infinite goodness brought our public Calamities and dangers (in all human probability) very near to a happy conclusion." He added: "The General has been surprised to find in Winter Quarters that the chaplains have frequently been almost all absent at the same time, under an idea their presence could not be of any utility at that season; he thinks it proper he should be allowed to judge of that matter himself, and therefore no future furloughs will be granted to chaplains except in consequence of permission from Headquarters..."

FAMILY TROUBLES

Almost invariably the bittersweet problems of Washington's family and domestic economy intruded, at even the happiest of times. His brother, Samuel, having had five wives, four of whom may have succumbed to tuberculosis, died in 1781, leaving seven children and stepchildren under fourteen along with numerous debts. His brother, John, wrote on November 12, 1782, giving the details. Washington replied the following January 16, referring first to Samuel, and then to complaints from his mother:

[Your letter] gave me extreme pain. In God's name how did my Brothr. Saml. contrive to get himself so enormously in debt? Was it by purchase? By misfortunes? Or sheer indolence and inattention to business? From whatever cause it proceeded, the matter is now the same, and curiosity only prompts the enquiry, as it does to know what will be saved, and how it is disposed of. In the list of his debts did it appear that I had a claim upon him for the purchase money of the Land I sold Pendleton on Bullskin? I have never received a farthing for it yet, and think I have been informed by him that he was to pay it.

I have lately received a letter from my Mother in which she complains much of the Knavery of the Overseer at the Little Falls Quarter, that She says she can get nothing from him. It is pretty evident, I believe, that I get nothing from thence, which I have the annual rent of between Eighty and an Hundred pounds to pay. The whole profit of the plantation, according to her Acct., is applied to his own use, which is rather hard upon me as I had no earthly inducement to meddle with it but to comply with her wish, and to free her from care. This, like every other matter of private concern with me, has been totally neglected; but it is too much while I am suffering in every other way (and hardly able to keep my own Estate from Sale), to be saddled with all the expence of hers and not be able to derive the smallest return from it. She has requested that I would get somebody to attend to it. I must therefore desire the favor of you to take it under your care. I know of none in whose hands it can be better placed, of none to whom it can be less inconvenient, and who is more interested in the good managemt. of the Land. For as it lyes directly in your Route to Berkley, and in the Neighbourhood of our friends, where you must always make a halt, it will give you very little additional trouble to provide an Overseer. Call upon him as you pass and repass, and settle the annual Accts. with him, so that I may have some knowledge of his transactions and a certainty that whatever is made goes towards payment of the Rent. I shall by this Post inform my Mother of this application to you...

While I am talking of my Mother and her concerns, I am impelled to mention something which has given, and still continues to give me pain. About two years ago a Gentleman of my acquaintance informed me that it was in contemplation that a move for a pension for her would reach the Virginia Assembly. That he did not suppose I knew of the measure, or that it would be agreeable to me to have it done; but wished to know my sentiments on it. I instantly wrote him that it was new and astonishing to me and begged that he would prevent the motion if possible, or oppose it if made; for I was sure she had not a Child that would not share the last farthing with her, and that would not be hurt at the idea of her becoming a Pensioner, or in other words receiving charity. Since then I have heard nothing of *that matter; but I learn from very good authority that she is, upon all occasions, and in all Companies complaining of the hardness of the times, of her wants and distresses; and if not in direct terms, at least by strong innuendos, inviting favours which not only makes <u>her</u> appear in an unfavourable point of view but <u>those</u> also who are connected with her. That she can have no <u>real</u> wants that may not be supplied I am sure of; <u>imaginary</u> wants are indefinite and oftentimes insatiable, because they are boundless and always changing. The reason of my mentioning these matters to you is, that you may enquire into her real wants and see what is necessary to make her comfortable. If the Rent is insufficient to do this, while I have anything I will part with it to make her so; and wish you to take measures in my behalf accordingly; at the same time I wish you to represent to her in delicate terms that impropriety of her complaints and acceptance of favours, even when they are voluntarily offered, from any but relations. It will not do to touch upon this subject in a letter to her, and therefore I have avoided it...*

The general had become well accustomed to shocks but the reports on his farms and property from Lund Washington, his wartime Mount Vernon manager, quite upset him. Lund had encountered great difficulties because his markets overseas and many needed supplies had been cut by hostilities. He was required to supply all goods needed by Martha Washington as well as take care of many problems of her son and Washington's mother. During the war years he had not written much about the financial results of Mount Vernon's operations. Washington, on the other hand, had drawn only his actual expenses from Congress for his services. When hostilities ceased, he became increasingly concerned about conditions at home. On January 29, Lund gave him a few figures on the 1782 corn crop, adding: "I generally put off writing... I had rather be employed in the most laborious way than copying any writing... It causes me to keep irregular accounts." He suggested he might be able to persuade himself to write something by the next mail. A chill blast was returned from the north on February 12:

You do not seem to have considered the force and tendency of the words of yr. letter when you talk of the probability <u>only</u> of sending me "the long promised account the irregularity of them"; not you add "for want of knowledge in keeping them but neglect"; your aversion to writing, &ca. &ca. These are but other words for saying "as I am not fond of writing, and it is <u>quite</u> immaterial whether you have any knowledge or information of your private concerns or whether the accts. are kept properly or not, I have delayed, and do not know how much longer I may continue to delay bringing you acquainted with these accts., irregular as they are."

Delicacy hitherto, and a hope that you long ago would have seen into the propriety of the measure, without a hint of it from me, has restrained me from telling you that the annual Accts. of my Crops, together with the receipts and expenditure of my money, state of my stocks, &ca. ought to have been sent to me as regularly as the year came about. It is not to be supposed that all the avocations of my public duties, great and laborious as they have been, could render me totally insensible to the <u>only means</u> by which myself and my family, and the character I am to maintain in life hereafter, is to be supported, or that a precise acct. of these matters would not have been exceedingly satisfactory to me. Instead of this, except the Acct. rendered at Valley Forge in the year 1778 I have received none since I left home; and not till after two or 3 applications in the course of last year could I get any acct. of the crop of the preceding one; and then only of the Corn by the Post on Sunday last.

I have often told you, and I repeat it with much truth; that the entire confidence I placed in your integrity made me easy, and I was always happy at thinking my Affairs were in your hands, which I could not have been, if they had been under the care of a common Manager; but this did not exempt me from the desires which all men have, of knowing the exact state of them. I have now to beg that you will not only send me the Account of your receipts, and expenditures of Specie; but of every kind of money subsequent to the Acct. exhibited at Valley Forge, which ended sometime in April 1778.

I want to know before I come home (as I shall come home with empty pockets whenever peace shall take place) how Affairs stand with me, and what my dependence is.

I wish to know also, what I have to expect from the Wheat of 1781 and 82, as you say the two Crops are so blended that they cannot be rendered separately. How are settlements to be made with and justice done to the several Parties interested under these circumstances?

Lund Washington provided a confusing reply, indicating he had once offered to send the accounts but the general had not specifically stated that he wanted them. He added: "It is painful to me to make excuses for bad crops, but owing to one cause or another, we have not made a good one in my remembrance." Lund wrote again, forwarding some accounts, which Washington did not find encouraging. He replied on June 11: "You seem to have an unconquerable aversion to going from home; one consequence of which is, I expect I shall lose all my rents; for in a letter from my brother John in Berkeley, are these words: 'I fear you are suffering *greatly* in your rents, as I am informed many of the tenants are gone into the Western country; and understand there are many arrears of rent due to you.'... If your own wages... have not been received by you… which does not appear by the Accts. you have lately rendered to me; I shall be more hurt than at anything else, to think that an Estate, which I have drawn nothing from for eight years… should not have been able for the last five years, to pay the manager. And that, worse than going home to empty coffers, and expensive living, I shall be encumbered with debt. It is disagreeable to me, because I dare say it will be so to you, to make these observations, but as my public business is now drawing to a close, I cannot avoid looking towards my private concerns, which do not bear the most smiling countenance." Lund subsequently advised the general that Mount Vernon was going to need a new roof. The French officers, before leaving America, had all expressed the hope that he would come to France, but his financial troubles were to rule out this possibility.

NEWBURGH AND NEAR MUTINY

In August 1782 Congress repealed the suspension of Gates from command, as well as its earlier recommendation for a court of inquiry on his conduct at Camden. He reported to Washington in October; the general received him cordially and assigned him command of the right wing. Although chastened, Gates had not quite lost his taste for intrigue. In his activities he operated through his aide, Major John Armstrong, Jr., and his former aide, Colonel Walter Stewart, who had been made the army's inspector general.

On January 6 a committee of officers, headed by General McDougall, appeared before Congress to present a respectful petition on their deplorable financial position. Alexander Hamilton, now in Congress, was appointed chairman of a finance committee to work out plans for a national revenue which would meet the needs of the army. In the ensuing discussions, which eventually brought the army close to open revolution, Hamilton played a constructive role in maintaining an authoritative line of communication between Congress and the commander in chief.

Congress, so Hamilton informed Washington, was split into factions. There were those who feared the army. There were pro-British and pro-French groups; some were for states' rights while others advocated a national power and revenue. The government was totally broke and what, unless the states showed more sense, could the army do? By February 7 Hamilton was writing Washington: "I will not conceal from your Excellency a truth which it is necessary you should know. An idea is propagated in the army that delicacy, carried to an extreme, prevents your espousing its interests with sufficient warmth. The falsehood of this opinion no one can be better acquainted with than myself, but it is not the less mischievous for being false. Its tendency is to impair that influence which you may exert with advantage, should any commotions unhappily ensue, to moderate the pretensions of the army and make their conduct correspond with their duty."

The rumors that flew between Philadelphia and Newburgh multiplied, each inflaming the other. When Congress passed some stopgap resolutions on February 6, reports reached Newburgh to the effect that Congress hoped quickly to dissolve the army and thus evade its financial obligations. Not long afterwards, rumors circulated in Congress that the army had voted not to disband and to use whatever force was necessary to establish its claims. By February 20 it began to be clear that a secret hand, that of Gates, was at work. Hamilton had never forgiven Washington but he thoroughly disliked Gates. The essence of his private statements was to trust Washington, at all costs, in the crisis. As Madison reported it, Hamilton said that:

> It was certain that the army had secretly determined not to lay down their arms until due provision and a satisfactory prospect should be afforded on the subject of their pay... The Commander was already become extremely unpopular, among all ranks, from his known dislike to every unlawful proceeding; that this unpopularity was daily increasing and industriously promoted by many leading characters; that his choice of unfit and indiscreet persons into his family was the pretext, and with some the real motive; but the substantial one [was] a desire to displace him from the respect and confidence of the army, in order to substitute General [Gates]... Mr. Hamilton said that he knew General Washington intimately and perfectly; that his extreme reserve, mixed sometimes with a degree of asperity of temper, both of which were said to have increased somewhat of late, had contributed to the decline of his popularity; but that his virtue, his patriotism and firmness... might be depended upon never to yield to any dishonorable or disloyal plans...

On February 27 Joseph Jones of Virginia informed Washington of the many reports reaching Philadelphia that dangerous combinations were being formed in the army. On March 4 the general wrote Hamilton: "The predicament in which I stand as Citizen and Soldier, is as critical and delicate as can well be conceived. It has been the subject of many contemplative hours. The sufferings of a complaining Army on the one hand, and the inability of Congress and tardiness of the States on the other, are the forebodings of evil... Unless Congress have powers competent to all *general* purposes... the distresses we have encountered, and the blood we have spilt in the course of an Eight years war, will avail us nothing..." In a veiled reference, which he knew Hamilton would understand, he noted that the ideas propagated against him in the army arose from an easily traced source. This was the "old leaven" of the cabal—General Gates—who was operating "under a mask of the most perfect dissimulation and apparent cordiality."

On March 8 Colonel Walter Stewart arrived in camp from Philadelphia. Until then, according to Washington, there had been no serious agitation. Stewart stirred up the whole camp with his report that Congress intended to disband the army without doing it justice. Two days later the first of three anonymous letters circulated within the army; these became known as the Newburgh addresses. They were written by Gates' aide, John Armstrong, and circulated by Stewart and his assistant, Major William Barber. Armstrong, only twenty-four, drew up a rather juvenile harangue which had its emotional impact:

> *After a pursuit of seven long years, the object for which we sought is at length brought within our reach... Peace returns again to bless—whom? A country willing to redress your wrongs, cherish your worth, and reward your services?... Or is it rather a country that tramples upon your rights, disdains your cries, and insults your distresses...*

> *Change the milk-and-water tone of your last memorial. Assume a bolder style... and suspect the man who would advise more moderation and larger forbearance... Let two or three men who can feel as well as write, be appointed to draw up your <u>last remonstrance</u>... Tell them that the slightest mark of indignity from Congress must now operate like the grave and part you forever... Nothing shall separate you from your arms but death. . .*

Armstrong further suggested that, even if war continued, the army should retire, under Washington's leadership, "to some unsettled country." If peace came, their swords would establish justice for themselves. Washington simply issued an order that the meeting, called by the faction for March 11, was not to be held; he added that he was sure no officer would respond to an irregular call from an unknown person. He ordered, in its place, a meeting of all general and field officers, together with one officer from each company, to meet on March 15 to discuss their representations to Congress. Armstrong immediately put out another anonymous letter, noting that the commander in chief, who had, to this time, only expressed "good wishes" for their success with Congress, was now on their side. Washington then issued to the army such congressional resolves as he had received, respecting their willingness to meet their commitments. He also talked individually with all his principal officers, asking for restraint; from them he heard that emotions had run wild. Contrary to his original intention, and probably mistrusting Gates, he showed up at the meeting.

A month previously, Washington, who had read and written so much over eight years, received a new pair of glasses from David Rittenhouse of Philadelphia. He thanked him on February 16: "The Spectacles suit my Eyes extremely well, as I am persuaded that the reading glasses also will when I get more accustomed to the use of them. At present I find some difficulty in coming at the proper Focus; but when I do obtain it, they magnify properly and shew those objects very distinctly which at first appear like a mist blended together and confused."

When all his officers were assembled, Washington entered and went to the lectern. He said he had not originally planned to come but he now had with him a written paper. As he pulled it from his pocket, he also took out the Rittenhouse glasses and said: "Gentlemen, you will permit me to put on my spectacles, for I have not only grown grey, but almost blind, in the service of my country." Those present noticed involuntary tears start in his officers' eyes. The audience was his. He proceeded:

> By an anonymous summons, an attempt has been made to convene you together; how inconsistent with the rules of propriety! how unmilitary! and how subversive of all order and discipline, let the good sense of the Army decide.

> In the moment of this Summons, another anonymous production was sent into circulation, addressed more to the feelings and passion, than to the reason and judgement of the Army. The author of the piece is entitled to much credit for the goodness of his Pen and I could wish he had as much credit for the rectitude of his heart, for Men see thro' different Optics, [as] induced by the reflecting faculties of the Mind... The Author of the Address should have had more charity than to mark for Suspicion, the Man who should recommend moderation and longer forbearance, or, in other words, who should not think as he thinks, and act as he advises. But he had another plan in view, in which candor and liberality of Sentiment, regard to justice and love of Country, have no part; and he was right to insinuate the darkest suspicion [in order] to effect the blackest design.

> ...This much, Gentlemen, I have thought it incumbent upon me to observe to you, to shew you upon what principles I opposed the irregular and hasty meeting... not because I wanted a disposition to give you every opportunity consistent with your own honor, and the dignity of the Army, to make known your grievances. If my conduct heretofore has not evinced to you that I have been a faithful friend to the Army, my declaration of it at this time would be equally unavailing and improper. But as I was among the first who embarked in the cause of our common Country; as I have never left your side one moment, but when called from you on public duty; as

*I have been the constant companion and witness of your Distresses, and not among
the last to feel and acknowledge your merits; as I have ever considered my own
Military reputation as inseparably connected with that of the Army; as my Heart
has ever expanded with joy when I heard its praises, and my indignation has arisen
when the mouth of detraction has been opened against it; it can <u>scarcely</u> <u>be</u> <u>supposed</u>,
at this late stage of the war, that I am indifferent to its interests. But, how are they to
be promoted? The way is plain, says the anonymous Addresser. If War continues,
remove into the unsettled Country; there establish yourselves, and leave an
ungrateful Country to defend itself. But who are they to defend? Our Wives, our
Children, Our Farms... If Peace takes place, never sheath your Swords, Says he,
until you have obtained full and ample justice; this dreadful alternative, of either
deserting our Country in the extremest hour of her distress... or turning our Arms
against it... has something so shocking in it that humanity revolts at the idea. My
God! what can this writer have in view, by recommending such measures?...*

*There might, Gentlemen, be an impropriety in my taking notice... of an anonymous
production, but the manner in which that performance has been introduced into the
Army, the effect it was intended to have, together with some other circumstances,
will amply justify my observations... With respect to the advice given by the Author,
to suspect the Man who shall recommend moderate measures and longer
forbearance, I spurn it, as every Man who regards that liberty and reveres that
justice for which we contend, undoubtedly must; for if Men are to be precluded from
offering their Sentiments on a matter which may involve the most serious and
alarming consequences, reason is of no use to us; the freedom of Speech may be
taken away, and dumb and silent, we may be led, like sheep, to the slaughter.*

*I cannot... conclude... without giving it as my decided opinion that [Congress]
entertain exalted sentiments of the Services of the Army, and, from a full conviction
of its merits and sufferings, will do it compleat justice...*

*For myself... a grateful sense of the confidence you have placed in me, a recollection
of the cheerful assistance, and prompt obedience I have experienced from you... and
the sincere affection I feel for an Army I have so long had the honor to Command,
will oblige me to declare in this public and solemn manner, that in the attainment
of compleat justice for all your toils and dangers, you may freely command my
Services to the utmost of my abilities.*

*While I give these assurances... let me entreat you, Gentlemen, on your part not to
take any measures which, viewed in the calm light of reason, will lessen the dignity,
and sully the glory you have hitherto maintained... Let me conjure you... as you*

value your sacred honor, as you respect the rights of humanity… to express your
utmost horror and detestation of the Man who wishes, under any specious
pretences, to overturn the liberties of our Country, and who wickedly attempts to
open the flood Gates [sic] of Civil discord, and deluge our rising Empire in Blood.
By thus determining and thus acting, you will pursue the plain and direct road to
the attainment of your wishes… You will give one more distinguished proof of
unexampled patriotism and patient virtue… And you will, by the dignity of your
Conduct, afford occasion for Posterity to say, when speaking of the glorious example
you have exhibited to Mankind, "Had this day been wanting, the World had never
seen the last stage of perfection to which human nature is capable of attaining."

Washington had once been considered no orator but he reached a peak here that he was to surpass on but few occasions. Leaving a stunned Gates in charge, Washington departed. Resolutions were quickly and unanimously passed expressing the confidence of every officer, including Gates, in Washington and Congress, and denouncing the "infamous" proposals of Armstrong.

One officer present, Major J. A. Wright, wrote: "[Washington] made a most excellent address; he appeared sensibly agitated, as the writer advises, 'to suspect the man who should advise moderation.' This expression… gave reason to suppose that it was a plan laid against his Excellency, as every one who knows him must be sensible that he would recommend moderation." Major Samual Shaw, who had seen him in battle and on many other occasions, said that he had never known him so truly great as at this meeting. "He stood single and alone. There was no saying where the passions of an army which were not a little inflamed, might not lead; but it was generally allowed that further forbearance was dangerous, and moderation had ceased to be a virtue. Under these circumstances he appeared, not at the head of his troops, but as it were, in opposition to them; and for a dreadful moment the interests of the army and its general seemed to be in competition. He spoke—every doubt was dispelled… What he says of the army may with equal justice be applied to his own character: 'Had this day been wanting, the world had never seen the last stage of perfection which human nature is capable of attaining.'"

Washington had forgiven Gates many times, but his sponsorship of the Newburgh addresses was too much. He considered the phrase, "Suspect the man who would advise moderation" as having originated with the second in command in the army. There is little doubt that Washington, who punned so often, deliberately inserted a plea to express detestation of "the Man who wickedly attempts to open the flood Gates of civil discord." Having thoroughly crushed Gates, Washington thereafter rarely spoke of him.

Major Armstrong had written that Washington expressed only good wishes that the army might get something. In fact, Congress and its executives had felt almost unbearable pressure from the commander in chief. Now Washington applied scalding heat. In transmitting the Newburgh resolves to the president of Congress on March 18, he said that they were "the last glorious proof of Patriotism [which] will not only confirm their claim to the justice but will increase their title to the gratitude of their Country." He continued, including a brief quotation from Armstrong:

> *If the whole Army has not merited whatever a grateful people can bestow, than have I been beguiled by prejudice, and built opinion on the basis of error. And "if" (as has been suggested for the purpose of inflaming their passions) "the Officers of the Army… are to grow old in poverty wretchedness and contempt," then shall I have learned what ingratitude is, then shall I have realized a tale which will embitter every moment of my future life. But I am under no such apprehensions, a Country rescued by their Arms from impending ruin, will never leave unpaid the debt of gratitude.*

Further letters followed in rapid succession to individual members, outlining the hunger, the cold, and the nakedness the army had suffered, the battles they had fought, and the jails they now faced if sent off penniless and in debt. Congress, on receipt of news of the great storm aroused by the Newburgh addresses had, with unexpected humor, appointed a committee, composed of those who opposed the army's claims, to meet their complaints. Soon, however, others took over, including two of Washington's former officers, Hamilton and Theodorick Bland. A makeshift revenue bill was presented to the states. In the end, the officers' and soldiers' claims were recognized, though they had to be content with treasury IOUs. These were funded into the national debt when Washington became president.

Washington also persuaded Congress to approve other rewards, which cost little but meant much to the army. All officers who had honorably served from January 1, 1776 on, were given a brevet one grade higher than they held at the conclusion of the war. Thus colonels could retire as brigadiers. For the enlisted men he proposed that the country make a free gift to them of the "arms and accoutrements" they had carried during the war. He wrote: "These constant companions of their Toils and Dangers, preserved with sacred Care, would be handed down from the present possessors to their Children, as honorable Badges of Bravery and Military Merit; and would probably be bro't forth, on some future Occasion, with Pride and Exultation… in the hands of Posterity." The final thing Washington did for his army was to sign all honorable discharges of officers and all badges of merit for enlisted men. Such signatures ran into the thousands.

PEACE

If Washington was interested in peace, so were his enlisted men. Private Joseph Plumb Martin, writing long afterwards, remembered the camp rumors as to what would be done with "General Washington's watch-chain." This was a 136-ton linked barrier across the Hudson at West Point which, as regularly as clockwork, was put in place when navigation opened in the spring and removed in the fall, before the river froze. That spring it was kept in the warehouse. On March 30 Washington had word of a general European armistice.

On April 6 Sir Guy Carleton informed Washington that he had just received the official peace intelligence from England. He would therefore declare a cessation of hostilities for April 8. Washington, in his turn, picked April 19, the eighth anniversary of the battle at Concord's rude bridge, for his proclamation. In joy as he wrote, he moved from army prose to a soaring flight of words, matched by no other founding father:

The Commander in Chief orders the Cessation of Hostilities between the United States of America and the King of Great Britain to be publickly proclaimed tomorrow at 12 o'clock at the New Building, and that the Proclamation [of Congress] which will be communicated herewith, be read tomorrow evening at the head of every regiment and corps of the army. After which the Chaplains with the several Brigades will render thanks to almighty God for all his mercies, particularly for his overruling the wrath of man to his own glory, and causing the rage of war to cease among the nations.

Although the proclamation before alluded to, extends only to the prohibition of hostilities, and not the annunciation of a general peace, yet it must afford the most rational and sincere satisfaction to every benevolent mind, as it puts a period to a long and doubtful contest, stops the effusion of human blood, opens the prospect to a more splendid scene, and like another morning star, promises the approach of a brighter day than hath hitherto illuminated the Western Hemisphere; on such a happy day, a day which is the harbinger of Peace, a day which completes the eighth year of the war, it would be ingratitude not to rejoice! It would be insensibility not to participate in the general felicity.

The Commander in Chief far from endeavouring to stifle the feelings of Joy in his own bosom, offers his most cordial Congratulations on the occasion to all the Officers of every denomination, to all the Troops of the United States in General, and in particular to those gallant and persevering men who had resolved to defend the rights of their invaded country so long as the war should continue. For these are the men who ought to be considered as the pride and boast of the American Army; And who, crowned with well earned laurels, may soon withdraw from the field of Glory, to the more tranquil walks of civil life.

While the General recollects the almost infinite variety of Scenes thro' which we have passed, with a mixture of pleasure, astonishment and gratitude; While he contemplates the prospects before us with rapture; he can not help wishing that all the brave men (of whatever condition they may be) who have shared in the toils and dangers of effecting this glorious revolution, of rescuing Millions from the hand of oppression, and of laying the foundation of a great Empire, might be impressed with a proper idea of the dignified part they have been called to act (under the Smiles of Providence) on the stage of human affairs; for, happy, thrice happy, shall they be pronounced thereafter who have contributed any thing, who have performed the meanest office, in erecting this stupendous Fabrick *of* Freedom *and* Empire *on the broad basis of Independence; who have assisted in protecting the rights of human nature and establishing an Asylum for the poor and oppressed of all nations and religions. The glorious task for which we first flew to Arms being thus accomplished, the liberties of our Country being fully acknowledged and firmly secured by the smiles of heaven on the purity of our cause and the honest exertions of a feeble people (determined to be free) against a powerful Nation (disposed to oppress them) and the Character of those who have persevered through every extremity of hardship; suffering and danger, being immortalized by the illustrious appellation of the* patriot Army; *Nothing now remains but for the actors of this mighty scene to preserve a perfect, unvarying, consistency of character through the very last act; to close the Drama with applause; and to retire from the Military Theatre with the same approbation of Angels and men which have crowned all their former virtuous actions..."*

THE ARMY MELTS AWAY

The address was much appreciated by the troops who failed to notice one of the concluding sentences: "Every considerate and well disposed soldier must remember that it will be absolutely necessary to wait with patience until peace shall be declared or Congress shall be enabled to take proper measures for the security of the public stores..." As Washington soon discovered, the soldiers could not distinguish between preliminary and final treaties. It was peace, they wanted to go home, and there was no way to stop them.

By the middle of June Washington was writing Lafayette: "We remain here in a listless state, awaiting the arrival of the definitive treaty; the uncertainty of which, added to the great expense of subsisting the Army, have induced

Congress to Furlough (which, in the present case is but another term for discharging) all the Soldiers who stood engaged for the War." Although Washington and Robert Morris tried to see that the soldiers had some small portion of their long missing pay in cash, they got only scrip. Many had to beg as they made their long hike from Newburgh to distant points. Washington had feared a clamor, and even a mutiny, but they went off quietly.

The situation was different in Lancaster, far from Washington's control. There, relatively new recruits, as he was careful to point out to Congress, complained about being discharged without pay. Eighty or so of them, under two sergeants, started for Philadelphia on June 17, in defiance of their officers. They intended to make their principal pleas, or threats, to the government of Pennsylvania, whose legislature shared Independence Hall with the Continental Congress. Hamilton, on behalf of Congress, appealed to the state's president, John Dickinson, to call out the militia but Dickinson refused. When the mutineers got to Philadelphia, they induced several hundred more men to join. On June 21 they surrounded the hall with fixed bayonets, shouting at both the state and national legislatures. Congress urgently asked Washington for help. He dispatched 1,500 troops under General Howe to Philadelphia. Before they arrived, Congress, muttering that the "majesty" of the United States had been "offended," removed itself to Princeton. The state government then called out its militia; with the approach of Washington's troops, the mutiny collapsed. Congress did not return to Philadelphia until 1790.

That autumn, in the congressional debates as to where the permanent capital should be, even Pennsylvania did not appear to want it in Philadelphia but offered Germantown. The majority of delegates appeared to think Maryland was more suitable and the choice should be between Annapolis and Georgetown.

PLEA FOR NATIONAL UNION

The commander in chief, his "sensibility" excited by seeing his veterans going off with pieces of paper they were expected to persuade the states to cash, decided on a plea to the whole country for a strong national government. On June 8 he finished a moving and forceful appeal under the modest title "Circular to the States." In it he announced his forthcoming retirement "for which I have never ceased to sigh through a long and painful absence." The address was lengthy:

> *The Citizens of America, placed in the most enviable condition, as the sole Lords and Proprietors of a vast Tract of Continent, comprehending all the various soils*

and climates of the World... are now acknowledged to be possessed of absolute freedom and Independence; They are, from this period, to be considered as the Actors on the most conspicuous Theatre, which seems to be peculiarly designed by Providence for the display of human greatness and felicity; Here, they are not only surrounded with every thing which can contribute to the completion of private and domestic enjoyment, but Heaven has crowned all its other blessings, by giving more opportunity for political happiness, than any other Nation has been favored with...

...Notwithstanding the cup of blessing... thus reached out to us, notwithstanding happiness is ours... yet... there is an option still left to the United States of America... whether they will be respectable and prosperous, or contemptible and miserable as a Nation; This is the moment when the eyes of the whole world are turned upon them, this is the moment to establish or ruin their Character forever, this is the favorable moment to give such a tone to our Federal Government, as will enable it to answer the ends of its institution, or this may be the ill-fated moment for relaxing the powers of the Union... exposing us to become the sport of European politics... for, according to the system of policy the states shall adopt at this moment, they will stand or fall... It is yet to be decided whether the Revolution was a blessing or a curse, not to the present age alone for, with our fate, will the destiny of unborn Millions be involved.

With this conviction of the importance of the present Crisis, silence in me would be a crime; there are four things... essential to the well being, I may even venture to say, to the existence of the United States as an Independent Power:

1st. An indissoluble Union of the States under one Federal Head

2dly. A Sacred regard to Public Justice

3dly. The adaption of a proper Peace Establishment, and

4thly. The prevalence of that pacific and friendly Disposition, among the People of the United States, which will induce them to forget their local prejudices and policies, to make those mutual concessions which are requisite to the general prosperity...

These are the pillars... Liberty is the Basis... It will be part of my duty, and that of every true Patriot to assert without reserve... that it is indispensable to the happiness of the individual States, that there should be lodged somewhere, A Supreme Power to regulate and govern the general concerns of the Confederated Republick without which the Union cannot be of long duration... Without an entire conformity to the Spirit of the Union, we cannot exist as an Independent

Power... It is only in our united Character as an Empire, that our Independence is acknowledged, that our power can be regarded, or our Credit supported...

...Honesty will be found on every experiment, to be the best and only true policy. Let us then as a Nation be just, let us fulfil the public Contracts, which Congress undoubtedly had a right to make... Let us strengthen the hands of Government and be happy under its protection; every one will reap the fruits of his labours, every one will enjoy his own acquisitions without molestation and without danger...

I now make it my earnest prayer, that God... would most graciously be pleased to dispose us all, to do Justice, to love mercy, and to demean ourselves with that Charity, humility and pacific temper of Minds, which were the Characteristicks of the Divine Author of our blessed Religion, and without an humble imitation of whose example in these things, we can never hope to be a happy nation.

The message's impact was immense. Governors and legislatures responded with their warmest thanks for Washington's services and advice to his country. Greene reported that Washington's words had a great impact in South Carolina, in contrast to the "feeble influence" of Congress. One newspaper said the report was "dictated by God." Even John Hancock wrote, which was perhaps his most unusual compliment.

Washington followed on November 2 with an address "To the Armies of the United States." This was his "affectionate farewell... of those he holds most dear." In it he recalled that the army had been originally composed of men who had been disposed to despise those from other sections, but they had become "one patriotic band of Brothers." He asked every officer and soldier to remember that the very existence of the nation, for which they had fought for so long, depended upon the country giving support and increased powers to the federal government. He asked them to exert every effort to effect "these great and valuable purposes." Twenty-three of the subsequent thirty-nine signers of the 1787 Constitution were to come from the revolutionary forces.

ORDER OF THE CINCINNATI

In May 1783 the organization of this society of revolutionary army officers created an uproar among those who were not eligible. The impetus for the society came from Knox, who sensed the strong desire among the officers that their friendships be maintained in the peace. Washington was automatically elected president. Its charter, as written by Knox, aimed to preserve the rights and liberties of the country, to work for national union, and to provide funds for the relief of widows and orphans of officers. Membership was to descend to the eldest male heir; this provision brought attacks from those who feared it might be an entering wedge to hereditary aristocracy. Its privileges were soon extended to the American navy and to France, which organized its own chapter.

The society, through the individual work of the order's members in the thirteen states, provided strong and constructive support to the calling of a national constitutional convention. Nine of the order signed the resulting Constitution, and two were in Washington's first cabinet.

PEACE ESTABLISHMENT

When Hamilton was appointed chairman of a congressional committee to propose a peacetime army, he asked Washington to submit his ideas. In his humorless way, Hamilton informed the general: "I will just hint to your Excellency that our prejudices will make us wish to keep up as few troops as possible."

Although Washington received the request towards the middle of April, he had ready a lengthy report for Congress on May 2. He suggested a small standing army of 2,631 officers and men, supplemented by an organization corresponding to Switzerland's "hardy and well organized militia service." He pointed out that the Swiss system had enabled her to retain independence and freedom for centuries.

Washington's far-ranging mind looked over the vast territories belonging to the United States. He advocated permanent forts at West Point, Penobscot, Lake Champlain, northern New England, Ticonderoga, Oswego, Fort Erie, Detroit, St. Mary's River, Fort Pitt, and the mouths of the Ohio, Kentucky, Illinois, and Scioto Rivers. He recommended that other posts in the Carolinas and Georgia be determined by those more familiar with the areas than he.

Washington in this paper and another which followed on September 7 outlined a peace policy providing for the orderly settlement and formation of new states, while assuring justice for the Indians. As he noted, there were huge areas of open land, hundreds of thousands of square miles, which the United States could not police. If the country neglected these, they would soon be overrun by land speculators and banditti, who would cause endless trouble with the Indians. He advocated that Congress establish a line beyond which no one could go without government approval. No further settlement should take place until there were satisfactory treaties with the Indians. Licensed traders only, checked for their integrity, should deal with them. Indian friendship should be gained by fair dealing.

In his proposal Washington also suggested that the land which is now Ohio should be the first to come under this policy. He sketched its boundaries, which come remarkably close to the present state lines. He thought that Detroit, though somewhat distant, should be included in the new territory because of the large number of French settlers there, who needed the protection of the American government. He also advocated opening the proposed new state to settlers from French Canada, who wanted to escape British rule, as well as to revolutionary veterans who had been promised land bounties. The latter would be useful in protecting the settlements.

As a part of his work on the peacetime military system, Washington sent General von Steuben to Quebec to confer with General Haldimand, the British commander in chief, and to arrange with him for the transfer of the western posts from British to American control. Haldimand, however, told Steuben that he had no instructions from London to yield them. The British did not give them up until Washington's second term as president.

CARLETON

Washington had much correspondence with Sir Guy Carleton on various terms of the peace treaty, which were not always clear to him nor to members of Congress. Washington particularly wanted New York evacuated, so he could go home. He had written to Chastellux in France on May 10: "We look forward with anxious expectation for the Definitive treaty to remove the doubts and difficulties which prevail at present, and our Country of our Newly acquired friends in New York... of whose Company we are heartily tired."

On May 6 Washington met Carleton at Tappan. Washington informed him that he had already given orders for the release of the German and British prisoners in American hands; they were to go to New York by land or by sea, as he preferred. Carleton said that he was doing everything he could to evacuate New York and had already sent some six thousand persons to Nova Scotia. He did agree to remove his troops from Westchester County, including what is now the Bronx. Becoming ill, Carleton returned to New York but not before his frigate had fired a seventeen-gun salute to General Washington and thus to the United States of America.

LETTERS FROM ENGLAND

Once the preliminary peace was signed, Washington's friends in England were free to write and many comrades from French and Indian War days sent him congratulatory letters. Strangers, some with unsurpassed gall, requested favors. On March 26 his old neighbor, George Fairfax, wrote from Yorkshire: "I cannot express the Joy, with which I take up my Pen to congratulate your Excellency upon the happy conclusion of the late diabolical war; my gratitude to Heaven exceeds all description… I wish you and your family may reap an ample harvest of honours and emoluments till time shall be no more. I have gloried in being called an American here, and I trust & hope, the People who have raised their reputation in the space of nine years from obscurity to the admiration of the world, will continue to act with Wisdom and moderation." Fairfax went on to say that one of his letters to Washington had been intercepted and sent to Lord North. It "like to cost me dear." He had fled Yorkshire, fearing arrest. Only his connections at court had saved him. He added: "Thank Heaven for you and my brave Countrymen, times are altered, and I am as much courted as I was despised as an American." People who had avoided him were now pressing for introductions to his distinguished friend, George Washington. To the letter the general replied on July 10:

With very sincere pleasure I receiv'd your favour… There was nothing wanting in this Letter to give compleat satisfaction to Mrs. Washington and myself, but some expression to induce us to believe you would once more become our neighbours. Your House at Belvoir, I am sorry to add, is no more, but mine (which is enlarged since you saw it) is most sincerely and heartily at your service till you could rebuild it.

As the path, after being closed by a long, arduous, and painful contest, is, to use an Indian Metaphor, now opened and made smooth, I shall please myself with the hope of hearing from you frequently; and till you forbid me to indulge the wish I shall not <u>despair</u> of seeing you and Mrs. Fairfax once more the Inhabitants of Belvoir, and greeting you both there, the intimate companions of our old Age, as you have been of our younger years…

I unite my prayers most fervently with yours, for Wisdom to these U States, and have no doubt, after a little while, all errors in the present form of their Government will be corrected and a happy temper be diffused through the whole; but like young heirs come a little prematurely, perhaps, to a large inheritance, it is more than probable they will riot for a while; but, in this, if it should happen, tho' it is a circumstance which is to be lamented (as I would have the National

character of America be pure and immaculate) will work its own cure, as there is
virtue at the bottom.

Washington said that it would hardly console Fairfax in the loss of his house
to know how much everyone in Virginia had suffered. He recalled a story of
an overseer employed by Mrs. Fairfax's father, who said the drought was so terrible he was like to starve but added: "Thank God my neighbours are as bad
off as I am."

Robert Stewart, another old comrade to whom Washington had lent
money so many years before, sent his "warmest and most sincere congratulations on that exalted fame which you so nobly won... The Poets and
Historians of After Ages shall vie with each other in endeavouring to represent it in its true brilliance." He was afraid, he said, that his remarks might
pain Washington's modesty but, although he was a British officer, he had
praised Washington to everyone and had opposed the war. Stewart spoiled
the letter by suggesting that he might like a job representing America at
some pleasant European court. Washington sent a warm and friendly reply
but noted that such appointments would go to those who had fought "with
Halters about their Necks."

Others who wrote included Jacob van Braam, who had translated the terms
of Washington's first and only surrender at Fort Necessity, and the Reverend
Jacob Duché, who had once written Washington that his cause was hopeless
but who now sent a moving appeal to be allowed to return to the United
States. Washington replied to Duché: "Personal enmity I bear none, to any
Man; so far therefore as your Return to his Country Depends on my private
Voice, it would be given in favor of it with cheerfulness." Washington pointed
out that the decision was up to the Pennsylvania state government.

A Scottish lady wrote to ask Washington to collect debts owing to her. He
replied politely that he could not do this but would send her letter to someone who might help her. The elderly Countess of Huntingdon, a devout
Methodist, wanted him to manage her scheme to convert the Indians. He
declined courteously. The Countess of Tankerville and her son, Lord
Tankerville, simply forwarded him a power of attorney to collect property they
believed to be due them in Virginia. Her ladyship seems to have assumed that
Washington would regard it as an honor to be her employee. He went to considerable trouble to find someone who could do the work.

INVITATION FROM FRANCE

The comte de Rochambeau sent Washington a charming note dated "à Paris le 13 Juillet 1783." He said:

Your letter, my dear General, of May 10 with which you honored me, gave me the greatest pleasure. I see you at the end of your long labors and with a desire to come to France. Try, my dear General, to carry out this project, let nothing prevent this idea, and come and receive, in a country which honors you and has always admired you, the great applause that we owe to a great man. You can count on a reception that will never be equalled. You will be received as you ought to be, after a revolution which has no parallel in history. Everyone is smiling in advance at the hopes you have aroused by your letter, and my heart already beats at the pleasure of embracing you.

It seems to me that you ought to leave in the first days of October, after the equinox, to arrive here at the beginning of November. You will find the Court returned from Fontainebleau, you will pass your winter in the midst of the <u>fetes</u> of Paris and the Court, and we will carry you to our estates in the spring. Come, my dear General, and satisfy the wishes of a nation whose hearts are yours. You will eclipse all England, who are now arriving here for a change of air. We receive them well because we are polite and proper, but the French heart will receive General Washington."

Washington had talked often of France, his wish to express his personal thanks for her aid, and his general desire to see the country, but he had now ruled out going to what he called "gayer scenes." He replied to Rochambeau on October 15:

With what words, my dear count, shall I express to you the sensibility of a heart which you have warmed by the flattering sentiments that are conveyed in your Letters of the 14th of April and 13th of July. Your Nation is entitled to all my gratitude. Your sovereign has a claim to my highest admiration, respect and veneration; and those Individuals of it who have been my companions in war, to my friendship and Love. Can it be surprizing then, that I should possess an ardent desire to visit your Country? But, as I observed to you in my Letter of the 20th of May, it is not yet clear to me, that I shall ever have it in my power to accomplish my wishes. My private concerns have been very much deranged by an absence of more than eight years, and require particular attention to put them in order.

THE CHEERFUL WASHINGTON

Though he was not to see the splendors of Versailles, Washington was unusually ebullient as the time for going home approached. Jefferson and others
commented that they had never seen him look happier nor more relaxed.
Some of his remarks appear in records as do tales at which he laughed. His
aide, Benjamin Walker, told everyone a story on himself. He had asked the
general for leave of absence, saying that the Quaker girl, to whom he was
engaged, had written that she would just die if he did not get it. Washington
said: "Women don't die for such trifles." Walker asked what he should tell her,
and Washington replied: "Why, tell her to add another page to the book of sufferings." To the man who said that Robert Morris, the finance minister, had
his hands full, Washington said he wished it were his pockets. He burst into
loud laughter at a story which, according to Dr. James Thacher, was told by Dr.
John Thomas in Yankee twang: "What do you think Chambeau's soldiers call
a hat? The tarnation fools, they call it a chapeau. Why, and be darn'd to them,
can't they call it a hat and be done with it?"

His principal officers weighed themselves on August 19. It is a little difficult
to see them as heads of a starving army, since the top nine weighed over a ton.

General Knox	280 pounds
Colonel Michael Jackson	252 pounds
Colonel Huntington	232 pounds
Colonel Henry Jackson	230 pounds
General Lincoln	224 pounds
Colonel Humphreys	221 pounds
Colonel Swift	219 pounds
General Washington	209 pounds
Colonel Cobb	186 pounds

General Huntington, at 132 pounds, was but a shadow at the bottom of the list.

Washington's boyish joy at returning home was reflected in the purchases
he made for Mount Vernon. With Martha beside him to tell him what replacements were needed after eight years of war, Washington ordered nails, paint,
glass, china, tea tables and urns, coffee pots, chairs and furniture of all sorts,
blankets, and such items as olives, anchovies, fruits, and nuts. For his own
reading pleasure, he chose from catalogues and advertisements, books which
reflected his tastes as soldier and citizen. Among the first were biographies
and memoirs of Gustavus Adolphus, Peter the Great, and Turenne. To these
he added works by Locke, Voltaire, and Goldsmith, dictionaries of the arts and

science; encyclopedias; histories of the world, Rome, and the Netherlands; travel books on France, Ireland, and Denmark; and—finally—a French grammar and dictionary, as though he had resolved on a heroic effort to acquire French. He asked Lafayette to procure china in France but cancelled this when he found that he could obtain what he needed in New York, at reduced prices, from forced sales by Tories and English merchants.

Although he had decided that he could not go to Europe, his curiosity about the great "empire," which Americans called their new country, was as great as when he was sixteen. He dreamed of a grand tour and invited Lafayette to come along, in a letter of October 12:

> *I have it in contemplation to make a tour thro' all the Eastern States, thence into Canada; thence up the St. Lawrence and thro' the Lakes to Detroit; then to Lake Michigan by land or water; thence thro' the Western Country by the river Illinois, to the river Mississippi, and down the same to New Orleans; thence into Georgia by the way of Pensacola; and thence thro' the two Carolina's home. A great tour this, you will say, probably it may take place no where but in imagination, tho' it is my <u>wish</u> to begin it in the latter end of April of next year; if it should be realized, there would be nothing wanting to make it perfectly agreeable but your Company.*

Such a trip would have been legendary, with Lafayette and Washington as an eighteenth-century Huck and Jim, paddling down the Mississippi, but it never came to pass. The British held on to the posts which they had agreed to surrender, and it was impossible to penetrate the area.

Washington's appetite for travel had been stimulated by the holiday trip he had taken north in July. He wrote Congress that he was bored with waiting for the peace treaty ("this distressing tedium") and with the many "troublesome demands" on him which he could not satisfy. With Governor Clinton to accompany him, he set out by horseback on July 18 and rode a little over 750 miles in nineteen days. He went as far north as Crown Point, returned to Schenectady, then rode along the Mohawk to Fort Schuyler, and on down to Lake Otsego. He returned to Newburgh by way of Albany. On his arrival, he found an invitation, which was in effect an order, to report to Congress at Princeton. He had to reply that his horses were so fatigued from his rapid journey that it might be a few days before they were rested enough for him to proceed south. Shortly afterwards, he wrote the president of Congress that Martha Washington had a fever and "is now in a very weak and low state." He noted that he had so many papers to pack that he would have further to delay his trip, and he hoped that Congress would forgive him. Not until twelve days after his return did he and his wife set out for New Jersey.

PRINCETON TO HARLEM

Washington received the usual addresses and praise from Congress upon his arrival in Princeton, but he found nothing to do. Congress was underrepresented and was unable to do anything effective about his recommendations for a peacetime army.

Washington learned in Princeton that Congress had unanimously passed an act for the erection of an equestrian statue of himself, to be designed "by the best artist in Europe." The act went on to say that the general was to be dressed in a toga, "holding a truncheon in his right hand, and his head encircled with a laurel wreath." Although it was now the law of the land that he appear in Roman dress, he did not care much for the idea. His August 1786 letter to Jefferson, who had asked how he wanted to be dressed for the Houdon statue, said, in effect, that he did not know much about art but "perhaps a severe adherence to the garb of antiquity might not be altogether so expedient as some little deviation in favor of the modern costume." He understood that Benjamin West's use of current dress "is received with applause."

Congress also decreed that the statue be erected "where the residence of Congress shall be established." Its members had already met in five cities and were debating several other possible locations. The irrepressible Francis Hopkinson suggested that it be placed on wheels, so that it could be hauled around wherever Congress moved.

Washington had to arrange to transfer his immense collection of war papers to his house. On October 8 he wrote Timothy Pickering that six wagons were available at Princeton to transport the papers, which were "very bulky." He could not yet estimate how many wagons would be required, but probably four or five. A biographer can only express the opinion that six wagons seem hardly enough but Jacob Hiltzheimer's diary for November 11 reported that number as passing through Philadelphia with the papers. Washington instructed Lieutenant Bezaleel Howe to take the wagons to Mount Vernon, located, he added, "ten miles below Alexandria." He said the papers were very valuable to him and Howe was not to use any ferries when the wind was high. Howe was ordered to have sentinels always on watch and the papers under lock and key at all times.

On the day following the dispatch of his papers, Washington set out for West Point to arrange with the state's governor to take over the administration of New York City when the British departed. On November 12 he received from Sir Guy Carleton his evacuation plan. On November 21 General Washington and Governor Clinton crossed the Harlem River onto Manhattan Island, his first return in seven years.

NEW YORK

The last redcoat left Manhattan November 25. The ever-faithful Knox, who had joined Washington eight-and-a-half years before as a twenty-four-year-old soldier, went ahead to the city, at the lower end of Manhattan, to take over its formal guard duties. Governor Clinton and Washington rode into town, wildly cheered by the citizens. They were accompanied by many New Yorkers, who had been exiled for more than seven years.

A long time before, in September 1777, a loyal Philadelphia lady, Deborah Logan, had written of the despair which gripped her heart when she saw the well-clad British troops march into her city and thought of the contrast between them and "our own poor, bare-footed, ragged troops." Now, a loyal New York lady wrote: "The troops just leaving us were as if equipped for show, and with their scarlet uniforms, made a brilliant display; the troops that marched in on the contrary, were ill-clad and weather beaten, and made a forlorn appearance; but then they were *our* troops, and as I looked at them and thought upon all they had done and suffered for us, my heart and my eyes were full, and I admired and gloried in them the more, because they were weather beaten and forlorn."

Washington resided in Fraunce's Tavern, which still stands, while waiting for Carleton to remove his troops from Staten and Long Islands. On November 28 the returning exiles gave Washington a dinner, as did the governor the following day. On December 2 fireworks were set off in the Bowery, a display which Washington called "splendid." On December 3 he nominated Knox to command what little was left of the American army. On December 4, informed that the British would quit the islands that day, Washington held a final lunch for his officers. His intelligence chief, Colonel Benjamin Tallmadge, who had gone on to the city in advance of the troops to secure all his agents, many of whom had been disguised as Tories, wrote of the farewell:

At 12 o'clock, the officers repaired to Fraunce's Tavern, in Pearl Street, where Gen. Washington had appointed to meet them... We had been assembled but a few minutes when His Excellency entered the room. His emotion, too strong to be concealed, seemed to be reciprocated by every officer present. After partaking of a slight refreshment, in almost breathless silence, the General filled his glass with wine, and turning to the officers, he said: "With a heart full of love and gratitude, I now take leave of you. I most devoutly wish that your latter days may be as prosperous and happy as your former ones have been glorious and honorable."

After the officers had taken a glass of wine, Gen. Washington said: "I cannot come to each of you, but shall feel obliged if each of you will come and take me by the hand";

Gen. Knox being nearest to him, turned to the commander-in-chief, who, suffused in tears, was incapable of utterance, but grasped his hand; then they embraced each other in silence. In the same affectionate manner, every officer in the room marched up to, kissed, and parted with his General-in-chief. Such a scene of sorrow and weeping I had never before witnessed, and hope I may never be called upon to witness again. It was indeed too affecting to be of long continuance... Not a word was uttered to break the solemn silence that prevailed... The <u>simple thought</u> that we were then to part from the man who had conducted us through a long and bloody war, and under whose conduct the glory and independence of our country had been achieved, and that we should see his face no more in this world, seemed to me utterly insupportable. But the time of separation had come, and waving his hand to his <u>grieving children</u> around him, he left the room and passing through a corps of light infantry who were paraded to receive him, he walked silently on to Whitehall, where a barge was in waiting. We all followed in mournful silence to the wharf, where a prodigious crowd had assembled... As soon as he was seated, the barge put off into the river, and when out in the stream, our great and beloved general waved his hat, and bid us a silent adieu.

SOUTH TO MOUNT VERNON

Washington's three remaining aides, David Cobb, David Humphreys, and Benjamin Walker, offered to accompany him to Mount Vernon, but at Philadelphia, Cobb was detached by Washington because of his distance from home.

The general, as they travelled south, had to hear and answer one tedious address after another from the citizens of New Brunswick, the legislature of New Jersey, the merchants of Philadelphia, the president and council of Pennsylvania, the general assembly of Pennsylvania, the militia of Philadelphia, the magistrates of Philadelphia, the trustees and faculty of the University of Pennsylvania, the learned professions of Philadelphia, the American Philosophical Society, the burgesses and common council of Wilmington, the citizens of Baltimore, the general assembly of Maryland, the governor and council of Maryland, and the mayor and council of Annapolis. He and his aides managed to find something new to say in each reply.

On December 23 Washington dictated to Walker his last letter as commander in chief. This was to von Steuben, to whom Washington expressed the hope he would be pleased to have "this last letter… in the service of my country." He offered him his highest praise for his "zeal… abilities… and faithful and meritorious services."

The new president of Congress, which had now been transferred to Annapolis, was Thomas Mifflin, who had participated in the Conway Cabal and whose record as quartermaster general had not been distinguished. Nevertheless everything passed off gracefully. Banquets were held for Washington in Annapolis on December 20 and 22. On the night of December 22 the statehouse was illuminated and the Maryland General Assembly gave him a ball. James Tilton, who was present, noted that "the General danced every set, that all ladies might have the pleasure of dancing with him, or as it has since been handsomely expressed, get a touch of him." At noon next day, Washington, flanked by his aides, entered an extraodinarily crowded hall to resign his commission. The president said that Congress was ready to receive his communication; Washington rose and spoke:

The great events on which my resignation depended having at length taken place, I have now the honor of offering my sincere Congratulations to Congress and of presenting myself before them to surrender into their hands the trust committed to me…

Happy in the confirmation of our Independence and Sovereignty… I resign with satisfaction the Appointment I accepted with Diffidence. A diffidence in my abilities to accomplish so arduous a task, which, however, was superseded by a confidence in the rectitude of our Cause, the support of the Supreme Power of the union, and the patronage of Heaven…

While I repeat my obligations to the Army in general, I should do injustice to my own feelings not to acknowledge in this place the peculiar services and distinguished merits of the Gentlemen who have been attached to my person during the War. It was impossible the choice of confidential officers to compose my family should have been more fortunate. Permit me, Sir, to recommend [them] as worthy of the favorable notice… of Congress…

I consider it an indispensable duty to close this last solemn act of my Official life, by commending the Interests of our dearest Country to the protection of Almighty God…

Having now finished the work assigned me, I retire from the great Theatre of Action; and bidding an Affectionate farewell to this august body under whose orders I have so long acted, I here offer my commission, and take my leave of all the employments of public life.

President Mifflin made a suitable reply, and Washington handed him his commission of 1775. After reaching Mount Vernon, he wrote to ask if he might have it back as a souvenir for his family. Charles Thompson, secretary of Congress, replied that a congressional committee was at work preparing to return it to him in a gold box with a suitable inscription. Such are the ways of committees that Washington never received the commission, nor the gold box, nor—for that matter—did the Continental Congress erect the statue to him for which its members had voted.

The general and his aides reached Mount Vernon on the eve of the birth of the Prince of Peace.

THREE

MOUNT VERNON TO PHILADELPHIA

1784–1787

WASHINGTON DID NOT, as he put it, "get translated into a private citizen," as easily mentally as he did physically. On February 20, 1784, almost two months after the ceremony at Annapolis, he wrote to General Knox:

I am just beginning to experience that ease, and freedom from public cares which however desirable, takes some time to realize; for strange as it may tell, it is nevertheless true, that it was not 'till lately I could get the better of my usual custom of ruminating as soon as I asked in the Morning, on the business of the ensuing day; and of my surprize, after having resolved many things in my mind, to find that I was no longer a public Man, or had any thing to do with public transactions.

I feel now, however, as I conceive a wearied Traveller must do, who, after treading many a painful step, with a heavy burden on his shoulders, is eased of the latter, having reached the Goal to which all the former were directed; and from his House top is looking back, and tracing with a grateful eye the Meanders by which he escaped the quicksands and Mires which lay in his way; and into which none but the All-powerful guide, and great disposer of human Events could have prevented his falling.

A particularly severe winter kept Washington largely indoors, and he chafed when he had insufficient exercise. He had usually been understaffed as a general. His aides suffered from the enormous amount of dictating, transcribing, and copying to which they were chained. Now Washington had no clerical staff. He found his accounts and papers in disorder. Many of his old problems as trustee and executor had never been settled. In addition, he had his six wagonloads of war papers to unload and sort out. They had been so hastily stuffed into boxes, during his frequent moves, that Washington called them "a mass of confusion."

Washington expected his friends to write and give him their gossip. If they neglected him, they got a humorous complaint, sometimes with a barb stuck in it. (He pleaded with Jefferson, in Congress, on March 3: "If you have any News that you are at liberty to impart, it would be charity to communicate a little of it, to a body.")

What Washington had not expected was the extent to which total strangers in Europe and America felt free to write. Some were distinguished and deserved and got polite answers. Others wanted favors, loans, or old records. Two persons wrote to accuse him of keeping money owed them by people of whom he had never heard. The Reverend Jonathan Boucher, quite like his old self, wrote to express his doubt that America would be as happy as it had been under the king. Washington replied to almost everyone, though in many cases he did not bother making file copies, as his aides had done during the war. Most tedious were the old estate and trustee matters, for he had to go through endless papers and, as he did for George Fairfax, make numerous handwritten copies of letters that the latter had not received during the war.

By February 7, 1785, the general, searching hard for a secretary, was describing his burden to David Humphreys who was now in Paris: "What with letters (often of an unmeaning nature) from foreigners. Enquiries after Dick, Tom, and Harry who *may have been* in some part, or at *sometime* in the continental service. Letters, or certificates of service, for those who want to go out of their own States. Introductions; applications for copies of Papers; references of a thousand old matters with which I *ought* not to be troubled, any more than the Grand Mogul, but which must receive an answer of some kind, deprive me of my usual exercise; and without relief, may be injurious to me as I already begin to feel the weight, and oppression of it in my head, and am assured by the *faculty*, if I do not change my course, I shall certainly sink under it." At the same time, Washington pointed out to Humphreys that he had sent but two short notes from France and his next letter had better not be so "laconic."

Practically everyone Washington had ever met considered himself an old and dear friend and welcome at Mount Vernon. Friends and acquaintances brought or introduced strangers, sometimes so many that Washington did not even catch their names and wrote that, among others, Mr.— and Mr.— had dined with him. Even worse were those who dropped in without introduction. He sourly recorded: "A Mr. Martel (or some such name) a Frenchman came in and dined... A Person calling himself Hugh Patten dined here... A Count de Cheize D'Artingnon (so calling himself)" dropped in unannounced and made himself at home for two days.

Not everyone was even grateful. A twenty-two-year-old Dutch boy, Karel van Hogendorp, sent on by Jefferson, wrote that he had been very well entertained at Mount Vernon, but he had not liked the general, who was a cold person and quite stupid. Hogendorp's unconsciously revealing account indicates the suffering he imposed. He wrote that he had to carry on almost all the conversations with Mrs. Washington and her friends. He did the same with her husband, noting that the more he showed "vivacity and enthusiasm" in his talks, the more the general looked embarrassed. Hogendorp added that Washington seemed to have difficulty in following his shifts in topics, from which it would appear that he had turned his mind to other matters.

Washington wrote his mother that he seemed to be running "a well-resorted tavern." His genuine friends were as welcome as their letters but he had an enormous amount of chaff with his wheat and a heavy expense. At times there were as many as eighteen house guests. With the fifteen or more house servants, the place, as Washington also noted to his mother, was pretty noisy. This induced him, as soon as he had a secretary, to spend as much time as possible out of doors.

TO PHILADELPHIA

Washington had called a first general meeting of the Society of the Cincinnati for May 1784. Though he disliked leaving his house, its president had no choice but to make the long trip to Philadelphia. He left Mount Vernon by carriage on April 26, arriving in Philadephia on May 1. This was the day the American army had devoted to celebrating King Tammany, the Delaware chieftan and friend of liberty. After the war, societies of St. Tammany were organized in various American cities. The Philadelphia sons were delighted with the opportunity of firing noisy cannon on his arrival and drinking numerous healths to George Washington.

Washington faced a difficult problem at the meeting. There had been a loud uproar, fairly nationwide, against the society because of its hereditary membership, fear of a veterans organization, and the admission of foreigners.

Washington's initial reaction was that the society should be disbanded, but he finally decided that its motives were pure and it was needed for charitable aid to the widows and orphans of officers. He consulted at length with Jefferson, who was most fearful of the men who had fought so long for their country. Washington then suggested various changes in the charter to make it acceptable to all Americans. He asked that any political phrases in the constitution be stricken out, the hereditary descent be cancelled, and a separate French society be organized. His fellow officers, who had been distressed and surprised by the clamor, generally went along with his views and made changes in the national constitution. The state charters were not amended; the hereditary proposals of 1783 prevailed. Contrary to the fears of Jefferson, the society never became a political organization.

On his return trip to Virginia, Washington visited Washington College at Chestertown. The students presented a play about Sweden's hero: *Gustavus Vasa*. A few lines were tacked on the end, drawing attention from "Swedish woes" to the "more than Danish" fury which America had suffered. The actor pointed out that a Potomac hero "gave us PEACE, where War and Rapine raged." According to the official college report, "tears rolled from every eye and applause from every heart."

On June 2, back home, Washington wrote General Knox to say how impatient he had been to get to Mount Vernon after leaving Philadelphia on May 18. However, such were the difficulties of travel then, that he had had to wait from eight in the morning of May 20 to the following evening before he could cross the Chesapeake by ferry.

LAFAYETTE RETURNS

When Washington wanted someone to visit him, he was likely to be persuasive. He wrote to Charles Thompson, January 22, 1784, asking him as one of his "late Masters" in Congress to come and stay. He added: "Mrs. Washington, if she knew I was writing to you in the stile of Invitation would, I am certain, adduce arguments to prove that I ought to include Mrs. Thompson; but before she should have half spun the thread of her discourse, it is more than probable that I should have nonplused her, by yielding readily to the force of her reasoning."

For Madame de Lafayette, Washington prepared an effusion nearly as gallant as a French courtier might have mustered:

Madam: It is now, more than ever, I want words to express the sensibility and gratitude with which the honor of your felicitations... has inspired me. If my expression was equal to the feelings of my heart, the homage I am about to render you would appear in a more favourable point of view, than my most sanguine expectations will encourage me to hope for...

Great as your claim is... as the wife of my amiable friend to my affectionate regards... the charms of your person, and the beauties of your mind, have a more powerful operation. These, Madam, have endeared you to me, and every thing which partakes of your nature will have a claim to my affections. George and Virginia (the offspring of your love), whose names do honor to my Country and to myself, have a double claim...

Mrs. Washington... feels very sensibly the force of your polite invitation to Paris, but she is too far advanced in life, and is too much immersed in the care of her little progeny, to cross the Atlantic. This, My Dr. Marchioness, is not the case with you. You have youth... and must have a curiosity to see the Country, young, rude and uncultivated as it is; for the liberties of which your husband has fought, bled, and acquired much glory. Where every body admires, every body loves him. Come... and call my Cottage your home... You shall taste the simplicity of rural life. It will diversify the Scene and may give you a higher relish for the gaieties of the Court, when you return to Versailles...

Lafayette's wife, with three small children, decided against the trip, but the marquis, now raised by Louis XVI to be major general in the French army, arrived in New York in August. On his way south to Mount Vernon, he had a triumph nearly as great as Washington received wherever he went. He reached Mount Vernon on August 17, with letters from Chastellux and Rochambeau, and the talk of Europe. He could tell Washington of the dinner he attended where all the marshals of France stood and drank a toast to General Washington. Lafayette stayed till the end of the month. There is little documentation on the visit except Washington's reference to the "round of company" which prevented him from answering letters.

Washington met Lafayette again at Richmond, after the general had returned from his western trip, and brought him back to Mount Vernon on November 24. He sent a note to Henry Lee at Stratford to say how anxious the marquis was to see him and to come over, as soon as convenient, "prepared to stay a few days." Since Lafayette was about to return to France, Washington prepared letters to his friends there, including one to Madame de Lafayette: "The Marquis returns to you with all the warmth and ardour of a newly inspired lover. We restore him to you in good health, crowned with wreaths of love and respect from every part of the Union." Another went to Virginia de

Washington's Western Tour

PENNSYLVANIA

MARYLAND

Will's Creek

Frostburg

Cumberland

Old Town

Bath

N. Br. Potomac River

S. Br. Potomac River

Martinsburg

Romney

Harper's Ferry
Charlestown

Leesburg

Moorefield

Petersburg

Shenandoah River

N. Fork, Shenandoah River

S. Fork, Shenandoah River

VIRGINIA

Alexandria

Washington

Mt. Vernon

Colchester

Elk Run

Staunton

Culpeper

September 1784

Lafayette: "Permit me to thank my dear little correspondent for the favor of her letter of the 18th of June last, and to impress her with the idea of the pleasure I shall derive in a continuation of them. Her papa is restored to her with all the good health, paternal affections and honors her tender heart could wish. He will carry a kiss to her from me (which might be more agreeable from a pretty boy), and give her assurances of the affectionate regard with which I have the pleasure of being her well-wisher." He accompanied Lafayette as far as Annapolis, taking his final farewell on December 1. A week later he sent him a gloomy note:

> *In the moment of our separation... and every hour since, I felt all that love, respect and attachment for you, with which length of years, close connections and your merits have inspired me. I often asked myself... whether that was the last sight I ever should have of you? And tho' I wished to say no, my fears answered yes. I called to mind the days of my youth, and found they had long since fled to return no more; that I was now descending the hill I had been 52 years climbing, and that tho' I was blessed with a good constitution, I was of a short lived family, and might soon expect to be entombed in the dreary mansions of my fathers. These things darkened the shades and gave a gloom to the picture, consequently to my prospects of seeing you again; but I will not repine, I have had my day...*
>
> *It is unnecessary, I persuade myself, to repeat to you, my Dr. Marquis, the sincerity of my regards and friendship, nor have I words which could express my affection for you...*

Along with the letter, he sent another for Lafayette to take to France and give to Luzerne. In flowery language he expressed his appreciation for the special invitation, which had been extended him by the king and queen of France, to visit Versailles. He wrote: "I fear my vows and earnest wishes are the only tributes of respect I shall ever have it in my power to offer them in return."

Lafayette answered Washington as he was about to sail: "No, my beloved General, our late parting was not by any means a last interview. My whole soul revolts at the idea, and could I harbour it an instant, indeed, my dear General, it would make me miserable. I well see you will never go to France. The unexpressible pleasure of embracing you in my own house, of well coming you in a family where your name is adored, I do not much expect to experience. But to you, I shall return... My firm plan is to visit now and then my friends on this side of the Atlantick, and the most beloved of all friends I ever had, or ever will have... Adieu, adieu... it is with unexpressable pain that I feel I am going to be severed from you... Adieu, adieu."

With a growing family and troubles in France, Lafayette did not return to Mount Vernon for forty years. Mrs. Washington's grandson, George Washington Parke Custis, who had been only three when Lafayette departed, was there to receive him. At Washington's tomb, Custis delivered what was intended to be a moving oration. With the Custis knack for saying the wrong thing, he referred to Lafayette as a "setting sun," and invited him, as soon as he had set, to join Washington in the sepulchre. Lafayette murmured, in reply, that he had no words with which to express his feelings.

TRAVELLER AND REPORTER

By the time he reached Philadelphia for the Congress of 1774, Washington had covered more American territory than any delegate there. His military activities in the revolution carried him to nine of the thirteen states. Between 1784 and 1799 his travels took him westward again to the Ohio region and from Maine to Georgia. His diaries, which he resumed in the fall of 1784, and his letters contain lengthy reports of the political sentiments of the people, but his notes on their daily life are often far more interesting. It would be possible, from these alone, to construct a quite complete account of the economic and social life of late eighteenth-century America.

Washington wrote that mail took three to four days from Philadelphia to Alexandria in 1785. Scheduled stage coaches ran three times a week from Norfolk as far north as Portsmouth, New Hampshire. The stage took ten to twelve days from Richmond to Boston. There was a good wagon road, 150 miles west, from Alexandria to Cumberland. Most people preferred to travel south of Virginia by ship, since the roads and inns were so bad in the Carolinas and Georgia. Washington noted in the mid-eighties that meat prices fluctuated seasonally from a minimum of 3-1/2 to 5-1/2 cents a pound, horses sold for $8 to $30, cows for $12, flour for $18 a barrel, while whisky was 40 cents a gallon at Pittsburgh. Land cost $10 an acre near Mount Vernon and $3 an acre in western Pennsylvania. One hundred shad in season could be bought at Alexandria for $2.50. Wages for workmen ran around a dollar a day. His records indicate what books the principal booksellers were advertising, and the prices for staples, gloves, furniture, wallpaper, and Peale portraits.

Washington's years on the frontier let him converse as an equal with frontiersmen and Indians. He could gossip extensively with the farmers of the country and certainly did so from a great variety of notes he made on agriculture wherever he travelled. He was able to talk with manufacturers, for he had made cloth, bricks, flour, and brandy. He could chat with ferrymen, for he owned a ferry, as well as with horsemen, hunters, carpenters, gardeners, fishermen, soldiers, sailors, surveyors, and inventors, whose activities he had touched at some point in his career.

SIMPSON, CANALS, AND THE WEST

More than thirty years before, Lawrence Washington had noted that the closeness of the Potomac and Ohio Rivers would be significant in the development of the West. George Washington thereafter had travelled over much of the region and, at twenty-two, canoed the Potomac from Cumberland to the falls above Georgetown. By 1769 he was endeavoring to promote a series of lock canals to improve transport and communications westward. Subsequently he went west to the Kanawha River and made the first attempt at organized settlement there. After buying land in western Pennsylvania, he spent much capital attempting to increase wheat growing and milling in the region. He now turned back to his old dreams.

Washington, in Cambridge, had referred to the extreme "stupidity" of Gilbert Simpson, the miller who had drained his pockets pretty heavily, while offering one excuse after another. Nine years later, hardly back at Mount Vernon, he requested an accounting from Simpson on February 13:

> It now behooves me to look into my own private business, no part of which seems to call louder for attention, than my concerns with you. How profitable our partnership has been, you best can tell…
>
> [My reports indicate] I ought to have a good deal of wealth in your hands… All agree that it is the best Mill, and has had more custom than any other on the west side of the Alleghany Mountains; I expect something very handsome therefore from that quarter. I want a full settlement of this Account from the beginning, clearly stated [and] a full and complete settlement of our Partnership accounts… supported by vouchers… The world does not scruple to say that you have been much more attentive to your own interest than to mine. But I hope your Accots. will give the lie to these reports… and that you have acted like an honest, industrious and frugal man…

On April 27 Simpson replied with a note quite like the old ones. He complained about everything, the prevalence of smallpox, the troubles he had, and his lack of cash. He said that he resented Washington's letter and was therefore asking for "a settlement and a separation." He hoped there would be a "crown of bliss and felicity" reserved somewhere for the general and his wife.

The existing documentation is scanty but it appears that Simpson may have come to Mount Vernon, for he wrote Washington from the mill on July 31: "I got safely home and found everything well... there has been no rane... which has almost don for our corn our winter crops are very light." There followed more complaints. Meanwhile Washington had written Simpson that he intended to let the mill and land to someone else, for he could no longer tolerate such "waste of property and losses, as I have hitherto sustained by my partnership with you." At the same time Washington made enquiries about his other Pennsylvania lands and found that squatters, taking advantage of his long absence, had settled down on them and were beginning to think of ways to get permanent possession.

In early March, Jefferson wrote Washington a long letter outlining his views on opening navigation to the Ohio. Many of these coincided with Washington's thoughts. Jefferson noted that he had written the Virginia Assembly, asking if a few thousand pounds could be set aside for this purpose. He feared that public bodies would be slow and wasteful. Could not Washington crown his achievements by taking the lead in this enterprise? Washington did not quite say no. He had Jefferson's proposal in mind when he decided that his western lands and the Simpson mill needed personal inspection. He spent a good deal of time that summer getting ready for a trip west and in arranging for supplies and boats for the Ohio River. He invited his old friend, Dr. James Craik; his nephew, Bushrod Washington; and Craik's son, William, to go along. Three servants and six horses for Washington's use were with the party. As he began the trip on September 1, he also resumed his diary.

The party proceeded via Falls Church and Leesburg to Charles Town. Though Washington had his rent collection and other business with his tenants in Berkeley County, he spent a good deal of time asking his old friend, General Morgan, and many of the leading citizens, about roads and rivers west. At Bath (now Berkeley Springs) and Martinsburg, he repeated his enquiries on the principal branches and runs leading into the Potomac, Monongahela, Little Kanawha, Ohio, and Youghiogheny rivers.

At Berkeley Springs, Washington was a fascinated watcher of an early experiment by James Rumsey in improving water transport. Rumsey shares with John Fitch credit for the first steamboats, which they launched separately in 1787. At this time Rumsey was still experimenting with water-current–induced propulsion. According to Washington's diary, Rumsey made him swear to keep his secret. He then demostrated his model, which Washington found to run "prety swift... it might be turned to the greatest possible utility in inland Navigation; and in rapid currents." Washington gave Rumsey a certificate that the invention appeared highly useful. This much annoyed John Fitch who trotted to Mount Vernon, the following year, with his designs.

As Washington moved north from Berkeley Springs, he went over ground he had covered during his first western expedition, his first diplomatic mission, and his subsequent battles with the French and Indians. There was no introspection in his diary, which records notes of every conversation he had on roads, paths, creeks, runs, rivers, and obstacles to navigation, but nothing about the past.

Washington's first stop was with the eighty-two-year-old Thomas Cresap. It had been over 36 years since Washington, the youth with his love of trees and good land, had first visited Cresap's house, where he wrote his account of the "comical" and liquor-inspired Indian "War Daunce." From Cresap's he rode to old Fort Cumberland, over whose status Dinwiddie and Loudoun had caused him so much anguish, then up the old Braddock Road, which he had travelled with the redcoated army. The party moved on through the Shades of Death to Laurel Hill, where Washington had once expressed his fear that the Forbes army would lose its laurels. On they rode to the house of Thomas Gist, brother of Christopher Gist, who had accompanied the twenty-one-year-old Washington to Fort Le Boeuf. At the Gist house a tired young Washington had rested on his way back to Williamsburg. In anticlimax to the ride through the great scenes of his younger years, the general reached Simpson's mill on September 13. He found, contrary to the reports he had received at Mount Vernon, that the situation was a mess. He summed it up:

> ...I do not find the land in _general_ equal to my expectation of it—some part indeed is as rich as can be, some other part is but indifferent—the levellest is the coldest and of the meanest quality—that which is most broken is the richest; tho' some of the hills are not of the first quality.

> The Tenements with respect to the buildings are but indifferently improved—each have Meadow and are arable, but in no great quantity—the Mill was quite destitute of water—the works and House appear to be in very bad condition—and no reservoir of water—the stream as it runs, is all the resource it has—formerly there was a dam to stop the water; but that giving way, it is brought in a narrow confined and trifling Race... In a word little Rent, or good is to be expected from the present aspect of her.

Washington held a public auction for the disposal of his share of the Simpson stock but was disappointed in the proceeds, about £47, towards his total investment in the enterprise of around £1,200. He was forced to let the land for shares in wheat. In addition Washington held conferences with the squatters on his land at Washington's Bottom, west of Pittsburgh. Many had been living there rent-free for years. When he visited the area, everyone refused to deal with him and said that he could try to sue to make them leave. Washington was forced to do this but it necessitated an intensive search of old records in Pennsylvania and Virginia. Some of the latter had been destroyed in Benedict Arnold's raiding expeditions, but Washington was eventually able to establish his full right to the land through a court order.

While he was conducting his business at the mill, the commanding officer at Fort Pitt confirmed rumors Washington had picked up that the Indians along the Ohio were in an ugly mood. He was warned against travelling there and promptly cancelled his trip to the Kanawha, where his previous settlements had presumably been knocked out by Indians. On the rest of his trip he pretty well confined himself to investigations of the area's transport and land use. He wrote in his diary that he found much of the intelligence given him to be unreliable, either from ignorance or design. He mentioned that information on the best and shortest route for portage or roads was always by way of the informant's property. He diligently checked and cross-checked every statement and, wherever possible, made personal observations.

At Gist's settlement, the general decided that he, his nephew, and a guide would set off across wild and often trackless country to examine the tributaries to the Potomac and Ohio Rivers. On September 25 Washington "lodged," as he put it, on the ground in a heavy storm with only his cloak to cover him. That morning he rode through heavy rain and a wet and gloomy forest to a farmhouse, where he could get only boiled corn for breakfast. He rode high up and over the Allegheny Mountains and down a steep and dangerous path to the valley. Three days later an exhausted Washington spent an entire day resting at Fort Pleasant, "having had a very fatiguing journey thro' the Mountains, occasioned not more from the want of accomodation and the real necessaries of life than the showers of Rain which were continually falling and wetting the bushes—the passing of which, under these circumstances was very little better than swimming Rivulets."

On the trip Washington discovered that the source of the north branch of the Potomac, which flowed into the Chesapeake and then to the Atlantic Ocean, was only ten miles from the head of the Youghiogheny River, which flowed to the Ohio and on into the Mississippi. This confirmed what his long-dead brother, Lawrence, had surmised.

In five more days of riding, marred frequently by rain, Washington reached Mount Vernon October 4, having covered, by his usually accurate measurements, 680 miles in a little over a month. While the trip was still fresh in his mind, he added to his diary notes extensive computations on the general geography and the distances from Detroit to Philadelphia and Detroit to Richmond. To these he added a series of "reflections" on the facts he had gained. He noted how enthusiastic he had become about navigation on the Potomac. Virginia stretched to the Ohio River; there was an immense fertile country between the Blue Ridge and the Allegheny Mountains, "but how trifling when viewed upon that immeasurable scale which is inviting our attention!"—the great Ohio Valley. To bring its trade to the Potomac would be cheaper and simpler than to any point to the north. Crops grew in the area with ease but the people had no incentive to grow more than they needed, without good inland transportation to the seaboard and thence to foreign markets. With it, the area would be of immense economic, commercial, and political importance.

The United States, he went on to himself, was occupied on its flanks and rear by formidable powers who would do anything to win the trade and allegiance of these people. The western settlers "from my own observation—stand as it were on a pivot—the touch of a feather would almost incline them any way" (to the United States, Great Britain, or Spain). They would meet the United States more than halfway, if their country did its part. "Our clearest interest... is to open a wide door, and make a smooth way for the produce of that Country to pass to our Markets..." In short, transport and communications would cement the settlers forever to the American union and promote the country's economic development to the fullest.

POTOMAC NAVIGATION COMPANY

In writing to Jefferson, March 29, 1784, Washington expressed keen interest in resuming his earlier work on improving navigation westward on the Potomac River. He noted that, before the war, because Virginia's funds were limited, he had proposed a private joint-stock company. The legislature would not approve even a private company, unless the James River were included as a sop to those with interests there. Virginia could not move without Maryland. His bill ran into opposition at Annapolis, when the merchants of Baltimore became alarmed, "perhaps not without cause, at the consequence of Water transportation to George Town of the produce which usually came to their Market."

Although he complained to Jefferson about his prewar difficulties, Washington, refreshed and enthusiastic from his trip, decided once more to try his dream scheme. He did not quite realize that, this time, whatever he wanted from a legislature, he was almost certain to get. What emerged was a pioneer public–private corporation to promote economic growth. As a by-product,

Washington devised a mechanism for bringing states to act together on matters of common interest. In stages that are perceptible, Washington launched himself from directing a canal company to heading a nation.

Washington polished his notes six days later into a long letter to Benjamin Harrison, Virginia's governor. He suggested that the state give consideration to forming, jointly with Maryland, a public or private corporation, and to the appointment of a Maryland–Virginia commission to survey all means to open navigation and trade westward to the Ohio. The governor answered at once that he not only liked the plan but that Washington's letter was "so much more explicit than I could be" that he had handed it directly to the assembly. The members, he reported, seemed so impressed that he thought the survey would be quickly authorized. By the middle of November, Washington was in Richmond with Lafayette and orally reported his findings to the assembly. On January 10, James Madison sent Thomas Jefferson, in Paris, a letter on Washington's efforts:

> *...The earnestness with which he espouses the undertaking is hardly to be described, and shews that a mind like his, capable of great views, and which has long been occupied with them, cannot bear a vacancy; and surely he could not have chosen an occupation more worthy of succeeding to that of establishing the political rights of his Country than the patronage of works for the extensive and lasting improvement of its natural advantages; works which will double the value of half the lands within the Commonwealth, will extend its commerce [and] link its interest with those of the [future] Western States...*

The bill to establish the Potomac Navigation Company provided for a joint-stock company, with 500 shares at $440 each, and authorized the company to collect tolls at various points. It was proposed, if Maryland agreed, that both states spend public funds on the road, from the end of navigation to the Cheat River. Pennsylvania was to be asked to cooperate on a road to the Youghiogheny. Virginia also authorized an intrastate company to develop the James.

Washington's ideas were speedily implemented. By December 13 the act had been approved in principle, and Virginia commissioners were appointed to discuss the bill in Annapolis. Washington was made chairman of the delegation whose other members were General Gates and Thomas Blackburn. The former, to say the least, was a surprising appointment, but the members of the Virginia Assembly could hardly know all the internal politics of the American revolutionary army. (Washington wrote privately to Knox: "My bosom friend Genl. Gates, being at Richmond, contrived to edge himself into the Commission.")

Blackburn did not appear. Gates and Washington went to Annapolis, where Gates fell ill, leaving Washington with the whole negotiation. Much of the talk was on the complex question of tolls, whether they should be by weight, value, or a combination thereof. In addition, he agreed to Maryland's suggestion, which had not been in the original bill, that each state bear 10 percent of the cost by buying shares. On December 28 Washington wrote to Madison in Richmond: "The Bill passed this Assembly with only 9 dissenting voices; and got thro' both Houses in a day, so earnest were the members of getting it to you in time. It is now near 12 at Night, and I am writing with an aching head, having been constantly employed in this business since the 22d. without assistance from my Colleagues: Genl. Gates having been Sick the whole time, and Colo. Blackburn not attending."

Since the legislature at Richmond was scheduled to adjourn in the near future, Washington himself galloped back to Virginia with the papers. He wrote to Samuel Chase of Maryland on Januray 5: "When I found your Express at Mount Pleasant, and was unable to procure another in Marlbro', I commenced one myself, got home before dinner, and dispatched one of my servants to Hooes Ferry immediately. He placed the packet into the hands of the Express there waiting, before nine o'clock next morning; on Friday the business with ease might have been laid before the Assembly..."

On January 4 the bill was ratified by Virginia, which placed in the act an unexpected clause, presenting to General Washington the state's 10 percent of the Potomac company shares, and fifty shares in the James River company, in gratitude for his wartime services and for promoting so beneficial an act. On February 8 the books of the new company were open to public subscription. By summer the needed sums, for all practical purposes, were subscribed. The directors elected Washington president of the company, a job at which he spent long and active hours. Washington was, however, very "agitated" by the act of the Virginia legislature in awarding him the shares, since he wanted neither to accept them nor to offend his state. On January 22, 1785, he wrote the governor:

The attention and good wishes which the Assembly have evidenced by their act... are more than mere compliment; there is an unequivocal and substantial meaning annexed. But believe me sir, notwithstanding these, no circumstance has happened to me since I left the walks of public life, which has so much embarrassed me. On the one hand, I consider this act... as a noble and unequivocal proof of the good opinion, the affection, and disposition of my Country [Virginia] to serve me; and I should be hurt, if by declining the acceptance of it, my refusal should be construed into disrespect... or that an ostentatious display of disinterestedness or public virtue, was the source of the refusal... Not content then with the bare consciousness of having, in all this navigation business, acted upon the clearest conviction of the political importance of the measure; I would wish that every individual who may hear that it was a favorite plan of mine, may know also that I had no other motive for promoting it, than the advantage I conceived it would be productive of to the Union...

How would this matter be viewed then by the eye of the world; and what would be the opinion of it, when it comes to be related that G W—exerted himself to effect this work and G W—has received 20,000 dollars, and £5,000 Sterling of the public money as an interest therein?

There was much more to the letter. Washington said he would take the views of all his friends, prior to the next meeting of the assembly. He did so in long letters. Knox made the sensible suggestion that the stock be used for the widows and orphans of revolutionary war men in Virginia. Washington accepted the idea of putting the shares to a charitable purpose, but he eventually decided they should go to educational institutions. The Virginia Assembly passed a subsequent act empowering Washington to place them in trust for this purpose.

Maryland and Virginia appointed commissioners of high caliber. They often dropped in on Mount Vernon, conveniently located between Annapolis and Richmond. By March they had agreed so amicably that they decided to continue the meetings, in order to discuss trade and other related questions. Some of these involved Pennsylvania and Delaware, and it seemed natural to ask them to participate. Other states became interested. Congress was too weak to act on general matters but there was nothing to prevent individual states from asking for a meeting. A majority soon did so, and Congress then ratified the proposal. Thus Washington had sliced America's Gordian knot. When a date was set for all the states to meet in Constitutonal Convention, it seemed only right to ask the president of the Potomac Navigation Company to attend.

FARMER

The various Mount Vernon farms, amounting at their peak to over 8,000 acres, composed a more complex operation and employed more people than the United States government in its initial stages under the new constitution.

Before the war Washington had tried to introduce at Mount Vernon a more systematic agriculture than was generally employed in Virginia. After the revolution he decided that American agricultural practices were, at best, crude and primitive.

The country could not progress unless scientific methods were introduced and information on them widely disseminated. When Arthur Young, England's foremost agricultural expert and editor of the *Annals of Agriculture,* opened correspondence with him, Washington was delighted. He wrote Young on August 6, 1786:

> *Agriculture has ever been amongst the most favourite amusements of my life, though I never possessed much skill in the art, and nine years total inattention to it, has added nothing to a knowledge which is best understood from practice; but with the means you have been so obliging as to furnish me, I shall return to it (though rather late in the day) with hope and confidence.*

> *The System of Agriculture (if the epithet of system can be applied to it), which is in use in this part of the United States, is as unproductive to the practitioners as it is ruinous to the land-holders. Yet it is pertinaciously adhered to. To forsake it; to pursue a course of husbandry which is altogether different and new to the gazing multitude, ever averse to novelty in matters of this sort, and much attached to their old customs, requires resolution; and without a good practical guide, may be dangerous... Your Annals shall be this guide. The plan on which they are published, gives them a reputation which inspires confidence; and for the favor of sending them to me, I pray you to accept my very best acknowledgments. To continue them, will add much to the obligation.*

Washington followed with other critical remarks to Young on American agriculture, many sounding remarkably like those applied by twentieth-century agricultural experts to underdeveloped countries. Virginia, he wrote on November 1, 1787, was as backward in agricultural matters as any place in America. Tobacco, given first preference, had ruined the soil. For other crops, corn was always grown first, followed by wheat on the same soil,

> *after which the ground is respited (except from weeds, and every trash that can contribute to its foulness) for about eighteen months; and so on, alternately, without any dressing; till the land is exhausted; when it is turned out without being sown with grass seeds, or any method taken to restore it; and another piece is ruined in the same manner. No more cattle is raised than can be supported by lowland meadows, swamps, &ca; as very few persons have attended to sowing grasses, and connecting cattle with their Crops...Our lands, as I mentioned in my first letter to you, were originally very good; but use, and abuse, have made them quite otherwise.*

Washington ordered special English plows from Young, which he found very satisfactory, and numerous varieties of seeds. He followed his advice on barn-building. On the basis of Young's articles and his own experiments, he introduced practices of later centuries, such as green manuring, the prevention of soil erosion, and crop rotation. He tried various types of fertilizer, from the usual dung to river bottom muck and plaster of Paris. He wrote of his great variety of crops, including some from the tropics, most unsuitable to Virginia: papaws, pepper, oats, buckwheat, rye, barley, wheat, millet, spelt, flax, corn, beans, sweet and Irish potatoes, cabbages, pumpkins, carrots, asparagus, peas, turnips, parsnips, and Jerusalem artichokes. He also grew clover, luzerne, and vetches. To his food and fiber crops he added such fruit trees as pear, crab-apple, cherry, apricot, apple, plum, fig, and sour oranges.

Washington hired a farmer from England, James Bloxham, as his manager, but he wrote to Young that the Englishman could not adapt very easily to American conditions. He made no allowances for eight years of war and destruction and for the generally primitive methods. Washington said that Bloxham had been hired to improve cultivation. Had America been as advanced as England he would not have been needed.

Washington was probably mistaken in thinking his soil had once been good but had been ruined by bad practices. It most probably had never been of more than mediocre quality though it had certainly deteriorated over the years. Washington had the usual problems with the American climate, late sharp frosts after he had planted, too-heavy spring rains, followed by long periods of severe heat and drought. These peculiarities increased plant diseases, and he complained of rust, cheat, and speck, together with chinch bugs and the Hessian fly (which had made its appearance about the time of the arrival of German troops who got the blame for it). The area was also a source of human diseases. A nearby "Hell Hole" was a breeder of malarial mosquitoes, and the general and his fieldhands alike suffered from "agues and fevers."

From his description of stock-feeding practices, it would appear that Washington was one of the first Americans to sow ground covers and grasses for cattle feeding. His inventory of November 1785 indicated that he had 130 horses, 336 cattle, and 283 sheep. He was never able to count his pigs, since they ran wild, but the number was substantial, for in December of the same year, he killed and dressed 128 hogs, to yield nearly eight tons of meat.

There is no accurate account of the total number of persons living and working at Mount Vernon, but probably close to four hundred had to be fed and clothed whether crops were good or bad. The working force consisted of free and indentured whites and of Negro slaves. Of the 322 Negroes on the place, not much more than a third formed the working force, the rest being old, sick, or children. As many as 30 percent were in the skilled or semiskilled class: cooks, waiters, bricklayers, overseers, seamstresses, weavers, gardeners, and stonemasons. The rest were field hands. Among the whites, some of whom were working out their passage to America, were millers, brewers, coopers, blacksmiths, tailors, bricklayers, carpenters, and cradlers (mowers). In addition, seasonal labor was hired for harvesting and fishing. One physician was kept on a retainer to treat the workers, while Washington's own physician, Dr. James Craik, and others, were called in from time to time on serious cases. Although he had had to fire his miller for constant drinking (with regret because he was a good one), Washington could tolerate a certain amount of it, and did so with a gardener, Philip Bater. Under an agreement, signed by Washington and Bater on April 23, 1787, the latter was to be allowed:

> *Four dollars at Christmas, with which he may be drunk 4 days and 4 nights; two Dollars at Easter to effect the same purpose; two Dollars also at Whitsuntide, to be drunk two days...*

GIFTS

Washington was given some French hounds by Lafayette, which he trusted to the care of future President J. Q. Adams. The latter did not at all relish being kennelmaster across the Atlantic, even for Washington, but the dogs did reach Mount Vernon. The king of Spain also sent a gift which Washington was exceedingly anxious to have—a pair of jackasses which could breed both their own race and mules for heavy labor.

The king, perhaps unintentionally, was thrifty enough to pay their freight only to England. One jackass died at sea and the other reached Gloucester, Massachusetts. Washington named it Jack Ass before its arrival and sent an overseer to Boston in October 1784 to bring it to Mount Vernon, with its Spanish groom. Eventually he had a very large bill both from the sea captain who got it to America and for the expenses of the trip to Mount Vernon. There Jack Ass was renamed Royal Gift.

---

* The following trees, shrubs, and plants were recorded by Washington as having been planted by him at Mount Vernon in 1784–1787. They do not include food and fiber plants, which are listed in the text: Holly, English walnut, oak, hemlock, aspen, linden, hickory, elm, ash, pistachio, mahogany, palmetto, poplar, hickory, locust, maple, cedar, spruce, white pine, redbud, dogwood, catalpa, honey locust, persimmon, horse chestnut, cypress, chestnut, filbert, acacia, weeping and yellow willows, sassafras, mulberry, buckeye, pecan, and magnolia. Also hollyhock, yew, mock orange, lilacs, fringe tree, laurel, jasmine, blackhaw, honeysuckle, boxwood, and spicebush.

Though Washington wrote very solemn letters of thanks to the Spanish minister to the United States, the American minister at Madrid, and the Spanish foreign minister, behind the scenes there was some pretty unroyal humor about the animal. The following April Washington informed his nephew, Bushrod, that, thus far, Royal Gift had shown little inclination to administer to a plebeian race. He wrote Lafayette in May:

> *The Jack which I have already received from Spain in appearance is fine; but his late royal master [Charles III, aged seventy], tho' past his grand climacteric, cannot be less moved by female allurements than he is; or when prompted, can proceed with more majestic solemnity to the work of procreation.*

To Colonel Fitzhugh, who enquired about having his mares bred, he replied that, like the king, the jackass could hardly "perform seldomer," but he hoped that when Royal Gift "becomes a little better acquainted with republican enjoyments, he will amend his manners, and fall into our custom of doing business." Richard Sprigg, who had a small jenny, which was not of as good quality as the Spanish, sent her over to the Washington farm. This time Royal Gift was successful. Washington wrote Sprigg on June 28: "Tho' in appearance quite unequal to the match, yet, like a true female, she was not to be terrified at the disproportionate size of her paramour, and having renewed the conflict twice or thrice, it is to be hoped the issue will be favourable." The Sprigg jenny foaled a jack, the first of this breed in America.

Washington asked a ship, which anchored off Mount Vernon in order to pick up flour for sale in Surinam, to buy a jenny for him there. This seems to have been the source of the one he acquired by late June. He noted that she finally inspired Royal Gift to administer to his mares and thus to breed mules for farm work. More jacks and jennies arrived from Malta, gifts of Lafayette, and Washington was able to advertise stud services. The new Washington breed performed more work, on less feed, than horses, and was invaluable to the new country.

LANDSCAPE ARCHITECT

Over the previous forty years Washington had often expressed his love of trees. (His references to birds, however, describe only their destructive work on his crops and fruit trees.) To Sir Edward Newenham, member of the Irish Parliament for Dublin, he wrote on April 20, 1787:

The manner in which you employ your time at Bell Champ (in raising nurseries of fruit, forest trees, and Shrubs) must not only contribute to your health and amusement, but it is certainly among the most rational avocations of life; for what can be more pleasing than to see the works of one's own hands, fostered by care and attention, rising to maturity in a beautiful display of those advantages and ornaments which, by the combination of Nature and taste of the projector... is always regaling to the eye...

I should have much pleasure in admiring your skill in the propagation and disposal of these things in a visit to Bell Champ, but declining health and an anxious wish to spend the remainder of my days in retirement will fix me to Mount Vernon.

Washington, from his wartime headquarters, had often sent anxious enquiries and instructions to Lund Washington on the planting of trees and shrubs around his gardens. With the spring of 1785, he was free to indulge the hobby which he called his "innocent amusement." Much of his diary records are devoted to his planting. His letters teem with polite requests to everyone he knew from New York to South Carolina and in Madeira, France, Ireland, and England to send him seeds for his botanical garden. With his artistic eye, he could blend the best of nature with the best of man. His views were practical— never move a tree or shrub that had grown in a forest, into the open, for it would not adjust—and esthetic—he thought his arrangement of white dog-wood in a circle around the flowering redbud or Judas tree to be "very pretty." He ended up with an extraordinary variety of trees and shrubs, though he mentioned few flowers.[*] Some were native plants which he used entirely for decorative effects. The more exotic ones he put into his botanical garden. To this he added a greenhouse, as well as a sweeping grass bowling green, in the middle of the carriage approach to Mount Vernon.

VISITORS

Visitors of infinite variety continued to pour in. "A Mr. Noah Webster" and Mason Weems, who were each to gain a certain immortality, came to call. John Fitch dropped by to explain his steamboat. Old army comrades, Lee and Lincoln, visited him; Madison and Monroe appeared to discuss state and national problems. The governors of Maryland and Virginia sought his advice. The head of the Pennsylvania Cincinnati brought him 250 diplomas to sign. The "celebrated Mrs. Macauley Graham," a formidable Whig authoress, arrived from England.

The writers who came failed to leave adequate impressions of Mount Vernon, but two visiting merchants did so. One was an Englishman, Robert Hunter, who came with Richard Henry Lee on November 16, 1785. Hunter, who considered Washington "the first man in the world," was enthusiastic about him as farmer and landscaper. He wrote:

I... took a walk about the General's grounds, which are really beautifully laid out. He has about 4,000 acres, well cultivated, and superintends the whole himself. Indeed, his greatest pride now is to be thought the first farmer in America. He is quite a Cincinnatus, and often works with his men himself; strips off his coat and labours like a common man.

The General has a great turn for mechanics. It's astonishing with what niceness he directs everything in the building way, condescending even to measure the things himself, that all may be perfectly uniform. The style of his house is very elegant, something like the Prince de Condé's at Chantilly... only not quite so large... He is making a most delightful bowling green before the house... The situation is a heavenly one, upon one of the finest rivers in the world. I suppose I saw thousands of wild ducks upon it...What makes it still more pleasing is the amazing number of sloops that are constantly sailing up and down the river...

By then, Washington had a secretary, William Shaw, who did not stay very long, but who told Hunter something about Washington's life. Shaw mentioned the astonishing numbers of letters that poured in from all over. Washington got up before sunrise and, after spending part of the morning answering them, rode out to superintend his farms. He dined at three and then spent two or more hours on his accounts and letters until tea time. He often worked thereafter until bed at nine. Because the Lees were there, Washington gave more than his usual time to relaxing in company. The delighted Hunter wrote:

At three, dinner was on the table... very neat and plain. The General sent the bottle about pretty freely after dinner, and gave success to the navigation of the Potomac for his toasts, which he has very much at heart, and when finished will, I suppose, be the first river in the world...

After tea General Washington retired to his study... If he had not been anxious to hear the news of Congress from Mr. Lee, most probably he would not have returned to supper but gone to bed at his usual hour, nine o'clock—for he seldom makes any ceremony. We had a very elegant supper about that time. The General with a few glasses of champagne got quite merry and, being with his intimate friends, laughed and talked a good deal…We had a good deal of conversation… about Congress, the Potomac, improving the roads, etc. At twelve I had the honour of being lighted up to my bedroom by the General himself.

An earlier visitor that year had been an American merchant, Elkanah Watson, who arrived on January 23. Watson had heard George III make the speech to Parliament, which had brought the king so much misery and Washington so much joy. He could hardly have failed to entertain the Washingtons with an account of it. Watson appeared when the family was dining and wrote: "This was the first time I had contemplated him in his private relations. I observed a peculiarity in his smile, which seemed to illuminate his eye; his whole countenance beamed with intelligence, while it commanded confidence and respect. I found him kind and benignant in the domestic circle, revered and beloved by all around him… Smiling content animated and beamed on every contenance in his presence."

Watson had arrived with a bad cold. When he got to bed that night he started coughing heavily. A little while later he noticed a lighted candle in his room. Washington was by his bedside with hot tea, a gesture which greatly moved the twenty-six-year-old Watson.

Washington talked at length of his canal schemes and of the need to open the West. Watson added: "Hearing little else, for two days, from the persuasive tongue of this great man, I was, I confess, completely under the influence of the canal mania, and it kindled all my enthusiasm." According to Washington's diary records, Watson stayed only one night at Mount Vernon but the effect was lasting. He became one of the leaders in the promotion of canals in New York State, helped to organize the Erie canal, and forty years after his visit wrote a history of his state's canal system.

Washington told Watson a funny story about one of his visitors, Joseph Wright, a minor artist, and son of the American, Patience Wright, who, during the war, ran both a wax museum and an intelligence service for Washington in London. Wright asked to make a medallion of Washington, and the rather reluctant general agreed to let his face be covered with plaster. Washington went on: "Whilst in this ludicrous attitude, Mrs. Washington entered the room, and seeing my face thus over spread with the plaster, involuntarily exclaimed. Her cry excited in me a disposition to smile, which gave my mouth a slight twist or compression of the lips, that is now observable in the busts Wright afterwards made."

Virginia and Congress had each decided that the best artist in Europe should be engaged to execute a statue of Washington but only the state carried the project to completion. Virginia's governor asked Jefferson to do the selecting, and he replied on January 12, 1785, that there was no question who should be employed, "the reputation of Monsr. Houdon... being unrivalled in Europe." He had consulted the sculptor who "was so anxious to be the person who should hand down the figure of the General to future ages, that without hesitating a moment he offered to abandon his business here, to leave the statues of kings unfinished, & to go to America to take the true figure."

The following October 2 Washington and his wife were awakened by a clatter downstairs. It was Jean-Antoine Houdon, who had arrived from Alexandria by water, with three assistants and an interpreter. Everyone knows the intelligent and sensitive face of Washington, as executed by Houdon, but neither the general nor the artist left more than scanty records of the meeting. Fortunately the visit made a lifelong memory for Nelly Custis, Martha Washington's six-year-old granddaughter. Martha had involuntarily exclaimed a little less than two years before, on seeing her husband covered with plaster by Joseph Wright. The horrified Nelly one day saw the general laid out on a table, covered with a sheet, and immediately assumed he was a corpse. She went into the room and found Houdon "engaged in putting on plaster to form the cast. Quills were in the nostrils. I was very much alarmed until I was told that it was a bust, a likeness of the general and would not injure him." This letter, acquired by Mount Vernon, was the first documentary evidence that their clay bust was made from a life mask.

On October 17 Houdon left by the stage for Philadelphia, and Washington for a meeting of directors of the Potomac Company. The two never met or corresponded again but Houdon's son-in-law stated the visit to Mount Vernon always shone for him "with special radiance." By the time his statue reached Richmond in 1796, Washington's national views had won him an intense hatred in his own state.

On July 30, 1785, Washington noted in his diary that he had "dined with only Mrs. Washington, which I believe is the first instance of it since my retirement from public life." On August 6, 1786, he wrote that he was "at home all day without Company."

On May 29, 1786, Tobias Lear, an honors graduate of Harvard, who had been cordially recommended by the president of the college and by General Lincoln, arrived at Mount Vernon. He had been engaged at a salary of $200 a year to be Washington's private secretary and tutor to Mrs. Washington's grandchildren. It was a fortunate choice for the general, since Lear stayed with him until 1793, and then returned to Mount Vernon after Washington's presidency.

LIFE AND DEATH

Death was ever-present in the eighteenth century, and it struck hard at the Washington family and friends. Four months after her husband returned to Mount Vernon, Martha Washington had news of the death of her mother and brother. On August 1, 1786, Washington wrote Jefferson in Paris:

You will probably have heard of the death of Genl Greene before this reaches you, in which case you will, in common with your Countrymen, have regretted the loss of so great and so honest a man. Gen. McDougall, who was a brave Soldier and a disinterested patriot is also dead... Colo. Tilghman, who was formerly of my family, died lately and left as fair a reputation as ever belonged to a human character. Thus some of the pillars of the revolution fall. Others are mouldering by insensible degrees. May our Country never want props to support the glorious fabrick!

In early 1787, Washington learned of the death of his favorite brother, John. He was always a little gloomy whenever he heard of the deaths of younger people and also when he fell ill. At the beginning of September 1786 he himself had a severe attack of malaria which he dosed heavily with quinine. It was accompanied by so bad an eruption on his face that, for days, he had to use scissors rather than a razor for his whiskers. This was followed soon afterwards by what he described as severe rheumatic pains which he had never previously experienced. These plagued him for months. Not long before he was to set off for the Constitutional Convention, he complained that he was hardly able to turn in bed or raise his hand to his head.

While death and illness were around, there were always new people coming up. Martha's grandchildren and quantities of nieces and nephews on both sides gave the general and his wife plenty to do, much joy, and many headaches. Martha Washington was totally maternal by instinct and spoiled all children, though her granddaughter, Nelly, complained that she was stricter with her than with her brother. Washington thundered at them when they did wrong and was extraordinarily kind and playfully humorous when they behaved. Nelly was his favorite. She wrote, after his death, how often she had made him laugh in "sympathy with my joyous and extravagant spirits." Her brother became a problem child, as his father had been before him, and Washington commented that he seemed to be able to command men, but not boys.

Washington saw to the education of two nephews, sons of his dead brother, Samuel, by placing them in school at Georgetown. They ran up such high bills that he removed them to Alexandria. One of them, George Steptoe

Washington, was subsequently reprimanded by his uncle for "disobedience, Perverseness, [and] disobliging conduct." Another nephew, Fielding Lewis, Jr., was chided for "your disrespectful conduct towards me, in coming into this country and spending weeks therein without ever coming near me." He summed up his niece, Harriott Washington: "She dabs her clothes in every hole and corner." Nonetheless, he spent a great deal of individual time and effort to see them brought up and educated. Another nephew, George Augustine Washington, who had served in the war as Lafayette's aide but had acquired the Washington family's tuberculosis, was sent on a long and expensive trip to the West Indies to recover his health. Washington was delighted when he married Martha Washington's niece, Fanny Bassett, and had them live at Mount Vernon. He also took care to see that another nephew, Bushrod, received the best legal education. Others were given loans or grants which Washington could not afford, plus advice or help.

Mount Vernon was something of a matrimonial bureau, for not only did Martha's niece marry George's nephew, and Tobias Lear marry two of Martha's nieces (one having died), but Martha also married her granddaughter to another nephew of Washington. Martha made sure there would always be a plentiful supply of babies for a growing country, leaving to her husband the task of achieving a peaceful nation in which they could grow up.

ENEMIES, FOREIGN AND DOMESTIC

No very certain figures exist of the number of American-born Tories who left for Canada, Nova Scotia, or Great Britain. Certainly many of the refugees were British-born officials, placemen, or merchants, while numerous Americans who fled to England during the war years returned quietly after the peace. They and others who had remained gradually forgot the past, settled down to be republicans, and intermarried with the patriots. Consequently many a daughter of the revolution is also a daughter of a united empire loyalist.

In determining policy for Quebec and Nova Scotia, the British government took care to see that no revolution could happen again. The existing inhabitants were given short shrift. In Nova Scotia Tories took command of the council and of the lower house. For Canada (a word largely meaning Quebec), the British government appointed a military governor, Sir Guy Carleton, former commander at New York, after making him Baron Dorchester. Lord Beauchamp remarked at the time: "Peers are made by dozens. The King, nobody knows why, has put Carleton into the list."

Carleton kept power in his hands, until he could arrange for its sharing with

Tories who could be trusted. He appointed lifetime councillors from their ranks. To free the crown and church from dependence on local revenues, he reserved one-seventh of the land for each of these bodies. He made additional generous land grants to those who fled the United States. By the time assemblies were permitted in upper and lower Canada, control was in the hands of crown, church, and gentry. British policies contrasted strongly with those established by Congress in the Northwest Ordinances of 1785 and 1787. These provided for the carving of new territories into acreage for public sale and settlement, the reservation of part of the land to finance public schools, and the establishment of new and fully equal states, when a territory had 60,000 people.

Lord Dorchester had an even more important task than setting back the Canadian clock. This was to reinstitute a hostile policy designed once more to keep Americans behind the Alleghenies. Britain had already refused to make a commercial treaty with the United States, while an order in council excluded American shipping from the West Indies trade. Dorchester, before leaving New York, had written that the United States seemed unlikely to survive as an independent power. George III, that same year, predicted that it would be many years before America, without a monarch, would have a stable government.

As governor of Canada, Dorchester commanded the British forts still held on American territory. Using these as cover, he promoted Indian attacks against the defenseless western settlements. John Jay, the American foreign secretary, remarked that Dorchester could easily outbuy the Indians, since the United States was so poor. Henry Knox, the war secretary, could do little, with his few hundred troops, to guard thousands of miles of frontier. When Prince William visited Canada in 1787, Dorchester took him to a great Indian council at Montreal. The prince wrote to George III that they said how pleased they were to see in him the same blood as their "Great Father in the East." They hoped he would again view them as his "favoured children," after the evil late rebellion in the south.

The only valid excuse which Britain could muster for holding forts on American territory lay in the failure to settle the prewar commercial debts owed by Americans to her merchants. When Jefferson visited Adams in London in 1786, the pair devoted much time to discussions with Duncan Campbell, chairman of the merchant group. Jefferson pointed out that America wanted to meet her just debts but the country had been ravished by a long war and needed time to pay. While there were differences on wartime interest, every sign appeared that they would reach an amicable agreement. Campbell went off happily to talk to the British secretary of state. He never again appeared. Jefferson assumed that the proposals had been overruled by the British government, which needed a reason to hold the posts.

Dorchester reestablished a British secret service system in the United States under his aide, Major John Beckwith, who had been assistant to John André. Its aim was to win friends for Great Britain, to get all useful intelligence, and to detach Vermont, Kentucky, and the territories north of the Ohio from American control. In 1787 Beckwith informed Quebec and London that William Smith, president of Columbia College and a member of Congress, told him the United States government was held in such contempt from Maine to Georgia that there was hardly an American who did not long to see monarchy restored.

In the meantime, while Spain was also holding American forts and stirring up Indian attacks in Tennessee and Georgia, a little American revolution broke out in New England, where British trade restrictions had caused a recession, Massachusetts, at the same time, reverted to a specie system which brought hardship to her western farmers who found their debts multiplying, while their produce sank in value. To the annoyance of Samuel Adams, now grown more conservative, the courts were closed, committees of correspondence were established, and armed rebellion, led by Daniel Shay, broke out. General Benjamin Lincoln, Washington's former officer, smashed the disorder with state militia. In New Hampshire, the state's president, General Sullivan, also had to call out the militia to establish peace. The Canadian government, carefully watching these developments, told the Indian nations to be patient and wait for the breakup of the American union.

WASHINGTON COMMENTS

Although the general wrote Jefferson in 1786 that he did not have much opportunity to get news, since he was mostly working on his canals and farms, this was only rhetoric. David Humphreys, who visited him the following year, said that Mount Vernon was the focal point for all New World intelligence. Washington kept himself well informed on domestic and international developments, while his own western visit had shown him how fragile were the ties of the settlers there to the United States.

As early as August 11, 1784, he noted to Jacob Read: "Tho' it is undoubted that the British Cabinet wish to recover the United States to a dependence on that Government; yet I can scarce think they ever expect to see it realized... unless *our* want of wisdom, and perserverance in error, should in their judgement render the attempt certain... Her prospect of success must diminish as our population increases, and the government becomes more consistent; without the last of which, indeed, anything may be apprehended... Nothing,

I confess, would sooner induce me to give credit to a hostile intention on the part of G. B., than their continuing (without the shadow of reason, for I really see none) to withhold the Western Posts... and sending... Sir Guy Carleton over as Viceroy..."

By June 30, 1785, he was writing George Fairfax in England: "With respect to the commercial system which G. B. is pursuing... the Ministers, in this as in other matters, are defeating their own ends, by facilitating those powers in Congress which will produce a counteraction of their plans, and which half a century without, would not have invested the body with. The restriction of our trade, and the additional duties which are imposed upon many of our staple commodities, have put the commercial people of this country in motion; they now see the indispensable necessity of a general *controlling* power, and are addressing their respective Assemblies to grant this to Congress." Following Knox's report to him of the troubles in Massachusetts, he replied on December 26, 1786:

> *I feel, my dear Genl. Knox, infinitely more than I can express to you, for the disorders which have arisen in these States, Good God! who besides a tory could have forseen, or a Briton predicted them! were these people wiser than others, or did they judge us from the corruption and depravity of their own hearts? The latter I am persuaded was the case, and that notwithstanding the boasted virtue of America, we are far gone in everything ignoble and bad...*

> *That G. B. will be an unconcerned Spectator of the present insurrections (if they continue) is not to be expected. That she is at this moment sowing the Seeds of jealousy and discontent among the various tribes of Indians on our frontier admits of no doubt, in my mind. And that she will improve every opportunity to foment the spirit of turbulence within the bowels of the United States, with a view to distracting our governments, and promoting divisions, is, with me, not less certain... We ought not therefore to sleep nor to slumber. Vigilance in watching, and vigour in acting, is, in my opinion, become indispensably necessary...*

CALL TO CONVENTION

Virginia, after its meeting with Maryland, invited other states to discuss trade regulations. Under the leadership of Madison, joined by Hamilton of New York, commissioners from Virginia, Pennsylvania, New Jersey, New York, and Delaware, met at Annapolis in September 1786. Washington, though ill, wrote Colonel John Fitzgerald on September 9: "Have the Commercial

Commissioners met? Have they proceeded to business? How long is it supposed their sessions will last? and is it likely they will do anything effectual?"

The meeting, five days later, called unanimously for a general convention of the states to meet the second Monday in May 1787 to "render the constitution of the federal government adequate to the exigencies of the Union." It was a successful call, so much so that seven states had selected their delegates, before Congress got around to approving the resolution in February.

On December 6 the new governor of Virginia, Edmund Randolph, notified Washington that Virginia was sending an exceedingly strong representation to Philadelphia. To lend the delegation, as Madison put it, "a very solemn dress and all the weight which could be derived from a single state," General Washington, by unanimous vote of the assembly, had been chosen chairman. When the list of delegates from America's largest state was printed throughout the country, HIS EXCELLENCY GENERAL WASHINGTON was automatically capitalized. The second largest state, Pennsylvania, selected its president, Benjamin Franklin, as her chairman, and the choices seemed good omens for the meeting.

Washington was not at all sure he would go. First and foremost in his mind was that, by odd chance, the triennial meeting of the Cincinnati had been called to meet in Philadelphia the first Monday in May 1787. On October 31 Washington had written to all the state societies, declining again to be president and explaining that he could not attend, since it was becoming more and more inconvenient for him to be absent from his farms:

> *The numerous applications... which are made to me in consequence of my military command; the multiplicity of my correspondences... the variety and perplexity of my private concerns... the arduousness of the task, in which I have been... engaged, of superintending the opening of the navigation of the great rivers in this State; the natural desire of tranquility and relaxation from business, which almost every one experiences at my time of life... and the present imbecility of my health, occasioned by a violent attack of the fever and ague succeeded by rheumatic pains... will, I doubt not, be considered as reasons of sufficient validity to justify my conduct in the present instance.*

The same reasons operated in Washington's mind when the governor's notification arrived. To these were added a recollection of his 1783 statement that he was withdrawing forever from public office, as well as the idea that his former officers would be greatly chagrined, if he attended one meeting and not the other. He sent a candid letter to Madison explaining also that the failure of many of the state societies of the Cinncinnati to amend their charters, to remove hereditary membership, made his situation especially "delicate."

Washington wrote Randolph on December 21 that in all probability he would not be able to attend and it would be better for Virginia to select someone else. The governor on January 4 replied that he and the council had decided to leave Washington's name as it was. "Perhaps the obstacles now in view may be removed before May; and the nomination of a successor, if necessary at all, will be as effectually made some time hence as now. Perhaps too (and indeed I fear the event) every other consideration may seem of little weight, when compared with the crisis, which may then hang over the United States."

Beyond every argument which he could convey to his friends was one he was too embarrassed to mention. He was in such critical need of money that he could not meet his taxes. His total efforts to restore his farms and income and to make up for nine years of neglect were far from succeeding. When his mother applied for money, he wrote her on February 15, 1787:

> *In consequence of your communication to George [Augustine] Washington of your want of money, I... send you 15 guineas, which believe me is all I have, and which indeed ought to have been paid many days ago to another...I have now demands upon me for more than 500, three hundred and forty odd of which is due for the tax of 1786; and I know not where or when, I shall receive one shilling with which to pay it... Those who owe me money cannot or will not pay it without suits, and to sue is to do nothing; whilst my expenses... for the absolute support of my family and the visitors who are constantly here, are exceedingly high; higher indeed than I can support without selling part of my estate, which I am disposed to do, rather than run in debt... but this I cannot do, without taking much less than the lands I have offered for sale are worth...*

In early March he was asking through his friends whether, if he did not go, he might be considered as not a warm republican. On March 28 he informed the governor that so many people seemed anxious for him to attend that, if his health permitted, he had about decided to participate. Once over the hurdle of decision, he was able to write to James Madison on March 31 with something of his old vigor: "It gives me great pleasure to hear that there is probability of a full representation of the States in Convention... My wish is that the Convention may adopt no temporizing expedient, but probe the defects of the constitution to the bottom, and provide radical cures; whether they are agreed to or not; a conduct like this, will stamp wisdom and dignity on the proceedings..."

On April 27, Washington wrote Knox that, though his arm was still in a sling, he had been getting ready to get to Philadelphia in time for the Cincinnati meeting. He had just had word of the critical illness of his mother and sister and was setting off for Fredricksburg and was therefore forwarding the papers needed for the meeting. The alarms turned out to be exaggerated, and he returned to Mount Vernon. On May 3 he rode over all his plantations with his nephew and new manager, George Augustine, explaining his management problems.

On May 9, 1787, shortly after sunrise Washington left Mount Vernon to cross the Potomac to Maryland. That night he recorded that he had a violent headache and sick stomach and had to rest at Elkridge. Two nights later high winds delayed his crossing of the Susquehanna, forcing him to spend the night at Havre de Grace. At Chester, May 13, he found the officers of the Cincinnati, who had been waiting impatiently to escort their president into Philadelphia.

FOUR

THE CONSTITUTION ADOPTED

1787–1788

I T IS PROBABLY not true that the only duty performed by the elect Light Horse Troop of Philadelphia was that of escorting General Washington into and out of the city. As they had done for twelve years, they welcomed and saluted him on May 13 as he rode into town with three of his revolutionary generals. The guns boomed, the church bells chimed, and great crowds were out at the boarding house of Mrs. House, where he had engaged rooms. He was mercifully spared any speeches. Mr. and Mrs. Robert Morris "warmly and kindly pressed" him to come and be more comfortable at their house a few doors away. He accepted; while his baggage was being removed to the Morris house, he rode off to call on the president of Pennsylvania, Doctor Franklin. This was their first meeting since 1775.

Washington had once before had a long and dreary wait in Philadelphia for Lord Loudoun, the British commander in chief. Now he passed boring days without his wife (who, he said, had become much too domestic to travel again), waiting for the various state delegations to show up. It had been a hard winter; the primitive roads were in bad condition, and travel was slower than ever. On his arrival only two states were represented—Pennsylvania and Virginia. The following day therefore he attended the Cincinnati, where he was unanimously reelected president.

By May 18 there was still no quorum. Washington recorded that he dined that day at a club, had tea with the Morrises, then went with Mrs. Morris "and some other ladies to hear a Mrs. O'Connell read (a charity affair). The lady being reduced in circumstances had had recourse to this expedient to obtain a little money. Her performance was tolerable." By Sunday he was reduced to visiting the Morrises' country farm. On Monday he dined "at Mr. Bingham's in great splendor." On May 23 he again rode into the country. In the afternoon he dined at Mr. Chew's and "drank tea there in a very large circle of ladies."

While waiting, Washington wrote long and anxious letters to George Augustine Washington, urging him, because of his health, not to work too hard, but at the same time forwarding detailed questions on every aspect of his farming operations. He added that he had bought and was forwarding Mrs. Washington's buckles and knives, and he asked George to send up his new umbrella.

THE CONVENTION

The representatives from states as far as South Carolina having reached Philadelphia, New Jersey managed to get its delegates across the Delaware on May 25. This made a quorum of seven states, and the convention proceeded to business.

The host state, Pennsylvania, had agreed to nominate Washington as president, with Franklin as sponsor. The latter was too ill to appear, and Robert Morris, Washington's host, had the honor. John Rutledge of South Carolina seconded the nomination and, since he was present, suggested that it not be discussed but be made unanimous. This was immediately done, and Morris and Rutledge escorted Washington to the president's seat. This was the chair, with its gilded sun on the back, used by every president of Congress and which is still in Independence Hall.

The country had as usual given a reluctant Washington a particularly gruelling job. This one was to last for almost four months, during one of the hottest summers on record. Some idea of what it involved may be gathered from Clinton Rossiter's estimate that the six delegates who talked the most made 900 speeches. Washington had to hear every one, many doubtless repetitive. Never has a future president received such an education in constitutional law and in diversity of opinion.

Washington made one of his usual little talks, expressing his thanks for the honor, his lack of qualifications, and his hope that the convention would indulge his errors. From then on he presided with grace and no known errors. The convention, after imposing total secrecy on its members, elected a committee composed of Hamilton, Charles Pinckney, and Chancellor Wythe to formulate rules and orders. Rhode Island, the smallest state, had refused to attend and, for its intransigence, was called Rogue Island in Boston. Other delegates subsequently straggled in. Not till June 2 were twelve states represented by a quorum of their delegates.

The French chargé d'affaires, Louis Otto, after reading a list of the members, informed the French foreign minister that even Europe had never seen "an assembly more respectable for the talents, knowledge, disinterestedness, and patriotism of those who compose it." Otto's observations were especially noteworthy, for France was also having a convention to consider constitutional and fiscal reform, the Assemblé des Notables, which Lafayette promptly dubbed the "not-ables."

The American convention was extraordinary for the diversity of experience of its members, who had often combined three or more careers. Thirty-two of the fifty-five had served in some capacity in the military forces, ranging from chaplain to commander in chief. Four had been on Washington's personal staff. Two were war governors of states devastated by the British. Forty-two men had served in the Continental Congress, and two had been its president. Eight had signed the Declaration of Independence. Practically every man from Washington down had also been in his colonial or state government, and many had worked on revising their own state constitutions after independence. A majority had enjoyed a college education at home or abroad. Princeton topped the list with nine graduates including James Madison, Jr., who had done much homework in preparation for the event. Harvard came in fourth after Yale and William and Mary.

New York State, then fifth in population, sent the oddest delegation. Washington's old and trusted friend, Governor George Clinton, was opposed to more than modest changes in the Articles of Confederation, since his state was happy in taxing products moving to the port of New York. Clinton arranged that two men, Robert Yates and John Lansing, Jr., who were opposed to any newfangled laws, be a majority for New York at the convention. In a complication arising from New York political intrigue, Alexander Hamilton was added to the group. Both Yates and Lansing did oppose the federal plan and then, seeing the convention move far from their position, withdrew in early July.

Hamilton, in his turn, made what was easily the most inept proposal to the convention. On June 18 he advocated a lifetime president to be elected by electors who, in turn, had been elected by electors, who had been chosen by the voters. The president was to appoint all state governors. Senators were to be elected for life by electors, while the lower house was to be chosen by the people. Congress was to be permitted to pass all "laws whatsoever," subject only to executive veto. Hamilton drew up a "constitution" modeled on his proposal which is noteworthy only for its clumsiness. There have been various conjectures as to why Hamilton left the convention on June 29, not to return again until August. It appears most likely that his effort at constitution making, having fallen with a dull thud, caused him to depart in high dudgeon. He remarked to Washington in a letter of July 10 that his attendance there seemed to be "a waste of time." From July 10 on New York was either unrepresented, or had but one man present, and therefore had no quorum and no vote.

With secrecy imposed, Washington's diary automatically became mum as to the proceedings. In the absence of news, some gazettes republished Washington's 1783 "Circular to the States," which pleaded for national union. A wild rumor appeared in the press that the convention had chosen a younger son of George III to be king. The convention authorized a public statement that a monarchy had never been considered. Benjamin Franklin got a mild chiding from one of the delegates for nearly revealing state secrets when, with others present in his garden, he exhibited a two-headed snake and began humorously comparing it with the problem of choosing one or two branches of Congress. In far-off Paris, Jefferson denounced the secrecy, perhaps because of an inordinate curiosity as to what was happening.

James Madison had brought to Philadelphia an outline of a proposed new constitution to substitute for the old Articles of Confederation. He discussed it point by point with the Virginia delegates. The plan was introduced into the convention by the state's governor on May 29. Thereafter Madison had the author's exquisite pain, which Jefferson had experienced with his declaration, of seeing it torn apart word by word. In the end, Madison put much of the flesh on his remade skeleton, which enabled it to grow into a living organism.

On June 4 Franklin predicted that whoever would be chosen to head the union "will be a good man," and everyone, with the possible exception of Washington, knew whom he had in mind. However, this was at a very early stage in the proceedings. Many still thought of "the National Executive" as a committee or council with a presiding officer. As the convention worked on, every delegate, including those who had never known him, had the fullest opportunity of observing and talking to the president. In the end the nation's presidency was tailored to the man who sat there "like patience on a monument," but the fullest safeguards were built around the office, in case his successors should be more ambitious or venal. Jefferson had once remarked that the horseflies from nearby stables tended to speed up debates in Independence Hall but they had no noticeable effect in 1787. Washington wrote Knox during a steamy August that any defects in the convention's work "cannot, with propriety, be charged to the hurry with which the business has been conducted."

SOCIAL LIFE

Washington had some social life after his duties, which generally occupied him six days a week. He attended a Roman Catholic Mass, and he heard Bishop William White preach. White, just consecrated by the Archbishops of Canterbury and York, had been chaplain of Congress and a leader in a revolution in the American branch of the Church of England. Washington dined with many prominent Philadelphians but also spent long hours reading and writing in his rooms. Mrs. Morris wrote later that she had never had a quieter guest nor one who gave less trouble. For the most part, days and nights were of a most routine nature, except for dinner parties and occasional rides to the country.

Washington inspected the most famous botanical gardens in America, belonging to William Bartram. As an experienced botanist and landscape designer, he did not think much of the garden, which he described as "not laid off with much taste, nor was it large." He also examined some experiments in using plaster of Paris as fertilizer on nearby farms. Having been told it should always be applied during a waxing moon, he added, "but this must be whimsical." Peale did his portrait once more.

During an interval from July 27 to August 6, the convention adjourned in order to give the Committee on Detail time to provide a first draft of a constitution. Washington went fishing, and his diary had a happier sound. He and Gouverneur Morris rode to a point near Valley Forge to catch trout. He examined his old encampment and found the works in ruins and woods growing where the army's log cabins had been. He made notes on raising buckwheat and its use in feeding cattle and laying "fat upon hogs." He continued fishing after Mr. and Mrs. Robert Morris came to join the party. They all returned to Philadelphia August 1. On August 3, in company with the three Morrises, he went over to Trenton to try the fishing there. He commented, "In the Evening fished, not very successfully." Next day he hooked some perch.

On August 5 he returned to Philadelphia and his grind. Thereafter, until September 15, little happened outside the convention. On August 19, a Sunday, he went to his old camp at Whitemarsh and dropped by the Chew house, the center of the Germantown battle. The only other item of interest he recorded was: "Visited a Machine at Doctr. Franklin's (called a Mangle) for pressing, in place of ironing, clothes from the wash. Which Machine from the facility with which it despatches business is well calculated for Table cloths and such articles as have not pleats and irregular foldings and would be very useful in all large families."

THE CONSTITUTION

Washington's highly discreet letters during the convention gave only hints of his feelings. To Jefferson he wrote on May 31: "The business of this Convention is as yet too much in embryo to form any opinion of the result. Much is expected of it by some; but little by others; and nothing by a few." On June 3 he wrote George A. Washington: "The sentiments of the different members seem to accord more than I expected they would as far as we have yet gone." On July 1 he informed David Stuart who had married Jacky Custis' widow: "I have had no wish more ardent, through the whole progress of this business, than that of knowing what kind of government is best calculated for us to live under... To inform the judgment, it is necessary to hear all arguments that can be advanced. To please all is impossible, and to attempt it would be vain... Demagogues, men who are unwilling to lose any of their state consequence, and interested characters in each, will oppose any general government." To Hamilton, who had left the convention, he wrote on July 10: "The state of the Councils which prevailed at the period you left this city... are now, if possible in a worse train than ever... I am sorry you went away. I wish you were back." On August 15 he told Lafayette: "There are seeds of discontent in every part of the Union; ready to produce other disorders if the wisdom of the present Convention should not be able to devise, and the good sense of the people be found ready to adopt a more vigorous and energetic government... "

Most of the work fell on the few who were hard working, able, and anxious to see a working union and constitution. Fewer than half the delegates attended consistently. The latter included Franklin, who came early to the state house in order to do duty as the state's president before the meeting. Death and illness, private or official business, called away others for short or long periods. Antiunionists quit the proceedings.

The first draft of the Constitution, presented by the Committee on Detail on August 6, was elephantine in comparison with the final version. The debates continued. Hours of meetings were lengthened. As the broiling heat of August persisted, speeches got shorter and compromises grew more acceptable. More antinational delegates departed, making it easier for the unionists to proceed.

The "National Executive" (some members having urged that three or more heads were better than one) slowly became "the president." An original proposal to give him a single seven-year term was beaten down to four. Though many objected, he could, in the end, be reelected. In a compromise between "national" and "state" interests, an electoral system was instituted for the president, rather than an election by Congress or popular vote. A proposal that judges and ambassadors be appointed by the Senate was fortunately changed, giving this power to the president, with the Senate reduced to advice and consent. Considering what all the delegates thought of George III, the president, who became chief of state and government as well as commander in chief, was a surprisingly strong figure. Nonetheless, everywhere in the documents were checks on his power by a strong Congress and an independent judiciary. The people could refuse to reelect the president. If they could not wait four years, a two-thirds vote in the House and Senate, under defined procedures, could remove him from office.

On September 8 a five-member Committee on Style was appointed to redraft the early version and to incorporate changes made by the voting states. Three committee members, Abraham Baldwin, James Madison, and Gouverneur Morris, all testified in later years that Morris was the man who did the drafting. In four memorable days he produced a masterpiece of clarity where intentions were clear and of ambiguity where the convention so determined. As an editor, Morris was notable. "We the People of the States of New Hampshire, Massachusetts, Rhode-Island and Providence Plantations, etc. etc." became "We the People of the United States," a change which brought howls from states' righters. Other wordy clauses were sharply cut. "The Executive Power of the United States shall be vested in a single person. His style shall be, 'The President of the United States of America'; and his title shall be, 'His Excellency,'" became "The Executive Power shall be vested in a President of the United States of America."

On September 17 the convention met for the last time. In a final motion to increase the size of the House of Representatives, in order to give more power to the people, the president rose and made his first speech. As indirectly quoted, Washington said that "the smallness of the proportion of Representatives had been considered by many members of the Convention an insufficient security for the rights and interests of the people. He acknowledged that it had always appeared to himself among the exceptional parts of the plan; and late as the present moment was for admitting amendments, he thought this of so much consequence that it would give much satisfaction to see it adopted." It was done immediately.

Two delegates, Edmund Randolph and George Mason of Virginia, the state which had started the whole business, announced they would not sign, as did Elbridge Gerry of Massachusetts. Hamilton stated that he would subscribe as New York's only delegate present. The first signature on the engrossed copy was "G. Washington—president and deputy from Virginia." He was followed by thirty-eight others from twelve states. Copies were ordered printed for dispatch to Congress and the states. The members then adjourned to await the anticipated uproar. Washington became a little more loquacious in his diary:

Met in Convention, when the Constitution received the unanimous assent of 11 States and Colo. Hamilton's from New York (the only delegate from thence in the Convention) and was subscribed to by every Member present except Govr. Randolph and Colo. Mason from Virginia, and Mr. Gerry from Massachusetts.

The business being thus closed, the Members adjourned to the City Tavern, dined together, and took a cordial leave of each other; after which I returned to my lodgings, did some business with, and received the papers from the Secretary of the Convention, and retired to meditate on the momentous work which had been executed, after not less than five, for a large part of the time six, and sometimes 7 hours sitting every day, except Sundays and the ten days adjournment... for more than four months.

TO MOUNT VERNON

Washington forwarded copies of the Constitution to Lafayette and Jefferson. He then exited from Philadelphia with as much haste as his packing and natural politeness permitted. The following morning he took "leave of those families in which I had been most intimate, dined early (abt. 1 o'clock) at Mr. Morris's... and reached Chester where we lodged, in Company with Mr. Blair, [delegate of Virginia] who I invited to a seat in my Carriage till we should reach Mount Vernon." The pair ran into a nasty accident at Christiana bridge, described by Washington:

The rain which had fallen the preceding evening having swelled the water considerably, there was no fording it safely, I was reduced to the necessity therefore of remaining on the other side or of attempting to cross on an old, rotten and long disused bridge. Being anxious to get on I preferred the latter, and in the attempt one of my horses fell 15 feet at least, the other very near following, which, had it happened, would have taken the Carriage with baggage along with him, and destroyed the whole effectually. However by prompt assistance of some people at a Mill just by, and great exertion, the first horse was disengaged from his harness, the

2d. prevented from going quite through and drawn off and the Carriage rescued from hurt.

Washington got to Mount Vernon September 22 "about sun set, after an absence of four months and 14 days." The following day, a Sunday, there were a dozen or so people for dinner and Washington did not go out to his farms. Early Monday morning he was out inspecting them, and he did this every day thereafter. There had been an exceptionally severe drought and his crops were meager. To add to his troubles there was an early and severe frost on October 14, which turned his buckwheat, peas, potatoes, and pumpkins "quite black."

Washington's acute financial position was much worsened by bad luck and weather. At the end of October he concluded that he would have to buy at least £500 in grains for his large but usually self-supporting establishment. On December 11 he wrote David Stuart "that at no period of my life have I ever felt the want of money so sensibly as now; among other demands upon me, I have no means of paying my Taxes."

From the time of his return from Philadelphia until the following summer, the greater part of his correspondence was devoted to trying to collect money owed him and to letters expressing anxiety about the ratification of the Constitution. Occasionally his two concerns overlapped. One of his largest debtors was John Francis Mercer, who had represented Maryland at Philadelphia. Mercer, an antifederalist, quit the convention in disgust when he saw the way things were moving. Before leaving, he informed Washington that as soon as he got home, he would send him £200 in part payment of his debts. The money never arrived, and Washington put increasing pressure on him to pay, so he could keep the sheriff away. While this was going on, Mercer's loud trumpetings against the Constitution were being carried across the Potomac to Mount Vernon, making him doubly irksome to the general.

With everything else on his mind, more impending trouble came in the form of a blunt letter, which David Humphreys sent him on September 28. This told Washington what everyone was expecting: "What will tend, perhaps, more than anything to the adoption of the new system will be an universal opinion of your being elected president of the United States and an expectation that you will accept it for a while." Washington was not one who generally tried to conceal the worst from his wife. He probably showed her the letter, since Humphreys announced he was coming for a long visit. She had borne a lot for her country, and there was now, apparently, more to come.

REVOLUTION BY DEBATE

The Constitution has meant many things to many people in the two centuries since its adoption. The five men most directly concerned with its operations in its first years differed widely on its meaning at the time of ratification. In his reply on October 10 to Humphreys, in which he ignored the comment about his being president, Washington wrote:

> *The Constitution that is submitted is not free from imperfections, but there are as few radical defects in it as could well be expected, considering the heterogeneous mass, of which the Convention was composed, and the diversity of interests that are to be attended to. As a Constitutional door is opened for future amendments and alterations, I think it would be wise in the People to accept...*

Adams wrote to Jefferson from London on November 10: "It seems to be admirably calculated to preserve the Union, to increase Affection, and to bring us all to the same mode of thinking... I hope the Constitution will be adopted..." Jefferson wrote Adams three days later from Paris: "How do you like our new constitution? I confess there are things in it which stagger all my dispositions to subscribe to it. The house of representatives will not be adequate to the management of affairs either foreign or federal. Their President seems a bad edition of a Polish king... Once in office, and possessing the military force of the union, without either the aid or check of council, he would not be easily dethroned..." Hamilton summed up his view to the convention September 6 when he said he disliked the whole scheme but he would vote for it. "It is better than nothing." John Jay wrote to Adams October 16: "[The Constitution] is much better than the one we have, and therefore... we shall be the gainers by the exchange, especially as there is reason to hope that experience and the good sense of the people will correct what may prove to be inexpedient in it. A compact like this, which is the result of accommodation and compromise, cannot be supposed to be perfectly consonant to the wishes and opinions of any of the parties."

The convention politely forwarded the Constitution to the Congress for approval and transmission to the states. In an unprecedented gesture, the delegates asked that the proposed Constitution "be submitted to a convention of delegates, chosen in each State by the people thereof... for their assent and ratification." This was an invitation to the most open free debate and to revolution by popular vote.

To say that the American people debated is to use understatement. Nothing else was discussed for months. Every gazette, legislature, dinner party, and tavern echoed with talk. For those who could not make head nor tail of the document, many papers pointed out that WASHINGTON and FRANKLIN had signed it, which should be sufficient guarantee of its goodness. It was the most bloodless revolution in history, though it is possible a few noses dripped red when feelings among a free and enlightened people ran high.

Washington's correspondence in the next eight months leaped to great volume as he moved to push ratification. The leading federalists in each state kept in the closest possible touch with each other. Letters in immense quantity were interchanged among Langdon in New Hampshire; Lincoln, Knox, and King in Massachusetts; Hamilton in New York; Madison in Virginia; and the Pinckneys in South Carolina. Washington was all unrestrained impatience to get news from any and all of them.

The first stages in the states were almost too easy. Delaware quickly and unanimously ratified, thus becoming "the first state," whose governor precedes all other state executives. New Jersey and Georgia ratified without opposition, while Pennsylvania and Connecticut approved by wide margins. The battle then grew harder. New York had been expected to be very troublesome, but Virginia also turned out to be difficult, while much opposition appeared in New Hampshire, Massachusetts, and North Carolina.

In New York State the battle was long. During his absence from the convention in July, Hamilton had attacked Governor Clinton in an unsigned article and impugned his motives. In a counterattack in September, a friend of Clinton wrote in the *New York Journal:* "I have also known an upstart attorney, palm himself upon a great and good man, for a youth of extraordinary genius, and under the shadow of such a patronage, make himself at once known and respected, but being sifted and bolted to the brann, he was at length found to be a superficial, self-conceited coxcomb, and was of course turned off, and disregarded by his patron." Hamilton wrote Washington that his feelings had been hurt by this, and he wanted a letter from him saying it was not true. Washington replied that he was much concerned at such a dispute between Clinton and Hamilton, for he had "the highest esteem and regard" for both. He added that the newspaper charges were "entirely unfounded." The quitting "was altogether the effect of your choice."

From all this, and the many attacks on the Constitution in the New York press, Hamilton decided on the more constructive approach of enlightening the people on what the document meant. He enlisted the help of James Madison and John Jay in developing the famous *Federalist Papers,* which appeared from September to May. Washington, after studying the writings with care, forwarded them to David Stuart, asking him to have them published in a Richmond paper. He also forwarded for publication a Pennsylvania speech by James Wilson, defending the new Constitution.

The federalist leaders in each state convention wrote those in other states, outlining the principal arguments of their opponents and how they were answered. They also revealed the use, when necessary, of political tricks. Massachusetts, determinedly democratic, had assembled nearly ten times as many delegates as signed the Constitution. John Hancock, the governor, whose sloth was exceeded only by his vanity, veered like a Boston winter weathervane, being for the Constitution one day and against it the next. The federalists informed him that Virginia, in all probability, would not ratify, and Washington could not therefore be president. Hancock, as the only man of stature next to him, would get his office. He decided for the Constitution, which carried by a rather small margin. Federalist express riders raced with the news to the neighboring capitals, Concord and Poughkeepsie.

Washington was exceedingly anxious to see Maryland ratify, as a good example to Virginia. The opponents there expected to use a tactic which had worked in New Hampshire—to vote to adjourn the state convention. Washington heard that this would also be tried in Virginia. He wrote his friends across the Potomac, under no circumstances should they permit this. On May 2, in glee, he informed Madison in Richmond that Maryland had approved by a huge majority: "Mr. Chace, it is said, made a display of all his eloquence. Mr. Mercer discharged his whole artillery of inflammable matter; and Mr. Martin did something; I know not what, but I presume with vehemence, but no converts were made, no, not one. So business after a very short Session, ended; and will if I mistake not, render yours less tiresome."

South Carolina quickly followed, and only one more state was needed to complete the nine necessary to union. It became a race between Virginia and New Hampshire. Washington had sent Tobias Lear, who came from the latter state, to report to him from Concord. By June 17 Washington had assurances from Lear that New Hampshire would ratify.

In Richmond the lineup was formidable for and against. Partly under Washington's prodding, the governor swung to support of the Constitution. Patrick Henry used all his flaming arguments against it. The quiet Madison displayed remarkable knowledge and debating skill. George Mason railed against the Constitution. It was ratified on June 25, though by but ten votes. Most of the opposition came from the western counties, now Kentucky and West Virginia, which voted, seventy-two years later, to stay in the Union. James Monroe, an opponent, wrote Jefferson that Washington's influence had carried the state. When it was over, Patrick Henry said he would support the union peaceably, as all good citizens should, and would work for changes within a constitutional framework. This gesture of magnanimity greatly pleased Washington. Alexandria held a celebration, after hearing the reports from Richmond, which was made even more cheerful by news that New Hampshire had ratified and ten states were in the Union. Washington reported to Lear on June 29:

> *Your letter of the 2d. instant came duly to hand and obliged me by its communications. On Friday last (by the stage) advice of the decision of the long and warmly (with temper) contested question, in the Convention of this State, was received, 89 ayes, 79 noes, without previous amendments; and in the course of that night Colo. Henley, Express from New York on his way to Richmond, arrived in Alexandria with the news of the ratification by the State of New Hampshire. This flood of good news almost at the same moment, gave, as you will readily conceive, abundant cause for rejoicing in a place, the Inhabitants of which are all federal. The cannon roared, and the Town was illuminated yesterday, as magnificent a dinner as Mr. Wise could provide (to which this family were invited and went), was displayed before the principal male Inhabitants of the Town; whose Ears were saluted at every quaff with the melody of federal guns. And on Monday, the business it seems is to recommence and finish, with fiddling and Dancing, for the amusement, and benefit of the Ladies.*

Only New York and North Carolina had yet to vote. The area around New York City sent a solid federal delegation to the state convention, while the opposition came from upstate. The New York convention, the longest of all, lasted nearly six weeks. Madison from Richmond and Langdon from New Hampshire sent urgent expresses to Hamilton, when their states ratified, in order to influence New York's vote. In the end, Hamilton carried the convention by the narrowest of all squeaks—three votes. This was done primarily by a threat that southern New York would secede from the state and join the Union. This, said Hamilton, would leave the upstate area without a friend, an ally, a port, or a source of taxes. Hamilton also made "Flag and mother" speeches when, according to his notes of July 17, he spoke of "Franklin… Washington… Heroes who have died… sister states… Mankind… Heaven." The economic threats doubtless carried greater weight. Washington wrote Hamilton on August 28, giving him high praise for the *Federalist Papers*:

> *As the perusal of the political papers under the signature of Publius has afforded me great satisfaction, I shall certainly consider them as claiming a most distinguished place in my Library. I have read every performance which has been printed on one side or the other… I have seen no other so well calculated… to*

produce conviction on an unbiased Mind, as the Production of your triumvirate.
When the transient circumstances... which attended this Crisis shall disappear,
That Work will merit the Notice of Posterity...

In anticlimax, North Carolina rejected the Constitution, but eleven states
were ready to start and Congress had taken steps to admit Kentucky to the new
Union. Washington had written John Armstrong on April 25, 1788:

Upon the whole I doubt whether the opposition to the Constitution will not
ultimately be productive of more good than evil; it has called forth, in its defence,
abilities which would not perhaps have been otherwise exerted, that have thrown
new light upon the science of Government, they have given the rights of man a full
and fair discussion, and explained them in so clear and forcible a manner, as
cannot fail to make a lasting impression upon those who read the best publications
on the subject.

The debates had certainly educated everyone. By the time they were over,
nearly every American considered himself an expert on constitutional law; it
was not going to be an easy country to govern. The great split was the beginning of a two-party system. Those who were against the Constitution formed a
large nucleus of an opposition party, while those who later disagreed with the
federal government's operations had a solid group with which to coalesce.

As the ratifications proceeded, the volume of letters pouring into Mount
Vernon rose sharply. Many came from disinterested persons who believed that
the country required Washington as president. Others expressed eagerness to
have office under him. He responded to all that he did not want to be president, it was too great a sacrifice once again to leave Mount Vernon, while there
was no assurance there would not be as great an opposition to his presidency
as there had been to the Constitution. To those who wanted office, he added
that, under the circumstances, a discussion of such matters was impossible.

FIVE

THE FIRST NATIONAL
ELECTION

1788–1789

I N THE MEANTIME, Great Britain had moved forward with policies
designed to confine Americans behind the mountains and to subordinate the Northwest Territory to Canada, two earlier grievances which had
helped to bring on revolution and war. The operations were directed by "His
Majesty's Government in America," the Canadian arm of Whitehall. Britain
was served by a large network of officials, army officers, Indian chiefs, traders,
unreconstructed Tories, and American friends and dupes. The seven forts
held by the British commanded the straits of Detroit, Mackinac, and Niagara,
as well as Lake Ontario, the Saint Lawrence River, and Lake Champlain. Lord
Dorchester had been commanded to hold them and, if attacked, to repel war
by war.

Dorchester was also ordered by London to support all Indian "rights" in
northern New York and west of Pittsburgh. This policy avoided open hostility,
while encouraging Indian warfare to prevent American settlements beyond
the mountains. The Indians were provided with gold, provisions, arms, and
ammunition. Numerous renegade Americans were employed to manage
them. They included Sir John Johnson in the Mohawk Valley as well as the
notorious Girty brothers and Alexander McKee and John Butler, who operated farther west.

London had further aims, to detach all American territory loosely tied to the confederacy, particularly Kentucky and Vermont. George Beckwith's espionage network employed Sir John Temple, British consul at New York; Peter Allaire, a New York merchant; Dr. John Connolly, who had spent four years in an American prison for intelligence work; as well as Dr. Edward Bancroft, who had been secretary to Franklin's Paris mission while on George III's payroll. Another member was Ethan Allen, who wrote Dorchester in 1788 that he was sure his 15,000 Vermont militia, leagued with the antifederalists, could prevent the ratification of the Constitution.

Connolly worked in Kentucky to attach it to Britain. This was a fertile area since most of its delegates had voted against ratification in Richmond. As early as 1786, Washington wrote Henry Lee that there were in Kentucky "many ambitious and turbulent spirits... who from the present difficulties in their intercourse with the Atlantic States, have turned their eyes to New Orleans, and may become riotous and ungovernable, if the hope of traffick with it is cut off by treaty."

In his negotiations with the Spanish minister, John Jay was unable to budge him on opening the Mississippi to American trade. The minister did agree to consider a commercial treaty, a move eagerly welcomed by New England, which was suffering a depression. Jay suggested that Congress set aside the question of navigation to New Orleans, in return for a trade treaty. There were not enough votes for this in Congress and the negotiations collapsed, but the proposal itself alarmed the Kentuckians.

While operating in Kentucky, Connolly picked up information on the activities there of another American, James Wilkinson, who was on Spain's payroll. Wilkinson, whose remarks about Gates and Conway had broken open the Conway Cabal, moved to Kentucky after the war. He began there an intrigue with the governor of Louisiana, who agreed to let Wilkinson move his goods to New Orleans and to have a pension, provided he would assist the Spanish to control the area east of the Mississippi. Wilkinson took the oath to Spain and returned to Kentucky to stir up the inhabitants against the United States. His address to the citizens there was forwarded by Connolly to Dorchester, with a note predicting that it could be detached from the United States if Britain could persuade Spain to open the river to Kentucky's products.

PAX VIRUMQUE

The general who had so long borne the arms of his country was the American who most loved peace. Between 1785 and 1789, particularly to his French friends, he expounded a consistently peaceful philosophy and a dream that

America would take the lead in making a better world for everyone. On July 25, 1785, he wrote Lafayette:

> *As the clouds which overspread your hemisphere are dispersing, and peace with all its concomitants, is dawning upon your Land, I will banish the sound of War from my letter. I wish to see the sons and daughters of the world in Peace and busily employed in the more agreeable amusement of fulfilling the first and great commandment, <u>Increase and Multiply</u>, as an encouragement to which we have opened the fertile plains of the Ohio to the poor, the needy and the oppressed of the Earth. Any one therefore who is heavily laden, or who wants land to cultivate, may repair thither and abound, as in the Land of promise, with milk and honey. The ways are preparing and the roads will be made easy...*

He followed with a further letter to Rochambeau on July 31, 1786:

> *It must give pleasure to the friends of humanity... to find that the clouds which threatened to burst in a storm of War on Europe, have dissipated... As the rage of conquest, which in times of barbarity stimulated Nations to blood, has in a great degree ceased; as the objects which formerly gave birth to Wars are daily diminishing; and as mankind are becoming more enlightened and humanized, I cannot but flatter myself with the pleasing prospect that more liberal policies and more pacific systems will take place amongst them. To indulge this idea affords a soothing consolation to a philanthropic mind, insomuch that, altho' it should be founded in illusion, one hardly wishes to be divested of an error so grateful in itself, and so innocent in its consequences.*

Washington happily congratulated Chastellux on April 25, 1788, on his unexpected marriage to a lady-in-waiting to the Duchesse d'Orléans:

> *In reading your very friendly letter... I was, as you may well suppose, not less delighted than surprised to come across those plain American words "my wife." A wife! Well my dear Marquis, I can hardly refrain from smiling to find you are caught at last. I saw, by the eulogium you often made on the happiness of domestic life in America, that you had swallowed the bait and that you would as surely be taken (one day or another), as you [are] a Philosopher and a Soldier... Now you are well served for coming to fight in favor of the American Rebels, all the way across the Atlantic Ocean, by catching that terrible Contagion, domestic felicity, which... like the small pox or plague, a man can have only once in his life... at least with us in America, I don't know how you manage these matters in France...*

While you have been making love, under the banner of Hymen, the great personages in the North have been making war... under the infatuation of Mars. Now, for my part, I humbly conceive, you have had much the best and wisest of the bargain. For certainly it is more consonant to all the principles of reason and religion (natural and revealed) to replenish the earth with inhabitants, rather than to depopulate it by killing those already in existence, besides it is time for the age of Knight-errantry and mad-heroism to be at an end.

He wrote again on November 27 to Chastellux, reintroducing Gouverneur Morris to him. Morris, in spite of having but one leg, was famous as a ladies' man. Washington therefore noted: "As for Mr. Morris only let him be once fairly presented to your French Ladies, and I answer for it, he will not leave the worst impression in the world, of the American character, for taciturnity and improper reserve." Chastellux never received the letter, for he died suddenly in October. Morris seems to have met all the French ladies he needed, without help. Jefferson sent him with a note to an old friend, Maria Cosway, in London, and got back her reply: "I am quite in Love with Mr. Morris. Are all Americans so engaging as those I know? Pray take me to that country."

Washington's French friends followed American political developments with close attention and as soon as they read the new Constitution they pushed for him as president. Rochambeau wrote that he longed to see Washington president of a strong confederation, while Lafayette said that he thought perhaps the president had too many powers but so long as Washington was to have the office, it would be all right. To Lafayette, on April 28, 1788, Washington gave the first indication that he might be forced to accept, against all inclination, but that it was not decent for him to talk about it, as there was always the story of the fox and the grapes. He followed this with another letter of June 19:

There seems to be a great deal of bloody work cut out for this summer in the North of Europe. If war, want and plague are to desolate those huge armies that are assembled, who that has the feelings of a man can refrain from shedding a tear over the miserable victims of Regal Ambition? It is really a strange thing that there should not be room enough in the world for men to live, without cutting one another's throats. As France, Spain and England have hardly recovered from the wounds of the late war, I would fain hope they will hardly be dragged into this...

I like not much the situation of affairs in France. The bold demands of the parliament, and the decisive tone of the King, shew that but little more irritation would be necessary to blow up the spark of discontent into a flame, that might not easily be quenched. If I were to advise, I would say that great moderation should be used on both sides. Let it not, my dear Marquis, be considered as a derogation from the good opinion that I entertain of your prudence, when I caution you, as an individual desirous of signalizing yourself in the cause of your country and freedom, against running into extremes and prejudicing your cause... It is a wonder to me that there should be found a single monarch, who does not realize that his own glory and felicity must depend on the prosperity and happiness of his People. How easy it is for a sovereign to do that which shall not only immortalize his name, but attract the blessings of millions...

... I expect that many blessings will be attributed to our new government... When the people shall find themselves secure under an energetic government, when foreign nations shall be disposed to give us equal advantages in commerce from dread of retaliation, when the burdens of war shall be in a manner done away by the sale of western lands, when the seeds of happiness which are somewhere shall begin to expand themselves, and when everyone... shall begin to taste the fruits of freedom, then all those blessings (for all these blessings will come) will be referred to as from the fostering influence of the new government. You see that I am not less enthusiastic than ever I have been in a belief that peculiar scenes of felicity are reserved for this country... Indeed, I do not believe that Providence has done so much for nothing...

... I hope, some day or another, we shall be a storehouse and granary for the world...

On January 29, 1789, as his presidency approached, he wrote Lafayette:

I will content myself with only saying that the elections have been hitherto vastly more favorable than we could have expected, that federal sentiments seem to be growing with uncommon rapidity and this increasing unanimity is not less indicative of the good disposition than the good sense of Americans. Did it not savour so much of partiality for my countrymen, I might add that I cannot help flattering myself that the new Congress on account of the... respectability and varied talents of its Members will not be inferior to any Assembly in the world...

... I can say little or nothing new, in consequence of the repetition of your opinion on the expedience there will be, for my accepting the office to which you refer... Nothing short of a conviction of duty will induce me again to take an active part in public affairs; and in that case, if I can form a plan for my own conduct, my endeavours shall be unremittingly exerted... to establish a general system of policy, which, if pursued, will ensure permanent felicity to the Commonwealth. I think I

see a path, as clear and direct as a ray of sunlight, which leads to the attainment of that object. Nothing but harmony, honesty, industry and frugality are necessary to make us a great and happy people. Happily the present posture of affairs, and the prevailing disposition of my countrymen promise to co-operate in establishing those four great and essential pillars of public felicity...

While you are quarreling among yourselves in Europe; while one King is running mad, and others acting as if they were already so, by cutting the throats of their neighbours, I think you need not doubt, my dear Marquis, we shall continue in tranquility here. And that population [growth] will be progressive so long as there shall continue to be so many easy means for obtaining a subsistence, and so ample a field for the exertions of talents and industry.

Washington's final word to France was to Rochambeau the same day:

Notwithstanding it might probably, in a commercial view, be greatly for the advantage of America that a war should rage on the other side of the Atlantic; yet I shall never so far divest myself of the feelings of a man interested in the happiness of his fellow-men, as to wish my country's prosperity might be built on the ruins of other nations. On the contrary, I cannot but hope that the Independence of America, to which you have so gloriously contributed, will prove a blessing to mankind. It is thus you see, My dear Count, in retirement, upon my farm, I speculate upon the fate of nations; amusing myself with innocent Reveries that mankind will, one day, grow happier and better.

WASHINGTON LEAVES THE PLOW

July 4, 1788, was celebrated throughout the nation as a day of hope. Enough states had ratified so that the new government was certain to come into being. That day, there were in all probability only two Americans (or three, if John Hancock is included) who did not hope the general would become president—Washington and his wife. A new song, "Great Washington shall rule the land," was first sung at York. In nearby Frederick, the Independence Day toast was "Farmer Washington—May he, like a second Cincinnatus, be called from the plow to rule a great people."

Cincinnatus was far from happy at the thought. He was having more difficulties that spring and summer than he had ever encountered with the Mount Vernon farms. The severe drought of the previous year, which had brought him so much financial loss, was followed by a wet and windy spring.

Washington's June diary noted the thinness of his wheat and buckwheat crops. That July 4 he was out all day in "dripping Rains," finding his grain crops too wet to cut and bind. Twenty days later there was a heavy, driving rain through the night. This was followed by a hurricane which lasted all day. Washington's trees were uprooted and felled, and many of his fences and crops were ruined. He noted that the Potomac tide, which rose four feet above any previous high-mark, drove all his boats onto the shore and drowned some of his shoreland. A miniature ship, *The Federalist*, which had been presented to Washington by the people of Baltimore, was smashed and sunk.

Washington's diaries for 1788 are the most extensive and the most tedious of any he kept during his life. No one on his farms was out for longer hours nor worked harder than he that year. It was as though he were trying, by sheer grit, to overcome personally all the difficulties that nature placed in his way, while blanking from his mind the imperious calls from the country. His financial condition grew worse. His January plea to John Francis Mercer to make his promised payments said that he had put the sheriff off three times on taxes. Though he had offered to finance the schooling of George Washington Craik, his physician's son, and had scraped together some money for this, he informed Dr. Craik on August 4:

> *I also send you Thirty pounds Cash for one year's allowance for the Schooling of your Son G.W. I wish it was in my power to send the like sum for the other year, which is now about, or near due; and that I could discharge your account for attendance and ministration to the Sick of my family; but it really is not; for with much truth I can say, I never felt the want of money so sensibly since I was a boy of 15 years old, as I have done for the last 12 months, and probably shall do for 12 Months more to come.*

A further drain on his purse was the schooling of the sons of his dead brother Samuel. He described this to another nephew, Bushrod Washington, on November 17: "What the abilities of my deceased brother Samls. Estate toward paying his debts may be, I am unable to say; but I much fear that the management of it is in very bad hands; as the hours of your Uncle Charles are, I have reason to believe, spent in intoxication... My Money (tho' it is exceedingly distressing to me to apply it that way) and my credit, is at stake for the board, the Schooling, clothing &ca. of George and Lawe. Washington, in Alexandria; without being able to receive from the Estate more than a little driblet now and then, entirely inadequate to the demand. My advance for them, at this time, in money and credit, is considerable..."

Congress, after a long summer's wrangle on where to locate the capital of the new government, decided on September 13 to leave it just where it was—in New York City. With this decision came a call for election of the president, vice-president, senators, and representatives, to meet and form the new government on March 4, 1789. Because of the slowness of communications, this did not give the faraway states too much time to organize their electoral machinery. New York, at the doorstep of Congress, did not even manage to vote for president.

Electioneering was intense for the vice-presidency and the twenty-two Senate and fifty-nine House seats. In general, the federalists thought in terms of John Adams as vice-president because he was a New Englander while Washington was a Southerner; Adams was also a Federalist, and had a long record of patriotic service. Another factor was that after his resignation as minister to Great Britain, he was out of a job.

Hamilton and others quickly discovered a flaw in the Constitution. If Adams received as many votes as Washington, then neither would be elected, and the new House of Representatives would have to decide who would be president. Hamilton therefore persuaded his neighboring states to give a few votes to other candidates, while providing a majority to Adams. Other states decided that they would compliment their own citizens by giving them a vote. Out of this chaos, Washington, as expected, received every vote, whereas Adams failed, by one, to have a majority, a result which he called "scurvy." No fewer than eleven men received votes for vice-president, including three from Massachusetts—Adams, Hancock, and Lincoln—and three exceedingly obscure Georgians.

Exactly when Washington faced the inevitable cannot be pinpointed. In October he informed Hamilton that the question filled him with gloom. That same month he repeated to Lincoln the despair he felt in facing "an unexplored field, enveloped on every side with clouds and darkness." He had hoped his public statement of 1783, that he would never again go into public office, would have been accepted by the people and thus give him "a last anchor of worldly happiness in old age." In early December he wrote John Trumbull, using the same phrase, "clouds and darkness," and indicating the sacrifice he would have to make. Nevertheless, in the same letter he noted how pleased he was by the selection of the first fourteen senators and the many distinguished people who were going into the House of Representatives. On December 19 James Madison arrived at Mount Vernon to spend six days in conference with Washington, while he made his final decision.

On January 29 Washington wrote to General Knox, the war secretary, in New York, that he had seen an advertisement in the *New York Daily Advertiser* for American broadcloth, the first manufactured in the country. He asked him to get enough cloth for a suit for himself and a riding habit for Mrs. Washington. On February 16, 1789, Knox replied that he had ordered the cloths from Hartford. "The moment they come to hand I will forward those for you and Mrs. Washington. It appears by the returns of elections hitherto obtained, which is as far as Maryland southward, that your Excellency has every vote for president…"

Virginia, with Patrick Henry an elector, also voted unanimously for Washington, though Henry and two others gave their votes to Clinton for vice-president. The votes from South Carolina and Georgia followed for Washington, and he was president-elect of the United States of America.

In early February, he received from Francis Hopkinson a book of music, dedicated to Washington, along with a humorous letter to which Washington replied: "We are told of the amazing powers of musick in ancient times; but the stories of its effects are so surprizing that we are not obliged to believe them unless they have been founded upon better authority than Poetic asser-tion… My dear Sir… you have not acted with your usual good Judgement in the choice which you have made of a Coadjutor, for should the tide of preju-dice not flow in favor of it (and so various are the tastes, opinions and whims of men that even the sanction of divinity does not ensure universal concur-rence) what, alas! can I do to support it? I can neither sing one of the songs, nor raise a single note on any instrument to convince the unbelieving…"

Washington wrote on May 13 that Hopkinson's subsequent reply made him "laugh heartily." It was obviously intended as advice to the president-elect, for Hopkinson wrote: "Orpheus was a legislator and civilizer of his country. In those days laws were promulgated in verse and sung to the harp, and the poets by a figure in rhetoric have attributed the salutory effects of his laws to the tunes to which they were play'd and sung."

On March 4 Washington wrote to Richard Conway in Alexandria to explain that he was terribly short of cash, he had not been able to sell his lands nor to collect money due him, and he was faced with the necessity of borrowing. Could Conway lend him £500 (which he later upped to 600)? Conway advanced the funds, enabling the president-elect to move to New York. On March 7 Washington rode to Fredericksburg to make a last call on his mother who was slowly dying of cancer.

The president-elect had now to wait while the House and Senate assembled with a quorum to make the official count. A severe winter delayed the new members in many states. Washington wrote to Knox on March 2 that the Virginia delegates were just about setting off. While waiting he drafted elabo-rate summaries of Mount Vernon's farm problems for his managers, as well as a proposed inaugural address. A report by Knox on the delays in New York was met with Washington's reply, April 1, that he considered them "a reprieve... My movements to the chair of Government will be accompanied by feelings not unlike those of a culprit who is going to the place of his execution... so unwilling am I, in the evening of a life nearly consumed in public cares, to quit a peaceful abode for an Ocean of difficulties, without that competency of political skill, abilities and inclination which is necessary to manage the helm... Integrity and firmness is all I can promise..."

On April 6 John Langdon, president of the Senate *pro tempore*, announced that both houses had met, the votes of all electors had been counted, and "His Excellency George Washington, Esq., was unanimously elected, agreeable to the Constitution, to the Office of the President of the said United States of America." Congress immediately dispatched Charles Thompson, who had been for fifteen years secretary of the old Continental Congress, to Mount Vernon, with the official notification and the duty of accompanying the president-elect to New York.

Thompson reached Mount Vernon shortly after noon on April 14 and read the document to Washington, who formally accepted. He wrote Senator Langdon that he would leave Mount Vernon for New York on April 16. In the meantime, by joint resolution, the Senate and House voted that the house lately occupied by the president of Congress, be prepared as the residence of the president of the United States.

THE TRIUMPHANT PROCESSION

Midmorning on April 16 Washington climbed into his waiting carriage. He recorded the event in his diary: "About ten o'clock I bade adieu to Mount Vernon, to private life, and to domestic felicity, and with a mind oppressed with more anxious and painful sensations than I have words to express, set out for New York in company with Mr. Thompson, and Colonel Humphreys, with the best disposition to render service to my country in obedience to its call, but with less hope of answering its expectations."

At Alexandria his fellow citizens had prepared a farewell dinner. The mayor, Dennis Ramsay, said that he would avoid the usual speech praising Washington as a great soldier and patriot, for his services to his neighbors had been "less splendid but more endearing... The first and best of citizens must leave us—Our aged must lose their ornament!—Our youth their model!— Our agriculture its improver!—Our commerce its friend!—Our infant Academy its patron!—Our Poor their Benefactor!—And the interior navigation of the Potowmack—an event replete with the most extensive utility, already, by your unremitted exertions, brought into partial use—its 'Institutor and Promoter'… Go, and make a grateful People happy… To that Being who maketh and unmaketh at will we commend you… May he restore to us again the best of men…" To this Washington replied:

Although I ought not to conceal, yet I cannot describe, the painful emotions which I felt in being called upon to determine whether I would accept or refuse the Presidency of the United States.

The unanimity of the choice, the opinion of my friends, communicated from different parts of Europe, as well as of America, the apparent wish of those who were not altogether satisfied with the Constitution in its present form, and an ardent desire, on my own part, to be instrumental in conciliating the good will of my countrymen towards each other have induced an acceptance.

Those who have known me best (and you, my fellow citizens, are from your situation, in that number) know better than any others that my love of retirement is so great, that no earthly consideration, short of a conviction of duty, could have prevailed upon me to depart from my resolution "<u>never more to take any share in transactions of a public nature</u>." For, at my age, and in my circumstances, what possible advantages could I propose to myself, from embarking again on the tempestuous and uncertain ocean of public life?

I do not feel myself under the necessity of making public declarations, in order to convince you Gentlemen of my attachment to yourselves, and regard for your interests. The whole tenor of my life has been open to your inspection; and my past actions, rather than my present declarations, must be the pledge of my future conduct.

In the meantime I thank you most sincerely for the expression of kindness contained in your valedictory address. It is true, just after having bade adieu to my domestic connections, this tender proof of your friendship is but too well calculated still farther to awaken my sensibility, and increase my regret at parting from the enjoyments of private life.

All that now remains for me is to commit myself and you to the protection of that beneficent Being who, on a former occasion, has happily brought us together after a long and distressing separation. Perhaps the same gracious Providence will again indulge us with the same heartfelt felicity. But words, my fellow-citizens, fail me: <u>unutterable sensations must then be left to more expressive silence; while from an aching heart, I bid you all, my affectionate friends and kind neighbours, farewell</u>!

According to the report of the *Pennsylvania Packet* from Georgetown,

> *The Most Illustrious the President of the United States of America... arrived at about 2 o'clock, on the banks of the Potomack, escorted by a respectable corps of gentlemen from Alexandria, where the George-Town ferry boats, properly equipped, received his Excellency and suite, and safely landed them under the acclamations of a large crowd of their grateful fellow-citizens, who beheld their Fabius in the evening of his days, bid adieu to the peaceful retreat of Mount Vernon, in order to save his country once more. From this place his Excellency was escorted by a corps of gentlemen... to Mr. Spurrier's tavern, where the escort from Baltimore took charge of him.*

The roaring Baltimore welcome included a speech containing the best single tribute paid Washington in his lifetime: "We behold an extraordinary thing in the annals of mankind, a free and enlightened People, choosing by a free election, without one dissenting voice, the late Commander-in-Chief of their Armies to watch over and guard their civil rights and privileges." Great crowds accompanied him to the Delaware line where that state's citizens took over, shouted their acclaim, and read an address to "The President General of the United States of America." At this point we can let the Reverend Mason Locke Weems take him as far as Trenton, where, seventy-two years later, Abraham Lincoln was to recall Weems' great impact on him as a boy:

> *"On reaching the western banks of Schuylkill," said a gentleman who was present, "I was astonished at the concourse of people that overspread the country, apparently from Gray's ferry to the city. Indeed one would have thought that the whole population of Philadelphia had come out to meet him. And to see so many thousands of people on foot, on horseback, and in coaches, all voluntarily waiting upon and moving along with* one *man, struck me with strangely agreeable sensations. Surely, thought I, there must be a divinity in goodness, that mankind should thus delight to honor it."*

> *His reception at Trenton was... planned... by the ladies... It was near this place that the fair sex in '76 suffered such cruel indignities from the enemy; and... it was here that Providence in the same year enabled Washington severely to chastise them for it... Under their direction, the bridge over the Sanpink... was decorated with a triumphal arch, with this inscription in large figures:*

> *DECEMBER 26, 1776*
> *THE HERO WHO DEFENDED THE MOTHERS*
> *WILL ALSO PROTECT THE DAUGHTERS*

He approached the bridge on its south side, amidst the heartiest shouts of congratulating thousands, while on the north side were drawn up several hundreds of little girls, dressed in snow-white robes, with temples adorned with garlands, and baskets of flowers on their arms. Just behind them stood long rows of young virgins, whose fair faces, of sweetest red, and white, highly animated by the occasion, looked quite angelic—and, back of them, in crowds stood their venerable mothers. As Washington slowly drove off the bridge, the female voices all began, sweet as the first wakings of the Eolian harp, and thus they rolled the song:

Welcome, mighty chief! once more
Welcome to this grateful shore...

While singing the last lines they strewed the way with flowers before him.

Completely charmed by this welcome, Washington wrote them from Trenton: "General Washington cannot leave this place without expressing his acknowledgements to the Matrons and Young Ladies who received him in so Novel and grateful a manner at the Triumphal Arch in Trenton, for the exquisite sensation he experienced in that affecting moment. The astonishing contrast before his former and actual situation at the same spot, the elegant taste with which it was adorned for the present occasion, and the innocent appearance of the *white-robed Choir* who met him with the gratulatory song, have made such impressions on his remembrance as, he assures them, will never be effaced."

At Elizabethtown there was a newly constructed barge, manned by twenty-six pilot-oarsmen dressed in white. Every ship in New York harbor was decorated with flags and bunting. Many followed the president-elect's barge, with singing and music. French, British, Spanish, and American ships fired salutes. Almost the entire population of New York had massed at the lower end of the island to roar a welcome. All the bells of the city rang. So heavy were the crowds that it was only with the greatest difficulty that Washington could get to the house prepared for him. The governor of New York gave him a formal dinner. That night the city was illumined but rain forced the cancellation of the fireworks planned by the Spanish and French missions. His former aide, Samuel Blatchley Webb, said he had never seen so much "joy" on every face. In the midst of his happy countrymen, one man, alone, viewed the delirium with a somber eye. The president-elect wrote in his diary: "The display of boats, which attended and joined on this occasion, some with vocal and others with instrumental music on board, the decorations of the ships, the roar of the cannon, and the loud acclamations of the people, which rent the sky as

I passed along the wharves, filled my mind with sensations as painful (contemplating the reverse of this scene, which may be the case after all my labours to do good) as they were pleasing."

SIX

THE GOVERNMENT
IS ORGANIZED

1789–1790

S INCE HIS EARLIEST days at Mount Vernon, when he discussed the
Ohio Company's plans with his brother, Lawrence, Washington's mind
had been concerned with the economic progress of Virginia, particularly in its western portions. More than four decades later, still at Mount
Vernon, he drafted a comprehensive program for the development of a new
nation with "an extent of fifteen hundred miles." It appears to have been
intended as his inaugural address as president. The original manuscript of seventy-two pages existed intact until the late 1820s, when it came into the hands
of an unscrupulous vandal, Jared Sparks, a managing editor. Finding it had
not been delivered, Sparks cut it into pieces, to give souvenirs to his friends.
The fragments, which have been put back together over the years, amount in
readable form to less than a quarter. From these, nonetheless, it is possible to
reconstruct a considerable portion of America's first economic development
program, which was also the first in the world.

As expected from his bitter years, when he had to fight without money,
Washington gave his first attention to the national credit and the "load of
debt… left upon us." In the government's initial planning, revenues would
have to come from import duties and excise taxes, for the support of the federal government and payments on the national debt. He hoped that these
could be made "as little burdensome on the people as possible." Fortunately,

an ocean separated America from Europe. The country could therefore avoid "the burden of maintaining numerous fleets and Armies… a singular felicity in our national lot." The federal government should, however, give every encouragement to the development of the merchant marine and the fisheries. Not only would these provide increasing national wealth but also be a source of sailors for the navy in any emergency. So long as the country was still impoverished by the war, he would not recommend an increase in the size of the regular army. However, there would be a need for arsenals, dockyards, and a well-trained and organized militia.

Washington then proceeded to his economic measures. He proposed national assistance to increase the production of wool, cotton, flax, and hemp to up to ten times the current level. While there would be a comparative advantage in importing the highest quality manufactures, the country should stimulate its own fabrication of agricultural products as well as leather, fur, iron, and wood, which were available in abundant supply. He advocated a great improvement in the postal system and in postroads to promote inter-state trade, which, he foresaw correctly, would be of much greater importance than international commerce. He proposed that the federal government carry newspapers and periodicals throughout the Union, without charge, in order to disseminate information to the people.

The president-elect also suggested federal assistance to institutions of higher education, a patent and copyright system, as well as uniform national coins, weights, and measures. He proposed a bill of rights. He advocated a federal judiciary system which would have "a supreme regard for equal justice and the inherent rights of the citizens."

The whole of the address was much broader and more inclusive but even the fragments suggest a constructive development program. Washington probably decided that he had best not present so sweeping a program as he entered office. His countrymen were still pretty sensitive to tyranny, and too much strong and apparent leadership at the beginning might be considered dangerous. He therefore cancelled the address and substituted for it a general statement. The plans remained, however, and were very largely carried through during his two administrations.

INAUGURATION

Washington's New York house had been hastily readied for him, though there were still some noisy repairs during his first days of residence. Visitors were an overwhelming problem since everybody dropped by, even before breakfast, "to pay their respects to the President." Washington realized that he would soon be nothing but the principal New York attraction for curiosity seekers. He made early restraining rules which aroused some outcries about royalty.

Congress set April 30 for Washington's oath of office. Since Great Britain had forbade colonial manufacturing, Washington, in conscious symbolism, put on a plain brown suit, which had been made at Mount Vernon from the American broadcloth ordered by Knox from Hartford. Its buttons bore the federal eagle, which was rapidly becoming a prominent feature of American decorative arts.

At nine in the morning the churches of the city opened for prayers for the president and government. At noon a committee of Congress, with an honor guard, almost all of whose officers had been revolutionary soldiers, arrived at Washington's house. He drove through the streets, lined with most of New York's thirty thousand people who were out to cheer him. Congress had always received him seated when he was a general, but all now rose as he entered. Having greeted them and sitting briefly, Washington was notified by the vice-president, John Adams, that they would proceed to the balcony of Federal Hall for the administration of the oath before the people.

As he came out onto the balcony, Washington could see every inch of space on the streets, in the windows, and on the roofs occupied by his people who applauded wildly when they saw him. He bowed to them and then faced the chancellor of New York, Robert Livingston, who was flanked by Vice-President Adams, Governor Clinton, and such old revolutionary companions as Steuben, Knox, St. Clair, Humphreys, and Webb.

Livingston, having handed the Bible to him, said: "Do you, George Washington, solemnly swear that you will faithfully execute the office of President of the United States and will, to the best of your ability, preserve, protect, and defend the Constitution of the United States?" Washington repeated the oath, adding, "So help me God." He then bowed to kiss the Bible. The chancellor turned to the people and said: "Long live George Washington, President of the United States."

Washington returned to the congressional chambers where he read his rather brief inaugural address. Fisher Ames of Massachusetts recorded an impression of his delivery: "His aspect grave, almost to sadness; his modesty, actually shaking; his voice deep, a little tremulous and so low as to call for close attention; added to the series of objects presented to the mind, produced emotions of the most affecting kind upon the members. I... sat entranced."

Washington's address was extraordinarily modest. It included a touching appeal to his countrymen not to look upon him as omnipotent or a deity. The deeply religious speech was also a call to virtue and unity among a people not always virtuous, and always fractious:

I was summon'd by my country, whose voice I can never hear but with veneration and love, from a retreat which I had chosen with the fondest predilection, and in my flattering hopes, with an immutable decision, as the asylum of my declining years, a retreat which was rendered every day more necessary as well as dear to me, by the addition of habit to inclination and of frequent interruptions in my health to the gradual waste committed on it by time. On the other hand, the magnitude and difficulty of the Trust to which the voice of my Country called me, being sufficient to awaken in the wisest and most experienced of her Citizens, a distrustful scrutiny into his qualifications, could not but overwhelm with despondence, one, who (inheriting inferior endowments from Nature and unpracticed in the duties of civil administration) ought to be particularly conscious of his own deficiencies. In this conflict of emotions, all I dare aver is that it has been my faithful study to collect my duty from a just appreciation of every circumstance, by which it might be affected. All I dare hope is that if in executing this Task, I have been too much swayed by a grateful remembrance of former instances or by an affectionate sensibility to this transcendant proof of the confidence of my fellow Citizens; and have thence too little consulted my incapacity as well as disinclination for the weighty and untried cares before me; my error will be palliated by the motives which misled me, and its consequence be judged by my Country, with some share of the partiality in which they originated.

It would be peculiarly improper to omit in this first official act, my fervent supplications to that Almighty Being who rules over the Universe, who presides in the Councils of Nations and whose providential aids can supply every human defect, that his benediction may consecrate to the Liberties and happiness of the People of the United States, a Government instituted by themselves for these essential purposes… No People can be bound to acknowledge and adore the invisible hand, which conducts the affairs of Men, more than those of the United States…

There is no truth more thoroughly established than that there exists in the economy and course of nature, an indissoluble Union between Virtue and Happiness, between duty and advantage, between the genuine maxims of an honest and magnanimous policy, and the solid rewards of public prosperity and felicity: Since we ought to be no less persuaded that the propitious smiles of Heaven, can never be expected on a Nation that disregards the eternal rules of order and right, which Heaven itself has ordained: And since the preservation of the sacred fire of Liberty, and the destiny of the Republican model of Government, are justly considered as deeply and finally staked on the experiment intrusted to the hands of the American people.

Following the address, Washington, with Congress and the invited guests, walked throughout the streets to St. Paul's Chapel, where the Right Reverend Samuel Provoost, Episcopal bishop of New York, conducted a brief worship, made the more blessed because he was not impelled to a sermon. Washington returned by carriage to his house. That evening he went with his secretaries, Humphreys and Lear, to watch the fireworks at the battery. So many people were out in the town that his carriage could not get back to his house at number three Cherry Street. The president walked home through the crowds.

Both Senate and House had been at work before Washington's arrival. The vice-president of the United States, John Adams, started his duties as president of the Senate with considerable seriousness. He had apparently assumed that, in the latter office, he would direct the proceedings and that his advice and counsel would be welcome at all times. It did not take very long for the Senate to indicate they expected him to be a silent and impartial presiding officer, voting only in a tie. This was a difficult task for an Adams. He complained how hard it was to listen without being able to talk back. The day after Washington's address, Senator William Maclay, a bitter little man from Pennsylvania, was on his feet in violent protest against his reference to the president's "most gracious speech." Adams, he said, was trying to make a king out of George Washington. Another senator replied that if Americans were never to use any British terms, they were going to be rather hard put to write or talk. The United States thus started its first day of operation with a quarrel, and a silly one at that, but the Senate's reply referred to the president's speech as "excellent" rather than "gracious."

In addition to a new House and Senate, some elements of the confederate government remained. The secretaries of foreign affairs and war, Jay and Knox, continued to act until new departments could be established by law. The old Treasury Board functioned, as did the Post Office. There were a handful of government clerks, an army of fewer than nine hundred men, and no money.

While many persons that spring and summer complained of the length of the debates and the slowness in organization, everything proceeded with what now appears to be remarkable speed. Washington had the aid of the noteworthy James Madison, a member of the House, with whom he had held so many discussions at Mount Vernon. Although, in deference to his countrymen's feelings about kingly rule, he had avoided presenting a solid initial program, he worked quietly and effectively with leaders of the Senate and House behind the scenes. There were divergencies in details on every measure that passed Congress but on broad aims there was general agreement and in fact little choice but to establish a revenue, permanent government departments, and a judiciary. The federalists generally were as anxious for a bill of rights as the antifederalists, the more so because it would serve to attach the latter more firmly to the Union.

WASHINGTON'S ILLNESS

Washington had come through the triumphant procession to New York in a rarely pessimistic and gloomy mood. This deepened as adulation approached mass hysteria. The newspapers spoke of "our adored ruler and leader" and, in one case, suggested that he was on the borderline between the human and divine. Published poetry referred to him as actually divine. Roman emperors might believe such claptrap, but for Washington, the thought that his countrymen expected him to be a living god served only to deepen his human worries. To Edward Rutledge of South Carolina he wrote six days after his inauguration:

> I cannot fail of being much pleased with the friendly part you take in every thing which concerns me; and particularly with the just scale on which you estimate this last great sacrifice which I consider myself as having made for the good of my Country. When I had judged, upon the best appreciation I was able to form of the circumstances which related to myself, that it was my duty to embark again on the tempestuous and uncertain Ocean of public life, I gave up all expectation of private happiness in this world. You know, my dear Sir, I had concentrated all my schemes, all my views, all my wishes, within the narrow circle of domestic enjoyment. Though I flatter myself the world will do me the justice to believe that, at my time of life and in my circumstances, nothing but a conviction of duty could have induced me to depart from my resolution of remaining in retirement, yet I greatly apprehend that my Countrymen will expect too much of me.

> I fear, if the issue of public measures should not correspond with their sanguine expectations, they will turn the extravagant (and I may say undue) praises which they are heaping upon me at this moment, into equally extravagant (though I will fondly hope unmerited) censures. So much is expected, so many untoward circumstances may intervene, in such a new and critical situation, that I feel an insuperable diffidence in my own abilities. I feel, in the execution of my arduous Office, how much I shall stand in need of the countenance and aid of every friend to the Revolution and of every lover of good Government. I thank you, my dear Sir, for your affectionate expressions on this point...

He said much the same thing more briefly in answer to an address from the city of New York on May 9: "The partiality of my Countrymen in my favor has induced them to expect too much from the exertions of an individual. It is from their cooperation alone, I derive all my expectations of success." Martha Washington, following her husband north, with her two grandchildren, arrived on May 28. She described the acclaim she had received in a letter to her niece on June 8:

My dear Fanny... In Philadelphia... [we] were met by the President of the state with the city troop of Horse... Was met on Wednesday morning by the President at Elizabethtown with the fine barge you have seen so much said of in the papers... Dear little Washington seemed to be lost in a maze at the great parade that was made for us all the way we came. The Governor of the state met me as soon as we landed. I thank God the President is very well... The House he is in is a very good one and is handsomely furnished... My first care was to get the children to a good school, which both are very pleased at... My Hair is set and dressed every day, and I have put on white muslin Habits for the summer. You would I fear think me a good deal in the fashion if you could but see me...

A week after Martha wrote this letter, the president took to bed with a serious illness. He had a fever which lasted for several days before a great and severely painful carbuncle formed on his thigh. He was attended by Dr. John Bard and his son, Dr. Samuel Bard, who were considered among the most eminent of New York's physicians. It was the younger Bard who summoned all his courage and, under his father's directions, performed the operation of cutting open the tumorous mass to drain the infectious matter. By July 4 Washington had improved sufficiently to receive the members of the Cincinnati, but he had to lie down in his carriage thereafter when he drove out for air.

On September 8 the president wrote his own physician, Dr. Craik: "My disorder was of long and painful continuance, and though now freed from the latter, the wound given by the incision is not yet closed... After the paroxysm had passed, I had no conception of being confined to a lying posture on one side six weeks, and that I should feel the remains of it more than twelve. The part affected is now reduced to the size of a barley corn, and by Saturday next (which will complete the thirteenth week) I expect it will be skimmed over. Upon the whole, I have more reason to be thankful that it is no worse than to repine at the confinement." The bill subsequently presented by the Bards indicates that he was under treatment until October 2.

The French minister at New York, the comte de Moustier, suggested, in a letter of June 24 to Jefferson in Paris, that Washington's illness was of emotional origin: "The President of the United States has run the risk of being the victim of his devotion to the good of his country. A complete change of life, a great preoccupation of mind... an unease caused by the novelty of a role difficult to play, especially when he wants to displease no one, something we of the more common sort believe to be impossible... Such circumstances have altered a vigorous health; fortunately the fire has gone to the surface."

Abigail Adams had arrived from Braintree to join the vice-president while Washington was sick. She called on Martha Washington, and the two women easily renewed their friendship. Abigail wrote to her sister: "She received me with great ease and politeness. She is plain in her dress but that plainness is the best of every article. Her hair is white, her teeth beautiful, her person rather short than otherwise... Her manners are modest and unassuming, dignified and feminine, not the tincture of hauteur about her... I found myself much more deeply impressed than I ever did before their Majesties of Britain." When Washington, propped up in bed, was able to receive Mrs. Adams, she wrote how pleased she was by his modesty and "easy affability." Later, when he was up and happily chatting with the ladies, Abigail noted that the president talked to them "with a grace, ease and dignity that leaves royal George far behind."

THE GOVERNMENT IS COMPLETED

Although Washington was ill much of the time, the executive and judicial systems were organized, and most of them in active operation by early October. Perhaps the most overworked of all persons were the secretaries to the president, especially Tobias Lear, for the presidential papers, all drafted in longhand, and copied for filing, ran into the thousands and presidential appointments into the hundreds. In addition, prior to the organization of the Department of State, the president was the chief means of communication with each of the states. Further, almost every college, religious society, city council, and state legislature, as well as innumerable citizens at home and abroad, felt impelled to write lengthy congratulatory letters and addresses, which were all politely answered. The most impressive of the private letters came from his former partisan officer, Colonel Armand, the Marquis de la Rouerie, who wrote from France that he wished Washington could command the whole world.

On June 8 the president asked the acting department heads—Foreign Affairs, War, Treasury, and Post Office—to provide him with as "clear account of their work... as may be sufficient... to impress me with a full, precise, and

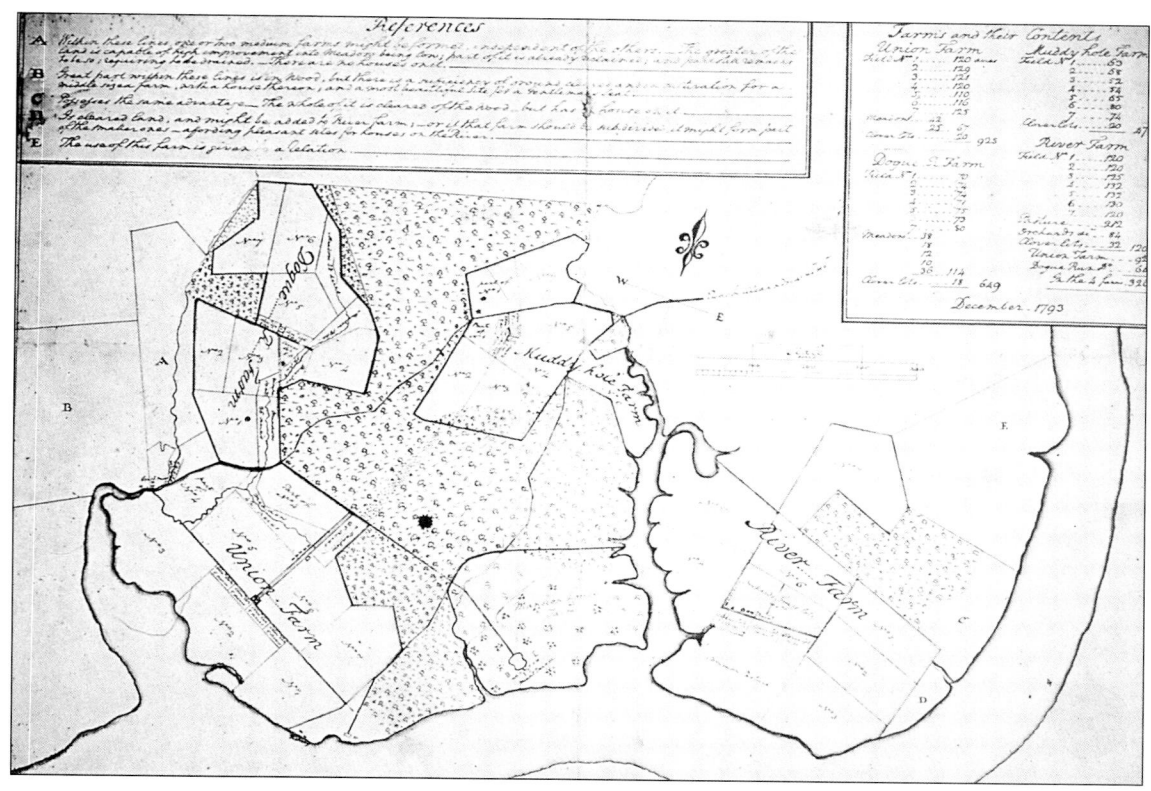

Washington's survey of his Mount Vernon farms (December 1793). *(Courtesy Huntington Library)*

John Adams, by John Trumbull, Vice President 1789–1797, President 1797–1801.
(National Portrait Gallery)

Thomas Jefferson, by Gilbert Stuart, Minister to France 1785–1789, Secretary of State 1790–1793, President 1801–1809. *(National Portrait Gallery)*

Henry Knox, by Charles Peale Polic, after Charles Wilson Peale, Secretary of War under the Confederation and the Constitution 1785–1794. *(National Portrait Gallery)*

John Jay, by John Trumbull, after Gilbert Stuart, Secretary of Foreign Affairs 1785–1789, Chief Justice of the United States 1789–1794, Special Envoy to Great Britain 1794, Governor of New York 1795–1801. *(National Portrait Gallery)*

Patrick Henry, by James Longacre, after James Sully. After early opposition to the new Constitution, Henry came to uphold it and was elected a Federalist Congressman in 1799, dying shortly thereafter. *(National Portrait Gallery)*

Gouverneur Morris, by James Sharples, Minister to France 1792–1794, reported faithfully to Washington on the Terror. *(National Portrait Gallery)*

James Madison, by Chester Harding, Member of Congress 1789–1797, President 1809–1817. *(National Portrait Gallery)*

James Monroe, by John Vanderlyn, Senator 1790–1794, Minister to France 1794–1796, President 1817–1825. *(National Portrait Gallery)*

John Quincy Adams, by George Bingham, appointed by Washington as Minister to the Netherlands 1794, President 1825–1829. *(National Portrait Gallery)*

distinct general *idea* of the affairs of the United States." Knox provided substantial information on the Indian situation, John Jay forwarded bulky reports on his foreign correspondence, while the postmaster general sent him a not too complete statement on postal finances. The most impressive document was provided by the Treasury Board, which forwarded, over a period of weeks, 250 folios, outlining the entire history of the currency after 1775, the current state of the national and state finances, and the foreign and domestic debts. This information was so complete that Hamilton was able to use it as a prime source for his subsequent report on the public credit.

On July 4, 1789, the president signed the first federal revenue act, a combination of *ad valorem* and specific tariff duties. Additional tonnage revenue acts, discriminating in favor of American-owned and -built vessels, followed. The states had adopted the British colonial port collector and naval officer system, which was now, in turn, nationalized. State officers became federal when authorizing legislation passed. On August 3 Washington nominated ninety-five collectors, surveyors, and naval officers, for ports ranging from Passamaquoddy, Maine, to St. Mary's, Georgia. Included on the list, as collector for Boston, was General Benjamin Lincoln, an appointment which, according to a friend of Lincoln, "renewed his youth and happiness."

One nomination precipitated the first conflict between the president and the Senate. Benjamin Fishbourne, appointed as naval officer at Savannah, was summarily rejected, without explanation, the only one on the list so treated. Washington wrote a dignified complaint, pointing out the reasons why he had nominated Fishbourne, which were to be his general criteria for all appointments. He had personally known him as a brave and resourceful revolutionary officer. He had been elected repeatedly to the Georgia Assembly which, in turn, had chosen him for the state council which elected him its president. Georgia had subsequently made him Savannah's naval officer. Washington noted that Fishbourne was endorsed for the office by numerous prominent Georgians. The Senate did not back down, and Washington nominated another officer. Subsequently the president learned that there had been charges made against his nominee in the state and these had been brought onto the Senate floor.

Legislation followed in rapid order. On July 27 the president signed the act to establish a Department of Foreign Affairs. The title was later changed to Department of State when a parsimonious Congress decided the occupant could administer both internal and external affairs. The War Department was approved on August 7. On August 18 Washington nominated a governor, General St. Clair, and a secretary and judges for the Northwest Territory, then, largely, Ohio. He also nominated commissioners to negotiate treaties with the

Indians. In September the acts establishing a federal judiciary, Treasury, and Post Office were signed by the president.

Between September 11 and 29 Washington made the most sweeping series of nominations ever made by a president of the United States when he sent to the Senate for confirmation the whole of the federal judiciary, the cabinet, and many other officers. On September 11 he designated Hamilton and Knox to head the Treasury and War departments, together with four principal officers of the Treasury, and the "surveyor of Town Creek." On September 24 he sent up nominations for a chief justice of the United States, John Jay, four associate justices, ten federal district judges, and twenty district attorneys and marshals. The following day he added two more district judges, four attorneys and marshals, and the names of Thomas Jefferson as secretary of state, Edmund Randolph as attorney general, and Samuel Osgood as postmaster general. On September 29 he named forty-five officers for commissions or promotions in the army. With a speed never equalled since, the Senate approved every nomination, and on September 29 both Houses adjourned. The United States government was in full operation and, for the first time, had proper officers and a revenue which began to accrue almost as soon as Washington forwarded commissions to the port collectors.

To add to an impressive beginning, which included the approval by Congress of constitutional amendments for a bill of rights, the United States enjoyed a summer of full crops, while Europe, including England, had grain shortages. Vessels streamed to America from Britain, France, Spain, and Portugal, buying wheat and flour at almost any price. In addition, according to William Short, chargé at Paris, over two hundred American ships went to France, Portugal, and the Baltic. In 1789 the port of New York alone reported the arrival of one thousand ships and smaller vessels. The government collected nearly $800,000 in the first five months of the new federal tariff. United States obligations rose by a third in the domestic money markets; at Amsterdam they went to par.

The costs of administration were smaller than the revenue.

Salaries and supplies were:

The President	$ 25,000
The Vice-President	5,000
Twenty federal judges	69,700
House and Senate	183,100
Treasury Department	28,000
Department of State	5,950

The army, with 887 officers and enlisted men, cost the government $160,887. The president's allowances had to cover his expenses as chief of state, his rent, entertaining, and travel, as well as the wages and board of four or five secretaries and as many as twenty servants. As usual, George Washington was to end up out of pocket from his public service.

SOCIAL LIFE

The first president, like all early heads of the republic, was supposed to be better than any king on earth, but no better than his commonest countryman. Unlike many of his successors, Washington could, with equal grace, sleep on a cold, wet hillside or preside at dinners made more cheerful by claret and champagne. As president he behaved pretty much as he always had, but with an eye to the dignity of the "United States," a term which he used on his letterheads. To conserve his time he established set social functions. He held a one-hour open-house for "respectable characters [male]" on Tuesday afternoon, while Mrs. Washington organized a similar affair for mixed company on Friday evenings. The Washingtons gave formal dinners each Thursday for members of Congress and the government. None of these affairs, which mixed up political enemies and strangers, was considered very lively. Washington kept Sundays free of official engagements to spend the day with his family.

In the middle of one of these dinners, September 1, when General von Steuben was at his most cheerful, a letter was delivered to the president announcing that his mother was dead of cancer. The *Gazette of the United States* announced that hers had been a life of "virtue, prudence and Christianity, worthy the mother of the greatest Hero who ever adorned the annals of history." Washington wrote his sister, Betty Lewis: "Awful and affecting as the death of a Parent is, there is consolation in knowing that Heaven has spared her to an age, beyond which few attain... When I was last at Fredericksburg, I took a final leave of my Mother, never expecting to see her more."

In a country where there was a movement to drop "Mister" as too formal a title, rumors circulated that the president's house was beginning to resemble a European court. These were stimulated to some extent by the social columns of the fawning *Gazette,* which relished reporting the names of titled guests who attended the Washingtons' receptions. Dr. David Stuart reported that stories about "the court" were being vigorously circulated in Virginia by opponents of the Constitution. Everyone was quoting Patrick Henry's early assertion that the document "squinted towards monarchy." It was also stated that Adams, who had suggested to the Senate that the president be called "His high mightiness," was using a state coach with a team of horses. Washington himself had become too snobbish to accept dinner invitations. The president replied on July 26:

Had I not adopted [rules], I should have been unable to have attended to <u>any</u> sort of business unless I had applied the hours allotted to rest and refreshment to this purpose, for by the time I had done breakfast, and thence till dinner, and afterwards till bed time I could not get relieved from the ceremony of one visit before I had to attend to another; in a word, I had no leisure to read or answer the dispatches that were pouring in upon me from all quarters... The late Presidents of Congress were involved in insuperable difficulties... for [their] table was considered as a public one, and every person, who could get introduced, conceived that he had a <u>right</u> to be invited to it. This, although the Table was always crowded (and with mixed company, and the President considered in no better light than as a Maitre d'Hotel) was in its nature impracticable and as many offences given as if no table had been kept...

So strongly had the citizens of this place imbibed an idea of the impropriety of my accepting invitations to dinner that I have not received one from any family (though they are remarkable for hospitality, and though I have received every civility and attention from them) since I came to the city, except dining with the Governor on the day of my arrival, so that, if this should be induced as an article of impeachment, there can be at least <u>one</u> good reason for my not dining out; to wit never having been asked to do so...

Washington added that, as far as he knew, John Adams never used more than two horses but he regretted that he had ever brought up the question of titles, for he foresaw that it would arouse great opposition.

Since Washington worked so hard, his wife found her life far less attractive than at Mount Vernon, as she wrote that fall:

I lead a very dull life here and know nothing that passes in the town. I never goe to any publick place. Indeed I think I am more like a state prisoner than anything else... I sometimes think the arrangement is not quite as it ought to have been; that I, who had much rather be at home, should occupy a place with which a great many younger and gayer women would be prodigiously pleased... I am still determined to be cheerful and to be happy, in whatever situation I may be; for I have also learned from experience that the greater part of our happiness or misery depends upon our dispositions, and not upon our circumstances.

Her husband, still athletic at fifty-seven, decided as soon as his recovery was complete, to get a lot more exercise. He also resumed his diaries on October 1. On October 3 he took a long walk. Two days later he was out on horseback for two hours and walked a further hour. On October 7 and 9 he again rode for two hours. On October 10 he went for a full day's excursion in the country. With John Adams and others, he took a barge to William Prince's fruit gardens and nurseries at Flushing. The comment by landscaper Washington was succinct: "These gardens, except in the number of young fruit trees, did not answer my expectations. The shrubs were trifling, and the flowers not numerous."

Washington also visited the Morrisania estate of Gouverneur and Lewis Morris, the latter the lord of the manor. The former had boasted to Washington about his barn. Farmer Washington was even briefer: "It was not of a construction to strike my fancy—nor did the conveniences of it all answer their cost." From there the party went to Harlem where Mrs. Washington, Mrs. Adams, and the Adamses' daughter, Mrs. Smith, were waiting. They dined at a tavern and returned to lower Manhattan.

In his diary, at this period, Washington noted the discussions he held on the possibility of sending a diplomat to London, to sound out the British on the peace treaty. He also discussed the desirability of a trip through the New England states, but in a *pro forma* manner because he had already made up his mind.

THE MORRIS MISSION

The president's policies, as he was to maintain them throughout his years in office, aimed to establish permanent peace with all nations. This would ensure domestic tranquility, and the steady growth of population, internal and external trade, and manufactures, until the country was strong enough to maintain its independence against any potential enemies. With strength, patience, and firmness, the United States would free itself of the British and Spanish occupying forces.

After numerous discussions with his cabinet, Madison, and Jay, the president determined on October 10 to send Gouverneur Morris to London as his personal representative, empowered to discuss the implementation of the 1783 treaty and to negotiate diplomatic representation and a treaty of commerce. Morris' instructions, which Washington drafted that day, were clear and succinct:

My letter to you, herewith enclosed, will give you the credence necessary to enable you to do the business, which it commits to your management...

Your inquiries will commence by observing that, as the present constitution of government, and of the courts established in pursuance of it, removes the objections heretofore made to putting the United States in possession of their frontier posts, it is natural to expect, from the asssurances of his Majesty, and the national good faith, that no unnecessary delays will take place. Proceed then to press a speedy performance of the treaty respecting that object.

Remind them of the article by which it was agreed that negroes, belonging to our citizens, should not be carried away, and the reasonableness of making compensation for them. Learn with precision, if possible, what they mean to do on this head.

The commerce between the two countries you well understand... You doubtless have heard that, in the late session of Congress, a very respectable number of both Houses were inclined to a discrimination of duties, unfavorable to Britain, and that it would have taken place but for conciliatory considerations and [to await negotiations for a commercial treaty].

Request to be informed, therefore, whether they contemplate a treaty of commerce with the United States... Let it be strongly impressed that the privilege of carrying our productions in our vessels to those Islands, and of bringing the production of those Islands, to our own ports and markets, is regarded here as of the highest importance; and you will be careful not to countenance any idea of our dispensing with it in a treaty. Ascertain, if possible, their views on this point; for it would not be expedient to commence negotiations without previously having good reasons to expect a satisfactory termination of them.

It may also be well for you to take a proper occasion of remarking that their omitting to send a minister here, did not make an agreeable impression...

It is, in my opinion, very important that we avoid errors in our system of policy respecting Great Britain; and this can only be done by forming a right judgment of their disposition and views. Hence you will perceive how interesting it is that you obtain the information in question, and that the business may be so managed that it may receive every advantage which abilities, address and delicacy can promise and afford.

Washington left the following morning for his New England tour. The secretary of the Treasury was among those who, as a mark of respect, accompanied the president part way out of town. Very probably that same day, he returned and began the extraordinary discussions and negotiations with the head of British intelligence in the United States, which have had no subsequent parallel.

THE YANKEE TOUR

No travel diaries of eighteenth-century America are as vivid as those of Washington on his five tours as president—to New England, through Long Island, to Rhode Island, south to Georgia, and to western Pennsylvania. In spite of the crowds, Washington was always able to look closely at the economy, noting what the farmers, merchants, seamen, and manufacturers were doing, and what the roads, inns, and people were like. In one way he had changed little since his youth, for he loved natural scenery, trees, good land, and beautiful women, and he found an abundance of these on his trips. There are few strictly political observations but he had a sharp and observing eye and ear for what the people liked and disliked. The tours were a great education for him, and they did an immense amount to cement the Union. Not until 1817 did any president venture so far out in the country.

CONNECTICUT AND MASSACHUSETTS

Washington began his trip on October 15 in the golden clear days of autumn. He was accompanied by two aides, William Jackson and Tobias Lear, and six servants. He crossed Kingsbridge, which separated Manhattan from the mainland, and spent the night in Rye at "the Tavern of a Mrs. Haviland… who keeps a very neat and decent Inn." He made copious notes as his party proceeded. The thirty-one miles from Manhattan north were "very rough and stony, but the Land strong, well covered with grass and a luxuriant crop of Indian Corn" mingled with pumpkins. He wrote that he had passed about 120 beeves and many sheep being driven to the New York market. The towns, East Chester, New Rochelle, and Mamaroneck, were scarcely distinguishable, as such, from the surrounding farming areas. Next morning he was again on stony roads which bounced his carriage around. He had breakfast at an inn which was only "tolerable good." He described the area from Horse Neck (Greenwich) to Fairfield:

Superb landscape… a rich regalia. We found all the Farmers busily employed in gathering grinding and expressing the Juices of their apples; the crop of which they say is rather above mediocrity. The average crop of Wheat… is about 15 bushels to the acre… often 20, and from that to 25. The Destructive evidences of British cruelty are yet visible both in Norwalk and Fairfield; as there are the chimneys of many burnt houses standing in them yet. The principal export from Norwalk and Fairfield is Horses and Cattle—salted Beef and Pork—lumber and Indian Corn to the West Indies, and in a small degree Wheat and Flour.

Washington crossed by the ferry at Stratford, recorded that vessels navigated the river up to Derby and that the town had established a factory for the manufacture of duck (a type of cloth), while there were grist and saw mills at Milford. He also noted "a handsome Cascade over the tumbling dam; but one of the prettiest things of this kind is at Stamford, occasioned also by damning the water for their mills; it is near 100 yards in width, and the water now being of a proper height, and the rays of the sun striking upon it as we passed, had a pretty effect upon the foaming water as it fell."

Leaving Milford the party was lucky enough to take the lower road. They thus missed a committee of the state legislature which had expected to read a long address to the president. They arrived in New Haven, free of officials, and walked at length around the town. They did not escape, however, for five hours later Washington had to stand and listen to them. They were followed by the Congregational ministers, the governor, the lieutenant governor, and the mayor of New Haven, who each said more or less the same things.

Since Washington arrived at New Haven on a Saturday afternoon, he was faced for the first time with Connecticut's laws against Sabbath travel. He spent Sunday in the town, attending the Episcopal Church in the morning and the Congregational in the afternoon. He invited the principal officers of the state and city to dine with him at his tavern, which he marked as "good." He questioned them about the manufacture of glass and linen.

At 6 A.M. Monday Washington rode to Wallingford where he examined the silkworm and mulberry tree experiments and samples of their heavy silk, which he pronounced "exceeding good." Going on to Middletown, he found the prospect from the heights over the Connecticut River to be "beautiful." He noted that the three principal towns on the river had around sixty-four trading vessels. "The Country hereabouts is beautiful." At Hartford Washington inspected the woolen manufactory and ordered another suit of broadcloth for himself, as well as bolts of a product called "Everlastings" for his servants' breeches. Washington rode on to Windsor where he inspected the United States arsenal and powder plant. There, a large party from Massachusetts waited to escort him to Springfield. As he left Connecticut, he recorded his impressons:

> *There is a great equality in the People of this State. Few or no opulent men—and no poor—great similitude in their buildings—the general fashion of which is a Chimney (always of Stone or Brick) and door in the middle, with a stair case fronting the latter, running up by the side of the former—two flush stories with a very good show of sash and glass windows—the size generally is from 30 to 50 feet in length, and from 20 to 30 in width, exclusive of a back shed, which seems to be added as the family increases.*

The farms, by the contiguity of the Houses, are small, not averaging more than
100 acres. These are worked chiefly by oxen (which have no other feed than hay)
with a horse, and sometimes two, before them, both in Plow and Cart. In their light
lands, and in their sleighs, they work Horses, but find them much more expensive
than oxen...

CONFUSION AT BOSTON

News that the president of the United States was on his way to Boston put the
state and city governments there in a frenzy. As Christopher Gore wrote
Tobias Lear: "The people of Boston are, beyond all conception, enraptured
with the idea of beholding their deliverer and protector." Gore, in response
to Lear's request, had engaged a house for the president, who had decided
always to stay at public inns or rented lodgings when travelling. Thus he did
not have to choose among clamorous hosts and hostesses nor subject them to
great crowds of curiosity seekers.

As it turned out, the vice-president, John Adams, the governor, John
Hancock, the lieutenant governor, Sam Adams, the executive council, the
state legislature, and the councils of Boston and Cambridge all worked to give
Washington a memorable welcome. They provided one he was scarcely likely
to forget.

Messengers galloped from Boston and Cambridge with invitations and
instructions. The governor asked Washington to stay at his house, the citizens
of Boston requested him to stay at another house, and an aide from the
Middlesex militia informed him they would escort him through the county to
a ceremonial reception at Cambridge. The governor had decided that the
president of the United States should make his first call in Boston on the
governor. He ordered, or Sam Adams and the state council volunteered, to go
and meet Washington and escort him from Cambridge to Hancock's house.
In the meantime the selectmen of Boston were working on their plans to
escort the president into Boston.

On Saturday, October 24, a raw New England day, the president and his
party set out at 8 A.M. from Marlborough, Massachusetts. Following his usual
pattern, Washington got out of his carriage at the Cambridge town limits and
mounted his horse to enable the people to see him better. He was in his place
at ten o'clock, punctually as planned, for his Cambridge reception. The militia that were to do honor to him did not show up until eleven. Washington
had to wait in the cold until they could perform their maneuvers. When these
were over, Lieutenant Governor Adams and the executive council of

Massachusetts moved to escort Washington across the neck to Boston. The selectmen of Boston had, however, determined that they were to do honors in the town. They appeared with their carriages and numerous schoolchildren to give Boston's official welcome, thus blocking the state party. The president had to sit patiently on his horse while the committees argued and brawled. Eventually the sheriff of Boston and his troopers broke through, scattering committees and children, and letting the president proceed.

In some sort of order, the city having won, the parade assembled, the state lined up behind the city, and the whole escorted the president to the Boston State House. Washington recorded seeing banners reading "To the man who unites all hearts," "To Columbia's favorite son," and "Boston relieved March 17, 1776." Washington climbed to the balcony where, as he wrote, "a vast concourse" was out to cheer him, many of whom, because of the contretemps, had waited hours in the cold.

When this was over, Samuel and John Adams, together with the state council, accompanied the president to his lodgings. Washington had agreed to go to dinner at the governor's house, but since the governor had not deigned to call on him (as Fisher Ames expressed it, Hancock did not like the idea that he had any "superior"), the president politely declined to go. Instead he dined in his own house with the vice-president of the United States. Governor Hancock, squirming, sent the lieutenant governor and members of the council to explain that he was too ill to call on Washington. The president replied that he would be glad to have the governor come when he recovered.

In the morning the president had begun to sneeze violently. Nonetheless, he attended an Episcopal service. When he returned to his lodgings, there was a note from the governor saying he was prepared to "hazard every thing, as it respects his health" to call on the man whom the governor referred to as "the President," a term borne also by the head of Harvard. With that glint which came often to his eye, Washington replied:

> *The President of the United States presents his best respects to the Governor, and has the honor to inform him that he shall be at home 'til two o'clock.*

> *The President of the United States need not express the pleasure it will give him to see the Governor; but, at the same time, he most earnestly begs that the Governor will not hazard his health on the occasion.*

The humorous Washington Irving could not bear to think that Washington was also humorous. His biography cautiously noted that the final sentence "almost savors of irony." Hancock appeared, his gouty foot carefully done up in cloth, as he was supported up the stairs by his servants. By the time he got back to his house, the rags were off and he skipped up the staircase without help. That afternoon the president attended a Congregational church and the vice-president again dined with him. Next day Washington was confined to his quarters with a bad cold and an inflamed eye. That evening, with even subtler irony, he presented them and himself at the governor's house.

On Tuesday, feeling a little better, he heard an oratorio at King's Chapel and received addresses from the town clergy, the governor and council, the town of Boston, the president of Harvard, the state Cincinnati, and others. During their meeting the town council requested that Washington sit for a picture so that it could be copied for various Boston ladies who wanted one in their houses. He promised that he would send a portrait from New York by John Trumbull, or another painter, since he did not have time to pose. The governor gave him a dinner that afternoon at Faneuil Hall. Hancock invited the vice-president also but in a manner which John Adams thought entirely too casual and he cut the dinner dead.

On October 28 Washington inspected factories. In one, he wrote, there were twenty-eight looms "and 14 girls spinning with Both hands (the flax being fastened to their waist). Children (girls) turn the wheels for them, and with this assistance each spinner can turn out 14 lbs. of Thread pr. day." The girls worked from eight in the morning to six at night. The whole factory produced thirty-two pieces of duck a week, each from thirty to forty yards long. Plans were under way to increase the number of workers and production. He told the manager that he had corralled all the best-looking girls in town. Washington also visited a factory where they made cards, including playing cards, which employed nine hundred hands.

In the evening, after visiting several ships, including French warships, he attended the Boston assembly where more than one hundred ladies were present. "Their appearance was elegant and many of them very handsome." This view of Boston was perhaps the best way to end a stay which had begun badly. John Adams, not often given to praise, was delighted with the president's trip and his popularity in his own state's capital. He wrote that Washington was very much "in character and consequently charming to all."

CAMBRIDGE TO NEWBURYPORT

After visiting Harvard, its library of 13,000 volumes, its laboratory and museum, Washington headed north. He found the bridges at Charlestown and Malden "useful and noble—doing great credit to the enterprising People of this State." He insisted on going to Marblehead which had not been on his itinerary. He wrote that 800 men and boys were engaged in commercial fishing in about 110 town vessels. He inspected the harbor and "their fish brakes for curing fish." Marblehead disappointed him: "The Houses are old; the streets dirty; and the common people not very clean."

At Salem the president was greeted by a Quaker chairman of the welcoming committee who merely said: "Friend Washington, we are glad to see thee, and in behalf of the inhabitants bid thee a hearty welcome to Salem." If Washington thought he was to be spared the full routine, he was mistaken, for singers stepped forth to sing an ode, after which he had to hear another long address. In the evening Salem did better, for the town held another dance for him "where there was at least an hundred handsome and well dressed Ladies. Abt. Nine I returned to my lodgings." He liked Salem, finding it "a neat Town and said to contain 8 or 9000 Inhabitants. Its exports are chiefly Fish, Lumber and Provisions. They have in the East India Trade at this time 13 Sail of Vessels."

The following morning Washington crossed the bridge to Beverley, commented on its handsome appearance, its length (nearly a third of a mile), and "the inconceivable low price at which it had been built"— about $11,000. He noted that all Massachusetts bridges of any importance had drawbridges and many had foot paths. At Beverley he inspected the "cotton Manufactory, which seems to be carrying on with spirit by the Mr. Cabots... They have the new Invented Carding and Spinning Machines... A number of Looms (15 or 16) were at work with spring shuttles, which do more than double work. In short, the whole seemed perfect and the cotton stuffs which they turn out, excellent of their kind; war and filling both are now of Cotton."

Newburyport, which he visited next, had prepared a noisy welcome, still remembered in its annals, which John Marquand recalled in *Timothy Dexter Revisited*. The local militia met him, the church bells rang, and the artillery fired the federal salute of thirteen guns. The smoke lifted to show a band and male chorus, as well as trumpeters, drummers, and cannoneers enthusiastically ready to serenade the president:

> *He comes! He comes! The HERO comes!*
> *Sound, sound your Trumpets [loud blasts] beat,*
>   *beat your Drums; [thunderous rolls]*
> *From port to port let Cannons roar [Boom, boom, boom]*
> *He's welcome to New England's shore.*
> *Welcome, welcome, welcome, welcome,*
> *Welcome to New England's shore.*

The second verse, with its line, "Loud, loudly rend the echoing air," probably barely conveys a sense of what happened when band, singers, trumpets, drums, and cannon all joined together. Marquand says that Washington was moved to tears. If so, this was the only sign he gave, as he sat on his white horse looking at the astonishing scene, that he was struggling not to laugh. Marquand continued:

> *Following the song a procession marched up the street, made up of all the social orders of the town. Following the musicians marched the selectmen, the marshal and the high sheriff. Then came the ministers, the physicians, the lawyers, the magistrates, the town officers, and the Marine Society. Behind the Marine Society were tradesmen, manufacturers, ships' captains, sailors, and finally schoolmasters with their scholars. Upon approaching the president, the parade divided its ranks to right and left, allowing the honored guest to pass through. Then they joined ranks again and followed him. The teachers, we are told, led four hundred and twenty scholars, each bearing his quill pen.*

At the Tracey house Washington was given an address of welcome to which he responded as usual with some graciously stilted words, and he was then given dinner. That night the militia came around and fired muskets under his windows. The citizens followed with fireworks including rockets. The next morning the president left Newburyport quietly.

NEW HAMPSHIRE

There was no Hancockian nonsense in New Hampshire. At the state line, October 31, the governor (General Sullivan), the lieutenant governor, members of the governor's council, both United States senators, the state marshal, as much of the state's cavalry as could be mustered, and "many officers of the Militia in handsome (white and red) uniforms of the manufacture of the State" were present to greet Washington, who wrote: "With this cavalcade, we proceeded and arrived before 3 o'clock at Portsmouth where we were received with every token of respect and appearance of cordiality, under a discharge of artillery. The streets, doors and windows were crowded there, as at all other Places; and alighting at the Town House, odes were sung and played in honor of the President."

Washington invited all the officials to dine with him at his tavern. Next morning, another Sabbath, he followed his usual custom, attending the Episcopal church in the forenoon and the Congregational in the afternoon.

After church he found time to write a few letters. He spent three more days in New Hampshire, which he recorded in some detail:

(November 2) "I went in a boat to view the harbour of Portsmouth; which is well secured from all winds; and from its narrow entrance from the Sea and passage up to the Town, may be perfectly guarded against any approach by water. The anchorage is also good... I stopped at Kittery [Maine]. From hence I went by the old Fort (formerly built while under the English government) on an Island, which is at the entrance of the harbour, and where the Light House stands... We were saluted by 13 guns... We proceeded to the Fishing banks, a little without the Harbour, and fished for Cod; but it not being a proper time of tide, we only caught two, with which... we returned to town. Dined at [Senator] Langdon's, and drank tea there, with a large circle of Ladies, and retired a little after seven o'clock...

(November 3) Sat two hours in forenoon for a Mr. [Gülager], A Painter, of Boston... Having walked through most parts of the town, returned by 12 o'clock, when I was visited by a Clergyman of the name of Haven, who presented me with an Ear and part of the stalk of the dyeing Corn, and several pieces of Cloth which had been dyed with it, equal to any colours I had ever seen... This Corn was blood red...

About 2 o'clock, I received an Address from the Executive of the State of New Hampshire, and in half an hour after dined with him and a large company, at their assembly room, which is one of the best I have seen anywhere in the United States. At half after seven I went to the assembly, where there were about 75 well dressed, and many of them handsome ladies—among whom (as was also the case at the Salem and Boston assemblies) were a greater proportion with much blacker hair than are usually seen in the Southern States. About nine, I retired to my quarter...

(November 4) About half after seven I left Portsmouth... without any attendance, having earnestly entreated that all parade and ceremony might be avoided... Before ten I reached Exeter, 14 miles distance. This is considered as the second town in New Hampshire, and stands at the head of the tide-water of Piscataqua River; but ships of 3 or 400 tons are built at it. Above (but in the town) are considerable falls, which supply several grist mills, 2 oil mills, a slitting mill, and a snuff mill. It is a place of some consequence, but does not contain more than 1,000 Inhabitants. A jealousy subsists between this town (where the legislature alternately sits), and Portsmouth; which, had I known it in time, would have made it necessary to have accepted an invitation to a public dinner, but my arrangements having been otherwise made, I could not.

MRS. COOLIDGE AND MR. TAFT

Washington proceeded south to Haverhill, Massachusetts, "in a beautiful part of the country," thence to Andover and on to Lexington to "view the spot on which the first blood was spilt in the dispute with Great Britain, on the 19th of April, 1775."

At this point the New England weather turned nasty and the president changed his route in order to pass the night at Watertown. There, he remarked, "We lodged at the house of a Widow [Mrs. Nathaniel] Coolidge, and a very indifferent one it is."

The president had no better luck the following day. Having covered thirty-six miles in threatening weather, over "amazingly crooked" road built, he said, to suit "the convenience of every man's fields," and having been given wrong directions which took him miles out of his way, the tired president was glad to stop for the night at the house of Samuel Taft at Uxbridge. Washington remarked that "though the people were obliging, the entertainment was not very inviting." He got out before dawn.

In his courteous way, Washington wrote a note of thanks next day, November 8, to Taft from Hartford, noting that he had been informed that he had named one son for the president and a daughter for Martha Washington, "and being moreover very much pleased with the modest and innocent looks of your two daughters, Patty and Polly, I do, for these reasons, send each of these Girls a piece of chintz. And to Patty, who bears the name of Mrs. Washington, and who waited upon us more than Polly did, I send five guineas, with which she may buy herself any little ornaments she may want... As I do not give these things with a view to have it talked of... the less there is said about the matter the better you will please me, but that I may be sure the chintz and money got safe to hand, let Patty, who I dare say is equal to it, write me a line thereof directed to 'The President of the United States' at New York."

Patty was more than equal to her task though it took her several weeks to figure out how to address a president. In Uxbridge, or elsewhere, she found a book from England which explained how to write to high personages. On December 28 she dispatched her letter:

May it please your Highness:

Agreeable to your commands, I, with pleasure, inform the President that, on the 20th inst., I received the very valuable present...

And I want to express gratitude to you, Great Sir, for the extraordinary favour &

honour, conferred on me and our family... while your Highness was pleased to honour my Papa's house with your presence...

My most ardent desires are that the light of heavens blessing may... ever rest on him who stands at the head of our United Empire... Papa and Mama with sincere thanks and duty desire to be remembered to your Highness... May it please your Highness...

Mercy Taft

Pray pardon me sir if I mention the mistake in my name, you see, sir, it is not Patty.

CONNECTICUT

As he moved south from the Tafts', Washington found an "intolerable bad road, and a poor and uncultivated country" on the Massachusetts side. On Sunday, November 8, he spent a peculiarly disagreeable day. He got breakfast at a bad inn on the Connecticut side and, finally, lodged Saturday evening at Ashford, which condemned him to pass the Sabbath there. He summed it up: "I stayed at Perkins' tavern (which, by the bye, is not a good one) all day—and a meeting-house being within few rods of the door, I attended morning and evening service, and heard very lame discourses from a Mr. [Enoch] Pond."

Talk of snows, worry about Mrs. Washington, and a general desire to get to New York to see what was going on caused the president to hurry home as rapidly as the bad roads permitted. On Monday, he travelled thirty-four miles to Hartford, twenty-four of them over "hilly, rocky, and disagreeable roads." He still found time to question the farmers about their crops and yields and where and what they marketed. Next day he reached New Haven where he met Elbridge Gerry, just arrived by stage coach from New York, who assured him his wife was in good health. On Wednesday he was nine miles beyond Fairfield and on Thursday at Rye. On Friday afternoon, November 13, "between two and three o'clock arrived at my house at New York, where I found Mrs. Washington and the rest of the family all well—and it being Mrs. Washington's night to receive visits, a pretty large company of ladies and gentlemen were present."

Shortly after returning, the president received an invitation from a minor, but rather pushy, New York family, to come to a burial service for a relative. He declined, feeling that if he went to Mrs. Isaac Roosevelt's service, he might be expected to attend too many others of people he did not know.

The trip did Washington great good. The gloom, with which he had moved to New York, and which had affected his health, seems to have entirely disappeared. The time he spent out-of-doors, riding and walking, brought renewed vigor. Though John Trumbull noted that he returned "all fragrant with the odor of incense," his own observations, rather than the public and tiring demonstrations, lifted up his spirits. He found the high caliber of his appointments to office had won universal admiration. People were pleased to have a respectable national government. Everywhere that Washington looked he could see strength and growth in the economy. The removal of the dead hand of colonialism had stimulated shipbuilding, manufacturing, and commerce. He heard reports of ships trading from New England to China and the Indies. He saw and talked with the people, egalitarian and prosperous, who were proud of their farms, handicraft, and new machinery. Washington sensed that the demonstrations of affection for the president had been their way of showing pride in themselves.

PROMOTING MANUFACTURING

Nine days after returning to his office, Washington wrote to Beverley Randolph, the governor of his own state, in an initial endeavor to get the south to move forward with New England:

From the original letters, which I forward herewith, Your Excellency will comprehend the nature of a prospect for introducing and establishing the Woolen Manufactory in the State of Virginia. In the present state of population and agriculture, I do not pretend to determine how far that Plan may be practicable and advisable; or in case it should be deemed so, whether any or what public encouragement ought to be given to facilitate its execution. I have, however, no doubt as to the good policy of encreasing the number of Sheep in every way. By a little Legislative encouragement, the Farmers of Connecticut have, in two years past, added one hundred thousand to their former stock. In my late tour through the Eastern States, I found that the Manufacturers of Woolens... preferred the Wool raised in Virginia for its fineness, to that raised in the more Northern parts of the Continent. If a greater quantity of Wool could be produced, and if the hands (which are often in a manner idle) could be employed in the manufacturing of it; a spirit of industry might be promoted, a great diminution might be made in the annual expenses of individual families, and the Public would eventually be exceedingly benefitted.

Under these impressions, I have thought proper to transmit the Proposal; and will only add that, if it should be judged expedient to submit the project to the Legislature, or if any private Company should engage in promoting the business, the necessity of keeping the Manufacturer's name concealed would undoubtedly occur: as a premature knowledge of it might not only frustrate the success of the Project, but also subject the person principally concerned to the most distressing consequences.

The United States, in its early development, did not have the technical and financial aid which it gave away so freely in the twentieth century. The reverse, in fact, was true as far as Great Britain was concerned. That country had passed legislation making it a criminal offense to export certain types of machinery and plans, or to encourage and promote the emigration of skilled engineers and mechanics. The laws were not entirely enforceable. Machinery, plans, and mechanics did cross the Atlantic but in a clandestine manner. One of Washington's most accomplished wartime intelligence officers, Thomas Digges, his friend and neighbor across the Potomac, aided in this traffic. Digges had operated from London during the revolution, sending out important intelligence. He had also helped American prisoners to escape, using them as couriers to convey information to Washington. The British so trusted him that they dispatched him as a peace emissary to John Adams in the Netherlands. Washington gave him high praise in 1794 for his work.

It is not clear whether the Virginia proposal came from Digges but it appears probable. He loathed slavery, as did Washington, and was anxious to promote manufacturing and European settlement in Virginia and Maryland. When Governor Randolph, much interested, asked the president's aid in getting the plans out of England, he had to reply that he had gone as far as he was able to do in sending the information. He could not actively assist in the violation of foreign laws.

SECRETARY HAMILTON

The first surviving letter by Hamilton was written at fourteen to Edmund Stevens: "To confess my weakness, Ned, my ambition is [so] prevalent that I contemn the grov'ling and condition of a Clerk... and would willingly risk my life tho' not my character to exalt my Station... I mean to prepare the way for futurity... We have seen such schemes successful when the Projector is Constant. I shall conclude saying I wish there was a War."

Hamilton's earlier experience as a shipping clerk was to be of value to the

United States, whose revenues, in the first years, came very largely from import duties. Much of his time after becoming secretary of the treasury was devoted to routine but complex matters. These included establishing forms and regulations for the customs collectors, deciding disputed points of law, building revenue vessels, and providing lighthouses and navigational aids. In addition, by order of the House of Representatives, he prepared a report on the public finances, providing for the settlement of the large internal and foreign debt.

By the time Hamilton took office, the government already had a revenue larger than its operating expenses. In addition, the president had obtained a very full documentation of the debt which he could give the secretary. What Hamilton formulated thereafter was a proposed debt settlement of great complexity, but a tax program to pay for it of utmost simplicity. In essence, the country's consumers of alcoholic beverages were to foot the bill. The secretary pointed out that such a tax was not only a dependable source of income but had a certain moral value as well. His estimate of the national consumption of spirits at that period is rather staggering. It was about three-and-a-half times per capita what it would be in the late twentieth century.

HAMILTON AND THE BRITISH

After the execution of John André, his deputy, George Beckwith, succeeded him as head of British intelligence. A much subtler operator than André, he remained with Sir Guy Carleton until the British departed New York in 1783. He reappeared in the United States in 1787 and 1788, getting such intelligence as he could, which would aid London in dividing the former colonies, and returning a large portion of the country to British control. While Washington was on his way north to take the oath as president in April 1789, Carleton, now Lord Dorchester, reported from Quebec to his home government that many settlers in Kentucky and Tennessee wanted independence. They would welcome English protection as well as an occupation of New Orleans, provided they could trade through that port. Dorchester noted that whoever controlled the navigation of the Mississippi would be master of the lands beyond the Alleghenies.

On June 7 Dorchester informed London that he intended to supply arms to Americans in the West, to assist their trade through Great Lakes ports, and to enlist their cooperation should the British attack New Orleans. While this proposal was being implemented, the English were studying a project to link Vermont with Quebec by a canal to the Chambly River. Ira Allen, a brother of Ethan, was working to bring Vermont back under English control. In

September 1789 Beckwith returned once more to New York, to direct the extensive activities of British intelligence. One of his first calls was on Senator Schuyler of New York, with whom he had previously held conversations. He insinuated that his government was not pleased with the American tonnage and revenue acts, which had passed before Hamilton assumed office. The British were quite prepared to take action.

When Schuyler reported this to Hamilton, the secretary of the treasury called Beckwith to his office. This talk and their most important future conferences were to take place while the president was away from the capital: in October 1789, from August to October 1790, and May to July 1791. In these, Hamilton was to endeavor to frustrate not only the president's policy of impartiality to all countries but his plans to develop the country's economic potentials by a great increase of manufactures and the merchant marine. In reporting to London and Quebec, Beckwith stated that Hamilton opened the talk by saying, "I have requested to see you on this occasion from a wish to explain certain points, relative to our situation, and from a desire to suggest a measure, which I conceive to be both for the interest of Great Britain, and of this country... I have always preferred a connexion with you, to that of any other country... We must be for years, rather an agricultural, than a manufacturing people, yet our policy has had a tendency to suggest the necessity of introducing manufactures... Doubtless their increase will be proportioned to your conduct... We wish to form a commercial treaty with you, to every extent, to which you may think it your interest to go..." In succeeding points, which are here rearranged to follow, in order, Washington's instructions to Morris, Hamilton observed:

> On our side there are... two points unadjusted, the Western Forts [two were on Lake Champlain] and the negroes, although as to the latter I always decidedly approved Lord Dorchester's conduct on that occasion... The reply of your cabinet to our application on that subject was perfectly satisfactory...

> We may have a matter of great importance to settle with Spain, I mean the navigation of the Mississippi; this is of the first moment to our territories to the westward, _they must have that outlet, without it they will be lost to us_... Our country is already sufficiently large, more so than prudence might wish, as its extent tends to increase our difficulties in certain points, and to weaken our government... Connected with you, by strong ties of commercial, perhaps of political friendships, our naval exertions, in future wars, may in your scale be greatly important and decisive. These are my opinions... which I have long entertained...

... I do think a treaty of commerce might be formed of advantage to both countries. I am of opinion, that it will be better for Great Britain to grant us admission into her Islands under certain limitations of size of vessels so as merely to enable us to [trade] there... and... under such restrictions as to prevent the possibility of our interfering with your carrying trade to Europe...

... The ideas I have thrown out may be depended upon, as the sentiments... of General Washington....

In the discussions Hamilton assured Beckwith the United States would never attack Canada, thus removing an important British fear. Hamilton indicated he was heartily against any commercial discrimination against Great Britain and intimated that Washington was also opposed. Beckwith said that Britain's national honor would force her to repel any trade hostility, even in opposition to Britain's own discrimination, and he blasted James Madison who had introduced the bill. Hamilton agreed that Madison had "little knowledge of the world" and that Britain would be acting wisely, and in honor, if she retaliated against the United States. Beckwith told Hamilton to make sure anyone the president chose to go to London had no French bias, a remarkable piece of impudence on the part of a military spy. At the end, Hamilton sought, and got, Beckwith's assurances that he would not repeat his conversation anywhere in the United States. He gave him full liberty to forward his views to the British cabinet.

When Gouverneur Morris appeared in London to present his case on behalf of the United States, which he did in exact accordance with the president's instructions, he was surprised at the cool contempt with which he was received. This was the first of the years in which Hamilton thwarted the president's efforts to achieve a peaceful settlement of all issues with Great Britain. Six days after Beckwith left New York, and before they heard of the appointment of Morris, the British cabinet forwarded to Lord Dorchester approval of his plan to form the western American settlements into a political unit, independent of the United States.

BACK TO WORK

Problems and correspondence had accumulated for Washington on his New England trip. Not all of his nominees to office accepted. His old secretary, Robert Hanson Harrison, whom he had placed on the Supreme Court, declined the post. In bad health, he died the following year. Washington went over the report of the commissioners whom he had sent to negotiate a peace treaty with the southern and warlike Indians. He noted: "Gave it one reading—and shall bestow another and more attentive one on it." Next day he held long conversations with the commissioners on their negotiations with the Creek chief, Alexander McGillivray, who was trying to play Spain and Great Britain against the United States, to find out who would bid highest.

On November 25 Washington went to the theater taking as his guests Mrs. Adams, the two New York senators and their wives, Senator and Mrs. Pierce Butler of South Carolina, Mr. and Mrs. Hamilton, and Mrs. Nathanael Greene. The theaters always trumpeted his appearance in a way to assure a full house. They had begun a custom of playing a tune on his entry, "The President's March," which later had the words, "Hail, Columbia." The *New York Daily Advertiser* wrote: "On the appearance of THE President, the audience rose, and received him with the warmest acclamations—the genuine effusions of the hearts of FREEMEN." The program included, as an epilogue, a short humorous sketch, *Darby's Return*, by William Dunlap, one of the first plays written by a native American. It was an account by a soldier, returned to Ireland, of the war in America and the new government. The humor has not stood the test of time but three lines on the Constitution had merit:

> *A revolution without blood or blows*
> *For as I understood, the cunning elves,*
> *The People all revolted from themselves.*

The president was a regular churchgoer and noted it each Sunday in his journal. He issued the first presidential Thanksgiving proclamation on October 3. On November 26 he wrote, probably without irony: "Being the day appointed for a thanksgiving, I went to St. Paul's Chapel, though it was most inclement and stormy—but a few people at Church." On December 11 he noted: "Being rainy and bad, no person except the Vice-President visited Mrs. Washington this evening." December 29 was worse: "Being very snowing, not a single person appeared at the Levee."

Though he made such notes, the president, from his diary comments, seems to have begun to enjoy his office more than he anticipated. He went on frequent walks, carriage rides with his wife and her grandchildren, and horseback rides as far as Harlem. His dinner parties included officers of the government, senators and representatives, old military comrades, governors, bishops and other clergy, and Péter Van Berckel, the Dutch minister who was the only fully accredited diplomat after the return of the French minister to Paris. When out on his horse he frequently stopped to call informally on various people who had come to his house.

The business which most occupied his attention was with Henry Knox, his war secretary. Reports in abundance reached the capital of Indian raids and atrocities from Pennsylvania to Georgia. Negotiations for peace treaties with the Indians bogged down. The president, in consequence, was greatly interested in revising the militia and defense system of the United States. He drafted his proposal himself after obtaining the views of Knox and von Steuben. He reviewed Hamilton's first report to Congress on the state of the public debt and shortly afterwards ordered Adam Smith's *Wealth of Nations*. He also wrote the first State of the Union message for delivery in January.

THE SECOND SESSION

Congress, scheduled to meet January 4, 1790, did not have a quorum that day. Washington sent a note to say that he would be glad to meet them at a time and place "convenient for Congress… to make some oral communications at the commencement of their session." Two days later Congress had its quorum, and Washington set January 8 for his message. He described the rather impressive ceremony in his diary:

> *According to appointment, at 11 o'clock, I set out for the City Hall in my coach, preceded by Colonel Humphreys and Majr. Jackson in uniform (on my two white horses) and followed by Mssrs. Lear and Nelson, in my chariot, and Mr. Lewis, on horseback, following them. In their rear was the Chief Justice of the United States and the Secretaries of the Treasury and War Departments, in their respective carriages, and in the order they are named. At the outer door of the hall I was met by the door-keepers of the Senate and House, and conducted to the door of the Senate Chamber; and passing from thence to the Chair through the Senate on the right, and House of Representatives on the left, I took my seat. The gentlemen who attended me followed and they took their stand behind the Senators; the whole rising as I entered. After being seated, at which time the members of both Houses also sat, I rose (as they also did) and made my speech… On this occasion I was dressed in a suit of clothes made at the Woolen Manufactory at Hartford, as the buttons also were.*

Though the speech was short, it contained much more meat than his inaugural address. Washington read it with a far clearer and more confident voice. Pleased with his country's progress, he now felt free to ask for a much broader program of national security and economic development:

> *I embrace with great satisfaction, the opportunity which now presents itself, of*

congratulating you upon the present favourable prospects of our public affairs. The recent acquisition of the important State of North Carolina to the Constitution of the United States (of which official information has been received)—the rising credit and respectability of our Country—the general and increasing good will towards the Government of the Union—and the concord, peace and plenty, with which we are blessed, are circumstances auspicious in an eminent degree, to our national prosperity...

Among the many interesting objects, which will engage your attention, that of providing for the common defense will merit particular regard.—To be prepared for War is one of the most effectual means of preserving peace.

A free people ought not only to be armed but disciplined—to which end a uniform and well digested plan is requisite. And their safety and interest require that they should promote such manufactories as tend to render them independent of others for essentials, particularly military supplies.

The proper establishment of the Troops, which may be deemed indispensable, will be entitled to mature deliberation. In the arrangements which may be made respecting it, it will be of importance to conciliate the comfortable support of the Officers and Soldiers, with a due regard to economy.

There was reason to hope that the pacific measures adopted with regard to certain hostile tribes of Indians would have relieved the Inhabitants of our Southern and Western frontiers from their depredations. But you will perceive from the information contained in the papers, which I shall direct to be laid before you (comprehending a communication from the Commonwealth of Virginia) that we ought to be prepared to afford protection to those parts of the Union, and if necessary, to punish aggressors.

The interests of the United States require that our intercourse with other nations shall be facilitated, by such provisions as will enable me to fulfill my duty in that respect... [with] a competent fund designated for defraying the expenses incident to the conduct of our foreign affairs.

Various considerations also render it expedient that the terms on which foreigners may be admitted to the rights of Citizens should be speedily ascertained by a uniform rule of naturalization.

Uniformity of the Currency, Weights and Measures of the United States is an object of great importance, and will, I am persuaded, be attended to.

The advancement of Agriculture, Commerce, and Manufacturing by all proper means, will not I trust need recommendation. But I can not forbear intimating to you the expediency of giving effectual encouragement as well to the introduction of new and useful inventions from abroad, as to the exertions of skill and genius in producing them at home; and of facilitating the intercourse between the distant parts of our country by due attention to the Post-Office and Post-Roads. Nor am I less persuaded that you will agree with me in opinion that there is nothing which can better deserve your patronage than the promotion of Science and Literature. Knowledge is in every country the surest basis of public happiness...

Whether this desirable objective will be best promoted by affording aids to seminaries of learning already established, by the institution of a national university, or by any other expedient, will be worthy of a place in the deliberations of the Legislature.

...Adequate provision for the support of public credit is a matter of high importance to the national honour and prosperity...

I have directed the proper Officers to lay before you such papers and estimates as regards the affairs, particularly recommended to your consideration and necessary to convey to you that information of the State of the Union, which is my duty to afford...

This was to be the longest legislative session of Washington's administration. In his quiet way the president presented the most comprehensive program which the federal legislature has ever received. Congress was to revise the general defense system, provide for payment of the national debt with new taxes, establish naturalization laws, uniform money, new weights and measures, a patent office, interstate roads, better postal service, a permanent foreign service, and aid to higher education and science. To these points in his message, Washington subsequently added proposals for copyright laws, a national census, the assumption of state debts, the establishment of a permanent national capital, and a national banking system. The executive was soon transmitting formal reports on treaties with the Indians, a proposal to reorganize the militia, the cession by North Carolina of lands to the federal government, a report on the public credit, and new nominations for federal offices.

In less formal language, Washington described to the enthusiastic English Whig, Catherine Macauley Graham, January 9, 1790, how the United States was doing:

On the actual situation of this Country under this new Government I will... make a few remarks. That the Government, though not absolutely perfect, is one of the best in the world, I have little doubt. I have always believed that an unequivocally free and equal Representation of the People in the Legislature, together with an efficient and responsible Executive, were the great Pillars on which the preservation of American Freedom must depend... So far as we have gone with the new Government (and it is completely organized and in operation) we have had greater reason than the most sanguine could expect, to be satisfied with its success.

Perhaps a number of accidental circumstances have concurred with the real effects of the Government to make the People uncommonly well pleased with their situation and prospects. The harvests of wheat have been remarkably good, the demand for that article from abroad is great, the increase of Commerce is visible in every Port, and the number of new manufactures introduced in one year is astonishing. I have lately made a tour through the Eastern States. I found the country, in a great degree, recovered from the ravages of War, the towns flourishing, and the People delighted with a government instituted by themselves and for their own good. The same facts I have also reason to believe, from good authority, exist in the Southern States. By what I have just observed, I think you will be persuaded that the ill-boding Politicians who prognosticated that America would never enjoy any fruits from her Independence, and that she would be obliged to have recourse to a foreign Power for protection, have at least been mistaken.

SEVEN

NEW YORK TO PHILADELPHIA

1790

ALTHOUGH HAMILTON'S BUDGET always placed his department ahead of the foreign office, the president considered the secretary of state to precede the head of the Treasury. When he originally offered the post to Jefferson on October 13, 1789, the latter, after examining his proposed responsibilities, replied: "When I contemplate the extent of that office, embracing as it does the principal mass of domestic administration, together with the foreign, I cannot be insensible of my inequality to it; and I should enter on it with gloomy forebodings."

Washington had received persuasive enough letters when he wrote in similar vein. He replied that he knew no one who could fill the post better than Jefferson. His appointment had given "extensive and very great satisfaction to the public." The domestic duties were, in fact, divided among the cabinet members. Adjustments would be made, if they were too great for the Department of State. It was Jefferson's option to return to Paris but Washington hoped Jefferson would report to the capital. The organization of the foreign service depended on his acceptance of the office.

When the secretary of state reached New York, he found that his entire staff was to consist of four clerks, a messenger, and an interpreter. Washington had underplayed the work involved. Jefferson found himself running the foreign office during war and revolution abroad, organizing a permanent diplomatic and consular service, administering the mint and the patent office, and working on weights and measures and a national census.

LEGISLATION

The president had now taken the lead, which he had originally planned to do in his inaugural address, in recommending legislation in widely varied fields of endeavor. The details were to be worked out either in Congress or in conferences between the legislative and executive branches. Many proposals were expected to be noncontroversial, but the census was originally rejected by the Senate as a form of make-work for bookkeepers. The president let the toughest major issues, where feelings ran high, be fought out in the Senate and House. He wrote that he occasionally signed legislation that he might have voted against, had he been in Congress. What he wanted, however, and what he got were generally in close agreement.

The first session of the First Congress had passed extensive legislation. The second was even more productive. Although Congress was criticized as dilatory, the laws came out with speed. Before Washington's first year in office was completed on April 30, North Carolina had been admitted to the Union and its federal officers appointed; the budget for 1790 ($551,491.71) had been approved; and acts had authorized a national census, uniform naturalization, a patent office, and a permanent army. Washington was disappointed that the regular army was set at only 1,680 officers and men, inasmuch as he faced trouble on many frontier points. Between May and August 1790, laws established a foreign and consular service, a territorial government south of the Ohio River, a Library of Congress, a copyright office, the placement of the permanent capital for the United States, and the admission of Rhode Island to the Union. Further legislation authorized the purchase of West Point, higher import duties, a revenue cutter service, and treaties with the Indians. In addition acts passed for the settlement of all United States debts.

Fiscal legislation was the most troublesome, but not all of it was controversial. The French finance minister, Jacques Necker, told William Short, the American chargé at Paris, that the United States ought to regard its war debts to France as the most sacred of all its obligations. No such reminder was needed. As a matter of national honor, all Americans agreed that the debt to France should have priority over payments to its own citizens. The Senate and House unanimously approved this at the beginning of debates which, on other parts of the debts, lasted for six months.

The internal debt of the old Continental Congress consisted of six types of obligations totalling, with arrears of interest, $40 million. The unsettled war charges owed by the various states were calculated at $18 million. Adding the foreign loans brought the total to $70 million. Hamilton's report on public credit recommended that the federal government assume the whole burden and raise taxes on spirits sufficiently high to pay the interest. In his first and subsequent reports, Hamilton added small taxes on sugar, salt, tea, and coffee. As nearly as can be calculated from Hamilton's reports, he urged taxes high enough to yield a federal revenue of $3.6 million. All but $600,000 was to be used for debt payments. His suggested settlements were clumsy but they were somewhat modified and improved in Congress.

Hamilton stated "the proper funding of the present debt will render it a national blessing," if "the creation of debt [is] always accompanied with the means of extinguishment." This was to be done by sinking funds. Hamilton, in his report to Congress, made two proposals, the first fraudulent and the second disingenuous. Hamilton proposed "that the net product of the post-office, to a sum not exceeding one million of dollars," be applied to debt redemption. The gross annual receipts of the Post Office at this time, as Hamilton knew, were only $29,000, and the service probably ran at a deficit. Hamilton also proposed that additional foreign loans be floated, to act as a sinking fund, thus implying that debts can be reduced by borrowing. His proposals for debt settlement, including the payment by the federal government of state war debts, nearly blew the Union apart. Neither the rich nor taxes were popular, and the proposals for the latter seemed designed to benefit the former. Speculation in federal and state securities had started almost as soon as it was clear that the new government would be organized under Washington. When Hamilton's proposals were announced (and, many thought even before, thanks to leaks to friends by Hamilton's assistant, William Duer), there were scrambles by foreign and domestic cash-holders to acquire securities, especially state obligations which had been selling as low as ten cents on the dollar.

No one had thought much about taking care of the soldiers during the war but politicians suddenly grew alarmed that those brave men who had been forced to sell their notes at discounts to speculators would thus have lost what was due them from the government. Madison proposed discriminating among the original and subsequent holders, but this failed of congressional assent. The individual states calculated how they would fare and were for or against assumption accordingly. New England was all for it and threatened to leave the Union if it did not pass. Virginia, which calculations some years later showed to have come out very well under assumption, was strongly against it, as a benefit to the north. There were cries throughout the Union against speculators as harpies and bloodsuckers. Even in such centers of commerce and banking as New York, Philadelphia, and Boston, which were supposed by many states to be the principal beneficiaries, there was violent newspaper opposition. The respected *Pennsylvania Gazette,* particularly indignant, attacked Hamilton in rhyme: "Soldiers and farmers don't despair—Untax'd as yet are earth and air."

Since much of the fiscal system was adapted from British practices, anti-English feelings came to the surface. There was also the fear, which Jefferson subsequently exploited, that the corrupting practices of the British government and Parliament would come to the purer air of America.

The president kept out of the controversy as much as he could. The Constitution had provided the Senate and House as the national cockpit and he was willing to accept what a majority finally determined. In his private letters he expressed regret at the warmth of the debates, the scurrility of the newspapers, and the narrowness of the margin by which, he predicted in April, a compromise would pass.

THE COMPROMISES

Jefferson, arriving in the midst of the discussions, followed them with interest. At this time, he still held on to a certain realistic objectivity and his reporting of events in these months has a degree of reliability. On April 6 he wrote William Short in Paris that Congress had approved a settlement of the foreign debt but the vote of the necessary funds had to await congressional determination of the domestic debt question. On May 3 he informed Washington that two of the American loans had gone above par at Amsterdam. On May 30 he told his son-in-law, Thomas Mann Randolph, that the question of removing the government to Philadelphia had been voted down in the Senate, 13–11, while assumption of state debts was "so equal on the former trial that it is very possible that with some modifications it may prevail." On June 6 he wrote his daughter that the House had voted to remove to Philadelphia; with the vice-president's vote, this might carry the Senate. On the same day Jefferson told Short that the senators who opposed a removal from New York were waiting for the new senators from Rhode Island to appear. To delay a vote they had referred the bill for a permanent capital to a Senate committee. He again noted that funds for the foreign payments were delayed by the assumption bill. On June 13 Jefferson wrote Elizabeth Eppes that the House had voted overwhelmingly to remove to Baltimore. "It is very doubtful whether the Senate will concur. However it may very possibly end in a removal either to that place or Philadelphia."

By June 13 Jefferson was writing to William Hunter that he thought the Baltimore vote might open the way to the government's temporary residence at Philadelphia and its permanent removal to Georgetown. The same day Jefferson informed George Mason that he thought there ought to be some compromise on the assumption of state debts: "I think it is necessary to give as well as take in a government like ours." By June 20 he was writing Monroe:

> *Congress has long been embarrassed by two of the most irritating questions that can be raised among them, 1. The funding of the public debt, and 2. The fixing on a more central residence... It has become probable that unless they can be reconciled, there will be no funding bill agreed to, our credit (raised by late prospects to be the first on the exchange at Amsterdam, where our paper is above par) will burst and vanish, and the states separate to take care everyone of itself... In the present instance I see the necessity of yielding for this time to the cries of the creditors in certain parts of the Union, for the sake of the Union, and to save us from the greatest of all calamities, the total extinction of our credit in Europe... It is proposed to pass an act fixing the temporary residence for 12 or 15 years at Philadelphia, and that at the end of that time it shall be transferred to Georgetown. In this way there will be something to displease and something to soothe every part of the Union, but New York...*

The compromise involved many of the states. The proposed debt settlements for Delaware, Virginia, and North Carolina were adjusted upwards. New England got the assumption it wanted. Pennsylvania was to have the capital for ten years. The South, meaning Maryland and Virginia, was to have the permanent capital on the Potomac. The residency bill passed in July and the debt settlement in August, although details of the states' debts were left for the next session.

Jefferson's letter mentioned that only New York failed to get what it wanted and had lost the national capital. This weakened Hamilton's New York political basis. It also played a role a few months later when Aaron Burr was chosen to replace Schuyler in the Senate. As it was to turn out, Hamilton had greatly underestimated the vigor of the country's economic development and growth. He had expected that as much as 80 percent of the federal revenue would be needed to service the national debt. By 1792 only a third of the federal receipts went to interest and principal. The great increase in the accruing revenues gave the president a needed flexibility in building the nation's maritime and military strength.

DOCTOR STUART

Washington continued to ask David Stuart to keep him informed on political conditions and sentiments in Virginia. What the president got were Stuart's views of Virginia politics, critical comments on everything he thought the federal government was doing, a physician's opinions on constitutional law, and a great deal of gossip. On March 15 he blasted the "eastern states" (New England) for acting in solid phalanx against Virginia. He disliked Madison's plan of discrimination in the debt settlement and denounced the proposed assumption of state debts as unconstitutional. On June 2 he wrote that he thought Congress was lazy, working only four hours a day, and, "like Schoolboys," taking Saturday as a holiday. Stuart sent on Patrick Henry's supposed remark that he did not wish to be a senator, for he was too old to learn all the fashionable graces expected at Washington's court. "From this expression I suspect the old patriot has heard some extraordinary representations of the etiquette established at your levees." He also quoted Colonel Theodorick Bland to the effect that there was more pomp at his house and "Washington's bows were more stiff" than anything that could be seen at the British court.

Washington took Stuart's rather humorless harangues more seriously than they deserved, very probably because Virginia was the largest state and his own. He replied on March 28: "If the southern States are less tenacious of their interest, or, if whilst the eastern move in a solid phalanx to effect their views, the southerners are always divided, which of the two is most to be blamed?... Common danger brought the States into confederacy, and on their union our safety and importance depend. A spirit of accommodation was the basis of the present constitution, can it be expected then that the Southern or Eastern part of the Empire will succeed in all their measures?" The president followed with another letter on June 15, acid in its humor:

Your description of the public Mind in Virginia gives me pain. It seems to be more irritable, sour and discontented than... in any other State in the Union, except Massachusetts; which, from the same causes, but on quite different principles, is tempered like it.

That Congress does not proceed with all that dispatch which people at a distance expect... is not to be denied... Can it well be otherwise in a country so extensive, so diversified in its interests? And will not these different interests naturally produce... long, warm, and animated debates? Most undoubtedly; and if there was the same propensity in Mankind to investigating the motives, as there is for censuring... it would be found the censure so freely bestowed is oftentimes unmerited and uncharitable, for instance, the condemnation of Congress for sitting only four hours in the day. The fact is, and this is, and has been for a considerable time, from ten o'clock in the forenoon until three, often later... after which the business is going on in Committees...

In a letter of last year, I informed you of the motives, which <u>compelled</u> me to allot a day for the reception of idle and ceremonious visits... That I have not been able to make bows to the taste of poor Colonel Bland (who, by the by, I believe never saw one of them) is to be regretted especially too, as (upon those occasions) they were indiscriminately bestowed, and the best I was master of; would it not have been better to throw the veil of charity over them, ascribing their stiffness to the effects of age, or to the unskillfulness of my teacher, than to pride and dignity of office, which God knows has no charm for Me?...

DEATH OF FRANKLIN

Benjamin Franklin, who had first entered public service in 1736, retired as head of Pennsylvania's government in 1788, after seeing the Constitution ratified. Hearing that the president had been ill, Franklin wrote him from his own sick bed on September 18, 1789:

For my own personal Ease, I should have died two years ago; but tho' those Years have been spent in excruciating Pain, I am pleas'd that I have liv'd them, since they have brought me to see our present situation. I am now finishing my 84th year and probably with it my career in this Life; but in what ever State of Existence I am plac'd hereafter, if I retain any Memory of what has pass'd here, I shall with it retain the Esteem, Respect, and Affection with which I have long been, my dear Friend, Yours most sincerely...

Washington replied a week later:

Would to God, my dear Sir, that I could congratulate you upon the removal of the excruciating pain under which you labour! and that your existence might close with as much ease, as its continuance has been beneficial to our Country, and useful to mankind!... If to be venerated for benevolence; If to be admired for talents; If to be esteemed for patriotism; If to be beloved for philanthropy, can gratify the human mind, you must have the pleasing consolation to know that you have not lived in vain; And I flatter myself that it will not be ranked among the least grateful occurrences of your life to be assured that, so long as I retain my

memory, you will be thought on with respect, veneration and Affection by Your
sincere friend.

Franklin's last public service was to send Jefferson, a few days before his death, a geographical description of a boundary in dispute between Great Britain and the United States. He died quietly on April 17, 1790, leaving a codicil to his will: "My fine crab-tree walking stick, with a gold head curiously wrought in the form of the cap of liberty, I give to my friend, and the friend of mankind, General Washington. If it were a sceptre, he has merited it and would become it."

THE PRESIDENT'S ILLNESS

On May 12 William Jackson, one of Washington's secretaries, sent an urgent letter to Clement Biddle, in Philadelphia, by express rider: "The inclosed letter from Doctor Bard to Doctor Jones is transmitted to you with a view to ensure secrecy, certainty, and dispatch in the delivery of it... I need not repeat the necessity of delivering the letter with Privacy, and keeping the object of it a secret from every person, even Mrs. Biddle. Doctor Jones may want your aid to accelerate his arrival at New York." Doctor Jones set off for New York the following day, two hours after he had received the letter.

Washington's illness was sudden and violent. He had written in his diary May 9: "Indisposed with a bad cold, and at home all day writing letters on private business." This developed into severe pneumonia. On May 12 his condition was critical, as three top New York physicians worked on him. Three days later he appeared to be worse, and Dr. Samuel Bard summoned Dr. Jones from Philadelphia. At the president's house that day everyone was in tears. Abigail Adams, knowing that only Washington could keep the still feeble government going, was badly shaken. Jefferson wrote his daughter, Martha Randolph, on May 16: "Yesterday the President was thought by the physicians to be dying. However about 4 o'clock in the evening a copious sweat came on, his expectoration which had been thin and ichorous, began to assume a well digested form, his articulation became distinct, and in the course of two hours it was evident he had gone thro' a favorable crises. He continues mending today, and from total despair we are now in good hopes of him." On May 27 Jefferson informed William Short in Paris that two of the three physicians present that day had considered that he "was in the act of death. A successful effort of nature relieved him and us. You cannot conceive the public alarm on this occasion. It proves how much depends on his life."

On June 7 the two tall Virginians, Washington and Jefferson, the latter having been suffering from severe headaches, went off on a three-day, deep-sea fishing trip. The *Pennsylvania Packet* carried a June 12 dispatch from New York: "The President... returned from Sandy Hook the fishing banks where he had been for the benefit of the sea air, and to amuse himself in the delightful recreation of fishing. We are told he had an excellent sport, having himself caught a great number of sea bass and black fish." Washington's physicians again urged him to get more exercise. His July diaries repeatedly note that he was out on horseback from five to seven every morning.

RELATIONS WITH GREAT BRITAIN

Washington's proposals to increase the army, in view of repeated Indian attacks, were reported to Quebec by British agents, in a manner calculated to alarm Lord Dorchester. The reports suggested that the United States intended to seize the frontier posts and other treaty rights by force. As a result George Beckwith came hurrying down from Canada in March to pick up military intelligence and to talk to his American contacts. From his conversations, Beckwith concluded, and so informed Dorchester, that the troops were being added primarily for defense against Indian attacks and to strengthen the hands of the federal government. Eventually they would operate offensively, but so far as he could see there would be no threat to the British-held posts that year.

During their conversations Hamilton warned Beckwith that Jefferson, the new secretary of state, had taken office the day before. This factor, he said, introduced a strongly pro-French element into the American government. In a further conversation, in which Beckwith sought assurances that the United States sincerely desired a close political and commercial connection with England, he asked Hamilton in mid-April whether the secretary's communications to him were, in fact, authorized by General Washington, the responsible chief of state. Hamilton replied: "I am not authorized to say to you in so many words, that such is the language of the President of the United States: to a gentleman who has no public character, such a declaration cannot be made but my honor and character stand implicated in the fulfillment of these assurances." While Hamilton thus destroyed whatever fragment of character and honor he claimed, he also introduced a very confusing situation for Dorchester and Beckwith. Lord Dorchester began pushing for a policy towards the United States, which was at variance with that of the British government.

THE MORRIS MISSION

On March 28 Gouverneur Morris, the president's emissary, presented Washington's letter of credence to the British foreign secretary, the Duke of Leeds. His Grace remarked astutely that America was quite far away. The question of sending a minister to New York was a difficult one, but Morris would hear something in due course. He was dismissed. At this time, the British government was concentrating its thoughts on an incident at Nootka Sound, in what is now British Columbia, and Spain had seized two ships in the territory she claimed as hers; the British were preparing to go to war over this, in order to break Spain's stranglehold in the Pacific.

The United States was considered of little importance, and official policy to the country had already been determined. The posts were to be held and treaties of commerce and friendship reserved for those areas which Great Britain planned to detach from the United States. Hamilton's assurances that there would be no American commercial restrictions against Britain, and no attack on British posts, had little real influence on British policy. A month after his initial interview and several subsequent written requests, Morris received a brutal note from Leeds: "We cannot but lament every circumstance which can have delayed the Accomplishment of those engagements (comprized in the Treaty) in which those States [the U.S.] were in the most solemn Manner bound and should the Delay in fulfilling them have rendered their final Completion impracticable, we have no Scruple in declaring our Object is to retard the fulfilling of such subsequent Parts of the Treaty as depend entirely upon Great Britain, until redress is granted… or a fair and just compensation obtained for the non-Performance of those Engagements on the part of the United States…"

Morris wrote a flawlessly diplomatic reply, in much better English. He asked the duke to be more precise in explaining British policy, which was exactly what the foreign secretary did not want to do. Morris wrote Washington that Leeds' "Confusion of Language… resembles the Stammering of one who endeavors to excuse a Misdeed which he has resolved to commit… It seems pretty clear they wish to evade a commercial treaty… I have construed into Rejection his Grace's abstruse Language leaving him the Option to give it a different Interpretation. I do not expect that he will, tho he may perhaps write an explanatory comment more unintelligible than the last."

A few days later a war crisis burst on London. The British had already directed a huge impressment of seamen, some of whom turned out to be Americans. In view of a probable war with Spain, the government instructed Lord Dorchester to send an agent to the United States to obtain military

intelligence and to see whether there was any chance of American cooperation in case of war. The navigation of the Mississippi, Dorchester was assured,
would be of much greater importance to the United States than the forts.

Morris' letter reached Leeds at a point when Britain did not want too many
enemies. By May 21 Morris was closeted with the prime minister and foreign
secretary. This time Morris played cold. When Leeds said that he had misinterpreted his letter and Britain was interested in discussing the possibility of a
commercial treaty, Morris replied that "it appeared idle to form a new treaty,
until the parties should be thoroughly satisfied about that already existing." A
long wrangle followed on violations, with Pitt maintaining that Britain had to
hold the posts as a guarantee that the United States would observe the treaty.
Morris replied: "We do not think it worth while to go to War with you for these
posts, but we know our rights, and will avail ourselves of them, when Time and
circumstances may suit."

While Morris' firmness had little immediate effect on British policy, the gov-
ernment took a few positive steps. Some impressed Americans were released.
Pitt also ordered Dorchester to restrain Indian massacres of American settlers.
Morris' warnings, planted at a suitable time, pushed the British government
along towards reaching its later decision to give up the posts, if war came.
Spain had been counting on French support but France, with revolution
spreading, could offer no help. By autumn Spain had knuckled under, and
Britain, for the moment, was triumphant.

In reporting to Washington on his May 21 conversation, Morris proposed
that, in case of war, Britain or Spain be forced to pay a high price for
American neutrality. He suggested that negotiations with Madrid proceed at
once. After receiving the letter, Jefferson worked on what was the beginning
of a neutrality policy designed to let the United States take the utmost advantage from the warring powers. In August he sent an American consul to
London, to obtain intelligence on British policy. He also ordered the
American chargé at Madrid, William Carmichael, to press Spain with full
force, if war broke out, to grant the United States the Mississippi navigation,
as well as a port of deposit at new Orleans. To give Carmichael support as well
as information on the new government's policies, the president dispatched his
secretary and former aide, Colonel David Humphreys, to Madrid. Jefferson
also wrote informally to the Portuguese ambassador at Paris to see if diplomatic relations could be established with Lisbon. Jefferson's most urgent
worry, frequently expressed, was that Britain might seize all Spanish territories
to the west and south and encircle the United States.

BECKWITH AND HAMILTON

On July 5, a Monday, the official celebration of American independence was held. Members of the government, House and Senate, the Cincinnati, and others called on Washington. The president went to St. Paul's Church, where Brockholst Livingston, according to Washington's diary, made an oration "to show the different situation we are now in, under an excellent government of our own choice, to what it would have been if we had not succeeded in our opposition to the attempts of Great Britain to enslave us; and how much we ought to cherish the blessings which are within our reach, and to cultivate the seeds of harmony and unanimity in all our public Councils. There were several other points touched upon in a sensible manner." Washington's diary the same day continued:

> *I was informed this day by General Irvine (who recd. the acct. from Pittsburgh) that the Traitor Arnold was at Detroit and had viewed the Militia in the neighborhood of it twice. This had occasioned much Speculation in these parts—and with many other circumstances—though trifling in themselves led strongly to a conjecture that the British had some design on the Spanish settlements on the Mississippi and of course to surround these United States.*

The British government had instructed Dorchester that his agents in the United States were to have no official or public character. The Canadian governor, in turn, gave secret orders to Beckwith to obtain intelligence on American relations with Spain and France, "the characters of military men… military arrangements… any increase of troops, their position and movements, the number and magnitude of deposits of military stores and provisions, and the arming of any ships for War…" Beckwith was instructed to be particularly attentive to Vermont and to the actions of French and Spanish agents.

In addition to his secret instructions, Dorchester handed Beckwith an open but rather caustic letter which he was permitted, at his discretion, to show to American authorities. In it he expressed the hope there would be no "alteration in the good disposition of the United States to establish a firm friendship and alliance with Great Britain." The same letter denounced America for its treaty violations and its "misrepresentations" of British activities, arising, he surmised, from the "unsettled state of their government" and from French influence. Dorchester expressed concern that the Spanish were stirring up the Indians, and he blasted anti-British statements by Americans in the Northwest Territory.

Beckwith and Hamilton conferred on the morning of July 8. In the course of the conversation, Beckwith showed Hamilton his nonsecret instruction, which he may have permitted him to copy. Hamilton decided at this point to make a partial disclosure to Washington of what he had been doing. In preparing his memorandum for the president, Hamilton doctored both Dorchester's letter and Beckwith's oral statements. He quoted the former's note referring to "the agency of Mr. Morris," but he added gratuitously that Beckwith had said that "Mr. Morris had not produced any regular credentials, but merely a letter from the President." Hamilton then stated that Great Britain and its cabinet were interested in an "alliance" with the United States and that Dorchester deplored both the Indian attacks and the "intemperate language" of Americans in the Northwest Territory. He inserted the unfounded remark that Beckwith suggested, with some indirection, that he was speaking for the British cabinet.

Washington was so interested in the Hamilton memorandum that he copied it as a whole in his July 8 diary. Dorchester, as Julian Boyd has pointed out, referred in his letter only to the "good disposition *of the United States*" (italics his) to form an alliance. The president of course had no such idea in mind. Neither Washington nor Jefferson were entirely fooled by Hamilton's memorandum, but their suspicions tended to be directed towards Great Britain rather than their colleague.

Washington commented in his diary that all the Beckwith communication signified was:

> *We did not incline to give any satisfactory answer to Mr. Morris, who was <u>officially</u> commissioned to ascertain our intentions with respect to the evacuation of the Western Posts within the Territory of the United States, and other matters into which he was empowered to enquire, until by this unauthenticated mode we can discover whether you will enter into an Alliance with us and make Common cause against Spain. In that case we will enter into a commercial Treaty with you and <u>promise perhaps</u> to fulfill what they already stand engaged to perform. However, I requested Mr. Jefferson and Colo. Hamilton, as I intend to do the Vice President, Chief Justice and Secretary at War, to resolve this matter in all its relations in their minds...*

Next day Washington recorded in his diary that troops and militia under General Harmar had moved from Kentucky into Ohio to prevent Indian raids, which he did not need to mention, were clearly instigated by Lord Dorchester. Subsequent to his conversations with various officials on July 14, the president instructed Hamilton, as he noted in his diary of July 14, "to treat [Beckwith's] communications very civilly—to intimate, delicately, that they carried no marks official or authentic nor in speaking of Alliance, did they convey any definite meaning… In a word, that the Secretary of the Treasury was to extract as much as he could from Maj. Beckwith and to report to me, without committing, by any assurances whatever, the Government of the U. States, leaving it entirely free to pursue, unreproached, such a line of conduct in the dispute as her interest (and honour) shall dictate."

It appears to have been an unfortunate error on the part of the president not to require the secretary of state to attend all discussions with Beckwith. Even the bifurcated tongue of Hamilton would have been hard put to cope in such a situation. The secretary of the treasury proceeded at once to violate the president's instructions. On July 15 he talked to Beckwith who recorded Hamilton's statements for his government:

I have communicated to the President, the subjects on which we have conversed… You must be sensible that official formality is wanting, but it is conceived that His Lordship would not have gone the length he has without being acquainted with the general views of your administration.

In the present stage of this business, it is difficult to say much on the subject of a Treaty of Alliance; Your rupture with Spain, if it takes place, opens a very wide political field; this much I can say, we are perfectly unconnected with Spain.

The Speeches… of any person whatever in the Indian Country… suggesting hostile ideas respecting the forts, are not authorized by this government.

Lord Dorchester's conduct with respect to the Indians is held by us to be a strong proof of His Lordship's disposition to harmony and friendship.

It appears to me that, from the nature of our Government, it would be mutually advantageous, if this negotiation could be carried out at our seat of Government, as it would produce dispatch and obviate misconceptions.

There is one thing more I wish to mention to you; I do it altogether as one gentleman to another, and I trust it will be so considered.

I have decided on doing it at this time from the possibility of my not having it in my power to come to such an explanation hereafter.

If it shall be judged proper to proceed on this business by the sending or appointing a proper person to come to this country to negotiate on the spot, whoever shall then be our Secretary of State, will be the person in whose department such negotiation must originate, and he in turn will be the channel of communication with the

President; in the turn of such affairs the most minute circumstances, mere trifles, give a favorable bias or otherwise to the whole. The President's mind I can declare to be perfectly dispassionate on the subject. Mr. Jefferson our present Secretary of State is I am persuaded a gentleman of honor, and zealously desirous of promoting those objects, which the nature of his duty call for, and the interests of his country may require, but from some opinions which he has given respecting Your government, and possible predilections elsewhere, there may be difficulties which may possibly frustrate the whole, and which might be readily explained away. I shall certainly know the progress of the negotiation from day to day, but what I come to the present explanation for is this, that in case any such difficulties should occur, I would wish to know them, in order that I may be sure they are clearly understood, and candidly examined; if none take place the business will of course go on in regular channels...

In this I am steadily following up what I have long considered to be the essential interest of this country...

Hamilton's report to the president did not mention most of what he had said to Beckwith. He prepared a twisted version of a portion of it for Washington, notably where he quoted Beckwith as repeating "assurances" of Lord Dorchester's "disposition to discourage Indian outrages." He suggested that Beckwith stated that Britain's efforts, in case of war with Spain, would be directed against South America. Hamilton also reported that he had told Beckwith: "As to alliance, this opens a wide field. The thing is susceptible of a vast variety of forms. 'Tis not possible to judge what would be proper or what could be done unless points were brought into view. If you are in a condition to mention particulars, it may afford better ground for conversation. I stopped here for an answer. Major Beckwith replied that he could say nothing more particular than he had done. This being the case (continued I) I can only say... we shall be disposed to pursue whatever shall appear under all circumstances to be our interest as far as may consist with our honor."

Beckwith did not confine his conversations to Hamilton, nor was he the only secret agent at work in America. The British government that summer and autumn was flooded with reports, some of such critical importance that they went directly to the prime minister. Beckwith forwarded the views of Thomas Scott, member of Congress for western Pennsylvania, who urged the British to take New Orleans. Their consul at Norfolk reported that western North Carolina was eager to raise men and to cooperate with the British in freeing the western areas from Spanish domination. Senator Johnson of Connecticut warned Beckwith that the British should never trust Jefferson.

Peter Allaire, a New York merchant, reported, in a message read by Pitt, that the whole great West and Florida would fall to England with a few thousand troops. One of the richest areas on earth could thereby be "forever" bound to Britain "in spite of Congress and all the world."

By early September Beckwith and Sir John Temple, British consul at New York, had written London that Colonel David Humphreys was on his way to Europe on some secret mission. Temple guessed that he might be going to France or Spain. Beckwith followed September 25 with an intimation from Hamilton that "in case of a rupture with Spain, the probable effect, which such an event may produce upon the navigation of the Mississippi, attracts the very particular attention of this government." On almost the same day Hamilton told Beckwith: "We consider ourselves perfectly at liberty to act with respect to Spain in any way most conclusive to our interests, even to the going to war with that power, if we should think it advisable to join you." This would have astonished the peace-loving president who was anxious to avoid war at almost any cost.

JEFFERSON ACTS

During Hamilton's last conversations with Beckwith, the president and secretary of state were absent in Virginia. Nevertheless instructions had gone out looking to the national interest. Washington and Jefferson felt that the gravest danger faced by the new federal Union was British encirclement. If that country, having posts in the North and the Midwest, and substantial control of the western Indians, moved to eject Spain from Louisiana and the Floridas, the United States would once again be surrounded by a hostile power controlling the seas.

Washington had two purposes in mind in sending Morris to London. He hoped he could negotiate a peaceful settlement with Britain. If not, he would be able to provide an accurate evaluation of the attitude of the British government, as a basis for American policy. Morris concluded that nothing could be done by negotiation. His assessment was based not only on conversations with the prime minister and the Foreign Office, but also with officials of the Board of Trade, members of parliament, the French ambassador, and Charles James Fox, leader of the opposition. John Adams, long experienced with the British, said that Morris had described exactly what could be expected. Having started negotiations with Lisbon and instructed Carmichael at Madrid to press for the opening of the Mississippi, Jefferson wrote to Gouverneur Morris on August 12:

You have placed their proposition of exchanging a Minister on proper ground. It must certainly come from them, and come in unequivocal form; with those who respect their own dignity so much, ours must not be counted at nought... Besides what they are saying to you, they are talking to us through Quebec; but so informally that they may disavow it when they please... They talk of a Minister, a treaty of commerce <u>and</u> <u>alliance</u>. If the latter object be honorable, it is useless; if dishonorable, inadmissible. These tamperings prove they view a war as very possible; and some symptoms indicate designs against the Spanish possessions adjoining us. The consequences of their acquiring all the country from the St. Croix to the St. Mary's are too obvious to you to need development. You will readily see the dangers which would then surround us. We wish you to intimate to them that we should contemplate a change of neighbours with extreme uneasiness; and that a due balance on our borders is not less desirable to us, than a balance of power in Europe has always appeared to them. We wish to be neutral, and we will be so, <u>if they will execute the treaty fairly, and attempt no conquests adjoining us</u>... If the war takes place, we would readily wish to be quieted on these two points, offering in return an honorable neutrality; more than this they are not to expect. It will be proper that these ideas be conveyed in delicate and friendly terms; but that they be conveyed, if the war takes place; for it is in that case alone, and not till it be begun, that we would wish our dispositions to be known; but in no case need they think of our accepting any equivalent for the posts...

So concerned was Washington that the British might move troops across the United States from Detroit to Spanish territory, that he took the unusual step on August 27 of asking the chief justice, the vice-president, and the members of his cabinet to send him written memoranda as to what should be done if the British requested permission to do this or, as more probable, if they did it without leave.

The answers were as varied as the personalities of the respondents. While Knox hedged, he made the shrewd guess that Spain would not go to war without France and that country might be too "convulsed" to join. Adams and Jefferson wanted strict neutrality with vigorous protests to the British court. The latter also thought America might be forced to join Spain and France, but this eventuality ought to be avoided as long as possible. Adams complained that Congress had provided too few funds for the foreign service. The United States badly needed first-class representatives at London, Paris, Madrid, and The Hague to forward intelligence. Hamilton was the slowest to reply and made the most involved explanation. He embedded in lengthy prose the suggestion that since "many of the best and ablest people" in the United States wanted an "intimate connection" with Great Britain, it might be better to side with her against Spain, navigation of the Mississippi was far more important than the British posts (a point made by the British cabinet), and more land possessions might never be desirable for the United States.

HAMILTON TIPS BRITISH INTELLIGENCE

Washington and Knox together planned a military expedition from Fort Washington (Cincinnati) to the Miami Villages (Fort Wayne) to check Indian raids south of the Ohio. The president asked Jefferson if Dorchester ought to be notified that the attacks were to be confined to raiding Indians and were not to touch British posts. The secretary of state said this was undesirable since it would certainly forewarn the Indians. The surprise presence of American troops in the Ohio region might also act as a deterrent to any moves planned by Dorchester against Spanish territory.

On August 20 General Arthur St. Clair, governor of the Northwest Territory, arrived in New York to discuss military plans with Knox and finance with Hamilton. The ubiquitous Beckwith was all eyes and ears to learn what was going on. Next day, while the president and secretary of state were in Rhode Island, Hamilton informed Beckwith of St. Clair's expedition. While Lord Dorchester himself did not receive the information until September 11, it was well within the bounds of Beckwith's capabilities to have sent the intelligence directly to British agents in the Ohio area. On August 24 Knox warned General Josiah Harmar, leader of the expedition, that "every possible precaution in the power of human foresight should be used to prevent surprise."

On November 10 Beckwith forwarded to Quebec a special intelligence report, rating St. Clair, Harmar, Wyllis, and Doughty the American officers in charge of the expedition. There was other information, but this dispatch was too late to be useful, for Harmar had already been ambushed and beaten. The man who supplied the information was a New Yorker experienced in military matters.

GOUVERNEUR MORRIS TRADUCED

Gouverneur Morris delivered the funeral eulogy over Hamilton in 1804. He might have enjoyed this more had he known what Hamilton had done to him in 1790. Just after the president left for Virginia, Hamilton talked to David Humphreys, Washington's special agent to Madrid, who had strict instructions to keep his mission secret at all costs. Humphreys, who was not too bright, reported to the president that he had had a very interesting conversation with

Hamilton and that he was glad to have his reasoning and to compare it with that "of other political characters. He said that Hamilton was not perfectly satisfied with the manner in which Morris had conducted the business in London" and had asked him to look into this while he was there. Humphreys complained that he did not see how he could do this and still keep himself secret.

In one of his interminable conversations with Beckwith, about September 25, Hamilton brought up his disapproval of Morris. Wording the conversation in such a way as to receive confirmation from Beckwith, he suggested that perhaps Morris had been so intimate with French Ambassador Luzerne in London that this might have brought about some reserve on the part of the British government. Beckwith said he had heard some of Morris' New York friends and relatives say that he had seen Luzerne and that Charles James Fox thought well of him. Hamilton picked this last name up in such a way as to extract from Beckwith the remark that "intimacies" with Fox, a member of the opposition, were not very desirable. Hamilton then indicated to Beckwith how much better it would be to have all negotiations transferred to New York—where he could keep an eye on them. Hamilton sent an arch letter to Washington on September 30:

> *I had lately a visit from a <u>certain</u> <u>Gentleman</u> the sole object of which was to make some observations of a delicate nature, concerning <u>another</u> <u>Gentleman</u> employed on a <u>particular</u> <u>errand</u>; which, as they were doubtless intended for your ear, and (such as they are) ought to be known to you, it is of course my duty to communicate.*

> *He began (in a manner somewhat embarrassed which betrayed rather more than he intended to discover) by telling me that <u>in</u> <u>different</u> <u>companies</u> where he had happened to be, in this City (a circumstance by the way very unlikely) he had heard it mentioned that that <u>other</u> <u>Gentleman</u> was upon terms of very great intimacy with the representatives of a certain Court at the one where he was employed and with the head of the party opposed to the [Prime] Minister; and he proceeded to say that if there were any symptoms of backwardness or coolness in the Minister, it had occurred to him that they might possibly be occasioned by such <u>an</u> <u>intimacy</u>... If this should be the case (said he) you will readily imagine that it cannot be calculated to inspire confidence or to facilitate free communication... Man, after all is but man; and though the Minister has a great mind, and is as little likely as most men to entertain illiberal distrust and jealousies, yet there is no saying what might be the effect of such conduct upon him...*

Having provided this imaginative version of what Beckwith did not say,

Hamilton added that *he* had told Beckwith: "I have never heard a syllable, Sir, about the matter you mention." He then put into Beckwith's mouth a phrase, "trifles often mar great affairs," a variant of what Hamilton had previously said to Beckwith, when he urged that negotiations take place in New York. Washington had sources of information, not known to Hamilton, and the secretary got back a rather short note, dated Mount Vernon, October 10:

> *Your letter came duly to hand. For the information contained in it I thank you, as I shall do for all others of a similar nature. The motives, however, by which the author of the communication to you was actuated, although they may have been pure and in that case praiseworthy, do also (but it may be uncharitable to harbor the suspicion) admit of a different interpretation and by an easy and direct clue.*

Washington thus left Hamilton to think about what the president knew. On November 4 the president dropped a note to the secretary of war, expressing his concern lest General St. Clair might have made a premature disclosure to the British of General Harmar's movements in the Northwest Territory. On November 19 he wrote further that he had forebodings of disaster.

LONG ISLAND, RHODE ISLAND, AND PHILADELPHIA

Washington made two special tours in 1790, the first before his illness, through much of Long Island. From Brooklyn he rode on April 20 to Utrecht, remarking that the farmers there grew twenty-five to thirty bushels of corn to the acre, and thirty or more bushels of wheat and rye. "This was the effect of Dung from New York (about 10 cart loads to the acre)... The land after crossing the Hills between Brooklyn and Flat Bush is perfectly level... All that end of the Island is a rich black loam... The timber is chiefly Hickory and Oak, mixed here and there with locust and Sassafras trees, and in places with a good deal of Cedar." He spent the night at "a pretty good and decent house" in Jamaica.

From Jamaica he drove ten miles to South Hempstead. He noted there was not a tree or shrub on the road except some rather poor fruit trees. The soil was "thin and cold, and of course not productive, even in Grass." He rode down to the ocean, observing "the small bays, marshes and guts, into which the tide flows at all times." He also observed a type of social distinction which had begun to appear in America, in the form of guesthouses. The owners maintained theirs were private houses, accepting paying guests, rather than taverns or inns, kept by common innkeepers. Washington appeared unable to discern any real difference. General de Chastellux had earlier guessed that they thus avoided paying license fees.

At Brookhaven Washington turned north to the sound. There the soil was also poor and indifferent. He circled around to Huntington and Oyster Bay, "to the House of a Mr. Young (private and very neat and decent where we lodged)." He noted that for nearly five miles out of Smithtown there was a bed of white sand and no trees taller than 25 feet. At Glen Cove he examined a grist mill and two paper mills. From thence he rode to Flushing and Brooklyn, again commenting on the productivity of New York City's manure on the fields. In general he found that this nearly doubled the crops but he also noted the use of such green manure as clover and timothy, which was plowed into the soil. He wrote that Long Island "fences" were often "growing trees, with the use of dogwood and white oak predominating."

When Rhode Island joined the Union, Washington was glad to have another excuse for a trip. On August 15, the day after Congress adjourned, Washington picked up Jefferson, Governor Clinton, and three secretaries and sailed for Newport, through Long Island Sound. Washington's own diary is missing but a congressman from South Carolina, William L. Smith, supplied the deficiency with his notes: "As we entered the harbor [Newport], a salute was fired from the fort and some pieces on the wharves; at our landing we were received by the principal inhabitants of the town, and the clergy who, forming a procession, escorted us through a considerable concourse of citizens to the lodgings which had been prepared for us..."

The president and his party walked to the heights above, followed by a large number of townspeople. At four o'clock everyone marched to the town hall, Smith said, adding: "The dinner was well dished up, and conducted with regularity and decency; the company consisted of about eighty persons; after dinner some good toasts were drank: 'may the last be first'... The President gave 'The Town of Newport' and... Judge Marchant gave 'The man we love' which the company drank standing."

Everyone then followed the president while he took another walk around the town. Next morning after breakfast, he received an address from the city council, which apologized for the fact that Newport, having suffered a long trade depression, was unable to offer as much hospitality as other towns.

The presidential party took seven hours to sail from Newport to Providence, where Smith described the reception:

The same salute took place as at Newport, but the procession up to the tavern was more solemn and conducted with a much greater formality, having troops and music. The Governor of the State was so zealous in his respects that he jumped aboard the packet as soon as she got to the wharf to welcome the President to Providence. The President... The Governor... [Senator] Foster... Governor Clinton... Mr. Jefferson... [Justice] Blair... Colonel Humphreys, Maj. Jackson and Mr. Nelson... followed the principal inhabitants of Providence... making a long file, preceded by some troops and music; the doors and windows for the length of a mile were all crowded with ladies and spectators. When we arrived at the tavern, the President stood at the door, and the troops and procession passed and saluted. In the procession were three negro scrapers [fiddlers] making a horrible noise. We then sat down to a family dinner. After tea, just as the President was taking leave to go to bed, he was informed... that the students of the college had illuminated it, and would be highly flattered at the President's going to see it, which he politely agreed to do, though he never goes out at night, and it then rained a little, and was a disagreeable night. We now made a nocturnal procession to the college, which indeed was worth seeing, being very splendidly illuminated...

Smith concluded by giving the heavy schedule for the president's last day in Rhode Island:

Thursday morning began with a heavy rain and a cold, easterly wind. It cleared at nine o'clock, and then the President, accompanied as before, began a walk which continued until one o'clock and which completely fatigued the company which formed his escort. We walked all around the town, visited all the apartments of the college, went on the roof to view the beautiful and extensive prospect, walked to a place where a large Indiaman of 900 tons was on the docks, went on board her, returned to the town, stopped and drank wine and punch at Mr. Clarke's, Mr. Brown's, Gov. Turner's, and Gov. Bowen's, and then returned home. As soon as the President was rested, he received the addresses of the Cincinnati, the Rhode Island colleges, and the Town of Providence, and then went immediately to dinner at the Town Hall. The dinner was attended by 200 persons, and an immense crowd surrounded the hall. After dinner several toasts were drank: the second was "The President of the United States," at which the whole company, within and without, gave three huzzas and a long clapping of hands. The President then rose and drank the health of all the company; he afterwards gave "The Town of Providence."... At the conclusion... the President rose, and the whole company, with a considerable crowd of citizens, walked down the wharf, where he and his suite embarked for New York.

The president arrived back in New York late on August 21. Very likely he was not entirely displeased at being away while there was a great deal of packing going on at his house. The faithful and much overworked Tobias Lear, now married, had the task imposed on him of moving all the president's furniture and papers to the new capital at Philadelphia. He also had to get the Robert Morris house ready for his permanent residence while the president had a vacation at Mount Vernon. In the meantime Lear had requested Clement Biddle in Philadelphia to engage temporary rooms there for the president and his wife, the two grandchildren, two secretaries, two maids, and four white and four black servants. His sixteen horses had also to be accommodated.

Lear stressed that Philadelphia should have "as little ceremony and parade as may be possible, for the President wishes to command his own time, which these things always forbid in a greater or less degree, and they are to him fatiguing and often times painful. He wishes not to exclude himself from the sight or conversation of his fellow citizens, but their eagerness to shew their affection frequently imposes a heavy tax on him." Nonetheless, the Philadelphia Light Horse Troop was out, and there were cannon shots and fireworks and a formal dinner for the President and his wife on September 2. Although Martha Washington was ill, both had to attend another dinner for two hundred people on September 4, where there were bands, songs, and endless toasts.

THE NATIONAL CAPITAL

The bargaining over the residence and assumption bills brought public commotion and discussion, letters to the newspapers, cartoons, squibs, and hints of corruption. New York was particularly annoyed at Robert Morris, the Philadelphia financier, who was accused of snatching the national capital for his own economic benefit.

The final residence act provided that the permanent capital might be placed anywhere along the Potomac River, from the Eastern Branch (the Anacostia) to the Conococheague River. The latter was a small stream across the Blue Ridge Mountains, which George Washington had first visited in his youth. To the city people of New York, Boston, and Philadelphia, it had the sound of the wilderness. The president probably had the name inserted as a ruse to keep the location secret from speculators but it soon became a national joke. Many assumed it really meant that Philadelphia was to be the permanent capital, but they did not know George Washington, the skilled professional surveyor and amateur architect. When Congress adjourned, the president proceeded to have a look at potential sites.

The *Pennsylvania Mercury* contains a subsequent report from Georgetown, September 11: "The President of the United States, his lady and suite [arrived] on their way to Mount Vernon. The members of the Potowmack company of Alexandria, and this place, met their illustrious President at Mr. John Suter's. Notwithstanding the fatigue of a long journey, his Excellency proceeded to business respecting the navigation of the Patowmack." If, in the course of business and dinner, the president asked a great many questions on land ownership and values, the condition of the harbor, and general facilities available, no one was surprised, since all had read the act for the establishment of the capital on the river.

Two days later Jefferson and Madison reached Georgetown. After examining the area from the Eastern Branch to Great Falls, they held conversations with various landowners on the possibility of buying a modest acreage for the federal buildings. On October 12 the president returned to Georgetown, thereafter travelling nearly eighty miles to the Conococheague itself. Ostensibly he was looking at the Potomac River and its navigational problems but in reality he was giving a false scent as to the area where the capital might be placed. One of the few surviving records of the trip indicates that he was at Elizabethtown (Hagerstown) on October 20. Even in the wilderness he was given an address which was literate and felicitous. The citizens suggested that their village might be the capital of the United States:

> We the inhabitants of Elizabeth Town... being deeply impressed with your illustrious character, and sensibly awake to your resplendent and innumerable virtues, hail you a hearty welcome.

> We are happy to find that, notwithstanding your perils, toils, and incessant cares and guardianship, you are still able to grant us this first, this greatest of all favors, your presence.

> We felicitate ourselves on your exploring our country—and, as you already reign in our hearts, we should think ourselves doubly blessed, could we have the honor to be included within your own especial command and jurisdiction—within the grand centre of virtues.

While the record is lacking, it can be assumed that the one-time surveyor and town-planner of Alexandria also carefully studied the topography from Rock Creek to the Eastern Branch and Alexandria. Everyone in the area was inordinately curious as to the results but the president kept his counsel until he issued a proclamation in January.

MOUNT VERNON

Except for the Potomac trip, Washington was at Mount Vernon from about September 12 to November 22. He was still short of cash, for when Charles Carter sent a note asking for a loan, Washington replied that he himself had tried to borrow from "Mr. Carroll of Carrollton, as the most likely, being the most monied man I was acquainted with, but without success."

The Washingtons had a visitor shortly after their arrival, a cheerful young gourmet, Thomas Lee Shippen. He wrote his father who had served in the revolutionary army's medical service, that he had met "my two valuable friends Messrs. Jefferson and Madison on the eastern shore of Maryland... We waited all day for want of a boat to take us over, and I never knew two men more agreeable than they were. We talked and dined, and strolled, and rowed ourselves in boats, and feasted upon delicious crabs... Mann's Inn at Annapolis is certainly to be placed among the most excellent in the world. I never saw so fine a turtle or so well dressed a dish as he gave us [with] Old Madeira... to season it..."

On September 16 he wrote again to his father from Mount Vernon: "I have been here two days... I have been treated as usual with every most distinguished mark of kindness and attention. The President exercises it to a superlative degree... and Mrs. Washington is the very essence of kindness. Her soul seems to overflow with it and her happiness is in exact proportion to the number of objects upon which she can dispense her benefits."

The president had to work on a great many of his old headaches, which had arisen from his too amiable past acceptance of trustees and other duties. As executor he was still trying to settle the estate of a Captain Colville, who had died twenty-three years before, as well as the affairs of his stepson, Jack Custis, nine years dead. The longest-lived case was that of Colonel Joshua Fry, who had been killed in a fall from his horse thirty-six years before. Eighteen years later he obtained for Fry's heirs the land bounty promised by Dinwiddie. Washington had gone to considerable expense on this. He asked Benjamin Harrison, November 21, to see if he could collect the amount which had been due him for yet another eighteen years:

It is a fact <u>well</u> known to most of the Patentees that had it not been for my exertions and decided conduct, the proclamation of Governor Dinwiddie... would never have been recognized... If the Gentleman claiming under Joshua Fry Esquire inclines to pay what is justly due me, the enclosed list of balances, which is original... will show what my advances are for his proportion of the land. If he pays this sum with interest since the year 1772, when the patents issued were paid for, and the title *became perfect, it will be no more than what is due in <u>gratitude</u>, and to <u>justice</u>. If he inclines to pay the principal only, let him do it and the matter will be closed. Or, lastly, if he chuses to do neither, preferring to receive the patents without paying any thing, e'en then let them go forth, for I shall not appear in a Court of law for this...*

Aside from routine correspondence with members of his cabinet, Washington concentrated heavily on his new house in Philadelphia. Here he was undoubtedly a trying husband, tenant, and chief, for he insisted on being his own interior decorator, builder, and steward. He had gone carefully over the Robert Morris house on his trip through Philadelphia. From then on numerous letters went off between September 5 and November 14 to Morris and Lear. His first letter to Lear assigned everyone his or her rooms:

First floor, two public rooms, and one for the upper servants.

Second floor, for Mrs. Washington, children and maids, leaving a small private dressing room and office for the President.

Third floor, one public room, one room for Mr. and Mrs. Lear, and two rooms for Washington's four to five male secretaries.

Garret, one room for the steward and wife, the rest for William and the other servants.

Over stable, assigned to groom and postilions.

Washington suggested building a back wing for a servants hall, with one or two rooms reserved for "servants who are coupled." In addition the smoke house might be more useful for servants than for smoking meat. Altogether some thirty people had to be squeezed in, while allowing some place for Washington to work and receive people. He asked Lear to see that his coach was repaired and ample firewood laid in. He wondered what to do with the washerwomen from New York who had families. He complained that the steward interfered with the cook's planning of meals; he thought she could make them "more tasty" if she had a freer hand.

Other letters followed. He reminded the Robert Morrises about putting in bow windows, getting the house painted, the back hall built, and the cow barn converted into stables. He was sorry it had to be done while they were still in the house. Washington was upset when Lear wrote from New York that people there had not commented too much on his moving into the house of the man everyone blamed for moving the capital to Philadelphia. Washington wrote back, in indignation, that the Philadelphia authorities had engaged the Morris house and he had had nothing to do with it. He worried further about the steward and his wife, feeling that their dining table was always as well loaded with liquors and fruits as his own. He had thought Samuel Fraunces (of Fraunces' Tavern) had been too expensive, but the new steward and his wife seemed even worse. He told Lear that he and Mrs. Morris had agreed to exchange mangles, since hers was already permanently attached in the house.

Lear, who had had to enter into extensive negotiations for the settlement of rent and other matters on the president's house in New York and to move eight servants and the president's furniture and fixtures to Philadelphia, was also instructed to look carefully into suitable schools for Washington's step-grandson, two nephews, and a niece. He was ordered to examine all the tradesmen in Philadelphia to find out where best to shop. On October 27 Washington acknowledged Lear's letters of October 6, 10, 14, and 17, the last two from Philadelphia advising the president he had arrived in good order. This caused the president to send up ample advice as to where to put each bit of furniture and all the ornaments. Washington added that he had not decided whether green or yellow curtains would look best in the hall.

By November 22 the president of the United States had assembled his wife, her two grandchildren, his secretaries and servants, carriage, and baggage wagons for a procession to Philadelphia. Four of the servants went by stage or boat, and the remainder, perhaps six, accompanied the Washingtons. A few miles below Baltimore, the president wrote an exasperated letter to Tobias Lear:

> *With some difficulty (from the most infamous roads that ever were seen) we have got to this place, and are waiting dinner; but have no expectation of reaching Baltimore to Night.*
>
> *Dunn has given such proofs of his want of skill in driving, that I find myself under the necessity of looking out for another Coachman. Before we got to Elizabeth Town we were obliged to take him from the coach and put him to the Waggon; this he turned over twice; and this Morning was much intoxicated. He has also got the Horses in a habit of stopping.*
>
> *Mrs. Washington's predilection for Jacob is as strong as my prejudices and fears are great. Yet in your enquiries after a Coachman ask something concerning Jacob. He wanted much it seems to return to us whilst we were in Philadelphia...*

Washington hurriedly sent the letter off by the regular stagecoach which was "at this instant starting." No time was lost by Lear and an assistant secretary.

They had an agreement prepared for another coachman, a Hessian, by the time the president reached the nation's new capital in November.

STATE OF THE UNION

Although the British had sent sufficient strength from Detroit to rout General Harmar on November 4 near the present Fort Wayne, the American commander had previously wrought great damage to the Miami villages. He destroyed the principal British trading posts of the area, three hundred loghouses and wigwams and many supplies. This show of strength was disturbing to the traders operating out of Detroit. The Indians looked to that fort for protection and support, and it was not going to be easy thereafter to maintain a policy of secret hostility to the United States, operating under a guise of friendship.

When Washington reached Philadelphia, no word had yet come of Harmar's defeat. He did have Morris' reports on the unwillingness of the British government to negotiate, and he well knew the extent of their support of Indian raids against the United States. He moved therefore to a stronger national policy in his brief address to Congress, December 8, on the State of the Union:

> *In meeting you again I feel much satisfaction in being able to repeat my congratulations on the favorable aspects which continue to distinguish our public Affairs. The abundant fruits of another year have blessed our country with plenty, and with the means of a flourishing commerce. The progress of public credit is witnessed by a considerable rise of American Stock abroad as well as at home and the revenues allotted for this and other national purposes have been productive beyond the calculations by which they were regulated...*

> *A loan of three million florins... has been completed in Holland...*

> *It has been heretofore known to Congress that frequent incursions have been made on our frontier settlements by certain banditti of Indians from the North West side of the Ohio. These, with some of the tribes dwelling on and near the Wabash, have of late been particularly active in their depredations; and being emboldened by the impunity of their crimes and aided by such parts of the neighboring tribes as could be seduced to join in the hostilities or afford them a retreat for their prisoners and plunder, they have, instead of listening to the humane overtures made on the part of the United States, renewed their violences with fresh alacrity and greater effect.*

The lives of a number of valuable citizens have thus been sacrificed, and some of them under circumstances peculiarly shocking; whilst others have been carried into a deplorable captivity.

I have accordingly authorized an expedition in which the regular troops in that quarter are combined with such drafts of Militia as were deemed sufficient. The event of the measure is yet unknown to me...

The disturbed situation of Europe, and particularly the critical posture of the great maritime powers, whilst it ought to make us more thankful for the general peace and security enjoyed by the United States, reminds us at the same time of the circumspection with which it becomes us to preserve these blessings. It requires also that we should not overlook the tendency of a war... to abridge the means of transporting our valuable productions to their proper markets. I recommend... such encouragements to our own Navigation as will render our commerce and agriculture less dependent on foreign bottoms...

The establishment of the Militia; of a mint; of Standards of weights and measures; of the Post Office and Post roads are subjects... which are abundantly urged by their own importance.

Lord Hawkesbury of the British Board of Trade, England's leading advocate of commercial and shipping restrictions against the United States, headed a committee on general policy towards this country. The preceding April 8 it had issued a secret report: "The Lords are of the opinion that, in a commercial view, it will be for the benefit of this country to prevent Vermont and Kentucky, from becoming dependent on the Government of the United States."

The president's message informed Congress that Kentucky had applied to be the fourteenth state. "The sentiments of warm attachment to the Union and its present Government, expressed by our fellow citizens of Kentucky, cannot fail to add an affectionate concern for their particular welfare..." There were some delays in forming a state constitution there. Vermont slipped in quietly as the fourteenth state in March 1791, and Kentucky became the fifteenth state in June 1792.

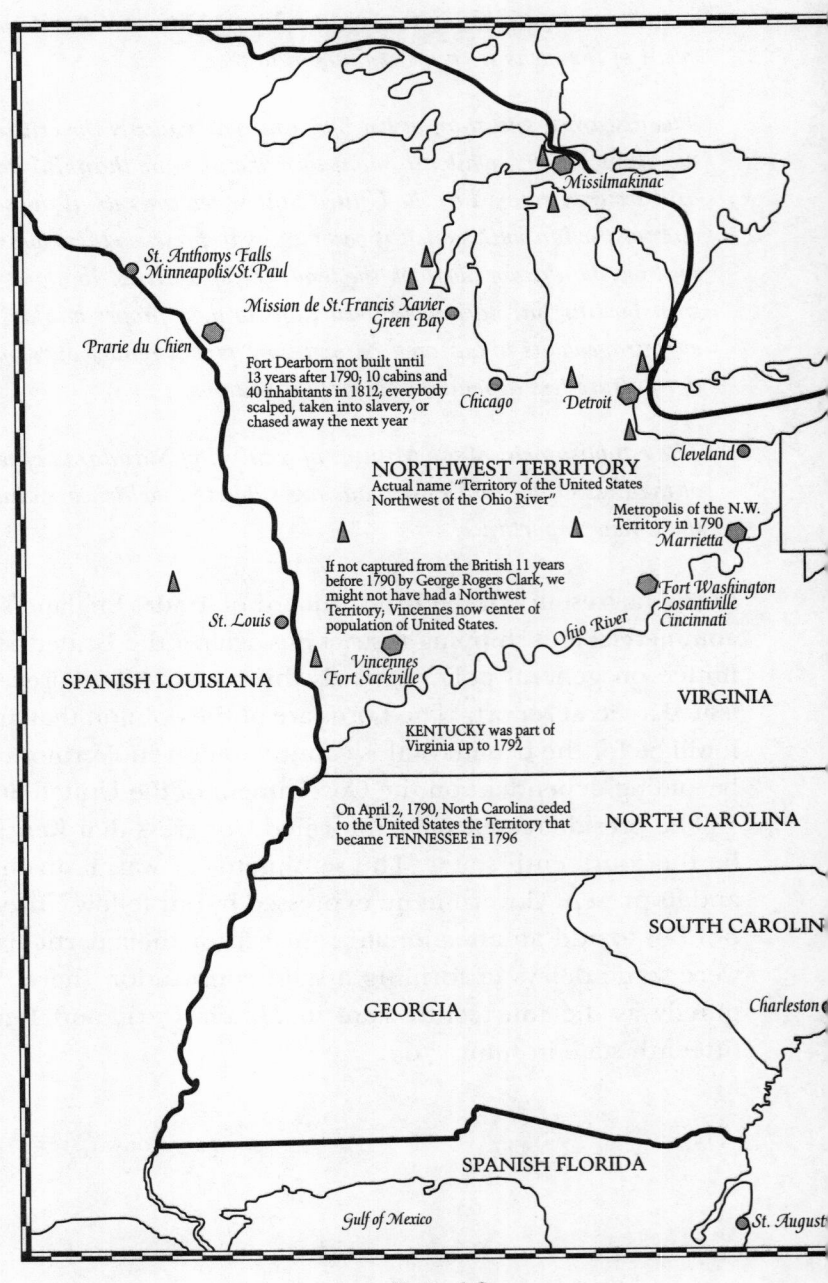

United States

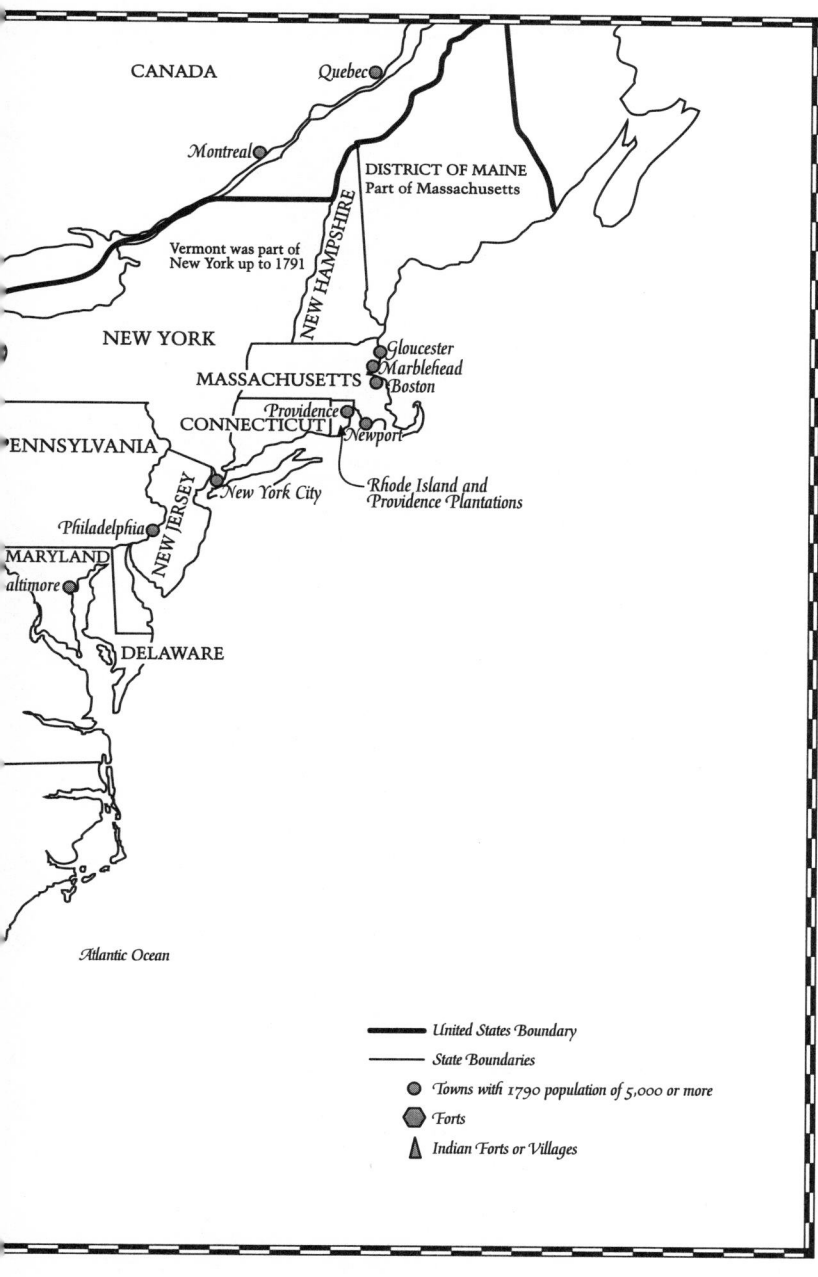

CANADA

Quebec

Montreal

DISTRICT OF MAINE
Part of Massachusetts

NEW HAMPSHIRE

Vermont was part of
New York up to 1791

NEW YORK

Gloucester
Marblehead
MASSACHUSETTS *Boston*

CONNECTICUT *Providence*
Newport

PENNSYLVANIA

NEW JERSEY

New York City

*Rhode Island and
Providence Plantations*

Philadelphia

MARYLAND

altimore

DELAWARE

Atlantic Ocean

─────── *United States Boundary*

─────── *State Boundaries*

⬤ *Towns with 1790 population of 5,000 or more*

⬡ *Forts*

▲ *Indian Forts or Villages*

1790

EIGHT

PHILADELPHIA— THE OLD CAPITAL

1790–1791

T HE ELECTIONS THAT fall and winter provided a large turnover in
Congress. In the House of Representatives twenty-seven of the sixty-five
members were replaced. Five senators, some of whom had drawn only
a two-year term, retired, mostly involuntarily. Two of these were among the principal American contacts of Beckwith—Schuyler of New York and Johnson of
Connecticut. In informing Hamilton of Aaron Burr's election in place of his
father-in-law, James Tillary of New York wrote in January 1791: "[Burr] is
avowedly your enemy, & stands pledged to his party, for a reign of vindictive
declamation against your measures. The Chancellor [Robert Livingston] hates,
& would destroy you." Those who were retiring from office continued to vote
until March 4. The session accomplished much. On March 16 the president
gave David Humphreys in Europe a brief account of new legislation:

> *Congress finished their session on the 3 of March, in the course of which they
> received and granted the applications of Kentucky and Vermont for admission into
> the Union; the former after August, 1792; and the latter immediately; they made
> provision for the interest on the national debt, by laying a higher duty than that
> which heretofore existed on spirituous liquors imported or manufactured; they
> established a national Bank; they passed a law for certain measures to be taken
> towards establishing a mint; and finished much other business of less importance,*

conducting on all occasions with great harmony and cordiality. In some few instances, particularly in passing the law for higher duties mentioned above, and more especially on the subject of the Bank, the line between the southern and eastern interests appeared more strongly marked than could have been wished; the former against and the latter in favor of these measures.

The tax on spirits, the foundation-stone of Hamilton's revenue system, was extended to cover both imported and domestically manufactured spirits. Even though the latter tax was small it was pretty unpopular, especially in the western areas where government operations, state or local, were characteristically limited.

Hamilton's proposal for a national bank, which passed the House by a wide margin, brought a split between South and North, as well as the first open cabinet debate on the extent of federal powers under the Constitution. Washington asked his three Virginia friends, Jefferson, Randolph, and Madison, to give him their opinions. The first two provided written negative legal opinions, and the third argued orally against the act. Madison, swinging away from the positions he had taken in the *Federalist Papers,* declared in the House that the Constitution was designed to protect the states by limiting the power of the national government. The president, who had listened to all the constitutional debates and had read the *Federalist Papers* with care, unhesitatingly signed the bill into law two days later.

Because of the defeat of General Harmar and the continued Indian raids, Congress at the end of the session voted to increase the standing army to 1,216 enlisted men. For economy's sake, their pay was cut from four to three dollars a month. The president could get almost anything he really wanted through Congress, except his unpopular militia proposals. He had asked for a universal militia system, which had been used from the days of the first settlement. This was too much for Congress, which preferred a poorly paid small army, which could enlist only society's dregs.

INDIANS

Washington, Jefferson, and Knox, in numerous memoranda and letters, agreed that fair treatment of the Indians was a prerequisite for peaceful internal development. The new Constitution gave treaty-making powers to the federal government, which were considered to override all state and local laws. The settled policy of the national government was to establish pacts with the Indians under which white settlement was forbidden in Indian-held territories and to license all trading with them. The aim was good in theory but difficult to enforce.

The Indians were divided into many tribes, ranging from the warlike and cannibal, to the gentle and domesticated. They were often at war with each other. Many were accustomed to migrating over hundreds of square miles, returning to small settlements in the winter. Hostile British and Spanish agents stirred many tribes to war. The state governments, often in opposition to the federal government, encouraged their citizens to extract land from the Indians. The frontiers were frequently overrun by criminals and unscrupulous American and British traders, who did not hesitate to murder Indians for gain. Innocent settlers were killed in retaliation. With a tiny army and a frontier stretching over 1,800 miles, policing was next to impossible.

Indian relations and treaty negotiations were under Knox's jurisdiction, thus giving the War Department an important voice in foreign policy. Here Washington, as he did with Europe, took a strong hand in all negotiations, especially when Indians came to see him in the capital.

Knox's extensive correspondence with Washington shows that Indian complaints of treaty violations or mistreatment were considered at length and seriously. The president signed letters to "Yockonahoma, great Medal Chief of Soonacoha, Yockehoopie, leading chief of Kaskooqua, Tobochoh, great Medal Chief of Congaltoo, Pooshemastubie, gorget Captain of Soungaro, and all the other medal and gorget Chiefs and Captains and Warriors of the Choctaw Nation" and to "Pearmingo, or the Mountain Leader, Head Warier and first Minister, and the other Chiefs and Warriors of the Chickasaw Nation." When the Senecas complained, Washington himself, after reading all the correspondence, speeches, and Knox's comments, wrote out a document of many pages which was signed by the president, the secretary of state, and the secretary of war:

The reply of the President of the United States, to the Speech of the Cornplanter, Half-town and Great-tree Chiefs and Counselors of the Seneka Nation of Indians.

I the President of the United States, by my own mouth, and by a written Speech Signed with my own hand, and Sealed with the Seal of the United States, Speak to the Seneka nation, and desire their attention, and that they would keep this speech in remembrance of the friendship of the United States...

I am not uninformed that the Six nations have been led into some difficulties with respect to the sale of their lands since the peace. But I must inform you that these arose before the present government of the United States was established, when the

Separate States, and individuals under their authority, undertook to treat with the Indian tribes respecting the Sale of their lands.

But the case is now entirely altered—the general government only has the power to treat with the Indian nations...

Hear well, and let it be heard by every person in your nation, that the President of the United States declares that the general government considers itself bound to protect you in all the lands secured to you by the Treaty of Fort Stanwix...

It appears upon inquiry of the Governor of New York that John Livingston was not legally authorized to treat with you, and that everything he did with you has been declared null and void...

In the future you cannot be defrauded of your lands—you possess the right to sell, and the right of refusing to sell your lands...

When you may find it necessary to sell any part of your lands, the United States must be present by their agent, and will be your security that you shall not be defrauded...

The murders that have been committed upon some of your people, by the bad white men, I sincerely lament and reprobate...

The Senekas may be assured, that the rewards offered for apprehending the murderers will be continued until they are brought to trial...

The problem of frontier control was so difficult that friendly Christian Senecas were killed near Fort Pitt, while Cornplanter and the other chiefs were returning, by way of the fort, to their nation. Washington, Jefferson, and Knox were outraged. Cornplanter sent a pathetic letter to the president from Pittsburgh on March 17:

When we raised from the great Council of the thirteen fires, we mentioned that we meant to have a Council with the Chiefs of the bad angry Indians.

Father!

Your promise to me was, that you would keep all your people quiet—but since I came here I find that some of my people have been killed—the good, honest people who were here trading.

Father!

We hope you will not suffer all the good people to be killed; but your people are killing them as fast as they can...

Father!

Our father and ruler over all mankind, now speak and tell me, did you order these men to be killed?

Father!

Our word is pledged to you that we would endeavor to make peace with all the warrior nations—If we cannot do it, do not blame us—You struck the innocent men first—we hope you will not blame us, as your people have first broke good rules, but as for our people they are friendly and as firm as ever.

Father!

We must now acquaint you with the man's name who did this murder at Beaver Creek—Samuel Brady, formerly a captain in your army, and under your command—also a Balden...

The murders aroused anger among all the Indians, friendly, neutral, and hostile, as well as great anxiety among the settlers.

Some hostile Indians attacked whites who, in retaliation, struck back at friendly Indians, nearly killing Cornplanter in the process. From Knox's reports it appears that Brady, the original murderer, was rounded up by the Pennsylvania authorities and tried but acquitted. Federal troops scheduled to take part against the Indians under British control soon reached Pittsburgh and restored some sort of order.

Washington summed up the situation to Tobias Lear on April 3: "Until we can restrain the turbulence and disorderly conduct of our borders it will be in vain I fear to expect peace with the Indians, or that they will govern their own people better than we do ours." The following day he complained to Hamilton not only about disorderly frontier people but of the work of land speculators, as well as interferences by the state governments in Indian affairs. What was particularly awkward was that he had been negotiating to have the aid of the six nations against the hostile Indians north of the Ohio. The actions of a few frontier desperadoes might set all Indians raging against the Americans. When he wrote to Knox to approve the measures he was taking to protect Cornplanter and the friendly tribes, he also wrote Jefferson from Mount Vernon on April 4:

You will readily agree with me that the best interests of the United States require such intimation to be made to the Governor of Canada, either directly or indirectly, as may produce instructions to prevent the Indians receiving military aid or supplies from the British posts or garrisons. The notoriety of this assistance has already been such as renders inquiry into particulars unnecessary. Colonel Beckwith seems peculiarly designed to be the channel of an indirect intimation... I wish it may be suggested... that certain information has been received of large supplies of ammunition being delivered to the hostile Indians, from British posts, about the commencement of last campaign. And, as the United States have no other view in prosecuting the present war against the Indians, than, in the failure of negotiation, to procure by arms, peace and safety to the inhabitants of their frontier, they are equally surprised and disappointed at such an interference by the servants or subjects of a foreign State... as seems intended to protract the attainment of so just and reasonable an object.

Washington had appointed Arthur St. Clair, governor of the Northwest Territory, as major general in command of the American army. He made Major General Richard Butler commander of the six-months' levies, and Brigadier Charles Scott head of the militia. Knox was ordered to raise sufficient auxiliary troops for St. Clair to undertake an expedition against hostile Indians in the Northwest Territory. Because Congress did not approve an increase in the army until March 3, the force was exceedingly slow in being organized. In the meantime, during the spring and summer, Knox received many reports of the continuing activities of Simon Girty, a notorious renegade white, Alexander McKee, the British deputy Indian commissioner, and Joseph Brant, the Mohawk chief who had participated in the Cherry Valley massacre. Their names struck terror into the hearts of peaceful settlers as well as of peaceful Indians.

THE FEDERAL CITY

Immediately after New Year's Day 1791, the president and the secretary of state went over the measurements which Washington had taken along the Potomac and his initial plans for the federal district. On January 24 the president proclaimed the new federal territory, extending from Georgetown to the Eastern Branch of the Potomac. He noted that the latter boundary was to be temporary until Congress passed additional legislation, permitting him to extend it to Alexandria. In forwarding his proclamation to William Deakins and Benjamin Stoddert of Georgetown, Washington asked them to give it wide publicity. The president, at the same time, appointed Thomas Johnson and Daniel Carroll of Maryland, and David Stuart of Virginia, as the first commissioners of the district, along with Andrew Ellicott as surveyor.

To get cheap initial land for the federal buildings and to foil speculators, the president displayed some of his old military skill at moves to deceive. Maryland and Virginia had guaranteed initial funds of $192,000 for the federal capital. With this as a reserve, the president asked Deakins and Stoddert to ascertain, "in the most perfect secrecy," how much land they could purchase in their own name for federal use. Washington said that his mind was perfectly balanced between Carrollsburg and "the lands on the river, below and adjacent to Georgetown." Deakins and Stoddert were to investigate the prices of various parcels but always to stipulate that no final decision could be made for two weeks. This would give them time to consult the president. He also suggested his particular interest in the property of David Burnes, along the Potomac, on which the president's house was eventually placed.

On March 2 Washington instructed Pierre-Charles L'Enfant, artist-engineer, to lay out plans for the public buildings between the Potomac River and the road from Georgetown to the Eastern Branch. To divert attention from the land to the west, L'Enfant was instructed to begin his work to the east. Not long afterwards, Thomas Jefferson handed the president his own sketch of a proposed capital, which was considerably cruder than the plan for Alexandria, which Washington had drawn at the age of seventeen. Jefferson scrunched the government buildings into an area of less than three hundred acres, adding the outline of a town perhaps four times as large.

When the president reached Georgetown on March 28, he saw L'Enfant who, eleven days later, wrote to Hamilton to describe his joy at what had happened. L'Enfant said he was always being accused of wanting to do more than his instructions permitted. Looking over the federal district, he had done this "without compunction," surveying the entire area. When the president arrived, he suggested having it all for the capital "and was fortunate enough to see it meet with his approbation." Washington then directed him "to delineate a grand and general plan" and to have it ready by the time he returned in June. Washington's diary continued the story; he described his meeting with the competing groups of land owners:

> *Finding the interests of the Landholders about Georgetown and those about Carrollburg much at variance... I requested them to meet me at six o'clock this afternoon at my lodgings...*

> *To this meeting I represented that the contention in which they seemed engaged, did*

not in my opinion comport either with the public interest or that of their own...
That neither the offer from Georgetown or Carrollburg, separately, was adequate to
the end of insuring the object. That both together did not comprehend more ground
nor would afford greater means than was required for the federal City; and that,
instead of contending which of the two should have it they had better, by combining
more offers make a common cause of it, and thereby secure it to the district; other
arguments were used to show the danger which might arise from delay and the good
effects that might proceed from a Union...

The parties to whom I addressed myself yesterday evening, having taken the matter
into consideration saw the propriety of my observations... and therefore mutually
agreed and entered into articles to surrender for public purposes, one half of the
land they severally possessed within bounds which were designated as necessary for
the City...

The business being thus happily finished and some directions given to the
Commissioners, the Surveyor and Engineer... I left Georgetown, dined in
Alexandria, and reached Mount Vernon in the evening.

At Georgetown, "on the thirtieth day of March in the year of our Lord 1791 and the independence of the United States the fifteenth," the president signed the proclamation extending the federal district to its full hundred square miles. Alexandria, Hamburg, Georgetown, and Carrollburg were now within the new territory. On April 4 he formally directed L'Enfant to plan a new city for the more than ten square miles between Rock Creek and the Eastern Branch. In forwarding the proclamation to the secretary of state, Washington said that he had persuaded the owners, "even the obstinate Mr. Burnes," to make all the land available, on condition that it be planned as a city. He had asked L'Enfant to design the capital, to locate the proposed federal buildings, and to lay out lots and streets. Under his agreement with the landholders, they were to own every other lot, alternately with the government, and to provide land for streets free of cost. Lands needed for public purposes could be purchased for $71.50 an acre.

His April 8 letter to Hamilton indicated that L'Enfant had begun work at once on the area which he described as "a most eligible one for to fix upon the capital of this extensive empire." He found it extremely fatiguing "surveying at so improper a season of the year." The area itself was a wilderness of forests and mud, streams and swamps, with small areas of cleared farmland. Nonetheless he persisted and in less than three months had ready an imaginative design for a great capital of the future. He broke up the normal rectangles of planned

American towns, by diagonal avenues, intended to add variety, as well as to give more rapid access from one part of the city to another. Included was his "grand avenue," subsequently named for Pennsylvania, which swept from the Eastern Branch to Georgetown. On it he placed the Capitol, atop Jenkin's Hill, and the president's house, at the Burnes farm. L'Enfant had been at the siege of Savannah. Probably influenced by that city's design, he subsequently added fifteen rectangles or squares, one for each state, to provide a further attractive form for the capital.

A draft plan and description was ready for the president on June 22. On June 28 Washington, L'Enfant, and Andrew Ellicott rode from Georgetown to examine the area and determine the final location of the two principal government buildings. Washington approved as perfect L'Enfant's choice for the capitol but he moved the president's residence to a higher nearby point. He seems subsequently to have reduced the number of avenues and to have suggested the addition of a public market. Then, recognizing the grandeur of L'Enfant's design, he gave it enthusiastic approval. The capital was thus designed and on its way within a year of the congressional vote.

While Washington was in the south, various landholders had second thoughts and some refused to part with their land. It took only brief persuasion by Washington to see they might spoil everything. Pennsylvania, alarmed about the capital's move from Philadelphia, had introduced a bill to build a capitol and president's house in Philadelphia. Washington wrote in his diary: "They readily waived their objections and agreed to convey to the utmost extent of what was required." When all the deeds had been signed on June 29, Washington showed them L'Enfant's plan for the city, noting certain expected changes in it. He wrote: "It was with much pleasure that a general approbation of the measure seemed to pervade the whole."

On September 8 the district commissioners, at a meeting attended by Jefferson and Madison, named the capital the city of Washington, and the district, the territory of Columbia.

THE SOUTHERN TOUR

The president left Philadelphia on March 20 for a planned absence of about three-and-a-half months in the southern states, a trip which would include his work on the national capital. Accompanying him were his secretary, Major Jackson; five servants; eleven horses; and a chariot and baggage wagon. Although the roads south of Philadelphia were poor and rutted, the procession encountered no trouble until it tried to cross the Chesapeake Bay by the Rock

Hall ferry four days later. A great part of the day was spent loading two boats. The president wrote:

> *Unluckily, embarking on board of a borrowed Boat because she was the largest, I was in imminent danger, from the unskillfulness of the hands, and the dullness of her sailing, added to the darkness and the storminess of the night. For two hours after we hoisted Sail, the wind was light and ahead, the next hour was a stark calm, after which the wind sprung up at [Southeast] and increased until it blew a gale. About which time, and after 8 o'clock P.M., we made the mouth of Severn River (leading up to Annapolis) but the ignorance of the People on board with respect to the navigation of it, ran us aground, first on [Greenberry] point from which with much exertion and difficulty we got off; and then, having no knowledge of the Channel and the night being immensely dark with heavy and variable squalls of wind, constant lightning and tremendous thunder, we soon grounded again on what is called Horne's Point where, finding all efforts in vain, and not knowing where we were, we remained, not knowing what might happen, till morning.*

The president described his rescue in his diary of March 25: "Having lain all night in my Great Coat and Boots, in a berth not long enough for me by the head, or much cramped, we found ourselves in the morning within about one mile off Annapolis and still fast aground. Whilst we were preparing our small boat in order to land in it, a sailing Boat came to our assistance, in which with the baggage I had on board I landed" to a fifteen-gun salute.

The governor of Maryland, John Eager Howard, had attempted the preceding night to meet the president on his passage across the bay but was driven back by the weather and spent an anxious night wondering about the president's safety. Howard met Washington as soon as he arrived at Mann's Inn, where young Shippen had so much enjoyed his turtle. The governor took him to see St. John's College, with its eighty students, and then back to a public dinner at the inn. The following day the president dined at the governor's house and then attended a dancing assembly in the evening. On the 27th, the president left for Georgetown and discussions on the capital. On March 31 he reached Mount Vernon.

After looking over his farms for a week, the president departed for the south on April 7. Almost immediately he encountered a further unpleasant experience with eighteenth-century travel:

> *In attempting to cross the ferry at Colchester, with the four horses hitched to the Chariot, by the neglect of the person who stood before them, one of the leaders got overboard when the boat was in swimming water and 50 yards from the shore—*

with much difficulty he escaped drowning before he could be disengaged. His struggling frightened the others in such a manner that one after another and in quick succession they all got overboard, harnessed and fastened as they were, and with the utmost difficulty they were saved, and the Carriage escaped being dragged after them... Providentially, indeed miraculously, by the exertions of people who went off in boats and jumped into the River... no damaged was sustained.

Richmond was illuminated the night of April 11 in honor of the president. Washington inspected the canal, sluices, and locks of the James River Canal Company, which he had been instrumental in forming. He took time to sound out Edward Carrington, federal marshal for the state, as well as others, on the political sentiment of Virginia. He was assured that the violent opposition in the Virginia Assembly to the assumption of state debts and to the tax on domestic spirits, was not representative of what the people of the state felt. In general they were very favorably disposed to the federal government but they needed more explanations of the measures, in order to support them.

Washington was accompanied from Richmond to Petersburg by large parties on horseback, intending to do honor to the president of the United States. They succeeded in enveloping him the whole way in clouds of choking dust. He found that more escorts were eagerly waiting to do the same thing south of Petersburg. When they asked him what time he planned to leave in the morning, the president replied that he "should endeavor to do it before eight o'clock; but I did it a little after five, by which means I avoided the inconveniences above mentioned."

While circling from Virginia to Georgia and back, Washington repeatedly commented on the poorness of the soils, region, roads, and inns. The trip was often as rough as his frontier travels. By the time he got to North Carolina, violent spring rains had turned the dusty roads not to mud, but "water, so level are the roads." The inns he encountered were so dirty and disagreeable that he had to travel as far as Halifax to find a place where he could stay.

As he travelled farther south in North Carolina, he observed the first cotton as well as flax and the usual corn. He was a fascinated observer of tar-rolling into barrels at Tarboro and Greenville. At New Bern, then the state capital, Washington had "good" lodgings. He attended a ball "at which there were abt. 70 ladies," at the governor's old palace, "a good brick building but now hastening to Ruins."

After New Bern Washington recorded that the inns were "indifferent" (his category for third-class), while the road from New Bern to Wilmington "passes through the most barren country I ever beheld." At Wilmington he had "very good" accommodations, his rare superlative. The town had "some good houses pretty compactly built." He examined the port which exported tobacco, corn, rice, flax seed, and pork. He attended a ball "at which there were 62 ladies—illuminations, Bonfires, etc."

Even indifferent inns disappeared as the president moved into South Carolina, where he was forced to accept private hospitality. The rice planta- tion of William Alston on the Waccamaw River was an oasis. Washington wrote: "His house which is large, new and elegantly furnished, stands on a sand hill, high for the Country, with his Rice fields below; the contrast of which with the lands back of it, and the Sand and piney barrens through which we had passed is scarcely to be conceived." At Alston's house he met Generals William Washington, a distant cousin, and William Moultrie, who had been famous in southern battles.

Washington travelled on to Georgetown where, he noted, many of the houses had been burned by the British. The town gave him a public dinner in the open and he then proceeded to a tea party with "50 ladies." Washington was further entertained at other plantations on his way to Charleston. That city, the most sophisticated in the south, had been looking forward with all the ardor of Boston to the president's visit but with much more careful prepara- tions. He was met at Haddrel's Point by various officials who had come to get him "in a 12 oared barge rowed by 12 American Captains of Ships, most ele- gantly dressed. There were a great number of other Boats with Gentlemen and ladies in them; two Boats with Music; all of whom attended me across, and on the passage were met by a number of others. As we approached the town a salute with artillery commenced, and at the Wharf I was met by the Governor, the Lt. Governor… the two Senators of the State, Wardens of the City, Cincinnati, etc. and conducted to the Exchange where they passed by in procession; from thence I was conducted in like manner to my lodgings, after which I dined at the Governors (in what he called a private way) with 15 or 18 Gentlemen." His lodgings, in a fine old Charleston house, he pronounced "very good."

Washington stayed a full week in the city and thoroughly enjoyed it. On his second day he "was visited about 2 o'clock, by a great number of the most respectable ladies of Charleston—the first honor of the kind I had ever expe- rienced and it was as flattering as it was singular." The following evening he went "to a very elegant dancing Assembly at the Exchange, at which were 256 elegantly dressed and handsome ladies." Washington failed to note in his diary that all the ladies wore ribbons with such legends as "Long live the President." The following evening he attended a concert, "at which there were at least 400 ladies, the number and appearance of which exceeded anything of the kind I had ever seen." Next night he danced at another ball at the governor's house "where there was a select Company of ladies." In their head-dresses were pictures of Washington or other references to him.

The president did not spend all his time dancing. He examined the fortifications of Charleston. In commenting on the 1780 battle in which Lincoln was captured, Washington thought that "the defense was noble and honorable, altho' the measure was undertaken upon wrong principles and impolitic." He visited the boys' orphan asylum, twice attended church services, rode through the town on horseback, found himself charmed by the view from Saint Michael's steeple, "the Gardens and green trees... adding much to the beauty of the prospect." He noted many good houses of brick or wood. "The inhabitants are wealthy, Gay and hospitable; appear happy and satisfied with the General Government." He wrote that Charleston's rice exports ranged from 80,000 to 120,000 barrels and tobacco from 5,000 to 8,000 hogsheads.

Savannah, much smaller than Charleston, had done its best to honor Washington, sending eight ships' captains to row him down the Savannah River. On his way he stopped to call on the widow of Nathanael Greene. Savannah was illuminated in his honor. On Friday, May 13, he attended "a dancing Assembly, at which there was about one hundred well-dressed and handsome ladies." There was a public dinner, attended by two hundred people, and fireworks. He inspected the defenses of Savannah, already largely obliterated, which made it impossible for him to judge how well d'Estaing and Lincoln had performed. The ladies of the town made a call on him after church on Sunday. He found walking in Savannah disagreeable because of the sand which filled the houses with dust when the wind blew. Three sides of the town were completely occupied by rice fields. Washington wrote that the principal exports were rice, tobacco, lumber, indigo, hemp, and cotton.

At Augusta, Georgia, a town described by the president as "well-laid out with wide and spacious streets," he was met by the governor, Edward Telfair, and the principal state officers. After dining at the governor's, he took "tea with many well-dressed ladies." The following day the citizens of the town gave a public dinner at the courthouse and, in the evening, Washington attended a ball "at the Academy." The following day he examined "the Ruins or rather small Remnant of the Works which had been erected by the British during the War and taken by the Americans." That same day he dined privately with the governor.

As he travelled north, Washington was rather depressed by the land, after the more luxuriant seacoast. "The whole Road [to Columbia, South Carolina]... is a pine barren of the worst sort, being hilly as well as poor. This circumstance added to the distance, length of the stages, want of water and heat of the day, foundered one of my horses very badly." Between Columbia and Camden lay "the most miserable pine barren I ever saw."

North of Camden Washington examined the areas where Greene fought Rawdon and Gates was beaten by Cornwallis. Of the former skirmish he wrote: "The ground had just been taken by [Greene] was well chosen, but he [was] not well established in it before he was attacked; which by capturing a Videt was, in some measure by surprise." On the latter he added: "As this was a night meeting of both Armies on their march, and altogether unexpected, each formed on the ground they met without any advantage in it on either side, it being level and open. Had Genl. Gates been 1/2 a mile further advanced, an impenetrable Swamp would have prevented the attack, which was made on him by the British Army, and afforded him time to have formed his owns plans, but having no information of Lord Cornwallis's designs, and perhaps not being apprised of this advantage it was not seized by him."

Not until Washington neared Charlotte, North Carolina, did the lands begin to lose their sandy appearance and "to assume a very rich look." Beyond Charlotte he noted the first meadows he had seen since he quit Virginia.

Washington was charmed by "the small but neat village" of Salem, North Carolina, a Moravian settlement. As he neared the town, according to its annals, he was serenaded with melodies, "played partly by trumpets and French horns, partly by trombones." Washington greeted everyone, as he always did, very affably, but the people were pleased that he was particularly attentive to the children who had come to see him. At dinner he said he would like some more music with his meal and this was quickly provided. The following evening he heard choral singing and instrumental music. He spent one more day in Salem than he had planned, partly to meet the governor of the state, but perhaps also because he enjoyed it so much.

Governor Martin of North Carolina confirmed what Washington had heard in Virginia, South Carolina, and Georgia. Opposition to the federal government was rapidly disappearing. Governor Martin supported, as did the governor of Georgia, the federal policy of peace and fair dealings with the Indians. This was of importance because both states bordered on Indian country. Washington later noted that, in his southern conversations, he found little opposition to the tax on domestic spirits, while almost no one had even mentioned the national bank act, which split his cabinet.

As soon as Washington crossed the Virginia line he summarized his none-too-enthusiastic impressions of southern conditions. His travels had taken him over more than 1,000 miles of North and South Carolina and Georgia. "Excepting the Towns (and some Gentlemens Seats along the Road from Charleston to Savannah) there is not within the view of the whole road... a single house which has anything of an elegant appearance... The accommodations... we found extremely indifferent... It is not easy to say on which road—the one I went or the one I came—the entertainment is most indifferent—but with truth it may be affirmed that both are bad."

Washington noted how much poor soil there was just inland from the sea, when it became "dead level and badly watered." In the low country, drainage and irrigation had made the soil productive for rice. Some land there was priced as high as $225 an acre whereas nearby piney soil sold for $1 an acre. Above the fall lines, land was often superior and capable of growing corn, tobacco, wheat, and hemp. In general, interior farms were too far from profitable markets. He thought inland water navigation could be widely developed at little cost. The rivers were great, with extensive lateral tributaries. The falls were low and easily bypassed by canals. With these, corn, tobacco, indigo, hemp, tar, pitch, timber, and other local products could be floated cheaply to market.

As Washington moved further north he noted that land and houses improved and the settlements were thicker. It took him a week to travel across Virginia to Mount Vernon. Next day, June 13, he dropped a note to Hamilton to say that his 1,700-mile trip had been uninterrupted by accidents, sickness, or bad weather. He had allowed eight days extra for "casualties," but he had not needed a single one of them. He planned to use the saved time to look over his farms.

In those happier days, the secretary of state had written the president on May 8: "The last week does not furnish one single public event worthy of communicating to you: so that I have only to say 'all is well.'" A week later Jefferson said: "We are still without any occurrence foreign or domestic worth mentioning to you."

Washington cleaned up a lot of business at Mount Vernon, left enough detailed written instructions to keep the whole staff at work till the snow fell, then set off for Georgetown to complete the business of the national capital. Still interested in seeing more, he decided to veer off into western Maryland and the Pennsylvania Dutch country. On June 30 he left Georgetown at 4 A.M. for Frederick, Maryland, covering the forty-three miles by sundown. The unexpected arrival of the president put the town into a frenzy. Citizens raced to ring the church bells and to load cannon. A band was hastily assembled to serenade him. The people asked if he could stay two days but he said he had to leave in the morning. Frederick managed to produce an address before he left, which they delivered practically at dawn, for the president set out at 7 A.M. for York, Pennsylvania.

As Washington moved north across Maryland and Pennsylvania, the contrast with the three southernmost states grew ever sharper. The president noted that, from Georgetown to Frederick, the soil was "rich and fine, the Country is

thicker settled and the farm Houses of a better kind than I expected to find."
North of Frederick "the lands... are remarkably fine... The farm houses are
good mostly of stone and the settlers compact, with good Barns and meadows."
He thought Hanover "a very pretty village with a number of good brick
houses... The country is exceedingly pleasant... The Country from York to
Lancaster is very fine, thick-settled, and well cultivated. About the ferry they are
extremely rich—the river Susquehanna at this place is more than a mile wide
with some pretty views on the banks of it."

Washington attended the Dutch Reformed Church, July 3, commenting
that as the sermon was "in a language not a word of which I understood, I was
in no danger of becoming a proselyte." The following day he celebrated
Independence Day with the good German people of Lancaster. By July 6 he
was back in Philadelphia. On July 28 he wrote a brief but cheerful account of
his trip to Gouverneur Morris: "In my late tour through the Southern States,
I experienced great satisfaction in seeing the good effects of the general government in that part of the Union... The Farmer, the Merchant and the
Mechanic have seen their several interests attended to, and from thence they
unite in placing a confidence in their representatives... Two or three years of
good crops, and a ready market for the produce of their lands, has put everyone in good humor; and, in some instances, they even impute to the government what is due only to the goodness of Providence."

CENSUS

In writing Morris, Washington corrected an earlier estimate he had sent him
of the population of the United States. "The estimate was then founded on
the ideas held out by the Gentlemen in Congress of the population of their
several States, each of whom, looking thro' a magnifying glass, would speak of
the greatest extent, to which there was any probability of their numbers reaching." He now indicated that the population would be just short of four million
but, as he had learned on his trip, many census officials had been negligent
in their counting, some people refused to report, thinking it was to be a base
for taxation, while others expressed some religious scruples against being
numbered. Europe, the president said, had always assumed that America had
a much smaller population. Now they might give her somewhat more weight
in the international scale.*

---

* These are rather rough estimates of the 1790 population of the main European powers:
Great Britain and Ireland, 14 million; France, 25 million; and Spain, 10 1/2 million.

AFFAIRS OF THE STATE

With the president being away from the capital for much of the first half of 1791, other founding fathers used the time to build up trouble for themselves and, subsequently, for Washington. Adams had been squelched by the Senate at its beginning. It consisted of only twenty-two members in its opening session. Not infrequently divided evenly, the vice-president cast the deciding vote, thereby always annoying eleven senators. Largely condemned to silence in his presiding role, the vice-president began writing for the newspapers. His long-winded "Discources on Davila," printed by the *Pennsylvania Gazette*, took a few critical flings at the French Revolution and the doctrine that one man was as good as another. Adams suddenly found himself the center of outraged cries that he, who had been so long at the Court of St. James', was a monarchist, aristocrat, and a hater of his own as well as the French Revolution. Adams complained that no one bothered to read what he had actually said.

It is not clear whether Jefferson's emotional reactions to events preceded or followed his migraine headaches. He had such headaches in May and may have had them in April. About April 5 he received Washington's plans for a great federal city, implying his faith in a strong national government. His own small plan was given short shrift. His July 10 letter to Monroe, flailing at "the federal town" and "certain schemes of manufactures," indicates that he was more upset than he indicated at the time. Not long afterwards, he began to fire at the leading figures of the government, omitting, in the initial stages, the president.

In late April or early May, having borrowed a copy of Thomas Paine's *Rights of Man*, which denounced Edmund Burke for attacking France and its revolution, Jefferson forwarded it, as requested, to the brother of a waiting printer. With it, he sent a note, welcoming its publication, adding a swipe at Adams' "political Heresies." The printer used this in his preface, joining to it praise of Jefferson. As a result of the ensuing uproar, the secretary of state wrote to the president to say that he was distressed that his letter had been used without permission. He himself was a good friend of Adams, in spite of his "apostasy to hereditary monarchy and nobility." In a polite letter to Adams, Jefferson explained how the situation had arisen. Adams met him openly, declaring that Jefferson was "wholly mistaken" as to the views ascribed to him. Jefferson then wrote Adams that he had not even had him in mind, a statement in direct contradiction to his letter to Washington.

Not long afterwards Jefferson and Madison went north to New York and New England, a trip which temporarily relieved Jefferson's headaches. Fortified by their belief in the extent of Virginia's sour opposition to many of the president's policies, the pair held conversations with leaders of similar thought in New York—George Clinton, Aaron Burr, and Robert Livingston. They also met with Philip Freneau, Madison's Princeton classmate. Leaving Madison in New York, Jefferson proceeded to Philadelphia. On July 10 he informed Madison that he proposed to "press on the President" the nomination of Paine, who had become a citizen of France, to be postmaster general of the United States. In August Freneau appeared in Philadelphia as translator for the Department of State. Along with this duty he edited the *National Gazette*, which was eventually to attack the president with fierce invectives. By July 28 Jefferson had added the names of the chief justice and the secretaries of the treasury and war, as plotting with Adams to overturn the government and Constitution, in order to have a king of America.

In the meantime Alexander Hamilton was engaged in actions and conversations of so complex a nature that they require a historian to unravel, nearly eighty-eight pages, much of it in fine print. These involved the apparent fabrication of documents by the secretary of the treasury.

RELATIONS WITH GREAT BRITAIN

Major Beckwith showed up in Philadelphia, not long after the government began its operations there. He settled into the same boarding house as Madison. This worried Jefferson who asked Madison to come and share his quarters. Beckwith also attended, quite freely, the president's receptions. He caused quite a lot of talk in New York and Philadelphia, because Sir John Temple, British counsel, wrote in April 1791 to the British foreign secretary: "Lord Dorchester has had one of his aides de Camp here and at Philadelphia, for the year past. The status of this Person about Congress hath indeed disgusted not a few who heretofore leaned towards Great Britain. An envoy, they say, from a Colony Governor... He can be considered in no other light than as a petty Spy!"

On the American side, the initial congressional bills for discrimination against British vessels had been a simple retaliation for Great Britain's restrictive practices. Washington's proposals, however, while they involved some of the same principles, had a far higher aim—the need to have an adequate merchant marine and fishing fleet for the national economy, as well as for the country's security. Senate and House had replied to the president that they would be prepared to support his requests with the necessary funds. Not long afterwards the president forwarded to Congress the correspondence of Gouverneur Morris with the British cabinet. His letter noted that the British government had declared "without scruple" that it did not mean to adhere to the treaty which it had signed.

Beckwith protested vigorously to Hamilton on February 16 that the president's messages had shown a French bias, they would prevent England from sending a minister to the United States, and they would check the "growing friendship" of Great Britain. Hamilton heard him without, as far as can be determined, raising a defense of the president. In private conversations in Philadelphia Beckwith declared that the trade of the United States was of no importance to Great Britain, a view which undoubtedly horrified the commercially minded British government when it reached London. The United States was, in fact, Britain's largest customer; British exports to the United States more than doubled from 1789 to 1791.

Beckwith's report to London on March 11 contained an appraisal of Washington and Jefferson:

> *The talents of General Washington are greatly overrated in the world. His public reputation has hitherto been supported by reserve, caution, temper, firmness, and a plain understanding, with a good choice of men around him; his present high station has lately become extremely embarrassing from a difference in the political opinion of the officers at the head of the executive departments... The great point of difference is on an English and a French connection; the gentleman at the head of the former, conceives the best interests of this country will be greatly promoted by a solid and permanent friendship with Great Britain... Mr. Jefferson is at the head of the latter, he is blindly devoted to a French interest... There are no lengths in his power to which he will not go to favor the interests of that kingdom.*

Beckwith's messages conveyed unintended warnings. Britain's carefully cherished commerce was being carelessly tossed around by a soldier-spy. There was also a growing danger in American commercial policy, which called for a diplomat rather than a soldier. The British government, not long after the receipt of Beckwith's dispatches, recalled George Hammond from the British Embassy at Madrid. He was ordered to proceed to Philadelphia as his majesty's minister. Washington and Jefferson had scored a first point.

Beckwith did not learn for some time of the British decision to establish a legation. He continued to try to influence policy, notably by suggesting to Hamilton a British "mediation" with the Indians. In essence, though it was not explained as such, the British would control the Indians west of the Ohio if Americans promised to stay out of this part of their territory. This proposal was too much even for Hamilton. He informed Beckwith that it was "inadmissible, and I could not submit such a paper to the President's consideration."

Though the British continued to refer such suggestions to Hamilton over the years, he was unshakable in his view that the United States was sovereign in the Northwest Territory. Beckwith, nonetheless, in further conversations with Hamilton in June and July attempted to persuade the secretary that the British government had nothing to do with the hostility of the Indians. Beckwith also protested against a law of Congress which located the new customs office for Vermont at Alburg, north of the British fortification which still existed in that state. Beckwith's last act, before leaving for London, was to forward to Hamilton a copy of an August 15 speech of Lord Dorchester to the Indians, which was supposed to indicate the pacific intentions of the British. In those parts which have been here underscored, they were quite to the contrary:

> When the King made peace and gave independence to the United States, he made a treaty in which he marked out a line between him and them... This line, which the King then marked out between him and the States, _even supposing the treaty had taken effect_, could never have prejudiced your rights. Brothers, the King's rights with respect to your territory were against the nations of Europe; these he resigned to the States. But the King never had any rights against you...

Dorchester's speech had been made to a group of confederated Indians at Quebec about six weeks after the British held extensive negotiations with them at the Maumee Rapids. That conference took an initial step towards the establishment of an extensive Indian buffer state. With no intended humor, the British government that winter, and the following spring, issued instructions and decrees for America, as though 1776 had never happened. They organized, on paper, a territory under British control, which was to cover the present states of Ohio, Indiana, Illinois, Michigan, parts of Minnesota, Vermont, and Pennsylvania, and nearly half of New York State.

FRENCH DEVELOPMENTS

Lafayette, not yet thirty, had taken the lead in the early stages of the French Revolution. As a member of the 1787 Assembly of Notables, he issued a call for the first French National Assembly. In 1789, as vice-president of the assembly, he secured passage of the Declaration of the Rights of Man. On March 17, 1790, he sent to Washington "a picture of the Bastille just as it looked a few days after I had ordered its demolition, with the main key of that fortress of despotism. It is a tribute which I owe... as a Missionary of Liberty to its Patriarch."

Lafayette was made head of the National Guard of Paris the day after the

Bastille fell. Shortly afterwards he designed the tricolore cockade of liberty. He subsequently rescued the queen from the Paris mobs and attempted to prevent the flight of the king and queen in 1791. Lafayette hoped to give France liberty and greater equality with orderly constitutional changes. As the Jacobin terror gained momentum, the moderate and liberal forces were swept aside. Lafayette himself, the following year, was declared an enemy to liberty and forced into exile.

The president and the secretary of state were warm in their sympathies with France but they viewed developments with different eyes. Washington, who had seen so much bloodshed, watched what was unfolding in France with realism and increasing apprehension. Jefferson gazed at the terror with equanimity and even joy. On the basis of almost the same information as Jefferson had, Washington wrote to Lafayette on July 24, 1791:

> *To a philanthropic mind, the happiness of 24 million [French] people cannot be indifferent... We must place a confidence in Providence... that right will ultimately be established. The tumultuous populace of large cities are ever to be dreaded. Their indiscriminate violence prostrates for the time all public authority, and its consequences are sometimes extensive and terrible. In Paris we may suppose these tumults are peculiarly disastrous at this time, when the public mind is in a ferment and when (as is always the case on such occasions) there are not wanting wicked and designing men, whose element is confusion, and who will not hesitate in destroying the public tranquillity to gain a favorite point. But until your Constitution is fixed, your government organized, and your representative Body organized, much tranquillity cannot be expected; for, until these things are done, those who are unfriendly to the revolution, will not quit the hope of bringing matters back to their former state.*

Thus, long before the real terror, Washington clearly foresaw the intense struggle that would develop between the forces of absolutism and the mobs led by evil men. Jefferson's mind, however, remained largely closed during the whole of the French Revolution. Four days previous to Washington's letter, he had written Edmund Pendleton: "The French revolution proceeds steadily, and is I think beyond the danger of accident of every kind. The success of that will ensure the progress of liberty in Europe, and its preservation here. The failure of that would have been a powerful argument with those who wish to introduce a king, lords & commons here, a sect which is all head and no body." Differences on foreign as well as domestic policy were basic to Jefferson's subsequent bitter hostility to Washington.

The French had been without a minister to the United States since the comte de Moustier had returned home in the autumn of 1789. On August 12, 1791, Jean-Baptiste Ternant presented his credentials to the president. The secretary of state was most unceremonious about this, dropping a note to the minister to say that he would be with the president in the early afternoon and Ternant could stop in at two-thirty.

Ternant had been an officer with Rochambeau's army and was probably hand-picked by Lafayette for his cordiality to America. When Washington and Jefferson subsequently left town, Hamilton called the French minister to his office to provide assurances almost the opposite of those he had given Beckwith—that any idea of a treaty of alliance with Great Britain was not admissible, and that the United States would insist on full rights for its shipping in the British West Indies.

STATE OF THE UNION

Washington appointed his nephew, George Augustine Washington, as over-seer of Mount Vernon, when he went to New York. The younger George had been an aide to Lafayette, and the president usually referred to him as "the Major." Since he married Mrs. Washington's niece both Washingtons took a special interest in him. He had the family tuberculosis and Washington often warned him not to work too hard. When his health deteriorated, he was forced to travel to Warm Springs, where his uncles had once gone, to attempt a cure. Because of this, Washington made an emergency trip to Mount Vernon on September 15.

On October 7 he asked Tobias Lear in Philadelphia to get material ready for his third State of the Union address. He requested him to examine his speeches and messages to the preceding sessions of Congress, to note everything he had recommended and what Congress had passed. He was to check with the clerks of the Senate and House on the status of proposals which had not yet received approval. Washington received a reply from Lear on October 14 telling him that Congress was scheduled to convene on October 24, not on the last day of the month as he supposed. The president replied that he was "distressed" to hear this. "I had no more idea of this than its being doomsday." He said he would return as rapidly as possible to the capital. He set out on October 17, pausing just long enough at Georgetown to order the sale of lots for the federal city and to confer with Jefferson and Madison. He spent the night at Bladensburg, was up writing notes at 5:30 in the morning, and started for Philadelphia at 6 A.M. in a heavy storm. He reached the city on October 21.

On October 25 the president delivered his third annual message to this, the

Second Congress. The president expressed pride in "the progressive state of Agriculture, Manufactures, Commerce and Navigation… and the… new and decisive proofs of the increasing reputation and credit of the nation." Revenues were proving so buoyant that no new taxes would be needed. The entire public stock issue of the Bank of the United States was sold in a single day. Most of the old holders of the domestic debt had subscribed to the new issues. The United States floated with ease a loan of eight and a half million florins in Amsterdam.

The president urged action on his past recommendations. The country needed a proper militia act and magazines and arsenals. More and better roads were required, especially new roads to the West and crossing outwards from the main northern and southern routes. Small change was scarce; a mint was urgently wanted. Provision was needed for the opening up and sale of public lands, at reasonable prices, to new farmers.

Indian affairs, he noted, were difficult. The government had concluded preliminary treaties with the Cherokees and Six Nations but many other tribes were still hostile. It was essential that the United States adopt, towards all Indians, a fair and enlightened policy, corresponding to its own principles of religion and philanthropy. They ought to have an impartial administration of justice and their land titles guaranteed by treaties, which the United States would enforce on its own citizens. Hostile Indians should be pacified under "offensive operations… conducted as consistently as possible with the dictates of humanity." Such enterprises were now under way. "It is sincerely to be desired that all need of coercion, in future, may cease; and that an intimate intercourse may succeed; calculated to advance the happiness of the Indians, and to attach them firmly to the United States."

NINE

REELECTION

1791–1792

WHEN CONGRESS, ALARMED by General Harmar's 1790 defeat, added to the ill-paid army, the secretary of war and the commanding general had severe organizational problems. Neither had direct experience with Indian warfare. Supplies for the western offensive had to be assembled in Philadelphia, Pittsburgh, and other staging areas for transport by wagon and boat to Fort Washington at what is now Cincinnati. The late passage of the act delayed the recruiting of regulars and militia. Desertions among the additions were frequent.

It was not until September 21, six months after the act was signed, that St. Clair was able to report to Knox that he had assembled 849 regulars and 1,538 militia, and was ready to start his campaign. Thereafter the reports by Knox and St. Clair expressed remarkable optimism about the anticipated results. St. Clair told Knox that he did not expect he would have to fight more than 1,200 or 1,500 Indians and he was sure of success. Knox, in turn, wrote to Washington that he presumed St. Clair's troops would be superior to any possible enemy force that could be assembled.

As St. Clair proceeded north, only fragmentary and delayed reports reached Philadelphia. As Washington had found when he was a frontier fighter, bad news always travelled fast. Reports of a disaster reached Philadelphia by various routes, well before St. Clair's own version arrived on December 9. This announced that he had reached Fort Washington with "the remains of my army." The mortified president learned that his defeat near the present Fort Wayne had been comparable to that of Braddock. Casualties numbered over 900 out of 1,400 Americans in battle. The survivors abandoned their guns and equipment and fled in panic to the Ohio River.

When Congress assembled three days later, the president gave them St. Clair's full report. He added that he had asked the secretary of war to provide complete information on all steps taken by his administration to secure peace with the Indians. The fact that nothing was concealed turned out to be wise. There was a good deal of "murmuring" in the country. Knox's and St. Clair's reputations suffered, but there was little criticism of the president. St. Clair resigned as commanding officer but retained his governorship of the Northwest Territory. A subsequent congressional inquiry did not attempt to place the blame on any person.

As Washington had learned during the revolution, it was easier to get Congress to improve the army after a defeat. Although Jefferson disapproved, Congress voted the first organic act for the United States army in March. This established a Legion of the United States, consisting of four infantry regiments, and cavalry and artillery battalions, with an authorized strength of around 4,500 officers and men. Hamilton and Knox estimated that the cost per year of the additional forces would be more than $650,000. Whatever his enemies thought of Hamilton, he was not lacking in courage. He proposed to Congress that the whole expense be covered by new taxes. Congress, which had been imposing so many imposts, balked at this suggestion. Fortunately the country's economy was developing rapidly. Government revenues for 1792 increased by more than enough to cover the additional military expenditures. Hamilton's November estimates indicated that the year's tax receipts would be $4.3 million, a sum ample to cover the civil list, payments on the national debt, and the revised budget of the secretary of war.

The president had a difficult time finding the right man to command the new army. By this time the surviving revolutionary generals were aging and often ill. Washington went over and over lists of those who might be competent and in good enough health to undertake a severe western campaign. After much consultation he made a choice which surprised many. On April 9, 1792, he sent to the Senate the name of Anthony Wayne, hero of Germantown and Stony Point, as major general and commanding officer of the troops of the United States. Wayne accepted this task with considerable reluctance, but he proved to be one of Washington's most fortunate appointments. He had once borne the name "Mad Anthony" for his impetuosity in attack, but this time he organized and trained the army with such caution and patience that there were to be many complaints of his inaction. In the end his policy was justified by success. Earlier, on October 31, Washington had nominated William Henry Harrison as ensign of the first Virginia regiment. Harrison subsequently became Wayne's aide, a first step on his long course upward to the presidency.

FAMILY PROBLEMS

Washington had always to turn from critical affairs of state to those of his relatives. Since the estate of his brother, Samuel, was insolvent, the president assisted in bringing up his three youngest surviving children. Although he could ill afford it, he dug into his own pockets for the education of Samuel's two sons, George Steptoe and Lawrence. He got them out of scrapes, complained of their extravagance, transferred them from school in Georgetown to Alexandria, and then to college in Philadelphia. Their sister, Harriott, a good-natured but careless child, was an especial source of worry to the president. He had hoped to leave her under the care of Fanny Washington, Martha's niece and wife of his manager, but this became too difficult when her husband grew very ill. The president did what he could, sending Harriott to his sister or to other relatives. He also took time to give advice freely and sometimes humorously. He wrote her on October 30, 1791:

I have received your letter of the 21st. Instant, and shall always be glad to hear from you...

At present I could plead a better excuse for curtailing my letter to you than you had for shortening of yours to me, having a multitude of business before me while you have nothing to do and delayed it until your Cousin was on the point of sending it to the Post-Office. I make this remark for no other reason than to shew you it is better to offer no excuse than a bad one... Occupied as my time now is, and must be during the sitting of Congress, I nevertheless will endeavor to indulcate upon your mind the delicacy and danger of that period to which you are arrived under peculiar circumstances. You are just entering into the state of womanhood, without the watchful eye of a Mother to admonish, or the protecting aid of a Father to advise and defend you; you may not be sensible that you are at this moment about to be stamped with that character which will adhere to you through life; the consequence of which you have not perhaps attended to, but be assured it is of the utmost importance that you should.

Your cousins with whom you live are well qualified to give you advice... but if you are disobliging, self-willed, and untowardly, it is hardly to be expected that they will engage themselves in unpleasant disputes with you, especially Fanny, whose mild and placid temper will not permit her to exceed the limits of wholesome admiration or gentle rebuke. Think then to what dangers a giddy girl of 15 or 16 must be exposed in circumstances like these. To be under little or no control may be pleasing to a mind that does not reflect, but this pleasure cannot be of long duration... Your fortune is small; supply the want of it then with a well cultivated mind; with dispositions to industry and frugality; with gentleness of manners, obliging temper, and such qualifications as will attract notice, and recommend you to a happy establishment for life....

Harriott as an orphan had no easy time, being shifted around from step-mother to uncle to aunt and to cousins, some of whom had little money to spare for her needs. She developed such an engaging way of appealing to the president, whenever she needed anything, that her "dear uncle," as she called him, always came through with her requested clothes, books, music, and finally, wedding dress.

WASHINGTON, THE FEDERAL CITY

Washington's nieces and nephews always assured their uncle they would follow his counsel at all times, whether they subsequently did so or not. The president also handed out good advice to emotional cabinet officers, as well as artists, who often paid him the same lip service. In the designer of the capital city he came up against a temperament too difficult to manage, though he explained to his district commissioners how to handle genius.

The commissioners very well understood the president's interest in the new capital and his desire to be consulted on every point. He did complain in April 1792 that they need not have sent him the specifications for the stone bridge between Georgetown and Washington, for he was a busy man, but the commissioners nonetheless continued to inform him of everything. This was to the good, since the president had superb taste and little would have been accomplished without his full support.

Washington, after choosing L'Enfant to lay out the capital, backed him in giving "imagination its full scope" and enthusiastically approved his subsequent draft plan. As everyone soon discovered, L'Enfant wanted to drive through to his objectives, without regard to the law, his superiors, or cost considerations. The commissioners squabbled often with him. The president, far from the scene, was repeatedly called upon to intervene. The first disagreement came when L'Enfant flatly refused to let his plans be used by the commissioners at the first public sale of lots because he did not wish to encourage speculators. They complained to the president that they could not sell the lots if no one could see what he was buying. Washington replied to them through David Stuart on November 21, 1791:

> *It is much to be regretted, however common the case is, that men who possess talents which fit them for peculiar purposes should almost invariably be under the influence of an untoward disposition… by which they plague all those with whom they are concerned. But I did not expect to meet with such perverseness in Major L'Enfant as his late conduct exhibited.*

> *Since my first knowledge of this Gentleman's abilities in the line of his profession, I have received him not only as a scientific man but one who added considerable taste to professional knowledge; and that, for such employment as his is now engaged in… he was better qualified than any one who had come within my knowledge…*

> *I had no doubts, at the same time, that this was the light in which he considered himself; and of course that he would be so tenacious of his plans as to conceive they would be marred if they underwent any change or alteration… The feelings of such Men are always alive, and where their assistance is essential, it is policy to humour them or put on the appearance of doing it…*

As he was to do the following year with Hamilton and Jefferson, Washington tried various tactics to soothe L'Enfant. He wrote a letter praising him and saying that his design was splendid. He pointed out, however, that the district commissioners were authorized by the law and the president to carry out the design and get the city going.

He had hardly dispatched this letter when more complaints reached him. Daniel Carroll, nephew of one of the commissioners, wrote that L'Enfant had abruptly threatened to pull down a house he was building, claiming that it intruded onto a platted but nonexistent street. Washington tried to soothe Carroll, L'Enfant, and the commissioners, but further letters arrived saying that L'Enfant had gone ahead and torn down the house. Carroll threatened to take him to court. Washington wrote the commissioners: "You are as sensible as I am of his value to us. But this has its limits, and there is a point beyond which he might be overvalued." He wrote a strong letter to L'Enfant, saying: "Having the beauty and regularity of your plan only in view, you pursue it as if every person and thing was *obliged* to yield to it." He insisted that L'Enfant heed both the law and the commissioners. He suggested to the latter that they see if there were some way to gratify L'Enfant's pride and ambition, while keeping a curb on him. He noted that he thought Carroll had been equally to blame with L'Enfant in not waiting for the architect's street plats. He urged everyone to try to adjust the disputes among themselves.

More letters reached Washington that winter on L'Enfant's intractable nature. The president finally took the trouble to send his private secretary, Tobias Lear, to Washington, but L'Enfant brushed him off with the remark that he had heard enough talk on the subject. This ended the president's patience, and L'Enfant was dismissed. He ordered Andrew Ellicott to proceed with the engraving of L'Enfant's plans and to lay out the principal streets and lots. Washington complained that Ellicott's wages of five dollars a day, including Sundays, were high but they had better get on with the job. He proposed that Congress pay a proper fee to L'Enfant for his work.

Washington was frequently in and out of Georgetown in 1792. He anxiously looked at the designs for the buildings which had been submitted in open competition. On July 30 he wrote Tobias Lear from Mount Vernon: "I found at Georgetown many well conceived and ingenious plans for the Public buildings in the New City: it was a pleasure indeed to find, in an infant Country, such a display of architectural abilities." He had selected James Hoban's plan for "The President's House" and men were already at work digging the cellars. Hoban was to supervise the work and also assist on the capitol. Washington probably did not know that one design he rejected was submitted anonymously by Jefferson. Washington also mentioned that two or three "elegant" drawings had been submitted for the capitol. On January 31, 1793, he wrote the commissioners that he liked Dr. William Thornton's plan best. "The Grandeur, Simplicity and Beauty of the exterior; the propriety with which the apartments are distributed; and the economy in the mass of the whole structure will, I doubt not, give it a preference in your eyes, as it has done in mine." The commissioners voted to accept it.

AMERICAN AGRICULTURAL SURVEY

The president had corresponded for several years with Arthur Young, the British agricultural expert. He continued this during his presidency, exchanging additional letters with Sir John Sinclair and James Anderson, Scottish agricultural writers and economists. Sinclair became president and Young secretary of the first British Board of Agriculture in 1793. Washington was so interested in their promotion of scientific agriculture and dissemination of information that he subsequently recommended to Congress that the United States establish a similar board. The inquiries by Young and to some extent, Sinclair, led to the first general, if rather haphazard, survey of American agriculture.

In early January 1791 Young asked the president for detailed information on American farming. He wanted to know the prices of lands and the portions of typical farms which were arable, pasture, and woodland. He inquired on yields of the principal grains, vegetables, and grasses. He requested the prices of farm animals and of marketed produce such as meat, butter, and cheese. Since the subject was dear to Washington's heart, he sent a circular letter to men he considered knowledgeable, asking them to make as detailed inquiries as they could.

Individual reports surviving among the president's papers cover Pennsylvania, New Jersey, southern Maryland, and northern Virginia. The reporters, who included Thomas Jefferson and David Stuart in Virginia, Richard Peters in Pennsylvania, and Thomas Johnson in Maryland, usually made very detailed replies. In general they were quite shocked at what they found. Jefferson said that agriculture practices in Charlottesville were "slovenly." David Stuart reported that he had never had a high regard for Virginia farming but after going over the situation his opinion was "certainly much lower than it was." He used almost the same phrase as Jefferson, speaking of the Northern Neck's "slovenly farmers." Thomas Johnson, who had been Maryland's governor, made one of the more interesting surveys. He, along with others, complained that farmers kept so few records they could not answer questions intelligently. He had therefore to do most of the work himself. He made careful comparisons of well-managed farms, where there was intensive cultivation and heavy manuring, and general Maryland practices. The yields in the former case were three to four times as much. His report on Montgomery County said that much of the land had been worn out by tobacco. Farming practices were so poor that no surplus food would be available for the federal city.

Washington read all the letters before forwarding copies to Young. He accompanied them with comments of his own. His letters of December 5, 1791, and June 18–21, 1792, indicated that he thought the area from Virginia to Pennsylvania best suited for agriculture, from the point of view of soil and climate. From what he had read of English soil, American land was inferior along the seacoast, but sixty to a hundred miles inland some of the world's richest agricultural areas were to be found. The Shenandoah Valley was one of the great agrarian regions of the world. Pennsylvania had the best managed agriculture in the Union, but it could well stand improvement.

Washington commented on the difference between the English intensive and the American extensive cultivation of land. This arose because laborers were better paid and fed than in England. "An English farmer must entertain a contemptible opinion of our husbandry, or a horrid idea of our lands, when he shall be informed that no more than 8 or 10 bushels of Wheat is the yield per acre; but this low produce may be ascribed… to a cause… namely, that the aim of the farmers in this Country (if they can be called farmers) is not to make the most from the land, which is, or has been cheap, but the most of the labour, which is dear, the consequence of which has been, much ground has been *scratched* over and none cultivated or improved as it ought to have been; Whereas a farmer in England, where land is dear and labour cheap, finds it to his interest to improve and cultivate highly… It requires time to conquer bad habits, and hardly anything short of necessity is able to accomplish it. That necessity is being approached by pretty rapid strides."

Young was so impressed that he asked the president for permission to reproduce his letters in the *Annals of Agriculture*. Washington replied that he had been writing as a friend. He would prefer that they not be published, especially as there were many strictures on his countrymen's practices.

FOREIGN INTERCOURSE

Although a few members of Congress regarded an American foreign service as tarnation foolishness, the Senate approved the president's recommended appointments to Madrid, London, Paris, and The Hague. His selections as chiefs of mission, along with Wayne as army commander, were among the most important of his administration.

George Hammond presented his credentials as the first minister from the Court of St. James' on November 11, 1791, after being assured that the president had selected a man for London. Washington's proposed nominee was Thomas Pinckney of South Carolina. In this, as in other diplomatic appointments, Washington informed but did not consult Jefferson about his choice. Pinckney had the broadest foreign education of any American diplomat. Before the revolution he had attended Westminster and Oxford. He also read law in London and passed a year of study in France. He returned to South Carolina to serve in the continental line and then as his state's governor. About all that could be said against his appointment was that he had no diplomatic experience but in this he was comparable to Franklin, Adams, and Jefferson when they took their posts.

Washington had to be sure of Pinckney's acceptance before sending his name to the Senate. It took several weeks to hear from Charleston. When Pinckney agreed to serve, Washington informed Jefferson that he was also nominating Gouverneur Morris to Paris and shifting William Short to the Netherlands. He sent the names to the Senate on December 9. Jefferson was most unhappy about Morris for he had hoped that his protégé, Short, would have the job.

The nominations brought lengthy debates in the Senate where some felt that there should be no diplomatic missions, others objected to The Hague alone, while several senators denounced Morris. In the end all were confirmed. On January 11 Washington sent to the Senate Jefferson's letter informing him that Spain, having agreed to discuss the navigation of the Mississippi, had requested that a commissioner be sent to Madrid. William Short, in addition to his Dutch duties, was designated one of two commissioners, along with William Carmichael, the American chargé at Madrid.

Gouverneur Morris was to be unique in being the only diplomat to stay in Paris through the whole Terror. In consequence Washington was probably the best informed chief of state at this period. Morris' information was invaluable as the continent broke into savage war and the stability of the new American nation was threatened by both Britain and France. The relatively narrow margin by which Morris was confirmed (16–11), plus the suspicions which Hamilton had once planted in Washington's mind, compelled the president to write him a friendly but forthright letter on January 28, 1792:

The official communications from the Secretary of State... will convey to you the evidence of my nomination, and appointment of you to... the Court of France; and my assurance that both were made with all my heart... I wish I could add that the advice and consent flowed from a similar source... Candour forbids it, and friendship requires that I should assign the cause...

Whilst your abilities... were adduced and asserted on the one hand; you were charged, on the other hand with levity and imprudence of conversation and conduct... In France you were considered a favourer of Aristocracy, and unfriendly to its Revolution (I suppose they meant Constitution.)... That in England you indiscreetly communicated the purport of your Mission in the first instance to the Minister of France, who... gave it the appearance of a movement through his Court. This... added to close intercourse with the opposition Members, occasioned distrust to the Ministry...

But not to go further into detail, I will place the ideas of your political adversaries in the light which their arguments have presented them to me... That the promptitude, with which your lively and brilliant imagination is displayed, allows too little time for deliberation... In a word, that it is indispensably necessary that more circumspection should be observed by our representatives abroad, than they conceive you are inclined to adopt...

In this statement... I give you a proof of my friendship... I have the confidence (supposing the allegations to be founded in whole or in part) that you would find no difficulty... to effect a change and thereby silence, in the most unequivocal and satisfactory manner, your political opponents...

Of my good opinion, and of my friendship and regard, you may be assured...

In June Washington hinted to Morris that, in the normal course of events, what he wrote would be communicated to the secretary of state. However, there might arise certain questions which of necessity should be for the president's eyes alone. Morris, in his discretion, was authorized to report directly and privately to him.

The British minister had arrived with rigid instructions. He was to fight any move to discriminate against British trade. Permission was given to initiate discussions about a commercial treaty but not to take further action without London's approval. He was ordered to point out to the Americans all their treaty violations. Hammond set out almost immediately to collect the facts on such alleged breaches but he took several months to do so.

Late in the winter he handed a document to Jefferson outlining all the errors of the Americans. A few days later, March 6, 1792, he wrote to his Foreign Office: "This statement will be found... to contain a body of proof so complete and substantial as to preclude the possibility of cavil and contradiction on the part of this government."

Jefferson never saw this comment by Hammond but he did have the paper. The secretary of state had been studying the peace treaty for years, and he had been in London to discuss the debt. He had already assembled a formidable documentation on the laws of the thirteen states. He added copiously to his files after receiving Hammond's letter. He spent much of the spring of 1792 drawing up a polemical but factual rebuttal. This quoted innumerable authorities on international law, acts of parliament directed against America, the laws of each of the states, and the negotiations over many years to obtain the frontier posts. Hamilton, when he read it, objected to some of its blunter statements. Jefferson accepted a few changes but refused to make more. Washington, after reading Hamilton's critique, overruled him. Jefferson delivered his letter to Hammond about the first of June.

Hammond acknowledged its receipt saying that he would send it to London. He assured Jefferson he had not intentionally misstated any facts. Jefferson and

Hammond thereafter had a long talk, in which the British minister said that the idea that his country had committed the first infractions would be entirely new to his ministry.

Hammond held an entirely different conversation with Hamilton at about the same time. He had not liked the "acrimonious" reply and complained to Hamilton of Jefferson's "extraordinary performance." Hammond reported to London: "After lamenting the intemperate violence of his colleague, Mr. Hamilton assured me that this letter was very far from meeting his approbation, or from containing a faithful exposition of the sentiments of this government. He added that at the time of our conversation the president had not had an opportunity of perusing this representation: For having returned from Virginia in the morning only on which it had been delivered to me, he had relied on Mr. Jefferson's assurance, that it was conformable to the opinions of the other members of the executive government."

The statement to Hammond was a flat lie on Hamilton's part. The president had read and approved the document and thereby made it the official view of the United States government. In spite of repeated subsequent inquiries by Jefferson, the only response that Hammond ever gave was that London was studying his document.

FIRST VETO

The completion of the first census required, in accordance with the Constitution, reapportionment of the House of Representatives. With this came fights in both Houses. The House had 69 members but the Constitution permitted an increase to 120. Each state wanted a little more than its share and New England managed proportionally to get the most. The bill passed the Senate by but one vote and the House by two votes. When it reached Washington's desk in March 1792, it was one of the first congressional acts seriously to disturb him. His general inclination was to accept compromises worked out in Congress but this one appeared unfair. Washington consulted the four members of the cabinet as to the act's constitutionality. Hamilton wrote a rather hasty opinion saying that he had not read the bill but it appeared to be permitted by the Constitution. Jefferson studied the bill more carefully. He did not go so far as to declare it absolutely unconstitutional but that it was, to say the least, "an inconvenient expression of its words," by giving several states more representation than one per thirty thousand, which is permitted by the organic document. Jefferson, by law, mathematics, and logic, was clearly in the right. The president followed his advice and returned it to

Congress unsigned, briefly giving his reasons. A new act was passed on a more equitable basis. This was one of many instances, as Washington later pointed out to Jefferson, in which his advice prevailed over that of Hamilton.

FAREWELL ADDRESS

Washington had optimistically hoped that, in one term, he could get the new government on its way and then retire. A clear hankering to be president was evident on the parts of Adams, Jay, Jefferson, Hamilton, Madison, and others while Washington wanted a peaceful life for his remaining years. None of the five main possible successors believed any of the other four as suitable as Washington, nor that the United States was yet strong enough to walk alone.

Washington talked with members of his cabinet on his desire to retire from office. He also discussed it with James Madison, whom he had always trusted, not realizing that the Philip Freneau who had so severely attacked his administration had been selected because he was Madison's old Princeton friend.

On May 20, 1792, Washington wrote Madison to ask his advice and help in drafting a farewell address to the American people. He summarized his thoughts, much of their substance appearing later in his farewell of 1796. Washington wrote that he wanted to tell Americans

> that we are all the Children of the same country; a Country great and rich in itself; capable, and promising to be, as prosperous and happy as any the Annals of history have ever brought to our view. That our interests, however diversified in local and smaller matters, are the same in all the great and essential concerns of the Nation. That the extent of our Country, the diversity of our climate and soil, and the various productions of the States consequent to both, are such as to make one part not only convenient, but perhaps indispensably necessary to the other part; and may render the whole, at no distant period, one of the most independent in the world. That the established government being the work of our own hands, with the seeds of amendment grafted in the Constitution, may by wisdom, good dispositions, and mutual allowances, aided by experience, bring it as near to perfection as any human institution ever approximated; and therefore, the only strife among us ought be, who should be foremost in facilitating and finally accomplishing such great and desirable objects; by giving every possible support, and cement to the Union. That however necessary it may be to keep a watchful eye over public servants and public measures, yet there ought to be limits to it; for suspicions unfounded, and jealousies too lively, are irritating to honest feelings; and oftentimes are productive of more evil than good.

Madison drafted several paragraphs for Washington but in the end the president was prevailed upon to accept a second term.

PANIC

The crisis in the money market in the spring of 1793 cannot be classified as the first of the business cycles which made a roller coaster of America's economic development. The United States was, in fact, reaping the combined benefits of a strong government and financial system, together with a high level of European demand for its products. The panic, however, shook the country's confidence in Hamilton and the administration; the opposition made the most of it.

William Duer, Hamilton's old associate, had quit the Treasury to engage in speculation. Duer used remarkably advanced techniques, rather like those employed in New York in the 1920s. He borrowed on an ever-expanding scale, paying higher and higher interest to the public, who were delighted to lend money to him. He pyramided his profits into more speculations, and he supported the market for his stock, while also selling short.

In January 1792 security prices fell abruptly. Duer was ruined and in prison by March. Many persons and institutions were dragged under, including Hamilton's own society for establishing useful manufactures, but the panic itself was short-lived.

Hamilton acted promptly to establish the Treasury's first open-market operations. Backed by cash and borrowings to the amount of $200,000, he successfully intervened to support the government's bonds and credit. He was attacked unmercifully for this, the *New York Journal* maintaining that he had substituted "the golden dreams of speculation" for the sacred words: "liberty and independence."

EXCISE TAX

The 1791 tax on domestically manufactured spirits turned out to be one of the most troublesome of the new imposts. It is difficult to write about from a modern point of view since the uproar concerned an excise of as little as two cents a quart on whisky distilled from domestic grain. It was originally proposed, as preferable to a land tax, by Madison, who had started out as a good federalist but had fallen under the thumb and spell of Jefferson. The latter made the most of the tax, weeping over the poor "ploughman" who supposedly had to pay it, though a plowman's land tax would have been worse.

On March 6, 1792, Hamilton submitted to the House of Representatives a "Report on the Difficulties in the Execution of the Act Laying Duties on Distilled Spirits." It was, in part, a hilarious comment on human foibles, which demolished every argument against the tax, except that it was not easy to collect. Hamilton took account of the many petitions against the act which had been submitted to the House. He noted that those who opposed it said that the tax contravened the principles of liberty, injured morals, and was ruining the distilling business.

Hamilton obviously enjoyed writing portions of it. He said that he could not quite grasp how an internal tax on "a consumable commodity [was] inconsistent with the genius of free government," while an import duty on the same commodity was not. He showed that the tax was higher on foreign whiskey, gin, or rum, and thus was a protective stimulus to the domestic industry. He could not see how filling out tax forms was such a hardship, since the distiller knew what he was doing and the government even gave him his ledger book. He said that the objection that an oath required on reports could hardly be said to be ruining morals, since he was sure most people were not committing perjury. He did not understand the complaints from western Pennsylvanians that the tax bore particularly hard on them. If so, they must be drinking too much and they ought to drink less. Their statement that they had to make the grain into spirits to save transport costs to distant markets made no sense as an objection since the consumer, not the farmer, paid the tax. The Pennsylvanians said they had little cash but Hamilton, as treasurer of the United States, noted that he was sending five times as much money to the area for its protection as he was getting back in excise receipts.

Hamilton summed up his whole argument by noting that, on the average, a family of six would consume about sixteen gallons of spirits a year, on which they would pay only a little over a dollar and a quarter in taxes. The federal government did not tax their lands, houses, or stock. Hamilton did, however, recommend to Congress administrative changes in the law to make it less objectionable.

In spite of Hamilton's reasoned statements, petitioning opposition in western Pennsylvania erupted into a small rebellion in the summer of 1792. Revenue officers were threatened with mayhem. When Hamilton reported this to the president at Mount Vernon, Washington replied on September 7: "Such conduct in any of the Citizens of the United States, under any circumstances that can well be received, would be exceedingly reprehensible; but when it comes from a part of the Community for whose protection the money arising from the Tax was principally designed, it is truly unaccountable, and the spirit of it much to be regretted." The president said he approved of the steps taken by Hamilton to get evidence against the offenders, in order to prosecute them in federal courts. He added: "But if, notwithstanding, opposition is still given to the execution of the Law, I have no hesitation in declaring, if the evidence of it is clear and unequivocal, that I shall, however reluctantly I exercise them, exert all the legal powers with which the Executive is invested, to check so daring and unwarrantable a spirit. It is my duty to see the Laws executed: to permit them to be trampled upon with impunity would be repugnant to it; nor can the Government longer remain a passive spectator of the contempt with which they are treated. Forbearance… seems to have had no other effect than to increase the disorder."

On September 15 a thunderous proclamation came from "George Washington, President of the United States," calling on "all persons whom it may concern, to refrain and desist from unlawful combinations and proceedings whatsoever having for object or tending to obstruct the operation of the laws aforesaid; inasmuch as all lawful ways and means will be strictly put in execution for bringing to justice the infractors thereof… "

In sending the proclamation to Jefferson for the signature of the secretary of state, he said that he knew that his actions would be "severely criticized; but I shall disregard any animadversions upon my conduct when I am called upon by the nature of my office, to discharge what I conceive to be a duty, and none, in my opinion, is more important than to carry the Laws of the United States into effect." To Hamilton he wrote that he expected strictures, but he added, what he did not say to Jefferson, that the government ought to use regular army troops only as a last resort, "otherwise there would be a cry at once, 'the Cat is let out; we now see for what purpose an Army was raised… '"

Some of the riotous leaders were indicted and brought to trial. For a while peace returned to western Pennsylvania. However, the opposition to the government later found a chance to revive the disorder and more trouble came in Washington's second term.

JEFFERSON'S COUNTER-REVOLUTION

When Jefferson read the new Constitution in Paris, his first appraisal was unenthusiastic. He missed Virginia's savage ratification fight where Patrick Henry, George Mason, Richard Henry Lee, and James Monroe lined up against Washington and Madison. An oft-reiterated complaint of the opposition was that the Constitution had no Bill of Rights, but when this was proposed by Washington and passed quickly by Congress, Virginia took nearly two years to ratify it. The objections were far deeper; many Virginians had a fundamentalist desire to maintain the state just as it was, a view quite different from that held by Virginia's greatest son.

Washington's influence had been responsible for the margin by which the state ratified the Constitution but this did not remove the fears of the national government which had been duly reported to him by Dr. Stuart. Most basic was apprehension that federal power might try to control or abolish slavery. There was a great uproar in Virginia in 1790, when the representatives debated a Quaker memorial, asking for the suppression of the slave trade. Another grievance was the use of federal courts to collect private debts due the British. The federal tax program and the assumption of state debts were a constant source of complaint from those who ill understood them.

When Jefferson returned from Paris to Virginia, the views he heard may have influenced his reluctance to enter Washington's cabinet. When he joined the administration, he sat with three men, Washington, Knox, and Hamilton, who had fought for freedom side by side at Harlem, White Plains, Trenton, Princeton, Brandywine, Monmouth, and Yorktown. Jefferson wrote that he soon found himself to be almost the only republican in governing circles. He defined the word as a belief that each state would "remain independent as to internal matters, and the whole form a single nation as to what was foreign only." What moved Jefferson to eventual frenzy was the sweep of Washington's national economic program. Washington believed that the country, stimulated and aided by an active federal government, should move forward in agriculture, commerce, industry, science, education, manufacturing, transport, and communications. Defense should be national, with a permanent American army. Jefferson, on the other hand, felt that farmers "are alone to be relied on for expressing the proper American sentiments." He was against banks and even paper money, feeling that gold and silver alone had value. Road building was too much even for a state government; Virginia, he thought, handled this properly by giving the function to the counties. A militia could do everything better than a trained army and would be much cheaper. In short, he wanted an ideal of farmer-philosophers watching over happy plantations and slaves.

A further fundamental divergence lay in Jefferson's lack of Washington's abounding faith in God and humanity. He persistently maintained that the people would elect corrupt men to Congress, the federal power in turn would corrupt the states, and all would end in tyranny. Washington's views, as he expressed them in his draft inaugural address of 1789, were that "this Constitution is really, in its formation, a government of the people; that is to say, a government in which all power is derived from them, and at stated periods reverts to them... The election of the different branches of Congress by the

Freeman… is the pivot on which turns the first Wheel of government… The exercise of this right to election seems to be so regulated as to afford less opportunity for corruption and influence than has usually been incident to popular governments. Nor can the members of Congress exempt themselves from the consequences of any unjust and tyrannical acts they may impose on others. For in a short time they will mingle with the people… Their re-election must always depend upon the good reputation they shall have maintained in the judgment of their fellow citizens… No government before introduced among mankind ever contained so many checks and such efficacious restraints to prevent it from degenerating into any species of oppression."

Jefferson saw conspiracy and intrigue in many government actions which were entirely well intended. Even as an old man he would repeat charges that von Steuben and Knox had conspired to set up a monarchy, that the Cincinnati was part of the plot, and that he alone had saved the republic. Washington suffered Jefferson during his four years in the cabinet with endless courtesy and patience although the secretary of state, orally and by letter, traduced his policies and vilified his motives. Along the way Jefferson was joined by James Madison, who had done so much to build the national government, as well as by James Monroe. Their home state of Virginia could not swing an election, but Jefferson found other allies farther south, and such New York supporters as Aaron Burr, George Clinton, and the Sons of St. Tammany. It took little calculation to show that the South and New York State with the extra votes given the South for its slaves would have enough electoral votes to capture the presidency.

In May of 1792 Jefferson wrote to the president, expostulating against his wish to retire at the end of his first term. Jefferson's plea that he continue in office probably arose from his fear that a successor would be much less "republican." He added a fervent though polite attack on the principal measures of the administration which, he said, were causing great public distress and worry. He implied that the president had nothing to do with the financial measures adopted by the government nor did he know of the stockjobbing and bribery in Congress, the split between North and South, and the move within the government to monarchy.

When he received the letter, Washington extracted the attacks on his policy and forwarded them to Hamilton with a statement that they represented the views of people not too friendly to the government, "among whom may be classed my neighbour and quondam friend, Colo. Mason." Hamilton made a strong and effective reply to Washington which ran many pages.

He demolished Jefferson's objection to the excise tax as an aristocratic concept by noting that there was, perhaps, "no article of more general and equal consumption than distilled spirits." He suggested that the Jeffersonian opposition was Tory and conservative while the government was Whig and progressive in its program. He added that the idea that anyone wanted a monarchy in the United States "is one of those visionary things, that none but madmen could meditate and that no wise man will believe."

In this letter, Hamilton pleaded with the president to remain in office, for enemies to the administration were making strenuous efforts to gain control of the government. The attorney general, Edmund Randolph, also urged him to serve a second term. If he did not, there would probably be civil war and Washington would be called on to suppress it.

While considering whether to remain in office, the president appealed to Hamilton, Jefferson, and Randolph to stop all dissension and bickering and to work for the common good. His letters to Jefferson and Hamilton were very similar but he made slight shifts of emphasis. He wrote Jefferson on August 23: "My earnest wish, and my fondest hope, therefore is, that instead of wounding suspicions, and irritable charges, there may be liberal allowances, mutual forbearances, and temporizing yieldings on all sides... Without them every thing must rub; the Wheels of Government will clog; our enemies will triumph, and by throwing their weight into the disaffected scale, may accomplish the ruin of the goodly fabric we have been erecting." He added that the many attacks on the government had filled him "with painful sensations; and cannot fail, I think, of producing unhappy consequences at home and abroad." In expressing similar sentiments to Hamilton, he added: "I cannot prevail on myself to believe that these measures are as yet the deliberate acts of a determined party." He hoped that "healing measures" would be applied everywhere in the Union.

Hamilton's reply was conciliatory, saying that he felt he was the deeply injured party but he would try to be as forbearing as possible. He thought the best thing would be for himself and Jefferson to quit the cabinet and thus give the president a free hand. He had recently, for the first time, begun a strong counterattack on subversive forces working to destroy the national government. He could not for the present recede but if Washington worked out a plan of reconciliation, he would at once desist. Jefferson, on the other hand, sent an insolent letter.

Jefferson said Washington had been duped by Hamilton on the assumption-capital issue, he denied that he had ever intrigued against the government, and he reiterated that Washington's financial system had corrupted the legislature. Congress had deserted the people, while the administration and Congress had subverted the Constitution and had even assumed power to legislate for the general welfare. He said that the long list of Treasury appointments throughout the nation (who had been almost entirely selected by the president) were an additional source of corruption. He defended his hiring of a State Department clerk to edit a paper attacking the government, adding that Hamilton's career was "a tissue of machinations" against the liberties of his adopted country.

The summer and fall of 1792 saw severe press attacks on Hamilton and Adams as well as Hamilton's counterattacks on Jefferson. The latter kept his hands clean of actual newspaper writing, but he had a host of others to do the work, including Freneau, Madison, and Monroe. No one emerged from the press debate, which took place under Latin pen names, with credit, and all concerned did great disservice to Washington. In the course of it, one Jeffersonian called Hamilton a "cowardly assassin," Monroe flung in an oblique reference to Hamilton's extramarital activities, Hamilton and William Smith were caustic about Jefferson's war record, while Hamilton made an obscene reference in print to Jefferson. The secretary of the treasury was always unsurpassed on the attack. In a strong position, pleading from a successful policy, he drove Jefferson into a frenzy. He described him as substituting "national disunion, National insignificance, Public disorder and discredit" for union, respectability, and order. On September 29, as "Catullus," he skewered the secretary of state:

> *Mr. Jefferson has hitherto been distinguished as the quiet, modest, retiring philosopher—as the plain simple unambitious republican. He shall now for the first time be regarded as the intriguing incendiary...*

> *There is always <u>a first time</u> when characters studious of artful disguises are unveiled; when the vizor of stoicism is plucked from the brow of the Epicurean; when the plain garb of Quaker simplicity is stripped from the concealed voluptuary; when Caesar <u>coyly refusing</u> the proffered diadem, is seen to be Caesar <u>rejecting</u> the trappings, but tenaciously grasping the substance of imperial domination.*

STATE OF THE UNION

The usual cheerful tone of Washington's earlier annual messages to Congress was replaced by a more somber note in his fourth report, delivered on November 6, 1792:

> *It is some abatement of the satisfaction with which I meet you on the present occasion that, in felicitating you on a continuance of the National prosperity*

generally, I am not able to add to it information that the Indian hostilities, which have for some time past distressed our western frontiers, have terminated.

Reiterated endeavors toward effecting a pacification have hitherto issued only in new and outrageous methods of persevering hostility... Besides the continuation of hostile appearances among the tribes North of the Ohio, some threatening symptoms have of late been revived among some of those south of it...

I have reason to believe that every practicable exertion has been made (pursuant to the provision by law for that purpose) to be prepared for the alternative of a prosecution of the war, in the event of a failure of pacific overtures. A large proportion of the troops authorized to be raised, has been recruited, though the number is still incomplete. And pains have been taken to discipline and put them in condition for the particular kind of service to be performed. A delay of operations (besides being dictated by the measures which we are pursuing towards a pacific termination of the war) has been in itself deemed preferable to immature efforts...

In looking forward to the future expense of the operations... I derive consolation from the information I receive that the product of the revenues for the present year, is likely to supersede the necessity of additional burthens on the community, for the service of the ensuing year.

I cannot dismiss the subject of Indian affairs without again recommending... laws for restraining the commission of outrages upon the Indians; without which all pacific plans must prove nugatory... If, in addition, an eligible plan could be devised for promoting civilization among the friendly tribes and for carrying on trade with them... under regulations calculated to protect them from imposition and extortion, its influence in cementing their interests with ours could not but be considerable.

Measures have been taken for employing some artists from abroad to aid in the establishment of our mint... Provision has been made of the requisite buildings... There has also been a small beginning in the coinage of half-dimes; the want of small coins in circulation calling the first attention to them.

The adoption of a constitution for the State of Kentucky has been notified to me.

Three new loans have been effected, each for three millions of florins—one at Antwerp... and the other two at Amsterdam... The rates of these loans and the circumstances under which they have been made, are confirmations of the high state of our credit abroad.

THE 1792 ELECTION

As the second presidential election approached, the Jefferson faction turned its fire from Hamilton to Adams. Not until the election was over did Jefferson's friends attack the president, who had been largely spared from direct bludgeoning.

It was not customary at that period for candidates for the presidency and vice-presidency to campaign. Neither Washington nor Adams did so. Nonetheless, the political enemies of both were exceedingly busy. They included a large number of Southerners plus Aaron Burr of New York and John Hancock and Samuel Adams in Massachusetts. Washington regarded the election as a test of confidence in his policies and he admitted that he would feel chagrin if there were a substantial decline in his previous unanimous electoral support.

The Jeffersonians chose George Clinton, who had fought the Constitution, as their candidate for vice-president. Adams, more pessimistic by nature than Washington, thought at one point that he would be defeated.

In 1788 only ten states voted in the national elections. In 1792 five additional states chose electors. Washington received all 132 electoral votes for president. John Adams lost three southern states and New York to Clinton, plus Kentucky to Jefferson. He, nonetheless, had a comfortable majority of seventy-seven, a stronger vote of confidence than he had received in 1788.

TEN

FOREIGN AND DOMESTIC STORMS

1792–1793

FRANKLIN HAD BEEN a fascinated watcher at the first Paris balloon ascension of 1783. Early in 1785 Jean-Pierre Blanchard, a Frenchman, and John Jeffries, an American physician, floated across the English channel. Washington read the initial reports from Paris with interest. On April 4, 1784, he wrote to General du Portail in France: "I have only news paper Accts. of the Air Balloons, to which I do not know what credence to give; as the tales related of them are marvellous, and lead us to expect that our friends at Paris, in a little time, will come flying thro' the air, instead of ploughing the Ocean to get to America." Washington's curiosity was finally satisfied when Blanchard appeared in Philadelphia near the end of his first term. On January 9, 1793, the president, attended by the secretary of state, went to the grounds at Walnut and Fourth Streets, to see Blanchard make his ascension. A large crowd of Philadelphians attended. The president handed Blanchard a special passport requesting every citizen to give him aid and friendship. Blanchard, displaying French and American flags from his balloon, rose in the air and soared over the Delaware. He landed less than an hour later in Woodbury, New Jersey, from which he returned to call on the president that evening.

MOUNT VERNON

The president, compelled by his unanimous countrymen to serve one more term, did relatively little public or private grumbling. The intensity of his feelings appeared in the extraordinary series of letters he sent to Mount Vernon from Philadelphia, beginning in October 1792 when he knew he would serve again, and continuing through June of 1793. More than 30 letters of instruction went out in his hand, most of them to his manager, Anthony Whiting. These were of such length that they would make a book of perhaps 150 pages. They displayed Washington's hope that by correspondence he could produce nearly as good management of the various Mount Vernon farms, as if he were there personally. Not until late spring did he learn that Whiting, like his previous manager, had been dying of tuberculosis during the period.

The letters indicate vividly that Washington had a photographic memory of the more than twelve square miles he owned on the Potomac. He knew also the individual capacities of his overseers, hired hands, indentured servants, and many of his slaves. He required weekly reports from his manager and overseers, and he had an eye for discrepancies.

In writing to Mount Vernon he explained how he accomplished a vast amount of work, suggesting that everyone else do the same. His manager was instructed to get a notebook and put down each Washington order so that he could check whether or not it was done. In preparing reports and letters, he was to make out a list of everything he wanted to tell the president and it would then be as easy for him as for Washington to write so many. The weekly orders from Philadelphia were so numerous and varied that it would have taken a corps of clerks to record and check them. Washington remembered them all, but not the poor manager. The president, who could address the nation gracefully, tended to lapse into clichés in writing his farm employees: "There is a season for all things; many a mickle makes a muckle; do not put off till tomorrow what you can do today; a penny saved is a penny got."

An index to the Whiting letters refers to such topics as water and wells; hospitality to Mount Vernon visitors; hedges, fences, and gates; grass, grain, and meadows; quarters and outhouses; barns and threshing; timber cutting; taxes; roads; thefts; house painting; censuses of stock; erosion and conservation of soil; fallow culture; the building of an icehouse and an experimental garden; protection of buildings against fire; the improvement of the fisheries; and work at the flour mill. From time to time Mrs. Washington added queries as to whether the potash was collected for the soap, why the seamstresses were making fewer shirts each week than when she was home, and what happened to the cart that had been ordered for one of her farms.

About the end of 1792, the president took time to design a barn and sheds, with their construction specifications, for the Dogue Run farm. The following year he described the plan to Arthur Young as "well calculated, it is conceived, for getting grain out of the straw more expeditiously than is the usual mode of threshing. There are good sheds... sufficient to cover 30 work horses and Oxen."

The president, when he was at Mount Vernon, had shared George Augustine Washington's agony as he coughed his health and life away. The younger George had at length gone to the house of his father-in-law, Burwell Bassett, in the autumn of 1792. In January Basset, Mrs. Washington's brother-in-law, died; George Augustine followed him to the grave the next month, two losses which greatly distressed Washington and his wife. The president, on February 24, 1793 (approximately the day he received a moving appeal from Madame de Lafayette for help for her imprisoned husband), wrote Frances Washington:

My dear Fanny: To you, who so well knew the affectionate regard I had for our departed friend, it is unnecessary to describe the sorrow with which I was afflicted at the news of his death... To express this sorrow with the force I feel it, would answer no other purpose than to revive in your breast, that poignancy of anguish, which, by this time, I hope is abated...

The object of the present letter is to convey in your mind the warmest assurances of my love, friendship, and disposition to serve you; These also I profess to have in an eminent degree, for your Children.

What plan you have contemplated... is unknown to me; and therefore I add, that the one which strikes me most favorably, by being best calculated to promote the interest of yourself and Children, is to return to your old habitation at Mount Vernon. You can go no place where you will be more welcome, nor to any where you can live at less expence, or trouble...

You might bring my niece, Harriet Washington, with you for a Companion; whose conduct, I hear with pleasure, has given much satisfaction to my sister... My affectionate regards attend you and your Children; and I shall always be your sincere friend...

Eventually Washington did over a house he owned in Alexandria for her occupancy. While he was still working on her problems, he received a warning from Dr. Craik that the successor overseer of Mount Vernon, Anthony Whiting, was quite ill and spitting blood. By June Whiting too was dying and Washington had to make a hasty trip to Mount Vernon, and found his affairs in bad order. He was soon recalled to Philadelphia by the French declaration of war against the Netherlands, Britain, and Spain. He appointed as temporary overseer one of a large supply of nephews, Howell Lewis, who had been an assistant secretary to the president.

INAUGURATION

As soon as it was certain that Washington would serve another term, the Jeffersonians opened up with violent attacks on him. These, to an extraordinary degree, were to parallel the abuse which France heaped on Washington during much of the period from 1793–1797.

The first move was a series of resolutions introduced in the House of Representatives by William Branch Giles of Virginia. These had been drafted in strong terms by Jefferson but were modified in the course of discussion. Several of them called on the president as well as Hamilton for information, thus making clear that the distinction previously maintained between the secretary of the treasury and the president had now been breached. The resolves accused Hamilton in effect of having violated the laws by manipulating the foreign loans entrusted to his care. Jefferson's draft resolution that Hamilton be dismissed from office and the Treasury be broken into two parts was never offered. The resolves failed completely, with only Madison and the Virginia delegation, together with a few other congressmen, voting for them. Even so, the main objective, to introduce into the country a suspicion as to the integrity of the administration, had been achieved.

The president's sixty-first birthday reception, February 22, 1793, a day which had long been celebrated by all Americans, was attacked by Freneau as a symbol of "royal pomp and power." The presidential diaries for that day noted: "The House of Representatives waited upon the President at 12 o'clock, in a body (excepting those who were opposed thereto,) to congratulate him on the anniversary of his birth." The president, who found ceremonies tedious, decided to take his second oath of office simply, within the Senate chamber, rather than before the people as he had done in 1789. Tobias Lear recorded in Washington's diary for March 4:

> At 12 o'clock the President went to the Senate Chamber to take the oath of office prescribed by the Constitution. The members of the Senate were present—and such of the House of Representatives as had not left the City—the Heads of the Departments—the foreign Ministers—and as large a number of other persons as could press into the Senate Chamber and adjacent Rooms. The oath was

administered by Judge Cushing—previous to which the president made the following short address to the Spectators:

"Fellow Citizens

"I am again called upon by the voice of my Country to execute the functions of its Chief Magistrate. When the occasion proper for it shall arrive, I shall endeavour to express the high sense I entertain of this distinguished honor, and of the confidence which has been reposed in me by the people of United America.

"Previous to the execution of any official Act of the President, the Constitution requires an Oath of Office. This oath I am now about to take—and in your presence—that if it shall be found during my administration of the Government, I have in any instance violated willingly, or knowingly, the injunctions thereof, I may (besides incurring Constitutional punishment) be subject to the upbraiding of all who are now witnesses of the present solemn Ceremony."

After the oath was administered the President withdrew from the Senate Chamber, and returned to his own house. The President, on this occasion, went alone in his carriage to the Senate Chamber—on his return he was preceded by the Marshal of the District and the High Sheriff of the County with their deputies, who had convened at the Senate Chamber to prevent any disturbance or inconvenience that might arise from the Crowd.

Senate and House recessed until December 2, leaving the president to direct the nation through a critical period. Much of Washington's work in the next weeks concerned preparations for peace negotiations with the Indians north of the Ohio River. A group of leading Philadelphia Quakers suggested that, because of their long and good relations with the Indians, they send a delegation with the official commissioners. The president gratefully accepted their offer.

Before he started for Mount Vernon, Washington had word that the Indians, backed by the British, were insisting that all Americans leave the Northwest Territory. He also had the news that Louis XVI had been executed, and he heard from Gouverneur Morris that France was mobilizing an army to attack Great Britain.

In no optimistic mood, with his personal affairs in disorder, the president left for Mount Vernon on March 27. At Georgetown he took time to try to settle a continuing squabble between Andrew Ellicott, engineer for Washington City, and the district commissioners. After hearing on April 12 from Hamilton and Jefferson that France had declared war on England, Spain, and Holland, he set out next day for Philadelphia. He wrote to the cabinet that the United

States should observe "Strict neutrality" and every effort should be made to prevent American privateers from embroiling the country in war. On April 17 he was back in Philadelphia to find his desk piled high with trouble.

NEUTRALITY

Washington returned with a resolve to prevent any action by American citizens, or others, which would bring the United States into a European war and thus destroy the country's growing economic and political strength. Members of the cabinet as well as the chief justice had worked on a proclamation for the president to study on his return. Randolph and Jefferson both disliked the word "neutrality," which was not used, though almost everyone soon called the proclamation by that name. In its final version, Washington asked all citizens to observe "impartial" conduct towards the belligerents, declaring those who violated the proclamation to be outside the protection of the government and subject to legal prosecution. The proclamation became the organic basis of America's historic policy of neutrality in European wars, broken in the nineteenth century only when Madison was in office. On the day that he signed the proclamation, April 22, 1793, Washington outlined to a friendly English admirer, the Earl of Buchan, his basic arguments for its existence:

> *The favorable wishes which your Lordship has expressed for the prosperity of this young and rising Country, cannot but be gratefully received by all its Citizens… One means to… its happiness is very judiciously portrayed in the following words of your letter "to be little heard of in the great world of Politics." These words I can assure your Lordship are expressive of my sentiments… I believe it is the sincere wish of United America to have nothing to do with the political intrigues or squabbles of European Nations; but on the contrary to exchange commodities and live in peace with all the inhabitants of the Earth… To administer justice to, and receive it from every power with whom they are connected will, I hope, be always found the most prominent feature in the Administration of this Country… Under such a system… the agriculture and Mechanical Arts, the wealth and population of these States will increase with that degree of rapidity as to baffle all calculation…*
>
> *I take the liberty of sending you the Plan of a new City… designed for the permanent seat of the Government; we are… deeply engaged and far advanced in extending the inland navigation of the River on which it stands… In 10 years, if left undisturbed, we shall open a connection by water with all the Lakes Northward and Westward of us… and an inland navigation in a very few years more from*

Rhode Island to Georgia… To these may be added the erection of Bridges over considerable Rivers, and the commencement of Turnpike roads…

GENET

In 1793 France renewed its efforts to reinstitute Vergennes' old plan, similar to that of Great Britain: to confine the United States to the Alleghenies. The first diplomatic agent of republican France was Edmond Charles Genet, just thirty, who had been his country's representative at St. Petersburg, until he was expelled by Russia as an emissary from revolutionary France. Genet was ordered to America, with instructions to organize attacks on Spanish-held Louisiana and Florida, to stimulate French privateer assaults on British shipping in the Atlantic and the Caribbean, and to establish French admiralty courts in American coastal states. He was also instructed to recruit American troops and seamen for the French forces. To finance and manage these schemes he was directed to apply to the secretary of the treasury for advance payments on the French war loans and to the secretary of war for guns. Genet landed at Charleston on April 8 and proceeded to commission the four armed privateers, which the French consul had purchased. He ordered the establishment of a French admiralty court in the city, empowered to condemn and sell all British ships taken at sea. Washington soon had word at Mount Vernon that preparations were under way by a foreign power to use American territory as a war base. Before Genet left Charleston, Senator Ralph Izard of South Carolina warned him that Jefferson and Madison were two ambitious men. They would work with him, so long as he furthered their interests, but would quickly drop him, if things went wrong.

John Marshall, who lived through the events, vividly described America's first reactions to Genet. The French declaration of war, he wrote, "restored full vivacity to a flame, which a peace of ten years had not been able to extinguish. A great majority of the American people deemed it criminal to remain unconcerned spectators of a conflict between their ancient enemy and republican France. The feeling upon this occasion was almost universal… Disregarding totally the circumstances which led to the rupture… and that the actual hostilities were first commenced by France, the war was confidently and generally pronounced a war of aggression on the part of Great Britain." Marshall noted that "extravagant marks of public attachment [such] as had never before been lavished on a foreign minister," were shown to Genet at Charleston and these continued on his way north to Philadelphia. At the capital, on May 16, Genet was welcomed with "transports of joy by the great majority of the inhabitants."

Two days later the minister presented his credentials to the president, whose desk had been burdened for weeks with reports of French violations of American sovereignty and laws. There were now three warring powers, operating with near impunity, in a peaceful neutral country.

JEFFERSON VERSUS WASHINGTON

In one of his final appraisals of the American government, Beckwith reported to London that the secretary of state "is blindly devoted to a French influence... and there are no lengths in his power to which he will not go to favor the interests of that kingdom." With the arrival of a minister from revolutionary France, Jefferson now began a policy of calculated deception and treachery which only his innate timidity and Washington's masterly control kept from bringing disaster to the country. The secretary soon developed his own definition of neutrality as "fair" when it favored France, whereas the president's aim was to meet all foreign intrigues with equal firmness. During his last months in the cabinet, Jefferson spoke on distinct levels, to the president with one voice, to Washington's opponents with another. Hardly any cabinet secret was safe, since he duly reported the substance of the discussions to Madison and Monroe. Genet later complained that the secretary of state conversed also with him in a private language and he found it and his public utterances hard to disentangle.

On May 5 Jefferson wrote Monroe: "All the old spirit of 1776 is kindling... A French frigate took a British prize off the capes of Delaware the other day, and sent her here. Upon her coming into sight thousands & thousands of the yeomanry of the city crowded and covered the wharves... When the British colours were seen reversed, & the French flying above them they burst into peals of exultation." Ten days later, the secretary of state informed the French minister that the vessel had been seized in American waters, in violation of American laws, and he was ordered to release the ship to the British.

On May 8 Jefferson wrote an ostensibly private letter, introducing Dr. Enoch Edwards to Jean-Pierre Brissot de Warville, leader of the Girondin party, which had forced an aggressive foreign war to offset economic and political difficulties at home. The secretary of state said: "We too have our aristocrats and monocrats, and as they float on the surface, they shew much... For their particular description, I refer you to Edwards... I continue eternally attached to the principles of your revolution. I hope it will end in the establishment of some firm government, friendly to liberty & capable of maintaining it. If it does not, I feel that the zealous apostles of English despotism will increase the number of its disciples."

Jefferson also requested Genet to forward to the French interior minister, a letter from James Madison, enthusiastically accepting honorary French citizenship and wishing France a triumph over all her enemies. Jefferson wrote Madison that his letter was precisely right in tone, though it was, in fact, a contemptuous disavowal of the president's neutrality proclamation.

The actions of the Philadelphia mobs, particularly those who cheered the capture of the British ship, were heady for the secretary and Genet. It is not hard to see Jefferson in Genet's early dispatch to Paris: "The voice of the people continues to neutralize the declaration of neutrality of President Washington." Jefferson was generally delighted with Genet in the first stages of their collaboration. On May 19 he wrote Madison: "It is impossible for anything to be more affectionate, more magnanimous than the purport of his mission… In short he offers everything and asks nothing." Eight days later, much annoyed, he reported to Madison that Hamilton suspected a trap in Genet's offer to negotiate a commercial treaty.

As the records now show, Genet hoped to subordinate the American economy to French interests. Genet was subsequently to report that Jefferson filled his mind with suspicions of the "monarchists" and "aristocrats" in the American government, whom Genet came to hate. While neither Jefferson nor Genet were trustworthy in their reports of conversations, the latter's 1797 letter to the former secretary, referring to what he said about the president, has a ring of truth: "You always spoke to me that unfortunately that excellent man was controlled by the English and the aristocrats, that you were the only one in the Cabinet who still took an interest in France, but that your voice was entirely powerless; that the people, however, was for us, that your friends would have a majority in the next Congress."

In June and July Genet handed to Jefferson a series of notes, which still rank as among the most insulting ever given an American secretary of state by a foreign diplomat. Genet said that neither "the public nor the private opinions of the President" were sufficient for him to change his course, for the government seemed to be directed by foreign (i.e., British) influence. He refused to comply with the president's orders against arming French warships or privateers in American ports. He asserted that France would alone determine whether her consuls acted as admiralty judges. He suggested that the president call Congress into session. He threw in phrases about America's "cowardly" abandonment of her friends. In July Genet wrote to France to complain that old man Washington ("le vieux Washington") was interfering with him "in a thousand ways." He had therefore determined secretly to order Congress to reassemble in Philadelphia.

Jefferson's duplicity reached its first peak in late June and early July when he compromised the president's neutrality policy as well as his own negotiations with Spain. On June 30 Jefferson asked the American commissioners at Madrid to protest vigorously against Spanish support of hostile Indian attacks in the south. The commissioners were to point out to the Spanish court: "We love peace and we value peace... We abhor the follies of war... Unmeddling with the affairs of other nations... we have, with sincere and particular dispositions, courted and cultivated the friendship of Spain."

Six days later the secretary of state extended his cooperation to Genet's plan to seize Spanish Louisiana. Genet informed Jefferson that he was sending a French agent, André Michaux, to Kentucky, to enlist Americans for war against Spain's territories. He mentioned that there were two Americans, George Rogers Clark and Benjamin Logan, who had been made French generals and would do the actual recruiting. Genet stated that he was issuing proclamations from the United States, encouraging the inhabitants of Louisiana and Canada to revolt. The secretary noted in his diary that the minister said he was telling these things, not to the secretary of state, but to "Mr. Jeff." The latter told Genet that the Americans might be hanged, if caught on Spanish territory, but "leaving out that article I did not care what insurrections might be excited in Louisiana." At Genet's request, Jefferson gave Michaux a letter of introduction to the governor of Kentucky, in which he noted that Michaux stood in high favor with Genet, implying that he also stood well with the American government. In July, when Washington asked Jefferson to supply him with an account of all his written and oral communications with Genet, the available evidence indicates that Jefferson failed to disclose his Louisiana-Canada conversation to the president.

FALL OF GENET

On order of the president, backed in full by his cabinet, Jefferson gave Genet a courteous refusal on the part of the United States to repay the French loan in advance or to provide arms. Genet persisted nonetheless with his demands. Thereafter the presidential diaries noted repeated instances of Genet's disregard of American laws and neutrality. Complaints were met with countercomplaints that American courts were interfering with French consuls, who were empowered to judge prizes. Genet protested that American marshals, acting "in the name of the President," had been outrageous in preventing the French from arming vessels.

The crucial test came for the government on June 22 when the president, according to his diary, received a letter from Governor Mifflin of Pennsylvania which "stated that a vessel called the *Little Sarah*, prize to the frigate *Ambuscade*, was equipping and fitting out as a privateer." This was being done in Philadelphia, almost under the president's nose. Washington asked the governor to investigate and report as soon as possible to the federal authorities. Two days later the president set out for a hasty trip to Mount Vernon because of the critical illness of his manager there. He returned to the capital on July 11, after Whiting's death, to face his severest diplomatic crisis.

On July 4 Hamilton received reliable word that the *Little Sarah,* renamed *Little Democrat,* had been heavily armed. The following day he met with Jefferson and Knox, who agreed that the cabinet should request the state's governor to prevent her sailing. Mifflin learned quickly that the ship was, in fact, ready to depart. He sent Alexander Dallas, secretary of the Governor's Council, to Genet late on the night of July 6 to warn him not to let the ship leave. Genet, in a rage, threatened to appeal at once to Congress and the sovereign people of the country. He said the ship would sail.

That same day Genet had gained Jefferson's cooperation in his Louisiana venture. During the conversation Genet informed the secretary that he intended to send two armed privateers to assist the enterprise. Jefferson did not record whether Genet mentioned that the *Little Sarah* was to be one of the two, but this was not hard to guess. The day after the dispute with Dallas, the secretary of state called on the French minister. Exactly what happened will never be known but it is clear that there was a violent altercation. Jefferson subsequently prepared two highly variant versions of the discussions. He wrote one immediately afterward on July 7 for Madison: "Never, in my opinion, was so calamitous an appointment made, as that of the present Minister of F. Here. Hot headed, all imagination, no judgment, Passionate & even indecent towards the [president] in his written as well as verbal communications, talking of appeals from him to Congress, from them to the people, urging the most unreasonable & groundless propositions & in the most dictatorial style &c.&c.&c. If ever it should be necessary to lay his communications before Congress or the public, they will excite universal indignation."

During the conversation Genet refused to delay the ship's departure until the president returned to the city, but he informed Jefferson that the *Little Sarah* might not be ready to sail. He added that any attempt to stop her by force would be met with force. He hinted too that a French fleet was about to arrive in American waters. Jefferson then persuaded the Pennsylvania governor to restrain the state militia, by assuring him the ship would not be ready to sail before the president arrived.

In his *Anas,* Jefferson noted a version of the conversation with Genet, which he gave to Mifflin, and which undoubtedly was similar to the report he subsequently gave the president. He said that Genet had talked so much he found it impossible to state the particulars of what he said. He added: "He did, in some part of his declamation to me, drop the idea of publishing a narrative or statement of transactions; but he did not on that, nor ever did on any other occasions in my presence, use disrespectful expressions of the President."

On July 8 there was a conference attended by the secretaries of state, treasury, and war, together with the governor of Pennsylvania. Hamilton, Knox, and Mifflin argued that the president's orders to stop the departure of vessels armed in the United States should be firmly supported. Mifflin proposed to send state militia to Mud Island, below Philadelphia, and Knox agreed to supply them with federal guns. Jefferson pleaded against this policy, fearful that the French would fire back. He claimed that France was "a most friendly nation" which was supporting "the most sacred cause that ever man was engaged in." The secretary of state managed to stymie action long enough for the *Little Sarah* to move downriver past Mud Island. He then took to his bed with a high fever and was still there when the president arrived in the capital on July 11. As soon as Washington read the correspondence, he wrote Jefferson:

> *What is to be done in the case of the <u>Little Sarah</u>, now at Chester. Is the Minister of the French Republic to set the Acts of this Government at defiance <u>with impunity</u>? and then threaten the Executive with an appeal to the people? What must the World think of such conduct, and of the Government of the U. States in submitting to it?*
>
> *These are serious questions. Circumstances press for decision, and as you have had time to consider them (upon me they come unexpected) I wish to know your opinion upon them, even before tomorrow, for the Vessel may then be gone.*

Jefferson pleaded with Genet to detain the ship until the president could study the legal problems, but the ship sailed to sea. Hamilton and Knox asked the president to request that France recall Genet immediately.

During the many crises of 1793, Knox, the huge secretary of war, was as fearlessly solid in international affairs as he had been on the battlefield. Throughout, and for the rest of his time in the cabinet, he was the president's strongest bulwark. His energetic attempt to prevent the escape of the *Little Sarah* risked Washington's displeasure, because he had given federal guns to state militia. Although the president on his return thought it an unfortunate precedent for other states, he approved the measure. Knox went farther than any other cabinet member in proposing the immediate suspension of Genet's functions. Knox's views greatly displeased Jefferson who called him a "fool" in his diary notes.

The cabinet struggled and fought, supposedly in secret, in the last days of July and the hot early days of August with the problems of France and Genet. Hamilton and Knox proposed that all correspondence with Genet be made public but Jefferson demurred. He suggested that this would set off a popularity contest between the president and the French minister: he gave his real reason to Madison—that such a revelation would weaken their faction in the country. The cabinet unanimously agreed that the French government be asked to recall Genet; all members but Jefferson wanted this to be peremptory. Jefferson suggested the request be made "with great delicacy." When the question arose as to whether Genet should be informed, Knox was for first telling him and then kicking him out of the country, whereas Jefferson thought it best not even to inform him, since "little differences" between friendly governments could be ironed out directly.

In the end Jefferson had to write to Gouverneur Morris to ask France to recall Genet. After a delay he also informed Genet that he was to be dismissed. Genet fired back in the press with a loud salvo against Jefferson. In the meantime, he had encouraged his consuls at New York and Boston to bring ashore forces from French warships to prevent American marshals from placing prizes under American jurisdiction.

By November, the president and Hamilton had swung over to Knox's view that Genet should be asked to leave the country. Jefferson opposed this, suggesting that Genet might not be willing to go. In the end, radical political changes in France caused that country to replace its minister.

THE HOT SUMMER AND FALL

The eleven months from June 1793 to April 1794 were the most perilous of Washington's presidency. In addition to trouble with France, almost everything else went wrong. The United States had no navy and its tiny army was almost entirely concentrated in the Ohio Valley. The country was far more sharply divided politically than during the revolution. In all the major seaports and in western villages, Jacobin clubs shouted for America to support France in its war. Hugh Brackenridge, in a July 4 speech in western Pennsylvania, declared that if France asked for American heroes and privateers, the United States should reply: "You shall have them... Our voice of war shall be heard with yours." On Bastille Day, Governor Mifflin, though his own authority had been defied by France, attended a dinner with Genet where speeches and toasts implied that those who would separate America from France were "Arnolds" and "traitors." The Jeffersonian press was soon calling

Washington a double-dealer and traitor; one cartoon placed the president's head under a guillotine and Philip Freneau composed a funeral dirge for George Washington.

While mobs shouted for war with England, the British government formulated policies which made it nearly impossible for the president to pursue a course of peaceful neutrality, General Wayne, from the field, wrote to Knox on July 2 that not only were the British using every tactic to prevent the American peace commissioners from treating with the northwest Indians, but they were sending agents to the southern Indians, in order to bring them into general league against the United States. A little later he reported that hundreds of Cherokees and Creeks were proceeding north to the Maumee Valley to meet British agents. These intrigues were directed by John Graves Simcoe, lieutenant governor of upper Canada. Simcoe had fought the Americans all during the revolution and had been captured by Washington at Yorktown. Not long before he had declared that he was determined once more to meet Washington on the field of battle and this time to defeat him. By the end of the year, the failure of peace negotiations made it clear that General Wayne would have to take the offensive against the Indians and risk war with England.

In June the British government issued an order-in-council, which provided for the seizure of all American ships carrying goods to France. This was reinforced in the autumn when the French Caribbean possessions were made a special target. Secret orders were issued to the Royal Navy in the West Indies, and their ships soon rounded up more than 250 American merchant vessels. Many of these were condemned in admiralty courts and their crews left penniless and starving.

Additional trouble for the president came from the South, where relations with both Spain and the Indians were critical. The hard-working Knox frequently brought to the president's desk his immense correspondence from American governors and agents in the area. A portion of the Creek nation was warring with other parts, the Cherokees were fighting the Creeks, while both engaged in raids on American settlements. Spanish agents continually worked to stir up the tribes to war on the Americans. As a further fillip to trouble, the French consul at Charleston organized a Franco-American expedition to proceed overland to attack Spanish settlements in Florida.

A number of Americans were in foreign pay. William Smith, the vice-president's son-in-law, was a French political and commercial agent, employed to press for money and arms for France. The second in command of the American army, General James Wilkinson, was in Spanish pay. Wilkinson tipped off the Spanish commissioners in Philadelphia that the French planned to invade their territory and that George Rogers Clark had been made a French general for this purpose. The Spaniards complained at once to the secretary of state. At the president's order, Jefferson, who had helped to promote the plot, was forced to write to the governor of Kentucky to warn him not to help the French. The governor replied that he did not understand why Jefferson should interfere when America's friends wanted to attack Spanish tyrants. To old and trusted friends, Washington reviewed his troubles with candid humor. He wrote Henry Lee, Virginia's governor, on July 21:

I should have thanked you at an earlier period for your obliging letter... had it not come to my hands only a day or two before I set out for Mount Vernon; and at a time when I was much hurried, and indeed very much perplexed with the disputes, memorials and what not, with which the Government were pestered by one or other of the petulant representatives of the powers at War: and because, since my return... I have been more than ever overwhelmed with their complaints. In a word, the trouble they give is hardly to be described.

The communications in your letter were pleasing and grateful to me; for, although I have done no public act with which my mind upbraids me, yet it is highly satisfactory to learn that the things which I do (of an interesting tendency to the peace and happiness of this Country) are generally approved...

That there are in this, as well as in all other Countries, discontented characters, I well know; as also that these characters are actuated by very different views: Some good... some bad, and (if I might be allowed to use so harsh an expression) diabolical; inasmuch as they are not only meant to impede the measures of that Government generally, but...to destroy the confidence, which it is necessary for the people to place... in their public servants; for in this light I consider myself, whilst I am an occupant of office; and if they were to go further and call me their slave, (during this period) I would not dispute the point.

But in what will this abuse terminate? The result, as it respects myself, I care not; for I have a consolation within, that no earthly efforts can deprive me of, and that is that neither ambitious nor interested motives have influenced my conduct. The arrows of malevolence, therefore, however barbed and well pointed, never can reach the most vulnerable part of me... The publications in Freneau's and [Bache's] papers are outrages on common decency; and they progress in that style, in proportion as their pieces are treated with contempt...

As we are told that you have exchanged the rugged and dangerous field of Mars, for the soft and pleasurable bed of Venus, I do in this, as I shall in every thing you may pursue like unto it good and laudable, wish you all imaginable success and happiness.

Earlier in the year Lee had asked Washington whether he should accept an offer to become a general in the French revolutionary army. The president, writing privately, warned him that conditions in France were too troubled and that he did not think it would be a very opportune time to go. Lee, instead, married Ann Hill Carter, who was to produce Robert E. Lee, who would vainly attempt to destroy the nation his father had worked so hard to build.

YELLOW FEVER

John Adams wrote to a friend in 1808 that if yellow fever had not appeared, the president would have been hauled out of his house in 1793 and roughly treated by the Philadelphia mobs, but this seems an Adams exaggeration. The epidemic did, however, bring government and politics almost to a halt. During its height, Martha Washington proved more strong-minded than the president for she forced him out of the city.

Philadelphia had been overwhelmed by French refugees from Santo Domingo where the fever flourished. A cabinet meeting in early July, while Washington was still out of town, discussed a letter from Henry Lee, which mentioned that the governor of South Carolina was worried that the French were bringing epidemic diseases from the West Indies. He asked for advice. The cabinet, having no information, did not take the letter seriously.

Yellow fever was first diagnosed by Dr. Benjamin Rush on August 19 as the cause of a number of deaths near the Philadelphia waterfront. Rush, who noted that mosquitoes were very troublesome that month, attributed the outbreak to rotting coffee brought from the West Indies. Washington's first written mention of the epidemic was contained in an August 23 letter to his temporary Mount Vernon manager, Howell Lewis, in which he said that Philadelphia was "very sickly and numbers dying daily." That same day Rush wrote his wife that the fever had taken a sudden and "alarming" spread and people were fleeing the city. He issued a statement on the disease to the public. It appeared in the *American Daily Advertiser* about the time the paper printed an unsigned letter recommending the use of oil on all stagnant waters to control the increase of mosquitoes expected after heavy August rains.

Alexander Hamilton and his wife both came down with the disease in early September. It was the secretary of the treasury who subsequently led a move for a more rational treatment of the disease than that used by Dr. Rush. Hamilton's old West Indies boyhood friend, Ned Stevens, to whom he disclosed his ambitions at fourteen, had settled into a Philadelphia medical practice, after taking an Edinburgh degree. Stevens' treatment was an essentially modern one, in which, where there is no specifically known cure, all support is given to nature. Yellow fever is highly debilitating and dehydrating; Stevens recommended that the patient stay quietly in bed, keep serene, and receive good nursing care, and that he eat well and drink many liquids, including Madeira. He recommended peppermint oils to relieve vomiting. Stevens deplored excessive evacuations which reduced the body's liquid. The Alexander Hamiltons recovered relatively quickly under Stevens' care.

Dr. Rush, assisted by various physicians and orderlies, sometimes treated as many as 150 patients a day. He used an entirely different procedure. He gave his patients severe purges more fit for a horse than a man. In addition, he bled them to excess, occasionally drawing more blood in five days than the amount normally contained in an adult human body. Both processes greatly increased debilitation and dehydration. There is no way to estimate how many deaths his methods caused but his letters to his wife contain the names (not all of them his patients) of 120 persons who died, including his sister, several of his student physicians, and numerous old friends. Others, outside his direct care, followed the Rush methods he gave out freely to the newspapers.

On September 11 Hamilton published a letter in the *Federal Gazette* and *Philadelphia Daily Advertiser* strongly praising Dr. Stevens' methods. As the disease spread and panic grew, Hamilton's letter was increasingly used to prove that Rush was wrong. In a final rationalization Rush stated he was being persecuted for having "republican" principles for which he could never be forgiven by such people as Hamilton.

The president, in late August, had written to his proposed new manager for Mount Vernon, William Pearce, that he planned to be at his farms on September 20. He asked Pearce to meet him there. Although the epidemic spread and the death rate went up sharply, the president decided to keep to his schedule. He suggested to his wife that she take her two grandchildren and proceed ahead of him to Mount Vernon. Martha Washington drew herself up to her five feet and announced that she would not leave the president in danger and the children would stay right there with him. He surrendered; on September 10 he climbed into the carriage with his wife and the children, and headed for Mount Vernon. On September 25, sounding a bit sheepish, he told the story to Tobias Lear. The president's departure meant that members of the cabinet, including Jefferson, and most government staffs, soon followed.

While at Mount Vernon, Washington's main concern was how he could get the government to function again and where Congress should meet. He made numerous constitutional inquiries to his widely scattered cabinet as well as to James Madison and the speaker of the House; he received sharply divergent advice in reply. In the end he decided to rent a house in Germantown, in ample time to prepare his fifth annual State of the Union message. With the first frosts the epidemic suddenly halted. On November 24 Washington wrote to Burges Ball that the fever had apparently entirely ceased in the city and he was now spending considerable time there. Shortly afterwards he was back in his old house.

During this period he outlined topics for Congress, which indicated that he had a lot on his mind—the western posts, British sea measures, negotiations with Spain, squabbles with Genet, American captives at Algiers, failure to attain peace with the Western Indians, troubles in Georgia and the Southwest, and a need for increased defense measures. His keynote point was to be: "The times are critical, and much temper and cool deliberate reflection is necessary to maintain Peace with dignity and safety to the United States." Washington had written Richard Henry Lee on October 24 to say that those who were attempting to subvert the government's peaceful measures were not genuinely concerned with France, nor liberty, for if war came they "would be among the first and loudest of the clamourers against the expense and impolicy of the measure."

STATE OF THE UNION

In view of the multiple problems to be presented to Congress, the president decided to cover many of them in separate messages. On December 3, 1793, at noon, Washington delivered his fifth annual message, his most forceful to date. He gracefully thanked the American people for their "affectionate partiality" in choosing him again for office, in spite of his "earnest wish for retirement."

He then stated bluntly that he intended to keep the country out of war. He had issued a neutrality proclamation, designed not only to keep Americans from committing belligerent acts but to impress on foreign nations that the United States was entitled to all the immunities of neutrality. He had not hesitated to prevent France from arming vessels within the United States, nor from retaining British merchant vessels captured within American territorial waters. He urged Congress to strengthen the federal laws in order to prevent *all* persons within the United States from committing hostile acts, assuming judicial powers, or organizing military expeditions. He continued:

I cannot recommend to your notice measures for the fulfillment of <u>our</u> duties to the rest of the world, without again pressing upon you the necessity of placing ourselves in a state of complete defence, and of exacting from <u>them</u> the fulfillment of their <u>duties</u> towards <u>us</u>. The United States ought not to indulge a persuasion that... they will forever keep at a distance those painful appeals to arms, with which the history of every other nation bounds. There is a rank due to the United States among Nations, which will be withheld, if not absolutely lost, by the reputation of weakness. If we desire to avoid insult, we must be able to repel it; if we desire to secure peace, one of the most powerful instruments of our rising prosperity, it must be known, that we are at all times, ready for War.

Two days later the president sent to Congress a special message on relations with France and Great Britain. With respect to the former, he wrote: "It is with extreme concern I have to inform you, that the proceedings of the person whom they have unfortunately appointed their Minister plenipotentiary here, have breathed nothing of the friendly spirit of the nation which sent him; their tendency on the contrary, has been to involve us in War abroad, and discord and anarchy at home... The papers now communicated, will more particularly apprize you of these transactions."

With reference to London, the president said: "The British Government, having undertaken by orders to the Commanders of their armed vessels, to restrain generally our commerce in Corn and other provisions to their own ports and those of their friends, the instructions now communicated were immediately forwarded to our Minister at that Court... I may expect to learn the result... in time to make it known to the Legislature during their present Session."

On December 16 the president delivered a further message on Spain. While, he said, his commissioners were treating at Madrid, the agents of their government were exciting "the hostilities threatened and exercised by the southern Indians on our border... It could not be conceived we would submit to the scalping knife and tomahawk of the savage without any resistance. I thought it time therefore to know... the views of their sovereign, and despatched a special messenger with instructions to our Commissioners, which are among the papers now communicated."

The president, in vigorous command of the foreign relations of the United States, proceeded, for the rest of the month, to dispatch messages to his manager and overseer at Mount Vernon. Included were complete plans for all major crops on his Mount Vernon farms for each of the years 1794 to 1799. If he could hold the peace, he would be back there to direct the last half of his six-year plan.

ELEVEN

PEACE IN THE WEST

1794

T HE PRESIDENT HAD expressed to Congress his feeling that a real, rather than a "fair," neutrality was "the powerful instrument of our rising prosperity." In an era where economic indices were few, the president could not know in the fullest detail the scope of the country's economic growth during his administration. His extensive travels and repeated conversations with members of Congress from various states, however, gave him a pretty good concept of it. In addition his Treasury reports showed that government revenue in 1793 was nearly two-and-a-half times the annual rate of 1789. By the end of 1793 gross national product had shown a gain of nearly 50 percent. Although the youthful population was growing with remarkable rapidity, real income per capita rose by an average of 9 percent a year.

Late in 1793 Jefferson reported to Madison that "the market," as he called the cost of living, had been going steadily upward in Philadelphia. Madison's boardinghouse charges would be higher at the new session of Congress. Jefferson blamed Hamilton for juggling the government bond market in order to raise prices and tax the farmer. In reality the American farmer was the principal beneficiary of the price rises of the 1790s, which seem to have been induced entirely by external causes. The revolution in France and the outbreak of a general European war brought food and raw material shortages and a constant rise in European demand. In consequence prices of American

exports increased much more rapidly than those of imports of European manufactured goods and West Indies tropical products. The terms of trade
became increasingly favorable for the United States. The effects were noticeable in several individual economic indices of the period. By 1793 Americans
were importing eight times as much coffee and nearly four times as much
sugar as in 1789; an indeterminate portion of this was, however, for re-export.
In a single year, excises paid on domestic whiskey jumped by nearly 60 percent, although some of the increase may have come from a better collection
of the tax. In 1789, after more than 170 years of settlement, the United States
had only 75 post offices; in the next four years, 131 were added. Government
revenues, thus far, generally covered the growth in military expenditures and
allowed for a planned further increase.

Even so the tax system was so light on the American farmer that
Washington could write to Sir John Sinclair on July 20, 1794: "Your system of
Agriculture, it must be confessed, is in a stile superior and of course much
more expensive than ours; but when the balance at the end of the year is
struck, by deducting [your] taxes, poor rates, and incidental charges of every
kind from the produce of the land in the two Countries, no doubt can remain
in which Scale it is to be found."

One person much hurt by the rising prosperity was the president himself.
His annual allowance of $25,000 to cover all the expenses of the presidency,
including rent, entertainment, secretaries, and domestic staff, remained
fixed, while prices continued to rise. In his last term, Washington's real
income was cut by a third and he had to sell land to meet his expenses.
Although he found a new manager for his Mount Vernon farms, William
Pearce, who turned out to be more competent than many of his previous managers, he complained that his farm income and outgo just about balanced.

Washington had trouble, like leaders of underdeveloped countries, in
finding men to fill positions with the government. His rigid standard precluded many, those whom he nominated frequently declined for various reasons—health or family, a preference for being important in their own state,
or, in the case of Supreme Court justices, an unwillingness to ride circuit. With
the growth of the pro-French faction in American politics, the field of choice
further narrowed. Out of necessity Washington picked Edmund Randolph,
his old friend and attorney, as secretary of state in place of Jefferson who
resigned at the end of the year. Randolph had at least the advantage of having sat through all the cabinet crises, but as secretary of state he was to be a
largely negative factor. William Bradford was appointed attorney general in
his place.

END OF GENET

Jefferson's old friend, Brissot de Warville, who had plunged France into war with England, was guillotined at the end of October 1793. Genet, a Girondin, in consequence lost his basis of political support in France. Even without the American request for his recall, he could not have lasted long.

On February 21 Jean Fauchet, the new French minister, arrived in Philadelphia with a group of aides and an order for the arrest of Genet and his return to France. David Cobb remarked that Genet would soon have been a head shorter, if the president had not offered him asylum. In 1797 Genet, still angry at Jefferson, wrote him: "Robespierre, acting upon your denunciations alone, [gave] orders not to allow me to arrive alive in Paris... This bloody request was rejected by Washington who declared that he had asked for my recall and not for my punishment; but Randolph, your friend... added confidentially that I still had many friends." Genet soon courted and married Cornelia Clinton, the daughter of the governor of New York.

On February 22, 1794, Washington's sixty-second birthday, Fauchet presented his credentials to the president. That evening, with Washington and members of the cabinet, he attended the Philadelphia Assembly Ball, held annually on the president's birthday. Fauchet was as much an intriguer as the other French diplomats who had been stationed in America, but his was a more subtle approach. He soon recalled the commissions given out by Genet, notably to George Rogers Clark, thus reducing the possibility that the United States would be involved in war with Spain.

JOHN JAY, SPECIAL MINISTER

In his 1793 and 1794 diaries the president made copious notes of correspondence handed him by members of the cabinet. He followed General Wayne's activities in the West with the closest attention. He wrote of the work of Clark in promoting the invasion of Louisiana, the intrigues of Simcoe, and the general disaffection to the federal government in Kentucky.

Washington also made summaries of reports from his diplomatic and other agents abroad, many quite unpleasant. On December 11, 1793, he wrote: "Letter... from Edwd. Church, Lisbon 8 October 93... thinks that sooner or later to *crush the U.S.* is the determination of Engd. & Spain... [Lisbon] October 12 containing the disagreeably important intelligence of a truce having taken place between Portugal and Algiers for 12 months—thro' the mediation of G. B. The Algerine fleet has therefore sailed out into the Atlantic...

Four American vessels have been captured... The view of the English being the injury of the U.S." The president shortly afterwards wrote that Portugal, alone of the European powers, had made a friendly gesture, in offering to convoy American ships, in spite of protests handed to the Portuguese court by the Spanish and British ambassadors.

On January 21 Washington had a letter from Thomas Pinckney, in which he quoted Lord Grenville, British foreign secretary, as assuring him that the government and people of Great Britain wanted to keep "on good terms" with the United States. Any illegal seizures of American ships in the Caribbean would be fully prosecuted. In January Britain did, in fact, greatly modify the earlier orders-in-council but the news took a long time to reach Philadelphia. In February the president started to receive reports of the many American ships that had been captured in the Caribbean. On March 25 he forwarded to Congress letters from the American consul at St. Eustatia, which stated that as many as 250 ships had been seized.

Ominous reports from Canada also reached the president. On March 10 Governor George Clinton of New York forwarded an account of a belligerent speech by Lord Dorchester to the Northwest Indians on February 10. The Canadian governor, recently returned from England, said that all efforts by Great Britain to establish peace had failed, and she and the United States would soon be at war. The Indians could then set their own terms within the neutral area which Britain would establish.

Although Dorchester's threat was real, and was soon followed by the establishment of a British fort on the Maumenee, the president viewed the situation with a far more experienced eye than most of his countrymen. He was aware that the British army under the Duke of York had suffered a defeat in the Netherlands, while the Royal Navy had been driven from Toulon. He wrote to Clinton on March 31 to say that the combined powers in Europe had suffered "disappointments." Lord Dorchester had reflected "the Sentiments of the British Cabinet at the period he was instructed. Foiled as that Ministry has been, whether it may not have changed its tone, as it respects us, is problematical." The United States should, nonetheless, be ready for any event. He asked Clinton to send agents to northern New York and Canada to obtain intelligence of British regular and militia troops, the state of the Canadian government, the opinions and dispositions of the Canadians, and to forward reports on American settlements and strength in the North.

General Knox, who accurately reflected Washington's thinking, wrote to General Wayne on March 31 stating that, following the January 8 changes in the British orders-in-council, there was "some hope that compensation and satisfaction will be made for the damages and injuries we have sustained..." In consequence, Wayne was directed to abstain "from every step or measure which could possibly be construed into any aggression on your part against either Spain or England... You are to consider that we are at peace with Great Britain and Spain and to act accordingly."

In Congress both Federalists and Jeffersonians lost their heads, temporarily, in reacting to the sea captures and Dorchester's speech. In early January Madison had introduced resolutions for commercial discrimination against Great Britain but these got nowhere. In the heat of the passionate feelings aroused by British policy, Madison had better luck with efforts to shut off foreign trade, a proposal similar to the futile and disastrous embargoes which Jefferson and Madison were to push forward in the early 1800s. Both Houses of Congress overwhelmingly voted a thirty-day stoppage of freight shipments from American ports. This hit American shipping severely while placing intolerable administrative burdens on the president. The questions poured onto his desk. Were state governors required to enforce federal orders? Should cutters take the news to southern ports? Could the British and French ministers be permitted to send out dispatches? Were passengers permitted to leave for the French West Indies? Were fishing vessels included in the order? Would ships in ballast be allowed to depart? Congress had passed the law, but the president was supposed to answer all the questions, his three lawyers in the cabinet not being very helpful.

Madison's embargo aroused furious approval and disapproval. The new French minister reported in admiration to Paris that Madison was "the Robespierre" of the American government. He was referred to as "Mr. Mad" by a disgruntled constituent of Senator King. Government forces and Jeffersonians thereafter split widely on the next steps to be taken. The Federalists followed Washington's views that arming for peace was the best assurance of keeping it. They introduced bills to establish the first navy under the new Constitution, to fortify the coastal cities, to increase the armed forces, to strengthen the militia, and to increase the number of arsenals. Madison, Monroe, and others of their party fought against these measures but went down to easy defeat. In turn, they attempted to break off intercourse with Great Britain and to sequester all debts owed to the British until she should yield.

The president had already advised Knox that he thought an agreement could be obtained with London. It is not possible entirely to reconstruct the subsequent events which led to the appointment of John Jay, particularly when the president kept his counsel even from his secretary of state. On March 12 Senator Ellsworth, representing several members of the Senate, called on the president to suggest that he send a special envoy to Great Britain. Ellsworth proposed Hamilton as the man best qualified for the mission. In one of his rare disclosures of opinion, Washington said that, while he had confidence in Hamilton, many in the country did not and he would have to take account of this. Two days later Edmund Randolph suggested that the president send an assistant to Pinckney to work on legal and other aspects of the British seizures.

The embargo took effect on March 26. On April 7 Senator King of New York called on the British minister, George Hammond, who stated a bit wryly that not many people came to his house these days and he was glad to see him. Hammond was encouraging. He wanted to see a special envoy proceed to London, for he too hoped for peace and friendly commercial intercourse between the two countries. He informed King that he did not believe that the Dorchester speech could possibly have had the approval of the British government. As proof, he pointed out that the orders-in-council, which had aroused so great a storm in America, were quickly revoked.

It was clear that an envoy extraordinary would have to be of high rank within the government to make the mission impressive. This left the choice among the vice-president, who was never seriously considered, the chief justice, and Hamilton. On April 14 Hamilton wrote the president, outlining his views of the problem in relation to Great Britain. In a forthright way, he said that there were too many objections in the country to his appointment. He strongly urged the chief justice for the position.

While this was going on, the secretary of state, probably with the nudging of Fauchet, endeavored to push Madison forward as special envoy, but this idea got nowhere. James Monroe, in a letter which the president clearly regarded as impertinent, wrote him on April 8 to say that sending Hamilton would be "injurious to the public interest." Washington replied the next day: "I request, if you are possessed of any facts or information, which would disqualify Colo. Hamilton... that you would be so obliging as to communicate them to me in writing... Colo. Hamilton and others have been mentioned and have occurred to me as an Envoy for endeavoring by negotiation, to avert the horrors of War. No one... is yet absolutely decided on in my mind... As I alone am responsible for a proper nomination, it certainly behooves me to name such an one as, in my judgment, combines the requisites for a mission so peculiarly interesting to the peace and happiness of this country."

On April 15, the day after his receipt of Hamilton's declination, the president sent a note to the chief justice, who by this time was well apprised of the situation and knew what was behind the invitation: "At as early hour this morning, as you can make convenient to yourself, I should be glad to see you. At eight o'clock we breakfast. Then, or after, as suits you best, I will expect to have the satisfaction of conversing with you on an interesting subject."

Jay, devoutly religious and possessing an integrity as great as the president's, was thoroughly realistic. He knew that he was being given the most difficult assignment of Washington's administration, the country was deeply divided, and too many persons wanted no treaty and no peace. He accepted, with feelings which he expressed to his wife: "I feel the impulse of duty strongly... On an occasion so important, I ought to follow its dictates, and commit myself to the care and kindness of that Providence, in which we both have the highest reason to repose the most absolute confidence."

On April 16 Washington sent a message to the Senate: "Peace ought to be pursued with unremitted zeal, before the last resource, which has so often been the scourge of nations and cannot fail to check the advanced prosperity of the United States, is contemplated; I have thought proper to nominate, and do hereby nominate John Jay, as Envoy Extraordinary of the United States to his Britannic Majesty."

The appointment of Jay set off a wild storm among a minority in the country. Jay was hanged or burned in effigy and denounced on the Senate floor. Washington was excoriated in the Jeffersonian press, being even accused of trying to spirit the chief justice out of the country so that he could not, as required by the Constitution, preside at the president's impeachment trial. Neither Washington nor Jay was ruffled, but Mrs. Jay had hard work to bear the attacks with the composure her husband encouraged her to show.

Before Jay accepted his mission, he noted to Washington that the turbulence in Congress had to be kept under control. He was in no position to negotiate if Congress cut off all trade with Britain and refused payment on commercial debts. The bill to break off intercourse with Britain passed the House; it was beaten in the Senate on April 28 by the veto of Vice-President Adams. This was the high point reached by those who wanted to interfere with the president's peaceful negotiations. A Senate bill to stop paying debts to Britain got only the votes of Virginia's senators. The embargo, after being extended a month, died unlamented in May.

Between April 19, when he issued his commission to John Jay, and May 6 the president worked intensively on instructions for the mission. These were contained in the official directive signed by Edmund Randolph. The letter, although long, was remarkably clear and simple. The president observed that "the solemnity of a special mission" bore the fullest evidence to the British that he wanted "to repel war, for which we are not disposed, and into which the necessity of vindicating our honor and our property may, but can alone drive us and at the same time, to assert, with dignity and firmness, our rights, and our title to reparation for past injuries."

Although the British minister had told Senator King that he did not believe there was the slightest chance that Parliament would vote compensation for seized American ships, the president made this the first order of business for Jay. If, and only if, this point were granted by Great Britain, Jay was directed, in point of order, then "to draw to a conclusion all points of difference between the United States and Great Britain, concerning the treaty of peace." Jay was especially urged to point out that retention of the posts, and the employment of British agents to stir up Indians, brought "much bloodshed on our frontiers."

The instructions reiterated that "vexations and spoilations" of American commerce were to be kept entirely separate from discussions of the 1783 treaty. Any settlement with respect to the latter was not to influence the former. If all these points were agreed to, then Jay, entirely at his discretion, was authorized but not directed to "listen to," or even broach the subject of a commercial treaty, as well as numerous related points, ranging from fisheries to control of piracy.

On May 12 Jay sailed from New York for London. The Society of St. Tammany at its dinner that day gave two not quite contradictory toasts: success to the Jay mission and success to the armies of France. While Jay was on his way across the seas, General Wayne reported further menacing developments in letters to the secretary of war:

> *It wou'd appear, that there is a perfect understanding & a constant communication between the Spanish Commandant at post <u>St. Louis</u> on the Mississippi, and the British at Detroit... The Spaniards... have taken post at the Chickasaw Bluffs... There are five Spanish Gallies now at the Mouth of the Ohio, carrying a Number of large Cannon, & Sixty men each. [May 26]*

> *Recent and well authenticated intelligence [indicates that I] may eventually have to oppose a Heterogeneous Army composed of British troops, the Militia of Detroit & all the Hostile Indians NW of the Ohio; now assembling at Roche de Bout at the foot of the Rapids of the Miami... under the Command of the Famous Governor Simcoe... His taking post in the Centre of the Hostile Indians & so far advanced within our acknowledged limits is most certainly an Aggression... [May 30]*

Although letters took a long time to reach Quebec, one of the earliest fruits of Jay's arrival in London was a July 5 British government reprimand to Lord Dorchester, so sharp in tone that he offered his resignation. The Canadian governor was directed to pull back immediately from the new post established at Roche de Bout, since the government expected to settle all issues with Mr. Jay.

In the meantime, Knox on June 7 had authorized Wayne to attack the Roche de Bout post, if necessary, but to treat the British and Spaniards with every courtesy. Knox, speaking for the president, added that he was convinced the British did not want war and he therefore hoped that "Mr. Jay... will be able to adjust all differences in an amicable and satisfactory manner."

JAMES MONROE, ENVOY EXTRAORDINARY

Within two months of his arrival in Philadelphia, Fauchet asked the secretary of state to recall Gouverneur Morris, the American minister, who had been a valuable and trusted informant to the president during the Reign of Terror. This placed Washington in a dilemma since he knew that the pro-French faction would want one of their adherents in the post. He at once asked Jay whether he would consent to be the permanent minister at London so that he could transfer Thomas Pinckney to Paris. Jay declined, and Washington offered the French post to Robert Livingston, the chancellor of New York. After Livingston refused, there was a wild scramble for the appointment. Hamilton suggested to the president that he ship Randolph to Paris, but this did not seem desirable. Randolph, in turn, pushed for Aaron Burr or James Monroe. In the end, Monroe was selected. This removed from the Senate an opponent of the president's policies but placed him in a position where he could damage his efforts to secure a British peace.

While Monroe was waiting to sail from Baltimore, Washington passed through the city on June 19. He tried to send a note by Monroe to Morris "to assure you that my confidence in, and friendship and regard for you, remains undiminished." Finding it had missed the ship, Washington wrote a longer letter from Mount Vernon on June 25, adding an appraisal of the political situation at home: "The affairs of this country *cannot go amiss*. There are so many *watchful guardians of them*, and such *infallible guides*, that one is at no loss for a director at every turn."

By the time Monroe got to Paris, Robespierre had been guillotined and there was some delay in accepting his credentials. Finally on August 15, while Jay was locked in strenuous negotiations with Lord Grenville, Monroe delivered a rapturous address to the French Convention, praising "the noble career of France... Whilst the fortitude, magnanimity and heroic valor of her troops command the admiration and applause of the astonished world, the wisdom and firmness of her councils unite equally in securing the happiest result." Monroe added that all America offered France "the most decided proof of her sincere attachment to the liberty, prosperity and happiness of the French Republic."

When the speech was completed, the president of the Convention embraced Citizen Monroe and kissed him on both cheeks. While neither the English cabinet nor public viewed these antics with any favor, Lord Grenville confined himself to an ironic little note, saying he was sure Jay did not envy Monroe. If, he implied, Monroe enjoyed being kissed in public, the British government could not very well object.

On September 25 the secretary of state, Edmund Randolph, who had vigorously opposed Washington's wish to instruct Jay to negotiate a treaty, wrote to Monroe: "Notwithstanding all the pompous expectations, announced in the gazettes, of compensation to the merchants, the prospect of it is, in my judgment, illusory; and I do not entertain the most distant hope of the surrender of the western posts. Thus the old exasperations continue, and new ones are daily added. Judge then how indispensable it is that you should keep the French republic in good humor with us."

OTHER DIPLOMATS

On May 27, when Washington nominated Monroe for Paris, he also sent to the Senate the name of William Short, minister at The Hague and commissioner to Spain, to be minister at Madrid. Short, the first American career diplomat, had served as Jefferson's secretary at Paris. Two days later, his voice shaking with pleasure, the presiding officer, John Adams, read a message from the president:

> *United States 29 May 1794*
>
> *Gentlemen of the Senate*
>
> *I nominate John Quincy Adams, of Massachusetts, to be Minister Resident of the United States of America, to their high mightinesses the States general of the United Netherlands.*

The Senate cheerfully and unanimously confirmed the nomination of Adams to the post which his father had held as the first United States minister.

The great expansion of American shipping and foreign trade brought with it a widened need for consuls. Presidential appointments were made that year to Gibraltar, Leghorn, Bremen, Amsterdam, Teneriffe, St. Petersburg, and Dublin.

HAMILTON'S TROUBLES

Samuel Flagg Bemis' *Jay's Treaty* maintained what is probably the oddest thesis ever put forth by a historian that, in 1794, Hamilton dominated American foreign relations, military affairs, and fiscal policy. The Washington presidential papers, which Bemis indicates in his bibliography he failed to examine, disclose, instead, that Hamilton was a rather apathetic administrator, who received sharp chastisement from Washington.

In his directives to Jay, the president largely ignored Hamilton's advice, since he thought a commercial treaty of minor importance in relation to the overriding issue of peace. When Congress recommenced an earlier inquest as to whether Hamilton had violated laws providing for the use of foreign loans only for payments on foreign debt, whereas some funds had been transferred to the Bank of the United States, Hamilton asked Washington for a letter stating that he had approved all the transactions. He got little satisfaction from the President who replied on April 8:

> *I cannot charge my memory with all the particulars which have passed between us, relative to the disposition of the money borrowed. Your letters, however, and my answers… speak for themselves…*

> *As to verbal communications, I am satisfied and… I do not doubt that it was substantially as you have stated in the annexed paper, that I have approved of the measures which you, from time to time, have proposed to me for disposing of the Loans, upon the condition that what was to be done by you, should be agreeable to the Laws.*

Since the statement with its last critical phrase went to Congress and was made public, it provided Jefferson and Madison an opportunity to jeer privately at the supposed ignorance of the president on fiscal matters. In fact Washington had so clear a memory that he wrote to Hamilton on April 22: "I wish to have some explanation of your letter of yesterday… [as to] whether the appropriation now proposed… will not in some measure be contrary to the appropriation contained in my power of the 8th of August 1793."

The president had advised nieces and nephews that no excuse was better than a weak one. The secretary of the treasury replied the next day: "When I wrote my letter of the 21st instant I had entirely forgotten the existence of your two powers of the 8 of August, owing probably to the effect upon my memory of my sickness which soon after ensued." Hamilton referred to the "embarrassments" he would encounter if he did not do things in his way. The president replied: "It may be well for you to state to me what the embarrassments are which you suppose will arise." Hamilton produced a very long statement which Washington answered by a short note on April 27. Hamilton was directed to follow the instructions of August 8. The president added that he would have no objections whatever if Hamilton went to Congress to explain the "embarrassments which you consider as probable."

On July 2 Hamilton was blasted by the president, in reply to a letter he wrote concerning compensation to the British for vessels seized by the French in American waters. This was a matter which Congress had rejected: "My understanding... of this business... differs very widely from your interpretation of it." He pointed out that Congress had not approved, his was a constitutional presidency, he had been exceedingly careful to give an opinion only to the British, and he could not stretch his powers, as Hamilton recommended. The only thing for him to do was to tell the British minister that Jay was authorized to discuss the matter in London.

Even on appointments within the Treasury Department, Hamilton was given little discretion by the president. In a letter of June 24, Hamilton suggested a nominee for the minor post of collector at Hampton, Virginia, adding the names of those who had forwarded recommendations. The president replied that he was going to Virginia, and he would discuss the matter with the governor of the state.

THE RISE OF SECRETARY KNOX

In the critical years, the strongest man of the cabinet was the secretary of war, who was much too sensible to try to dominate his colleagues. Knox was a gifted and totally loyal administrator who followed the president's instructions and wishes as closely as possible. His great hulk absorbed any amount of work, even the crushing load imposed upon him in 1794. A check of the presidential diaries for the first half of the year indicates the president saw or corresponded with Knox about four times as often as with Hamilton and nearly always on much more complex business.

Knox administered within his department a great deal of what were considered to be foreign affairs. He had worked out treaties with the Creeks and Cherokees, which had been duly ratified by the Senate. He was endlessly engaged in establishing federal authority in the West under Indian treaties of the Confederation. He managed an extended, if weak, army-militia system along the frontiers, in cooperation with the state governors. He directed the Legion of the United States, the American army operating north of the Ohio.

He controlled a network of agents employed to pacify the Indians or to provide intelligence.

In 1794 Knox rose to his full strength. He had complete confidence in the president's judgment that there would be peace with Great Britain. His instructions to the army and to his agents were to avoid aggression and trouble at any cost. At the same time the congressional votes to expand the army, to establish a navy, and to provide defenses for the country's seaports, greatly increased his responsibilities.

On March 18 Knox made an effective suggestion to the president. He noted that, in general, the operations of the federal government had lessened the "patronage... influence... and dignity" of the state governors. The president had also frequently imposed on them "unpleasant duties" in enforcing federal neutrality laws. He suggested that it might "be a conciliatory and grateful measure to them, as Commanders of their Militia, to be the agents of the United States, in a certain degree, of the proposed fortifications... The Engineers might be directed to consult and take the opinions of the Governors upon the points most proper to be fortified... The Governors might also be requested to appoint some suitable person to superintend the erection of the works and also of the mounting of such Cannon... as are to be furnished by the respective States... By an arrangement of this sort it is conceived that the Governors would be kindly brought to act by system to support the general government."

Washington approved this plan, and the governors, many of whom had been revolutionary officers, responded with enthusiasm. Two states, Pennsylvania and New York, went so far, in fact, as to pass special acts for their defense, thus raising embarrassing constitutional questions. In New York, General von Steuben, long in retirement, volunteered a plan for fortifying the city of New York. He was subsequently appointed by the state as chairman of a committee to provide for northern defenses. Undoubtedly Knox's proposal influenced the subsequent hearty support to Washington from nearby governors, when he moved to break an insurrection in western Pennsylvania.

Both the president and Knox were anxious to have Indian delegations visit the capital that year, and many came. On June 14 the president wrote in his diary: "Had a meeting with the Chiefs of the Cherokee Indians, now in Philadelphia, at my house. The Secretaries of State, Treasury & War & Colo. Pickering were present. The great pipe was smoked by all. Delivered a speech to them in writing. Several of them spoke & after having eaten and drunk plentifully of cake & wine, they departed seemingly well pleased... being referred to Genl. Knox for further communication."

On July 11 the president received Paimingo, chief of the Chickasaws, and other chiefs. According to John Quincy Adams, who was present, a peace pipe, twelve to fifteen feet long, was brought out and everyone took whiffs from it. The president read a speech which was interpreted sentence by sentence. Then all had wine, punch, and cake. A few days later, at Knox's request, the president formally presented them with signed commissions.

Knox, in addition to handling armories, army, fortifications, and Indians, also worked on the authorized navy. He provided information and recommendations with great speed, and the president acted on them with decision. Following Indian attacks in Tennessee, Knox wrote the president that regular troops ought to be sent there but they could not be spared from Wayne. He therefore proposed that the president call into service the local militia, to be paid by federal funds and supplied with federal arms. On April 12 Washington wrote: "Your report dated the 11th instant, respecting the defense of Mero district is approved, and the Governor of the South Western Territory may be authorized to carry it into effect."

On April 15 Knox submitted to the president the first formal proposal for an American naval force. After he had discussed the matter with numerous shipbuilders and former naval officers, Knox recommended a program for construction of four ships of forty-four guns and two of thirty-six. He expressed prices, rather curiously, in pounds rather than dollars. His first preliminary estimate was that the larger ships would cost £34,100 each and the smaller, £27,300. Knox added that since the government was "of the whole people and not just a part only" it seemed proper to distribute the building among the ports of Charleston, New York, Boston, Philadelphia, Baltimore, and Norfolk. The following day Washington wrote Knox: "As soon as the most important points on which the master-builders have differed, are settled... and you can obtain means for carrying the law into effect, it is my desire that the work may be entered upon without delay."

On June 3 the president nominated and the Senate confirmed the first six captains of the regular navy: John Barry, Samuel Nicholson, Silas Talbot, Joshua Barney, Richard Dale, and Thomas Truxton. All had been revolutionary naval heroes who were to supervise ship construction. On July 25, long before there could be any ships, the captains met and designed uniforms for officers of the navy and the marine corps. Knox struck out the proposed "embroidery" as not suitable for a republican fleet.

Knox, his small salaried income steadily cut by price increases, was forced to think of resigning in order to provide for his large family. He asked the president for leave of absence in August, assuring him that things were under control and Hamilton could manage such business as the department's staff could not handle. He left for Maine on August 8 and thus missed receiving a rather immodest dispatch from General Wayne, dated August 28, which had been the goal of years of planning by General Knox:

> *It's with infinite pleasure that I now announce to you the brilliant success of the Federal army under my command with the combined force of the Hostile Indians & a considerable number of the Volunteers & Militia of Detroit on the 20th Instant, on the Banks of the Miamis, in the vicinity of the British post & Garrison.*

At Fallen Timbers, the last battle of the revolutionary war, Wayne, immensely cautious in preparing against any possible enemy surprises, attacked with such sudden force and fury that in an hour's battle, the astounded Indian, British, and Canadian army was totally annihilated as a fighting force. More impressive was the fact that Wayne beat over 2,000 of the enemy with fewer than nine hundred men. The nearby British garrison watched, helpless, as Wayne destroyed all the cornfields, as well as the houses and stores of Colonel Alexander McKee, the British agent in Ohio. Among those who received Wayne's special mention for bravery was Lieutenant William Henry Harrison.

MOUNT VERNON AND OTHER PROBLEMS

Sounding faintly offended, though this was not his intention, the president on July 13 wrote to his new Mount Vernon manager, William Pearce, who had complained of his numerous instructions: "I am sensible that I express my wishes faster than they can be accomplished; but by keeping them steadily in view you will fulfill them as fast as time and seasons will permit and this is all I can expect or do desire; but in order that my directions, when given, may not escape you, read my letters over frequently... or take from them at the time they are received such parts by way of memoranda to refresh your memory, as are necessary." The letters to Mount Vernon, picturing his acres in his mind as he wrote his instructions, appear to have been Washington's principal diversion from presidential duties.

Family problems, some trivial, plagued Washington. He had forwarded detailed instructions to Pearce to prepare a house in Alexandria for Fanny Washington. She wrote to the president to say that the cellar was damp and needed paving. He asked Pearce to do this work, adding: "This job will afford another week for Davis and his attendants, when one man in this City would begin and finish it... in half a day." It was an accurate guess. Washington learned from a subsequent report that the job had required six days.

Burges Ball asked his uncle to send down from Philadelphia "2 or 3 bushels of Chocolate Shells such as we've frequently drank Chocolate at Mount Vernon, as my Wife thinks it agreed with her better than any other Breakfast." The president politely replied that he would order the chocolate and have it placed on a ship to Virginia.

The president was once more brought into the troubled estate and family problems of Samuel Washington, his long-dead brother. Samuel's son, George Steptoe, had eloped in Philadelphia, the preceding year, with Lucy Payne, thereafter bringing his bride to his father's house, Harewood, at Charles Town. In September Dr. David Stuart informed Washington that there was to be a forced sale of Samuel's properties. He suggested that the president lend the estate a thousand pounds to prevent this. Washington replied on September 21: "The estate of my brother Samuel being involved, and left under wretched management, has already proved a heavy tax on me. Land which I sold twenty years ago... falling into his hands, and he thereby becoming paymaster to me, has... sunk me more than £800. For the board, education, and other expenses of his two sons, I am in a further advance for it, upwards of £1000 more, besides the support of his daughter Harriot." He added that giving a further thousand pounds would be a great hardship for him. He thought that Samuel's two sons had been extravagant, they had a mistaken idea of what their property was worth, and they seemed not to be "sensible, I believe, of the inconveniency of the advances I have made for their accommodation." If every other resource failed, Stuart was directed, nonetheless, to lend the money. The president did not, at this time, know of a footnote to this story. Six days previously Lucy Washington's recently widowed sister, Dolley Todd, had married, at Harewood, a rather troublesome member of Congress, James Madison.

"CREATED FREE"

Washington viewed slavery as abhorrent as well as uneconomic. His was a troublesome dilemma for he owned more slaves than his land could support. He noted that their productivity was but a fraction of that of white labor in Philadelphia. Unlike Jefferson, he had long refused to sell any of his slaves, no matter how pressing his financial problems, in order to avoid breaking up families. Sometime in 1793, in the midst of all his other problems, he resolved on a solution for his dilemma. So far as can be determined, he confided the plan to free all his slaves only to his family and to Tobias Lear.

After Arthur Young informed Washington that many farmers in the British Isles wanted to settle in America, the president in December 1793 provided

Young with a detailed report of all his Potomac holdings. He expressed a desire to rent to good farmers all Mount Vernon farms, except for the land around the mansion house. On May 6, 1794, he sent a copy of the letter to Tobias Lear in England, indicating that he would also like to sell all his western land holdings. He asked Lear to inquire in England for potential buyers. He added his reasons for selling or leasing most of his properties:

> *I have no scruple to disclose to you, that my motives for these sales (as hath been, in part, expressed to Mr. Young) are to reduce my income... to specialties [contractual income] that the remainder of my days may, thereby, be more tranquil and free from cares; that I may be enabled (knowing precisely my dependence) to do as much good with it as the resource will admit; for although, in the estimation of the world, I possess a good and clear estate, yet so unproductive is it, that I am oftentimes ashamed to refuse aids which I cannot afford unless I were to sell part of it to answer the purpose. (Private) Besides these, I have another motive which makes me earnestly wish for the accomplishment of these things, it is indeed more powerful than all the rest, namely to liberate a certain species of property which I possess, very repugnantly to my own feelings; but which imperious necessity compels... until I can substitute some other expedient by which expenses not in my power to avoid (however well disposed I may be to do it) can be defrayed.*

In Washington's mind, judging by his final directives, the problem was far more complex than that of giving them freedom, suffering a capital loss, and then forgetting about them. The older or sick workers who could not support themselves were to have pensions or other assured support. Those who wanted to work as free laborers had to be given employment. Children were to be educated and taught trades in order to prepare them for the future.

Washington's plan, had he been able to carry it out while living, might have had an enormous impact on the future of American society. Death came before he could provide this leadership but his will ordered his plan for freedom to be carried to completion.

WESTERN INSURRECTION

While called the Whiskey Rebellion, its supposed cause, the tax of as little as two cents a quart on domestic whiskey, was the flimsiest of pretexts for revolt. Hamilton had already demolished the arguments from western Pennsylvania, by his jocular declaration that if the tax hit the people of the area harder than anywhere else in the Union, they ought to try to be more temperate.

The insurrection, which extended from western Pennsylvania through Kentucky, had multiple causes, not all ignoble. Even before the 1776 revolution, friction existed between "the West" and the East. There were not infrequent complaints that taxes flowed eastward and no corresponding government benefits returned. When officials did appear, there was even more indignation as debtors were made to pay, the lawless were jailed, and squatters were kicked off land not theirs.

The federal government, after 1789, became an especial target as it moved to assert its sovereign authority over Indian affairs. The lawless, who had been accustomed to defrauding Indians of their land and to shooting them at will, were increasingly checked by federal officers; this aroused cries for liberty and the rights of man. British, Spanish, and French agents took advantage of the situation and freely circulated propaganda along with money and arms. The Jacobin or democratic societies were especially active in promoting both war with Britain and secession from the United States. The societies focused their attention, and eventually murderous tactics, not on their real objectives but on minor and unarmed officials of the federal government, the collectors of the alcohol tax.

On February 24 the president, according to his diary, "signed a Proclamation, offering a reward of 200 dollars for apprehending certain unknown persons who violently entered the office of the Collector of Revenue for the Counties of Westmoreland and Fayette in Pennsylvania and forced from him his commission." He had earlier noted therein that the "Collector for Bourbon" (County) in Kentucky had been having trouble.

In July disorders suddenly spread. While Hamilton was en route to Albany, Knox reported to the president on July 26 that Governor Mifflin of Pennsylvania was taking steps to suppress "the commotion in Allegheny county." It was soon evident to the president from numerous reports that armed rebellion against the federal government had broken out. He had no hesitation in signing a powerful proclamation, on August 7, 1794:

> And whereas the said combinations, proceeding in a manner subversive equally of the just authority of Government and of the rights of individuals, have hitherto effected their dangerous and criminal purpose... by endeavors to deter those who might be so disposed, from accepting offices... through fear of injury to persons and property, and to compel those who had accepted such offices, by actual violence to surrender or forbear the execution of them; by circulating vindictive menaces... [and] injuring and destroying the property of persons who were understood to have complied [with the law]; by inciting cruel and humiliating punishments upon private citizens... appearing to be friends of the law; by

intercepting the public officers on the highway, abusing, assaulting, and otherwise ill-treating them; by going to their houses in the night, gaining admittance by force, and committing other outrages, employing for these unwarrantable purposes the agency of armed banditti...

And whereas... the endeavors of the executive officers to conciliate a compliance with the laws, by explanations, by forbearance and even by particular accommodations... have been disappointed of their effect by the machinations of persons whose industry to excite resistance has increased with every appearance of disposition among the people to relax in their opposition and acquiesce in the laws, insomuch that many persons in the said Western parts of Pennsylvania have at length been hardy enough to perpetrate acts which I am advised amount to treason, being overt acts of levying war against the United States; the said persons having... proceeded in arms to the house of John Neville, inspector of revenue... having repeatedly attacked the said house with the persons therein, wounding some of them; having seized David Lenox, marshal of the district of Pennsylvania, who previous thereto, had been fired upon, while in the execution of his duty, by a party of armed men...

The president then quoted the act authorizing him to call out the militia "to execute the laws of the Union, suppress insurrections, and repel invasion." He noted that Associate Supreme Court Justice Wilson had declared that the laws were being opposed by such combinations of force as to render the usual processes of law no longer effective. Washington had therefore determined to order out the militia, since "the very existence of Government" was involved. He called on all "insurgents" to return to their abodes by September 1 or face the consequences.

On August 10 Washington acknowledged receipt of Charles Mynn Thruston's report of deep trouble in Kentucky. That state was moving to have its own war with Spain. The president said that he knew that the Jacobin societies were spreading disaffection there, in spite of "the unwearied endeavors of the General government to accomplish... what they seem to have most at heart, viz., the navigation of the Mississippi." They would be "dissatisfied under any circumstances, and under every exertion of government (short of a war with Spain, which must eventually involve one with Great Britain)." In referring to the Pennsylvania insurrection, he added:

If the laws are to be trampled upon, with impunity, and a minority (a small one too) is to dictate to the majority, there is an end put, at one stroke, to republican government, and nothing but anarchy and confusion is to be expected thereafter; for Some other man, or society, may dislike another Law and oppose it with equal

propriety until all Laws are prostrate, and everyone (the strongest I presume) will
carve for himself.

The president added that he was sure there would be people around who would be horrified equally by law-breaking and efforts to enforce the laws. As it turned out, the best example was the secretary of state, Edmund Randolph. He doubted whether Justice Wilson's letter had legal validity since it mentioned no particular laws that were violated. He opposed the use of force, fearing this would disrupt the Union. It was especially bad policy, he said, to draw militia from one state to enforce federal laws in another. He was afraid that Kentucky would secede, while western Pennsylvania would not only destroy the federal forces but would then turn against Wayne's army in Ohio. He foresaw a simultaneous civil war and war with England.

Randolph stood quite alone in the cabinet. The president directed that the militia of Pennsylvania, Maryland, Virginia, and New Jersey stand by in readiness. Governor Henry Lee of Virginia responded, offering the fullest support to Washington in suppressing rebellion and pledging that the president could count on him to lead the state's militia in person. Lee added that Patrick Henry had been much hurt by a story carried to him that Washington believed him to be "a factious seditious character." Lee thought this was unfortunate, for Henry was not only an able man but was now well disposed to the federal government. Washington's August 26 letter thanked Lee for his support and asked him to assure Patrick Henry that he had always "respected and esteemed him." He would be delighted to have him in the federal government, in any employment that he regarded as suitable, subject only to certain established practices, such as not having too many appointments in particular areas from a single state.

After issuing his proclamation, the president dispatched the attorney general and two federal agents, along with two Pennsylvanians, representing the state's governor, to negotiate with the insurgents. They were to be assured of full amnesty provided they submitted within the time set by the proclamation. By early September negotiations had failed, and Washington called the militia to active duty on September 9.

On September 25 he issued a final proclamation:

Whereas, from a hope that the combinations against the Constitution and laws of
the United States would yield to time and reflection, I thought it sufficient, in the
first instance, rather to take measures for calling forth the militia than immediately
to embody them; but the moment is now come... when every form of conciliation not
inconsistent with the being of Government has been adopted, without effect; when the

well-disposed in these countries are unable by their influence and example, to reclaim the wicked from their fury, and are compelled to associate in their own defense; when the proffered lenity has been perversely misinterpreted into an apprehension that citizens will march with reluctance; when the opportunity of examining the serious consequences of a treasonable opposition has been employed in propagating principles of anarchy, endeavoring through emissaries to alienate the friends of order from its support, and inviting enemies to perpetrate similar acts of insurrection; when it is manifest that violence would continue to be exercised upon every attempt to defend the laws; when, therefore, Government is set at defiance, the contest being whether a small proportion of the United States shall dictate to the whole Union, and at the expense of those who desire peace, indulge a desperate ambition.

Now, therefore, I GEORGE WASHINGTON, President of the United States, in obedience to that high and irresistible duty, consigned to me by the Constitution, "to take care that the laws be faithfully executed"; deploring that the American name should be sullied by the outrages of citizens on their own Government; commiserating such as remain obstinate from delusion; but resolved, in perfect reliance on that gracious Providence, which so signally displays its goodness towards this country, to reduce the refractory to a due subordination to the laws; do hereby declare and make known that, with a satisfaction which can be equaled only by the merits of the militia summoned into service from the States of New Jersey, Pennsylvania, Maryland, and Virginia, I have received intelligence of their patriotic alacrity, in obeying the call... that a force, which according to every reasonable expectation, is already in motion to the scene of disaffection...

That same day, Washington, on the basis of his intelligence reports, wrote to Burges Ball:

The Insurrection in the Western counties of this State is... the first <u>ripe fruit</u> of the Democratic Societies. I did not, I confess, expect their labors would come to maturity so soon; though I never had a doubt that such conduct would produce some such issue if it did not meet the frown of those who were well disposed to order and good government, in time; for can anything be more absurd, more arrogant, or more pernicious to the peace of Society, than for self-created bodies, forming themselves into <u>permanent</u> Censors, and under the shade of <u>Night</u>, in a conclave, resolving [that] the acts of Congress which have undergone the most deliberate and solemn discussion by the Representatives of the people... [are] unconstitutional [or] pregnant of mischief; and that all who vote contrary to their dogmas are actuated by selfish motives or under foreign influence; nay in plain terms are traitors to their Country... The Democratic Society of this place (from which the others have

emanated) was instituted by Mr. Genet for the express purpose of dissension, and
to draw a line between the people and the government, after he found the Officers
of the latter would not yield to the hostile measures in which he wanted to embroil
this Country.

THE COMMANDER IN CHIEF

General Washington's call to arms for defense of the Union met with an over-whelming response. It was the more impressive because Pennsylvania filled its quota of half the troops entirely from volunteers. Altogether at least 15,000 men assembled, more Americans than Washington had ever commanded, except for fleeting moments in the revolution. The governors of Pennsylvania, New Jersey, and Virginia placed themselves directly under the orders of the president. Well-known regiments such as the Philadelphia Light Horse and the Jersey and Macpherson Blues appeared. The officers included several revolutionary generals and colonels: Morgan, Lee, Irvine, and Hand. No fewer than five officers were nephews of the president. Henry Lee, newly created major general and second in command to Washington, wrote him that the federal union had to be preserved "at the risk of our lives and for-tunes." Marching through a sullen Virginia countryside to Cumberland, Maryland, Lee there joined the troops of his neighboring state. Pennsylvania and New Jersey troops went to a rendezvous at Carlisle, Pennsylvania.

On September 30 George Washington assumed his constitutional duties as "Commander in Chief... of the Militia of the several States, when called in to the actual service of the United States." At 10:30 that morning, accompanied by Alexander Hamilton and his secretary-nephew, Bartholomew Dandridge, he set out for Carlisle.

For the president, while the business was deadly serious, it was also some-thing of an outing. He spent as much time looking at the economy of the country as into military matters. The success of his call assured him that he had a force more than sufficient to battle down the insurgents, who had threatened to sweep across Pennsylvania and seize Philadelphia. Washington's first night on the road was further cheered when Knox's chief clerk galloped up with Wayne's dispatch announcing his great victory at Fallen Timbers. Ohio was now safe, and Pennsylvania, he knew, soon would be.

On October 2 the president examined a canal, under construction, to con-nect the Susquehanna and the Schuylkill Rivers. Its four brick locks he pro-nounced to be "admirably constructed." On October 13 he made diary notes on the country as far as Williamsport, Pennsylvania. From Philadelphia to

Reading, he found the whole road "very pleasant" and the farms "tolerably well cultivated." From Reading to Lebanon: "The country is extremely fine—The lands rich—The agriculture good, as the buildings also are, especially their barns, which are large and fine and for the most part good." As far as Carlisle the lands were good but not so well cultivated as in the Pennsylvania Dutch country. Turning south to Shippensburg, he found "thin and dry soil," but where it was better, "[t]he improvements along the road were mean—The farms scattered; the houses but indifferent—and the husbandry apparently bad." As they continued to Williamsport, the president noticed consistently better farming.

As he travelled, Washington reviewed various detachments of forces marching west. Approaching Carlisle, he found the governors of Pennsylvania and New Jersey awaiting him, their cavalry and infantry drawn up in honor of the commander in chief. For six days he worked to organize the militia who had arrived "in a very disjointed and loose manner; or rather I ought to have said in urging General Mifflin to do it; as I no otherwise took the command of the troops than to press them forward, and to provide them with necessaries for their March." Here Washington established the ranking officers in command: Lee, Mifflin, and Richard Howell, New Jersey's governor. General Edward Hand, his old revolutionary adjutant general, was here given the same assignment in this new national force.

On October 9 two deputies from the insurgents, William Findley and David Redick, were interviewed by the president. He recorded in his diary that Findley remarked there was now more disposition to submit in the West but that it had been not just the excise law that was opposed but "all law, and Government." Redick said that those who supported the government had, in fear of their lives, slept with "their Arms by their bed sides every night." Findley reported that the people of western Pennsylvania had presumed that opposition to the tax was universal in the country, that no troops could therefore be raised, and that rumors of an army coming were false. As soon as its reality became apparent, many of the leaders of the insurrection signed a submission and received amnesty.

The president noted that he had tried every form of conciliation and used force as a last resort. Now great expense had been incurred, winter was approaching, and he had to have "the most unequivocal <u>proofs</u> of absolute submission." The army would otherwise proceed as planned. Next day the two deputies asked if they could assemble a meeting in the counties to discuss submission. The president said that he saw no objection if everyone were unarmed. They were to be sure no gun was fired since the troops would then be forced to act. The army, he assured them, was not there to execute the laws nor to institute military trials, but simply to support the authority of civilian judges and marshals.

On October 10 the Pennsylvania and New Jersey troops began their march for Bedford. The president spent two days seeing them off, then drove south to Cumberland. There he found that nearly 6,000 Maryland and Virginia troops were in Pennsylvania or approaching the area. He interviewed deputies from Fayette County, Pennsylvania, who informed him that the people in the West were "very much alarmed at the approach of the army; but though submission is professed, their principles remain the same; and that nothing but coercion will reclaim and bring them to a due and unequivocal submission to the Laws."

After fixing the southern army's marching routes to Bedford, the president set out for that town on October 19 accompanied by General Lee. He recorded in his diary that they travelled over a road "opened by troops under my command in the Autumn of 1758." That afternoon the president and the three state governors met in Bedford to review the situation with Judge Richard Peters (who had stolen the British naval signals in 1781) and the federal attorney for Pennsylvania. While he was there the president received a letter from John Jay expressing optimism that he would reach agreement in London. In forwarding it to the secretary of state, Washington said that he presumed there would have to be a good deal of "give and take" between Jay and Grenville.

On October 20, having arranged the routes of all the armies westward, the president pressed their officers "to prepare with all the Celerity in their power for a forward movement." The army was ordered to march on October 23. Washington thereupon handed the command to General Lee, with a letter to be read to the troops:

> *There is but one point on which I think it proper to add a special recommendation. It is this, that every officer and soldier will constantly bear in mind that he comes to support the laws and that it would be peculiarly unbecoming in him to be in any way the infractor of them; that the essential principles of a free government confine the provinces of the Military to these two objects: first, to combat and subdue all who may be found in arms in opposition to the National will and authority; secondly, to aid and support the civil Magistrates in bringing offenders to justice. The dispensation of this justice belongs to the civil Magistrate and let it ever be our pride and our glory to leave the sacred deposit there unviolated... Being about to return to the seat of government, I cannot take my departure without conveying through you to the Army under your command the very high sense I entertain of the enlightened and patriotic zeal for the constitution and laws which has lead them cheerfully to quit their families and homes and the comforts of private life, to*

perform a long and fatiguing march and to encounter and endure the hardships and privations of a Military life...

No citizens of the United States can ever be engaged in a service more important to the Country. It is nothing less than to consolidate and to preserve the blessings of that Revolution which, at much expense of blood and treasure, constituted us a free and independent Nation...

Days of heavy rain followed, falling on the troops moving west and the president travelling east. On October 26, after crossing the Susquehanna, he wrote Hamilton: "I rode yesterday thro' the rain from York Town to this place, and got twice in the height of it hung... on the rocks in the middle of the Susquehanna, but I did not feel half as much for my own situation as I did on acct. of the Troops on the Mountains, and of the effect the rain might have on the roads through the glades." He hoped that Hamilton had arranged to ship the two or three ringleaders, already captured, to Philadelphia "for their winter quarters." Hamilton almost daily reported to the president the progress of the army westward in spite of the rains.

By November 17 some 150 insurgents had been rounded up and turned over to the federal court for trial. At that time Lee and Hamilton concluded that, with most of the rebels having signed submissions or being under arrest, the disorders had been smashed. Hamilton soon found ample evidence that the Jacobin societies had been the principal instruments of revolt against the government. The troops gradually returned home, leaving a small garrison under General Daniel Morgan in the west. In December Lee and his troops returned to Virginia after learning that his efforts to support the Union and Washington had received the disapproval of the Virginia Assembly. The Jeffersonians had chosen a new governor in his place.

STATE OF THE UNION

The president hurriedly returned to Philadelphia to attend the opening session of Congress set for November 3. More than two weeks elapsed thereafter before Congress had a quorum. This gave the president time, now that the west was peaceful, to turn his attention to John Jay, to Mount Vernon, and to his annual message. To Jay he wrote at the beginning of November:

[Your letter] of the 5th of August dawns more favorably upon the success of your mission than any that had preceded it; and for the honor, dignity and interest of

this country; for your own reputation and glory; and for the peculiar pleasure and satisfaction I should derive from it, as well on private as on public considerations, no man more ardently wishes you <u>complete</u> success than I do... So to deserve success, by employing the means with which we are possessed to the best advantage, and trusting the rest to the all wise disposer, is all that an enlightened public and the virtuous and well-disposed part of the community, can well expect... Against the malignancy of the discontented, the turbulent and the vicious, no abilities, no exertions, nor the most unshaken integrity, are any safeguard.

As far as depends upon the Executive, measures preparatory for the worst, while it hopes for the best, will be pursued; and I shall endeavor to keep things in status quo, until your negotiation assumes a more decisive form, which I hope will soon be the case, as there are many hotheads and impetuous spirits among us, who can, with difficulty, be kept in bounds...

The Self-created societies... have been the fomenters of the Western disturbances but, fortunately, they have precipitated a crisis for which they were not prepared... This has afforded an occasion for the people of this country... to show their attachment to the Constitution and the laws; for I believe that five times the number of militia that was required, would have come forward, if it had been necessary...

A subsequent note to Jay on December 18 pointed out that "the western insurrection has terminated highly honorably for this country... without spilling a drop of blood. In the eyes of foreigners among us, this affair stands in a high point of view."

On November 2 the president resumed his long weekly letters to his Mount Vernon manager. This letter made clear that William Pearce, more than any of the long preceding line to whom he had entrusted his affairs, had won his full confidence: "As the accident I met with in June last, prevented my riding about my farms when I was last at home, I should have been very glad to have made another visit to it, in the course of last month, knowing if I did not do it then, it would not be in my power to do it before April, as Congress will, more than probably, sit till March, and the roads during that month will be in no condition to travel. The perfect confidence, however, which I place in your care, judgment and integrity, makes me quite easy under the disappointment, which I should not have been, if my affairs were in the hands of a person of whom I did not entertain the same favorable opinion." There followed a summary of the main objectives he hoped to achieve by his six-year plan for Mount Vernon, together with numerous detailed suggestions.

On November 19, at noon, Washington delivered his sixth annual message on the state of the Union. The president, strong in his success, delivered his speech with such force and feeling that his highly critical audience heard him with "the utmost reverence and attention." He praised General Wayne for his victory and announced the first successful coinage by the United States mint (which had sent a silver dollar to him while he was with the troops). He noted that lawless American marauders on Creek lands had been thrown out through the efforts of the United States and Georgia. A proposed settlement at what is now Erie, Pennsylvania, had been stopped at the request of the Six Nations, in order to bring them to a peaceful feeling.

On the western insurrection, Washington was, as he had informed Jay he intended to be, "prolix." His was a thorough and documented account of the origin and course of the revolt. He threw down the gauntlet, in stronger terms than he had ever used publicly, to those of the opposition who, claiming to be democratic or republican, were, in fact, neither. He spoke of the "self-created societies," operating among the law-abiding citizens of western Pennsylvania, who stirred up the "vicious and turbulent," not over a particular law but against "all order." In high praise of the troops and of the cooperating states, the president said:

> *It has been a spectacle, displaying to the highest advantage, the value of republican Government, to behold the most and the least wealthy of our citizens, standing in the same ranks, as private soldiers; preeminently distinguished by being the army of the constitution, undeterred by a march of three hundred miles over rugged mountains, by the approach of an inclement season, or by any other discouragement...*

> *To every description, indeed, of citizens, let praise be given. But let them preserve in their affectionate vigilance over that precious depository of American happiness, the Constitution of the United States...*

> *Having thus fulfilled the engagement which I took, when I entered into office, "to the best of my ability to preserve, protect and defend the Constitution of the United States," on you gentlemen, and the people by whom you are deputed, I rely for support.*

George Thatcher, congressman from Maine, wrote his wife that, at this point of the speech, "I felt a strange mixture of passions that I cannot describe. Tears started into my eyes, and it was with difficulty I could suppress an involuntary effort to swear that I would support him." Elizabeth Smith shortly afterwards described her feelings; "It really seemed as tho' we were addressed by a far superior being than any here below."

Although the president was not to learn of it for months, John Jay and Lord

Grenville, a few hours before he delivered this message, had signed a treaty which declared that "there shall be a firm inviolable and universal peace, and a true and sincere friendship between His Britannic Majesty, His Heirs and Successors, and the United States of America." On December 14 Jay wrote to Tench Coxe, revenue commissioner of the Treasury: "The best disposition towards us prevails here… Next to the king, our President is more popular in this country than any man in it."

In 1765 when George Grenville introduced the Stamp Act which taxed the American colonies, his youngest son, William, was only five years old. At thirty-five, in an act of great statesmanship, William, Lord Grenville, thus terminated nearly thirty years of intervening hostility and bitterness. In America the document which he signed bears Jay's name but it might more aptly be called Grenville's treaty.

TWELVE

PEACE WITH
GREAT BRITAIN

1795

TWO DAYS AFTER delivering his annual message, Washington turned to another vexing problem, relations with Spain. On November 21, 1794, he informed Congress that, while the American commissioners at Madrid had made every effort to reach agreement, he had received intimations from Spain that they would prefer another negotiator. He was amenable to this idea, in spite of his confidence in the Americans at Madrid. He was therefore nominating "Thomas Pinckney, to be Envoy Extraordinary of the U. S. to his Catholic majesty, for the purpose of negotiating of and concerning the navigation of the river Mississippi, and such other matters relative to the confines of their territories and the intercourse to be had thereon, as the mutual interests and general harmony of neighborhood and friendly nations require should be precisely adjusted and regulated, and of and concerning the general commerce between the said United States and the Kingdoms and Dominions of his said Catholic majesty."

Behind this clumsy verbiage lay the fact that Spain had been procrastinating for years. When, as an additional means of delay, Spain complained that the American envoys were not of high enough rank, Washington took the court at its word and dispatched the American minister at St. James' to Madrid. Jay's letter of August 5 to the president, outlining the major points on which agreement was expected with the British, had inserted a phrase "for 'there is a *tide* in human affairs,' of which every moment is precious." Jay added that this was for the president's "private satisfaction." This was an apparently prearranged signal from Jay to Washington to say the British would back American claims to navigation of the Mississippi, in which, by the 1783 treaty, they would share. If Spain made trouble, she would have no support from Canada. Washington's reply of November 1, carried by a friendly hand to London, said: "As it has been observed, there is a 'tide in human affairs' that ought always to be watched." Thus Pinckney was informed he was to proceed to Spain, in accordance with Jay's judgment. With the Spanish garrisons isolated, the president could lead from strength.

The president also took steps to keep the turbulent Kentuckians in line so they would not start a private war with Spain while Pinckney was en route to Madrid. He dispatched Colonel James Innes to the state capital to outline the long and serious efforts made by the federal government to secure the navigation of the Mississippi. On April 17, 1795, the secretary of state informed the president that Innes had sent a report from "Washington court-house... By a letter from the Governor of Kentucky to him, it is clear that his mission has been accepted most cordially and that it has had its full effect; as well proving its policy as engaging the Executive on the side of your measures. Shelby expresses himself in strains of high compliments to you for your exertion on the subject of the Mississippi." Randolph, in addition, mentioned that he had received a letter from Washington, Pennsylvania, which praised the good conduct of the army troops, stationed there because of the insurrection.

RESIGNATION OF KNOX

Henry Knox, risen from bookselling to head the American artillery, succeeded George Washington as commander of the fragment of the army which he left behind in December 1783. As secretary at war he became the first permanent member of Washington's cabinet, but soon his title changed from "at" to "of war." The ablest and most effective of all Washington's cabinet officers, he served the longest. He was as steadfastly loyal to country and president as he had been to country and general in the war. Before he retired, he provided the president with information on the progress of the navy (slow), the coastal fortifications (going forward well), and the size of the army. There were 3,629 noncommissioned and private men in the forces, of whom 369 were assigned to Atlantic forts. Most of the remainder were in Ohio. On December 29 Knox handed Washington a final report on Indian affairs:

To retrace the conduct of the Government of the United States toward the Indian tribes since the adoption of the present Constitution, cannot fail to afford satisfaction to every philosophic and humane mind. A constant solicitude appears to have existed in the Executive and Congress not only to form treaties of peace with the Indians upon principles of Justice, but to impart to them all the blessing of civilized life, of which their condition is susceptible. That a perseverance in such principles and conduct will reflect permanent honor upon the national character cannot be doubted. At the same time it must be acknowledged that the execution of the good intentions of the public, is frequently embarrassed with perplexing considerations.

The desires of too many frontier white people to seize by force or fraud the neighboring Indians' lands, has been and still continues to be an unceasing cause of jealousy and hatred on the part of the Indians... This appears to be a principal cause of Indian wars... An adequate police force seems to be wanting either to prevent or punish the depredations of the unruly. It would afford a considerable pleasure could the assertion be made on our part, that we have considered the murders of Indians the same as the murders of whites, and have punished them accordingly. This however is not the case. The irritated passions on account of savage cruelty are generally too keen in the places where trials are had, to convict and punish for the killing of an Indian... An adequate remedy ought to be provided...

It is certainly an evil to be involved in hostilities with tribes of savages amounting to two or three thousand, as is the case north west of the Ohio. But this evil would be greatly increased were a general Indian war to prevail south of the Ohio, the Indian warriors of the four nations in that quarter not being much short of fourteen thousand...

It seems that our own experience would demonstrate the propriety of endeavoring to preserve a pacific conduct in preference to a hostile one with the Indian tribes... There is a responsibility of our national character, that we should treat them with kindness and even liberality. It is a melancholy reflection that our modes of population have been more destructive to the Indian nations, than the conduct of the conquerors of Mexico and Peru. The evidence of this is the utter extirpation of nearly all the Indians in the most populous parts of the Union. A future historian may mark the causes of this destruction of the human race in sable colours. Although the present Government of the United States cannot with propriety be involved in the opprobrium, yet is seems necessary, however, in order to render their attention upon this subject strongly characteristic of their justice, that some powerful attempts should be made to tranquilize the frontiers...

Upon the most mature reflection... arising from the experience of several years, [the subscriber] humbly conceives all attempts to preserve peace with the Indians will be found inadequate, short of an arrangement somewhat like the following:

That a line of military posts... be established upon the frontiers within the Indian boundary and out of the jurisdiction of any State, provided consent can be obtained for the purpose from the Indian tribes [and] garrisoned with regular troops... If any murder or theft be committed upon any of the white Inhabitants by an Indian, [his] tribe shall be bound to deliver him to the nearest military post, in order to be tried and punished by Court Martial... All [white] persons who shall be assembled or embodied in arms on any lands belonging to Indians... for the purpose of warring against the Indians or of committing depredations upon any Indian town or persons or property, shall thereby become liable and subject to the rules and articles of War...

On December 30 Washington wrote to Knox to accept his resignation, wishing "that it was otherwise. I cannot suffer you, however to close your public service, without uniting with the satisfaction which must arise in your own mind from a conscious rectitude, my most perfect persuasion that you have deserved well of your Country. My personal knowledge of your exertions, while it authorizes me to hold this language, justifies the sincere friendship which I have ever borne for you, and which will accompany you in every situation of life, being with affectionate regards, always yours."

To replace Knox, Washington followed the policy, first established, rather unwillingly with Edmund Randolph, of promotion from within the government. Timothy Pickering, who had been Washington's rather ineffective quartermaster general during the revolution, was advanced from head of the post office to the War Department. Pickering, in little over four years at his previous job, had added thousands of miles of post roads and increased the country's post offices from 89 to 450. In addition to these duties, Pickering, whose benevolent attitude to the Indians was well known, was repeatedly chosen by the president, from 1789 onwards, as special peace commissioner to the Indians. In this work he reported directly to Henry Knox. A man of the utmost integrity, Pickering was highly qualified to complete Knox's efforts to establish peace with all the tribes. As secretary of war, Pickering proved so able that, in August, Washington also assigned him duties as secretary of state. This was a fast rise to responsibilities greater than those which had been borne by Jefferson, Hamilton, or Knox.

Pickering's clear and sharp reports to the president indicate that he possessed unusual administrative ability. In at least one area he improved on the methods of Knox, who was inclined to bundle up voluminous correspondence and send it, undigested, to the president. Pickering made summaries or abstracts, and where correspondence or proposed legislation was extensive, he pointed out the crucial points which required the president's reading. Washington expressed his gratification at this considerate approach. Pickering enlivened his letters to the president with dry New England humor: "The writer, David Campbell of the Southwestern territory, begged [this] might be presented; otherwise the Secretary of War would not have troubled the President with its perusal. It contains merely an eulogy on Gov. Blount… He aims at the poetic style, perhaps very properly, as poets deal in fiction." In reporting an officer's resignation, he added: "From the information heretofore received by the Secretary, the resignation is not to be regretted." He summed up his job to the British minister as long hours of drudgery, for pay so low he had to live on "mutton, mush and cold water."

On January 8 and 9, just after Pickering assumed office, the Senate ratified treaties with the Cherokees, the Six Nations, and the Oneida. The first had been negotiated by Knox, the latter two by Pickering, in the preceding year. Soon thereafter Wayne reported to the War Department that representatives of seven of the principal tribes north of the Ohio had requested peace talks. He added that British agents were at work, stirring up murders by Indians, and he feared that this would once again inflame Kentucky against the Union. Pickering prepared lengthy instructions to Wayne on his negotiations. The Indians were to be assured, above all, that they owned their land and that no American was permitted by law to purchase it, or otherwise come into its possession, without approval of the federal authorities. In March Pickering informed Wayne, in confidence, that the British had agreed to withdraw all garrisons from American territory.

HAMILTON ALSO

The Syrett edition of Hamilton's letters contains an undated, unaddressed note written by Hamilton in 1794, to someone in Europe, conceivably his sister-in-law, Angelica Church, saying that he was "heartily tired" of his situation in the cabinet and that he intended to resign. Before leaving he gave the president the unpleasant news that there would be a budget deficit for the year of more than $2 million and the Treasury would have to borrow to cover it. He informed Washington of an attempt by the French consul, J-B. Petri, at the direction of the French minister, to violate the American laws against arming privateers. He added: "I fear that agents of France have not ceased to countenance proceedings which not only contravene our neutrality but may prove a source of very serious expense to the United States."

Hamilton resigned effective January 31, 1795, and Washington wrote him two days later: "In every relation which you have borne to me, I have found that my confidence in your talents, exertions and integrity, has been well placed. I the more freely render this testimony of my approbation because I speak from opportunities of information which cannot deceive me, and which furnish satisfactory proof of your title to public regard. My most earnest wishes for your happiness will attend you in your retirement and you may assure yourself of the sincere esteem, regard and friendship of, dear Sir, your affectionate…" The president appointed as his successor, Hamilton's able and hard-working assistant, Oliver Wolcott, Jr., who was about the same age as Hamilton was when he was originally appointed.

THE JAY TREATY

On February 23, 1795, Jay replied to the president's November 1 letter, "Your remarks relative to my negotiations are just and kind. I assure you nothing on my part has been wanting to render the conclusion of them as consonant as was possible to your expectations and wishes. Perfectly apprised both of my duty and responsibility I determined not to permit my judgment to be influenced by any considerations but those of public good under the direction of my instructions."

The British foreign minister, Lord Grenville, received Jay promptly upon his arrival in London on June 15. He was soon dining with the cabinet, the prime minister, and the lord chancellor. King George III, clearly delighted that Washington had stood up so well to the French, was more than cordial. By July 21 Jay could inform the president that Simcoe had been ordered out of Ohio. He presumably did not hear of the cabinet's letter to Lord Dorchester, saying that the government expected to settle all issues with Mr. Jay, but the king himself told Jay he could count on a successful mission. By August 1 he had assurances that the British government would render "complete and impartial justice," in the case of the captured ships. Although the British minister at Philadelphia had expressed doubts that his government ever would pay damages, Grenville agreed that, where the processes of British law were insufficient, the government itself would pay the claims which were to be processed by a joint commission. This assured the first objective of the president.

The surrender of the British forts was easily negotiated but, as Jay wrote, the British could not avoid pressing the merchants' claims for American debts. Jay worked out a simple *quid pro quo* along exactly the line of the ship claims. The United States would pay, where American law processes failed. Jay, who hated slavery, described the southerners' claims to compensation for slaves who had escaped to freedom, as "odious." He simply ignored the matter.

The negotiations took five months. When the treaty was signed, Jay wrote to Lord Grenville: "To use an Indian figure, may the hatchet be buried for ever, and with it all the animosities which sharpened, and which threatened to redden it." Jay wrote of Grenville, as he might well have done of himself: "Few men would have persevered in such a dry, perplexing business, with so much patience and temper as [he] has done."

On March 6, 1795, Jay expressed to the president his considered opinion that the British government had been so persuaded of the inevitability of war, by the violent American clamors and the reception to Genet, that orders to prepare for it had gone to Lord Dorchester. The president's subsequent decision to send the chief justice of the United States to London was taken as proof of his firm desire for peace. "The perfect and universal confidence reposed in your personal character excluded every doubt of your being sincere." The British government had determined, therefore, "to give conciliation a fair experiment, by doing us substantial justice and by consenting to such arrangements favourable to us, as the national interests and habitual prejudices would admit... to admit us into their East and West India dominions, and into all their continental American territories, were decided deviations from their former policy, and tended to shock ancient prejudices... Whatever the American opinion of it may prove to be, the administration here think it very friendly to us; and it could not in the present moment have been made more so, without exciting great discontent and uneasiness in this country." Jay continued:

> *You have doubtless heard that the merchants concerned in the American trade gave me a dinner. The principal Cabinet Ministers were present, and about two hundred merchants. Many toasts were given. When 'The President of the United States' was given, it was proposed to be with three cheers, but they were prolonged (as if by preconcert, but evidently not so) to six.*

> *I have great reason to believe that the king, the Cabinet, and nation were never more unanimous in any system than that of conciliation with us...*

> *This system rests principally on their confidence in the uprightness, independence, and wisdom of your conduct... The idea which everywhere prevails is, that the quarrel between Britain and America was a family quarrel, and that it is time it*

should be made up. For my part, I am for making it up, and for cherishing this
disposition on their part by justice, benevolence, and good manners on ours. To cast
ourselves into the arms of this or any other nation, would be degrading, injurious
and puerile; nor, in my opinion, ought we to have any political connection with
any foreign power.

Two copies of the Grenville treaty were lost at sea, owing to action by French privateers. A third copy, after long delays, was delivered to the president on March 7. As he read it, he could clearly see the care with which Jay had followed his instructions and how much he had accomplished for the public good. First and foremost, he had achieved peace and British goodwill, the points nearest the president's heart. Second, the British agreed to make compensation for all seized vessels. Third, all British military posts were to be handed over to the United States in 1796, thus freeing the country of endless bloodshed and expense. Finally, financial claims on both sides were to go to two joint commissions. While this process was to take a long time, the United States paid $2.8 million to settle its prewar debts, and Great Britain handed over more than $10 million for the seized ships. Vague boundary lines were to be settled by a joint survey team and a joint commission. For the first time the British opened the West Indies to small American vessels and their East Indies ports to all American ships. Although potential sources of friction still remained between the United States and Great Britain, a maritime power at war, the British navy now became an important shield against aggressive France.

The Grenville treaty of 1795 provided a far more satisfactory recognition of American independence than the pact which Jay had negotiated thirteen years before. Europeans then expected that the thirteen former colonies could not hold together and would eventually fall into French or British hands. Now Great Britain conceded not only that the United States was entirely sovereign but was too strong ever to be a French or English satellite. The United States had become Britain's most important customer, as well as a vitally needed supplier of provisions to the West Indies, and food and raw materials to a Great Britain at war. Washington's peaceful measures in the Northwest clearly indicated that the United States had no desire to attack Canada, while, as a strong country, she would be an effective buffer against any threats to Canada from Spanish territories.

On March 3, just before Congress adjourned, the president issued a summons to the Senate to reconvene on June 8. He swore the secretary of state to secrecy on the treaty. With this diplomatic triumph in his pocket, the president could devote his mind to other matters.

A NATIONAL UNIVERSITY

Washington's work in promoting the James and Potomac River canals had brought him, in 1785, a Virginia grant of shares in the two canal companies. Since they had a face value of $32,000, he had been much embarrassed by the gift. He subsequently requested the governor and legislature to permit him to hold them in trust for educational institutions to be selected by him. This provision was ratified by the Virginia Assembly. The president's first annual message to Congress asked for federal aid to higher education and suggested the desirability of a national university. By 1794 Washington was telling John Adams that such a university had been long "talked of" but nothing had been done. What impelled Washington to further work on the matter was a proposal sent to John Adams to transfer the faculty of the University of Geneva to America because of disorders in Europe.

On January 28, 1795, Washington in a more refined manner wrote to the district commissioners to say that a university for the federal city "has frequently been the subject of conversation." He felt that it was a pity so many young Americans had to study in Europe where they were exposed to "principles unfriendly to republican government." He asked the commissioners to look into the cost and to draw up proposals.

On February 15 Thomas Jefferson wrote to the president about the Geneva proposal, indicating that its sponsorship had been turned down by the Virginia legislature. He suggested that the canal shares held by Washington might be used for this purpose. Washington replied on March 16 that he had never expected his shares to form more than part of the cost of a university and, in any case, "not to induce an entire college to emigrate." He now planned to donate his shares to a new national university which he preferred to have on the Virginia side of the federal territory. The central location within the Union would help bring together boys from all the states. The students would have the advantage of being able to study the operations of government. Washington could not resist inserting a little jollity at Jefferson's expense. He was not certain whether bringing the Genevans over was such a good idea for "having been at variance with the levelling party of their own country, the measure might be considered as an aristocratical movement by those who, without any just cause that I have been able to discover, are continually sounding the alarm bell of aristocracy."

On March 16 the president outlined his plans to Governor Robert Brooke of Virginia. He pointed out, as he had done to Jefferson, the desirability of having the fullest educational facilities at home, rather than sending young Americans abroad. He continued:

The time is therefore come, when a plan of Universal education ought to be adopted in the United States. Not only do the exigencies of public and private life demand it; but if it should ever be apprehended that prejudice would be entertained in one part of the Union against another; an efficacious remedy will be, to assemble the youth of every part under such circumstances, as will, by the freedom of intercourse and collision of sentiment, give to their minds the direction of truth, philanthropy, and mutual conciliation.

It has been represented, that a University, corresponding with these ideas, is contemplated to be built in the federal city; and that it will receive considerable endowments. This position is so eligible from its centrality, so convenient to Virginia, by whose legislature the shares were granted, and in which part of the federal district stands, and combines so many other conveniences, that I have determined to vest the Potomack shares in the University. [*]

The president then said that he thought it might be more agreeable to the Virginia legislature if his James River shares went to a college ("seminary") to be established within Virginia. From the college, students could proceed to further work at the national university. It would be better if all the shares were concentrated in a single institution but he wanted to "give a particular attention to Virginia," with these shares. The Virginia Assembly subsequently ducked the issue, requesting Washington to give them to such an institution as he saw fit. The shares eventually ended up as a portion of the endowment of what became Washington and Lee University.

WASHINGTON CITY

On May 24, Washington wrote to Alexander White, whom he had just appointed as commissioner of the District of Columbia:

The year 1800 will be soon upon us. The necessity therefore of hurrying on the public buildings, and other works of a public nature; and executing of them with economy; the propriety of preventing idleness in those who have day, or monthly wages, and

---

[*] From the history of Washington appearing in *The Georgetowner,* June 6, 1968: "November 13, 1874. Columbian College has opened as Columbian University this fall... It now seems unlikely we will ever see the federally sponsored university envisioned by John Quincy Adams, since there is a great deal of opposition to it, led by President Eliot of Harvard." This university was subsequently named for George Washington.

imposition by others, who work by measure, by the piece, or by contract, and seeing that all contracts are fulfilled, with good faith, are too obvious to dwell on, and are not less important then to form plans, and establish rules for conducting and bringing to a speedy and happy conclusion this great and arduous business.

A severely troublesome problem of the capital site was its thick forests. The avenues and streets in the L'Enfant plan had to be chopped out slowly, day by day, with hand labor and axes. Even after several years, this work was far from complete. From the descriptions of travellers who wandered through the mazes in 1795 and 1796, it seems to have been a miracle that L'Enfant could have penetrated some of the areas, have surveyed them so carefully and quickly, and have dreamed of a better Versailles in such a wilderness.

To a certain extent Washington had pushed the enterprise, trusting to heaven, nerve, and luck. Philadelphia, in the meantime, complacently went on building a permanent house for the president. Since sales of individual lots in Washington were slow, the commissioners had drawn in speculators, including Robert Morris, under terms which would provide monthly construction money for the capitol, president's house, and streets. The speculators were overextended; by September they were far behind in their payments and the commissioners begged Washington for help. He wrote to Morris on September 14 urging him to meet his commitments. He added: "There are many valuable Stone cutters and other workmen now engaged; a number of laborers are employed on the public buildings… Everything seems to progress as well as can be reasonably expected under the embarrassments which have been encountered… Without the aid required… the workmen *must* be discharged… the buildings will be left not only in a stagnant state but in a hurtful situation; involving consequences which are too obvious to need enumeration."

The last thing Washington wanted was to ask Congress for funds, for it would revive all the old controversy as to where the capital should be. As the winter drew on and there was a continuing shortage of money, Washington and the commissioners agreed that an approach would have to be made to the state of Maryland for loans to the federal government. The president said that if that failed he would try Congress, because he did not intend to abandon the capital.

SALES OF WASHINGTON LANDS

Though benumbed by work, the president pursued with vigor his attempts to sell his land holdings so that he could present to the nation a program leading to a voluntary abolition of slavery. As was only too soon to be evident, the

temper of Virginia and of the South in general with regard to the federal government and slavery, was too sour to be touched by anything but example.

The president's extensive acres were scattered through New York, Ohio,
Pennsylvania, Maryland, Virginia, and Kentucky. He had never been a specu-
lator, having held most of the land he began to acquire at eighteen until his
presidency. Many farms had been settled on long leases or were in troubled
areas, which made their sale difficult. There were no proper estate agents, and
Washington had to pick from old friends or, from their recommendations,
those who might persuade people to buy. Washington's correspondence was
enormous to all points of the compass. It resulted that year in a reduction of
a few thousand acres of his holdings but this was only a small beginning.

MONROE

When Jay wrote to Washington to express his own and the British displeasure
at Monroe's behavior in Paris, Washington replied that perhaps Monroe's
praise of France displeased the British but her enemy's stress over her
American alliance might have helped to expedite Jay's negotiations.

The reactions to the Jay treaty by the American ministers at The Hague and
in Paris were markedly different. Young John Quincy Adams wrote to Jay on
January 9: "The value of peace and neutrality is nowhere more forcibly felt
than at this moment in the country where I am. Its situation becomes more
and more critical from day to day. In the terrible agitation between the dismal
alternative of conquest or civil war, it feels at the same moment all the terrors
of a torrent rushing from without, and a volcano bursting from within."
Adams noted that bad weather alone seemed to be holding the French armies
from their attack on Holland.

Monroe, on the other hand, wrote Jay of French uneasiness about the
treaty. He demanded a copy for their government. Jay replied that the French
did not seem to have the "confidence in the honor and good faith of the
United States which they certainly merit." He pointed out the United States
was entirely independent and sovereign and the agreement contained a
clause stating that the pact did not affect any previous treaties, including the
one with France. He had negotiated under the promise of secrecy, and it
would not be becoming to deliver it without permission nor to have it submitted to the "judgment of the councils of a *foreign nation*." Not until late in
the summer did Monroe receive the text, whereupon he set to work to defeat
its major aims of peace and neutrality.

RATIFICATION OF THE JAY TREATY

Washington, that spring after the congressional adjournment, made a quick trip to Mount Vernon, returning to Philadelphia on May 2. There he found Randolph and Fauchet, the French minister, almost at sword's point. Randolph had informed James Monroe in Paris that Fauchet's behavior was terrible. He had raked up every charge he could find against the United States, which he presented in an "indecent" letter, a term employed by Jefferson in writing of Genet. The worst, however, was to come; in the middle of the Senate negotiations on the Jay treaty, a new French minister, Pierre Adet, appeared in Philadelphia to take Fauchet's place and to break the peace with England. Adet was to be the most ill-mannered of the ministers sent by France to America during Washington's presidency.

While the Senate was assembling, the Jeffersonian press bitterly attacked the president on the treaty, though none of the papers knew its provisions. Washington gave the Senate the documents on June 8, including the text of his instructions to Jay. Resolutions to make the treaty and its accompanying papers public were quickly voted down. The clause concerning commerce with the British West Indies, which permitted small American vessels for the first time to trade there but which forbade re-export of colonial products, including cotton, aroused much debate and many of the president's supporters found this provision objectionable. They resolved therefore to approve the treaty without this clause, while asking the president to hold further negotiations with Great Britain on the West Indies trade. During debate the southern states moved their objections to Jay for having failed to provide compensation for freed slaves, but only southern senators voted affirmatively. On June 24 the treaty carried, without the offending clause, by a vote of twenty to ten, with seven southern senators voting no.

About the first of July the secretary of state, possibly without the knowledge or approval of the president, provided the French minister with a copy of the Jay treaty. It appeared shortly thereafter, in full, in the Philadelphia opposition press, with the explanation that Senator Thomson Mason of Virginia had determined to give it out, in order to prevent false reports from circulating. The president himself was about ready to make it public but he was forestalled by a few days. Nevertheless, it was made to appear that a "patriot" had acted to let Americans know of a secret treaty, dangerous to their welfare.

Washington took advantage of the presence of the Senate in Philadelphia to make a number of appointments, including army officers and port collectors as well as consuls for Algiers, Tripoli, and Tunis. He also sent in the names of Benjamin Hawkins, George Clymer, and Andrew Pickens as commissioners to negotiate a treaty with the Creek Indians, who were causing much damage in Georgia and the Cumberland region.

John Jay returned to America to find that he had been elected governor of New York. He therefore resigned from the Supreme Court. In his place, Washington offered the nomination to John Rutledge, chief justice of South Carolina, but his reply could not reach the capital before the Senate adjourned.

ARMAGEDDON

Shortly after Jay was selected for his mission, Adams wrote to Jefferson that, while he did not expect Jay to achieve a brilliant success, he hoped that he could at least obtain peace. Like Washington, Adams tried a little humor on the former secretary of state. He said that a war would add $200 million to the national debt, force the building of a big army, and perhaps eventually bring in a monarchy: "Those who dread Monarchy and Aristocracy and at the same time advocate War are the most inconsistent of all Men."

Once the treaty terms were made public, there began a bitterly divisive struggle in America. It was a curious spectacle, for most of the old revolutionary generals and colonels lined up solidly for peace, while those who sought war included Madison and Jefferson who had never served in the armed forces.

The mobs again swung into action in the principal seaports. Jefferson reported to Madison on August 3: "Hamilton... spoke on its behalf in the meeting at New York, and his party carried a decision in favor of it by a small majority. But the Livingstonians appealed to stones & clubs and beat him & his party off the ground." The treaty and a British flag were burned in Charleston by a mob which included many Frenchmen. Other French joined a Philadelphia group in throwing rocks at the British minister's house after listening to inflammatory orations by followers of Jefferson.

Petitions poured in on the president from groups and individuals. It cannot be said that the American people did not read the treaty. From the length of many of the petitions, which took it apart clause by clause, it is clear that citizens read it in great detail. They also reviewed the Declaration of Independence and the Constitution, inserting therefrom appropriate phrases. The literary quality throughout the country was impressive. Many petitions noted that the Constitution required that Congress (i.e., both Houses) regulate commerce and therefore the representatives had also to approve the treaty. The president replied politely to most letters, saying that he had to do his constitutional duty and what he thought was right for the country. To those who were against, he added that he regretted the division of opinion; he thanked those who were for the treaty for their "approbation." Four of the petitions, three from the South, were scandalously abusive. The president marked them as "too rude" or "too indecent" to merit an answer. A highly emotional plea against the treaty came from Richmond, where the chairman of the meeting was George Wythe. The mayor of the city said that he was forwarding the document to the president "with pleasure."

An assessment of the petitions indicates that twenty-eight out of the forty against it were from the South, the bulk of them written in Virginia and South Carolina. Only a single voice of support for the president came from below the Potomac. General Daniel Morgan rallied the citizens of Frederick County in hearty approval of the treaty. It was probably about this time that the president made a remark later quoted by Edmund Randolph. If, said Washington, the North and South split, he intended to move to the North.

John Jay, who, of all the founding fathers, most nearly resembled Washington in strength of character, was subjected to unparalleled denunciations in the Jeffersonian portion of the press. He bore it with fortitude and a comment on its cause to James Duane on September 16:

> *The opposition to which you allude, except as to the degree of malignity, was not unexpected...*
>
> *The Constitution [is] a rock of offence to the Antifederalists; and the funding system, by affording support to the government, had become exceedingly obnoxious to that party. It was evident, then, That a treaty with Great Britain, by preventing war, would disappoint the Southern debtors of the receipts in full, which they flattered themselves from a war.*
>
> *That it would displease the French, by lessening our supposed dependence on them for protection against Great Britain, by diminishing their influence in our councils, and by making us friends with their enemies.*
>
> *That it would discontent the Antifederalists, by disarming them of their affected complaints against the government on account of the posts, and commerce, etc., and by giving additional strength to the administration.*
>
> *Hence there was reason to apprehend that a treaty with Great Britain would become a signal to the Antifederalists, the debtors, and the French, to unite their efforts to prevent its taking effect, and to embarrass its execution if ratified, and to conduct*

their opposition in a manner most injurious to the Constitution and to the administration...

Strenuous efforts will be made to gain and mislead a majority of the House of Representatives at the ensuing session of Congress; and if they succeed, many perplexities and embarassments may be expected... While moral evil remains in the world it will constantly generate political ones.

Jay put his finger on a major source of trouble, the House of Representatives. The southern vote there (and in the electoral college) was padded by the constitutional proviso that a slave was to count as three-fifths of a person, for the purpose of representation. In consequence fifteen congressmen represented slaves.

Jefferson, in a series of letters to Monroe in Paris, did all he could to encourage the French government to action by assuring Monroe the treaty was opposed by all the American people who would break it in the House. He wrote on September 6: "Mr. Jay's treaty has at length been made public. So general a burst of dissatisfaction never before appeared against any transaction. Those who understand the particular articles of it, condemn these articles. Those who do not understand them minutely, condemn it generally as wearing a hostile face to France. This last is the most numerous class, comprehending the whole body of the people, who have taken a greater interest in this transaction than they were ever known to do before. It has in my opinion completely demolished the monarchical party here... We do not know whether the President has signed it or not. If he has, it is much believed the H. of representatives will oppose it as constitutionally void, and thus bring on an embarrassing and critical state of government." Jefferson subsequently pushed Madison hard to defeat the treaty in the House, with the aid of southern members who held 43 percent of the seats.

TREATY OF GRENVILLE

General Anthony Wayne began negotiations for a peace treaty with the Northwest Indians in the spring of 1795. He reported to Pickering that the British were working to subvert the peace but that the Indians had lost all confidence in them after the Battle of Fallen Timbers, "because they remained idle spectators & saw their best and bravest Chiefs & Warriors slaughtered before their faces, and under their great Guns without attempting to assist them—hence they consider the British not only liars—but also Cowards."

After receipt of the Jay treaty, Pickering had given Wayne the confidential information that the British would evacuate their posts in the territory. Since the treaty was under a veil of secrecy, he could provide no further information until it was published. Wayne had therefore to negotiate in the dark until summer. He nonetheless satisfactorily concluded his treaty. On August 9 he wrote to the secretary of war: "It is with infinite pleasure I now inform you, that a treaty of peace between the United States of America & all the late hostile tribes of Indians North West of the Ohio, was Unanimously and Voluntarily agreed to, & chearfully signed by all the *Sachems* & *War Chiefs* of the respective Nations, on the 3rd & exchanged on the 7th Instant a copy of which I have now the honor to transmit."

Wayne added that he had seen the text of the Jay treaty in newspapers, which had just arrived, as well as the "violent and ungenerous attacks upon it... I however hope and trust... that our Great & virtuous President will once more save this Country from ruin, by ratifying that treaty... In the name of God what do these intemperate resolutions tend to? are they meant to provoke a War with Great Britain? where is our Marine or Naval force...? Will... the Virtuous thinking Citizens... wantonly precipitate & involve America in an unequal contest with a powerful Marine Nation, at a Crisis—when we are so ill prepared—to repel force by force, on that Element where she is clearly predominant! I believe not. At the same time I clearly foresee one very unpleasant consequence of those intemperate proceedings, i.e., a procrastination of the surrender of the Western posts & possibly—a renewal of the Indian War."

THE PRESIDENT SIGNS THE TREATY

Early in July American newspapers carried sketchy reports that the British, in expectation of grain shortages, had issued a new provision order to the Royal Navy. This permitted the navy to carry foreign grain ships, proceeding to France, into British ports where the cargo was to be purchased. The order was well within the letter but hardly within the spirit of the Jay treaty. John Trumbull, who had been Jay's secretary in London, protested to the British government in July that this was not a very politic move, while the treaty was under consideration, especially as the United States would be happy to sell directly any needed grain. The ministry assured Trumbull they intended to proceed with absolute fairness and to pay at once. The order was repealed not long afterwards.

Hamilton, out of the cabinet in 1795, turned from his previous apathy to great strength. He did more for the president during his ordeal over the treaty than any member of the government. At Washington's request, he examined every aspect of the treaty and wrote a powerful paper of great length, pointing out the treaty's many strengths and relatively few weaknesses. In his appraisal, Hamilton stated that the new British provision order, while not happily conceived, was within the existing law of nations as well as clause XVIII of the treaty. He strongly urged the president to sign. Hamilton forwarded his views to Washington, who received them a day or two before setting out for Mount Vernon.

Washington had also asked the secretary of state to appraise the treaty, in fullest detail. Randolph provided his own shorter report on July 12 which the president took with him to Mount Vernon on July 15. Randolph summarized the treaty as follows:

Advantages	Disadvantages
1. Old bickerings settled; except as to impressment and provisions	*1. Loss of Negroes*
2. Indian Wars at an end, at least those countenanced by G. Britain	*2. Assumption of debts due to creditors in certain cases*
3. New opportunities for extending trade in Canada	*3. The lands which may be taken from the U.S. by the indulgence of British settlers [within the restored bounds of the U.S.]*
4. Posts surrendered	*4. The situation of provisions*
5. Captures compensated	
6. Gr. Britain interested in securing to us the Mississippi	

Randolph noted that the treaty would secure peace, and the United States, in consequence, would not be "thrown into one set of European politics by an abhorrence of the outrages of another." He added that Jay had not exceeded his authority, there seemed little chance of obtaining a better treaty, and rejection would have a serious effect on national morale, while causing Britain to postpone the surrender of the posts. Finally, the twenty senators who had voted for it would be subjected to a savage public assault if the president rejected it.

Had the gods been kind to Edmund Randolph, they would have stopped his pen at this point but, with almost no transition, he inserted the sudden statement that "the order for capturing provisions is too irreconcileable with a state of harmony, for the treaty to be put into motion during its existence." He said that if there were no other way out, "the treaty ought to be absolutely broken up." He advised the president to take no further action. The war might end soon, people's passions would subside, and perhaps the British courts would order compensation for vessels previously seized. Negotiations could be resumed with Great Britain at some later date. The president should buy time by asking Randolph to tell the British minister that he would not sign the treaty until the order for recission had reached Philadelphia. Ratifications could then be exchanged at the American capital, if the president still wanted to sign it.

The secretary of state had placed strong doubts in Washington's mind on the provision order before he left for Mount Vernon. On the strength of this, Randolph, deliberately, or through a failure to understand, wrote on July 21 to the American legations in Europe to say that he believed that the president would not sign, so long as the order stood and perhaps never, even if it were repealed. At Mount Vernon, Washington read Hamilton's appraisal and compared it with Randolph's proposal to wreck the treaty. Shortly afterward, convinced by Hamilton that the British, while exasperating, were not willfully in violation of the treaty, the president changed his mind about the provision order and decided that he had no choice but to ratify, in the form that the Senate advised. On July 29 Washington informed the secretary of state that the violent opposition which had been manifested to the treaty would probably induce him to return rather quickly to the capital. Randolph was not to come to Mount Vernon, as he had planned to do. He continued:

I view the opposition which the treaty is receiving from the meetings in different parts of the union in a very serious light: not because there is_more_ weight in _any_ of the objections which are made to it, than were foreseen at first; for there are _none_ in _some_ of them; and _gross_ _misrepresentation_ in _others_; nor as it respects myself personally, for this shall have no influence on my conduct, plainly perceiving, and I am accordingly preparing my mind for it, the obloquy which disappointment and malice are collecting to heap upon me. But I am alarmed on account of the effect it may have on, and the advantage the French government may be disposed to make of the spirit which is at work to cherish a belief in them, that the treaty is calculated to favor G. Britain at their expence. Whether they believe or disbelieve these tales, the effect it will have on the nation, will be nearly the same; for whilst they are at war with that Power, it will... be their policy... to prevent us from being on good terms with G. B.

On July 31 the Cabinet sent an urgent request to Washington to return to Philadelphia, the secretary of war privately adding that there was a "*special reason*" which made it desirable that he come "with all convenient speed." At the same time Washington wrote Randolph that "this government in relation to France and England may be compared to a Ship between the rocks of Scylla and Charybdis. If the Treaty is ratified, the partisans of the French (or rather of war and confusion) will excite them to hostile measures, or at least to unfriendly Sentiments; if it is not, there is no foreseeing *all* the consequences which may follow as it respects G. Britain." On August 1 Pickering wrote to Wayne to say that the president would ratify the treaty within a few days. On August 3 Washington informed Randolph that only "imperious" circumstances could shake his determination to sign the treaty.

Torrential rains delayed both the president's departure and his trip north. He found the roads muddied and flooded and bridges washed out. He arrived in Philadelphia on August 11 and was soon inquiring after Pickering's special reason. Pickering explained that the British minister had given him a copy of a Fauchet dispatch to Paris, which had been intercepted by the Royal Navy and forwarded to Philadelphia by the foreign office. Hammond, the British minister, had shown it to Oliver Wolcott, who, in turn, had consulted with Bradford and Pickering. It was soon clear to the president why he had been asked to return to town as soon as possible. The letter, which contained typical French praises of Jefferson, Madison, and Monroe, indicated that the secretary of state had made "valuable disclosures" to Fauchet. He added that Randolph, fearing civil and foreign war, had been very disturbed by the president's plan to issue a proclamation against the insurgents in western Pennsylvania. He suggested that Fauchet bribe certain persons in the state to forestall their cooperation with the federal government. The president read the letter and then indicated to the three cabinet members that they should continue to keep it secret.

Next day the cabinet met. Randolph introduced the memorial which he had sent to Mount Vernon, advising that the government tell the British minister that Washington would not sign the treaty. Many points needed adjustment and negotiation, and the British king was to be "invited" to consider them. The president asked the cabinet for their opinion.

Wolcott, Bradford, and Pickering advised him to sign immediately. Randolph, up to this time convinced that he had smashed the treaty, expostulated and protested. The president said that he would sign it without stipulation. He ordered Randolph so to inform the British minister in a memorandum. On August 14 Randolph delivered it to George Hammond, expressing his chagrin at having to do so. The minister was too polite to say that he knew that the president had entirely rewritten Randolph's original text. Hammond, who had been recalled to the foreign office, left for London with an assured peace. That same day Pickering wrote to Jay:

> *No man can be more anxious for the fate of the treaty with Great Britain than you; and the wanton abuse heaped upon you by enemies of their country, gives you a right to the earliest possible relief. The treaty will be ratified. This day the president finally sanctions a memorial announcing it to the British minister Mr. Hammond. The ratification will conform to the advice and consent of the Senate, unembarrassed with any other condition.*

On August 17 Jay replied to Pickering: "I think the President, with the blessing of Providence, will be able to carry his country safe through the storm, and see it anchored in peace and safety; if so, his life and character will have no parallel." On August 18 the president and secretary of state formally signed the treaty. A month later, still pursuing peace, the president wrote to Pickering to say that he had received the summary of the Wayne treaty with the northwest Indians. He asked him to dispatch at once the Indian agent in the Southwest to negotiate peace between the Cherokees and the Creeks. "It would be a pleasing circumstance not only to be enabled to say, at the meeting of Congress, that we were at peace with *all the Indian nations*, but by the mediations of the U States, we had settled the differences between the tribes above mentioned."

On August 19, in the presence of Pickering and Wolcott, Washington showed Randolph the Fauchet letter. There was discussion and some lame discourse by the secretary of state who then resigned. An additional burden for the president came when the attorney general, William Bradford, died four days later. The president encountered extraordinary difficulty for months in filling both posts. During the interim, Pickering handled, with great effectiveness, both the State and War Departments.

ABUSE OF THE PRESIDENT

Washington had written Hamilton in early July that he was greatly in need of relaxation. In addition he found the "intense" heat of Philadelphia "suffocating." He reported a "hot and disagreeable ride" to Mount Vernon from whence he was recalled to Philadelphia during another unpleasantly humid season. On September 8 he started once again for Mount Vernon for a month's rest, though he was not spared trouble while at home.

Hamilton, under the name "Camillus," had followed his private letter to the president with a series of brilliant articles in the *New York Argus* in defense of the treaty and in attack on the opposition. Washington praised the articles highly, while Jefferson wrote to Madison that Hamilton had become a "colossus" of the "anti-republican" (republican) forces. Hamilton squarely placed on Jefferson the blame for the general mob scenes and national disorders. He noted the immense abuse which had been heaped on Jay for his two successes, the peace and the ejection of a Jeffersonian from the governorship of New York. Hamilton won few southern hearts when he proclaimed that attempts by Virginia to lure back to slavery Negroes who had escaped to freedom during the revolution were "odious and immoral." He accused Virginia and South Carolina of deliberately evading, by acts of their legislatures, payments on private debts owing to British merchants, in violation of a national treaty. This forced the federal government to pay them, as a matter of honor, in order to regain the posts. Hamilton's arguments had a profound impact in the North; Jefferson, in alarm, wrote to Madison in September that he was even persuading many southerners of the treaty's merits.

During the period from the summer of 1795 through 1796, Jefferson managed an underground movement within the government, which operated against the treaty, even after its proclamation by the president had made it the supreme law of the land. He worked through Tench Coxe, commissioner of revenue in the Treasury, through whom he wrote letters to Monroe in vitriolic denunciation of the treaty. He urged Madison and other Virginia members of Congress to work to overthrow the peace. He also encouraged the Virginia Assembly, where his son-in-law was a member, to censure the president for having signed it.

The effectiveness of Hamilton was such that the Jeffersonian faction and press turned not on Hamilton, but on Washington with a savagery which would have been unbecoming in a jungle. Edmund Randolph wrote a number of harassing letters to the president, which Washington considered full of "innuendoes." He nonetheless gave Randolph permission to publish any and every letter he had written, even if private and confidential, or to quote anything he had said if they would help him to vindicate himself from the "suspicious" circumstances surrounding his resignation. Randolph, ungrateful, informed Madison on November 1 that Washington was a "Tiberius" and an "assassin." Washington dismissed Randolph's subsequent "vindication" as simply an "accusation."

In October the Jeffersonian press began an all-out assault on Washington's record as general and as president. That same month the *Aurora* of Philadelphia accused the president of having overdrawn his salary and asked for his impeachment. This information probably came from Tench Coxe. The distortions of fact here were remarkable. The president had been forced to move to a larger house in New York in 1790, and he then had to move his whole staff to Philadelphia at enormous expense. He received a Treasury advance to cover these extra expenses, which he subsequently covered from his own pocket, Congress having been too penurious to vote the necessary funds. In November a New York paper began printing the old forged Washington letters, prepared by the British at the beginning of the revolution, in which Washington was shown to have made treasonable comments. The French minister, Adet, eagerly seized on these and forwarded them to France as evidence of what Washington was really like.

In the midst of the uproar and after the Virginia Assembly had overwhelmingly adopted resolutions reflecting on the president and the treaty, the Maryland House and Senate, about November 27, unanimously passed a resolution condemning the "insinuations" and "invectives" of the Jeffersonians and expressing gratitude to Virginia's greatest son for his "*integrity, judgment, and patriotism.*" Washington replied to Governor John Stone on December 6:

At any time the expression of such a sentiment would have been considered as highly honorable and flattering; at the present, when the voice of malignancy is so high-toned, and no attempts are left unessayed to destroy all confidence in the Constituted authorities of this country, it is peculiarly grateful to my Sensibility; and coming spontaneously, and with the unanimity it has done, from so respectable a representation of the People, it adds weight as well as pleasure to the Act.

I have long since resolved (for the present time at least) to let my calumniators proceed, without taking notice of their invectives myself, or by any other, with my participation or knowledge. Their views, I dare say, are readily perceived by the enlightened and well disposed part of the Community; and by the Records of my Administration and not by the voice of faction, I expect to be acquitted or condemned hereafter.

STATE OF THE UNION

In spite of the abuse hurled at him, the president had so much good news to report that he made an unusually cheerful presentation of the state of the country on December 8, 1795:

I trust I do not deceive myself, while I indulge the persuasion, that I have never met

*you at any period when, more than at present, the situation of our public affairs
has afforded just cause for mutual congratulation; and for inviting you to join
with me in profound gratitude to the Author of all good, for the numerous and
extraordinary blessings we enjoy.*

*The termination of the long, expensive and distressing war in which we have been
engaged, with certain Indians Northwest of the Ohio, is placed in the option of the
United States, by a treaty which the Commander of our Army has concluded... In
the adjustment of the terms, the satisfaction of the Indians was deemed an object
worthy no less of the policy than of the liberality of the United States, as the
necessary basis of durable tranquillity...*

*The Creek and Cherokee Indians... have lately confirmed their pre-existing treaties
with us, and were giving evidence of a sincere disposition to carry them into
effect... But we have to lament, that the fair prospect in this quarter, has been once
more clouded by wanton murders, which some Citizens of Georgia are represented to
have recently perpetrated on hunting parties of the Creeks... Measures are
persuing... to avert general hostility...*

*A letter from the Emperor of Morocco announces to me his recognition of our Treaty
made with his Father... With peculiar satisfaction I add that information has been
received from... Algiers... that the terms of a Treaty... authorize the expectation of
a speedy peace, and the restoration of our unfortunate fellow-citizens from a
grievous captivity.*

*The latest advices from our Envoy at the Court of Madrid, give moreover, the
pleasing information that he had received assurances of a speedy and satisfactory
conclusion of his negotiation...*

*A Treaty of Amity, Commerce and Navigation has been negotiated with Great
Britain and... the Senate have advised and consented to its ratification... I have
added my sanction...*

*If by prudence and moderation on every side, the extinguishment of all the causes
of external discord, which have heretofore menaced our tranquillity, on terms
compatible with our rights and honor, shall be the happy result—how firm, and
how precious a foundation will have been laid for accelerating, maturing and
establishing the prosperity of our country!*

*While many of the nations of Europe... have been involved in a contest, unusually
bloody, exhausting and calamitous, in which the evils of foreign war have been*

aggravated by domestic convulsions and insurrection... [and] a scarcity of subsistence has embittered others' sufferings... our favored country, happy in a striking contrast, has enjoyed general tranquility... Our Agriculture, Commerce and Manufactures prosper beyond former example... Our population advances with a celerity which, exceeding the most sanguine calculations, proportionately augments our strength and resources, and guarantees our future security... With Governments founded on genuine principles of rational liberty, and with mild and wholesome laws, is it too much to say, that our country exhibits a spectacle of national happiness never surpassed if ever before equalled?

The president noted that he had pardoned all offenders in the western insurrection, including those who had been sentenced to death. Although it was his sworn duty to enforce the laws, it was also desirable to "mingle in the operations of government, every degree of moderation and tenderness, which the national justice, dignity and safety may permit."

Washington told Congress that he would forward separately the government's plans to provide fair treatment for the Indians, as well as reports on the progress made by the mint, and in the building of the navy and coastal fortifications. He added a final word to his countrymen: "Temperate discussion... and mutual forbearance where there is a difference of opinion, are too obvious and necessary for the peace, happiness and welfare of our country, to need any recommendations of mine."

FIRST PLACE

Lord Grenville had generously written to Jay after his departure: "You are happy in America if you can avoid, as I trust you will, the dangers of the war and the peace." He extended his sincere wishes for the country's prosperity.

Washington reported to his Mount Vernon manager during the year the price increases of one of the most important American exports, flour, as it moved from $8 to $10 and then to a record high of $12 a barrel. With the Jay treaty assuring peace and increasing shortages of food developing in the world, American exports rose by a third over the previous year. The American merchant marine had more than tripled in size since Washington assumed the presidency. In 1795 the fleet alone earned a larger sum in foreign exchange than the total value of all American exports in any year, when the states were colonies.

On a per capita basis the United States moved easily ahead of the mother country into first place in world trade. America's imports of goods and services in 1795 were 60 percent higher, per head, than those of the world's greatest commercial and industrial nation. While consumption was growing rapidly, it was clear that Americans were investing huge sums in shipping and insurance, fisheries and industries, canals and bridges, post offices and post roads, and schools and colleges. With the Indians at peace, hundreds of thousands of people began to move across the mountains into the land of milk and honey, carrying with them the Bible and the Constitution of the United States.

THIRTEEN

PEACE WITH SPAIN

1796

T HE LAST FOURTEEN months of Washington's presidency were triumphant on almost every front. Troubles with France, stimulated by her American supporters, alone scarred the scene.

Washington began 1796 with a New Year's Day speech to the French minister, composed in all probability by his droll secretary of state. Citizen James Monroe presented an American flag to the French Assembly, which ordered it displayed alongside the tricolore. That body then voted to present a French flag to the citizen representatives of the United States whom it persisted in trying to label as the American government. Pickering deftly intercepted the presentation to Congress; the French minister agreed to hand it to the president. In his speech Adet said that the flag was a symbol of terror to France's enemies but not to those with whom she had established close relationships. The president replied with disarming bombast. He referred to the French as "Wonderful People! Ages to come will read with astonishment the history of your brilliant exploits... [and your] interesting revolutionary movements." He concluded:

The transaction will be announced to Congress; and the colours will be deposited with the archives of the United States, which are at once the evidences and the memorials of their freedom and independence. May these be perpetual! and may the friendship of the two republics be commensurate with their existence.

Nine days later the French minister discovered the significance of the para-graph indicating that the symbol of terror would be filed. He fired a furious but futile note of complaint to Pickering.

APPOINTMENTS

Finding the right man for office became increasingly irksome for the presi-dent. To add to his troubles, the chief justice, John Rutledge, who had been appointed *ad interim* to the Court while Congress was in recess, thereafter spent much of his time denouncing the Jay treaty. The Senate, which had ratified it by a vote of two to one, had no hesitation in booting him out of office. Since another judge had resigned, the president had to find two Supreme Court justices and two cabinet members from the limited supply of able personnel. He included, as a new potential appointee, Patrick Henry, who had swung to support of the Constitution while Madison turned away from it. Washington sounded out five men, including Henry, for the post of secretary of state. All declined, at least one saying he did not care to undergo the abuse heaped on the administration. In the end, Pickering, who had dis-played great abilities and loyalty as head of the War Department (including the navy) and as acting secretary of state (including the foreign office, mint and patent office), got the job.

This left the war office open. Washington never tried to conceal from those whom he asked to take office that he had previously offered it to oth-ers. On January 20, 1796, he wrote to James McHenry, his aide during the revolution: " ...Will you suffer me to nominate you to the Office of Secretary of War? That I may give you evidence of the candour I have possessed above, I shall inform you that, for particular reasons (more fit for an oral, than a written communication) this office has been offered to Genl. Pinckney of So. Carolina, Colo. Carrington of Virginia, and Govr. Howard of Maryland, and that it would now give me sincere pleasure if you would fill it." McHenry accepted. This left the office of attorney general to fill. The president offered this post to John Marshall of Virginia. He declined, and Washington appointed Charles Lee, brother of Henry Lee, of a Virginia family noted for its devotion to the federal Union.

The appointments of Senator Oliver Ellsworth of Connecticut and Samuel Chase of Maryland as chief and associate justices completed Washington's most important assignments. It was noticeable that the president was increasingly forced to make most of his appointments from north of the Potomac in order to be sure of his men. The previous October 9 he had written to Edward

Carrington that it would be "an act of governmental suicide" to bring into high office a man "unfriendly to the Constitution and laws which are to be his guide."

TREATY WITH SPAIN

Next only to the Jay treaty, the agreement with Spain, officially known as the Treaty of San Lorenzo el Real but more usually called the Pinckney treaty, was the greatest diplomatic triumph of Washington's administration. It was gained by unorthodox methods, similar to those the president employed when he sent the chief justice to supercede the regular minister at London. Washington, in turn, transferred Pinckney to Madrid, as a special emissary to meet the procrastinating challenge of the Spanish government. The timing of his arrival was perfect; Pinckney appeared just as an aggressive French army was crashing into Spain. With assurances of secret British support in his Mississippi negotiations, Pinckney could lead from even greater strength than Jay.

Spain's astonishing first concession was a surrender of her previous claims to a large portion of present-day Alabama and Mississippi, as well as parts of Georgia, Tennessee, and Kentucky. Title to these areas had been transferred to the United States by Great Britain, in a secret clause of the 1783 treaty, but Spain had refused to recognize previous British claims thereto. The Mississippi River was divided between the United States and Spain. Americans were permitted to establish the trading post at New Orleans, which had been so much wanted by Kentucky. Spain agreed to withdraw all her garrisons from east of the Mississippi and north of the thirty-first parallel.

John Jay had sailed for London on May 12, 1794. Pinckney signed his treaty on October 27, 1795. In less than eighteen months, the president had broken forever the designs successively of Great Britain, France, and Spain to make the Alleghenies the western boundary for Americans. The sovereignty of the United States had more than tripled, with about 600,000 square miles added, covering parts or all of fourteen existing and future states. Today the world's most important agricultural and industrial area, it holds perhaps eighteen times the entire population of the country in 1790.

Wayne's Grenville treaty was unanimously ratified by the Senate in December 1795. On February 26, 1796, the president sent the Spanish treaty to the Senate which, six days later, also unanimously voted its approval. On March 1, having received a copy of the Grenville-Jay treaty signed by George III, the president formally proclaimed it in effect.

On April 8 the president transmitted to Congress the request of "the territory south of the Ohio" to be admitted as the sixteenth state. On June 1

Tennessee, now extending to the Mississippi, joined the Union. Andrew Jackson, the state's first congressman, was to be the last revolutionary war veteran to serve in the White House.

JEFFERSON

As the president moved from success to success, Thomas Jefferson, hidden away, endeavored with increasing emotion to block and baulk him, employing formidable weapons for the purpose. Virginia held nearly 20 percent of the seats in the House of Representatives. Aided by some New York and Pennsylvania votes, the deeper South, and the extra seats allotted for slaves, the democrats held a working majority in the lower chamber. Jefferson repeatedly urged Madison and his associates to use this power to wreck the Jay treaty. On March 27 he told Madison that the agreement was "a conspiracy with the enemies of our country," in which "the honor and faith of our nation are so grossly sacrificed." He had already added the Pinckney treaty to his proscribed list, writing to Madison, in early March, that the Spanish treaty "will have... eternal broils, instead of peace and friendship." Jefferson felt that Spain should have given up "vastly more," but it is difficult to see what else that country could have handed over, unless it were the crown jewels. Soon, with more accuracy than he intended, he was dividing Americans into "honest men" and "rogues."

Jefferson also kept up his correspondence with Monroe in Paris. He assured him that only Hamilton, in the entire United States, had the "effrontery" to defend the Jay treaty. The "public pulse" against it beat in more "universal union" than it had ever done since the Declaration of Independence.

While these intrigues were proceeding, the Jeffersonian press accused Washington of senility and of being both under British influence and subject to manipulation by his cabinet and Hamilton. In addition, Bache published in the *Aurora* a secret memorandum from the president to his cabinet, written just before he issued his 1793 neutrality proclamation.

This brought on the last known exchange of letters between Jefferson and Washington. The former, using a disclaimer that he was Bache's source, as an excuse for writing his letter of June 19, moved quickly to his real purpose which was to destroy the president's faith in Henry Lee. Lee had informed Washington two years earlier that Jefferson had been referring sarcastically to the president's advisers and to his supposed attachment to Great Britain. Washington replied to Lee that Jefferson's remarks seemed to be "enigmatical... or spoken ironically; and in that case they are too injurious to me, and

have too little foundation in truth, to be ascribed to" the former secretary of
state. When Jefferson heard of the Lee letter, he added Lee to his list of enemies. In writing Washington on June 19, 1796, he said of Lee:

> *I learn that this last has thought it worth his while to try to sow tares between you
> & me, by representing me as still engaged in the bustle of politics, & in turbulence
> & intrigue against the government. I never believed for a moment that this could
> make any impression on you, or that your knowledge of me would not outweigh the
> slander of an intriguer, dirtily employed in sifting the conversations of my table,
> where alone he could hear of me; and seeking to atone for his sins against you by
> his sins against another, who had never done him any other injury than that of
> declining his confidences... But enough of this miserable tergiversator, who ought
> indeed to have been of more truth, or less trusted by his country...*

Jefferson signed the letter in a Benjamin Rushlike manner: "With great & sincere esteem & respect." Washington replied on July 6 to the effect that he had
never had any suspicion that Jefferson had given a cabinet secret to the press.
He could easily "conjecture" the source (Randolph), and he knew that two
Virginia congressmen had been bandying it about the halls of Congress. He
then noted that the opposition press had used every opportunity to weaken
the confidence of the people in the government by using existing documents,
presented in a twisted form, as well as papers which had been forged for the
purpose of publication. He continued:

> *It would not be frank, candid, or friendly to conceal, that your conduct has been
> represented as derogatory from that opinion I had conceived you entertained of me.
> That to your particular friends and connexions you have described, and they have
> denounced me, as a person under a dangerous influence; and that, if I would
> listen more to some other opinions, all would be well. My answer invariably has
> been that I had never discovered anything in the conduct of Mr. Jefferson to raise
> suspicions, in my mind, of his insincerity; that if he would retrace my public
> conduct while he was in the Administration, abundant proofs would occur to him,
> that truth and right decisions, were the sole objects of my pursuit; that there were as
> many instances within his own knowledge of my having decided against, as in
> favor of the person [Hamilton] evidently alluded to; and moreover, that I was no
> believer in the infallibility of the politics, or measures of any man living. In short,
> that I was no party man myself, and the first wish of my heart was, if parties did
> exist, to reconcile them.*

> *Until within the last year or two ago, I had no conception that Parties would, or*

even could go, the length I have been witness to; nor did I believe until lately, that it was within the bounds of probability, that, while I was using my utmost exertions to establish a national character of our own, independent, as far as our obligations and justice would permit, of every nation on earth; and wished, by steering a steady course, to preserve this Country from the horrors of a desolating war, that I should be accused of being the enemy of one Nation, and subject to the influence of another; and to prove it, that every act of my administration would be tortured, and the grossest and most insidious mis-representations of them be made (by giving one side only of a subject, and that too in such exaggerated and indecent terms as could scarcely be applied to a Nero; a notorious defaulter; or even to a common pickpocket). But enough of this; I have already gone farther in the expression of my feelings, than I intended.

Just before receiving this letter, Jefferson had written the most savage indictment of Washington and his administration which had yet appeared. He sent this to Phillip Mazzei, a French sympathizer living in French-occupied Tuscany. It would be difficult not to believe that Jefferson expected his letter to be published in Europe as, indeed, it soon was. He wrote on April 24:

The aspect of our politics has wonderfully changed since you left us. In place of that noble love of liberty, & republican government which carried us triumphantly thro' the war, an Anglican monarchical, & aristocritical party has sprung up, whose avowed object is to draw over us the substance, as they have already done the forms, of the British government. The main body of our citizens, however, remain true to their republican principles; the whole landed interest is republican, and so is a great mass of talents. Against us are the Executive, the Judiciary, two out of three branches of the legislature, all the officers of government, all who want to be officers; all timid men who prefer the calm of despotism to the boisterous sea of liberty, British merchants & Americans trading on British capitals, speculators & holders in the banks & public funds, a contrivance invented for the purpose of corruption, & for assimilating us in all things to the rotten as well as the sound parts of the British model. It would give you a fever were I to name to you the apostates who have gone over to these heresies, men who were Samsons in the field & Solomons in the Council, but who have had their heads shorn by the harlot England.

The letter, published in Italy at the end of the year, was reprinted in the French government's official newspaper, along with an editorial which declared it to be a complete justification for having broken diplomatic relations with the United States. This act, the paper further observed, was intended to effect "a triumph to the party of good republicans, the friends of

France," in the presidential elections. When Washington read the letter, which was reproduced by many American newspapers in 1797, he learned all that he needed to know of Jefferson.

THE MEANING OF THE WORDS

The Constitutional Convention of 1787 had proclaimed that "this Constitution for the United States of America" was ordained and established by "the people of the United States in order to form a more perfect Union, establish justice, insure domestic Tranquility, provide for the common defence, promote the general Welfare, and secure the blessings of Liberty to ourselves and our Posterity." To make certain that it was, in fact, the American people who ordained it by democratic process, the convention provided for its ratification not only by their representatives in Congress but by additional popularly elected special assemblies called for that purpose in each state. In transmitting the Constitution to Congress, the president of the convention, George Washington, wrote on September 17, 1787:

> *The friends of our country have long seen and desired, that the power of making war, peace, and treaties, of levying money and regulating commerce, and the correspondent executive and judicial authorities should be fully and effectually invested in the general government of the Union…*

> *It is obviously impracticable in the federal government of these States, to secure all rights of independent sovereignty to each, and yet provide for the interest and safety of all. Individuals entering into society, must give up a share of liberty to preserve the rest…*

> *In all our deliberations… we kept steadily in our view, that which appears to us the greatest interest of every true American, the consolidation of our Union, in which is involved our prosperity, felicity, safety, perhaps our national existence. This important consideration, seriously and deeply impressed on our minds, led each State in the Convention to be less rigid on points of inferior magnitude than might otherwise have been expected; and thus the Constitution, which we now present, is the result of a spirit of amity, and of that mutual deference and concession which the peculiarity of our political situation rendered indispensable.*

> *That it may promote the lasting welfare of that country so dear to us all, and secure her freedom and happiness, is our most ardent wish.*

In 1796 Jefferson began to diverge ever more sharply from Washington on the Constitution. To describe the Union he introduced, for the first time, the word "confederacy." Joined by Madison, who knew better, Jefferson began to call the Constitution a "compact" or, its slighter form, "pact." The transition from there to nullification and secession was easy and direct. Washington's Union, the "consolidation" of the American people into one nation, became the evil against which the sovereign and independent states were obliged to fight.

MADISON

In the months that followed Washington's message to the Senate on the Jay treaty, there was a marked shift in public opinion as the treaty's merits won increased acknowledgment. Even Benjamin Rush noted in January 1796: "All is peace in our country. General Washington is still esteemed by a great majority of our citizens and his treaty with Great Britain becomes less unpopular in proportion as it is understood." By March Rush was sure that the House of Representatives would vote its support.

Nonetheless the Democrats, under Madison, charged to the attack on the treaty, in confidence that they could overturn it. Their first assault took place on March 24, when, by a vote of sixty-two to thirty-seven, the House called for all the treaty papers, although this request was modified to exclude any documents the president considered "improper" to become public. Six days later the president replied with one of the bluntest statements he had ever sent to Congress:

> To admit... a right in the House of Representatives to demand, and to have as a matter of course, all the Papers respecting a negotiation with a foreign power, would be establishing a dangerous precedent.

> Having been a member of the General Convention and knowing the principles on which the Constitution was formed, I have ever entertained but one opinion on this subject... The power of making treaties is exclusively vested in the President, by and with the advice and consent of the Senate, provided two-thirds of the Senators present concur, and that every treaty so made, and promulgated, thenceforward became the Law of the Land.

> As therefore it is perfectly clear to my understanding, that the assent of the House of Representatives is not necessary to the validity of a treaty: as the treaty with Great Britain exhibits in itself all the objects requiring legislative provision; and on these the papers can throw no light: And as it is essential to the due administration of

government, that the boundaries fixed by the Constitution between the different departments should be preserved: A just regard to the Constitution and to the duty of my office, forbids a compliance with your request.

The president then forwarded to the Senate nominations for boundary commissioners under the Jay treaty, for which the House would have to vote funds. The representatives blustered, threatened, and then asserted, by a vote of fifty-seven to thirty-five, the right to pass on all treaties. At this point the voice of the country began to be heard. A great Boston town meeting voted almost unanimous approval of the treaty. Petitions and letters poured into the House, in huge volume, asking the members to vote approval. "Washington and Peace" became a byword.

For a month the debate continued; Madison found his supporters drifting away, one by one. On April 30 a further vote was held. Although eighteen of Virginia's representatives voted against the president, one congressman, George Hancock of the Shenandoah Valley, sided with Washington. Opponents from north of the Potomac, disturbed by the public clamor for the treaty, deserted Madison in such numbers that the House, in committee of the whole, voted forty-nine for and forty-nine against an appropriation. The Speaker, on whom Madison had previously relied, broke the tie in favor of the treaty.

The president had won, as Madison's twenty-five-vote majority shriveled into a three-vote minority. Peace was secure; Madison was not to have his war for another sixteen years. In June Jefferson complained to Monroe that "the people" had overruled their representatives, who knew more than they did.

MONROE

The French minister had suggested to the president of the United States on New Year's Day that France's flag was a symbol of terror. This was true in Europe, as French armies swept across Belgium and the Netherlands and into Germany, Austria, and Spain. Jefferson's new hero, "that wonderful man," Bonaparte, was leading a horde of pillaging French across the plains of Italy, taking ransom from pope and princes alike. The Washington who had held off the British empire for so many years was not terrorized, and, accordingly, he was blindly hated by France.

In his generally hilarious 1798 comments on Monroe's defense of his actions in France, Washington wrote that Monroe forwarded all complaints by the French government to Philadelphia but delivered American protests against French ship seizures so weakly they had no effect. Monroe's intrigues with "the French party" in the United States—Jefferson and Madison in Virginia, and Benjamin Bache and George Logan in Pennsylvania—finally forced the president to recall him. On July 2, 1796, three members of the cabinet urgently wrote to Washington at Mount Vernon:

> We think the great interests of the United States require that they have near the French government some faithful organ... Our duty obliges us to be explicit. Altho' the present Minister plenipotentiary of the United States at Paris has been amply furnished with documents to explain the views and conduct of the United States, yet his own letters authorize us to say, that he has omitted to use them, and thereby exposed the U States to all the mischiefs which could flow from jealousies and erroneous conceptions of their conduct. Whether this dangerous omission arose from such an attachment to the cause of France... or from mistaken views of the latter, the evil is the same...

> In confirmation of our opinion of the expediency of recalling Mr. Monroe, we think the occasion requires that we communicate a private letter which came to our hands since you left Philadelphia. The letter corresponds with other intelligence of his political opinions and conduct. A minister who has thus made the notorious enemies of the whole system of government his confidential correspondents, in matters which affect the Government, cannot be relied on to do his duty to the latter. The private letter we received in confidence. Among other circumstances that will occur to your reflection, the anonymous letters from France to Thomas Blount and others are very noticeable... These... are proofs of sinister designs, and shew that the public interests are no longer safe in the hands of such men.

> The information contained in the confidential communication... on the project of the French Government relative to the Commerce of the U States, is confirmed by the open publication of the same substantially and more minutely in the News-papers.

The letter, enclosed by the cabinet, had been written by Monroe to George Logan, forwarding material to be inserted in Bache's newspaper. Monroe promised to send further reports for this purpose. After consulting the attorney general, who was in Alexandria, Washington wrote to Pickering on July 8 to say he would recall him but he would have difficulty in finding a successor loyal to the government and acceptable to France. He again approached Patrick Henry and John Marshall, but neither were induced to go. Once again he turned to a Pinckney, Charles Cotesworth, brother of the minister at London. Pinckney accepted, but the French Directory subsequently refused to receive his credentials. Monroe, before his recall, informed the French government that there would be American presidential elections in 1796 and these would provide a leadership more friendly to France.

FRENCH WAR MEASURES

Spain, which had been fighting alongside Great Britain, had turned a flipflop. By 1796 she was allied with the French aggressor, this was to be the eventual undoing of the Spanish empire. For the United States its most immediate impact was a delay in surrender of the Spanish posts in Mississippi, but not in Tennessee and Alabama. Almost unnoticed, during the House flurry over the Jay treaty, was an amendment to it which the Senate ratified in 1796. It was presented as covering British traders in the Northwest Territory but so worded as to specify that the treaty would not affect or be affected by other commercial treaties which had been signed by the United States. This ensured that Britain would share the navigation of the Mississippi, as provided by the 1783 treaty. Spain did not like this at all but the clause assured warm British support for the United States, if there were to be any contest over the point. To this extent, therefore, the Jeffersonians were right in declaring that the United States had become, in fact, a limited ally of Great Britain.

In the meantime France increased her aggressive seizures of American merchant vessels, in a manner calculated to force the United States to war. Diplomatic relations were broken off towards the close of the year, the French foreign minister declaring to Monroe that the United States had become a vassal state of France's enemy. There were some 30,000 Frenchmen in the principal seaports of America, prepared to uphold France at all costs. The French resumed arming privateers in America to prey, not on British, but on American commerce.

France also resumed her dream of rebuilding a great empire in North America. She put pressure on Spain, weak and torn, to restore Louisiana to France. French agents, too, were busy in Canada and in French settlements in the Northwest Territory, planning to gain control of Canada, Louisiana, and all of the United States west of the Alleghenies. General Wayne, who had spent four arduous years fighting the British and Indians, wrote numerous dispatches to the War Department, outlining the activities of the country's newest enemies, operating under the orders of the French minister in Philadelphia.

On May 25, at the president's direction, McHenry informed Wayne that the government had positive and reliable intelligence that French spies were proceeding to Pittsburgh and the West, "to gain knowledge of our military posts in the Western country, and to encourage and stimulate the people in the quarter to secede from the Union, and form a political and separate connexion with a foreign power." He identified them as General Georges De Collot, Thomas Powers (a Frenchman of Irish descent), and a man named Warin, formerly an engineer in the American service. They expected to visit all the American posts in Kentucky and the Northwest, as well as the old French settlements of Vincennes and Ste. Genevieve.

Wayne soon confirmed that all three had been in Pittsburgh. He added that there was a fourth Frenchman, Constantin Volney, associated with them. Although neither Wayne nor McHenry knew it, Volney had just spent three weeks with Jefferson at Monticello, presumably not confining his discussions to philosophy. Wayne reported that De Collot carried with him "bushels" of introductory letters from leading Democrats in the Senate and House. Aaron Burr, who was to be associated with Wilkinson's future conspiracies, was among the writers. Wayne added that Judge Benjamin Sebastian of Kentucky was apparently also involved with the French and Spanish. Although Wayne could not know the details, subsequent documentation showed that Sebastian, Harry Innes, a federal judge of Kentucky; and George Nicholas were engaged in a conspiracy to turn Kentucky and Tennessee over to Spain.

Wayne reported that the French agents, who all spoke English fluently, were loud in their indiscretions. They denounced the Jay treaty everywhere, saying that it completely justified France's seizures of American ships. The agents described the president as "timid." They informed the Westerners that France was ready to force Spain to break the treaty opening the Mississippi and to return Louisiana to France. It was high time for that part of the United States west of the Alleghenies to secede from the Union, otherwise the Mississippi would be forever shut to them. Wayne particularly noted that De Collot was "busy in Electioneering for Mr. Jefferson & advises a *proper* choice of Electors for that purpose." He also wrote that the three principal agents issued a violent diatribe against the federal government in Kentucky. De Collot had then proceeded onward, making an accurate survey of defenses of the Ohio and of the Mississippi to the Kaskaskias River. Volney moved north to inspect the fortifications at Niagara, which would be of vital importance if France seized Quebec and the Saint Lawrence River.

Although Wayne, at the president's orders, made efforts to capture De Collot and his papers, the Frenchman escaped. Wayne did intercept letters from Adet which clearly showed that the mission had been sent for purposes of espionage, insurrection, and election intimidation.

THE FRIENDLY BRITISH

John Jay had reported from London that Washington was the foreigner most admired by the British people. Benjamin West was soon to hear from the king's own lips that this included George III as well. In the spring and summer of 1796 Washington had the new experience of being the subject of cordial enquiries on the part of Lords Dorchester and Cornwallis, as well as being toasted by British officers in Canada.

On May 13 Thomas Twining, returning to England after serving on the staff of Cornwallis, the governor general of India, called on the president. Mrs. Washington received him and engaged him in conversation. Twining reported: "The door opened and Mrs. Washington and myself rising, she said, 'The President,' and introduced me to him. Never did I feel more interest than at this moment, when I saw the tall, upright, venerable figure of this great man advancing towards me to take me by the hand. There was a seriousness in his manner which seemed to contribute to the impressive dignity of his person, without diminishing the confidence and ease, which the benevolence of his countenance and the kindness of his address inspired... So completely did he look the great and good man he really was, that I felt rather respect than awe in his presence. I mentioned the particular regard and respect with which Lord Cornwallis always spoke of him. He received this communication in the most courteous manner, inquired about his lordship and expressed for him much esteem." The president invited Twining to dinner but, to his distress, the latter had to decline because of another engagement.

Just before this visit, Washington and his secretary of war had discussed their approach to Lord Dorchester, requesting the formal surrender of all posts. The British had been understandably nervous at the loud cries of the Democrats, and had held them to a point where they could not be evacuated before June 1, the required treaty date. Not long afterwards McHenry sent a Captain Lewis (possibly Howell Lewis, the president's nephew) to Quebec with a letter to Dorchester. On June 27 the secretary of war wrote to the president at Mount Vernon, enclosing copies of the orders he had received from "Adjutant General Beckwith" (the old spy) for the evacuation of Fort Miamis, Detroit, Michilimackinac, Oswego, and Niagara. Next day he reported to Washington:

Capt. Lewis says he was treated with much civility by Lord Dorchester's family (staff). That the People seemed every where pleased at the prospect of a friendly intercourse with our Citizens. Lord Dorchester was particular in his inquiries respecting your health, and seemed pleased to learn that you were well and looked well. I believe his Lordship is himself about seventy. Lewis could have dined out for a Month at Quebec. The first toast the King of Great Britain, the second, invariably, the President.

Dorchester had resigned as governor of Canada after being reprimanded by the British government for his actions in Ohio. He sailed for England and retirement after ordering the graceful transfer of the posts he had worked so long to hold.

In the meantime Wayne, on the frontier, had been worried that the Chippewas and other tribes were again moving towards hostilities, stimulated by the Canadian Indian department, which had been fearful that the "Virulent Opposition" in Congress would cause the treaty to fail. As soon as it was secure the British were prompt and magnanimous in handing over the posts. On July 11 Wayne wrote to McHenry that his troops were now at Detroit and Miamis. The British had been "polite and friendly" and had acted in a manner "truly worthy to British Officers [doing] honor to them & the Nation to which they belong." By August 28 Wayne himself was in Detroit. On September 20 he reported that the posts of Michilimackinac, Niagara, and Oswego had been transferred to the Americans "in the most polite, friendly & accommodating Manner." He continued:

An event that must naturally afford the highest pleasure & satisfaction to every friend of order & good Government, & I trust will produce a conviction to the world—that the Measures adopted & pursued by that great & first of men, the President of the United States—were founded in Wisdom, & that the best interests of his country have been secured by that unshaken fortitude, Patriotism & Virtue, for which he is so universally & justly celebrated (a few Democrats excepted—& even they in their hearts must acknowledge his worth).

On October 3 Wayne forwarded to McHenry a list of the Indian chiefs who were proceeding to Philadelphia, "to see & converse with their great Father the President of the United States of America, agreeably to the Unanimous request of all the Chiefs who signed the Treaty of Green Ville." Accompanying them were three army officers as interpreters for the tribes. On November 29 Washington received warriors from the Wyandots, Delawares, Shawanoes, Ottawas, Chippewas, Potawtimes, Miamis, Weeas, Kickapoos, Piankashaws, and Kaksaskias. In greeting them Washington referred to "my great warrior, General Wayne." By then Wayne was seriously ill from overwork. He died in Erie, Pennsylvania, on December 15, 1796.

Andrew Jackson, by Ralph Earl, elected to Congress 1796 and to the Senate in 1797, serving only to 1798, President 1829–1837. *(National Portrait Gallery)*

William Henry Harrison, by Rembrandt Peale, served in the Army 1791–1798, President 1841. *(National Portrait Gallery)*

By Amos Doolittle after Joseph Wright, shows the seals of the United States and the thirteen original States linked in strong union by Washington. *(Courtesy of Mount Vernon Ladies' Association of the Union)*

The Washington family by David Edwin after Edward Savage. *(Courtesy of Mount Vernon Ladies' Association of the Union)*

Bushrod Washington by Henry Benbridge; nephew of George Washington, who was appointed to the Supreme Court by President Adams in 1798. *(Courtesy of the Mount Vernon Ladies' Association of the Union)*

George Washington Laying the Cornerstone of the United States Capitol, Sept, 18, 1793

(Courtesy of John Melius, artist)

Plan of the city of Washington to be the federal capital in 1800.

Martha Washington, by Robert Field.
(Courtesy of the Mount Vernon Ladies'
Association of the Union)

Pastel portrait of
Martha Washington's
granddaughter, the
"Beautiful Nelly" Custis,
who married George
Washington's nephew,
Lawrence Lewis. *(Courtesy
of the Mount Vernon Ladies'
Association of the Union)*

Memorial Engraving *Pater Patriae* by Enoch Gridley after John Coles, Jr., and Edward Savage, circa 1800. *(Courtesy of the Mount Vernon Ladies' Association of the Union)*

LAFAYETTE

To Washington's continuing sorrow, Lafayette had been imprisoned since 1792 in a series of European fortresses, finally being incarcerated at Olmutz, Moravia. The president had a difficult role to play as an old friend of Lafayette and as chief of state. Washington and Lafayette were considered by the French government as enemies to France, while the European autocracies thought of Lafayette as a wild revolutionist who deserved imprisonment. Washington for years had requested his ministers, Morris, Monroe, and Pinckney, to make informal appeals to Franz II to permit Lafayette's release to the United States. In May 1796 Washington himself addressed a direct and moving request to the emperor to parole him, under any restrictions thought necessary.

The Marquise de Lafayette, having decided to appeal personally to the emperor to permit her and her daughters to join Lafayette in Olmutz prison, dispatched her fourteen-year-old son, George Washington, to the president with a note saying that she was placing "this dear child under the protection of the United States... and... the special protection of their President whose sentiments for his father are well known to me." Madame de Lafayette requested that her son be permitted to live an obscure life in America and to resume the education which had been stopped by the Reign of Terror.

Young Lafayette's arrival in Boston in early September 1795, with a tutor, Felix Frestel, placed Washington in what he considered to be an embarrassing dilemma. He wrote at once to Senator Cabot: "To express all the sensibility which has been excited in my breast by the receipt of young Fayettes letter, from the recollection of his fathers merits, services and sufferings, from my friendship for him, and from my wishes to become a *friend* and *father* to his Son, are unnecessary. Let me in a few words, declare that I *will be his friend;* but the manner of becoming so, considering the obnoxious light in which his father is viewed by the French government, and my own situation, as the Executive of the U. States, requires more time to consider... than I can bestow at present; the letters not having been in my hands more than an hour, and I myself on the point of setting out for Virginia..." Washington asked Cabot to assure young Lafayette that he would be a *"Father, friend, protector"* to him. He suggested that Cabot enroll Lafayette in Harvard, at Washington's expense, until he could plan his future more clearly. He pointed out that the president and the boy had to act with prudence because of difficult relations with France and the fact that his mother and many of his relatives had been imprisoned by the French government. In November the president sent young Lafayette a warm and affectionate letter, suggested that he proceed to New York, where Alexander Hamilton, his father's old friend, would take care of him until it was possible for the president to see him. By April the president's personal feelings for Lafayette and his son finally overruled any hesitation he had in regard to political consequences. George Lafayette and his tutor thereupon joined the Washington household, staying until news came of General Lafayette's release from prison.

LEAR AND CUSTIS

Tobias Lear, secretary to and friend of Washington, had left his post with the president not long after the sudden death of his first wife in 1793. His small son, Benjamin Lincoln, was placed in the care of Lear's mother while he went to Europe. When Lear settled in business in Georgetown in 1794, Washington offered him the post of district commissioner, which he declined. Washington continued to use him for various business matters including work with the Potomac Canal Company. On December 12, 1794, Washington asked Lear to get the master key to his papers from Fanny Washington, Mrs. Washington's widowed niece. The Alexandria widow and the Georgetown widower were married a few months later. Fanny Lear had the tuberculosis which had so long plagued the Washington family, and she died in March 1796, leaving Lear again a widower, this time with his own child and three stepchildren, Anna Maria, George Fayette, and Charles Washington. On March 30 the president and his wife wrote Lear:

> *Your former letters prepared us for the stroke, which that of the 25th instant announced; but it has fallen heavily notwithstanding...*
>
> *To say how much we loved, and esteemed our departed friend, is Unnecessary. She is now no more! but she must be happy, because her virtue has a claim to it.*
>
> *As you talked of coming to this place of business, let us press you to do so. The same room that serves Mr. Dandridge and Washington is large enough to receive a Bed also for you; and it is needless to add, we would be glad of your company. The change may be serviceable to you; and if our wishes were of any avail, they would induce you to make your stay here as long as your convenience would permit.*
>
> *At all times, and under all circumstances, we are, and ever shall remain, Your sincere and Affectionate friends*
>
> *G. Washington*
> *M. Washington*

In spite of his national problems, the president took a great deal of time and trouble to help Lear arrange for the care of the four children. He wrote to Burwell Bassett, Lear's brother-in-law, informing him that Lear had arrived in Philadelphia and they had had many conversations. At first Lear had wanted to keep all the children but he then decided that Maria, the daughter, should live with the Bassetts. The president said that he and his wife had always wanted to raise Fayette but now that the two boys had neither father nor mother, it seemed best to keep them together, at least until the president's forthcoming permanent retirement from government.

On June 3 the president wrote to Lear who had returned to Georgetown: "The chief design of my writing to you by this Post, is to inform you that your good Mother, and lovely son, arrived in this city on Tuesday evening; and left it yesterday about ten o'clock on their way to the Federal City. Mrs. Lear is very well, and Lincoln as sprightly as ever; but both disappointed at not meeting you here. It was with great difficulty a Carriage could be procured to take her on; for it so happened, that Congress closed their Session yesterday, that the members were struggling for, and bidding on each other for conveyances; and your Mother's anxious desire to get to you, would not permit her to wait. At length, after some unavailing attempts, Mr. [George Washington] Craik succeeded in getting a Carriage and a pair of horses, which I hope will take her safe down..."

Maria, also ill with tuberculosis, gave her stepgrandmother a difficult time. Martha Washington wrote Mary Lear on November 4:

> *As soon as we came to town the President sent Mr. Dandridge to enquire of the Minister of the Moravian church, if he could get Maria into the school at Bethlehem. I am sorry to tell you that the answer was that the school was full, so that it would be some time before she could be taken in. The President says he will write to Bethlehem and endeavor if its possible to get her in... I have been told there is a very good boarding school in Georgetown...*

> *I was extremely sorry to be told, after Maria went from Mr. Law's, how ill she had behaved to you. Had I known it before, I should have reprimanded her very seriously. She has always been a spoiled child, as indeed they were all... I loved the child's mother and I love her. It gives me pain to think that a child as circumstanced as she is, should not have a disposition to make herself friends. Her youth will plead for her.*

In addition to looking after Maria's welfare, the president took time to write to and about George Washington Custis, his wife's grandson, who was turning out to be a model of his father. Colonel George Washington had tried, with almost no success, to give John Parke Custis a good education. With rueful foresight the president wrote to Tobias Lear on November 20: "Washington Custis has got settled at Princeton College, and I think under favourable auspices, but the change from his former habits is so great and sudden; and his hours for study so much increased beyond what he has been accustomed to that though he promises to be attentive, it is easy to be perceived he is not at all reconciled to it yet. That of getting up an hour before day, to commence them, I will venture to pronounce not the least irksome to him."

ESTATE TROUBLES

In 1767 Washington's good nature had trapped him as executor of the Colville estate, bringing him thirty-one years of trouble. In 1796 Washington asked Bushrod Washington, his lawyer nephew, to make a final settlement of the business. His letter of February 10 to Bushrod referred to an "extraordinary devise" in the Colville will, adding that he hardly knew where to begin or end a story which had involved him in such "unexpected vexation and trouble." He continued:

> You must know then that in a visit to Colo. Thos. Colville on his death bed (an unlucky one I have ever since deemed it) he informed me, that he had appointed me one of his Executors. I told him that my numerous engagements of a similar kind, would not permit me to discharge the duties of one. He urged; I refused; he pressed again, assuring me that all the trouble would be taken off my hands by his wife and Mr. Jno. West (who married his niece) that he wished only for my name, and I would now and then only inquire how matters were conducted by those first named. Unwilling to make the last moments of a worthy and respectable character uneasy, I yielded to his request; and having done so I would not be worse than my word and qualified accordingly.

Washington then mentioned that he had gone off to the wars. Years later he returned to find Mrs. Colville and West dead and everything relating to the estate "enveloped in darkness." He thereupon engaged a lawyer to go through the whole of the papers so that a final settlement, for which he was responsible, might be made. The letter went on:

> I ought to have mentioned in an earlier part of this detail, that one of the first acts of the Executors was to publish in the English papers an extract of the Will of Colo.

Thos. Colville making the nearest relations of his Mother, the residuary legatees.
The bequest and publication raised a host of claimants, one of whom, through the
medium of General Howe, while he commanded the B. forces in America, <u>demanded</u>
in an open impudent and imperious letter, which passed through the hands of that
officer, the restitution of an Estate worth <u>Forty thousand</u> pounds which he said was
the Surplus of the Estate and due to him; altho the very clause under which he
claimed expressed a doubt of there being any surplus at all.

The president asked his nephew to submit the whole of the matter to the chancellor of Virginia so that the court could order a proper distribution based on the surplus, as finally calculated. Two more years of trouble were involved thereafter for Washington, including the writing of a reply to the clerk of the peace in Durham, England. He patiently explained to the clerk, on September 10, 1797, that it had been a long and trying business to find "the nearest relations of [Colville's] mother, by the names of Stott, Wills, Richardson and Catherine Smith, of Durham, or their descendants." The court of chancery of Virginia had now decreed a distribution. No doubt the heirs would be disappointed at the smallness of the amount involved, a little over $3,000. Washington had asked the Virginia court to determine it, for so many claims were handed in and many were either vague or "accompanied by such unjust and indecent insinuations" that only a court order could clear the mess up. Everyone in Durham now knew where to write to present their documents; he had "nothing more to do in the matter [himself]." Washington's share of the Colville estate correspondence ceased in 1798.

GILBERT STUART

A further unlucky event for Washington was the arrival in Philadelphia that winter of the portrait painter, Gilbert Stuart. Senator William Bingham of Pennsylvania and his wife had promised to present an oil of Washington to the Marquess of Lansdowne, the former British prime minister. On April 11, 1796, the president dropped a line to Stuart: "I am under promise to Mrs. Bingham to sit for you tomorrow at nine o'clock, and wishing to know if it be convenient to you that I should do so, and whether it shall be at your own house (as she talked of the State House), I send this to ask for information."

This was the only completed portrait of Washington which Stuart made directly from his subject and the result was disastrous. The face was devoid of all Washington's intelligence, charm, and humor, and aged far beyond his years. Benjamin Latrobe, the artist-architect, who saw him three months later, reported that "he is about 64 but appears some years younger." The stiff, ungainly figure was painted in later, as were the waxlike hands, by unskilled assistants of Stuart. The artist dashed off many copies of the Lansdowne and the unfinished Antheneum portrait, thereby providing a long line of American schoolchildren with an unpleasant image of the father of their country. The pitching of all Stuart portraits of Washington into Boston Harbor would be appropriate.

The comparison of Washington's real face to his portraits was noted by Charlotte Chambers. In writing her mother, February 21, 1795, about a visit to the Washingtons, she said, "The President, soon after, with that benignity peculiarly his own, advanced, and I arose to receive and return his compliments, with the respect and love my heart dictated." She added how little a portrait on the wall resembled him. The various pictures she had seen looked much more like each other than they did the president.

THE NATIONAL UNIVERSITY

In his last year in office, the president pushed, so far as his time allowed, his favorite object of a national university. By 1796 he had, perhaps because of Virginia's contumacy, decided that the university belonged in Washington, rather than in Alexandria. He was encouraged by reports from the district commissioners that investors and speculators intended to make substantial donations to the university. That year he selected a large site for it, west of the president's house, on which part of the present George Washington University is located. This included land that he owned and which he expected to give to the university as an addition to his Potomac Canal shares.

On July 16 Benjamin Latrobe visited Washington at Mount Vernon. He wrote that after breakfast next morning, the president talked for an hour: "His subject was principally the Establishment of the university at the Federal City. He mentioned the offer he had made of giving to it all the interest he had in the City on condition that it should go on in a given time, and complained that though magnificent offers had been made by many speculators for the same purpose there seemed to be no inclination to carry them into Effect." In December Washington entrusted Madison to carry legislation in the House, authorizing the university, for which he made a strong plea in his last address to Congress.

On September 15 Washington notified the governor of Virginia that he was presenting his James River Canal shares to Liberty Hall Academy in Lexington, Virginia. The institution changed its name to Washington Academy. It subsequently became Washington College and, in the course of time, Washington and (Robert S.) Lee University.

THE CITY OF WASHINGTON

Speculators, described by Washington as "men one day and mice the next," continued to give trouble to the Washington City commissioners. The commissioners' repeated appeals to Robert Morris and his associates were met by promises but no cash. The president approved of their alternate plans to advertise the sale of lots throughout the country and to apply for a loan in Holland, but he warned that the loan application in Europe would take six months to complete. He also endeavored to sound out a Philadelphia bank on the subject but without success.

Washington's letters repeatedly urged the commissioners to devote full time to their work and to live in the city itself. All preferred the amenities of Georgetown to the rigors of the capital's forests. On July 4, 1795, Washington wrote to commissioner Gustavus Scott:

> *I must be explicit in declaring that, not only to obviate the suspicions and jealousies which proceed from a residence of the Commissioners without the City, or in a remote corner of it, not only that they may be where the busy and important scenes are transacting and that they may be the judge of the conduct of others, not from <u>Reports Only</u>, but from ocular proof, as the surest guide to Economy and dispatch; Independent, I say of these considerations... I should view the Residence of the Commissioners... and their Officers... in some central part of it as a nest egg (pardon the expression) which will attract others...*

The finances of the city plagued the commissioners all summer; Washington told them it would be highly impolitic for him to go to Congress for money unless all else failed, since it would revive all the squabbles over the location of the capital. In November the president signed an application to Maryland for a loan; in December he added an urgent personal appeal to the state's governor for funds. On December 25, replying to Scott, who informed him that the Maryland Assembly was about to agree to a loan of $100,000 provided the commissioners personally guaranteed the federal government's note, Washington expressed his gratitude for Maryland's action but commented on the required endorsement: "The necessity of the case justified the obtaining of it on almost any terms, and the zeal of the commissioners... in making themselves liable for the amount, as it could not be had without, cannot fail of approbation… At the same time I must confess that the request has a very singular appearance, and will not, I should suppose, be very grateful to the feelings of Congress." He assured them they would suffer no loss.

THE FAREWELL ADDRESS

The president appears to have verbally informed John Adams in the spring that he would retire at the end of his second term. He gave the same assurance to John Jay by letter in May. No doubt others were told; his anticipated retirement was soon common knowledge, though the president made no formal announcement until September.

When Washington originally planned to retire at the end of his first term, he discussed a farewell address with Madison and gave him a letter indicating the topics he wanted to cover in a valedictory to the people. Madison drafted several introductory paragraphs for the proposed speech, based on their conversations and Washington's letter. Around February 1796, when Hamilton was in Philadelphia, Washington told him that he had been working on a proposed new valedictory, which he would like Hamilton to "redress."

Following his custom with state and private papers, and along the lines of his frequently repeated advice to farm managers and cabinet officers, the president made extensive notes of all the major points he intended to cover. Some of these were in the form of full paragraphs, others, brief outlines:

> *Cherish good faith, justice and peace with other nations:*
>   *1. Because religion and morality dictate it*
>   *2. Because policy dictates it.*
> *Our separation from Europe renders standing alliances inexpedient.*

In his first draft Washington quoted what Madison had said before he moved to the opposition, but this reference was subsequently removed. In preparing his outline the president wrote out his introductory paragraphs, added a rewrite of the Madison draft, and then introduced his major points. It was probably this outline which he showed to Hamilton and from which he expected to write his final paper. Subsequently he added to it his own draft of an address. Though this latter document was rather quickly written and not polished, it is often more moving than the final version:

> *I am every day more sensible that the increasing weight of years renders the private walks of it, in the shade of retirement, as necessary as they will be acceptable to me.*

May I be allowed to add that it will be among the highest as well as the purest enjoyments that can sweeten the remnant of my days, to partake, in a private station, in the midst of my fellow citizens, of that benign influence of good laws under a free Government, which has been the ultimate object of all my wishes, and... the happy reward of our cares and labours.

In contemplating the moment at which the curtain is to drop forever on the public scenes of my life... my sensations... do not permit me to suspend the deep acknowledgments required by the debt of Gratitude which I owe to my beloved country for the many honors it has conferred upon me... All the returns I have now to make will be in those vows which I shall carry with me to my retirement and to my grave, that Heaven may continue to favor the people of the United States with the choicest tokens of its benificence...

...I ask your indulgence while I express... the following most ardent wishes of my heart...

That party disputes, among all the friends and lovers of their country may subside, or, as the wisdom of Providence has ordained that men, on the same subjects, shall not always think alike, that charity and benevolence... may... banish... invectives...

That we may be always prepared for War, but never unsheath the sword except in self-defence, so long as Justice and our <u>essential</u> rights are preserved... If this country can remain in peace 20 years longer: and I devoutly pray that it may do so to the end of time; such in all probability will be its population, riches, and resources, when combined with its peculiarly happy and remote Situation... as to bid defiance, in a just cause, to any earthly power whatsoever.

That our Union may be as lasting as time; for while we are encircled in one band, we shall possess the strength of the giant and there will be none who can make us afraid...

... I leave you with undefiled hands, an uncorrupted heart, and with ardent vows to heaven for the welfare and happiness of that country in which I and my forefathers to the third or fourth progenitor drew our first breath.

When Hamilton reminded Washington in May that he had asked him to review the work and he would need time for it, the president put together all his notes and drafts, requesting Hamilton on May 15 to make a workable second draft from them. In late June Hamilton completed this, and at

336 ALL CLOUDLESS GLORY

Washington's request, went over the whole of the material with John Jay, who subsequently wrote the president about some matters he considered delicate.

It is not possible to determine how many times thereafter Washington rewrote the second draft. In a late August letter to Hamilton he referred to several intensive revisions. From then to the middle of September the paper had further reviews by the president as well as by the entire cabinet.

Washington was unsurpassed as editor and writer. He cut out masses of heavy paragraphs and phrases. He shifted material about, rewriting and transforming as he went. "Cherish good faith and justice towards, and peace and harmony with, all Nations" (Hamilton's version of Washington) became "Observe good faith and justice towards all Nations. Cultivate peace and harmony with all." The final Washington testament, Pauline in its injunction to keep the faith and to love one another, was also a powerful political document, warning against foreign intrigue and domestic anarchy and disunion.

Washington offered "unceasing vows that Heaven may continue to give you the choicest tokens of its beneficence—that your Union and brotherly affection may be sacredly maintained—that its administration in every department may be stamped with wisdom and virtue—that, in fine, the happiness of the people of these states, under the auspices of Liberty, may be made complete, by so careful a preservation and so prudent a use of this blessing as will acquire to them the glory of recommending it to the applause, the affection and adoption of every nation which is yet a stranger to it."

The Union and the Constitution—with its twin supports, religion and morality—had brought to America full independence, peace, liberty, tranquillity, and prosperity. Nevertheless there were grave dangers ahead. "Internal and external enemies... (though often covertly and insidiously)" would batter away against the national Union. He warned that parties were splitting up into northern, southern, and even western factions. In the West, great suspicions had been excited against the federal government which had now opened up the Mississippi River to the whole nation.

The president foresaw that mobs and factions would attempt to overthrow the constitutional government of all the people. Through them, "cunning, ambitious and unprincipled men will be enabled to subvert the power of the people and to usurp for themselves the reins of Government, destroying afterwards the very engines which have lifted them to unjust dominion." The spirit of faction, too, opened the highest councils of government "to foreign influence and corruption." "Habitual hatred, or habitual fondness" for foreign nations would make America, to some degree, "a slave" and provide "ambitious, corrupted, or deluded Citizens (who devote themselves to the favorite nation) facility to betray, or sacrifice the interests of their own country...

gilding, with the appearances of a virtuous sense of obligation, a commendable deference for public opinion, or a laudable zeal for public good, the base or foolish compliances of ambition, corruption or infatuation… Against the insidious wiles of foreign influence (I conjure you to believe me, fellow-Citizens) the jealousy of a free people ought to be <u>constantly</u> awake… Real patriots, who may resist the intrigues of the favourite, are liable to become suspected and odious, while its tools and dupes usurp the applause and confidence of the people, to surrender their interests."

Europe, he continued, had its own primary concerns having only a remote relation to those of the United States. "Why, by interweaving our destiny with that of any part of Europe, entangle our peace and prosperity in the toils of European ambition, rivalship, interest, humour, or caprice?" The neutrality proclamation had been the entire, open, and clear foundation of Washington's foreign policy. If it continued to be the basis of American policy, the United States would have entire "command of its own fortunes."

The president's diary for September 19 noted: "Address to the People of the United States was this day published in Claypoole's paper notifying my intention of declining being considered a Candidate for the Presidency of the United States of America… Left the City this morning on my way to Mount Vernon."

THE REACTIONS

Washington never conceived that his last farewell would be looked upon by his countrymen as if it had come from Mount Sinai. He expressed in it only the modest hope that "counsels from an old and affectionate friend… may be productive of some partial benefit, some occasional good; that they may now and then recur to moderate the fury of party spirit, to warn against the imposture of pretended patriotism." Nonetheless, for many Americans, the address, reproduced at the time from one end of the country to another by press and pamphlet and so often reprinted since, became almost as sacred as the Constitution itself.

The legislatures, in all cases unanimously, of Vermont, Rhode Island, Massachusetts, New Jersey, Pennsylvania, Delaware, Maryland, and North and South Carolina passed lengthy resolutions of praise for all aspects of Washington's conduct, as well as his final "paternal" advice to his countrymen. The warmest and most enthusiastic response came from Maryland, to which the city of Baltimore added its acclaim. Berkeley County in what is now West Virginia and Frederick County in Virginia also expressed their appreciation, first in prose, and then by ejecting their Jeffersonian representative from Congress. In his stead they chose General Daniel Morgan, who considered Democrats "a parsell of egg-sucking dogs." Abigail Adams wrote that his farewell found Washington "covered with glory... the first of heroes and greatest of benefactors to mankind." Jacob Hilzheimer expressed the hope that all good Americans would remember his words "to the end of time." Senator Cabot of Massachusetts, with Bostonian enthusiasm, declared the address to be "excellent." *The Times* of London said that Washington, the old revolutionist, was as far removed from the "wild and wicked revolutionists" of Europe as the "altar" was from "sacrilege."

Virginia did not quite ignore the Farewell Address but its assembly issued a resolution so brief, so grudging, and so sharply in contrast to Maryland's, that Washington, who responded warmly to messages from all the states and cities, answered Richmond: "Be pleased to accept my acknowledgment." Conspicuously absent from the state rolls were Georgia, Kentucky, and Tennessee, whose boundaries had been greatly widened by Washington's diplomacy. Madison thought the president's message, which asked for friendship with all nations, showed pro-British feelings and an unexpected "rancor" towards the French. Jefferson dismissed it as "the adieu." The French minister, in forwarding it to his foreign office, termed the address "insolent" and immoral.

THE 1796 ELECTION

The subsequent presidential election was a mess, in part because of the unfortunate constitutional provision whereby each elector had two votes. Both counted equally; the president-elect had to have a majority of half the electoral votes while the vice-president merely had to have the second highest total. Where letters took weeks to travel, it was difficult for the Federalist electors, in states as far apart as New Hampshire and South Carolina, to coordinate their plans in the brief period before the election.

The French played their part. In addition to his agents who electioneered for Jefferson in western Pennsylvania and Kentucky, the French minister issued a series of threatening letters in late October and in November, designed to sway the election. He timed his first letter just before Pennsylvanians went to the polls. The letters were ostensibly addressed to Pickering, the secretary of state, who received them after Bache had published them. Adet termed the proclamation of neutrality "insidious" and he called on Americans to unite to smash the Jay treaty. He threatened many evils if they did not do so. He denounced the Washington administration in the strongest terms, after claiming that the United States had violated its treaty with France. Until the United States returned to the alliance, France was breaking diplomatic relations, which would be restored only when the American government changed its neutral policy. "Let your government return to itself, and you will find in Frenchmen faithful friends and generous allies."

The Federalist candidates were John Adams, along with Pinckney who had not only secured the Spanish treaty but had the additional virtue of being a southerner. In both North and South, some electors hated to vote for both men, fearful that a tie would throw the election into the House of Representatives. In several states there were favorite sons or others who gained the approving votes of individual electors.

In the end no fewer than thirteen persons received votes, four Democratic and nine Federalist-Republicans. The total electoral vote was a triumph for the Federalists, who received more than a third of the votes south of the Potomac and 86 percent in the North. French activities were sufficient to give Pennsylvania to the Democrats by 235 popular votes. Except for this narrow popular margin in that state, the Federalists would have had almost every vote north of the Potomac.

The split in the vote among nine Federalists bore the fatal result that, while Adams was elected by a bare majority, Jefferson, with a minority, jogged in right behind him as vice-president. Adams himself had 80 percent of the electoral votes in the North, a sharp increase over his total in 1789 and 1793. Jefferson obtained only 15 percent of the electors above the Potomac, but this was sufficient to place him in an office, with limited responsibilities and unlimited opportunities for mischief.

THE STATE OF THE UNION

Washington returned from Mount Vernon to find awaiting him a French declaration of belligerency, accompanied by intolerable interference in America's internal affairs and elections. It was France's reply to the Farewell Address.

In that autumn crisis Washington consulted his cabinet as well as the two most experienced men outside the federal government, Hamilton and Governor Jay of New York. In asking Hamilton's advice he wrote on November 2: "There is in the conduct of the French government... an inconsistency, a duplicity, a delay, or a something else, which is unaccountable upon honorable grounds... As I have very high opinion of Mr. Jay's judgment, candor, honor and discretion... it would be very pleasing to me if you would shew him this letter... and let me have, for consideration, your joint opinion on the several matters therein stated." The president added that he was "fatigued with this and other matters which crowd upon me." Washington mentioned that the second letter from Adet to Pickering, issued a few days before his return, had been published in its entirety by "Claypool, at the government's suggestion." The Jeffersonian press had been giving it out piecemeal, and the government thought it best to make it known as a whole. Washington remarked that the French government was "disposed to play a high game. If other proofs were wanting, the *time* and *indelicate mode and stile*, of the present attack on the Executive, exhibited in this laboured performance, which is as unjust as it is voluminous, would leave no doubt as to the primary object it had in view."

Hamilton's advice to the president was judicious. He deplored Pickering's open reply to Adet in the newspapers, suggesting that it was undignified. The government should make such communications only to Congress. Complaints in regard to French actions ought to be presented to the French Directory by the American minister, in as calm and reasoned a manner as possible. Every possible effort should be made to secure peace. The United States should offer to negotiate all outstanding issues. Hamilton made it clear that France had certain justifiable causes of complaint; these should be adjusted by treaty, as had been done with Great Britain.

Washington, before writing Hamilton, had already determined to give Congress the whole story of the relations with France and to transmit a copy of all the documents to the American minister at Paris. He ordered Pickering to assemble material for a special message to follow his remarks on France in his State of the Union message.

On December 7, at noon, George Washington, with his cabinet in attendance, made his last address to the Congress. He stated that the House delay in voting for the Jay treaty "necessarily procrastinated the reception of the Posts stipulated to be delivered, beyond the date assigned for that event. As soon, however, as the Governor General of Canada could be addressed with propriety on the subject, arrangements were cordially and promptly concluded for their evacuation." American and British commissioners were already at work on the Canadian boundary and on compensation for the captured vessels.

The president said that, to protect "the active external Commerce" of the United States, a naval force was essential. "The most sincere neutrality is not a sufficient guard against the depredations of Nations at War. To secure respect to a Neutral flag, requires a Naval force, organized, and ready to vindicate it from insult or aggression. This may even prevent the necessity of going to War, by discouraging belligerent Powers from committing such violations of the rights of the Neutral party, as may, first or last, leave no other option."

The president then turned to the economic development of the country, adding further recommendations to those which he had previously proposed to Congress:

> *Congress have repeatedly, and not without success, directed their attention to the encouragement of Manufactures. The object is of too much consequence, not to insure a continuance of their efforts, in every way which shall appear eligible. As a general rule, manufactures on public account are inexpedient. But where the state of things in a Country leaves little hope that certain branches of Manufacture will, for a great length of time obtain; when these are of a nature essential to the furnishing and equipping of the public force in time of War, are not establishments for procuring them on public account, <u>to the extent of the ordinary demand for public services</u>, recommended by strong considerations of National policy, as an exception to the general rule?...*

> *It will not be doubted that, with reference either to individual, or National Welfare, Agriculture is of primary importance. In proportion as Nations advance in population, and other circumstances of maturity, this truth becomes more apparent; and renders the cultivation of the Soil more and more an object of public patronage. Institutions for promoting it, grow up, supported by the public purse; and to what object can it be dedicated with greater propriety? Among the means which have been employed to this end, none have been attended with greater success than the establishment of Boards, composed of proper characters, charged with collecting and diffusing information, and enabled by premiums, and small pecuniary aids, to encourage and assist a spirit of discovery and improvement. This species of establishment contributes doubly to the increase of improvement, by stimulating to enterprise and experiment, and by drawing to a common centre, the results everywhere, of individual skill and observation; and spreading them thence over the whole Nation. Experience accordingly has shown that they are very cheap Instruments, of immense National benefits.*

> *The Assembly to which I address myself, is too enlightened not to be fully sensible how much a flourishing state of the Arts and Sciences, contributes to National prosperity and reputation. True it is, that our Country, much to its honor, contains many Seminaries of learning, highly respectable and useful; but the funds upon which they rest, are too narrow to command the ablest Professors in the different*

departments of liberal knowledge, for the Institution contemplated, though they would be excellent auxiliaries.

Amongst the motives to such an Institution, the assimilation of the principles, opinions and manners of our Countrymen, by the common education of a portion of our Youth from every quarter, well deserves attention. The more homogeneous our Citizens can be made, in these particulars, the greater will be our prospect of permanent Union; and a primary object of such a National Institution should be, the education of our Youth in the science of <u>Government</u>. In a Republic, what species of knowledge can be equally important? and what duty, more pressing on its Legislature, than to patronize a plan for communicating it to those who are to be the future guardians of the liberties of the Country?

The Institution of a Military Academy is also recommended by cogent reasons. However pacific the general policy of a Nation may be, it ought never to be without an adequate stock of Military knowledge for emergencies... War might, often, not depend on its own choice... Whatever argument may be drawn from particular examples, superficially viewed, a thorough examination of the subject will evince, that the Art of War, is at once comprehensive and complicated; that it demands much previous study; and that the possession of it, in its most improved state, is always of great moment to the security of a Nation. This, therefore, ought to be a serious care of every Government; and for this purpose, an Academy, where a regular course of instruction is given, is an obvious expedient...

The Compensation to the Officers of the United States... appears to call for Legislative revision. The consequences of a defective provision are of serious import to the Government.

If private wealth is to supply the defect of the public contribution, it will greatly contract the sphere within which the selection of Characters for Office, is to be made; and will proportionately diminish the probability of a choice of Men, able as well as upright. Besides that it would be repugnant to the vital principles of our Government, virtually to exclude from public trusts, talents, virtues, unless accompanied by wealth.

The president then turned to France, where "circumstances of a very unwelcome nature have lately occurred. Our trade has suffered, and is suffering, extensive injuries in the West Indies, from the Cruisers and Agents of the French republic; and communications have been received from its minister here, which indicate that danger of a further disturbance of our Commerce, by its authority." He noted that he had been constant and sincere in his wish to have peace and harmony with France. "The wish remains unabated... Nor will I easily cease to cherish the expectations that a spirit of justice, candour and friendship on the part of the Republic will eventually ensure success."

The president noted that he would send a special message on the subject to Congress. In his subsequent January 4 directive to the secretary of state, Washington wrote: "I have no doubt you have taken care, and will continue to be assured of your facts; for as this business will certainly come before the public, not only the facts, but the candour also, the expression, and the force of every word will be examined with the most scrutinizing eye, and compared with everything that will admit of a different construction, and if there is the least ground for it, we shall be charged with unfairness, and an intention to impose on, and to mislead the public judgment."

REPLIES BY CONGRESS

It had been customary, throughout the first years of the republic, for each House to send a committee to thank the president for his message and to declare its sentiments on the various issues raised. The Senate quickly passed a warm-hearted message of gratitude for all Washington's services; this was delivered by John Adams on December 12. A similar message ran into trouble in the House, which shortly afterwards turned down the proposal for a national university by a single vote. Williams Branch Giles, a Virginia congressman, made a savage attack on the president. He asked that the reference to his "moderation, wisdom, and firmness" be stricken out. Giles said Washington lacked these qualities, and the United States was thereby being dragged into a calamitous crisis. He, for one, was glad the president was retiring from office. Giles' resolution received only twelve votes. On December 16 the House delivered an affectionate final message to the president.

FOURTEEN

MOUNT VERNON

1797–1798

DURING THE FEDERALIST era, 1789–1801, the United States achieved what appears to have been the most rapid rate of economic development of any country in history. George Washington, who left the presidency two-thirds of the way through this period, could take justifiable pride in the country's progress.

Between 1789 and 1796 the value of American exports quadrupled. In real terms—that is, deducting price rises—the 1796 export volume was up two and a half times. Gross national product rose a phenomenal average of nearly 30 percent a year. American per capita income was, in all probability, the highest in the world by 1801.

In 1796 the American merchant marine, which in colonial times, had been largely confined to the coastal and Caribbean trade, was sailing to most of the principal seaports of Europe, Africa, and Asia. The fleet had more than doubled in size; its earnings were up threefold. In 1789 the consular service consisted of a few agents only; by 1796 there was a worldwide network from Cadiz to St. Petersburg in Europe, and from Tangier to Calcutta and Canton in Africa and Asia.

Individual economic data showed impressive gains. The seventy-five post offices of 1789, all that existed after 182 years of settlement, had $29,000 in revenues. By 1801 there were 1,025 post offices; the great increase in the postal system's net revenues was devoted to a rapid expansion of the nation's post roads. Though proper data are lacking, it appears that wages rose much more rapidly than prices. John Adams complained that he paid his farm labor four times as much as he had given them earlier.

POLITICAL AND GEOGRAPHICAL GROWTH

The eleven states that formed the 1789 Union had increased to sixteen, stretching to the Mississippi. The country was extraordinarily youthful. The median age was sixteen in a population highly fecund. Although mortality rates were more than double those of today, the high birth rates carried the net population growth to around 3.5 percent a year. There were some 3.8 million Americans in 1789; nearly a million had been added by the time Washington returned to Mount Vernon. Younger sons and daughters were travelling by hundreds of thousands into new farms in western Pennsylvania, Virginia, and New York. Kentucky, Tennessee, and even far away Ohio were filling with energetic settlers.

The United States of America had become a thoroughly viable and vigorous country under strong leadership. An efficient and honest federal customs and revenue system operated to provide an increasing range of domestic and foreign services. The once bankrupt country had achieved the highest of the world's credit ratings in Amsterdam. A federal judiciary system, remarkably high in quality, was in operation in the national capital and in the sixteen states. The country had conducted its first census and established a mint, a decimal coinage system, and active copyright and patent offices. The federal government had greatly expanded the number of lighthouses, beacons, buoys, and public piers. There was a national sea-rescue system under the new coast guard. State and local road building added to the new national network of post roads, although the quality had apparently shown little improvement. The United States had its first national banking system and an efficient national army. A naval fleet was under construction. An imaginative new capital was well past the planning stage; major government buildings and private houses and hotels were pushing towards completion. The single diplomatic envoy at the capital, the representative of France, had been joined by several colleagues, as Great Britain, the Netherlands, Spain, and Portugal recognized the increasing importance of this newest republic. Nearly a dozen institutions of higher learning, many subsequently great universities, were established during Washington's presidency.

THE FINAL TWO MONTHS

As the end of his term approached, the Jeffersonians increased the fury of their attacks on the president. Thomas Paine's psychotic diatribe, which had been sponsored by Monroe, was published in Philadelphia in December. It was industriously circulated in the country, along with the French minister's aspersions on the administration. With relief in sight, Washington could view the situation with disdain in his January 8 letter to David Stuart:

> *A large party under real, or pretended fears of British influence, are moving heaven and earth to aid [French minister Adet] in his designs… Finding a Neutral conduct has been adopted, and would not be relinquished by those who administered the government, the next step was to try to rally the people… Several presses and many Scribblers have been employed… This not working as well as was expected, from a supposition that there was too much confidence, and perhaps personal regard for the present Chief Magistrate and his politics, the batteries latterly have been levelled at him particularly and personally and, although he is soon to become a private citizen, his opinions are to be knocked down, and his character reduced as low as they are capable of sinking it, even by resorting to absolute falsehoods. As an evidence whereof, and of the plan they are pursuing, I send you a letter from Mr. Paine to me, Printed in this City and disseminated with great industry. Others of a similar nature are also in circulation.*
>
> *To what lengths the French Directory will ultimately go, is difficult to say; but that they have been led to the present point by our own People, I have no doubt…*

As the attacks grew in intemperance, the people of Philadelphia determined to show Washington how much the great majority of the country loved and admired him. Weeks of planning and preparation went into the celebration of his last birthday as chief of state and government. According to Washington's diary, February 22 opened with rain, followed by a cloudy forenoon. Thereafter it was "clear and very fine." The whole city was on holiday. There were parades and the firing of cannon; all ships in the harbor were decorated with flags and pennants. Immense crowds gathered near the president's house to watch the dignitaries who called on him and his wife between noon and three—the vice-president, the cabinet, the diplomatic corps, members of the Senate and House, officers of the army and navy, and representatives of the Cincinnati.

That evening 1,200 persons attended a ball, which the president described as "elegant." Claypoole's newspaper expressed the opinion that for "Splendor, Taste and Elegance [it] was, perhaps, never excelled by any similar entertainment in the United States." James Iredell wrote to his wife that it was much too crowded and there was "such scrambling to go to supper that there was some danger of being squeezed to death." He reported that the applause for the president and his lady was so overwhelming that Mrs. Washington broke into tears and her husband found the tribute such that "his emotions were too powerful to be concealed."

The president was overburdened with business during his last two months in office, some of it time-consuming trivialities. A federal judiciary was established in Tennessee. Army officers were promoted. Consuls were nominated for North Africa, Italy, and Sweden. Patents were signed, including one for artist Charles Wilson Peale, who had developed "a new and useful improvement in making Bridges." Treaties with the Six Nations and the Cherokees were forwarded to the Senate and duly ratified. The president signed letters of credence for Minister John Quincy Adams, promoted from The Hague to Madrid, as well as David Humphreys, his old secretary, who became minister at Lisbon. On March 3, 1797, he nominated Anthony White to be surveyor of New Brunswick, New Jersey, and the Senate approved it the same day. This was Washington's last appointment to office but his work, thanks to the slowness of Congress, piled up to the end. He wrote to Jonathan Trumbull on March 3:

> When I add that, according to custom all the Acts of the Session, except two or three very unimportant Bills, have been presented to me within the last four days, _you_ will not be surprised at the pressure under which I write at present; but it must astonish _others_ who know that the Constitution allows the President ten days to deliberate on _each_ Bill that is brought before him, that he should be allowed by the Legislature less than half that time to consider _all_ the business of the Session; and in some instances, scarcely an hour to resolve the most important. But as the scene is closing with me, it is of little avail _now_ to let it be with murmurs.

On the afternoon of March 3 the Washingtons gave a dinner for the president-elect, the members of the cabinet who were to stay in office, and the diplomatic corps. That night the president of the United States slept very well.

MARCH 4, 1797

The president-elect, as he wrote his wife, had a very bad night, thinking he might very well faint next day in front of the whole world. The morning sight of a cheerful Washington, his face, according to Adams, "as serene and unclouded as the day," did nothing to aid his morale, for he thought the general was indicating how glad he was to be out of that office. Another observer, Charles Biddle, noted that Washington appeared happier than he had ever seen him before, while William Duer wrote that his face was "radiant."

President Adams was sworn in by the chief justice before Washington, Jefferson, the cabinet, the House and Senate, and all who could crowd into the chamber. Adams went through the ordeal very well after all. He made an excellent, strong, and forthright speech, echoing many of Washington's general principles of government as well as his Farewell Address. Without a trace of false sentimentality, Adams managed to be particularly graceful in referring to the "great example" of his predecessor in office. The whole occasion—the retirement of Washington, the easy transfer of power, and Adams' speech—brought tears to the eyes of almost everyone. The president noted that there was scarcely a dry eye to be seen anywhere, except for George Washington. The president was roundly cheered as he concluded his speech and moved through the throng. Jefferson waved to Washington to follow the president. Firmly but politely Washington indicated that the vice-president of the United States preceded a private citizen. The transfer of power was thus symbolically complete.

The former president called on the president, shortly after the speech, to wish him "a happy and successful and honorable" administration. Mrs. Washington had already told Adams how pleased she and her husband had been by his election, a remark which surprised the president-elect, coming as it did from a woman who had been notably discreet through the presidential years. Philadelphia gave a farewell dinner to Washington that afternoon. The Washingtons spent the next few days in packing and saying goodbye.

The Jeffersonian press hurled their final abuse at Washington, embellishing their insults by extolling John Adams. In England, however, there were other appraisals. On March 5, after acknowledging receipt of the Stuart portrait, Lord Lansdowne wrote to William Jackson: "I cannot express to you the satisfaction I have felt in seeing the forts given up… General Washington's conduct is beyond all praise. He has left a noble example to sovereigns and nations, present and to come. I beg you will mention both me and my sons to him in the most respectful terms possible. If I were not too old, I would go to Virginia to do him homage." Shortly afterwards his one-time enemy, George III, gave George Washington the most generous tribute of his career. The king told Benjamin West, the American painter who was a personal intimate, what he thought, in a conversation which West reported to Rufus King, the American minister, on May 3:

Mr. West said things respecting America had changed very much; that people who could not formerly find words of unkindness enough now talked in a different language; that the King had lately spoken in the most explicit manner of the wisdom of the American Gov. and of the abilities and great worth of the characters they produced and employed...

In regard to General Washington, he told him since his resignation that in his opinion "that act closing and finishing what had gone before and viewed in connection with it, placed him in a light the most distinguished of any man living, and that he thought him the greatest character of the age."

Although the former president was exceedingly anxious to get home, the logistics of moving family, house guests, servants, and an eight-year accumulation of papers, furniture, and general whatnots was complex. President Adams had agreed to occupy the Morris house, which the Washingtons previously rented. The former president himself wrote out a seven-page inventory of its contents. He informed Adams that he would leave all furniture for which the government had paid. He had originally planned to take the best of his own pieces home and sell the rest, but this seemed ungracious to Adams. He therefore offered to sell such contents of the house as he might want, but the new president eventually declined to buy any. Washington then sold at auction some of the pieces and gave others as presents to close friends. He asked Lear and Dandridge, his two secretaries, to see to the packing and shipment of all the rest. From Lear's letter to Washington, after his departure, it appears that they sent by sea to Mount Vernon more than 170 crates, boxes, trunks, and assorted packages of merchandise.

Early in the morning of March 9, with the temperature disagreeably cold, the Washingtons, Nelly Custis, George Lafayette, and his tutor, with assorted servants, carriages, and newly acquired horses, set out for the long journey to Mount Vernon. That evening Washington wrote to Lear from Chester: "On one side I am called upon to remember the Parrot, on the other to remember the dog. For my own part I should not much pine if both were forgot."

To add to the miseries of the bad roads, the bitter winds, and occasional snow, Mrs. Washington had a severe cold. In consequence, Washington tried to avoid all delaying ceremonies, but Baltimore, which had given him so hearty a welcome in 1789 and had since so ardently supported his presidency, could not be denied. The Washingtons were escorted into town by a troop of horse and, according to the Baltimore paper, were greeted by "as great a concourse of people as Baltimore ever witnessed." On alighting at the Fountain Inn, the General was saluted with reiterated and thundering huzzas from the spectators. The mayor and council delivered an address after which the Washingtons "dined and lodged" at the inn. On March 14 the couple drove through the city of Washington. The *Washington Gazette* reported next day:

Yesterday George Washington (God bless him) passed through the city on his way to Mount Vernon. When he reached the Capitol the company of Artillery, under the command of Captain Hoban, welcomed him by a discharge of cannon. After dining in the City , he was escorted to George Town by several of our most respectable Citizens. As he passed the President's house, a salute of 16 guns was fired by the said company and followed by repeated huzzas, dictated by hearts sensibly alive to his merits.

Washington dined in Washington with his wife's granddaughter, Eliza Law. The Washingtons spent the night with Martha Peter, another married granddaughter. Next day he received addresses from the city of Georgetown, as well as from its college, which had begun instruction the year he took the oath as president. The former president was welcomed at the Alexandria ferry by old friends and neighbors who escorted him to Mount Vernon. On March 19, four days after their arrival, Nelly Custis wrote to the wife of the secretary of the treasury that it had been a "fatiguing" trip. She added a sentence which Washington himself clearly dictated: "Grandpapa is very well and much pleased with being once more 'Farmer Washington.'"

MOUNT VERNON

Mrs. Washington's cold hung on until April but she recovered in the spring in her own house. The family's letters for the rest of the year had a note of good cheer, which was marred only by the death of Washington's sister, Betty Lewis, at the end of March. Mrs. Washington wrote that she and the general felt like children just released from school. They loved having old friends call but begrudged sparing any of their time for strangers, who dropped in to have a look at the general. The Washingtons, however, welcomed with interest three young Bourbon brothers who appeared on April 5, to stay four days. The Duc d'Orléans, once a Jacobin, was to be king of France thirty-three years later. Washington gave them a map and recommendations for their explorations in Kentucky and Tennessee.

On April 3 Washington sent a note to James McHenry, asking him occasionally to spare any news from the seat of government, which was "not contrary to the rules of your official duty to disclose." He added:

I find myself in the situation, nearly, of a young beginner, for although I have not houses to build (except one, which I must erect for the accommodation and security of my Military, Civil and private Papers which are voluminous, and may be interesting) yet I have not one or scarcely anything else about me that does not require considerable repairs. In a word I am already surrounded by Joiners, Masons, Painters, &ca. and such is my anxiety to get out of their hands, that I have scarcely a room to put a friend into or to set in myself, without the Music of hammers, or the odoriferous smell of Paint.

I am indebted to you for several unacknowledged letters; but ne'er mind that; go on as if you had them. You are at the source of information and can find many things to relate; while I have nothing to say, that could either inform or amuse a Secretary of War in Philadelphia.

I might tell him that I begin my diurnal course with the Sun; that if my hirelings are not in their place at that time I send them messages expressive of my sorrow for their indisposition; then having put these wheels in motion, I examine the state of things further; and the more they are probed, the deeper I find the wounds are, which my buildings have sustained by an absence and neglect of eight years; by the time I have accomplished these matters, breakfast, a little after seven o'clock... is ready. This over, I mount my horse and ride around my farms, which employs me until it is time to dress for dinner; at which I rarely miss seeing strange faces; come, as they say, out of respect to me. Pray, would not the word curiosity answer as well: and how different this, from having a few social friends at a cheerful board. The usual time of sitting at Table; a walk, and Tea, brings me within the dawn of Candlelight; previous to which, if not prevented by company, I resolve that, as soon as the glimmering taper supplies the place of the great luminary, I will retire to my writing Table and acknowledge the letters I have received; but when the lights are brought, I feel tired and disinclined to engage in this work, conceiving that the next night will do as well; the next comes and with it the same causes for postponement, and effect, and so on.

This will account for your letter remaining so long unacknowledged; and having given you the history of a day, it will serve for a year... but it may strike you that in this detail no mention is made of any portion of time allotted for reading; the remark would be just, for I have not looked into a book since I came home, nor shall be able to do it until I have discharged my Workmen; probably not before the nights grow longer; when possibly I may be looking in doomsday book...

Washington found not only that his buildings had been neglected but his farm production had greatly diminished. His 1797 yield of wool per sheep was less than half what it had been in 1789; he set about purchasing good rams to improve his breed. He did the same for his cattle, buying an expensive bull from John Threlkeld of Georgetown. In July he wrote to William Strickland, an English farmer who had made a tour of America, including Mount Vernon, to say that his observations of poor American fencing practices were just. He had tried in absentia to prevent the wasteful way his managers cut down trees to build fences, by asking them to plant living fences. They had not done as he directed; old as he was and even if he did not live to see them grow, he was determined to use cedars extensively, as natural fencing for his farms.

On July 31 Washington sent a note to Lear to say that the house was empty. "Unless someone pops in, unexpectedly—Mrs. Washington and I will do what I believe has not been done within the last twenty years by us—that is sit down to dinner by ourselves." Fortunately, the great majority of visitors who poured into Mount Vernon that summer and autumn for meals and, sometimes, bed, were old friends and relatives. They included the grand- and great-grandchildren of Martha, assorted nieces and nephews of the general, along with their children, as well as his great Virginia supporter, Henry Lee, and his wife and daughter. The Spanish and British ministers to Philadelphia appeared, as did various British treaty and colonial officials. In addition there were strangers whose names were listed as "a Mr. X" if Washington got the name or simply appeared as blank in his diary.

It was partly the mass of visitors but also the general's inherent kindness which led him to write on August 4 to the widowed Lawrence Lewis, whose mother had died in March, inviting him to make Mount Vernon his residence. He indicated that he could not pay him a salary as he was too overburdened with staff but he would be glad if, in return for bed and board for himself, a servant and a horse, Lawrence could take over some social and clerical duties. "As both your aunt and I are in the decline of life, and regular in our habits, especially in our hours of rising and going to bed, I require some person (fit and Proper) to ease me of the trouble of entertaining company, particularly of nights, as it is my inclination to retire (unless prevented by very particular company, always do retire) either to my bed, or to my study, soon after candle-light. In taking these duties (which hospitality obliges one to bestow on company) off my hands, it would render me a very acceptable service, and for a little time to come, only, an hour in the day, now and then, devoted to the recording of some Papers, which time would not allow me to complete before I left Philadelphia... If you have inclination for it [your other time] might be devoted to Reading, as I have a great many instructive books, on many subjects, as well as amusing ones..." Lawrence Lewis appeared on August 31 and helped the general until his death.

Washington declined an invitation to attend the marriage of another nephew, Lawrence Augustine Washington, saying that "as wedding assemblies are better calculated for those who are *coming in to*, than to those who are *going out of* life, you must accept the good wishes of your Aunt and myself in place of personal attendance, for I think it is not likely that either of us will ever be more than 25 miles from Mount Vernon again."

Washington, who had played so great a role in national and international affairs, now took particular interest in the growth and development of Alexandria and Washington. In a chatty June 26 note to David Humphreys at Lisbon, he wrote:

> *The Public Buildings in the Federal City go on well; one wing of the Capitol (with which Congress might make a very good shift) and the President's house, will be covered in this autumn, or to speak more correctly perhaps, the latter is <u>now</u> receiving its cover, and the former will be ready for it by that epoch. An elegant bridge is thrown over the Potomack at the Little Falls, and the navigation of the River above will be completed, nearly, this season; through which an immensity of Produce must flow to the Shipping Ports thereon.*

> *Alexandria you would scarcely know; so much has it increased since you [were] there; two entire Streets where Shallops then laded and unladed are extended into the River, and some of the best buildings in the Town erected on them. What were the commons are now all inclosed and many good houses placed on them.*

> *As my circle is <u>now small</u>, my information will be, of course, contracted; as Alexandria and the federal city will probably be the extent of my perambulations.*

When rumors reached Mount Vernon that Lafayette, after five years in prison, was about to be released, young George Washington Lafayette could not be restrained from returning to France. General Washington thought it imprudent to return on the basis of a rumor. He told young Lafayette that he could not be sure of conditions in France and his parents might very well be coming to America for refuge. On October 12 Washington rode to Georgetown with Lafayette and his tutor, Felix Frestal, in order to put them on the stage to New York. He accompanied their coach as far as the city of Washington. Having given them $300 to defray their return to France, Washington wrote to Alexander Hamilton in New York, asking him to procure their passage and to advance them any further funds they needed. As it turned out, young Lafayette's instincts were sound. His father, mother, and sister had been released into the hands of the American consul at Hamburg. Madame de Lafayette, who had spent much time in French and Austrian prisons, was too ill to travel to America. Young Lafayette joined his family in February.

LAWYER WASHINGTON

Washington complained that his lack of legal knowledge made the presidency particularly irksome. He was daily faced with intricate constitutional and international legal problems, with only a part-time lawyer, on a retainer basis, as his attorney general and counselor. When it came to land titles, however, his nearly fifty years of experience gave him as good knowledge as a member of the bar. When an overly smart attorney found what he thought to be a title flaw in land Washington had bought thirty-five years previously and subsequently sold, lawyer Washington got busy. To William Triplett, a purchaser of similar land, he wrote on September 24 to say that the testimony of the principal witness, Grafton Kirk, "is not *quite immaculate*, but so much the reverse as [he proves] to be always a ready witness upon all occasions." Washington never hesitated to get the best legal advice but he clearly hated paying lawyers. He asked two future Supreme Court justices, John Marshall and Bushrod Washington, to handle his case, if he had to appeal. He explained the situation to his nephew, Bushrod, in a letter of October 9, which was a mixture of irony, humor, legal language, and Latin and English puns:

Mr. Thomas Pearson, heir entail to Simon Pearson, his Brother, has brought suit… for the lands which the latter sold to Wm. Triplett, George Johnson and myself, five and thirty years ago.

I understand from Colo. Simms, who is Pearson's Lawyer, that his complaint is founded upon some irregularity in the proceedings of the Jury, who met on the land to value the same, pursuant to a Writ of ad quod damnum. And the examination of the evidence to prove these irregularities went (for I attended) to the establishment of two points: 1st. that there was no survey of the premises in presence of the Jury, at the time of their enquiry into the value of the land and 2ly, that the said Jury did not explore it sufficiently to ascertain with exactness what the real value of the land was.

This is the amount of Grafton Kirk's evidence, who was one of the jurors and who, from your practice in Fairfax county you may have learnt, is a rare hand at all obsolete claims that depend much on a good memory*.*

Let me ask your opinion on the following points:

Does the Law providing for the Docking of Entails, by a writ of ad quod damnum, make a survey in the presence of the Jury an essential part of the proceedings? The Writ itself (of which I retained a copy)… requires no such thing.

*Who is to judge of the mode by which a Jury on Oath is to report their Opinion of
the value of the land, if they are not to do it themselves?...*

*Whether, as Simon was lawfully married and never legally divorced, the children of
the woman, though begotten (no matter by whom) in the state of separation from
him, is not a bar to the claim of Thomas?*

*What operation will the Act of Assembly of Virginia for Docking all entails. . .
passed many years before the death of Simon Pearson, which happened only last
Spring, have in this case...*

*Whether I had better interest myself in defending the suit, already commenced in the
County court, or await the decision there and take it up in the dernier resort, if it
should be adverse... I wish also... to be informed (confidentially) whether, in your
opinion, Mr. Swan's demand for defending the suit [$200] is not unreasonable?...*

*You may think me an unprofitable applicant in asking opinions and requiring
services of you without dousing my money, but pay day may come. If the case
should go to the higher courts, I shall expect you to appear for me, and Mr.
Marshall also...*

*P. S. Whether Colo. Simms has any thing in petto [up his sleeve] I am unable to
say, I am told however, that he is sanguine and some add that he is to go snacks
[divvy up the loot taken from Washington].*

Washington made only a brief further reference in his correspondence to the
suit, which presumably never got beyond the lower court.

GEORGE WASHINGTON CUSTIS

Martha Washington's grandson, born less than six months before her husband's Yorktown victory, grew to become his stepgrandfather's adolescent
plague. He received Washington's best advice, always promised his faithful
adherence to it, and as invariably defaulted. Custis was to be a double
dropout, fit, as his stepgrandfather finally decided, only for the army. Custis
entered the college at Princeton in 1796, to which the president addressed
long letters of counsel and good cheer. On November 15 he forwarded ten
dollars "to purchase a gown, if proper... I advise you not to provide this without first obtaining the approbation of your tutors; otherwise you may be distinguished more by folly, than by the dress." All Custis' letters to Washington

have disappeared, probably owing to the indulgence of his grandmother or Washington heirs. Their general tenor, particularly as to how well he was doing, may be deduced from the president's constantly encouraging tone:

It affords me pleasure to hear that you are agreeably fixed; and I receive still more from the assurance you give of attending closely to your studies... Endeavor to conciliate the good will of all your fellow students, rendering them every act of kindness in your power. Be particularly obliging and attentive to your chambermate, Mr. [John] Forsyth [later Secretary of State], who, from the account I have of him, is an admirable young man and strongly impressed with the importance of a liberal and finished education. But above all, be obedient to your tutors, and in a particular manner, respect the president of the seminary who is both learned and good... Never let an indigent person ask, without receiving something, if you have the means, always recollecting in what light the widow's mite was viewed. (November 15, 1796)

You are now extending into that stage of life when good or bad habits are formed. When the mind will be turned to things useful and praiseworthy, or to dissipation and vice. Fix on whichever it may, it will stick by you... This admonition proceeds from the purest affection for you; but I do not mean by it, that you are to become a stoic, or to deprive yourself in the intervals of study of any recreations or manly exercise, which reason approves. 'Tis well to be on good terms with all your fellow-students, and I am pleased to hear you are so, but while a courteous behavior is due to all, select the most deserving only for your friendships and before this becomes intimate, weigh their dispositions and character well. I would guard you too, against imbibing hasty and unfavorable impressions of any one... To speak evil of any one, unless there is unequivocal proof of their deserving it, is an injury for which there is no adequate reparation... Keep in mind that scarcely any change would be agreeable to you at first from the sudden transition, and from never having been accustomed to shift or rough it. And, moreover, that if you meet with collegiate fare, it will be unmanly to complain. (November 28, 1796)

I presume you received my letter covering a ten dollar bill to pay for the gown, although it is not mentioned. To acknowledge the receipt of letters is always proper, to remove doubts of their miscarriage... The pleasure of hearing you were well, in good spirits, and progressing as we could wish in your studies, was communicated by your letter of the fourteenth... to your grandmama; but what gave me particular satisfaction, was to find you were going to commence a course of reading with Doctor Smith... 'tis to close application and constant perseverance, men of letters and science are indebted for their knowledge and usefulness... You... know how anxious all your friends are to see you enter upon the grand theatre of life, with the advantages of a highly cultivated mind, and a proper sense of your duties to God and man. (December 19, 1796)

Your letter of the 22n. inst. received. The affectionate sentiments contained in them are highly pleasing to me. But that which affords a still higher gratification is to hear that you are not only attentive to your studies but pleased with them also... (February 27, 1797)

It gives me singular pleasure to hear that your time has been so well employed during the last winter, and that you are so sensible of it yourself. (April 3, 1797)

The serene picture was suddenly shattered for the former president when, in May, he received a stern letter from the Reverend Samuel Stanhope Smith, president of the college. This has also not been found, but Washington's reply indicates its nature: "Your favor of the 18th instant was received by the last post, the contents of which, relative to Mr. Custis, filled my mind (as you naturally supposed it would) with extreme disquietude. From his infancy I have discovered an almost unconquerable disposition to indolence in everything that did not tend to his amusements; and have exhorted him in the most parental and friendly manner, often, to devote his time to more useful pursuits. His pride has been stimulated, and his family expectations and wishes have been urged as inducements thereto. In short, I could say nothing to him by way of admonition, encouragement, or advice, that has not been repeated over and over again."

Washington Custis followed up Smith's report with a long, remorseful letter, expressing his sorrow at his "late contest with the passions," apparently an outburst against the college authorities for trying to get him to study. Grandfather Washington sat down and wrote him on June 4: "Your letter... eased my mind of many unpleasant sensations and reflections on your account... If your sorrow and repentance for the disquietude occasioned by the preceding letter, your resolution to abandon the ideas which were therein expressed, are sincere, I shall not only heartily forgive, but will forget also, and bury in oblivion all that has passed... You must not suffer this resolution you have recently entered into, to operate as the mere result of a momentary impulse, occasioned by the letters you have received from hence."

On July 10, 1797, Washington wrote to Custis: "If it has been usual for the students of Nassau college to go to the balls on the anniversary of the Declaration of Independence, I see no reason why you should have avoided it, as no innocent amusement or reasonable expenditure will ever be withheld from you." Custis then developed a correspondence with a Yale tutor, who gave him advice on his studies, which were not in accord with those of Smith. Washington replied to Custis on July 23: "With regard to Mr. Z. Lewis, [he] was educated at Yale college, and as is natural, may be prejudiced in favor of the mode pursued at that seminary; but no college has turned out better scholars, or more estimable characters, than Nassau." He followed with another letter of August 29: "Your letter of the 21st instant… as usual, gave us pleasure to hear that you enjoyed good health, were progressing well in your studies and that you were on the road to promotion… I shall make all fears [that he would not return to Princeton after his vacation] yield to a firm persuasion that every day convinces you of the propriety and necessity of devoting your youthful days in the acquirement of that knowledge which will be advantageous, grateful and pleasing to you in your mature years, and may be the foundation of your use-fulness here and happiness hereafter. Your grandmamma.… has been a good deal indisposed by swelling on one side of her face but it is now much better. The rest of the family within doors are all well, and all unite in best regards to you, along with your sincere friend and affectionate… G. Washington."

His calm was once more interrupted by a series of letters from the president of Princeton. These no longer exist among the Washington files but his October 9 reply implies that Custis was asked to leave the college:

Dear and Revd. sir: I have duly received your several letters of last month; but as an expression of my regret at the conduct and behavior of young Custis would avail nothing, I shall not trouble you by the attempt.

I am persuaded that your conduct towards him, has been such as friendship inspired, and the duties of your important trust required. And, as you have seen, he will have himself only to upbraid for any consequences which may follow and this perhaps come too late.

Washington sent funds by young Lafayette to Smith to pay the final bills at Princeton. On January 7 he once more attempted to bring young Custis, now back at Mount Vernon, to a sense of order and discipline. He gave him a written memorandum, particularly asking him to stop wasting his time "running up and down stairs" and also engaging in "conversation any one who will talk to you." He then urged him to get up early and make it a habit. He was to engage in studies from breakfast till afternoon dinner. Thereafter he could walk till teatime and then resume his studies until bedtime. Above all he was to be punctual for meals, since the servants had "to be running here and there, and they know not where, to summon you." Saturdays he was to have for hunting or other relaxation.

These directives had little effect. On January 22, he informed Custis' step-father, Dr. Stuart, that he had been "disappointed and my mind much dis-turbed by his conduct." He asked Stuart to find out from him, while he was visiting his mother, what the boy really wanted to do. He himself had always thought Harvard was the best place in the country for him, since it was the largest institution and had the highest moral standards. Having him far away would be "a heart-rending stroke" for Mrs. Washington. He doubted that William and Mary would be satisfactory, even if Custis were placed in Bishop James Madison's own house. The following month, Washington conferred with an uncle, George Calvert of Annapolis. Calvert recommended St. John's College, assuring Washington there was little dissipation in the state capital, because of the "strictness of the police." Dr. Stuart agreed to enroll him there.

Once again grandpaternal letters went to Custis. On March 19 Washington wrote how pleased he was to find him "disposed to prosecute your studies with zeal and alacrity." His next letter said he was happy that "you are... going on well in your studies. Prosecute these with diligence and ardor and you will, sometime hence, be more sensible than now of the rich harvest you will gather from them." On May 10 he chided Custis for asking to whom he should apply for more money. "You were provided very plentifully... with necessaries when you left this house (two months ago only)... I am at a loss to discover what has given rise to so early a question. Surely you have not conceived that indulgence in dress or other extravagances are matters that were ever contemplated by me as objects of expense; and I hope they are not so by you." On June 15 he wrote: "It is now near five weeks since any person has heard from you... Knowing how apt your grandmamma is to suspect that you are sick, or that some accident has happened to you, how could you omit this?" When vacation time approached, Washington Custis finally cracked Washington's monumental patience by inquiring whether, now that he had completed a course in geometry, he was to quit school. Back went the answer from Mount Vernon on July 24: "Your... question... really astonishes me! For it would seem as if nothing I could say to you made more than a momentary impression. Did I not, before you went to that seminary, and since by letter, endeavor to fix indelibly on your mind, that the object for which you were sent there was to finish a course of education?" Washington's letter had induced Custis to leave his effects in Annapolis, while he came home for vacation. On August 13 the general wrote Stuart: "If you or Mrs. Stuart could, by indirect means, discover the State of Washington Custis's mind, it would be to be wished. He appears to be moped and stupid, says nothing, and is always in some hole or corner, excluded from Company. Before he left Annapolis, he wrote to me desiring to know whether he was to return there, or not, that he might pack up accordingly; I answered that I was astonished at the question! And that it appeared to me that nothing that could be said to him had the least effect. Whether this, by thwarting his views, is the cause of his present behavior, I know not." By September 6 he was writing the president of St. John's that Custis would be paying a brief visit to settle his accounts and pick up his books and clothing.

TROUBLES IN PHILADELPHIA

As John Adams' biographer, Page Smith, expressed it, the president had entered "into a goodly heritage. Washington had made the presidency a strong office and Adams intended to keep it so." Adams' inaugural address noted that for eight years the country had been administered by a citizen who, "by a long course of great actions" had brought "unexampled prosperity" and "the highest praise of foreign nations." After a brief recession in 1797, when peace hopes temporarily disappeared in Europe, the United States began to climb to yet higher prosperity.

John Adams had long and diversified experience. He had been in the Massachusetts legislature and the Continental Congress. He had achieved diplomatic triumphs in the Netherlands and France. For eight years he was Washington's loyal vice-president, thereafter as president, retaining Washington's entire cabinet, including Pickering and Wolcott, who had been in the federal government almost since its beginning. He could also rely on the remarkably able group of American diplomats abroad, who had been appointed by Washington. They included John Quincy Adams, considered by the first president to be the most competent of all.

There were offsets to these advantages. Adams did not have the stability and calm of his predecessor, and he realized he would never enjoy more than a fraction of Washington's popularity. In the crisis with France, now grown to dangerous proportions, he could count on the opposition of a large and powerful group of Jeffersonians, ready to thwart whatever he tried to do. His popularity with the Democrats, pleased as they were with the departure of Washington, lasted ten weeks. The president was surprised only that he escaped criticism that long. In the end, in trying to straddle the chasm between the Federalists and Democrats, he fell into the widening gap between them.

Adams later wrote his wife that the presidency was "a peck of troubles [arriving] in a large bundle of papers… every day." The reports from the legation in France were among the earliest to appear. Therein the president read the obsequious speech of Monroe to the French Directory, remarkable for its first person praise of France's revolution and aggressive armies. The farewell to Monroe, by the head of the Directory, was surly and insulting to the United States, but complimentary to the American minister, who represents "the true interests of your country. Depart with our regrets." The director refused to receive General Pinckney as a successor, threatened subsequently to place him under the jurisdiction of the police minister, and finally gave him written orders to leave the country. In European practice, this was the normal prelude to a declaration of war. Adams thereupon summoned Congress into special session. In his message of May 19, 1797, the president gave the full story but indicated that he intended to maintain the policies of Washington:

> *It is my sincere desire… to preserve peace and friendship with all nations: and believing that neither the honor nor the interests of the United States absolutely forbid the repetition of advances for securing these desirable objects with France, I shall institute a fresh attempt at negotiation, and shall not fail to promote and accelerate an accommodation on terms compatible with the rights, duties, interests and honor of the nation. If we have committed error, and these can be demonstrated, we shall be willing to correct them; if we have done injuries, we shall be willing on conviction to redress them; and equal measures of justice we have a right to expect from France and every other nation.*

On May 31, as evidence of his sincerity, Adams nominated General Pinckney, Francis Dana of Massachusetts, and John Marshall of Virginia "to be jointly and severally envoys extraordinary and ministers plenipotentiary to the French republic." When Dana was unable to go, Adams chose Jeffersonian Elbridge Gerry, an old personal friend, over the objections of his cabinet. Gerry had defended Monroe in correspondence with Adams and even urged the president to send him back to France. Adams replied that he thought Monroe was "dull and stupid." He denied Gerry's claim that France was republican, saying a republic there was likely to last as long as a snowball in a Philadelphia summer.

Adams' efforts to negotiate, while arming for defense, brought him into immediate conflict with the Democrats. Jefferson wrote to Madison to say that Adams wanted war and he himself would therefore work to defeat all defense measures. In subsequent letters Jefferson praised the "splendid" victories of Bonaparte as a deterrent to Adams' war plans. He reported conversations he held with the French spy, Constatin Volney. He repeatedly referred to the "folly" of Adams in calling Congress into session during a crisis. By June Jefferson was writing Aaron Burr that the president's speed had been "inflammatory," it was a declaration of war, and Adams wanted negotiations to fail, since two of his nominees were not "strongly attached" to the French alliance. "War then was intended." He called on Burr to rally the people of New York and the eastern states against the government. To Gerry, in expressing "infinite joy" at his appointment, Jefferson wrote that "peace even at the expense of [French] spoliations past & future," had to be secured. To Edward Rutledge he expressed the view that "Great Britain… is going down irrecoverably, & will sink us also, if we do not clear ourselves." It is well that Jefferson never knew that George III told the American minister in London how much he liked Adams' speech.

On June 28 James Monroe arrived in Philadelphia, indignant not at the French but at the American government. He was warmly greeted by Jefferson, who had been all impatience for his presence. On July 1 the vice-president sponsored a public dinner in his honor. Attending were some of Washington's enemies—Horatio Gates, Thomas Mifflin, and Aaron Burr. The presence of many Virginians caused a Federalist newspaper to refer to that state as the "land of debts," a reference to the fury of Virginians at having to pay what they had long owed to their English creditors. Jefferson himself had overdue more than $30,000 to his British creditors. His bitterness towards the federal government, the Jay treaty, and Great Britain had the same root causes as the attitude of other citizens of his state.

Thus publicly supported, Monroe began an open controversy with the secretary of state, from whom he demanded the reasons for his recall as minister to France. He received a forthright reply: "It is not true that removal from office implies actual misconduct. It may merely imply a want of ability." Pickering said that the president could not be expected to provide reasons for actions taken by his predecessor. At Adams' insistence, the cabinet informed Monroe that he could see the papers on his recall. Monroe, however, did not appear at Pickering's office to inspect the documents. On July 3, in the midst of these commotions, the president sent to the Senate an intercepted letter written to James Carey, an Indian agent, by William Blount, Democratic senator from Tennessee. It disclosed the surface of a conspiracy by western Democrats to attack Spanish possessions in the Southwest and Florida, with the aid of the British and Indians. Since Spain, at war with England, had heard of this plan, that country had been holding on to her last two posts on American soil. Blount asked Carey to inform the Indians that George Washington was responsible for their boundary problems. "This sort of talk will be throwing all the blame off me upon the late President, and as he is now out of office, it will be of no consequence how much the Indians blame him." Blount was not present when Jefferson read the letter to the Senate; upon his return, it was read again. Blount immediately departed the chamber and Philadelphia. On July 8 the Senate expelled him from office.

The two straightlaced Puritans in the president's house, John and Abigail, watched this sordidness and bore the press attacks with as much composure as they could muster. Adams at least had the satisfaction of seeing most of his recommended program for national defense, including twelve new frigates, succeed in Congress, in spite of Jefferson's determined opposition. The president was well aware of his activities, writing that Jefferson was "weak, confused, uninformed and ignorant." Mrs. Adams put it differently: "We are in perils by land, and we are in perils by sea, and in perils from false brethren."

"A TRICK SO DIRTY AND SHABBY"

Jefferson's Mazzei letter, severely blasting Washington, was published in the American press two months after Washington's retirement from office. "It became immediately," as John Marshall put it, "the subject of universal conversation." Since Washington subscribed to various newspapers, he had a copy in fairly short order. He made no mention of it in his correspondence. Jefferson, for his part, discussed with Madison, Monroe, and others, whether he should acknowledge the letter and what he should say in extenuation. Monroe urged him to avow it, while Madison thought it better to say and do nothing publicly. Jefferson followed the latter policy but privately disseminated the idea that he had been mistranslated or misquoted.

Whatever shred of faith Washington retained in Jefferson's integrity vanished after reading this letter written while Jefferson was professing esteem and attachment; from it the general learned that the vice-president was probably involved in a scheme to entrap him. In early October Washington received a letter from a stranger, John Langhorne of Warren, a small town south of Charlottesville. The writer praised Washington as "eminently just and virtuous" and commiserated with him for having borne such "unmerciful calumny." Washington returned a polite note of thanks on October 15. He said that attacks on a government elected "by the people" could result in no good and much evil for the country. He continued: "So far these attacks are aimed at me, personally, it is, I can assure you, Sir, a misconception if it be supposed I feel the venom of the darts. Within me, I have the consolation which proves an antidote against their utmost malignity, rendering my mind in the retirement I have long panted after, perfectly tranquil."

The arrival at a tiny post office of a letter from General Washington aroused much interest; this intensified when no one had heard of "Mr. Langhorne." The postmaster apparently asked the county clerk, John Nicholas, whether he knew anyone by that name. Nicholas said that there was a Mr. Langhorne in a neighboring county, who had fought in "Braddock's war" and might thereby have known Washington. In reporting to Washington, on November 18, Nicholas said that he asked a friend to deliver the letter to Mr. Langhorne. To his great surprise, it had been claimed by a county resident "closely connected with some of your greatest and bitterest enemies, as being intended for him, tho' his name was very different indeed from Langhorne... The only conclusion I can draw from this strange circumstance, is that certain men, who are resolved to stick at nothing to promote their wicked and inglorious views, have fallen on this last miserable deceptive means... to entrap you." He warned Washington to be exceedingly careful, for he knew the real dispositions towards him at "the headquarters of Jacobinism."

The name "Nicholas" had unpleasant connotations for Washington because of four brothers, John, George, Wilson, and Philip, devout Jeffersonians. John Nicholas, a congressman, had been a gadfly during the ratification of the Jay treaty. Washington consulted Dr. Stuart about John Nicholas, when the former stayed overnight at Mount Vernon on November 29. Having been assured by Stuart that this John Nicholas, a cousin, was a strong Federalist and "a respectable man," Washington wrote to express thanks for Nicholas' "obliging favour." He said that he had a high regard for his father, with whom he served in the Virginia Assembly and that he would be glad to see him if he were ever in the neighborhood of Mount Vernon. He forwarded copies of the Langhorne letter and his reply, asking Nicholas to find out whether there was any "nefarious plan" being developed at Charlottesville against the government. If he found nothing, he was to destroy the papers. He added that his only feeling about "Mr. Langhorne" had been that he was "a pedant who was desirous of displaying the powers of his pen."

On December 9 Nicholas forwarded to Washington a copy of a note, written by Peter Carr, in which he claimed to be "Mr. Langhorne" and "entitled to that letter." Nicholas added, in case Washington did not recognize the name, that Carr was "a favorite nephew of your very sincere friend Mr. Jefferson, raised and educated by himself from a child, a constant dependent and resident in his house from that period almost to the present; and entertaining sentiments, I do assure you of my own personal knowledge, very different indeed towards you from those contained in his letter." Nicholas sent a further report on February 22 which indicated he had not, as yet, been able to determine Jefferson's role in the attempted entrapment but the man who brought Carr's note and picked up the Langhorne letter was a Monticello servant. He learned that Jefferson encouraged and helped Monroe with his book attacking the former president. Nicholas had heard Jefferson say that Washington premeditated the destruction of Monroe, by appointing him minister to

France. Since Nicholas mentioned that he was a friend of Bushrod Washington, the general sent his March 8 reply to his nephew for review and an evaluation of Nicholas, adding that, knowing the political views of most of his family, he had little esteem for them. He was almost alone in his family in support of the government "but does not stand less firm on that account." Bushrod said that he had heard of "the virulence" of Peter Carr's feelings about Washington. He had therefore forwarded his uncle's letter, which follows, to Nicholas:

> Nothing short of the Evidence you have adduced, corroborative of intimations which I had received long before, through another channel [General Lee], could have shaken my belief in the sincerity of a friendship which I had conceived was possessed for me by the person to whom you allude. But attempts to injure those who are supposed to stand well in the estimation of the People and are stumbling blocks in their way (by misrepresenting their political tenets), thereby to destroy all confidence in them, is one of the means by which the Government is to be assailed and the constitution destroyed. The conduct of the Party is systematized and everything that is opposed to its execution, will be sacrificed, without hesitation or remorse, if the end can be answered by it.

> If the person whom you _suspect_, was really the Author of the letter under the signature of John Langhorne, it is not at all surprising to me that the correspondence should have ended where it did; for the penetration of _that_ _man_ would have perceived at the first glance of the answer, that nothing was to be drawn from _that_ mode of attack. In what form the next insidious attempts may appear, remains to be discovered. But as the attempts to explain away the constitution and weaken the government are so open... it is hardly to be expected that a resort to covert means to effect these ends, will be longer retarded...

> As to [Monroe's] propriety in exposing to public view his private instructions and correspondence with his own government, nothing need be said: for I should suppose that the measure must be reprobated by the well informed and intelligent of _all_ Nations; and not less so by his abettors in this country, if they were not so blinded by Party views and determined at all hazards to catch at any thing that, in their opinion, will promote them. This mischievous and dangerous tendency of such a practice, is too glaring to require a comment.

> If the Executive, in the opinion of the gentlemen you have alluded to, is chargeable with "premeditating the destruction of Mr. Monroe in his appointment"... it is to be hoped that he will give it credit for its lenity to that Gentleman for having

designated several others (not of the Senate) as victims to this, before the sacrifice of Mr. Monroe was ever in contemplation.

Somehow Jefferson's spies got word of Bushrod's role. In informing his uncle of this on August 7 Bushrod said there was a mention of him by Peter Carr in "Davis's paper of the 24th. July," calling him "an informer." He added that he well knew "that Mr. Langhorne was a scoundrel: but I did not suppose he would ever be so stupid as to provoke a publication of his own Villainy." John Nicholas, he continued, now wanted to publish an account of the whole affair. Washington replied on the 12th that, if Jefferson were the "real Author or abetter, it would be a pity not to expose him to Public execration, for attempting in so dishonorable a way to obtain a disclosure of Sentiments of which some advantage could be taken… If a *trick* so *dirty* and *shabby* as this is supposed to be, could be clearly proved, it would, in my opinion, be attended with a happy effect at this time." Washington warned, however, that unless it were not only fully substantiated and all documents in the case published, the report would recoil on the author.

The activities of the Jeffersonians were to react on themselves, since they brought Washington back to an active political role. He asked Bushrod and John Marshall, who were to sit for many years on the Supreme Court together, to come for an early conference at Mount Vernon. "The Crisis is important. The temper of the People of this State in many… places is so violent and outrageous, that I wish to converse with Genl. Marshall and yourself on the elections which must soon come."

FARM LIFE

If Mr. and Mrs. Washington felt they had too many strange guests, they seem to have made life more interesting for Martha's granddaughter, the happily disposed Nelly Custis. Her high spirits, Nelly later wrote, brought frequent hearty laughs from the general. Shortly after Christmas she informed Mrs. Wolcott: "We have spent our summer and autumn very happily here… Have had many agreeable visitors and are now contentedly sitting around our winter fireside, often speaking of and wishing to see again our good friends in Philadelphia, but never regretting its amusements or a life of ceremony. I stay very much at home, have not been to the city for two or three months… I never have a dull or lonesome hour…"

The general and his wife carried on a cheerful correspondence with Elizabeth Powel in Philadelphia. Washington had sold her his secretary-desk before leaving the city. She wrote him that, on opening it, she found a packet of love letters addressed to the president in a lady's handwriting. Lear had absolutely refused to touch them but she would see that he received them back in good order. He replied with thanks for her delicate handling of the matter; he was afraid that any reader might have been disappointed that Martha didn't write with more passion. On December 18 he asked his wife to tell Mrs. Powel that "neither his health nor his spirits were ever in greater flow, notwithstanding he is descending and has almost reached the bottom of the hill, or in other words, the shades below."

Washington's plan to free his slaves envisioned the sale of most of his western lands and the rental of his farms near Mount Vernon. In carrying out his 1793 plan, he undertook to establish centralized dwellings, barns, cribs, and storehouses at Union, Dogue Run, Muddy Hole, and River farms. He subsequently made repeated enquiries in England for suitable British migrants; in 1796 he also advertised the farms in various parts of the United States. The responses were not, on the whole, very encouraging. The applicants did not have the necessary knowledge or capital, or they could not use such large areas. In addition, as he discovered, uncleared western land, which could be bought cheaply, was more attractive than rented Virginia farms, even though they were fenced, cleared, settled, and in effective operation. Washington had therefore to turn back to managing his vast enterprises, with his usual difficulties in finding suitable overseers. In 1797 he drew up and studied an alternate plan to use his farms for grazing rather than crops.

Washington's supervision of more than twelve square miles of property was a heavy burden for a man of sixty-five. On December 3 he wrote to William Vans Murray, American minister to The Hague: "I rarely stir from home, never beyond Alexandria or the Federal city; indeed, if my inclinations were more extensive, my business would restrain them; for at no period of my life have I been more closely engaged... than during the months I have been home. Hardly a resident for the last five and twenty years at this place... I have found upon an examination into the state of my buildings that time and want of attention... have caused such depredations thereon and everything connected with them, and have so deranged all matters of private concern, that, what with the plague and trouble proceeding from the number of workmen I have been obliged to employ... I have been occupied from the 'rising of the sun to the setting of the same,' and which, as the wise man has said, 'may be all vanity and vexation of spirit,' but as I did not seek it as a source of happiness, but entered upon it as a case of necessity, a line may be drawn between his disappointments and mine."

He wrote to John Marshall on December 4: "A very severe winter has commenced. Since the first of November we have hardly experienced a moderate

Day; heavy rains following severe frosts have done more damage to the winter grain, now growing, than I ever recollect to have seen. At this moment and for several days past, all the Creeks and small waters are hard bound with Ice, and the Navigation of the River, if not entirely stopped is yet very much impeded by it."

Washington resumed various other duties. He followed closely the work of the Potomac Canal Company and did not hesitate to ask the governors of Maryland and Virginia for financial aid to keep the work going. His interest in the city of Washington remained keen though he himself had no further responsibility for the work. When he heard from Alexander White, a district commissioner, that the president thought the offices of cabinet members should be located near the capitol for the convenience of Congress, he replied on March 25 that his opinion, "as an individual is a matter of Moon-shine." He had placed the cabinet offices near the president's house for directly opposite reasons. The cabinet had to see the president daily. His officers constantly complained they could get no work done when Congress was in session. Senators and representatives dropped by so freely for conversation, or to ask for documents, that "they have been obliged, often, to go home and deny themselves, in order to transact the current business." After the commissioners declared that more houses should be built in the city for the accommodation of the government, Washington, even though overextended, engaged William Thornton to build two rental houses close by the capitol.

After the Washingtons learned that their old friend, Bryan Fairfax, now an Episcopal minister and eighth Lord Fairfax, was going to England on business, they took occasion on May 16 to renew their correspondence with his sister-in-law, Mrs. George Fairfax. Washington recalled the "happy moments, the happiest in my life, which I have enjoyed in your company… It is a matter of sore regret, when I cast my eyes toward Belvoir, which I often do, to reflect that the former inhabitants of it, with whom we lived in such harmony and friendship, no longer reside there." He and Martha strongly urged Mrs. Fairfax to return to her own country to pass her final years. As an inducement thereto, Washington added a report on how greatly the country had progressed during the years since she had left. A capital city was building on the Potomac which, "if the country keeps united, in a century might be of a magnitude inferior to few others in Europe… A situation not excelled for commanding prospect, good water, salubrious air, and safe harbor by any in the world; and where elegant buildings are erecting, and in forwardness, for the reception of Congress in the year 1800. Alexandria, within the last seven years (since the establishment of the General Government) has increased in buildings, in population, in the improvement of its Streets by well executed pavements, and in the extension of its wharves, in a manner of which you can have very little idea. This shew of prosperity… is owing… to the extension of the Inland navigation of the Potomack River; now cleared to Fort Cumberland… If this country can steer clear of European politics, stand firm on its bottom, and be wise and temperate in its government, it bids fair to be one of the greatest and happiest nations in the world."

WASHINGTON'S BIRTHDAY

The celebration of Washington's sixty-sixth birthday was as noteworthy for confusion as national joy. Alexandria honored it by the old-style calendar, whereby Washington was born February 11, 1731/32. As this date fell on a Sunday, the city held a birthday ball on February 12. Washington wrote in his diary that he and his family, presumably his wife and two stepgrandchildren, attended the dance.

A similar ball planned for February 22 in Philadelphia, caused the president and his lady to lose their aplomb. Abigail was furious that there should be a dance in honor of Washington, when there was now a new president. Adams thought it unfortunate that honor was to be paid to a private citizen. The Adamses sent a discourteously abrupt refusal. Jefferson, also invited, declared that there might be some sense in paying honor to General Washington but none to President Washington. As soon as he learned that Adams refused to attend, he also declined. Abigail Adams mistakenly thought the vice-president did this in deference to the president. Instead Jefferson was chortling at the fury of the Washingtonians and the discomfiture of the "Adamites."

On his birthday, Washington wrote to Senator Martin of North Carolina to thank him for forwarding some dramatic poetry. He added: "Lamentable and much to be regretted indeed it is, that in a crises like the present, when all hearts should be united and at their post, ready to rejoice at the good, or repel the evil which awaits us, that nothing but internal dissensions and political hostilities are to be found in the Councils of our common Country. Although no longer an Actor on this Theatre myself, I cannot but view these things with deep concern."

THE MONROE AND FAUCHET REPORTS

In 1796 and 1797, pamphlets and books were published which further extended the Franco-American attacks on the United States government. The most important were those written by James Monroe, Joseph Fauchet, the former French minister, William Duane, who went out of his way to defend the Mazzei letter by speech and pamphlet, and Albert Gallatin, a member of Congress.

On January 12 Washington requested Timothy Pickering to send him the works of Fauchet and Monroe. At the end of the month he wrote to acknowledge their receipt. He said that he had read Bache's "malignant falsehood... exhibited against you in the Aurora. Satisfied as I am of the motive and the end, intended to be answered by the publication, I have read with much gratification your explicit disavowal." He noted that Fauchet had accused him, Washington, of carrying on secret negotiations with "the Pretender" (Louis XVIII), who had sent a Mr. Antoine-Omer Talon to Philadelphia for that purpose. Washington called this an "impudent, wicked and groundless assertion." He could not remember any M. Talon, though it was always conceivable he might have been among the numerous strangers present at receptions.

When Monroe's lengthy treatise, greatly swelled by its inclusion of secret government dispatches, appeared, it bore a ponderous title which Jefferson had advised Monroe to shorten and improve: "A view of the conduct of the Executive in the foreign Affairs of the United States, connected with the Mission to the French Republic during the Years 1794, 5 & 6." The vice-president, after sending copies of the Paine letter and the Fauchet pamphlet to Virginia, informed Monroe that Bache would soon ship two or three hundred copies of his book to Richmond. He said that it was "irresistible" and that Fauchet had reinforced the story of Washington's "duplicity." Jefferson wrote to Madison that "Monroe's book is considered as masterly... and unanswerable."

Sometime that winter Washington read Monroe's publication and commented on it in the margins. Jefferson, in late years, tried to portray Washington as growing senile after 1793, but his mind was sharper than ever. By turns humorous and satirical, the former chief executive of the United States ripped James Monroe to pieces. Washington's masterpiece was not published for nearly a century thereafter. Because of its length, it is not possible to reproduce more than short extracts.

Monroe said that France and the United States had been in process of "being thrown wholly apart... Upon my arrival in Paris... I found that the work of alienation... had been carried further than I had before even suspected." Washington: "Why? Because one nation was seeking redress for violations and injuries committed by the other... If we had submitted to them without remonstrating, we should still have been their dear friends and Allies."

Monroe: "My first note to the committee of public safety... combatted copiously... the conduct of France in thus harassing our commerce against the stipulations of certain articles in our treaty." Washington: "But he finally told [the committee] (contrary to instructions) that if it was not convenient to comply… the Government and People of the U. States would give them up with pleasure…"

Monroe: "Such was my conduct upon the above occasion, and such the motives of it." Washington: "And extraordinary indeed it was!"

Monroe: "Had [the Jay] treaty then never passed… what might we not have expected from [France's] friendship?" Washington: "Nothing if she did not perceive some advantage to herself in granting it."

Monroe wrote that there had been "a spontaneous and almost universal disapprobation" of the Jay treaty "throughout the United States as soon as it was seen." Washington: "He should have said before it was seen; for it is a well known fact that the opposition from the French Party in the U.S. began… as soon as it was known that a Treaty had been concluded and before one article therein was known…"

Monroe: "With respect to the declaration that we were an independent people and had a right to decide for ourselves… I did not perceive how it applied…" Washington: "None are more dull than those who will not perceive."

Monroe wrote that he had considered resigning as minister to France, on which Washington scribbled: "Curious and laughable… His recall was a second death to him."

It is pointless to quote further from a Monroe who expressed himself in elephantine circumlocution. Washington's further observations were crisp and usually brief:

When a rational answer and good reason cannot be given, it is not unusual to be silent.

If the cap did not fit, why put it on?

What! Declare to the world in a public speech that we were going to treat with this and that Nation, and that France was to assist us! Insanity in the extreme!

Could this repeal be announced before it was known?

Declined for the best reason in the world because he had none that would bear the test of examination.

Self importance appears here.

Of all the mistakes he has made, and bold assertions, none stands more prominent than this.

None but a person incompetent to judge, or blinded by party views, could have misconstrued as he did. But had France a right to be acquainted with the Private instructions of our Ministers?

For this there is not better proof than his own opinion; whilst there is abundant evidence of his being a mere tool in the hands of the French government, cajoled and led always by unmeaning assurances.

As he has such a happy knack of determining, he ought not to have let this opportunity escape him.

Here is a pretty smart compliment paid himself, at the expense of the Administration; but the truth of the case is...

That is to say, if we would not press them to do us Justice, but have yielded to their violations, they would have aided us in every measure that would have cost them: Nothing.

The sufferings of our Citizens are always a secondary consideration when put in competition with the embarrassments of the French.

In his closing documentation, Monroe quoted the head of the French Directory as declaring that France would always welcome "loyal explanations... above all, citizen Minister, when they shall be made through you." Washington added: "The treatment of our minister, General Pinckney, is a pretty evidence of this. The thought of parting with Mr. Monroe was unsupportable by them."

XYZ AFFAIR

Washington received reports from Philadelphia, through Alexander White, that Democratic members of Congress had written to the French Directory to suggest that it refuse to receive the accredited ministers of the United States but "on the contrary, to menace us with hostile appearances, and they might rely on bringing the U. States to their feet." There was no subsequent evidence of this, although Democrats often wrote their friends in France, denouncing their country's policy. In this case, certainly, Jefferson did not sponsor such a scheme. In January he stated that Talleyrand, the foreign minister, had assured Joseph Letombe, the French consul-general at Philadelphia, that the American ministers had arrived safely in Paris and "they will be well received, & that every disposition exists on the side of France to accommodate their differences with us."

The American delegates, Marshall and Gerry, left the United States in July. While Jefferson and Monroe had been praising France for its friendship, that country had seized nearly 350 American ships, with a value in excess of $55 million. This figure was more than five times the amount of French monetary aid to America during the revolution. While thus engaged in piracy, the French government never failed to remind Americans of their ingratitude for France's earlier generosity.

On December 4 Washington wrote to John Marshall to express his appreciation of a letter announcing his safe arrival at The Hague and to say that the press had now reported that he was in Paris. He hoped he would have an honorable and successful mission. If, however, the French Directory proceeded on the assumption that the Federalist and Democratic parties were nearly equal in strength and that the latter would rally to the French standard, "they will greatly deceive themselves; for the Mass of our citizens require no more than to understand a question to decide it properly and an adverse conclusion of the Negotiation will effect this."

Thereafter, everyone from Adams and Washington to Jefferson and Madison waited with impatience to hear from Paris. A terrible silence followed. Washington grew anxious; he wrote the secretary of war on January 28: "Are there no accounts yet from our Envoys?" He followed with another enquiry on March 4: "Are our Commissioners guillotined? Or what else is the occasion of their Silence?" That same day the president opened the bulky coded reports of the mission. As they were deciphered, he read a tale of intrigue, deception, and greed, which approached in sordidness the affair of the diamond necklace, involving the queen and cardinal of France a few years before. Included were reports on Talleyrand's agents, denominated X, Y, and Z (Hottenguer, Bellamy, and D'Hauteville) and others, including a lady who was intended to charm the Americans out of their money. John Marshall himself wrote what is perhaps the best summary of the transactions for his biography of Washington:

> *History will scarcely furnish the example of a nation, not absolutely degraded, which has received from a foreign power such open contumely, and undisguised insult, as were, on this occasion, suffered by the United States in the person of their ministers.*
>
> *It was insinuated that their being taken from the party which supported the measures of their own government furnished just cause for umbrage and, under*

slight pretexts, the executive directory delayed to accredit them as the representatives of an independent nation. In this situation, they were assailed by persons… exhibiting sufficient evidence of the source from which their powers were derived, who, in direct and explicit terms, demanded money from the United States as the condition which must precede… any negotiation…

A decided negative was given to the preliminary required [Pinckney said, 'No! No! Not a sixpence.']… but they returned to the charge with wonderful perseverance… The immense power of France was painted in glowing colours, the humiliation of the house of Austria was stated, and the conquest of Britain was confidently anticipated… The fate of Venice was held up to warn her of the danger which awaited those who incurred the displeasure of the great republic. The ministers were assured that, if they believed their conduct would be approved in the United States, they were mistaken. The means which the Directory possessed, in that country, to excite odium against them, were great, and would unquestionably be employed…

This degrading intercourse was at length interrupted by the positive refusal of the envoys to hold any further communications with the persons employed in it.

Meanwhile, they urged the object of their mission with persevering but unavailing solicitude. The Directory still refused to acknowledge them in their public character; and [Talleyrand], at unofficial visits which they made him, renewed the demand which his agents had unsuccessfully pressed.

The American ministers made a last effort to execute the duties assigned to them. In a letter addressed to [Talleyrand], they entered at large into the explanations committed to them by their government, and illustrated, by a variety of facts, the uniform friendliness of its conduct to France. Notwithstanding the failure of this effort… they continued, with a passiveness which must search for its apology in their solicitude to demonstrate to the American people the real views of the French republic, to employ the only means in their power to avert the rupture which was threatened, and which appeared to be inevitable.

During these transactions, occasion was repeatedly taken to insult the American government; open war continued to be waged by the cruisers of France on American commerce; and the flag of the United States was a sufficient justification for the capture and condemnation of any vessel over which it waved.

At length, when the demonstration became complete, that the resolution of the American envoys was not less fixed, than their conduct had been guarded and temperate, various attempts were made to induce two of them voluntarily, to relinquish their station; on the failure of which they were ordered to quit the territories of the republic. As if to aggravate this national insult, the third, who had been selected from that party which was said to be friendly to France, was permitted to remain...

Marshall noted in a footnote that the masterly letter to Talleyrand, which he had drafted, had received a bitter and angry reply. The French government forwarded this to Bache, who had it before it reached the secretary of state in Philadelphia. Bache promptly published the reply but not the letter by the American mission.

Adams' first reaction was rage and a willingness to ask Congress to declare formally the state of war, which existed de facto. The president drafted a war message but with a divided cabinet and country, he decided on caution and to hold back the offensive dispatches. He informed Congress, March 19, 1798, that the mission had made every effort to bring about a pacific settlement with France but their attempts had been unsuccessful. He asked the Senate and House "to adopt with promptitude, decision and unanimity... measures... for the protection of our seafaring and commercial citizens, for the defense... of our territories... and to provide such efficient revenue as will be necessary to defray extraordinary expenses." He announced that he had authorized the arming of merchant vessels.

The vice-president told Madison that the president had delivered "an insane message." He informed Monroe that the Democrats would seek to override the authorization to arm merchant vessels and would introduce resolutions to adjourn Congress, so that no defensive measures might be passed. The Democrats needed to stall for time while France landed troops in England. In addition Jefferson wrote that he believed Adams had kept back the whole story, as too unfavorable for his war plans. His party would therefore call for all the secret papers of the American mission to Paris. The Bache-type press soon redoubled its attacks on Adams. So many threatening letters arrived at the president's house that Abigail Adams feared for her husband's safety.

In formal debate, at the beginning of April, the House took up a Democratic resolution asking the president to provide all relevant papers of the French mission. The president watched with interest as Federalists quietly added support. When the vote came, it was overwhelmingly in favor. The president, with ill-concealed satisfaction, forwarded to both Houses the whole of the story. The effects were shattering. The House Democrats attempted to stop their release but the Senate ordered the printing of 50,000 copies for distribution throughout the country.

PUBLIC REACTION

Washington's letter to Marshall had correctly anticipated what the feeling of the great mass of Americans would be, if the Directory broke off negotiations. A rush of support for the president brought him the highest degree of popularity ever achieved by an Adams. Addresses and letters poured in by the hundreds from town and country meetings, state legislatures, militia companies, old soldiers, Harvard, Princeton, and Dartmouth students, and the first president of the United States.

Joseph Hopkinson, son of Washington's old friend, Francis, having been asked to produce words to "The President's March," wrote "Hail Columbia," with its chorus, "firm united let us be, Rallying round our Liberty." With Mrs. Adams present, Gilbert Fox, accompanied by a chorus and orchestra, sang it in the Chestnut Street Theatre, to the enthusiastic shouts of the audience, who called for it again and again. On its last rendition the audience joined in. A few days later, when the president and his wife attended the theater, they were greeted with wild applause. The tune was again sung by the audience, band, and chorus. On May 9 Hopkinson sent a copy to Washington, saying that it was being played night after night, in theaters in New York as well as Philadelphia, "and men and boys sing it in the streets as they go." It became, in fact, a national serenade for John Adams.

Jefferson wrote that the XYZ message had produced "shock and dismay" among the Democrats. Several of them departed the House of Representatives to return home, while others rallied to Adams. On April 26 Congress authorized the establishment of a separate Navy Department, to which Adams appointed Benjamin Stoddert as its first secretary. Other measures, including the raising of 10,000 men for the army, as well as new taxes, passed Congress without much trouble.

Adams did not sponsor them, although he gladly signed two important measures for the national security. The first gave the president power, in case of war, to seize or deport all enemy aliens. Jefferson complained that this act seemed to be particularly directed at "Collot and Volney," the two French spies who had travelled through the West, drawing maps for France and electioneering for Jefferson. The pair quickly left the country, along with many other Frenchmen. A second act provided fines and imprisonment for those who engaged in insurrection or plots against the United States government, in seditious libel, or in hostile acts, on behalf of a foreign government, against the officers of the United States. In libel cases, a jury trial was required; malice and intent had to be proved by the government, and truth was a full defense. The first man indicted was Benjamin Bache.

John Marshall's masterly role in Paris won him wide popular acclaim in the United States. His June 18 arrival in Philadelphia was a signal for a popular demonstration greater than even Washington had received in the city. Jefferson, feeling the tide against him, had expected to leave the city but stayed for Marshall's arrival to see what intelligence he could acquire. Three days later he wrote Madison that Marshall "was received here with the utmost éclat. The Secretary of State and many carriages, with all the city cavalry, went to Frankfort to meet him, and on his arrival here in the evening, the bells rung till late at night, & immense crowds were collected to see & make part of the show, which was circuitously paraded through the streets."

Jefferson did not mention the dinner for Marshall which was attended by members of the Supreme Court, most congressmen, the Episcopal and Catholic bishops, and numerous others. Toasts were given to the president, the nation, General Washington, General Pinckney, the army, and the navy. It was Robert Goodloe Harper, congressman from South Carolina, who raised his glass and gave the famous words: "Millions for defense, but not one cent for tribute."

Jefferson's report to Madison noted an uproar in the press over Dr. George Logan, who had sailed for France and was reported to be a secret emissary "from the Jacobins here to solicit an army from France, instruct them as to their landing, & c. This extravagance produced a real panic among the citizens." Jefferson did not mention that Logan carried a letter of introduction from him. Shortly afterwards, the vice-president of the United States set out for Virginia, determined to bring the force of his state against the Constitution which he had sworn to protect and defend.

Adams, after ordering Gerry recalled from Paris, announced to Congress, June 21, that he would never send another minister to France "without assurances that he will be received, respected and honored as the representative of a great, free, powerful and independent nation." Talleyrand's eventual indirect reply, employing the president's own words, was to be the key by which Adams crowned the Washington peace policy with a French treaty.

On June 17 Washington, who had heard that the president planned an inspection trip to the federal city, where he was to move in 1800, politely asked him to make Mount Vernon his headquarters while in the area. He added: "I pray you to believe that no one has read the various approbatory Addresses, which I have done; nor are there any who more sincerely wish that your Administration of the Government may be easy, happy, and honorable to yourself, and prosperous for the Country."

A POLE VISITS MOUNT VERNON

Few of the hundreds of guests at Mount Vernon left useful surviving descriptions of family life there. A notable exception was Julian Niemcewicz, Polish poet, soldier, statesman, and dramatist, whom the Washingtons encountered rather accidentally in Washington city. He had been adjutant to General Kosciuszko, a former officer of Washington's revolutionary army, who subsequently led the Poles in an unsuccessful revolt against their Russian rulers. Niemcewicz recorded not only the domestic scene but Washington's reactions to the XYZ affair.

On May 19 the Washingtons left Mount Vernon for a week's visit to Martha's descendants. They spent a night at the house of David Stuart, whose wife had been the widow of John Custis. In Washington they spent several days at the houses of Martha's two granddaughters, Mrs. Thomas Peter and Mrs. Thomas Law. Niemcewicz was at the Law house. He recorded that he was struck dumb at meeting the general. He soon relaxed for Washington was very cheerful. When Law asked him if he had seen the account from New York of the duel in which the Democrat, Brockholst Livingston, killed John Jones, a Federalist, Washington replied: "They say that [Jones] shot off a piece of his nose. How could he miss it? You know Mr. Livingston's nose and what a first-rate target it is." Niemcewicz, who had much humor of his own, expressed his delight. His diary recorded that Martha Washington was "charming, bright and gay." Niemcewicz, in his turn, seems to have charmed the Washingtons who asked him to make an extended stay at Mount Vernon. In company with Law he arrived a few days later; thereafter he missed nothing.

"June 2… We arrived at the foot of a hill where the Washington properties begin. We took a road newly cut through a forest of oaks. Soon we discovered still another hill, at the top of which stood a rather spacious house, surmounted by a small cupola, with mezzanines and blinds painted in green… All kinds of trees, bushes, flowering plants, ornament the two sides of the court… Near the ends of the house are two groves of locusts… The ground where they are planted is a green carpet of the most beautiful velvet…

"We entered the house. General Washington was out on his farm. Madame appeared after a few minutes, welcomed us most graciously and had punch served. At two o'clock the General arrived, mounted on a gray horse. He shook our hand, dismounted, gave a cut of the whip to the horse, which went off by itself to the stable…"

While the general went to dress for dinner, Mrs. Washington took Niemcewicz on a tour of the house. After providing a minute description of the mansion, he wrote of "the most beautiful green" lawn to its front and "perhaps the most beautiful view in the world," from the piazza. The arrival of Nelly Custis diverted the poet's attention from the river. According to Washington's diary, Nelly was accompanied by a "Miss Lee of Greenspring." Niemcewicz said she "was not beautiful at all" but he was enchanted by Nelly: "A young woman of the greatest beauty... one of those celestial figures that nature produces only rarely, that the inspiration of painters has sometimes divined and that one cannot see without ecstasy. Her sweetness is equal to her beauty... She plays the harpsichord, sings, draws better than any woman in America or even in Europe."

That light June evening Washington took Niemcewicz around his gardens to complete his day: "The garden, the plantations, the house, their perfect form, show that a man born with natural taste can divine the beautiful without having seen the model. The General has never left America. After seeing his house and gardens one would say that he had seen the most beautiful examples of the great old houses of England..."

In the next couple of days, accompanied by Washington or Law, Niemcewicz rode over much of the land. He was astonished at the extent of the farms and the great fields of peas, rye, corn, wheat, flax, and alfalfa. He examined the flour mill, with its newly invented machine for aerating flour, and the large distillery, capable of turning out 12,000 gallons of whiskey (mainly rye) a year. He commented: "If this distillery produces poison for men, it offers in return the most delicate and succulent feed for pigs. They keep 150 of them of the guinea type ... [which are] so excessively bulky that they can hardly drag their big bellies on the ground. They looked to me like so many priors in our Dominican monasteries. We saw here and there flocks of sheep. The General has between six and seven hundred..." Niemcewicz examined his cattle, "super bull," Lafayette's jackasses, and some fifty mule descendants. Washington also showed him an ingenious plow which he had invented as well as the new octagonal barn that he had designed. From this point on (June 5) Niemcewicz turned increasingly to recording his impressions of the Washingtons:

At table, after the departure of the ladies, or else in the evening seated under the portico, he often talked with me for hours at a time. His favorite subject is agriculture, but he answered with kindness all questions that I put to him of the Revolution, the armies, etc. He has a prodigious memory. One time in the evening he listed all the rivers, lakes, creeks and the means to procure a communication between these waters, from Portsmouth as far as the Mississippi...

Since his retirement he has led a quiet and regular life. He gets up at 5 o'clock in

the morning, reads or writes until seven. He breakfasts on tea and [corn muffins]
spread with butter and honey. He then immediately goes on horseback to see the
work in the fields; sometimes in the middle of a field he holds a council of war with
Mr. Anderson [his manager]. He returns at two o'clock, dresses, and goes to dinner.
If there are guests, he loves to chat after dinner with a glass of Madeira in his
hand. After dinner he diligently reads the newspapers, of which he receives about
ten of different kinds. He answers letters, etc. Tea at 7 o'clock; he chats until nine
and then he goes to bed. Mrs. Washington is one of the most estimable persons that
one could know, good, sweet, and extremely polite. She loves to talk, and talks very
well about times past.

June 9. Mrs. Washington made me a gift of a china cup with her monogram and
the names of the States of the United States. Miss Custis gave me my monogram in
flowers, which she had herself painted…

June 13… On our return [from fishing] we found a notable and unexpected
company from Alexandria. The table in the great hall was set with a Sèvres
porcelain service with places for twenty. The General, in high spirits, was gracious
and full of attention to everybody. Among the guests were the young Randolphs. I
do not know whether both their ages would add up to 38 but they are already the
parents of three children. Mrs. [William Fitzhugh], who in corpulence and girth
gives way only to the late [Empress Catherine], was in a gay humor and had an
enormous appetite. As she swept through one plate after another, her husband
laughingly encouraged her with these words: 'Betsy, a little more, a little more.'

In the evening, after the departure of the company, the General, sitting with Mr.
Law and me under the portico, read us a letter which he had just received from a
friend [almost certainly John Marshall] in Paris. This letter, written with sense,
dispassion and a sound knowledge of the situation in France and of the politics of
those who rule her, gave us an opportunity for conversation about the wrongs
suffered by America at French hands, and about the bloody struggle which might
shortly break out between the two countries. This conversation aroused the
passionate wrath of the venerable citizen and commander. I have never heard him
speak with so much candor, nor with such heat.

"Whether we consider the injuries and plunder which our commerce is suffering (50
million dollars) or the affront to our national independence and dignity, in the
rejection of our envoys, or whether we think on the oppression, ruin and final
destruction of all free people, through this military government, everywhere we
recognize the need to arm ourselves with a strength and zeal, equal to the dangers
with which we are threatened. Continued patience and submission will not deliver

us, any more than submission delivered Venice or others. Submission is degrading. Rather than allow herself to be insulted to this degree, rather than having her freedom and independence trodden under foot, every American, including myself though old, will pour out the last drop of blood in his veins.

"They censure Mr. Adams for haste in deeds and excessive boldness in words; from the moment that I left the administration, I have not written a word to Mr. Adams [Washington did write four days later] nor have I yet received a word from him except the despatches which we have seen in our papers; I do not know what are those other sources of information on which he acts: with all this I am certain, as a reasonable and honest person and as a good American, that he cannot do other than he does. In his place, I would perhaps be less vehement in expression but I would prepare myself steadily and boldly in the same fashion."

The strong and noble feelings of this man pierced my heart with respect and emotion.

June 14. In the evening, for the last time, pretty Miss Custis sang and played on the harpsichord. The next day, having risen before the dawn, I walked for the last time about the green groves of Mount Vernon and looked out over the clear and beautiful Potomac river. Then, at six in the morning, with gratitude for the hospitable welcome and with sorrow, silent and unexpressed, I took my leave of the noble Washington, his worthy wife and the beautiful, good and kind Miss Custis. *

Niemcewicz had greatly pleased the family at Mount Vernon. He wrote a graceful letter of thanks from the "City of Washington." Washington's affectionate reply of June 18 said that "the pleasure this family derived from the favour of your company... could only be equaled by the regret we felt at parting with you." If his prayers for Poland's liberty had been answered, Niemcewicz would now be as happy under his own fig tree as the American people were. He hoped he would come again to Mount Vernon where they would try to show him attentions which would "alleviate the poignancy" of his feelings for Poland's tragedy. Washington thus indicated the tact and sympathy with which he and his family handled the despair gripping Niemcewicz after letters from Polish friends were delivered at Mount Vernon.

---

* Two translations exist from the original Polish, one by W. M. Kozlowski, the other by Metchie J. E. Budka. Both are used here, the latter more extensively. In neither is the English perfect, and each has received minor editing.

JULY 4, 1798

In the crisis years, 1775, 1787, and 1789, the nation turned, as a matter of course, to George Washington. President Adams in his June 22 answer to the invitation to stay at Mount Vernon, replied that Congress had authorized a great expansion in the army and he was faced with deciding whether to call on the old generals or to pull in "a younger set." Washington's name was worth more "than many an army." The secretary of war four days later asked if he would "accept the command of all our armies."

By chance the twenty-second anniversary of American independence turned out to be a hectic day for Washington. The nearest post office, Alexandria, was nine miles away. As president he had sent for letters on each post day but as a farmer he felt less need to do so. As a result the president's and secretary's letters did not reach him at Mount Vernon until July 3, a day when he was entertaining ten to dinner. With little time for reflection, he got up very early next morning to reply.

To Adams Washington wrote that when he left office, he had no idea there could ever be a threat of invasion but it seemed to be "reserved for intoxicated and lawless France… to slaughter its own citizens, and to disturb the peace of the World besides." He himself could not easily decide what he ought to do. In case of an "actual invasion by a formidable force, I certainly should not entrench myself under the cover of Age and retirement, if my services should be required by my country." Immediate preparations should be undertaken to repel invasion, if the government's information justified it. Yet he could not believe that the French would actually plan for an invasion "after such a uniform and unequivocal expression of the sense of the People, in all parts, to oppose them with their lives and fortunes."

Washington added that the "old set of Generals" would hardly be a suitable source of officers for an active army. Instead they should be chosen from the most "experienced and intelligent Officers of the late Army, without respect to Grade." The most important nominations would be in the general staff, and the heads of artillery, engineering, and hospitals.

To McHenry Washington wrote at greater length and with candor. He had entirely retired from public life; if he appeared once more therein, the opposition would denounce it as a "restless Act" by one who could not really leave power alone. He was convinced that no actual invasion would take place, even though French partisans in America had deluded the Directory into thinking that a show of force would lead to an uprising. The country might well want younger generals, particularly as the French always chose those "of juvenile years to lead their Armies" (Napoleon was twenty-eight). In addition, he was not himself convinced that his advanced age made it "advisable to commit so important a trust to my direction." He expanded further on the need for a good general staff. He added that the "pain" he would feel if, once more he had to accept a command, "cannot easily be expressed." He was prepared to help his country but only in case of an actual invasion or of knowledge of such "a design… as cannot be mistaken." Even then the country's call for his services had to be demonstrated to him "unequivocally." He would also have to be entirely free to select his staff.

Washington, having made his position clear, set off to celebrate Independence Day in Alexandria, in the uniform of general of the American revolutionary army. He arrived there at ten o'clock in the morning, presumably carrying with him the letters for mailing. He was escorted into town by troops and warmly cheered and greeted by the people in that strongly Federalist city. He watched the parades and celebrations. After attending Christ Church, he "dined in the Spring Gardens… with a large company of the Civil and Military of Fairfax County."

What he did not know was that the president, without awaiting his reply, had signed a commission, hastily ratified by the Senate, appointing George Washington "Lieutenant General and Commander-in-Chief of all the Armies raised or to be raised for the Service of the United States." In nominating him, the president reduced him a grade below the rank he held from 1775 to 1783.

The United States at the Close of the Federalist Period

FIFTEEN

COMMANDER IN CHIEF
OF THE ARMIES

JOHN ADAMS CONTINUED, in words, Washington's policy of building
the nation's strength as the surest means to peace, but his actions lagged
far behind. In nominating Washington to command, the president presumably intended to give France clear warning that the United States would
repel attack. For an extended time, however, he failed to produce the
expanded army, although required by law to do so. His unilateral decision to
send Washington's name to the Senate, without consulting anyone, annoyed
many of his supporters. Further dissension appeared when the Senate
attempted to restore Washington's previous rank. The president bluntly
rebuffed this by the statement that he was the constitutional commander in
chief of the armed forces.

Adams was aware of a move among the Federalists to make Hamilton commander of the army, if Washington refused, or second in line, if he accepted.
When it was apparent that the president would nominate Washington,
Hamilton wrote to him to express his willingness to be inspector general with
a line command. It is not clear to what extent Hamilton thereafter directly
engaged the support of Federalist senators but many put pressure on the secretaries of state and war to place him just below Washington. The first intimation of this reached Mount Vernon in July when Pickering informed
Washington that the president (who, with reason, mistrusted Hamilton)

appeared disinclined "to place Colo. Hamilton in what we think is his proper station, and that alone in which we suppose he will serve you: The Second to You; and Chief in your absence." Pickering said that even his political enemies "would repose more confidence in him than in any other military characters... The appointment of Colo. Hamilton... appears to me of such vast importance to the welfare of the country, that I am willing to risque any consequences of my frank and honest endeavours to secure it."

Washington replied at once that he did not know what the president thought but he himself certainly hoped Hamilton would be in the army. In his own mind, however, he wanted General Charles Cotesworth Pinckney as his second. "If the French should be so mad as openly and formidably to invade these United States... I conceive there can hardly be two opinions respecting their Plan, and that their operations will commence in the Southern quarter 1. because it is the weakest 2. because they will expect, from the tenor of the debates in Congress, to find more friends there 3. because there can be no doubt of their arming our own Negroes against us and 4. because they will be more contiguous to their Islands, and to Louisiana, if they should be possessed thereof, which they will be, if they can." He continued:

> *If these premises are just, the inference I am going to draw, from placing Colo. Hamilton over General Pinckney, is natural and obvious. The latter is an officer of high military repute; fond of the Profession, spirited, active and judicious; and much advanced in the estimation of the Public by his late Conduct as Minister and envoy at Paris. With these pretensions and being senior to Colo. Hamilton, he will not, I am morally certain, accept a junior appointment... His connections are numerous, powerful and more influential than any other in the three Southern States.*

Washington's reply was mailed in Alexandria by the coachman, who had been ordered to pick up the arriving James McHenry, secretary of war. McHenry, sent by Adams to Mount Vernon to deliver his letter and commission, proceeded to press on Washington, not the president's views, but those of Hamilton, Pickering, and himself. With Adams' letter, he also carried one from Hamilton which warned Washington that Adams knew little of military policy. The president believed in "routine [seniority,]" whereas active and energetic officers were needed for the new army. As if to confirm Hamilton's statements, Adams suggested as the order of senior officers: "Lincoln, Morgan, Knox, Hamilton, Gates, Pinckney, Lee, Carrington, Hand, Muhlenberg, Dayton, Burr, Brooks, Cobb, Smith."

The list was notable for its military ineptness and general tactlessness. Lincoln and Morgan were too old at sixty-five and sixty-four. The former, never a very competent general, seems to have been placed there because he was a Massachusetts man and a friend of Adams. Morgan was neither qualified for the second post nor was he in good health. He had, however, warmly supported Adams as a Federalist congressman from Virginia. Knox, younger but much more experienced than the first two, was placed third. Hamilton was well down the list. Two old enemies of Washington, Gates and Burr, were included. The last man, William Smith, was Adams' rather disreputable son-in-law, who had once been a French agent.

No record has been found of the discussions which took place between Washington and McHenry from July 11 to 14. An approximation can be deduced from what Washington wrote before and after the meeting. It is clear that the president's hasty action had placed him in a difficult position. If Washington refused his commission, it would be embarrassing for the president; if he accepted, he would be accused by the Democrats of once more wanting power. What he apparently did was to ask McHenry to inform the president of his many objections to serving. If he were to accept, it was to be clearly understood that he was not to be called to active service, except in a national emergency. He also had to have senior officers of judgment on whom he could fully rely. He emphasized that he did not want to interfere with the president's prerogatives of appointment but that none should receive a commission unless the commanding general found him suitable. In a memorandum which he gave McHenry, Washington suggested that there should be no hurry in appointing the senior officers or in calling them to active duty. The first task was to establish possibilities by consulting with the proposed nominees, to see if they would be available in a crisis. Orally, and probably in writing, he expressed his preference for Pinckney as senior major general, with Hamilton as inspector general and Knox as third major general. If any of the three declined, Washington's next choice was Henry Lee. The most important task, for the moment, as Washington saw it, was to commission recruiting officers to enlist men and field and company officers to train them.

In further work with McHenry, Washington provided from memory the names of more than fifty men in ten states, whom he considered as good officer material. He also suggested his preference for Edward Hand as adjutant general, Edward Carrington as quartermaster general, and Dr. James Craik as director of hospitals.

The precise nature of what McHenry advised the president on his return to Philadelphia cannot be established, but it is clear that Adams bears the responsibility for the next precipitous action. The House of Representatives had adjourned but the Senate waited for McHenry's return. Adams, contrary to Washington's advice, at once sent to the Senate for ratification the names of Hamilton as inspector general and major general, along with Pinckney and Knox as major generals. It is likely that McHenry failed to tell Adams, with sufficient precision, Washington's own preferences. None of the three officers was consulted on the matter.

In placing Hamilton first on the list, Adams clearly thought, and said so afterwards, that this did not give him a line command. McHenry and Pickering, on the other hand, believed that the order determined respective ranks. Clearly many in the Senate also thought so, for, as Knox later reported to Washington, voices were raised there in protest against his low seniority. Knox also wrote that the Senate was thereupon informed, presumably by the war office, that this had been Washington's choice and there could be no change. Adams added two major generals, Henry Lee and Edward Hand, to the list. He ignored Washington's request to make the latter his adjutant general and substituted his own son-in-law, William Smith.

In the meantime, Washington, not expecting Adams' action, wrote to Hamilton to explain candidly why he preferred Pinckney as his number two man. In any case, as he pointed out, the prerogative of choice rested with the president. The good of the country was all that mattered, and he himself wished that either Pinckney or Hamilton had been chosen in his stead. Two days later, Washington wrote to Knox. He said that he had intimations from Congress and the cabinet that they preferred Hamilton to all others for second in command. He himself, for the reasons he had given McHenry and Hamilton, preferred Pinckney. He hoped that the only contention among all would not be about rank but as to who would serve with the greatest zeal. He noted that he had discussed everything with the secretary of war, who would convey his views to the president for decision.

Hamilton's reply greatly surprised Washington, for he disparaged Pinckney and said he would not serve under him; it was too great a sacrifice. Hamilton also blasted McHenry as unfit for his office. The same post brought a long cry of outrage from Knox. This included a flat refusal to serve under either Hamilton or Pinckney. He said that he should have been "previously consulted on an arrangement in which my feelings and happiness have been so much wounded; or that I should not have been dragged forth to public view at all, to make the comparison so conspicuously odious." He was ready to shed his last drop of blood for the country but it would be a final touch of malignant irony if he were excluded from service by "a constant sense of public insult and injury." He had always held a high sense of friendship for Washington and believed that he stood well in his opinion, as friend and military man. Now he thought he had passed twenty years in "perfect delusion." While he had no official notifications from the secretary of war, his answer would be negative.

The president and McHenry had thus placed Washington in an extraordinarily difficult position. Washington had not wanted to serve at all, feeling that the place should go to "younger" men. He had been appointed without his knowledge or consent. Washington had been conspicuously reduced a grade. He had asked McHenry to see to it that no general officer was nominated until the main persons concerned had met with the president in Philadelphia. The army commander in chief now had two highly aggrieved men on his hands. Hamilton was furious with McHenry. He was soon to be equally so with Adams, when he found the president considered him number three on the list. Washington could not explain his own position to Knox without criticizing the president.

On August 9 Washington wrote to both Hamilton and to Knox. He expressed agreement with the former that McHenry had not shown capacity for his office. He had not received a single word as to the status of the army, nor what action had been taken since he had gone back to Philadelphia. He made no mention of Hamilton's position nor of his unwillingness to serve under Pinckney, knowing that nothing would keep Hamilton out. He sent him a copy of Knox's letter and his reply.

Washington wrote a very careful letter to his old artillery chief. Without in any way criticizing the president, he drafted it in a manner to enable Knox, if he read carefully between the lines, to understand what had happened. He himself, he wrote, had been hastily nominated without advance notice and it had been equally impossible for him to consult Knox. As for Hamilton, the appointment had been represented to him as Congress' most earnest wish, but it had not been made by him. He wanted all three to serve with equal heart. He did not think that New England should regard it as an outrage to have the "third" major general. All officers of that grade were of equal stature. Massachusetts, Knox's state, alone was to have two of the five major generals. He assured Knox that his friendship for him was as "warm and sincere" as ever.

The tempest grew worse when Knox went to see the president in Quincy, prior to receiving Washington's letters. There appears to be no record of their conversation but Knox was not in an amiable mood and Adams was not General Washington. The interview might have been worse for Adams, had Knox known that Adams had also placed him third in seniority. It is probable that Knox followed more or less the same argument he used with Washington. His previous rank and long service entitled him to far better treatment, and he should not be ordered to serve under officers, previously his juniors. The argument which carried most weight with Adams was that New England had been humiliated. That area would doubtless furnish a large proportion of the needed troops, but they were to have only a "third" major general.

During this period, Abigail Adams, the president's wife, was critically ill. Adams wrote that his "depression and anxiety" rendered him scarcely fit to think or to handle problems. Knox's agitation threw Adams into further loss of judgment. On August 14 the president wrote the secretary of war: "You may depend upon it, the five New England states will not patiently submit to the humiliation that has been meditated for them." General Knox was legally entitled to be first and Pinckney to be second. Hamilton must therefore be third. If General Washington would consent to this arrangement, the officers could be called to service.

McHenry was appalled by the president's letter. He had not adequately informed Adams of Washington's views: a) he preferred Pinckney, for urgent military and political considerations but b) the choice was up to the president. McHenry replied, with too little regard for the truth, that "the order of ranking proceeded originally and exclusively from General Washington." Adams answered that General Washington could have the presidency if he wished, but so long as he held the office, he would make the decisions. He had determined the order, and he did not intend to change. There had already been too many "intrigues" in the matter. McHenry protested against this last remark. Adams' reply indicated that he had guessed a good portion of the truth: "I have suspected that extraordinary pains were taken to impress upon your mind that the public opinion and the unanimous wish of the Federalists, was that General Hamilton might be first and even commander-in-chief; that you might express this opinion to General Washington more forcibly than I should have done and that this determined him to make the arrangement as he did." The arrangement, in fact, was McHenry's own.

The announcement that General Washington was once again commander of the army brought with it the usual upsurge in mail to Mount Vernon. Volunteers wanted to go immediately into service, many of them on Washington's staff. It was particularly gratifying to Washington to hear from old comrades or their sons: Tallmadge, Marshall, Carroll, Cadwalader, Nelson, and Izard. With the single exception of William Heth, he declined to consider any person as an aide until he entered on active duty.

Martha Washington and Nelly Custis were asked to be sponsors of the Alexandria regiments, which brought an amusing correspondence with the secretary of war. Washington wrote him on July 27:

The Greyheads of Alexandria, pretty numerous it seems, and composed of all the respectable old People of the place; having formed themselves into a Company [the Silver Greys] for the defense of the Town and its Vicinity, are in want of Colours: and it being intimated that the Presentation of them by Mrs. Washington would be flattering to them; I take the liberty of requesting the favour of you to have them made and sent to me. Handsome but not more expensive than becomes Republicans (but not Bachite Republicans) is required. If you think a Motto would be proper, the choice of one 'chaste and unassuming,' is left to your own judgment. Send the cost and the money shall be remitted by Yours always...

Nelly selected "Conquer or die" as the words for her volunteers' banner. McHenry told her that it was a pretty bloody motto for a young lady to choose. When her standard did not arrive from Philadelphia, Nelly grew impatient. She sent the secretary a letter, which was undoubtedly drafted by her "Grampa" who had used the same pun during the revolution. In it she said: "My troop are all uniformed and waiting for that Standard, which they are determined to defend with a bravery never excelled... I am afraid their patience (which is already *threadbare*) will be entirely *worn out*... Not having 'Conquer or Die' before their eyes... their patriotic ardor may be exchanged for a resolution... that it is better to stay at home."

WASHINGTON'S ILLNESS

Washington's request to have Tobias Lear commissioned as his aide, secretary, and lieutenant colonel took much time to win approval. It went to McHenry in Philadelphia who, in turn, had to forward it to the president in Quincy. Before this authorization "at length" reached Mount Vernon, the badly over-worked general had fallen into a critical illness. Washington on August 5 esti-mated his weight at 210 pounds, practically unchanged from the days he and his generals weighed themselves, fifteen years before. A few weeks later he was down to 190 pounds.

On August 27 Washington described the initial stages of his sickness to his nephew, Bushrod: "On the 18th at night I was seized with a [malarial] fever, of which I took little notice until the 21st; when I was obliged to call for the aid of Medicine; and with difficulty a remission thereof was so far effected, as to dose me all night on Thursday, with bark [quinine] which has stopped it, and weakness only remaining, will soon wear off, as my appetite is returning."

On August 30 Washington informed Lear that his appointment had been confirmed. He added that the secretary of war "having thrown a mass of Papers upon me which I have not looked into... I should be glad if you would now come and take your station. Yours always and affectionately." On September 3 he wrote McHenry that the War Department could not expect him to be as active as "you probably have counted on." His illness had made him "too much debilitated to attend much to business." Nonetheless he added several pages on the problems of the southern military district. Included were numerous directives and questions. On September 14 he informed Alexander Spotswood that he was down twenty pounds but his fever had gone and not returned. "I am recovering my flesh fast, nearly a pound and a half a day; at which rate if I should hold it for a twelve Month I shall be an overmatch for Major Willis."

General Washington increasingly complained of the difficult position in which he had been placed. The president was in Quincy for months, while the government drifted and decisions on the army command were changed and shifted. The cabinet tended to look to Washington for leadership but he was not the president and could not fill the vacuum. In turn the secretary of war was proving ineffectual and giving him no information. Though still weak, he wrote to McHenry on September 14:

> No plan is yet decided on that I can discover for recruiting the augmented force, or even for appointing the officers therefor.
>
> … It is for the Executive to account for this delay. Sufficient it is for me to regret, and I do regret it, sorely; because that spirit and enthusiasm which was inspired by the Dispatches from our Envoys… are evaporating fast… The law passed before the middle of July, was positive; and the middle of September has produced no fruit from it. This to me, is inconceivable.
>
> I must once more, my dear McHenry, request that your correspondence with me, may be more full and communicative. You have a great deal of business I must acknowledge; but I scruple not to add, at the same time, that much of the important and interesting part of it will be transacted with the Commander in chief of the Armies of the U. States, from whom there ought to be no concealment or want of information. Short letters, therefore, taking no notice of suggestions or queries, are unsatisfactory and distressing. Considering the light in which I think my sacrifices have placed me, I should expect more attention from the Secretary of War, but from Mr. McHenry, as a friend and Coadjutor, I certainly shall look for it. Compare then my letter to you of the 3d inst., which I wrote in much pain, from the debilitated state into which the fever had thrown me, with your acknowledgment thereof dated the 7th, and judge yourself whether I could derive any satisfaction therefrom, on the score of business… Nor to this moment… and my asking the question in direct terms, what there was in the Report of Colo. North's nomination to the Office of Adjutant General, has there been the least notice taken of the matter since.

I will defer saying anything on the President's new arrangement of the three Major Generals until you have communicated the result of Colo. Hamilton's answer to me.

But in the name of the Army, what could have induced the nomination of Walton White to the rank of Brigadier... I formerly asked the same question with respect to Severe [Sevier] to which no reply was made.

White's name was placed in the list of Field Officers... merely as one that might be considered in that grade, when the general organization came on; but I had no idea when you left this place, that General Officers would be appointed at the time they were, for the Provisional Army... Of all the characters in the Revolutionary Army, I believe one more obnoxious to the Officers who composed it could not have been hit upon for a Genl. Officer than White, especially among those to the Southward, where he was best known, and celebrated for nothing but frivolity, dress, empty show, and something worse; in short for being a notorious [Liar]... As to [Sevier] the only exploit I ever heard of... was the murder of Indians.

What measures, if any, are pursuing, to provide Small Arms, I know not;... If any other article of foreign manufacture are needed, not a moment is to be lost in the Importation...

On September 16 Washington received from McHenry the determination the president had made with respect to the rankings of the three major generals. Washington replied that since this was only a private letter, he could take no action. He was informed that the cabinet would make a respectful representation to the president. Washington was not sure the president would change his mind and, therefore, he was prepared to return his commission. McHenry, much alarmed, wrote to Adams, who replied with a brief note to the effect that he had signed the three commissions on September 30. This action gave no one priority and settled nothing.

As soon as Washington heard that the president knew of his reactions, he wrote, September 25, a long, dignified, and respectful letter to Adams. He realized that what he had to say was "delicate." He had no desire whatever to lessen the power of the president nor to increase his own. Nonetheless his appointment to the command had placed him in a difficult position. He had not wanted it and accepted with "sorrow at being drawn from my retirement." He had explicitly declared to the secretary of war his express condition that the nominations of general officers must have his concurrence.

It had been Washington's understanding, when McHenry left Mount Vernon, that no general officers were to be nominated for some time.

Nonetheless the names of three officers had been sent to the Senate, in order, Hamilton, Pinckney, and Knox, and it was the Senate's understanding that this was the president's choice and that their commissions would so issue. Now Adams had reversed the first and last. The president had, further, nominated five brigadiers, one of whom had no military experience and another whose appointment had given "the greatest disgust." While Washington made no direct mention of the fact that Adams had appointed his own son-in-law as adjutant general, he noted that two nominations had gone forward without the least intimation to him. He would hope that the president would understand that all he aimed at in finding the ablest coad-jutors, was the public good. If war broke out with France, conditions would be entirely different than in the revolution. From 1775 to 1781, the country had to buy time until it could train troops. Now the United States would have to move immediately to the attack, to prevent the French from gaining any foothold in the country. They would probably aim at the South because there were so many disaffected persons there and the area was near their Caribbean Islands. Working with McHenry, he had suggested certain arrangements with respect to the generals, hoping that everyone could meet with the president in Philadelphia, before final arrangements were made. He was subsequently presented with an accomplished fact. He had learned from many New England congressmen that they preferred Hamilton to Knox. The president had the prerogative of making any appointments he wished but he now wanted to change everything.

Washington further explained to Adams that he had especially wanted General Pinckney, for reasons he had previously given in detail to the secretary of war. He had never expected General Knox to make so many difficulties. Washington then pointed out that four months had gone by and there had not been a single recruit for the army nor any battalion officer appointed. If France were to attack the United States, he would have to meet veterans "with Militia or raw recruits; the consequence of which is not difficult to conceive or fore-tell." He concluded: "I have addressed you, Sir, with openness and candour, and I hope with respect, requesting to be informed whether your determina-tion to reverse the order of the three Major Generals is final, and whether you mean to appoint another Adjutant General, without my consideration."

The president replied that any determination of ranks desired by Washington would be supported by him. He was instructing the secretary of war to commission whomever General Washington wished as adjutant gen-eral. Although the battle was thus technically over, the president thereafter displayed little enthusiasm for the army or for General Hamilton and Secretary McHenry.

The only happy note in the commotion was struck by General Pinckney. When Washington heard that Pinckney had reached New York, he wrote to Pickering, October 18, that he hoped "he will not play the second part of the difficulty created by General Knox." General Pinckney turned out to be the perfect southern gentleman. He said that he was delighted with the choice of Hamilton and would be pleased to serve under him. He intimated to General Knox that he would be glad to give way to him, so that he could be second. General Knox had since stated that he would not serve under Pinckney and he could not repeat the offer. Nevertheless if the president wished to change the ranks, he would neither be dissatisfied nor resign. Washington was highly pleased to find one general who placed his country first.

When the secretary of war asked Washington to attend a November conference of the senior generals, probably to be held in Trenton because of a renewed outbreak of yellow fever in Philadelphia, he replied on October 21:

> *I hardly think it will be in my power to attend... 1st because I am yet in a convalescent state (although perfectly recovered of the fever) so far at least as to avoid exposure and consequent Colds, 2dly, My Secretary (Mr. Lear) had had a severe fever, and is now very low... and 3dly, and principally, because I see no definitive ground to proceed upon... from anything that has hitherto appeared...*
>
> *If General Pinckney could be prevailed upon to remain with you, and there was a moral certainty of meeting Generals Hamilton and Knox, I would, maugre the inconveniences and hazard I might run, attempt to join them for the valuable purpose of projecting a Plan in concert with you...*

At the same time he wrote to Knox, who offered to serve as his aide, to plead for his reconsideration: "We shall have either no War or a severe contest with France; in either case, if you will allow me to express my opinion, this is the most eligible time for you to come forward. In the first case to assist with your council and aid in making judicious provisions and arrangements to avert it. In the other case, to share in the glory of defending your Country; and by making all secondary considerations yield to that great and primary object, display a mind superior to embarrassing punctilios, at so critical a moment as the present." Knox declined his commission, and Henry Lee became the third ranking major general of the American army.

VIRGINIA AND KENTUCKY RESOLVES

There was no mistaking the man Washington had in mind when he wrote to Colonel William Heth on July 18: "I think with you that all secret enemies to the peace and happiness of this Country should be unmasked, for it is better to meet two enemies in the open field than one coward behind the curtain." Generals Washington and Lee held similar views, for the latter wrote: "The real enemies of the Republic are Vice-President Jefferson and his henchmen. Like rodents they gnaw at the very foundations of our system of government at a time when our liberty itself is in peril."

Well hidden behind a protective curtain of secrecy, Jefferson was at work that summer, to see that his views would prevail or the Union perish. Making Wilson Nicholas his confidant, he drew up a series of resolutions designed to establish the states as superior to the federal government. Nullification of the federal laws was his first aim. Should this fail then it logically followed that a state could secede, even if this meant civil war and bloodshed. Jefferson's correspondence clearly indicated that he was prepared to go to the ultimate extreme of 1861. Nowhere in the wording does such a concept as "the people of the United States" appear. Instead, the Constitution is defined as a compact among states, who assigned certain defined powers to the general government, "reserving, each state to itself, the residuary mass of right to their own self-government... Whensoever the General Government assumes undelegated powers, its acts are unauthoritative, void and of no force." The state government alone could act for its citizens and not the people within the state.

Jefferson declared that the first unconstitutional act passed by Congress was "to punish frauds committed on the banks of the U.S." This act was void and of no force. The second was the sedition act which was also invalid. The third was control of alien immigration and emigration. Only the states had the right to admit or eject persons, not the national government. Fourth, "the power... to pay the debt and provide for the common defense and welfare... and to make all laws necessary" thereto, although in the Constitution, did not mean what the Constitution said. The federal government did not possess such rights. While, Jefferson continued, the people chose their representatives and had the right to change them this was not a sufficient defense for the Constitution. Where their representatives went beyond it, each state legislature had the right "to nullify of their own authority," whatever act had been passed by the people of the United States, in Congress assembled. The states, in communication with each other, were the sole authority "to judge in the last resort of the powers exercised" in the Constitution. Congress was a mere creature of a pact formed by the states.

The American people had already voted unconstitutional acts which were driving "these states into revolution and blood." In cooperation with their sister states, Virginia and Kentucky therefore declared "these acts void and of no force, and will each take measures of its own for providing that neither these acts, nor any others of the General Government, not plainly and intentionally authorized by the Constitution shall be exercised within their respective territories."

Although the resolves which Jefferson forwarded to Kentucky were modified, and references to war and bloodshed were stricken out, some even stronger language was used in the actual resolutions which passed the Kentucky legislature and were signed by the governor on November 16. Similar but more restrained resolves, prepared by Madison for the Virginia legislature, introduced the long-lived but ineffective doctrine of "interposition." So effectively did Jefferson conceal his part in the Kentucky action that it was to be nearly sixty years before his original words saw print. If he expected other states to swallow his constitutional line, he was disappointed. None joined Kentucky and Virginia. Eight legislatures denounced the resolves in varying degrees of horror. Maryland, as usual, was the most outspoken of all.

TO PHILADELPHIA

By the time General Washington started for his conference, frosts had killed the yellow-fever–bearing mosquitoes and the talks were reset for the national capital. Not yet fully recovered, Washington set out with Lear from Mount Vernon on November 5. Troops escorted him into Alexandria where a sixteen-gun salute was fired. Five Georgetown men carried him by yawl to their city, which rendered him honors. The Georgetown cavalry escorted him to Washington. There, having some business to transact, he stayed the night with his wife's granddaughter.

Baltimore turned out a cavalry escort, as well as the huge throngs which always greeted him when he passed through the city. As he proceeded north, he had another triumphant procession but not as fervid as he had experienced in going to the presidency. Once again the Philadelphia Light Horse escorted Washington into the capital and deposited him at his boarding house. Church bells rang as they had so often done when he came to the city. For the next three days all Philadelphia seems to have called on him, for he recorded in his diary that he had spent the time "receiving many visits."

On November 13 Washington had one unwelcome visitor when the Reverend Dr. Blackwell was announced. When he came downstairs, he found that he had been tricked; standing with Blackwell was George Logan, the self-appointed Jeffersonian emissary to France. Washington recognized him but failed to acknowledge his presence because he had used a cover in attempting to talk to him. Logan mentioned his own name as if it were not well known. Washington subsequently wrote that he offered Dr. Blackwell a chair, "the other took a seat at the same time. I addressed all my conversation to Dr. Blackwell, the other all his to me. I only gave negative or affirmative answers, as laconically as I could, excepting asking how Mrs. Logan did." When Blackwell rose to take his leave, Washington got up and went to the door, expecting Logan to follow. The latter stayed, however, and rambled on about meeting Lafayette, which "he had mentioned before... As I wished to get quit of him, I remained standing and showed the utmost inattention to what he was saying." When Logan mentioned that the purpose of his trip to France had been to improve relations, "this drew my attention more pointedly to what he was saying and induced me to remark that there was something very singular in this." Washington's comments grew sharper:

> That he who could be viewed as a private character; unarmed with proper powers; and presumtively unknown in France; should suppose he could effect what these gentlemen of the first responsibility in our country, specially charged under the authority of the Government, were unable to do. With this observation, he seemed a little confounded; but recovering, said that not more than five persons had any knowledge of his going; that he was furnished by Mr. Jefferson and Mr. McKean with certificates of his citizenship. That Mr. Merlin, President of the Directory of France had discovered the greatest desire that France and America should be on the best terms. I answered that he was more fortunate than our Envoys, for they could neither be received nor heard by Mr. Merlin or the Directory. That if the Powers of France were serious... they [could] repeal the obnoxious arrets by which the commerce and Rights of the country had been invaded... A conduct like this would speak more forcibly than words... He said that the directory was apprehensive that this Country... was not well disposed towards France... I asked what better evidence could be given in refutation of this opinion, than its long suffering of the outrageous conduct of the Nation towards the U States. He said that the attempt at a Coalition of European Powers against France would come to nothing; that the Directory were under no apprehensions... and that Great Britain would have to contend alone; insinuating, as I conceived his object at the time to be, that we should be involved in a dangerous situation if we persisted in our hostile appearances. To this I finally replied that we were driven to these measures in self defense and asked him if the Directory looked upon us as worms; and not even allowed to turn when trod upon?... I hoped the

Spirit of the country would never suffer itself to be injured with impunity by any nation under the sun...

Awaiting Washington in Philadelphia was a memorandum from McHenry proposing conferences with the secretaries of war and treasury but leaving the subjects vague. Washington asked him to be more explicit so that he could study the topics to be discussed. He thought it best they provide written data, in advance for him to review. He added: "I find also that the documents referred to in your letter of the 1ost inst. did not accompany it. As these will be necessary in forming an opinion... I must beg you to furnish me with them without delay." He noted that six papers on the major dispositions of the troops, artillery, and stores of the United States were missing as enclosures.

Washington did not comment on the long absence of the president, nor did he make any further written remarks on the poor preparation of the War Department for the conference. His diary records are scanty, indicating only where he dined. It is not possible to determine when serious talks got under way but it can be surmised that it was not at an early date. Not until the first two weeks in December was there really hard work, with Washington conferring from ten in the morning until late at night. During this period he accepted no dinner invitations.

On December 8 the president delivered his annual address to Congress on the state of the union. General Washington attended, flanked by Generals Hamilton and Pinckney, as well as Colonel Lear. Adams hinted that he thought France was moving towards a conciliatory policy, yet her warlike acts continued. Nothing should cause the United States "to change or relax our measures of defense. On the contrary, to extend and invigorate them is our true policy." The United States still desired peace "but to send another emissary without more definite assurances that he would be received would be an act of humiliation to which the United States ought not to submit." Adams called for an increase in the navy which had already done able service in protecting American commerce. He added a point at which Washington might well have raised an eyebrow: "Various circumstances have concurred to delay the execution of the law for augmenting the military establishment, among these the desire of obtaining the fullest information to direct the best selection of officers. As this object will now be speedily accomplished, it is expected that the raising and organizing of the troops will proceed without obstacle and with effect."

Washington's final work consisted of two documents, more than 8,000 words long, which he gave the secretary of war on December 13. He transmitted them with a note: "I am really ashamed to offer the letters... with so many erasures, etc., but it was not to be avoided unless I had remained so much longer as to have allowed [Lear] time to copy the whole over again... My impatience to be on my return homewards on account of the Season—the Roads—and more especially the passage of the Susquehanna—would not admit of this."

Although his time had been short, Washington produced two of his most incisive state papers. After reviewing the problem of allocating officers to the states, he analyzed the whole of American relations with Europe and the compelling need for a defense system that would assure peace or, if France pushed to an extreme, a quick victory in war:

The law for augmenting the army is peremptory in it provisions... The voluntary suspension of execution could not be justified but by considerations of decisive cogency. The existence of any such considerations is unknown.

Nothing has been communicated respecting our foreign relations to induce the opinion that there has been any change... as to external danger, which dictates an abandonment of the policy of the law... It need not be examined how far it may be at any time prudent to relinquish measures of security... merely because there are probable symptoms of approaching accommodation... [These] may be ascribed to the measures of vigour adopted by the Government; and may be frustrated by a relaxation in those measures, affording an argument of weakness and irresolution... Hitherto nothing is discoverable in the conduct of France which ought to change or relax our measures of defense...

Though it may be true that some late occurrences have rendered the prospect of invasion by France less probable or more remote... Yet, duly considering the rapid vicissitudes of political and military events... it can never be wise to vary our measures of security with the continually varying aspect of European affairs... Standing, as it were, in the midst of falling empires, it should be our aim to assume a station and attitude, which will prevent us from being overwhelmed in their ruins...

It has been very properly the policy of our Government to cultivate peace. But in contemplating the possibility of our being driven to unqualified War, it will be wise to anticipate that frequently the most effectual way to defend is to attack. There may be imagined instances of very great moment to the permanent interests of this Country, which would certainly require a disciplined force. To raise and prepare such a force will always be a work of considerable time...

The sound conclusion, viewing the subject in every light, is conceived to be that no unavoidable delay ought to be incurred in appointing the whole of the Officers and raising the whole of the men, provided for by the act... It cannot be relied upon that troops will be raised and disciplined in less than a year. What may not another year produce? Happy will it be for us if we have so much time for preparation and ill-judged indeed if we do not make the most of it.

The general then made specific recommendations. He proposed that all officers hitherto selected be called immediately into active service and ordered to recruiting duty. General Washington then outlined a needed reorganization of the United States army. An engineer should report on all Great Lakes posts. The western army needed reinforcements. Artillery was to be located in the West and at eleven named seaports on the Atlantic. He selected five major points for new recruiting depots, as far away as possible from the larger cities. The army magazines were to be placed at three principal points, Springfield, Harpers Ferry, and Rocky Mount, as central to the three subdivisions of the country. He added four other towns, Pittsburgh, West Point, Trenton, and Fayetteville, for substations. He entered into detail on the organization of the infantry and cavalry regiments, clothing for the men (remarking there did not seem to be any), and rations. Washington noted how much the French armies depended on their artillery and engineers. He suggested numerous methods to improve the deficiencies of the American army in this regard.

On December 14, for the last time, General Washington left Philadelphia for home. In Chester that night he remembered that he had asked the secretary of war for the appointment of Washington Custis, as a cornet in Lawrence Lewis' regiment. He wrote the secretary to be sure to make no public announcement, until he had the approval of Mrs. Washington and Mrs. Stuart. The following day, held from crossing the Susquehanna by ice and winds, he turned to weightier matters. He informed McHenry that he intended to adhere to his original decision not to take command unless there were an emergency. The two senior officers could do the main work. He would like to see all southern states up to the Potomac under the command of Pinckney, aided by Wilkinson in Tennessee, and William Washington in South Carolina and Georgia. In the North Hamilton would be in immediate command, as well as in charge of the national recruiting drive. On December 19 Washington reached Washington, where he passed the night. He arrived at Mount Vernon the next day.

During Washington's stay in Philadelphia the most conspicuous absentee was the vice-president of the United States. He was expected, in his official station, to be present for the opening of Congress on December 3. Not daring to see General Washington in person, he remained in Charlottesville. On the day that Washington reached Washington, Thomas Jefferson started for the national capital, where he arrived three-and-a-half weeks late.

POLITICS

Although John Adams was to be negligent in carrying out his military recommendations, the general remained his most important political bulwark. Washington had occupied public offices almost continuously for fifty years. He had never been a politician on a party basis, but the attitude of many Virginians towards the federal government brought him into active political work. Aside from bandying doctrines of nullification and secession, Virginia had gone so far as to decree that no member of the state legislature could hold a post in the federal government. John Taylor, a Virginia state senator, who was nominated to a majority in the dragoons, explained to Washington his difficulty of choice. Washington strongly advised him to stay in the Senate where, as a Federalist, he was much more urgently needed.

From the middle of 1798 Washington actively urged the ablest Virginians to seek elective federal and state office. He well remembered that only one of the twenty-one Virginia senators and representatives supported his efforts to secure peace with Great Britain. His first aim was to capture a majority of the state delegation in the House of Representatives, as well as to increase Federalist representation in Virginia's legislature. In this work, the Lee brothers rallied to him, as did John Marshall, John Nicholas of Charlottesville, Daniel Morgan, and the old libertarian, Patrick Henry. Washington expressed his general political and military concerns to Bartholomew Dandridge. The latter, secretary to the American minister at The Hague, was offered an appointment in London as well as a captaincy in the army. Washington wrote that the choice between the diplomatic and military services had to be made by him:

> *Both are attended with uncertainties… The augmented Corps, in which you are appointed, are by Law, to exist no longer than the dispute with France shall continue; but how long this will continue, will require more wisdom than I possess to foretell; and you know, without information from me, what a bug-bear a standing Army (as a few regiments with us are called, though liable to be disbanded at any moment, by withholding the application for their support) is, in the eyes of all those who are continually raising Spectres and Hobgoblins, to affrighten themselves and to alarm the People: and how certain it is that ours (with their consent) will not exist a moment longer than it can be avoided by their endeavors; whether the cause which gives rise to it ceases, or not…*

> *Lawrence Lewis is appointed Captn. in the Corps of light Dragoons… Washington Custis is made Cornet in Lewis's troops for it was found unpracticable to keep him*

longer at College... so great was his aversion to study... The Army, generally, will be very respectably officered.

The General Assembly of this State is in Session; and, by accounts of its proceedings, running into every kind of opposition to the measures of the General government, and into all the extravagant resolutions, which folly can devise...

Patrick Henry had declined the highest appointive offices in the federal government and had refused re-election as governor of Virginia. His political days, he often said, were finished forever. George Washington's appeal of January 15, 1799, changed his mind:

It would be a waste of time, to attempt to bring to the view of a person of your observation and discernment, the endeavors of a certain party among us, to disquiet the Public mind... with unfounded alarms...

Unfortunately, and extremely do I regret it, the State of Virginia has taken the lead in this opposition...

It has been said that the great mass of the Citizens of the State are well affected... to the General Government and the Union; and I am willing to believe it, nay do believe it: but how is this to be reconciled with their suffrages... both to Congress and their State Legislature...

One of the reasons assigned is, that the most respectable and best qualified characters amongst us, will not come forward...

Vain will it be to look for Peace and happiness, or for the security of liberty or property, if Civil discord should ensue; and what else can result from the policy of those among us who, by all the means in their power, are driving matters to extremity...

I come now, my good Sir, to the object of my letter, which is to express a hope, and an earnest wish, that you would come forward at the ensuing Elections (if not for Congress, which you may think would take you too long from home) as a candidate... in the General Assembly...

With great and very sincere regard and respect...

Henry did agree to run for the assembly and thereby gained Jefferson's malignant hatred. At one point Washington felt sure that he would win eleven of the nineteen Virginia seats in the House of Representatives. In the end eight Federalists were elected. In three additional districts, the election was so close as to give the Jeffersonians a scare. John Marshall became representative from Richmond and Henry Lee from the district which covered Washington's own Fairfax County. Lee's brother, Richard Bland, was elected as Fairfax delegate to the assembly at Richmond. Although disappointed at not attaining a majority, Washington had achieved a remarkable comeback for the national party, in the state where opposition was greatest.

Shortly after receiving news of Patrick Henry's defection, Jefferson remarked to Benjamin Rush in Philadelphia that only two men stood between him and the presidency: George Washington and Patrick Henry. Their deaths would make his election "*speedy* as well as *certain.*" On March 12, 1801, Rush reminded Jefferson of his grisly prophecy.

WASHINGTON'S BIRTHDAY

Lawrence Lewis did not accept his commission for reasons which Washington gave to the secretary of war: "The enclosed letter from Major Lawrence Lewis requires explanation and it is the purpose of this letter to give it. He had, it seems, been making overtures of Marriage to Miss Custis some time previous to the formation of the Augmented Corps... without any apparent impression, until she found he was arranged as a Captain in the Regiment of Light Dragoons, and was about to try his fortune in the Camp of Mars. This brought into activity those affections for him, which *before* she conceived were the result of friendship only. And I believe the condition of Marriage is, that he is to relinquish the field of Mars for the sport of Venus."

That year, 1799, when Washington was sixty-seven, he again had two attractive celebrations. Alexandria gave him "an elegant ball and supper" on the old style date, February 11. He was accompanied into town by three companies of dragoons who, with other troops, conducted maneuvers before the general.

Nelly Custis chose February 22 for her marriage, in special compliment to her stepgrandfather. The Reverend Thomas Davis of Alexandria appeared at Mount Vernon, in time for afternoon dinner. Washington's diary recorded that "Miss Custis was married about Candle light to Mr. Lawrence Lewis." Once again George and Martha Washington's blood relatives were united. Mount Vernon appears to have celebrated the event for an extended time. There were twelve guests for dinner on the 25th and eight more the following day. The bride's mother and three Stuart half-sisters and her sisters, Mrs. Lewis and Mrs. Peter, stayed at the mansion until March 3. It appears from the somewhat uncertain account in Washington's diary that another sister, Mrs. Law, was there for an even longer time. On March 5 the bride and groom went to Washington to spend a little over two weeks on their honeymoon.

The general, at sixty-seven, had more than enough to do, managing his extensive properties, keeping abreast of national and international politics, as well as the army, the inland navigation, and the city of Washington. He wrote McHenry on March 25 that he was still trying to get his affairs in order after his sixteen years' absence. "But this is not all, nor the worst, for being the Executor, the Administrator, and Trustee of and for other Estates, my greatest anxiety is to leave all these concerns in such a clear and distinct form, so that no reproach may attach itself to me, when I have taken my departure for the land of Spirits."

INLAND NAVIGATION

When Washington was twenty-two, his natural curiosity made him canoe down more than 170 miles of the Potomac. He began at a point just below Cumberland and continued within two miles of Great Falls, noting where channels might be cut or rocks dug out to permit boats to pass the falls and other obstacles to navigation. Forty-six years later, he was as keen as ever to see his early ideas move to completion.

On July 21 he wrote to Charles Carroll, the last to die of the Signers, hoping that all Potomac Company shareholders, including himself and Carroll, would attend the next meeting. He added:

Greatly is it to be regretted that an Undertaking productive of, or rather promising such immense advantages to the States of Maryland and Virginia... should be suffered to progress so limpingly, as this work has done for some years back.

If this Navigation was completed, and it is susceptible of being so in a short time; and the Shenandoah opened... I would predict... that it would be found one of (if not) the most productive funds (with the least risk to the Stockholders) of any Legalized Institution in the United States...

It might be as unjust as improper to censure the conduct of the Directors... but if the means can be obtained, I shall declare for having the residue of the Work executed by Contract...

Washington attended the stockholders' meeting which prepared an appeal to

Maryland and Virginia for more capital funds. That night he spent with the Thomas Laws at their house near Jenkins Hill, atop of which the wing of Dr. Thornton's national capitol building was nearing completion.

On August 12 the general wrote to William Berkeley, treasurer of Virginia, to urge the state to come forward with financial help. "To dilate on the benefits which would result from improving the great *high way* which nature has marked out as the easiest and most direct communication with the Western World (maugre all the endeavours of Pennsylvania and New York to divert it into other Channels) would be a mere waste of time... But it must be acknowledged at the same time that habits and customs are not easily over-come. Consequently if the produce of the upper Ohio and the Lakes should settle in either of the channels above mentioned, it will require time as well as inconvenience, to bring it back to the course which nature has ordered... "

By December 1, Maryland, always more farsighted than Virginia, had sub-scribed to new funds for the canal. Washington wrote to Dr. Thornton: "I am glad to hear that the legislature of Maryland have acted favourably on the application made by the Potomac Company. Your information of this event is the first I had received. It is to be hoped that the Legislature of this State will 'go and do so likewise.' Neither would be backward in promoting this useful undertaking if the measure was impartially investigated and the welfare of the respective States duly considered."

The first part of the Potomac Company's work, the canal around the Great Falls, was completed in 1802. Other sections as far west as Harpers Ferry were finished a few years later. In 1828 Washington's organization was merged into the Chesapeake and Ohio Company, which, by 1850, had extended the canal from Georgetown as far as Cumberland. Thus George Washington's dream was completed 96 years after his canoe trip down the Potomac. Although never a profitable enterprise it served inland commerce for many years there-after. Now part of the national park system, it is one of the most attractive of all monuments to the farseeing young colonel.

WASHINGTON, THE CAPITAL

Dr. William Thornton was a gifted and busy man. He was an inventor, painter, architect of the capitol, and commissioner of the territory of Columbia. In this last office, he worked night and day to get the city ready for the expected transfer of the government from Philadelphia in 1800. Dr. Thornton was also the physician who treated Tobias Lear as well as co-architect of the two houses which Washington ordered built on Capitol Hill. Washington admired, liked, and trusted Thornton and saw him frequently at Mount Vernon or in the federal city.

When Thornton queried him about the city's plan, Washington replied on June 1 that, since he had left the presidency, he had never intermeddled "in any public matter which did not immediately concern me." Thornton's question, however, seemed to refer to his own earlier directives "on which I presume my Letters were not as clear and explicit as it was my intention to be. I have no hesitation in declaring... that it has always been my invariable opinion, and remains still to be so, that no departure from the *Engraved* plan of the City ought to be allowed, unless *imperious* necessity should require it, or some great public good is to be promoted thereby." He added that the plan had been circulated throughout Europe, to induce purchasers to buy lots. They might well complain "of deception and injury," if the plans were arbitrarily changed without their knowledge.

Washington, jointly with Thornton, worked out designs for two elegant federal houses, with "united Doors in the Center, a Pediment in the roof and dormer windows on each side." The houses could be joined in the interior to form, if needed, a single house. Washington added a feature from Mount Vernon. This consisted of blowing fine sand on painted wooden exteriors, to give them the appearance of stone. The sand also acted as a preservative. In 1943 Ralph Cole Hall, an architect, and Stephen Dorsey, an architectural writer, after jointly examining Washington's plans, praised "the deep perception and judgment" of his designs.

As the buildings progressed, there was constant correspondence between Washington and Thornton. The general frequently came into town to inspect the work. On November 9 he examined them, then dined with the Thomas Laws and spent the night with the Peters at what became 2618 K Street. This was the last time that Washington slept in Washington. Nine days later he made a typical comment to Thornton: "I have no objection to Mr. Blagden's frequent calls for money; but I fear the work, which is not enumerated in the contract with him, is pretty smartly whipped up in the price of it."

Thornton continued to appeal to Washington's judgment on the city's development. On December 8 the general wrote him: "... I know not on what ground the Attorney General of the United States has founded the opinion communicated in your letter, of the insufficiency of the President's Powers to authorize the Commissioners of the City to accept a loan, for the purpose of carrying on the public works in that place. Under the original Act empowering the President to establish the permanent Seat of the Government on the Potomac, no doubt ever occurred to my mind, nor I believe to the Minds of any of the Officers thereof... of a want of this Power.

But by the obstructions continually thrown in its way, by *friends* or *enemies*, this City has had to pass through a fiery trial. Yet, I trust it will, ultimately, escape the Ordeal with éclat."

AGRICULTURE

On January 20, 1799, Washington wrote to Sir John Sinclair, the former head of the British Board of Agriculture: "No one is more impressed than I am with the importance of National encouragement to Agriculture. No one can approve more of such an Institution, as you have been the promoter of, than myself. Nor no one wishes more ardently than I do, to see such a measure adopted in the United States but we must look, I fear, to a more tranquil period for the accomplishment of it. Endeavouring in the meanwhile, to draw all the advantages we can from the labours of others." It was given to Lincoln, Washington's first great successor in office, to establish a small Bureau of Agriculture in 1862. Washington's dream of a national system of roads to unite the country and to promote western economic development, lay far longer in abeyance. For an extended period the Braddock and Forbes roads of 1755 and 1758 were the major connections to Ohio.

When his father died, George Washington inherited about 2,500 acres in Deep Run, in addition to his father's farm. He kept the former tract throughout most of his life, giving it to a nephew, Robert Lewis, in 1795. The additional lands he acquired from subsequent inheritance, purchase, or military service, he also held, for the most part. Occasionally, he exchanged properties for more convenient locations. At other times he sold lands to meet debts and obligations arising from his long periods of public service. Over the years his holdings increased until they totalled about ninety-six square miles. These lands were situated in New York, Pennsylvania, Maryland, Virginia, North Carolina, the District of Columbia, and the present states of West Virginia, Ohio, and Kentucky.

Washington's desire to sell large portions of this land, in order to free his slaves, had not been successful. In fact, his plan had become costly. He had resolved never to sell a slave who was to be freed. In his view at least half of the slaves were of no use to him but they had to be fed and clothed. He ran each year a large cash deficit which he estimated over several years to be in excess of $50,000. He was able to sell just enough acreage to break even.

LAST WILL

On July 9 George Washington drew up a will, disposing of the lands, shares, and other properties he possessed. With some exceptions, his wife was given a life interest in his property.

The next and most important provision was to free all his slaves, in a manner conforming to the laws of Virginia. Washington's will provided that all who were old or infirm were to be supported with full room, board, and clothing for the rest of their natural lives. Those who were not of age and had no parents were to be apprenticed to those who would teach them reading, writing, and a proper trade. He added: "And I do hereby expressly forbid the Sale or Transportation out of the said Commonwealth of Virginia, of any Slave I may die possessed of, under any pretense whatever. And I do moreover most pointedly, and most solemnly, enjoin it upon my Executors... to see that *this* clause respecting Slaves, and every part thereof, be religiously fulfilled... without evasion, neglect or delay... particularly as it respects the aged and infirm; seeing that a regular and permanent fund be established for their Support as long as there are subjects requiring it; not trusting to the uncertain provision to be made by individuals."

Succeeding clauses were devoted to education. Washington had been contributing an annuity to the Alexandria Academy for the education of orphans. In lieu thereof, he bequeathed the academy twenty shares in the Bank of Alexandria. He confirmed his previous donation of one hundred James River Company shares to the institution which was to become Washington and Lee University. A final educational clause looked to the great national university which Washington had planned for years. When he first laid his proposal before Congress, the opposition press severely attacked it. The congressional bill authorizing the acceptance of donations, was defeated by a single vote, thanks to Virginia's congressmen. Washington's will repeated and extended remarks which he had so often made:

> *It has been my ardent wish to see a plan... to spread systematic ideas through all parts of this rising Empire, thereby to do away with local attachments and State prejudices... from our National Councils. Looking anxiously forward to the accomplishment of so desirable an object... my mind has not been able to contemplate any plan more likely to effect the measure than the establishment of a UNIVERSITY... for education in... literature, in arts and sciences, in acquiring knowledge in the principles of Politics and good Government; and (a matter of infinite Importance in my judgment) by associating with each other, and forming friendships in juvenile years, to be enabled to free themselves from those local*

prejudices and habitual jealousies which... when carried to excess, are never failing sources of disquietude to the Public mind, and pregnant of mischievous consequences to this country.

For the establishment of a university in the territory of Columbia, Washington bequeathed the fifty Potomac Company shares, which had originally cost the state of Virginia $43,000. Washington had confidence in the future of the enterprise if it were well managed, and he expected the profits to be large and the value of the shares to increase. His will provided that all dividends be reinvested in bank stocks and added to the principal until the institution was established and the funds were needed.

The history of Washington's plan after his death is one of America's ironies. He assumed that the federal government would give such a national university a fostering hand. Jefferson ignored the proposal. Madison took up the suggestion with Congress in 1809 and 1815 but got nowhere. In 1816, Benjamin Latrobe, remembering Washington's enthusiasm and expecting a success for Madison's efforts, made an elegant sketch and design for the university to be located on the Mall, southeast of the president's house. The proposal was not acted upon, and Jefferson appropriated Latrobe's general design for the University of Virginia. The shares eventually became worthless. Some amends were made, six years after the Civil War, when Columbia College, in the nation's capital, was renamed the George Washington University.

Washington's further individual bequests were in excess of fifty, although a few were tokens of esteem rather than of value. Around forty nieces and nephews, grandnieces and nephews, and Martha Washington's four grandchildren shared in the estate. The most important bequest was to Bushrod Washington, associate justice of the Supreme Court, who received the Mount Vernon mansion house, 4,000 acres around it, and all of Washington's papers and books. Lawrence Lewis, married to Martha's granddaughter, got title to the 2,000-acre Dogue Run farm, on which Woodlawn was later built. Charles and George Washington, as grandnephews of both George and Martha Washington, were given a 2,077-acre tract, subsequently known as Collingwood. A portion of this, 360 acres, was reserved for their stepfather, Tobias Lear, as a lifetime free tenancy. Washington Custis was bequeathed approximately 1,200 acres near Alexandria, not far from his father's estate, which came to be known as Arlington. With the exception of certain other specific bequests, the remaining property was divided into twenty-four parts which were assigned, after the sales of property, to various heirs, some included in the preceding distribution. This portion Washington estimated as worth $530,000. He made no attempt to evaluate the whole estate.

A little over two months after he wrote his will, Washington informed Lawrence and Nelly Lewis that he was leaving them the Dogue Run farm. They had expressed a desire to settle near the general, who would be happy to rent them the property, so that they could build a house there. They would thus not have to buy expensive land but still have assurance that the rented property would pass to them as a gift, if they gave no displeasure to their uncle. Washington hastily added a reassurance that he had no reason to expect this, it was just his way of making certain about everything.

UNITED STATES ARMY

Although Washington had made it clear that he would not assume an active command until an emergency developed, he was nonetheless overworked and sometimes overwhelmed with army business. On February 25 he wrote to Hamilton that he thought the delay in recruiting was "unaccountable; and baffles all conjecture on reasonable grounds." If the winter were thus allowed to pass idly away, there would soon be heavy demands for agricultural workers and recruiting would be greatly hampered. The army would have to pick up "the riff-raff of the Country and the Scape gallowses of the large Cities." He followed this on March 25 with a forthright letter to Secretary of War McHenry:

You will not only consider this letter as a private one, but as a friendly one from G:W to J:M. And if the sentiments which you will find in it are delivered with more freedom and candour than are agreeable, say so; not by implication only, but in explicit language; and I will promise to offend no more...

Thus premising, let me, in the name and behalf of the Officers who have been appointed, ask what keeps back the Commissions; and arrests the Recruiting Service? Be assured that both, among the friends of Government, excite astonishment and discontent. Blame is on every mind, but it is not known where to fix it. Some attach it to the P., some to the S. of W., and some, fertile in invention, seek for other causes. Many of the appointed Officers have quit their former occupations... Others, who were about to enter into business... stand suspended... Applications are made by numbers to me, to know what the cause of the delay is, what they are to expect, and what they ought to do.

What could I say? Am I not kept in as much ignorance as they are themselves? Am I advised of any new appointments?... Any of the views or designs of the Government relatively to the Army?... Nothing short of a high sense of the Amor

Patriae could have placed me in my present situation; and though I stand bound by, and will obey the call of my Country whenever it is made... none will regret the event with more poignancy...

I have been thus full, as it relates to myself, in order to shew you that information in all matters of a military nature, are necessary for my Government; thereby having a prospective view of things, I may prepare accordingly; and not, though detached from the Army until the exigencies of our Affairs may require my presence with it, appear as a person just dropped from the clouds, when I take the Command: nor will it, without doing great violence to the concerns of others, equally with my own, be in my power to "take up my bed and walk" at an unexpected requirement...

The augmented Corps... must have been intended as a well organized and disciplined body of Men... Will this be the case if the enemy should invade this Country? Far from it! What better, in the first instance, are Regiments so composed than Militia?

The two Major Generals and myself were called to Philadelphia in November last, and there detained five weeks very inconveniently to all of us, at an inclement season, in wading through volumes of applications and recommendations to Military Appointments; and I will venture to say that it was executed with as much assiduity and under as little influence of favor or prejudice, as a work of that sort... ever was accomplished; and what has followed? Why any member of Congress who had a friend to serve, or prejudice to indulge could set them at nought?

Thus prodded, McHenry issued a release to the gazettes, which explained that officers would be paid from the date of acceptance of their commission. On April 23 Washington wrote to the secretary to say that this had removed one cause of discontent among those who had quit their occupations, "but if these Officers are not speedily employed in the Recruiting Service, a clamour will soon arise in another quarter, for it will be asked why they are in actual pay and unemployed." In a subsequent private letter to Hamilton, Washington expressed agreement with Hamilton's argument for the promotion of Brigadier James Wilkinson, who had been commander of the American army. Having seen this letter, McHenry then asked Washington to give him a formal recommendation. Washington replied on July 7:

I am always willing to give publicity to any statement, which I have expressed in this way, if circumstances should require or render it proper. But as the appointment of other Officers of high rank has been made, not only without my recommendation but even without my knowledge, I cannot see the necessity… of my writing an official letter… Permit me, moreover to say that it would seem as if when doubts or difficulties present themselves, I am called upon to sanction the measure and thereby take a responsibility upon myself: and, in other cases, to which no blame may be attached, my opinions and inclinations are not consulted.

From great issues Washington was pulled back into trivia—the complaints of Washington Custis. The commander in chief wrote one week later to the secretary of war: "The young Cornet (in my family) is anxious to receive his Military equipments. Daily fruitless enquiries are made of me to know when they may be expected. Perhaps if you were to jog Mr. Francis, the *Purveyor*, the sooner they might be *Purveyed*, and the young gentleman gratified."

In 1798 Washington accepted two months active-duty pay, a little over $500 a month. On September 14, 1799, he declined the offer of the secretary of war to add a further sum, since he was living at Mount Vernon. He noted, however, the troubles his "inactive" command had brought him that year: "Applicants, recommenders of applicants, and seekers of information, with their servants and horses (appear at Mount Vernon) to aid in the consumption of my forage, and what, to me, is more valuable, my time." He would nonetheless draw only actual expenses, since he did not want those "who are always on the lookout for something to cavil at," to be able to say he was enjoying a lucrative retirement.

A remarkable feature of Washington's tenure as army chief was his sound advice on naval matters. He recommended to the secretary of the navy, on September 26, 1798, the establishment of a federal naval shipyard in the territory of Columbia. The opening of navigation of the Potomac, beyond tidewater, would provide, he said, the best naval timber in the country. Above the head of the Potomac was "an abundant supply of the largest and best white pine trees for Masts… No part of the U.S. affords better cedar and locust than the lands about this River. You know that iron of the best quality can be furnished from the works on the river, and as cheap as from any part of the U.S., and the establishment of a public foundry and Armory [at Harpers Ferry] will afford no small advantage in arming the ships. The articles of Tar, Pitch, live Oak, can be brought here upon as good terms as to any place North of this." Washington also noted that hemp could probably be grown cheaply and easily in the Ohio Valley. The government should encourage this, to avoid foreign dependence. He further advocated careful soundings of the Potomac and the deepening of its channels, in order to accommodate ships of the line.

The secretary of the navy followed Washington's advice and established a navy yard, which was subsequently destroyed during Madison's war.

The same letter pointed out how the national capital could be made impregnable to sea attack. "Should proper works be erected on Digge's Point... it would not be in the power of all the navies in Europe to pass that place... for every vessel, in passing up the River, must, from the course of the channel (and the channel is so narrow as to admit of but one vessel going abreast) present her bows to that point long before she comes within gun shot of it, and continue in that direction until she comes directly under the point, from whence shot may be thrown upon her deck, almost in perpendicular direction. Should she be so fortunate as to pass the works, she must expose her stern to the fire from them, as far as the shot can reach. Thus exposed to be raked fore and aft, for such a distance, without once being able to bring her broadside to bear upon the fort, you can readily see how impossible it will be for a vessel to pass this point; provided it be properly fortified and well supplied. And what makes it more important is that it cannot be attacked by land with any prospect of success... From the heights about Cedar Point... no Vessel can enter the River undiscovered, and by means of signals established on the prominent Eminences between that place and the site just mentioned, and the Federal City, notice thereof and of the number and descriptions of the Vessels may be conveyed to those places in a few minutes." Jefferson established a feeble fort at this point which Madison and Monroe continued to keep weak and useless. The British fleet easily captured it and the city of Alexandria in 1814.

One other point was made by the commanding general to the secretary of the navy: "If the British are resolved to keep up armed Vessels on the lakes, I presume it will be expedient for us to do the same; but in time of peace a better way, in my opinion, is for neither one to have any." Years later this became a firm pillar of Anglo-Canadian-American policy.

In September Washington received the news that General Pinckney, in charge of the army south of the Potomac, had taken his critically ill wife to Newport for her health. In consequence, Washington, the only high-ranking officer south of Philadelphia, had to assume aspects of command in September and October which he could otherwise have avoided. Most of it concerned instructions to three regiments, who were establishing cantonments and building new barracks at Harpers Ferry, or elsewhere. This involved extensive correspondence with the commanding officer of the regiments, the governor of Maryland, and others.

Washington's final letter on military affairs was written to Hamilton, who had forwarded to the secretary of war an overly elaborate plan for a national military academy. On December 12 he noted: "The Establishment of an Institution of this kind... has ever been considered by me as an Object of primary importance to this Country; and while I was in the Chair of Government, I omitted no opportunity of recommending it, in my public Speeches, and otherways, to the attention of the Legislature." He did not propose now, to go into the details of such a plan.

INTERNATIONAL DEVELOPMENTS

On February 18, 1799, the president of the United States transmitted to the Senate the nomination of William Vans Murray, American minister at The Hague, to be minister plenipotentiary to the French republic. Enclosed with the nomination was a letter from Talleyrand to the secretary of the French legation at The Hague, which declared that the French government would receive a minister from the United States "with the respect due to the representative of a free, independent and powerful nation." This phrase was the condition which, Adams had previously informed Congress, had to be met before he sent the French another minister. Under senatorial pressure, Adams subsequently made Murray one of three commissioners.

Adams had consulted no one on this measure and kept the Cabinet and Senate in the dark. Long afterwards, Timothy Pickering, secretary of state, surmised, probably correctly, that it was Adams' own idea, as a way to outflank Jefferson and win the Democrats over to his administration. He succeeded only in turning many horrified supporters against him. Jefferson, in reading the message to the Senate, noted the "mortification" and "dismay" of the Federalist senators. He immediately issued to Madison and Monroe the official party line. The Federalists had been concealing all along the true position of France. The French had always wanted peace, the Democrats were right, and it had been only provocation on the part of the United States which had caused trouble. With such a line, Adams could gain nothing politically. A few days previously Jefferson had written of the burden of defense, that the existing budget was already costing one-third the value of American exports and would soon take half. In fact, the then total federal expenditure was less than 10 percent of American exports and shipping earnings and perhaps a little over 1 percent of the gross national product. Once Adams announced peaceful overtures, the Jeffersonians returned with renewed angry attacks on any American defense system.

Washington viewed Adams' impetuous gesture with great concern. He wrote to the secretary of state on March 3 that he had been

informed there had been no <u>direct</u> overture from the Government of France... On the *contrary that Mr. Talleyrand was playing the same loose and round-about game he had attempted the year before with our Envoys; and which, as in that case, might mean anything or nothing, as would subserve his purpose best. Had we approached the ante-chamber of this Gentleman when he opened the door to us and there waited for a formal invitation into the Interior, the Governments would have met upon equal ground; and we might have advanced, or receded, according to circumstances. In plainer words, had we said to Mr. Talleyrand, through the channel of his communication, we still are, as we always have been ready to settle by fair Negotiation, all differences... upon open, just and honourable terms; and it rests with the Directory (after the indignities with which our attempts to effect this, have been treated, if they are equally sincere) to come forward in an unequivocal manner, and prove it by their acts. Such conduct would have shown a dignified willingness on our part to Negotiate; and would have tested their sincerity, on the other. Under my present view of the subject, this would have been the course I should have pursued; keeping equally in view the horrors of War, and the dignity of the Government.*

Jefferson returned to Charlottesville in March to work on national and state elections. By this time he was counting on Pennsylvania to go Democratic which, with the South, would be sufficient to carry him to the presidency. The intrusion of Patrick Henry in support of the Federalists was particularly galling to him. He wrote on May 21 that whenever a man wanted public office, "a rottenness begins in his conduct. Mr. Henry has taken the field openly; but our legislature is filled with too great a mass of talents and principle to be now swayed by him... Still I fear something from his intriguing and cajoling talents, for which he is still more remarkable than for his eloquence." The elections of Patrick Henry and eight Federalist congressmen Jefferson found "extremely to be regretted."

Patrick Henry died on June 6, to the shock of Washington. Ten days later he wrote to John Marshall: "In the Death of Mr. Henry... not only Virginia but our country at large has sustained a very serious loss. I sincerely lament his death as a friend; and the loss of his eminent talents as a Patriot I consider as peculiarly unfortunate at this critical junction of our affairs." Yet Washington sensed there had been a move to moderation, even in the South. To the painter, John Trumbull, who was in London (and whom he asked to give his best respects to Benjamin West) Washington wrote on June 25: "The public mind has changed, and is yet changing every day with respect to French principles. The people begin to see clearly that the words and actions of the governing powers of that Nation can not be reconciled... The late changes in the Congressional Representation sufficiently evince this: for of the two sent from the State of Georgia, one certain, some say both are Federal characters; of six from South

Carolina, five are decidedly so; of ten from North Carolina, seven may be counted upon; and of nineteen from this state (Virginia) eight are certain, a ninth doubtful, and, but for some egregious mismanagement, eleven supporters of Governmental measures would have been elected." Washington also wrote:

> No well informed and unprejudiced man, who has viewed with attention the conduct of the French Government since the Revolution in that Country, can mistake its objects or the tendency of the ambitious plans it is pursuing. Yet, strange as it seems, a party, and a powerful one too, among us, affect to believe that the measures of it are dictated by a principle of self preservation; that the outrages of which the Directory are guilty, proceed from dire necessity; that it wishes to be upon the most friendly and amicable terms with the United States; that it will be the fault of the latter if this is not the case; that the defensive measures which this Country have adopted, are not only unnecessary and expensive, but have the tendency to produce the evil which, to deprecate, is mere pretence, because War with France they say is the wish of this Government; that on the Militia we should rest our Security... [All this is done] with all the arts of sophistry, and no regard to truth, decency or respect to characters, public or private, who happen to differ from themselves in Politics...

The dissensions within the Federalist party brought many leaders to look for another candidate in 1800. Washington seemed to be the one man who could again unite the country and save the Union. John Trumbull's brother, Jonathan, governor of Connecticut, was one of the first to sound out the general on the subject. Washington replied forcefully on July 21:

> It would be a matter of sore regret to me if I could believe that a serious thought was turned towards me as his successor; not only as it respects my ardent wishes to pass through the vale of life in retirement... unless called upon to defend my country... but on public grounds also... I am thoroughly convinced I should not draw a <u>single</u> vote from the Anti-federal side; and of course should stand on no stronger ground than any other Federal character, well supported; and when I should become a mark for the shafts of envenomed malice, and the basest calumny to fire at; when I should be charged not only with irresolution, but with concealed ambition, which waits only on occasion to blaze out; in short, with dotage and imbecility. All this... ought to be like dust in the balance when put in competition with a <u>great</u> public good... But as no problem is better defined in my mind than that principle, not men, is now, and will be, the object of contention... Any other respectable Federal character would receive the same suffrages that I should; at my time of life (verging towards three score and ten) I should expose myself without rendering any essential

service to my Country, or answering the end contemplated. Prudence on my part must arrest any attempt at the well meant, but mistaken views of my friends, to introduce me again into the chair of Government.

Washington then took up a problem which sorely vexed the Cabinet and everyone concerned with the operations of government in crisis: the fact that the president was so long away from the capital. He "would give him to understand that his long absence from the Government in the present critical conjecture, affords matter for severe animadversion by the friends of government, who speak of it and set it down as a favourable omen for themselves. It has been suggested to me to make this Communication; but I have declined it, conceiving that it would be better received from a private character, more in the habits of social intercourse and friendship."

In a further letter on August 11 to the secretary of war, Washington referred to various matters, including the charges by the Jeffersonian press that federal officials had been receiving bribes:

I think you wisemen of the East have got yourselves in a hobble... Whom will you offend?... But to be serious, I think the nomination and Appointment of Ambassadors to treat with France would, in any event, have been liable to unpleasant reflections... and, in the present state of matters in Europe, must be exceedingly embarrassing. The President has a choice of difficulties... If he pursues the line he marked out, all the consequences cannot be foreseen. If he relinquished it, it will be said to be of a piece with all the other Acts of the Administration; unmeaning if not wicked, deceptions & ca... and will arm the opposition with fresh weapons to commence new attacks upon the Government... I come now to the Scene of Bribery.

And pray, my good sir, what part of the $800,000 have come to your share? As you are high in Office, I hope you did not disgrace yourself in the acceptance of a paltry bribe. A $100,000 perhaps. But here again I become serious. There can be no medium between the reward and punishment of an editor who shall publish such things as Duane has been doing for sometime past... I hope and expect that the Prosecutors will probe this matter to the bottom.

Is the President returned to the seat of Government? When will he return? His absence (I mention it from the best motives) gives much discontent to the friends of government, while its enemies chuckle at it...

In the meantime, keeping his hand entirely secret, the vice-president further dabbled in treasonable activities by declaring the right of any state to secede, the doctrine by which Jefferson was to father the eventual civil war. In once more dispatching Wilson Nicholas to Kentucky to induce its pliant legislature to pass further resolutions, Jefferson wrote, September 5, asking Kentucky to reply to the many states who had denounced the earlier Virginia and Kentucky resolves. He complained bitterly that they had, in effect, endorsed the work of the national Congress and their actions were therefore unconstitutional. Kentucky should protest vigorously, "*reserving* the right to make this palpable violation of the federal compact the ground of doing in future what we might now rightfully do," that is to secede from the Union. Jefferson used the term "scission" rather than secession. Virginia would never surrender "the rights of self-government." Rather, as he had pointed out a few days earlier to Madison, we ought to "sever ourselves" from the Union.

While Jefferson was plotting to dissolve the Union and reports reached Philadelphia that Virginians were arming in defiance of the federal government, the president stayed quietly in Quincy from March to October. That year saw more revolutionary changes in France as most of the Directory were overthrown and the Terror briefly renewed. To numerous Federalists this French instability made it even less desirable that a mission proceed. In October the president reached Trenton where he stayed temporarily to avoid yet another yellow fever epidemic in the capital. As Pickering reported to Washington, October 24, the president ordered the secretary of the navy to prepare a frigate to carry the two American commissioners to France. Adams told the secretary that he had not consulted the cabinet because his mind was "unchangeable."

When Washington heard from Hamilton of the presidential decision, he replied on October 27: "I was surprised at the *measure*, how much more so at the manner of it? This business seems to have commenced in an evil hour, and under unfavourable auspices; and I wish mischief may not tread in all its steps, and be the final result of the measure. A wide door was open, through which a retreat might have been made from the first faux-pas; the shutting of which, to those who are not behind the Curtain, and are as little acquainted with the Secrets of the Cabinet as I am, is, from the present aspect of European affairs, incomprehensible." He wrote in a somewhat similar vein to McHenry, expressing the hope that "good will come from the Mission, which is about to depart... These are my wishes, and no one is more ardent in them; but I see nothing in the *present* aspect of European Affairs on which to build them. Nor no possible evil under the same circumstances, that could result from delay in forwarding it."

On November 10 McHenry replied with a long, gloomy, and as events turned out, quite accurate appraisal of the political situation. It was to be the last letter of importance on national affairs which Washington received.

McHenry explained that the French mission had been appointed without consultation with Congress. Most of the Federalist members disapproved. They regarded the move as ill timed, made on too slight grounds, and likely to be hurtful to the United States. In addition, Adams' action tended to encourage French and Jeffersonian principles. That summer, members of the Cabinet had written to the president, pointing out that the changes in the Directory and the successes of the British and their allies made it desirable to suspend the mission. The president made no reply but on his arrival simply ordered the Cabinet to prepare instructions for the mission, which was to depart on November 3. Three of the Cabinet, the secretaries of state, treasury, and war, regarded the move as "impolitic and unwise." The president, in consequence, was highly displeased with them, and there was a probability one or more would be dismissed. In McHenry's view, "good and able" substitutes could easily be found, but this would not remedy the evil. The mission had become such "an apple of discord" among the Federalists as to jeopardize the ensuing election for the presidency. Pennsylvania had already gone Democratic. The Jeffersonians were making progress elsewhere.

McHenry could see only danger ahead. The secretaries of state and treasury, able men both, had been made "cyphers... I see rocks and quicksands on all sides and the administration as a sinking ship. It will depend... upon the President whether she is to weather or go down." On November 17 Washington replied:

Your confidential and interesting letter... came duly and safely to hand. With the contents of which I have been stricken dumb; and I believe it is better that I should remain mute than express any sentiment on the important matters which are related therein.

I have, for sometime past, viewed the political concerns of the United States with an anxious and painful eye. They appear to me, to be moving by hasty strides to some awful crisis; but in what they will result, that Being, who sees, foresees, and directs all things, alone can tell. The Vessel is afloat, or very nearly so, and considering myself as a Passenger only, I shall trust to the Mariners whose duty it is to watch, to steer it into a safe Port.

On December 6 the Virginia legislature, where James Madison was a delegate, elected James Monroe as governor. Not long afterwards they steered through an act to give all Virginia's electoral votes to the man having the majority of votes in the state. He would clearly be Thomas Jefferson, facing a divided party under a nominal leader, John Adams.

THE FINAL AUTUMN

In late August 1799 Mrs. Washington fell seriously ill with malaria. She was in bed for several weeks. During this period Washington heard of the death of Charles, his brother. He wrote to Burgess Ball on September 22: "I was the *first*, and am now the *last*, of my father's Children by the second marriage who remain. When I shall be called upon to follow them, is known only to the giver of life. When the summons comes I shall endeavour to obey it with a good grace."

After Martha's recovery life was generally cheerful at Mount Vernon. On November 12 the general wrote to the managers of the Alexandria dances: "Mrs. Washington and myself have been honoured with your polite invitation to the Assemblies in Alexandria this winter; and thank you for this mark of attention. But alas! our dancing days are no more; we wish, however, all those who relish so agreeable and innocent an amusement, all the pleasure the season will afford them." Five days later he rode the nine miles to Christ Church, Alexandria, for his last church service.

Thereafter there was frequent company at Mount Vernon, largely family or old friends. These included Doctors Craik and Stuart and Colonel Carrington with their wives. On November 27 Dr. Craik was summoned from Alexandria; that morning Nelly Lewis gave birth to a daughter, Frances, who was the general's great-niece and his wife's great-granddaughter. Thirteen days earlier Martha Peter had given birth in the city of Washington to Mrs. Washington's great-grandson, John Parke Custis Peter.

On December 7 Washington rode to Mount Eagle to dine with Lord Fairfax, his friend of more than fifty years. On December 9 Howell Lewis and his wife set out for home, and Lawrence Lewis and Washington Custis for New Kent, none of the four thinking they would never again see George Washington. Lawrence Lewis later recalled the last sight of his uncle: "It was a bright, frosty morning. He had taken his usual ride, and the clear healthy flush on his cheeks and his sprightly manner brought the remark from both of us that we had never seen the General look so well. I have sometimes thought him decidedly the handsomest man I ever saw; and when in a lively mood, so full of pleasantry, so agreeable to all with whom he associated, that I could hardly realize he was the same Washington whose dignity awed all who approached him."

On December 13 three Fairfaxes, two Washington relatives, and John Herbert dined at Mount Vernon. That night the general noticed "a large circle around the Moon." Next morning "about 10 o'clock it began to snow, soon after to Hail and then to a settled cold Rain." In spite of the bad weather, Washington went out on horseback for his usual farm inspection. A little after three he returned to the mansion house, his neck wet and snow on his hair. Since dinner was waiting he went to the table without stopping to change. The following morning there was a heavy snow and Washington stayed indoors. He complained of a sore throat but nonetheless walked out on the grounds in the afternoon. That evening Lear noticed that he was hoarse but "he made light of it, as he would never take anything to carry off a cold, always observing 'let it go as it came.'"

In the evening General and Mrs. Washington sat with Lear, reading the newspapers which had come from the post office. About nine Mrs. Washington went upstairs to see how her granddaughter was doing. The general, Lear noted, "was very cheerful; and when he met with anything which he thought diverting or interesting, he would read it aloud as well as his hoarseness would permit. He desired me to read to him the debates of the Virginia Assembly on the election of a Senator and Governor; which I did and, on hearing Mr. Madison's observations respecting Mr. Monroe, he appeared much affected and spoke with some degree of asperity on the subject... On his retiring to bed, he appeared in perfect health, excepting the cold before mentioned, which he considered as trifling, and he had been remarkably cheerful all the evening."

Sometime before four in the morning of December 14 Washington awakened his wife to tell her he had a chill and fever and was very sick. Mrs. Washington noticed that he could scarcely speak and that he breathed with the greatest difficulty. Much alarmed, she wanted to get up and awaken the household but he told her not to leave her bed or she might catch cold. As soon as a servant appeared to light a fire in the early morning, Mrs. Washington sent for Lear, asking him to order George Rawlins, the farm overseer, to come to the house. Lear after looking at the general, ordered a servant to ride with all possible speed to Alexandria, to bring Dr. Craik to Mount Vernon.

Lear and Martha Washington, while waiting, prepared a drink to soothe his throat "but he could not swallow a drop. Whenever he attempted it he appeared to be distressed, convulsed and almost suffocated." When the overseer appeared, the general ordered himself bled according to the medical custom of the times. Mrs. Washington was worried about this, not thinking it proper and tried to stop it. She asked him to take only a little blood. At her entreaty, Rawlins desisted after drawing a half pint. Mrs. Washington then asked Lear to send for Dr. Gustavus Brown of Port Tobacco, Maryland, whom Dr. Craik had recommended if he were not available.

Dr. Craik appeared at Mount Vernon in midmorning. Dr. Brown arrived at 3:30 in the afternoon and Dr. Elisha Cullen Dick, summoned from Alexandria by Dr. Craik, joined them shortly afterwards. There has been, since that time, an endless but unnecessary controversy over Washington's medical treatment.[*] Before his colleagues arrived, Dr. Craik, his intimate friend since the French and Indian War, "employed two copious bleedings; a blister was applied to the part affected, two moderate doses of calomel were given, an injection was administered which operated on the lower intestines, but all without perceptible advantage." There was further bloodletting in the afternoon as well as administration of a strong emetic. These treatments, while very uncomfortable for the patient, may have hastened but did not affect the final outcome of the illness.

Dr. Dick, the last to arrive, at once favorably impressed his older colleagues with his diagnostic knowledge. As Brown subsequently wrote Craik: "You remember how, by his clear reasoning and evident knowledge of certain symptoms, he assured us it was not really quinsy, which we supposed it to be, but a violent inflammation of the membranes of the throat, which it had almost closed, and which, if not immediately arrested, would result in death."

Dr. Brown noted also that Dr. Dick proposed to halt further bleeding, as a means to conserve Washington's remaining strength. Dr. Dick himself on January 10, 1800, reported to Thomas Semmes, his further counsel: "I proposed to perforate the trachea as a means of prolonging life, and of affording time for the removal of the obstruction to respiration in the larynx, which threatened speedy dissolution." He would take all responsibility for failure. Dr. Craik appears to have at first agreed but was finally persuaded by Dr. Brown to oppose the measure.

Although he could scarcely speak, Washington's mind remained clear to the end and his politeness as natural as ever. He noticed that Christopher, his servant, had been standing all day and he motioned to him to sit. He asked Mrs. Washington to bring his two wills to the bed. After looking at them, he ordered one put in the fire, giving her the other. He informed Lear that he was dying and asked him to arrange all his military papers and accounts. He asked if Lear had any final question. He said he could think of nothing except to hope that it was not fatal. Washington smiled and said that it was the debt

---

[*] Dr. Heinz H. E. Scheidenmandel of Annandale, Virginia, made the first persuasive diagnosis in his "Did George Washington Die of Quinsy?" (Arch. Otolaryngol; 102: 519–521, September 1976). Dr. Scheidenmandel wrote: "The clinical findings in George Washington's case are identical to those produced by acute epiglotitis... a fearsome entity that does not respond well to medical treatment and that can lead to death within a few hours. It requires emergency tracheotomy or intubation in almost every case. If Dr. Dick would have prevailed, a rapidly performed tracheotomy or possibly cricothyreostomy would have led to immediate total airway obtrusion in his by then advanced case, and an airway would have to have been established within three to five minutes to avoid cardiac arrest." The epiglottis is the leaf-shaped plate of cartilage at the root of the tongue which covers the trachea when swallowing.

that all must pay. When the physicians once more appeared to look at their patient, he essayed his last little joke. After making several attempts to speak, he prayed them not to give themselves any further trouble.

Washington's final moments were subsequently recorded by Lear:

About ten o'clock he made several attempts to speak to me before he could effect it. At length he said, "I am just going. Have me decently buried, and do not let my body be put into the vault in less than three days after I am dead." I bowed assent for I could not speak. He then looked at me again and said "Do you understand me?" I replied, "Yes Sir." "It is well," said he. About ten minutes before he expired his breathing became much easier. He lay quietly. He withdrew his hand from mine and felt his own pulse. I spoke to Dr. Craik who sat by the fire. He came to the bedside. The General's hand fell from his wrist. I took it in mine and laid it upon my breast. Dr. Craik put his hand on his eyes and he expired without a struggle or Sigh. While we were fixed in silent grief, Mrs. Washington, who was sitting at the foot of the bed asked, with a firm and collected voice, "Is he gone?" I could not speak but held up my hand as a signal that he was. "It is well" said she in a plain voice. "All is now over. I have no more trials to pass through. I shall soon follow him."

MARTHA WASHINGTON

It had been less than twenty-seven hours since Martha Washington had seen her husband, cheerful and happy, as she sat with him in the quiet Mount Vernon parlor. "Taught," as she subsequently wrote the president of the United States, "by the great example, which I have so long had before me," she bore his sudden death with Christian fortitude. It was she the following morning who asked Lear to order the coffin from Alexandria. She also requested that a door be placed on the family vault rather than having it sealed, repeating that she would soon follow him. Mrs. Washington gave instructions as to all the family and old friends who were to be invited to the funeral. She read the will and asked Lear to notify all executors. Soon letters poured out from Mount Vernon to the president of the United States, Generals Hamilton and Pinckney, members of the Washington family, the Laws, Peters, Howell Lewises and Lawrence Lewis, and Washington Custis.

On the afternoon of December 18, burial took place in the old family vault at Mount Vernon. Eleven pieces of artillery and a schooner had been sent from Alexandria to fire minute guns. Five clergymen, three Episcopal and two Presbyterian, were present, led by the Reverend Thomas Davis and including the Reverend Lord Fairfax. There were troops, cavalry, and foot, and a large delegation of Masons. After Davis read the Episcopal burial service and delivered a short eulogy, the Masons conducted their ceremony and the body of George Washington was placed in the vault. The mourners then retired to the Mount Vernon mansion house for the refreshments which Mrs. Washington had ordered.

Martha Washington's composure held until letters reached her from her old friends, John and Abigail Adams. The president's wife later learned through Lear that, although their letters were not long, it had taken Mrs. Washington two hours to read them through her tears. It was to Abigail Adams that Martha finally poured out her anguish. Martha Washington was given the grace, however, to be able to console those who mourned with her. The governor of Connecticut, Jonathan Trumbull, when writing, enclosed extracts of the moving letter he had received from her husband when his own father, the revolutionary governor of Connecticut, had died. Martha Washington replied on January 15, 1800, in phrases strongly reminiscent of her husband.

> *When the mind is deeply afflicted by those irreparable losses which are incident to humanity, the good Christian will submit without repining to the dispensations of Divine Providence, and look for consolation to that Being who alone can pour balm into the bleeding heart, and who has promised to be the widow's God. But in the severest trials, we find some alleviation to our grief in the sympathy of sincere friends; and I should not do justice to my sensibility, was I not to acknowledge that your kind letter of condolence of the 30th of December was grateful to my feeling. I well knew the affectionate regard which my dear deceased husband always entertained for you, and therefore conceive of what you have given of what was written to you on a former melancholy occasion, is truly applicable to this. The loss is ours; the gain is his.*

> *For myself, I have only to go with humble submission to the will of that God who giveth and who taketh away, looking forward with faith and hope to the moment when I shall be again united with the partner of my life. But, while I continue on earth, my prayers will be offered up for the welfare and happiness of my friends, among whom you will always be numbered, being, Dear Sir, Your sincere and afflicted friend...*

On November 11 of that year Mrs. Washington wrote to Mrs. Tobias Lear, Sr., to say that she had often been ill and never expected to be well, as long as she was in this world. On May 24, 1802, Martha Washington, who had also served her country with grace and distinction, was laid to rest beside the general in the Mount Vernon vault.

EPILOGUE

LATE IN THE summer of 1798, the American minister to The Hague, William Vans Murray, wrote to the secretary of war in Philadelphia: "The energy and great respectability of the United States have produced a State of Things in the Directory at Paris, from which we may see the rights of neutral Nations, in general, respected. It would dilate every artery in you to see the glory which is spreading over the U. S. at this moment in the eyes of Europe… She plants her foot with firmness—France recoils… Be firm and persevering… France will recoil, we shall triumph."

President Adams had indicated he thought that General Washington's name was worth many army divisions and perhaps it was to France. It was to be the navy, founded by Washington and Knox, on which Adams primarily relied. American frigates and armed privateers drove the French from the coastal areas of the United States, while navy squadrons also patrolled the Caribbean. More than eighty French armed ships were captured in less than two years. By September 1800 France had recoiled and concluded a convention with the United States, which restored the peaceful *status quo ante*. The question of reparations for ship seizures by France was still unsettled when Adams left office.

With the United States at peace with all the world, her 1801 exports reached a level four times as high as those of 1789. The country that year attained a per capita income greater than it was to enjoy for about seventy years. The twelve federalist years had shown an average increase in America's gross national product of nearly 20 percent per annum.

In 1801 Jefferson, who loathed the revolution's military heroes, moved into the presidency, thanks to the extra electoral and lower House votes given the South for its slaves. In turn the electoral machinery in the southern states was closely controlled within the state by the slave-owning coastal sections, which held a disproportionate share of the seats in the state legislatures.

Jefferson proceeded, as rapidly as feasible, to demolish the financial and military strength, of the national government. He also began an unsuccessful assault on the federal judiciary. The army and foreign service were greatly reduced in size and the navy practically junked. With the savings Jefferson used the federal budget as a sharply depressing deflationary device. Excess receipts were devoted to reducing the national debt rather than to developing the country's resources. In 1803 when Napoleon handed Jefferson what Henry Adams correctly termed his "trebly invalid" title to Louisiana, its "bargain" price was largely at the expense of American shipowners who received only trifling sums for their heavy losses. The new lands were added by Jefferson to the nation as slave territory.

After a temporary peace, the European powers resumed their war in 1803. This time, with American defense forces cut to the bone, the belligerents could afford to ignore the American president. He did make an attempt to revive a "navy" with the building of small boats, armed with one or two guns. He added to this feeble threat an embargo on American exports. Established at the end of 1807, it had limited effect on the belligerents but it nearly ruined the American economy. The embargo was dropped as Jefferson was leaving office. At the end of eight years America's per capita income was down by a third.

Things grew worse under Madison. Unlike Jefferson, he occasionally announced that there ought to be a constitutional amendment to permit the government to assist the country's economic development. This was rhetoric to cover his failure to use the powers already existing. In taking office in 1809, Madison moved once more to reduce defense expenditures which, by 1811, he had cut a further 22 percent. By then he had also destroyed the national bank and had begun a series of attacks against the Indians, which eventually brought the country into conflict with most of the tribes from Wisconsin to Florida. The Indians complained that their "great father, Washington" had promised them perpetual peace and the solemn observance of their treaties. Nonetheless there were more than twenty major battles with them from 1811 to the end of Madison's presidency.

In 1814, after hearing of the burning of Washington by the British, Philadelphia diarist Thomas Cope recalled that "with an empty treasury—six frigates and no army—we declared war against a nation... possessing the greatest naval force ever known... having more than one thousand ships of war..." Jefferson had written Kosciusko, ten days after the declaration of war: "Our present enemy will have the sea to herself, while we shall be equally predominant on the land... We have nothing to fear from their armies." Two months later, the British were in possession of Mackinac, Detroit, and Chicago, all American troops in the area having been killed or captured. Jefferson recommended to Madison that he shoot General Hull, who had been given orders from Washington to seize upper Canada with 1,500 militia. Further American attempts to attack that country were thrown back repeatedly and, it must be added, comically.

In August 1814 the war reached its climax of ineptness when the Royal Navy chased Jefferson's gunboats up the Potomac and Patuxent rivers. The president had provided no effective defense, and he and Monroe scampered ignominiously, much as Jefferson had done in 1781, to hide from the small British army which captured Washington and burned the principal public buildings. By the time Madison and Monroe returned to the capital, they found that other forces had captured Alexandria. At this point the British retired from the Washington area, having punished Madison for the burning of the capital of upper Canada.

By 1814 America's export and shipping earnings were down to 15 percent of what they had been when Adams left office in 1801. Per capita income had dropped sharply. The one continual series giving an indication of general prosperity, the consumption of coffee and sugar, declined by two-thirds in fourteen years. In the four war and postwar years, 1812–1815, the deficit in the federal budget of $68 million was slightly larger than the entire federal government expenditures in the twelve Federalist years. Thus the party of limited or no national government had engaged in reckless war and a feckless waste of lives and resources. This was a sharp reversal of the Washington-Adams era of frugal government and rapid economic growth in the private sector. Never again would the federal government operate so efficiently.

By the time Monroe, the least competent of the Virginia dynasts, had finished his first term in 1821, slavery had metastasized up both banks of the Mississippi, as far as Missouri. The great dreams of George Washington of permanent national union, continuous economic growth, and the abolition of slavery were now safely buried.

INDEX

Abercromby, Major General James, I:93, 100, 130

Act of Oppression. *See* Stamp Act

Adams, Abigail, I:213, 219, 224; II:3; and celebration of G. Washington's birthday, II:370; friendship with M. Washington, II:134; on husband's problems on assuming presidency, II:364; illness of, II:392; letter to M. Washington on G. Washington's death, II:427; and President Washington's farewell address, II:338; reaction to President Washington's illness, II:168; and the XYZ affair, II:376

Adams, Charles Francis, Jr., I:263

Adams, Henry, II:430

Adams, John: absence from capital as president, II:420; on adoption of the Constitution of the United States, II:108; appointment of Washington as commander in chief (1798), II:383-384; attack on John Dickinson, I:228-229; on British troop movements across the United States to Spanish territory (1790), II:177; chairman of the Board of War and Ordnance, I:263; complaints of congressional deterioration, I:318; continuation of Washington's policy of building the nation's strength, II:387-393, 395-396, 404; and the Conway cabal, I:358-360; criticism of Brigadier Sullivan, I:276; description of Charles Lee, I:224; "Discourses on Davila," II:209; discussions of war debts with Campbell, II:92; dispatching of U.S. commissioners to France, II:421-422; effort to dismiss Schuyler from command, I:329; and election of 1796, II:339; at First Continental Congress meeting, I:196, 208; inauguration of, II:348-349; introduction of resolution to discipline troops, I:284; and the Jay Treaty, II:300; Jefferson's criticisms of, II:209-210; letter to M. Washington, on husband's death, II:427; as minister to France, I:508-509; Morris house as presidential residence of, II:350; on Morris' mission, II:176; nomination as minister to the Netherlands, II:268; nomination of minister plenipotentiary to France, II:417-418; and Paris peace talks, II:23, 24, 25, 27-29; as possible presidential candidate (1792), II:228; as president of the Senate, II:131, 209; as president of the United States, II:339, 348-350, 361-364, 374,

444 / INDEX

Constitutional Convention, II:99; crop yields, I:149; on departing Mount Vernon for New York and presidency, II:122; draft treaty at Yorktown, I:545; expense accounts, I:89-90; farming difficulties at Mount Vernon, II:119; first meeting of Continental Congress, I:196; illness in Barbados, I:29; on Independence Day (1790), II:172; instructions to intelligence agents, I:517; land agreements, I:148; mission to French fortifications, I:34-35, 36; siege of Yorktown, I:542; travel records, I:147; II:141-151, 180-181, 202-208, 280-281; visitors to Mount Vernon, I:187-188; on welcome to New York as president-elect, II:125-126; western trip, I:22-24, 174-176; II:73, 78
Dick, Charles, I:82
Dick, Dr. Elisha Cullen, II:424-426
Dickinson, John, I:228-229; II:50
Dickinson, Major General Philemon: in Battle of Monmouth, I:402, 405; in New Jersey, I:397
Dieskau, Baron de, I:76
Digby, Rear Admiral Robert, I:526-527, 539; II:9, 18
Digges, Thomas, II:152
Dilworth, Pennsylvania, I:334
Dinwiddie, Lieutenant Governor Robert, I:12; actions after France constructs forts, I:33-34, 37-38, 40; appointment of Innes as commander in chief of four colonies, I:48; appointment of Washington as commander in chief of Virginia Regiment, I:46, 79; attack on behavior of Washington's officers, I:95-96, 97; attempt to get Indian support, I:43, 45; attempts to assist Washington at Winchester, I:98-100; battle reports from Washington, I:46-47, 48; breach between Dinwiddie and Washington, I:54-56, 120-121; first meeting with Washington, I:31; governor's conference, I:61; illness, I:100, 109, 120; land bounty promised to Fry's heirs by, II:185-186; opposition to closing of Fort Cumberland, I:108-109, 110, 111; orders that reduced morale of Virginia Regiment, I:118-119; partner in Ohio Company, I:18; reaction to Braddock's defeat, I:75; refusal to surrender French prisoners, I:53
"Discourses on Davila," II:209
Dismal Swamp Company, I:153-154

District of Columbia. *See also specific locations, e.g.,* Washington, D.C.: creation of, II:198-201, 209
Dobbs Ferry, New York, I:291, 474-475, 476, 483, 521
Dogue Run farm, II:241, 368, 412, 413
Domestic debt. *See* Economic issues
Dorchester, Baron. *See* Dorchester, Lord
Dorchester, Lord: admiration for Washington, II:325; and American treaty with Great Britain, II:292-293; and British designs on Spanish territory in the United States, II:178; and British intelligence, II:153, 170-171, 172-175, 210; and British postwar policy, II:91-93, 113; reaction to Washington's proposals to increase the U.S. army, II:169; resignation of, II:266, 326; speech to Indians, II:212, 262
Dorchester Heights, Massachusetts, I:248-249
Dorsey, Stephen, II:409
Doughty (American officer), II:178
Drake, H.M.S. (ship), I:418
Duane, James, I:470; II:12; and the Jay Treaty, II:301
Duane, William, II:371
Duc de Bourgogne (ship), I:512
Duché, Jacob, I:348-349; II:56
Duer, William, II:163, 229, 349
Dumas, Guillaume Mathieu, Comte, I:512, 524
Dunbar, Colonel Thomas, I:59, 66, 70-71, 75, 76
Dundas, Lieutenant Colonel Thomas, I:509, 545
Dunkirk: France request for return of, II:26
Dunlap, William, II:156
Dunmore, Earl of. *See* Murray, John, Earl of Dunmore
Dunmore, Lady. *See* Murray, Elizabeth, Lady Dunmore
Dunn, (Washington's coachman), II:187
Dunning, John, I:441
Duponceau, Pierre, I:385
Duquesne, Fort. *See* Fort Duquesne, Pennsylvania
Dutch Reformed Church, II:208

East Chester, New York, II:141
East India Company, I:173, 189, 190
East Indies, II:294
East River, I:257, 272
Economic issues. *See also* Continental army;

All Cloudless Glory

All Cloudless Glory

THE LIFE OF
GEORGE WASHINGTON

FROM YOUTH TO YORKTOWN

Harrison Clark

REGNERY PUBLISHING, INC.
Washington, D.C.

Clark, E. Harrison
    All cloudless glory : the life of George Washington / E. Harrison Clark
       p.   cm.
    Includes bibliographical references (p.   ) and index.
    Contents: v. 1. From youth to Yorktown
    ISBN 0-89526-466-8 (v. 1)
    1. Washington, George, 1732–1799. 2. Presidents—United States—Biography.
 3. Generals—United States—Biography. 4. United States. Continental Army—Biography.
I. Title.
E312.C56   1995
973.4'1'092—dc2   95-37393
[B]   CIP

Published in the United States by Regnery Publishing, Inc.
An Eagle Publishing Company
422 First Street, SE, Suite 300
Washington, DC 20003

Distributed to the trade by National Book Network
4720-A Boston Way
Lanham, MD 20706

Printed on acid-free paper.
Manufactured in the United States of America

10 9 8 7 6 5 4 3 2 1

Books are available in quantity for promotional or premium use. Write to Director of Special Sales, Regnery Publishing, Inc., 422 First Street, SE, Suite 300, Washington, DC 20003, for information on discounts and terms or call (202) 546-5005.

Designed by Dori Miller
Maps by Chris Capell Computer Graphics

Endpapers: Paintings of Mount Vernon attributed to Edward Savage, 1792. Front: the west front with the circular driveway in the foreground. Back: the east front overlooking the Potomac. (Courtesy of the Mount Vernon Ladies' Association of the Union)

George Washington had thanks and naught beside,
Except the all-cloudless glory (which few men's is)
To free his country.

Byron *Don Juan*, Canto the Ninth.

For
Agnes Mason Clark

CONTENTS

LIST OF MAPS

ACKNOWLEDGEMENTS

THE AUTHOR IS indebted to many for advice and help, not least to those who critically reviewed the manuscript at Mount Vernon and elsewhere. His thanks go to Dr. William B. Allen, the late John A. Castellani, Professor North Callahan, Mrs. Ellen McCallister Clark, Mr. Frank Hammond, the late Edgar M. Hinchcliffe, Professor Codman Hislop, the late Colonel Francis Pickens Miller, Mrs. Helen Hill Miller, Mr. Robert Nash, Mr. John P. Riley, Dr. Heinz H. E. Scheidemandel, Mrs. Clara J. Schleh, Mrs. Robert Channing Seamans, Jr., Mr. Paul G. Sifton, the late Charles C. Wall, and the late Mathilde Williams. His particular thanks go to Mr. John Augustine Washington, the late Frank E. Morse, Mr. Franz M. Oppenheimer, and Miss Barbara McMillan.

The following institutions kindly provided copies of their original documents: the Boston Public Library, the Houghton Library of Harvard University, the Historical Society of Minnesota, the Historical Society of Pennsylvania, the Manuscript Division of the Library of Congress, the Mount Vernon Ladies Association of the Union, the Virginia State Library, the Alderman Library of the University of Virginia, and the George Washington Birthplace National Monument.

All Cloudless Glory

PART ONE

FAMILY AND BOYHOOD
1657–1748

ONE

THE ANGLO-AMERICAN WASHINGTONS

1657–1732

T HE ENGLISH WASHINGTONS, an ancient gentry family and dutiful
subjects of their Tudor and Stuart monarchs, gained rewards suitable
to their stations. In 1539 Lawrence Washington, a former mayor of
Northampton, purchased from the Crown for a modest sum a priory at
Sulgrave, where he built a house. Two generations later, another Lawrence
Washington of Sulgrave produced seven sons to serve their sovereigns. One
died in Spain while page to the Prince of Wales. Two were knighted, one
becoming the father of Colonel Sir Henry Washington, hero of the armies of
Charles I. Sir William, Henry's father, married an aunt of the duchess of
Richmond. From this it appears that it was another kinsman, George
Washington, who was recorded under Charles I as "waiting on the Duke of
Richmond to be sworn of the Privy Chamber to the King."

The Reverend Lawrence Washington, the only cleric among these seven
sons, was to suffer in mind, body, and estate for his loyalty to church and
Crown. An Oxford graduate, he became in 1633 the "modest, sober" rector
of All Saints Church in Purleigh, Essex. When civil war broke out in 1642,
he supported the sovereign and denounced the "Traytors" of the parliamentary army. Shortly after the second Lord Fairfax broke the cavaliers'
siege of Hull, Parliament ejected the "Malignant Royalist," as it called
Lawrence, from his parish. Parliament added the common Puritan charge

that he was guilty of a "beastly vice, dayly tippling" in alehouses, in which he encouraged others to participate.

Lawrence found haven with friendly royalists in nearby Maldon. Sometime thereafter Thomas Roberts, lord of Little Braxted Manor, five miles away, permitted him to preach in his small parish church. So impoverished was the family that Lawrence's wife and children were forced to move in with her stepfather at Tring. Lawrence died in 1653, four years after the king's execution; he was buried in All Saints Church in Maldon. His widow survived him only until 1655. Her oldest son, John, after obtaining authority in 1656 to administer her estate, set out to make an adventurous living.

The following year John Washington signed as second officer aboard the *Sea Horse of London,* a ketch carrying cargo to Danzig, Lübeck, and Copenhagen. Part of the cargo was tobacco; from his subsequent deposition filed in Virginia, it is known that he traveled overland to sell the weed in Elsinore. The ship thereafter sailed directly for Virginia to pick up more tobacco. It arrived there late in 1656 or early in 1657. On February 28, 1657, the ship ran aground on an inland shoal of the Potomac River, later sinking in a violent storm with the loss of all cargo. John helped to raise and repair the ship but this ended his career in the merchant navy. He stayed in Virginia and founded a family.

After a dispute over his share of the wages and profits, John filed an attachment against the ship's master, Edward Prescott. In May the case was heard before the justices of the peace of Westmoreland County. Its final disposition is not known but one of the justices was Nathaniel Pope, a Virginia burgess, who had previously served in the Maryland Assembly, and had a daughter named Anne. Sometime the following year John married her. Pope gave his son-in-law seven hundred acres at Bridges Creek, on the Potomac River, and lent him enough money to start farming. Bridges Creek was to be, for several generations, the seat of the Washingtons in Virginia. John's brother Lawrence, after making several trips between England and Virginia between 1659 and 1665, also settled permanently in the area.

John, twenty-five when he married, set out vigorously to improve his position. He became a vestryman, burgess, justice of the peace, and, as a militia colonel, helped to suppress Bacon's Rebellion. Washington Parish, with its upper and lower churches, was named for him, a rare instance of an individual being so honored. In his twenty years in the colony, he added more than 8,000 acres to the land deeded by his father-in-law, including among his purchases what he and his immediate descendants described in their wills as 2,500 acres at Hunting Creek, much farther up the Potomac, in near wilderness. Three generations later, its meticulous heir, George

Washington, surveyed his Mount Vernon farm and found that it contained 2,126 acres.

John's will assigned his property to his wife, his daughter Martha, and two sons, Lawrence and John. Lawrence, the elder, inherited the original Pope land at Bridges Creek as well as the Hunting Creek tract.

Lawrence Washington, in the course of his rather short life, added only modestly to his inherited acreage. Like his father, he served in the House of Burgesses, and like his father made a good marriage, to Mildred, daughter of Augustine Warner, once speaker of the House of Burgesses. He died in 1698 at about thirty-seven.

Although the documentation is uncertain, around 1690 Lawrence may have erected a small house at Hunting Creek, which may have been enlarged over the next century into the Mount Vernon mansion house. Lawrence's 1698 will mentioned that two women were then living at the farm, though it is not known whether they were in this house or elsewhere on the property.

Within a year or so of her husband's death, Lawrence's widow—and George Washington's grandmother—Mildred Washington married George Gale of an English tobacco-importing family, with whom she soon moved to Whitehaven, England, along with her children by Lawrence: John, Augustine (Gus), and Mildred. In 1701 George Gale enrolled the two boys, John, age ten, and Augustine, seven, at the Appleby Grammar School in Westmorland, but in 1704, in response to a Virginia court order, he returned the three Washington children to the colony. In accordance with their father's will, his cousin John assumed the guardianship of the two boys and their sister.

AUGUSTINE WASHINGTON

The younger boy, Gus, whose English education was brief, grew into a tall young man, of whose characteristics only tradition remains. His fourth son, George, had a vague memory of him as a blond and husky man who was very fond of his children. He was a county judge at twenty-two, the age at which George was to be Virginia's commander in chief. Subsequently he became a vestryman, church warden, militia captain, and sheriff. He farmed, bought and traded land, and promoted iron ore mining and smelting through the Principio Company. Among his land purchases was the Hunting Creek property, which he acquired from his sister in 1726.

In 1715, probably the year he came of age, Gus married his first wife, Jane Butler, by whom he had four children: Butler and Jane, who died in infancy and youth, and Lawrence and Augustine (Austin). Perhaps feeling that his own English schooling at Appleby had too quickly ended, Gus gave Lawrence and Austin the advantages of a full English public school education.[*]

Richard Appleby stressed the classics. Although the school was small, headmaster Richard Yates took pride in its library, which he continued to expand during his fifty-eighty-year tenure. It was well-equipped in such diverse fields as history, mathematics, geography, and theology. Among the books were Addison's *Cato* and two copies of a Latin translation of Baldassare Castiglone's *Il Libro del Cortegiano*, first published in Venice in 1528, containing rules for courtly manners. The students read *The Spectator* of Addison and Steele and also used it as a basis for translations into Latin. By the time the brothers returned to Virginia, they were well-equipped to supervise the education of their stepbrother, Mary Ball Washington's oldest son.

MARY BALL WASHINGTON

When Augustine Washington returned to Virginia in 1730 from a trip to England, he learned that his first wife, Jane, had died the previous November. On March 6, 1730, the widower, about thirty-seven, married Mary Ball, who was around twenty-one.

Joseph Ball, George's maternal grandfather, was a relatively prosperous farmer who served as burgess, vestryman, and justice of the peace. A widower

---

[*] Thanks to an intensive search of its archives by Edgar Hinchcliffe, late master and librarian of the school, it is possible to give an approximation of the curriculum of the era as well as the dates the brothers were enrolled in and taught at the school.

Richard Yates, Appleby's headmaster for fifty-eight years (1723-1781) was, according to Hinchcliffe, "a remarkable man, a scholar of no mean ability, who made the School the most notable Grammar School in the North at the time." Surviving correspondence indicates that Gus Washington and his two sons were on the friendliest of terms with Yates for many years. It appears to have been in 1729 that Gus took Lawrence with him on a trip to England, in connection with his colonial iron works, and enrolled him at Appleby School where, for the next three years, he was on the honor rolls. Lawrence is also recorded as having donated a half-guinea to Yates' library fund on December 4, 1732. The manuscript is too defaced to determine whether, at this time, he returned for a visit to Virginia.

In 1732, the year of George Washington's birth and probably after the event, Austin joined Lawrence at Appleby, where he was recorded as being on the honor rolls in the ensuing years. No further documentation was found for Lawrence, although it appears probable that Gus saw his two sons at Appleby in 1737. Since the brothers were there well beyond the usual school-leaving age, Hinchcliffe concluded that, as honor students, they had become "ushers" (assistant masters) for what was a customary three-year term. His statement was supported by two facts: (1) Austin, about twenty-one or twenty-two, gave the library fund a half-guinea, December 3, 1741, "on his leaving the school," and (2) Yates wrote to Lawrence at Mount Vernon in the humorous terms used to a colleague rather than as a headmaster to a former pupil.

approaching sixty, he married a widow, Mary Johnson, sometime before 1709, fathered Mary Ball, and died while his daughter was still in infancy. Her mother survived only until she was entering her teens. The orphaned child became the ward of George Eskridge, the lawyer who had unsuccessfully defended George Gale in the action brought to return his Washington stepchildren to their Virginia relations. One of the boys sent back from Westmorland, England, to Westmoreland, Virginia, became her husband. When Mary Ball came of age, she had substantial inheritances in land, live-stock, and slaves from her father, mother, and brother. No portraits of Mary Ball are extant and perhaps none was ever made, but there is little reason to doubt the statement given to Mason Weems by John Fitzhugh, a longtime friend of Mary's, that she had been a famous beauty in her youth.

During the Victorian period, Mary Ball Washington tended to be canonized by American and even English writers. In reaction, perhaps, a few twentieth-century historians and writers have tried to paint her as something of a monster, unloved by George and her other children. Her slim surviving correspondence, however, indicates the warmth of her feeling for all her family. To her oldest son she wrote: "I am, my dear George, your loving and affectionate mother." He, in turn, publicly referred to her as "my revered Mother; by whose Maternal hand (early deprived of a Father) I was led from childhood." A cousin of his recalled how "very kind" she was yet sufficiently forceful to keep the young "mute as mice" when she was nearby. Her grandson, Lawrence Lewis, when in his sixties, gratefully remembered his walks with her to see the beauties of the Rappahannock, while she urged him to express his love to the God who had given them to the world. On behalf of her neighbors, the mayor of Fredericksburg, addressing her oldest son, called her "amiable," a word often applied to George Washington.

Mary Ball Washington had a difficult life, early orphaned and, at thirty-five, widowed with five children, the oldest age eleven. In 1781, sick and well past her threescore and ten, she traveled over the Blue Ridge Mountains, appar-ently on the news that her son, Samuel, was dying. She stayed on through a hard winter to help care for his seven children and stepchildren, all under age fourteen. In so doing, she missed seeing another son, George, on his way north from Yorktown. She wrote him how much this distressed her, for she might never again have the pleasure of seeing him.

The earlier tradition that she was a Spartan mother was based on fact. She lived a longer life than her parents, children, or grandchildren. Her forty-six-year widowhood almost equalled her husband's life span of forty-nine years. Her firstborn, George, the last of her children to die, clearly inherited his robust constitution from her, outliving his half brothers and four preceding Washington forebears by nearly two to three and one-half decades. Mary Ball Washington added a needed vigor to the previously short-lived Washington stock.

TWO

THE EARLY YEARS

1732–1748

I N 1798, MARTHA WASHINGTON, sitting by her tea service at Mount Vernon, recalled to a Polish visitor the primitive Virginia of her childhood. She remembered, nearly but not quite accurately, that there had been only one carriage in the entire colony, and that she and her friends always traveled by horseback. There was little trade except in and for tobacco. A package of tea was considered "a very great present."

The Virginia of 1732, the year George Washington was born, contained about 125,000 people, three-quarters of them white. The residents were confined, for the most part, to the tidewater regions. Specie was scarce, and tobacco was the principal medium of exchange. And yet Virginia had been self-governing for 113 years. Its legislature, the second-oldest parliament, functioned almost uninterruptedly during the years when its London mother was frequently suspended. Virginia also appears to have been the most fecund of the colonies. British travelers before the revolution commented on the numbers of children to be seen everywhere. From 1732 to 1775 Virginia's population quadrupled to nearly 500,000, though immigration was not large and slaves were imported at a rate averaging a thousand or so a year. Long before the idea of revolution entered the head of any American, Virginia was producing a surplus of vigorous young, accustomed to self-government, who began moving westward in increasing numbers. George Washington was born while the movement inland was gaining momentum. By the time he was twenty-three, Governor Dinwiddie was reporting to London that the colony wanted all the land to the west, including California.[*]

THE FAMILY

Gus Washington's ten children were not unusually numerous by Virginia standards. George, fifth of the ten to appear in approximately twenty-three years, was born near Pope's Creek, Washington Parish, Westmoreland County. Though a bill exists for a house built by Gus Washington some ten years before, there is no certainty that this was the house of George's birth. He himself wrote of his "numerous" relatives who had reproduced for several generations in the area.

A family Bible at Mount Vernon records the births of Mary Washington's six children and the deaths of a daughter and stepdaughter. Written by some unknown person, the information is of such a character as to appear that it came from Mary Washington. George was baptized on April 5. The unsubstantiated story that George was named for his mother's guardian, George Eskridge, has been frequently repeated, but the possibility lingers that George II was the inspiration. The Bible thereafter records the births of Betty in 1732, Samuel in 1735, John Augustine in 1736, Charles in 1738, and Mildred in 1739. In 1735 Jane, Gus' child by his first wife, died; in 1740 his last-born, Mildred, was buried.

Gus traveled to England, probably in 1736, to discuss his iron ore mining and smelting operations. He returned to Virginia and fathered Charles, who was born on May 1, 1738. In October he purchased from the widow of Anthony Strother a 260-acre farm on the Rappahannock. Mason Weems noted, in the early 1800s, that it was "a plantation... opposite to Fredericksburg. It lifts its low and modest front of faded red, over the turbid waters of Rappahannock." He added that it was an object of pilgrimage, many thinking it was George Washington's birthplace.

In 1739 Great Britain declared war on Spain and, subsequently, France. George II's later refusal to commission Americans was to annoy George Washington, but, at this period, the king encouraged colonials to serve the Crown by granting them regular British commissions. In calling for three

---

* In 1849, Benjamin Franklin Washington, great-grandson of Samuel, born in 1734 at Bridges Creek, settled in California. The tenth Lord Fairfax may have migrated there about the same time since he is recorded in *Burke's Peerage* as speaker of California's lower house in 1853.

thousand American reinforcements of British troops in the Caribbean, the king, in April 1740, forwarded to Sir William Gooch, acting governor of Virginia, and to the proposed commander, Major General Alexander Spotswood, company grade commissions for officers selected. Lawrence Washington, George's elder half-brother, was quick to abandon farming for military service, carrying to Gooch all the recommendations he could accumulate. He was the first officer chosen, thereby becoming senior captain in the Virginia contingent. When Spotswood died, Gooch assumed command of the American Regiment.

Lawrence received his commission August 6, 1740. William Byrd's diary indicates that the Virginia Assembly called on Gooch near the end of the month to say farewell, presumably not long before he sailed. The American Regiment joined the land forces of Major General Thomas Wentworth, operating with the British fleet under Vice Admiral Edward Vernon. The expedition, to capture Spanish-held Cartagena, was to be the first of the two major military disasters in which the Washington brothers participated on the British side, the other being Braddock's defeat.

Lawrence spent much of his time on Admiral Vernon's flagship. He was the hero of an early British attack on Panama's Puerto Bello, which he had dashingly captured in two days' fighting. When the fleet arrived off Cartagena on March 3, Wentworth, to Vernon's dismay, temporized for three weeks before he undertook a land assault. The Spanish were given ample time to prepare, and the result was a bloody rout for the British, who were forced to retire to Jamaica. In a letter home dated May 30, Lawrence Washington estimated that six hundred men had been killed in battle but tropical diseases had decimated the fleet and army in even greater number. A further attempt to capture Santiago, Cuba, was soon abandoned. The American Regiment was ordered broken up.

In October 1741, the headmaster of Appleby wrote to Gus to commiserate with him on his "late calamity suffered by fire," which no one has satisfactorily identified. At the same time, he congratulated Gus on Lawrence's escape at Cartagena, where so many had died. Yates added that Austin, who was finishing his teaching term, had set his heart on studying law, but he was a boy of such "goodness" that he would reconcile himself to another career if his father thought best. Joseph Deane, of Whitehaven, a friend of the Washington boys at Appleby, informed Lawrence in the Caribbean that his brother had become "a pretty [fine] young fellow." Austin returned to Virginia in 1742, while his family was still concerned about Captain Lawrence Washington.

Lawrence may have reached Virginia about the end of the year or perhaps in early 1743. Although he had not been in the shore fighting, his long volunteer service made him a hero to the colony, while his British commission was to give him half-pay for life. He subsequently became adjutant general of Virginia's militia with the rank of major.

AUGUSTINE WASHINGTON'S DEATH

Gus Washington had sent his two oldest sons to England for schooling when they reached the age of about eleven or twelve. In later life George Washington claimed that plans for sending him also to England changed with the sudden death of his father. According to the family's recollections to Weems, George was visiting cousins in Choptank, in the next county, when he was called back to his dying father's bedside.

On April 11, 1743, the day before he died, Gus drafted—hastily and rather loosely—an extensive will providing for the distribution of property to his wife and seven living children. This was complicated because he owned many square miles of land scattered through Maryland and four counties of Virginia.

As the oldest son, Lawrence received title to all Gus' ironworks, together with the land at Little Hunting Creek. Along with this went the house, live-stock, and watermill on the property. This indicates that what was to be Mount Vernon was a farm in full operation. Austin, next in seniority, inherited the lands between Bridges and Pope's Creeks, subject to the clause that Gus' widow be given "the Liberty of working my Land at Bridges Creek Quarter for the term of five years next after my Decease during which time she may fix a Quarter on Deep Run." John, the fifth living son, received most of Gus' remaining peninsular land between Bridges and Mattox Creeks, amounting to seven hundred acres.

George inherited the Strother farm on the Rappahannock, described by his father as "the Land I now live on." In addition he and his brother Samuel were given half of Gus' lands on Deep Run, which George later estimated to amount to five thousand acres, and George received three lots in Fredericksburg, two with houses. Other farms, totaling some twenty-four hundred acres, went to Samuel, Austin, Charles, and John.

Shortly after Gus' death, Lawrence renamed his newly inherited house "Mount Vernon," in respect of the marks of favor he had received from his former commanding admiral. The first documented use of the term is in Lawrence's July 19 letter to Richard Yates at Appleby. In it he announced that he was married that day to Anne Fairfax, daughter of William Fairfax, who owned Belvoir, the next large plantation down the Potomac River. His former headmaster replied to Lawrence in November with a Latin pun on Mount Vernon and his marriage.

Although the onset of Lawrence's tuberculosis, from which he suffered an early death, cannot be determined with precision, the probability is that he had the disease when he was married and that he had contracted it in the ship's close quarters in the Caribbean.

GEORGE WASHINGTON'S EDUCATION

Following Gus' death, Mary Washington and her five surviving children, ages three to eleven, returned to her husband's Bridges Creek plantations, where so many of the children's relatives lived. It had one of the few schools beyond the elementary, available to planters' sons. In addition Austin had returned to the area after his three years' teaching at Appleby Grammar School.

Mason Weems, who interviewed many members of the Washington family as well as George's old schoolmates, reported that Mary sent her oldest son to live with Austin, now married to Anne Aylett. This provided him with the nearest approach to the English public school education that his father had planned for him prior to his death. He also attended Henry Williams' school, located by the National Park Service as on or near the Mattox Creek lands inherited by John. It seems that he took practical courses under Williams, while being tutored in the finer arts by Austin.

Old schoolmates told Weems that Williams taught "reading, spelling, English grammar, arithmetic, surveying, book-keeping and geography." Their statements are confirmed by George's notebooks, which show that he studied arithmetic, geography, geometry, trigonometry, and surveying. He learned bookkeeping in the form he would use all his life for his personal and official accounts. Numerous exercises in penmanship resulted in his graceful handwriting, so easy to read two centuries later. As an exercise he copied out the Italian rules of civility, a Latin version of which had been in the Appleby library. Probably Austin lent an English translation to Williams. George's schoolmates remembered how the powerful youth beat them all in running, wrestling, pole vaulting, weight throwing, and broad jumping.

George made notes on his studies in history and literature, presumably in Austin's library and under his direction. These show he read English history, most of the *Spectator*, as well as Addison's *Cato*, a play which greatly influenced American eighteenth-century writing, including George's. His later letters and general library indicate that he was a fast reader who absorbed writers as diverse as Goldsmith, Voltaire, Sterne, Adam Smith, and

Arthur Young. In his middle teens he studied military history, strategy, and tactics with his brother Lawrence.

George thus had the advantage of two substitute fathers as friendly guides in his development to manhood. He probably spent the greater part of his adolescent years at the house of one or the other. He easily absorbed the social graces. His superb horsemanship and dancing skill, his charm and humor, made him welcome everywhere.

Further developments in George's education were undoubtedly connected to his brother's marriage to Anne Fairfax and to the claims of her father's cousin to the Northern Neck of Virginia. Charles II had granted the vaguely defined neck to seven men who had defended his father, Charles I, against Cromwell and the Fairfaxes. In the course of time, the proprietary claims passed to Lord Culpeper, whose daughter married Thomas, fifth Lord Fairfax. These, in turn, were inherited by his son, Thomas. The sixth lord vigorously pressed his claim to a territory far more extensive than the Virginia government considered justified by the original grant. Lord Fairfax's 1736-1737 survey was made in order to present his claim to the privy council in London. Virginia fought Fairfax thereafter for years, but he was well provided with friends at court.

After long study, the council handed down its decision in April 1745, confirming most of his claim. The sixth Lord Fairfax became the assured proprietor of eighty-one hundred square miles of Virginia and what is now West Virginia. The territory extended from below the point where George was born to the headwaters of the Potomac and Rappahannock Rivers in the Allegheny Mountains. Larger than Wales, the domain was subject only to his recognition of earlier grants made by Virginia. Lord Fairfax's agent in Virginia was his cousin, William Fairfax, father-in-law of Lawrence Washington.

How soon George or Lawrence heard of the council's decision is not known but the news reached the governor at Williamsburg in June 1745. Shortly thereafter, in August, George undertook an intensive course in surveying, a skill that would be much needed in the Fairfax grants. His course lasted at least until the following March. He wrote his notebooks in duplicate. The first were neat working papers. The second were models of esthetic and professional accuracy and are the first evidence of George's precocity and early maturity. Among his extant surveys is one of the ancestral lands at Bridges Creek.

Not long after he completed this course and before he did advanced surveying, there was a curious episode in which Lawrence suggested that George go to sea. England was still at war. Lawrence had admired the Royal Navy and he or his Fairfax connections obtained a midshipman's berth for George. William Fairfax was engaged by Lawrence to tell his brother about the plan.

Fairfax's September 9, 1746, letter to Lawrence produced George's first quoted statement that "he will be steady and thankfully follow your advice as his best friend." Lawrence also engaged Robert Jackson to intercede with Mary Washington but he reported nine days later: "I am afraid Mrs. Washington will not keep to her first resolution. She seems to intimate a dislike to George's going to sea and says several persons told her that it is a very bad Scheme. She offers several trifling objections such as fond and unthinking mothers suggest, and I find that one word against his going has more weight than ten for it. Colo. Fairfax seems desirous he should go and desired me to acquaint you with Mrs. Washington's sentiments." Colonel Fairfax's own midshipman son, Thomas, had been killed in action the preceding June, which was not a heartening inducement for a mother to send her son to war.

In December Mary Washington wrote her half-brother, Joseph Ball, then in England, about two problems: the coming end of her tenure at Bridges Creek and George's proposed maritime career. His May 19 reply scorned the idea of her oldest son going to sea. If George entered the merchant marines, he would be subject to impressment in the Royal Navy, which would "cut him and staple him and use him like a Negro, or rather, like a dog. And as for any considerable preferment in the Navy, it is not to be expected, there are always too many grasping for it here, who have interest and he has none." He added that any planter, if he were industrious, lived much better than a master of a Virginia ship. He included some sound advice, which George did not follow for a long time: "Neither must he send his Tobacco to England to be sold here, and goods sent him; if he does, he will soon get in the merchant's debt, and never get out again. He must not be hasty to be right; but must go on gently and with patience as things will naturally go. This method, without aiming at being a fine gentleman before his time, will carry a man more comfortably and surely through the world than going to sea, unless it be a great chance indeed. I Pray God help you and yours... Your Loving Brother J. B."

The year 1747, when George may have completed his formal schooling, was noteworthy for the arrival of the lord proprietor at Belvoir. At about this time young Washington's professional skill was checked by James Genn, one of Lord Fairfax's principal surveyors. George earned his first fees thereafter from private landowners in the neck. Cryptic notes among his papers indicate he may have traveled that year as far afield as Frederick Town (now Winchester).

Possibly this same year Mary Washington moved to her own land, where she built a house big enough to accommodate her five children, ranging in age from nine to fifteen. The only surviving document referring to this is the May 19, 1747, letter to her from Joseph Ball. This disclosed that, in addition to discussing the proposal to send George to sea, she had written about her future plans. He wrote: "I think you are in the Right to leave the house where you are, and to go upon your own Land; but as for Timber I have scarce enough for my own plantations; so can spare you none of that; but as for stone, you may take what you please to build you a House." The letter was addressed to her "nigh the falls, Rappahannock River," indicating that she was building a house north of Falmouth.

Her eldest son, mature beyond his years, was soon off to make his living. Later George was to give endless praise to the joys of farming, but its drudgery clearly repelled him in his youth when he set out for western adventures. From 1747 on, he passed part of each year with Lawrence and Anne Washington at Mount Vernon. To the list of clothing he made for a trip he added at the top, as an afterthought, "Razor," to emphasize his growing manhood. Being with his brother was ideal for an ambitious youth. His surveying services were soon employed by Lord Fairfax, William and George William Fairfax, and Lawrence Washington, the most important people of the Northern Neck and of great influence in the colony itself. William Fairfax was a member of the governor's council and later its president. His son George, Lawrence's brother-in-law, was burgess for Frederick County, where he had large land holdings. Lawrence, Virginia's adjutant general, represented Fairfax County in the Virginia Assembly and was also a justice of the peace. In addition, he and his friends, who included the lieutenant governor, Robert Dinwiddie, had organized a company to promote land purchases and settlement in the Ohio Valley, beyond the Fairfax grants.

That autumn and winter Lord Fairfax and James Genn planned new surveys in the western portion of his territory. It was undoubtedly Genn, highly experienced in wilderness survey work, who recommended the inclusion of young Washington in the team he was to head. Since George does not appear to have been paid for this, it may have been a field internship, qualifying him to be a registered surveyor. Both Lawrence Washington and George Fairfax gave him special assignments in addition to his work for Genn. Lawrence did not live to see it but his half-brother, barely sixteen when he first went over the mountains, was to become commander of Virginia's military forces six years later.

PART TWO

FRONTIERSMAN
1748–1758

THREE

YOUTH

1748–1753

T HE IMPORTANT ROLE of the Fairfaxes in opening up settlement of the West has never received adequate attention. George joined them in an active capacity when their work was already well advanced.

In mapping his claimed domain in 1736 and 1737, Lord Fairfax ordered the territory surveyed to the headwaters of the Rappahannock and the Potomac. The headspring of the latter was traced to the Allegheny Mountains. In 1742, while Fairfax's appeal to the privy council was still pending, a party of Virginians penetrated what is now West Virginia and Kentucky. At the Mississippi, they were captured by the French and imprisoned at New Orleans.

In 1744 the governments of Virginia, Maryland, and Pennsylvania entered into a treaty at Lancaster, Pennsylvania, with the Six Nations, the loose confederacy of Indian tribes who were often called "Iroquois." Through a long process of extermination or conquest of weaker tribes, the Six Nations had extended their claims well into the Ohio Valley regions. There, tributary Shawnees and Delawares settled after 1720. During the negotiations, the Iroquois claimed that they had conquered all the tribes along the Susquehannah and the Potomac, as well as those who had settled on the lands far beyond these rivers. They did admit that the English had beaten one tribe and had a justifiable claim to a portion of the area. In the end, the Indians sold the lands that Virginia wanted, with the understanding that further territories could be purchased as needed.

In 1746, Colonel William Fairfax led a new surveying party to map the western boundary of the Fairfax territory, from the Rappahannock to the headwaters of the Potomac. It was while he was en route that he stopped to tell George Washington of the plan to send him to sea. Colonel Fairfax had with him numerous attendants, his own son George, and James Genn. The Fairfax party, which placed a still extant headstone at the originating spring of the Potomac, found that a nearby stream apparently flowed into a tributary of the Ohio River which, in turn, joined the Mississippi. This close link between the two fired Lawrence Washington's imagination.

In 1747 the Ohio Company was organized to promote trade and settlement beyond the Fairfax domain. Lawrence Washington was one of its original organizers. Over the next years additional shareholders included Thomas Lee, who, as head of the governor's council, was called the president of Virginia, Austin Washington, various other Lees, and George Mason, who in 1758 moved to Gunston Hall near Mount Vernon.

In 1748 France and England signed a peace treaty. These powers, by long habit, passed peaceful years aggressively pushing territorial claims in a way as to ensure further war. The Ohio Valley was one such place where they were moving to collision. France had been far ahead of England in the area between the Alleghenies and the Rockies. La Salle had claimed the Mississippi and all its tributaries for France as early as 1682, effectively adding the whole area to Canada. By 1748 French priests and soldiers had astonishingly accurate maps of the Great Lakes, the Mississippi, and the river which they called "l'Oyo" or "la Belle Rivière." They were well aware of the important strategic point where the Allegheny and the Monongahela joined to become the Ohio, which they named "Trois Rivières." There, on French-claimed territory, Lawrence Washington hoped to establish a British fort and trading post.

TO THE MOUNTAINS

George Washington began both his first extended trip westward and a lifelong diary on March 11 (O.S.), 1748, with two passages scarcely designed to ring down through the ages:

> *Began my Journey in Company with George Fairfax, Esqr.; we travell'd this day 40 Miles to Mr. George Neavels in Prince William County.*

This Morning Mr. James Genn the surveyor came to us. We travell'd over the Blue Ridge to Capt. Ashby's on Shannondoa River. Nothing remarkable happen'd.

From this date, the previously unknown George Washington emerges with vigor. The wit and humor, which bubble through his writings, appear for the first time. In echoing his mother's love for natural beauty, he began to develop a theme which was to recur in his presidential diaries more than forty years later.

Genn's surveying party stopped first at Lord Fairfax's quarter, marked on its original survey as the Manor of Leeds, in honor of an English family holding. Fairfax's house, built the following year, was given the name Greenway Court. In riding up the Shenandoah Valley, George wrote that "we went through the most beautiful Groves of Sugar Trees & spent the best part of the Day in admiring the Trees & richness of the Land." Next day, on their way to Frederick Town, Washington again commented on the land as "exceeding Rich & Fertile all the way produces abundance of Grain Hemp Tobacco." That day the surveyors laid off lots. George continued the following day:

15th We set out early with Intent to Run around the said Land but being taken in a Rain & it Increasing very fast obliged us to return, it clearing about one oclock & our time being too Precious to Lose, we a second time ventur'd out & Worked hard till Night & then return'd to Penningtons. We got our Suppers & was lighted into a Room & I not being so good a Woodsman as the rest of my Company stripped myself very orderly & went into the Bed as they called it when to my Surprize I found it to be nothing but a Little Straw-Matted together without Sheets or any thing else but only one thread Bear blanket with double its Weight of Vermin such as Lice Fleas ec. I was glad to get up (as soon as the Light was carried from us) & put on my Cloths & Lay as my Companions. Had we not been very tired I am sure we should not have slep'd much that night I made a Promise not to Sleep so from that time forward chusing rather to sleep in the open Air before a fire as will appear hereafter.

16th We set out early & finish'd about one oClock & then Travell'd up to Frederick Town where our Baggage came to us we cleaned ourselves (to get Rid of the Game we had catched the Night before) & took a Review of the Town and thence return'd to our Lodgings where we had a good Dinner prepar'd for us Wine and Rum Punch in Plenty & a good Feather Bed with clean Sheets which was a very agreeable regale.

18th We Travell'd about 35 Miles to Thomas Berwicks on Potomack where we found the River so excessively high by Reason of the Great Rains that had fallen up about the Allegany Mountains, so they told us, which was then bringing down the melted Snow & that it would not be fordable for several Days it was then above Six foot Higher than usual and was rising. We agreed to stay till Monday.

23d Rain'd till about two oClock & Clear'd when we were agreeably surpris'd at the sight of thirty odd Indians coming from War with only one Scalp. We had some Liquor with us of which we gave them Part it elevating there Spirits put them in the Humour of Dauncing of whom we had a War Daunce. There manner of Dauncing is as follows Viz They clear a Large Circle make a Great Fire in the Middle then seats themselves around it the Speaker makes a grand speech telling them in what Manner they are to Daunce after he has finished the best Dauncer Jumps up as one awaked out of a Sleep and Jumps about the Ring in a most comical Manner he is followed by the Rest then begins there Musicians to Play. The Musick is a Pot half of Water with a Deerskin Stretched over it as tight as it can go & a goard with some Shott in it to Rattle & a Piece of an horses Tail tied to it, to make it look fine, the one keeps Rattling and the other Drumming all the while the others is Dauncing.

The surveyors rode through the cold spring rains up the South Branch of the Potomac. By March 29 they were surveying acreage and laying off lots to be sold by Fairfax's agents. On April 3 a gusty storm blew their tent away and they had to lie the rest of the night in the open. The next day they were watched by German-speaking curiosity seekers. Many Germans had poured into the Fairfax grant with Virginia titles or as squatters. This group may have been among those whose settlement was arranged by Joist Hite, who refused to recognize Lord Fairfax's ownership. He raised so much commotion that in 1749 Lord Fairfax temporarily closed his Frederick County land office.

In continued spring rain the Genn surveying party moved on, occasionally stopping to shoot wild turkeys weighing as much as twenty pounds. On April 8 George wrote:

We rode down below the Trough in order to Lay off Lots... The Trough is [a] couple of Ledges of Mountain Impassable running side and side together for above 7 or 8 Miles & the River down between them you must Ride Around the back of the Mountain for to get below them. We Camped this Night in the Woods near a Wild Meadow where was a Large Stack of Hay. After we had Pitch'd our Tent and made a very Large Fire we pull'd out our Knapsack in order to Recruit ourselves. Every[one] was his own Cook, our Spits was Forked Sticks, our Plates was a Large Chip, as for Dishes we had none.

On April 9 the party began the return trip, reaching Frederick Town two days later. Washington wrote briefly of the last stage to Mount Vernon: "12th We set off... in order to go over Wms. Gap about 20 Miles and after Riding about 20 miles, we had 20 to go for we had lost ourselves... This day [we] see a Rattle Snake the first we had seen in all our Journey. Wednesday the 13th of April 1748 Mr. Fairfax got safe home and I myself safe to my Brothers which concludes my Journal."

APPOINTMENT TO OFFICE

While George, aided by his own ability as well as by powerful friends, was rising into trusted and active work, his half brother Lawrence, full of dreams of the future, was increasingly ill from chronic tuberculosis. His four children apparently caught it also, for each died in infancy. Thus five tragedies were to make George Washington the eventual owner of Mount Vernon. In December 1749, nine months after the survey party returned, Lawrence asked for sick leave from the House of Burgesses. George spent at least part of that winter with his ill brother at Mount Vernon. On May 5, 1749, George wrote to Lawrence in Williamsburg, where he had resumed his seat, to express the hope that his cough was mending and that he would not have to go to England. He had hoped to meet him in the capital to register some deeds, but his horse, through lack of fodder, was too weak to make the journey.

That same month William Fairfax engaged George as assistant surveyor to lay out what was to be the most important town in the Northern Neck, Alexandria, north of Mount Vernon and Belvoir. Either before or during this period Lawrence sailed for England on Ohio Company business. William Fairfax wrote his son-in-law from Mount Vernon on July 17 that he was there with Lawrence's wife, his brothers Austin and George, and his sister Betty. They had been joined by Mr. Carlyle and Sarah (Fairfax's daughter) as well as George Fairfax and his wife and a "Miss Molly" [McCarthy]. This large house party toasted the success of Lawrence in England. Colonel Fairfax mentioned that George was writing him to enclose his plat of Alexandria and his ideas as to the proposed sale of lots.

With the completion of his apprenticeship, George rode to William and Mary College at Williamsburg. There, on July 30, 1749, he received his formal commission, at seventeen, as surveyor for Culpeper County. He went to his new post almost immediately to take his oaths and conduct his first licensed survey. Thereafter his notebooks show rough notes for each survey, which he converted into the elegant designs he had learned to draw. From the date of receipt of his commission, he signed himself "G. Washington SCC." Generally he had with him a crew of two chainmen and a marker.

For the next months, until winter cut his work short, George did surveying over a vast area. He spent time with Lord Fairfax, receiving instructions about work Lord Fairfax wanted performed. An undated note, found among his papers, is a request to "Mr. Washenton" to look for a lost horse with a white face and bell, on the South Branch of the Potomac. This and other evidence indicate that he was far afield, north of what was to be the frontier post of Cumberland and up the Shenandoah to Augusta County. Some idea of the roughness of his life is contained in an undated letter (probably November) which he wrote to "Robin," possibly a Washington cousin:

> The receipt of your kind favour of the 2d of this Instant afforded me unspeakable pleasure... I receiv'd it amongst a parcel of Barbarian's and an uncooth set of People... Since you receiv'd my Letter in October Last I have not sleep'd above three Nights or four in a bed after walking a good deal all the Day. I lay down before the fire upon a Little Hay Straw Fodder or bairskin whichever is to be had with Man Wife Children like a Parcel of Dogs or Catts... Happy's he that gets the Birth nearest the fire... Nothing would make it pass off tolerably but a good Reward. A Dubloon is my constant gain every Day that the Weather will permit my going out and sometimes Six Pistoles. The coldness of the weather will not allow my making a long stay as the Lodging is rather too cold... I have never had my cloths off but lay and sleep in them like a Negro except the few nights I have lay'n in Frederick Town.

George's fees were high, since six pistoles equalled around twenty-two Spanish dollars; land in the Shenandoah Valley could be bought for less than a dollar an acre. George waited carefully to find good farms. When he was eighteen, he began buying in quantity, picking up nearly fifteen hundred acres in 1750 and 1751.

George's first signs of illness appeared during this frontier surveying. In writing that autumn to his sister-in-law, Anne Washington, he said how glad he was to hear that his brother had arrived safely "*in health*" in England. The fever and ague which he himself had "to Extremety" prevented him from calling on her at Mount Vernon. Though his description might cover malaria, his close association with Lawrence makes it more likely that this was the initial onset of George Washington's own long battle with tuberculosis.

THE OHIO COMPANY

Late in 1749 Lawrence returned from a successful trip to London. George received from him a full report of the proposed operations of his company, which had been granted five-hundred thousand acres in the Ohio Valley. Lawrence prepared a rough map of the area, indicating how he thought the Potomac and Ohio Rivers might nearly interlock. Years later, George, inspecting the area, confirmed that their headwaters were only a few miles apart. Along with his map, Lawrence sent to England a letter describing the area beyond this point as "vastly rich."

English traders, he added, had not been able to penetrate because of a lack of goods. Once the Ohio Company established its post at the junction of the Allegheny and Monongahela Rivers, they could travel hundreds of miles into the interior. The Virginians had a great advantage over the French, since they could supply goods by way of the Potomac, while the Saint Lawrence was at a much greater distance and frozen for a large part of the year. He added: "The further we extend our Frontier, the safer we render the interior Dominions, and the French, having possession of the Ohio, might easily invade Virginia, for our mountains are not so formidable as to be much security... The Indians are our Friends... Nothing can more contribute to keeping them our Friends than contriving them the necessaries of Life at the easiest rates... The Indians... esteem those honestest who sell the cheapest."

Lawrence also pleaded that the new area be entirely free in religion in order to attract settlers: "Restrictions on conscience are cruel in regard to those on whom they are imposed and injurious to the country imposing them... This Colony was greatly settled in the latter part of Charles the First's time and during the usurpation, by the zealous churchmen; and that spirit which was then brought in, has ever since continued... What has been the consequence? We have increased by slow degrees while our neighboring communities, whose natural advantages are greatly inferior to ours, have become populous."

While Lawrence greatly underestimated the growth of Virginia's population, which his friends and relatives were stimulating, his views were remarkable for their vision and tolerance. Lawrence's dreams influenced his brother, who became the first Washington to reach the Monongahela, go down the Ohio River, and own land in that valley.

In 1750 Thomas Lee, president of the Ohio Company, died, and Lawrence became his successor. That same year Dr. Thomas Walker and a party of Virginians explored as far west as Kentucky. Shortly afterwards, the company dispatched Christopher Gist, long experienced in work with the Indians, on an extended trip through present-day Ohio, Indiana, and Kentucky. He found the Indians averse to any settlement north of the Ohio. In consequence Gist was dispatched in 1751 and 1752 on another extensive investigation along the southern areas of the valley, as far as the present Wheeling, West Virginia. He wrote long reports for the Ohio Company, which were available to George at Mount Vernon.

The Ohio Company built its first storehouse in 1750 at Will's Creek (Cumberland). The following year the company started construction of a road to the forks of the Ohio River. In 1752 the governor of Virginia empowered Christopher Gist to hold treaty talks with the Indians at Logstown, about thirteen miles from the junction of the three rivers. Gist successfully negotiated title to lands south of the Ohio. In the meantime, the French were also active. They had charted the Ohio River in 1746, burying plates at various points, claiming the territory for France. By 1752 the French had plans for a series of forts south of Lake Erie. The most important of these was to be at the forks of the Ohio, the proposed terminus of the Ohio Company's road. The stage was being set for conflict and for Washington's early rise to international fame.

TO BARBADOS

Meanwhile, Lawrence Washington's active tenure as president of the Ohio Company was cut short as his health grew steadily worse. In July 1750, George took Lawrence to the warm waters at Bath, Virginia (now Berkeley Springs, West Virginia), but they did him no good. In 1751 Lawrence decided, as a last desperate remedy, to proceed to Barbados which, though hot and sticky, had a favorable reputation for pulmonary disorders. His wife, Anne, at home with her one surviving child, a sickly girl of about eleven months, could not travel. George became Lawrence's companion.

The trip to Barbados would be George's only venture outside of continental America. The brothers sailed from Fredericksburg for Bridgetown towards the end of September 1751. George was gone for four months, nearly half the time at sea. His diary survives only in mutilated form but enough remains to provide an indication of their activities.

George had spent most of his early years on or near rivers. Now he spent much of his first five weeks on a larger ship, learning as much more as he could of seamanship. His extant papers include a ship's log in his neat handwriting, wherein he recorded every two hours the course, latitude and longitude, the distance run, and the wind and weather. His curiosity as powerful as his intellect, George was soon writing learnedly of reefing and double-reefing the sails and of hauling the foresail.

The voyage in hurricane season was unmercifully rough. Between October 16 and 22 the ship passed close to what the ship's officers assumed was "a violent hurricane." George wrote first of a "Strong wind" and then over several days of a "Hard gale and a disturb'd and large Sea which imminently endangered our Masts... Hard Squalls of Wind and Rain... The Compass not remaining two hours in any point. The Seamen seemed disheartend confessing they had never seen such weather... A Constant succession of hard Winds, Squalls of Rain... a large Tumbling Sea."

On the twenty-second the wind lightened enough for the sailors to repair the damaged rigging. The next day the sun came out, and George remarked that it showed that the bread "was almost Eaten up by Weavels & Maggots." By October 30 there was "a certain & steady trade Wind which after near five Weeks buffiting and being toss'd by a fickle & Merciless Ocean was gladening news." They landed at Bridgetown on November 3 or 4.

Upon arrival they were greeted by Major Gedney Clarke, a member of the Barbados governor's council and a relation of the first husband of Mrs. William Fairfax. He recommended a physician who, after examining Lawrence, was quite optimistic as to a cure. Thus encouraged, George gave his attention to the scenery as they rode in search of a house to rent. Barbados, in its wet season, was lush, and George records himself as "perfectly ravished by the beautiful prospects which on every side [were] presented to our View. The fields of Cain, Corn, Fruit Trees, &c., in a delightful Green."

Major Clarke invited the Washingtons to breakfast and dinner with him. George recorded going without much enthusiasm, since there was a case of smallpox in the house. By the eighth, the brothers had rented a house for the "extravagantly dear" price of fifteen pounds per month. Lawrence found the hot and humid climate very trying, and was forced to keep mainly to the house except early in the morning or in the cool of the evening.

George, however, now nineteen, blossomed in his new life. His natural charm, about which so many persons were to comment in later life, made him a sought-after guest. With his brother he was invited to the Beefsteak and Tripe Club, which met each Saturday night at the house of a member. Thereafter George was asked everywhere. He dined with the military, judges, and the surveyor general. He attended church as well as the theatre. On November 17 the gay life abruptly stopped. His December 12 diary made a brief note of what happened:

Was strongly attacked with the small Pox: sent for Dr. Lanahan whose attendance was very constant till my recovery, and going out which was not 'till thursday the 12th of December.

Not another word did he write of the miseries of two sick brothers far from home. George was soon dining out again, with a commodore, a general, members of the governor's council, and the governor of Tortola. He took everyone in stride, and poked into everything in Barbados. He inspected the island fortifications. He read a natural history of the island. He noted all the local produce, particularly the fruits, which he sampled: granadella, sapodilla, pomegranate, orange, lemon, forbidden fruit, apple, guava, pineapple, avocado, yam, plantain, potato, rice, and Guinea corn. He enjoyed most the taste of fresh pineapple. He commented on the richness and blackness of much of the soil and expressed wonder that so many people could be in debt when the farms were more productive than those of Virginia. He made notes on manuring practices. The women, he wrote, were very agreeable but behaved rather too much like negroes. The men had florid complexions. The climate was healthy for those who stayed temperate. He attended a trial for rape. He remarked on the behavior of the governor, who stayed too aloof from the people. Barbadians, too, complained of the rapacity of British officials, whose fees were regarded as far out of line with the work they performed.

Lawrence Washington subsequently informed William Fairfax that the climate was too hot for him and he proposed to proceed to Bermuda. George sailed on the *Industry* for Virginia on December 22, very probably with instructions to give Anne Washington news of her husband and to bring her and her daughter, if it seemed desirable, to Bermuda. This sea trip home was even rougher than his outward voyage. Though Christmas Day was "fine and clear and pleasant with moderate Sea," and the occasion for a feast of goose and roast beef, on the last day of the year the *Industry* ran into "violent winds... with excessive rain [and] mountainous running [seas which prevented] carrying Sail." On the third and fourth of January there were more storms and heavy seas. On the eighth the ship was marooned; next day there were such huge winds and seas that the ship had to proceed with masts almost bare. Soon snow and hail were added to the rain. On January 16 the *Industry* encountered HMS *Glasgow*, which had been trying for two weeks to make the Virginia coast in the storms. They also met a merchant vessel, which had been five weeks on its way from Saint Kitts to Philadelphia.

On January 23 George wrote that the mate, with the weather moderating, was "inticed... from his Cabbin (as a snail enlivened by the genial heat of the Sun) who since the third or fourth day after leaving Barbados has been coop'd up with a fashionable disorder contracted there." On January 26 the waters grew shallower, and birds and marsh weed appeared; late that night the ship reached the mouth of the York River. Upon landing, George proceeded to Williamsburg to deliver his brother's letters to Governor Dinwiddie.

This was the first encounter between the sixty-year-old governor (technically lieutenant governor) and the nineteen-year-old youth, whom he was soon to make Virginia's military commander. George wrote that Dinwiddie received him "Graceously. He enquired kindly after the health of my Brother and invited me to stay and dine." It is a reasonable surmise that George raised the question whether, since Lawrence's health made it desirable that he resign as adjutant general, he could have the job. If the governor expressed surprise, history has no record of it.

Shortly after his return, George rode west to Frederick County to resume surveying. While there, he increased his landholdings at Bullskin Creek, not far from the present-day Charles Town, which was to be named for his youngest brother. He returned to the tidewater in the spring, as increasingly worried letters from Lawrence reached Mount Vernon. If Lawrence had any hope of recovery, he would stay in Bermuda and ask George to bring his wife and baby there. If not, he would return to Mount Vernon "to my grave."

George had heard that the Virginia adjutancy, held by his brother, was considered too large a task for one man. In consequence, at least three district adjutants were to be appointed. Colonel William Fitzhugh, who was living in Maryland, was under consideration for the Northern Neck. George stopped in Maryland to call on Fitzhugh to see whether he wanted the job. The colonel gave him a letter to forward to the governor, stating conditions to be met if he were to accept. On June 10 George sent Fitzhugh's letter to Dinwiddie, requesting at the same time that, if the colonel were not appointed, he might have the Northern Neck adjutancy. If Fitzhugh got it, he would be happy to have one of the other districts. George added that he would "take the greatest pleasure in punctually obeying, from time to time, your Honour's commands; and by a strict observance of my Duty, render myself worthy of the trust reposed in me: I am sensible my best endeavors will not be wanting, and doubt not, but by a constant application to fit myself for the Office, could I presume Your Honour had not in view a more deserving person."

Very shortly afterwards, Lawrence, a dying man, reached Virginia. Mary Washington and her children went to Mount Vernon to see him. Lawrence rewrote his will, as quickly and loosely as his father had done. He left Mount Vernon to his daughter, or to George in the event of her death (a possibility he mentioned three times in his will), subject to his wife's life tenancy. Lawrence died on July 26, 1752. His daughter lived for only a short time thereafter and George became the heir about 1754.

On November 6 the governor of Virginia, by and with the advice and consent of his council, appointed George Washington major of militia and adjutant for the southern district. Major Washington was sworn in just before his twenty-first birthday. Although Dinwiddie could not foresee this, the young officer was to be his principal interest and irritant for the next five years.

FOUR

LIEUTENANT COLONEL WASHINGTON

1753–1754

MAJOR WASHINGTON AT twenty-one had presumably reached his full height of six feet, two-and-one-half inches. He was a giant in an age when Americans were much shorter on the average. A tabulation of the heights of 1,134 men in Virginia's colonial regiment showed that two-fifths were between four feet eleven inches and five feet five inches. Only one man exceeded Washington in height; probably none did in strength. He had an unusually powerful build, with hands that Lafayette and Timothy Pickering described as the largest they had ever seen on a man. He was very light in coloring with eyes described by Weems as cerulean blue. Dr. James Craik recalled in later years that when he and Washington attended church in the frontier days, the eyes of the ladies were more likely to be on Washington than on the preacher.

The governor-in-council had defined the adjutant's duties as "instructing the officers and soldiers in the use and exercise of their arms... bringing the militia to a more regular discipline, besides improving the meaner people." The young major, in addition to his military reading at Mount Vernon, had attended his brother in some of his duties as adjutant. Washington's training in mathematics, topography, and surveying would also be helpful.

The construction in 1752 of two French forts in what is now western Pennsylvania abruptly brought Washington into high responsibility. Dinwiddie, increasingly alarmed, reported France's action to London in June. The British government reacted with uncharacteristic speed. In August, George II approved the construction of forts by Virginia and announced that British ordnance supplies were on their way. The king ordered Dinwiddie diplomatically to request all intruders to depart peaceably. Should they be answered with force, Dinwiddie was to drive the French out of the territory. He was assured that the British government would give him the fullest backing.

In October of 1753, shortly after the governor received his instructions, Major Washington was in Williamsburg, volunteering to proceed to the French forts. With the council's approval, Dinwiddie drafted Washington's orders and handed him a passport as well as a letter to the commander of the French forces in the territory. Without experience in war or diplomacy, Washington faced a difficult and dangerous mission that included intelligence work, since the governor instructed him to find out all he could of French fortifications and numerical strength.

Washington started north on October 31. In Fredericksburg he picked up the Dutch-born Jacob van Braam, who had some knowledge of French. In Alexandria and Winchester the pair purchased supplies and horses. At Will's Creek, Christopher Gist, the experienced agent of the Ohio Company, joined them, along with four Indian traders and servants. From November 15, the party picked its way through the forbidding passes of the Alleghenies. On November 22, sixteen months after his brother's death, George reached the forks of the Ohio, where Lawrence had planned to establish his trading post. He wrote:

> *I spent some time in viewing the Rivers and the Land in the Fork which I think extremely well situated for a Fort, as it has the absolute Command of both Rivers. The Land at the Point is 20 or 25 Feet above the common Surface of the Water; and a considerable Bottom of flat, well-timbered land all around it, very convenient for Building: The Rivers are each a Quarter of a Mile, or more, and run here very near at right Angles; Aligany bearing N. E. and Monongahela S. E. The former of these two is a very rapid and swift running Water; the other deep and still, without any perceptible Fall.*

Washington spent the days of November in discussions with Indians friendly to the English, including an Oneida and Mingo chief, Monakatoocha, and a Seneca chief, the Half-King, so-called because of allegiances he owed the Six Nations. The Half-King informed Washington that he had complained to the French of their movements in the region and they had treated him with contempt. He, the Shanoahs, and Delawares promised therefore to support the English. He offered Washington an escort on his visit to the French commander, which was gladly accepted, and the expedition resumed its progress:

[Venango, December 4.] This is an old Indian Town, situated at the Mouth of French Creek on Ohio... We found the French Colours hoisted at a House which they drove Mr. John Frazier, an English Subject, from; I immediately repaired to it, to know where the Commander resided: There were three Officers, one of whom, Capt. Joncaire, informed me that he had the Command of the Ohio, but that there was a General Officer at the near Fort, where he advised me to apply for an Answer. He invited us to sup with them, and treated us with the greatest Complaisance. The Wine, as they dosed themselves pretty plentifully with it, soon banished the Restraint which at first appeared in their Conversation, and gave a License to their Tongues to reveal their Sentiments more freely. They told me, That it was their absolute Design to take Possession of the Ohio, and by G— they would do it; For that altho' they were sensible the English could raise two Men for their one; yet they knew their Motions were too slow and dilatory to prevent any Undertaking of theirs. They pretend to have an undoubted Right to the River, from a Discovery made by one LaSalle 60 Years ago; and the Rise of this Expedition is to prevent our settling on the River or Waters of it, as they had heard of some Families moving-out in Order thereto.

7th Monsieur La Force, Commissary of the French Stores, and three other Soldiers came over to accompany us up [to Fort Le Boeuf near Waterford, Pennsylvania]... At 11 oClock we set out for the Fort, and were prevented from arriving there till the 11th by excessive Rains, Snows and bad Travelling, through many Mires and Swamps... We passed over much good Land... and through several extensive and very rich Meadows...

12th I prepared early to wait upon the Commander... I acquainted him with my Business, and offered my Commission and Letter: Both of which he desired me to keep till the arrival of Monsieur Riparti [de Repentigny]... At 2 oClock... [he] arriv'd, when I offered the Letter, &c. again; which they receiv'd, and adjourn'd into a private Apartment for the Captain to translate, who understood a little English; after he had done it, [Legardeur de Saint Pierre,] the Commander, desir'd I would walk in, and bring my Interpreter to peruse and correct it, which I did.

13th The chief Officers retired, to hold a Council of War; which gave me an Opportunity of taking the Dimensions of the Fort, and making what Observations I could.

Washington estimated that the fort held about a hundred men. He instructed his guides and Indians to count all canoes. They numbered 220, with others building. By December 14 snow was falling heavily and the horses grew so weak Washington had them sent on ahead. The next day the commandant gave him a reply to Dinwiddie, along with ample supplies and liquor for his trip. He also attempted to bribe his Indians to desert. Washington commented: "I can't say that ever in my life I suffer'd so much Anxiety as I did in this Affair." Washington then made what he described as "a very fatiguing passage" upriver by canoe. He wrote that a number of times they were

> *nearly staved against Rocks, and many Times were obliged all Hands to get out and remain in the Water Half an Hour or more, getting over the Shoals. At one Place the Ice had lodged and made it impassable by Water; therefore we were obliged to carry our Canoe across a Neck of Land, a quarter of a Mile over. We did not reach Venango, till the 22nd, where we met with our Horses.*

The horses however "were now so weak and feeble," and the progress of the main party so slow over snow and ice-bound roads that Washington became "uneasy to get back to make Report of my Proceedings to his Honour the Governor," and "determined to prosecute my Journey the nearest Way through the Woods, on foot." Setting out with Gist alone, the two men were the very next day waylaid by "a Party of French Indians," one of whom "fired at Mr. Gist or me, not 15 steps off, but fortunately missed." The next day the two men reached the Allegheny River, which they had hoped vainly to find frozen so they could walk across it. Instead they built a raft with but "one poor Hatchet" for a tool. "Just after Sun-setting, after a whole Day's Work; we got it launched, and on board of it, and set off; but before we were Half Way over, jammed in the Ice, in such a Manner that we expected every Moment our Raft to sink, and ourselves to perish; I put out my setting pole to try to stop the Raft, that the Ice might pass by, when the Rapidity of the Stream threw it with so much Violence against the Pole, that it jerked me out into ten Feet Water." Washington fortunately saved himself by catching hold of one of the raft logs. But the travellers could not get the raft to either shore and were forced to swim for an island.

Gist had all his fingers and some of his toes frozen. By morning the river was solid and they made for John Frazier's house. There they met "20 Warriors who were going to the southward to War, but coming to a Place upon the head of the Great Cunnaway [Kanawha], where they found seven People killed and scalped, all but one Woman with very light hair, they turned about and ran back, for Fear the Inhabitants should rise and take them as the

Authors of the Murder... By the Marks that were left, they say they were French Indians of the Ottaway Nation."

Obtaining horses, they made a visit to "Queen Aliquippa, who had expressed great Concern that we passed her in going to the Fort. I made her a Present of a Matchcoat and a Bottle of Rum, which latter was thought much the best Present of the Two." In the face of continued extreme weather the two men made Belvoir by January 11 and Williamsburg January 16, where Washington "waited upon his Honour the Governor with the Letter I had brought from the French Commandant."

The December 15 letter from Legardeur de St. Pierre, which Washington delivered to the governor, was politely blunt:

I have the honor, Sir, to be commander-in-chief here. Monsieur Washington transmitted to me the letter which you wrote to the commandant of French troops.

As for your summons to me to retire, I do not feel any obligation to do so, whatever may be your instructions. I am here by orders of my general and I beg you, Sir, not to doubt for an instant that I have the fixed resolution to conform to them with the exactness and firmness expected of the best officer.

I made it my particular duty to receive Monsieur Washington with a distinction, equal to your position and to his own quality and great merit."

The letter achieved the distinction, which was to be rare among the French, of spelling Washington's name correctly.

Although the House of Burgesses had adjourned without voting defense funds, the council was in session when George returned. The governor asked him to prepare a report of his trip, giving him only twenty-four hours to do so. Dinwiddie was sufficiently impressed to subsequently order it printed for the Virginia Assembly. He gave Major Washington barely enough time to write a preface, in which Washington apologized for the "numberless imperfections" that were consequent on the haste with which he had written it. He was given no time for redrafting nor had he even known it was to be printed until the Assembly, called for February 14, was already in session. He added: "There is nothing can recommend it to the Public, but this. Those Things which came under the Notice of my own Observation, I have been explicit and just in a Recital of. Those which I have gathered from Report, I have been particularly cautious not to augment, but collected the Opinions of the several Intelligencers, and selected from the whole, the most probable and confident Account."

The printed version omitted Washington's careful drawing of the whole region from the Alleghenies to Lake Erie, which he had made from his compass reckonings. Later surveys showed the map to be remarkably accurate, considering the primitive conditions under which his notes were made. The drawing contained designs of the existing French forts, with an outline of their further plans: "The French are coming from their Forts on and near the Lake Erie to Venango [at the junction of French Creek and the Allegheny River] to erect another Fort. From thence they design to the Forks of the Monongahela and to the Logs Town and so to continue down the River building at the most convenient places in order to prevent our Settlements, &ca. NB. A little below the Shanapin Town [Pittsburgh] in the Forks is the place where we are going immediately to Build a Fort as it Commands the Ohio and Monongahela."

Dinwiddie sent copies of the printed document to members of the council and House and to other colonial governors. He also transmitted a copy to London where it was immediately reprinted. Thus the twenty-one-year-old major became known for the first time internationally. The report indicated that he was a tough, resourceful officer and an acute observer who could gather and accurately evaluate intelligence under unusually adverse conditions.

While waiting for the House to convene, Dinwiddie dispatched Washington to the Shenandoah Valley to recruit militia for service at the forks of the Ohio. Washington, on his return, reported that the militia system was a paper organization and little recruiting had taken place, although Lord Fairfax himself was the county lieutenant. When the Assembly reconvened, the governor urged immediate action to provide funds for defense of the frontier, using the Washington report as his most powerful argument. The Assembly itself promptly voted praise and fifty pounds to the young major for his mission.

In spite of the clear emergency, the governor had no easy time getting funds for a regular military force. There were outcries in the House of Burgesses that the ten thousand pounds he requested was for the protection of a private enterprise, the Ohio Company. Questions were raised as to whether the forks of the Ohio were in Virginia or Pennsylvania. This was important since Virginia law forbade the militia (needed to reinforce the regular troops) to serve outside the colony. Others wondered whether the territory was even British. Since Dinwiddie had direct orders from London to protect the frontiers, the debates made him very uneasy. In the end, the burgesses voted the money but appointed a committee to control its expenditure jointly with the governor. Dinwiddie signed the act but complained bitterly to London that it was unconstitutional. The governor, as the Crown's representative, had the clear prerogative of allocating supplies.

Washington had asked Dinwiddie to appoint him adjutant of the Northern

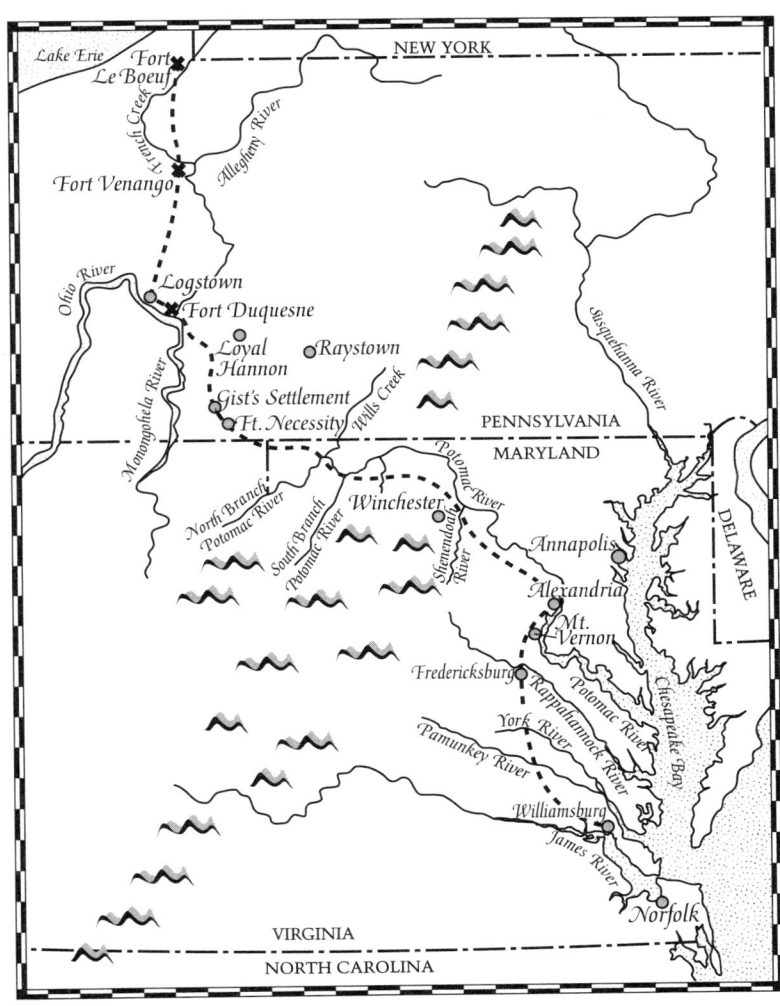

Washington's Journey to Fort Le Boeuf, 1753

Neck if he did not find a man more suitable for the position. During Washington's absence in the Ohio regions, the governor transferred him there. Once the military bill authorizing the recruiting of three hundred men passed, young Washington made known to Richard Corbin, of the governor's council, his desire to join the regular military service. As John Marshall put it, Corbin's reply was laconic: "Dear George—I enclose you your commission. God prosper you with it."

Dinwiddie, who was to complain of the shortage of experienced officers in the colony, selected Joshua Fry as colonel and commander of what was to become the Virginia Regiment. Fry, a surveyor and mapmaker, had been a county lieutenant in charge of militia, with additional experience in Indian negotiations. Shortly thereafter Washington, who described Fry many years later as "old and corpulent," was appointed lieutenant colonel and second in command, a commission he held in addition to his majority in the militia. Other appointments included George Muse as major and Christopher Gist and Adam Stephen as captains. James Craik joined as physician. In order to reward the officers, and to stimulate the recruitment of enlisted men, the governor authorized a future grant to them of two hundred thousand acres of land in the Ohio Valley. The officers were ordered to various points to recruit: Fry to the tidewater region, Washington to Alexandria, and Stephen to Winchester.

Before Washington reached Alexandria, a company under Captain William Trent, largely composed of frontiersmen, had begun to erect the first fort at the Ohio forks. On March 20 Washington received urgent orders from the governor to proceed immediately there with such men as he had enlisted. Dinwiddie had a dispatch from Trent to the effect that he anticipated a French attack. Washington reported to the governor that he and others had assembled around seventy-five soldiers, many of the "loose, idle" type who often had no shoes or shirts. The commissary, Major Carlyle, was prepared to clothe them, if the colony could guarantee credit and the men would gladly repay from their wages. As soon as wagons could be assembled, Washington set off for his first military venture. On April 2, with around 150 officers and men, he began the march to Winchester, which he completed in about seven days.

At Winchester a few men under Captain Adam Stephen joined Washington. From this frontier post the young lieutenant colonel had to get his men and supplies to Will's Creek and thence over the Allegheny Mountains to the Ohio River. He stretched his impressment powers, as he wrote the governor, to the limit, to get wagons. He thought his authority would not "be questioned, unless some busybody interferes." In spite of all efforts he could gather only ten of seventy-four requisitioned wagons. At Will's Creek, while Washington held council with the Indians, Ensign Edward Ward, who had been left in charge of the Ohio fort, arrived with the news that he and thirty-three soldiers had surrendered to French forces, which he estimated to be at least one thousand. Neither Captain Trent nor his lieutenant had been present at the time of the surrender, though Ward had informed them that Indian scouts had seen the French moving down the river in overwhelming force. Washington, with a handful of untrained troops, was now the entire force of the British empire opposing French control of the Ohio Valley.

FIVE

COLONEL WASHINGTON
PUSHES WAR

1754

A T THIS CRITICAL PERIOD, there were no British troops in Virginia and relatively few elsewhere in the colonies. Although George II had commanded Dinwiddie to use force to eject the French from the Ohio if they did not depart peaceably, and had promised the fullest military support, for an extended time this remained a paper assurance. London moved slowly in crises. Nearly five years would elapse before Washington led a British army into Fort Duquesne. His military service during the period was to be as long as that from Long Island to Yorktown and proved a rehearsal for the main event, when once again he would struggle with inadequate supplies and funds, undisciplined militia, provincial jealousies, and long marches with infrequent battles. His experience now with guerrilla tactics and British commanders and troops was to be of the greatest future value to him.

Ensign Ward reported to Washington that their Indian ally, the Half-King, had been among those captured at the forks. He brought with him the Half-King's letter, renewing his loyalty and expressing his readiness to "fall upon" the French. He added: "If you do not come to our assistance now, we are entirely undone... I speak with a heart full of grief." Washington replied with some exaggeration that his troops were clearing the roads for "a great number of our warriors, who are ready to follow us, with our great guns, our ammunition and provisions." He signed himself "George Washington

Conotocarious," an Indian name meaning 'towntaker,' which had been conferred on him by the Half-King.

Washington dispatched Ward to Williamsburg with a letter for Dinwiddie. He informed the governor that he would do his best for the "good of my country; whose rights, while they are asserted in so just a cause, I will defend to the last remains of my life." He had determined to push ahead to Redstone Creek, a tributary of the Monongahela, some thirty-seven miles from the fort the French had taken. He continued:

I doubt not that we can maintain a possession there, till we are reinforced, unless the rising of the waters shall admit the enemy's cannon to be conveyed up in canoes, and then I flatter myself we shall not be so destitute of intelligence, as not to get timely notice of it, and make a good retreat.

I hope you will see the absolute necessity for our having, as soon as our forces are collected, a number of cannon, some of heavy metal, with mortars and grenades to attack the French, and put us on an equal footing with them.

Washington suggested that Dinwiddie make every effort to induce the Cherokees, Catawbas, and Chickasaws to come to his assistance, as well as to conclude a treaty with the English allies, the Six Nations. He also informed him that he was writing for help directly to the governors of Pennsylvania and Maryland because of the time it would take to get mail to their capitals by way of Williamsburg.

Washington's letters to Governor Horatio Sharpe of Maryland and to Governor James Hamilton of Pennsylvania recapitulated much of the information given to Dinwiddie, stressing the strong French forces already in the area as well as the intelligence that additional French troops were on the way and would be joined by six hundred Indians. To Sharpe he added:

I ought first to have begged pardon of your excellency for this liberty of writing... It was the glowing zeal I owe my country that influenced me to impart these advices and my inclination prompted me to do it to you as I know you are solicitous for the public weal and warm in this interesting cause; that should rouse from the lethargy we have fallen into, the heroick spirit of every free-born English man to attest the rights and privileges of our king (if we don't consult the benefits of our selves) and resque [rescue] from the invasion of a usurping enemy, our Majesty's property, his dignity, and land.

I hope, sir, you will excuse the freeness of my expressions, they are the pure
sentiments of the heart.

On May 9, twelve days after Washington had written to the neighboring governors, he reported again to Dinwiddie. He complained that the horses
Captain Trent had promised for his arrival at Will's Creek were not there and
that they had had to send forty miles for wagons. His men were building and
widening the road north. So difficult was the task they were able to move only
two to four miles each day. Intelligence from traders fleeing the French indicated their increasing reinforcements, with a heavy concentration fortifying
Duquesne. A few days later he wrote Fry that he had canoed thirty miles down
the Youghiogheny River, to see if it were navigable, but he had encountered
two miles of rapids and then a forty-foot fall. He asked for trading goods to
give to the Indians whose "friendship is not so warm as to prompt them to
services gratis."

FIGHT WITH THE FRENCH

On May 27 Washington learned that Dinwiddie had gone to Winchester, hoping to see the Half-King and other chiefs. Washington transmitted to the governor, verbatim, the following message, which he had received from the
Half-King:

To the forist [first of], his Majesties Commander Offiverses to hom this meay concern:

On acc't of a freench armey to meat Miger Georg Wassiontton therfor my Brotheres I
deesir you to be awar of them for deisin'd to strik ye forist English they see ten days
since they marchd I cannot tell what nomber the half King and the rest of the Chiefs
will be with you in five dayes to consel, no more at present but give my serves to my
Brothers the English

The Half-King
John Davison (interpreter)

Washington noted that he was writing from Great Meadows, eighteen miles
beyond his previous camp, and that French scouts had been seen: "We have,
with Nature's assistance, made a good Intrenchment, and, by clearing the
Bushes out of these Meadows, prepar'd a charming field for an encounter."
He added that his previous intelligence on the size of the French forces had

probably been exaggerated. The next day Washington encountered the French. He wrote immediately to Colonel Fry, saying:

> *I send to inform you, that Yesterday I engag'd a party of French, whereof 11 were killed and 20 taken, with the loss of only 1 of mine killed and 2 or 3 wounded... By some of their Papers we can discover, that large detach'ts. are expected every day, which we can reasonably suppose are to attack us, especially since we have began.*

He asked for immediate reinforcements. Colonel Fry died after being thrown from his horse two days after this was written. At twenty-two Washington became acting and then commissioned colonel and commander in chief of His Majesty's Virginia Regiment. The same day George wrote a full account of the battle to Dinwiddie:

> *I had detach'd a party of 75 Men to meet with 50 of the French, who, we had Intelligence, were upon their March towards us to Reconnoitre, &ca. Ab't 9 O'clock the same night, I receiv'd an express from the Half King, who was Incamp'd with several of his People ab't 6 Miles off, that he had seen the Track of two French Men X'ing the road, and believ'd the whole body were lying not far off, as we had an acc't of that number passing Mr. Gist's.*

> *I set out with 40 Men before 10, and was from that time till near Sun rise before we reach'd the Indian's Camp, hav'g March'd in [a] small path, a heavy Rain, and a Night as Dark as it is possible to conceive.*

> *When we came to the Half King, I council'd with him, and got his assent to go hand in hand and strike the French... When we came to the place where the Tracks were, the Half King sent two Indians to follow their tracks, and discover their lodgement, which they did ab't half a mile from the Road, in a very obscure place surrounded with Rocks. I thereupon... form'd a disposition to attack them on all sides, which we accordingly did, and, after an Engagement of ab't 15 minutes, we killed 10, wounded one, and took 21 Prisoners. Amongst those that were killed was Monsieur Jumonville, the Commander, princip'l Officers taken is Monsieur Druillong and Mons'r La force, who your Honour has often heard me speak of as a bold Enterprising Man, and a person of great sublity and cunning.*

> *These Officers pretend they were coming on an Embassy; but the absurdity of this pretext is too glaring, as your Honour will see by the Instructions and Summons inclos'd. These Instructions were to reconnoitre the Country... to get intelligence which they were to send Back by some brisk dispatches.*

The Half King... has declared to send these Frenchmen's Scalps with a Hatchet to all the Nations of Indians in union with them.

I shall expect every hour to be attack'd, and by unequal numbers, which I must withstand if there are 5 to 1 or else I fear the Consequence will be we shall lose the Indians if we suffer ourselves to be drove Back... I doubt not if you hear I am beaten, but you will at the same [time] hear that we have done our duty in fighting.

This small skirmish, which followed the French seizure of a British fort, was often wrongly credited as the cause of the ensuing war between France and Britain, which spread to Europe and as far east as India. Horace Walpole called it a "trifling incident, but one which gave date to the war," while Voltaire expressed surprise that "a cannon-shot fired in America could give the signal that set Europe in a blaze." Washington was sufficiently pleased with his success to describe it further in a letter of June 3 to Dinwiddie:

If the whole Detch't of the French behave with no more Resolution than this chosen Party did, I flatter myself we shall have no g't trouble in driving them to Montreal. Tho' I took 40 Men under my com'd when I marched out, yet the darkness of the night was so great, that by wandering a little from the main body 7 were lost, and but 33 ingag'd. There was also but 7 Indians with arms, two of which were Boys, one Dinwiddie, your Honour's God Son, who behav'd well in action. There were 5 or 6 Indians who served to knock the poor, unhappy wounded in the head, and bereiv'd them of their scalps.

We have just finish'd a small pallisado'd Fort, in which, with my small numbers, I shall not fear the attack of 500 men.

Following Dinwiddie's appeal for aid, London ordered the governors of South Carolina and New York to send regular troops to Virginia. North Carolina added a regiment of provincials. The New York companies were much delayed in reaching Virginia. When they finally arrived, Dinwiddie found them not only undermanned but many too old to march. In addition, they had thirty women and children along but were lacking in provisions, tents, and blankets. The North Carolinians arrived with insufficient arms and money. When their payroll stopped, the units disbanded before getting near the front. Only the South Carolina regulars under Captain James Mackay saw action; they would join Washington just in time to be beaten.

Dinwiddie had appointed Washington a full colonel and commander of the Virginia Regiment in early June of 1754. To coordinate the troops from the four colonies Dinwiddie chose as commander in chief a fellow Scot, Colonel James Innes, with whom Lawrence Washington had served at Cartagena. Washington was to rank second, while Dinwiddie gave brevet commissions as lieutenant colonels to the regular captains from New York and South Carolina. This was ingenious but unworkable. The holders of a king's commission, however low, maintained they outranked even a colonel appointed by a provincial governor. About June 10 Washington wrote Dinwiddie a long letter balanced between appreciation and complaints:

> *I... return your Honour my hearty thanks for your kind congratulations on our late success, which I hope to improve without risquing the imputation of rashness... I rejoice that I am likely to be under the command of an experienced Officer and Man of Sense, it is what I have most ardently wished for. I shall here beg leave to return my grateful thanks for your favour in promoting me to the Command of the Regiment.*
>
> *I hope Captain McKay will have more sense than to insist upon any unreasonable distinction, tho' he and His have Commissions from his Majesty... yet we have the same Spirit to serve our Gracious King as they have; and are as ready and willing to sacrifice our lives for our Country's good.*
>
> *Since writing the foregoing, Captain McKay with the Independent Company has arrived... Having Commissions from the King, they look upon themselves as a distinct Body.*
>
> *It now behooves, Honourable Sir, that you lay your absolute commands on one or another to obey. This is indispensably necessary.*

Then Washington went to a major point which was to rankle him in all his associations with the British army until he retired from this war. As he pointed out to Dinwiddie, British officers would automatically order "a Regular attack which would expose us to almost immediate death without hope of damaging them, as the French all fight in the Indian method which, by this, we have got some experience in." The Americans under Washington had begun to learn from the French and Indians and hence knew better than the British how to deal with them. The youthful Washington could never persuade his British superiors on this point; more than two decades later he would drive the point home somewhat more effectively.

LETTERS FROM TIDEWATER

Some cheerful letters from friends reached Washington on the frontier, conveying the respect he had won throughout Virginia. Colonel Charles Carter, father-in-law of Light Horse Harry Lee, said that he was "charmed" by the bravery of Washington in his first engagement with the French. Daniel Campbell wrote that his victory "gave me and your other friends such satisfaction as is only felt by those who have hearts full of mutual affection and friendship." Major Carlyle explained what he was doing to get supplies to the troops. He added: "We have great Rejoicings on Yr Good Success." William Fairfax enclosed two *Gazettes*, "wherein you'l observe, your mem'ble Acts are not forgot." Some of the letters were still on their way to him when Colonel Washington suffered his first military defeat.

SIX

"SOUNDLY BEATEN"

1754

T HE YOUNG VIRGINIA COLONEL, with too few troops, guns, and even supplies to maintain an adequate defense, decided to undertake the kind of high-risk offensive against superior forces that would later earn a reprimand from General Washington.

The Virginia garrison, in its "small palisado'd Fort" at Great Meadows, had fewer than three hundred men. When Captain Mackay refused to cooperate, the Virginians established two forward posts, one at Redstone Creek, which flowed into the Monongahela, the other thirteen miles from Great Meadows at the house of Captain Christopher Gist. Washington hauled guns and supplies to Gist's house and began negotiations with the Shawnees, Delawares, and Six Nations. He was assisted by the Half-King and Andrew Montour, friendly Indians, and George Croghan, a frontier trader. Washington had only meager presents and not much apparent strength. The Indians were shrewd at guessing the size of opposing forces and one by one they disappeared. Even the Half-King slipped back to Fort Necessity. A friendly Indian warned George that twelve hundred French and allied Indians were on their way to attack him.

Washington asked for the help of Mackay, who moved to Gist's house with his detachment. Their council of June 28 concluded that they should "decamp directly" to Fort Necessity. Once they arrived they worked rapidly at the small, hastily constructed fort, building defensive trenches, but the enemy allowed them little time. The French and Indians, nine hundred or so in number, swiftly moved south on June 26 from Fort Duquesne. Their commander, Coulon de Villiers, a brother of Jumonville, wanted particularly to punish Washington. By July 2 they were at Gist's settlement and next morning at Fort Necessity, which Coulon described as advantageously situated. Washington's 1786 summation from memory was brief and reasonably accurate:

> *About 9 Oclock on the 3d. of July the Enemy advanced with Scouts, and dismal Indian yells to our Intrenchment, but was opposed by so warm, spirited and constant a fire, that to force the works in that way was abandoned by them. [T]hey then, from every little rising tree, stump, Stone, and bush kept up a constant galling fire upon us; which was returned in the best manner we could till late in the Afternoon. [Then] fell the most tremendous rain that can be conceived, filled our trenches with Water, Wet not only the Ammunition in the Cartouche boxes and firelocks, but that which was in a small temporary Stockade in the middle of the Intrenchment called Fort Necessity... and left us nothing but a few (for all were not provided with them) Bayonets for defence. In this situation and __no__ prospect of bettering it, terms of capitulation were offered to us by the enemy which, with some alterations that were insisted upon were the more readily acceded to, as we had no Salt provisions, and but indifferently supplied with fish; which from the heat of the weather, would not keep; and because a full third of our numbers, Officers as well as privates were, by this time, killed or wounded. The next Morning we marched out with the Honours of War, but were soon plundered contrary to the Articles of capitulation of a great part of a our Baggage by the Savages.*

The main fighting took place between 11 A.M. and 8 P.M. when the French called to talk. Washington had with him only two French-speaking officers, the chevalier de Peyroney who had been wounded and Jacob van Braam, the Dutch-born officer whose French was limited. The French offered their terms which van Braam then had to translate into English. The fact that neither French nor English were van Braam's first language would later be a source of some confusion. After discussions and changes in the wet night, Mackay and Washington signed for the English and Coulon for the French.

The fight, the capitulation, and the surrender brought Washington into international controversy, and earned him severe criticism from some sources. The governor of Virginia said Washington was undoubtedly brave, but he should not have pushed towards the Redstone Creek without waiting for the additional troops and supplies that had been ordered. The governor of Maryland, Horatio Sharpe, made some tart comments. Sir William Johnson, a well-known Indian agent in New York, said Washington appeared to be too anxious for glory. Horace Walpole said he was a fanfaron. The loudest complaints came from France.

The articles of capitulation included a statement, twice repeated, that the killing of Jumonville, bearer of a diplomatic letter, was a murder. The French had outmaneuvered the translator who, according to Washington, rendered this as "loss" or "death." The French court published the capitulation, with an edited version of Washington's papers and diaries, and circulated them throughout Europe. They called their future ally "the cruel Washington," while a minor poet, Antoine Thomas, added an epic denunciation of the killing of Jumonville at "l'Oyo."

The British ambassador to Versailles, Lord Albemarle, was also titular governor of Virginia. (Titular governorships were an old British custom to give court favorites extra income. The real governor, in this case Dinwiddie, did all the work but bore the title of lieutenant governor and shared his salary with the ambassador.) Albemarle, after receiving the French protests, complained about Washington to Dinwiddie. The lieutenant governor defended him, saying that the translator had been incompetent and a poltroon, and had misled Washington.

The ambassador also wrote to the colonial secretary: "Washington and many such may have courage and resolution but they have no knowledge or experience in our profession; consequently there can be no dependence on them. Officers and good ones, must be sent to discipline the militia and to lead them... We may then (and not before) drive the French back to their settlements and encroach on them as they do at present upon us." Albemarle penned this in September. He died in December, a few months before the Braddock disaster.

Another controversy developed around Article VII in the capitulation, which provided that the prisoners taken in the "murder" of Jumonville would be returned. Van Braam and Robert Stobo were left with the French as hostages until this could be arranged.

When the treaty reached Dinwiddie, he declared that Washington had no authority to surrender French prisoners and refused their release. In consequence van Braam and Stobo spent several years in a Canadian prison. Stobo's exploits were legendary. While still a prisoner at Fort Duquesne, he drew a map of the fort with an estimate of its garrison and smuggled it to Virginia. These papers were found in Braddock's baggage and Stobo was sentenced to death in Quebec. He escaped instead with valuable information that he gave to Wolfe. He returned to Virginia in 1759 to a hero's welcome. Van Braam was released when the English took Quebec in 1760.

FRICTION WITH DINWIDDIE

Though criticism was widespread outside Virginia, his fellow countrymen regarded Washington as their greatest military hero. He had stood off nine hundred French and Indians with a third that number throughout a day's fighting until his ammunition had been lost in heavy rains. Virginians believed, incorrectly, that each side had lost a third in killed and wounded and that the numerical advantage in enemies struck was greatly on the side of the local regiment.

Virginians made their feelings about Colonel Washington abundantly clear in the ensuing months. The chevalier de Peyroney wrote from Williamsburg that there was praise for Washington "from every mouth," and all the burgesses united to vote additional funds for his regiment. Nevertheless a breach had developed between Dinwiddie and Washington that widened over the years. Washington never realized that Dinwiddie had secret dreams of military glory. The governor had asked London for a royal commission for himself but, to this time, none for the local colonel.

Washington reached Williamsburg about two weeks after the battle. Captain Mackay, who went with him, mentioned that he was not a very gay companion on the return journey. The remnants of Washington's troops gradually drifted into Alexandria. The governor and council gave a reward of one pistole to each man who had fought the French.

On July 20 Dinwiddie ordered Colonel James Innes to build a fort at Will's Creek large enough to hold six months' provisions, advising him that he ought to have sufficient troops, food, and ammunition before attempting to remount an offensive against the French. Some days later Dinwiddie abruptly changed his mind. He wrote Washington on August 1 that his "Forces should immediately start over the Allegheny mountains either to dispossess the French at Fort Duquesne or to build a new fort in the area." He ordered him to raise his regiment to its authorized strength of 300, to march immediately such troops as he had to Will's Creek, and to proceed from there "with despatch" to destroy the French corn supplies at Logstown, northwest of Duquesne. This strange order may be attributed to what Dinwiddie described as the "monstrous fatigues" he had undergone. Washington mulled over the letter for a week or more and then complained to his friend, William Fairfax. After quoting the governor in full, he said:

> Thus, Sir, you will see I am ordered, with the utmost dispatch, to repair to Will's Creek with the regiment; to do which, under the present circumstances, is as impracticable, as it is... to dispossess the French of their fort.

Consider, I pray you, Sir, under what unhappy circumstances the men at present are; and their numbers, compared with those of the enemy, are so inconsiderable, that we should be harassed and drove from place to place at their pleasure... Before our force can be collected, with proper stores of provisions, ammunition, working-tools, &c., it would bring on a season in which horses cannot travel over the mountains on account of snows, want of forage... high waters... Neither can men, unused to that life, live there, without some other defence from the weather than tents. This I know of my own knowledge, as I was out last winter... The cold was so intense that it was scarcely supportable.

I have orders to compleat my regiment, and not a 6d. is sent for that purpose. Can it be imagined, that subjects fit for this purpose, who have been so much... alarmed at our want of provisions, which was a main objection to enlisting before, will more readily engage now without money, than they did before with it?... [There are] great deficiencies of Men, Arms, Tents, Kettles, Screws (which was a fatal want before), Bayonets, Cartouche-Boxes, &c., &c.,... Scarcely a man has either shoes, stockings, or hat. These things the merchants will not credit them for; the country has made no provision; they have not money themselves... There is not a man that has a Blanket.

If we depend on Indian assistance, we must have a large quantity of proper Indian goods to reward their services... It is by this means alone, that the French command such an interest among them, and that we had so few. This, with the scarcity of Provisions, was proverbial; would induce them to ask, when they were to join us, if we meant to starve them as well as ourselves.

Washington also informed Captain Mackay of his orders, to which the captain whimsically, if bitterly, replied:

I was favour'd with yours of the 15 Inst. by Mr. Cowper which was the first I heard of the Sudden Resolves. [Y]our being So Well provided to enable you to Comply wt. your Instructions gives grate hope of the Success of the Interpraise what ever it is. Not doubting but that every other thing upon which an expedition of Such Importance depends Will be equely taken care of; Some days ago we had 12 head of Cattle but they went away and I Suppose after the example of the No. Carolina Regt. have gon home but this is not all our dependance for we have about 40 lb of Bacon and 3 Milk Cows one of which we have caught this day. So if we go Soon on this new Sceam there is no doubt of our being well supplyed there being Such large provision made for it.

So far as is known Washington did not express his displeasure directly to the governor. He did take up the affair with Innes, who said he was unable to countermand the orders to proceed to Will's Creek. Innes could settle the vexing problem of Washington's rank, since he held a king's commission as captain, which was senior to the other regular officers. He was thus in a position to keep the Virginia command independent of the others.

Dinwiddie's scheme collapsed following a dispute with the House of Burgesses. In older days the governor had been entitled to a fee for signing each land patent but this had gone into abeyance. After Dinwiddie reinstituted its collection, the house protested and sent an agent to England to argue the matter. When the governor asked for twenty thousand pounds for the colony's defense, the burgesses tacked onto the supply bill a clause paying the agent's expenses. The governor refused to sign and dissolved the house. He suggested to London that the British Parliament pass an act "to compel the subjects here to obedience to His Majesty's commands."

Thereafter Dinwiddie wrote Washington: "No doubt You have heard that our Assembly is prorogu'd without granting any Supplies; Under this unexpected disappointment, I fear we are not Numbers sufficient to attack the Fort taken from Us by the French." Instead he directed Washington to send Captain Lewis and forty or fifty men to protect the frontier from Indian raiding parties. With the rest of the regiment, Washington was ordered "to march to Will's Creek, to join the other forces in executing such Orders as I may see proper to direct... The late Disappointment from the Assembly has entirely defeated the Operations I had proposed."

COLONEL WASHINGTON RESIGNS

Shortly after Dinwiddie cancelled his orders, the House of Burgesses passed a resolution commending Washington, his officers, and men "for their late gallant and brave Behaviour in the Defence of their Country." Washington replied:

> *We, the Officers of the Virginia Regiment, are highly sensible of the particular Mark of Distinction, with which you have honoured Us... and can not help testifying our grateful Acknowledgements for your high <u>sense</u> of what We shall always esteem a Duty to our Country and the best of Kings.*

> *Favoured with your Regard, We shall zealously endeavor to deserve your Applause, and, by our future Actions, strive to convince the Worshipful House of Burgesses,*

how much We Esteem their Approbation; and, as it ought to be, Regard <u>it</u>, as the Voice of our Country.

Whether the underlining of "it" can be considered a slap at the royal governor cannot now be determined. It is of some significance in view of the dispute that had developed between Dinwiddie and both burgesses and troops. All the officers of the regiment except Muse and van Braam were individually mentioned in the resolution. Muse had retreated from the French fire and was considered a coward. Van Braam came under a cloud because of his interpretation from the French, which many thought treacherous. The assembly made amends years later when van Braam returned to the colony.

It is not entirely clear who was responsible for Washington's resignation from the Virginia Regiment. In October Governor Sharpe of Maryland received a king's commission and was given authority over the armed forces of the continent. This was understood to be temporary until a general officer could come out from England. Dinwiddie broke the regiment into companies and informed Washington that he was to have captain's rank until the question of royal commissions for Americans could be settled. Washington blamed Dinwiddie and the machinations of the regular officers stationed at Will's Creek for this demotion. In this he may have been wrong, for not long afterwards an order arrived, signed by George II, decreeing that all officers appointed by colonial governors were to rank below those having the king's commission. Even general officers, when joined to regular troops, if holding provincial commissions, were to have no recognized rank above that of captain. Colonel Washington resigned; he would not submit to officers whom he had previously commanded.

Governor Sharpe attempted to persuade Washington to continue. Although Washington wrote to Colonel William Fitzhugh, the governor's assistant, that his inclinations were "strongly bent to arms," he declined, adding:

You made mention in your letter of my continuing in the Service, and retaining my Colo's Commission. This idea has filled me with surprise; for if you think me capable of holding a commission that has neither rank nor emolument annexed to it, you must entertain a very contemptible opinion of my weakness... I must be reduced to a very low command, and subjected to that of many who have acted as my inferior Officers. In short, every Captain, bearing the King's Commission, every half-pay Officer, or other, appearing with such a commission, would rank before me... I shall have the consolation of knowing, that I have opened the way when the smallness of our numbers exposed us to the attack of a Superior Enemy; that I have hitherto stood the heat and brunt of the Day, and escaped untouched in time of

extreme danger; and that I have the Thanks of my Country, for the Services I have
rendered it.

Within a few months Washington's actions at Braddock's defeat would bring
him Virginia's unanimous recall to service.

SEVEN

THE BRADDOCK DEFEAT

1755

O N FEBRUARY 20, 1755, Edward Braddock, a Scot newly elevated
from colonel to major general in the foot guards, arrived in Virginia
as commander in chief of His Majesty's forces in America.
Dinwiddie wrote to the Scots-Irish governor of North Carolina to say that he
was "mighty glad" that Braddock had come.

Braddock had with him two regiments under Colonels Sir Peter Halkett
and Thomas Dunbar. His aides, Captains Roger Morris and Robert Orme, and
his military secretary, Captain William Shirley, son of the governor of
Massachusetts, were to become Washington's good friends when he joined
Braddock's staff. Two other officers, Horatio Gates and Thomas Gage, would
later play important roles during the revolution. A teamster grandson of a
baronet, Daniel Morgan, was to be an outstanding American guerrilla leader.

Braddock seems to have been selected for his reputation as a strict disciplinarian, an asset with British troops but less so with the more undisciplined
Americans. He was also a brusque no-nonsense man who could get things
done. But things did not get done so easily in America, and this evoked his
belligerence. He possessed a good deal of European military knowledge, an
innate kindness in dealing with his staff and an unshakable bravery and self-
confidence. He came to admire only two Americans, Washington and
Franklin, which indicates good judgment of men. Franklin's verdict that he

would have made "a good Officer in some European war" is perhaps the most just that has been made.

WASHINGTON RETURNS TO DUTY

After resigning his commission Washington returned to farming. His sister-in-law, the widow of Lawrence Washington, had a life tenancy of Mount Vernon but she had remarried and was living elsewhere. George rented the property from her in December 1754. It remained his permanent residence until his death.

Although retired, the twenty-two-year-old former soldier followed the news of British moves with intense interest. As soon as he heard of Braddock's arrival Washington sent him a note of congratulation. Three weeks after his twenty-third birthday, he received a polite reply from Captain Orme, Braddock's aide: "The General having been inform'd that you exprest some desire to make the Campaigne, but that you declin'd it upon the disagreableness that you thought might arise from the Regulation of Command, has order'd me to acquaint you that he will be very glad of your Company in his Family [on his staff] by which all Inconveniences of that kind will be obviated. I shall think myself very happy to form an acquaintance with a person so universally esteem'd." Farmer Washington replied enthusiastically:

Mount Vernon, March 15, 1755

Sir: I was not favoured with your agreeable letter, (of the 2d) till yesterday, acquainting me with the notice his Excellency is pleased to honour me with, by kindly desiring my Company in his Family. It's true, Sir, I have ever since I declined a command in this Service express'd an Inclination to serve the Ensuing Campaigne as a Volunteer; and this believe me Sir, is not a little encreased, since its likely to be conducted by a Gentleman of the General's great good Character...

I shall do myself the pleasure of waiting upon his Excellency, as soon as I hear of his arrival at Alexandria.

It appears that Washington first met Braddock at Alexandria late in March 1755, explaining that he was eager to serve but had to arrange for the management of his property. Braddock agreed that there was no pressing need for Washington to join him before he moved his troops to Will's Creek.

THE GOVERNORS' CONFERENCE

Under the leadership of Braddock, a conference was held at Alexandria in April consisting of Captain Augustus Keppel, his naval commander, and the governors of Virginia, Maryland, Pennsylvania, New York, and Massachusetts. This was an all-British conference to discuss strategic plans devised in London. The ablest man present was William Shirley of Massachusetts. English-born, he had lived for nearly a quarter of a century in America and got along well with the colonists and his legislature. Shirley's planning had earlier been responsible for a major British victory at Louisburg, using New England troops. Franklin said of him: "Tho Shirley was not a bred soldier, he was sensible and sagacious in himself, attentive to good Advice from others, capable of forming judicious Plans, quick and active in carrying them into Execution." Shirley had been designated a major general and second in command to Braddock.

The conference approved a four-pronged attack against the French. Braddock was to take Fort Duquesne and then proceed north to Niagara. Shirley and William Pepperell, the New England hero of Louisburg who had received a baronetcy and a royal commission as major general, were to proceed west to Niagara to meet Braddock. A third force was designated to proceed to Crown Point on Lake Champlain, while a fourth was assigned to retake Louisburg, which to the annoyance of New England had been returned by the British to the French. On April 23 Washington wrote from Mount Vernon to William Fairfax to tell him of the conference:

> *I have had the honour to be introduced to the Governors; and of being well receiv'd by them all, especially Mr. Shirley, whose character and appearance has perfectly charmed me, as I think every word and every action discovers the Gent'n. and great Politician. I heartily wish something of such unanimity amongst us, as appear'd to Reign between him and his Assembly.*

Washington's brother John agreed to take charge of his affairs while he was on Braddock's staff. The brothers visited his Bullskin plantation across the Blue Ridge, and George then proceeded to Frederick, Maryland, where he found Braddock in a frenzy. Braddock had dispatched one regiment through Maryland and the other through Virginia hoping to speed the troops on separate routes, but the Maryland road on which Braddock had come with the regiment sent through that state ended at Frederick. The troops had to backtrack across the Potomac to get to Winchester. Contractors failed to deliver supplies. Wagons, horses, and forage were scarce. The roads were dreadful, and the heat had turned un-English. Braddock began to curse the Americans, especially the assemblies of Pennsylvania, Maryland, and Virginia, which he felt were not cooperating with him on roads or supplies.

BENJAMIN FRANKLIN

Washington appears to have reached Frederick after Benjamin Franklin had left. Franklin was then an important member of the Pennsylvania Assembly as well as deputy postmaster general of the colonies. During the initial stages of trouble in the Ohio River region, Pennsylvania had contributed little in the way of money or provisions. This was partly a reflection of Quaker pacifism but more the result of friction between the Quaker-dominated Assembly and the proprietaries who, Franklin noted, refused with "incredible Meanness" to let "their vast Estates" be taxed. The Assembly in turn refused to pass defense bills unless the proprietaries were taxed, and a permanent deadlock ensued. Hearing of Braddock's low opinion of Pennsylvania, the Assembly sent Franklin, ostensibly in his capacity as deputy postmaster, to confer with him. In his autobiography, Franklin described this trip, on which his son accompanied him:

> We found the General at Frederick Town, waiting impatiently for the Return of those he had sent thro' the back Parts of Maryland and Virginia to collect Waggons. I staid with him several Days, Dined with him daily, and had full Opportunity of removing his prejudices, by the Information of what the Assembly had before his Arrival actually done and were still willing to do to facilitate his Operations. When I was about to depart, the Returns of Waggons to be obtained were brought in, by which it appeared that they amounted only to twenty-five, and not all of these were in serviceable Condition. The General and the Officers were surprised, declared the Expedition was then at an End, being impossible, and exclaimed against the Ministers for ignorantly sending them in a Country destitute of the Means of conveying their Stores, Baggage, &c., not less than 150 Waggons being necessary.

> I happened to say, I thought it was a pity they had not been landed in Pennsylvania, as in that Country almost every Farmer had his Waggon. The General eagerly laid hold of my Words, and said, "Then you, Sir, who are a Man of Interest there, can probably procure them for us; and I beg you will undertake it."

Franklin and Braddock settled on terms for horses and Conestoga wagons. Braddock provided eight hundred pounds as an advance. Franklin and his son went to York, Lancaster, and Cumberland and placed advertisements in the local gazettes, offering to hire on a per diem basis men, horses, and wagons. In offering the king's gold and silver Franklin added that Sir John St. Clair, "the Hussar," a word chosen to strike terror into the German farmers, was prepared to enter Pennsylvania to seize what he needed. Within two weeks Franklin had 150 wagons and 259 horses ready for Braddock. He had given his personal bond to the farmers guaranteeing them against losses. This action caused him much subsequent trouble. He also made cash advances from his own pocket, only part of which he ever recovered.

Braddock was overjoyed with Franklin's effectiveness and wrote to London to say that he had done his job "with great punctuality and Integrity, and [it] is almost the only Instance of Ability and Honesty I have known in these provinces." There were those who later complained that Franklin was too efficient and that Braddock's army should not have been burdened with so heavy a supply train. Franklin did not stop with wagons. The army also received 6,000 bushels of oats and corn for fodder. In addition, after hearing that the British officers lacked amenities, he got the Pennsylvania Assembly to provide food parcels for them consisting of tea, coffee, sugar, biscuits, condiments, chocolate, rice, raisins, cheeses, plus 40 hams, 400 pounds of butter, 40 gallons of rum, and nearly 500 bottles of old Madeira.

Franklin's autobiography, written years after the event, noted another conversation with Braddock:

> He [gave] me some Account of his intended Progress. "After taking Fort Duquesne," says he, "I am to proceed to Niagara; and, having taken that, to Frontenac, if the Season will allow time, and I suppose it will; for Duquesne can hardly detain me above three or four Days; and then I see nothing that can obstruct my March to Niagara."... I had conceived some Doubts and Fears of the Campaign. But I ventured only to say, "To be sure, Sir, if you arrive well before Duquesne, with these fine troops so well provided with Artillery, that Place, not yet compleatly fortified, and as we hear with no very strong garrison, can probably make but a short Resistance. The only Danger I apprehend of Obstruction to your March, is from Ambuscades of Indians, who, by constant practice, are dextrous in laying and executing them. And the slender Line, near four Miles long, which your Army must make, may expose it to be attacked by Surprize on its Flanks, and to be cut like a Thread into several Pieces, which, from their Distance, cannot come up to support each other."

> He smiled at my Ignorance, and replied, "These Savages may indeed be a formidable Enemy to your raw American Militia, but upon the King's regular and disciplined Troops, Sir, it is impossible they should make any Impression." I was

conscious of an Impropriety in my Disputing with a military Man in Matters of his Profession, and said no more.

In 1786, in a brief memoir, Washington indicated that he had said almost the same thing: "He... used every proper occasion... to impress the Genl. and the principal officers" with the need to take defensive measures suitable to the tactics the Canadian French, and their Indians would use against a column of British regulars on the "March through the Mountains and covered Country." But "so prepossessed were they in favr. of *regularity* and *discipline* and in such absolute contempt were *these people held*, that the admonition was suggested in vain."

THE NEW ADC

On May 10 Washington was "appointed Aid-de-Camp to His Excellency General Braddock." Washington, without a command, enjoyed himself. The serious, lengthy, and complaining letters he had written as colonel were replaced by lighthearted notes. He wrote his mother from camp: "I am very happy in the General's Family, and I am treated with a complaisant Freedom which is quite agreeable." His letter to Major Carlyle said that he had "infinite satisfaction" that Braddock had had to turn his troops back to Virginia from Maryland. Washington had apparently warned him that this would happen. He also informed Mrs. George Fairfax that he had found out why General Braddock regarded Mrs. Wardrop much more favorably than Mrs. Fairfax, for Mrs. Wardrop had sent him a present of cake and "potted woodcocks." He wrote his brother John that it was "quite the mode" to wear boots in the army. His wore out, and he asked for another pair. After telling about his trip, he said: "I shou'd be glad to hear you live in Harmony and good fellowship with the family at Belvoir, as it is in their power to be very serviceable upon many occasions to us, as young beginners. I would advise your visiting often... To that Family I am under many obligations, particularly to the old Gentleman [Colonel William Fairfax]." He then asked his brother to fish around "with indifference and unconcern" to see what George's prospects might be and how much support he would get from the leading citizens if he decided to run for the House of Burgesses from Fairfax. He had heard in Williamsburg that the county was to be divided and two new seats would soon be available.

THE ARMY MOVES FORWARD

Washington may have been the only cheerful person around the camp. William Shirley, Braddock's secretary, wrote gloomily to his friend, the governor of Pennsylvania:

> *We have a general most judiciously chosen for being disqualified for the service he is employed in, in almost every respect. He may be brave for aught I know, and he is honest in pecuniary matters. But as the King said of a neighboring governor of yours [Sharpe of Maryland] when proposed for the command of the American forces about a month ago & recommended as a very honest man though not remarkably able... "A little more ability & a little less honesty upon the present occasion might serve our turn better." It is a joke to suppose that secondary officers can make amends for the defects of the first... As to these I don't think we have much to boast. Some are insolent, others capable, but rather aiming at showing their abilities than making a proper use of them. I have a great love for my friend Orme. I think it uncommonly fortunate for our leader that he is under the influence of so honest and capable a man. But I wish for the sake of the Public that he had some more experience in business, particularly in America... You will think me out of humour. I own I am so. I am greatly disgusted at seeing our expedition (as it is called) so ill concerted originally in England & so ill appointed; so improperly conducted since in America.*

Washington, in a letter to Colonel Fairfax, described Braddock's state of mind: "The General, by frequent breaches of contracts, has lost all degree of patience... [I]nstead of blameing the individual as he ought... he... looks upon the Country... as void of both Honour and Honesty; we have frequent disputes on this head which are maintained with warmth on both sides, especially on his, who is incapable of Arguing with't; or giving up any point he asserts."

Washington thought the expedition had too many wagons and too few packhorses. He noted an increase in dysentery among the twenty-six hundred men of the army. As the expedition proceeded, June heat, chiggers, and flies added to the discomfort. Friendly Indians appeared but, covered as they were with greasepaint and smelling to heaven, they failed to cheer the English. They became drunk on the general's rum and did what the British described as horrible dances with barbarous yells. Nor were the English regulars' dispositions improved by the not-so-tall American tales of Indian atrocities; stray English soldiers were found scalped.

WASHINGTON'S ILLNESS

George missed most of the army's march. On June 14 he came down with an acute attack of what may have been tuberculosis. Two weeks later, still very weak, he wrote his brother John, explaining that he had been left behind to wait for the rear group under Colonel Dunbar.

The rear detachment had been formed in part because of Washington's own advice to Braddock. Alarmed that the column's three- to four-mile wagon train was an invitation to ambush, he urged Braddock to move ahead quickly with a strong force of men and the artillery but only the most necessary supplies. The train, adequately guarded, could then come on at its own pace. The plan was adopted, at least in theory, Braddock moving on with roughly half the men and fewer than "30 Carriages... and all of those strongly Horsed; which was a prospect that convey'd the most infinite delight to me tho' I was excessively ill at the time." Very soon, however, Washington became disenchanted with the British notion of a quick march. "[A]ll my sanguine hopes [were] brought very low when I found, that instead of pushing on with vigour, without regarding a little rough Road, they were halting to level every Mole Hill, and to erect Bridges over every Brook; by which means we were 4 Days gett'g 12 miles." In any event Washington was now too sick to travel at all and "was left by the Doct'r's Advice and the Genl's absolute orders" to follow later with the rear guard. Meanwhile the main column continued nervously having "had frequent Alarms, and several Men scalp'd."

In spite of his problems, the irascible general looked after his young aide like an old mother hen; on June 19 Roger Morris wrote to Washington to say that it was "the general's positive Commands to you are not to stir but by the advice of the person under whose care you are."

On June 30 Washington informed Orme that he was still with the rear of Colonel Dunbar's detachment, adding: "My Fevers are very moderate, and I hope are near a Crisis; when I shall have nothing to encounter but excessive weakness, and the difficulty in getting to you; which I wou'd not fail in doing ere you reach Duquesne, for £500."

THE BATTLE

On July 8, a wagon with Washington lying in it arrived at Braddock's camp. He was hardly strong enough to get up and ride but he did so the next day in time for the fight. He bore up thereafter for thirty or more sleepless hours of activity.

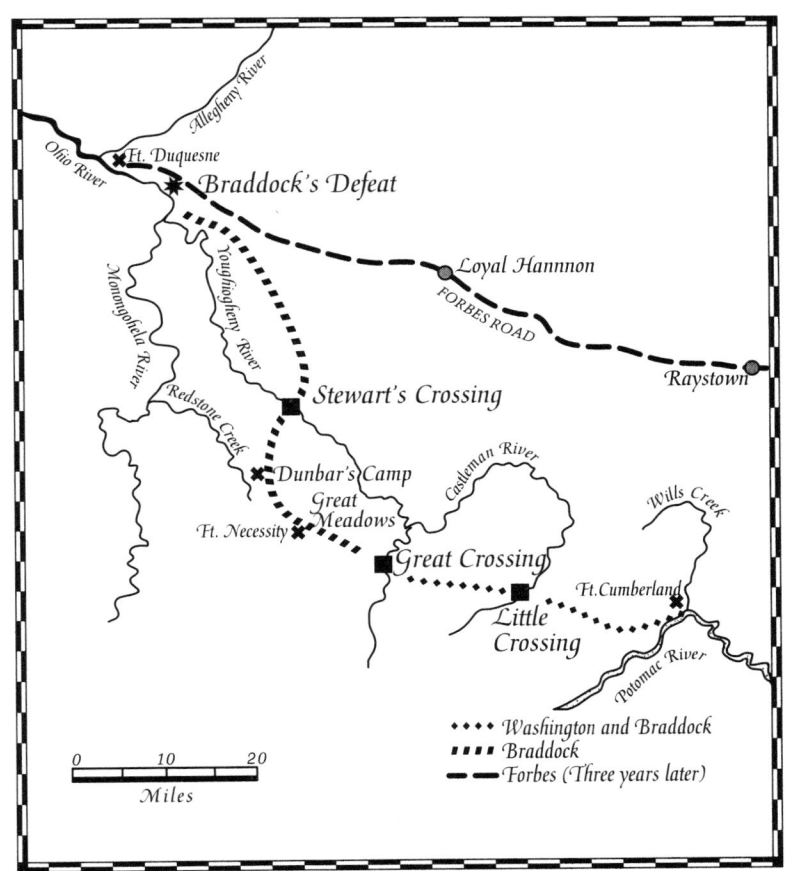

Braddock's Defeat, 1755

Approximately 1,400 British troops were assigned to the attack on Fort Duquesne. The total number at the fort is not exactly known but it may not have exceeded 400 French and Canadians, of whom perhaps 100 were untrained boys. In addition about 800 Indians (termed "savages" or "Americans" by the French) had gathered from many tribes to help their French brothers. Despite such odds, the audacity of a few French officers who knew the terrain was to win the day. The Sieur de Contrecoeur, who had taken the fort from the English, received daily reports of the advance. He knew that they were in sufficient force to take Duquesne by siege. The Indians were alarmed at their numbers, and for a while there was a serious question as to whether they would fight or run.

At the suggestion of young Captain Daniel Beaujeu, who had reached Duquesne with reinforcements, Contrecoeur decided to send out most of his troops and Indians to ambush and attack Braddock at one of the two crossings of the Monongahela. The Indians took a great deal of persuasion to join and it appears that Beaujeu told them he would have to fight without them. They agreed to go, but by the time they had held their war dances and prepared themselves emotionally, it was too late to cut off the British at the river itself. Beaujeu and his men therefore improvised.

The attacking party consisted of Captains Beaujeu, Dumas, and Ligneris, a few subalterns, slightly over 200 French and Canadians, and fewer than 650 Indians. The British plan of march called for two crossings of the Monongahela through shallow fords. Washington recalled in detail, more than thirty-three years later, the subsequent events as he saw them:

> About 10 Oclock... after the Van had crossed the Monongahela the <u>second time</u>... and the rear yet in the River, the front was attacked, and by the unusual Hallooing and whooping of the enemy, whom they could not see, were so disconcerted and confused, as soon to fall into irretrievable disorder. [A British officer later wrote: "The yell of the Indians is fresh on my ear, and the terrific sound will haunt me till the hour of my dissolution."] The rear was forced forward to support them but, seeing no enemy, and themselves falling every moment from the fire, a general panic took place among the [English] troops, from which no exertions of the Officers could recover them.

Gage's forward troops succeeded in killing the French commander, Beaujeu, and turning cannon on the French and Indians. Many Canadians fled and the Indians wavered, but Dumas, who took over the command, directed them to spread out on both flanks of the British. Numerous Indians took command of a hill above the main British forces where they could see but not be seen.

When some Virginians, under Captain Thomas Waggener, moved up the hill in Indian fashion, the British troops fired on them, bringing down many. Washington continued:

Before it was <u>too late</u>, and the confusion became general, an offer was made by George Washington to head the provincials, and engage the enemy in their own way, but the propriety of it was not seen, until it was too late for execution. After this, many attempts were made to dislodge the enemy from an eminence on the Right, but they all proved ineffectual, and fatal to the Officers who, by great exertions and good examples, endeavoured to accomplish it. In one of these the General received the Wound of which he died but, previous to it, had several horses killed and disabled under him. Captains Orme and Morris, his two Aids de Camp, having received wounds which rendered them unable to attend, George Washington remained the sole Aid throughout the Day. He also had one horse killed and two wounded under him. A ball [went] through his hat and several through his clothes, but [he] escaped unhurt. [Here Washington named various officers killed or wounded.] No person knowing, in the disordered State things were, nor who the surviving Senior Officer was, and the Troops by degrees going off in confusion, without a ray of hope of further opposition from those that remained, George Washington placed the General in a small covered cart, which carried some of his most essential equipage, and in the best order he could, with the best Troops... brought him over the <u>first</u> ford of the Monongahela. There they were formed in the best order circumstances would admit, on a piece of rising ground, after which, by the General's orders, he rode forward to halt those who had been earlier in the retreat. Accordingly, after crossing the Monongahela the <u>second time</u> and ascending the heights, he found Lieutenant Colonel Gage engaged in this business, to whom he delivered the General's order, and then returned to report the situation he found them in. When he was again requested by the General, whom he met coming on in his litter, with the first halted troops, to proceed (it then being after sundown) to the second division under the command of Colonel Dunbar, to make arrangements for covering the retreat, and forwarding on provisions and refreshments to the retreating and wounded Soldiery.

To accomplish this, for the second division was 40 odd miles in the rear, took up the whole night, and part of the next Morning, which from the weak state in which he was, and the fatigues and anxiety of the [previous] 24 hours, rendered him in a manner wholly unfit for the execution of the duty he was sent upon, when he arrived at Dunbar's camp. To the best of his power, however, he discharged it, and remained with the second division, till the other joined it. The shocking Scenes which presented themselves in this Nights March are not to be described. The dead, the dying, the groans, lamentation, and crys along the Road of the wounded for help... were enough to pierce a heart of admanant, the gloom and horror of which was not a little encreased by the impervious darkness occasioned by the close shade of thick woods which in places rendered it impossible for the two guides which attended to know when they were in, or out of the track but by groping on the ground with their hands.

The British killed and wounded 977 out of 1,469 troops present. French and Indian casualties were probably no more than 50. Fortunately, as Washington noted, the Indians did not follow or the remaining survivors would have been massacred. They had stopped to scalp the wounded and the dead (including eight women) and to gather all the loot they could before retiring in triumph to Duquesne. That night the French fort was a joyful place. The Indians burned twelve of their English prisoners at the stake, their dying screams mingling with the delighted yells of the Indians. The next day they abandoned the French, fearing the British would attack again.

Bad news traveled fast even in a wilderness. News of the defeat had reached Dunbar's camp before Washington's arrival. Colonel Innes at Will's Creek had a garbled version the following day, whereupon he sent out dispatches "To whom this may concern," a phrase that later provoked Washington's sarcasm. Dunbar's version reached Dinwiddie in Williamsburg on July 14. Shirley, the new British commander in chief, whose son was killed in the battle, learned of it in Albany on July 22.

Washington found Dunbar's camp in a state of panic. Though the rear camp was far from the enemy, many of the men fled when "To Arms" was beaten. Washington was too fatigued to do more than deliver Braddock's request for help. Braddock arrived in camp the next night after a terrible ordeal. Colonel Dunbar immediately ordered the destruction of all guns, most supplies, and the Pennsylvania farmers' wagons, to speed the retreat. The still-large army, seventeen hundred strong, marched off rapidly for Cumberland. Braddock died on July 13, his last words were: "We shall better know how to deal with them another time." Washington saw to his proper burial and had wagons driven over the grave, to obliterate it. Dunbar did not tarry long, even at Will's Creek, 100 miles from Duquesne. Not until he reached Philadelphia, some 350 miles by the route he took, did he set up a permanent encampment. There, as Franklin put it, he felt safe, knowing that the inhabitants would protect him.

The news of Braddock's defeat spread horror in Pennsylvania, Maryland, and Virginia. Not for some time did these colonies hear that Dunbar had abandoned the frontier upon which, as Parkman wrote, there will burst "a storm of blood and fire." The British army had provided a most convenient road across the mountains for the French and Indians.

EIGHT

MR. WASHINGTON IS
REAPPOINTED COLONEL

1755

WITHIN A WEEK the bulk of the surviving Virginia troops were in
Cumberland. After two days' rest, Washington sent Dinwiddie an
account of the proceedings at the Monongahela. Because the
French and Indians had kept so well hidden, Washington and the other par-
ticipants greatly underestimated the size of the opposing force:

*We were attacked (very unexpectedly I must own) by abt. 300 French and Ind'ns;
Our numbers consisted of abt. 1300 well arm'd Men, chiefly Regulars, who were
immediately struck with such a deadly Panick, that nothing but confusion and
disobedience of order's prevail'd amongst them: The Officers in gen'l behaved with
incomparable bravery, for which they greatly suffered, there being near 60 kill'd
and wound'd. A large proportion out of the number we had! The Virginian
Companies behav'd like Men and died like Soldiers; for I believe out of the 3
Companys that were there that day, scarce 30 were left alive; Captn. Peyrouny and
all his Officers, down to a Corporal, were kill'd; Captn. Polson shar'd almost as
hard a Fate, for only one of his Escap'd: In short, the dastardly behaviour of the
English Soldier's expos'd all those who were inclin'd to do their duty to almost
certain Death; and at length, in despight of every effort to the contrary, broke and
run as Sheep before the Hounds, leav'g the Artillery, Ammunition, Provisions, and
every individual thing we had with us a prey to the Enemy; and when we*

endeavour'd to rally them in hopes of regaining our invaluable loss, it was with as much success as if we had attempted to have stop'd the wild Bears of the Mountains... I luckily escap'd with't a wound tho' I had four Bullets through my Coat and two Horses shot under me. It is supposed we left 300 or more dead in the Field; about that number we brought off wounded; and it is imagin'd... that two thirds of both... received their shott from our own cowardly English Soldiers who gather'd themselves into a body contrary to orders 10 or 12 deep, wou'd then level, Fire and shoot down the men before them.

I tremble at the consequence this defeat may have upon our back settlers, who I suppose will all leave their habitations unless there are proper measures taken for their security.

Colo. Dunbar, who commands at present, intends so soon as his Men are recruited at this place, to continue his March to Phila. into Winter Quarters: so that there will be no Men left here unless it is the poor remains of the Virginia Troops.

Washington wrote a similar letter to his mother, adding that after the other aides were wounded, "I was the only person left to distribute the Genl's. Orders which I was scarcely able to do, as I was not half recovered from a violent illness... I am still in a weak and Feeble cond'n."

Captain Orme, severely wounded in the thigh, also sent letters to Governors Dinwiddie, Morris, and Shirley, which because of his weakness he dictated. In his letter to Morris of Pennsylvania, which was similar to the one to Dinwiddie, he said:

The Officers were absolutely sacrificed by their unparalleled good behaviour, advancing some times in bodies and sometimes separately hoping by such examples to engage the soldiers to follow them, but to no purpose. The General had five horses killed under him, and at last received a wound through his right arm into his lungs of which he died the 13th instant. Poor Shirley [William Jr., the governor's son] was shot through the head. Mr. Washington had two horses shot under him, and his clothes shot through in several places behaving the whole time with the greatest courage and resolution. Sir Peter Halkett was killed upon the Spot. Colonel Burton and Sir John St. Clair wounded.

In writing Governor Shirley, Orme said it had been his understanding that the continental command devolved on him, whereas Dunbar maintained that he had a status independent of Shirley. He noted that all the general's papers had been lost on the battlefield. These were to give the French the British plan of campaign against them.

DUNBAR MOVES DECISIVELY

Dinwiddie received Washington's and Orme's letters on July 24. They were his first official reports and necessarily a shock. He told Orme he had read his letter with tears in his eyes, and he offered him a room at the governor's house for his convalescence. In replying to Washington, Dinwiddie first congratulated him on his gallant behavior and then chided him for his remarks about Dunbar. "Surely you must mistake. Colonel Dunbar will not march to winterquarters in the middle of summer... No, he is a better officer, and I have a different opinion of him." Nonetheless, the governor was sufficiently perturbed to write to Dunbar, referring to British honor and to his "character as a brave officer." Dunbar replied that he was leaving the next day for Philadelphia. Dinwiddie called this "monstrous," a cry quickly echoed in Pennsylvania and Maryland. Dinwiddie complained that Dunbar was removing not only his own troops but the independent companies that had arrived long before Braddock.

At this point the difficulties of long-distance command became apparent. William Shirley was moving from Albany to Lake Ontario, to conduct the offensive that had been planned at Alexandria. Since he was in New York, that province pressed him for additional troops and he ordered Dunbar to proceed north. When urgent appeals rolled in from the colonies to the south, however, Shirley ordered Dunbar to return to the attack on Duquesne. But he left a loophole through which Dunbar would crawl. Shirley noted that if it were "absolutely impracticable" to do so, then Dunbar was to bring his troops to Albany. Since he had already decided this at Fort Cumberland, Dunbar ignored the order to return to Duquesne and stayed in Philadelphia for a month.

While there he and his officers gave a ball at the State House to celebrate the victory of American troops at Crown Point. He then moved north, but so slowly that Shirley complained that he arrived too late to do any good there either. He was eventually relieved of his command and sent to Gibraltar. He died a lieutenant general. John Shirley, William's son, whose brother William Jr. had been killed with Braddock and who was himself to die three months later in the campaign against Oswego, wrote to the governor of Pennsylvania: "Col. Dunbar's retreat is tho't by many here to be a greater Misfortune than the late Genl. Braddock's unhappy defeat. What Dishonour is thereby reflected on the British army."

THE INQUEST

William Shirley had earlier received instructions from London to make "Enquiry into the Causes and Circumstances of the late bad Behaviour of the King's Troops upon the Monongahela." When Dunbar reached Albany in October, Shirley ordered him and Gage to prepare a report. Their document was without value. In an understatement, Shirley said that it "doth not seem so distinct and clear as it might be." He himself, as a trained lawyer and a man with some military experience, interviewed the surviving officers. He also instructed an engineer, Patrick Mackellar, who had been at the battle, to draw maps of the terrain and the positions of the troops. These have been regarded as the most reliable documents of the engagement. Two major points were brought out by Shirley in his report dated November 5. The first concerned the destruction of the supplies that had been hastily ordered by Dunbar:

> As to the Consequences of the General's Defeat, after his Troops who were concerned in that Action, had join'd the Division, I find that _now_ the immediate Destruction of great Quantities of the Artillery Stores and Provisions is Condemned by some of the Field Officers. The Copy of an Order from the late General, signed by Capt. Dobson his fourth Aid de Camp hath been produced to me by Col. Dunbar in his own Justification, yet it seems difficult to say how that Order, which was given out from the General at a time, when the Colonel looked upon him, as he says, as a dying man, and consequently incapable of Command, came to be so readily complied with.

Shirley further commented on Braddock's defeat: "The Baron de Dieskau [a German-born French general captured at Lake George by American troops] in speaking of General Braddock's defeat, said that none of their Officers were in the least Surprized at it, as it was a Maxim with them never to Expose Regulars in the Woods, without a sufficient number of Indians and Irregulars for any Attack that might be Expected. The inclosed Extract of a Paper dated at Montreal July 25th will further shew, Sir, what use the French make of Irregulars, when join'd with Regulars in Marching through the Woods; Vizt. for Scouts, Ranging Parties and Outguards upon their Flanks to prevent Ambuscade or Surprize, which Services, the French call 'la petite Guerre.'" Less than ten percent of the forces at the Braddock defeat were French regulars.

WASHINGTON GOES TO MOUNT VERNON

On the day he wrote Dinwiddie, Washington informed his brother John: "As I have heard since my arriv'l at this place, a circumstantial acct. of my death and dying speech, I take this early opportunity of contradicting both... We have been scandalously beaten by a trifling body of men." From Mount Vernon on June 28 he dropped a note to Orme: "It is impossible to relate the difft. accts. that was given of our late unhappy Engagem't; but all tend'd greatly to the disadvantage of the poor deceas'd Gen'l., who is censured on all hands." To this Orme replied a month later from Philadelphia:

My dear George:

Your letter gave me infinite Pleasure as every Mark of your Friendship & Remembrance ever will do... The Part of your Letter mentioning the Reflections upon the General gives me much uneasiness tho' I feel a Contempt for the Detractors. I know the ignorant and rascally C D (Dunbar) is one promoter through Resentment and Malevolence, and the thick head Baronet [St. Clair] another intending to build his Character upon the Ruins of one much more amiable than his can be. For my Part I judge it a Duty to vindicate the Memory of a Man whom I greatly and deservedly esteemed... I am convinced the Affection he bore you as well as your Integrity and good Nature will make you assiduous in removing these abominable Prejudices... I am...

> *My dear George*
> *Yr. most affectionate friend*
> *Robert Orme.*

The salutation and conclusion are unusually warm for letters between military men and indicate the esteem Washington had won. Orme soon thereafter returned to England and resigned his commission.

CONGRATULATIONS

Despite the defeat, Washington received various letters of congratulation for his own behavior and that of the colonial troops. Joseph Ball, his uncle, who had lived in England for many years, commended Washington on his "Martial Spirit," and added: "We have heard of General Braddock's Defeat. Every body Blames his Rash Conduct. Every body Commends the Courage of the Virginia and Carolina Men: which is very Agreeable to me." Charles Lewis wrote of the "good Opinion the Governour Assembly &c. entertain of Yr. Conduct, I assure you Sir scarce anything else is talked of here," while Philip Ludwell said that he had told the governor that he ought to give a new command to Colonel Washington who "deserved everything his Country could do for him."

As magazines and newspapers arrived from England, to his embarrassment Washington found that they were sometimes too enthusiastic about the colonists. One account said that after the regulars fled, three hundred Virginians held off sixteen hundred French and Indians for three hours and then successfully brought Braddock off the field.

Still quite ill during his sojourn at Mount Vernon, Washington expressed bitterness about his military life and his treatment by Innes and Dinwiddie, blaming the latter for his demotion from colonel to captain. His August 2 letter to his brother Austin, a member of the House of Burgesses, summed up his feelings in a way that appears to have been intended for the legislature:

> *I am always ready and always willing, to do my Country any Service that I am capable of; but never upon the Terms I have done, having suffer'd much in my private fortune, besides impairing one of the best of Constitutions.*
>
> *I was employed to go a journey in the Winter (when I believe few or none wou'd have undertaken it) and what did I get by it? my expenses borne! I then was appointed with trifling Pay to conduct an handful of Men to the Ohio. What did I get by this? Why, after putting myself to a considerable expence in equipping and providing necessarys for the Campaigne I went out, was soundly beaten, lost them all—came in, and had my Commission taken from me or, in other words my Com'd reduced, under pretence of an Order from home. I then went out a volunteer with Genl. Braddock and lost all my Horses and many other things, but this being a voluntary act, I shou'd not have mentioned it, was it not to shew that I have been upon the losing order ever since I enter'd the Service, which is now near two year's; so that I think I can't be blam'd, shou'd I, if I leave my Family again, and end'vr. to do it upon such terms as to prevent my sufferg., (to gain by it, is the least of my expectation).*
>
> *You ask whether I think the forces can March this Fall. I must answer, I think it impossible, for them to do the French any damage (unless it be by starv'g) for want of a proper train of Artillery.*

On August 14 Washington wrote to Warner Lewis to say that if he were to accept any command he would have to have the final say on the selection of his officers. Appointments made without his advice and consent had brought him unnecessary trouble.

COMMANDER IN CHIEF AGAIN

Washington's mother quickly got word, four weeks after his worrisome letter from Cumberland, that he might be off again to fight the French and Indians. She wrote, asking him not to go, but he replied on August 14: "If the Command is press'd upon me by the genl. voice of the Country, and offer'd upon such terms as can't be objected against, it would reflect eternal dishonour upon me to refuse it and that, I am sure must, or ought, to give you greater cause of uneasiness." That same day Dinwiddie finished drafting his "Instructions for Colonel George Washington, Commander-in-Chief of the Virginia Regiment."

Washington arrived in Williamsburg on August 27 to discuss the matter with the governor and the Assembly. He knew exactly what he wanted and was tough enough, at twenty-three, to express his demands. He got almost everything he asked. The Assembly had voted forty thousand pounds for a regiment of one thousand men to be divided into sixteen companies. Dinwiddie had already appointed many of the company captains by the time Washington got to Williamsburg. He insisted that he nominate all field officers and that he be provided with an adjutant, an aide-de-camp, and proper batmen. He also demanded a good salary and allowances. The governor and the Assembly yielded all along the line. His pay was set at thirty shillings a day against his earlier 12/6, and he was given a table allowance of one hundred pounds a year. He also seems, then or possibly somewhat later, to have been given a commission of 2 percent on all the funds he handled for the regiment. Having won his points, Washington agreed to take the command and the governor gave him his commission about September 1. Washington quickly appointed Adam Stephen as lieutenant colonel and Andrew Lewis as major. Captain George Mercer became his aide.

Colonel Washington was again in command of His Majesty's principal force in defense of the Virginia frontiers. His was a slim enough command, with probably no more than two hundred men on active duty. He was now supposed to recruit eight hundred more troops, equip and train them, and erect defenses along an enormous border country open to Indian attacks at any point.

NINE

COMMAND TROUBLES

1755–1756

S HORTLY AFTERWARDS THE governor wrote to London in an attempt
to get Washington a royal commission. In his letter to Sir Thomas
Robinson, he said:

*I have granted commissions to raise sixteen companies, to augment our forces to one
thousand men, and have incorporated them into a regiment. The command thereof
is given to Colonel George Washington, who was one of General Braddock's aides-
de-camp, and I think a man of great merit and resolution. Our officers are greatly
disturbed for want of his Majesty's commissions, that, when they join the regulars
they may have some rank; and I am persuaded it would be of infinite service, if his
Majesty would graciously please to honour them with his commissions, the same as
General Shirley's and Sir William Pepperell's regiments; and I am convinced, if
General Braddock had survived, he would have recommended Mr. Washington to
the royal favour, which I beg your interest in recommending.*

Washington remained hopeful for some time that he would get his royal commission, particularly as the undeclared hostilities between Britain and France
were giving way to full-scale war. With his governor's commission only, he
quickly ran into trouble with a captain holding a British commission who
turned out to be more annoying than Captain Mackay.

DIFFICULTIES

Washington took over the new command with his usual seriousness, but the tasks facing him were more wearisome than those of 1754. Recruiting turned out to be the most troublesome problem of all. Every prospective soldier had heard in fullest detail of the Braddock defeat and of Indian atrocities; even the jobless preferred starvation to service on the frontier. A few unemployed were rounded up in Fredericksburg, but they caused so much commotion that they were jailed. Their friends broke in to release them. At the first Alexandria recruiting not a single man volunteered. Officers had to be sent into Maryland and Pennsylvania to look for recruits.

George's commissary, Charles Dick, decided he did not want to continue in a thankless post, complaining that he had not received his pay and had not even been reimbursed for supplies purchased from his own pocket. He informed Washington that he was being sued for having trusted the government. He added: "As this is the Case besides 50 things more too tedious to mention, I leave you to Judge what Man can bare such usage."

Officers were given strict and detailed orders by Washington, but, as he wrote to Dinwiddie, some of them paid not the least attention to them. He was soon writing to the governor to complain of a lack of "Tents, Kettles, Arms, Ammunition, Cartridge, Paper, &c."

On August 14 Washington had reported that he was still in a "weak and feeble condition." Once reappointed to command, however, he came to full and vigorous life. In September and early October he galloped some twelve hundred miles throughout Virginia and its frontiers, inspecting, advising, commanding, and exhorting. His route took him from Williamsburg to Fredericksburg, Alexandria, Winchester, Cumberland, back to Winchester, up the Shenandoah Valley to Augusta Court House (now Staunton), then across the Alleghenies to Fort Dinwiddie (five miles west of Warm Springs), and thence to the Greenbrier River in what is now West Virginia. He then retraced his route via Winchester and Alexandria to Williamsburg.

From Augusta westward, Washington got his first glimpse of what the Indian raids meant to settlers in the far areas of Virginia. The farms lay deserted and the corn was unharvested. A few weeks before his arrival the Indians had attacked a group of settlers at a fort on the Greenbrier River, killed a dozen of them, and captured two girls. They also burned a dozen farmhouses. Before he got back to Williamsburg he received an urgent dispatch from Adam Stephen, in command at Fort Cumberland. Stephen had been reporting increased Indian patrols and scouting expeditions around the fort. The situation had suddenly worsened. He wrote worriedly to Washington on October 4:

> *Matters are in the most deplorable Situation at Fort Cumberland—Our Communication with the Inhabitants is Cut off—By the best Judges of Indian affairs, it's thought there are at least 150 Indians about us—They divided into Small parties, have Cut off the Settlement of Paterson Creek, Potomack. Above Cresops, and the People on Town Ck about four miles below his house—They go about and Commit their Outrages at all hours of the Day and nothing is to be seen or heard of, but Desolation and murder heightened with all Barbarous Circumstances, and unheard of Instances of Cruelty. They Spare the lives of the Young Women, and Carry them away to gratify the Brutal passions of Lawless Savages. The Smoke of the Burning Plantations darken the day, and hide the neighboring mountains from our sight—*
>
> *Unless Relief is Sent to the Back inhabitants immediately None will Stay on this side Monocasy or Winchester—*
>
> *The Magazine is Secured, and a Watch Set about on the Fort—So many Alarms prevented the Work Going on with dispatch. I have reason to believe Capt Dagworthy will look upon himself as Commanding Officer after You have joined the troops... The Province he Serves has 30 effective men in the Service. I was attacked by the Indians on my way down, and lost a man. I saved my Bacon by retreating to the Fort.*
>
> *I was apprisd of the Indians design to Attack, and Sent to My Lord Fairfax for 200 militia—alarming the South Branch and all the Neighborhood... I heard my Lord was very Urgent, and assiduous in the Affair, but there is only a few sent up under Capt. Vorne—Had my directions been observed by Harry Vanmeter, or the Militia Come from Frederick, The Lives and Liberty of 100 people would have been saved.*

The Indians, according to Washington's reports, killed or captured some seventy settlers and burned a number of houses. Washington took prompt action with his tiny command and such additional militia as he could raise. He dispatched sixty officers and men from Fredericksburg to Cumberland, but as this was a two weeks' march, he decided to go himself to the latter post with the few recruits available in Alexandria and, on the way, pick up Shenandoah militia. He reported to speaker of the house John Robinson that he intended to "Repair to Winchester with all imaginable Dispatch, and full hopes of having it in my power to Repel those Barbarous and insolent Invaders, of our Country." From Winchester, on October 11, he sent Dinwiddie a graphic account of the panic produced by Indian raids and the compounding influence of rumors:

> *I rid post to this place, passing by Lord Fairfax's who was not at home, but here, where I arrived Yesterday about noon, and found everything in the greatest hurry and confusion, by the back Inhabitants flocking in, and those of the Town removing out, which I have prevented as far as it was in my power. I was desirous of proceeding immediately, at the head of some Militia, to put a stop to the Ravages of the Enemy; believing their Numbers to be few; but was told by Colo. Martin, who had attempted to raise the Militia for the same purpose, that it was impossible to get above 20 or 25 Men; they having absolutely refused to stir; choosing as they say to die, with their Wives and Familys... In all things I meet with the greatest opposition. No Orders are obey'd, but what a Party of Soldiers, or my own drawn Sword, Enforces; without this, a single Horse, for the most urgent occasion cannot be had: to such a pitch has the Insolence of these People arrived, by having every point hitherto submitted to them; however, I have given up none where his Majesty's Service requires the Contrary, and where my proceedings are justified by my Instructions; nor will I, unless they execute what they threaten, i.e., "to blow out my Brains."*

Washington complained to the governor about the lack of a proper military law, which made it impossible to take action against "the Indolence" of the officers and "the growing Insolence" of the enlisted men. He had again thought of resigning, since he could "never answer one expectation of the Assembly." He noted that legislation was also needed to provide fines and corporal punishment for civilians who harbored deserters. He reported one comic interlude:

> *Last night at 8 o'clock, arriv'd an express, just spent with fatigue and fear, reporting that a party of Indians were seen about the plantation of one Isaac Julian ab't 12 Miles off and that the Inhabitants were flying in the most promiscuous manner from their dwellings... This morning, before we could parade the Men, to March upon the last Alarm, arrived a Second Express, ten times more terrified than the former, with information that the Indians had got within four Miles of the Town, and were killing and destroying all before them; for that he had heard constant Firing, and the Shrieks of the unhappy Murder'd! Upon this, I immediately collected what Force I could which consisted*

of 22 Men, recruited from the Rangers, and 19 of the Militia and Marched therewith directly to the place where those horrid Murders were said to be committed. When we came there, whom shou'd we find occasioning all this disturbance but 3 drunken Soldiers of the Light-Horse, carousing, firing their Pistols, and uttering the most unheard-of Imprecations; Those we took and Marched Prisoners to Town, where we met the Men I sent out last Night, and learned that the party of Indians, discovered by Isaac Julian, proved to be a Mulatto and Negro, seen hunting of Cattle by his Son, who alarmed the Father, and the Father the Neighbourhood.

Washington reported that he was taking all available militia and rangers to Fort Cumberland, although he had received information that the Indians, who had been killing and harassing settlers in the area, had probably departed. He also informed the governor that Captain Waggener, who had brought recruits from Alexandria, could hardly pass over the Blue Ridge Mountains "for the Crowds of People, who were flying as if every moment were death... they firmly believing that Winchester was in Flames." In consequence he ordered public notices posted informing the people that no Indians had been seen for about ten days. He urged everyone to return home, especially as this was harvest time.

On the march to Cumberland the colonel saw unpleasant evidence of the Indian raids. One farmhouse had been burned and the owner killed. Neighbors had buried the body but wolves had dug it up and eaten it. Not far away they found the body of a woman who had been scalped, and nearby a dead boy and young man. On arriving at Cumberland, Washington took immediate steps to assist the settlers. Where farms were deserted, he ordered his troops to gather the crops for public use. He assigned armed guards to farmers who were afraid to work their fields. Burial and scouting parties were organized. He ordered Captain Christopher Gist to Harris's Ferry (Harrisburg) to raise Indian allies against the enemy and to recruit "Woods-men." Gist had been in Philadelphia and reported to Washington on October 15 the impression he had made. "Yr. Name Is More talked of in Pennsylvania than any Other person of the Army and everybody Seems willing to Venture under Your command and if you could Send Some descreet person doubt not but They will Inlist a good Nomber... The Assembly of Pennsylvania is now Sitting and for a fortnight. Mr. Franklin and Indeed Mr. Peters both Told me if you was to write a pressing letter to them informing them of the Damage and Murder and Desire their Assistance you would now get it Sooner than any one in America."

Captain Hog, stationed at the lonely outpost of Camp Dinwiddie, southwest of what is now Staunton, wrote that he had no salt, iron for axes, or nails, and winter had reached the valley. With the humor of the frontiersman, he described his experience with the local militia on October 13:

> *The Louisa Company under Capt. Fox marched out from Dickison's fort abt 10 days ago, with 4 of the Inhabitants of Green Briar and the first night after they got there one of the Country Men was killed and scalped, Supposed by the Indians. They continued 2 or 3 days there & returned complaining of Hunger and Hardships after devouring 2 beeffs & a sufficient quantity of potatoes this is all the good they have done... notwithstanding they were fired with Military Courage & greatly desirous of doing something Glorious for their King and Country, when Mr. John Todd preached to them a Military Sermon.*

Washington continued, burdened with details. He issued strict orders to control looting by his troops. He had to arrange for wagons, barrels, flour, pork, and beef and to meet the ever-present need for salt to preserve meat. He was concerned with cartridges, powder, and scarce paper for making cartridges. He stressed the need to be careful and sparing of supplies. He was watchful of such minor details as windows insufficiently secured on powder magazines.

The problem of cooking kettles involved even the governor. Captain Hog wrote to Washington: "I did not gett any kettles at Fredericksburg and the Men suffer prodigiously for want of them." Colonel Stephen appended a simple footnote to one of his reports: "Memoranda, We want Kettles much." Eventually the governor wrote Washington: "I hope by this You have more Camp Kettles &c. from N York which were forwarded from Hampton ten days ago."

The governor agreed fully with Washington as to the need for a military law and called a special Assembly for this purpose. He asked Washington to come to Williamsburg to present his views. Washington made it in seven days' hard riding. His proposals had been conveyed verbally to Colonel William Fairfax and by letter to the governor and speaker. The law, as passed, was inadequate from Washington's viewpoint but it did provide the death penalty for desertion, mutiny, and other military offenses. The governor had to approve all executions before they could be carried out. At Washington's request, Dinwiddie gave him signed blank warrants for his use.

WASHINGTON IN POLITICS

When Washington, as Braddock's aide, went to Williamsburg he picked up a rumor that Fairfax County was to be divided; this would mean two additional seats in the House of Burgesses. He immediately wrote to his brother to see what support he could get were he to run. When a seat unexpectedly became vacant in Frederick County on the frontier, Washington's friends entered his name at the last minute for the December election. He drew only forty votes in this first try for elective office. He was never defeated thereafter.

THE CASE OF CAPTAIN DAGWORTHY

In his October 4 letter to Washington, Adam Stephen hinted that Captain John Dagworthy would attempt to take command at Fort Cumberland. His prediction was correct and Dagworthy caused George much misery.

Dagworthy was an American-born officer who, for a brief period, had held the king's commission as captain. He was then put on half-pay, which he settled for a lump-sum payment. When Braddock came to America, Governor Sharpe of Maryland appointed Dagworthy head of a company that joined Braddock's forces. Dagworthy showed Braddock his old royal commission, which for some reason he had not been required to surrender. Braddock said that he would have to recognize him as a senior captain. This laid the groundwork for later trouble. When James Innes took leave as governor of Fort Cumberland, he handed the command to Lieutenant Colonel Adam Stephen of the Virginia Regiment. Around the beginning of October Dagworthy turned up at Cumberland with around thirty men of his Maryland company. He claimed the overall command as holder of the king's commission, though his orders came from Maryland's governor. Dagworthy was able to make his claim stick for a surprising length of time, in spite of the outrage expressed by Washington, Stephen, Dinwiddie, and the Virginia Assembly. Dagworthy went so far as to commandeer the provisions supplied the fort by Virginia and to say that none could be used without his express order. Washington, totally fearless in battle, quivered at the royal commission and refused thereafter to go near Fort Cumberland, leaving the burden of the dispute to Stephen.

The officers at Cumberland took sides; at least one Virginia officer refused to obey Stephen, asserting only Dagworthy could issue orders. Washington made urgent appeals to Dinwiddie, who wrote to Shirley, the British commander in chief. Shirley in turn asked Sharpe to settle the matter. Sharpe instructed Dagworthy that he was in command of the fort but not of the Virginia troops. But Dagworthy gave out only that part of Sharpe's letter that referred to the fort.

ORDERS AND COMPLAINTS

From the beginning of November until early February Washington sent a series of letters, orders, and memoranda to his officers and to the governor. These cover sixty pages of print. They were dated from Williamsburg, Fredericksburg, Mount Vernon, Alexandria, and Winchester but never from Cumberland. They included issues great and small. He wrote his paymaster to deduct sixpence each month from the pay of the drummers for their instruction and the repair of their drums. He informed him that the pay of any man who died was to continue for twenty-eight days in order to pay for his coffin. He begged the governor for copies of the military act. The governor replied that the printer had been so busy making paper money for the troops that he had not had time to print the bill but the governor would send copies when this was done.

Washington frequently chided delinquent officers. He informed Captain Hog: "The Governor complains of your laying in provisions for twenty months, instead of the twelve which I ordered; and takes notice of an extraordinary charge of ten pounds, for a Trough, which amazes me: the like sure was never heard of." To Captain John Ashby he wrote on December 28: "I am very much surprized to hear the great irregularities which were allowed of in your Camp... There are continual complaints to me of the misbehaviour of your Wife; who I am told sows sedition among the men, and is chief of every mutiny. If she is not immediately sent from the Camp, or I hear any more complaints of such irregular Behaviour upon my arrival there; I shall take care to drive her out myself, and suspend you."

Washington wrote to Stephen that the various officers he sent out for recruiting had returned after more than a month's absence. "Yesterday being the time appointed to Rendezvous here, came in ten Officers, with twenty recruits; which make up the number at this place, twenty-five. Great!" He ordered Stephen to see that officers chose proper men for new sergeants in their companies. "I think there are many more of the new ones that will grace the Officers better than the old dirty ones." He ordered his commanders to read the mutiny bill to the men and to inform them that if they deserted they would be hanged, even if they returned voluntarily.

Throughout the dispute with Dagworthy his desire for a king's commission preyed much on his mind. To Stephen he wrote:

> I shall wait [at Alexandria] a few days, in hopes of receiving the express from General Shirley, who the Governor sent to for commissions for the Field Officers... We have advices [these turned out to be mistaken] the King return'd to London from

Hanover on the 25th. of September, that War was Proclaim'd the 29th., and that we
have already taken 5 of their Men of War and 120 Sail of Merchant Men; a bold
stroke by jove; a glorious beginning... The Man of War mention'd in my last is not
yet arriv'd, tho' hourly expected; it is said... that she has commissions for us... I have
sanguine expectation's we shall soon receive them... The express that was sent to
Genl. Shirley returned without seeing him... The Governor is very strongly of
opinion that Captn. Dagworthy has no right to contend the Command... He is not
there by order of his Majesty... He can have no better pretention's than a visiting
half pay Officer who transiently passes thro' the Camp, to assume the Com'd. I wish
you would sound him out on this h'd, and hear how he will answer these things.

TO BOSTON

Washington thus passed the problem to his subordinate, who got nowhere
with Dagworthy. Washington then appealed to Dinwiddie for permission to
present his case (along with a letter from the governor and a memorial from
his officers) to Shirley in Boston. Dinwiddie, as annoyed as Washington,
approved the request and wrote a kindly letter on his behalf to Shirley. To this
point, except for his voyage to Barbados, numerous visits to Williamsburg, and
trips to Frederick and Annapolis, Washington had seen little but rough frontier country. Now, with Dinwiddie's leave, he was able to visit the north and its
three major towns.

Washington began the long ride in early February, accompanied by his
aide, Captain George Mercer; another favorite officer, Captain Robert
Stewart; as well as two batmen, John Alton and William Bishop. Mercer's
appointment had caused some Virginia talk about the twenty-three-year-old
colonel. Dinwiddie said he had never before heard of a man below general's
rank having an aide, while William Fairfax remarked that the Burgesses found
it extraordinary that he had not only an aide but a secretary.

Washington kept no diary of his trip but his expense accounts give clues to
his activities. In Philadelphia, America's largest town, he spent twenty-four
pounds at the tailors and hatters. He remained there for four or five days
before moving on to New York, carrying introductory letters to two prominent
men, Oliver De Lancey and Beverley Robinson, who were to uphold the
British cause in the revolution. He seems to have passed part of his time at the
house of Robinson, a son of Virginia's speaker. He noted in his accounts that
he took "ladies," presumably Mrs. Robinson and her sister, Mary Philipse, to
see "that elaborate and celebrated piece of mechanism, called the Microcosm,
or the World in Miniature," as the press called it. This had moving ships, birds,

coaches, and other objects. He also lost at cards, bought three horses, and properly tipped the servants.

Washington and his officers reached Boston about February 27. How often he saw Shirley is not known but the governor informed Sharpe that he had taken some days to make up his mind on the Dagworthy affair. While waiting, Washington played cards at the governor's house and again lost money. He bought a hat, gloves, and quantities of silver lace for the uniforms of himself and his Virginia officers, and paid a tailor's bill. On March 5 Shirley gave Washington the paper for which he had come so far:

> *Governor Dinwiddie at the Instance of Colonel Washington having referred to me concerning the right of Command, between him and Capt. Dagworthy, and desiring that I would determine it, I do thereupon give it as my Opinion that Capt. Dagworthy who now acts under a Commission from the Governor of the Province of Maryland, and where there are no regular Troops join'd, can only take Rank as Provincial Captain and of Course is under the Command of all Provincial Field Officers, and in case it shall happen, that Col. Washington and Capt. Dagworthy should join at Fort Cumberland. It is my Orders that Colonel Washington should take the Command.*

Instead of directly confronting Dagworthy as Dinwiddie had advised, Washington, with great expenditure of time and money, had won a minor victory but had gained no major objective. While in Boston he heard that Shirley had appointed Governor Sharpe of Maryland, whom George did not very much like, as commander of all the southern forces. Shirley wrote to Sharpe on February 23 outlining his campaign plans against the French. He proposed that the provinces of Pennsylvania, Maryland, Virginia, and South Carolina raise 7,300 men, keeping 4,000 for their own defenses and shipping 3,300 men north. He expressed the view that smashing the enemy at Niagara and Lake Ontario would stop supplies to the French and Indians in the Ohio Valley. Shirley concluded:

> *As it is necessary that an Officer of Rank in his Majesty's Army should be appointed to take upon him the Command of all the Forces rais'd in the Colonies of Pennsylvania, Maryland, and Virginia and South Carolina to be emply'd in the Expedition against Fort Duquesne, I have appointed you, Sir, to that Command, and now inclose your Commission.*

When Dagworthy heard of Sharpe's appointment, Stephen wrote Washington, "He is by with Hopes and Expectations, Exults for Joy at the Change, Struts like a Bull Frog." What Sharpe, Dagworthy, Dinwiddie, and Washington did not know was that Shirley's days of power were ending. He had many enemies in New York, including the De Lancey family and the Indian commissioner, Sir William Johnson. A month after Washington saw him, Shirley learned that he was to be relieved both as commander in chief and as governor of Massachusetts. In his place Lord Loudoun was appointed commanding general; he was also made titular governor of Virginia. Loudoun was to be one of the most blundering generals ever sent to America, and this meant more trouble for the British forces as well as for Colonel Washington.

Washington headed south for Williamsburg, returning somewhat more rapidly than he had ridden north. He reached the Virginia capital on March 30. He had hardly arrived before expresses came from the frontier to say that, with spring, strong Indian attacks had begun and he was urgently needed in the West. Three days later he was on his way back to his command.

TEN

FORT BUILDING

1756

WASHINGTON HAD BEEN annoyed by the appointment of Governor Sharpe as head of the southern military forces. He planned to resign his commission as soon as he got to Williamsburg. The news of renewed Indian attacks on the frontier made this impossible. Instead, he wrote to Sharpe and Shirley asking to be made second in command. Washington's letter, dispatched on April 4 to Sharpe, was forwarded by him to Shirley on April 14 with a generous endorsement: "As Mr. Washington is much esteemed in Virginia and really seems a gentleman of merit, I should be exceedingly glad to learn that Your Excellency is not averse to favoring his application and request."

By the time Sharpe's letter reached Shirley, the latter had learned that he was to be relieved as commanding general. He was informed that a Colonel Daniel Webb, just raised to major general, would be coming to assume temporary command until General James Abercromby or Lord Loudoun could arrive. If Abercromby came before Loudoun he was to take command from Webb until Loudoun's arrival. This was a confusing situation for Shirley, who was given no inkling of their proposed plans. In the meantime, Pennsylvania, Maryland, and Virginia had rejected his proposal that they assign troops to the northern campaign. They could barely raise enough men for their own defense, they said. Shirley wrote Sharpe that under the circumstances it seemed useless to consider an attack against Fort Duquesne. He added kind words about Washington:

> *In the mean time I beg you would be pleas'd to acquaint Col Washington, that the Appointment of him to the second Command in the propos'd Expedition upon the Ohio, will give me great satisfaction and pleasure; that I know no Provincial Officer upon this Continent, to whom I would so readily give it as to himself; that I shall do it, if there is nothing in the King's Orders, which I am in continual expectation of, that interferes with it; and that I will have the pleasure of answering his Letter immediately after my receiving them.*

The situation with respect to Dagworthy settled itself quite independently of Washington's trip to Boston. Colonel James Innes returned in April from North Carolina. He was reconfirmed by Sharpe as commander of the fort, which he then took from Dagworthy. Stephen reported to Washington that Innes did not thereafter interfere with the Virginia troops.

PANIC AT WINCHESTER

Washington returned to Winchester to find endless troubles. On April 7 he wrote separate letters to Dinwiddie and to Robinson:

> *I arrived here yesterday, and though not a little fatigued, and incessantly hurried by the afflicting news from the back inhabitants, who are hourly importuning me for assistance, which is not in my power to give... The people in general are greatly intimidated, and so apprehensive of danger, that I really believe the Blue Ridge Mountains will in time become the Frontiers of Virginia. If the <u>fears</u> of the people do not magnify <u>numbers</u>, those of the Enemy are not inconsiderable. They have made many ineffectual attempts upon several of our Forts; destroyed Cattle, burned Plantations; and this in defiance of our smaller parties, while they dextrously avoid the larger.*

> *Our Detachments, by what I can learn, have sought them diligently; but the cunning and vigilance of Indians in the woods are no more to be conceived, than they are to be equalled by our people. Indians are the only match for Indians; and without these, we shall ever fight upon unequal terms.*

> *I find it impossible to continue on to Fort Cumberland, until a body of men can be raised, in order to do which I have advised with Lord Fairfax, and other officers of*

the militia... in hopes that this expedient may meet with wished-for success. If it should, I shall, with such men as are ordered from Fort Cumberland to Join these, scour the woods and suspected places, in all the mountains, valleys, &c. on this part of our frontiers.

It seemed to be the sentiment of the House of Burgesses when I was down, that a chain of forts should be erected on our frontiers, for the defense of the people. This expedient, in my opinion, without an inconceivable number of men, will not answer their expectations.

Your Honour may in some measure penetrate into the daring designs of the French by their instructions, where orders are given to <u>burn</u>, if possible, our magazine at Conococheague, a place that is in the midst of a thickly settled country.

The people of this town are under dreadful apprehension of an attack, and all the roads between this and Fort Cumberland are much infested.

Washington's acute intellect enabled him in a day to take in all aspects of a bad situation throughout western Virginia. On April 16 he wrote again to Dinwiddie to say that all his hopes of raising men to scour the mountains had vanished. Only fifteen had shown up in response to orders. As the officers put it, their exhortations to the militia had failed. He therefore had to wait for reinforcements from Cumberland. Having heard that the Assembly had voted funds to raise two thousand men, he proposed that the size of companies be raised from fifty to eighty-seven enlisted men. This followed the British pattern and would be less expensive than the Virginia system. He pointed to the need for drafting men who would be under military laws, but Landon Carter, his friend and supporter, wrote back: "Should we talk of obliging men to serve the Country, you are sure to have a fellow mumble over the words Liberty & Property a thousand times."

HIS OFFICERS ACCUSED

The expresses ran almost continuously between Williamsburg and the valley that spring and summer. On the day that Washington sent his first gloomy reports back, the speaker and governor were preparing letters that were to cause Washington great anguish. The speaker referred to "complaints... of the Behaviour of some of the Officers of the Fort," while Dinwiddie said: "I hope the Affairs of the Regimt. are not in so bad a Condition as represented here. The

Assembly were greatly inflamed being told that the greatest Immoralities & Drunkenness have been much countenanced and proper Discipline neglected." Even his loyal old friend, William Fairfax, worried him: "It's talked of among the Burgesses that an Enquiry is intended relating to the Misbehaviour of some of your Officers." Speaker Robinson, after receiving Washington's letter on the desperate situation in the Winchester area, replied that he thought that it was partly caused by the bad conduct of the officers at Fort Cumberland.

While his friends and supporters were cutting at his morale, Washington received word that Indians had attacked Edward's Fort, only twenty miles from Winchester where Washington had but a small garrison. Three families were murdered by hostile Indians at Patterson Creek. When George assigned a force under Captain John Mercer to search Warm Springs Mountain for Indians, they halted at Edward's Fort, which suffered a further attack. Mercer, his ensign, and fifteen men were killed and scalped.

In the midst of all the alarums and excursions, at a time when Washington did not know whether Winchester would be the next objective, he sat down on April 18 and wrote the governor and speaker agonized letters concerning the charges from Williamsburg against the officers at Fort Cumberland. To Robinson he said:

> It gave me infinite concern to hear by several letters, that the Assembly are incensed against the Virginia Regiment; and think they have cause to accuse the officers of all inordinate vices; but more especially of drunkenness and profanity! How far any <u>one</u> individual may have subjected himself to such reflections, I will not pretend to determine, but this I am certain of; and can with the highest safety call my conscience, my God! and (what I suppose will still be a more demonstrable proof, at least in the eye of the World) the Orders and Instructions which I have given, to evince the purity of my own intentions and to shew on the one hand, that my incessant endeavours have been directed to discountenance Gaming, drinking, swearing, and other vices, with which all camps too much abound... I have been more explicit, Sir, on this head than I otherwise shou'd, because I find that my own character must of necessity be involved in the general censure, for which reason I can not help observing, that if the country think they have cause to condemn my conduct, and have a person in view that will act; that <u>he</u> may do. But who will endeavour to act more for her Interests than I have done? It will give me the greatest pleasure to resign a command which I solemnly declare I accepted against my will.
>
> For which reasons I shou'd ever be content in retirement, and reflect with no little pleasure, that no sordid views have influenced my conduct, nor have the hopes of

unlawful gains swerved me in any measure from the strictest dictates of Honour! I have diligently sought the public welfare; and have endeavoured to inculcate the same principles on all that are under me. These reflections will be a cordial to my mind so long as I am able to distinguish between Good and Evil.

Washington sent a copy of the governor's letter to Adam Stephen, who made a dignified reply and defense. The whole affair was a temporary tempest in a winecup but it had been mishandled in Williamsburg at a critical moment in the colony's history. The threat of resignation brought immediate and encouraging letters. Landon Carter said: "I find by your letter to Colo. Carter that you have suffered yourself to be affected with some reflections that at most were only hinted at, some few of the Officers who perhaps may have behaved like disorderly young men. When you can't but know that it can only be the want of more power in your Country to have added every honr. & reward that even Perfect Merit could have entitled itself to, how we are grievd. to hear Colo. George Washington hinting to his country he is willing to retire Sir Merit begets Envy... No Sir rather let Braddocks bed be your aim than anything that might discolour those Laurels that I promise my self are kept in store for you... A whole crowd of Females have ordered me to tender their best wishes for yr. success & I don't doubt but this night will in a great measure be dedicated to heaven for yr. protection."

Charles Carter wrote: "The House of Burgesses have the greatest expectations from your personal appearance on our Frontiers and are so far from imputing any mistakes or irregularities of the Officers to you that I am satisfied they would have resented it to your satisfaction if any person had... From my constant attendance in the House I can with great truth say I never heard your conduct questioned. Whenever you are mentioned tis with the greatest respect. I hope you will therefore arm your Self with patience." And William Fairfax, who had sent a note that disturbed George, wrote: "Your good Health and Fortune is the Toast at every Table, Among the Romans Such a general Acclamation and public Regard shown to any of their Chieftains were always esteemd a high Honour and gratefully accepted."

Dinwiddie did not apologize for his letter but replied: "I observe Colo. Stephen's Letters vindicating his Character, & I hope the Reports were without Foundation & [of] course malitious." There the matter rested and Washington continued attempting to defend the frontiers. Later in the year a gazette in Williamsburg published an attack on the Virginia Regiment using similar material, and this brought about the threatened resignation of the entire officers' corps.

MORE PANIC

In letters of April 22 and 24 Washington further described to Dinwiddie the conditions in and around Winchester:

This encloses several letters... Your Honour may see to what unhappy straits the distressed inhabitants, as well as I, am reduced. I am too little acquainted, Sir, with pathetic language, to attempt a description Of the people's distresses, though I have a generous soul, sensible of wrongs and swelling for redress, But what can I do? If bleeding, dying! would glut their insatiate revenge, I would be a willing offering to savage fury, and die by inches to save a people! I see their situation, know their danger, and participate in their sufferings, without having it in my power to give them further relief than uncertain promises, In short, I see inevitable destruction in so clear a light that, unless vigorous measures are taken by the Assembly, and speedy assistance sent from below, the poor inhabitants that are now in forts, must unavoidably fall, while the remainder of the country are flying before the barbarous foe.

(Two days later) Not an hour, nay scarcely a minute, passes, that does not produce fresh alarms and melancholy accounts... The inhabitants are removing daily, and in a short time will leave this country as desolate as Hampshire, where scarcely a family lives. Three families were murdered the night before last, at the distance of less than twelve miles from this place; and every day we have accounts of such cruelties and barbarities, as are shocking to human nature... No road is safe to travel.

I have just been informed that numbers about the neighborhood hold councils and cabals to very dishonourable purposes... They talk of capitulating and coming upon terms with the French and Indians, rather than lose their lives and fortunes through obstinacy.

Dinwiddie's letters show that he was as shocked by events as Washington was. Never during his term of office did he work harder to get help to the man on the front. On April 29 he sent an express to Washington to say: "Your letter of the 24th was delivered to me by Capt. Peachy, which Letter with his Information gives me great Pain and Uneasiness for the back Settlements, & your present distress'd Situation, I have and continue to do every Thing in my Power for Your relief. The Militia of ten Counties are ordered to march directly for Winchester, Small Arms, Powder, Shott &c. have been sent from this to Fredericksburg two Days ago... Commissary Walker is sent up to forward the Ammunition to You, to provide Provisions & any other necessary

Services... The Cherokees left this on Monday for Augusta Court House, & I send an Express to Major Lewis to hasten them to Winchester."

Further letters from Dinwiddie informed Washington that he was pushing a new military bill through the Assembly; he was sure that if Washington used army provisions for the relief of distressed civilians, he would receive full government approval; and he had obtained Assembly consent to build a fort at Winchester. He was sending more powder and small arms. "I have ordered everything in my Power that I cou'd conceive necessary for Your relief." He added that no less a person than the attorney general of the province planned to accompany "one hundred Gentlemen" who would gallop to his aid. Such action "will give great Spirits to our Common People." Washington's letters, however, make no reference to their having arrived.

Washington's appeals for militia help through the county lieutenants who attended his meetings were almost too effective. Dinwiddie too sent urgent orders and their efforts brought unexpected results when the militia poured in. On April 29, 86 men arrived and Washington was informed 100 more were nearing town. On May 2 he had 173, and more came each day. On May 8 he ordered a detachment of 200 men to halt outside the town, as Winchester was full and the militia had begun quarreling. On May 10 more than 200 officers and men arrived to which were added 262 the following day.

On May 17 expresses arrived reporting that the Indians were attacking three nearby forts. Though this was a false alarm the militia fled as fast as they had come. By morning Washington found that he had only a handful left. Sixty-four of 70 men from the Louisa company departed, 50 of the 58 in the Stafford company, and so it went down the line. Not only farmers panicked; Washington had the distressing task of telling the governor of the militia's retreat.

Fortunately about this time the Indians left as quickly as the militia. Washington informed the governor that they had returned to Duquesne: "The roads over the Allegany Mountains are as much beaten, as they were last year by General Braddock's army. From these and other circumstances we may judge their numbers were considerable. Whether they are gone for the season, or only to bring in a larger party, I am at a loss to determine."

Remembering the comments from Williamsburg on his troops, Washington issued orders that any soldier fighting or quarreling was to be given five hundred lashes. The penalty for being drunk was set at one hundred. Shortly afterward he decreed that the use of profane language should cost the offender twenty-five strokes. In addition he ordered a court-martial for a sergeant who had retreated at Edward's Fort. He was sentenced to death. Two deserters received the same sentence.

A new military law had passed authorizing a regiment of fifteen hundred men but it had defects. Men were to be drafted but could obtain exemption on payment of ten pounds. Many paid and, in consequence, Washington got the colony's dregs. Draftees were not to be sent out of the colony, which meant they could not serve at Cumberland, on the Maryland side of the Potomac. Finally, they were to be released on December 1 after relatively short service.

The law authorized the commander to build a series of small forts from Will's Creek southward to the North Carolina border. With few men and tools, Washington complained he was given inadequate instructions. He heard from Williamsburg that (since he had designed the fort at Winchester) they had left the decisions to him. With the valley grown temporarily more peaceful, he rode down to the capital for further discussions.

Washington had been kept somewhat posted on the expected arrival in America of three additional British generals, with reinforcing troops, and, it was hoped, the long-sought royal commissions for Americans. Colonel Gage, who had been in Braddock's command, wrote on May 10 that Shirley was in Albany, waiting for them. He added a description of his American soldiers: "The greatest Boasters and werst Soldiers on the Continent... I never Saw any in My Life So infamously bad as those that come from New England." This was a bit unkind, since Gage's English troops had panicked at Braddock's defeat, while New England troops at Beauséjour had won one of the only two British victories of 1755. Twenty years later, when Washington took command of the New England troops who held Gage in a tight net in Boston, his first impression of them, which soon vanished, was not much higher.

Dinwiddie had written to General Abercromby to try to obtain Washington's royal commission, even before the inevitable plea to do so came from the colonel: "Good Sir, give me leave to pray your interest with his Lordship in favour of Colonel George Washington, who, I will venture to say, is a very deserving gentleman, and has from the beginning commanded the forces of this dominion. General Braddock had so high an esteem for his merit, that he made him one of his aides-de-camp, and, if he had survived, I believe he would have provided handsomely for him in the regulars. He is a person much beloved here, and he has gone through many hardships in the service, and believe he can raise more men here, than any one present I know."

By the time Washington's later letter reached his desk, the governor could reply: "You need not have wrote me to recommend You to the Earl of Loudoun." The Virginia Assembly also petitioned the king for his royal favor to the officers of the Virginia Regiment. When Washington subsequently saw Dinwiddie in Williamsburg, he found him at the beginning of an illness that forced his retirement the following year. He had suffered paralytic disorders which, with the fatigue of his work, made him less and less capable of directing affairs.

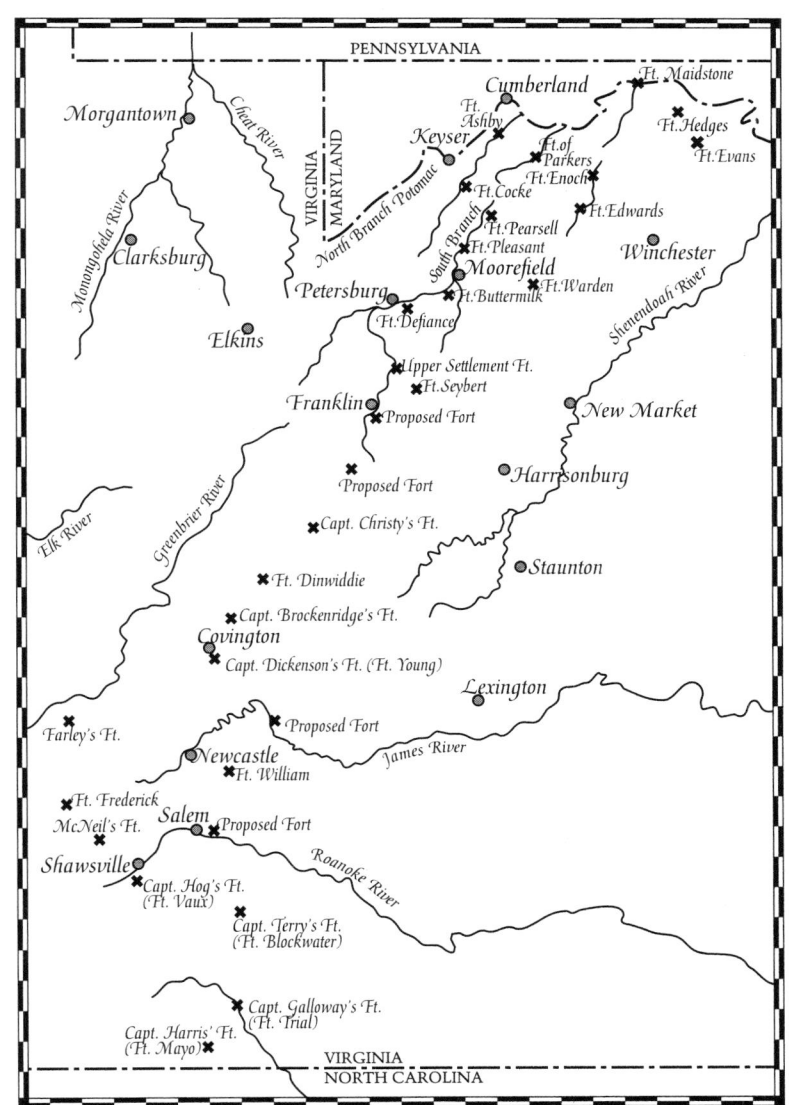

The Virginia Frontier, including Washington's Proposed Forts,
1756–1758

On his return to Winchester, Washington reappraised the situation for the governor's benefit. In May the Virginia Regiment had only 321 regulars. The draft law had added 246 men but some of these had deserted and others were unfit for service. With the scarcity of tools and the few men available, fort building was a slow process. Since each had not only to be built but garrisoned, he could erect only one at a time. It is probable that all the forts were personally designed by Washington. On July 21 he wrote to Captain Waggener: "I now enclose you the plans promised in my last; which if you observe, you can not possibly err. The one shows the Ground-Work of foundation of the Fort. The *other*, the Houses and conveniences therein; with such plain and easy directions for constructing these Buildings, that you can not mistake the design." By August 4 the colonel could report progress to the governor:

> *Giving the necessary orders and directions, about the chain of forts to be built on the frontiers, has kept me so closely employed, that I could not write fully to your Honour until this. But I have got that trouble now pretty well off my hands.*
>
> *By the enclosed council held at Fort Cumberland, you will see our determination... where it is necessary to erect the forts. Although we have not kept strictly to the act of Assembly, I hope it will be overlooked, as I am sensible this will be the best chain that can possibly be erected for the defense of the people, and that the Assembly aimed at that, but, being unacquainted with the situation of the country, had fallen into an error.*
>
> *I could wish we were clear of Fort Cumberland. It takes a great part of our small force to garrison it, and I see no service it is to our colony; for since the Indians have drove the inhabitants so low down, they do not hesitate to follow them as far as Conogochiege and this place. There have been several families murdered within two miles of the mouth of the Conogochiege, on the Maryland side, this week; and Fort Cumberland is now so much out of the way that they seldom hear of these things within a month after they are done.*

DECLARATION OF WAR

On May 17, 1756, London announced the long-expected war with France, pretending as the cause the French seizure two years previous of the forks of the Ohio. Washington asked the governor how to announce it to his troops. Dinwiddie replied: "The method, you are to declare war, is at the head of your companies, with three vollies of small arms for his Majesty's health and a successful war." In addressing his troops on August 15, after paraphrasing the pompous statements of the royal proclamation, Washington added: "Let us show our willing obedience to the best of kings, and, by a strict attachment to his royal commands, demonstrate the love and loyalty we bear to his sacred person." Twenty years later he wrote to Joseph Reed from Cambridge: "Do not neglect... to bring us the shirts, medicines, &c. from New York; they are much wanting here, and cannot be had, I should think, upon better terms than on a loan from the best of Kings, so anxiously disposed to promote the welfare of his American subjects."

ELEVEN

AFFAIRS AT
FORT CUMBERLAND

1756

TO BUILD CIRCULATION the *Virginia Gazette*, Williamsburg's only newspaper, engaged in a series of attacks on the government. They were written under the head of "The Virginia-Centinel." The tenth article, taking the Virginia Regiment apart, was published on September 3, 1756. It appeared just after Washington's August 29 appeal to Lord Fairfax for immediate help in saving "the most valuable and flourishing part of this country from immediate destruction." The *Gazette* said in part: "When raw Novices and Rakes, Spendthrifts and Bankrupts... are honoured with Commissions in the Army... and... give their Men an Example of all Manner of Debauchery, Vice and Idleness; when they lie sculking in Forts... instead of searching out the enemy... when nothing brave is so much as attempted... when Men whose Profession it is to endure hardships, and encounter Dangers, cautiously shun them, and suffer their Country to be ravaged... Censure cannot be silent nor can the Public receive much Advantage from a Regiment of such dastardly Debauchees. Their country calls; and see! the Heroes run / To save her—if the Game or Dance is done."

The entire officers' corps exploded and presented an ultimatum to Colonel Stephen, demanding "Publick Satisfaction" for such "groundless and barb'rous Aspersions." They said that otherwise they would hand in a mass resignation. They added that "The Printer wou'd never have dar'd to insert such a Paper" without the governor's approval.

The officers also drew up a petition to the Assembly, noting their long service and many battles and their endeavors to build new forts under difficult conditions. They pointed out that, unlike regular British troops, they never went into winter quarters. They also referred sarcastically to their "luxurious and dainty living," adding that the authors of the article were "malicious, wilfull and (as they fear to discover themselves) cowardly Lyars." They demanded that the Assembly give them a vote of thanks in order to wipe out the stain. Although his letters have been lost, it appears that Washington wrote to his brother Austin, as well as others, to see whether he ought to resign. His brother replied:

> *It is [the Speaker's] opinion, mine & all your friends you ought not to give up your commission, as your country never stood more in need of your assistance & we are all apprehensive if you give up Innes will succeed & then only consider how disagreeable it will be to the whole Colony (a few Scotchmen excepted) & I must believe as much so to you as any in particular... I hope Sir for the above reasons you will calmly consider of it & not at this time of imminent danger give up your commission in doing of which it will in some measure be giving up your Country... You will give a handel to that Scandalous Centinel. I am sensible you will be blamed more for that than every other action of yr. life.*

Having been persuaded to forget the matter by numerous letters from Williamsburg, Washington succeeded in calming the ruffled feelings of his officers.

VALLEY TOUR

The colonel repeatedly complained to the capital about the ineffectiveness of the fortifications he had been ordered to garrison. He disliked Cumberland because it was an ill-defended storage point that took 150 men from more active scenes of war. He decided that it was a waste to have small troop units in a long chain of posts in the Shenandoah Valley. He advocated combining them into three or four large forts, each with a garrison strong enough for ranging, scouting, and defensive and offensive action.

On hearing of new Indian action near Augusta, Washington set off on September 28 to examine his chain of posts. On this trip southward, he came within a few miles of the North Carolina border. He was almost ambushed near what is now Christiansburg by Indians who shortly afterward killed and scalped two men at the spot. His reports were full of gloom. He wrote Stephen on October 23: "Last night I returned from a very long and troublesome jaunt on the Frontiers, as far as Mayo; affairs seem to be in a dangerous situation: and to add to our misfortunes, I find our neighbourhood here on the wing; you and your Garrison in great distress and danger; the Enemy ravaging the country about Conogochieg, Stony-Run, and South Branch; loud and general complaints for protection; few or no men to send abroad for any Service. In short, so melancholy a scene, without the power of changing it to our satisfaction and interest, fills me with the greatest anxiety and uneasiness." Washington wrote to Speaker Robinson on November 9 pointing out weaknesses of the militia system:

1st. The bad order of the Militia and the insufficiency of defending the Inhabitants by them... The difficulty of collecting them in time of danger is so prejudicial, that the Enemy have every opportunity to plunder, kill, scalp and escape before they appear.

2nd. The Garrison I found weak for want of men; but more so thro' indolence and want of order. None I saw were in a posture of defence; and few that might not be surprized with the greatest ease. An instance whereof happened at Dickerson's fort; when the Indians ran down, caught several children playing under the Walls, and had got to the Fort gate before they were discovered. Thus Vass's fort was surprized and lost with the Garrison... Their diligence and resolution in pursuit are exemplified in Capt. Hunt... who was persuaded by Capt. McNeil, on seeing a poor man inhumanly massacred... to go in search of the Savages. They followed the tracks, and came to a run, thro' which they had just passed... Here the Captain stopped, and finding he came up fast with them, thought proper to desist.

From these and other circumstances too tedious to mention, it must appear a very natural conclusion, that the situation of the Frontiers is much to be pitied... The ruinous state of the frontiers, and the vast extent of land we have lost since this time twelvemonth, must appear incredible to those who are not eye-witnesses of the desolation. Upwards of fifty miles of a rich and (once) thick-settled country is now deserted and abandoned, from the Maryland to the Carolina lines.

THE EARL AND THE TROUBLED WATERS

To add to Washington's problems, the question of Fort Cumberland now arose to plague him further. His proposal to abandon the outpost, for which he advanced cogent reasons, was overruled by Lord Loudoun. This was only a tiny fraction of Loudoun's continent-wide bumbling, but it caused much misery to Virginia and to Washington. Washington had written on August 5 to John Robinson, the speaker, who was on the house committee for military affairs, to explain why he considered Cumberland a liability:

> I could heartily wish the governor and Committee would resolve me, whether Fort Cumberland is to be garrisoned with any of the Virginia forces or not. It lies in a most defenceless posture, and I do not care to be at expence in erecting _new_, or repairing the old works, until I am satisfied on this point.

> This place [Cumberland] at present contains all our provisions and valuable stores, and is not capable of an hour's defence, if the enemy were to bring only one single half-pounder against it; which they might do with great ease on horseback. Besides, it lies so remote _now_ from this, as well as the neighbouring inhabitants, and at the same time is not a whit more convenient than Cocke's Fort, on Patterson's Creek, to the enemy, which is twenty five miles nigher this way, that it requires as much force to keep the communication open to it, as a fort at the Meadows would do, and employs 150 men, who are a _dead_ charge to the country, as they can be of no other use than just to protect and guard the stores, which might as well be lodged at Cox's; indeed better, for these reasons—it would then be more contiguous to this, to the inhabitants, and to the enemy, if we should ever carry an expedition over the mountains, by opening a road the way the Indians have _blazed_. A strong garrison there would not only protect the stores, but also the few remaining inhabitants on the Branch, and at the same time waylay, and annoy the enemy as they pass and repass the mountains. Whereas, those at Fort Cumberland, lying out in a corner, quite remote from the inhabitants, to where the Indians always repair to do their murders, can have no intelligence of any thing that is doing, but remain in total ignorance of all transactions. When I was down, I applied to the Governor for his particular and positive directions in this affair. The following is an exact copy of his answer. "Fort Cumberland is a King's fort, and built chiefly at the charge of the colony, therefore properly under our direction, until a governor is appointed." Now whether I am to understand this ay or no, to the plain simple question asked, vizt. "Is the fort to be continued or removed?" I know not. But in all important matters I am directed in this ambiguous and uncertain way.

Robinson took up Washington's letter with his committee, which supported his case, but Dinwiddie overruled it. Washington said that Dinwiddie was unclear but the governor's letter was to the point. He had written: "As to Fort Cumberland, its a King's Fort & a Magazine for Stores, its not in my Power to order it to be deserted, & if we did it wou'd encourage the Enemy to be more audacious; when Lord Loudon comes here... he has full Powers to do what he thinks proper & a Representation to him will be regular, at present it must be properly supported with Men."

On Washington's repeated insistence, Dinwiddie reconsidered, writing on September 30 to say that he thought it would be "disagreeable... to me to give up any Place of strength, as it would raise the Spirits of the Enemy... but as You are on the Spot & You think it very prejudicial to the Service to keep that Fortress, I desire You may call a Council of Officers & consult whether the most adviseable to keep it or demolish it." He added that if the decision were made to abandon the fort the officers should be most explicit in their reasoning since Dinwiddie would report it to Loudoun. But before the council had time to meet, the governor received a letter from Loudoun: "[I] do hope & trust the Government of Virginia will not suffer the Post of Fort Cumberland to be wrested from them."

Washington did not participate in the war council of his Cumberland officers. After two days' deliberation their report questioned the use of the fort in its current state but proposed additional works and an increased garrison if it were to be maintained. The officers suggested that the three neighboring provinces contribute to its support. This was quite different from what Washington had in mind but he forwarded the decision to the governor with his own comments and recommendations on November 2. The governor placed them before his council. In doing so Dinwiddie noted that additional troops would be needed to fortify Cumberland properly and persuaded the council that this was what was really required. He then sent a peremptory command to Washington: "I hereby order You immediately to march one hundred Men to Fort Cumberland, from the forces you have at Winchester, & make the Place as strong as You can in Case of an Attack... These orders I expect you will give due obedience to."

Dinwiddie had been increasingly ill; this partly explains an approach to Washington quite different from his past treatment. For some reason, not clear now, he suspected Washington of ingratitude and snapped at phrases in his letters that he felt reflected upon his judgment.

The letter reached Washington in Alexandria about November 24. In response to his orders he hurried immediately to Winchester. There he found that, with all draftees scheduled to be released December 1, he had only eighty-one men to meet the governor's order and to protect both Winchester and Cumberland. The governor had mistaken the size of the garrison because he had included draftees in his count. Washington reported to Dinwiddie that the "late and unexpected order has caused the utmost terror and consternation in the people. The stores of every kind have all been brought from Fort Cumberland, save those indispensably necessary there, at a very great expense, and lie in the court-house and other public buildings... I am convinced, if your Honour were truly informed of the situation of this place, of its importance and danger, you would not think it prudent to leave such a quantity of valuable stores... In the next place... the works, which have been begun and continued with labor and hardship... [will be] in a manner totally abandoned." The governor, prodded by Lord Loudoun, now further intervened to make the situation more wretchedly complicated. He wrote Washington on December 10:

The Returns of Your Strength at Fort Loudoun surpriz'd me... I tho't You might have march'd 100 Men from thence for reinforcing Fort Cumberland, & left a sufficient Garrison at Fort Loudoun, but as Capt. Mercer's Information was wrong, I on receipt of Yr. Letter call'd the Council, not caring to act in an Affair of that Consequence without their Advice, Copy of the Minutes, of Council You have enclos'd; by which You may observe, that it's tho't absolutely necessary to reinforce Fort Cumberland; at same Time to leave a proper Garrison at Winchester; in order thereto it's further thought proper to call in the Forces from the Stockade Forts, to qualify You to march a proper Number of Men to Fort Cumberland, & to leave a proper Garrison at Fort Loudoun with Officers suitable, also to appoint a Person to command, who may continue the Finishing of the Fort.

I rec'd a letter from Ld. Loudoun, a Paragraph thereof in regard to Fort Cumberland is as follows. "As to the Affair of Fort Cumberland; I own it gives me great Uneasiness, & I am of the same opinion with You, that it was very material to have supported that Fort this Winter, & after that, we cou'd easily have made it a better Post than ever it has been, from what I hear of it; I cannot agree with Col. Washington in not drawing unto him, the Posts from the Stockade Forts, in order to defend that advanced one; & I shou'd imagine, much more of the Frontier will be expos'd, by retiring Your advanc'd Posts near Winchester, where I understand he is retired, for from Your Letter, I take it for granted, that he has before this executed his Plan, without waiting for any Advice; If he leaves any of the great Quantity of Stores behind, it will be very unfortunate; & he ought to consider, that it must lie at his own door—This Proceeding, I am afraid will have a bad Effect as to the Dominion; & will not have a good Appearance at Home [England]."

Washington quickly forwarded to Dinwiddie his comments on Loudoun's obtuse appraisal: "I have read over that paragraph in Lord Loudoun's letter... over and over again, but am unable to comprehend the meaning of it. What scheme it is, I was carrying into execution without awaiting advice, I am at a loss to know, unless it was building the chain of forts along our frontiers, which I not only took conformably to an act of Assembly, and by your own orders... If, under these circumstances, my 'conduct is responsible for the fate of Fort Cumberland,' it must be confessed, that I stand upon a tottering foundation indeed. I cannot charge my memory with either proposing, or intending, to draw the forts nearer to Winchester... Nothing gives me greater uneasiness and concern, than that his Lordship should have imbibed prejudices so unfavourable to my character."

The governor, doubly afraid of Loudoun, who was titular governor of Virginia and British commander in chief, had overreacted to Loudoun's thoughtless remarks. Sick and distracted, he tended to hide behind Loudoun and his council. He had forced the issue of Cumberland against the advice of his field commander. He then ordered a new garrison to Cumberland larger than the number of men at Winchester. To correct his initial mistakes he compounded them by requesting Washington to strip the forts in the Shenandoah Valley. As Dinwiddie became more foolish, Washington turned icily polite and more willing than ever to obey orders if he could decipher them:

> *I am at a little loss to understand the meaning of your Honour's orders, and the opinion of the Council, when I am directed to evacuate all the stockade forts, and at the same time to march only one hundred men to Fort Cumberland, and to continue the like number here to garrison Fort Loudoun. If the stockade forts are all abandoned, there will be more men than are required for these two purposes, and the communications between them, of near eighty miles, will be left without a soldier, unguarded and exposed. But I mean nothing more by asking the question, than to know your Honour's intentions, which I would willingly pay strict obedience to.*

Dinwiddie now ordered that any surplus men be retained for the frontier posts. This backing and filling by royally appointed officials, their disregard of Washington's advice, and the callous treatment of the Shenandoah Valley's inhabitants created much resentment in Williamsburg. Speaker John Robinson wrote Washington on December 31, 1756:

> *I am truly concerned at the uneasiness you are under in your present Situation, and the more so, as I am sensible You have too much reason for it. The Resolution of defending Fort Cumberland, and evacuating the other Forts was taken before I knew... any thing of the Matter... I took the Liberty to expostulate with many of the Council upon it, who gave me for Answer that Lord Loudoun had insisted that*

Fort Cumberland be preserved at all Events; and as we had so few troops, it could not be done without breaking up the small Forts... It was no Purpose to tell them that our Frontiers would thereby be intirely exposed to our Cruel and Savage Enemy, and that they could receive no protection from Fort Cumberland... in another province, and so remote from any of our inhabitants... They persisted in their Resolution without any other reason for it than it was in pursuance of Lord Loudoun's desire, it can't be any difficult matter to guess who was the Author and Promoter of this Advice and Resolution, or by whom my Lord Loudoun has been persuaded the Place is of such importance.

The affair of Fort Cumberland was not finally corrected until a meeting of royal governors in Philadelphia determined that Maryland should garrison the fort. It was nearly summer before that province provided the needed troops. Although Dinwiddie had given far more attention to the views of the British commander in chief than to those of Virginia, this did not prevent Loudoun from subsequently trying to have Dinwiddie removed from office.

TWELVE

FORT LOUDOUN

1757

WILLIAM PITT CAME to power in late 1757 but not until the following year was he able to recall Lord Loudoun from the
American command. Loudoun had lost a major battle at Oswego
in August 1756, shortly after taking over from Shirley. He subsequently
endeavored to place the blame for the disaster on his predecessor. He
scrapped Shirley's strategic plans, which were very similar to those that
would be adopted by Pitt and his generals. Loudoun concentrated, instead,
on taking Louisburg, far from the northern French fortresses at Niagara,
Oswego, and Ticonderoga, and farthest of all from Duquesne. Washington,
patiently hoping for a visit from the commander in chief, waited in vain.
Nonetheless, he kept to a simple faith that Loudoun had the power to save
Virginia. In January 1757, Washington drafted a letter to him which is ten
pages long in print. He reviewed the history of relations with the French
from the days of his expedition to Fort Le Boeuf down to the time of writing. It was Washington's finest state paper to date, dispassionate and without
rancor, although at times he was emotional about the sufferings of the
Virginia Regiment. The letter bears evidence of careful polishing and
redrafting, but he slipped in some soldier's slang in referring to his men
thinking they were "bubbled" (swindled) when they failed to receive their
pay. Washington described his troops thus:

However, under these disadvantageous restraints, I must beg leave to say, that the Regiment has not been inactive; on the contrary, it has performed a vast deal of work, and has been very alert in defending the people, which will appear by observing, that, notwithstanding we are more contiguous to the French and their Indian allies, and more exposed to their frequent incursions, than any of the neighbouring colonies, we have not lost half the inhabitants, which others have done, but considerable more soldiers in their defence. For in the course of this campaign, since March, I mean, (as we have had but one constant campaign, and continued scene of action, since we first entered the service), our troops have been engaged in upwards of twenty skirmishes, and we have had near an hundred men killed and wounded, from a small regiment dispersed over the country.

Washington said that the regiment had experienced "a dawn of hope" when it heard of Loudoun's appointment and of his high character. He enclosed a memorial from his officers, which, in calling Loudoun their noble patron, expressed "the deep sense We have of His Majesty's great WISDOM and paternal care for His Colonies, in sending your Lordship to their protection at this critical juncture."

Washington received a polite acknowledgement from Loudoun's aide, who said that the general "seems very much pleased with the Accounts you have given him." Since they were uniformly gloomy, this indicated that Loudoun had not bothered to read the letter. Nine months later, Washington wrote to the speaker of the House of Burgesses, suggesting means by which "we may be able to draw a little of Lord Loudoun's attention to the preservation of these colonies."

Washington, having heard that various colonial governors would meet with Loudoun in Philadelphia to discuss southern military affairs, asked Dinwiddie for permission to attend. The governor replied: "I cannot conceive what service you can be of in going there, as the plan concerted will in course be communicated to you and the other officers. However, as you seem so earnest to go, I now give you leave."

THE CONFERENCE

Washington arrived in Philadelphia around February 21, the day before his twenty-fifth birthday. He was accompanied by Captain Robert Stewart and by his servant, Thomas Bishop. Franklin's autobiography said that indecision and procrastination were Loudoun's most characteristic features. He quoted a messenger as telling him that the general was "like St. George on the Signs always on horseback, and never rides on." The governors of Maryland, Virginia, and North Carolina, to say nothing of Colonel Washington, consequently had a tedious wait until his excellency appeared on March 14.

Washington met Franklin briefly in Philadelphia and appears to have heard him speak in the Assembly. His expense account notes bottles of wine he shared with Governor Sharpe of Maryland. Washington also learned while there that his old notes and diaries (which had been captured by the French at Fort Necessity who then translated and published them in French) had been retranslated into English and were in process of publication. He subscribed to a copy.

Loudoun was quite secretive with the governors about his northern plans. He was in Philadelphia primarily to get as many troops as he could and he had little interest in southern problems. The governors were told that he had no plan for an attack on Duquesne in 1757, and they were urged to raise additional troops for defensive purposes. Because an assault by the French on South Carolina was feared, Loudoun persuaded Dinwiddie to send four hundred men from the small Virginia regiment to Charleston. In return he got Sharpe of Maryland to agree to take over Fort Cumberland.

Washington presented carefully drafted facts about Virginia to the conference but his work was largely wasted. He won a concession at Cumberland but lost a part of the Virginia troops needed for frontier defense. And he obtained no recognition from Loudoun for himself or for the officers of the Virginia Regiment.

During this period the Pennsylvania Assembly appointed Benjamin Franklin its agent in London. Shortly afterwards Loudoun ordered all shipping along the coast and outward to cease in order to maintain secrecy for his northern expedition. Franklin had to wait almost three months in New York and nearly ran out of money. His encounters with Loudoun, his endeavors to be reimbursed for his expenses in raising horses and wagons for Braddock, and his comments on the Louisburg expedition are recorded in his autobiography:

> *While I was... detained at New York, I received all the Accounts of the Provisions,*
> *&c., that I had furnished to Braddock... I presented them to Lord Loudoun,*
> *desiring to be paid the balance. He caused them to be examined by the proper Officer*
> *who, after comparing every Article with its Voucher, certified them to be right, and*
> *the Balance due, for which his Lordship promised to give me an Order on the*
> *Paymaster. This, however, was put off from time to time; and, tho' I called often for*
> *it by Appointment, I did not get it. At length, just before my Departure, he told me*
> *he had on better consideration concluded not to mix his Accounts with those of his*

Predecessors. "And you," said he, "when in England, have only to exhibit your Accounts at the Treasury, and you will be paid immediately."

I mentioned, but without Effect, a great and unexpected Expense I had been put to by being delayed so long at N. York, as a Reason for my desiring to be presently paid; and on observing, that it was not right I should be put to any further Trouble or Delay in obtaining the Money I had advanced, as I charged no Commission for my Service. "O, Sir," says he, "you must not think of persuading us that you are no Gainer. We understand better those Affairs, and know that every one concerned in supplying the Army finds means in the doing it to fill his own Pockets." I assured him that this was not my Case, and that I had not pocketed a Farthing; but he appeared clearly not to believe me... As to my balance I am not paid it to this Day.

At length the Fleet sailed, the General and all his Army on board, bound to Louisburg, with Intent to besiege and take that Fortress; all the Packet Boats in Company, ordered to attend the General's Ship ready to receive his Despatches when those should be ready. We were out 5 Days before we got a Letter with Leave to part... The other two Packets he still detained, carried them with him to Halifax, where he staid some time to exercise the Men in sham Attacks upon sham Forts, then altered his Mind as to besieging Louisburg, and returned to New York, with all his Troops, together with the two Packets above mentioned, and all their Passengers. During his Absence the French and savages had taken Fort George on the Frontier of that Province, and the Savages had massacred many of the Garrison after Capitulation... On the whole I wondered much how such a Man came to be Entrusted with so important a Business as the Conduct of a great Army... General Shirley, on whom the Command of the Army devolved upon the Death of Braddock, would in my opinion if continued in Place, have made a much better Campaign than that of Loudoun in 1757, which was frivolous, expensive, and disgraceful beyond Conception.

DINWIDDIE REBUKED

Virginia was the only province that deliberately ignored Lord Loudoun's embargo. The Virginia Assembly begged Dinwiddie for permission to export current crops of wheat and tobacco, some of which were already on ship-board, saying that the province's entire livelihood was at stake. The Assembly strongly hinted that they could not afford to pay taxes for defense unless this was done. With the advice and consent of his council, Dinwiddie ordered the embargo lifted. Lord Loudoun was so furious at this breach of orders that he endeavored to have Dinwiddie recalled by London. Eventually this storm blew over but it did not improve Dinwiddie's disposition.

BACK TO THE FRONTIER

In early April Washington was again on his weary frontier beat. He described it to his English tobacco agent, Richard Washington, in a letter dated April 15: "I have been posted then for twenty Months Past upon our cold and Barren Frontiers, to perform I think I may say impossibilitys that is, to protect from the cruel Incursions of a Crafty Savage Enemy a line of Inhabitants of more than 350 Miles in extent with a force inadequate to the task, by this means I am become in a manner an exile and Seldom inform'd of those oppertunitys which I might otherwise embrace, of corrisponding with my friends."

Virginia's commander now ran into more trouble with Fort Cumberland. Maryland's independent-minded Assembly declared that the British commander in chief had no right to give orders to the province's own troops. Lord Loudoun's cry of outrage was instantly seconded by Dinwiddie. Washington was caught in a bind when Virginia's governor ordered him on April 5 and 7 to detach two hundred men, under Colonel Stephen, and send them from Cumberland via Fredericksburg for further shipment to Charleston, South Carolina. The governor, more querulous than ever, was now always determined that all his commands be obeyed instantly. Maryland delayed sending in its forces, leaving Washington in a position of risking the fort or the governor's displeasure. Not long after the redoubtable Captain John Dagworthy took the Cumberland command, he alarmed the whole frontier with false reports that the French were coming in great force to attack his fort. Washington, back at Fort Loudoun in Winchester, was forced to send urgent letters to Dinwiddie, his forward posts, and the militia. He was disgusted once more at Dagworthy, when it turned out that Dagworthy had misunderstood what his Indians had reported.

Dinwiddie now issued orders whose effect was further to reduce the morale of the Virginia Regiment. It seems to have been his answer to a lengthy petition sent by the officers on April 16. They complained that they had been the longest in wartime service of any troops in the colonies, yet they had no regular status nor the perquisites of British officers. To emphasize this, they continued: "We can not conceive that because we are Americans, we shou'd therefor be deprived of the Benefits common to British subjects, nor that it shou'd lessen our claim to preferment. And we are certain, that no Body of regular Troops ever before served three bloody Campaigns, without royal notice." Complaining of "the great expence" of the officers to the colony, Dinwiddie ordered all but seven captains to be reduced to lieutenant's rank. He also cut Washington's allowances and the number of his servants. He directed Washington to have nothing further to do with Indian affairs, indicating he had appointed Edmund Atkin for this purpose.

On June 16 Washington reported to the governor that his regiment, exclusive of those who had gone to Charleston, consisted of 384 men stationed at nine forts distributed over 200 miles of territory. Since he estimated that the whole frontier was 350 miles in length, this meant slightly over one man to the mile. To add to his burdens, he had trouble with friendly as well as hostile Indians. Atkin was slow in arriving, and the allied Indians complained they were not getting their goods. The colonel informed the governor on May 24: "A party of Cherokees under Warhatchie is come in with 4 Scalps and 2 Prisoners: They are much dissatisfied that the presents are not here. Look upon Capt. Mercers going off [to South Carolina] as a trick to evade performance of the promise that has been made to them; will not believe that Mr. Atkin is coming; and in short, they are the most insolent, most avaricious, and most dissatisfied wretches that I have ever had to deal with. If any thing shou'd detain Mr. Atkins arrival, it will not be in my power to convince them that it is not a mere *hum* [humbug]."

After Atkin's arrival Washington said that the Indians seemed to be both more pleased and more displeased than ever. Washington had sent out scouting parties to search for the French and their Indian allies. One group killed two French officers and brought back another officer and an Indian as captives. This produced a quarrel between Atkin, who claimed the sole right to question Indians, and the officers of the Virginia Regiment. Both sides complained to Washington. Atkin said that the officers had dared to question the authority of "his Majesty's Agent & Superintendent of Indian Affairs," while they in turn said that they "imagin'd he had been better acquainted with the Rules of good Manners than to send such a Message to Gentlemen who from their Station in Life their Births & Education ought to be treated with Respect."

Washington intervened to soothe everyone and then questioned the prisoners in the company of the agent. Atkin, later suspecting some of the Cherokees, had them arrested and confined in prison. Their brethren immediately sent out messengers ordering a general Cherokee uprising, to free them. Washington again had to straighten out this situation.

Since Stanwix's Pennsylvania command extended to the southern British forces, Washington was technically under his orders. He asked Dinwiddie how he should act with respect to Stanwix. The governor replied that Washington was to obey Stanwix without regard to orders that might have originated with him. However, the governor continued to send instructions as though Stanwix did not exist. In one instance Washington asked both for urgent leave for some private affairs. Stanwix sent a polite reply saying that it was unnecessary to ask him as he knew that Washington would never take time off unless there were an emergency. Dinwiddie denied the request.

NEWS FROM CHARLESTON

During the summer Captain George Mercer, who had been Washington's aide, wrote from Charleston to tell him how the Virginia detachment fared. He praised the Swiss-born British commanding officer, Colonel Henry Bouquet, as "a good natured, sensible Man, very obliging to all under his Command." The following year Bouquet was transferred to Pennsylvania; Washington was to serve under him in the final campaign against Duquesne.

Mercer reported that the Virginians got along well with the regular British officers. They had expected to see a parcel of disorderly people "like the rest of the Provincials," but they found that the Virginians "made a good and soldierlike Appearance and performed in every particular as well as could be expected from any Troops." The English, having found Washington's officers to be gentlemen, became very friendly. They stopped calling them "provincials," referring to them instead as "the Detachment of the Virginia Regiment." Captain Mercer summed up Charleston:

> *I never... was so much disappointed. The Town Is little larger than Williamsburg no buildings in it to compare with our public ones. The town is on a point of land... There are some very good houses [there.] The rest of the Town is indifferently improved, many very bad low clapboard House upon their Principal Streets which are in general narrow & confined... I have not yet mentioned the fair Ones I wish I could call Them so, I assure you they are very far inferior to the Beauties of our own Country, & as much on the Reserve as in any Place I ever was, occasioned by the Multiplicity of Scandal which prevails here; for the chief of your Entertainment even in the best Houses & as the first Introduction is upon that agreeable Subject. Then you hear the Termagant & the Inconstant, the Prude & the Coquette the fine Gent & the fine Lady laid off in their most beautiful Colours.*

Mercer added that he was sure that Washington would hardly believe that Colonel Stephen, who had been so long at the frontier post of Cumberland, "never appears here but in full dressed laced Suits—so great a change has

Carolina produced." The Virginia detachment, having encountered no enemy, returned to Washington's command in time for the campaign of 1758 against Duquesne.

DINWIDDIE AND WASHINGTON QUARREL

The governor and his commander had worked together since late 1753, when Dinwiddie had appointed the young man as major. Now the governor was sick and testy, and Washington himself, during the latter part of the year, became desperately ill. Their final relationship ended on an unhappy note. Early in June the colonel wrote to the speaker of the house: "I am convinced it would give pleasure to the Governor to hear I am involved in trouble, however undeservedly, such are his dispositions towards me."

In July Dinwiddie complained of the slowness in building Fort Loudoun and of Washington's failure to transmit information he had received from Stanwix. On August 13, a sharp letter reached the colonel from Williamsburg. The governor said Washington was very loose in sending his accounts. He added that Washington had not mentioned the number of men sent to Augusta, nor did he acknowledge receipt of small arms, and he had failed to report trouble with the friendly Indians. "You must allow this is a loose way of Writing & it's Your Duty to be more particular to me." Washington replied on August 27:

I must beg leave, however, before I conclude, to observe, in justification of my own conduct, that it is with pleasure I receive reproof, when reproof is due, because no person can be readier to accuse me, than I am to acknowledge an error, when I am guilty of one; nor more desirous of atoning for a crime, when I am sensible of having committed it. But, on the other hand, it is with concern I remark that my best endeavours lose their reward, and that my conduct, although I have universally studied to make it as unexceptionable as I could, does not appear to you in a favourable light. Otherwise your Honour would not have accused me of <u>loose</u> behaviour and remissness of duty, in matters where, I believe, I have rather exceeded than fallen short of it. This, I think, is evidently the case in speaking of Indian affairs at all after being instructed not to have any concern with or "management of Indian affairs"... I really thought it unnecessary to say more than that "the detachment for Augusta was marched," because your Honour gave me a copy of the council held at Philadelphia, which directed one hundred and fifty men to be posted at Dickinson's, and one hundred at Vauses, which direction I observed, and thought it would be sufficiently understood when I wrote as above... I should have acknowledged the receipt of the arms had they come, but they were not arrived when

my last was wrote... However, if I have err'd in these points, I am sorry for it, and
shall endeavour for the future to be as particular and satisfactory, in my accounts
of these things, as possible.

The Indian agent, provided by Dinwiddie, had proved so ineffective that he turned many friendly Indians against the English. On September 17 twenty settlers were killed twelve miles from Fort Loudoun. Fifteen more were massacred a few days later. On September 24 Washington informed Dinwiddie that the inhabitants of the valley were "terrified beyond expression. Some have abandoned their plantations, and many are packing... Another irruption into the heart of this settlement will be fatal. The only method of effectually defending such a vast extent of mountains covered with thick woods, as our frontiers, against such an enemy, is by carrying the war into their country." On being denied leave to come to Williamsburg, the colonel wrote the governor on October 24 that he wanted to go to the capital to beg for help in his dire straits; the Virginia Assembly, Lord Loudoun, or Colonel Stanwix had to do something. If no farmers were left in the valley, there would be no food for the garrison.

On November 2 the governor wrote Washington: "I am much indisposed." It probably reached headquarters after the colonel's collapse with a dangerous illness. It was a recurrence of tuberculosis on top of severe dysentery with which he had suffered off and on, since August 1. The long relations between the two ended, with both men very sick.

THE RETURN TO MOUNT VERNON

On November 9 Captain Robert Stewart wrote to Dinwiddie from Fort Loudoun: "For upwards of three Months past Colo. Washington has labour'd under a Bloody Flux, about a week ago his Disorder greatly increas'd attended with bad Fevers the day before yesterday he was seiz'd with Stitches & violent Pleurtick Pains upon which the Doctor Bled him and yesterday he twice repeated the same operation... The Doctor has strongly recommended his immediately changing his air and going some place where he can be kept quiet (a thing impossible here) being the best chance that now remains for his Recovery, the Colo. objected to following this Advice before he could procure Yr. Hons. Liberty but the Doctor [Craik] gave him such reasons as convinc'd him it might be too late and he has at length with reluctance agreed to it; therefore has Directed me to acquaint Yr. Honr. (as he is not in condition to write himself) of his resolution of leaving this immediately."

Dinwiddie promptly replied to Stewart: "The violent Complaint Colo. Washington labors under gives me great Concern, it was unknown to me or he shou'd have had Leave of Absence sooner, & I am very glad he did not delay following the Doctor's advice, to try a Change of Air, I sincerely wish him a speedy Recovery."

Harboring a chronic disease, and worn down by fatigue, criticisms, and frustrations, Washington collapsed. For five months he was unable to resume his command.

THIRTEEN

BRIGADIER WASHINGTON REACHES DUQUESNE

1758

G EORGE WASHINGTON HAD moved into his brother's tubercular household when he was about sixteen. His first severe illness occurred the following year. His next bout with the disease appears to have taken place not long after his twentieth birthday. He was again ill for several months when he was twenty-three. Midsummer of 1757 was the beginning of the longest serious illness of Washington's life. Even near the end of his bitter fight, he missed death by the narrowest margin. When he realized that he was finally free of the disease, perhaps in late 1762, he was a changed man whose goal was no longer glory but the happiness of living.

When Washington returned to Mount Vernon he received as good medical advice as could be given even in a much later age. James Craik, though he had followed the barbarous practice of bleeding a very sick man, wrote to him at Mount Vernon to say that God was the best of all physicians. Nothing would be more conducive to his recovery than complete rest and quiet and turning his mind from all public business. At home he was under the care of a remarkable man, Charles Green, a physician who had taken Holy Orders and was also his rector. Green confined Washington to strict rest, told him to avoid meats, and assigned a bland diet of jellies, tea, and wine mixed with gum arabic.

Washington's brother John and his wife, who were taking care of Mount Vernon, were away when he returned. He therefore appealed to Mrs. George

Fairfax, his neighbor, for help. William Fairfax, who so long supported Washington, had died two months previously. George Fairfax was in England to settle his father's estate and perhaps to look into other matters, for he was now in line for the family title, after Lord Fairfax's aging brother.

Shortly after Christmas Washington had sufficiently recovered to write a few letters to his London merchants. He soon indicated that he wanted to return to his post. He may have been influenced by a report he received of a Christmas night brawl that his regiment had started at Winchester. The details are obscure, but from a January 30 letter to Washington by John Baylis, a militia major, it appears that Washington's soldiers beat up a man they thought was Baylis, and Lord Fairfax was threatened with mayhem, with the result that numerous soldiers were jailed. At least one duel was subsequently offered. The news that he was struggling to return to his post reached his neighbor George Mason, who chided him on January 4: "I hope You will comply with the Opinion & Advice of all Your Friends, & not risque a Journey to Winchester till a more favourable Season of the Year, or a better State of Health, will permit You to do it with Safety; & give Me Leave Sir to mention another Consideration, which I am sure will have Weight with You—in attempting to attend the Duty of Your Post at a Season of the Year when there is no Room to expect an Alarm, or anything extraordinary to require Your Presence, You will, in all probability, bring on a Relapse, & render Yourself incapable of Serving the Public at a time when there may be the utmost Occasion; & there is nothing more certain than that a Gentlemen in Your Station owes the Care of his Health & Life not only to Himself & his Friends, but to his Country."

Around February 11 Washington made an attempt to travel to Williamsburg to talk to John Blair, acting governor after Dinwiddie's departure, but he had such severe pains and fevers that he returned to Mount Vernon and to bed. It was almost three weeks before he could go south again. In March he was at the capital, combining business with a fast and successful courtship.

MRS. CUSTIS

Washington was 27 in February. He knew that his condition was so critical that if he resumed service at all, it could be for only a short period. It was better for him, therefore, to have a wife who could help restore his health. With her he could go back to farming, adding public service on the side.

He unerringly picked the right woman, though reliable details as to how he did it are lacking. She was a widow, a few months older than he, with two small children. From all the later descriptions of Martha Dandridge Custis it is possible to surmise why she accepted the colonel. She spoke of herself as "a fine, healthy girl... cheerful as a cricket and busy as a bee." Others said of Martha that "her soul overflows with kindness." She was never happier than when she could nurse sick people, children, servants, and soldiers to health. Sometime that March, five-foot-high Martha agreed to take the towering colonel as her husband. A year later he wrote of the happiness he had with the "agreeable Partner" who was finally to restore him to health.

BACK TO BATTLE

On March 4 Washington resumed correspondence about the war with France. Lord Loudoun had forwarded to Colonel Stanwix the proposal of a Major John Smith to take Detroit. Stanwix sent the letter to Washington for comment. He replied:

> *You condescend to ask my opinion of Major Smith. Pray, does not his plan sufficiently indicate the man? Can there be a better index to his abilities, than his scheme for reducing the enemy on the Ohio? and his expeditious march of a thousand men to Detroit? Surely, he intended to provide them with wings to facilitate their passage over so mountainous and extensive a country, or what way else could he accompany it in?*

> *I have not had the pleasure of seeing Major Smith, though I have been favoured with a letter from him, in which he politely professes some concern at hearing of my indisposition, as it prevented him from seeing me at Winchester; but desires, at the same time that I will <u>attend him at his house</u> in Augusta, about two hundred miles hence! or in Williamsburg by the 20th instant, when, I suppose he intends to honour me with his <u>orders</u>.*

> *I have never been able to return to my command, since I wrote to you last, my disorder at times returning obstinately upon me, in spite of the efforts of all the sons of Aesculapius. At certain periods I have been reduced to great extremity.*

> *I am now under a strict regimen, and shall set out tomorrow for Williamsburg to receive the advice of the best physicians there. My constitution is certainly greatly impaired, and as nothing can retrieve it, but the greatest care and the most circumspect conduct, as I now have no prospect left of preferment in the military*

way, and as I despair of rendering that immediate service, which my country may require from the person commanding their troops, I have some thoughts of quitting my command, and retiring from all public business, leaving my post to be filled by some other person more capable of the task, and who may, perhaps, have his endeavours crowned with more success than mine have been. Wherever I go, or whatever becomes of me, I shall always possess the sincerest and most affectionate regard for you.

Colonel Stanwix, throughout their association, always treated Washington with great consideration and politeness, which Washington warmly recipro-cated. While in Williamsburg the colonel learned of new developments in the French war. Pitt had recalled Loudoun and assigned Jeffrey Amherst to take Louisburg. The brilliant Lord Howe was ordered to smash Ticonderoga while an unknown Scot, John Forbes, was selected to capture Fort Duquesne. Pitt promised the Americans that the British would provide arms, ammunition, and equipment, and the colonies need only raise and pay their soldiers. He removed a great American grievance in which colonial field officers, when with regular British troops, were reduced to captain's rank. They were now permitted to retain their rank through colonel. Pitt appealed with generosity to Americans who responded with enthusiasm.

Virginia, like England, sprang into fresh life. On April 7 the colony voted to increase its forces to two thousand men, to add three ranger companies and a second regiment, and to call up additional militia for local defense. The colony agreed to send the regiments wherever they were needed. Colonel William Byrd III was appointed to command the second regiment. On April 5, two days before the act passed the Assembly, Colonel Washington was back at Fort Loudoun.

John Forbes, just created brigadier general, took over his command in Philadelphia in March. It consisted of Scots Highlanders on their way from Britain, the Royal Americans, and provincial regiments from Pennsylvania, Maryland, Virginia, and North Carolina. To these were added the detachment of the Virginia Regiment that had been in South Carolina.

Washington at once began his usual maneuvers to assure his becoming an important figure in the campaign. He wrote to Stanwix, just promoted to brigadier, on April 10:

Permit me, at the same time I congratulate you... upon the promotion you have met with and justly merited, to express my concern at the prospect of parting with you. I can truly say, it is a matter of no small regret to me! and that I should have thought myself happy in serving this campaign under your immediate command...

I... Beg that you will add one more kindness, and that is, to mention me in favorable terms to General Forbes... not as a person who would depend upon him for further recommendation to military preferment, for I have long conquered all such expectancies... but as a person who would be gladly distinguished in some measure from the <u>common run</u> of provincial officers, as I understand there will be a motley herd of us.

Washington also requested Colonel Thomas Gage, with whom he had served in the Braddock campaign, to put in a good word for him with the southern commander in chief. All this showed the kind of modesty on which people were to comment for years after he had won international fame. Forbes, in fact, had heard all about him and, not long after assuming command, wrote of him in complimentary terms to the acting governor of Virginia. When Blair forwarded the letter to the colonel, Washington dropped a line to Forbes: "Permit me to return you my sincere thanks for the honour you were pleased to do me, in a letter to Mr. President Blair, and to assure you that, to merit a continuance of the good opinion you have therein expressed for me, shall be one of my principal studies. I have no higher ambition than to act my part well during the campaign, and if I should *thereby* merit your approbation, it would be the most pleasing reward for the toils I shall undergo." He added that his men were scattered over some two hundred miles of territory and he would have considerable trouble assembling them after his orders arrived.

Washington stressed repeatedly to Forbes, St. Clair, and Bouquet the importance of their Indian allies, the need to encourage them with gifts, and the desirability of frequently counselling with their chiefs. Forbes was new to America but St. Clair had long experience in the country. This time the British worked with patience to secure Indian support, thereby delaying the campaign so long that Washington chafed with impatience.

To replace the men of the Virginia Regiment, who were scheduled to go north, the law authorized the governor or the commander in chief of the regiment to call out the militia. The acting governor suggested that Washington do this but he felt it politically too delicate and believed that such orders should come from Williamsburg; hence Blair took on the responsibility.

On April 27 Washington wrote to St. Clair that Blair had ordered the Virginia Regiments placed under Forbes' command and that he expected his companies from South Carolina shortly. He thanked St. Clair for his good opinion saying that "the Esteem of my Friends" would be his only reward other than the consciousness of doing his duty. St. Clair dropped a line on May 7 to say he would proceed to Winchester to help Washington in any way he could. In the meantime, he was "busy about Roads, Hay, Oats, Indian Corn,

& Waggons." He asked Washington to arrange for a room in Winchester. Washington replied: "I have engaged Lodgings for you at Mr. P. Buchby's, much the best House in this Town."

Increasingly Washington urged training and discipline for his officers and men. He asked Major Lewis to read as widely as he had done to qualify for his majority. He enjoined his officers to put the men through exercises, to see that their arms were well repaired, they had adequate target practice, and their uniforms were carefully mended. He took time to procure leggings for his men, as well as a hair-trunk, a traveling writing case, cups and saucers, and English saddles for himself.

When St. Clair came to Winchester he gave Washington orders for his regiments to march. He also sent him to Williamsburg for supplies and pay for the troops. Washington left Winchester about May 24, returning on June 13 by way of Martha Custis' house. The new governor, Francis Fauquier, reached the capital just after Washington's departure. Washington dropped him a note of welcome and congratulations from Winchester.

The first Virginia Regiment set off on June 24 from Fort Loudoun for Fort Cumberland, with the second marching the following day. Washington reached Cumberland on July 2. There he had to sit and wait in agony while the entire summer slipped away. He wrote to Bouquet that his officers and men were short of regimental uniforms. He therefore proposed putting them into the hunting shirt and leggings of the woodsmen. Bouquet, more flexible than most British officers—having seen men of Major Lewis' Virginia detachment in this dress—gave his approval. In thanking Bouquet, Washington said this would save many pack horses for the expedition to Duquesne.

THE NEW BURGESS

Since 1755 Washington had wanted to be in the House of Burgesses. Now that his military career was ending he was more anxious than ever to win a seat. Though it was difficult for him to campaign in Frederick County while he was in Cumberland, he entered his name for the July 24 election.

Bouquet gave Washington permission to campaign, but Washington decided to leave the election in the hands of his friends. His managers, however, urged him to return since his absence gave a handle to talk that he could not be fighting and representing the district at the same time. They added that the promises of the common herd to vote for him could not be trusted and that he should personally see them. Others reported that his friends were pushing everything with the greatest ardor, "even... Will the Hatter and his

Oyly Spouse Show the greatest Spirit in the Cause." Old friends such as John Carlyle and his brother-in-law, George Fairfax, came up from Alexandria to assist. Lord Fairfax also helped and was recorded as voting for Washington. Letters soon reached Fort Cumberland headed "Dear Burgess," informing him that he had won by a wide margin. Lieutenant Charles Smith of his command said: "I have the Happiness to Inform You your Friends have been Very Sincere So that you were carried by a Number of Votes more than any Candidate... Colo. James Wood Sat on the Bench, and Represented Your Honour, and was Carried round the Town with a General applause, Huzawing Colo. Washington." The Virginia Assembly had not yet forbidden the candidates to give out liquor during the campaigns. Washington asked his managers to spare no expense on this. His bills showed they distributed seventy-two gallons of rum, thirty-four of wine, and forty-six of beer.

The balloting was open and by voice. Washington later copied out the names and choices of all voters. A few selected only one of the four men running. It would appear that, without a single speech or public appearance, the young colonel received 309 votes, or 78 percent of the total. The other successful candidate, Thomas Bryan Martin, nephew of Lord Fairfax, had 239 votes. Captain Robert Stewart wrote Washington that it was a remarkable display of confidence in one who had "so long Commanded the whole of that Country in the worst of times."

Washington's frontier constituents and military officers were a tough and skeptical lot but they expressed an equally high faith in him. From letters of his officers, it appears that he had the knack of making each one feel that he was his particular friend. Strangers who visited the camp at Fort Cumberland were treated with such courtesy that Colonel Washington's hospitality became legendary throughout the frontier posts of Maryland and Pennsylvania.

Following his election, the colonel dropped numerous letters of thanks to his campaign managers and friends. To James Wood he wrote that his heart was full of "joy and gratitude... I don't like to touch upon our Public Affairs... I will therefore say little... Backwardness appears in all things but the approach of Winter—that jogs on apace."

COLONEL WASHINGTON VERSUS THE BRITISH ARMY

When Washington was born, Americans thought themselves English and the British armies invincible. When George was nine, Captain Lawrence Washington, R. A., watched the Cartagena disaster, the result of fumbling by the British army command. Four years later, New Englanders, led by the

American general William Pepperell, successfully brought off the siege and capture of Louisburg. At twenty-two, Washington became the only American aide to General Braddock, British commander in chief in America. When disaster struck down Braddock, and his English troops panicked, the little glory of the day was reserved for Washington and his Virginians. Braddock's defeat and Dunbar's flight opened Virginia's frontiers to bloody Indian attacks, which Colonel Washington had to fight off with pitifully small means. He then had to bear bumbling interference in his operations by the succeeding British commander in chief. Lord Loudoun subsequently failed in the mismanaged siege of Louisburg.

The new commander in chief, Major General James Abercromby, to whom Brigadier John Forbes reported, had been planning an attack on Ticonderoga in 1758, while Bouquet was moving on Duquesne. When the American Lieutenant Colonel John Bradstreet offered to lead a simultaneous expedition against Fort Frontenac (Kingston, Ontario), Forbes overruled him but was persuaded by his war council to permit Bradstreet to have a small force. Abercromby moved north with about fifteen hundred troops, the majority American. After his second in command, the popular Lord Howe, was killed, the British were humiliatingly beaten by Montcalm's French army, which was a quarter its size. Abercromby fled southward in a manner that was to be as long remembered in New England and New York as Dunbar's flight was in the middle colonies. Colonel Washington had this news at approximately the time he received the election returns from Winchester. He was now to encounter an even lower level of competence in the commander in chief of the southern forces of North America, General Forbes, who had been Lord Loudoun's adjutant general. On June 25 Francis Halkett, Forbes' brigade major, informed Washington that the general did not "debar any body from telling their way of thinking, when at the same time he only makes use of that part of their way of thinking, which corrisponds with his own."

It is not clear why Forbes landed at Philadelphia, which was much farther from Fort Duquesne than Alexandria, Virginia, but it can be presumed to have been a blunder by the war office in London. Nearly everyone assumed that, in spite of this initial mistake, he would march his fourteen hundred regulars to Fort Cumberland to join the more than five thousand troops from Pennsylvania, Maryland, Virginia, and the Carolinas. There a road existed almost to Duquesne itself. Forbes was dilatory, taking nearly three months to reach Carlisle, Pennsylvania, one hundred miles to the west. There he fell seriously ill, far too much so to lead an expedition, where speed, strength, and stamina were required. Nonetheless he persisted in maintaining his command, moving slowly by litter with frequent stops for rest.

About the time Washington reached Cumberland at the beginning of July, rumors floated through Maryland and Virginia that General Forbes planned to go straight across Pennsylvania to Duquesne. Even Pennsylvanians found this difficult to believe. Their own western trade went through Cumberland, since little more than Indian trails existed from a point ten miles west of Shippensburg across the rest of the colony. The planned direct western course required that more than 162 miles of road be hacked through wilderness and over numerous mountain ridges. Reports to Washington by his own officers indicate that it sometimes took a day to clear a half mile of wagon roads.

Colonel Washington, having been ordered to move his two regiments to Cumberland and to detach approximately five hundred men under Lieutenant Colonel Adam Stephen to Ray's Town (Bedford) in Pennsylvania, was himself asked to proceed to Ray's Town, but this order was subsequently cancelled. In the meantime the Virginia troops were ordered to work on the roads leading east from Ray's Town and northeast from Cumberland to that place. Soon loud howls were heard from Virginia's volunteer troops that they were being made day laborers for Maryland and Pennsylvania. They were also engaged, as they knew, in building roads away from the enemy. At one point, Bouquet did instruct Washington to repair the Braddock road, but the Virginia colonel replied that all the troops he could spare were working elsewhere.

Although mountain frosts were only three months off, Bouquet sent men out in July to reconnoitre the paths westward. On the fourteenth he informed Washington that he was unacquainted with the country and asked whether Washington thought an expedition could be sent against the Indians in the Ohio Valley. Washington replied that such an undertaking with a large body of troops and provisions was not feasible. The Indians would quickly discover them and the enterprise would fail. Washington had early discerned the plans of Forbes (along with most other unbelieving Virginians), but he was among the last to be officially informed. Bouquet's letter of July 24 giving Washington a hint is missing, but the colonel's reply suggests its contents:

> *I shall most chearfully proceed on any Road; pursue any Route; or enter upon any service; that the General or yourself can think me usefully employ'd in; and shall never have a Will of my own, when a duty is required of me; but since you desire me to speak; permit me to observe this that after having convers'd with all the Guides, and been convinced by them and every other who has knowledge of the Country, that a Road comparable to General Braddock's (or indeed fit for any Service at all even for carrying Horses) cannot be made... I shou'd be extremely glad of one hours conference with you and that when the General arrives.*

About July 30 Washington saw Bouquet in Ray's Town. It was a frustrating meeting for him, since Bouquet not only showed no understanding of the issues raised by the colonel, who had fought and traveled over the area for six years, but also reported sourly on his plans to Forbes. Upon his return to camp at Cumberland, Washington composed one of his most able papers, with only a day or two of work. His brilliant mind enabled him to summarize the situation with respect to the roads as well as to prepare a plan to move nearly seven thousand troops and three months' reserve supplies of food, to build fortified deposits along the way, and to capture Duquesne within fifty-two days.

Washington's letter, dispatched on August 2, pointed out that the Cumberland-Duquesne road had been selected by Pennsylvanians and Virginians after long discussions with experienced Indians who knew every inch of the land. All having agreed that it was the best route to the Ohio, its construction had begun five years earlier. His own and Braddock's troops had put it into good shape to a point near Duquesne. Washington emphasized that it was not practical or possible to construct so good a road west from Ray's Town over "such monstrous Mountains, covered with woods and Rocks." Time pressed because the troops of the middle colonies would be out of service in the autumn. How, he asked, could the argument be advanced that it was easier to build the one hundred miles of road, still needed, than to use a road already existing. He pointed out, further, that Cumberland was a central point for supplies from Virginia and Maryland, which could come by water as well as road. Washington then came to the heart of his proposal, to achieve success in a little over seven weeks:

1. The troops should never be divided, and proposals to use both roads would not work. However, the existing trails over the mountains of Pennsylvania could be used for the quick return of unloaded packhorses, which could then bring supplies down the regular road. Scarce forage would thereby be saved.

2. Since time was short, the building of fortified places of deposit along the way had to be limited. Washington proposed the first fort at the Great Crossing. He suggested that fifteen hundred men could march there immediately, with wagons loaded to carry about thirty days of supplies for six thousand men. The remaining army would follow with ample provisions. He inserted detailed calculations of the number of wagons required for food supplies. For the march and the erection of a fort, he estimated that twenty-six days would be required.

3. At Salt Lick, his next proposed fort, thirty-five miles and four days' march beyond, he suggested sending 2,500 men to build a strong work. From this point, 3,000–4,000 men could be sent on to investigate Duquesne. In the meantime, packhorses would be returning over the mountains to bring more supplies.

Washington's final calculation was that the whole army could move in thirty-four days to the two forts and on to Duquesne, with nearly three months' supplies on hand. This would be an overwhelming reserve for a siege, which should not require more than eighteen days to complete.[*] At the outside, even allowing for errors, everything would be finished by October 15. With his papers is a file copy of a note that Washington may or may not have sent to Forbes' brigade major, Halkett, to say that if the other route were taken, they would be stopped at "Laurel Hill this Winter; not to gather Laurels, by the by."

It is safe to say that Forbes had never before, during his British army career, encountered brilliance. Moreover, it was displayed by a colonial colonel who not only thought carefully of logistics, strategy, and tactics, but who was also quite prepared to lead the whole enterprise while the general rested at a point far from the scene. Before his letter was forwarded to Forbes, Bouquet simply told Washington the general had ordered the Pennsylvania road built. Forbes was subsequently furious at Washington and eventually took his umbrage out on all American officers and men. Washington, he wrote, was "taking the lead in this ridiculous way" and "his behavior about the roads was no ways like a soldier." More than three months later, Forbes voted to abandon the expedition at Laurel Hill, but it was Colonel Washington who saved him from this final humiliation.

To Bouquet, Washington wrote further on August 6: "The General's orders... will, when once given, be a Law to me. I shall never hesitate in obeying them; but, till this Order came out, I thought it incumbent upon me to say what I cou'd... If I am deceived in my opinion, I shall acknowledge my Error as a Gentleman, led astray from judgment, and not by prejudice, in opposing a measure so conducive to the Publick Weal as you seem to have conceiv'd this to be. If I unfortunately am right, my conduct must acquite me of having discharg'd my Duty on this Important occasion; on the good Success of which, Our All, in a manner, Depends."

From this point on, Washington, still doomed to inactivity at Cumberland, received conflicting intelligence. Bouquet, euphoric, wrote him on August 10: "The Road will be cut tomorrow night to the foot of the mountain." He

---

[*] For those interested in parallels, the siege and conquest of Yorktown were to take nineteen days.

followed on August 26: "The first division of the artillery is over the Allegheny and had no Stop or difficulty to go over the Gap; The Road will be cut tonight to the foot of L. Hill and in three days Sir John promises to be over to Loyal Hannon. The second division will follow immediately and I expect with impatience the arrival of the General to move on myself. We must shortly enter upon action, and I know that we have time enough to carry our Point, if we meet with no new difficulties."

At the same time, William Ramsay, a Virginian in Bouquet's camp, said that even Pennsylvanians thought the road from Shippensburg to Ray's Town was far worse than anything on the Cumberland-Duquesne route, and that the British were encountering great difficulties in constructing the advance portion. "The road up the Allegheny Mountains is Steep, Stony & of very difficult access, even Alpine difficulties attend the lightest carriages." He added that he did not see how artillery could ever be taken over this or the next large ridge. In the meantime, General Forbes was resting at Shippensburg, with what he called "a most violent and tormenting distemper."

On August 19 Ensign Coleby Chew of the Virginia forces reported that he had reconnoitered Fort Duquesne and found that its French and Indian garrison was much weaker than the British thought. Washington had subsequent confirmatory reports from his Indian scouts. He concluded that the total enemy force was around eight hundred, towards which an army of nearly seven thousand was inching forward.

Nine days later Washington received abrupt orders from General Forbes to move forward on the Braddock road and to take a position at Salt Lick, a procedure that Washington had previously termed fatal. At the same time Forbes asked to see him in Ray's Town, towards which Forbes was proceeding so slowly that he did not reach there until September 15. On September 2 Washington gave the governor of Virginia, Francis Fauquier, an objective appraisal of the situation, including his own arguments for the Cumberland road and the progress that had been made to that point on the Pennsylvania road. He noted that Forbes had made it appear to everyone that the Virginians "were the partial people." He said he heard that the contractor was ordered to lay in supplies for four thousand men that winter at Loyal Hannon, at the foot of Laurel Hill. He added: "I think *now* nothing but a miracle can procure Success." Sometime thereafter he received a letter from Joseph Chew, dated New York, September 11, informing him that the American Colonel Bradstreet had taken Fort Frontenac and thereby cut all French communications with their western forts and settlements. He hoped this would make the conquest of Duquesne easy. This was to be, in fact, one of the two miracles supplied by Americans that saved the expedition.

On September 16, two American gentlemen, Colonels George Washington and William Byrd, appeared before Forbes in Ray's Town. The commanding general was in an ugly mood. During the preceding two weeks, he had denounced Americans to Bouquet as "scoundrels." He wrote to Pitt, the British prime minister, that the Virginia and Pennsylvania Regiments were a disappointment. American officers were, with a few exceptions, "a collection of broken inn-keepers, horse jockeys and Indian traders," while the enlisted men were "scum." Now he coarsely chided Washington for being a provincial partisan whose sole objective in wanting the Cumberland road was Virginia's good. He said he did not care "twopence" for colonial jealousies and suspicions. He cancelled his previous order to proceed up the Braddock road. Washington was commanded, instead, to march to Ray's Town, now a backwater post. As Forbes' additional punishment, Washington had to wait there for more weeks of inaction combined with further schooling in British army methods.

NOT TO REASON WHY

On September 13, very shortly after his arrival at Ray's Town, Washington received news of a major disaster devised by Bouquet and Major James Grant of the Highlanders in which sixty-seven Virginia officers and men were killed and many wounded. As he was soon to find out, Forbes had no idea the battle was even to take place, so Washington was not in a position to complain that no one had consulted him. On September 25 he informed George Fairfax:

I greatly bewail the misfortune that gives rise to the following relation. Major Grant... with a chosen detachment of 800 Marchd from Our advancd Post at Loyal Hannon the 12th Instt. for Fort Duquesne what to do there I cannot certainly say, but it is reported and I suppose justly, to Annoy the Enemy and to gain Intelligence. In the Night of the 13th, he took Post with his Troops in several Columns on a Hill just above the Fort, from whence he sent out to Reconnoitre the Works, this they did, and burnt a Log House just by the Walls. Not content with this Success Majr. Grant must needs send an Engineer in full view of the Fort next morning with a covering Party to take a Plan of the place... and while this was doing causd the Reveille to beat in different places; which caused the Enemy to Salle upon them in great numbers.

Washington did not then know the extent to which the Highlanders had panicked. The Virginians, under Major Lewis, who had been left as baggage guards, pushed forward on hearing the firing. They were caught in the retreating tide but succeeded in partly saving the situation. Washington noted that General Forbes had "complimented me publickly on their good behaviour, and that every Mouth resounds their Praises." Forbes himself reported to Amherst that the Virginians alone had saved the day. Majors Lewis and Grant were captured and sent to Montreal. The disaster did not prevent Grant's subsequent rise to full general in the British army. In reporting the battle to the governor on September 25, Washington mentioned that Major Lewis had been very much opposed to the whole idea but "there was no dissuading Colonel Bouquet." He thought that this affair added "a greater gloom than ever" to the campaign.

Not long afterwards, the Virginia Assembly, fed up with British army bungling, nearly voted to abolish the Virginia Regiments. At the last minute they were saved but ordered back to the colony by December 1.

DUQUESNE FALLS

In the meantime Washington continued at Ray's Town, ten days' march from the forward post at Loyal Hannon. His only known activity was a brisk memorandum to General Forbes, instructing him on how to march troops through wooded country while protecting themselves against Indian or French attacks by promptly heading for the trees. There is no indication that Forbes paid him much attention, for he was too busy with the increasing difficulties of the road beyond Loyal Hannon, fifty miles from Duquesne. By October 15 Forbes was writing Bouquet that his descriptions of the road pierced him to the soul. On October 20 he reported to Pitt that heavy rains and snow had made the road a morass. "If the weather does not favour, I shall be absolutely locked up in the mountains." On October 13 Washington began the march for Loyal Hannon, arriving there on October 23. On November 11 Forbes and his war council agreed that the expedition had to be given up as hopeless. The next day Washington barely escaped being killed. In 1788, still remembering it vividly after thirty years, he described what happened:

> During the time the Army lay at Loyal haning a circumstance occurred which involved the life of G W in as much jeopardy as it had ever been before or since. The enemy sent out a large detachment to reconnoitre our Camp, and to ascertain our strength; in consequence of Intelligence that they were within 2 miles of the Camp a party commanded by Lt. Colo. Mercer of the Virginia line (a gallant and good officer) was sent to dislodge them between whom a severe conflict and hot firing ensued which lasting some time and appearing to approach the Camp it was

conceived that our party was yielding the ground upon which G W. with
permission of the Genl. called (for dispatch) for Volunteers and immediately
marched at their head to sustain, as was conjectured the retiring troops. Led on by
the firing till he came within less than half a mile, and it ceasing, he detached
Scouts to investigate the cause and to communicate his approach to his friend Colo.
Mercer, advancing slowly in the meantime. But it being near dusk and the
intelligence not having been fully disseminated among Colo. Mercer's Corps, and
they taking us, for the enemy who had retreated approaching in another direction
commenced a heavy fire upon the relieving party which drew fire in return, in spite
of all the exertions of the Officers, one of whom and several privates were killed and
many wounded, before a stop could be put to it. To accomplish which G W never
was in more imminent danger by being between two fires, knocking up with his
sword the presented pieces.

In addition to this miraculous escape, Washington had the good luck to capture three of the enemy. These, according to his November 26 letter to the
governor, indicated how weak the enemy fortress was, and that provisions
were running low. A new note of cheer appeared in camp, and the decision
was made to go forward. Here at last Washington came into his own. Forbes
assigned him the advance brigade, honoring him with the short-lived title
"Brigadier Washington." In the meantime, Virginia's governor, unaware of
the decision to halt and fearing criticism if Washington's troops were recalled,
summoned the Assembly to meet. On November 13 the speaker sent an
express to Washington to tell him that the Assembly had proceeded with a dispatch never before known and in three days "passed an Act to empower the
Govr. to continue the Forces in the Pay of this Colony" until January 1. This
was done "not from any Expectation many of us had that an Attempt would
be made, after so many repeated delays, to rescue the Fort at this Season, but
as I said before that the blame might not lie at our door... I heartily pity our
poor men who must be now very illy provided to stand the severity of the
Season."

As he advanced over the last of the mountains, Washington wrote dispatch
after dispatch to Forbes and Bouquet. From Chestnut Ridge he reported that,
though it was nearly midnight on his arrival on the fifteenth, he had ordered
out working parties for the road. He urgently asked for more axes. Two days
later he reported that constant labor from daybreak till nightfall had opened
seven or eight miles of road. The next day he wrote of more progress, informing the general that he would set out, with a thousand men, at three the next
morning. He asked for additional meat for his hard-working soldiers and
assured the general that he was sending out scouting parties to prevent

surprises. He reported that they were still about thirty miles from Duquesne.

On November 24 returning Indian scouts reported that they had seen great columns of smoke arising from the fort. The French, in accordance with orders previously received, had abandoned Duquesne rather than risk a siege. They destroyed such provisions and arms as they could not carry away. On November 28 Washington wrote to Governor Fauquier to say: "I have the pleasure to inform you, that Fort Duquesne, or the ground rather on which it stood, was possessed by his Majesty's troops on the 25th instant... The possession of this fort has been a matter of great surprise to the whole army." General Forbes promptly renamed it Fort Pitt in honor of the man who had made the victory possible, he said, thereby placing "this noble, fine country, to all perpetuity, under the dominion of Great Britain."

With characteristic generosity, Washington reported to the governor of Virginia: "General Forbes has great merit (which I hope will be rewarded) for the happy issue which he has brought our affairs to, infirm and worn down as he is." Bouquet, on the other hand, wrote to William Allen, chief justice of Pennsylvania: "After God, the success of this expedition is due entirely to the General... Yielding to the urging instances for taking Braddock's Road... would have been our destruction."

Washington had carried himself through the five months of strain on adrenaline alone. Almost the moment he reached Duquesne and planted the British colors, he fell back into illness. To maintain the fort through the winter, Forbes asked that a detachment of Virginians be stationed there. Since they were ragged and ill equipped, as usual, he requested Washington to proceed immediately to Williamsburg to arrange for supplies. Washington began the long exhausting ride from Fort Pitt to Virginia's capital about December 1, stopping en route at Mount Vernon. He arrived in Williamsburg before the year's end. After taking care of Forbes' affairs he tendered his resignation as commander in chief of the Virginia Regiments.

THE REGIMENT'S ADDRESS

On December 31 twenty-seven officers of the first Virginia Regiment drafted a memorandum on his retirement and sent it to Washington by officer messenger. It said, in part:

To GEORGE WASHINGTON, Esqr. Collo. of the Virginia Regiment &
Commander of all the Virginia Forces —

*We your most obedient and affectionate Officers, beg leave to express our great
Concern, at the disagreeable News we have received of your Determination to resign
the Command of that Corps, in which we have under you long served.*

*The happiness we have enjoy'd, and the Honour we have acquir'd, together with
the mutual Regard that has always subsisted between you and your Officers, have
implanted so sensible an Affection in the Minds of us all, that we cannot be silent
on this critical occasion...*

*Judge then, how sensibly we must be Affected with the loss of such an excellent
Commander, such a sincere Friend, and so affable a Companion. How rare it is to
find these Amiable Qualifications blended together in one Man? How great the loss
of such a Man?... We with the greatest Deference, presume to entreat you to suspend
those Thoughts (of Retirement) for another Year, and to lead us on to assist in
compleating the Glorious Work of extirpating our Enemies, towards which so
considerable Advances have already been made. In you we place the most implicit
Confidence. Your Presence only will cause a steady Firmness and Vigour to actuate
in every Breast, despising the greatest Dangers, and thinking light of Toils and
Hardship, while led on by the man we know and Love.*

Captain Robert Stewart, formerly Washington's aide, said it more simply in his
letter of January 16: "The regret, dejection and grief your Resignation has
occasion'd in the whole Corps is too melancholy a Subject to enter on."
Washington replied to his officers and men with an emotional appreciation of
their letter and services. In 1788, after he had received endless praise, he
remembered their salute well: "The solicitation of the Troops which he commanded to Continue, their Affectionate farewell address to him, when they
found the Situation of his health and other circumstances would not allow it,
affected him exceedingly and in grateful sensibility he expressed the warmth
of his attachment to them on that, and his inclination to serve them on every
other future occasion."

PART THREE

FARMER
1759–1775

FOURTEEN

MARRIAGE AND PEACE

1759–1765

EIGHTEENTH-CENTURY AMERICANS of the governing class, in contrast to their British cousins, led generally pure private and public
lives. Such exceptions as Daniel Parke and his son-in-law, William
Byrd, were the more memorable on that account. Parke, the American aide to
Marlborough, who brought the news of Blenheim to Queen Anne, received
numerous rewards from her, including the governorship of the Leeward
Islands. He was murdered in Antigua in 1710, as a consequence of one of his
liaisons. His complex will provoked decades of litigation among his legitimate
and unsanctified descendants in the courts of Antigua, England, and Virginia.
Parke's two legitimate daughters married William Byrd and John Custis of
Virginia. Byrd's diary contained enough scandalous passages about his stay in
London for his descendants to hide it many years. The eccentric Custis,
before his death, ordered a famed epitaph, still on Virginia's Eastern Shore:
"John Custis... aged 71 years, and yet lived but seven years, which was the space
of time he kept a bachelor's home... This inscription put on his tomb was by
his own positive orders." Shortly before John's death in 1749 his son, Daniel
Parke Custis, a bachelor of thirty-eight, married the eighteen-year-old Martha
Dandridge. Daniel died in 1757, leaving his widow and two surviving children,
John Parke (Jacky) and Martha (Patsy or Pat), who were then around two-and-
a-half and a few months old, respectively.

Martha Dandridge Custis had been a widow for about eighteen months when she remarried. Her union with George Washington, which was to last nearly forty-one years, took place on January 6, 1759, at the White House, her country farm some thirty miles from Williamsburg. The absence of any extant correspondence on the part of Washington until May makes it appear probable that his wife made him rest as much as possible until they settled at Mount Vernon.

The myth that Martha was rich, and that this was an attraction for her new husband, has persisted down the years. Since Daniel Custis died intestate, she received by law only one-third of his estate. A portion of her share of $40,000 or so was for life only. The inheritance was subject to severe shrinkage if continuing litigation against it were successful. Suit for around $43,000 had been filed, including interest, but plus costs. In addition Martha had paid extensive legal fees for the defense of her children's and her interests. By an April court order Washington became administrator of the estates of Jacky and Patsy. He managed these without charge over the years, doubling their values in about fifteen years. No adverse judgment materialized against the Custis properties.

Washington was sworn in as Burgess for the frontier county of Frederick on his twenty-seventh birthday. Four days later the House voted its thanks to him "for his brave and steady behaviour, from the first Encrouchments and hostilities of the French and their Indians, to his resignation, after the happy Reduction of Fort Duquesne." He was assigned to the committee on propositions and grievances but his main work was on military matters. The new British commander in chief, Jeffrey Amherst, had called on Virginia for troops to assist him in taking French Canada. A bill for this passed the House in April. Washington, still ill, then asked for leave to return to Mount Vernon.

The colonel, who had ridden so long on the frontier with his hard-bitten officers, was now leader of a different flock: Martha, and two little children who had begun to call him "Poppa." On his way home, Washington sent a note ahead to his overseer, John Alton, asking him to get the key to the house from George Fairfax; make fires and air the place; set up beds; polish the tables, chairs, and stairs; and buy eggs and chickens.

The Washingtons reached their house on April 6, as the early spring blossoms were at their height. Mount Vernon had been raised a story the preceding year, but it lacked the wings and waterfront piazza that the master subsequently added. Its furnishings were presumably of the spare kind suitable for a bachelor officer. It was soon made a hospitable place, as indicated by Washington's August 9 note to Colonel Henry Churchill: "I was in hopes we should have had the pleasure of seeing you at Mount Vernon. Mrs. Washington impeaches you of a breach of promise in failure of this, and I don't know a better method of atonement, than coming soon and doubling the intended times of staying."

PLANTER

At this point Washington had to take on an essentially new career. He had left farming for other work in early youth. Mount Vernon, still rented from Lawrence Washington's widow, had little chance to attain efficiency, even by rather low Virginia standards. Gus Washington lived there only briefly, turning it over to Lawrence who soon went off to the wars. When George first leased it, he too departed for five years' military service. His brother John looked after the farm until his marriage, when he moved to his own quarters. The outbuildings, fencing, stock, and lands showed signs of long neglect.

Farming became for Washington the most absorbing of all his lifelong interests. With the zest which led him to read all he could on military management, he set out to be what was rare in the colonies, a man who studied the latest advances in British agricultural sciences. For the next forty years Washington lavished—insofar as his long absences permitted—hard work, intense study, and much capital on his property.

In the years before the revolution, Washington corresponded extensively with his London agents who sold his crops and sent him the goods he needed. He wrote his principal agent, Robert Cary, on May 1, enclosing copies of his appointment as administrator of the Custis estates. Mrs. Washington was clearly not satisfied with the sparseness of the furnishings. In addition to lists of wanted clothing, grass seed, and treatises on agriculture, gardening, and horses, Washington ordered a tester bedstead, curtains, carpets, and a firescreen. On May 7 he wrote to Richard Washington: "I have quit a Military Life; and Shortly shall be fix'd at this place with an agreeable Partner, and then shall be able to conduct my own business with more punctuality than heretofore as it will pass under my own inspection; a thing impracticable in the Publick service."

A great deal of Washington's London correspondence thereafter was given over to complaints of low tobacco prices and of shoddy goods shipped in return. Some of the clothing sent from London, he wrote his merchants, might have been worn by his forefathers. As early as June 12, in his first spring at Mount Vernon, he complained to Capel and Osgood Hanbury of London that they had got poor prices for him, though tobacco was scarce, while they had sent no accounts since the death of Colonel Custis. He informed them that these were particularly necessary now that he had to make twice yearly trustee reports to the General Court of Virginia.

On September 20 he wrote to Cary, asking him to set up three accounts, one for himself and one for each of his stepchildren. "The whole will remain under my management whose particular care it shall be to distinguish always either by Letter or Invoice from whom Tobacco are ship'd, and for whose use Goods are Imported in Order to prevent any mistakes arising." He continued:

> *I am possess'd of several Plantations, on this River (Potomack) and the fine Lands of Shenandoah, and shou'd be glad if you wou'd ingenuously tell me what prices I might expect you to render for Tobacco's made thereon of the same seed of that of the estate's and managed in every respect in the same manner as the best Tobacco's on James or York River's are. I ask this question for my own private Information, and my Shipping of these Crops will be govern'd in a great measure by the answer you may give; therefore you will excuse me I hope, if I again desire the favour of you to take some pains to inform yourselves exactly, because shou'd the prices differ from those of the Estate I might possibly think myself deceiv'd and be disgusted of Course.*
>
> *Please to send the Goods contain'd in the Inclos'd Invoices and charge them as there directed. I flatter myself that particular care will be taken in choosing them, the want of which gives some Tradesmen an oppertunity of Imposing upon us most Vilely.*

There followed a shopping list running to more than six printed pages. A sampling of this huge market basket indicates the difficulties early Americans had where the supplier was at such distances:

- *Food*—Cheese, tea, anchovies, capers, olive oil, raisins, almonds, sugar, oats for oatmeal, candy, mustard, pepper, and biscuits.

- *Household and Farm*—Starch, bluing, candles, pins, soap, medicines, blankets, saws, axes, scythes, hinges, chisels, compasses, gimlets, files, thread, playing cards, brushes, bridles, scissors, and writing paper.

- *Clothing*—Suits, hats, handkerchiefs, aprons, hose, and shoes for the Washington household, including the servants. Toys and dolls for the children were added.

Washington also ordered busts of various military heroes, including Alexander, Caesar, Charles XII, Marlborough, and the King of Prussia

(Frederick the Great). The art dealer to whom this order was referred regretted that he had none of these, but offered in their place Virgil, Homer, Shakespeare, Milton, Locke, and Newton.

On November 25 Washington wrote to Cary in London that he was shipping between fifty and sixty hogsheads of tobacco (usually averaging a thousand pounds each). On November 30 a further letter commented that his long shopping lists had gone by ships that had probably foundered and he was forwarding duplicates. He added that he needed a neat grate (for coal or wood) for his fireplace, saying that he understood grates were now made of steel. He thanked them for their "polite Congratulations on my Marriage, as I likewise am for your Dispatch of my Goods." On the same day he wrote to another London merchant to suggest the shoes they sent were of "Dog leather," for the two pairs he received had worn out in four days.

THE DIARY

Washington had started a diary when he first went over the mountains at sixteen. At twenty-seven he began a new one which ran, with gaps, until the day before his death. Many of his notes are of trivial events and weather changes, but others reflect Washington's humor and inquiring mind. Some of the best travel records of eighteenth-century America are contained in them. Washington's neighbor Daniel French received this opening comment on January 1, 1760: "Visited my Plantations and receiv'd an Instance of Mr. French's great Love of Money in disappointing me of some Pork, because the price had risen to 22/6 after he had engaged to let me have it at 20/." Washington was forced to accept, since he needed the meat for his overseers and other personnel. The hogs arrived on January 8, Washington noted, "one being lost on the way—as the others might as well have been for their goodness." The animals, when killed, weighed 751 pounds as dressed meat. In spite of his complaints, he bought seventeen more hogs from French on the twenty-second.

Washington noted homely items. They were out of butter; an oysterman, tied up at his dock, plagued him with "disorderly behavior," and Washington had to order him away "in the most pre-emptory manner." Mrs. Washington had measles and several of the household caught the disease. The Reverend Charles Green, who had ministered to him when he was laid up with dysentery and tuberculosis, treated Mrs. Washington. Mrs. Fairfax came over from neighboring Belvoir to look after her. She stayed till evening and Washington sent her home in a carriage. He complained that she did not return it the next day, Sunday, until it was too late to go to church. The opening pages included much humor:

> We spent a very lonesome Evening at Colo. Champe's, not any Body favouring us with their Company but himself... Found Richd. Stephen's hard at Work with an ax—very extraordinary this... Went to a ball at Alexandria, where Musick & Dancing was the chief Entertainment. However in a convenient Room detach'd for the purpose abounded great plenty of Bread and Butter, some Biscuits with Tea, & Coffee which the Drinkers oft coud not Distinguish from Hot water sweeten'd. Be it remembered that pocket handkerchiefs serv'd the purposes of Table Cloths & Napkins... I shall... distinguish this Ball by the Stile of the Bread & Butter Ball... Doctr Laurie came here. I may add Drunk.

Much of his time was spent looking after sick slaves. "Cupid," ill of pleurisy at the Dogue Run plantation, was brought to Mount Vernon for better care. Washington sent for Dr. Laurie to take care of "Beechy." Two other slaves were ordered blooded or "physicked." A smallpox epidemic reached his Bullskin farm. He rode there, ordered the sick slaves placed in his own rooms, and employed a nurse to look after them.

Washington wrote of moving out his tobacco crops and of purchasing corn, hay, tallow, and shingles. He mentioned that he had made more than a thousand bottles of cider. He set a horse's broken leg in accordance with directions in a handbook he had. After placing the leg in a sling that did not hold, he had to destroy the horse.

Washington noted that he made an agreement with his neighbor William Clifton to buy 806 acres of his land for 1,150 pounds sterling, subject to Mrs. Clifton's approval. Later Clifton came by to say that his wife had refused but "his shuffling behaviour on the occasion convinced me of his being the trifling body represented." A few days later Washington learned that Clifton had sold the land to Thomson Mason for 1,200 pounds. In his diary he called Clifton "a thorough paced Rascall, disregardful of any Engagements of Words or Oaths." Eventually after "much discourse," Washington offered him 50 pounds above Mason's price, saying the land had been promised him. The case was settled on this basis.

Washington resurveyed his lands, finding many inaccuracies in the deeds. With his blacksmith he tried, unsuccessfully, to design a new type of plow. However, he continued working at it; some of his later inventive experiments succeeded. Shortly after this, he began grafting cherry and plum trees, and then "a pretty little pearky June Pear." Subsequently he grafted apples.

In April Washington was out plowing and seeding lucerne, rye grass, oats, and barley. He experimented with compost on marked fields, mixing in various combinations earth, sand, mud, marl, and black loam with horse, cow, and sheep dung to "a tolerable degree of fineness & jumbling them well together in a cloth." From these experiments he went on to animal breeding and sheepshearing.

Washington's diaries include long tables of tobacco, corn, and wheat yields from various fields, the rent paid him from his many properties; and records of his tobacco shipments. On April 3, 1761, he wrote Robert Cary to complain that he had been paid only 11d. for his tobacco while other planters got 12d. He added: "Certain I am no Person in Virginia takes more pains to make their Tobo. fine than I do and tis hard then I should not be as well rewarded for it."

THE WAR

The Seven Years' War, which George Washington had a role in starting, continued for more than four years after his retirement to Mount Vernon. While he was haggling over tobacco prices, the British were achieving great victories on the American continent. His former officers Robert Stewart and George Mercer sent him welcome reports of their frontier service.

Mercer, commanding at Fort Pitt, informed Washington in September that the French, after burning the posts at Venango and Le Boeuf, which he had visited as Dinwiddie's emissary, had retired to Detroit. The British were building a brick fortress at Pittsburgh large enough to hold a garrison of four thousand.

Stewart, also stationed at Fort Pitt, said that the Shawnee and Delaware tribes were still so angry at Washington, whom they considered to be the cause of all their misfortunes, that they always spoke of him as "The Great Knife." Stewart was enraptured by Pittsburgh: "A view of three glorious Rivers, and the many Beauties Nature has been so lavish in adorning this place... A most delightful prospect, terminated by many high, romantic Mountains... The more I see of this charming Country, the more I'm enamoured with it." He asked what had happened to the bounty lands along the Ohio River that had been promised those who had volunteered to serve Virginia in 1754.

In July Ticonderoga and Crown Point fell to Amherst. In September Wolfe captured Quebec, ending French rule in Canada. Billy Fairfax, Washington's neighbor and prospective heir to the Fairfax title and lands, died with Wolfe. On September 20, before he had news of this victory, Washington wrote his London correspondent, Richard Washington: "The Scale of Fortune is turn'd greatly in our favour, and Success is become the boon companion of our Fortunate Generals." He added that his brother Austin, who had gone to

England for his health, had not benefited from his trip. He himself longed to see the great metropolis of London, "but I am now tied by the Leg and must set Inclination aside."

TWO DEATHS

At the end of 1760, word reached Virginia of the death of George II. The new monarch, George III, young and well-meaning, though not very bright or well-educated, was warmly greeted in England. He inserted into his first speech to Parliament the phrase "Born and educated in this country, I glory in the name of *Britain*." Some of the older courtiers regarded the sentences as slightly unkind to his German-born predecessors, while others thought the word "Britain" was too deferential to the Scots. His subjects generally viewed it for what it was, a simple declaration of pride in country. A few years later an American newspaper predicted that not many generations would elapse before the royal family would move to the center of the growing empire and the monarch would declare: "Born and educated among you, I glory in the name of AMERICA."

On February 11, 1761, Governor Francis Fauquier proclaimed the new king in the capital of Virginia, "amidst the joyful acclamations of the people, at the capitol, the market place, and the college." On March 5 he appeared before the Burgesses to say that there was "the greatest reason to form the most sanguine expectations of enjoying the blessing of freedom, in the same full latitude we experienced under his grandfather, in the person of his successor, his present Majesty." No sooner was the king crowned and sanctified, however, than he moved to displace Pitt from power, thus beginning twenty years of personal reign.

Washington was not present at this session of the Burgesses. He may have been detained because of the critical illness of Lawrence Washington's widow, Anne Fairfax, wife of George Lee. She died on March 14, very probably from the disease that had killed her first husband and four children. By her death Washington became the sole owner of Mount Vernon, which he had previously leased.

ELECTION

The succession of a new king led to the automatic dissolution of the House of Burgesses and a new election. This meant additional trouble and expense for

Washington, who represented a frontier constituency. Thomas Bryan Martin, Lord Fairfax's nephew, decided not to run again in Frederick. Two men, Adam Stephen, Washington's former lieutenant colonel, and George Mercer, his one-time aide, announced their candidacy. Stephen was the more aggressive and energetic of the two and quickly got to work. This provided an additional complication for Washington since he mistrusted Stephen and liked Mercer. It also meant a more active campaign than he would have had to make with only two candidates.

Captain Robert Stewart soon warned Washington that Stephen was making headway. He "is incessantly employ'd in traversing this County and... practices every method of making Interest with it's Inhabitants for Electing him their Representative in Assembly, his claims to disinterestedness, Public Spirit and genuine Patriotism are Trumpeted in the most turgid manner." Stephen proposed to introduce "various Commercial Schemes, which are to diffuse Gold & opulency thro' Frederick, and prove... as Sovereign a Remedy against Poverty and Want as Glen's red root was in removing hunger and imbecility from our Horses in Campaign 58... He has attracted the attention of the Plebeians, whose unstable Minds are agitated by every Breath of Novelty." Stewart urged Washington to come to Frederick as soon as possible.

Washington followed this advice in May 1761. He attended a cockfight and a wedding, and made long, rough rides through his enormous constituency. For reasons that are now obscure, Washington was furious at Stephen. He wrote to Captain Van Swearingen, the sheriff, to say:

> *Col. Stephens proceedings is a matter of the greatest amazement to me. I have come across sundry of his letters directed to the Freeholders wherein he informs them that he acquitted himself of what was charged to him in the Streets of Winchester while you were present, and goes on to draw Comparisons to prove his Innocence... However His conduct throughout the whole is very obvious to all who will be convinced, but I find there are some that do not choose to have their Eyes opened.*
>
> *I hope my Interest in your Neighbourhood still stands good, and as I have the greatest reason to believe you can be no Friend to a Person of Colo. Stephens Principles; I hope, and indeed make no doubt you will contribute your aid towards shutting him out of the Public trust he is seeking.*

The election, held on May 18, 1761, resulted in 505 votes for Washington (88 percent), 399 for Mercer, and 299 for Stephen. The first two were declared the Frederick Burgesses.

ILLNESS

The strenuous campaign brought Washington what seemed at first to be a feverish cold. He soon became acutely ill from what was the most severe of his many tubercular attacks. He consulted Drs. Craik and Laurie and the Reverend Charles Green. He sent an account of his illness and symptoms to Captain Stewart in Philadelphia, who there saw a Dr. Macleane, whom Stewart called the ablest physician in America. Macleane advised Washington to proceed to Philadelphia. At Dr. Green's advice, he went instead to Warm Springs (Berkeley) where he had once taken his very ill brother, Lawrence. On August 26 he wrote to Green of the waters and of his disagreeable trip:

> *We found of both sexes about 200 people at this place, full of all manner of diseases and complaints... The Springs... are situated very badly on the East side of a steep Mountain, and inclosed by hills on all sides, so that the afternoon's Sun is hid by 4 o'clock and the fogs hang over us till 9 or 10 which occasion great damps, and the mornings and evening to be cool.*

> *I was much overcome with the fatigue of the ride and weather together. However, I think my fevers are a good deal abated, although my pains grow rather worse, and my sleep equally disturbed. What effect the waters may have upon me I can't say at present, but I expect nothing from the air—this certainly must be unwholesome.*

Washington stayed there about three weeks and then returned to Mount Vernon. The exact course of the disease is not now known, but he referred to the fact that he had been critically ill in a letter of October 20 to Richard Washington: "Since my last of the 14th. July I have in appearance been very near my last gasp; the Indisposition then spoken of Increased upon me and I fell into a very low and dangerous State. I once thought the grim King would certainly master my utmost efforts and that I must sink in spite of a noble struggle but thank God I have now got the better of the disorder and shall soon be restor'd I hope to perfect health again."

In early November Washington thought he had recovered sufficiently to attend the House of Burgesses. On November 9 he informed Peter Stover that he had introduced the bill to establish Stover's Town (now Strasburg) in the valley, but he had been so ill he had to withdraw from the House. He asked another Burgess to manage it for him.

There is little documentation on the next months of his illness. It is known that he paid rather large bills to two Williamsburg physicians. Thereafter it can be assumed that he returned to Mount Vernon for a long period of Mrs.

Washington's nursing care. His full recovery took many months. This is indicated by the fact that not until May 28 did he answer long accumulated correspondence from Robert Cary and Company in London. He noted that he was responding to their letters of the previous June, August, September, and October. In the spring he attended the funeral of his half brother Austin. About all that can be said from the evidence available is that Washington's longest critical illness lasted from May of 1761 to about May of the following year.

Washington brushed close to death during this period but his strong heart pulled him through and enabled him forever to break the hold of tuberculosis. In passing through the valley of the shadow of death he changed greatly. The Colonel Washington of thirty was a man mature beyond his years, mellow, humane, and happy to be alive.

On August 28, 1762, long recovered, he wrote to Burwell Bassett, who had married Martha Washington's sister, the kind of sprightly letter he usually confined to close friends:

> *I was favoured with your Epistle wrote on a certain 25th of July when you ought to have been at Church, praying as becomes every good Christian Man who has as much to answer for as you have; strange it is that you will be so blind to truth that the enlightening sounds of the Gospel cannot reach your Ear, nor no examples awaken you to a sense of Goodness; could you but behold with what religious Zeal I hye me to Church on every Lords day, it would do your heart good, and fill it I hope with equal fervency; I am told you have lately introduced into your Family, a certain production which you are lost in admiration of... It is thought you will have little time to animadvert upon the prospect of your crops; pray how will this be reconciled to that... vigilance which is so essentially necessary at a time when our growing Property, meaning the Tobacco, is assailed by every villainous worm that has had an existence since the days of Noah... Perhaps you may be as well off as we are; that is, have no Tobacco for them to eat and there I think we nicked the Dogs, as I think to do you if you expect any more... I shall see you I expect about the first of November.*

THE GREAT DISMAL SWAMP AND THE MISSISSIPPI

After his recovery, Washington's great energy could not be entirely channelled into being a farmer, head of household, churchman, and legislator. He engaged in two ventures as far apart as the eastern Virginia swamps and the Mississippi River.

In June 1763 he became one of the fifty sponsors and organizers of the Mississippi Company. Its charter authorized the dispatch of an agent to

London to obtain a Crown grant of 2.5 million acres along the Mississippi River. The royal proclamation line prohibiting settlement beyond the Alleghenies, established later in the year, killed this scheme, but Washington's interest in obtaining land as far west as the Mississippi continued for years.

The second Washington venture was a proposal to drain and irrigate land in the Great Dismal Swamp. Washington made his first examination in May 1763. He found some very rich land and farmers already established on higher ground. He made a further trip in October. The Dismal Swamp Company was chartered by the Virginia Assembly and given canal access rights across privately owned lands. The company itself acquired some forty thousand acres, and Washington bought additional acreage for himself. Nothing productive ever came of this venture though a start was made on canal digging.

DIVERSIFICATION

Washington was one of the first American farmers, and perhaps the first on a large scale, to experiment with crop diversification and to plan his crops in accordance with future market demands. As early as 1763 his livestock included sheep, pigs, cattle, and horses. He caught substantial supplies of herring and shad. His fruit trees consisted of apples, peaches, plums, pears, and cherries. He grew turnips, peas, and, a little later, potatoes. His grain crops included wheat, barley, and spelt, a form of wheat. According to his diary, he also planted around 180,000 stands of corn. He produced cider and brandy. All of this was in addition to tobacco.

What eventually made Washington a modestly prosperous farmer was his decision to abandon tobacco growing. Tobacco was Virginia's largest cash crop, which provided the sterling exchange needed for necessities and luxuries. Washington's continued complaints to his London merchants on the prices they obtained indicate his dissatisfaction with its handling. His tobacco was not as good quality as he thought and his 1762 crop was skimpy. In 1763, Washington signed a seven-year contract with Carlyle and Adams, merchants of Alexandria, for sales of wheat to them at a fixed price. From 1765 on, after initial experiments with small crops, he rapidly expanded his wheat acreage. Later he entered the milling business for his own and for others' grain and found that his diversification program provided greater stability of income than a single cash crop.

The advantages of American economic subordination to Great Britain were not entirely one-sided. Britain offered bounties on American flax and hemp.

Washington experimented with these crops, and, although conditions for them at Mount Vernon were not ideal, he did collect some small hemp bounties.

By 1763, Washington had worked four years to build up his family's farms and fortunes. An April 27, 1763, letter to Captain Robert Stewart indicates how far he still had to go. Stewart had served long and honorably with the Virginia Regiment, which had been disbanded. He asked Washington to lend him four hundred pounds so that he could purchase a captain's commission in the British army. Washington replied:

I wish my dear Stewart that the circumstances of my Affairs wou'd have permitted me to have given you an order... for £400 with as much ease and propriety as you seem to require it, or even for twice that Sum if it would make you easy; but alas! to shew my inability in this respect, I inclose you a copy of Mr. Cary's last Acct. currt. against me, which upon my honour and the faith of a Christian is a true one, and transmitted to me with the additional aggravation of a hint at the largeness of it.

...I doubt not but you will be surprized at the badness of their condition unless you will consider under what terrible management and disadvantages I found my Estate when I retired from the Publick Service of this Colony; and that besides some purchases of Lands and Negroes I was necessitated to make adjoining me (in order to support the Expenses of a large Family), I had Provision's of all kinds to buy for the first two or three years; and my Plantation to stock in short with every thing; Buildings to make, and other matters, which swallowed up before I well knew where I was, all the money I got by Marriage nay more, brought me in Debt, and I believe I may appeal to your own knowledge of my Circumstances before.

I do not urge these things my dear Sir in order to lay open the distresses of my own Affairs, on the contrary they should forever have remained profoundly secret to your knowledge did it not appear necessary at this time to acquit myself in your esteem, and to evince my inability of exceeding £300 a sum I am now labouring to procure by getting money to purchase Bills of that amt. to remit to yourself, that Mr. Cary may have no knowledge of the transaction, and for which my regard for you will disappoint him. A Regard of that high nature that I coud never see you uneasy without feeling a pain and wishing to remove the cause; and therefore when you complained of the Mortification of remaining a Subaltern in a Corp you had frequently commanded the Subs of, I wanted you out, and hope it might be effected; but I shall have done on the Subject giving me leave to add only that in case you shoud not have a call for the money (and your Letter speaks of this) you will then be so good as to pay it to Mr. Cary to whom I believe it will be no disagreeable tender and advise me thereof.

Stewart subsequently had a rather checkered career, but in 1768 he was appointed collector of customs at Kingston, Jamaica. From there he wrote to Washington saying that he could now draw on London "for the amount of the money you was generously pleas'd in the handsomest and most Friendly manner to advance to me... for which and your invariable and polite attention to my welfare my heart will never cease to glow with the most lively ardour of the strongest Friendship and genuine gratitude."

Washington, though he himself had to pay interest on his London debits, drew only the principal amount, but he ran into difficulties in collecting it. He complained about this to Robert Cary, his London merchant, noting that he had loaned the money many years before without security. This matter was finally settled, and Stewart wrote to Washington: "I observe with the utmost Gratitude that you have Drawn only for the Principal... I really want words to convey the Ideas of what I feel on this *Noble Act* and fresh mark of your uncommon Friendship... Accept my dear Friend of my most Gratefull Thanks."

PEACE AND HIGHER TAXES

An England at the height of glory signed the 1763 peace treaty by which all French Canada became British. George III's government proceeded that year, and in the two following, to irritate his American subjects into near-rebellion. Virginia, praised in 1762 by Fauquier as composed of "loyal, faithful and dutiful subjects... dear to your royal Sovereign" and in 1763 by Amherst, the British commander in chief, as a "public-spirited colony, full of Honour," was the first to suffer. This brought from Burgess Washington his first known outcry against London's directives.

Although peace had come to Europe, the French-oriented Indians in North America rose up in fury against their new British rulers. Included among the rebellious tribes were the Shawnees and Delawares, who had singled out Colonel Washington as the source of their woes. An Indian war, led in the West by Pontiac, broke out almost simultaneously with the peace. The Indians seized many of the British posts in Pennsylvania, Indiana, Ohio, and Michigan, and nearly captured Detroit and Fort Pitt. Washington reported to Robert Stewart on August 13, 1763, that "another tempest has arose upon our Frontiers, and the alarm spread wider than ever... No families stand above the Conogocheage road... In Augusta many people have been killed, and numbers fled, and confusion and despair prevails in every Quarter."

Virginia had been financing its defense by forced loans in the form of emissions of treasury bills that were to be redeemed from future taxes. Virginia's currency was far below sterling, and British merchants were afraid they would be paid in depreciated pounds rather than in sterling. Accordingly, they persuaded the British government to order Virginia to desist. Washington had reported this to Stewart on May 2: "Our Assembly is suddenly called, in consequence of a Memorial of the British Merchts. to the Board of Trade representing the Evil consequences of our Paper emissions, and their Lordships report and orders thereupon which I suppose will set the whole Country in Flames; this stir of the Merchts. seems to be ill timed and cannot be attended with any good effects."

In August, after reporting the Indian troubles to Stewart, Washington said that he had expected the Assembly would be called to provide for the province's defense. Since it was to be "an Assembly without money," the governor had not summoned it and had relied instead on militia "under the Command of Colo. Stephen whose Military Courage and Capacity (says the Governor) is well established."

Virginia felt aggrieved again when George III issued a proclamation on October 2, 1763, establishing the Allegheny Mountains as a limit beyond which no American settlement could take place and forbidding private or provincial purchases of Indian lands without the king's permission. Trading with the Indians was to be by license. All the area from Florida to the Great Lakes and from the Atlantic watershed to the Mississippi was declared out of bounds to settlers. Virginia claimed all of the territory involved, from Tennessee north to the Great Lakes. The proclamation was regarded as an intolerable interference in Virginia's domestic affairs and by none more than those who hoped for riches from land speculation. It was also well-known that the British government was so corrupt that those close to the king could still get land. Americans paid only modest heed to the proclamation. Within seven years of its issue, some seventeen thousand settlers were in Kentucky and Tennessee.

As early as 1762 the British government had decided to keep an army of ten thousand men in America, though standing armies had been unpopular in England and almost unknown in the colonies. Captain Stewart, in a chatty note of early 1764, gave Washington a forecast of what was next in store: "It is said I'm afraid from too good authority that the Colonies will be saddled with a Tax of not less than three hundred thousand Pounds Sterling per annum in order to support the Troops Judg'd necessary for their Defence." The revenue act of 1764 increased duties paid in America on such luxury imports as silk and Madeira and raised the tax on non-British sugar, much needed by New England for its rum manufactures. This feature aroused particular opposition in Massachusetts. Samuel Adams, a radical, and Thomas Hutchinson, a Tory, thought the act impolitic and unconstitutional.

On March 22, 1765, the House of Commons passed a stamp act introduced by George Grenville, the king's first minister, which placed excises in English, not depreciated colonial, pounds on all American legal documents, licenses, and publications, as well as on cards and dice. The tax hit at everyone but hardest at the two most strident groups of society, lawyers and newspaper publishers. The reactions to the 1764 tax had been mild in Virginia but not so to that of 1765. Virginia had been self-governing and self-taxing for almost a century and a half. This blow, following the proclamation line and the prohibition against paper money, brought the first Virginia moves towards rebellion.

Two months after the Stamp Act passed, a new member, Patrick Henry, took his seat in the House of Burgesses. Henry, youthful and rustic, had already won a famous case, the Parson's Cause, in which he objected to the Crown overruling acts of the Virginia Assembly. Some of his remarks to the jury at that time had brought cries of "treason" from the spectators. The older Burgesses, until now, had held the House under tight control. The speaker, John Robinson, also treasurer of the colony, was one of Virginia's most influential persons. It was not then known, or not to most people, that he had used the provincial treasury as a loan office for his friends. When he died the next year, his accounts were found to be a hundred thousand pounds short. Three days or so after Henry became a Burgess, a bill was introduced to establish a Virginia land loan office, to be financed by borrowing in London. Very probably this proposal was connected with Robinson's peculations. Henry rose to oppose it. Jefferson, who heard him speak, reported his saying that it had been indicated that "men of property had contracted debts which, if exacted suddenly, must ruin them and their families, but with a little indulgence of time, might be paid with ease. What, Sir, is it proposed, then, to reclaim the spendthrift from his dissipation and extravagance by filling his pockets with money?" While the House passed the bill, the council, the upper body, refused assent.

Hardly had Patrick Henry engaged the enmity of the controlling group than he proceeded again to the attack. A copy of the proposed stamp act had reached the Burgesses. With many members absent, including, in all probability, Washington, the House formed itself into a committee of the whole to consider what measures to take. On his twenty-ninth birthday, Henry rose to introduce the Virginia Resolves: that Virginians had all the basic privileges of Englishmen, that they had uninterruptedly governed themselves since ancient times, and that the Virginia Assembly had the sole right to tax Virginians. Debate in the House, as Jefferson later reported, was "most bloody." The older members cried out against the resolves; Henry received a great deal of personal abuse. On the second day, in an impassioned harangue against the Stamp Act, Henry made his legendary statement: "Caesar had his Brutus;

Charles the First, his Cromwell, and George the Third..." At this point Speaker Robinson shouted "Treason" and the cry was echoed by the speaker's supporters. Jefferson, who had been enthralled by Henry's "sublime eloquence," heard him conclude, "and George the Third may profit by their example. If this be treason, make the most of it." He then apologized to the House for his language. Five of his resolves passed by a small margin, and Henry left for western Virginia. The older members, as soon as he was gone, struck out the fifth resolve, but the essential deed was done.

The royal governor of Massachusetts, Francis Bernard, wrote to London: "Two or three months ago, I thought this people would have submitted to the Stamp Act... But the publishing the Virginia Resolves, proved an alarmed bell to the Disaffected." The British commander in chief, now General Gage, called them a signal for a general outcry throughout the continent. "The Lawyers," he added, "are the Source from whence the Clamours have flowed in every Province."

The governor of Virginia, Francis Fauquier, dissolved the House and ordered new elections. This proved a blessing for Washington. A seat became vacant in Fairfax County where he lived, and he ran there instead of Frederick. He was elected without difficulty; he thus severed his political connections with the frontier, which he had represented for seventeen years.

WASHINGTON COMMENTS ON THE STAMP ACT

Washington, who had missed the debate, remained calm about the act. One of his few known references to it was in a September 20 letter to the portrait painter Francis Dandridge, his wife's uncle who lived in England.

The Stamp Act Imposed on the Colonies by the Parliament of Great Britain engrosses the conversation of the Speculative [i.e. philosophical] part of the Colonists, who look upon this unconstitutional method of Taxation as a direful attack upon their Liberties, and loudly exclaim against their Violation; what may be the result of this and some other (I think I may add) ill judged Measures, I will not undertake to determine; but this I may venture to affirm, that the advantage accrueing to the Mother Country will fall greatly short of the expectations of the Ministry for certain it is, our whole Substance does already in a manner flow to Great Britain and that whatsoever contributes to lessen our Importations must be hurtful to their Manufacturers. And the Eyes of our People, already beginning to open, will perceive, that many Luxuries which we lavish our substance to Great Britain for, can well be dispensed with whilst the necessaries of Life are (mostly) to

be had within ourselves. This consequently will introduce frugality, and be a
necessary stimulation to Industry.

COLONEL MERCER RETURNS TO AMERICA

George Mercer, Washington's old aide and friend, had left Virginia in 1763 to
seek political preferment in England. There is no reason to suppose he particularly sought the post of stamp distributor for Virginia, but having been
offered it, he accepted. Captain Stewart wrote to Washington from London,
on August 18, 1765, to report: "As for News I beg leave to refer you to the
Bearer Colo. Mercer who returns to Collect a Tax upon his native Land, the
Mode of Imposing which, we are told, the people of America in general, and
the Virginians in particular, look on as in infringement of their Priviledges,
which has occasioned such a ferment that a Majority of their Representatives
in a Legislative Capacity, made some Very warm and bold Resolves, Printed
Copies of which are handed about in this place but it is asserted that the last
and most violent of them is spurious."

The resolve to which Stewart refers was most probably the one which was
stricken out as soon as Patrick Henry left town. By the time Mercer got to
Virginia, nine of the colonies had met in Congress in New York to pass resolutions more restrained than those of Virginia, requesting Parliament to
repeal the act.

Colonel Mercer arrived in Virginia two days before November 1, the date
the act was to take effect. As soon as his presence was known, an immense
crowd assembled. The governor, who was popular with Virginians and noted
for his tact, handled the situation with such skill that there was no violence.
He reported to London that there had been a "concourse of people, I should
call a mob, did I not know that it was chiefly if not altogether composed of
gentlemen of property." After discussions and negotiations lasting two days,
Mercer resigned and soon thereafter returned to England. When no litigants
appeared at the general court, the governor adjourned it.

In New York and Massachusetts mob violence got out of hand. The first
stages of revolution had begun. Soon, Virginia as well as the other colonies
had their "Sons of Liberty," a term first employed in Parliament by Colonel
Isaac Barré in a speech opposing the stamp tax. Eleven years later, Patrick
Henry, who had precipitated the disturbance, became the first republican
governor of Virginia.

FIFTEEN

RELATIVE TRANQUILITY

1766–1769

T HE STAMP ACT, described by the British minister, George Grenville, "as an experiment towards further aid," that is, American financial aid to Britain, casually passed an indifferent Parliament in March 1765. The king was then in a state of illness, diagnosed by Paul Wold, professor of pathology, University of California, San Diego, as "the congenital metabolic disease, acute intermittent porphyria. This condition causes agonizing abdominal pain, manic overactivity, skin rash, red urine, paralysis, delirium and psychosis." The king was unfit to make important decisions.

The king snapped out of it in time to encounter Parliament's consternation at the ferocity of American opposition. By then Lord Rockingham's Whig cabinet, more sympathetic to Americans, was in power but holding on precariously. In December 1765, George III wrote to General Henry Seymor Conway, the cabinet's manager in the House of Commons: "I am more and more grieved at the accounts from America. Where this spirit will end is not to be said. It is undoubtedly the most serious matter that ever came before Parliament. It requires more deliberation, candour, and temper, than I fear it will meet with." The king saw the situation correctly, but this did not prevent his own bumbling interference.

The reactions in Parliament ranged from those who wanted to dispatch the British army and navy instantly to America to enforce the laws, to those who asked for immediate repeal and a declaration that Britain would never again impose such a tax. The Whigs devised a bad compromise that carried both houses. Parliament first resolved that the king "by and with the advice and consent of the Lords Spiritual and Temporal and Commons of Great Britain in Parliament Assembled, had, hath, and of Right ought to have full power and authority to make Laws and Statutes of sufficient force and validity to bind the Colonys and People of America, subjects of the Crown of Great Britain, in all cases whatsoever."

Ensuing resolutions contained much talk of "the power and dignity" of Great Britain, the violation by Americans of the laws and authority of that country, and of the passage by American legislatures of resolutions derogatory to "the legal and constitutional dependency of the colonys." One resolution, instructing the British governors in America to bring the offenders to "condign punishment," was stricken out. Practically the only opposing voices in either house were those of Pitt and Lord Camden. The House of Commons did not even divide on the resolves. Only four lords, one of whom was Earl Cornwallis, voted with Camden. The House of Commons, with practical unanimity, also refused to receive the petition of the Stamp Act Congress.

Rockingham and Conway supposed that the assertion of Parliament's absolute authority over America would clear the way to an easy repeal of the stamp tax, but the bill ran into trouble. Grenville was all for using force in America but he was voted down. The king wavered and wobbled. Rockingham had the king's assurance that he favored repeal, but when Lord Strange, a friend of Grenville, asked him whether he was for repeal, enforcement, or modification, the king said modification. Rockingham was in great distress, but George III, after a brief nervous collapse, said he was for modification as opposed to repeal or enforcement; however, if he had to choose between the latter two, he was for repeal. Conway finally carried it through Commons, but Rockingham had a rough time before the House of Lords passed it over vigorous opposition, on its third reading, March 17, 1766.

The king and Pitt became great heroes to America. New York erected a statue of George III, which stayed on the Bowery, until July 9, 1776, when it was wrecked and large portions melted into bullets for use against the king's troops. On July 21, 1766, Washington, in one of his letters of complaint to Robert Cary and Company, London (they had, he said, sent too many shoes, their scythes and chisels were often crooked, while the hoes they forwarded were as bad as those he had returned the year before), added:

the Repeal of the Stamp Act, to whatsoever causes owing, ought much to be rejoiced at, for had the Parliament of Great Britain resolv'd upon enforcing it the consequences I conceive wou'd have been more direful than is generally apprehended both to the Mother Country and to her Colonies. All therefore who were instrumental in procuring the Repeal are entitled to the Thanks of every British Subject and have mine cordially.

Washington's letter reduced the constitutional issue to its element. Was Parliament supreme in the empire, as the Declaratory Act implied, or was it, as Washington called it, "the Parliament of Great Britain"? Already that year, Richard Bland, his colleague in the House of Burgesses, had written a pamphlet which called the king sovereign in America but not the king and Parliament.

For the next three years, except for a 1767 reference to the stamp tax as an "Act of Oppression," Washington's scanty surviving correspondence takes little note of political affairs. Then, in writing to George Mason, he said that Americans might yet, as a last resort, have to take up arms in defense of their rights.

DEPENDENCE ON BRITAIN

Mature politically, America was still highly economically dependent on England. Washington's London shopping lists included the most elemental manufactures, as well as luxury items that could be sacrificed without essential harm. The increased attention to spinning and weaving on Washington's farms after 1765 was an effort to reduce British imports. His decision to grow no tobacco at Mount Vernon in 1766, while part of a long-range plan of diversification, was influenced by British measures to tax the colonists. It reflected a general American desire to lessen the economic ties that, more than the political, kept the country tied to mother's apron strings.

Later agreements not to import British goods, in which Washington took the lead in Virginia, were almost universally supported. For Virginians they had the added advantage that many planters had lived beyond their means. This had been fashionable, but it became equally so to dress and live simply. In 1770 there was a feminine declaration of independence when the ladies at the governor's ball in Williamsburg all dressed in homespun rather than in London silks. In many ways it was a fortunate movement. Nearly ten years before the war, America began increasingly to make its own cloths, hats, shirts, and, finally, muskets and gunpowder. The Washington plantations were among the first to participate, spinning, weaving, milling, distilling, and, when required, giving up goods taxed by Britain.

The growth of American population, instead of being a source of pride to

England, alarmed many Englishmen who could see America deigning to "wrestle with us for Preeminence." As early as 1766, the increase of population led them to think independence was on its way unless "we wisely take the power out of their hands." Keeping settlers behind the Alleghenies and controlling American trade were two weapons. Americans, including Washington, were already thinking in terms of destiny. A favorite game was to estimate future population. Americans believed they were doubling roughly every twenty-five years and would eventually catch up with England. It was only a matter of time before hordes of Americans would go smashing over the mountains whatever London might order.

MRS. WASHINGTON'S CHILDREN

Washington tried to provide his stepson, Jacky Custis, with a good classical and general education; in this program he had rather limited cooperation from Jacky. Mrs. Washington's daughter ("my little Patt") was more worrying because her epileptic fits occurred more frequently as she grew older. The Washingtons consulted physicians in Williamsburg, Fredericksburg, and Alexandria. They also took her to the waters at Warm Springs and even tried a man who attached an iron ring to her to bring out the devil.

Late in 1761, Washington engaged a tutor, Walter Magowan, who stayed with the family until 1768 when he left to take Holy Orders in England. Washington, after his marriage, ordered books from London for a child just learning to read and then, in 1761, a more impressive array, which included works by Horace and Terence, and Latin grammars and dictionaries. Washington wrote to his subsequent tutor that Jacky had read Virgil by the time he was twelve. Young Martha Custis was not fit for intense study. She received some tutoring from Magowan, but when he left, instruction, except in music and dancing, appears to have been abandoned.

When Jacky was fourteen, Washington persuaded his wife that Jacky ought to go to a school where disciplined study could be enforced. He selected the school of the Reverend Jonathan Boucher in Caroline County, Virginia. On May 30, 1768, he wrote to Boucher:

Mr. Magowan who lived several years in my Family, Tutor to Master Custis (my Son-in-Law and Ward) having taken his departure for England leaves the young Gentleman without any master at this time. I should be glad therefore to know if it would be convenient for you to add him to the number of your Pupils. He is a boy of good genius, about 14 yrs. of age, untainted in his morals, and of innocent manners...

Now Sir, if you incline to take Master Custis I should be glad to know what conveniences it may be necessary for him to bring, and how soon he may come. For as to Board and Schooling (provender for his Horses he may lay in himself) I do not think it necessary to enquire into and will cheerfully, pay Ten or Twelve pounds a year extraordinary to engage your peculiar care of and a watchful eye to him as he is a promising boy; the last of his Family and will possess a very large Fortune; add to this my anxiety to make him fit for more useful purposes, than a horse Racer.

Washington was too honest not to imply that Jacky Custis was a bit of a problem child. Boucher, then about thirty and having a struggle to survive, was delighted to add such a pupil.

The Church of England, through the bishop of London who had charge of American branches, tended to ship out clergymen who were not suitable for appointment to an English parish. Boucher had not received a rectorship to his liking in Virginia and turned to teaching. When he replied to Washington that he wanted Jacky very much, he noted that he might be moving the school to Maryland where he hoped for a parish. After asking Washington to send him down "immediately," he concluded:

Ever since I have heard of Mastr. Custis, I have wish'd to call Him one of my little Flock; and I am not asham'd to confess to You, that, since the Rect. of yr. Letter, I have wished it much more. Engag'd as I have now been upwards of seven Years in the Education of Youth, You will own it must be mortifying to Me to reflect, that I cannot boast of having the Honr. to bring up one Scholar. I have had, 'tis true, Youths, whose Fortunes, Inclinations and Capacities all gave Me room for the most pleasing Hopes: yet I know not how it is, no sooner do They arrive at that Period of Life when They might be expected more successfully to apply to their Studies than They either marry, or are remov'd from School, on some, perhaps even still, less justifiable motive.

Boucher's letters to Washington tended to be as candid as this expression of his failures as a teacher. Jacky arrived at the school in early July. Boucher wrote back that the boy had had stomach trouble, adding "it might be owing to Worms." Two weeks later he wrote that Jacky had malaria, but, as he later noted, malaria "easily gives way to Vomits and Bark."

Mrs. Washington was so devoted to her children that she could barely let them out of her sight. Her ease of mind could hardly have been improved by this correspondence. Boucher also wrote that while Jacky was of "exceedingly mild & meek a Temper," he was "far from being a brilliant Genius." Boucher noted that he had not misunderstood the remark about Jacky's fortune, and he promised to give "more vigilant Attn. to the Propriety and Decorum of his Behvr., & the restraining. Him fr. many Indulgences... allowg. Him more frequently to sit in my Company, & being more careful of the Company of Those, who might probably debase or taint his Morals."

Boucher restored Jacky to his parents about the beginning of September. Washington reported back to him on Sept. 4:

> *Master Custis was so much disordered by an intermitting fever attended with bilious vomitings, that we were obligd... to send for Doctr. Mortimer... He is now better, but not clear of slow fevers, and very weak and low (being much reduced) which induces his Mamma to take him home with us, till he is perfectly restored.*

Boucher wrote that perhaps he should have told Washington more about Jacky's illnesses, which he attributed to eating too many cucumbers.

Jacky stayed under the watchful care of his mother until quite late in the school year. Washington dispatched him back to Boucher on January 26, 1769, with a note: "After so long a vacation, we hope Jacky will apply close to his Studies, and retrieve the hours he has lost from his Books, since your opening School, he promises to do so, and I hope he will." By July, Boucher could write Washington: "I have a Pleasure in informing You that I please Myself with thinking We now do much better than formerly."

On July 25, following his return to Mount Vernon, Washington ordered from London a large library for Jacky's use. It included nearly fifty authors, many in large sets: the works of Cicero (twenty volumes); Livy and Grotius; the Greek New Testament; Greek and Latin grammars; the poetry of Thomson and Milton; histories of Rome, England, and Scotland; and various geographies. Jacky's was a good basic library for the eighteenth century but it was not destined to be extensively used.

THE GOOD LIFE

Between 1762 and 1768, Washington added numerous public duties to his work as Burgess. The first was his election in October 1762 as vestryman of Truro Parish, an office once held by his father. The Anglican church was established by law, and the vestry were responsible not only for church administration but for the care of the parish orphans and the poor. In 1766 he became warden of the parish. As such he was the principal officer to choose a site in 1767 for the new Pohick Church, which he helped to design. Washington,

George Mason, and George Fairfax were on the committee that supervised its building and assigned the family pews.

In 1766, the year he was elected churchwarden, he was also chosen trustee (councilman) for the town of Alexandria. In 1768 he became justice of the Fairfax county court and of the court of oyer and terminer. As Washington added city, church, and court duties to his work at the provincial capital, a note of increasing contentment and happiness appears in his diaries. Paradoxically, for the first time in his life, he began to allow himself more leisure. His daily horseback riding—to check every detail of fencing, seeding, ploughing, reaping, and milling on his farms—was frequently replaced by days devoted entirely to hunting. He went sport fishing and duck hunting. He went to several balls in Alexandria and wrote that he twice stayed up all night to dance. He went to the horse races and took Jacky with him to dine with the governor. Much company came to dinner and cards at Mount Vernon. They included Lord Fairfax as well as his brother Robert and their cousin Bryan, who were later the seventh and eighth lords. The Washingtons also dined out often. By 1770 they were going frequently to plays in Alexandria and Williamsburg. In 1768 Washington ordered a handsome new coach from England for his family. He mentioned, from time to time, staying home all day to write to his London agents or to balance his books. Most of his time, when the weather permitted, was spent out of doors building the strength on which he was to rely during more than eight years of war. He noted only occasional illnesses, usually mild forms of malaria and dysentery.

THE WESTERN LANDS

While king and Parliament in London were busy debating the best means of handling their possessions, Americans went on developing the country in their own way. Washington, who had helped to open the West, took two steps to obtain land beyond the Alleghenies. As he wrote to Colonel John Armstrong of Pennsylvania, who had been with the Forbes army: "I would most willingly possess some of those Lands which we have labord and Toild so hard to conquer." For this work he engaged an old companion of his youthful days in Winchester, Captain William Crawford, who had settled on the Youghiogheny River. He made a proposal to him on September 21, 1767: "I wrote to you a few days ago in a hurry... I then desird the favour of you (as I understood Rights might now be had for the Lands, which have fallen within the Pennsylvania Line) to look me out a Tract of about 1500, 2000 or more Acres somewhere in your Neighbourhood."

Washington wrote also to Armstrong for help in acquiring acreage, saying he had heard Armstrong was to set up a land office in Carlisle. Armstrong said that no such bureau was planned. The Penn Proprietors kept land under such strict control that it was difficult to buy any. Two years later Pennsylvania did start to sell land and Washington got his acreage. Crawford wrote subsequently that he had obtained several choice pieces of land and had them surveyed. Washington did not get out to the wild west of western Virginia until two years later than he had expected.

Washington's views were often well ahead of their time. His opinion that the proclamation line of 1763 was bound to give way was confirmed in 1768 when the British signed treaties with the Iroquois and Cherokees, extending British territory to what is now West Virginia and to the Kanawha and Ohio Rivers. Washington resolved to claim from this territory the 200,000 acres of land promised by Dinwiddie to the three hundred or so volunteer officers and men of 1754. In May 1769, he brought up the subject in conversation with Lord Botetourt who had succeeded Francis Fauquier as governor. On December 8 of that year he formally presented to Botetourt the facts of the soldiers' claims. With the governor's encouragement, he prepared to make his farthest trip west, surveying lands suitable for the bounty.

A NEW BRITISH TAX

Some months after the repeal of the Stamp Act, the king asked Pitt to form a new government. He accepted not only the job but the earldom of Chatham. This lost the Great Commoner much of his popularity. Walpole observed: "That fatal title blasted all the affection which his country had borne to him." Shortly afterwards he fell into a mental disorder, although he did not give up office until 1768.

Pitt's illness left England without a firm guiding hand. His chancellor of the exchequer, Charles Townshend, brilliant and unstable, unguardedly mentioned in Parliament one day that he knew how to tax the Americans without making them angry. Upon a challenge by Grenville, he agreed to make good his words. Many Americans, including Franklin, had argued that Parliament could lay no internal tax in America but that it could levy an external tax. The subsequent Townshend Act, passed in mid-1767, imposed duties on glass, paper, paints, and tea exported from Britain to America. According to the Duke of Grafton, these taxes were presented to Parliament over the objection of every member of the cabinet. They passed without the knowledge of Pitt and with hardly a dissent. After getting the tax through in May, Townshend died in September, leaving a weak government to meet the roar of outrage from America. Lord North was appointed in place of Townshend; in 1770 he succeeded Grafton as the king's first minister.

Massachusetts was the first province to react, since the law established a new customs board at Boston. That colony drew up "a humble, dutiful and loyal petition to the king" and addressed a moderate letter to the legislatures of the other provinces. Lord Hillsborough, the excitable American secretary, ordered Massachusetts to rescind the letter but its legislature refused. Hillsborough then asked the king for troops, which were sent from Halifax. Rioting and general trouble ensued at Boston. In early 1769 Hillsborough proposed to replace the elected Massachusetts council with royal appointees and to threaten the province with revocation of its charter if it questioned an act of Parliament. The king, more moderate and sensible, slapped Hillsborough down:

> *The vesting in the Crown the Appointment of the Council of Massachusetts Bay may from a continuance of their conduct become necessary; but till then ought to be avoided as the altering Charters is at all times an odious measure.*

> *The second Proposition is of so strong a nature that it rather seems calculated to increase the unhappy feudes that subsist than to asswage them.*

The French had followed the growing rift between America and Britain with great interest. In 1767, not long after the Stamp Act's repeal, French diplomats in London got in touch with Benjamin Franklin, praising him as a man of science, and invited him to Paris. There he met Louis XV and many scientists and philosophers.

In 1768 the count du Chatelet reported from London to the French foreign minister: "The ties that bind America to England are three-fourths broken. She must soon throw off the yoke. To make themselves independant, the inhabitants want nothing but arms, courage and a chief... Perhaps this man exists. Perhaps nothing is wanted but happy circumstances to place him upon a great theatre." On April 5, 1769, Washington, who had been studying the economic boycott of Britain adopted in Maryland and Pennsylvania, wrote his neighbor George Mason:

> *At a time when our lordly Masters in Great Britain will be satisfied with nothing less than the deprication of American freedom, it seems highly necessary that some thing should be done to avert the stroke and maintain the liberty we have*

derived from our Ancestors; but the manner of doing it to answer the purpose effectively is the point in question.

That no man should scruple, or hesitate a moment to use arms in defence of so valuable a blessing, on which all the good and evil of life depends; is clearly my opinion; yet Arms I wou'd beg leave to add, should be the last resource... Addresses to the Throne, and remonstrances to Parliament, we have already it is said, proved the inefficacy of; how far then their attention to our rights and privileges is to awakened or alarmed by starving their trade and manufactures, remains to be tryed.

The northern Colonies, it appears, are endeavouring to adopt this scheme. In my opinion, it is a good one, and must be attended with salutory effects, provided it can be carried pretty generally into execution... That there will be difficulties attending the execution of it every where, from clashing interests, and selfish designing men... cannot be denied; but in the Tobacco colonies where the Trade is so diffused, and in a manner wholly conducted by Factors for their principals at home, these difficulties are certainly enhanced.

The more I consider a Scheme of this sort, the more ardently I wish success to it, because I think there are private, as well as public advantages to result from it; the former certain, however precarious the other may prove; for in respect to the latter I have always thought that by virtue of the same power (for here alone the authority derives) which assumes the right of Taxation, they may attempt at least to restrain our manufactories; especially those of a public nature; the same equity and justice prevailing in the one case as the other, it being no greater hardship to forbid my manufacturing, than it is to order me to buy Goods of them, loaded with Duties, for the express purpose of raising a revenue. But as a measure of this sort will be an additional exertion of arbitrary power, we cannot be worsted I think in putting it to the Test.

He concluded by noting that many Virginians were in debt to England and they could only benefit by reducing their expenditures. Washington had already begun to develop political clairvoyance as to the outcome of issues that were still developing. Because of this, his views expressed to Mason were more radical than those of any other leading American. Six years before the outbreak of war, he foresaw that armed hostilities were inevitable if other measures failed. He also stated that Parliament had no more right to interfere with American manufacturing than it had to tax Americans. Probably no American, from Franklin down, would have agreed with him, since they considered the British economic measures to be within their rights. Pitt, the stout defender of America, said that if they overthrew Britain's economic controls, he would be the first to move to crush the Americans.

Mason replied the same day to Washington. He made no mention of Washington's radical ideas, but he did send him a redraft of the Pennsylvania nonimportation agreement that he had adapted to Virginia conditions. Washington had it with him when he arrived in Williamsburg on May 3.

VIRGINIAE DUX

When the Burgesses assembled in 1769, it was the 150th anniversary of this first American parliament, which had met under nine sovereigns and Oliver Cromwell.

Lord Botetourt was an even more popular governor than Francis Fauquier and handled the Burgesses with tact and skill. Nonetheless, he had direct instructions from London to dissolve the Burgesses if they supported the circular letter of Massachusetts. Botetourt's welcoming address was made in a cordial spirit and the Burgesses moved to answer with the same good will. A new delegate, Thomas Jefferson, was assigned to draft a response, but his work was not well-regarded and older members were given the task.

It was Washington who took the lead in persuading his fellow Burgesses to join the nonimportation agreement of the northern colonies and to support the circular letter of Massachusetts. After debate, the House affirmed its exclusive right to tax in Virginia and its resolve to support Massachusetts.

Though the resolutions were worded with care, Botetourt had no choice but to dissolve the House. Washington, who had dined twice with the governor during the legislative meetings, took the Burgesses over to the Raleigh Tavern to discuss the proposed nonimportation agreement. His diary records for May 17, 1769, only this: "Dined at the Treasurer's and was upon a Committee at Hay's [owner of the tavern] till 10 o'clock." There they formed the Virginia Non-Importation Association, which was signed by 94 Burgesses. They then drank loyal toasts to the king and queen, to the governor, and to "the constitutional British liberty in America." On May 19 Washington and his fellow Burgesses attended a ball at the governor's palace, celebrating the queen's birthday.

After this, his first major political move, Washington returned to Mount Vernon on May 22 and noted in his diary that day: "Found my Wheat much better in general than ever it was at this Season before, being Ranker, better spread over the ground, and broader in the Blade than usual."

On July 25, he wrote to Robert Cary, his London agent, ordering various goods, adding that if there were any prohibited goods on the list, "it is my express desire and request that they may not be sent, as I have very heartily entered into an Association... not to Import any Article which now is or hereafter shall be Taxed... until the Acts are repeal'd... I am fully determined to adhere religiously to it."

SIXTEEN

WASHINGTON LOOKS WEST AND EAST

1770–1775

T HE AMERICAN BOYCOTTS broke down when Great Britain again
        moved to mollify her colonies. On March 5, 1770, Lord North intro-
        duced a bill removing all Townshend duties except on tea. An amend-
ment to repeal the tea tax failed adoption by a small parliamentary margin; it
was retained as a matter of principle. George III and Lord North wanted
peace with America while most Americans viewed the remaining threepence-
per-pound tea tax as no great hardship.

On the day that North moved his bill, a large mob of Boston roughnecks,
described by John Adams as a "motley rabble of saucy boys, negroes and
mulattoes, Irish teagues and outlandish jack tars," attacked a group of British
soldiers with oyster shells, icy snowballs, stones, and clubs. The infuriated soldiers eventually fired on them, killing five. Samuel Adams, Paul Revere, and
the Boston press attempted to picture the affair as a British massacre but
John Adams and Josiah Quincy, Jr., defended the men in court. A jury of honest countrymen acquitted all but two soldiers and effectively acquitted the
remaining two, who were branded on the thumb. Thereafter all was calm for
more than three years until Lord North, in an offhand way, introduced a
measure intended to assist the East India Company to provide cheaper tea
for America. To his and the king's surprise, the Boston mobs once again went
into action.

With repeal, Americans rushed to buy British goods. Imports which had fallen from £2.2 million in 1768 to £1.4 million in 1769, increased to more than £4 million in 1771. Even taxed tea was imported in increasing volume: 55 tons in 1770 and 370 tons in 1773. The Washingtons again drew up their London shopping lists: fashionable clothing for themselves and Jacky Custis, handkerchiefs, bonnets, many pairs of shoes, hunting caps, brooms, decanters, silver spurs, pencil cases, tea and coffee cups and saucers, hairpins, powder boxes, and food such as walnuts, salad oil, spices, sugar, currants, and figs.

WESTERN LAND

With relations between mother country and colonies once more peaceful, Washington turned again to acquiring western lands. In particular he looked to his share of the 200,000-acre land bonus in the Ohio Valley that Dinwiddie had promised the Virginia Regiment in 1754. He also hoped to make additional land purchases in western Pennsylvania and Virginia. In 1770 Lord Botetourt and the Virginia council gave a favorable report on the soldiers' bonus land claims. In consequence Washington invited his former officers to meet him in Fredericksburg in August to draw up plans. He volunteered to go to the Ohio Valley to look for the best land available and suggested that the officers and men contribute pro rata to the expenses. Court duties and harvesting delayed his trip until autumn. On October 5, 1770, Washington, Dr. Craik, and three servants set out from Mount Vernon for what was to be the farthest inland trip of Washington's life.

After visiting his brother Samuel at Harewood (near the present Charles Town)—a house still owned by a descendent—the party moved toward the northwest. On October 13 they reached Great Meadows, where Washington had capitulated to the French in 1754. It was quite good land, and he bought his old battlefield as a farm in December. They rode across Laurel Hill down "to the Plantation of Mr. Thos Gist [where] the Land appeared charming; that which lay level being as rich & black as any thing could possibly be." Next day, they inspected a mine which produced "Coal of the very best kind, burning freely, & abundance of it." He then recorded their travel to and stay at Pittsburgh:

Monday 15th. Went to view some Land which Captn. Crawford had taken up for me near Yaughyaughgane distant about 12 Miles. This Tract which contains about 1600 Acres Includes some as fine Land as ever I saw, a great deal of Rich Meadow... This Tract is well watered, and has a valuable Mill Seat...

The Lands which I passed over to day were generally Hilly, and the growth chiefly white Oak, but very good notwithstanding; & what is extraordinary, & contrary to the property of all other Lands I ever saw before, the Hills are the richest Land; the soil upon the Sides and Summits of them, being black as Coal, & the Growth, Walnut, Cherry, Spice Bushes, &ca...

Wednesday 17th. Docr. Craik & myself with Captn. Crawford and others arrived at Fort Pitt, distant from the Crossing 43 1/2 Measurd Miles... We passed over a great deal of exceeding fine Land...

We lodgd in what is calld the Town, distant at 300 yards from the Fort at one Mr. Semples who keeps a very good House of Publick Entertainment. These Houses which are built of Logs, & rangd into Streets are on the Monongahela, & I suppose may be abt. 20 in Number, and inhabited by Indian Traders, &ca.

The Fort is built in the point between the Rivers Alligany & Monongahela, but not so near the pitch of it as Fort Duquesne stood. It is 5 sided & regular, two of which (next the Land) are of Brick, the other Stockade. A Mote incompasses it. The Garrison consists of two Companies of Royal Irish Commanded by one Captn. Edmonson.

Thursday 18th. Dind in the Fort with Colo. Croghan & the Officers of the Garrison. Suppd there also, meeting with great civility from the Gentlemen, & engagd to dine with Colo. Croghan the next day at his Seat abt. 4 miles up the Alligany.

Friday 19th. Recd. a Message from Colo. Croghan that the White Mingo & other Chiefs of the 6 Nations had something to say to me... I went up and received a Speech with a String of Wampum from the White Mingo to the following effect:

That as I was a Person who some of them remember to have seen when I was sent on an Embassy to the French, and most of them had heard of; they were to come to bid me welcome to this Country, and to desire that the People of Virginia woud consider them as friends & Brothers...

To this I answered (after thanking them for their friendly welcome)... that I was sure nothing was more wishd and desired by the People of Virginia than to live in the strictest friendship with them...

After dining at Colo. Croghan's we returned to Pittsburgh... Engagd an Indian calld the Pheasant, and one Joseph Nicholson an Interpreter to attend us the whole Voyage. Also a young Indn. Warrior.

Saturday 20th. We Imbarked in a large Canoe with sufficient Stores of Provisions and Necessaries.

CANOEING

The canoe, probably a *Canot du nord*, could hold eight persons, plus supplies. The party drifted rather slowly down the Ohio River, stopping at various points for meals and to inspect properties. Colonel Croghan was offering part of his land for sale. Washington thought it fine and rich, but noted that the country was in too unsettled a state for him to think of buying. The party ran into a snowstorm though it was still only October. When they were seventy-five miles from Pittsburgh, they stopped at an Indian village, Mingo Town (Mingo Junction, Ohio), which had twenty cabins. Washington noted an abundance of ducks, geese, and turkeys, with excellent shooting along the river. They soon passed Wheeling Creek where that city is now located. On the Virginia side, he encountered an old friend who was out hunting:

> *We found Kiashuta and His Hunting Party incamped. Here we were under a necessity of paying our compliments, as this person was one of the Six Nations Chiefs, & head of them upon this River. In the person of Kiashuta I found an old acquaintance, he being one of the Indians that went with me to the French in 1753. He expressed a satisfaction in seeing me, and treated us with great kindness; giving us a Quarter of very fine Buffalo. He insisted upon our spending that Night with him, and in order to retard us as little as possible movd his Camp down the River... After much Councelling the overnight, they all came to my fire the next Morning, with great formality; when Kiashuta rehearsing what had passed between me & the Sachems at Colo. Croghan's, thanked me for saying that Peace & friendship was the wish of the People of Virginia... and again expressed their desire of having a Trade opend with Virginia... The tedious ceremony which the Indians observe in their Councellings and speeches, detained us till 9 Oclock.*

SURVEYING

Washington continued down the river to the big bend of the Ohio and to the junction of the Great Kanawha River, now Point Pleasant, West Virginia. For the first time he saw lands worth patenting for his former soldiers. He also became the first president to go buffalo shooting. He noted:

The young Washington as surveyor. *(The Bettmann Archive)*

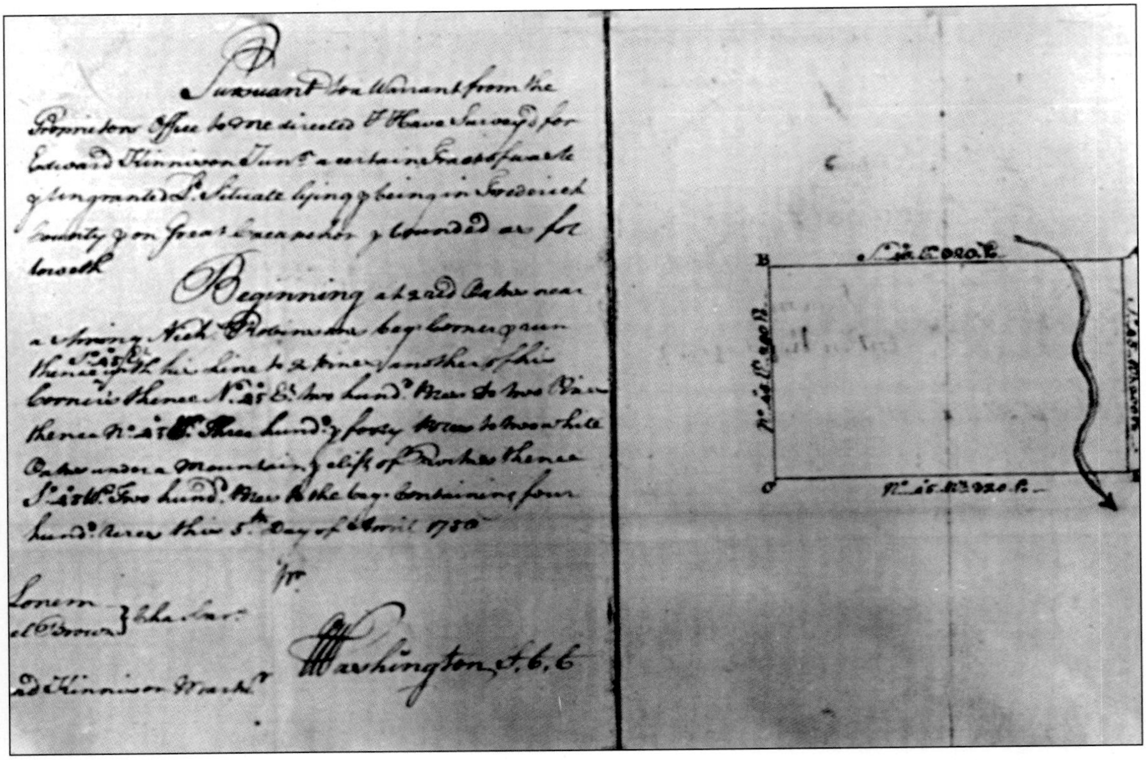
Pursuant to a Warrant from the
Proprietors Office to me directed I Have Survey'd for
Edward Kinnison Jun. a certain Tract of waste
& ungranted L. Situate lying & being in Frederick
County & on Great Cacapehon & bounded as fol-
loweth
Beginning at 2 red Oakes near
a Strong Neck [illegible] beg. Corner & run
thence S 25 W [illegible] his Line to 2 [illegible] another of his
Corners thence N 25 E two hund. Poles to two Oa[illegible]
thence N 25 W Three hund. & forty Poles to two white
Oakes under a Mountain & clift of Rocks thence
S 25 W Two hund. Poles to the beg. Containing four
hund. Acres this 5th Day of April 1750
pr
G Washington S.C.C.

One of Washington's surveying accounts, this one from Frederick County, Va., presumably written in his own hand. It is dated April 5, 1750. *(The Bettmann Archive)*

Washington, delivering an ultimatum to the French for Virginia's Colonial Governor Robert Dinwiddie, being escorted to Fort Le Boeuf in 1753. *(The Bettmann Archive)*

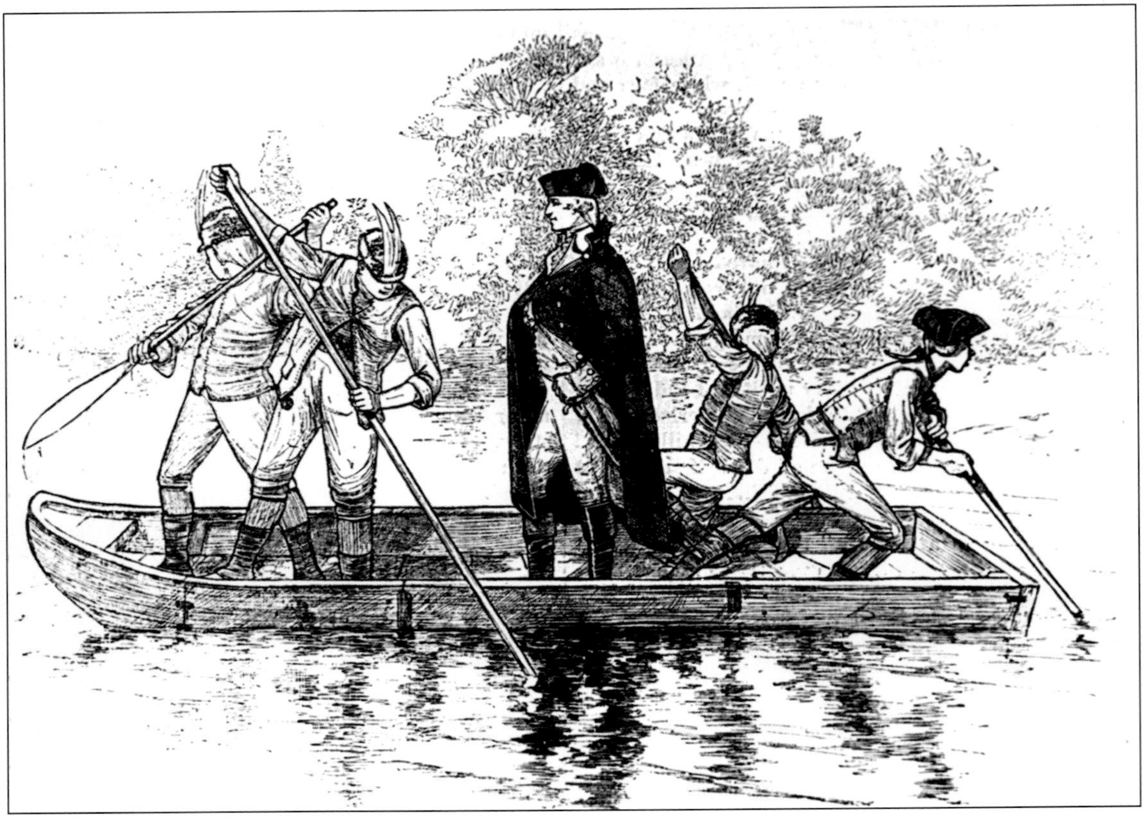

This first portrait of Washington, at age forty wearing his British Colonial uniform, was painted by Charles Wilson Peale (1772). *(The Bettmann Archive)*

Martha Washington by Charles Wilson Peale (1776). *(Courtesy of the Mount Vernon Ladies' Association of the Union)*

Washington, a dedicated planter, directs work on the Mount Vernon plantation (Lithograph, 1853, after a painting by Stearns). *(The Bettmann Archive)*

Carpenters' Hall,
Philadelphia, where the first
Continental Congress
convened in 1775. *(The
Bettmann Archive)*

Carpenters Hall Phila in which the first
U S Congress sat in 1775

A typical day in the rapidly
growing city of Philadelphia
in the late 18th century.
(The Bettmann Archive)

After being named General and Commander-in-Chief by the Continental Congress, Washington took command of the Continental Army in Cambridge, Massachusetts. *(The Bettmann Archive)*

John Adams of Massachusetts. Although lacking a military background, Adams was a critic of Washington's generalship. *(The Bettmann Archive)*

Portrait of General Washington by John Trumball, who served briefly as one of
Washington's aides. *(The Bettmann Archive)*

Wednesday 31st. I sent the Canoe along down to the Junction of the two Rivers abt. 5 Miles, that is the Kanawha with the Ohio, and set out upon a hunting Party to view the Land. We steered nearly East for about 8 or 9 Miles, then bore Southwardly, & Westwardly, till we came to our Camp at the confluence of the Rivers.

November 1st… We set off with our Canoe up the River, to discover what kinds of Lands lay upon the Kanawha. The Land both sides this River just at the Mouth is very fine; but on the East side when you get towards the Hills… it appears to be wet & better adapted for Meadow than tillage…

Novr. 2d. We proceeded up the River with the Canoe about 4 Miles more, & then incampd and went a Hunting; killd 5 Buffaloes & wounded some others… This Country abounds in Buffalo & Wild Game of all kinds as also in all kinds of wild fowl, there being in the Bottoms a great many small grassy Ponds or Lakes which are full of Swans, Geese & Ducks.

Saturday 3rd. We set off down the River on our return homewards, and Incampd at the Mouth; at the Beginning of the Bottom above the Junction of the Rivers, and at the Mouth of a branch on the East side, I mark'd two Maples, an Elm, & Hoopwood Tree as a Cornr. of the Soldiers Ld. (if we can get it) intending to take all the bottom from hence to the Rapids in the Great Bend into one Survey. I also marked at the Mouth of another Gut lower down on the West side… an Ash and hoopwood for the Beginning of another of the Soldiers Survey.

Washington marked off the course of the Ohio and Kanawha Rivers by means of his compass and recorded them in his diary. In company with Captain Crawford, he walked eight miles across the neck of land, which he described as "generally good; and in places very rich. The growth in most places is beach intermixed with walnut… but more especially with poplar… The land towards the upper end is black Oak, & very good; upon the whole a valuable Tract might be had here, & I judge the quantity to be about 4000 acres."

Washington returned slowly to Pittsburgh, spending some two weeks going upriver. He again encountered Kiashuta. Floods and heavy rains delayed him. He used this time to estimate the distances, from point to point, which he had travelled, as 266 miles from Pittsburgh to the mouth of the Great Kanawha.

Washington noted that the Shawnees, Delawares, and Mingos had received little compensation when the English purchased lands from the Six Nations and were, in consequence, quite annoyed at the settlers who were moving in. He wrote that Indian women were as skilled as men in handling canoes. The Indians had camps and cabins all along the river. They hunted during the winter, sometimes moving two hundred or three hundred miles, returning in the spring to their settlements. The women then did all the planting while the men sold furs, gossiped, and led an easy life.

At Mingo Town, Washington obtained horses and crossed the land stretch to Pittsburgh rather than go around by water. On December 1 he was back at Mount Vernon "after an absence of 9 Weeks and one Day."

Upon his return he learned that Lord Botetourt had died while Washington was paddling upriver more than a hundred miles from Pittsburgh. This meant that another governor would come out, and Washington would have to explain anew the situation of the soldiers' land. He also learned of the possibility of trouble from a British group, headed by Thomas Walpole, who were demanding land in the area where Washington had been surveying. Although Washington did not know it at the time, his efforts on behalf of his former officers and men were to involve him in trouble and expense practically the rest of his life. His correspondence in regard to the claims continued for twenty-eight years.

In March 1771, Washington met again with his officers to explain what he had accomplished on his trip and the complications. The governor and council had put an arbitrary limit of 20 tracts to cover the whole 200,000 acres. With Washington's efforts and subsequent surveys by Captain Valentine Crawford, 10 tracts had been found, for a total of 62,000 acres. Over the succeeding two years the remaining acreage was found within the prescribed additional 10 serves. Washington's own share of the land, plus acreage he bought up as a speculation from his former soldiers, increased his holdings in the Ohio Valley to around 24,000 acres. Most of it was far from known civilization and had to be seated, that is, worked as a farm, within a reasonable period. His endeavors to comply with Virginia laws on this cost him more than the land was worth inasmuch as he purchased the claims for around eleven cents an acre.

When the land was being distributed in 1773 in accordance with the patents approved by the governor and council, George Muse, who had been forced to resign from the Virginia Regiment for cowardice at the battle of Fort Necessity, felt that he had been defrauded of a few acres by Washington. Muse sent him an abusive letter. Washington waited only twenty-four hours and then replied on January 29, 1774:

Sir: Your impertinent letter of the 24th ulto. was delivered to me yesterday by Mr. Smith. As I am not accustomed to receive such from any Man, nor would have taken the same language from you personally, without letting you to be cautious in writing me a second of the same tenour; for though I understand you were drunk when you did it, yet give me leave to tell you that drunkeness is no excuse for rudeness; and that but for your stupidity and sottishness you might have known, by attending to the public Gasettes... that you had your full quantity of ten thousand acres of land allowed you... whilst I wanted near 500 acres of my quantity... But suppose you had really fallen short 73 acres of your 10,000, do you think your superlative merit entitles you to greater indulgences than others? or that I was to make it good to you, if it did?... If either of these should happen to be your opinion, I am very well convinced you will stand singular in it; and all my concern is, that I ever engag'd in behalf of so ungrateful and dirty a fellow as you are... I wrote... a few days ago... proposing an easy method of dividing our lands; but since I find in what temper you are, I am sorry I took the trouble of mentioning the Land, or your name in the Letter, as I do not think you merit the least assistance from G. Washington.

In 1775, Lord Dunmore attempted, in one of the last acts of royal authority in the colony, to set aside the land grants on a technicality. The state of Virginia, however, subsequently ratified the transaction and, because of the war, waived the time requirement for seating the lands.

DEVELOPMENT ECONOMIST

a. Canals

Washington, possessing some thirty-seven miles of western land, much of it earned in the service of his country, worked before the revolution to develop it as well as to open up the West to general settlement. Some of his proposals were beyond the existing technical and financial capacity of the country.

As early as 1754 Washington canoed the Potomac from near Cumberland to Great Falls, not far from Georgetown, making extensive notes. By the 1760s, England had begun to build toll canals. After learning of this development, Washington in 1769 drew up a plan for a privately financed system of locks on the Potomac from Georgetown to Cumberland. The old Braddock road thence led to Pittsburgh, from which there was relatively easy water communication with points along the Ohio and on down the Mississippi.

In 1770 Washington sponsored a bill in the Virginia Assembly to promote the navigation of the Potomac; this passed in 1772. It required Maryland to enact similar legislation. He worked actively to promote the company, but political difficulties after 1774 forced the temporary abandonment of the scheme. It was revived after the war, and Washington became president of the company. At the time he made a western trip on which he wrote a brilliant political–economic analysis of the development problems of the new union.

b. Flour Mills

Washington, with a first-class flour mill on his Mount Vernon property, decided to build another on his property on the Youghiogheny River in Pennsylvania. He engaged Gilbert Simpson to settle there and build the mill, thereby acquiring problems that pursued him for many years.

Late in 1772, Washington and Simpson arranged for servants, tools, and necessities for clearing the land, raising grain, and building a mill. By the following April, Simpson was on the land but full of complaints. His cabin, he said, was "leekey Smooke." He told Washington he would stay till fall and then quit. His wife had not wanted to come, and he hated the place. In June he left but assured Washington he had everything in good order and had given directions to his workers. He said he might return in September when there were fewer flies. Washington wrote him a sharp letter, which is now lost, and Simpson replied that he was "Reyley Sorrey," but it was all the fault of his wife, the worthless hands that Washington had sent, the flies, the bad housing, and the colds and boils from which he suffered. Somehow, Washington persuaded him to go back, and Simpson then began asking for money and more helpers, nails, salt, and flour.

The following year war with the Indians broke out. This added to the troubles of Simpson and Washington. More than a thousand fleeing settlers retreated across the Monongahela near Washington's mill property. With wars, interruptions, lack of material, and general inefficiency, Simpson wrote Washington that his mill would probably cost around £700, a figure higher than he had anticipated. He asked for £250 immediately. Simpson acknowledged receipt of the money saying, "I am Sorrey you Should Think the Cost of Your Mill So high." Two months later Simpson asked for a further £300. Washington sent this money and Simpson replied: "I am heartyly Sorrey to heare your uneaseyness Concerning Mills Costing so Much... She has alreydy Cost you double the Money I ever Expect She Was to Cost and She Will Cost a Great Deel More yet." Simpson added that it had been so much trouble he would never do it again; but said he agreed with Washington that gold did not grow on trees but he was doing great service in opening the country to poor people.

In February 1775, Simpson asked for more money, and again said he was sorry but hoped that God would bless Washington, who was doing so much for "the good of Amerecay." On August 20 General Washington wrote from Cambridge to Lund Washington at Mount Vernon after Simpson had requested further funds: "Although I never hear of the Mill under the direction of Simpson, without a degree of warmth and vexation at his stupidity, yet if you can spare the money from other Purposes, I could wish to have it sent to him, that it may, if possible, be set agoing before the Works get ruined and spoilt, and my money perhaps totally lost."

Simpson did get the mill in operation and kept it working during the war, but he seems to have kept no accounts, and he offered a settlement in worthless continental currency. Washington figured in 1784 that he had lost some £1,200 on the deal.

c. Land Settlement

Washington was scrupulous in following the Virginia laws relating to settling and clearing land, although the difficulties in attending to this from a great distance were immense.

In March 1774, he got together some twenty slaves and indentured servants and a great quantity of equipment and provisions to send to his lands in the Ohio Valley. The Indian war, known as Lord Dunmore's war, broke out at this time, and the intended settlers fled, abandoning the equipment and leaving Washington considerably out of pocket. On October 10 the battle of Point Pleasant took place near Washington's Kanawha lands.

In 1775 he tried again. The first expedition to settle his lands within the three years required by law cost Washington about three hundred pounds. The second settlement was, temporarily, more successful. On April 2, 1776, his overseers filed at Fincastle a statement of all the improvements made on Washington's lands in the summer of 1775. This showed they had erected four large houses, a barn, and eight smaller cabins. They had also cleared twenty-eight acres and planted corn, potatoes, and turnips as well as two thousand peach stones that Washington had ordered. These improvements were valued at eleven hundred pounds for tax purposes. No record has been found as to the final fate of this enterprise, but it can be assumed that, during the revolution, it was destroyed by Indians.

BOUCHER AND JACKY CUSTIS

While Washington worked on diverse problems, he continued his efforts to provide Jacky Custis with an education. This he did more or less against Jacky's wishes and despite the ineffectual Reverend Jonathan Boucher, who had moved his school to Maryland.

In early 1770, Boucher appears to have been in some financial difficulties. He endeavored to persuade Washington to let him borrow money from Custis' estate. Washington did not like this proposal, and Boucher dropped it. He then took another tack, proposing to take Jacky on a two-year Grand Tour of Europe at Jacky's expense. Boucher's letter of May 9, 1770, assured Washington "it will not be thought that I can possibly have any interested Views in this Matter." The plan was entirely for Jacky's benefit, though Boucher did admit that he wanted to see England again. On May 21 Boucher wrote an exceedingly long amplification of his earlier views, again urging its great advantage to Jacky. He estimated the trip would cost a thousand pounds a year, of which half would be allocated to Mr. Boucher.

Washington replied that he thought travel would be advantageous to Jacky provided that he first had a good classical education. He noted that he was Jacky's trustee and he had to manage Jacky's affairs wisely. Jacky's estate was not too profitable because feeding and clothing the slaves was a very heavy charge, and the lands were of a rather low yield. Having been informed of the possible cost by Boucher, Washington had consulted others who had travelled. Washington wrote that the trip might cost a great deal more than the estimate, and Jacky would have to "break into the capital." To do this, Washington needed court approval.

Boucher persisted with his plan. He asked the governor of Maryland, Robert Eden, for leave to travel and wrote that the governor had granted this in order to oblige Washington and Jacky. He had discussed the value of the estate with the governor, estimating it at a thousand to twelve hundred pounds per annum, which the governor thought would cover their expenses.

On July 9, 1771, Washington sent Boucher a letter to which he had given much thought. He noted that his friends and advisers had conflicting views on the matter. The trip would be expensive, and he had to account to the general court for "every farthing." He then said:

> *His education, from what I have understood of his improvement... is by no means ripe enough for a travelling tour; not that I think his becoming a mere scholar is a desirable education for a gentleman; but I conceive a knowledge of books is the basis upon which other knowledge is to be built; and that it is men and things more than books he is to be acquainted with by travelling. At present, however well versed he may be in the principles of the Latin language (which is not to be wondered at, as he began the study of it as soon as he could speak), he is unacquainted with several of their classical authors, which might be useful to him to read. He is ignorant of Greek... knows nothing of French... little or nothing acquainted with arithmetic, and totally ignorant of the mathematics; than which, so much of it at least as*

relates to surveying, nothing can be more essentially necessary to any man possessed of a large landed estate…

I should think myself wanting in candour, if I concealed any circumstances from you… Before I ever thought myself at liberty to encourage this plan, I judged it highly reasonable and necessary, that his mother should be consulted. I laid your first letter and proposals to her, and desired that she would ponder it well, before she resolved, as an unsteady behaviour might be a disadvantage to you. Her determination was, that, if it appeared to be his inclination to undertake this tour, and it should be adjudged for his benefit, she would not oppose it, whatever pangs it might give her to part with him. This declaration she still adheres to, but in so faint a manner, that I think, what with her fears and his indifference, it will soon be declared that he has no inclination to go.

Boucher did not get his trip, nor did he succeed in advancing Jacky's education very much. He was, however, successful in getting him inoculated against small-pox. Washington wanted this done, but the operation had to be concealed from his mother. Washington asked Boucher to write him about it "in a hand not your own… I am sure she cou'd not rest satisfied without knowing the Contents of any Letter to this Family of your writing." Jacky was sent secretly to Baltimore, but he was in such a funk he nearly failed to go through with it. Martha Washington, finally informed of the result by the normally courageous but in this case rather timid Washington, was relieved that her son was now immune.

Washington returned Jacky to school, with a note dated December 16, 1770, which said that his "mind is a good deal released from Study, & more than ever turn'd to Dogs Horses and Guns; indeed upon Dress and equipage, which till of late, he had discovered little Inclination of giving into." He asked Boucher not to let him ramble "about of Nights in Company with those, who do not care how debauched and viceous his Conduct may be." Boucher, though a man of the cloth, was himself rather addicted to drinking, and there is some indication that he had an affair with his housekeeper. For awhile he did watch Jacky, but he then drifted off to more interesting things, including his own courtship and marriage.

In June of 1771 Washington wrote to Boucher to tell him that Jacky had learned very little and that he was giving insufficient attention to his studies. Washington's August letter to his stepson seems to have been lost, but he apparently chided him for inattention and bad spelling. Jacky replied on August 18:

I am exceedingly thankful for your Remarks on my Letters, which I am sorry to say, are but too just. It is however really true, that I was in a hurry, when I wrote; and though undoubtedly I might have found time, I am obliged to own, that I am one of those who put every thing to the last. And how it should or does happen, I know not, but so it is, that tho I can certainly write as good English, & spell, as well as most people yet when hurried I very seldom do either, I might perhaps account for it in a manner less reproachfully to Me, but, as you have attributed it to Carelessness alone, & as Appearances are so much against me, I suppose it is so. All therefore that I can do now is promise to be more attentive & watchful for the future; your gentle yet very striking observations shall have their due weight with me.

By fall Washington was in touch with Dr. John Witherspoon, president of the college at Princeton, who indicated that he thought Jacky Custis was deficient in his education. Washington wrote to his stepson, who showed the letter to Boucher. Witherspoon was a Presbyterian minister and a Whig, while Boucher was an Anglican minister and a Tory. The latter reacted with emotion in his letter to Washington of November 19, 1771:

I have seen your Letter to your Son, &, I will own to You, it has given Me a sensible Concern. That my Attention to Him has not lately been so close nor so rigid, as I wish'd, or, as it ought to have been, is a Truth I will not attempt to deny. The Peculiarities of my Circumstances & Situation, as well as of my Temper & Disposition, are All I have to offer in my Excuse... I know that I might have taught him more than I have... Dr. Witherspoon says I <u>ought</u> to have put Him in Greek. Now, how much Deference soever I owe to his Authority, I will venture to say, that this Declaration, at least, must have been made much at random... I neither have attended, nor dare I promise that I can attend, to Him with the Regularity of a School-Master. But, Sir, tho' the little unessential Minutia of School-Learning may have sometimes been neglected, & thro' my Fault; I think I know You to be too observant & too candid a Man to believe that he has been wholly unattended to... Remiss as I am, or seem to be, I doubt not, in due Time, to deliver Him up to You a <u>good</u> Man, if not a very learned one...

If, after all, You resolve on removing Him, all I have to add is a Request, that it may not be to Princeton.

Washington looked into William and Mary and, not finding it to his satisfaction, decided to send Jacky to King's College (Columbia) in New York. Before he got him placed, there was a new development. George and Martha Washington had visited Annapolis to see Jacky. There they dined with Benedict Calvert and his daughters. Calvert was an illegitimate son of the fifth Lord Baltimore who, in turn, descended from an illegitimate daughter of

Charles II; he had married a distant cousin, Elizabeth Calvert, daughter of a one-time governor of Maryland. In early 1773, when Jacky was eighteen, he abruptly announced that he was engaged to Eleanor (Nelly), their daughter.

The Washingtons were considerably shocked since an engagement was then considered an absolute promise to marry. Boucher heard from the governor of Maryland that the Washingtons blamed him. He protested to Washington that he had not had "the most distant suspicion of any such Thing's being in Agitation." George wrote Benedict Calvert a lengthy letter on the matter, indicating the size of Jacky's estate, saying they would not oppose the marriage but hoped that he would go to college first.

Jacky agreed to enter King's College, then under the direction of the Reverend Myles Cooper, a Tory who, not long afterwards, fled to England. Included on its staff was the Reverend John Vardill, who became a British spy during the revolution. On their way to New York, Washington took Jacky to Annapolis, where they stayed with Eden, whose wife was a sister of the sixth Lord Baltimore. Eden accompanied Washington and Jacky as far as Philadelphia, where they dined with Governor Penn. Washington attended the Philadelphia Assembly ball and met various persons, such as Robert Morris, who would aid him in the revolution.

At New York on May 27, Washington attended a dinner given by the city for General Gage, British commander in chief in North America. Gage had been his old companion-in-arms at Braddock's defeat. A few days later Washington dined privately with him; slightly over two years later they were to face each other as enemies. On Washington's return trip, having deposited Jacky and a hundred pounds in cash at the college, he toured the Pennsylvania Dutch country. After visiting Haverford, Lancaster, and York, he proceeded by way of Baltimore to Mount Vernon.

Washington was always fond of and close to Burwell Bassett, who had married a sister of Martha Washington. To him he wrote letters of cheer and sorrow. On February 15, 1773, he dropped Bassett a note: "Our celebrated fortune, Miss French, whom half the world was in pursuit of, bestowed her hand on Wednesday last, being her birthday (you perceive I think myself under a necessity of accounting for the choice) upon Mr. Ben Dulany, who is to take her to Maryland in a month from this time. Mentioning of one wedding puts me in mind of another, tho' of less dignity. This is the marriage of Mr. Henderson... to a Miss More... remarkable for a very frizzled head, and of good singing, the latter of which I shall presume it was that captivated our merchant."

Not long afterward, tragedy struck the Bassett and Washington households when both families lost daughters. On April 25, Washington wrote to Bassett: "That we sympathize in the misfortune, and lament the decree that has deprived you of so dutiful a child, and the world of so promising a young lady, stands in no need, I hope, of argument to prove; but the ways of Providence being inscrutable, and the justice of it not to be scanned by the shallow eye of humanity, nor to be counteracted by the utmost efforts of human power or wisdom, resignation, and as far as the strength of our reason and religion can carry us, a cheerful acquiescence to the Divine Will, is what we are to aim; and I am persuaded that your own good sense will arm you with fortitude to withstand the stroke, great as it is, and enable you to console Mrs. Bassett, whose loss and feelings are much to be pitied." On June 20, only a few days after his return from New York, Washington again wrote Bassett:

> It is an easier matter to conceive, than to describe the distress of this Family; especially that of the unhappy Parent of our Dear Patsy Custis, when I inform you that yesterday... the Sweet Innocent Girl Entered into a more happy and peaceful abode than any she has met with in the afflicted Path she has trod.
>
> She rose from Dinner about four o'clock in better health and spirits than she appeared to have been in for some time; soon after she was seized with one of her usual Fits, and expired in it, in less than two minutes without uttering a word, a groan, or scarce a sigh. This sudden, and unexpected blow, I scarce add had almost reduced my poor Wife to the lowest ebb of misery; which is encreas'd by the absence of her son... and want of the balmy consolation of her Relations; which leads me more than ever to wish she could see them, and that I was Master of Arguments powerful enough to prevail upon Mrs. Dandridge to make this place her entire and absolute home. I should think as she lives a lonesome life (Betsey being married) it might suit her well, and be agreeable, both to herself and my Wife, to me most assuredly it would.

The death of Patsy Custis brought a division of her estate between her brother and Martha Washington, her share going to her husband. Washington received some eight thousand pounds in British bonds, which roughly balanced his British debts. Jacky Custis, on being informed of the death of his sister, wrote moving letters to his mother and stepfather. Almost inevitably, he decided it was time to quit school, and in September he returned to Mount Vernon. He was married the following February to Nelly Calvert.

After Jacky left for college, Boucher wrote Washington to say that he had to forego a planned trip to Mount Vernon, adding that "I have often owned with shame and terror that I did not do so much for him as I could or ought... It is peculiarly vexing to be... disappointed in the pleasure I had promised myself from this visit to a family and some friends, I am proud to rank by far the nearest to me."

In 1775 Boucher took flight for England. He wrote the American commander in chief a farewell note: "You are no longer worthy of my friendship. A man of honour can no longer without dishonour be connected with you." Washington simply noted in his account book a loss of four pounds ten shillings owed him by Mr. Boucher who had "removed" to England.

In his native country Boucher wrote a book about his adventures in Virginia. He said of the man he had troubled so much: "I did know Mr. Washington well... I cannot conceive how he could... have ever been spoken of as a great man. He is shy, silent, stern, slow and cautious, but has no quickness of parts, extraordinary penetration, nor an elevated style of thinking. In his moral character he is regular, temperate, strictly just and honest... excepting... he has lately found out that there is no moral turpitude in not paying what he confesses he owes to a British creditor."

WASHINGTON AND PEALE

Boucher performed one good service in persuading Charles Wilson Peale, who had returned to Maryland after studying in London with Benjamin West, to visit Mount Vernon. Peale arrived at Washington's house with Custis on May 18, 1772. Washington was delighted to have him and to order miniatures of Mrs. Washington, Jacky, and Martha Custis. They promptly got after the colonel to have his portrait made in the uniform of the Virginia Regiment. To his family, to Boucher, and to Peale, therefore, the country is indebted for the first painting of Washington made when he was forty years old. Washington's diary notes on Peale were succinct:

18. In the Evening Mr. Peale and J. P. Custis came to Mount Vernon.
20. I sat to have my Picture drawn.
21. I set again to take the Drapery.
22. Set for Mr. Peale to finish my Face.

Washington described the experience to Boucher on May 21: "Inclination having yielded to Importunity, I am now contrary to all expectations under the hands of Mr. Peale; but in so grave—so sullen a mood—and now and then under the influence of Morpheus, when some critical strokes are making, that I fancy the skill of this gentleman's pencil, will be put to it, in describing to the World what manner of man I am."

For many years thereafter, the reluctant Washington was dragged before the easel by all sorts of painters, good and bad. He sat for Peale at least seven times. In May of 1785, when he was painted by Robert Pine, who had also painted George II, Washington wrote the witty Francis Hopkinson:

> *In for a penny, in for a pound is an old adage. I am so hackneyed to the touches of the Painters pencil, that I am now altogether at their beck, and sit like patience on a Monument whilt they are delineating the lines on my face.*

> *It is a proof among many others of what habit and custom can effect. At first I was as impatient at the request, and as restive under the operation, as a Colt is of the Saddle. The next time, I submitted very reluctantly with less flouncing. Now no dray moves more readily to the Thill than I do to the Painters Chair.*

Washington's diary mentions other houseguests who were at Mount Vernon with Peale. Several of the younger men were out pitching an iron bar when, as Peale related it: "Suddenly the Colonel appeared among us. He requested to be shown the pegs that marked the bounds of our effort; then, smiling, and without putting off his coat, held out his hand for the missile. No sooner did the heavy iron bar feel the grasp of his mighty hand than it lost the power of gravitation, and whizzed through the air, striking the ground far, very far, beyond our utmost limits. We were indeed amazed, as we stood all stripped to the buff, with shirt sleeves rolled up, and having thought ourselves very clever fellows, while the Colonel, on retiring, pleasantly observed, 'When you beat my pitch, young gentlemen, I'll try again.'"

LORD DUNMORE

Virginia had been fortunate in two royal governors, Fauquier and Botetourt, who had been genuinely mourned after their deaths in office. John Murray, earl of Dunmore, was of a different stripe. He was not by nature inclined to be conciliatory like his predecessors; the increasing opposition to British policies served only to raise his natural choler. Although the dispute with Britain began to take a more serious turn after 1773, Washington got along well enough personally with Dunmore, with whom he dined frequently at the palace. Dunmore was interested in acquiring western lands. Washington was about the only Virginian of prominence who had been far west. Dunmore questioned him at length about the area and asked Washington to accompany him on a tour. Washington agreed to this but the death of his stepdaughter forced him to cancel the trip.

In 1774, Dunmore, fearing that the Pennsylvanians would seize Fort Pitt, which Virginia claimed, sent a garrison to that post. There was an Indian uprising shortly afterwards in much of the area over which Washington had travelled in 1770. Dunmore ordered out the militia under Colonel Andrew Lewis. In October 1774, Lewis defeated the Indians at Point Pleasant. By then the colony was in an uproar over British measures in Massachusetts, and Dunmore found Virginians more troublesome than Indians.

THE TEA PARTY

When the East India Company, a pet of the British government, ran into financial trouble, London proposed to allow its surplus of tea to pass through England free of the shilling-a-pound duty. It could then be sold in America with only a threepenny tax and be cheaper than before. Whether Lord North discussed the proposal with the king is not known, but if so it was probably only in passing. There is only a brief reference to it in George III's correspondence in a note by North: "The House went... into the East India Committee, where they came into three resolutions, concerning the Exportation of Tea to America and foreign parts; There was some debate, but the questions passed without a division."

By greatly reducing the price of tea, the act placed the East India Company in the strongest competitive position to the dismay of such a smuggling merchant as John Hancock, who was pro-Tory or pro-Whig, depending on the way the wind blew for John Hancock. Under the leadership of the wooly-minded Samuel Adams, a Boston mob pitched 342 chests of tea into the town harbor on December 16, 1773. Other cities did much the same. These senseless acts, deplored by Franklin and Washington, cast a long shadow on the efforts of Americans to appear responsible and reasonable arguers of constitutional law. They greatly strengthened the hands of English Tories who wanted far stricter control of the colonies. When news of the mob's work reached London, General Gage, the commander in chief in America, called on the king who recorded their conversation in a note to Lord North, dated February 4, 1774:

Since You left me... I have seen Lieutenant General Gage, who came to express his readiness though so lately come from America to return at a day's notice if the conduct of the colonies should induce the directing coercive measures... He says they will be Lyons, whilst we are Lambs but if we take the resolute part they will undoubtedly prove very meek; he thinks the four Regiments intended to Relieve as many Regiments in America if sent to Boston are sufficient to prevent any disturbance; I wish You would see him and hear his ideas as the mode of compelling Boston to submit to whatever may be thought necessary; indeed all men seem now to feel that the fatal compliance in 1766 has encouraged the Americans annually to encrease in their pretensions that thorough independence which one State has of another, but which is quite subversive to the obedience which a Colony owes to its Mother Country.

The king was not a wicked or an ill-intentioned man, but he was wrapped up in cotton wool, away from the world. It is not known that he ever saw or talked with an American other than a royal appointee. Franklin, who was intensely loyal to Britain, was in London for years without ever being questioned about America by George III. The king got his ideas from his royal governors or from army men like Gage, and they were always prejudiced and almost always wrong.

Franklin in London wrote that America never had so few friends in England as after the destruction of the tea. The king, North, and Parliament proceeded to be lions by punishing at once the guiltless majority in Massachusetts as well as the Hancock–Sam Adams mobs. The Boston Port Act, blockading the port and removing the customs house to Salem, passed without a division. This act was to continue in force until the East India Company was reimbursed and the king satisfied that Boston had returned to obedience.

In triumph North then rammed through a series of frontal attacks on all of Massachusetts. The acts bore remarkably innocent titles. A bill for the better regulation of the government of Massachusetts Bay abolished the elected council and established royally appointed councillors, judges, magistrates, and sheriffs. A bill for the impartial administration of justice permitted the governor to send indicted persons outside the province for trial. One of the few voices of protest in Parliament was that of Thomas Pownall, a former royal governor of Massachusetts and a friend of Franklin, who informed North in debate: "I tell you the Americans will oppose the measures, now proposed by you, in a more vigorous way than before. The Committees of Correspondence in the different provinces are in constant communication... As soon as intelligence of these affairs reaches them, they will judge it necessary to communicate with each other. It will be found inconvenient and ineffectual to do so by letters. They must confer. They will hold a Conference; and to what these committees, thus met in congress; will draw up, I will not say. Should recourse be made to arms, you will hear of other officers than those appointed by your governor."

The king closely followed the bills as they moved through first, second, and third readings. At each stage he dropped little notes to Lord North: "Infinitely pleased... Infinite satisfaction... much pleasure." The king informed North that perseverance and firmness were the only sure guides to administering public affairs successfully.

The king had his final pleasure when the Quebec bill became law. From the American point of view this act was ominous because it extended south to the Ohio River the boundaries of Quebec, thus blotting out the ancient charter claims of several American colonies. The act also abolished the Quebec Assembly and established a system of internal and external taxes for that province. The lord chancellor stated that it was the kind of charter the American colonies should have been given originally.

To enforce the new acts the king appointed General Gage, commander in chief of the British army in America, as governor of Massachusetts. On July 1, after talking to Thomas Hutchinson, Gage's predecessor, George III wrote North: "I am now well convinced they will soon submit; he owns the Boston Port Bill was the only wise effectual method... for bringing them to a speedy submission... One of the Regiments arrived the 1st of June the day he sailed, and the People of Boston seem much dispirited." On September 11 he again wrote North: "The dye is now cast, the Colonies must either submit or triumph; I do not wish to come to severer measures but we must not retreat; by coolness and an unremitted pursuit of the measures that have been adopted I trust they will come to submit."

VIRGINIA REACTS

The Boston Port Act, designed to close the harbor on June 1, 1774, and to starve the people into submission, brought a violent wave of reaction throughout the continent. Everywhere, efforts were made to send supplies, food, and money to the city, not only from the other American colonies, but even from Quebec and England itself. Israel Putnam drove 130 sheep from Connecticut to Boston. Washington subscribed fifty pounds to funds for the city.

On May 12, Washington set off for Williamsburg, stopping in Fredericksburg to see his mother. He arrived in the capital on the sixteenth and dined with Governor Dunmore. About the nineteenth, the news of the Boston Port Act reached the Burgesses. On May 24, after they had had a few days to consider it, Robert Carter Nicholas, the colony's treasurer, introduced a resolution:

> *This House, being deeply impressed with Apprehension of the great Dangers to be derived to British America from the hostile Invasion of the city of Boston... whose Commerce and Harbour are, on the 1st Day of June next, to be stopped by an armed Force, deem it highly necessary that the said first Day of June be set apart, by the Members of this House, as a day of Fasting, Humiliation and Prayer, devoutly to implore the divine Interposition, for averting the heavy Calamity which threatens*

*Destruction to our civil Rights, and the Evils of civil War; to give us one Heart
and one Mind firmly to oppose, by all just and proper Means, every Injury to
American Rights; and that the minds of his Majesty and his Parliament, may be
inspired from above with Wisdom, Moderation and Justice, to remove... all Cause
of Danger from a continued Pursuit of Measures pregnant with their Ruin.*

This was a stronger resolve than had ever passed the Burgesses. The British
government had assumed that a few regiments would overawe Boston, while
other colonies would ignore the measures. Two days after its passage, the governor, saying the resolution reflected highly on the king and Parliament,
ordered the House dissolved. Landon Carter noted in his diary that it seemed
to be the first time that a prayer asking that king and Parliament might have
wisdom, justice, and moderation, a phrase modelled on the Prayer Book, was
thought to be derogatory.

The Burgesses moved to the Raleigh Tavern and there passed even stronger
resolutions, the most important of which was a call for a congress of all the
colonies. They then adjourned to attend a ball for Lady Dunmore at the
palace. On May 29 Washington went to Divine Service in the morning and
afternoon. On the same or the following day, urgent dispatches reached
Williamsburg containing the calls of Massachusetts, Pennsylvania, and
Maryland for united action. Virginia, in turn, forwarded them to North
Carolina. On June 1, Washington wrote in his diary: "Went to Church and
fasted all day." Landon Carter recorded that his rector the same day omitted
the usual "God Save the King" and asked God, instead, to preserve the rights
and liberties of America.

On August 5 the Burgesses, now calling themselves a convention, voted to
send seven men to the general congress of the colonies scheduled to meet at
Philadelphia in September. They were Peyton Randolph, speaker of the house,
Richard Henry Lee, George Washington, Patrick Henry, Richard Bland,
Benjamin Harrison, and Edmund Pendleton. The die was indeed cast;
Governor Pownall's prediction of a congress was fulfilled in a matter of months.

From the Virginia convention, a rumor sped through the continent that
Washington, in a dramatic speech, had said: "I will raise one thousand men,
subsist them at my own expense and march myself at their head for the relief
of Boston." There is no evidence that he ever said it, though it may have been
a garbled version of something he did say. It was quoted from New England
to Charleston and served to recall to many the legendary Colonel Washington
of the French and Indian wars.

WASHINGTON'S VIEWS

On June 10, 1774, Washington wrote to George Fairfax who, though resident in England, was strongly pro-American:

> *Our Assembly met at this place the 4th... and was dissolved the 26th for entering into a Resolve... which the Governor thought reflected too much upon his Majesty and the British Parliament... This Dissolution was as sudden as unexpected for there were other resolves of a much more spirited nature ready to be offered to the House wch. would have been unanimously adopted respecting the Boston Port Bill... The day after this Event the Members convend... at the Raleigh Tavern and enterd into the Inclosd Association... the Ministry may rely on it that Americans will never be tax'd without their own consent that the cause of Boston the despotick measures in respect to it I mean now is and ever will be considerd as the cause of America (not that we approve their conduct in destroyg. the Tea) and that we shall not suffer ourselves to be sacrificd by piece meals though god only knows what is to become of us, threatend as we are with so many hoverg. evils as hang over us at present; having a cruel and blood thirsty Enemy upon our Backs, the Indians... with whom a general War is inevitable whilst those from who we have a right to seek protection are endeavouring by every piece of Art and despotism to fix the Shackles of Slavery upon us... Since the first Settlement of this Colony the Minds of people in it never were more disturbed, or our Situation so critical as at present... arising from an Invasion of our rights and Priviledges by the Mother Country; and our lives and properties by the Savages.*

While George Fairfax was supporting the Americans in England, his brother, Bryan, who remained in America, was Loyalist in sympathy. Since he was neither active nor dangerous, Washington saw to it that he was not molested during the war. Early in 1774, he had suggested that Bryan run for the House of Burgesses but the latter declined, feeling, as he explained, that he was almost alone in the county in opposing strong measures. He gave his views to which Washington replied on July 4, 1774:

> *As to your political sentiments, I would heartily join you in them, so far as relates to a humble and dutiful petition to the throne, provided there was the most distant hope of success. But have we not tried this already? Have we not addressed the Lords, and remonstrated to the Commons? And to what end? Did they deign to look at our petitions? Does it not appear, as clear as the sun in its meridian brightness, that there is a regular, systematic plan formed to fix the right and practice of taxation upon us? Does not the uniform conduct of Parliament for some years past confirm this?... Is not*

the attack upon the liberty and property of the people of Boston, before restitution of the loss to the India Company was demanded, a self-evident proof of what they are aiming at? Do not the subsequent bills (now I dare say acts), for depriving the Massachusetts Bay of its charter, and for transporting offenders into other colonies or to Great Britain for trial where it is impossible from the nature of the thing that justice can be obtained, convince us that the administration is determined to stick at nothing to carry its point? Ought we not, then, to put our virtue and fortitude to the severest test?

FAIRFAX RESOLVES

The dissolution of the House required new elections. Washington again stood in Fairfax where he was unopposed. George Mason, in consultation with Washington, drew up a series of resolutions to be discussed and approved by the county voters, subsequent to the election for the House. They were sharp in tone, stating that Americans were subjects and not slaves of the British government. Americans possessed all the rights of Englishmen and of the British constitution and had the sole right to tax themselves through their assemblies. British action to tax them, "if continued," would result in "the most grievous and intolerable species of tyranny and oppression that was ever inflicted on mankind." The resolves then called for nonimportation, a general congress of all the colonies, and a final petition to the king from whom "there can be but one appeal." This last phrase may have been inserted by Washington.

Bryan Fairfax wrote a temperate letter to Washington just before the meeting in which he pointed out that Americans had often been inconsistent. They had said Parliament had no right to tax them, but that in other measures Parliament was supreme. Now they were moving to deny any parliamentary right over America. They should accept the Constitution and petition only. He asked Washington to present his views; Washington handed his letter around, but he informed Fairfax afterwards that no one seeemed to be interested in them. He added:

That I differ very widely from you... I shall not hesitate to acknowledge... I see nothing... to induce a belief that the Parliament would embrace a favourable opportunity of repealing acts, which they go on with great rapidity to pass, and in order to enforce their tyrannical system...

The conduct of the Boston people did not justify the rigour of their measures unless there had been a requisition of payment and refusal of it; nor did that measure require an act to deprive the government of Masachusetts Bay of their charter, or to exempt offenders from trial in the place where offences were committed, as there was not, nor could not be, a single instance produced to manifest the necessity of it. Are not all these things self evident proofs of a fixed and uniform plan to tax us? If we want further proofs, do not all the debates in the House of Commons serve to confirm this? And has not General Gage's conduct since his arrival, (in stopping the address of his Council, and publishing a proclamation more becoming a Turkish bashaw than an English governor, declaring it treason to associate in any manner by which the commerce of Great Britain is to be affected,) exhibit a testimony of the most despotic system of tyranny, that was ever practised in a free government?... What hope then from petitioning... Shall we, after all this, whine and cry for relief, when we have already tried it in vain? Or shall we supinely sit and see one province after another fall a prey to despotism?

As to the resolution for addressing the throne, I own to you, Sir, I think the whole might well have been expunged. I expect nothing from the measure, nor should my voice have accompanied it, if the non-importation scheme was intended to be retarded by it; for I am convinced, as much as I am of my existence, that there is no relief but in their distress; and I think, at least I hope, that there is public virtues enough left among us to deny ourselves every thing but the bare necessities of life... This we have a right to do, and no power upon earth can compel us to do otherwise, till they have first reduced us to the most abject state of slavery that ever was designed for mankind.

Had Washington's letters been published at the time, they would have made a stirring appeal to his countrymen, but his best efforts were reserved for private letters to his friends. On August 5, Washington wrote from Williamsburg to Thomas Johnson in Maryland to inform him that Virginia had agreed to send delegates to Philadelphia on September 5, though they had hoped the meeting would be somewhat later and that it would take place in Lancaster. He noted that they had never had so full an attendance at the legal Assembly as they did at the illegal convention of the same men. On August 7 he wrote to his fellow delegate, Richard Henry Lee, to ask him to obtain from the customs houses figures on commerce with Great Britain. He also mentioned that he would be glad to have Lee's company on the way to Philadelphia. On August 24 he again wrote to Bryan Fairfax to say that he was sure the unanimity of the colonies had been entirely unexpected in Britain, as indeed it was, and that he was also sure that the quiet behavior of the people of Massachusetts Bay was more disconcerting to Gage than anything else could have been. He put in as a lightly needling postscript: "Pray what do you think of the Canada Bill?"

FIRST CONTINENTAL CONGRESS

On August 30, two Virginia delegates, Patrick Henry and Edmund Pendleton, arrived at Mount Vernon. George Mason came over from Gunston Hall to confer with them. The next day Washington recorded in his diary: "With Colo. Pendleton and Mr. Henry, I set out on my journey for Phila. and reached uppr. Marlbro." On September 4 the three men arrived at Philadelphia. Next day the Continental Congress came formally into session under the presidency of Speaker Randolph of Virginia.

Washington's diary records for the Congress are of almost no import. On September 6 he wrote: "Dind at the New Tavern, after being in Congress all day." He noted various people who later served in the revolution, such as Thomas Mifflin and Joseph Reed. He did not mention, though, that he met John Adams, Samuel Adams, Robert Treat Paine, and others from Massachusetts. Adams referred to Washington but once in his diary when he described the speech that he was supposed to have made at the Virginia convention. In his autobiography years later he expanded his notes from memory:

> On the 5th of September Congress assembled in Carpenters Hall. The Day before I dined with Mr. Lynch a Delegate from South Carolina, who, in conversation on the Unhappy State of Boston... after some Observations had been made on the Eloquence of Mr. Patrick Henry and Mr. Richard Henry Lee, which had been very loudly celebrated by the Virginians, said that the most eloquent Speech that had ever been made in Virginia or any where else, upon American Affairs had been made by Colonel Washington. This was the first time I had ever heard the Name of Washington, as a Patriot in our present controversy, I asked who is Colonel Washington and what was his Speech? Colonel Washington he said was the officer who had been famous in the late French war and in the Battle in which Braddock fell. His Speech was that if the Bostonians should be involved in Hostilities with the British Army he would march to their relief at the head of a Thousand Men at his own expence. This Sentence, Mr. Lynch said, had more Oratory in it, in his Judgment, than any that he had ever heard or read. We all agreed that it was both sublime, pathetic and beautiful.

Much of the time was spent by delegates in assessing each other. Tories and Whigs were represented, and those who wanted accommodation with Britain and those who, like Washington, called for radical measures. Washington's common sense and his knowledge of the country gained him wide influence. He had travelled through nine of the thirteen colonies and farther west than any other delegate. Patrick Henry wrote: "Colonel Washington, who has no pretensions to eloquence, is a man of more solid judgment and information than any man on the floor."

One effort was made by the British, perhaps at the instance of General Gage, to woo Washington to their viewpoint. Captain Robert Mackenzie, a former officer of the Virginia Regiment who had purchased a British commission and was then stationed with Gage in Boston, wrote to urge an accommodation with Britain. Mackenzie said Massachusetts was in an unhappy state, its policies aimed at independence, and therefore abler heads and better hearts were needed to draw a line for the guidance of the province. He called the people rebellious and their attacks on authority scandalous while he stressed Gage's efforts to establish full military authority. Washington wrote to Mackenzie (and thus perhaps indirectly to Gage) on October 9, 1774:

Permit me with the freedom of a friend (for you know I always esteemed you) to express my sorrow, that fortune should place you in a service, that must fix curses to the latest posterity upon the diabolical contrivers, and, if success (which, by the by, is impossible) accompanies it, execrations upon all those, who have been instrumental in the execution.

...When you condemn the conduct of the Massachusetts people, you reason from effects, not causes; otherwise you would not wonder at a people, who are every day receiving fresh proofs of a systematic assertion of an arbitrary power, deeply planned to overturn the laws and constitution of their country, and to violate the most essential rights of mankind, being irritated, and with difficulty restrained from acts of the greatest violence and intemperance... You are led to believe by venal men, for such I must take the liberty of calling those new-fangled counsellors, which fly to and surround you, and all others, who, for honorary or pecuniary gratifications, will lend their aid to overturn the constitution, and introduce a system of arbitrary government... Give me leave, my good friend, to tell you, that you are abused, grossly abused, and this I advance with a degree of confidence and boldness... having better opportunities of knowing the real sentiments of the people you are among, from the leaders of them... than you have from those whose business it is, not to disclose truths, but to misrepresent facts... It is not the wish of that government, or any other upon this continent... to set up for independency; but this you may at the same time rely on, that none of them will ever submit to the loss of those valuable rights and privileges, which are essential to the happiness of every free state...

Give me leave to add as my opinion, that more blood will be spilt on this occasion, if the ministry are determined to push matters to extremity, than history has ever yet

*furnished instances of in the annals of North America, and such a vital wound
given to the peace of this great country as time itself cannot cure, or eradicate the
remembrance of.*

This was stronger language than almost any used at the congress but
Washington had long moved to the most radical of positions. Congress,
though having to compromise divergent views, accomplished a great deal.
The members endorsed the resolves of Suffolk County in Massachusetts,
which said the coercive acts were illegal and therefore need not be obeyed.
Congress issued a declaration of American rights, approved an economic boycott of Great Britain, and threatened to cut off American exports in 1775 if
the coercive acts were not repealed.

Washington left Philadelphia on October 27 and reached Mount Vernon on
October 30. On November 17 he wrote to William Milnor in Philadelphia to
order treatises on military discipline and a hundred muskets. He followed with
orders for drums and fifes. By the time he returned to Virginia, numerous county
committees had organized armed companies, and George Washington was
invited by many to be their commander. His own county, Fairfax, adopted the
Whig colors, buff and blue, which General Washington wore through the ensuing war.

BRITAIN REACTS

Massachusetts largely ignored General Gage, the governor and commander in
chief, who remained in Boston. Its legislature moved to Concord, elected
John Hancock its president, and proceeded to take over the government of
the rest of Massachusetts. Independent companies were ordered, trained, and
drilled. A system of espionage was established and relief supplies were
ordered for Bostonians. Boston, with its port shut, saw its merchants in ruins,
unemployment high, and friends of Britain suffering with the rest. Under
their pressure Gage pleaded with London to let him drop the Port and other
acts. The king wrote North on November 18, 1774: "His idea of Suspending
the Acts appears to me the most absurd that can be suggested; the people are
ripe for mischief upon which the Mother Country adopts suspending the measures she has thought necessary this must suggest to the Colonies a fear that
alone prompts them to their present violence; we must either master them or
totally leave them to themselves and treat them as Aliens."

Although the king so wrote, many in England spoke up for the Americans.
The secretary at war, Lord Barrington, wrote to the secretary for the colonies,

Lord Dartmouth, who was Washington's fourth cousin, to say that the contest would bring no gain to Britain. It involved a single point of honor that could not be enforced and was leading to a serious civil war. This could only be won at enormous expense and would thereafter have to be maintained by extensive armies and fleets. In the House of Lords on January 20, 1775, Pitt introduced a resolution to remove all the troops from Boston:

I wish, my lords, not to lose a day in this urgent, pressing crisis; an hour lost in allaying ferments in America, may produce years of calamity...

The glorious spirit of Whiggism animates three millions in America; who prefer poverty with liberty, to guilded chains and sordid affluence; and who will die in defense of their rights as men, as freemen...

...I trust it is obvious to your lordships, that all attempts to impose servitude upon such men, to establish despotism over such a mighty continental nation, must be vain, must be fatal. We shall be forced ultimately to retract; let us retract while we can, not when we must. I say we must necessarily undo these violent oppresive acts: they must be repealed—you will repeal them; I pledge myself that you will in the end repeal them.

Pitt's resolution was voted down 68 to 18. The king was so pleased with his support that he wrote Lord North: "Nothing can be more calculated to bring the Americans to a due submission than the very handsome Majority." Four days later, on January 27, 1775, Lord Dartmouth sent secret orders to General Gage informing him that the king considered the colonies in rebellion, force should be met by force, and reinforcements were on the way for Gage's four thousand or so effectives, including seven hundred Marines, three regiments of infantry, and one of light dragoons from Ireland. Gage, said Dartmouth, had been too long on the defensive; he added:

It is hoped however that this large Reinforcement to your Army will enable you to take a more active & determined part...

...It is the Opinion of the King's Servants in which His Majesty concurs, that the first essential step to be taken towards re-establishing Government, would be to arrest and imprison the principal actors & abettors in the Provincial Congress... If the steps taken upon this occasion be accompanied with due precaution, and every means be devised to keep the Measure Secret until the moment of Execution, it can hardly fail of Success, and will perhaps be accomplished without bloodshed; but

however that may be I must again repeat that any efforts of the People, unprepared to encounter with a regular force, cannot be formidable; and though such a proceeding should be, according to your own idea of it, a Signal for Hostilities yet, for the reasons I have already given, it will surely be better that the Conflict should be brought on, upon such ground, than in a riper state of rebellion.

On February 9, Parliament pledged to the king its support:

We beg leave, in the most solemn manner, to assure Your Majesty, that it is our fixed resolution, at the hazard of our lives and properties, to stand by Your Majesty against all rebellious attempts in the maintainence of the just rights of Your Majesty and the two Houses of Parliament.

PART FOUR

GENERAL AND FARMER
1775–1781

SEVENTEEN

COMMANDER IN CHIEF

1775

L ONDON'S INSTRUCTIONS to General Gage were an order for war. So long as it had to come, the timing for America was, to some extent, lucky. Britain was already advancing into the industrial revolution, which was to make her the world's most formidable power. The growing financial and political troubles of France, under its new weak king, in the course of time might well have made her more cautious about war.

The American War of Independence is often called a civil war, since it split nearly all classes of society in both Great Britain and America. Estimates of those who were Tories in America vary widely. It does appear that, in the initial stages of the war, as high as 40 percent of Americans were opposed to it and to independence. By its end, confirmed Tories may have declined to as low as 10 percent. In England, the opposition at the start was mainly among the better classes. Towards its close, supporters were the king and a few of his friends, with nearly the whole nation in opposition to the war's continuance.

Josiah Quincy, Jr., who was in London as an agent of Massachusetts, talked with so many Englishmen who told him that Americans were fighting their common battle for liberty, that he came to believe that a majority were for the colonies. His diary for January 23, 1775, noted:

Attended a long debate in the House of Commons on American Affairs.

Speakers for the Americans: Burke, Johnston, Charles Fox, T. Townshend, Lord J. Cavendish, Captain Lutterell, Alderman Sawbridge, &c—eighty two. Against the Americans: Sir William Meredith, Lord North, Lord Clare, Sir George Macartney, Sir. G. Eliot, Lord Stanley, &c.—total, one hundred and ninety-seven.

This debate and division show that if King, Lords and Commons can subdue America into bondage against the almost universal sentiment, opinion, wish, and hope of the Englishmen of this island, the deed will be done.

The split affected all of England. Nearly a third of Parliament stood by the Americans. Boswell and Johnson quarreled over the issue, with Tory Boswell for America. The memoirs of the prodigal rake, William Hickey, describe a yachting trip with several Englishmen, including George Dempster, a member of Parliament, Lord George Gordon, and Sir Charles Bingham. Each night on their yacht, renamed *Congress*, they drank treasonable toasts: "Success to the Americans." The generals and admirals divided—Amherst, Cavendish, Pitt, and Keppel, among others, refused to fight them. Other high officers such as Henry Seymour Conway and the duke of Richmond vigorously attacked the war in Parliament. The dukes of Cumberland and Gloucester were against the policy of their brother, the king, the former voting with Pitt on his plan for reconciliation. In the cabinet, too, there was dissension.

THE MINISTRY

The three men principally responsible for the war effort were Lord North, the king's first minister, Lord George Germain, the secretary for American affairs, and Lord Sandwich, first lord of the Admiralty. North, bearing a courtesy title as eldest son of an earl, sat in Commons. He was in power from 1770 to 1782. Short, rotund, and pop-eyed like his king, he was a good-natured man, famous for his wit and debating skill. George III complained that North was lazy and often careless with his accounts. His main drawback for the king, as it turned out, was that he had a conscience in a conscienceless court. He ran a well-oiled machine of corruption, spent the king's money to win elections, and distributed offices, sinecures, titles, and contracts to keep Lords and Commons happy. He himself drew twenty thousand pounds from the treasury, with the king's permission, to pay his personal debts. Yet his scruples were such that, after the battle of Saratoga, he repeatedly told the king the American policies had been wrong and disastrous. He urged the negotiation of peace at almost any price.

Lord George Germain, whose family name was originally Sackville, had served George II as an officer at the battle of Minden, where Lafayette's father was killed. There Germain was accused of cowardice and court-martialed. The probably unjustified verdict was that he was "unfit to serve his Majesty in any military capacity whatever." George III restored him to favor and, at the end of November 1775, following an undignified cabinet dispute over honors, put him in charge of the American colonies. John Montagu, earl of Sandwich, was sufficiently licentious that, even in the freewheeling English eighteenth century, he was regarded as without morals. He was later severely castigated in Parliament, with considerable reason, for corruption and mismanagement in the naval office.

Sandwich was an effective if savage debater. In replying to Pitt's speech on reconciliation with the colonies, he termed Franklin "one of the bitterest and most mischievous enemies this country has ever known," and he said of Americans:

> *The noble Lord [Pitt] mentions the impracticability of conquering America; I cannot think the noble Lord can be serious on this matter. Suppose the Colonies do abound in men, what does that signify? They are raw, undisciplined, cowardly men. Believe me, my Lords, the very sound of a cannon would carry them off... as fast as their feet would carry them.*

Four years later, during the Keppel riots in London, the mob stormed the Admiralty. In Walpole's words, "Lord Sandwich, exceedingly terrified, escaped through the garden *with his mistress*, Miss Ray, to the Horse Guards, and there betrayed a most manifest panic."

On March 2, 1775, just before war began, George Fairfax provided Washington with his appraisal of the situation in England: "What can, or dare I say, about the unhappy difference between this country and America. That you are condemned by the Ministry, and their dependents, and much aplauded by every welwisher to the Antient and Constitutional Rights of Englishmen, whether on this, or the other side of the Atlantic; of which there are a great majority in this County [Yorkshire]. You'll hear probabelly before this reatches you... about the much talked of Motion... I rather think they find they have gone far enough, that the Americans are not so easily duped, and that a War across the Atlantic will be the most expences they have had... It is pretty certain that the Minister has lost ground... A change must soon take place... God grant that it may be for the better, worse I think it cannot be... Yet I fear it never will happen while the Premier has so many lucrative places in his disposal. We can... very justly say that the law is on our side, for all the Law

Lords that do not fill some high office, and many great disinterested Getn. in the Commons, are in support of America."

The king regarded the opposition as personal enemies, if not traitors. He termed them a "motley crew" and "wicked" men. His invective was especially directed at William Pitt, whom he called "a trumpet of sedition."

WASHINGTON IN CONVENTION AND CONGRESS

The Virginia Burgesses met once again in convention on March 20, 1775. Not all the forbidding news from England had reached them, nor could they know of the secret orders to Gage to begin war. It was Patrick Henry who rose to propose measures to put Virginia in a state of defense. He introduced the notion, startling to many but not to Washington, that they might soon have a fight on their hands. Once his resolves carried, Washington was assigned to the military committee for work on recruiting troops in each of the colony's counties. On March 25, he was reelected as delegate to the Second Continental Congress. That same day he wrote his brother John:

> I had like to have forgot to express my entire approbation of the laudable pursuit you are engaged in of Training an Independant Company. I have promised to review the Independant Company of Richmond sometime this Summer, they having made me a tender of the Command of it. At the same time I could review yours and shall very cheerfully accept the honr. of Commanding it, if occasion requires it to be drawn out, as it is my full intention to devote my Life and Fortune in the cause we are engaged in.

Everyone in Virginia with an interest in defense turned automatically to Washington for advice. Two half-pay British officers, Horatio Gates and Charles Lee, who had served with Braddock, came to call at Mount Vernon. The latter, on his second visit, was accompanied by young Harry Lee (not related), who later commanded a troop of light horse.

When, on April 21, a hostile move was made by Governor Dunmore, who removed the powder from the Williamsburg magazine to a British ship, Hugh Mercer, George Weedon, and Alexander Spotswood of the Spotsylvania militia sent an express to Washington to say that "this first Public insult is not to be tamely submitted to," and they proposed to march on Williamsburg. The Prince William and Albemarle companies wrote much the same letters to Washington. The Speaker, Peyton Randolph, however, intervened to stop the use of force while he appealed to the governor. On April 30 Spotswood informed Washington that they had cancelled the proposed march but that he was sure Congress would now want an army. "Their is not the least doubt But youl have the Command of the Whole forces in this Collony." Spotswood assured Washington that he was ready to serve "in the Glorious cause of liberty, at the Risk of my life and fortune Gratis."

LEXINGTON AND CONCORD

Expresses with the news of the battles at Lexington and Concord were ordered to carry the news south while fighting was still in progress. Each town marked its time of arrival. It is possible to trace the news almost hour by hour as the expresses reached Worcester, Norwich, New London, Saybrook, Guilford, New Haven, Fairfield, New York, New Brunswick, Philadelphia, and then south to Annapolis and Alexandria, where the intelligence was forwarded to Williamsburg and the Carolinas. Washington had word of the April 19 battle only a day or two after he heard of Dunmore's actions. This made his trip to Philadelphia the more urgent, as war had begun.

PHILADELPHIA

On May 4, 1775, George Washington left his wife and house for what he hoped would be a rather short absence. He was building a south extension to Mount Vernon, as well as planning to add a front porch, or piazza. He wrote Bryan Fairfax that he always felt the work went a little better when he was around to supervise it. Except for a few days on the way to and from Yorktown in 1781, Washington did not see his house again until Christmas 1783.

Washington was unofficial head of Virginia's troops, through his election as commander of the most important independent county regiments. Automatically he wore his Fairfax County uniform to Philadelphia as a symbol that Virginians would fight alongside their Massachusetts brethren.

At their invitation, Washington reviewed the Baltimore troops on his way north. On May 9 he and his fellow Virginians were escorted into Philadelphia by a band as well as many officers and men of the local volunteer companies. The church bells rang and crowds cheered. The New Englanders, on their arrival, were greeted in the same way. Samuel Curwen, a Loyalist, wrote in his diary that he met Colonel Washington at a dinner. He was "a fine figure and of a most easy and agreeable address." Curwen added that he could find no disposition among the delegates at Philadelphia to make an accommodation with Britain.

Two men were present with firsthand information—Benjamin Franklin, who could give an accurate account of the temper of king and Parliament, and John Adams, who had toured the battlefields of Concord and Lexington and had talked to the American army before Boston. For the first time, Washington, Adams, and Franklin were together, in a war that began near Adams' and Franklin's birthplaces and effectively ended some fifty miles from the farm where Washington was born.

Congress moved swiftly to business. Joseph Warren, physician and soldier, and acting head of the Massachusetts Provincial Congress, rose to say that his colony had voted to raise 13,500 men and that other New England governments were cooperating to establish an American army. The defense of New York came into early focus, and Washington was made chairman of a committee to examine the question.

The delegates were intensely interested in reports on Lexington and Concord and the rapid retreat of the British regulars, who were saved only by the skilled work of the earl of Percy, who was ordered out with relief troops. Lord Percy complained that the Americans fired from behind walls. Washington liked to quote Franklin's subsequent comment that walls had two sides. Franklin wrote Joseph Priestly in England to say the British had had "an *expedition* back again. They retreated twenty miles in six hours." It did not come out at this time what bad shots the embattled farmers were. They scored fewer than three hundred hits out of some ninety thousand rounds expended. Had they been trained marksmen, the effects would have been devastating. Congress examined many affidavits that tended to show that the British fired first but, as Governor Pownall had already observed in Parliament, once blood was shed, it mattered little whose was the first shot. Washington read the affidavits, got as much information as he could, and wrote on May 31 to George Fairfax in England:

> *Before this Letter can reach you, you must, undoubtedly, have received an Account of the engagement in the Massachusetts Bay between the ministerial Troops (for we do not, nor cannot yet prevail upon ourselves to call them the King's Troops) and the Provincials... I inclose you several Affidavits...*

> *General Gage acknowledges, that the detachment under Lieutenant Colonel Smith was sent out to destroy private property; or, in other Words, to destroy a Magazine which self preservation obliged the inhabitants to establish. And he also confesses, in effect at least, that his Men made a very precipitate retreat from Concord,*

notwithstanding the reinforcement under Lord Piercy, the last of which may serve to convince Lord Sandwich (and others of the same sentiment) that the Americans will fight for their Liberties and property, however pusillanimous, in his Lordship's Eye, they may appear in other respects.

From the best Accounts I have been able to collect… if the retreat had not been as precipitate as it was (and God knows it could not well have been more so) the Ministerial Troops must have surrendered, or been totally cut off: for they had not arrived in Charlestown (under cover of their Ships) half an hour before, a powerful body of Men from Marblehead and Salem were at their heels, and must, if they had happened to have been up one hour sooner, inevitably have intercepted their retreat to Charlestown. Unhappy it is thought to reflect, that a Brother's Sword has been sheathed in a Brother's breast, and that, the once happy and peaceful plains of America are either to be drenched with Blood, or Inhabited by Slaves. Sad alternative! But can a virtuous man hesitate in his choice?

When Washington had finished his recommendations for the defense of New York, he was made chairman of a committee composed of Philip Schuyler, Thomas Mifflin, Samuel Adams, Silas Deane, and Lewis Morris, representing colonies from Massachusetts to Virginia, to look into the all-important question of providing ammunition in a country with pitifully little manufacturing. John Adams noted that "Washington… by his great experience and abilities in military matters, is of much service to us."

Congress proceeded slowly but eventually decided to sponsor the New England army serving in Massachusetts, to assist in its financing, to ask for additional recruits from other provinces, and to draft regulations for the new army. Washington moved as chairman from the committee for the defense of New York to ammunitions, then to army finance, and finally to the committee for the regulation of the army. There was only one more step to go.

On May 24 Peyton Randolph was recalled to Virginia to meet with the Assembly called by Lord Dunmore. John Hancock was elected president of Congress in his place. Thomas Jefferson, still on his Charlottesville farm, rode to Williamsburg to join the Burgesses, who, according to Dunmore, displayed such "violence of temper," that he retired to a British warship at sea. Jefferson helped draft resolutions opposing Lord North's conciliatory proposals and then took off, as Randolph's alternate, for Philadelphia. He arrived shortly before Washington left Congress.

On the day after Randolph quit Philadelphia, British reinforcements, including no fewer than three major generals, arrived in Boston on the

Cerberus, a frigate named for the three-headed dog guarding hell. At once a Boston verse was circulated:

> *Behold the Cerberus the Atlantic plough,*
> *Its precious cargo Burgoyne, Clinton, Howe—*
> *Bow! Wow! Wow!*

CONGRESS ADOPTS AN ARMY

The early settlers of America brought with them a strong Anglo-Saxon aversion to a permanent standing army. In part, they disliked the expense, but, more than that, long experience had shown that an army could be instrumental in suppressing liberty. Sending British troops to Boston had done much more to arouse the continent than the imposition of taxes. A citizen militia that could be summoned at need and then disbanded was something else again. The dislike of a permanent army persisted on each side of the Atlantic and hampered the war efforts of both countries. Britain's land and sea forces, which numbered more than 300,000 in the Seven Years' War, had shrunk to 34,000 by the beginning of 1775.

The American army at Boston, consisting of volunteers from four New England provinces, was without a chief. Artemas Ward was general in command of Massachusetts troops only. Other colonies had their own commanders. On June 2 Massachusetts asked Congress to determine how civilian control of the troops could be maintained and to make regulations for the army. When Congress authorized raising troops outside New England, it directed that they be under the commander in chief of the army. Someone therefore had to be selected for this post. John Adams' autobiography suggests that he was the main and almost sole instrument whereby Washington was chosen. His version seems as questionable as his statement that John Hancock was mortified that he was not elected to head the army. About all that seems historically certain is that Washington was chosen by Congress as chairman of all the committees dealing with military affairs. Serving with him were representatives of six provinces outside Virginia. He won the liking and admiration of his committeemen as well as of most of the other delegates. Massachusetts looked to the national congress to assure the fullest help of its sister colonies. Washington had been discussed in Massachusetts as a possible commander in chief and this had won wide approval. Elbridge Gerry wrote on June 4 to the Massachusetts delegation at Philadelphia to say that he was sure that the New England generals would welcome as their generalissimo "the beloved Colonel Washington" from their "sister colony" of Virginia. Gerry added that Dr. Joseph Warren, acting head of the Massachusetts congress, who had been chosen a general of the provincial forces, concurred in his view. It is difficult to believe that so important a letter was not known to Hancock.

There is little doubt that Adams admired Washington and that he, along with his cousin, Samuel Adams, took the lead in presenting his name. John Adams proposed on June 14, in response to the desire of Massachusetts, that Congress adopt the army before Boston. The meeting adjourned, and the talk continued in the lobbies and courtyards, and at dinner tables. On the following day the delegates, probably on the formal nomination by Thomas Johnson of Maryland, unanimously chose George Washington to be general and commander in chief of the armies of the United Provinces. Almost simultaneously Congress authorized the raising of rifle regiments in Pennsylvania, Maryland, and Virginia. By this action Congress intended to show that in choosing a general they were also prepared to give continental military support to New England. What was extraordinary was the ability of a body representing the disparate people and interests of thirteen colonies to choose so unerringly a man who would stay a rugged and foggy course for more than eight-and-a-half years. The hand of Providence clearly worked its wonders in this. Congress did not do so well in selecting his first major generals but the field of choice was narrow.

Washington was so concerned at his lack of qualification for the command that he told Patrick Henry privately that he was not only risking his reputation but that he expected to lose it. Nonetheless, at the official notification of June 16, 1775, he accepted with a modest statement that he read to Congress:

Mr. President: Tho' I am truly sensible of the high Honour done me in this Appointment, yet I feel great distress from a consciousness that my abilities and Military experience may not be equal to the extensive and important Trust: However as the Congress desires I will enter upon this momentous duty, and exert every power I possess in their Service for the Support of the glorious Cause: I beg they will accept my most cordial thanks for this distinguished testimony of their Approbation.

But lest some unlucky event should happen unfavourable to my reputation, I beg it may be remembered by every Gentn. in the room, that I this day declare with the utmost sincerity, I do not think my self equal to the Command I am honoured with.

As to pay, Sir, I beg leave to Assure the Congress that as no pecuniary consideration would have tempted me to accept this Arduous employment at the expence of my domestic ease and happiness I do not wish to make any profit from it: I will keep an

exact Account of my expences; those I doubt not they will discharge and that is all
I desire.

At dinner that day, the leaders stood and drank a toast "To the Commander-in-Chief of the American Armies." The next day the delegates unanimously pledged their "lives and fortunes" to the support of Washington.

When he heard about the election, Horace Walpole, who had first mentioned Washington as far back as 1754, wrote to a friend on August 3: "The Congress, not asleep, have appointed a Generalissimo, Washington, allowed a very able officer, who distinguished himself in the last war. Well! we had better have gone on robbing the Indies. It was a more lucrative trade." To another friend, after noting that Washington had declined to take any pay, he wrote: "If these folks will imitate both the Romans and the Cromwellians, in self-denial and enthusiasm, we shall be horribly plagued with them."

PAY

Washington kept as exact a record of his expenses as his frequently rapid moves permitted. Since each state had its own currency and the Continental Congress also issued notes, the complications were considerable. Taking the real value of the depreciating paper dollar, together with the expenditures in hard money, the general's headquarters costs, which included those of his staff and the secret service, averaged a little over $6,000 per year. Not only did Washington draw no pay for his services, but his first outlays in the amount of $2,000 were met from his own pocket. He was not reimbursed for eight years. In addition, during the darkest days of the war years, 1778–1780, he lent the government the equivalent of a further $8,000 in hard money, which he did not get back for many years.

During his long absence, Washington's farm and other properties deteriorated through neglect and mismanagement. In addition, many debts due him were paid in depreciating or worthless currency, while he met his own obligations at full value. He emerged from the army a very much poorer man who had the greatest difficulty in meeting his taxes for a long period after the war. By contrast the British commanders in chief were exceedingly well paid. Sir Henry Clinton received more than $57,000 a year in untaxed salary and allowances, and he had, in addition, almost unlimited secret service funds. He was able to save enough, during his years in America, to live comfortably for the rest of his life.

JOHN WRITES ABIGAIL ADAMS

On June 17 John Adams, much pleased, dropped a line to his wife in Braintree: "I can now inform you that the Congress have made choice of the modest and virtuous, the amiable, generous and brave George Washington, Esquire, to be General of the American army, and that he is to repair, as soon as possible, to the camp before Boston. The appointment will have a great effect in cementing and securing the union of these colonies." Abigail met Washington after his arrival in Cambridge, and wrote back to John:

> *You had prepared me to entertain a favourable opinion of him, but I thought the half was not told me. Dignity with ease & complacency, the Gentleman and the Soldier look agreeably blended in him. Modesty marks every line & fiture of his face. Those lines of Dryden instantly occu'rd to me:*
>
> > *"Mark his Majestic fabrick; he's a temple*
> > *Sacred by birth, and built by hands divine.*
> > *His soul's the Deity that lodges there.*
> > *Nor is the pile unworthy of the God."*

John Adams was annoyed by later attempts to deify Washington, whom he had helped to put in office, but his own wife thought the general more than human when she first saw him.

GEORGE WRITES MARTHA WASHINGTON

Washington had a much harder letter to write to his wife for, as he told his brother John, he knew his appointment would "be a cutting stroke upon her." Only two letters from George to Martha Washington appear to survive, both written in Philadelphia in June of 1775. In the first, of the eighteenth, Washington wrote of his concern for the uneasiness his selection would cause his wife. He hoped she would summon her whole fortitude and try to pass her time as agreeably as possible. He mentioned the will he had just drawn up. He was sending her two suits of "the prettiest muslin" he could find.

In the next couple of days he wrote his stepson, Jacky, asking that he and his wife spend as much time as possible at Mount Vernon, as this was "absolutely necessary for the peace and satisfaction of your mother." He also asked Martha's brother-in-law, Burwell Bassett, to go with his wife to see Martha or to ask her to visit them at their house. He also requested John

Washington and his wife to call on Martha, if at all possible. To the captains of the Virginia independent companies, who had elected Washington their commander, he wrote on June 20:

Gentlemen: I am now about to bid adieu to the companies under your respective commands, at least for a while. I have launched into a wide and extensive field, too boundless for my capabilities, and far, very far, beyond my experience. I am called, by the unanimous voice of the Colonies, to the command of the Continental Army; an honour I did not aspire to; an honour I was solicitous to avoid, upon a full conviction of my inadequacy to the importance of the service. The partiality of the Congress, however, assisted by a political motive, rendered my reasons unavailing, and I shall to-morrow set out for the camp near Boston.

I have only to beg of you, therefore before I go, (especially as you did me the honour to put your companies under my direction, and know not how soon you may be called upon in Virginia for an exertion of your military skill,) by no means to relax in the discipline of your respective companies.

To his brother he wrote the same day: "That I may discharge the Trust to the Satisfaction of my Imployers, is my first wish; that I shall aim to do it, there remains as little doubt of, but this I am sure of, that in the worst event I shall have the consolation of knowing (if I act to the best of my judgment) that the blame ought to lodge upon the appointers, not the appointed, as it was by no means a thing of my own seeking, or proceeding from any hint of my friends."

In the same letter he noted that Artemas Ward, head of the Massachusetts troops, was made a major general, along with Charles Lee, Philip Schuyler, and Israel Putnam. Horatio Gates was appointed his adjutant general. Washington and Gates were thus to go to Boston to oppose General Thomas Gage, with whom they had served in the Braddock campaign. On June 23 Washington again wrote his wife:

My dearest,

As I am within a few Minutes of leaving this City, I could not think of departing from it without dropping you a line, especially as I do not know whether it may be within my power to write again till I get to the Camp at Boston. I go fully trusting in that Providence which has been more bountiful to me than I deserve, & in full confidence of a happy meeting with you sometime in the Fall. I have not time to add more, as I am surrounded with Company to take leave of me. I retain an unalterable affection for you, which neither time or distance can change. My best love to Jack and Nelly, & regards for the rest of the Family concludes me with the utmost truth and sincerity

Yr. entire G. Washington

Martha Washington, about whom George worried, turned out to be of stout stuff. When Lord Dunmore raided the coastal towns of Virginia and rumor rose that he would try to capture the general's wife, she remained the most composed person in the colony. And that fall and every autumn for eight years, she climbed into a carriage at Mount Vernon and rode over the rough and icy colonial roads, through rain, snow, and sometimes blizzards, to see the general at his headquarters. Altogether she spent almost two-thirds of the war not only by his side but taking care of the sick and wounded.

Shortly after writing his farewell to Martha, General Washington, accompanied by Generals Lee and Schuyler, and two members of his personal staff, Thomas Mifflin and Joseph Reed, rode off to Boston. John Adams and, probably, Thomas Jefferson saw the departure of the man who would determine whether they would be hanged by a thoroughly offended majesty. Adams wrote, after he watched the glamorous procession: "Such is the Pride and Pomp of War. I poor Creature, worn out with scribbling, for my bread and my Liberty, low in Spirits and weak in Health, must leave others to wear Laurels which I have Sown." Adams soon pulled himself together and not long afterwards proceeded to push America's first authorized naval force through Congress.

EIGHTEEN

CAMBRIDGE

1775

JOHN BURGOYNE, one of the three newly arrived British generals, was a minor playwright. At General Gage's request, he drew up a proclamation designed to subdue the rebellion by dramatic force. As issued by Gage on July 12, it said:

Whereas, the infatuated multitude, who have long suffered themselves to be conducted by certain well known, incendiaries and traitors... have at length proceeded to avowed Rebellion; and the good effects which were expected to arise from the patience and lenity of the King's Government have been often frustrated, and are now rendered hopeless, by the influence of the same evil counsels...

A number of armed persons, to the amount of many thousands, assembled on the 19th of April last, and from behind walls and lurking holes, attacked a detachment of the King's Troops... Since that period, the rebels... have added insult to outrage; have repeatedly fired upon the King's ships and subjects with cannon and small arms... and with a preposterous parade of military arrangements they affected to hold the army besieged...

...I avail myself of the last effort within the bounds of my duty to spare the effusion of blood... I hereby, in his Majesty's name, offer and promise his most gracious

pardon to all persons who shall forthwith lay down their arms... excepting only... Samuel Adams and John Hancock, whose offenses are of too flagitious a nature to admit of any other consideration than that of condign punishment.

Many English laughed with the Americans at the document. A London paper commented that the Americans had certainly "effected" a siege, while Walpole asked: "When did you ever read before of a besieged army threatening military execution on the country of the besiegers?"

Gage had taken a very different view in a private dispatch to Lord North, written two days previously. He said that he would need at least thirty-two thousand troops at Boston, New York, and Lake Champlain, and that he saw no possibility of any accommodation. On the same day, a letter, probably written by General William Howe, went to London. It said: "The Situation these wretches have taken in forming the Blockade of this Town is Judicious and Strong, being Well Intrenched... Their Numbers are great... Upon the Alarm being Given, they come from far & near, & the Longer the Action Lasts, The Greater their Numbers Grow... In this State, The General has not Judged it prudent to attack them."

BUNKER HILL

Before Washington left Philadelphia, reports reached the city that there had been another bloody engagement with the British. This was the battle of Bunker Hill, fought at Breed's Hill and Charlestown. Howe mentioned in his letter that he thought Gage should have occupied both Dorchester Neck, south of Boston, and Charlestown, on a peninsula to the north. When the committee of public safety got word that Gage planned to occupy Charlestown, reinforcements were sent to fortify Bunker Hill, near the exit from that town to the mainland.

The five leading American officers who carried the plans through were among the oldest that ever fought a battle. Seth Pomeroy was about 69, Richard Gridley 65, Israel Putnam 57, William Prescott 49, and John Stark 47. All had military experience, some going as far back as the 1745 siege of Louisburg. Joseph Warren, a physician who had been appointed provincial major general and who arrived on the scene as a volunteer, was 34. Putnam commanded the Connecticut troops and Stark those of New Hampshire who joined Prescott's Massachusetts men. Probably owing to the advance of Putnam, the small group, which originally amounted to twelve hundred men and to which were added roughly three hundred later arrivals, decided to fortify Breed's Hill, some six hundred yards farther south than Bunker Hill. Working all night, they had, by morning, constructed a substantial redoubt. According to General Howe's report, the British sentries heard the Americans at work but did not bother to report their activity. The first Gage knew of it was when British ships began firing on the American defense.

With a fort directly threatening Boston, Gage had no choice but to act. At a council of war, General Clinton suggested landings south and north of the redoubt, to encircle it, but his advice was rejected. Gage ordered Howe to make a direct frontal attack under cover of the British fleet in the harbor.

During the course of the battle, the British fleet trained guns on Charlestown and burned it. An American corporal, Amos Farnsworth, wrote afterwards: "The town... supposed to contain about 300 dwelling-houses, a great number of which were large and elegant, besides 150 or 200 other buildings, are almost all laid in ashes by the barbarity and wanton cruelty of that infernal villain Thomas Gage." Abigail Adams and her small son, John Quincy, watched the destruction of Charlestown, the first of a long line of defenseless towns to be burned by the enemy.

Altogether Howe led some 2,400 trained men against the American garrison of 1,500. All afternoon, the British bravely tried to take the American position, which the Americans defended with equal courage and vigor until their water, ammunition, and food ran out. General Warren was killed. The Americans retreated. The British had won but at a terrible price. When the casualties were totaled, the Americans had around 440 killed and wounded, and the enemy 1,054, including 89 officers. It was a staggering loss for the British and, in consequence, General Howe reported to London that he had faced 4,500 to 5,000 Americans and, he said, he had even heard the figure of 6,000 mentioned.

REPERCUSSIONS

The effects of Lexington, Concord, and Bunker Hill were extraordinary. Gage's offensive plan to occupy Dorchester and Charlestown and then to attack the American troops at Cambridge collapsed. There was recrimination and dissension within the British high command; some of the younger officers threatened to resign, having found distasteful the task of killing their fellow subjects.

Shortly after the battles of Lexington and Concord, the Americans dispatched a fast ship to England with the news. It reached there before Gage's dispatches. The king and cabinet simply disbelieved the reports since they were contradictory to the government's statements that Americans would run from a few British regiments. Lord George Germain noted that the opposition was full of smiles. The Whigs attacked the government, both for the disaster and for concealing it, but the government had not yet had confirmation from its own army.

The city of London promptly addressed a petition to the king which, though it was labelled a "humble Address," was perhaps the most insulting one ever handed a reigning British sovereign. The city expressed its "abhorrence of the tyrranical measures pursued against our fellow-subjects in America," referred to "despotism" and "arbitrary power," and declared that American resistance was "their indisputable duty to God." The petition claimed that Gage had begun a civil war, described the king's minister as "notoriously bribed to betray their constituents and Country," and asked the king to dismiss them and dissolve Parliament, for having "by various acts of cruelty and injustice... manifested a spirit of persecution against our brethren in America."

Since the ministers had been wrong in their policy, their orders to Gage, and their assessment of American resistance, they had to find scapegoats. Lord George Germain wrote that the defeat of Gage at Lexington and Concord was similar to that of Braddock and it was obvious he held a command "of too great importance for his talents." The axe was ready for him, even before the news of Bunker Hill reached London. Gage had complained about Admiral Samuel Graves, in sea command at Boston. By fall, both officers were recalled.

The news of Bunker Hill forced the king and cabinet to face a war of a scope beyond anything for which they were prepared. They had believed their own statements; now Britain, with relatively few troops, had to face an enemy willing to fight. To win, desperate measures were required. Thus, in the summer of 1775, Britain undertook policies embracing (a) bribery, treachery, and corruption; (b) burning defenseless towns; (c) hiring foreign troops; and (d) arming Indians and negroes as allies. General Burgoyne, "Gentleman Johnny," was the first to propose such measures to London. As Franklin predicted in 1776, these policies were to make it very difficult for the British to forgive the Americans after the war for having frustrated their knavish tricks.

The news of Lexington, Concord, and Bunker Hill spread through Europe. The reports were cheered at Versailles. The ladies of the court abandoned the English "Whist" to play a new card game, "Boston." The foreign minister, Charles Gravier, comte de Vergennes, followed the reports with satisfaction. In consultation with his king and prime minister, he dispatched two agents, Pierre Caron de Beaumarchais, who continued to write *The Barber of Seville* while going back and forth on secret missions to London, and the aptly named Monsieur Bonvouloir, to Philadelphia. Beaumarchais' dispatches exaggerated the dissension in England, as well as the size of the American armies, but this did the coming United States no harm. After Bonvouloir's arrival in Philadelphia, Congress moved to establish a foreign affairs committee and to dispatch the first American agent to Paris. Another Frenchman, a young king's officer who heard the reports with joy in his heart, was Gilbert Motier de Lafayette, who bore the name of his famous ancestor, a marshal of France who, with Joan of Arc, had driven the English from Orleans.

George III found himself with few friends in Europe. The French and Spanish had long hated England. The king's attempt to rehire Scot troops who had been of the Patriot Party declared that the Americans were "a brave people, defending in a becoming, manly and religious manner those rights which, as men, they derive from God, not from the legislature of Great Britain." Even that towering autocrat, Empress Catherine, rejected British attempts to obtain Russian troops. George III complained to North that she did it in not too "genteel a manner... She... has thrown out some expressions that may be civil to a Russian Ear but certainly not to more civilized ones."

In opening Parliament on October 26, the king declared that a "desperate conspiracy" existed in America, their protestations of loyalty were only meant to "amuse" (trifle) and it was time to increase the army and navy in order to put a quick end to the disorders.

The Whig opposition jeered at the Crown ministers. They threw back at them their speeches saying that Americans were cowards and a few regiments would pacify them. They asked how a physician (Warren) leading a horde of peasants could have done so much damage to the king's troops. If it took a thousand men to capture one hill, they continued, how many hills were there in America? Lord John Cavendish denounced the king's speech as full of falsehoods. Charles James Fox declared that Lord North had lost more territory in one campaign than Caesar, Alexander, and Pitt had ever gained. The heaviest blow came when the duke of Grafton, a member of the cabinet and a former first minister, attacked the government. In Walpole's words, "The Lord Privy Seal deserted and fired on them." Nineteen peers signed a protest that the "ministers have deceived Parliament, disgraced the nation, lost the Colonies... and upon the most unjustifiable grounds, wantonly spilled the blood of thousands of our fellow-subjects."

Nonetheless the king and North proceeded with their policies. Above all, the king wanted a quick war and a cheap war, and these aims were contradictory. In August orders went from London to Gage and, through him, to Sir John Johnson, the British Indian agent, to engage the Indians to attack the colonists. In October, the Royal Navy burned Falmouth (now Portland, Maine). In November, Lord Dunmore issued a decree for the purpose of establishing "peace and good order," calling on all slaves to revolt and be armed as part of His Majesty's troops, thereby gaining their freedom. The decree was perhaps made less effective by being issued on board a ship "off Norfolk."

To get troops as cheaply as possible, a point he emphasized over and over, George III began to recruit and hire Germans. Since he was also king of Hanover, he was quickly able to order 2,355 troops from that country to relieve British garrisons in Gibraltar and elsewhere. By fall intensive negotiations were under way in Hesse-Cassel, Brunswick, Hesse-Hanau, and three smaller states for the purchase of troops, a move that shocked most of Europe. Since close to two-thirds of the nearly 30,000 Germans eventually came from the two Hesses, the term "Hessian," a word ranking with Hun in America, was indiscriminately applied to all of them.

Nevertheless, there was something pathetic about the king's efforts to raise men. Here was a ruler with great power who wrote out in his own handwriting lengthy lists and returns of individual regiments, noting where each was, how many men were sick, or how many men were needed for their full complement. When Lord North asked for two thousand men to begin a campaign in the southern provinces, the king replied on October 15 that it was going to be very hard to find that many but he would try to scrape them together, mainly from Ireland, since "every means distressing America must meet with my concurrence as it tends to bringing them to feel the necessity of returning to their Duty." The difficulties of raising men in Britain and Ireland and the cheapness of the Germans forced this foreign recruiting in order to shorten the time needed to crush America. No policy could have been better calculated to harden resistance.

GENERAL WASHINGTON PROCEEDS TO THE COMMAND

When Washington returned from Boston to Williamsburg in 1756, he was urgently recalled to the frontier to repel French and Indian attacks. In short order, after arriving at Winchester, he absorbed the problems facing his scattered defense command. After reaching Cambridge he wrote reports to Congress and the provincial governors and legislators, reports that showed a similar quick insight into his problems, some quite insoluble under existing conditions.

Washington formulated, almost immediately, the philosophies that carried him through the war years and beyond. The first was that the people were sovereign, they chose their civilian rulers, and military officers were subordinate to them. Within the military, however, discipline and order were necessary. This was a clear distinction but it was difficult to apply in New England, where the men not only voted for their public officials but elected their company and field officers. Washington also set to work to weld the various provincial armies into a single force as a first step towards building a nation. In practice, this proved the most difficult policy of all to execute, but eventually he achieved it to a remarkable degree. Congress had hoped that he might be a resourceful commander. No member could have foreseen the patience, diplomacy, and tact with which he was to handle thirteen sovereign governments, jealous and sometimes treacherous generals, a Congress with few defined powers, and a war effort finally involving armies and navies from the most sophisticated court of Europe.

When Washington arrived in New York on his way to Cambridge, the provincial legislature congratulated him on his appointment, but hastened to add a sentence expressing common Anglo-Saxon concern about an army. They hoped, they said, that as soon as an accommodation with Britain was reached, he would "cheerfully resign" his post. Washington might have been annoyed at such a request, coming only eleven days after his appointment, but he made a graceful reply that quickly circulated through the country: "When we assumed the Soldier, we did not lay aside the Citizen; and we shall most sincerely rejoice with you in that happy hour when the establishment of American Liberty... shall enable us to return to our Private Stations in the bosom of a free, peaceful and happy country."

Washington reached Cambridge on July 2, a quiet Sabbath. The following day he took command without much ceremony. On July 4 he announced to the army that Artemas Ward, Charles Lee, Philip Schuyler, and Israel Putnam had been appointed major generals in "the American Army," the first official use of the term. Thomas Mifflin was made his aide, and Joseph Reed his secretary. He added:

> *The Continental Congress having now taken all the Troops of the several Colonies, which have been raised, or which may be hereafter raised for the support and defense of the Liberties of America; into their Pay and Service. They are now the Troops of the UNITED PROVINCES of North America; and it is hoped that all Distinctions of Colonies will be laid aside; so that one and the same Spirit may animate the whole.*

The general ordered discipline, the observance of the articles of war, "a punctual attendance on divine Service" by all officers and men, and cleanliness of person and camp. To Jonathan Trumbull, the only provincial governor who embraced the American cause and who had been reelected by the Connecticut Assembly, he wrote on July 18: "The uncorrupted Choice of a brave and free people, has raised you to deserved eminence; that the Blessings of Health and the still greater Blessings of long continuing to Govern *such* a People may be yours, is the Sincere Wish of, Sir... G. Washington."

His public letters were tactful and polite and often similar in spirit, but his private communications to friends become ever sharper as he looked at the problems with which he had been so abruptly saddled.

GENERAL PROBLEMS

Washington's first perplexities involved his top officers. He knew that his own appointment had political motivations, although congressional trust in him was perhaps more important. His obvious integrity, military knowledge, friendliness, handsome appearance, and past war record played their part in the delegates' judgment. Congress had to pick other officers by guesswork.

As a matter of politics and courtesy, Artemas Ward of Massachusetts, supplying a majority of the troops, was placed second in command. Ward had been a lieutenant colonel of militia in the French and Indian War and thereafter was often in ill health. He was a colorless leader who failed to appear at Bunker Hill, even though he was head of his colony's forces.

Charles Lee, the third major general, neurotic and unstable, had more extensive military experience than Washington. As a British officer he had been in the battles of Ticonderoga, Niagara, and Montreal. Thereafter he served under Burgoyne in Spain, proceeding finally to Poland where he was an aide to the king and a major general. He subsequently returned to America to settle on his British half-pay. John Adams described him to James Warren: "You observe in your letter the Oddity of a great Man. He is a queer creature. But you must love his Dogs if you love him, and forgive a thousand whims for the Sake of the Soldier and the Scholar." The British captured this letter and made it public. Lee, unoffended, thanked Adams, since everyone now fussed over his dogs, while Abigail Adams wrote that she was made to shake the paw of one of the hounds her husband had made famous.

Philip Schuyler was the only one of the four major generals with a claim to aristocracy. From a patroon family, his was a generous and decent nature but his manners constantly annoyed the New England levellers. He had fought at Oswego, Crown Point, and Frontenac. Washington always trusted him as a man of integrity and judgment. Israel Putnam, last of the four appointed major generals, was by far the oldest. He had been in the French and Indian wars with Roger's Rangers. His bravery at Bunker Hill was not duplicated thereafter. None of the first four major generals served for an extended time. Coming up behind them were unknowns who were to stay with Washington for the entire war: Greene, Knox, Wayne, Morgan, Glover, and many others.

Washington encountered immediate problems with other general officers. Congress had too little knowledge of their ranks in provincial commands. In handing out commissions, men were advanced or demoted without a rational basis. John Thomas of Massachusetts, for example, who outranked two others, found himself below them as a brigadier. Joseph Spencer, who preceded Putnam, was placed under him. The new commander in chief, as he was often to do during the war, had to assuage the hurt feelings of his officers. On July 23 he wrote a long letter to Thomas, pleading with him not to resign:

> *The Retirement of a general Officer possessing the Confidence of his Country and the Army at so critical a Period, appears to me big with fatal Consequences... I think it my Duty to use this last Effort to prevent it... In such a cause as this, where the Object is neither Glory nor extent of territory, but a defense of all that is dear and valuable in Life, surely every post ought to be deemed honourable in which a Man can serve his Country... I admit, Sir, that your claims and services have not had due respect, it is by no means a singular case... For the sake of your bleeding Country, your devoted Province, your charter rights, and by the memory of those brave men who have already fallen in this great cause, I conjure you to banish from your mind every suggestion of anger and disappointment; your country will do ample justice to your merits.*

Thomas accepted his demotion gracefully and soon rose to be major general. Spencer retired, but eventually he, too, returned to the army at his previous rank.

OTHER TROUBLES

As Washington looked around him day after day, the problems seemed to multiply. Field and company grade officers had been selected by the provinces, not by Congress. The size of companies and regiments differed among the colonies, and it was difficult to weld them into a whole. The commander in chief might order everyone to forget provincial distinctions, but practically no one did. Washington became so exasperated that he, too, lapsed briefly into being a provincial Virginian. According to informal reports given him on his arrival, he had 18,000 to 20,000 troops. Almost his first command was to order returns from all headquarters. He later said that he expected them to reach him by nightfall. After a week of repeated orders and complaints, he began to get his reports but many were so faulty they had to be redone. When they were tabulated, he had only 16,000 men, of whom but 14,500 were fit for duty. This was his first shock. His second came when he asked for the supplies of powder on hand and was informed that there were 308 barrels of this most scarce commodity. On checking further, he found only 36 barrels; the returns had included the amounts expended at Breed's Hill and elsewhere. With this powder, and the supplies available in Connecticut and Rhode Island, he had hardly enough for nine rounds per man. According to John Sullivan, Washington sat in stunned silence for a half hour after receiving the corrected report.

Some of Washington's problems were temporary and concerned the long lines established around Boston, but many he mentioned that early July of 1775 continued year after year. They included shortages of engineers, artillery, ammunition, money, and clothing; provincial jealousies; the temporary nature of militia duty; the difficulties of dealing with local officials as well as committees of Congress; and a general air of amateurishness that pervaded the army. Washington did not, at this point, have an intelligence or supply organization, or a paymaster or medical director. As he wrote his brother John on July 20, the troops were fairly numerous but there was "very little command, discipline or order." The British had entire control of the waters and could move their forces to any point on short notice. "Our situation is a little unfavourable, but not so bad but I think we can give them a pretty warm reception if they think proper to make any advances towards us."

Washington slowly began to beat a sense of order into his young army. The camps were cleaned up and the sentries forced to alertness. By July 22 he had formed the forces into three divisions, each consisting of two brigades, under Generals Ward, Lee, and Putnam. His new brigadiers included Nathanael Greene, who was eventually to be commander of the southern army. Washington's order of July 23 revealed one problem: "As the Continental Army have unfortunately no Uniforms, and consequently many inconveniences must arise, from not always being able to distinguish the Commissioned officers, from the non Commissioned, and the non Commissioned from the private; it is desired that some Badges of Distinction may be immediately provided. He ordered field officers to wear red or pink cockades; captains, yellow or buff; and subalterns, green. Sergeants were distinguished by red cloth on their sleeves, and corporals by green. This followed an earlier order by which Washington was to be recognized by a blue ribbon worn across his breast and other general officers by a pink ribbon.

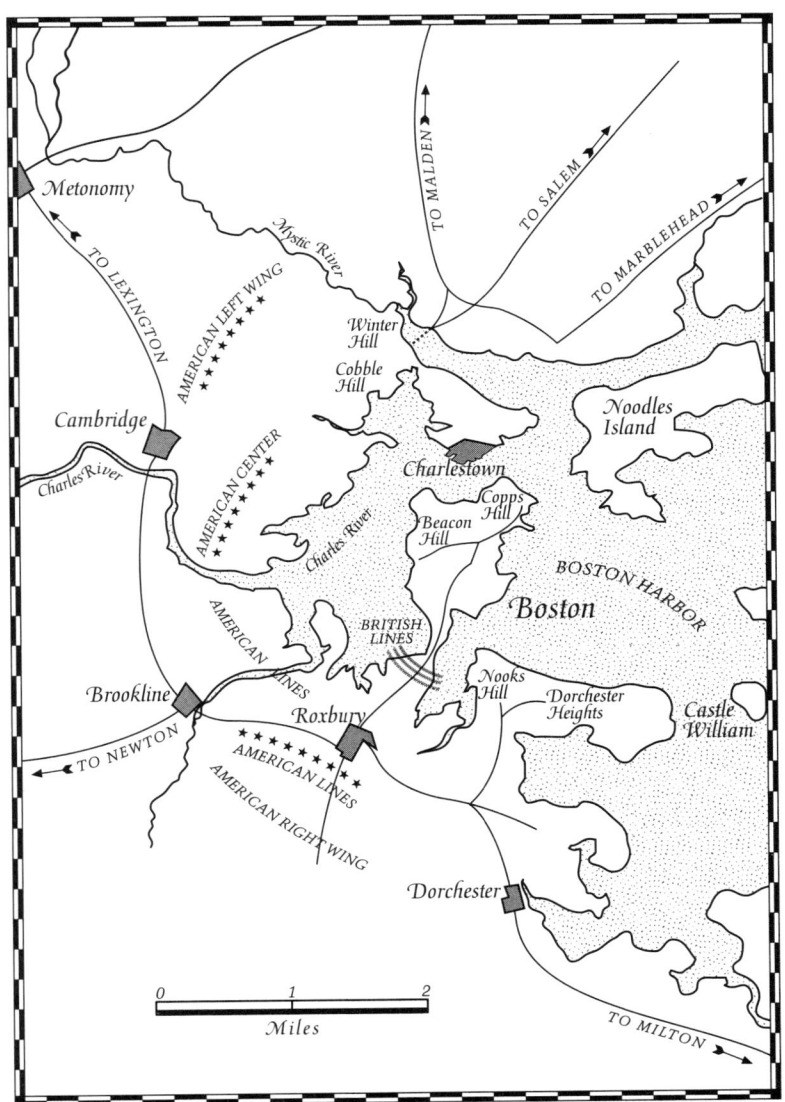

The Siege of Boston, 1775–1776

To introduce discipline and a certain amount of fear into his officers and men, Washington set up a system of courts-martial for offenses, some of which had been committed before he took command. He was particularly angry at any sign of cowardice and dishonor in an officer. The men, rustic and youthful as they often were, were treated with greater leniency. They were fined, whipped, or reprimanded for offenses for which officers were cashiered. He complained to Lund Washington on August 20 of the character of his command:

> *The People of this government have obtained a Character which they by no means deserved; their officers generally speaking are the most indifferent kind of People I ever saw. I have already broke one Colo. and five Captains for Cowardice and for drawing more Pay and Provisions than they had Men in their Companies; there is two more Colos. now under arrest, and to be tried for the same offences; in short they are by no means such Troops, in any respect, as you are led to believe of them from the accts. which are published, but I need not make myself Enemies among them by this declaration, although it is consistent with truth. I dare say the Men would fight very well (if properly Officered) although they are an exceedingly dirty and nasty people.*

When he wrote this, Washington had been in command only seven weeks. The burden of organizing a proper defense, without the backing of an effective government, had fallen on him. He was worried about Mount Vernon and the rumors that Lord Dunmore would try to capture Martha Washington. In addition, sanitary arrangements at the camps were primitive, and this offended his senses of decency and military discipline. In spite of his comments, only one officer in a hundred or so, and one enlisted man in a thousand, were dismissed from the American army during 1775. This was not a bad record for an army of amateurs. Thereafter, except for an occasional outburst, Washington tended more often to praise than to condemn.

CONGRESS

Although it had unanimously voted an army to protect its liberties, Congress was still divided as to procedures. Under the lead of John Dickinson, that body passed another humble petition: "Most Gracious Sovereign: We, your Majesty's faithful subjects..." Even John Adams signed this but most unwillingly.

Adams, in letters, attacked such "Puerilities." He complained to his wife that they should not be wasting their time that way. "We have a Constitution to form... a country to fortify, millions to arm and train, a naval power to begin." On July 24, in a private letter to James Warren, Adams expressed his opinion of Dickinson: "A certain great Fortune and piddling Genius, whose Fame has been trumpeted so loudly, has given a silly Cast to our whole Doings. We are between Hawk and Buzzard. We ought to have had in our Hands a month ago, the whole Legislative, executive and judicial of the whole Continent... to have raised a naval Power; to have arrested every Tory to be found on the continent, and then, perhaps, to have been ready to discuss peace with Britain."

The British captured this letter and published it in order to divide Congress. This worked to some extent, for Dickinson cut Adams dead on the street, and many other members indicated they thought he had been indiscreet. He had pulled the rug out from the humble petition. The reply to it was a thundering London proclamation calling the rebels "wicked and desperate persons," to be brought to "condign punishment."

Congress adjourned on August 1, leaving no central authority with which Washington could deal. Thereafter, for some time, he had to wheedle what he could from the New England provinces. Washington wrote to the president of Congress on August 31 and September 7. Winter was approaching; shelter was required; enlistments were about to expire. He pleaded more urgently but still politely on September 21:

> *It gives me great Pain to be obliged to sollicit the Attention of the Hon. Congress to the State of the Army, in Terms which imply the Slightest Apprehension of being neglected: But my Situation is inexpressibly distressing to see the Winter fast approaching upon a naked Army, The time of their Service within a few Weeks of expiring, and no Provision yet made for such important Events. Added to this the Military Chest is totally exhausted. The Paymaster has not a single Dollar in Hand.*

This letter caused Congress to appoint a committee to attend him at his camp, but it took several weeks until they reached Cambridge. While pleading with Congress, Washington received a rather tart note from Jonathan Trumbull, the able governor of Connecticut, who normally gave him every assistance. On September 2 and 8 Washington ordered the new Connecticut levies, raised for continental duty, to march immediately to Cambridge to replace other troops sent to Canada. The governor protested that the British were raiding Stonington, Connecticut, and asked that the troops remain there, but Washington let his orders stand. Trumbull then wrote him: "I am surprised that mine of the 5th instant was not received, or not judged worthy of Notice, as no mention is made of it... I am, with great Esteem and Regard for your personal character..." Washington replied on September 21 to Trumbull:

It gives me real concern... that you should think it Necessary to distinguish between my Personal and Public Character and confine your Esteem to the former.

...I have long been sensible that it would be impossible to please, not Individuals merely, but particular Provinces, whose Partial Necessities would occasionally call for assistance; I, therefore, thought myself happy, that the Congress had settled the Point, and apprehended I should stand excused to all, for acting in the Line which not only appeared to me to be that of Policy and Propriety, but of express and positive Duty; If, to the other Fatigues and Cares of my Station, that is to be added that of giving Reasons for all Orders, and explaining the grounds and Principles on which they are formed; my Personal Trouble will perhaps, be of the least Concern, the Public will be most affected.

The subject was not so new to me as to require long Consideration; I had occasion fully to deliberate upon it in Consequence of applications for troops from Cape Ann, Machias, New Hampshire, and Long Island... I wish I could extend Protection to all; but the numerous Detachments necessary to remedy the Evil, would amount to a dissolution of the Army, or make the most important Operations of the Campaign depend upon the Piratical Expeditions of 2 or 3 Men of War and Transports.

Trumbull promptly apologized and thereafter always gave Washington fullest support. In December, Joseph Reed, Washington's military secretary, picked up a report in Philadelphia that the Massachusetts officials were much annoyed because Washington had been insufficiently attentive to them. Washington wrote on December 15 to Reed to say: "I cannot charge myself with incivility... to the gentlemen of this colony; but if such my conduct appears, I will endeavour at a reformation, as I can assure you, my dear Reed, that I wish to walk in such a line as will give most general satisfaction. You know, that it was my wish at first to invite a certain number of gentlemen of this colony every day to dinner, but unintentionally I believe by anybody, we somehow or other missed of it. If this has given rise to the jealousy, I can only say that I am sorry for it; at the same time I add, that it was rather owing to... too much attention to other matters, which caused me to neglect it." While writing this, he was watching much of his army vanish.

WASHINGTON AND GAGE

Though Washington might be far from having all he wanted to make him happy, his opponent, General Gage, was in a worse moral position. The British commander in chief of all America was barely able to hold on to a single port and unable to risk a counterattack for fear of losing the war in one stroke. It was he who had told the king what he wanted to hear, that a few regiments would suppress the rebellion. Now he could only attempt to uphold the Crown's dignity by words. The two former companions-in-arms, Washington and Gage, had an acrimonious correspondence on the treatment of prisoners. The American led off on August 11:

> *Sir: I understand that the Officers engaged in the Cause of Liberty and their Country, who by the Fortune of War have fallen into your Hands, have been thrown, indiscriminately into a common Gaol appropriated for Felons; That no Consideration has been had for those of the most respectable Rank, when languishing with Wounds, and Sickness; that some have been even amputated, in this unworthy Situation.*

> *Let your Opinion, Sir, of the Principle which Actuates them, be what it may, they suppose they act from the noblest of all Principles, a Love of Freedom, and their Country: But political Opinions I conceive are foreign to this Point; the Obligations arising from the Rights of Humanity, and Claims of Rank are universally binding... These, I should have hoped, Would have dictated a more tender Treatment of those Individuals, whom Chance of War had put in your Power. Nor can I forbear suggesting its fatal tendency, to widen that unhappy Breach, which you, and those Ministers under whom you act, have repeatedly declar'd you wish'd to see forever closed.*

> *If Severity and Hardship mark the Line of your Conduct (painful as it may be to me) your Prisoners will feel its effects.*

Gage replied on August 13, in a letter addressed rather contemptuously to "George Washington, Esqr.":

> *To the Glory of Civilized Nations, humanity and War have been compatible; and Compassion to the subdued is become a general system. Britons, ever preeminent in Mercy, have outdone common examples, and overlooked the Criminal in the Captive. Upon these principles your Prisoners, whose Lives by the Law of the Land are destined to the Cord, have hitherto been treated with care and kindness, and*

more comfortably lodged than the King's Troops in the Hospitals; indiscriminately it is true, for I acknowledge no Rank, that is not derived from the King. My intelligence from your Army would justify severe recrimination... I would willingly hope, Sir, that the Sentiments of liberality, which I have always believed you to possess, will be exerted to correct these misdoings. Be temperate in political disquisition; give free Operation to truth, and punish those who deceive and misrepresent... Should those, under whose usurped Authority you act, controul such a disposition, and dare to call severity retaliation, to God who knows all hearts, be the appeal for the dreadful consequences. I trust that British Soldiers, Asserting the rights of the State, the Laws of the Land, the being of the Constitution, will meet all events with becoming fortitude... and... will find the patience of Martyrs under misfortune. Till I read your insinuations in regard to Ministers, I conceived that I had acted under the King.

Washington's lengthy riposte of August 30 attempted to outdo Gage in bombast and the result was something of a syntactical mess:

Whether British or American Mercy, Fortitude, and Patience are most preeminent, whether our virtuous Citizens, whom the Hand of Tyranny has forced into Arms to defend their Wives, their Children, and their Property, or the mercenary Instruments of lawless Domination, avarice and Revenge, best deserve the Appelation of Rebels, and the Punishment of that Cord, which your affected Clemency has forborne to inflict: whether the Authority, under which I act, is usurped, or founded upon the genuine Principles of Liberty, were altogether foreign to the Subject. I purposely avoided all political Disquisition; nor shall I now avail myself of those Advantages, which the sacred Cause of my Country, of Liberty, and human nature, give me over you... I am embarrassed with the Numbers, who crowd to our Camp, animated with the purest Principle of Virtue... You affect, Sir, to despise all Rank, not derived from the same Source with your own. I cannot conceive one more honourable than that which flows from the uncorrupted Choice of a brave and free People.

WASHINGTON'S FLEET

Late in the summer Washington turned from his land operations to organize a small naval force that could tap British supplies. At his urging, the governor of Rhode Island, Nicholas Cooke, sent an armed vessel to Bermuda to seize British powder but this operation failed. In early September, stretching his powers as army commander to the limit, Washington instituted America's first armed naval vessels. On October 16 he issued orders to Captain Nicholas Broughton:

> *You being appointed a Captain in the Army of the United Colonies of North America, are hereby directed to take the Command of a Detachment of said Army and proceed on Board the <u>Schooner Hannah</u>, at Beverly, lately fitted out & equipp'd with Arms, Ammunition and Provisions at the Continental Expence.*
>
> *You are to proceed as Commander of <u>Sd. Schooner</u>, immediately on a Cruize against such Vessels as may be found on the High Seas or elsewhere, bound inward and outward to or from Boston, in the Service of the Ministerial Army, and to take and seize all such Vessels, laden with Soldiers, Arms, Ammunition, Provisions for or from sd. Army.*

Provision was made for prize money for the captain and crew. Broughton was particularly warned not to try to engage British men-of-war. Shortly afterwards the general appointed the enterprising John Manley captain of the *Lee*, and subsequently the fleet's commodore. Manley was to make the first important capture of a British vessel in 1775 and the last seizure of the war in 1783.

In October John Adams led a move in Congress, which encountered bitter opposition, to establish a continental navy. The feeling of many was that any attacks on the British navy or merchant marine would bring retaliation against the coastal towns. Nonetheless Adams won by a small margin and was then put on a committee to draft the fleet's rules and regulations.

Almost at the same time, Congress sent Washington hastily drawn instructions to form a marine corps out of his army. Washington replied on November 10, complaining that he would have to upset his entire existing arrangement "which has cost us so much Time, anxiety and pains to bring into any tolerable form. Notwithstanding any Difficulties which will arise, you may be assured, Sir, that I will use every endeavour to comply with [the] Resolve." Congress then amended the instructions to provide that the corps be enlisted independently of the army.

WASHINGTON IS LIKED

Even working night and day, Washington could scarcely begin to cope with the infinite variety of problems thrust upon him. To trusted friends such as Joseph Reed, Richard Henry Lee, and John and Lund Washington, he poured out his feelings. He wrote to Lee on August 29, less than two months after taking command:

> *There has been so many great, and capital errors, and abuses to rectify—so many examples to make—and so little Inclination in the officers of inferior Rank to contribute their aid to accomplish this work, that my life has been nothing else (since I <u>came here</u>) <u>but</u> one continued round of <u>annoyance</u> and <u>fatigue</u>; in short, no pecuniary <u>recompense</u> could induce me to undergo what I <u>have</u>, <u>especially</u> as I expect, by shewing so little <u>countenance</u> to irregularities and publick <u>abuses to</u> render myself very obnoxious to a <u>greater</u> part of these People.*

This was like old times when young Colonel Washington, out on the cold barren frontier, was the whole force of the British empire. Tired and often discouraged, he wrote to his friends who rallied around him with praise and comfort. Lee, too, replied on September 26: "I assure you, that so far as I can judge from the conversation of Men, instead of there being any who think you have not done enough, the wonder seems to be that you have done so much... Your labours are no doubt great, both of mind and body; but if the praise of the present and future times can be any compensation you will have a plentiful portion of that."

In July, Henry Knox of Massachusetts, soon to be head of Washington's artillery, wrote to his brother: "General Washington fills his place with vast ease and dignity, and dispenses happiness around him." James Warren, president of the Massachusetts legislature, wrote of the "great satisfaction" that Washington gave. A Pennsylvanian, who visited the American camps, wrote a letter on August 9, which appeared in the *Pennsylvania Gazette* of August 23: "We waited on General Washington, who I have the pleasure to inform you is much beloved and admired for his polite condescension and noble deportment. His appointment to the chief command has the general suffrage of all ranks of people here, which I think is no bad omen."

NINETEEN

CAMBRIDGE AND BOSTON

1775–1776

O N SEPTEMBER 26 General Gage received orders to hand his American command to his subordinate, General William Howe, who was an even more determined enemy of the American revolt than his predecessor. On leaving England he stated his belief that most Americans were loyal to the king and only a "frantic" few were prepared to revolt. What was particularly galling to the colonists, including Washington, was that they had greatly admired his elder brother, Lord Howe, who was killed at Ticonderoga. Massachusetts had placed a memorial to him in Westminster Abbey. Shortly after his arrival, Howe led the bloody charge up Breed's Hill. A few days after he assumed command, his forces shelled and burned Falmouth, Maine, destroying 130 houses and the church, library, and town hall. He followed this with an order for the summary execution of any Bostonian caught leaving the city. Later he permitted some of the poorer citizens to depart. Since some had smallpox, Washington believed that he thus attempted to infect the American army. Washington had no illusions about his opposite number but held Howe in personal respect, as he wrote Howe on October 18:

> *Permit me to add Sir, that we have all here the highest regard and reverence for*
> *your great personal Qualities and Attainments, and that the Americans in general*

esteem it not as the least of their Misfortunes, that the name of Howe; a name so dear to them, should appear at the Head of the Catalogue of Instruments, employed by a wicked Ministry for their destruction.

CANADA

On June 25, on his way through New York City, Washington ordered General Schuyler to take command in the province of New York, obeying therein all instructions of the Continental Congress. He asked him to forward regular reports on his activities as well as any important intelligence. He noted that he could not himself command at so great a distance and Schuyler's own "good sense" would have to govern his actions. When Schuyler complained of the numerous difficulties he was encountering, Washington replied sympathetically on July 28: "Mine must be a portrait in full length of what you have had in Miniature... However we mend every Day, and I flatter myself that in a little Time, we shall work up these raw Materials into good stuff. I must recommend to you what I endeavour to practise myself, Patience and Perseverance."

Having raised an army for the support of American liberties that it was unable to equip, feed, clothe, or pay properly, Congress now pushed a campaign for the conquest of Canada. In so doing, that body nearly wrecked America's defenses before the Declaration of Independence was signed. Two men, later to be on George III's payroll, Ethan Allen and Benedict Arnold, appear to have been principally responsible for persuading Congress that capturing Canada would be as easy an operation as Ticonderoga. The argument for invasion was not put forth as a naked aggression. Instead it was argued, with some justification, that the French of Canada were to be freed and British aid to Indian attackers would be stopped. The subsequent operation, nominally under Schuyler's direction but, in fact, under the command of his subordinate, Richard Montgomery, was so bungled that its main objective, an attack on the fortress of Quebec, took place in a Canadian winter.

There is no evidence that the American commander in chief was consulted about the proposed attack to the north. Since he reacted strongly against a similar New England proposal for the conquest of Nova Scotia, it is reasonable to assume Washington would have argued as persuasively against Congress' plans to attack Quebec. He explained to the Massachusetts committee of public safety on August 11: "As to the Expedition proposed against Nova Scotia by the Inhabitants of Machias, I cannot but applaud their Spirit and Zeal; but, after considering the Reasons offered for it, several objections occur, which seem to me unanswerable. I apprehend such an Enterprize inconsistent with the General Principal upon which the Colonies have proceeded. That Province has not acceded, it is true, to the Measures of Congress;... But they have not Commenced Hostilities... To attack *them*, therefore, is a Measure of Conquest, rather than Defence... It might, perhaps, be easy, with the Force proposed, to make an Incursion into the Province... but the same Force must Continue to produce any lasting effects." Washington added that, in any case, he had no powder to spare for such an expedition.

When Arnold appeared in Cambridge, he proposed that an additional force of Americans proceed into Quebec from New England. In outlining this plan to Schuyler, Washington suggested it might be an important "Diversion that would distract Carleton and facilitate your Views." When Schuyler heartily approved, Washington sent Arnold off with a thousand men by way of the Kennebeck River and thence into Quebec province. Washington's instructions were more complete and detailed than those issued by Congress or Schuyler. He stressed the diplomatic difficulties of Arnold's task; Arnold was to turn back immediately if the Canadians resented the invasion. He was to respect absolutely their property and religion. There seems little doubt that the Canadians, under alien rule, felt general sympathy with the Americans. Arnold, in total disregard of orders, was to turn them into enemies. Washington's September 14 instructions stated:

> *You are by every Means in your Power, to endeavour to discover the real Sentiments of the Canadians towards our Cause, and particularly as to this Expedition, ever bearing in Mind, that if they are averse to it, and will not co-operate... it must fail of Success... In this Case you are by no Means to prosecute the Attempt...*

> *...You will... observe the strictest Discipline and good Order, by no Means suffering any Inhabitant to be abused, or in any Manner injured, either in his Person or Property... You are to endeavour... to Conciliate the affections of those People... convincing them that we come... as the Friends and Supporters of their Liberties, as well as ours...*

> *...Crush... every attempt to plunder even those who are known to be Enemies to our Cause...*

> *Spare neither Pains or Expence to gain all possible Intelligence on your March, to prevent Surprizes...*

> *In the case of an Union with General Schuyler... you are to put yourself under him and follow his Directions...*

If Lord Chatham's son [General Pitt] should be in Canada and in any Way fall in your Power, you are enjoined to treat him with all possible Deference and Respect. You cannot err in paying too much Honour to the Son of so illustrious a Character and so true a Friend to America...

You will be particularly careful, to pay the full Value for all Provisions or other Accommodations which the Canadians may provide for you on your March... Amply compensate those who voluntarily assist you...

As the Season is now far advanced, you are to make all possible Dispatch, but if unforeseen Difficulties should arise or if the Weather shou'd become so severe as to render it hazardous to proceed in your own Judgment and that of your principal Officers, (whom you are to consult)... you are to return...

As the Contempt of the Religion of a Country by ridiculing any of its Ceremonies or affronting its Ministers and Votaries has ever been deeply resented, you are to be particularly careful to restrain every Officer and Soldier from such Imprudence and Folly... You are to protect and support the free Exercise of the Religion of the Country and the undisturbed Enjoyment of the rights of Conscience in religious Matters.

Arnold's expedition pushed forward through such adverse circumstances as to have rendered it prudent, in accordance with his instructions, to have returned. When Washington was facing great difficulties with a vanishing army at the end of the year, he learned that Arnold had joined Montgomery in time to meet disaster at Quebec.

GUNS FOR BOSTON

Although Arnold and many another officer were to give Washington pain, others coming up were prepared to aid him beyond the call of duty. Two were longtime friends: Nathanael Greene, thirty-three, a limping Quaker from Rhode Island, and Henry Knox, twenty-five, a huge Bostonian who had lost two fingers from his left hand. They were both of an agreeable disposition and were alike in their omnivorous reading of military textbooks. Knox had also studied engineering and had seen service with Boston's artillery militia.

When Washington assigned Knox to the artillery, Knox asked him where it was. The commander in chief had to tell him there really wasn't any. Knox said that he would go to Ticonderoga and get some. In doing so, he was to perform one of the great feats of the Revolutionary War. He left Cambridge about November 18. According to his diary of expenses, he had, by late January, delivered to the general fifty-five guns weighing a total of sixty tons, having hauled them for three hundred miles over snow and ice.

DR. CHURCH

One of the many disputes that came to Washington was between Benjamin Church, director general of the hospital, and the regimental surgeons. On September 7, Washington ordered a court of inquiry. Church at once offered his resignation but Washington refused it on the grounds that he could not be spared.

Church was considered a strong patriot. As a member of the Massachusetts legislature, he was sent to Philadelphia to explain the military situation at Boston. He was also chosen to greet Washington on his arrival in the province. Subsequently the general selected Church as his chief medical officer.

Before the court of inquiry could report, a strange tale came to Washington. A woman had attempted, through an acquaintance in Newport, to smuggle a letter to Boston. The person receiving it consulted another patriot and they opened it. The letter, addressed to Major Cane, aide to General Gates, was in code. The woman was brought to headquarters and questioned by Washington. She eventually admitted that it had been written by Church and that she was his mistress. The letter, when decoded, turned out to have somewhat exaggerated information on the American military forces, a note on the planned invasion of Canada, and an appeal to Britain to remove all the oppressive acts.

Church denied any attempt at treason. Washington, uncertain of his authority to try him by court-martial, asked Congress for advice. That body ordered him confined in a Connecticut jail. After two years' imprisonment, Church was permitted to leave for the Caribbean, where he was lost at sea.

Not until many years afterward was it learned from Gage's papers that Church was a paid British spy. He had informed Gage of the cache of American arms at Concord. This brought Gage's hasty action to seize them, thus precipitating war. The British later pensioned Church's widow.

The medical profession, vital to Washington's sick and wounded troops, remained troublesome throughout the war. No sooner had he got rid of Church than he had to cashier a regimental surgeon from Connecticut. His next medical director, John Morgan, quarreled with his fellow physicians and was dismissed from the service by Congress. Morgan's successor, William Shippen, Jr., in turn, was court-martialed. Benjamin Rush, surgeon general of the middle department, having resigned from the army after a dispute, tried to have Washington dismissed from his command.

SECRETARIES AND CORRESPONDENCE

Because of what he said were commitments to his clients, Joseph Reed, a lawyer and Washington's military secretary, returned to Philadelphia in late October. Washington considered Reed's services so important that he intervened with Benjamin Chew, chief justice of Pennsylvania, to see whether Reed's cases could be postponed. The judge replied that the court was not in session and he was sure that Reed could arrange his affairs in order to be able to rejoin his staff. Washington, on hearing this, wrote Reed on November 28: "I could wish, my good friend, that these things may give a spur to your inclination to return; and that I may see you here as soon as convenient; as I feel the want of your ready pen, &c. greatly." This followed a letter he had written on November 20:

> *The hint contained in the last of your letters, respecting your continuance in my family, in other words, your wish that I could dispense with it, gives me pain... You cannot but be sensible of your importance to me; at the same time I shall again repeat, what I have observed to you before, that I can never think of promoting my convenience at the expense of your interest and inclination. That I feel the want of you, yourself can judge, when I inform you, that the peculiar situation of Mr. Randolph's affairs obliged him to leave this soon after you did; that Mr. Baylor, contrary to my expectation, is not in the slightest degree a penman, though spirited and willing; and that Mr. Harrison, though sensible, clever, and perfectly confidential, has never yet moved upon so large a scale, as to comprehend at one view the diversity of matter, which comes before me, so as to afford that ready assistance, which every man in my situation must stand more or less in need of. Mr. Moylan, it is true, is very obliging; he gives me what assistance he can; but other business must necessarily deprive me of his aid in a very short time. This is my situation; judge you, therefore, how much I wish for your return, especially as the armed vessels, and the capital change (in the state of this army) about to take place, have added an additional weight to a burthen, before too great for me to stand under with the smallest degree of comfort to my own feelings. My mind is now fully disclosed to you, with this assurance, sincerely and affectionately accompanying it, that whilst you are disposed to continue with me, I shall think myself too fortunate and happy to wish for a change.*

There were further pleas to Reed, one on January 23: "Real necessity compels me to ask you, whether I may entertain any hopes of your returning to my family?... At present my time is so much taken up at my desk, that I am obliged to neglect many other essential parts of my duty. It is absolutely necessary, therefore, for me to have persons that can think for me, as well as execute orders." Reed did not return at this time, although he continued in the affection of the commander in chief.

Washington, lacking ammunition, clothing, and, often enough, money to keep his troops contented, had to carry on correspondence with Congress; with the provinces of New Hampshire, Massachusetts, Connecticut, Rhode Island, and New York; and with Arnold in Canada and Schuyler in New York. He prepared addresses to the citizens of Canada and Bermuda; organized and reorganized an army, with all the paperwork involved; and wrote of his personal affairs to his wife, Lund Washington, and others. Though overburdened, the man who had made the phrase "When we assumed the Soldier, we did not lay aside the Citizen" continued his epigrammatic comments. His letters and general orders had crisp, fresh phrases not customary with generals. A few follow:

For God's sake hurry the signers of money, that our wants may be supplied. (to R. H. Lee)

Whilst we have Men therefore who in every respect are superior to mercenary Troops, that are fighting for two pence *or* three pence *a day: Why cannot we in appearance also be superior to them, when we fight for Life, Liberty, Property and our Country?* (General Orders)

I am told that Captain Wallace's [Royal Navy] Ships have been Supplied for some time with provisions by the town of New Port... We need not expect to Conquer our Enemies by good Offices. (to the Governor of Rhode Island)

Our Treasury is almost exhausted, and the demands against it, very considerable; a constant supply of money... would much promote the good of the Service; in the common affairs of Life, it is useful: In War, it is absolutely necessary and essential. (to Congress)

I hope it has... enabled the Congress to bestow a little more attention to the affairs of this army, which suffers exceedingly by their overmuch business, or too little attention to it. We are now without any money in our treasury, powder in our magazines, arms in our stores. We are without a brigadier (the want of which has been twenty times urged), engineers, expresses (though a committee has been appointed these two months to establish them), and by and by, when we shall be called upon to take the field, shall not have a tent to lie in. Apropos, what is doing with mine? (to Reed)

The reflection on my situation, and that of this army, produces many an uneasy hour when all around me are wrapped in sleep... I have often thought how much happier I should have been, if, instead of accepting a command under such circumstances, I had taken my musket on my shoulder and entered the ranks, or, if I could have justified the measure to posterity and my own conscience, had retired to the back country, and lived in a wigwam. (to Reed)

On reading the Copy of Genl. Wooster's Letter I was much surprised to find, that he had granted Furloughs to the Connecticut Troops under his Command, in Preference of Discharges. What Advantage could he imagine they would be to the Continent, when they were at their own Homes? (to Schuyler)

I received your Favour... and am exceedingly sorry to hear, that Congress countermanded the embarkation of the two Regiments, intended against the Tories on Long Island... Our Enemies from the other Side of the Atlantic, will be sufficiently numerous. It highly concerns us to have as few internal ones as possible. (to General Lee)

No man upon Earth wishes more ardently to destroy the nest in Boston, than I do. (to Congress)

The Clouds gather fast, where they will burst, I know not, but we should be armed at all points. (to Congress)

I observe what you say in respect to my... travelling wagon... I have no doubt but that the Treasury, by application to Mr. Hancock, will direct payment thereof, without any difficulty, as Congress must be sensible, that I cannot take the field without equipage, and after I have once got into a tent I shall not soon quit it. (to Reed)

I have heard of no other valiant son of New England waiting promotion, since the advancement of Frye... At present he keeps his room, and talks learnedly of emetics, cathartics, &c. For my own part, I see nothing but a declining life that matters him. (to Reed; Frye lived until 1794)

MRS. WASHINGTON AND MOUNT VERNON

Washington found time to write to Williamsburg with regard to the Ohio Valley lands, which he had endeavored to seat in accordance with the law. He asked for help in their registration, noting that he might find them useful as an asylum. He also wrote to Lund Washington in regard to the additions under way at Mount Vernon. Lund's reply stated he did not know how much building he ought to be doing, since the British might come at any time and burn the place down.

Many Virginians were fearful for Martha Washington's safety, though Washington wrote that he did not believe Dunmore would act "so low and unmanly a part" as to seize Mrs. Washington. Lund informed him that Martha was not worried and everyone in Virginia had offered either to take her in for protection or to march to defend Mount Vernon. She eventually went to her old family house at New Kent. While she was there, Washington suggested to her that she join him in Cambridge. He also wrote on October 13 to his brother John:

> *I am obliged to you for your advice to My Wife, and for your Intention of visiting her; seeing no great prospect of returning to my Family and Friends this Winter I have sent an Invitation to Mrs. Washington to come to me, altho I fear the Season is too far advanced (especially if she should, when my Letters get home, be in New Kent, as I believe the case will be) to admit this with any tolerable degree of convenience. I have laid a state of the difficulties, however, which must attend the journey before her, and left it to her own choice.*

According to report, Martha, on receiving George's letter, had to be restrained from setting off without even taking time to pack. The messenger who brought her husband's letter was directed to proceed to Mount Vernon to order a supply of Virginia hams and various delicacies that she could haul to Cambridge to cheer the general's Christmas. Mrs. Washington left the next day, accompanied by her son and daughter-in-law, for a trip that took nearly a month. She was escorted into and out of Philadelphia by troops of light horse and infantry; in Newark the church bells rang on her arrival. As she wrote home later, there was as much pomp for her as if she had been a "some body."

Just before she reached Cambridge, Captain Manley, Washington's naval commodore, captured a ship from London, the *Jenny*, bringing supplies for the king's troops, including limes, lemons, oranges, sweetmeats, and pickles. The general asked Manley politely, through his aide, if he could buy a small portion, so that Mrs. Washington would have them on her arrival.

THE VANISHING ARMY

To get firsthand information on Washington's problems, Congress sent a committee of three to Cambridge in October. Its members were Benjamin Franklin, Thomas Lynch, and Benjamin Harrison, of Pennsylvania, South Carolina, and Virginia, respectively. Its southern composition raised New England eyebrows; General Greene wondered why only "strangers" were sent.

The committee spent many days conferring with Washington, his staff, and representatives of the four New England provinces. Congress had forwarded a number of questions as to the size and pay of his army. Washington, after consulting with his council, had the answers ready when the committee arrived. The army needed a force of 20,372 men; this was a larger number than any Washington had had to date. There were urgent matters of barracks, winter clothing, and firewood to consider. The most troublesome problem was that all enlistments, beginning with the Connecticut troops in early December, were about to expire. Washington had asked how many expected to reenlist; a majority wanted to return home.

Washington took up with the committee the problem of whether, if he attacked Boston, he should destroy the city if necessary. The committee felt that so important a question could be decided only by Congress. As the committee was concluding its work, the news of the destruction of Falmouth reached camp. The committee's report gave support to most of Washington's recommendations, which Congress in turn approved. The resolutions merely gave him authority to try to solve his problems.

The Connecticut troops decided they could not, as they put it, "tarry." Washington and his officers pleaded with them, on every patriotic ground, to stay at least a few extra days until hastily summoned troops from Massachusetts and New Hampshire could take their place. Some went off without leave, others said they might stay a little longer if they got extra money. At this time, Washington was desperately trying to get firewood and blankets, build barracks, and lay in winter supplies, while keeping an eye on the enemy in Boston, who knew from their spies that his army was disintegrating. Washington expressed his feelings in a letter to Reed on November 28:

> *Such a dearth of public spirit, and want of virtue, such stock-jobbing, and fertility in all the low arts to obtain advantages of one kind or another, in this great change of military arrangement, I never saw before, and pray God I may never be witness to again. What will be the ultimate end of these manoeuvres is beyond my scan. I tremble at the prospect. We have been till this time enlisting about three thousand*

five hundred men. To engage these I have been obliged to allow furloughs as far as fifty men a regiment, and the Officers I am persuaded indulge as many more. The Connecticut troops will not be prevailed upon to stay longer than their term (saving those who have enlisted for the next campaign, and mostly on furlough), and such a dirty, mercenary spirit pervades the whole, that I should not be at all surprised at any disaster that may happen.

The first sentence has often been quoted as if it were a denunciation of all New England, but it related to particular circumstances. According to General Lee, the cold and homesick Connecticut farm boys, as they went off, were "so horribly hissed, groaned at and pelted, that I believed they wished their aunts, grandmothers and even sweethearts, to whom the day before they were so much attached, at the Devil's own place." When they got home, they found aunts, sweethearts, and grandmothers so indignant that many were glad to return to Cambridge.

New Englanders understood both themselves and their general. Governor Trumbull wrote that Connecticut had received the reports with "grief, surprise, and indignation." He explained that it was difficult for New Englanders, "high for liberty," to be subordinate to anyone. He had immediately called the Assembly into special session. "You may depend on their zeal and ardor to support the common cause, to furnish our quota, and to exert their utmost strength for the defence of the rights of these colonies. Your candor and goodness will suggest to your consideration, that the conduct of our troops is not a rule whereby to judge of the spirit of the colony." General Greene wrote to Samuel Ward, Rhode Island delegate in Congress, on December 18:

His Excellency is a great and good man. I feel the highest degree of respect for him. I wish him immortal honor. I think myself happy in an opportunity to serve under so good a general... But his Excellency, as you observe, has not had time to make himself acquainted with the genius of this people. They are naturally as brave and spirited as the peasantry of any other country; but you cannot expect veterans, of a raw militia of only a few months's service... The sentiment of honor, the true characteristic of a soldier, has not yet got the better of interest. His Excellency has been taught to believe the people here a superior race of mortals; and finding them of the same temper and dispositions, passions and prejudices, virtues and vices of the common people of other governments, they sink in his esteem. The country round here set no bounds to their demand for hay, wood and teaming. It has given his Excellency a great deal of uneasiness that they... extort... such enormous prices.

Washington's army was pouring out nearly $275,000 a month in unbacked currency for the maintenance of the troops and additional sums for munitions and equipment. Prices were inevitably rising.

The Massachusetts and other enlistments ran out at the end of the year. On Christmas Day, Washington wrote Congress that recruits for the new army were only some 8,500 men—about 40 percent of his authorized strength. This figure was optimistic; a count of January 10 showed that, while his nominal strength was 8,212, only 5,582 men were present and fit for duty. The treasury was almost empty. As Washington wrote Reed on January 4: "It is easier to conceive than to describe the situation of my mind for some time past, and my feelings under our present circumstances. Search the vast volumes of history through, and I much question whether a case similar to ours is to be found; to wit, to maintain a post against the flower of the British troops for six months together, without powder, and at the end of them to have one army disbanded and another to raise within the same distance of a reinforced enemy. It is too much to attempt... For more than two months past, I have scarcely emerged from one difficulty before I have plunged into another."

1776

As America entered upon her most famous year, Montgomery lay dead at Quebec. Arnold was wounded. The Americans had suffered a bloody repulse. On New Year's Day, Lord Dunmore began the shelling and burning of Norfolk, Virginia, nearly obliterating the town. That same day, the commander in chief issued orders to the new army besieging Boston:

This day giving commencement to the new Army, which, in every point of View is entirely Continental, The General flatters himself, that a laudable Spirit of emulation will now take place, and pervade the whole of it; without such a Spirit, few Officers have ever arrived to any degree of Reputation, nor did any Army ever become formidable: His Excellency hopes that the Importance of the great Cause we are engaged in, will be deeply impressed upon every Man's mind, and wishes it to be considered, that an Army without Order, Regularity and Discipline, is no better than a Commission'd Mob; Let us therefore, when every thing dear and valuable to Freemen is at stake; when our unnatural Parent is threat'ning us with destruction from every quarter, endeavour by all the Skill and Discipline in our power, to acquire that knowledge, and conduct, which is necessary in War—Our Men are brave and good; Men who, with Pleasure, it is observed, are addicted to fewer Vices than are commonly found in Armies; but it is Subordination and Discipline (the

*Life and Soul of an Army) which next under Providence, is to make us formidable
to our enemies, honourable in ourselves, and respected in the world.*

THE SIEGE OF BOSTON

Washington's inability to attack the British was most irksome of all. He consulted his council of war on all important questions, usually sending advance
written questions to his officers for study. He had often done this in the
French and Indian wars, and he continued this policy in obedience to his
instructions by Congress. The council's decisions often had to be approved by
Congress, which, at times, intervened by sending independent orders. In addition, Washington frequently had to call provincial officials into consultation.
This was an inefficient system; some of the indecision attributed to
Washington at the time was due to the complex maze erected about him.

Washington held councils in September and October 1775 to decide
whether to attack Boston. They voted, each time, that it was too risky. The
October meeting, held when the congressional committee was in Cambridge,
had raised the question of the destruction of Boston. Not until December 22
did Congress make its determination: "If General Washington and his council
of war should be of opinion, that a successful attack may be made on the
troops in Boston, he may do it in any manner he may think expedient,
notwithstanding the town and property in it be destroyed." John Hancock,
one of the richest men of Boston, forwarded the resolve with a note: "May
God crown your attempt with success. I most heartily wish it, though individually I may be the greatest sufferer." This resolve did not give the commander
in chief, but only his council, the final authority.

Washington was unable to attack, but his fury at the British increased. His
letters spoke of the cruelty and barbarity of the enemy. On January 31, referring to the destruction of Norfolk, he told Reed that he hoped this would
"unite the whole country in one indissoluble band against a nation which
seems to be lost to every sense of virtue, and those feelings which distinguish
a civilized people from the most barbarous savages. A few more of such
flaming arguments, as were exhibited at Falmouth and Norfolk, added to the
sound doctrine and unanswerable reading contained in the pamphlet
Common Sense will not leave numbers at a loss to decide upon the propriety of
a separation." He wrote again on February 10 to Reed:

*With respect to myself I have never entertained an idea of an accommodation, since
I heard of the measures, which were adopted in consequence of the Bunker's Hill*

fight. The king's speech has confirmed the sentiments I entertained upon the news of that affair; and if every man was of my mind, the ministers of Great Britain should know, in a few words, upon what issue the cause should be put. I would not be deceived by artful declarations, nor specious pretenses; nor would I be amused by unmeaning propositions... I would tell them, that we had borne much, that we had long and ardently sought for reconciliation upon honorable terms... that the spirit of freedom beat too high in us to submit to slavery, and that, if nothing else could satisfy a tyrant and his diabolical ministry, we are determined to shake off all connexions with a state so unjust and unnatural. This I would tell them, not under covert, but in words as clear as the sun in its meridian brightness.

Colonel Knox arrived at Framingham on January 25 with his guns. These weapons gave renewed interest to the attack on Boston. With its harbor frozen, Washington presented an urgent plea to his council on February 16 to approve an attack by ice on the city, adding, "a stroke well aimed at this critical juncture might put a final end to the War." His officers voted him down. A disappointed Washington reported two days later to Congress that the vote was "almost unanimous," meaning, probably, that only Washington voted aye. He explained:

The Result... I must suppose to be right although, from a thorough conviction of the necessity of attempting something against the Ministerial Troops, before a Reinforcement should arrive and while we were favour'd with the Ice, I was not only ready, but willing and desirous of making the Assault; under a firm hope, if the Men would have stood by me, of a favourable Issue, notwithstanding the Enemy's advantage of Ground, Artillery, &ca.

Perhaps the Irksomeness of my situation, may have given different Ideas to me, than those which influenced the Gentlemen I consulted, and might have inclin'd me to put more to the hazard than was consistent with prudence. If it had, I am not sensible of it, as I endeavourd to give it all the consideration that a matter of such Importance required. —True it is, and I cannot help acknowledging, that I have many disagreeable Sensations, on Acct. of my Situation; for to have the Eyes of the whole Continent fixed, with anxious expectation of hearing some great event, and to be restrain'd in every Military Operation for want of the necessary means of carrying it on, is not very pleasing, especially, as the means used to conceal my weakness from the Enemy conceals it also from our friends and adds to their Wonder.

As an alternative to a direct attack, the council proposed that Dorchester Heights, commanding Boston and its harbor, be fortified in order to draw the enemy out. Washington wrote Reed that he would follow this plan, though he was still disappointed, "after waiting all the year for this favourable" opportunity, at being told that his plan was "too dangerous!" Now, he said, he would have "to try if the enemy will be so kind to come to us."

In the next few days, Washington formulated a complex plan, involving the placement, as a feint, of guns at points far from Dorchester, planning the kind of fortification that could be erected overnight on the Heights and preparing an amphibious assault on Boston, to be carried out as soon as the British moved to attack Dorchester. This involved an immense secret movement of troops, guns, fortification materials, and boats.

Lieutenant Colonel Rufus Putnam, who was soon thereafter promoted to chief of engineers, devised a prefabricated fort that required little digging into the frozen earth. It consisted of timber frames (gabions) into which were placed tied logs (fascines), hay, and baskets of earth. These could be transported by ox cart from Roxbury and quickly assembled at night. Barrels filled with rocks and earth were added, to be placed in front of the fortification; they could also be an offensive weapon when rolled downhill against attacking troops.

To divert British attention from his plans, Washington ordered the mounting of heavy guns at Lechmere's Point on Philip's farm, opposite Charlestown, and on Cobble Hill to the north. These were on the left of the American lines. Other guns were mounted at Roxbury on the right wing. Four thousand men, under Putnam, were assigned to brigades under Sullivan and Greene, and ordered to prepare an amphibious attack on the British in Boston. All American leaves were cancelled, and militia from nearby areas were summoned. Regimental physicians were ordered to Cambridge to prepare for care of the wounded. Signal flags for a general alarm were established.

On March 2, the Americans began a bombardment of Boston from Lechmere's Point and Cobble Hill. This continued a second night and the British guns replied. On the third night, General John Thomas and a working and armed party of 3,000 men and 360 ox carts, moved onto Dorchester Heights, where they erected the planned fortifications with great gusto. The works were complete on the morning of March 5. General Washington, there with his troops, waited joyfully for action.

GENERAL HOWE FUNKS OUT

As dawn came to Boston, there was tension in the American lines, but little anxiety, since the operation had been carried out exactly as planned. The Americans watched for the British reaction, which was slow in coming.

Admiral Molyneux Shuldham sent at once to General Howe to say he could not keep his ships in the harbor under the guns and that Howe had either to take the fortifications or remove his army to the navy's ships. Howe attempted a bombardment but could not sufficiently elevate his guns. He determined to attack and summoned a force of more than twenty-four hundred men. The Americans heard the general alarm and watched the great movements in the town. The British missed the tide. Late in the afternoon, when rain began, Howe held another council of war, at which most of his officers advised against further action. Howe, who had fought at Breed's Hill and knew, though British honor was at stake, how bloody the assault would be, agreed with his officers. They decided to abandon Boston. That night, around midnight, there arose a storm of near-hurricane proportions that lasted all night. This enabled Howe to announce to his troops that only the intervention of Providence prevented him from dislodging the Americans.

In writing to London on March 21, Howe said that the fortifications erected by the Americans were so strong that they must have required "the employment of at least twelve thousand men." Howe then explained that he had ordered an attack "but the wind unfortunately coming contrary and blowing very hard... the attempt became impracticable." He had therefore decided to leave and thus comply with the king's orders that, when practicable, he sail from Boston.

Howe's reports to London were not precisely truthful, but the British government made them less so by announcing that Howe's troops had embarked for Halifax in good order. The duke of Manchester commented in Parliament that it was a lucky thing that the navy was there to save the British from utter disgrace since it was clear they had been forced out of Boston. Washington had waited in vain for the British to attack. Two days later, on March 7, he expressed his disappointment to Congress:

> It is much to be wished that it had been made. The event I think must have been fortunate, and nothing less than victory and success on our side, as our Officers and men appeared Impatient for the appeal, and to have possessed the most animated Sentiments and determined Spirit... In case the Ministerial Troops had made an Attempt to dislodge our Men from Dorchester Hills, and the number detached upon the occasion, had been so great as to have afforded a probability of a successful attack's being made upon Boston, on a signal given from Roxbury... four thousand men... were to have embarked at the mouth of Cambridge River in two divisions... The first was to land at the Powder House and gain possession of Beacon Hill and Mount Horam. The second at Barton's Point, or a little south of it, and after securing that post, to join the other divisions and force the Enemy's Works and Gates for letting in the Roxbury Troops. Three floating batteries were to have proceeded... and kept up a heavy fire on that part of the

Town where our men were to land... I had reason to hope for a favourable and happy issue.

The evacuation was a difficult task for Howe and Shuldham. There were nearly nine thousand British—including troops, wives, and civilians—to embark, while more than a thousand Tories pleaded to accompany Howe. He permitted them to come, but they took so many possessions that many of the king's stores had to be abandoned. Twelve days were needed to get everyone aboard.

The Boston selectmen appealed to Howe not to destroy the city. He replied that if Washington agreed not to molest the embarkation he would spare the city. The selectmen sent a flag of truce to Washington with this message, but since there was nothing official in it from Howe, he could not reply. Apparently Washington and Howe understood this to be an informal agreement. It was a sad coincidence for the many Irish officers and men among Howe's troops that it was on St. Patrick's Day that the last man embarked and the British set out to sea. On the same day American troops moved into Boston.

March 17 was a Sabbath, and Washington attended church in Cambridge. The Congregational minister took as his text: "The Egyptians said, Let us flee from the face of Israel, for the Lord fighteth for them against the Egyptians."

Washington had last left Boston on March 5, 1756, on the trip occasioned by his annoyance at having to take orders from a former British army captain. Twenty years and thirteen days later he entered the city, according to the posted proclamations, as "His Excellency, George Washington, Captain General and Commander-in-Chief of the Forces of the Thirteen United Colonies," after forcing out an army with five British generals and a Royal Naval force of 150 or more ships. He described the city's condition to John Washington on March 31:

> *The Enemy left all their Works standing in Boston, and on Bunker's Hill, and formidable as they are, the Town has shared a much better Fate than was expected, the damage done to the Houses being nothing equal to report, but the Inhabitants have suffer'd a good deal by being plunder'd by the Soldiery at their departure... King's property [was left] in Boston to the amount... of thirty or £40,000 in Provisions, Stores, &ca. Many Pieces of Cannon, some Mortars, and a number of Shot, Shells... Baggage-Wagons, Artillery Carts... were found destroyed, thrown into the Docks, and drifted upon every shore. In short, Dunbar's destruction of Stores after Genl. Braddock's defeat, which made so much noise, affords but a faint idea of what was to be met with here.*

In the letter, he made one of his rare grumbles about Providence: "That this remarkable Interposition of Providence is for some wise purpose, I have not a doubt: but as the principal design of the Manouvre was to draw the Enemy to an Ingagement under disadvantages... and seemed to be succeeding to my utmost wish... I can scarce forbear lamenting the disappointment."

HONORS

On March 28 Washington was again in the colony's capital to receive the thanks of the province and city. A very Boston account said: "This day, the Thursday lecture, which was established and has been observed from the first settlement of Boston, without interruption until within these few months past, was opened by the Rev. Dr. Eliot."

General Washington attended the lecture and Divine Service and then went to "an elegant dinner... Joy and gratitude sat in every countenance and smiled in every face." The following day, New England reserve further faded when the legislature of Massachusetts expressed its appreciation: "May future peaceful generations, in the enjoyment of that freedom, the exercise of which your sword shall have established, raise the richest and most lasting monuments to the name of Washington." He thanked them for their approval, adding:

> That the metropolis of your colony is now relieved from the cruel and oppressive invasions of those who were sent to erect the standard of lawless domination, and to trample on the rights of humanity... must give pleasure to every virtuous and sympathetic heart; and its being effected without the blood of our soldiers and fellow-citizens must be ascribed to the interposition of that Providence, which has manifestly appeared in our behalf through the whole of this important struggle...

> May that being, who is powerful to save, and in whose hand is the fate of nations, look down with an eye of tender pity and compassion upon the whole of the United Colonies.

On April 3, Harvard awarded its Doctorate of Laws to "GEORGIUS WASH-INGTON, Armiger, Imperator praeclarus, cujus Scientia et Amor Patriae undique patent; qui propter eximias Virtutes, tam civiles quam militates." However, it reached him too late to find him at Cambridge, for he was off again to the wars.

Byron said that Washington got, from his countrymen, "thanks, and naught else beside," but his warm-hearted nature welcomed them. Washington wrote his brother on March 31 that the Boston addresses showed "a pleasing testimony of their approbation of my conduct, and of their personal regard, which I have found in various other Instances; and which, in retirement, will afford many comfortable reflections." He still hoped that peace and retirement might not be far off.

On March 25 Congress received the news from Boston and, after resolving its thanks to Washington and to the army, ordered a gold medal struck to commemorate the evacuation of the city. Because of war conditions, Washington did not get it until 1786. In forwarding the resolution, John Hancock wrote Washington on April 2: "It gives me the most sensible pleasure to convey to you, by order of Congress, the only tribute which a free people will ever consent to pay, the tribute of thanks and gratitude to our friends and benefactors... As a peculiar greatness of mind induced you to decline any compensation for serving them, except the pleasure of promoting their happiness, they may without your permission bestow upon you the largest share of their affections and esteem."

In a polite reply, Washington expressed his appreciation and, using a phrase of Hancock, said that he had issued the thanks of Congress to his officers and men. "I am happy in having such an opportunity of doing justice to their Merit. They were indeed, at first, 'a band of undisciplined Husbandmen,' but it is (under God) to their bravery and attention to duty, that I am indebted for that success which has procured me the only reward I wish to receive; the affection and esteem of my Countrymen."

TO NEW YORK

Washington concentrated not on honors but on New York, which he assumed would be Britain's next objective. He had ordered General Lee there in January after receiving intelligence of British troop and fleet movements out of Boston. Now that the whole of the enemy forces were out of that city, there were only two ports where they could go—New York or Halifax. For ten days the fleet stayed just outside Boston, in Nantasket Road. Washington had no explanation of this, though his spies reported that repairs were needed on the king's ships before they got under way. His men watched the ships, manned the fortifications, and prepared to repulse any landings. On March 27 the fleet sailed for Halifax. Washington reported its departure to Congress, as well as the fact that he had ordered six regiments, under Sullivan, to march immediately for New York. The rest, except for five regiments left for Boston's defense, would follow shortly. The Massachusetts legislature offered Washington three hundred teams to be added to the British wagons taken at

Boston; these he assigned to Knox to move his artillery and powder. Washington departed Cambridge on April 5. On his way to New York he stopped to call on the governors of Rhode Island and Connecticut and to watch some of his troops leave Connecticut by water. He arrived in New York on April 13; his wife joined him there four days later. On its way to meet him at New York was a British fleet twice the size of the Spanish armada. Admiral Lord Howe commanded this mission with full powers to pardon all offenders and to restore the king's peace.

TWENTY

NEW YORK

1776

ALTHOUGH NEITHER THE king nor his government had expected the rebellion to be so extensive, they moved to mobilize with speed. No expense was spared. British garrisons at home and abroad were stripped. Treaties were negotiated with six German states for nearly thirty thousand troops. The Irish Parliament voted to send four thousand men from that country. Transports were hired and food supplies purchased wherever they could be found. Thousands of men were impressed for the navy from civilian life or the merchant marine. Britain's war expenditures more than doubled from 1775 to 1776. In order to finance the interest on its new debt, the government placed additional taxes on newspapers, deeds, cards, and dice—imposts that Americans had refused to pay in 1765.

In defending the hiring of Germans, Lord North told Parliament this was a quicker and more efficient way of getting troops than any other. Britain, he said, could not stand idly by in the face of an "unprovoked rebellion." He continued: "I believe there is no person in this House who is not firmly persuaded, that the whole united strength of America will not be able to oppose the force which is to be sent out early in the spring. I have the strongest and most confident hopes, that America will submit as soon as she is convinced that Great Britain is determined to act with resolution and vigour."

NEW YORK

London might be aroused but business was going on as usual in New York. The Royal Navy's ships were kept supplied with fresh provisions. British sentries were in cheerful communication with the people and not much was being done about defense. Within six days of his arrival, Washington put a stop to trading with the enemy. On April 17 he wrote to the New York committee on public safety to say that he always wanted to cooperate with civilian bodies but the needs of the country came first. If he took measures that caused pain, he would do so reluctantly, but do it he would. He added:

> That a continuance of the intercourse... between... this Colony and the Enemy, on board the Ships of War, is injurious to the Common Cause, requires no extraordinary abilities to prove... We are to consider ourselves either in a state of peace or War, with Great Britain. If the former, why are our Ports shut up, our Trade destroyed, our property seized, our Towns burnt, and our worthy and valuable Citizens led into captivity and suffering the most cruel hardships? If the latter, my imagination is not fertile enough, to suggest a reason in support of the intercourse.

> ...To tell you, Gentlemen, that the advantages of an intercourse of this kind, are altogether on the side of the Enemy... would be telling what must be obvious to every one... Besides their obtaining supplies of every kind... it also opens a regular Channel of intelligence... It would, Gentlemen, be taking up too much of your time, to use further arguments in proof of the necessity of putting an immediate and Total stop to all future Correspondence with the Enemy. It is my incumbent duty to effect this...

> In effecting the Salutory purposes above mentioned, I could wish for the Concurrence and support of your honorable Body; It will certainly add great weight to the Measures adopted, when the Civil authority Co-operates with the Military.

The committee resolved, two days later, to prohibit sending supplies to the British. Washington added a military proclamation to the same effect. These measures, plus the erection of fortifications, forced the enemy fleet to move thirty miles to Sandy Hook.

DEFENSE

New York's defense problems bore some similarity to those that had faced Howe in Boston. Manhattan was an island connected by a single bridge with the mainland. Boston was a peninsula with a narrow land connection. Brooklyn Heights dominated the city as those of Dorchester did Boston. There the similarity largely ended. New York harbor had many more large and small islands, bays, and sounds. The British could approach from Long Island Sound as well as through the Narrows. Washington had to plan to fight an army and a fleet. The Royal Navy had ships of the line and frigates that were mobile forts. These, with their transports, could move troops rapidly from one point to another under protective firepower. With no naval force of his own, Washington could only divide his small army.

Washington's plan to have General Charles Lee look to the city's defense while he was in Cambridge had been frustrated when Congress ordered Lee to the south. The senior officer at New York, a brigadier, William Alexander, earl of Stirling, took command. He was a collateral descendant of the first earl, a favorite of James I, who, in a fit of generosity, gave him most of eastern Canada and part of Maine. Among his numerous titles was that of Lord Canada. Alexander, with the aid of the duke of Argyll, had successfully established his descent and claim to the earldom by Scottish law. His subsequent efforts to win the approval of the House of Lords, in order to regain his vast ancestral holdings, were blocked in London by powerful interests.

Washington, after taking the command from Stirling, and in the time he could spare from a heavy administrative burden, toured Manhattan, Staten Island, and Brooklyn; the mainland north of the city as far as Tappan Zee on the Hudson; and Long Island Sound up to Mamaroneck. He also looked at Amboy, New Jersey. This was an enormous coastline. Washington ordered street barricades built on lower Manhattan and fortifications at the Battery and in the northwest, at Washington Heights. To prevent the British fleet from sailing up the East River, he added gun emplacements at Governor's Island and at two points in Brooklyn. On the Hudson River, he ordered further fortifications on the Jersey side, at Paulus Hook (now Jersey City) and across from Fort Washington (as it came to be called) at Fort Lee. He also established chevaux-de-frises (wooden barricades with iron points) built on hulks between the two forts on the Hudson and in the channels separating Manhattan from Brooklyn. He ordered further works at King's Bridge leading out of the city to the Bronx, and at points farther north. Every workman who could be hired, as well as most of his troops, were put to building and digging.

A serious problem in regard to defense was the large number of Tories in the city. Some, openly loyal to the king, were known, but others had been secretly recruited as spies or as king's soldiers. In addition, there were many neutrals who were prepared to jump to whichever side proved the stronger. The flame of revolution burned rather low in Manhattan. It was nearly nonexistent on Long Island and Staten Island, or in the Bronx and Westchester.

At Washington's urging, the New York legislature appointed secret committees in May to supervise county subcommittees, empowered to watch or arrest Tories. These committees also channeled intelligence to Washington. Where practicable, Washington preferred to have local governments who knew their people handle the roundup of suspected civilians, leaving the army to deal with military offenders. In emergencies both acted.

One of the first cases involved the mayor of New York and many others, including a member of Washington's bodyguard. The royal governor, William Tryon, after fleeing to the British fleet, sent agents ashore to recruit soldiers for the British army. These were to appear in uniform against the Americans as soon as the British landed. Washington's guard, an Irishman named Thomas Hickey, was convicted by court-martial as a member of the recruiting ring and hanged in view of the American army.

CANADA AND THE SOUTH

Charles Lee, dispatched by Washington to New York to look over its defenses, had arrived there in early February. Congress almost immediately ordered him to the command in Canada. As Adams wrote Lee: "We want you at N. York—We want you at Cambridge—We want you in Virginia—But Canada seems of more importance than any." Rumors then reached Philadelphia that the British would attack in the south. His Canadian orders were countermanded, and he was directed to head a new southern department of the army, stretching from Virginia to Georgia. When Lee went to Virginia, Washington wrote his brother John on March 31, just before leaving Cambridge:

> *General Lee, I expect, is with you before this. He is the first Officer in Military knowledge and experience we have in the whole Army. He is zealously attach'd to the Cause, but rather fickle and violent I fear in his temper. However as he possesses an uncommon share of good Sense and Spirit I congratulate my Countrymen on his appointment to that Department.*

Lee settled down in the governor's palace in Williamsburg from which Dunmore had been ejected. From this pleasant place, he was ordered south.

The British plan for southern operations had been sent by Lord George Germain to Governor Robert Eden of Maryland. The document, captured by the Americans, revealed that the first landing was to be in North Carolina. The plan went awry when violent storms damaged the vessels bringing troops from Ireland that were to meet additional forces under General Clinton proceeding from Boston. By the time the fleets met, North Carolina had scored a great victory over the Scottish Loyalists at Moore's Creek on February 27. Nearly nine hundred of the enemy were killed, wounded, or captured. This ended any chance for a Loyalist uprising in the province. After hovering awhile off the North Carolina coast, the British decided to attack Charleston.

Lee had gone to Wilmington, North Carolina. Learning that the enemy had departed, he guessed that Charleston would be next and hurried there. South Carolina troops, though not yet continental, were promptly placed under his command by Governor John Rutledge. The British fleet arrived off Charleston about the time Lee got there. Lee's role was largely confined to rather rough treatment of the southern troops and to criticism of their fortifications. He did, however, provide some useful suggestions and encouragement in the fighting. The South Carolinians had constructed their forts well; enemy shells sank softly into the local palmetto wood.

The British forces were routed on June 28. Admiral Sir Peter Parker lost one ship, as well as his breeches when he was wounded in the backside. A number of other ships were badly damaged. There were more than two hundred British casualties as compared with thirty-seven among the Americans. Washington, in his July 21 order to his troops, highly commended Lee and the South Carolinians:

> *The General has great pleasure in communicating to the officers, and soldiers of this Army, the signal success of the American arms under General Lee at South Carolina. The Enemy having attempted to land at the same time that a most furious Cannonade for* <u>twelve</u> *hours was made upon the Fortifications near Charlestown: both fleet and Army have been repulsed with great loss by a small number of gallant troops just raised. The Enemy have had one hundred and seventy two men killed and wounded... two capital ships much damaged, one Frigate of Twenty-eight Guns entirely lost... The firmness, Courage and bravery of our Troops, has crowned them with immortal Honor. The dying Heroes conjured their Brethren never to abandon the Standard of Liberty, and even those who had lost their Limbs, continued at their posts... This glorious Example... the General hopes will animate every officer, and soldier, to imitate, and even out do them, when the enemy shall make the same attempt upon us.*

When Lee later arrived in Philadelphia, Congress covered him with laurels and also advanced him $30,000 so that he could pay off his debts. From this point on, Lee, raised to an eminence greater than his psychic resources could bear, began the erratic moves that were to destroy his reputation and himself.

The battle of Charleston was the only good news the Americans had after the evacuation of Boston. In Canada, after the death of Montgomery and the failure at Quebec, the situation deteriorated steadily. Canada became a morass into which Congress, alarmed by the reports it received, poured endless troops, supplies, and provisions. In February, Congress resolved to send commissioners there: Benjamin Franklin, Charles Carroll, and Samuel Chase. They were accompanied by John Carroll, a Jesuit priest, who was later to be the first American archbishop. The commissioners did not reach Montreal until the end of April, when they found the situation too desperate to accomplish anything. Franklin, ill from the long journey, had to return before the others.

Washington had issued careful instructions to American troops going to Canada that they were on a mission which was to be as much diplomatic as military. He ordered them to treat the Canadians with the greatest respect and to safeguard absolutely the Canadians' religion and property. His instructions were ignored. The behavior of the twelve hundred or so men who remained in the country after the defeat at Quebec was described by Colonel Moses Hazen, a Massachusetts man living there, in his letter of April 1 to General Schuyler:

> You are not unacquainted with the friendly disposition of the Canadians, when General Montgomery first penetrated into the country; the ready assistance which they gave on all occasions, by men, carriages, or provisions, was most remarkable... His most unfortunate fate, added to other incidents, has caused such a change in their disposition, that we no longer look upon them as friends... The clergy... have been neglected, perhaps in some instances ill-used... The peasantry in general have been ill-used. They have, in some instances, been dragooned with the point of the bayonet to supply wood for the garrison at a lower rate than the current price. For... many articles furnished, certificates have been given, not legible, without signatures... And in a more material point, they have not seen sufficient force in the country to protect them.

Colonel Hazen soon reported to Schuyler that the Canadians were arming against the Americans. He added: "We have brought about by mismanagement, what Governor Charelton himself could never effect." The plan for the conquest of Canada had been Congress' baby. Now that it had failed and the situation was desperate, Congress took further measures without consulting Washington or waiting for the reports of its commissioners. These stripped the commander in chief of a large portion of his best officers and troops, without saving the situation in the north.

In March Congress ordered Brigadier John Thomas, who had brilliantly executed the fortification of Dorchester Heights, to Quebec to command with the rank of major general. This removed one of Washington's best officers. Thomas died of smallpox in June. Subsequently six additional regiments under Brigadier John Sullivan were detached from Washington for Canadian duty. Washington replied no when he was asked if he could spare even more troops.

In June the delegates at Philadelphia ordered Horatio Gates—Washington's adjutant general, on whom he relied for organization and discipline—to proceed to Canada, raising him to major general. When Gates and Schuyler subsequently quarreled over who was in charge, Washington suggested to Congress that he could very well use one of them. He was ignored; by the time Congress got through meddling there were more continental troops engaged on the Quebec expedition than in New York. The commander in chief was left with only the oldest major general in the army and a handful of brigadiers of varying quality.

Early in May General John Burgoyne arrived in Quebec with nearly eight thousand reinforcements. The American army, suffering from smallpox, dysentery, and every kind of shortage, was quickly harried out of the country. According to Gates, American losses there—by death, capture, or desertion—numbered five thousand.

When Arnold's troops left Montreal, they looted the town, thus adding to Canadian enmity. This led to subsequent quarrels between Arnold and Hazen, and between him and Lieutenant Colonel John Brown, who had married Arnold's cousin. In April of the following year Brown published a handbill against Arnold, in which he charged him with many misdeeds. He added: "Money is this man's god, and to get enough of it, he would sacrifice his country."

NERVE CENTER

Although he had been stripped of many of his general officers and troops, Washington resolutely continued to function as the active center of continental military and naval operations. Some indication of their extent is contained in his request of April 23 to Congress for more pay for his aides:

I take the liberty unsolicited by, and unknown to my aid de Camps to inform your Honorable body, that their pay is not, by any means, equal to their trouble and confinement.

No person wishes to save money to the public more than I do... but there are some cases where parsimony may be ill placed...

I give into no kind of amusements myself, consequently those about me can have none, but are confined from Morn' 'till Eve hearing, and answering the applications and Letters of one and another; which will now, I expect, receive a pretty considerable addition as the business of the Northern and Eastern departments... must... pass through my hands. If these Gentlemen had the same relaxation from duty as other Officers have in their common Routine, there would not be so much in it, but to have the mind always upon the stretch, scarce ever unbent, and no hours of recreation, makes a material odds; knowing this, and at the same time, how inadequate the pay is, I can scarce find Inclination to impose the necessary duties of their Office upon them.

Congress raised their pay from $33 to $40 per month. By July 25 Washington was asking for more aides. "The augmentation of my Command, the Increase of my Correspondence, the Orders to give; the Instructions to draw, cut out more business than I am able to execute in time, with propriety. The business of so many different departments centering with me, and by me to be handed on to Congress for their information, added to the Intercourse I am Obliged to keep up with the adjacent States and incidental Occurrences, all of which requiring confidential (and not hack) writers to execute, renders it impossible in the present State of things for my family to discharge the several duties expected of me with that precision and despatch that I could wish. What will it be then when we come into a more active Scene, and I am called upon from twenty different places perhaps at the same Instant?" Congress authorized one more aide.

Washington's burden can only be understated. He made appeals for militia to New York, New Jersey, Pennsylvania, and Connecticut, and helped to organize flying camps (mobile forces) in New Jersey. He ordered the Loyalist governor of New Jersey arrested. He was involved in endless problems of discipline and order among his troops who found New York more exciting than New England. He saw congressional delegations and asked for more troops and general officers. The correspondence and instructions to the army in northern New York and Canada went through his hands. The commander in chief had to provide boat transportation for the troops ordered north, as well as salt, powder, tools, and meat for their use. He hired carpenters, boat builders, painters, and axemen for work on the New York fortifications. Washington was concerned with shortages of arms, engineers, and working tools such as spades and shovels. He dispatched whaleboats to patrol New York harbor and to intercept messages and supplies for the Royal Navy. He ordered the building of flat-bottomed boats for troop transport to and from Long Island and New Jersey. He supervised naval operations extending to the Bahamas.

THE BOARD OF WAR AND ORDNANCE

Washington had frequently suggested that Congress appoint a war board with which he could deal directly. The board was established June 12 under the chairmanship of John Adams. His colleagues were Roger Sherman, Benjamin Harrison, James Wilson, and Edward Rutledge. Its membership ranged from New England to South Carolina.

The board having met, its members asked not what they could do for Washington, but how they could impose more paperwork on him. They requested him "as speedily as possible" and "for the more speedy and effectual despatch of military business" to prepare "forthwith" returns of all his troops, being sure that they were fully detailed as to the colonies from which they came, and their time and period of enlistment. Washington was ordered to send these periodically and to conduct "a constant and regular correspondence." This dispatch reached him as the first sails of the British armada came into sight of New York harbor.

The board's next business seems to have been to order three of the five continental regiments stationed at Boston to proceed, not to New York, where they were vitally needed, but northward to Canada. The board gave Washington discretion on ordering the remaining two regiments to New York. On July 6, 1776, the board made a detailed inquiry as to the pay and allowances of drum and fife majors and quartermaster sergeants.

WASHINGTON ASKS FOR CAVALRY

Washington, who had ridden so long as a frontier officer, knew how valuable cavalry could be for reconnaissance and mobile troop support. Though this might seem obvious, a long line of historians has chided him for failing to understand and use cavalry at the August battle of Long Island. The most bitter attack on Washington for negligence was made by Charles Francis Adams, Jr., writing in the twentieth century.

On June 21 Washington requested authority from Charles' great grandfather, John Adams, to enlist a troop of cavalry which, he said, would be "extremely useful... in reconnoitering the Enemy and gaining Intelligence...

and... have it in their power to render many other important benefits." John Adams pigeonholed the request by filing it for later consideration.

On July 22 Washington repeated his request for cavalry authorization, but again he got no answer from Adams. By September, despairing of Congress, he had to turn to temporary Connecticut mounted militia for reconnaissance work. Washington received his authorization to establish a continental cavalry force in December while Adams was on a long holiday.

VIRGINIA VOTES FOR INDEPENDENCE

In the spring of 1776, county meetings were held throughout Virginia for the purpose of advising their delegates at Richmond on whether to vote for a final separation from Great Britain. The results were unanimous. Cumberland County, for example, instructed its representatives "that you solemnly abjure any allegiance for His Britannick majesty and bid him good-night forever." On May 15 the Virginia Convention in turn unanimously asked its congressmen at Philadelphia to vote to forswear all allegiance to the British crown. Washington received this news from his brother John. He replied on May 31:

> I am very glad to find that the Virginia Convention have passed so noble a vote, and with so much unanimity, things have come to that pass now, as to convince us, that we have nothing more to expect from the justice of G. Britain; also, that she is capable of the most delusive Arts, for I am satisfied that no Commissioners ever were design'd, except Hessians... The Idea was only to deceive... Many Members of Congress... are still feeding themselves on the dainty food of reconciliation...

> To form a new Government, requires infinite care, and unbounded attention; for if the foundation is sadly laid the superstructure must be bad, too much time therefore, cannot be bestowed in weighing and digesting matters well... My fear is that you will all get tired and homesick, the consequences of which will be, that you will patch up some sort of Constitution as defective as the present; this should be avoided, every Man should consider, that he is lending his aid to frame a Constitution which is to render Millions happy, or Miserable, and that a matter of such moment cannot be the work of a day.

Eleven years after he wrote this paragraph, he was elected chairman of the convention called to draft the Constitution of the United States.

CONGRESS VOTES

On June 7, Richard Henry Lee of Virginia—who had entered the House of Burgesses just before Washington and who had, the following year, introduced a bill to end the "iniquitous and disgraceful" slave trade—rose in Congress and offered its most famous resolution:

> *Resolved, That these United Colonies are, and of right ought to be, free and independent States, that they are absolved from all allegiance to the British Crown, and that all political connection between them and the State of Great Britain is, and ought to be totally dissolved.*

When the first vote was taken on July 1, only nine provinces could command a sufficient majority among their delegations in favor of the resolution. South Carolina and Pennsylvania voted no, Delaware was evenly split, and New York lacked authorizing instructions. The next day, with the arrival of a fresh delegate from Delaware, the abstention by two Pennsylvanians, and a reversal by South Carolina, twelve states voted for it. New York subsequently approved. While this was technically unanimous, it was hardly so in spirit. On July 4 Congress approved "A Declaration," as it was called. In it, reliance was firmly placed "on the Protection of Divine Providence." Although the declaration did not so state, Congress had also to rely on George Washington; his one major general, "Old Put" Putnam; and nine thousand troops present and fit for duty in New York. The delegates had reduced Washington's effective force as much as 40 percent for the abortive Canadian expedition, leaving him to face an enemy with six or more times his numerical strength. On July 9 he issued general orders to his troops.

> *The General hopes and trusts, that every officer and man, will endeavour so to live, and act, as becomes a Christian Soldier defending the dearest Rights and Liberties of his country.*

> *The Hon. The Continental Congress, impelled by the dictates of duty, policy and necessity, having been pleased to dissolve the Connection which subsisted between this Country, and Great Britain, and to declare the United Colonies of North America, free and independent STATES: The several brigades are to be drawn up this evening on their respective Parades, at Six OClock, when the declaration of Congress, shewing the grounds and reasons of this measure, is to be read with an audible voice.*

The General hopes this important Event will serve as a fresh incentive to every
officer, and soldier, to act with fidelity and Courage, as knowing that now the peace
and safety of our Country depends (under God) solely on the success of our arms.

That evening a joyful mob, many of them soldiers, clambered over the statue of George III, hitched ropes to it, and pulled away; down it came. George's head was hacked off and rolled along the ground.

The next day, Washington issued a reprimand: "Tho the General doubts not the persons, who pulled down and mutilated the Statue, in the Broadway, last night, were actuated by Zeal in the public cause; yet it has so much the appearance of riot, and want of order, in the Army, that he disapproves the manner, and directs that in future these things shall be avoided by the Soldiery, and left to be executed by proper authority." Revolution or no, its leader wanted law and order.

A SUBSTITUTE

When Rip Van Winkle woke from his twenty-years' sleep through the revolution and beyond and returned to his native village, he found many puzzling changes. On the old tavern sign he recognized "the ruby face of King George, under which he had smoked many a peaceful pipe, but even this was singularly metamorphosed. The red coat was changed for one of blue and buff, a sword was held in the hand instead of a sceptre, the head was decorated with a cocked hat, and underneath was painted in large characters, GENERAL WASHINGTON." Washington Irving thus symbolized the change that was to come to the new nation, though it did not take place immediately. It came the easier because, as Benjamin Rush noted in a letter which was reproduced by a London paper in 1776, every king in Europe, by the side of Washington, would have looked like his valet.

"OUR WORKS ARE MANY, AND THE TROOPS BUT FEW"

In thus appealing to Connecticut for more militia, Washington summed up his situation, but even he had no idea of the size of the opposing force he would face.

On June 25 General Howe arrived in New York from Halifax with three ships. On June 29 Washington reported to Congress that more than 150 ships (though the number was probably somewhat less) had joined Howe. On July

21 Admiral Howe, in his flagship, with another 150 ships, arrived with troops from England. On August 1, Admiral Sir Peter Parker, with 40 ships, and Generals Clinton and Cornwallis hove to off Sandy Hook. On August 8 still another fleet came in. On August 12, 34 more men-of-war and troop transports reported to the Howes. Lord Dunmore, with a small force, also showed up. In September 65 more transports arrived.

Lord Sandwich reported to the king in June that half his naval force of 30,000 had gone to duty in American waters and all but a few small frigates were on the way there. The warships and their transports, many hired in Europe, came from Halifax, Charleston, Glasgow, Emden, Cork, Portsmouth, Spithead, Hamburg, and elsewhere. Altogether around 450 vessels with more than 15,000 sailors and 43,000 troops and marines, all superbly equipped and ready for battle, showed up by September to beat back the rebellion. Included among the officers were no fewer than twenty members of Parliament. On July 7 General Howe described his situation to Lord George Germain in a letter with which Washington would have been in disgusted agreement:

> *I have the satisfaction to inform your Lordship, that there is great reason to expect a numerous body of the inhabitants to join the army from the provinces of New York, the Jerseys, and Connecticut, who in this time of universal apprehension only wait the opportunities to give proofs of their loyalty and zeal for government. This disposition among the people makes me impatient for the arrival of Lord Howe, concluding the powers with which he is furnished will have the best effect at this critical time; but I am still of the opinion, that peace will not be restored in America until the rebel army is defeated.*

Howe quickly disembarked more than nine thousand troops on Staten Island, a Tory stronghold. Tory or not, women were fair game for the British, so long as they were Americans. Francis, Lord Rawdon, a young Irish officer, wrote to his uncle, Lord Huntingdon, on August 5: "The fair nymphs of this isle are in wonderful tribulation, as the fresh meat our men have got here has made them as riotous as satyrs. A girl cannot step into the bushes to pluck a rose without running the most imminent risk of being ravished, and they are so little accustomed to these vigorous methods that they don't bear them with the proper resignation, and of consequence we have the most entertaining courts-martial every day." Lord Howe's secretary, Ambrose Serle, described the fleet's arrival on July 12:

> *We passed Sandy Hook in the afternoon, and about 6 o'clock arrived off the east side of Staten Island. The country on both sides was highly picturesque and*

agreeable. Nothing could exceed the joy that appeared throughout the fleet and army upon our arrival. We were saluted by all the ships of war in the harbour, by the cheers of the sailors all along the ships, and by those of the soldiers on the shore... What added to their pleasure was that this very day about noon the Phoenix of 40 guns and the Rose of 20, with three tenders, forced their passage up the river, in defiance of all their vaunted batteries, and got safe above the town, which will much intercept the provisions of the Rebels.

As soon as we came to anchor, Admiral Shuldham came on board, and soon after Genl Howe... We learnt the deplorable situation of His Majesty's faithful subjects, that they were hunted after and shot at in the woods and swamps, to which they had fled for these four months to avoid the savage fury of the Rebels... and that deserters and others flocked to the King's army continually. We also heard that the Congress have now announced the Colonies to be independent States, with several other articles of intelligence that proclaim the villainy and the madness of these deluded people. Where we anchored was in full view of New York, and of the Rebels' head quarters under Washington, who is now made their generalissimo with full powers.

The forcing of the Hudson was only too true. Washington was furious at his soldiers who gaped at the ships as they passed. His general order the following day said: "The General was sorry to observe yesterday that many of the officers and a number of men instead of attending to their duty at the Beat of the Drum; continued along the banks of the North River, gazing at the ships... A weak curiosity at such a time makes a man look mean and contemptible." Washington dispatched orders to Brigadier James Clinton in the Hudson Highlands to keep a close lookout, since he did not know whether the ships carried troops.

The Howes decided to wait for most of their expected forces to arrive before taking action against the rebels. Many came later than planned. This was of some help to the Americans as the British did not like to fight in the winter. The ship movements up the Hudson were the first and most successful probe of the American defenses. Aside from the alarms they produced in the city and state, their most immediate effect was to force Washington to order the three regiments on their way from Boston to Canada to proceed by land, rather than by water, from Norwich to New York and then to Albany. Washington expressed regret that the men had to march in the summer heat over so long a distance.

The Howes now began their probe of American political defenses. On July 12 a signal came from the British fleet that a messenger would come to the city under a flag of truce. Washington sent Joseph Reed, now back on his staff as adjutant, General Henry Knox, and an aide, Samuel Webb, to meet the officer messenger. The messenger brought with him a letter from Lord Howe addressed to "George Washington, Esq.," which they would not accept because Washington was not addressed officially. Four days later, the British offered another letter for Washington, which added several "et ceteras" after "esquire." This too was refused, and Serle fumed in his diary at the "insolence and vanity" of Washington, "a little paltry Colonel of Militia." On July 17 Lord Howe signalled to ask if Washington would receive his adjutant general. Washington agreed to do so. On July 20 Lieutenant Colonel James Paterson came ashore and called on General Washington. He was excessively polite, addressing Washington as "Your Excellency" with each breath. He assured him that no disrespect had been intended. Colonel Knox described the subsequent talk in a letter of July 22 to his wife:

> He [Paterson] said Lord and General Howe lamented exceedingly that any errors in the transcription should interrupt that frequent intercourse between the two armies which might be necessary in the course of the service. That Lord Howe had come out with great powers. The General said he had heard that Lord Howe had come out with very great powers to pardon, but he had come to the wrong place; the Americans had not offended, therefore they needed no pardon. This confused him.
>
> After a considerable deal of talk about the good disposition of Lord and General Howe, he asked, "Has your Excellency no particular commands with which you would please to honour me to Lord and General Howe?"
>
> "Nothing, sir, but my particular compliments to both." General Washington was very handsomely dressed and made a most elegant appearance. Colonel Paterson appeared awe-struck, as if he was before something supernatural. Indeed I don't wonder at it. He was before a great man indeed.

Colonel Paterson politely refused refreshments, saying that the brothers would be anxious to hear about the interview. Howe had also sent letters to various American officials, including Franklin, whom he called his "worthy friend." Franklin replied on July 20:

> The official despatches to which you refer me, contain nothing more than what we had seen in the act of Parliament, viz., offers of pardon upon submission, which I am sorry to find, as it must give your lordship pain to be sent so far on so hopeless a business. Directing pardons to be offered the colonies, who are the very parties injured, expresses indeed that opinion of our ignorance, baseness, and insensibility,

which your uninformed and proud nation has long been pleased to entertain of us; but it can have no other effect than that of increasing our resentment.

It is impossible that we should think of submission to a government that has with the most wanton barbarity and cruelty burnt our defenceless towns in the midst of winter, excited the savages to massacre our farmers, and our slaves to murder their masters, and is even now bringing foreign mercenaries to deluge our settlements with blood. These atrocious injuries have extinguished every remaining spark of affection for that parent country we once held so dear; but were it possible for us to forget and forgive them, it is not possible for you (I mean the British nation) to forgive the people you have so heavily injured...

I consider this war against us... as both unjust and unwise; and I am persuaded that cool, dispassionate posterity will condemn to infamy those who advised it; and that even success will not save from some degree of dishonor those who voluntarily engaged to conduct it. I know your great motive in coming hither was the hope of being instrumental in a reconciliation; and I believe, when you find that impossible on any terms given you to propose, you will relinquish so odious a command, and return to a more honorable private station.

Franklin's letter was delivered to Lord Howe by Americans who had gone aboard his flagship to discuss the handling of prisoners. Howe commented that he expressed himself very warmly. Franklin's remarks were wasted on the Howes, who were so convinced that the great majority of Americans were loyal to the king that they did not take him too seriously. They were not completely wrong, for less than three weeks before, three states had voted against independence. General Howe's intelligence reports that large groups of citizens in New York and New Jersey were ready to help the British were accurate. Ambrose Serle noted in his August 13 diary entry that many Irish soldiers had already deserted to them from Washington's army.

General Howe had correctly predicted that the British would have to beat the rebel army. However, this attempt could not take place until most of the troops reached New York. When a large fleet arrived on August 12, preparations for attack got under way.

A SKIRMISH ON LONG ISLAND

On August 7, in a further appeal for militia and other help from Governor Trumbull of Connecticut, Washington disclosed that the enemy had 30,000 men ready to attack Long Island and New York. (His intelligence later raised this to 32,000.) He said that much of his army was sick, few levies of new troops had shown up, and he had an enormous extent of ground to defend. He felt that the disgrace to the British arms in the South, plus the fact that the season for fighting was getting short, would force their army and navy to exert every effort against him. He added that he had on hand 10,514 men fit for duty, plus about 3,000 "on command," that is, on detached service. "By this, you will see, we are to oppose an Army of 30,000 experienced Veterans, with about one third the Number of Raw Troops, and these scattered, some 15 miles apart." In his assessment Washington did not mention the enemy's great naval strength. At this point, General Clinton expressed the prevailing British view that the Americans would soon take a drubbing and peace negotiations would quickly follow.

Brigadier John Sullivan returned to New York in early August. He had been dispatched north to take command in Canada and he had then been replaced by General Gates. He left the command in a huff and hurried to Philadelphia to express his resentment and to offer his resignation. Some cooler heads prevailed on him to withdraw it before Congress could act. He was ordered to New York. He had almost no time to assess the situation before going into battle.

On August 12 Washington announced to the army that three of his four brigadiers, Heath, Spencer, and Greene, along with Sullivan, had been made major generals. Shortly thereafter, Greene, who had been in charge of the Brooklyn defense, came down with a serious illness and fever. Washington reported that many of his field officers were also stricken and some regiments had none capable of duty.

Additional reinforcements from Pennsylvania, Massachusetts, and Maryland arrived in New York, as well as some eight thousand Connecticut militia. By the time the British attacked, Washington's paper strength was probably close to nineteen thousand, but many of the additions were farm boys with little or no training.

On August 13 Washington announced to his troops that most of the enemy reinforcements had arrived and they could soon expect battle. He asked them to "be ready for action at a moments call; and when called to it, remember that Liberty, Property, Life and Honor, are all at stake; that upon their Courage and Conduct, rest the hopes of their bleeding and insulted Country... The enemy will endeavour to intimidate by shew and appearance, but remember how they have been repulsed, on various occasions by a few brave Americans; Their Cause is bad; their men are conscious of it, and if opposed with firmness, and coolness, at their first onset, with our advantage of Works, and Knowledge of the Ground, Victory is most assuredly ours."

On August 22 General Howe moved fifteen thousand troops from Staten Island to Gowanus Bay, on Long Island, and landed them without difficulty. On August 25 he sent over five thousand Hessians. On August 27 Lord Howe added two thousand marines. Present on Long Island were Lieutenant Generals Howe, Clinton, Cornwallis, and Percy—four of Britain's top command—plus the experienced German Major General von Heister. In addition, there was Major General James Grant, the officer who had made the foolish attack on Fort Duquesne in 1758 that had cost the lives of many of Washington's Virginians. The four top British officers had suffered humiliation of one sort or another from the Americans. Now they had not only twice the Americans' total strength in Brooklyn alone, but they were a far more effective combat force.

When Howe landed, there were about four thousand Americans in the Brooklyn area. A small Pennsylvania detachment watched the enemy arrive and reported to Washington that there were eight thousand British on the island. This report was so inaccurate that for two or three days Washington groped in the dark, unable to determine whether this was a feint to cover a main landing on Manhattan. He dispatched some eighteen hundred militia to Brooklyn; two-thirds of these were hastily assembled rural volunteers. From time to time, he sent additional troops to Long Island. Their number has been so variously estimated that there seems no possibility of arriving at exactness. The maximum American strength at any point appears to have been more than 10,500, of whom only a third engaged in battle with the 22,000 British troops and marines.

The main American army was stationed on Brooklyn Heights, which commanded, along with guns on Red Hook, Governor's Island, and on lower Manhattan, the entrance to the East River. There was also a series of redoubts and fortifications that extended from Wallabout Bay to a marsh ranging nearly to Gowanus Bay. All the British forces landed south of this area. To reach Brooklyn Heights, they had to pass through, or around, the Heights of Guan, which stretched inland from a point near the bay to central Queens. Along these heights were posted some thirty-five hundred men under Sullivan. They guarded three of the four passes through Guan, but there was only a small mounted patrol at the fourth.

On August 23 Washington went to Long Island to inspect the situation. On August 25 he gave the overall command to his senior general, Israel Putnam, who knew little of military tactics. In his instructions to Putnam, he chided the troops for sporadic and wasteful fire, and asked Putnam to control this. Noting that militia were "most indifferent Troops," he ordered that they be used only in fortified works, leaving the more experienced men for outside

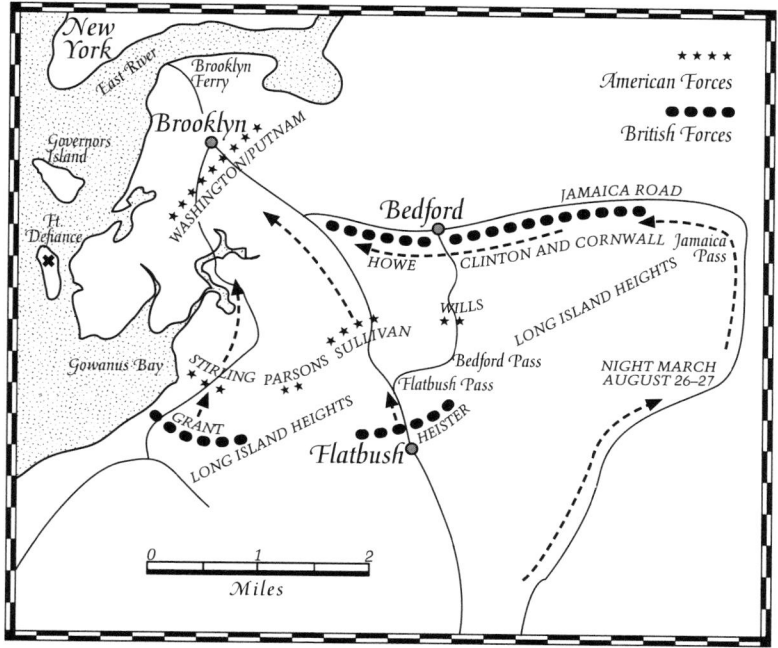

The Battle of Long Island, August 27, 1776

guard and patrol duty. Washington also instructed Putnam to "form a proper line of defence, round your Encampment and Works... The Woods should be secured by Abbatis &c. where Necessary to make the Enemy's approach, as difficult as possible; Traps and ambuscades should be laid for their Parties, if you find they are sent out after Cattle &c." There was little time to do all this.

Guided by Tories, and no doubt by the maps of Captain John Montresor, Howe's aide, who had lived many years in New York, the British under Clinton simply planned to go around Sullivan's forces, through the Jamaica pass.

On August 26 Washington again went to Long Island, where he stayed until the thirtieth. Sullivan remained in command of Guan, with Stirling posted at the Gowanus road along the shore, the only access that did not go through Guan Heights. On the night of the twenty-sixth, Clinton captured a patrol at Jamaica and then, in the early morning of the twenty-seventh, with half the British army, marched through it to outflank the small American detachments under Stirling and Sullivan. Sullivan and his men fought vigorously but were quickly overwhelmed. Some were forced to surrender but many escaped.

On the British left, Stirling with some fifteen hundred men held off seven thousand British troops and marines for an extended period. When Cornwallis came up on his rear with fresh troops, Stirling ordered two-thirds of his men to retreat through the marshes. With the remaining five hundred men, he turned to attack Cornwallis. Five times they fought through until, overwhelmed by a superior force, they surrendered. Many of Stirling's other men got to the American lines, though under the greatest of difficulty.

American battle casualties were about four hundred, mostly killed. The British losses were approximately the same, but perhaps a quarter only were dead. The British took about nine hundred prisoners, including two generals, Sullivan and Stirling.

Ambrose Serle, who was on the flagship, reported that the navy "made a feint of attacking... Many of the principal men of war got under way and sailed backwards and forwards" as a diversion. General Howe received no other naval aid from his brother's ships except for the landing of new supplies of munitions. Washington's planned defense of the East River held throughout the engagement, and his communications with his command post on Manhattan remained secure.

Washington now had nine thousand or more troops—the majority fresh—who held Brooklyn Heights, which could be taken only by direct assault or by siege. Howe and Clinton had had too much experience at Breed's Hill with the cost of an assault, and Howe had refused to attack Washington at Dorchester Heights for the same reason. Had the American defense not kept the British fleet from participating, the Howes might have engaged in a successful combined land and sea operation. Lord Howe could not help, and General Howe therefore moved to his only alternative. To avoid any possible disaster to the British army, he established a siege in the hope of eventual naval support. At some point during this time of decision, Washington received word that a part of the British fleet, unable to get through the East River, had gone around Long Island and was approaching from the north.

The shortage of American supplies, especially tents and food, made their position militarily tenable for only a limited period. The British siege redoubts had moved close to the American lines. On August 29 Washington's council of war approved his move for the return of all troops to Manhattan. That night, John Glover and his regiment of Marblehead fishermen and seamen brought over every available boat from Manhattan. Beginning late in the evening, the entire American army, with practically all its provisions and cannon, was moved quietly across the river. When the British saw the American lines the next morning, they were empty. It was one of the most skillful maneuvers in military history, conducted in the face of an army several times as large and an immense British naval force only a few miles off.

Long Island was a technical defeat for the Americans. Twenty-two thousand troops under famous British generals, including a collateral descendent of Hotspur, had managed to surround thirty-five hundred peasants, two-thirds of whom escaped the trap. Howe reported to London that he had beaten ten thousand Americans and had captured or killed some four thousand of them. The king was so pleased with this amphibious operation that he made Howe a knight of the Bath. It was a victory but not precisely an Agincourt.

Now Washington's army, with its hard core of good troops, was whole again on Manhattan, while the British army was divided. Howe had already been two months in New York harbor but not a single British soldier had set foot on Manhattan.

THE BRITISH WILL NEGOTIATE

When Washington received returns of prisoners from Howe, he was surprised to find more than he had estimated. The discrepancy came in part because additional American militia, operating independently on Long Island under Brigadier Nathaniel Woodhull, were captured after the fight at Brooklyn Heights. According to tradition, when Woodhull surrendered and handed his sword to a Tory officer, he was so badly slashed with it that he died a short time later. Probably because of this, his nephew, Abraham Woodhull, later volunteered to head Washington' s intelligence service during the British occupation of New York.

Stirling and Sullivan, as general officers and in accordance with military custom of the eighteenth century, were entertained by Lord Howe at dinner aboard his flagship. Now that the rebels had apparently been given a crushing blow, Howe returned to his peace mission. Whether Howe misled Sullivan, or Sullivan misunderstood Howe, is not now clear. According to Sullivan, Howe asked him to proceed to Congress to tell them that he could set aside all offensive acts of Parliament and effect a peace settlement. Sullivan agreed to go, and Washington, considering this a political matter, gave him permission to proceed to Philadelphia. John Adams was most annoyed at Sullivan and called him Howe's "decoy duck." He also expressed the opinion that it was too bad that one of the British bullets had not gone through Sullivan's head. After long debate, Congress agreed to send Franklin, Adams, and Rutledge to meet Howe on September 11 at Staten Island.

From his own point of view, Howe was exceedingly tactful in dealing with rebels. He explained that he could talk with them only as individuals, not as congressmen, but this did not matter, since, as soon as peace was declared, Congress would disappear. The irrepressible Adams said Howe could look upon them in any way he wanted but not as British subjects. Howe ruffled a bit at this. The conference got nowhere. At the end Franklin said that Howe seemed still to want unconditional submission and Howe said this was not the case at all. They parted in a polite manner, and the Howes returned to the war. Sullivan did not gain many kudos from this affair but, in the interim, Howe agreed to exchange Stirling and Sullivan. Washington a little later had his two generals back.

GENERAL HOWE ATTACKS NEW YORK

The strain Washington had undergone is noted in his letter to Congress of August 31:

> *Inclination as well as duty, would have induced me to give Congress, the earliest information of my removal of the Troops from Long Island and its dependencies to this City, the night before last; but the extreme fatigue, which myself and family have undergone (as much from the Weather as any thing else) since the incampment of the 27th. rendered me entirely unfit to take a pen in hand. Since Monday, we have scarce any of us been out of the Lines, till our passage across the*

East River was effected yesterday Morning, and for the 48 hours preceeding that; I had hardly been off my horse and I had never closed my Eyes, so that I was quite unfit to write or dictate till this Morning.

Our Retreat was made without any loss of Men or Ammunition and in better order than I expected, for Troops in the Situation ours were, we brought off all our Cannon and Stores, except a few heavy pieces, (which in the condition the Earth was, by a long continued rain) we found upon tryal impracticable... I have inclosed a Copy of the Council of War held previous to the Retreat, to which I beg leave to refer Congress for the reasons...

When Washington was appointed to his command, he received instructions from Congress. His written commission ordered him "punctually to observe and follow such orders and directions... as you shall receive from... Congress... or a Committee of Congress for the purpose appointed." A subsequent directive authorized him "advising with your council of war, to order and dispose of the said army under your command." The first clause, to obey Congress, was clear. The second was less so but Washington understood it to mean that he had to act with the advice and consent of his council. This was not clarified until the spring of 1777, when Congress resolved that Washington was not obliged to follow the recommendation of his general officers. Because he had interpreted the phrase to mean what Congress probably originally intended it to be, he sent them the council's opinion on removing from Long Island. With continued congressional interference in the army and frequent division in his council, he was not fully free in his command until later in the war.

Once both Brooklyn Heights and Governor's Island, from which Washington also withdrew, were in enemy hands, the British fleet was free to operate and New York could be defended for but a short period. The British needed the city for military quarters. Washington posed to Congress the question he had once before asked about Boston: Should the city be destroyed? In the former case, Hancock, a Bostonian, had replied for Congress: Destroy if necessary. This time, Congress, much less brave, hurriedly ordered Washington to leave the city intact.

The remaining question, whether to abandon New York to the enemy, he put to his war council. Washington had informed Congress that he had found the militia so unreliable—they were deserting in such droves—that any hopes he had for the city's defense had almost vanished. The minutes are missing, but the first vote was to defend New York. On September 8 Washington sent Congress the appraisal that he had reached with his council of war. In it, he referred to the "country," meaning the mainland, since American and British forces were still on islands. He wrote:

> *Before the landing of the Enemy on Long Island, the point of attack could not be known... It might be on Long Island, on Bergen or directly on this City, this made it necessary to be prepared for each, and has occasioned an Expence of Labour which now seems useless and is regretted by those who form a Judgement from after Knowledge... By such Works... we have not only delayed... the Campaign, till it is too late to effect any capital Incursion into the Country, but have drawn the Enemy's forces to one point... It is now extremely obvious, from all Intelligence... they mean to enclose us on our Rear, while the Shipping effectually secures the Front, and thus either by cutting off our communication with the Country, oblige us to fight them on their own terms, or surrender at discretion, or by a brilliant Stroke endeavour to cut this Army to pieces...*

> *...On every side there is a Choice of difficulties and every Measure... to be formed with some Apprehension that all our Troops will not do their duty...*

> *History, our own experience, the advice of our ablest friends in Europe... demonstrate, that on our side the War should be defensive. It has even been called a War of costs. That we should on all Occasions avoid a general Action, or put anything to the risque, unless compelled by necessity, into which we ought never to be drawn.*

> *...With these views, and being fully persuaded that it would be presumption to draw out our Young Troops into open ground, against their Superiors both in number and Discipline; I have never spared the Spade and Pick Ax; I confess I have not found that readiness to defend even strong Posts, at all hazards, which is necessary to derive the greatest benefit from them... We are now in a strong Post, but not an impregnable one, nay acknowledged by every man of Judgement to be untenable... To draw the whole Army together in order to arrange the defence proportionate to the extent of Lines and works, would leave the Country open to an Approach and put the fate of this Army and its Stores on the hazard of making a successful defense in the City... On the other hand to abandon a City... on whose Works much Labour has been bestowed, has a tendency to dispirit the Troops and enfeeble our Cause. It has also been considered as the Key to the Northern Country.*

Washington made a point ignored by most subsequent historians that his elaborate defense system for New York, though on a weak troop basis, had thrown away all British plans to take it quickly. Now, he explained, he proposed to move his stores and the large number of sick out of the city, and to concentrate the defense at Fort Washington and King's Bridge to the north and across the river at Fort Lee. His council divided as to holding or abandoning the city. They had worked out a compromise, based on a belief of the majority, that Congress expected them to hold New York at all costs. They therefore planned to leave five thousand men in the city and remove nine thousand. From Washington's letter, it may be guessed that an acrimonious dispute developed among his general officers over leaving any part of the army in the city. Those who were opposed thought the enemy, with naval support, could attack at any point and these five thousand would be lost. Since Congress had resolved the city should not be destroyed and the army could not defend it, the only thing that could be done would be to delay the enemy's taking over. Even this presented problems, since six thousand of the eight thousand Connecticut militia had deserted after the battle on Long Island.

After studying his letter, on September 10 Congress clarified its resolve: Washington was informed that he need hold the city no longer than he thought necessary. However, on October 10, Congress passed a further resolve that Washington, "by every art, and at whatever expense," should prevent the enemy from passing the Hudson River between Fort Washington and Fort Lee on the Jersey side. Washington's war council concluded that Congress had directed that Fort Washington on Manhattan "be retained as long as possible." This congressional backing and filling was to be of serious consequence in a major American disaster.

On September 12 the council resolved that the army should remove from the city to the north, but there were so many supplies and such a shortage of wagons that the task was difficult. The sick alone came to a quarter of the army. They were taken out first. Before the stores could be got out, the enemy struck in force.

KIP'S BAY

On September 15, five British frigates drew up in Kip's Bay, at that time an indentation in Manhattan, running from about the present Thirtieth to Fortieth Streets, and extending in to Second Avenue. The ships began a heavy firing on the rather shallow entrenchments of the militia. In Harlem, Washington, who had expected the enemy to land in the Bronx, heard the sounds. As he wrote Congress the next day:

As soon as I heard the firing, I road with all possible despatch towards the place of landing, when to my great surprize and mortification, I found the Troops that had been posted on the Lines, retreating with the utmost precipitation, and those ordered to support them... flying in every direction... I used every means in my power, to rally and get them into some sort of order, but my attempts were fruitless and ineffectual and on the appearance of a small party of the Enemy... they ran away...

...We are now encamped at... Harlem, where I should hope the Enemy would meet with defeat in case of an Attack, if the generality of our Troops would behave with tolerable resolution, but experience, to my extreme affliction, has convinced me that this is rather to be wished for than expected.

At this point, Washington's factual report merges into legend. The legend is reported by enough persons to bear the mark of fact. Washington rode up, found the troops demoralized, and ordered them behind ditches and walls, and into cornfields. As they continued to flee, he pulled out his riding whip and tried to strike them back into line. No one escaped. Privates, field officers, and even a brigadier got a lashing of whip and tongue. All fled so fast that Washington himself was left, abandoned. His aides forced the stunned general to turn his horse around; he rode back to Harlem to write this comment on his troops.

Putnam was dispatched south to move his troops on the double out of the threatened city. They marched up the West side while the British and the Hessians were pouring in from the East River. The British moved east to Murray Hill to await reinforcements before going north. There Howe called on Mrs. Robert Murray and enjoyed a glass of wine.

HARLEM

Putnam moved rapidly to Harlem, having been forced to abandon many American supplies. Howe also moved north. There was some skirmishing that day but not until next day did the forces meet. The Americans were dug into modest entrenchments on the plateau of Morningside Heights, in the neighborhood of what is now Columbia University. What came close to a major engagement quickly developed.

Washington sent out a small patrol under Colonel Thomas Knowlton to scout the British defenses. They were soon discovered by a body of enemy infantry, who pursued them, blowing an insulting fox-hunting call. Washington added a newly arrived unit of Virginia troops under Major

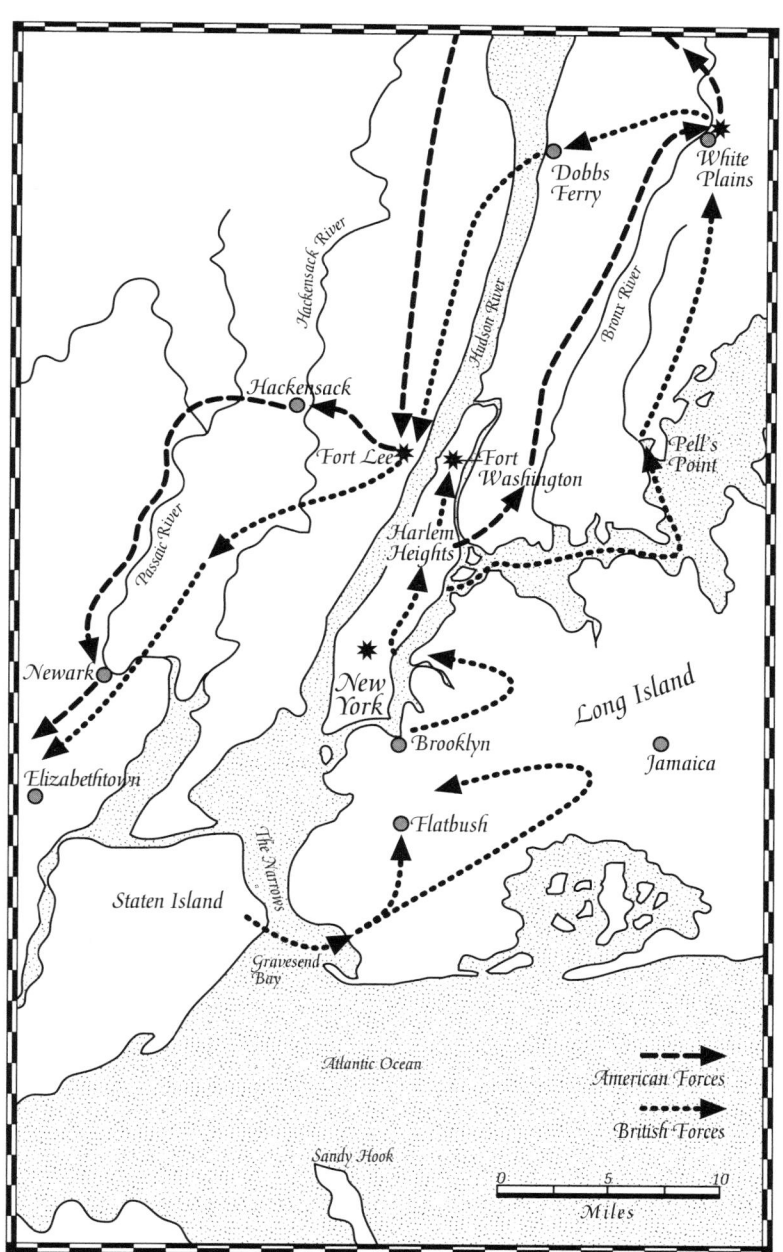

The New York Campaign, 1776

Andrew Leitch to encircle the British, while sending further detachments, as a feint, to hit them in the center as they advanced. Though there were blunders, and the Americans attacked on the flanks instead of the rear, the British were driven back for more than a mile. It was cheering for Americans to see the backs of redcoats and the Black Watch regiment as well as the Hessians. Washington added more troops, singling out particularly the New Englanders who ran at Kip's Bay. They moved forward and when the enemy finally stopped, they fought as vigorously as the rest. For the first time in the war, Americans from New England to Virginia were on the firing line together and successfully. Howe finally had to send in five thousand troops, and Washington, not wanting a general engagement, ordered his men back to the lines. Americans had around sixty casualties, including Knowlton, who was killed, and Leitch, who later died of his wounds. The British lost nearly three hundred men. Howe reported to London that he had engaged three thousand Americans, though the number who drove back his troops was only a few hundred. It disturbed Howe to be beaten in the open for the first time, and he began to be more cautious.

This affair greatly cheered Washington after the disaster at Kip's Bay. His general order of September 17 said: "The Behaviour of Yesterday was such a Contrast to that of some Troops the day before, as must shew what can be done, where Officers and Soldiers will exert themselves.—Once more therefore, the General calls upon officers, and men, to act up to the noble cause in which they are engaged." Washington also referred to "the gallant and brave Colonel Knowlton, who would have been an Honour to any Country."

Many army tents had been lost in New York because Washington had given priority to moving out several thousand sick troops. Many of his men were now without shelter. He directed his colonels "to store their men thicker in their tents, and lend all they can spare, to their suffering fellow-soldiers."

FIRE AT NEW YORK

About midnight on the night of September 20, 1776, a great fire broke out at several places in New York. It seems to have been set by Americans, probably New Englanders, but whether this was done from patriotic motives, or to cover looting, or both, cannot be determined. Washington watched the city burn. He wrote about this on October 6 to Lund Washington:

Had I been left to the dictates of my own judgment, New York should have been laid in Ashes before I quitted it; to this end I applied to Congress, but was

absolutely forbid; that they will have cause to repent the Order, I have not a
moments doubt... It will be next to impossible for us to dispossess them of it again
as all their Supplies come by Water, whilst ours were derived by Land... By leaving
it standing, the Enemy are furnished with warm and comfortable Barracks, in
which their whole Force may be concentrated, the place secured by a small garrison
(if they chuse it) having their ships round it, and only a narrow Neck of Land to
defend, and their principal force left at large to act against us, or to remove to any
other place for the purpose of harrassing us. This in my judgment may be set down
amg. one of the capitol errors of Congress.

In speaking of New York, I had forgot to mention that Providence, or some good
honest Fellow, has done more for us than we were disposed to do for ourselves, as
near One fourth of the City is supposed to be consumed. However enough of it
remains to answer their purpose.

General Howe had to call in many of his troops, as well as sailors from the
ships, to put the fires out. When it was over, more than a quarter of the town
had gone up in flames. This was a great disadvantage to the British, who had
to house not only thousands of Tories, but the British armed forces, many
naval officers, and the British civil authority.

NATHAN HALE

On September 22, Howe's aide, Captain John Montresor, came to
Washington's camp under a flag of truce to arrange for the exchanges of
Generals Stirling and Sullivan. In passing, he mentioned that they had captured and that day hanged a spy, Captain Nathan Hale of Knowlton's regiment. Hale had volunteered to go to Long Island and get information.
Though the documentation is not too clear, he may have been captured while
nearing the American lines. Hale was hanged without trial directly after the
fire at New York. The British may have thought he was involved in it.
Montresor reported, at a later date, that Hale had murmured as he was going
to the gallows, "What a pity it is that we can die but once to serve our country," a line from Joseph Addison's *Cato*.

Washington made no written comment on Hale's death, which indicates
that he probably had no knowledge of his selection, although he may have
encouraged Knowlton to find someone to go to the enemy lines.

WASHINGTON AND THE BOARD OF WAR

Washington again had to face his old problems: shortages of tents and winter clothing in an army of soldiers many of whose enlistments were shortly to expire. His strength of men fit for duty had dwindled to fourteen thousand or fewer. Many of these were short-term militia, ungovernable and without discipline. The board of war continued to function. As the army was going into battle in October, the board requested from Washington a detailed list of all his ordnance. A polite reply was returned to the effect that the guns were being used on the enemy and they were a little difficult to count. Washington went on to suggest that the board might bestir itself to provide more ordnance.

When John Adams rode to Staten Island to see Howe, he noticed on the way many soldiers loitering and hanging around taverns. This offended him. He induced Congress to pass a resolution that "the commander in chief... be directed... that the troops may, every day, be called together, and trained in arms... and inured to the most exemplary discipline." On its receipt, Washington, on September 24, sat up late in order to write a letter to Congress, giving them the facts:

> From the hours allotted to Sleep, I will borrow a few Moments to convey my thoughts on sundry matters to Congress...
>
> It is in vain to expect, that any... part of this Army will again engage in the Service on the encouragement offered by Congress... As the War must be carried on systematically, and to do it, you must have good Officers, there are, in my Judgment, no other possible means to obtain them but by establishing your Army upon a permanent footing; and giving your Officers good pay... They ought to have such allowances as will enable them to live like, and support the Characters of Gentlemen; and not be driven by a scanty pittance to the low, and dirty arts which many of them practice, to filch the Public of more than the difference of pay would amount to... Besides, something is due to the Man who puts his life in his hands...
>
> With respect to the Men, nothing but a good bounty can obtain them upon a permanent establishment; and for no shorter time than the continuance of the War, ought they to be engaged... If this encouragement is given to the Men, and such Pay allowed the Officers as will induce Gentlemen of Character... to engage... We should in a little time have an Army able to cope with any that can be opposed to it...
>
> To place any dependence upon Militia, is, assuredly, resting upon a broken staff. Men just dragged from the tender Scenes of domestick life; unaccustomed to the din of Arms; totally unacquainted with every kind of Military skill... when opposed to

Troops regularly train'd, disciplined and appointed... makes them timid and ready to fly from their own shadows... To bring Men to a proper degree of Subordination is not the work of a day, a Month or even a year...

The Jealousies of a Standing Army, and the evils to be apprehended from one, are remote... but the consequence of wanting one... is certain and inevitable Ruin.

John Adams did, at times, appear rather foolish. Aside from asking Washington to discipline troops in daily battle, he suggested the officers take time to study military history and science. They ought to be able, like Sallust, to write great reports where "You see the combatants, You feel the ardor of battle. You see the blood of the slain, and you hear the wounded sigh and moan."

Washington's long letter aroused Congress, which began to face the issues for the first time. Adams said it was a lot easier to get action after a couple of defeats than it had been before. Congress authorized a permanent army of eighty-eight regiments, raised the pay of officers, gave bonuses and clothing to enlisted men, and otherwise attempted to introduce major reforms. Unfortunately this was paper legislation for a paper army, backed by paper money, and it did not materially help Washington for some time to come. Having got these measures through, Adams then took a long vacation from his labors and left Congress on October 13. Jefferson had already resigned, leaving the implementation of the Declaration of Independence to others.

Washington did not complain of one aspect of his command, that he had to be chief of staff of the American army, as well as a field commander, without ever having a day of rest. The generals with the best reputations, though they were not necessarily the best officers—Gates, Schuyler, and Lee—were elsewhere, while Sullivan and Stirling were not released from captivity until October. Washington's devoted associates recognized this problem. Colonel John Haslet of Delaware wrote on September 4: "The General I revere, his Character... Patience and Fortitude will be had in Everlasting Remembrance, but the Vast Burthen appears to be too much his own... w'd to Heaven Genl Lee were here is the Language of officers and men." General Knox wrote his brother on September 23: "The general is as worthy a man as breathes, but he cannot do everything nor be everywhere. He wants good assistants. There is a radical evil in our army—the lack of officers."

Another appraisal of Washington's command was made on September 25 by General Howe in a report to Lord George Germain: "The enemy is too strongly posted to be attacked in front, and innumerable difficulties are in our way of turning him on either side... [I have] not the smallest prospect of finishing the combat this campaign." Howe requested further recruits from

Europe, more seamen to manage his boats, and an additional ten ships of the line. Since king and cabinet had scraped the bottom of the military, naval, and money chests in order to provide a knockout blow to the rebellion, this was rather poor thanks from Howe. Although the British commander had received two setbacks, he could still count on further reinforcements, which were already on their way. On October 12 more British and Hessian troops arrived, bringing the grand total of all ranks of enemy soldiers, sailors, and marines who crowded New York and its harbor to nearly seventy thousand. This contrasts with the approximately thirty thousand men in Philip II's Armada. George III wrote to Lord North on November 4: "Nothing can have been better planned nor with more alacrity executed than the taking of the city of New York and I trust the Rebel army will soon be dispersed." The rebel army was, in fact, soon dispersed, but not for long.

TWENTY-ONE

HARLEM TO MORRISTOWN

1776–1777

T HE DAY AFTER Howe reported to Germain that the American defenses were too strong to attack, Washington wrote to Brigadier Hugh Mercer, head of the flying camps in New Jersey: "If the Troops at this Post, can be prevailed upon to defend it, as they should do, it must cost General Howe a great many Men to carry it, if he succeeds at all. If this should happen to be *his* Opinion there is scarce a doubt but that he will turn his thoughts another way, as inactivity is not to be expected from him."

Washington indicated that Howe might move to New Jersey and Philadelphia or even attack farther south. He asked Mercer to get all the intelligence he could and to keep a close watch from the coast on all ship and troop movements. He added: "In doing this Money may be required, and do not spare it." While waiting to see what Howe would do, Washington began to plan a counterattack on Long Island, where the enemy was getting food supplies and many recruits for its army. When Howe landed in the Bronx, Washington abandoned this scheme.

Washington urged Congress to give greater attention to his need for troops. He said that the enemy now offered a bounty of ten pounds to each American recruit and he was afraid that Howe might be more successful in getting enlistments than he was. On October 4, he pointed out to its president that, while Congress had authorized a larger army, there was a difference between voting men and raising them. "Give me leave to say, Sir, I say it with due deference and respect... that your Affairs are in a more unpromising way than you seem to apprehend." He pointed out that he was likely to lose his most valuable officers for lack of pay and that letting states appoint officers, subject to ratification by Congress, brought him men who, too often, owed their appointment to politics, or to their ability to recruit, rather than merit. In congratulating Patrick Henry on October 5 for his election to the governorship of Virginia, Washington gave him lengthy advice on choosing Virginia officers for continental regiments. He said that officers needed character, honor, and martial spirit, and should have a good reputation that they would not want to lose. In his letter, Washington referred to Virginia as "your Colony," an indication of his newly national senti- ment. Independence was so recent that he forgot to call it a state.

Jonathan Trumbull, governor of Connecticut, approached the question with his usual good sense. He asked if Washington could get his generals to supply a merit rating of Connecticut officers, which would then be used in determining promotions. In forwarding these to Trumbull, Washington expressed his gratitude for so novel a scheme, which put merit ahead of poli- tics. He added that he was pleased that the governor's son, Joseph Trumbull, had been given particular praise. The general subsequently suggested to Massachusetts and Rhode Island that they adopt a similar plan.

On October 5 Washington wrote to his brother Samuel, who said that he had read in the gazettes of all the militia coming to his camp: "The pompous Acct. of the Marches, and Counter Marches of the Militia, tho' true so far as relates to the Expence, is false with respect to the Service, for you could nei- ther get them to stay in Camp or fight when they were there, in short, it may truely be said they were eternally coming and going without rendering the least Earthly Service, altho' the expence of them surpasses all description." He added that he had heard from others that Howe's troops "were scarce a mouthful for us," which was hardly true.

By the early part of October, the first of a long line of French volunteers— some men of character, others soldiers of fortune—had begun to arrive in camp. Washington wrote Congress that he did not know what to do with them. Officer appointments were made by the states and not by him. He asked advice on a problem that later became most serious.

FROG'S NECK TO WHITE PLAINS

On October 12, Howe finally attempted the mainland, landing at Frog's Neck (now Throggs Neck). Washington reported to Congress that this was effected

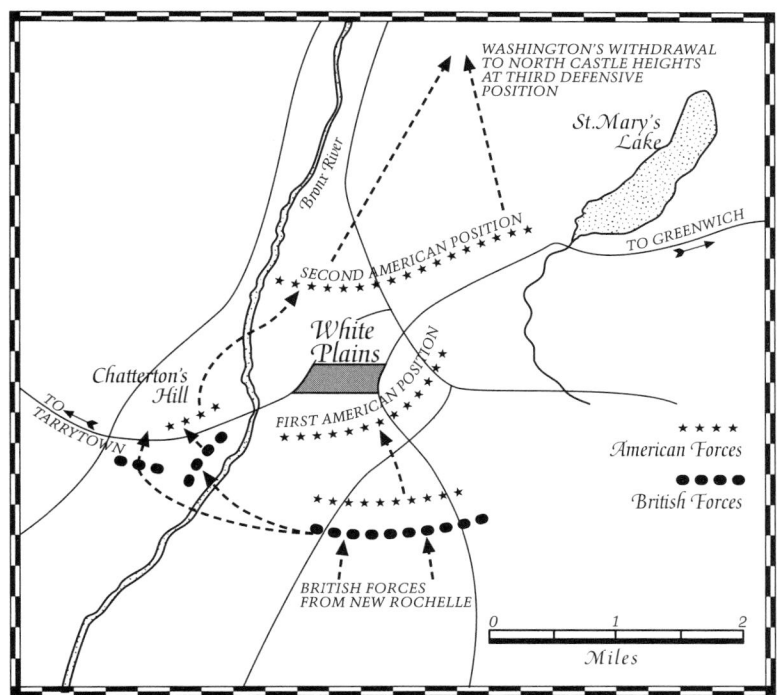

Battle of White Plains, October 28–29, 1776

in order to cut off American communications at King's Bridge. He added that the area, with many stone walls, was strongly defensible, so that Howe's army and artillery could advance only on the main road. He assured Congress his men posted there were in good spirits.

Howe, with 10,000 men, had not, as he expected, landed on the mainland itself. In effect, Frog's Neck was an island, isolated by a brook and marshes. The Americans, under Colonel Edward Hand, had removed the planking from its only bridge connection and proceeded, with 225 men, to hold off the whole British army. Additional American reinforcements came up and Howe and Cornwallis were held for six days in this ridiculous position.

At this point, General Lee was on his way back from Philadelphia. On October 12 he wrote from Amboy to Congress to warn them that the British would not attack Washington's army; instead they would probably move into New Jersey to take Philadelphia. He told Congress to start raising men immediately for defense of the city. On October 12 Lee reached New York. He was assigned to command north of King's Bridge, which Washington expected to be a focal point for the British attack.

On October 9 two enemy ships of the line and a frigate sailed up the Hudson, past Forts Washington and Lee, going easily through the secret channel within the chevaux-de-frises. Tory spies may have given the British sufficient information to make a move that greatly annoyed Washington. Two days later Washington received the directive of Congress that ordered him "by every art, and whatever expense, to obstruct effectually the navigation of the river, at the two forts on the Hudson." His war council of October 16 voted that, in view of this directive, Fort Washington should be retained as long as possible. At the same time, the council voted against holding Harlem because the troops might be cut off by the British. The army, leaving a garrison of about twelve hundred men at Fort Washington, moved north. A further garrison of three thousand men was ordered across the river to New Jersey. Forts Lee and Washington were placed under the command of General Greene, who had a further source of reserves in New Jersey's flying camps.

On October 18 the British moved from Frog's Neck to Pell's Point, south of New Rochelle. They were held there temporarily by 750 Americans under the command of Colonel John Glover, who subsequently received high praise from Washington. By October 21 the American commander in chief was in Westchester and on October 23 the main American army was heading towards White Plains in a move to outflank Howe. Four days later, the enemy was on the way there.

By then the Americans were placed along a line of low hills, south of the village, with their right on Chatterton's Hill. As the British moved towards that point, Washington increased the force to 1,500 men. Howe advanced 4,000 British and Hessians who easily stormed the hill. Though called the battle of White Plains, it was no more than a skirmish, in which each side suffered about 250 casualties.

After this, Washington pulled the Americans back to a stronger and higher position on Northcastle Heights. Howe's troops, now numbering some twenty thousand men, waited for several days, probing the American defenses. On November 2 William Demont, a lieutenant and adjutant of a Pennsylvania regiment, escaped from Fort Washington, carrying with him to the enemy a plan of the fort, an estimate of the strength of the garrison, and, presumably, a list of the valuable stores located there. On November 4, Howe's army began to withdraw from White Plains towards Dobbs Ferry and Manhattan. Howe made preparations for an assault on Fort Washington and then for a crossing to New Jersey, while Washington waited in Westchester.

FORT WASHINGTON FALLS

Washington had left Greene in charge of the key points on the Hudson when he moved north on October 16. He now had to make a number of decisions in the light of Howe's unexpected retreat. Washington was certain that Howe would move on Fort Washington, but he had to guess whether Howe would also move north on the Hudson or cut into New Jersey. He decided to leave General Lee with half the army at White Plains and to move General Heath with four thousand men farther north to Peekskill. On November 7 Washington sent an urgent warning to Greene to watch for an attack on Fort Washington and for a possible move into Jersey. On November 8 he followed with a further letter:

> *The late passage of the 3 Vessels up the North River... is so plain a Proof of the Inefficacy of the Obstructions we have thrown into it, that I cannot but think, it will fully Justify a Change in the disposition which has been made. If we cannot prevent Vessels passing up, and the Enemy are possessed of the surrounding Country, what valuable purpose can it answer to attempt to hold a Post from which the expected Benefit cannot be had; I am therefore inclined to think it will not be prudent to hazard the men and Stores at Mount Washington, but as you are on the Spot, leave it to you to give such Orders as to evacuating Mount Washington as you Judge best... The best Accounts obtained from the Enemy, assure a considerable Movement among their Boats last Evening... From various sources of Intelligence, they must design a Penetration into Jersey and fall down upon your Post. You will*

therefore immediately have all the Stores &c removed, which you do not deem
necessary for your defence.

Greene replied the next day from Fort Lee:

The passing of the ships up the river is, to be sure, a full proof of the insufficiency
of the obstructions to stop the ships from going up; but that garrison employs a
double the number of men to invest it, than we have to occupy it. They must keep
troops at Kingsbridge to prevent a communication with the country, and they dare
not leave a very small number for fear our people should attack them. Upon the
whole, I cannot help thinking that the garrison is of advantage; and I cannot
conceive it to be in any great danger. The men can be brought off at any time, but
the stores may not so easily be removed. Yet I think they can be got off in spite of
them, if matters grow desperate. This post is of no importance, except in
conjunction with Mount Washington. I was over there last evening. The enemy
seems to be disposing matters to besiege the place; but Colonel Magaw thinks it will
take them till December expires before they can carry it. If the enemy do not find it
an object of importance, they will not trouble themselves about it; if they do, it is a
full proof that they feel an injury from our possessing it. Our giving it up will open
a free communication with the country by way of Kingsbridge.

On November 10 Washington wrote Lee that, in view of the enemy's probable
move to New Jersey, he would go there with a small body of troops. The command of the army near White Plains devolved upon Lee, who was warned to be
on guard, since any British moves across the Hudson might be a feint. If they
crossed in force, Lee was to join him "with all possible despatch." The next day
Washington and Heath examined the passes and terrain of the Hudson
Highlands. He was instructed to remain there with his troops, to guard the area
and its three forts, but to be ready to aid Lee, should he be attacked.

Late in the evening of November 13, Washington reached Hackensack near
Fort Lee. There he consulted with Greene who, repeating his firm conviction
that Fort Washington could be held, indicated that he had not removed the
supplies but had strengthened the garrison. He referred to the order of
Congress to hold these guardians of the Hudson, Forts Lee and Washington,
at almost any cost. Putnam, in charge of the Manhattan fort's engineering,
supported Greene. Colonel Magaw, in command at Fort Washington, had
already indicated his certainty that the fort could hold until December. To
order it abandoned at the last minute, Washington would have had to over-
rule the senior officers who had been on the spot, as well as disobey Congress'
directives. Even so he hesitated but it was soon too late for decision.

On November 15, the day Howe demanded that the garrison surrender, Washington set out across the Hudson. On the way he met Generals Putnam and Greene, who informed him that the troops were "in high Spirits and would make a good Defence." The next day Washington, Greene, Mercer, and Putnam crossed the river but battle had begun and they returned to the Jersey shore. Howe sent 8,000 troops smashing in, with a full knowledge of the defense system. While the fort was under attack, Washington sent a messenger to tell the defenders that if they could hold till dark, he would try to bring them all out. By this time the outer works had fallen and the messenger was nearly captured. Shortly afterwards the fort surrendered. The troops on the outside had fought bravely, but inside many of the militia panicked in the crowded edifice. Magaw had to surrender in order to avoid their complete slaughter by British artillery. The British lost 450 men, killed and wounded, and the Americans around 150. The British captured 2,800 rebels, one of the most serious losses of the war. These, with the prisoners taken on Long Island, added up to more than 4,000 in enemy hands. They were confined in close ship's quarters or crowded prisons and brutally mistreated; many died. Washington protested vigorously to Howe on his lack of humanity. Three years later Washington wrote that his anguish at the loss of the fort was made far more "poignant" by the sufferings of the prisoners.

In addition the Americans lost much of their ordnance and munitions and such scarce supplies as tents and flour. Demont, English born, received sixty pounds for his treason but it took him seventeen years to collect from the British government. Greene, the day after the loss of the fort, expressed his feeling to Knox: "I was afraid of the fort. The redoubt that you and I advised was not done... This is a most terrible event; its consequences are justly to be dreaded." On November 19 Washington finished a letter to his brother John, which he had begun thirteen days previously at White Plains: "This is a most unfortunate affair, and has given me great Mortification... I had given it... as my opinion to Genl Greene, under whose care it was, that it would be best to evacuate the place; but as the order was discretionary, and his opinion differed from mine, it unhappily was delayed too long, to my great grief, as I think Genl Howe, considering his army and ours, would have had but a poor tale to have told without it and would have found it difficult... to have reconciled the People of England to the Conquest of a few pitiful Islands, none of which were defensible, considering the great number of their Ships."

There was little time to mourn. On the night of November 19, Lord Cornwallis and a British force of four thousand crossed the Hudson and raced to Fort Lee to capture Washington and Greene. An American warned Greene just in time and he informed Washington. Before departing in great haste,

Washington wrote to Congress asking them to get clothing and blankets to the prisoners at New York.

TREASON ON THE STAFF

Although Washington, Greene, and Putnam were chagrined at the quick fall of the fort, they had no hesitation about going on fighting. The new adjutant general, Colonel Joseph Reed, however, was totally shaken by the event; even a month later he was writing to Washington of the desperate plight of the army, and his worry about his wife and children and the poverty and ruin that he faced. Reed proceeded, almost immediately after the fort fell, to acts of treason. Treason is defined in the Oxford dictionary as "betrayal of... trust; breach of faith; treachery." Had he succeeded, the war might have quickly ended with the capture of Washington.

Some parts of the action and correspondence are missing, but enough is available to reconstruct events. On November 16 Washington sent to Lee a factual account of the surrender of Fort Washington. At the same time, Reed wrote to Lee complaining about Greene's influence on Washington, which had led to the loss of the fort. Lee, after hearing from Reed, wrote to Washington on the nineteenth: "Oh, General, why would you be over-persuaded by men of inferior judgement to your own? It was a cursed affair." This phrase about men of inferior judgement very probably came from Reed, who, in a later letter of December 22 to Washington, used an almost identical sentiment urging him not to be subject "to the Influence of Opinions of Men in every Respect your Inferiors."

When the British landed in New Jersey, Washington asked his aide, William Grayson, to send Lee a quick order. Grayson much too politely informed Lee that Washington now thought it "advisable" for Lee to cross the Hudson.

On November 21 Washington asked Reed to draft further orders to Lee. Reed sent them to Lee that day. The first two paragraphs, with the probable exceptions of the first sentence and the last two sentences, are in Washington's unmistakable style. The two paragraphs, with the orders to Lee, were entirely rewritten by Reed. In the file copy at the Library of Congress, they are on the inside of a four-page folded sheet:

With respect to your Situation, I am very much at a Loss what now to determine, there is such a Change of Circumstances since the date of your Letter, as seems to call for a Change of Measures. Your Post undoubtedly will answer some important Purposes; but whether so many or so great as your Removal... is well worthy of

Consideration... Upon the whole therefore, I am of Opinion and the Gentlemen about me concur in it, that the publick Interest requires your coming over to this side...

My reasons for this measure and which I think must have weight with you, are, that the Enemy are evidently changing the Seat of War to this side of the North River... It is therefore of the utmost Importance, that at least an Appearance of Force should be made, to keep this Province in the Connection with the others, if that should not continue, it is much to be feared, that its Influence on Pennsylvania would be very considerable... Unless therefore some new event should occur... I would have you move over by the easiest and best Passage... Perhaps it may not be agreeable to the troops [but it] will at least have an effect to discourage the desponding here.

With this letter, Reed enclosed another of his own to Lee. The first sentence indicated that the "order" had been written by Reed rather than Washington, but this may easily have been overlooked by Lee, in reading what his military secretary had to say: "The letter you will receive with this contains my sentiments with respect to your military situation. But besides this I have some additional reasons for most earnestly wishing to have you where the principal scene of action is laid. I do not mean to flatter, nor praise you at the expense of any other, but I confess I do think it is entirely owing to you that this army and the liberties of America, so far as they are dependent on it, are not totally cut off. You have decision, a quality often wanting in minds otherwise valuable, and I ascribe to this an escape from York island—from Kingsbridge and the Plains—and I have no doubt had you been here the garrison at Mount Washington would now have composed a part of this army... I ardently wish to see you removed from a place where there will be little call for your judgement and experience to the place where they are likely to be so necessary... Every gentleman of the family [Washington's staff]... have a confidence in you."

Reed continued: "Col. Cadwalader... has been liberated from New York without any parole. He informs us that the enemy... hold us very cheap in consequence of the late affair at Mount Washington where both the plan of defense and execution were contemptible... General Washington's own judgment, seconded by representations from us, would I believe have saved the men and their arms, but unluckily General Greene's judgment was contrary; this kept the general's mind in a state of suspense until the stroke was struck. Oh! General—an indecisive mind is one of the greatest misfortunes that can befall an army—how often have I lamented it this campaign. All circumstances considered we are in a very awful and alarming state... As soon as the season will admit I think yourself and some others should go to Congress and form the plan of the new army."

As the army left Hackensack, Reed scribbled a hasty note to Lee: "We are flying before the British." By his actions, Reed warned Lee, who had already formed such an idea in his mind, that Washington was weak, timid, and indecisive. When Lee first saw Grayson's note, he told Heath that it almost seemed an order to move. He demanded that Heath, as the officer nearest the ferrying point, send two thousand of his men to Washington. Heath properly refused; he informed Lee that Washington had ordered him to keep his men there. Furious, Lee asked Heath if he thought he held an independent command. Washington, he said, was far away, and Greene was the officer to be obeyed. "By your mode of reasoning, the General's injunctions are so binding that not a tittle must be broke though for the salvation of the General and his army."

The harassed Heath did his duty. He replied with the sharp implication that Lee himself was disobeying orders: "Be my mode of reasoning as it may, I conceive it my duty to obey instructions... The least recommendation from him, to march my division or any part of them, over the river, should have been instantly obeyed, without waiting for a positive order."

On November 23 Lee wrote to James Bowdoin, president of the Massachusetts council, to say that he had always assumed, even before the fall of Fort Washington, that there should be separate American armies, each "on its own bottom," on the west and east sides of the Hudson River. Now, he said, it was "absolute insanity" for him to move across the river. The next day, having received the Washington order drafted by Reed, he sent extracts of it to Bowdoin, saying he could make his own comment on it. Lee added that "the resolves of the Congress must no longer too nicely weigh with us... There are times when we must commit treason against the State, for the salvation of the State." He asked for reinforcements for "his" army.

While all this was going on, Reed had become so concerned for the safety of his wife and children that Washington sent him to Burlington on November 23 to look after them, and also to appeal to the governor of New Jersey for assistance. Totally unaware of Reed's treachery, Washington opened a letter from Lee to Reed, dated November 21, which said that Washington had recommended his moving across the river but that his troops would be too late "to answer any purpose... I have therefore ordered General Heath who is close to the only ferry which can be passed to detach two thousand men, to apprize His Excellency, and wait his further orders, which I flatter myself will answer better what I conceive to be the spirit of the orders... Withdrawing our troops from hence would be attended with some very serious consequences which at present would be too tedious to mention."

Washington at once wrote sharply to Lee: "From your letter to Colo. Reed, you seem to have mistaken my views entirely, in ordering Troops from Genl Heath... Colo. Reed's second Letter, will have sufficiently explained my intention... that it was your division I want to have over." In response to a further equivocal letter from Lee, Washington wrote him on the twenty-seventh: "My former Letters were so full and explicit, as to the Necessity of your Marching, as early as possible, that it is unnecessary to add more on that Head. I confess I expected you would have been sooner in motion." Washington also commended Heath for obeying the instructions of the commander in chief.

Lee at last reluctantly crossed the Hudson on December 2, after engaging in a quarrel with Heath. He slowly ambled into New Jersey while Washington and Congress sent him impatient letters. About November 27, Washington, who had retreated to Brunswick, opened a letter to Reed from Lee, which said: "I received your most obliging, flattering letter—lament with you that fatal indecision of mind which in war is a much greater disqualification than a stupidity or even want of personal courage—accident may put a decisive blunderer in the right—but eternal defeat and miscarriage must attend the man of the best parts if curs'd with indecision." On November 30 Washington forwarded the letter to Reed, who by then had resigned as adjutant general, with an accompanying note:

> *The enclosed was put into my hands by an Express from the White Plains. Having no Idea of its being a Private Letter, much less suspecting. This, as it is the truth, must be my excuse for seeing the contents of a Letter, which neither inclination or intention would have prompted me to.*
>
> *I thank you for the trouble and fatigue you have undergone in your Journey to Burlington... My best to Mrs. Reed.*

It is well that the governor of New Jersey, William Livingston, wrote Washington a letter on November 27, which arrived shortly after the letter from Lee to Reed: "I can easily form some Idea of the Difficulties under which you labour and particularly of one for which the public can make no allowances because your Prudence and fidelity to the Cause will not suffer you to reveal it to the public, an instance of Magnanimity superior perhaps to any that can be Shewn in Battle. But depend upon it, my dear Sir, the impartial world will do you ample Justice before Long. May God support you under the Fatigue both of Body and Mind to which you must be constantly exposed."

ACTION ELSEWHERE

While Washington was fighting in the New York area, there were important developments elsewhere. In March Congress sent Silas Deane to Paris as the first American agent. With the help of the French government, Beaumarchais and Deane quickly set up a secret dummy trading corporation to supply arms and ammunition to Washington's troops. In October 1776, Franklin left America for France. In early 1777 the American army began to receive some foreign supplies as well as a number of adventurers, to whom Deane promised commissions as general and field officers in the American army. Washington needed officers but not the type who, too often, came.

Meanwhile Britain had built up its forces in Canada to thirteen thousand troops under the command of General Guy Carleton, aided by John Burgoyne. In September British troops moved southward into the United States. This action indicated the strategy being developed at Whitehall to cut the United States in half in 1777 through joint operations with Howe in New York. The British movements were delayed by the need to build vessels to bring troops and guns southward on Lake Champlain. Benedict Arnold, who had some merchant marine experience, moved urgently to build a small defensive fleet. In October he met the British in battle and was quickly swept from the lake. He and his men escaped to Fort Ticonderoga. However, Arnold had delayed the British sufficiently for Carleton to feel it was too late in the season to attack the fort. The British retired to winter quarters in Canada. An encouraged Congress permitted Washington to order Gates, with six regiments, to march to the defense of Philadelphia.

Washington's rapid retreat across New Jersey convinced Howe that he could now release troops for an additional offensive. At the end of November he ordered General Clinton and Admiral Peter Parker, the mismated pair who blamed each other for the failure at Charleston, to take Newport. This was easily done in December. Newport provided an additional base for Lord Howe's fleet and a possible staging area for operations against New England when the British again moved south from Canada in their next offensive.

HACKENSACK TO MORRISVILLE

Washington had somewhat more than four thousand men under his command when he left Hackensack on November 21, but the number dwindled rapidly during his retreat across New Jersey. Lord Rawdon, who saw the mess left by the retreating Americans at Fort Lee, commented that "their army is all broken to pieces." By November 29, Washington was at Brunswick. Many enlistments were to expire at the end of the month; other enlistees had deserted before their time was up. Washington, in writing to Congress, now referred to his forces as a "handful." On December 1 he again appealed to Lee to hurry, or he might be too late. On the same day he appended a post-mark to his letter to Congress: "½ after 1 o'clock P.M. The Enemy are fast advancing, some of 'em are now in sight. All the Men of the Jersey flying Camp under Gen Herd being applied to, have refused to continue longer in service."

He immediately appealed to Governor Livingston for whatever men he could send and asked him to secure every boat on the Delaware for his troops. The news that Cornwallis was moving fast threw Philadelphia into a panic; all roads west were crowded with people and wagons. That evening Washington informed Congress that he could not hold New Jersey and would cross the Delaware. On December 2 he was at Princeton, the next day at Trenton. He reported to Congress that he had not had a word from Lee for a week and had dispatched an officer to find him.

On December 3 Washington sent his sick into Philadelphia. He took time to repeat his complaints to Congress about militia and short-term enlistments. If, he said, any troops had rallied around him while crossing New Jersey, he was sure he could have made a stand there. He urged a larger standing army that, when trained, would no longer be "a disorderly Mob." He reported that General Howe and Lord Howe had issued a joint proclamation, offering pardons to everyone in New Jersey who would submit to the king within sixty days.

The British now moved so fast that Washington ordered all troops to Pennsylvania. The tiny American army crossed the Delaware on December 7 and 8 to what is now Morrisville. Every boat was secured on the west side to prevent the enemy from following. On December 9 Washington finally heard from Lee, who was at Morristown but doubtful that he could join Washington. He thought, however, that he might be able to make some diversion on Howe's flanks and would let Washington know. By this time, Washington's troops were down to three thousand, but Pennsylvania militia came in to add a little strength.

Washington advised Congress to fortify Philadelphia immediately, adding that he was sending Generals Mifflin and Putnam to the city to assist in the work. Cornwallis, having reached the Delaware and finding no transportation, established his headquarters at Pennington. Howe, who had posted British and Hessian troops at all important towns from Amboy to Trenton and Burlington, now ordered his army into winter quarters. He was induced to do this by the increasingly severe weather, the weak and broken state of

Washington's army, and because thousands of Jerseyans were flocking to take the oath of allegiance to the king in response to his amnesty proclamation. Howe reported to London: "I conclude the troops will be in perfect security."

A fast ship carried to London the news of Cornwallis' movements across New Jersey. On January 1 George III dropped one of his usual little notes to Lord North. He said he was sorry that General Howe had received such bad bread and flour from the European contractors who supplied the army. "I trust Sir William Howe is now in possession of so extensive a Country that he will not require to be entirely provided from Europe; I have seen a private letter from the General that his posts will extend from the River Delaware to Rhode Island consequently my opinion seems well grounded."

On December 10 Washington again asked Lee to move because he had only "weak and feeble forces... Do come on, your arrival may be happy, and if it can be effected without delay, may be the means of preserving a City, whose loss must prove of the most fatal consequences to America." He wrote to Lund Washington on the same date: "I tremble for Philadelphia. Nothing... but Gen. Lee's speedy arrival... can save it... It is next to impossible to guard a shore for sixty miles." On December 11 he asked Lee to "push on with every possible succour you can bring."

That day he sent Major Elisha Sheldon of the Connecticut volunteer cavalry to Congress to plead once again for an authorization for continental cavalry regiments. In his letter he said: "I can only say the Service of himself and his Troop, has been such as merits of the public, and deserves a handsome Compensation for their Trouble... From the Experience I have had this Campaign, of the Utility of Horse [cavalry], I am convinced there is no carrying on the war without them." Congress, now thoroughly scared, at once granted a request that had been lingering in Adams' committee for six months. Immediately thereafter Congress fled to Baltimore.

On December 16 Washington gave Sheldon his commission as "Lieut. Colo. Commandant of a Regiment of Horse." That dark December day, the United States cavalry service was born on the banks of the Delaware.

On December 14 the exasperated Washington wrote again to Lee: "I am much surprized that you should be in any doubt respecting the Route you should take, after the information you have had upon that Head... Let me once more request and entreat you to march immediately for Pitts Town." The letter did not reach Lee, who the day before had finished a letter to General Gates:

> *The ingenious maneuver of Fort Washington has unhinged the goodly fabrick we had been building. There never was so damned a stroke. Entre nous, a certain*

great man is most damnably deficient. He has thrown me into a situation where I have my choice of difficulties. If I stay in the Province I risk myself and army, and if I do not stay the Province is lost for ever...

In short unless something which I do not expect turns up we are lost. Our counsels have been weak to the last degree... If you think you would be in time to aid the General I would have you by all means go.

Lee had just enough time to get the letter out to Gates before he was captured. He had gone three miles away from his army to an inn, for reasons that have never been satisfactorily determined. Colonel William Harcourt, leading a body of British cavalry, captured American soldiers who told him, under threats of death, where Lee could be found. Harcourt was instantly on the trail to get him. To the British, it was a great triumph to capture the man who had become second in command of the American army after the resignation of Ward; to the Americans it seemed the severest of a long series of misfortunes. The capture, however, turned out to be a blessing for Washington. Once rid of Lee, Sullivan, next in command, marched his troops straightway to Washington.

In his letters, Washington occasionally hinted at a "stroke" he had in mind. With almost no army, no equipment, no supplies—and while waiting for Lee and Gates—Washington had been constantly turning in his mind an attack on the enemy. Before he heard of Lee's capture, he told Gates to hurry to Pittstown. "I expect Genl. Lee will be there this Evening, or tomorrow, who will be followed by Genl. Heath and his Division. If we can draw our forces together, I trust, under the smiles of providence, we may yet effect an important stroke." To Heath, who had been ordered from Peekskill, he wrote on December 14: "If we can collect our forces speedily, I should hope we may effect somthing of importance."

Enlistments for nearly the whole Continental Army were to expire on December 31. George wrote Lund Washington that he was less afraid of Howe's army than of total disaffection to the cause in New Jersey and Pennsylvania. Unless he could get a new army and support from these states, the game was pretty well up. Already two former Pennsylvania members of Congress had taken the oath to George III. He asked Lund to send all his personal papers from Mount Vernon to Berkeley County, in what is now West Virginia. He told Reed in November that, if necessary, he would go into the Shenandoah Valley to continue fighting, and beyond that he was prepared to retreat over the Alleghenies. The flame of revolution, so long as he was alive, was never to be allowed to flicker out. He wrote his brothers on December 18 and 19 that, knowing the cause was just, "I cannot entertain an Idea that it will finally sink tho' it may remain for some time under a cloud."

On December 19, Thomas Paine, who had followed the retreating army across New Jersey, published a famous pamphlet with the now-familiar opening words:

These are the times that try men's souls...

...No great deal is lost yet. All that Howe has been doing for this month past is rather a ravage than a conquest, which the spirit of the Jerseys, a year ago, would have quickly repulsed, and which time and a little resolution will soon recover.

...In the fourteenth century the whole English army, after ravaging... France, was driven back like men petrified with fear; and this brave exploit was performed... by a woman, Joan of Arc. Would that heaven might inspire some Jersey maid to spirit up her countrymen.

I shall not now attempt to give all the particulars of our retreat to the Delaware... Both officers and men, though greatly harassed and fatigued... bore it with a manly and martial spirit. All their wishes centred in one, which was that the country would turn out and help them drive the enemy back.

Voltaire has remarked that King William never appeared to full advantage but in difficulties and in action; the same remark may be made of General Washington... God has given him a mind that can even flourish upon care.

The pamphlet circulated from hand to hand in the army and throughout the new nation in its darkest hours.

On December 20 Washington wrote a lengthy letter to Congress, asking what had happened to his October requests for corps of engineers and artillery. He had not been able to wait any longer and he had ordered the enlistment of three artillery regiments. Congress, on leaving Philadelphia, had given him emergency powers; with these he had ordered Knox to raise his artillerymen. He urgently asked Congress to authorize additional infantry regiments and a corps of engineers, authority to pay a bonus to keep his men past the end of the month, and better pay, a clothing department, a commissary of prisoners, magazines, tents, small arms, and officers on the national establishment. General Greene wrote to Congress on December 21: "Greater powers must be lodged in the hands of the General... Time will not permit nor circumstances allow of a reference to Congress... There never was a man that might be more safely trusted, nor a time when there was a louder call."

On December 30 Congress, in "perfect reliance on the wisdom, vigor and uprightness of General Washington," gave him everything he asked, including full powers to raise additional regiments of infantry and to appoint the officers, and to enlist three thousand cavalry, three regiments of artillery, and a corps of engineers. Before he received his directives, Washington stretched his powers to offer a ten dollar bonus to men who would stay six weeks beyond their enlistment period.

Sullivan brought about two thousand men to camp, while Gates arrived with another six hundred, bringing Washington's total forces to six thousand. Gates, who had been warned by Lee that Washington was "damnably deficient," refused to accept a command at Bristol. Pleading illness, he went to Baltimore to try to persuade Congress to move the army to the south. As it turned out, his timing was most inept. Washington's "stroke" was already set in his mind.

TRENTON

On the night of December 24, the American commander in chief held a conference with his general officers in a house not far from what is now Washington's Crossing. Those present included Greene, Stirling, Sullivan, Knox, Mercer, and St. Clair. He outlined plans that called for crossing the river with twenty-four hundred troops, then moving south to Trenton. Brigadier James Ewing, with a thousand militia, would go over at a point below Trenton and move north. Colonel John Cadwalader, with a few hundred men, would cross still further down in a diversionary attack on the Hessians at Mount Holly and Burlington.

Washington's troops assembled after dark on Christmas night. His tiny army was remarkably national, with ten out of thirteen states represented. It included future presidents Washington and Monroe, cabinet members Hamilton and Knox, and Chief Justice Marshall. Colonel John Glover and his Marblehead fishermen, who had ferried Washington's troops across the East River on a hot August night, were there with Durham boats used for river freight. These were forty to sixty feet long, of very shallow draft, and capable of holding up to fifteen tons. They easily carried the horses and Knox's seventeen guns. It was bitterly cold, snow alternating with sleet, and ice cakes forming in the river.

Washington was giving orders, which Knox relayed in his bullhorn voice. Wind, river ice, and sleet delayed the crossing some three hours longer than planned. Although Washington did not know of it until later, Ewing was unable to get over to New Jersey, while Cadwalader moved some troops but not his guns. Washington therefore had to improvise new plans.

The troops had a nine-mile march to Trenton. The command was split, going on two roads of an approximately equal distance, with Greene on the left, Sullivan on the right. The severity of the weather had called off the Hessians' usual morning patrol. Washington's restrained report of the action was sent to Congress the next day:

> *The quantity of Ice, made that Night, impeded the passage of the Boats so much, that it was three O'Clock before the Artillery could all get over, and near four, before the Troops took up their line of march.*

> *This made me despair of surprizing the Town, as I well knew we could not reach it before the day fairly broke, but... I determined to push on... The upper Division arrived at the Enemys advance Post, exactly at Eight O'Clock, and in three Minutes after, I found, from the fire on the lower Road, that that Division had also got up. The out Guards made but small Opposition, tho' for their Number, they behaved very well, keeping up a constant retreating fire from behind Houses. We presently saw their main Body formed, but from their Motions, they seemed undetermined how to act Being hard pressed by our Troops, who had already got possession of their Artillery, they attempted to file off by a road on their right leading to Princetown, but perceiving their Intention, I threw a Body of Troops in their Way which immediately checked them. Finding from our disposition that they were surrounded, they agreed to lay down their arms.*

This modest summary failed to convey that it had been a brilliant encircling movement, devised after he found that Ewing's force had not arrived. Washington sent his troops to choke off the only escape route, while others surrounded two Hessian regiments. These regiments surrendered after their commander, Colonel Johann Roll, was mortally wounded. The third regiment, driven to a creek, held out only a short time thereafter.

More than a thousand Hessians were killed, wounded, or captured. Included was a brass band that was to play for the Americans the following July 4 in Philadelphia. American casualties numbered perhaps four wounded. On January 1, Washington, replying to congratulations from Robert Morris, said: "The Accounts you give me... of the good effects that are likely to flow from our Success at Trenton, add not a little to the Satisfaction I have felt on that occasion. You are pleased to pay me many personal Compliments as if the Merit... was solely due to me; but I assure you, the other General Officers, who assisted me in the plan and Execution, have full as good a right to your

Encomiums as myself." He wrote Congress that everyone had behaved with "the highest honour.

Washington was especially pleased with Knox and his artillerists, singling them out for praise. Before the news of Trenton could reach Congress, that body had ratified Knox's promotion to brigadier. In sending Colonel George Baylor, his aide, to Congress with his victory dispatch, Washington added a particular commendation of the bearer. Congress voted Baylor a fully equipped horse and a cavalry command. Washington thus lost a badly needed aide but told Baylor that he "cheerfully" acquiesced.

PRINCETON

On December 27 the general wrote to Cadwalader that they should follow up the success at Trenton as soon as possible by beating up all the enemy's posts on the Delaware. He suggested an early conference, but Cadwalader, heading militia, had shown unexpected enterprise by saying he had already planned a crossing and suggested that Washington join him there. Cadwalader had done this in spite of the equivocal role played by Joseph Reed. The latter had been assigned to Cadwalader's forces because of his special knowledge of the Burlington area. Reed had forwarded a pessimistic report from Philadelphia to Washington on Christmas Day, but the general wrote Cadwalader that this would not influence his plans. The next day, while Washington was counting his Trenton prisoners, Reed appeared in Bristol. According to Cadwalader's later account, Reed stated how discouraged he was. There were only "the remains of a broken army," he had a family to take care of, and General Howe's amnesty would soon expire. He said that he had advised his brother in New Jersey to seek British protection if necessary. Inasmuch as a letter had already arrived at camp from the Hessian commander who agreed to see Reed, Cadwalader's suspicions were aroused. He said that he thought Reed ought to have been placed under arrest, but he was afraid of the discouragement this would give to his troops. He took Reed with him to New Jersey but kept an eye on him.

On the other side Cadwalader found that the Hessians in posts below Trenton had panicked and fled. He wrote Washington that if they could all be driven "from west Jersey, the success will raise an army by next spring." The general's troops were exhausted from the two river crossings and the battle at Trenton, but this possibility of regaining much of New Jersey made him spring to action. He wrote to Heath, on his way south from Peekskill, to hurry as fast as possible to Hackensack. He asked McDougall at Morristown to order out all the Jersey militia. With help, he could drive "the Enemy from the whole province of Jersey."

Washington, desperately short of food and money, appealed to Robert Morris, who had been left by Congress in Philadelphia as caretaker of its business. In this period Morris was the commander's stoutest supporter, saying he would assume powers rather than let the cause suffer. He got him the food needed and on December 31 forwarded £124 7s. 6d. to Washington, in gold and silver coins, which he had borrowed, so that Washington could pay his New Jersey spies. With it was a note saying, "The year 1776 is over. I am heartily glad of it, and hope you, nor America will never be plagued with such another." Washington's further request for $50,000 in paper money, to pay his promised bonus to his troops, reached Morris late that night. The next day Morris forwarded the money, saying he had gotten up early the next morning and awakened everyone in town to get it. When Washington made out his accounts at the end of the war, he remembered the £124 7s. 6d. exactly, "the time and circumstances of it being too remarkable ever to be forgotten by me."

On December 30 Washington again crossed the Delaware with even worse weather and ice conditions than those of Christmas night. From Trenton he issued a proclamation announcing that the American army was back in the province and calling on the whole population and the militia to rise against the enemy. On January 1 when Mifflin joined him with sixteen hundred men, Washington had a total force of around thirty-four hundred men.

Trenton had shocked the British into counteraction. Cornwallis cancelled his planned leave to England and raced across Jersey with seven thousand men. Although harassed and delayed by American troops along the way, he reached Trenton late on January 2, with darkness setting in. That night, using intelligence gathered by his and Cadwalader's spies, including a map of Princeton, Washington determined to counterattack the forces left by Howe and Cornwallis at Princeton. After he ordered the army's baggage moved to Burlington and leaving all the campfires brightly lit at Assunpink Creek, the army quietly decamped on the Sandtown road. Circling around Cornwallis, they advanced against Howe's regiments at Princeton, quickly defeating them. On January 5 Washington reported to Congress:

> We found Princeton about Sunrise with only three Regiments of Infantry and three Troops of Light Horse in it, two of which were upon their March for Trenton; these three Regiments (especially the two first) made a gallant resistance and in Killed, wounded and Prisoners must have lost near 500 Men...
>
> The rear of the Enemy's army Laying at Maidenhead (not more than five or Six

Miles from Princeton) were up with us before our pursuit was over, but as I had the
precaution to destroy the Bridge over Stony Brook (about half a Mile from the field
of Action) they were so long retarded there, as to give us time to move off in good
order for this place. We took two Brass field pieces from them, but for want of Horses
could not bring them off. We also took some Blankets, Shoes, and a few other
trifling Articles...

My original plan when I set out from Trenton was to have pushed to Brunswick,
but the harassed State of our own Troops (many of them having had no rest for two
Nights and a day) and the danger of losing the advantage we had gained by aiming
at too much, Induced me, by the advice of my Officers, to relinquish the attempt, but
in my judgement Six or Eight hundred fresh Troops upon a forced March would
have destroyed all their Stores, and Magazines; taken (as we have since learnt) their
Military Chest containing £70,000 and put an end to the War...

...The Militia are taking Spirit, and, I am told, are coming fast from this State;
but I fear those from Philadelphia will scarce Submit to the hardships of a Winter
Campaign much longer, especially as they very unluckily sent their Blankets with
their Baggage to Burlington; I must do them the justice however to add, that they
have undergone more fatigue and hardship than I expected Militia (especially
Citizens) would have done at this Inclement Season. I am just moving to
Morristown where I shall endeavour to put them under the best cover I can,
hitherto we have lain without any, many of our poor Soldiers quite barefoot and ill
clad in other respects.

As usual, others present had to report on Washington's personal bravery, which encouraged his troops but made them concerned for his safety. At Princeton were three enemy troops of light horse and three regiments, the first two of which were already on the march to aid Cornwallis. Having heard firing the preceding night from Trenton, their initial surprise was complete.

Brigadier Hugh Mercer was sent to the left, with orders to destroy Stony Brook Bridge and then to join Washington and the remainder of the troops who were proceeding by the back road to Princeton. They soon encountered a British regiment which, not expecting Americans there, was driven back. They rallied and Mercer received a wound that was to be fatal. Washington forwarded additional militia under Cadwalader, but both forces were driven back rapidly. Washington himself came up with the greater part of his men. Charging ahead on his horse he rallied the Americans, telling them to hold their fire. The enemy shot first and there was a great cloud of smoke around the general. One aide put his hands over his eyes, afraid to see the commander in chief fall. Then

Washington called the order to charge and fire and the British lines broke. Washington and his cavalry pursued them, while others chased the enemy as far as four miles on foot.

A part of a second British regiment nearby retreated to Princeton, where the other enemy forces had taken a position in Nassau Hall. After the artillery was turned on them, the majority surrendered. The remainder escaped to the north. Cornwallis, having pursued the enemy up from Trenton, reached the Princeton area as the tired Americans were on their way north to Morristown. Afraid for his supply depot and his seventy-thousand-pound treasure at Brunswick, the British commander moved eastward. British casualties at Princeton amounted to about four hundred, while the Americans lost forty, including Mercer and Colonel John Haslet, who had been commended by Washington for his bravery at Harlem.

Within a few days the British abandoned every post in New Jersey except Brunswick, Amboy, and Paulus Hook. On January 6 the Americans captured Hackensack, the point from which Washington had fled across the state not quite seven weeks before. It had taken the general and his ragged, often shoeless, army from Christmas to Twelfth Night to beat an enemy with forces numbering, in their entirety, nearly twelve times his combat forces, and to drive them back to what he had once described as their "pitiful islands." The British suffered fourteen hundred casualties in the period, the Americans around forty-five.

Not quite four years later the chevalier de Chastellux, a French general who tried to visit all of Washington's battlefields, went to Princeton with Colonel Stephen Moylan, Washington's aide. He was immediately seized by President Witherspoon, who engaged him in conversation in bookish French about his college. Chastellux wrote: "I confess... that I was rather impatient to seek out the traces of General Washington, in a country where every object recalled his successes, I passed rapidly therefore from Parnassus to the field of Mars, and from the hands of President Witherspoon into those of colonel Moylan. They were both upon their own ground; so that while one was pulling me by the right arm, telling me 'Here is the philosophy classroom' the other was plucking me by the left, telling me 'This is where one hundred and eighty English laid down their arms.'"

MORRISTOWN

By the time he reached his new headquarters in Morristown on January 6, Washington was already thinking of attacking New York. He wrote to General Heath the next day, ordering him and General Lincoln to move towards the city to blockade it and, if possible, to prepare for an assault upon it. His hopes, however, were dashed when Heath marched against Fort Independence in the Bronx on January 18. Heath demanded that the fort surrender within twenty minutes or take the consequences. The British ignored this and fired at him. Heath attempted a siege but the British sortied ten days later and drove him off. Heath got a lot of ridicule and Washington sharply reproved him.

Washington took some pleasure in writing to Lord Cornwallis on January 8 to say that his army would not molest convoys of money and stores intended for the German and British prisoners at Trenton and Princeton. But, he added, he could not answer for the militia of the state, who were "exceedingly exasperated at the treatment they have met with, from both Hessian and British troops." He therefore would send one of his officers to escort the convoy across New Jersey, indicating thus that Cornwallis' men would not otherwise be safe.

In moving across New Jersey, the British, but far more the Hessian troops, had ravaged, plundered, and raped on such a scale as to turn the state from Tory or neutral to Whig. The Hessians took no account of the difference between loyal and rebel inhabitants. The fact that the king could not give protection to those who had sworn allegiance to him made a great difference in the attitude of the population. The militia swarmed into Washington's camp, a change from the days when Washington could raise no more than one hundred men when he was retreating across New Jersey. British foraging and raiding parties were regularly attacked by continentals and militia. On January 7, a German foraging party was set upon and around fifty killed, wounded, or captured. Throughout the spring, guerrilla operations of this kind continued against the enemy. Washington used the original French term, *la petite guerre*, for these actions. George III's hope that Howe could now draw on the country for provisions was not fulfilled.

Washington had hardly arrived in Morristown before he wrote to Robert Morris and his friends to get the gun foundry at Philadelphia going again. He would need "a large number of field pieces" for the spring campaign.

REED

On January 13 Washington announced that Colonel George Weedon, once a captain in his Virginia Regiment, had been made adjutant general, *pro tempore*, in the place of the resigned Joseph Reed. The commander in chief soon offered the post to General Gates, who declined on the ground that this would be a comedown after having a northern command. He did not disclose his real reason that, following the work of Reed and Lee, he had developed a deep mistrust of Washington. Gates subsequently persuaded Congress to send him to the north, far from the commander in chief.

That spring Washington offered the command of the cavalry service to Joseph Reed, who declined to serve. In June he wrote Washington, apologizing for his letter to Lee, assuring him there was nothing in it that was "inconsistent with that respect and affection" he had always borne to the general. The statement was false, but Washington, not knowing it to be so, answered by thanking Reed for his "friendly and affectionate sentiments." He added that he had always unreservedly welcomed Reed's "advice on any point in which I appeared to be wanting. To meet with any thing, then, that carried with it a complexion of witholding that advice from, and censuring my conduct to another, was such an argument of disingenuity, that I was not a little mortified at it. However, I am perfectly satisfied that matters were not as they appeared from the letter alluded to."

PRISONERS

The reports that Washington received of the Howes' mistreatment of prisoners brought him almost to tears. An American officer described them as "miserable starved objects... mere skeletons, unable to creep or speak in many instances."

Washington wrote separate letters to the Howe brothers on January 13. To General Howe, he said: "I am sorry that I am again under the necessity of remonstrating to you upon the Treatment which our prisoners continue to receive in New York. Those, who have lately been sent out, give the most shocking Accounts of their barbarous usage, which their Miserable, emaciated Countenances confirm. How very different was their Appearance from that of your Soldiers, who have lately been returned to you, after a Captivity of twelve months; And, whether this... was owing to a difference of treatment, I leave it to you... to determine... If you are determined to make Captivity as distressing as possible, to those whose Lot it is to fall into it, let me know it, that we may be upon equal terms, for your Conduct must and shall mark mine." To Lord Howe, he wrote: "I hope that, upon making the proper Inquiry, you will have the matter so regulated, that the unhappy Creatures, whose Lot is Captivity, may not in future have the Miseries of Cold, disease and Famine, added to their other Misfortunes." An acrimonious correspondence continued between Washington and the British for an extended period. On June 10 he wrote General Howe:

To prove that the Prisoners did not suffer from any ill treatment...

you say "they were confined in the most airy Buildings and on Board the largest Transports in the fleet"...

That airy Buildings were chosen to confine our Men in, is a fact I shall not dispute. But whether this was an Advantage or not in the Winter Season, I leave you to decide. I am inclined to think it was not; especially as there was a general Complaint, that they were destitute of fire...

...I wish their sufferings may not have been increased in the Article of clothing, by their being deprived of what they had thro' the rapacity of too many of their Captors...

...You ask "How is the Cause of debility in Prisoners to be ascertained?" This seems to be considered as a perplexing Question. For my part, I cannot view it as involving any great difficulty. There is no more familiar mode of reasoning than from Effects to causes... In the Subject before us, the appearance of the Prisoners and what eventually happened, proved that they had been hardly dealt with.

In this last sentence, Washington referred to the fact that many prisoners had been so weakened that they died shortly after reaching the American lines. By October of 1777, there were far more British in American hands than the other way around, and Washington had greater leverage in his negotiations.

In April, Benjamin Franklin appealed, in turn, to Lord Stormont, British ambassador at Paris, to obtain better treatment for American prisoners in England. Stormont returned the letter with a note saying that he would receive no letters from rebels unless they came to implore "his Majesty's mercy." Franklin returned it to Lord Stormont, with a note saying that it was a matter of common humanity "between two nations, Great Britain and the United States of America," and Stormont's reply was "*indecent.*" Franklin complained again by a message that reached Lord North and was forwarded by him to George III. The king, with his usual astuteness, replied that Franklin's letter was an obvious trick to gain recognition and perhaps to have some propaganda value, since no British officer would ever act with cruelty, even to rebels. He added: "If they have erred I should rather think it has been in too much civility towards them."

LEE

Lee was the top prisoner of the British and a favorite of Congress, which took great interest in his welfare and the possibility of his being exchanged. Howe at first tried to consider Lee a deserter from the British army and wrote home for instructions. London suggested that he be sent to Britain for trial, but Congress' threat to retaliate caused a change in directives. Lee's reported bad treatment complicated Washington's negotiations, since Congress ordered a British officer, Colonel Archibald Campbell, and several Hessian officers kept to close confinement. Washington protested and eventually got this changed. He maintained a policy of treating British and Hessian prisoners well, not only for humanitarian reasons but on the simple ground that this was a much easier way to obtain enemy deserters.

Contrary to reports to Congress, Lee was handled more as a prisoner of state than of war. Some of the British officers were old friends and he had them to dine. The Howes again tried to get Congress, through their captive, to send negotiating commissions but, though Lee begged them to do so, Congress refused. Lee, feeling the American cause was all but hopeless and that—as he later explained to Elias Boudinot, Washington's agent to the prisoners—American troops could not stand up to British forces, wrote out and gave to Henry Strachey, General Howe's secretary, a long plan whereby the Howes could obtain the submission of the United States. Howe paid it little heed. Congress continued to apply pressure for Lee's exchange and unfortunately succeeded the following year.

FORGED LETTERS

Sometime late in 1776 a series of letters—purportedly written by Washington to his wife, stepson, and Mount Vernon manager—were printed in London and subsequently republished in New York. Washington guessed they were composed by John Randolph, once attorney general of Virginia, who had gone to England. Possibly a more likely candidate was Randolph's brother, Beverley, since they show considerable knowledge of activities at Washington's headquarters and his problems. Beverley Randolph was on active duty with the British forces in New York and knew something of Virginia politics and Washington's family affairs. The letters are not especially vicious, but they have a despondent Washington protesting both his loyalty to the king and worry about his wife's suspicions. The London press expressed doubt that they were genuine. They were republished by the Jeffersonian press in 1796. Other forgeries appearing in New York thereafter described lewd behavior on the part of Washington. Since his conduct was open to all, they made no impression.

SICKNESS AND SPRING

A new aide, the twenty-two-year-old Alexander Hamilton, was appointed on March 1 and, like all who held that post, bore the rank of lieutenant colonel. He had gone from New York to White Plains and on to Trenton and Princeton with the army. He entered the general's family just before Washington's first illness of the war.

Washington, who had been nearly two years without a day's rest, came down with a severe peritonsillar abscess. Hamilton and the other aides had to keep visitors and business from him, and to act as nursemaids to a general who was highly aggrieved at being in bed. Washington became very sick; the household and staff passed through agony, hearing the general's difficult breathing. Before he fully recovered, Martha Washington arrived in camp from Mount Vernon and helped to put him on his feet again.

For the first time in the war, with Mrs. Washington around to see to it, Washington began to take better care of himself and to get the exercise and sport he had too long denied himself. With the British beaten back to New York, he became—for a little while—the old cheerful, smiling Washington, taking long horseback rides and playing ball with his officers. This was a form of the "base-ball" enjoyed as a boy by George III, an early patron of the game. Colonel Theodorick Bland of Virginia came with his wife, Martha, to join Washington. She wrote a fine, gossipy letter to her sister, Frances Randolph:

> *Now let me speak of our noble and agreeable commander (for he commands both sexes) one by his excellent skill in military matters, the other by his ability, politeness and attention. He is generally busy in the forenoon—but from dinner till night he is free for all company. His worthy lady seems to be in perfect felicity while she is by the side of her Old Man, as she calls him. We often make parties on horseback—the General, his lady, Miss Livingston, and his aides-de-camp… at which times, General Washington throws off the hero, and takes on the chatty, agreeable companion. He can be downright impudent sometimes.*

As for Martha Washington, one of the matrons of Morristown told of visiting her with several ladies. They had heard that she was a very grand person. "So we dressed ourselves in our most elegant ruffles and silks… And don't you think we found her knitting and with a (checked) apron on… There we were, without a stitch of work, and sitting in state, but General Washington's lady with her own hands was knitting stockings for herself and husband. She seems very wise in experience, kind-hearted and winning in all her ways. She talked much of the poor soldiers, especially the sick ones." Washington was to have only a brief taste of domestic bliss before the spring campaign.

MARCH 17, 1777

It had been a year since Washington had driven Howe out of Boston and, in the interim, New Jersey. Howe held two seaports and a bit of the mainland, and that was all. In New York, Lord Rawdon and his Irish troops made a brave showing as they marched up Broadway in a Saint Patrick's Day parade. On the same day Colonel William Harcourt, who had captured Lee and who was later to be a field marshal, wrote to his father, Lord Harcourt, lieutenant of Ireland: "Though it was once the fashion of this army to treat them in the most contemptible light, they are now become a formidable enemy. Formidable, however, as they may be, I flatter myself as we are a good deal more so, and I have therefore little doubt that, provided affairs continue quiet in Europe, and the expected reinforcements arrive in good time, we shall soon bring this business to a happy conclusion."

Lord Howe's secretary, Ambrose Serle, who had been calling Americans "poor mad Quixotes," wrote in his March 28 diary that he expected "a speedy termination of the war." He added that he and Joseph Galloway, a Pennsylvania Tory, agreed that in the future Americans should have little to say about their government, since they could not be trusted with power.

By March the news of Washington's victories at Trenton and Princeton had spread through Europe. Every foreign and war office began to scramble for maps and to ask, who is General Washington? Frederick the Great, regarded with awe as the greatest soldier of his time, told his ambassador in London that, in his view, Americans could be expected to gain their independence. Howe had informed his government that there was no possibility of ending the war with the 1777 campaign. Everyone in Europe watched, with no little malice, to see what George III and Lord North would do now.

TWENTY-TWO

MORRISTOWN TO VALLEY FORGE

1777

DUPLICITY WAS A common practice in European diplomacy, but those who used it were often duped by others. In 1775 the comte de Vergennes, French foreign minister, told the British ambassador to Versailles that his government regarded the American rebellion as deplorable and France would do nothing to help an insurrection against a lawful sovereign. Although the British cabinet had reason to doubt such assurances, North repeatedly declared to Parliament that there was no possibility of war with France. By 1776, trusting both Vergennes and their own ability to crush the rebellion quickly, the British had the bulk of their armed forces in America. In the same year, France and Spain began sending secret arms and supplies to America. These arrived in some quantity in 1777.

Silas Deane, the first American representative in Paris, worked closely with Beaumarchais in setting up the trading company that purchased arms, ammunition, and clothing for the rebels. He was rather too sharp a trading Yankee and some government purchases managed to end up as his own. In addition he may have tried to charge Congress for goods given free by the French. Using his private knowledge of French plans, he also speculated on the London stock exchange, through Edward Bancroft and Mrs. Jacobus van Zandt, American spies on George III's payroll. By 1781, or perhaps earlier, Deane was also a paid agent of the British king.

Benjamin Franklin in Paris was surrounded by intrigue. The French police and court agents kept their eyes on his doings. The British also spied on him through their secret service in Europe, headed by William Eden, brother of the last royal governor of Maryland. Eden's French agent was Paul Wentworth, a New Hampshire Tory who enlisted the services of Bancroft, secretary to the American legation, and a Major Thornton, secretary to Arthur Lee of the mission. Wentworth later brought Deane into the network. For his money the king got some remarkably bad intelligence, such as the information that Congress had been advised by Franklin not to ratify the treaty with France. Where the information was accurate it was often too painful for the king to believe. He also mistrusted his spies who, he correctly thought, were too often "stockjobbers" (speculators).

Arthur Lee, after joining Franklin as the third United States commissioner in Paris, quickly suspected Deane and Bancroft. In this he was remarkably astute; his suspicions were confirmed but not until many years had gone by and archives were opened. Franklin, much more interested in high level international politics than in business details, paid insufficient attention to Lee's complaints. Lee finally suspected that Franklin, too, was involved, and he may well have been justified. Lee complained to Congress about Deane, who was recalled from France. John Adams took his place.

The news of Trenton and Princeton had been well received by the French, who quickly gave Franklin further secret funds in the amount of $400,000. In England, the situation became acute for the king because he and his government were in financial difficulties with victory nowhere in sight. Lord North had some very unhappy times with his Parliament that spring.

In April of 1777 North announced that the king was more than £600,000 short in his accounts, and Parliament would have to vote the sums necessary. It was a sad picture, for the palace servants and fuel bills were unpaid. Most—and probably all—of the money had been spent for such purposes as the bribery of press and Parliament. The immensity of his debts is shown by the fact that before the war, the British budget, other than the king's civil list, had been less than £5 million a year. Parliament not only had to vote him £600,000 but also an extra £100,000 a year for purposes that were not disclosed but that were well known to Parliament.

The House of Commons passed the requisite acts only after lengthy debates and a call by the Whigs for a full statement of the facts. The king, pleased at the passage, told North the money had been voted because he had placed the management of Commons in "the most able and honest hands." When the king went to Parliament to assent to the bills, the speaker rose, addressed his majesty, and said:

At a time of public distress, full of difficulty and danger, their constituents labouring under burdens almost too heavy to be borne, your faithful Commons... have not only granted to your Majesty a large present supply, but also a great additional revenue; great, beyond example, great beyond your Majesty's highest expense. All this, Sir, they have done in a well-grounded confidence that you will apply wisely what they have granted liberally.

This was a first sign of parliamentary revolt. The House of Commons not only subsequently unanimously approved the statement but then congratulated the speaker on having said it. The king complained to North that this tended to spoil everything, "for the manner may enhance or diminish any gift."

Not long afterwards North had to turn to Parliament for £5 million more in supplementary war expenditures, which meant new taxes and loans. All this became a part of Britain's system of corruption. To the bribes and pensions from the king's purse, and the titles and ribbons he could give, were added lucrative war contracts that often went to George III's friends in Parliament. In addition, loans at exorbitant rates were placed through the same channels. Yet, at the same time, there were increasing signs of a popular desire to return to the old British standards of decency and honor that had been brought to America by the early settlers.

DEANE AND THE FRENCH OFFICERS

Silas Deane was plagued after his arrival in Paris by visitors who wanted something from Americans: intelligence, supply contracts, or jobs. Many who came to his office were adventurers or retired officers who saw a chance to advance in the only war going on at the time. They often exaggerated their military rank, added nonexistent hereditary titles to their names, and pretended to more knowledge than they had. Without much discrimination, Deane hired many and promised them they would be generals or colonels as soon as they got to America. This became a source of great embarrassment to Congress, and to Washington, when that body unloaded them onto him.

Deane selected some good officers, including Johann Kalb, who, calling himself a baron, came as an ostensible volunteer, but he was engaged in a plan to make the comte de Broglie commander in chief of the American army. Another man he chose was Gilbert Motier, marquis de Lafayette, connected by marriage, as Deane knew, to the great house of Noailles, which had enough field marshals, governors, and ambassadors in the family to be itself a small empire.

Lafayette's father was killed at Minden, the battle that resulted in the cashiering of Lord George Germain. His son had already had a precocious career; he was a military cadet at age twelve, married and a captain in the French army at sixteen, and a father at eighteen. He too was promised a major general's commission in America. The romantic stories about him are well known: his visit to the English court where the marquis de Noailles was ambassador; his introduction to George III and Germain; his return to France and the purchase of his own ship; and his escape from his king's police after being ostensibly forbidden to go to America. Congress, having had their fill of adventurers, treated him rudely when he arrived at Philadelphia in July, but his dignified plea that he had the right to volunteer, without pay, won him his commission as major general just before his twentieth birthday. Shortly after receiving his July 31 commission, he met Washington in Philadelphia. Lafayette found him impressively tall and majestic and his welcome most friendly. Nonetheless he embarrassed Washington, the more so because he said he only came to learn and, of course, to fight. Washington asked Congress on more than one occasion what they intended for Lafayette. He considered Lafayette's appointment as a general officer honorary, while Lafayette did not think it such at all. "The Marquis," as he was soon called by everyone, earned his field command by sheer persistence and personal bravery. He turned out to be a good soldier who improved as the years passed. Six months after his arrival he was writing to his wife, Adrienne: "My presence... is more necessary to the American cause than you can think... In the place that he occupies one may be surrounded by flatterers or secret enemies; he finds in me a sure friend to whom he can open his heart, and who will always tell him the truth."

CONGRESS

The great Congress, which had assembled in Philadelphia, soon deteriorated. Washington had left even before independence and Franklin and Jefferson not long after, the former to assume his important duties in Paris. By May of 1777, Adams was complaining to Jefferson that Congress consisted of only "twenty hands," all that were still on deck to do the work. He added: "Your country is not yet quite secure enough to excuse your retreat to the delights of domestic life." Jefferson did not return until the war was securely won. Adams himself departed for Paris before the year was out.

The weakness of Congress became a recurring complaint of the army. By 1778 Hamilton was asking the governor of New York why his state was not represented by men of the stature of Livingston and Jay. That same year

Washington asked Benjamin Harrison about Virginia's representation: "Where is Mason, Wythe, Jefferson, Nicholas, Pendleton, Nelson and another I could name?" meaning the letter's recipient.

The small representation, in a Congress divided into numerous committees, had one advantage for the commander in chief. In 1775 and 1776, its members had interfered at numerous points, directed an invasion of Canada, and stripped him of officers, troops, and supplies. By 1777 Congress was too weak to try to control overall strategy and left its management very largely where it belonged. As a result, American military planning was much more efficient in the third year of the war than it had been at first. Congress meddled in more minor matters and often struck at the morale of the officers' corps.

STRATEGY

On February 25 Congress suggested to Washington that he should keep the enemy confined, stop further supplies from reaching them, and beat Howe before additional reinforcements arrived from Europe. He replied on March 14 that he would be happy to do just this but, at the moment, he had exactly 981 continentals with him, plus militia who were engaged only till the end of the month.

Two days earlier Washington had informed General Schuyler, who held the northern command, that American operations would have to continue on the defensive. He planned to station his forces in post "so central to the theatre of War, that they may be sent to the support of any part of the country. It is a military observation, strongly supported by experience, 'that a superior Army may fall sacrifice to an inferior, by an injudicious division.'" Americans ought therefore to avoid "being beaten in detachments."

Washington went on to say that there should be a garrison at Ticonderoga to prevent a penetration from Canada. The principal defensive point, however, was to be the Hudson Highlands. The force there would act to prevent the enemy from moving up the Hudson. It could promptly march north if an incursion came from Quebec province or south to New Jersey, if the British moved across the state, to attack Philadelphia. Troops could easily reach Peekskill from New England, and then shift north or south as required. This, with variations taking place that year, remained the core of his strategy. It involved keeping the various parts of the American army in full communication. The British were to be attacked "if they formed an injudicious division."

The original British plan for the conquest of America projected an invasion from Canada to join with the forces taking New York. These would then cut off New England. Washington had upset them by grimly holding onto Manhattan until the fall of 1776 and then by stopping Howe at White Plains. The Canadian portion of the British plan had also stalled in the north. The original plans were changed in 1777 when Howe decided to take Philadelphia, leaving New York with only a defensive garrison. Washington quickly learned from his agents in Philadelphia that Howe was trying to recruit pilots with a knowledge of the Delaware. At least a part of Howe's army would be coming by sea, if this plan were to be executed.

Washington did not know that Howe had requested heavy reinforcements—fifteen thousand troops—from England so that he could make a combined attack across New Jersey and up the Delaware. His failure to receive the needed men and ships, along with Washington's New Jersey defenses, made him eventually decide to take his troops on the sea route.

That winter General John Burgoyne had sold the king and Germain on a plan for a new enterprise from Canada that would involve fifteen thousand men of all ranks. Leaving behind a garrison in Quebec, Burgoyne himself would descend into the United States by Lake Champlain. An additional force would sail up the Saint Lawrence and then move across New York's Mohawk Valley from Lake Ontario. No one in authority bothered particularly about the long supply lines involved. Burgoyne's operations seem to have been planned and approved independently of General Howe's schemes to go south. As it was to turn out, there were six separate British armies operating in 1777: three maintaining stations in Quebec, Newport, and New York; a fourth moved eastward across New York state; a fifth marched south from Montreal; and a sixth wallowed for weeks at sea before landing at the head of the Chesapeake. Throughout, Washington's strategic plans held until they were, in part, wrecked by the vainglory of General Gates. Nonetheless, by the end of the year, at least twelve enemy general officers had been killed, captured, or driven from the country. In addition, the British commander in chief offered his resignation to London.

By early May Washington had reports of the invasion projected from Canada. He automatically assumed that Howe would cooperate with it and that an attack on Philadelphia seemed less probable. He ordered General McDougall to survey all sources of food on both sides of the Hudson, in case he brought his troops north. He urged each of the northern states to raise more men, particularly to reinforce Ticonderoga. He detached six of his brigadiers for northern service and ordered eight Massachusetts regiments, recently recruited, to Peekskill. He also asked Greene, Knox, and Wayne to examine and strengthen the fortifications of the Hudson Highlands.

In mid-May Sullivan was assigned to Princeton, with instructions to keep a close watch for any movements by Howe. If Howe headed for the Delaware, he was to harass and impede Howe's movements but to be ready at all times to retreat to hilly country. If the enemy moved to Morristown or the Hudson, they were to be annoyed night and day by small parties. Sullivan was ordered always to have his troops ready to march at a moment's notice and never to risk a general engagement.

General Howe had spent the winter comfortably in New York with his mistress, Mrs. Elizabeth Loring, wife of Howe's Loyalist commissary of prisoners. Her fame became lasting because of various verses that circulated, including one from Francis Hopkinson's "Ballad of the Kegs," which is, perhaps, the most widely quoted of revolutionary rhymes:

> *Sir William, he, snug as a flea,*
> *Lay all this time a-snoring*
> *Nor dreamed of harm, as he lay warm*
> *In Bed with Mrs. Loring.*

Another poem commented: "Awake, Sir Billy... leave your little filly, and open the Campaign." As spring began, Sir Billy did, in fact, make numerous moves to open it, but it was not till July that his campaign to take Philadelphia was under way. In March, British troops attacked Peekskill and did substantial damage before being driven off. In April an expeditionary force burned many houses and barns in Danbury, Connecticut. Brigadier Benedict Arnold, who helped to repel the enemy, was promoted by Congress.

GENERAL PROBLEMS

The commander in chief worked hard attempting to keep his top officers happy. On February 24 he wrote Sullivan: "Do not, my dear General Sullivan, torment yourself any longer with imaginary slights... No other officer of rank, in the whole army, has so often conceived himself neglected, slighted and ill treated, as you have done, and none I am sure has had less cause." Lord Stirling and his sister-in-law got into a squabble over a house she rented from him, and she complained to Washington, who asked him to treat her with all the respect due her sex. Stirling replied, in a rather persuasive letter, that she had caused all the trouble. Washington had assuaged Arnold's feeling of annoyance at not being made a major general prior to Danbury. Others of his command threatened to resign over their treatment by Congress, and

Washington was kept busy with their grievances. In turn John Adams complained they were scrambling for promotion, like apes after nuts.

Meanwhile Gates had gone to Ticonderoga, believing he was to take command in the north. Subsequently Congress reaffirmed that Schuyler was in command, to the annoyance of Gates, who was told he could report either to Schuyler or to Washington. Prior to that time, Gates had sent his reports of enemy movements to Congress only, from which source they belatedly reached the commander in chief. Washington complained to Gates, saying Howe would concert his actions with those of Burgoyne, and it was vital that he have the earliest intelligence of all British activities. Subsequently Gates told Washington he was depriving the northern army of tents and should not keep everything for himself. He added that he would appeal to Congress, "the common parent body of all the American armies," thus attempting to establish that he was independent of the commander in chief, who was holding back his needed supplies.

Washington was further plagued by the French, who demanded high rank and command. As early as February, Washington asked Gates, then still in Philadelphia, "to stop the shoals of French Men that are coming on to this Camp... For these ten days past, it has taken up half my time to hear their pretensions." Later, exasperated, he told Richard Henry Lee that many were adventurers whose effrontery was far greater than their merit. They often impressed Congress, however, and John Adams was particularly taken in by them. On June 19 Washington wrote to James Warren: "We have three capital characters here, Monsr. de Coudray, General Conway and Monsr. de la Balme. These are great and learned men. Coudray is the most promising officer in France." As it turned out, all were intriguers who made trouble for the American commander in chief.

Phillippe Tronson du Coudray had helped Beaumarchais to select artillery for America. He then arranged with Deane to proceed to the United States as a major general and inspector general of engineers and artillery, with a commission dated to make him senior to every officer in the army except Washington. Hearing of this, Washington wrote to John Hancock, protesting that this might cost him the valuable services of Henry Knox, who had labored so long with the American artillery service. When rumor reached camp that Congress had confirmed the appointment, Knox, Greene, and others threatened to resign. Congress was furious, and John Adams wrote angrily to Greene, saying that many members wanted the generals arrested or dismissed from the service. This storm blew over but resentment continued in Congress; this eventually spewed over onto Washington. Congress made du Coudray a major general but subsequently appointed him inspector general of ordnance, which was intended as a staff rather than a line appointment. When Washington informed du Coudray that some of the artillery sent from France was too cumbersome to move and he was having it recast, du Coudray wrote tartly, implying that Washington was ignorant of the subject and had been too easily influenced by another French officer, the chevalier du Plessis. Washington sent a long, polite reply to du Coudray outlining in detail the reasons the guns could not be easily transported "through the Mountainous and Woody country in which our operations most commonly are." He added: "I am at a loss to conceive how you could imagine that I had been governed in my determination in this matter by the advice of Monsieur Du Plessis... It can hardly be supposed that either Genl. Knox or myself would repose so implicit a confidence in his representations and counsels, as to regulate our measures entirely by them, in an affair of so much consequence." Du Coudray was drowned in September while crossing the Schuylkill River, to the ill-concealed relief of many in the American army. Even the kindly Lafayette called it "a happy accident."

Augustin de la Balme got Congress to appoint him inspector general of cavalry. After creating difficulties and doing nothing, he resigned in October. Conway, an Irishman in the service of France, was made a brigadier and then a major general, following which he attempted to oust Washington from the army in order to get the command for Gates.

BOUND BROOK

From January to May Washington continued his partisan attacks on British foraging parties. Hamilton estimated that as many as five hundred British were killed or wounded that spring, with relatively light American losses. In addition the enemy suffered greatly from sickness and desertion. Howe's army was less formidable than it had been the preceding year and few reinforcements came from England.

By the middle of May Washington had built his strength in New Jersey to about nine thousand men, in addition to the regiments that he had stationed from Peekskill to Ticonderoga. On May 28 he marched them to Middle Brook, in order to give them exercise and training after the long winter at Morristown. The army soon saw some action when Howe and Cornwallis endeavored to bring them to a general engagement. As Hamilton, reflecting Washington's views, wrote at the time, this was the only way the British could win the war, but it was the one thing the Americans had to avoid. Their army was increasing while time was diminishing the enemy forces, but Washington was still too weak for a major battle. As long as the American army existed, the British could hold only one or two posts; if they held more, they had to divide and the Americans could then attack.

Howe sent eighteen thousand men to New Jersey on June 12 to try to draw Washington's army, half its size, into battle. Howe and Cornwallis did all they could for nearly three weeks to draw Washington into a trap, but he eluded their maneuvers. At the end of June, Howe gave up and withdrew all British troops from New Jersey to Staten Island. On July 24 Lord North sent the king a report "by which his Majesty will see that Sir Wm. Howe has found Mr. Washington's camp too strong to venture to attack it, & has embarked his troops as Lord North supposes for Chesapeake Bay in order to attack Philadelphia." Howe's embarkation was so slow that he did not set sail until the day before the king received this letter.

TICONDEROGA

In the meantime, Gentleman Johnny Burgoyne had set out from Canada with high hopes and many Indian braves to restore the king's peace to the United States. Burgoyne had drafted the proclamation issued by General Gage from besieged Boston. Now, on his own, he produced another, which resulted in even more laughter in America and England and a parody by Francis Hopkinson. On June 23, 1777, he announced to Americans: "By John Burgoyne, Esq., etc., etc., Lieut. General of his Majesty's Forces in America, Colonel of the Queen's Regiment of Light Dragoons, Governor of Fort-William in North-Britain, one of the Representatives of the Commons of Great-Britain in Parliament, and commanding an Army and fleet in an Expedition from Canada etc. etc. etc... At the Head of Troops in the full Powers of Health, Discipline, and Valour, determined to strike where necessary, and anxious to save where possible, I, by these Presents, invite and exhort all Persons, in Places where the Progress of this Army may point, and by the Blessing of God I will extend it FAR, to maintain such a Conduct as may justify me in protecting their Lands, Habitations, and Families... If notwithstanding these Endeavors and sincere Inclination to assist them, the Phrenzy of Hostility should remain, I trust I shall stand acquitted in the Eyes of God and Men in denouncing and executing the Vengeance of the State against the wilful Outcast. The Messengers of Justice and of Wrath await them in the field, and Devastation, famine and every concomitant Horror." Hopkinson's parody said, in part:

I Issue This My Manifesto
By John Burgoyne and Burgoyne, John, Esq.
And Graced with titles still more higher,
For I'm Lieutenant-general too,
Of George's troops both red and blue...
And furthermore, when I am there,
In House of Commons I appear
(Hoping ere long to be a Peer),
Being a member of that virtuous band
Who always vote at North's command...
And all my titles to display,
I'll end with thrice et cetera...
I will let loose the dogs of Hell,
Ten thousand Indians, who shall yell
And foam and tear, and grin and roar,
And drench their moccasins in gore...
They'll scalp your heads, and kick your shins,
And rip your —, and flay your skins...
If after all these loving warnings...
You shall remain as deaf as adder...
I swear by George and by St. Paul
I will exterminate you all.

John Burgoyne commanded king's troops, who wore red coats; Hessians, who wore blue; and Indians, who largely wore skin—altogether some nine thousand officers and men. With them were an enormous baggage train and many women, ranging from officers' wives to prostitutes. Baroness von Riedesel, wife of the general in command of the Germans, wrinkled up her nose at Burgoyne, who, she wrote, spent his nights in his tent drinking champagne with his mistress.

At Ticonderoga, the American defenders had thirty-four hundred troops under General St. Clair, many inexperienced militia. When General Gates inspected Ticonderoga, a proposal was made to him to fortify Sugar Loaf Mountain, a mile from the fortress, but he ruled out this scheme as impracticable. The British, more skilled in military matters, quickly seized Sugar Loaf when they got to Ticonderoga and mounted guns on it. By this maneuver, they drove out St. Clair and the Americans on July 6 for an easy victory. This was a heavy blow to morale in the north.

Germain received the dispatch announcing the fall of Ticonderoga on August 23 and sent it with a note to the king: "Lord George Germain has the honour of Congratulating your Majesty upon the great and Glorious success of Lt. General Burgoyne in taking Ticonderoga, in destroying vessels Boats, Stores, Artillery &c &c &c."

WASHINGTON MOVES NORTH

On July 1 Washington reported to Congress that the British had evacuated New Jersey. Throughout July Washington continued to assume that Howe, in all probability, would go up the Hudson to make a juncture with Burgoyne. During this period General Henry Clinton was, in fact, trying to argue Howe into this plan. Washington's counter-strategy continued the policy of maintaining the Hudson Highlands as the key to an American defense system that would be flexible enough to meet any British moves.

After Howe abandoned Amboy, Washington urgently warned the American General George Clinton in the Highlands to be on a sharp lookout for an attack. He asked that militia be ordered out immediately: "the least delay may be productive of the most fatal consequences." He also ordered two regiments to proceed at once to Peekskill. He asked General John Nixon and four regiments to proceed north, to reinforce Schuyler as soon as the two new brigades got to Peekskill. Washington continued to think there was a preconcerted plan between Burgoyne and Howe, though none existed in reality. On the other hand, he could never be certain that Burgoyne's moves might not be a feint to enable Howe to attack Philadelphia. By July 4, Washington had moved his army to Morristown in order to be ready to march north if Howe attacked there. He put troops on the alert and ordered his officers to strip themselves of heavy baggage. "If after this second notice, they continue to fill and encumber wagons with old tables, chests, chairs, &c., they are not to be surprised if they are left in the field."

Shortly afterward, Washington dispatched Sullivan to the Highlands to get intelligence of possible enemy movements. By July 7, on the basis of his information from Staten Island and Manhattan, he began to question whether Howe really planned to go north. At this time Henry Clinton was still trying to argue Howe into so doing but his commander was unshakable. When Howe heard that Washington had sent more troops into upper New York, he was determined to take an additional brigade with him to Philadelphia.

Washington learned from Schuyler on July 12 that Ticonderoga had fallen to Burgoyne. At Schuyler's request he immediately sent cannon, entrenching tools, kettles, and gunpowder, and regretted that he had no tents or further regiments to spare. However, he added, he had some reserve troops who could go north in an emergency. Soon thereafter, Washington moved his army to Smith's Clove, near Haverstraw, in order to head off any move by Howe. From there he wrote to Schuyler not to despair over Ticonderoga. He added: "I hope a Spirited Opposition will check the progress of General Burgoyne's Arms and that the confidence derived from his success, will hurry him into measures, that will in their consequence be favourable to us." He requested Schuyler to send down every boat from Albany so that he could move troops north by water if necessary.

The next day he informed Schuyler he had decided to order Benedict Arnold, an aggressive officer, to help him. Arnold, he said, knew the country; he was a New Englander, and he would give spirit to New England troops. A few days later he wrote to Schuyler to suggest that Arnold might be especially useful in western New York, if the enemy attacked Fort Schuyler. This turned out to be an accurate forecast.

Washington made other efforts to help the northern army. He wrote to Schuyler on July 22 that he had found some tents and was sending them on; he had also decided to send General Glover and his Marblehead regiment north. He ordered General Lincoln, who was popular with the Massachusetts militia, to take charge of similar forces in Vermont. He advised Schuyler that it was particularly important to attack Burgoyne's left flanks from that area. By August Burgoyne was complaining to London that the militia on his left were like "a gathering storm." In sending three New England officers, Washington recognized that New England disliked Schuyler. He gave both political and military support, in the expectation that New York and New England would then work together to destroy Burgoyne. He appealed to Massachusetts and New Hampshire to add all the militia they could. Washington wrote further to Schuyler on July 22:

> *I yet look forward to a fortunate and happy change. I Trust General Burgoyne's Army will meet, sooner or later an effectual check, and I suggested before, that the success, he has had, will precipitate his ruin. From your accounts, he appears to be pursuing that line of conduct, which of all others, is most favourable to us; I mean acting in Detachment... Could we be so happy, as to cut one of them off, supposing it should not exceed four, five or six hundred Men. It would inspirit the people and do away with much of their present anxiety... They would fly to Arms and afford every aid in their power.*

On July 24 Washington received confirmed intelligence that Howe had sailed with an armada of 260 warships and transports. The fleet was observed off Sandy Hook; this meant that it was heading south. Washington wrote that he found it "unaccountable" that Howe had abandoned Burgoyne, but he moved immediately to defend Philadelphia. He and his army raced south and, by July 31, they were again crossing the Delaware.

This was one of the more peculiar periods of the war and totally nerve-wracking for Washington and his army. From July 23 until August 25, the greater part of the British army rolled around the Atlantic Ocean and Chesapeake Bay. Washington could never be sure of what would happen, whether Howe would turn north again or go farther south. Howe was sighted off Delaware on July 30 and then his fleet disappeared. Washington was uncertain whether Howe would head back to the Hudson. On August 10, the fleet appeared off Maryland and then for a long period again disappeared. Washington was now in Pennsylvania but nearly two weeks went by with no news. Howe was again sighted, this time coming up the Chesapeake. On August 25 he anchored at Head of Elk (Elkton) in Maryland and began to disembark his troops. Howe was now farther from Philadelphia than he had been in Amboy two months before, but the terrain was much easier for him than it was in New Jersey. Washington would have found it militarily preferable to have attacked New York, held by Clinton with only seven thousand troops, but to do so meant abandoning the capital and Congress to the enemy. Politically this was impossible, and Washington was forced to fight the main British army with inferior forces.

The campaigns from August to November 1777 were one of the two most extensive campaigns the British undertook in America. Fighting ranged from Maryland and Delaware in the south to the New York Highlands, the Mohawk Valley, Ticonderoga, and into Vermont in the north. In the end, American strategy, employing forces inferior to those of the enemy, bent but never broke. Britain gained a single limited objective, Philadelphia, but her strategy lay in the dust.

BATTLES IN NEW YORK AND VERMONT

Schuyler made every effort to obstruct Burgoyne's march southward by destroying all bridges and felling trees along the roads. He also pulled out all cattle, food, and forage along the way, leaving the country bare. Burgoyne himself decided to cut a road from Skenesborough to Fort Edward rather than go by water. This delayed him more than three weeks.

In the meantime the second invading army of some eighteen hundred men under Brigadier Barry St. Leger moved eastward from Fort Oswego, on Lake Ontario, through the Mohawk Valley to Fort Stanwix, near the present Rome.

There two American forces, one in the fort under Colonel Peter Gansevoort, and the other militia under Brigadier Nicholas Herkimer, held St. Leger until Schuyler could send Benedict Arnold with relief. Arnold's timely approach forced St. Leger to raise the siege on August 22. He retreated to Lake Ontario and Canada. One of the six British armies of 1777 was knocked out of the war. Burgoyne could no longer count on a junction with St. Leger.

Burgoyne, desperate for food, forage, and transport, largely because of Schuyler's actions, dispatched into the New Hampshire grants (now Vermont) a force of Hessians and Indians to get horses, meat, and grain. A party of militia under Colonel John Stark (who had been refused a promotion by Congress) killed or captured almost all of the enemy at the battle of Bennington on August 16. A relief party sent to their aid by Burgoyne was also badly mauled. Altogether Burgoyne lost more than nine hundred men. Congress quickly promoted Stark to his brigadiership.

The Indian allies of Burgoyne were considered a particular threat both to the army and to the inhabitants of upper New York. To counteract them, on August 22 Washington ordered his best partisan regiment, Colonel Daniel Morgan's corps of riflemen, north to fight them on their own terms. He also added additional regiments from New York to the northern forces.

Schuyler did not reap the benefits of Washington's efforts on his behalf. New Englanders in Congress savagely attacked him for the loss of Ticonderoga, which was more properly attributable to Gates. In an atmosphere that Washington on August 4 called "Suspicion and Fear," John Adams led a successful move to dismiss Schuyler from his command. In a gesture, Congress asked Washington to nominate a successor but he sidestepped this as a political trap. Congress then chose the man New England wanted, Horatio Gates. He was an enemy of Washington and the choice was to have unfortunate consequences. Schuyler bore the outrage with dignity and continued his efforts to help the American forces. Gates took over the command on August 19, after the victory of Bennington and just before St. Leger was beaten. Schuyler's successes brought such an accretion of militia to Gates' camp that he soon had twelve thousand men, while Burgoyne's army had fallen to fewer than five thousand effectives.

For the first time Washington asked Congress to define his authority if he moved north to join Gates. His August 4 letter noted that the northern department had always been considered by Congress as "under their direction." On August 21 he repeated his request to define his powers. On August 23 Congress resolved that they had never intended, by setting up a departmental command, "to Supercede the power of General Washington as the Commander-in-Chief of all the Continental Land Forces within the United

States." This did not mean quite what it said. Congress, at Gates' request, did subsequently and unfortunately circumscribe the powers of Washington with relation to Gates.

THE BATTLE OF BRANDYWINE

Washington was now back in Pennsylvania, the state with the largest percentage of Tories. Philadelphia was the capital of the confederacy. These were two factors that led Howe to choose it for attack. Washington decided, in consequence, to march his army in strength through Philadelphia in order to give pause, if not to the Tories, at least to those who wanted to save their skins by being on the winning side.

The ten thousand men made as brave a show as they could on August 24 as they marched through the capital. Their uniforms, ragged and worn, had been washed or brushed. Every man wore a sprig of green in his hat. Washington, impeccably uniformed, rode with Lafayette by his side, and the young marquis got his first cheers and taste of glory. The parade took two hours to pass the watching Congress and only John Adams complained, undoubtedly correctly, that they didn't quite look like soldiers or quite march in step.

Howe took a long time to unload his troops, baggage, and horses. Many of his men were sick, while the draft and cavalry horses that had survived the trip were weak from lack of fodder. Howe took his time getting fresh meat, provisions, and forage, a task quite easy in the cooperating Quaker country of southern Maryland. Washington, along with Greene and Lafayette, reconnoitered Head of Elk on the next two days. Thereafter he ordered out Delaware and Maryland militia to harass Howe's flanks as his army marched and to remove all cattle and forage from the enemy's paths. He reported to Congress that Captain Henry Lee and his cavalry had captured twenty-four British prisoners.

On September 5 Washington issued general orders to the army. In these he indicated that this was the enemy's "last attempt" to take Philadelphia. They had tried to capture it the preceding year and failed. They had begun another campaign to cross New Jersey that summer and that, too, failed. Howe's attempt to come up the Delaware had been frustrated by American fortifications on the river, and he had been forced to use the longer Chesapeake route. Howe would now gamble on taking Philadelphia. If he were beaten "the war is at an end... One bold stroke will free the land from rapine, devastations and burnings, and female innocence from brutal lust and violence... If we behave like men, this third Campaign will be the last... The eyes of all America, and of Europe are turned upon us, as on those by whom the event of the war is to be determined."

By September 6 the British army was on the move, its baggage left behind. Washington too ordered his army to travel light to meet an expected "speedy and rapid movement" of the enemy. Lord Howe's fleet put down the bay in order to return up the Delaware and meet the army at Philadelphia. On September 9 the two armies were two miles apart. Washington reported to Congress that Howe had started to move, his obvious plan was to flank his right, to cross the Brandywine, and to make straight for Philadelphia. To off-set this, he proposed to cross the river, and take post on the high ground at Chadd's Ford.

Washington took a few minutes out, while waiting for battle, to direct Putnam, commanding at Peekskill, to move part of his forces down to New Jersey to prevent an expected attack by Clinton on that state. He added that the enemy was advancing but he trusted "under the smiles of Providence... that we shall give them a repulse or at most... a painful and dear bought victory."

The best description of the battle was written three years later by the French general, the chevalier de Chastellux. He spent many hours at the Brandywine battlefield with French and American officers who had fought there. The terrain had not changed in any essential detail; Chastellux noted that many trees still bore the marks of bullets and cannon shot. Prior to his visit he discussed the battle in detail with Generals Washington, Wayne, Sullivan, and Lafayette. In tracing the movements of the armies, he used a copy of Howe's map of the battle. Chastellux commented, after his inspection of December 7, 1780:

The English, having finished their debarkation, were ready to advance into the country; [Washington's] right flank was exposed, and he was leaving both Philadelphia and the whole of Lancaster County uncovered. It was determined therefore that the army should cross back over Brandywine Creek and encamp on the left [eastern] bank of this river. The position chosen was certainly the best that could be taken to dispute the passage. The left of the position was very good and was supported by thick woods extending as far as the junction of the creek with the Delaware... A battery of cannon with a good parapet was pointed towards Chadd's Ford, and everything appeared secure on that side; but to the right the ground was so covered that it was impossible to judge of the movements of the enemy... The only precaution that could be taken was therefore to place five or six brigades in echelon, to watch that sector. General Sullivan had the command of these brigades; he received orders to keep abreast of the enemy, should they march by their left; and on the supposition that they would unite their forces near Chadd's Ford, he was himself to cross the river and make a powerful diversion of their flank.

When a general has foreseen everything, when he has made the best possible dispositions, and when his activity, judgment, and courage in the action are equal to the wisdom of his measures, has he not already triumphed in the eyes of every impartial judge? And if by some unforeseen misfortunes, the laurels he has merited drop from his hands, is it not for History to gather them up carefully and replace them on his brow?... Let us now observe how such wise dispositions were upset by the mistakes of a few officers and by the inexperience of the troops.

On the 11th of September, General Howe occupied the heights on the right [west] of the creek; he there formed part of his troops in line of battle and had batteries placed opposite Chadd's Ford, while his light troops were attacking and driving before them a corps of riflemen, who had crossed over the right bank to observe his motions more closely. General Washington seeing that the cannonade was continuing without any disposition on the part of the enemy to cross the river, concluded that they had another object. He was informed that a great part of their army had marched up the creek and was threatening his right; he realized how important it was to keep an attentive eye on all movements of this corps; but the country was so covered with thickets, that the patrols could discover nothing; It must be observed that General Washington had only a very small number of horsemen, and that he sent these to the right towards Dilworth to scout that sector. He ordered an officer, whom he judged an intelligent one, to cross the river and inform himself accurately of the route Lord Cornwallis was taking, for it was Cornwallis who commanded this separate corps. The officer returned and assured him that Cornwallis was marching by his right to join Knyphausen, in the direction of Chadd's Ford... Another officer was then sent, who reported that Cornwallis had changed his direction, and that he was rapidly advancing by the road to Jefferies's Ford, two miles above Birmingham Church. General Sullivan was immediately ordered to march thither with all the troops of the right. Unfortunately the roads were badly reconnoitred, and not all open: with great difficulty General Sullivan got through the woods, and when he came out of them to gain a small eminence near Birmingham Church, he found the English columns were coming up the same height on the opposite side. It was no easy matter to range into order of battle such troops as his; he had neither the time to choose his position nor to form his line. The English reached the eminence, drove the Americans back on the woods, and pursued them to the edge of these woods, where they finally dispersed them.

During the short time that this rout lasted, Lord Stirling and General Conway had time to form their brigade on rather advantageous ground: this was a sort of hillock, partly covered by the woods which backed it up. Their left was protected by these same woods, and on the right of this hillock, but a little in the rear, was the Virginia line, which had been ranged in battle formation, on slightly rising ground and on the edge of a sort of grove. The left column of the enemy, which had not been engaged with Sullivan, deployed rapidly and marched against these troops with as much order as vivacity and courage. The Americans made a very smart fire, which did not check the English, and it was not till the latter were within twenty yards of them, that they gave way and plunged into the woods. Lord Stirling, M. de La Fayette, and General Sullivan himself, after the defeat of his division, fought with this body of troops, whose post was the most important, and who resisted the longest. It was here that M. de La Fayette was wounded in his left leg, while rallying the troops who were beginning to waver. On the right, the Virginia line made some resistance; but the English had gained a height, from which their artillery took them obliquely.

General Knyphausen heard the firing... He descended from the heights in two columns, one at Jones's Ford, which turned the battery of the Americans, and the other lower down at Chadd's Ford. The latter marched straight to the battery of General Wayne, whose brigade was in line of battle, the left on a height and the right inclined towards the battery, withdrew his right and strengthened the heights, thus operating a sort of change of front. In a country where there are neither open columns, nor successive positions to take in case of misfortune, it is difficult to make any provision for retreat. The different corps which had been beaten all rushed headlong into the Chester Road... At nightfall, General Wayne also took the road, but in better order.

Chastellux's description makes clear a point that subsequent historians have overlooked, that the country was so thickly wooded that reconnaissance was extremely difficult. Chastellux could not know that the flanking turn over the ford to the north of Washington's army was led by Pennsylvania Tories, headed by Joseph Galloway. In effect, Washington was in enemy territory, and he found intelligence hard to get from local farmers. By midnight most of the American army was at Chester. Though overcome with fatigue, Washington reorganized his troops, and he found the strength to report to Congress:

I am sorry to inform you, that in this day's engagement, we have been obliged to leave the field. Unfortunately the intelligence received of the enemy's advancing up the Brandywine, and crossing at a ford about six miles above us, was uncertain and contradictory, notwithstanding all my pains to get the best. This prevented my making a disposition, adequate to the force with which the Enemy attacked us on the right; in consequence of which the troops first engaged, were obliged to retire before they could be reinforced. In the midst of the attack on the right, that body of the Enemy which remained on the other side of Chad's Ford, crossed it, and attacked the division there under General Maxwell who, after a severe conflict, also retired... Though we fought under many disadvantages, and were from the causes, above mentioned, obliged to retire, yet our loss of men is not, I am persuaded, very considerable, I believe much less than the enemy's. We have also lost about seven or eight pieces of cannon.

Notwithstanding the misfortunes of the day, I am happy to find the troops in good spirits; and I hope another time we shall compensate for the losses now sustained. The Marquis La Fayette was wounded in the leg, and Genl. Woodford in the hand.

History has rightly given the victory to Howe but has failed to second Chastellux's award of laurels to Washington for his placement of troops. The American army that fought at Brandywine had not read the future verdicts and many thought they had won against a much larger British army. Their morale was high. This was unlike the battle of Long Island where the army thought it was worse beaten than it was and despair caused nearly a third of the troops to desert. Casualties for the British were under six hundred, and for the Americans around one thousand. The wounded Lafayette, who had just passed his twentieth birthday, emerged as a hero to the Americans.

On September 13 Washington issued a general order from Germantown: "The Honble. Congress, in consideration of the gallant behaviour of the troops on Thursday last, their fatigue since and from a full conviction they will manifest a bravery worthy of the cause they have undertaken to defend, having been pleased to order thirty hogshead of rum to be distributed among them... the Commander in Chief... orders the Commissary... to deliver to each officer and soldier, one gill [4 oz.] per day, while it lasts."

Congress and Washington had given much thought to the defenses of the Delaware River and here French engineers were most helpful. Washington had no more continentals to spare for the river's defense and informed Congress that militia would have to be used. While watching Philadelphia, he also kept an eye on the Hudson. As soon as Sir Henry Clinton made a sortie into New Jersey, he asked Putnam to dispatch reinforcements to the state. At the same time he warned him they might also move up the Hudson and Putnam could not be "too vigilant."

Washington reported to Congress on September 15 that Howe and the main body of the British were at Dilworth, "not far from the field of Action where they have been busily employed in burying their Dead." He added that he was moving northwest and would recross the Schuylkill to prevent the enemy "from turning our right flank, which they seem to have a violent inclination to effect, by all their Movements."

This letter referred also to the case of General Sullivan, who had conducted an earlier and abortive raid on Staten Island. At that time Congress had suggested a court-martial for him. Now, much annoyed at his failure to spot Cornwallis' flanking move at Brandywine, Congress ordered Washington to hold the court. The commander had been adopting an increasingly tough approach to Congress; he firmly said this was impossible. "We are now most probably on the point of another Action, and to derange the Army by withdrawing so many General Officers from it, may and must be attended with many disagreeable, if not ruinous, Consequences... How can the Army be possibly conducted with a prospect of Success, if the General Officers are taken off, in the moment of Battle?... I am obliged to observe... that I cannot be answerable for the consequences."

A near-battle with the British the next day failed to materialize when heavy rains poured down on both armies. Much of Washington's ammunition was made useless, and he marched his men to the powder magazine at Warwick Furnace. From there the army moved towards Valley Forge. An American detachment stationed at Paoli under General Wayne was routed when British troops caught them in ambush. By this time Howe had moved to White House Tavern, west of Philadelphia.

On September 18 Alexander Hamilton urgently warned Congress that Howe was able to send troops into Philadelphia in greater force than any militia stationed there and its members should leave the capital. Aroused between midnight and three in the morning, they fled the city angry and dispirited. Their chagrin they later took out on Washington. John Adams let out a bellow in his diary of September 21. This has often been quoted for its blast at Washington, usually omitting his even more bitter comment on Gates in the north. Adams criticized Washington for his false alarm (the British did not occupy Philadelphia until September 26) and for maneuvering his army very injudiciously. He remarked that a brigade from him, along with the town's militia, could have cut Howe's army to bits. Adams added that he thought Gates was acting "the same timorous, defensive Part, which has involved us in so many disasters.—Oh Heaven! grant Us one great Soul!" Congress, after its dispersion, settled first at Lancaster and then York, where Adams complained that their quarters were too crowded. Not long afterward, he requested and was given leave by Congress. He went home intending to resign.

Before leaving, Adams informed everyone that the eighteen thousand troops that Howe had brought with him were, in reality, only half that number. On his part, Washington had been putting out greatly exaggerated figures of his strength in order to fool Howe. It is doubtful that Washington succeeded with the British but he seems to have persuaded many Americans. In consequence of Adams' and Washington's statements, members of Congress and others thought Washington far stronger than Howe, and they bitterly resented his defensive tactics and the fact that he had been beaten.

To augment his army, Washington ordered reinforcements from New Jersey that had gone to the state to meet an expected attack by Sir Henry Clinton. These arrived in time to induce Washington to attack the British at Germantown. On September 19 Washington recrossed the Schuylkill. Two days later Howe moved to Valley Forge and then north along the river. Washington followed in a parallel column on the other side. Washington had two fears: that Howe would try either to turn his right flank or try to capture Reading, where the major American army stores were located. Howe's march had been a feint. He suddenly backtracked and crossed the river on September 22 to Germantown. This placed him between Washington's army and the capital. A few days later he sent Cornwallis into the city with advance troops who received many welcoming cheers from the Tories.

FREEMAN'S FARM

On the day that Congress left Philadelphia a major battle took place in the north. A few days before, Burgoyne had crossed the Hudson and moved south with his dwindling forces and supplies. He met Gates' army at Freeman's Farm, where Gates had entrenched on Bemis Heights, north of Stillwater. Gates intended to hold this position and wait for the enemy to attack, but Arnold and Morgan persuaded him to send them and their men forward on the left flank. Morgan and his crack riflemen broke up an advancing group of Indians and provincials, but they were temporarily pushed back by British regulars. Arnold came up with his troops to help and then asked for more men from Gates. These were refused and angry words were exchanged between them. German reinforcements came in and drove Arnold back. By night the indecisive battle was over, but Burgoyne received a message from Sir Henry Clinton saying he could make an attack on the Hudson Highlands to provide a diversion if Burgoyne so desired. Burgoyne asked him to do so with all urgency.

WASHINGTON MOVES

While Burgoyne waited for Clinton, and Gates for Burgoyne, Washington began a march towards Philadelphia. On September 26 he advanced from what is now Pottstown to the present town of Schwenksville. He also moved to reinforce, as fast as he could, the forts on the Delaware in order to prevent Lord Howe from coming up the river to join his brother. He informed Congress that he was having difficulty in marching his army because 10 percent of his men were barefoot. On September 28 he issued orders to the army:

> *The Commander in Chief has the happiness again to congratulate the army on the success of the American Arms, at the northward. On the 19th. instant an engagement took place between Gen. Burgoyne's army and the left wing of ours under Gen. Gates... our troops fighting with the greatest bravery and not giving an inch of ground... A detachment from the northern army under Col. Browne... have got possession of the old French lines at Ticonderoga.*

The same day he called a council of war and informed it that he would soon have about eight thousand continentals and three thousand militia. According to his best estimate, Howe had only eight thousand men at Germantown, the remainder being in Philadelphia with Cornwallis. He asked if they should now attack the enemy. The council voted ten to five against but suggested that the army move closer to them. He so informed Congress, adding his opinion that "we may count upon the total ruin of Burgoyne." He wrote to Putnam on October 1 to say that he did not think Clinton planned an attack in the Highlands because of Burgoyne's perilous situation. This was written while Clinton was preparing such an action. Washington soon learned, however, that Clinton had received reinforcements from Europe and this changed his opinion. He urgently requested the governor of Connecticut to send militia reinforcements to Putnam, from whom he had drawn a substantial force. On October 2 he issued a further order to his army: "The whole army are to strike their tents tomorrow morning at 8 O'clock, and get ready to march. At *nine* the march is to begin."

The four days from October 4 to 7 were among the most critical of the war for the American and British armies. Around fifty thousand troops of both sides engaged in battle from Pennsylvania to northern New York. The enemy, led by six British and German lieutenant generals, won two Pyrrhic field victories and lost one army. Within a few weeks the British were shut up in Philadelphia and in the area around New York City. Except for Newport with its small garrison, the rest of the country was liberated and Versailles was free to take advantage of Britain's difficulties.

GERMANTOWN — OCTOBER 4

On October 3 Washington's orders to his troops further praised Gates' successes in the north. He also mentioned a victory by the American frigate *Randolph*, which had taken four out of the five enemy ships it had met. He went on:

> *This army, the main American army, will certainly not suffer itself to be outdone by their northern Brethren; they will never endure such disgrace... Covet! my Countrymen, and fellow soldiers! Covet! a share of the glory due to heroic deeds!... Let the enemy no longer triumph. They brand you with ignominious epithets. Will you suffer the wound given to your Country to go unrevenged... The term of <u>Mercy</u> is expired, General Howe has, within a few days proclaimed all who had not then submitted, to be beyond the reach of it, and has left us no choice but <u>Conquest</u> <u>or</u> <u>Death</u>... My fellow soldiers!... Be firm, be brave; shew yourselves men, and victory is yours!*

Washington's war council now unanimously approved an immediate attack on the British forces at Germantown, which were somewhat greater than Washington's intelligence had estimated. Though his plans came fairly close to succeeding in the subsequent battle, they were nonetheless very complex for inexperienced troops and officers. Chastellux was much more critical of them than of his plan at Chadd's Ford. Accidents, ineptness, and fog threw them awry. Some idea of what they involved is shown by his orders the day before the battle:

> *The divisions of Sullivan and Wayne to form the right wing and attack the enemy's left; they are to march down the Monatany road. The divisions of Green and Steven to form the left wing and attack the enemy's right; they are to march down the Skippack Road, General Conway to march in front of the troops that compose the right wing, and file to attack the enemy's left flank. General McDougall to march in front of the troops that comprise the left wing, and file off to attack the enemy's left flank. General Nash and General Maxwell's brigade to form the corps de reserve and to be commanded by Major General Lord Stirling. The Corps de reserve to pass down the Skippack Road. General Armstrong to pass down the ridge road, pass by Leverings Tavern and take guides to cross the Wissahikon creek up*

the head of John Vandeering's mill-dam so as to fall above Joseph Warner's new house. Smallwood and Forman to pass down the road by a mill formerly Danl. Morris and Jacob Edges mill into the White marsh road at the Sandy run: thence to Whitemarsh Church, where take the left hand road, which leads to Jenkin's tavern, on the old York road, below Armitages, beyond the seven mile stone, half a mile from which turns off short to the right hand, fenced on both sides, which leads through the enemys incampment to German town market house. General McDougall to attack the right of the enemy in flank. General Smallwood and Forman to attack the right wing in flank and rear.

General Conway to attack the enemy's left flank and General Armstrong to attack their left wing in flank and rear.

Washington further wrote that each column should be within two miles of the enemy by 2 A.M. All were to attack simultaneously at five in the morning. The plan, more simply put, called for the army to march sixteen miles in the dark, two columns on main roads, and two partly across country, using rather vague landmarks. All were supposed to arrive at the same time, but one never got to Germantown, and a second reached there as the Americans began their retreat. Washington accompanied Sullivan and the left wing, perhaps because of congressional criticisms of that general's moves at Brandywine. The main army, moving along what is now Germantown Avenue, saw the sun rise as Chestnut Hill was crossed.

At Mount Airy, near Germantown, there was a first encounter with the enemy, which quickly developed into full-scale battle as British reinforcements moved up. The Americans determinedly used the bayonet, forcing a British retreat. Howe himself came up but was forced by the Americans back to Germantown. A morning mist soon turned to fog, making operations thereafter difficult for both sides. At this point of their retreat, the British, under Colonel Thomas Musgrave, got into the Benjamin Chew house on the Germantown road, quickly turning it into a small fortification.

The Americans had now to decide whether to go around or attack the house; the latter decision was made, primarily at Knox's urging. His artillery was unable to demolish a house built in the solid stone of Pennsylvania. From this point on, trouble developed for the Americans. Howe sent in further reinforcements and ordered Cornwallis to come from Philadelphia. In the meantime, Adam Stephen, Washington's mistrusted companion from the French and Indian War days, turned off from Greene's approaching column and headed for the firing. He had taken on too much rum against the morning chill and, seeing men in the fog, he ordered his command to fire on them.

They were Wayne's troops, from Sullivan's division, and they returned the fire. Each side retreated from the supposed enemy.

While this was occurring, Sullivan's men, who had carried out a major part of the attack, were running out of ammunition. They were forced to retire. Greene's fresher men took on the enemy, now reinforced by Cornwallis and his cavalry. Greene fought as long as he could, but he too had to retreat. Washington had taken personal command, exposing himself to every kind of danger, as he had often done before, but he could not rally his men. The tired army, which had marched all night and fought all morning, began its weary retreat. By noon they were at Chestnut Hill, from which they moved on twenty miles to Schwenksville.

Green forces had done well in attacking, without hesitation, well-led professionals and they had scented at times the near-proximity of victory. Americans killed, wounded, or missing totalled around one thousand, although the losses included a fair number of deserters. Each side had a general officer killed. Four days later, Howe expressed his opinion of the battle by writing urgently to Sir Henry Clinton in New York to send down four thousand reinforcements. Two weeks after that he pulled his army back from Germantown to Philadelphia and began to erect fortifications.

Washington's report to Congress on the following day is nearly as complicated as his line of march. His summary conclusion seems justified, for the Americans thought they had done well. Washington went out of his way to praise Sullivan, who was on Congress' black list. He wrote:

Upon the whole it may be said that the day was rather unfortunate than injurious. We sustained no material loss of Men and brought off all our Artillery, except one piece which was dismounted. The Enemy are nothing the better by the event; and our Troops, who are not in the least dispirited by it, have gained what all young troops gain by being in Action...

In justice to Genl Sullivan and the whole right wing of the Army, whose conduct I had an opportunity of observing... I have the pleasure to inform you, that both Officers and Men behaved with a degree of Gallantry, that did them the highest honor.

On October 6 the American commander sent a note to his British counterpart: "General Washington's compliments to General Howe. He has the pleasure to return him a dog, which accidentally fell into his hands, and by the inscription on the Collar, appears to belong to General Howe."

The news of Germantown reached Versailles before that of Saratoga. Vergennes, the foreign minister, remarked to the American commissioners, perhaps with diplomatic tact, that he was much impressed that Washington could build up a brand-new army that year and then go out and attack the British. That, he said, promised everything. Congress, too, congratulated Washington for attacking the enemy.

FORTS MONTGOMERY AND CLINTON
OCTOBER 5 AND 6

The day after Germantown, a battle took place in which the British general Henry Clinton faced the American generals, George and James Clinton, for possession of Fort Clinton, which was named for George Clinton. It was the only one of the three battles of the four days in which British naval forces participated.

When Sir Henry Clinton received reinforcements from England and an appeal from Burgoyne to do something, he moved with considerable speed to establish his diversion on Gates' rear. Forts Montgomery and Clinton were located on the west bank of the Hudson near Bear Mountain, across from Fort Independence and Peekskill. Putnam was stationed near Peekskill with some fifteen hundred troops, a garrison much reduced by Washington's urgent call for men. About six hundred men were on the west bank.

Sir Henry Clinton left New York with four thousand men in troopships guarded by three frigates and moved up the Hudson. On October 5, in the same kind of fog that had belabored Howe and Washington, he landed troops on the east bank as a feint to Putnam and his main force, who retired into prepared positions. The next day, the main British force of about twenty-one hundred men landed across the river and, without too much difficulty, took the two forts. The British destroyed these and then Fort Independence across the Hudson. Clinton sent his naval forces further up the river to burn Esopus (Kingston), the temporary state capital. They retired after receiving news of Burgoyne's surrender. Soon Clinton received Howe's urgent request for four thousand troops. He abandoned the Hudson Highlands and retired to New York.

BEMIS HEIGHTS—OCTOBER 7

The battle of Bemis Heights, more widely known as that of Saratoga, took place between an American army, commanded by an Englishman of the servant class, and an English army containing six officer members of the Houses of Lords and Commons.

Gates, with all his faults, had some of the patience of Washington and a willingness to let the enemy make mistakes. He told Governor Clinton of New York that Burgoyne, whom he had known in London, was a gambler. He would wait for him to stake his all. Arnold and others violently opposed this policy, which caused further dissension between Gates and Arnold. While he waited, additional strength poured into his camps. General Lincoln's militia were north of Burgoyne, busily cutting his supply lines and setting siege to Fort Ticonderoga. Other militia forces were operating to the east and west of Burgoyne's lines in a slowly strangling network.

Burgoyne's only hope was that Sir Henry Clinton's forces, moving north to attack Gates' rear, would force him to detach troops to the south, but the Highlands were far away and Gates did not swallow the bait. Clinton's messages of encouragement to Burgoyne were captured by the Americans. Forage for his horses and food for his troops became ever scarcer. There was no longer a possibility of retreat. Burgoyne had to fight or surrender.

On October 7 the British general determined on the gambling attack that Gates had awaited for more than two weeks. He ordered out a reconnaissance force of sixteen hundred, a mixed bag of Germans and British. Gates sent in only a portion of his forces, mainly Morgan's riflemen, keeping most of his troops in reserve. Burgoyne's right was rolled back, leaving the center open. At this point, Arnold, grumbling in his tent, dashed out, got on his horse, and took command in the center and helped to drive the enemy back. British General Simon Fraser was killed by Morgan's riflemen and Gates sent more men into the attack. Gates himself stayed in his quarters, a move that gained him no honor among his fighting men. Arnold and Morgan swept into the redoubt on the British right, killing its commander. Burgoyne's casualties were 600, the Americans' 150, including Generals Arnold and Lincoln, who were wounded. Burgoyne ordered a retreat towards Saratoga.

On October 13 Burgoyne opened a parley with Gates, who was now worried about Sir Henry Clinton's moves up the river. Gates somewhat weakly accepted a convention rather than a full surrender. This allowed Burgoyne's army to return to Great Britain after agreeing not to serve again in America. On October 17 the British army surrendered fifty-seven hundred prisoners, seven general officers, and a large quantity of guns and small arms. The tonic effect on the morale of the new United States was extraordinary and Gates became a great hero.

The convention caused endless complications, with both sides claiming breaches of faith. The captured forces were expected to sail from Boston, but Howe endeavored to change this to New York. There he hoped to exchange them for American prisoners, thus saving endless time and expense to the

British in sending replacements. Although Congress could not know this, they suspected some trick and asked that the British government and king ratify the terms. With one delay and another the captured army was not returned to Europe till after the war.

Gates' deplorable actions subsequent to the battle have tended to obscure a superb aspect of his achievement. By building his strength and patiently waiting, in spite of the outrage of some of his subordinates, for Burgoyne to take rash and impetuous action, he secured the surrender of an army at a cost, in final battle, of only one hundred fifty American casualties. This feat was not duplicated by any other commander, British or American, in the war.

The enemy garrisons at Ticonderoga and elsewhere in northern New York soon retired to Canada. Clinton had brought his men back from the Highlands, leaving all of the Hudson-Champlain area from the Canadian border to Westchester County clear of the British. Howe, with the major part of his forces, including the Royal Navy, was still struggling to clear the Delaware. Washington now saw that he could get back from the north a large portion of the regiments he had dispatched to Schuyler, in order to make the northern victory possible.

THE HESSIANS AND THE AMERICANS

The Continental Army has been so often pictured as ragged and shoeless that it is sometimes forgotten that it contained a remarkably large and tough breed of men in comparison to Europeans. The Germans who served with Burgoyne were much impressed. One officer wrote: "The colonists are... big, handsome, sinewy, strong, healthy men." Another commented on the Americans at Saratoga: "Nature had formed all the fellows who stood in rank and file so slender, so handsome, so sinewy, that it was a pleasure to look at them, and we were all surprised at the sight of such a finely built people. And their size!... Quite seriously, English America excels most of Europe in respect to the stature and beauty of its men."

The Hessians who went with Howe to Pennsylvania, Maryland, and New Jersey were even more impressed with the well-stocked and fertile farms, particularly those of the Pennsylvania Germans. They also picked up some new notions of equality and freedom. While Howe was showing the old flag there, the state was displaying itself to the Germans. Desertions by Hessians and Brunswickers became increasingly common thereafter. By the end of the war, nearly 17 percent of the German army (which had cost Great Britain almost £5 million) had deserted.

COLONEL HAMILTON ON MISSION

There was no flicker of jealousy in Washington's remarks on Gates' victory, of which he and Schuyler had been the principal architects, but he was thoroughly displeased that Gates reported it to Congress and not to him. This intelligence was crucial to the operations of the army from Peekskill to Philadelphia. Gates was dilatory in sending the information, even to Congress; this upset the exiled legislators. In the excitement, they tended to overlook his casualness.

On October 18 Washington received indirect news of the victory from Generals Putnam and Clinton, and he notified Congress. He also announced it to the army, ordering small arms fired in celebration. Six days later he wrote anxiously to Congress that he had received no confirmation or communication from Gates. When that body had the northern commander's letter on October 30, Washington was informed. He immediately wrote Gates:

> *By this Opportunity, I do myself the pleasure to congratulate you on the signal success of the Army under your command, in compelling Genl. Burgoyne and his whole force to surrender themselves prisoners of War. An event that does the highest honor to the American Arms, and which, I hope, will be attended with the most extensive and happy consequences. At the same time, I cannot but regret that a matter of such magnitude and so interesting to our General Operations, should have reached me by report only.*

The letter further advised Gates that Washington was sending Alexander Hamilton north to explain the needs of his army and the enemy dispositions. If he sent them by post, the facts might reach the British. What Washington did not know was that, a few days before, Gates had received a letter from Brigadier Thomas Conway, the Irish officer admired by John Adams. This letter followed the old Reed–Lee argument that Washington was weak and incompetent, and served further to minimize Gates' already feeble desire to cooperate with his commander in chief.

Hamilton, only twenty-two, had the disagreeable task of negotiating with the fifty-year-old Gates, now exalted into eminence. In doing so, he displayed some of the same toughness and resourcefulness that Washington had once displayed as a twenty-one-year-old emissary to the French. While Hamilton was en route north, Congress voted Gates a gold medal and limited the number of troops Washington was permitted to draw from him.

On arriving at Peekskill, Hamilton ordered continental troops under Putnam's command to march south immediately. He reported to Washington that Morgan's riflemen were already on their way. The more delicate task began at Albany. From there, about November 6, he wrote that Gates was very uncooperative. He had told Hamilton that the intelligence that additional troops were being sent from New York to Philadelphia was unconfirmed; Sir Henry Clinton might again come up the Hudson, and he had to defend New York and New England. Hamilton added that he had done all he could, without avail, to persuade Gates: "I felt the importance of strengthening you as much as possible, (but) on the other hand I found insuperable inconveniences in acting diametrically opposite to the opinion of a gentleman whose successes have raised him to the highest importance. General Gates has won the intire confidence of the Eastern States; if disposed to do it, by addressing himself to the prejudices of the people he would find no difficulty to render a measure odious... General Gates has influence and interest elsewhere."

Gates finally agreed to send a brigade. Hamilton wrote him on November 5: "By inquiry, I have learned that General Patterson's brigade, which is the one you proposed to send is by far the weakest of the three now here." After further discussion, Hamilton got Gates to add Glover's brigade to those ordered south. When Hamilton got to the Highlands, he wrote Washington that he found that Putnam had been negligent in sending on continental troops, since he had in mind an attack on New York. At the advice of Governor Clinton, Hamilton ordered Putnam "in the most emphatic terms" to send the troops. He added that he had written Gates again, giving him a full account of the situation in New York and the departure on November 5 of troops from the city to aid Howe against Washington. By this, he said, he hoped to "extort from him a further reinforcement... I doubt whether you would have had a man from the Northern Army, if the whole could have been kept at Albany, with any decency."

While Hamilton had got brigades from Gates and hurried on the men from Putnam's command, the bulk of them did not arrive in time to keep Howe from smashing the Delaware fortifications. On the trip Hamilton learned of the existence of a Gates faction that was opposed to Washington. This he duly reported to his commander. Washington always remembered that Hamilton had done his duty very well on this occasion.

HOWE OPENS THE DELAWARE

Though he had occupied the American capital and received his additional troops from Clinton, Howe was still in a dangerous position. His brother's ships were cut off from Philadelphia by American forts on the Delaware while the city was besieged by the rebel army. Washington thought that if northern reinforcements arrived in time, he could force Howe out of Philadelphia by holding the river forts, but his troops present were too few to do this for more than a brief period.

In early October Lord Howe's fleet moved up the Delaware to cooperate with Sir William. On October 21, Count Carl von Donop led some two thousand Hessians against Fort Mercer on the Jersey side. Its commander was Colonel Christopher Greene, the general's cousin, who had only four hundred men. Before the attack was over, Americans had killed or wounded an equal number of Hessians including von Donop, their commander, who later died of his injuries. Two British warships went aground and were blown up the next day by the Americans. The strong defense delayed the British advance. Not for a month could the enemy bring up enough naval and armed forces to destroy Fort Mifflin on Mud Island and to clear the river for the Royal Navy. On November 22 the Americans evacuated Forts Mifflin and Mercer; the Howes had control of the access by sea.

Just as the forts fell, the most important of the northern regiments reached the Philadelphia area. On November 26 Washington wrote his brother John "Had the reinforcement from the Northward arrived but ten days sooner it would I think have put it in my power to have saved Fort Mifflin which defended the Cheveaux de Frieze, and consequently have rendered Philadelphia a very ineligible situation for them this winter."

On November 25, with added forces, Washington proposed an attack on Philadelphia but the great majority of his general officers strongly opposed such a risk. General Knox was among those who voted against it. Knowing that Washington was being severely criticized for waiting tactics, he wrote to him on November 26 that he was certain his reputation would not suffer if he avoided rash action. He added: "I know to the contrary, the people of America look up to you as their Father, and into your hands they entrust their all, fully confident of every exertion on your part for their security and happiness and I do not believe there is any man on earth for whose welfare there are more solicitations at the Court of Heaven, than for yours."

On December 4 Howe moved with most of his army from Philadelphia to Germantown, to tempt Washington into battle. Although his forces were far larger, he did not himself try to attack the rebel positions, which, he concluded, were too strongly entrenched. Howe's ploy failed, and he returned to spend the winter in Philadelphia. The Americans then had to decide where to station their men.

On the day that Howe suffered his disaster at Fort Mercer, he forwarded to London his resignation as commander in chief of the British forces in

America. He did not say that he had been continuously outmaneuvered by Washington for more than two years, but he complained that he had never had sufficient forces and support from Britain. This was a tacit admission that he could not beat him. The battle of Brandywine was the last time in the war that a British army attempted to attack Washington and his army.

LAFAYETTE GETS A COMMAND

Lafayette, after being wounded in the leg at Brandywine, was taken to Bethlehem where he was cared for by Moravian sisters. On October 16 he wrote his wife: "Let us talk then of the wound... The surgeons are astonished by the promptness with which it healed. They go into ecstacies every time they dress it, and pretend that it is the most beautiful thing in the world. That depends on taste." Lafayette added that he was getting the best of care thanks to the orders of General Washington, "that inestimable man, whose talents and virtues I admire." He told his wife to explain to everyone in Paris that Washington's army had been much smaller than Howe's but that he would soon retake Philadelphia.

While Lafayette was recuperating, Conway came to see him and told him how marvelous Gates was as a soldier. Lafayette sent Gates a letter of congratulation, noting that he was anxious to meet him. This was Conway's opening move to maneuver Lafayette into an anti-Washington position, but the young Frenchman was too clever to be trapped.

Lafayette, not fully recovered, returned to Washington's army and begged to join General Greene, who was protecting southern New Jersey from Cornwallis. There he asked Greene to let him go on a reconnaissance mission to Gloucester. As Washington reported to Congress on November 26, Lafayette was "not inactive" there. He quoted a letter from Greene to himself of the same date:

> *The Marquis with about 400 Militia and the Rifle Corps, attacked the Enemie's Picket last Evening, killed about 20, wounded many more and took about 20 prisoners. The Marquis is charmed with the spirited behaviour of the Militia and Rifle Corps. They drove the Enemy above half a Mile and kept the ground till dark. The Enemeys Picket consisted of about 300 and were reinforced during the skirmish. The Marquis is determined to be in the way of danger.*

Lafayette's action had, in fact, brought out Cornwallis and much of the British army to save the fleeing Hessians. Darkness made both sides withdraw.

Lafayette added to his éclat by sending a modest little note to the new president of Congress, Henry Laurens: "I was there almost nothing but a witness, but I was a very pleased one in seeing the behavior of our men."

Washington had issued general orders on November 20 appointing Lieutenant John Marshall to be deputy judge advocate and James Monroe to be aide to General Stirling. The orders also approved the court-martial verdict cashiering Adam Stephen for misbehavior at Germantown.

Lafayette had strongly urged Washington to give him a line command and threatened to return to France unless he got it. His social and political connections there were such that this would have been unfortunate. Now that he had proved his devotion at Brandywine and in New Jersey, Washington recommended to Congress that Lafayette be given his command. Congress responded enthusiastically and on December 4 Washington issued orders: "Major General, the Marquis La Fayette is to take the command of the division lately commanded by General Stephen." It was fitting that Lafayette, who tried to emulate Washington, should command Virginia troops.

DUCHÉ AND HOPKINSON

On October 15, two days before Burgoyne's surrender, Washington received a letter from Jacob Duché, an Anglican clergyman of Philadelphia, who had been chaplain to Congress. He wrote: "Your harbours are blocked up, your cities fall one after another; fortress after fortress, battle after battle is lost. A British army, after having passed almost unmolested through a vast extent of country, have possessed themselves with ease of the capital of America. How unequal the contest now! How fruitless the expense of blood!" Duché attacked Congress, referring to its members as "dregs," adding that America had no navy, while the army had let Washington down. With Great Britain united, there was no further hope for the cause. He asked Washington to negotiate an accommodation "at the head of your army... 'Tis to you, and you alone, your bleeding country looks... May Heaven inspire you." Washington, calling it a "ridiculous, illiberal performance," sent the letter to Congress. Duché's brother-in-law, Francis Hopkinson, a Signer, was shaken by the plea. On November 14 he forwarded an open letter to Washington, which he asked to be forwarded to Duché:

> *Words cannot express the grief and consternation that wounded my soul at the sight of this performance. You have by a vain and weak effort attempted the integrity of one whose virtue is impregnable to the assaults of fear or flattery; whose judgment needed*

not your information and who, I am sure, would have resigned his charge the moment he found it likely to lead him out of the paths of virtue and honour.

Although Duché had gone over to the Tories and Hopkinson remained a patriot, both looked to Washington as the one man to save the country. This was increasingly the national opinion, but there were those ready to increase their denunciations of Washington for timidity, indecision, and incompetence. Their deadliest attacks were to be made while he kept together his half-starved army at Valley Forge.

TWENTY-THREE

BITTER WINTER

1777–1778

W HILE WASHINGTON AND his staff were settling into a crowded
Valley Forge farmhouse, the palaces at London, Versailles, and
Madrid churned with the news from the wilderness. Philadelphia's
fall was depressing to Franklin, whose town it was, but he put on a good front
for the French as he received Vergennes' congratulations for Germantown. The
news of Burgoyne's capture reached Paris on December 4, a day or two after
London had the news. The French, who had been waiting for just such an event,
moved quickly. Two days later Conrad Alexandre Gérard, an official of the foreign ministry who was to be the first diplomatic representative to the United
States, called on Franklin. He asked the Americans to resubmit their earlier proposal for a treaty of alliance. On December 17 Vergennes informed Franklin
that the French government would accept the treaty but would not formally ratify it until Spain had expressed its opinion. From December to March Franklin
received an extraordinary number of callers from London offering whatever he
wanted if America would choose anything but independence.

On February 6, 1778, France and the tiny new nation, its Congress in exile,
signed the treaty. On March 20 Franklin, cheered by all Paris, formally called
on Louis XVI, a scene too well known to need another telling.

For George III this was a trying winter but he bore it with a fortitude worthy of a better cause. Parliament had been in an uproar even before Saratoga.

Governor Pownall, who had accurately forecast events, told Parliament: "I tell this House and this Government that the Americans never will return to their subjection to this country." Pitt was in a fury in the Lords over the use of Hessians and Indians as allies:

> As to conquest, my Lords, it is impossible! You may swell every expense and every effort, still more extravagantly; pile and accumulate every assistance you can buy or borrow; traffic and barter with every little prince that sells his subjects to the shambles of a foreign Prince; but your efforts are for ever vain and impotent... If I were an American, as I am an Englishman, while a foreign troop was landed in my country, I never would lay down my arms—never—never—never!

> But, my Lords, who is the man that—in addition to these disgraces and mischiefs of our army—has dared to authorize and associate to our arms the tomahawk and scalping-knife of the savage?... My Lords, these enormities call aloud for redress and punishment... [They are] a violation of the Constitution... They shock every sentiment of honour.

On December 1 Lord George Germain reported to the king that Washington's army was "still in force" and that Sir William Howe, claiming he had had insufficient support from home, wanted to resign. The next day Lord Sandwich forwarded the "unpleasant accounts" of Saratoga. When the news was reluctantly announced in Parliament, the Whigs turned on the ministers with such scorn that Lord North was moved to tears. Two days after receiving the news, the king, who had a sense of military strategy, told North that henceforth British military activity in America would have to be defensive. George III dismissed the capture of Philadelphia as of little significance. The king gave more tribute to Washington than he intended, for it had been only fifteen months since the latter had said that the Americans would have to fight a defensive war. That same day Lord North gave his first hint to the king that it would be better if he resigned. On December 18 the king received news of the success at Mud Island. This offered him a brief ray of hope that Howe would be able to defeat Washington in a general engagement.

When Parliament met on January 20, the government lost a vote on a motion to call for papers relating to the failure of Burgoyne's expedition. The opposition split on the question of American independence, Pitt being against and Lord Rockingham for it. British recognition of independence was the only way in which a long and expensive war with France could have been averted. North was in a dilemma. The king had recognized that America could not be conquered unless Great Britain redoubled its efforts, and this could not be done with France ready to go to war. The strain on North was such that he wrote the king that "the anxiety of his mind for the last two months [has] deprived Lord North of his memory and understanding... The whole of this matter had been an additional proof to Lord North of his incapacity for the high and important office in which he has been placed. A pacifick proposition appears to him necessary both for this country and America." He again strongly suggested that he retire.

Although Lord North had been wholly on the king's side in willingness to crush America, by January 1778 he realized that the policy had been fruitless. There began a long struggle between North and the king over his retirement that did not end until 1782. The king cajoled, threatened, praised, and bribed Lord North to keep him. He appealed to his "honour," a word that did not have quite the same connotation to the king as it did to Washington. North, often weary and embittered, continued in office at the command of a king who had the hand but not the heart of his prime minister. George III was just clever enough a politician to realize that war with France would be much more popular than war with America. He was correct since many of the Whigs and others who opposed the American policy heartily joined him in fighting the trans-channel enemy. The king reluctantly agreed that North should introduce measures in Parliament to pacify America so that Britain could concentrate its forces against France. If that country were beaten, any concessions to America could be quickly scrapped.

On February 17 Lord North rose in Commons to say: "The forces of Washington are not sufficient to make him quit his defensive plan. Our army is great, our navy is great, our men in health, in spirits, and well supplied; but the resistance of America is greater, and the war has lasted longer, than was at first apprehended." He added that the government was prepared to grant everything that America had asked for—in 1775. The tea and other taxes were to be repealed, many concessions were to be made, and commissioners were to go to America with the usual power to grant pardons. (The offer of pardons always irked Americans. Governor Trumbull of Connecticut said they needed to ask God for pardon every day but they needed none from the English king.) After North introduced these proposals, Charles James Fox rose to ask if Lord North knew that the Americans had signed a treaty with France. Fox suggested that Versailles had beaten North by ten days and the house was in an uproar. Walpole made his usual tart comment: "Such... criminality, ignorance and incapacity in the Ministers has never been equalled." Even the bills introduced by North stated that nothing signed by the peace commissioners would be binding unless ratified by Parliament. This maintained the principle over which America had revolted.

The bills passed handily but everyone knew their chance of succeeding was slim. With the prospect of war with France, the British nation almost to a man called for Pitt, who had once before led Britain to victory. When North suggested him to the king, George III answered: "No advantage to this country nor personal danger can ever make me address myself for assistance either to Lord Chatham or any other branch of the Opposition honestly I would rather lose the Crown." To the king's great relief Pitt died soon afterwards.

The treaty with France made Britain hurry the peace commissioners to America. They were instructed to head off the French envoy and prevent ratification of the pact. A remarkably ill-assorted mission was chosen. Lord Carlisle, its chairman, was a macaroni, gambler, and poetaster. William Eden had been head of the secret service, while George Johnstone was a naval officer who had been governor of West Florida. Secretaries, servants, wine, and mountains of baggage accompanied them. The expedition brought John Wilkes' comment: "To captivate the rude members of Congress, and civilize the wild inhabitants of an unpolished country, a noble peer was very properly appointed chief of the honourable embassy. His lordship, to the surprise and admiration of that part of the new world, carried with him a green ribbon, the gentle manners, winning behaviour, and soft insinuating address of a modern man of quality and a professed courtier. The muses and graces with a group of little laughing loves were in his train, and for the first time crossed the Atlantic."

As the peace commissioners sailed up the Delaware they were fired at from every point. They did not know that orders to abandon Philadelphia had already gone out from London. By the time they arrived, the British forces were packing and Congress had ratified the French treaty.

On March 17, Madame de Lafayette's uncle, the French ambassador in London, handed a note to the foreign secretary. It was couched in the bantering Shakespearean humor of the dauphin's gift of tennis balls to Henry V. The note declared that, in view of the good relations between the two countries, France was pleased to forward information that Great Britain would find "interesting." Since the United States of America were "in full possession of their independence," France had concluded a treaty of friendship and commerce with them. Inasmuch as the United States had reserved the right to negotiate such treaties with other countries, the note suggested Great Britain might approach the Americans, requesting a similar pact.

PENNSYLVANIA AND THE ARMY

Pennsylvania, the most Tory or neutral state, gave Washington the least help of any. In writing to his brother John on October 17, he said: "This State acts most infamously, the People of it I mean as we derive little or no assistance from them." On the same day he complained bitterly to the president of the Pennsylvania council, Thomas Wharton, Jr., that, although the main British army was in Pennsylvania and had occupied the capital, the state's continental regiments were less than half full. Only twelve hundred of the local militia had come to his aid. He pointed out that Pennsylvania was the richest and most populous of the northern states but was doing far less for him than New England had done for Gates. While he did not mention that most of the continental troops on the river defenses were from Rhode Island, he wrote his brother that Virginia had as many troops in the state as Pennsylvania.

Nothing pained the Quaker general, Nathanael Greene of Rhode Island, more than the attitude of the Pennsylvania Quakers. He was exasperated by their eagerness to provide food and provisions to Howe for gold and silver, their refusal of continental currency, and their lending money to Howe. Washington complained that, in some areas of the state, he could get no help or information from the inhabitants, while some of them went out of their way to give information to the enemy. Howe's victory at Brandywine was in part owing to the intelligence he was able to obtain from local citizens.

Pennsylvania might have been last in war but it was first in criticism. When the decision was taken to send the army to Valley Forge, the state's legislature complained angrily that the army was retiring to winter quarters, away from battle, leaving the state to be ravaged. In fact, Washington had reluctantly chosen this site as the nearest defensive post to Philadelphia, even though it was in an area short of supplies. Three days after he received the letter from Congress, December 20, he wrote a reply from Valley Forge designed to take the skin off the senders.

We have, by a field return this day made, no less than 2898 Men now in Camp unfit for duty because they are bare foot and otherwise naked... Our whole strength amounts to no more than 8200 In Camp fit for duty. Notwithstanding which, and that, since the 4th Instt., our Numbers fit for duty from the hardships and exposures they have undergone, particularly on Acct. of Blankets (numbers being obliged and do set up all Night by fires, instead of taking comfortable rest in a natural way) have decreased near 2000 Men. We find Gentlemen without knowing whether the Army was really going into Winter Quarters or not (for I am sure no resolution of mine would warrant the remonstrance) reprobating the measure as if they thought Men were made of Sticks or Stones and equally insensible of frost and Snow and moreover, as if they conceived it practicable for an inferior Army, under the disadvantages I have described ours to be, which is by no means exaggerated, to confine a superior one (in all respects appointed and provided for a Winter's Campaign) within the city of Phila., and cover from depredation and waste the States of Pensa., Jersey, &ca., but what makes the matter still more extraordinary in my eye is, that these very Gentn., who were well apprized of the nakedness of the Troops from ocular demonstration… advised me near a Month ago to postpone the execution of a Plan I was about to adopt for seizing Cloathes under strong assurance that an ample supply would be collected in ten days, agreably to a decree of the State, not one article of which by the bye is yet come to hand, should think a Winters Campaign, and the covering these States from an invasion of an Enemy so easy a business. I can assure these Gentlemen it is a much easier and less distressing thing to draw remonstrances in a comfortable room by a good fireside than to occupy a cold bleak hill and sleep under frost and Snow without Coats or blankets; however, although they seem to have little feeling for the naked and distressed Soldier, I feel superabundantly for them, and from my Soul pity those miseries.

THE WINTER ENCAMPMENT

When Washington decided to move his troops to a point twenty miles from Philadelphia, he explained it to the army in general orders of December 17:

The Commander in Chief, with the highest satisfaction, expresses his thanks to the officers and soldiers for the fortitude and patience with which they have sustained the fatigues of the Campaign. Altho' in some instances we unfortunately failed, yet upon the whole Heaven hath smiled on our Arms and crowned them with signal success; and we may upon the best grounds conclude that, by a spirited continuance of the measures necessary for our defence we shall finally obtain the end of our Warfare, Independence, Liberty and Peace… Every motive therefore irresistably urges us, nay commands us, to a firm and manly perseverance in our opposition to our cruel oppressors… The General ardently wishes it were now in our power, to conduct the troops into the best winter quarters. But where are these to be found? Should we retire to interior parts of the State, we should find them crowded with virtuous citizens, who, sacrificing their all, have left Philadelphia… To their distresses, humanity forbids us to add. This is not all, we should leave a vast extent of fertile country to be despoiled and ravaged by the enemy… Many of our firm friends would be exposed to all the miseries of the most insulting and wanton depredation… These conditions make it indispensably necessary for the army to take such a position, as will enable it most effectually to prevent distress and to give the most extensive security… With activity and diligence Huts may be erected that will be warm and dry… [The General] will share in the hardships, and partake of every inconvenience.

Washington thus warned they were going to a hardship post. On December 19 the troops marched to Valley Forge and began to erect log cabins. Designed by the commander in chief, they were fourteen by sixteen feet. The supply services were disorganized; shortages of food, clothing, and fodder grew increasingly acute. On Christmas Day four inches of snow fell. That same day Washington worked on a plan for a surprise attack on Philadelphia. This was where his heart lay but the task was not possible. The capital was too well fortified and his men were as worn out as their uniforms and shoes. The general's energy had to be diverted to keeping his army alive; in this he only partly succeeded.

The winter at Valley Forge is so great a part of American life that it is worth telling again because it was worse than the legend. Typhus was common, and the scant supplies of drinking water were often polluted. From January on, heavy snows blocked delivery of supplies. The hospital and medical services were primitive and inefficient. Provisions were so scarce that, for days on end, the only food was firecake, a mixture of flour and water baked on stones. Twenty-five hundred or more soldiers died that winter. Fodder was so scarce that some five hundred horses died and could not be buried in the frozen ground. Some two thousand men decamped to the British and took the king's oath. Most were foreign born, the majority Irish. The remaining soldiers who lived stayed on in camp, to the amazement of the French officers, including Lafayette.

Joseph Galloway, Tory superintendent of police in Philadelphia, prepared a memorandum for George III in January 1779 during the British occupation. In it he took pride in the degree to which Pennsylvania had cooperated with the British. He estimated that Philadelphia had nearly 26,000 inhabitants who had not fled the city prior to Howe's arrival. "The above number of 25,767 People with the British Army and Navy supposed in the whole to amount to near 55,000 persons were fed and supplied with all manner of fresh provisions and every other necessary that the Country usually produced in great plenty by the well affected Inhabitants from without Sir William Howe's Lines; though Washington's Patroles and Picquets continually cirrounded these Lines… At the same Washington's Army both Foot and Horse were starving."

On the last day of 1777 Washington wrote to the governor of New Jersey: "Our difficulties and distresses are certainly great and such as wound the feelings of Humanity. Our sick naked, our well naked, our unfortunate men in captivity naked!" Five days later one of his officers, John Brooks, wrote to a friend in Massachusetts:

> *You make me smile when you observe that you are not so sanguine about matters in this quarter at present as you were. My dear friend, whatever made you sanguine?... Could a large superiority of numbers on the side of Mr. How through the whole campaign have made you sanguine?*

> *...For a week past we have had snow, and as cold weather as I almost ever knew at home. To see our poor brave fellows living in tents, bare-footed, bare-legged, bare-breeched, etc., etc., in snow, in rain, on marches, in camp... is really distressing... Another thing which has been the occasion of much complaint is the unequal distribution and scanty allowance of provisions... The cursed Quakers and other inhabitants are the cause of the latter... Our regiment has never received but two months pay for twelve months past... In my opinion nothing but virtue has kept our army together...*

> *The States of Pennsylvania and Maryland do not seem to have any more idea of liberty than a savage has of civilization... They have ever supposed (till wofull experience taught them otherwise) that the King's troops were as kind, mercifull and just as they represented themselves to be. But now the tone is altering fast. Even some of the Thees and Thous, who have had their wives ravished, houses plundered and burned, are now ready... to take their arms and oppose them.*

THE CONWAY CABAL

The ill-bred Thomas Conway comes down in history with his name attached to a plot against Washington. The paradox arises because Conway was to complain of the cabal that, in the end, formed against him. This included nearly the whole of Congress and the army.

Two strands of thought, the first developed by John Adams and the second by Joseph Reed, met and fused in the cabal. Conway, described by Washington as an "incendiary," tossed a match into highly flammable material.

Although no trace of complaint of John Adams by name can be found in Washington's reports and papers, it is clear that, as head of the board of war, he was a considerable cross. When Adams issued his directive of September 1776 to Washington to "Call his troops in every day and discipline them," he was much hurt by Washington's tart reply. He sent a lengthy complaint to Colonel William Tudor that there were imperfections in the American generals and any indiscipline or cowardice among the men was the fault of the officers. He mentioned to Tudor the need for a great mind in the army. On October 1, 1776, he wrote to Colonel Hitchcock that the army was mismanaged. By February 1777, Adams was complaining to Congress of the "superstitious veneration that is sometimes paid to General Washington." In the summer he praised Conway and other troublesome foreign officers. In October Adams spread the word that Howe had only half the number of troops that he had, in reality, brought to Pennsylvania and that Washington was acting in a timorous and defensive way. On October 26 he wrote his wife that he was pleased that Gates' victory at Saratoga had not been "immediately due to the commander in chief. If it had been, idolatry and adulation would have been unbounded; so excessive as to endanger our liberties."

Just before the battle of Trenton, Joseph Reed informed Dr. Benjamin Rush that all the troubles of the army were the fault of Washington, who was not fit to command a regiment. He had written to Washington, as he had to Lee, that he was too much influenced by men of inferior judgement. Reed, in turn, knew Conway, and it is of some significance that Conway also wrote to Washington to complain that he had a "confidence in men who are much inferior to you in judgement."

Charles Lee had blasted Washington to Gates, declaring America's counsels "weak to the last degree." Gates refused thereafter to serve directly under Washington, and he told Benjamin Rush that Patrick Henry had declared him to be unfit for his job. Thomas Mifflin, the army's quartermaster, had, in turn, been miffed with him for neglecting Philadelphia's defense, when he was uncertain where Howe would land, and for criticizing the management of his department. Mifflin spent little time with the army, and the supply services broke down.

In the middle of this backbiting, the battles of Brandywine, Germantown, and Saratoga took place; Congress fled to York; and Philadelphia fell to the enemy. General Conway thereupon tossed his match. In a letter to Gates praising his leadership, Conway wrote a strong critique of Washington's generalship. Gates cordially responded that his views seemed to confirm reports he had from others. Gates was not very discreet in showing Conway's letter around camp, and word of it soon reached Pennsylvania. Gates mentioned to General Morgan at Saratoga that there was great dissatisfaction with Washington, and many officers had threatened to resign unless he were replaced. Morgan, however, told Gates never again to bring up such a subject, for he would serve under no other commander in chief.

While this was going on, Dr. Benjamin Rush was active in Pennsylvania. Having heard of the Conway correspondence, he added his own criticisms in an October 13 letter to John Adams: "We lost a city, a victory, a campaign... General Conway wept for joy when he saw the arder with which our troops pushed the enemy from hill to hill... But when he saw an officer low in command give counterorders to the Commander in Chief... his distress and resentment exceeded all bounds. For God's sake do not suffer him to resign... He is moreover the idol of the army... Some people blame him for calling some of *our generals* fools, cowards, and drunkards... But these things are proofs of his integrity... Be not deceived, my dear friend. Our army is not better than it was two years ago." Eight days later Rush followed with another letter to Adams:

> *General Gates' unparalleled success gave me great pleasure, but it has not obliterated the remembrance of the disorders I have seen in the army in this department... I have heard several officers who have served under General Gates compare his army to a well-regulated family. The same gentlemen have compared General Washington's imitation of an army to an unformed mob. Look at the characters of both! The one on the pinnacle of military glory... the other outgeneraled and twice beated, obliged to witness the march of a body of men only half their number through 140 miles of a thick-settled country, forced to give up a city the capital of a state, and after all outwitted by the same army in a retreat...*
>
> *"A great and good God," says General Conway in a letter to a friend, "has decreed that America shall be free, or [Washington] and weak counselors would have ruined her long ago."*
>
> *General Mifflin must not be suffered to resign... If he is you will soon receive a hundred others.*

Before Washington learned of Conway's critiques, he heard that Congress was considering making Conway a major general. He wrote to Richard Henry Lee on October 17: "If there is any truth in a report which has been handed to me, Vizt., that Congress hath appointed, or, as others say, are about to appoint, Brigadier Conway a Major General in this Army, it will be as unfortunate a measure as ever was adopted... I must speak plain... General Conway's merit, then, as an Officer, and his importance in this Army, exists more in his own imagination than in reality... For it is a maxim with him, to leave no service of his untold, nor to want any thing which is to be obtained by importunity... Allowing him every thing his warmest Friends will contend for, I would ask why the Youngest Brigadier (for I believe he is so) should be put over the heads of all the Eldest... This truth I am very well assured of... that they will not serve under him... These Gentlemen have feelings as Officers... All our Officers are tired out: Do not, therefore, afford them good pretexts for retiring... I have been a slave to the service: I have undergone more than most Men are aware of, to harmonize so many discordant parts, but it will be impossible for me to be of any further service, if such insuperable difficulties are put in my way."

Lee informed Washington, mistakenly, as it turned out, that he was sure Conway would not be promoted over the army's objections. On October 27, James Wilkinson, Gates' aide, passed through Reading with the victory dispatch. In what seems to have been a drinking bout, Wilkinson mentioned the Conway letter to the aide of Lord Stirling. The latter, calling it "wicked duplicity of conduct," forwarded the information to Washington. Wilkinson then went on to Congress which, upon Gates' recommendation, promoted him to brigadier. On November 9 Washington dropped a note to Conway:

Sir: A Letter which I received last Night, contained the following paragraph.

In a Letter from Genl. Conway to Genl. Gates he says: "Heaven has been determined to save your Country; or a weak General and bad Councellors would have ruind it."

I am Sir Yr, Hble Servt. G. Washington.

The effects of the note were to be out of all proportion to its length. There were quarrels, recriminations, duels, and the tarnishing of reputations. When it was all over, Washington was undisputed commander in chief of all the American armies. On November 13 he wrote to Patrick Henry: "I was left to fight two Battles, in Order, if possible, to save Philadelphia, with less numbers than composed the Army of my Antagonist, whilst the world had given us at least double. This, though mortifying in some points of view, I have been obliged to encourage; because, next to being strong, it is best to be thought so by the enemy... My own difficulties, in the course of this Campaign, have been not a little encreased, by the extra aid of Continental Troops which the gloomy prospect of our affairs in the North... induced me to spare... If the cause is advanced, indifferent it is to me, where, or in what quarters it happens."

After receiving Washington's November 9 note, Conway wrote him, repeating twice that he was governed by men of inferior judgement. At the same time he offered his resignation to Congress, which postponed action on it. He also consulted Mifflin, who sent Gates a warning that, although Conway had expressed "just sentiments," the northern commander should have been more discreet. When Wilkinson returned to his headquarters, he found Gates in an ugly temper, claiming that Alexander Hamilton had stolen letters from his files. He added that he intended to disgrace both the stealer and the receiver, Washington. Wilkinson, who had tossed out Conway's incriminating remarks over a bottle, always claimed he had no recollection of having done so. He gave Gates no information on his own actions but suggested that Robert Troup, a staff member who had been a college roommate of Hamilton, might have passed along the information. Gates wrote to Conway for help in finding out who stole the letters, and he asked which one had been copied. He also wrote to Washington on December 8: "I conjure your Excellency to give me all the assistance you can in tracing out the author of the infidelity which put extracts from General Conway's letters to me into your hands. Those letters have been *stealingly copied...* I shall have the honour of transmitting a copy of this to the President of Congress." Gates added that he did not know whether an officer or a member of Congress had given him the information.

After his victory Gates received numerous letters of congratulation, some noting the contrast, expressed by Rush, between his victories and Washington's defeats. Joseph Reed wrote that Saratoga would "enroll him with the happy few who shine in history... I have for some time volunteered with this army, which, notwithstanding the labors and efforts of its amiable chief, has yet gathered no laurels." James Lovell, head of Congress' foreign affairs committee, said: "You have saved our northern hemisphere... We have had a noble army melted down by ill judged marches... How much are you to be envied, my dear general! How different your conduct and fortune... Conway [and] Mifflin [have] resigned... This army will be totally lost, unless you come down... We want you most near Germantown... Come to the Board of War if only for a short season." Among Conway's words to him were: "What a pity there is but one Gates! But the more I see of this army, the less I think it fit for general action under its actual chiefs and actual discipline... I wish I could serve under you."

Some who wrote to Gates complained that Washington was too much idolized. Not all the criticism was of the commander in chief. Those who complained of his "council" referred mainly to his principal advisor, Nathanael Greene, whose responsibility for the loss of Fort Washington had not been forgotten. Conway, as Rush pointed out, had been publicly denouncing Washington's officers as drunks, fools, and cowards.

For some time Congress had been considering the appointment of a board of war not composed of members of Congress. This was a first step towards the organization of an executive body. Because of congressional backing and filling, the old and new boards overlapped. Gates was elected president, although he did not appear at congressional headquarters until January 1778. Mifflin was placed on it; thus, Washington had a board with two men who mistrusted him. Also on the board were Joseph Trumbull; Richard Peters, who had been secretary of the old board; and Timothy Pickering.

On December 13 Congress raised Thomas Conway to the rank of major general and appointed him inspector general. Congress soon received the protests of brigadiers from seven states who said they represented all the brigadiers in the army. Their dissent was approved and forwarded by Major General Greene. At almost the same time forty-seven colonels of the line denounced the promotion of Colonel Wilkinson.

When Washington received Gates' letter, he gave him a candid version of events, quoting exactly the correspondence he had obtained from Stirling and the information the latter had received through Wilkinson. He included a copy of his letter to Conway. He assured Gates that no one except Lafayette, outside his personal staff, had seen the correspondence, since it was his duty to conceal from the enemy all signs of internal dissensions. He expressed surprise that Gates had sent Congress a copy of his letter. He would therefore have to do the same. He continued:

> *Thus, Sir, with an openess and candour which I hope will ever characterize and mark my conduct have I complied with your request; the only concern I feel upon the occasion... is that... I have necessarily been obliged to name a Gentn. whom I am persuaded (although I never exchanged a word with him upon the Subject) thought he was rather doing an act of Justice, than committing an act of infidelity; and sure I am that till Lord Stirlings Letter came to my hands, I never knew that General Conway (who I viewed in the light of a stranger to you) was a corrispondant of yours, much less did I suspect that I was the subject of your confidential Letters; pardon me then for adding that... I considered the information as coming from yourself; and given with a friendly view to forewarn, and consequently forarm me, against a secret enemy; in which character, sooner or later, this Country will know General Conway.*

As the controversy developed, the army rallied around Washington. They showed their feelings in vigorous protests to Congress against the promotions of Conway and of Gates' favorite, Wilkinson, and in extensive correspondence. General Knox gave his opinion to Elbridge Gerry, a member of Congress from his own state: "Every military character on this continent, taken collectively, vanishes before him." General Greene wrote to his brother, Jacob: "A horrid faction has been forming to ruin his Excellency... Mifflin has quarelled with the General because he would not draw off the force to the southward last summer... before the enemy's object was ascertained... Mifflin thought Philadelphia was exposed by it, and went there and raised a prodigious clamour against the measure, and against me for advising it. But the General, like the common father of all, steadily pursued the great Continental interest without regard... to the discontents of individuals... General Conway is a man of much intrigue and little judgment." Colonel Hamilton summarized the situation to New York governor George Clinton, who had informed him in November that a plot was brewing against Washington: "All the true and sensible friends to their country, and of course to a certain great man, ought to be on the watch to counter the secret machinations of his enemies. Have you heard anything of Conway's history?... There does not exist a more villainous calumniator and incendiary." Dr. Craik, assistant director of the medical services, wrote to Washington: "Notwithstanding your unwearied diligence and the unparalleled sacrifice of domestic happiness and ease of mind which you have made for the good of the country, yet you are not wanting in secret enemies who would rob you of the great and truly deserved esteem your country has for you... The method they are taking is by holding General Gates up to the people, and making them believe that you have had a number three or four times greater than the enemy; that Philadelphia was given up by your management, and that you have had many opportunities of defeating the enemy. It is said they dare not appear openly as your enemies; but that the new Board of War is composed of such leading men, as will throw such obstacles and difficulties in your way as to force you to resign." Colonel Morgan had already declared to Gates his absolute loyalty to Washington and Stirling had shown it by his actions. General Varnum wrote to Greene: "Next to God Almighty and my country, I revere General Washington and nothing fills me with so much indignation as the villainy of some who dare speak disrespectfully of him." Mercy Warren summed it all up in telling her husband that the soldiers' toast was "Washington or no army."

Conway had been arrogant with Congress. In putting forth his claims to promotion he listed all his merits and demanded an immediate reply. Now he proceeded to handle the commander in chief in similar fashion. He informed Washington that his new rank was absolutely essential for his inspector generalship. Washington replied on December 30:

Your appointment of Inspector General... I believe has not given the least uneasiness to any Officer... By consulting your own feelings upon the appointment of the Baron de Kalb you may judge what must be the Sensations of those Brigadiers, who by your Promotion are Superceded... For my own part I have nothing to do in the appointment of Genl. Officers... nor have I any other wish on

*that Head, but that good attentive officers may be chosen, and no Extraordinary
promotion take place, but where the Merit of the Officer is so generally
acknowledged as to Obviate every reasonable cause of Dissatisfaction thereat.*

To this Conway answered the following day: "What you are pleased to call an
extraordinary promotion is a very plain one. There is nothing extraordinary
in it, only that such was not thought of sooner. The general and universal
merit, which you wish every promoted officer might be endowed with, is a rare
gift. We see but few men of merit so generally acknowledged. We know but the
great Frederick in Europe and the great Washington on this continent. I certainly was never so rash as to pretend to such a prodigious height... I do not
mean to give you or any officer in the army the least uneasiness therefore I am
ready to return to France."

Washington forwarded the correspondence to Congress, but Conway was
not through putting the commander in chief in his place. He wrote him on
January 10: "I remain in a state of inaction until such time as your Excellency
will think fit to employ me... I cannot believe, Sir, neither does any other
officer in your army believe, that the objection to my appointment originates
from any body living but from you." Washington never again wrote to Conway,
who had thus implied he was a liar. His aides, however, were livid with rage.

LAFAYETTE'S SUPPORT OF WASHINGTON

The twenty-year-old marquis moved through these troubled scenes with a sure
touch and understanding. There was nothing he was not prepared to do to
help America and Washington. From his cold hut at Valley Forge, he forwarded plans to the French prime minister on ways to hurt Great Britain. He
also sent his father-in-law, lieutenant general the duc d'Ayen, a message that
he knew would circulate at the highest court levels:

*Our General is a man truly made for this revolution, which could not be
successfully accomplished without him. I see him more closely than any man in the
world and I see that he is worthy of the adoration of the country. His tender
friendship and his entire confidence in me in regard to all military and political
subjects, great and small which occupy him, place me in a situation to judge of all
that he has to do, all that he has to conciliate and overcome. I admire him more
each day—the beauty of his character and of his soul. Certain foreigners, offended
at not having been placed, although that in no wise depended on him, and some
whose ambitious plans he was not willing to serve, certain jealous caballers, have*

tried to tarnish his reputation; but his name will be revered in all ages by all lovers of liberty and humanity.

Friend and father confessor to the commander in chief, Lafayette was equally the friend of his soldiers and dug into his own pockets to try to get them food and clothing. He was often miserable and homesick, missed his family, and wrote to Paris that Valley Forge was about as gay as a dungeon. He told his wife he wanted to go home but honor required him to stay by Washington's side. "So many foreigners... have made powerful cabals. They have tried by all sorts of traps to disgust me with this revolution and with him who is its chief. They have spread about, as much as they could, that I was going to leave the continent... The English have announced it openly. I cannot, in all conscience, make it appear that they are right. If I leave... many Frenchmen, useful here, will follow my example. General Washington would be truly grieved... His confidence in me is greater than I dare to avow, because of my age... Adieu, adieu; love me always, and do not forget for an instant the unhappy exile who thinks always of you with a new tenderness." Lafayette found the intrigues in Congress distressing and the work of Conway even more so. He poured out his feelings in a letter of December 30, 1777, to Washington:

When I was in Europe, I thought that here almost every man was a lover of liberty, and would rather die free than live a slave. You can conceive my astonishment when I saw that Toryism was as apparently professed as Whigism itself... There are open dissensions in Congress; parties who hate one another as much as the common enemy; stupid men who, without knowing any thing about war, undertake to judge you, to make ridiculous comparisons. They are infatuated with Gates, without thinking of the different circumstances, and believe that attacking is the only thing necessary to conquer. These ideas are entertained by some jealous men, and perhaps secret friends to the British government, who want to push you, in a moment of ill humour, to some rash enterprise upon the lines, or against a much stronger army.

[Conway] calls himself my soldier, and the reason such behaviour for me is that he wishes to be well spoken of at the French court, and his protector, the Marquis de Castries, is an intimate acquaintance of mine; but since the letter of Lord Stirling I inquired in his character. I found that he was an ambitious and dangerous man. He has done all in his power, by cunning maneuvers, to take off my confidence and affection for you. His desire was to engage me to leave this country... I have the warmest love for my country and for every good frenchman; their success fills my heart with joy; but, sir, besides Conway is an irishman I want countrymen who

deserve, in every point, to do honour to their country... I am now fixed to your fate, and I shall follow it and sustain it as well by my sword as by all means in my power.

Washington responded the next day:

Your favour of Yesterday conveyed to me fresh proof of the friendship and attachment which I have happily experienced since the first of our acquaintance... It will ever constitute part of my happiness to know that I stand well in your opinion... Happy, thrice happy, would it have been for this Army and the cause we embarked in, if the same generous spirit had pervaded all the Actors in it. But one Gentleman, whose Name you have mentioned, had, I am confident, far different views... How far he may have accomplished his ends, I know not, and but for considerations of a public Nature, I care not. For it is well known that neither ambitious, nor lucrative motives led me to accept my present Appointments; in the discharge of which I have endeavored to observe one steady and uniform conduct, which I shall invariably pursue, while I have the honour to command, regardless of the Tongue of slander or the powers of detraction. The fatal tendency of disunion is so obvious that I have, in earnest terms, exhorted such officers as have expressed their dissatisfaction at General Conway's promotion, to be cool and dispassionate... We must not, in so great a contest, expect to meet with nothing but Sun shine. I have no doubt but that everything happens for the best; that we shall triumph over all our misfortunes, and shall, in the end, be ultimately happy; when, My Dear Marquis, if you will give me your company in Virginia, we will laugh at our past difficulties and the folly of others.

When Gates took over as head of the war board, he and Congress went back to the old chimerical vision of the capture of Canada. Ignoring Washington, they developed another scheme for a midwinter invasion without advance planning or supplies. This expedition may have originally been intended to provide a command for Conway, but his increasing unpopularity and the marquis' renown gave Gates a chance to detach Lafayette from Washington. He was offered the command directly by Gates, with Conway to be his second. Washington refused to give Lafayette advice on what to do. The young officer leaped at this chance to revenge the British capture of French Canada. Though dazzled, he kept his head. He informed Congress that he would accept only on condition that he serve under Washington. He went to York and explained further, by a superficially naive but very clever letter to Henry Laurens, that he had Washington's permission to go to Canada, but he was surprised that he had not had the orders from the general himself. No doubt, he went on, it was ridiculous the way he sometimes misinterpreted things, for he knew Congress meant him to be directly under Washington, and in any case he would find it a much higher honor than having an independent command. Furthermore, said Lafayette, *all Frenchmen* felt exactly the same way. He also indicated he wanted Johann Kalb as his second in command, and if Congress would kindly approve all this, he would then return to camp to take leave and "the last orders of my general."

Congress might push Washington around, but Lafayette could put that body in its place. On the eve of the expected French alliance the representatives surrendered completely. That day Gates gave a dinner for the marquis followed by the usual toasts. Lafayette rose and said that they seemed to have forgotten one which he would give: "To the Commander-in-Chief of the American Armies!" Lafayette later wrote of the look of pain on some faces as the men got to their feet.

Conway was sent on ahead of the main group. Lafayette, Kalb, and several other French officers departed in the middle of the winter, with Gates' promises of all the soldiers, supplies, and money that would be waiting for them in the northern country. For fourteen days they travelled across frozen rivers and landscapes to Albany where Schuyler and Arnold told Lafayette that it was a mad scheme, for there were few soldiers and no money or supplies. Lafayette wrote to Washington: "Why am I so far from you, and what business had the board of war to hurry me through the ice and snow without knowing what I should do, neither what they were doing themselves... Your excellency may judge that I am very distressed by this disappointment... It will soon be known in Europe... I am afraid it will reflect on my reputation and I shall be laughed at." Washington replied on March 10:

> *I... hasten to dispel those fears respecting your reputation, which are excited only by an uncommon degree of Sensibility... It will be no disadvantage to you to have it known in Europe, that you had received so manifest a proof of the good Opinion and confidence of Congress... and I am persuaded that every one will applaud your prudence in renouncing a Project... in which you would have attempted Physical Impossibilities. Indeed, unless you can be chargeable with the invariable effects of natural causes, and be arraigned for not suspending the course of the Seasons... the most prone to slander can have nothing to found blame upon... Your Character stands as fair as ever it did.*

Three days later Congress authorized Washington to recall Lafayette and Kalb to commands in his army. Henry Laurens, president of Congress, wrote John Rutledge on March 11 that he remembered only three votes, in addition to his own, in opposition to "that indigested romantic scheme" but now everyone was remarking: "I never liked that Canada expedition." Its failure did not enhance Gates' reputation.

THE COLLAPSE OF THE CABAL

While this was going on, the Pennsylvania council, which had given the minimum cooperation to Washington's campaigns and the maximum criticism of his going to Valley Forge, decided that action should be taken against Howe. The state determined to organize its militia and drive Howe out of Philadelphia. Benjamin Rush busied himself with trying to persuade Gates to place his friend Mifflin at the head of the enterprise, but nothing came of this. Rush was also engaged in a quarrel with his superior medical officer and had taken his case to Congress.

While operating in this manner, Rush sent two letters to Washington, one on December 25, which he signed "With the most perfect esteem," the other February 25, which he concluded "with the warmest sentiments of regard and attachment." In between he wrote an anonymous letter on January 12 to Patrick Henry. What induced him to try to bring Henry into the coalition seems to have been Gates' remark that Henry considered Washington unfit for his command. It is certain that he never made such comment. Rush said to Henry:

> *America can only be undone by herself. She looks up to her councils and arms for protection, but alas! where are they?... But is our case desperate? By no means... The northern army has shown us what Americans are capable of doing with a GENERAL at their head. The spirit of the southern army is in no ways inferior to the spirit of the northern. A Gates, a Lee, or a Conway would in a few weeks render them an irresistible body of men. The last of the above officers has accepted of the new post of inspector general of the army in order to reform abuses. But the remedy is only a palliative one.*

In another letter to a friend Rush wrote, "A great and good God hath decreed America to be free, or the [commander in chief] and weak counselors would have ruined her long ago."

Three days later Rush wrote his wife: "As there is a rupture between General Gates and General Washington, it is feared no great things will be accomplished by this proposed army reform. Conway has banished himself from Headquarters by speaking disrespectfully of the Commander in Chief. These things occasion great uneasiness to all the true whigs, who foresee from General Washington's coolness to the two first officers in his army a

continuation of all the calamities under which we have groaned... The
Congress act a prudent part. They consult General Washington in every-
thing, but they are determined to support the authority and influence of
Gates and Conway."

Not long afterwards an anonymous document was found in the halls of
Congress demanding a change in generals and detailing many reasons for it.
When this was placed in the hands of Henry Laurens, president of Congress,
he forwarded it to Washington with a note of apology. He was an exceedingly
strong partisan of Washington but at the same time anxious to heal any split
in the army. Two weeks or so after Gates arrived in York on January 19,
Laurens informed him of some of Conway's actions, including his sarcastic
comparison of the great Washington and Frederick the Great. Gates began to
view Conway with distaste and made efforts to conciliate his commander.
Washington replied to Laurens on January 31:

> *I cannot sufficiently express the obligation I feel to you for your friendship and
> politeness upon an occasion in which I am so deeply interested. I was not unapprized
> that a malignant faction had been for some time forming to my prejudice; which,
> conscious as I am of having ever done all in my power to answer the important
> purpose of the trust reposed in me, could not but give me some pain on a personal
> account; but my chief concern arises from an apprehension of the dangerous
> consequences, which internal dissentions may produce to the common cause.*

> *As I have no other view than to promote the public good, and am unambitious of
> honours not founded in the approbation of my Country, I would not desire in the
> least degree to suppress a free spirit of enquiry into any part of my conduct that
> even faction itself may deem reprehensible.*

> *The anonymous paper handed you exhibits many serious charges, and it is my wish
> that it should be submitted to Congress; this I am the more inclined to, as the
> suppression, or concealment, may possibly involve you in embarrassments hereafter;
> since it is uncertain how many, or who may be privy to the contents.*

> *My Enemies take an ungenerous advantage of me; they know the delicacy of my
> situation, and that motives of policy deprive me of the defence I might otherwise
> make against their insidious attacks. They know I cannot combat their
> insinuations, however injurious, without disclosing secrets, it is of the utmost
> moment to conceal. But why should I expect to be exempt from censure; the
> unfailing lot of an elevated station: Merits and talents, with which I can have no
> pretensions of rivalship have ever been subject to it.*

Patrick Henry, after receiving Rush's anonymous letter, wrote on February 20 to Washington: "You will, no doubt, be surprised at seeing the enclosed letter... I am sorry there should be one man who counts himself my friend, who is not yours. Perhaps I give you needless trouble in handing you this paper. The writer of it may be too insignificant to deserve any notice... But there may possibly be some scheme or party forwarding to your prejudice... Believe me, Sir, I have too high a sense of the obligations America has to you, to countenance so unworthy a proceeding. The most exalted merit has ever been found to attract envy. But I please myself with the hope, that the same fortitude and greatness of mind, which have hitherto braved all the difficulties and dangers inseparable from your station, will rise superior to every attempt of the envious partisan. I really cannot tell who is the writer of this letter... The handwriting is altogether strange to me."

When Gates arrived in Pennsylvania, he found Washington's January 4 letter awaiting him. On January 23 he replied in the devious manner he often employed with the army's head. "[Your] letter... has relieved me from unspeakable uneasiness... The paragraph which your Excellency has condescended to transcribe, is spurious. It was certainly fabricated to answer the most selfish and wicked purposes. Conway's letter was perfectly harmless." Gates went on to say that it ought not be shown "to those who stand most high in the public esteem... Honour forbids it." He added a tortuous explanation as to why he had sent a copy of his own letter to Congress. He called Wilkinson treacherous, in having first made an unscrupulous forgery and then accusing Troup of having tipped off Hamilton. Washington delayed a reply until February 9, informing Gates that he had been engaged in more urgent business. He then demolished the victor of Saratoga:

> *It is my wish to give implicit credit to the assurances of every Gentleman but... I am sorry to confess, there happen to be some unlucky circumstances, which involuntarily compel me to consider the discovery you mention, not so satisfactory and conclusive as you seem to think it.*

> *I am so unhappy as to find no small difficulty in reconciling the spirit and import of your different Letters, and sometimes of the different parts of the same Letter. It must appear somewhat strange that the forgery remained so long undetected; and that your first Letter to me from Albany of the 8th. of Decemr. should tacitly recognize the genuineness of the paragraph in question; while your only concern at that time seemed to be "the tracing out the author of the infidelity..."*

> *Throughout the whole of that Letter, the reality of the extracts is by the fairest*

implication allowed... Your Letter of the 23d. Ulto. to my great surprize, proclaims it "in words as well as in substance a wicked forgery."

It is not my intention to contradict this assertion, but only to intimate some considerations, which tend to induce a supposition, that though none of Genl. Conways Letters to you contained the offensive passage mentioned, there might have been something in them too nearly related to it, that could give such an extraordinary alarm... If this were not the case, how easy in the first instance, to have declared there was nothing exceptionable in them, and to have produced the Letters... Concealment in an affair, which had made so much noise, tho' not by my *means, will naturally lead men to conjecture the worst... The anxiety and jealousy you apprehended from revealing the letter, will be very apt to be increased by suppressing it.*

You are pleased to consider General Conway's Letters as of a confidential nature... Permit me to enquire, whether, when there is an impropriety in communicating, it is only applicable with respect to the parties, who are the subject of them... Your not knowing whether the Letter... "came to me from a Member of Congress, or from an Officer," plainly indicates that you originally communicated it to at least one of that honorable body; and I learn from General Conway... it had been communicated to the perusal of several of its members, and was afterwards shewn by himself to three more. It is somewhat difficult to conceive a reason, founded in generosity, for imparting the free and confidential strictures of that ingenious Censor, on the operations of the Army under my command to a Member of Congress.

Washington clearly indicated that many members of Congress had seen Conway's correspondence, and it is reasonable to suppose, Congress not being very adept at keeping secrets, that Washington knew precisely what Conway had been writing and saying. Wilkinson himself later wrote to Washington that his quotation had been nearly exact. At this point, Henry Laurens, much distressed by the dispute, intervened and implored Gates to end it. Gates washed his hands of Conway in a letter to Washington:

I earnestly hope not more of that time, so precious to the public, may be lost upon the subject of General Conway's letter... I have no personal connection with him, nor have I any correspondence, previous to his writing the letter... He therefore must be responsible; as I heartily dislike controversy, even upon my own account, and much more in a matter in which I was only accidentally concerned... I solemnly declare that I am of no faction... After this, I cannot believe your

Excellency will either suffer your suspicions or the prejudices of others to induce you to spend another moment upon this subject.

Washington immediately replied: "I am as averse to controversy as any Man and had I not been forced into it, you would never have had occasion to impute to me, even the shadow of a disposition towards it... Your Solemnly disclaiming any offensive views... makes me willing to close with the desire, you express, of burying them in silence... My temper leads me to peace and harmony with all Men; and it is particularly my wish, to avoid any personal feuds or dissensions with those who are embarked in the same great National interest with myself."

Patrick Henry followed his first letter with another. Jacky Custis had called on him and told him that General Mifflin had been working against Washington. Henry said: "It is very hard to trace the schemes and windings of the enemies to America. I really thought that man its friend; however, I am too far from him to judge of his present temper. While you are facing the armed enemies of our liberty in the field, and by the favor of God have been kept unhurt, I trust your country will never harbor in her bosom the miscreant who would ruin her best supporter. I wish not to flatter; but when arts, unworthy of honest men, are used to defame and traduce you, I think it not amiss, but a duty, to assure you of that estimation in which the public hold you... I cannot help assuring you... of the high sense of gratitude which all ranks of men in this our native country bear to you... I do not like to make a parade of these things, and I know you are not fond of it; however, I hope the occasion will plead my excuse... your ever affectionate friend." Washington's responses to Henry's first and second letters were dispatched in the same outgoing mail of March 28:

Your Friendship, Sir, in transmitting me the Anonymous Letter you had received, lays me under the most grateful obligations...

I have ever been happy in supposing that I had a place in your Esteem, and the proof you have afforded on this occasion, makes me peculiarly so. The favourable light in which you hold me, is truly flattering, but I should feel much regret, if I thought the happiness of America so intimately connected with my personal welfare as you so obligingly seem to consider it. All I can say is, that she has ever had, and I trust she ever will have, my honest exertions to promote her Interest. I cannot hope that my services have been the best. But my heart tells me, they have been the best I could render...

The Anonymous Letter... Was written by Doctor Rush so far as I can judge from a similitude of hands. This Man has been elaborate, and studied in his professions of regard for me; and long since the letter to you.

My caution to avoid any thing, that could injure the service, prevented me from communicating, but to a very few of my friends, the intrigues of a faction, which I know was formed against me, since it might serve to publish our internal dissensions; but their own restless Zeal to advance their views has too clearly betrayed them, and made concealment, on my part fruitless... It appeared in general, that General Gates was to be exalted, on the ruin of my reputation and influence. This I am authorised to say, from undeniable facts in my possession... General Mifflin, it is commonly supposed, bore the second part in the Cabal; and General Conway, I know was a very Active and malignant Partisan; but I have good reasons to believe that their machinations have recoiled most sensibly upon themselves.

Washington thus accurately appraised the cabal. Its subsequent collapse can be summarized as follows.

WILKINSON

When this officer learned that Gates had attempted to make him the scapegoat of the affair, he demanded an apology for a slur on his honor. Gates replied with a tart note, enclosing a copy of Washington's letter. Wilkinson challenged Gates to a duel. According to the latter's unconfirmable version they met; Gates assured him that he had not meant it, and the affair ended with Gates in tears. Later, while Wilkinson was secretary of the war board, he asked to see Washington's correspondence with Gates on Conway. After reading it, he immediately resigned his post with the board, in a letter to the president of Congress: "After the acts of treachery and falsehood in which I have detected Major General Gates, the president of that board, it is impossible for me to reconcile it to my honor to serve with him."

RUSH

This physician carried his bitter dispute with Dr. William Shippen, Jr., to Congress but got nowhere with his complaints. He resigned in disgust at the end of January. He assured Shippen: "You have supposed that I am busy in traducing you. Far from it. I declare solemnly I feel no personal resentment against you." Before and after this note Rush wrote severe castigations of

Shippen to Washington, John Adams, Nathanael Greene, and others. He continued to make bitter comments on Washington in some of his letters but had no further role in the war. Washington was so anxious to keep dissensions quiet that, though he saw Rush on many occasions over the years, he never mentioned his letter. In 1804 Rush learned with horror that John Marshall had received it from Bushrod Washington and planned to publish it in his life of Washington. Rush protested; Marshall published it without his name, thus preserving the anonymity.

GATES

The general's behavior in the Conway affair did not increase his esteem in Congress. After the collapse of the Canadian campaign he was invited by that body to leave the board of war and place himself under the command of General Washington.

MIFFLIN

Mifflin, as quartermaster of the army, had not exercised his functions and the army suffered greatly. He resigned his commission but was persuaded to retract and go on the board of war. He was one of the principal movers of Gates' election as the board's president. After the army's roar of support for Washington, Mifflin quickly retreated and denied that he had any role in wanting to displace him. He too was taken off the board of war and put under Washington's orders. Washington was not cheered by this addition to his army. He wrote Gouverneur Morris on May 18:

> *I was not a little surprized to find that a certain Gentleman who some time ago (when a cloud of darkness hung heavy over us and our affairs looked gloomy) was desirous of resigning, now stepping forward in the line of the Army. But if <u>he</u> can reconcile such conduct to his own feelings as an <u>Officer</u> and Man of Honour and Congress hath no objection to his leaving his Seat in another department, I have nothing <u>personally</u> to oppose it, yet I must think, that Gentleman's stepping in, and out, as the Sun Happens to beam forth or obscure is not <u>quite</u> the thing, nor <u>quite</u> just with respect to those Officers who take the bitter with the sweet.*

Congress not long afterwards ordered an inquiry into Mifflin's management of the quartermaster's department, and he resigned his commission.

CONWAY

This Irishman soon had Congress and practically all the army, including Gates and the French officers, against him. The only position the inspector general could obtain was third in command of the small Canadian expeditionary force under Lafayette. When this failed, Congress ordered the two top officers to return, leaving Conway wandering around upstate New York. Conway wrote protesting letters to Congress and to Washington. The latter informed Gouverneur Morris on May 18: "I am told that Conway (from whom I have receiv'd another impertinent letter... *demanding* the comd. of a division of the Continental Army) is, through the medium of his friends, solliciting his commission again. Can this Be?" In writing Congress, Conway offered to resign if his complaints were not remedied. Morris replied to Washington: "[I] took the earliest opportunity to express [in Congress] in the very strongest terms my satisfaction my joy at the receipt of the letter from him and of consequence to assign the reasons why this event gave me so much pleasure... No opposition was made... [to] accepting his resignation."

Conway, protesting that he had not meant to resign, hurried down to York. From there he wrote to Gates, who had left the war board: "I never had a sufficient idea of Cabals until I reached this place my reception, you may imagine was not a warm one... Mr. Carroll from Maryland upon whose friendship I depended is one of the hottest of the Cabal. He told me a few days ago almost literally, that any body that displeas'd or did not admire the commander in chief ought not to be kept in the army. Mr. Carroll might be a good papist, but I am sure the sentiments he expresses are neither roman nor catholick."

Conway continued to give out sentiments hostile to Washington. In return General John Cadwalader expressed his opinion that Conway had been a coward at Germantown. Conway challenged Cadwalader to a duel and the latter shot him in the mouth. Conway recovered and hung around the United States till the end of the year. He then disappeared from American history until he turned up in Lafayette's house in Paris to claim the Order of the Cincinnati along with Rochambeau and the French officers who had won at Yorktown. Lafayette wrote Washington that he had given it to him; otherwise Conway would have claimed that there was a plot by Washington and Lafayette against him.

TWENTY-FOUR

HOPEFUL SPRING

1778

ASIDE FROM HAVING to bear the attacks of treacherous American generals and congressmen, Washington had also to manage an army and conduct a war from Valley Forge. He maintained his sense of humor although on one occasion he found it unappreciated. General William Smallwood had captured two British vessels near Wilmington, with arms, ammunition, food supplies, and a number of British officers' wives. The news of the captives made an impression in camp. Lafayette wrote his father-in-law that the wives were dreadfully afraid they were to be put to servicing the American army. Washington congratulated Smallwood and said if there were any supplies of liquor aboard, not to forget "the poor fellows" in his camp.

When the wives were released, Smallwood asked how he should account for their food rations. Washington replied on February 23: "With respect to the board of the Officers' Wives, it is a matter you must determine yourself. I imagined they had been sent to Philadelphia, soon after the prize was taken. I do not suppose that the public will suppose themselves liable for it... and it might be deemed ungenerous to make the Ladies pay it themselves... As you and your Officers only have had the pleasure of their company and conversation, I believe you must adjust the matter among you."

Smallwood replied with heavy earnestness: "Even had I have enjoyed the pleasure of their company and conversation I should not have thought myself liable... Upon reflection you must be conscious I have been fully employed in a less agreeable way [with] little relaxation and leisure to enjoy the ladies' company if I discharge my duty which I have endeavored to do."

Washington replied on March 6: "I... am sorry to find that what I meant merely as a joke, has been taken by you in a serous light. I can assure you I never had the least suspicion that any part of your time was sacrificed or your duty neglected, on account of the Ladies who fell into your hands... The Board... in my opinion properly becomes an incidental charge, to be deducted from the gross amount of the prize."

Congress and its board of war were supposed to negotiate for troops and clothing with the individual states but, as a practical matter, Washington was forced to send pleading letters to individual governors. He wrote politely on January 18 to the president of Pennsylvania, the state that had toyed with the idea of raising its own militia to capture Howe and thus show up Washington. He noted again that the state's regiments were very depleted in numbers and had little clothing. Previously he had told their officers to go out in the state to buy clothing. A committee of the state legislature asked him to desist for they had sent out commissioners for this purpose. Washington added: "What these Commissioners have done I do not know, but no clothing has come to the army thro' their hands." He suggested that, since so many of the inhabitants were staying home because of their principles, they might be able to do weaving and spinning. He also sent appeals for clothing to North Carolina, Virginia, Delaware, Connecticut, and New Jersey.

On New Year's Day 1778, Washington complained to Congress that he had long been without a quartermaster general. His first draft noted that General Mifflin had quit the post in July. He had pleaded indisposition but recovered on being offered a post on the board of war.

When a congressional committee was appointed to look into the army's problems, Washington prepared a thirty-eight-page document for them. He particularly asked for a pension plan, explaining that the men had made great financial sacrifices and that there was no provision for their families in case of disability or death. He discussed the need for more cavalry, which had proven invaluable for intelligence purposes. He proposed eighty regiments for the army with a total of forty thousand rank and file. He asked for a provost marshal, with mounted troops, for the maintenance of order and discipline, camp security, and counterintelligence. He requested an assistant inspector general for each regiment, in order to institute a uniform system of training. He complained that the congressional methods of promotion had brought so much bickering and so many resignations that he had to spend too much time on officers' grievances. The commissary department needed reorganization. The army, he said, lived "from hand to mouth if I may be allowed the phrase." The hospital department was in a deplorable condition, partly because of the lack of supplies but also because of the constant quarreling among the physicians in charge. He asked for extra pay for his engineers, who were often in great danger, building or blowing up fortifications in the face of the enemy. He wanted more riflemen for guerrilla purposes.

Many of the requests and plans Washington made were far in advance of army practices of the time, while others such as pensions were copied from the British army. In his organizational thought, he was always ahead of the country and he was now thoroughly professional. The amateur critics in Congress continued to maintain that he needed only a few thousand temporary extra militia from the farms to beat a trained and formidable enemy. His proposed pension plan aroused almost implacable opposition on the ground that it would establish a favored class in society.

By the middle of February, the army was so close to starvation that Washington was begging, in the word's most literal sense, the governors of Maryland, Virginia, Connecticut, New Jersey, and New York for food, informing them the army was naked and starving. He appealed to the loyal citizens of Pennsylvania and the neighboring states to provide what food they could to keep the army together. He sent out such fighting officers as Greene, Wayne, and Henry Lee to forage. Washington expected the army to revolt or leave him but there were only plaintive murmurings. One French officer heard a man say: "No bread, no soldier."

On March 1 Washington expressed his gratitude to those who stuck by him through the hardships: "The Commander-in-chief again takes occasions to return his warmest thanks to the virtuous officers and soldiery of the Army for that persevering fidelity and Zeal which they have uniformly manifested in all their conduct... The recent Instance of uncomplaining Patience during the scarcity of provisions in Camp is a fresh proof that they possess in an eminent degree the spirit of Soldiers and the magnanimity of patriots... Defects in the Commissaries department, Contingencies of weather and other temporary impediments have subjected and may again subject us to a deficiency for a few days, but soldiers! American soldiers! will despise the meanness of repining at such trifling strokes of adversity, trifling indeed when compared to the transcendent Prize... Glory and Peace."

On March 24 Washington announced that Major General Greene was appointed his quartermaster general. This unexpected assignment of one of his ablest general officers had taken all of the commander in chief's very persuasive powers to accomplish. Greene had remarked: "No one ever heard of a quartermaster general in history." This turned out not to be true. He handed in a brilliant performance before returning to a field command. He later wrote Washington that he had taken the job "out of compassion" for the commander in chief, who was acting as quartermaster general as well.

Washington's next problem was the army's urgent need for training and discipline. Had Conway not made so many enemies, Washington would have welcomed him for this task. In January, while he was wrestling with the Conway intrigues, he had a note from Baron Frederick von Steuben, who had arrived at Portsmouth, New Hampshire, with an introductory letter from Franklin. This described him as a lieutenant general and former aide to Frederick the Great. Steuben wrote Washington:

> *The object of my greatest ambition, is to render your country all the services in my power and to deserve the title of a citizen of America by fighting for the cause of your liberty…*

> *If the distinguished ranks in which I have served in Europe should be an obstacle, I had rather serve under your Excellency as a volunteer, than to be an object of discontent to such deserving officers as have already distinguished themselves amongst you…*

> *…I could say moreover (were it not for the fear of offending your modesty) that your Excellency is the only person under whom (after having served under the King of Prussia) I could wish to pursue an art to which I have wholly given up myself.*

Much has been made of the fact that Steuben seems to have had no higher rank than major in the Prussian army. However, the rank of lieutenant general, which corresponded with that of the English brigadier, may have been conferred on him—as his barony was—by one of the minor German courts. It is of little importance since Steuben was immediately liked by Congress and, after arriving at Valley Forge, made himself indispensable.

On February 27 Washington wrote to Henry Laurens, president of Congress: "Baron Steuben… appears to be much of a Gentlemen, and as far as I have had an opportunity of judging, a man of Military knowledge and acquainted with the World." A few days later, John Laurens informed his father that he thought Steuben would make an ideal inspector general. Training and discipline were so badly needed that, however "obnoxious" Conway had been to the whole army, it would have been better to have had him than no one. The baron was liked by everyone and it might be just the job for him. Washington's letters and orders thereafter were full of praise for Steuben's ability, zeal, cheerfulness, and intelligence. By March 8 John Laurens was writing his father: "The Baron Steuben has had the fortune to please uncommonly, for a stranger, at first sight. All the general officers who have seen him, are prepossessed in his favour, and conceive highly of his abilities."

Though Steuben was horrified at conditions in camp, he plunged into his duties with tact and understanding. As he wrote to a friend in Europe, he quickly found that American soldiers could not be ordered around as soldiers were at home. Once the need for doing things was explained to them, however, they responded with alacrity.

On March 17 Washington chose one hundred men for drilling. Steuben found an assistant, Captain Benjamin Walker, who translated for him. Soon he acquired the ability to swear a little in English, mixed with French and German, and this put the army in good humor. He had the ability to make drilling, marching, and musket drill seem like games, and those who passed through his command emerged proud of their new abilities. The army clamored to take part. Soon Washington was appointing inspectors in each brigade and ordering everyone to take the drills. Steuben himself sat up late at night composing manuals of training and discipline. Washington quickly extended the system to troops in New Jersey and Delaware. On April 30 Washington warmly praised Steuben to Congress and asked that he be appointed inspector general. On May 8 after the army had paraded in celebration of the French alliance, Washington announced in general orders:

> *The Commander in Chief takes particular pleasure in acquainting the Army that their Conduct yesterday afforded him the highest Satisfaction; The Exactness and order with which their movements were performed is a pleasing Evidence of the Progress they are making in military Improvement... The General at the same time presents his thanks to Baron Steuben and the Gentlemen under him for the indefatigable Exertions in the duties of their Office, the good effects of which are already so apparent.*

On May 9 Washington informed the army that Congress had made Steuben major general and inspector general.

An exasperated Washington had written to Congress on April 10 in reply to a resolve authorizing him to call in five thousand militia from Pennsylvania, Maryland, and New Jersey. He pointed out that he needed an army, not militia. That winter he had been able to raise fewer than one thousand militia in Pennsylvania to help him against the enemy and usually there were no more than one hundred. A congressional committee had visited him and extensively gone over his problems. They had reached agreement as to his needs but nothing happened. The committee had led him to expect that Congress would support him with forty thousand troops, but he had heard nothing further of these. His requests for pensions for officers had been ignored; many officers were so dissatisfied they had resigned. His urgent needs for "the horse establishment, Companies of Sappers, Provost Marshalseys &ca., &ca., &ca. as agreed to by the Committee, and recommended for Congress's consideration, are entirely at a stand."

Shortly afterwards he received a letter from John Banister, a new Virginia member of Congress and an old acquaintance. Banister was optimistic that Congress would establish a pension scheme for officers. Washington replied on April 21 that he was pleased but that he regretted the long delay. He added: "I find it a very arduous task to keep the officers in tolerable humour." Washington then analyzed congressional attitudes towards the army:

> The other point is, the _jealousy_ which Congress unhappily entertains of the Army, and which, if reports are right, some Members labour to establish. You may be assured, there is nothing more injurious, or more unjustly founded. This jealousy stands upon the common, received Opinion, which under proper limitations is certainly true, that standing Armies are dangerous to a State... The prejudices in other Countries has only gone to them in time of _Peace_... It is our policy to be prejudiced against them in time of _War_; though they are Citizens having all the Ties, and interests of Citizens, and in most cases property totally unconnected with the Military Line. If we would pursue a right System of Policy... there should be none of these distinctions. We should all be considered, Congress, Army, &c. as one people, embarked in one Cause, in one interest; acting on the same principle and to the same End. The distinction, the Jealousies set up, or perhaps only incautiously let out, can answer not a single good purpose. They are impolitic in the extreme... The very jealousy, which the narrow politics of some may affect to entertain of the Army, in order to assure a due subordination to the supreme Civil Authority, is a likely mean to produce a contrary effect... It is unjust, because no Order of Men in the thirteen States have paid a more sanctimonious regard to their proceedings than the Army; and, indeed, it may be questioned whether there has been that scrupulous adherence had to them by any other... [At this point in the draft letter, Washington's feelings in regard to the army got the upper hand. In redrafting it he inserted the following addition.] ...for without arrogance, or the smallest deviation from truth it may be said, that no history, now extant, can furnish an instance of an Army's suffering such uncommon hardships as ours have done, and bearing them with the same patience and Fortitude. To see Men without Cloathes to cover their nakedness, without Blankets to lay on, without

Shoes, by which their Marches might be traced by the Blood from their feet, and almost as often without Provisions as with; Marching through Frost and Snow, and at Christmas taking up their Winters Quarters within a day's March of the enemy, without a House or Hutt to cover them till they could be built and submitting to it without a murmur, is a mark of patience and obedience which in my opinion can scarce be parallel'd.

Washington went on to say that from time to time the army had remonstrated against certain measures taken by Congress. Only slaves would be denied the right to petition and Congress should not consider this as an infringement of civil authority.

Washington's remark that the legislature seemed to dislike having a standing army, when the country was at war for its liberties, was a severe condemnation of a body that was fearful of a starving army whose bare feet had bloodied the snows of Valley Forge. Washington did not need to add to Banister that he bore the brunt of the attacks, though he had gone far out of his way to support civil authorities, maintained in office only by the existence of the army itself.

It is worth noting that whereas Congress remained throughout the war as the supreme authority, the British allowed only military control in occupied areas. The single exception was thinly populated Georgia, where a royal governor was reinstalled. The American Tories frequently protested that the British did not trust them or permit them to reestablish civil government, but their complaints were ignored.

On April 22 Washington received copies of Lord North's reconciliation bills from William Tryon, last royal governor of New York, who had become a major general of Tory troops. He sent them to Congress with a letter saying that Tryon had made the "extraordinary and impertinent request" that he communicate them to his army. Congress then passed a resolution requesting the states offer pardons to all Tories who should surrender prior to June 10. Washington replied on April 26 to Tryon:

I had had the pleasure of seeing the Draughts of the two Bills... I can assure you they were suffered to have a free currency among the officers and men under my command, in whose fidelity to the United States, I have the most perfect confidence...

I take the liberty to transmit you a few printed copies of the resolution of Congress of the 23d. instant, and to request, you will be instrumental, in communicating its contents... to the persons who are the objects of its operation. The benevolent purpose, it is intended to answer, will, I persuade myself, sufficiently recommend it to your candour.

On the day he had the note from Tryon, he received a resolve of Congress that he call a general council of his officers to devise plans for the ensuing campaign. Washington had already, through memoranda circulated to his senior officers, asked their opinions whether to attack Philadelphia or New York, or to adopt a waiting policy. Very roughly (though some voted for more than one policy), a third of his generals wanted him to attack New York, a third Philadelphia, and a third asked him to wait till the army was better trained.

The resolution authorized Generals Gates and Mifflin to attend the council. Gates was ordered to the command in New York State but placed under Washington's orders. He and Mifflin were to appear at camp when directed by the commander in chief. In forwarding the resolves, Gouverneur Morris strongly suggested that his council's decisions not be sent to Congress, which could never keep a secret. This was a clear hint not to let the members interfere with military strategy. Washington was now, in fact as well as by commission, commander in chief of all the armies and his authority was never again in serious question.

JOLLITY

While the cabal was collapsing, Mrs. Washington arrived at headquarters after a long, rough trip in a blizzard. She wrote Mercy Warren on March 7: "The General's apartment is very small; he has had a log cabben built to dine in which has made our quarters much more tolerable than they were at first." A miniature of her husband made by Major Nicholas Rogers was presented to Martha that month. John Laurens wrote his father, probably reflecting her views, that he had made the general too aged. His associates thought, in fact, that he had begun to look a great deal older, but Mrs. Washington did not care to notice this.

An effort was made to keep up a little social life in the waste of Valley Forge. The army band played for the commander in chief on February 22. He gave them some of his small personal stock of hard money. There was singing in the evening over cups of tea or coffee, and this was almost the only entertainment. General Greene's wife, Kitty, could speak French and found herself a center of attraction for the French officers. She was more active in promoting the French alliance than some thought proper. Baron Steuben allowed his aides to have a dinner in his quarter, to which all American officers were invited who had not a whole pair of breeches. His aide, Pierre Duponceau, described it as a meal of tough beefsteak and potatoes, the drink "salamanders," liquor set on fire then drunk "flame and all. Such a set of ragged and at the same time merry fellows were never brought together. The Baron loved to speak of that dinner, and his sans-culottes." Mrs. Washington herself had to patch the breeches of John Laurens, the general's aide, so he could be fit for duty.

SPRING

Washington tried several times to attack British ships frozen in the Delaware. By the end of February he wrote that the thaw in the river had made this impossible. There was more snow in March, but on the twenty-third the weather began to turn warm. By the middle of April spring was in full bloom. Schools of patriotic shad raced past the British fortifications and up the Schuylkill to feed the army. The camp was thoroughly cleaned. Washington ordered his men to wash their clothes even though they were but "rags." The lean, tough, and disciplined army, which had survived the winter, had a vital élan that promised well.

On May 1 maypoles were erected throughout the camp and the day was given up to celebrating King Tammany, the old Delaware chieftain who was a symbol of resistance to oppression. The procession was led by a sergeant dressed as an Indian chief. The soldiers who wore blossoms in their hats paraded and cheered. The enlisted men were all given a drink of whiskey. In the evening the officers held a dance in honor of their own chief.

That day Washington received the news of the French alliance and immediately sent word to Congress, adding: "I believe no event was ever received with a more heartfelt joy." Although he did not announce it officially to the army until Congress had acted, his delight and gratitude clearly appeared in his general orders of Saturday, May 2:

> *The Commander in Chief directs that divine Service be performed every Sunday at 11 oClock in those Brigades to which there are Chaplains; those which have none, to attend the places of worship nearest them. It is expected that Officers of all Ranks will by their attendance set an Example to their men.*

> *While we are zealously performing the duties of good Citizens and soldiers we certainly ought not to be inattentive to the high duties of Religion. To the*

distinguished Character of Patriot, it should be our highest Glory to add the more distinguished Character of Christian. The signal Instances of providential Goodness which we have experienced and which have now almost crowned our labours with complete Success, demand from us in a peculiar manner the warmest returns of Gratitude and Piety to the Supreme Author of all Good.

Congress received the news too late for action on Saturday, and on the Sabbath it did not meet. The treaty was read on Monday, May 4, and ratified that afternoon. The following day Washington announced it to the army:

It having pleased the Almighty Ruler of the Universe propitiously to defend the Cause of the United American States and finally by raising us up a powerful Friend among the Princes of the Earth to establish our liberty and independence upon lasting foundations, it becomes us to set apart a day for gratefully acknowledging the divine Goodness and celebrating the important Event which we owe to his benign Interposition.

The French officers were smothered with congratulations and joy. The following day the whole army paraded in celebration after prayers. Two French officers, Kalb and Lafayette, were given preferred positions. The men marched with unusual precision. Thirteen cannon were discharged. The infantry then fired in a running line from right to left on the front line and from left to right on the second line. There were cheers by the whole army: "Long live the king of France" and "God save the American states." A discharge of thirteen cannon finished the ceremony. The enlisted men were given a gill of rum. All military prisoners were released and two soldiers under sentence of death were pardoned by Washington.

After the ceremony Washington gave a dinner for all his officers and such of their wives as were in camp. The army band played. According to John Laurens, Washington was given "such proofs of the love and attachments of his officers as must have given him the most exquisite feelings." The general, in fact, suddenly looked years younger. One officer noted that his face had a look of "uncommon delight." When he left the table the whole assembly rose and cheered, and as he rode off the shouts continued and hundreds of hats were flung into the air. The general returned the greetings with great waves of his hat and "huzzaed" back several times.

Throughout the country a new anthem was being sung to an old tune: "God Save Great Washington," ending with a rousing "God Damn the King."

PHILADELPHIA

The well-fed British army stayed comfortably in the nation's capital all winter. Balls, plays, dinners, and cards kept the officers contented, but some of their doings had not been previously known in quiet Philadelphia. The British and their mistresses were much frowned upon by the Quakers in whose houses they were billeted.

The previous December George III had taken no joy in the capture of Philadelphia. On March 23 he wrote North that, with a French war certain, "it is a joke to think of keeping Pennsylvania for we must form from the Army now in America a corps sufficient to attack the French Islands." It had not been an easy winter for the king. A few days before, he had written North: "I am fairly woren down."

North continued to offer his resignation so that "*new* and *able* men" could take over the government, but the king replied that North's "Honour and Integrity" were at stake. The king added that North was too diffident of himself. At this point, on March 25, Lord North, the only man in the kingdom who dared to do so, bluntly gave George III the facts:

> *From the situation of public and private credit, Lord North doubts very much whether this country can borrow for two years more… The power of borrowing has been hitherto the principal source of the greatness and weight of Great Britain.*

> *…The condition of the country as to its facilities is deplorable. It is totally unequal to a war with Spain, France, and America, and will, Lord North fears, be over match'd if the contention is only with the House of Bourbon, and, therefore, although the offence received from France is great He owns that he should be glad if an accommodation with America would prevent for the present moment, a war with France, as he thinks that Great Britain will suffer more in the war, than her enemies, He does not mean, by defeats, but by an enormous expense, which will ruin her, and will not in any degree be repaid by the most brilliant victories. Great Britain will undo herself while she thinks of punishing France.*

> *Lord North begs leave to trouble his Majesty for a moment on a disagreeable subject, but in which he is bound to speak the truth, the bad situation of affairs will with great appearance of reason be attributed to the obstinate perseverance in the American War… Ld. North's diffidence of himself is grounded upon seven years' experience, and will for ever render it fatal to his Majesty to continue him at the head of affairs. His Majesty's own sentiments will make him prefer the salvation of this country to every personal consideration, impress'd as he is, with that*

affectionate regard to his people which becomes a good Prince. Lord North having said this much, is silent, but this much he could not, with peace of mind, refrain from saying.

Lord North has received the obloquy of history but it has not been a just appraisal. At this critical stage of world affairs North appealed for reason and sanity. Had the king listened, five more years of bloodshed in America, a war with France, and the French revolution might have been averted. The king's only reply to North was that it was necessary to end the war with America "to be enabled with redoubled ardour to avenge the faithless and insolent conduct of France." To do so, he was prepared even to open "the channel of intercourse with that insidious man," Benjamin Franklin. North continued to plead to be allowed to quit, saying his abilities and memory were greatly impaired, and he could no longer continue. In the modern world North would have resigned, but in the eighteenth century the king had the means to force him to stay as he dragged his kingdom and North down to destruction. So long as the war had to continue, it was at least good for America that a halfhearted man conducted it. The king shortly thereafter made him warden of the Cinque Ports, a sinecure that added £ four thousand a year to his income.

The news that France had dispatched to America a fleet under the comte d'Estaing caused great commotion in the cabinet and in Parliament. The Royal Navy was totally unprepared for this sudden move, and the king himself went to Portsmouth to try to expedite a relief fleet. Its commander was Admiral Byron, uncle of Lord Carlisle, peace commissioner. They were the grandfather and cousin of the poet, who described Carlisle's rhyming as "paralytic puling," but wrote of Washington:

> *... The first — the last — the best —*
> *The Cincinnatus of the West, ...*
> *To make man blush there was but one!*

On May 8 the king received correct but belated reports that there had been many desertions in Washington's army and that "they are sickly and in want of cloathing, and not above six thousand in camp." Two days earlier the wholly cheerful American army had paraded in celebration of the French alliance.

On May 13 General Burgoyne arrived in England on parole. Washington had been particularly desirous that he be allowed to return since his only defense for his defeat would be to describe the overwhelming strength of the Americans. Burgoyne was not allowed a court of inquiry, for Lord George

Germain was not anxious that Parliament look into the war office. He was coldly received and stripped of the offices in which he had taken so much pride in his American proclamation: colonel of the Queen's light dragoons and governor of Fort William. He was forced to turn to producing dramas and illegitimate children. In this latter enterprise he fathered a son who became a field marshal 146 years after his father's birth.

On April 9 Sir William Howe was recalled to England. He was the second of the three unlucky generals who had arrived in Boston in May 1775 to join the unfortunate Gage. Now he and Burgoyne were on their way home to be scapegoats, leaving Sir Henry Clinton, the last of the trio, to be the final sacrificial goat offered up for London's sins. As the new commander in chief, he reached Philadelphia from New York on May 8. The following day he received the king's instructions to abandon the city and retire to New York and permitting him a further retreat to Halifax. He was informed that peace commissioners were on the way, but Clinton clearly saw that America was not likely to accept terms when the British were giving up a major post.

On the eve of General Howe's departure, the British gave him a regatta and a great ball called the "Meschianza." Letters went to London praising the glory of it. Ladies in Turkish costume were attended by knights of the blended rose and of the burning mountain who jousted in tournaments. Magnificent arches led into a ballroom decorated with 85 mirrors and 34 sconces covered with flowers and ribbons. The 430 guests dined in a brilliant supper room adorned with 56 more mirrors and more than 700 candles. Toasts were given to the king, queen, army, and navy, and to the knights and their ladies. Dancing continued till four in the morning.

In his life of Washington, Washington Irving could not restrain his contempt for "this tawdry and somewhat effeminate pageant... this silken and mock heroic display [when] the number of British chivalry in Philadelphia was nineteen thousand five hundred and thirty, cooped up in a manner by an American force at Valley Forge, amounting according to official returns, to eleven thousand eight hundred men. Could any triumphal pageant be more ill-placed and ill-timed." It was especially so for the American Tories who had been risking their property, liberty, and even lives, in order to maintain the king's cause in America. The ball, held just before the British abandoned the capital, greatly shocked them, the more so as General Howe rather casually suggested they ought to make their peace with the rebels. Joseph Galloway, according to Lord Howe's secretary, Ambrose Serle, was filled with "horror and melancholy." Serle tried to console him but noted in his diary: "Nothing remains for him but to attempt reconciliation with (what I may now venture to call) the United States of America." Less than two years before Serle had described the "villainy and madness" of the Americans for rebelling. Now he thought, as did Howe, that they had won de facto independence. Clinton, however, was now in command, and he feared that the provincial Tory troops in New York might give up unless the Philadelphia Loyalists were protected. He offered to take them to New York by ship. Since there were so many, he was forced to march the main part of his army across New Jersey and this gave Washington an opportunity for action.

When Sir William Howe saw the king on July 3 he pledged his support. George III drafted for Lord North a little memorandum of this talk: "I had a very long conversation with him... the Substance of which was his very strongly declaring nothing shall make either His Brother or Him join Opposition, but that Lord G. Germaine and His Secretaries Nox and Cumberland have everywhere loaded him with obloquy that he must therefore be allowed some means of justifying himself."

General Howe was not allowed what he thought a proper defense and he and his brother finally swung over to the opposition. Nonetheless, he lost his seat in the house at the next election, his constituents showing their disapproval of the American war and his part in it.

CHARLES LEE

The Americans had more good news on top of the French alliance. After long negotiations, they succeeded in swapping General Richard Prescott, another unlucky British general who had been captured twice, and once before exchanged, for General Charles Lee, the ranking major general of the American army.

Lee had been taken in the darkest days of the war and since then had been under strong British influence. He had a low opinion of Washington at the time of his capture, and he had not been with the army since it had acquired a wholly different spirit from that following the fall of Fort Washington.

General Lee was received in May with great ceremony by Washington, who rode out four miles from camp with his principal officers and an army band to meet him. He was given all military honors and escorted to camp, where the general and his wife gave him a splendid dinner with music. Lee soon told Elias Boudinot, Washington's commissary of prisoners, who had arranged his transfer, that he thought the army was in deplorable condition and that Washington was unfit to be a sergeant. He later told others that the army could never stand up to British professionals.

When Lee was asked to sign the oath to the United States, including a renunciation of his allegiance to George III and his successors, he put his hand on the Bible and then took it away. When asked why, he said he was glad to abjure his allegiance to George III but he had some scruples about the Prince of Wales. This was taken as a joke by the army, which knew nothing of Freudian interpretations of wit. Lee had told Sir Henry Clinton in March that he thought the war would end by negotiation and if he and Clinton were at the heads of the armies there would soon be an accommodation.

On May 3 Lee wrote to British General Robertson that America should forget about independence. After Sir Henry took command, Lee dropped him a note from Valley Forge on June 4: "General Lee presents his most sincere and humble respects to Sir Henry Clinton. He wishes him all possible happiness and health and begs, whatever may be the event of the present unfortunate contest, that he will believe General Lee to be his most respectful and obliged humble servant."

On the following day, Lord Howe's confidant, Ambrose Serle, recorded in his diary that Lee had told a member of a British flag party that "he was very unhappy in and very averse to the present course of affairs, and that he might assure Lord Howe that he had acted entirely as he had promised him and wished for nothing so much as to promote every idea of peace."

Serle, who undoubtedly reflected the views of the British high command, loathed Lee. His diary refers to him as "a damned scoundrel" and "as ill-looking a rebel in appearance as he really is." While Lee was committing treason to be on the winning side, Serle had come to a different conclusion as to their position. After learning that the British army was to abandon Philadelphia, he wrote on May 21: "I now look upon the contest as at an end."

LAFAYETTE AND BARREN HILL

Washington's spies were so active that, days before the Philadelphia Tories learned the bad news, he heard that the enemy appeared ready to abandon the city. He assigned Lafayette the command of an advanced unit of twenty-two hundred troops to proceed to Barren Hill, about half way between Valley Forge and Philadelphia. His orders of May 18 to his young commander were:

> *...To be a security to this camp and a cover to the country between the Delaware and the Schuylkill, to interrupt the communication with Philadelphia, obstruct the incursions of the enemy's parties, and obtain intelligence of their motives and designs... You will endeavour to procure trusty and intelligent spies, who will advise you faithfully of whatever may be passing in the city.*

A variety of concurring accounts make it probable the enemy are preparing to evacuate Philadelphia. This is a point, which it is of the utmost importance to ascertain; and if possible the place of their future destination...

You will remember that your detachment is a very valuable one, and that any accident happening to it would be a severe blow to this Army. You will therefore use every possible precaution for its security, and to guard against a surprise. No attempt should be made nor anything risked without the greatest prospect of success and with every reasonable advantage on your side.

Lafayette's troops included infantry, militia for patrol duty, detachments of cavalry, and fifty Indians he had persuaded to come with him from his expedition to Canada. The enemy got word of his movements as he approached Barren Hill. As a last gesture before quitting America, Howe decided to lead out nearly half the British army under Clinton, Grey, and Grant to capture him. They were so confident that they invited their officers to dinner that night "to meet General Lafayette." They set out on what was to be a brilliant encircling movement, surrounding Barren Hill on three sides, with Lafayette trapped at the river. On the nineteenth, General Grant marched a roundabout way through Whitemarsh to arrive to the north. Grey was assigned to go through Germantown to hit the center, while Clinton was to take a road along the river. Lafayette had posted militia along the Whitemarsh Road to watch for the British but they simply disappeared. Grey reached his position. Clinton and Howe were spotted and Lafayette was warned. British cavalry came unexpectedly on the Indians. They let out such loud whoops of fear that the dragoons beat a hasty retreat, while the Indians moved off rapidly in the opposite direction.

Below Barren Hill was a road unknown to the British that was concealed by thick woods. Lafayette, after sending out a few guards to divert the enemy, got all his men safely down this road, across the Schuylkill, and back to Washington and Valley Forge. British columns under Clinton and Grant raced from opposite sides to the top of the hill and encountered each other. They glared, cursed, and returned to Philadelphia. Lafayette, who hardly needed it, had more acclaim then ever.

THE PEACE COMMISSION ARRIVES

The three commissioners—Carlisle, Eden, and Johnstone—sailed up the Delaware, astonished at the American siege, and landed at Philadelphia on June 6. They found four hundred or so British transports being loaded with baggage and Tories, and all preparations under way for flight. They considered their government had made fools of them. Their instructions for public behavior were such that they could only continue to look foolish, but privately Lord Carlisle and William Eden viewed the situation objectively. Carlisle wrote his wife: "We all look grave, and perhaps we think we look wise... I don't see what we have to do here." To George Selwyn in London he noted: "I have this morning at five o'clock been taking a ride into the country, about ten miles; grieved I am to say, eight miles beyond our possessions." William Eden wrote a friend: "It is impossible to see even what I have seen of this country and not to go nearly mad at the long train of misconducts and mischances by which we have lost it."

Though the commissioners were pessimistic they pleaded with Clinton not to leave Philadelphia until they had approached Congress. His orders from London were so positive that he could not delay. The commissioners complained of the "perfidy" of the ministers, yet it is possible that the cabinet had deluded itself into thinking that the Americans would accept their offers. Lord George Germain had indicated to Clinton that "the generous terms now held out... will be gladly embraced, and... a negociation will immediately take place upon the arrival of the New Commission, and be so far advanced before the season will admit of military operations as to supersede the necessity of another campaign. So speedy and happy a termination of the war could not fail to give the greatest pleasure to the King."

The commissioners asked Washington for permission for their secretary, Dr. Adam Ferguson, professor of natural philosophy at Edinburgh, to proceed to York. Washington sent the request to Congress, which refused to receive him. This forced the commission on June 13 to write to His Excellency, the President of Congress, thereby formally recognizing Congress as an official body. They expressed the desire to avoid further bloodshed and to re-establish "the tranquillity of this once happy empire." The letter offered everything that was in the limit of their instructions, including American seats in Parliament and internal freedom of legislation and government in America. There was more than a hint that Britain recognized the military importance of America, which, after reconciliation, would act "in peace and war, under our common sovereign." The commissioners attacked "the insidious interposition of France," an enemy to both Britain and America. They concluded by threatening calamities, horrors, and devastations if America did not submit.

Before Congress could reply, the commissioners had to scurry to join the British fleet retreating to New York. President Laurens sent them an answer on June 17, which did not reach them for nearly three weeks:

Nothing but an earnest desire to spare the further effusion of blood could have induced [Congress] to read a paper containing expressions so disrespectful to his most Christian majesty, the good and great ally of these states, or consider propositions so derogatory to the honour of an independent nation.

The acts of the British parliament, the commission from your sovereign, and your letter suppose the people of these states to be subjects of the crown of Great Britain, and are founded on the idea of dependence, which is utterly inadmissible.

I am further directed to inform your excellencies that Congress are inclined to peace, notwithstanding the unjust claims from which this war originated and the savage manner in which it hath been conducted. They will, therefore, be ready to enter upon the consideration of a treaty of peace and commerce not inconsistent with treaties already subsisting, when the king of Great Britain shall demonstrate a sincere disposition for that purpose. The only solid proof of this disposition will be an explicit acknowledgement of the independence of those states, or the withdrawing of his fleet and armies.

The commissioners on July 11 asked Congress by what authority it dared to sign a treaty with France. They threatened to appeal over their heads to the American people. Congress ignored the letter, which reached them after the arrival in Philadelphia of Conrad Gérard, his most Christian majesty's minister to the United States.

On June 8 Martha Washington left for Mount Vernon, having received what her husband liked to call her "marching orders." Washington had picked Benedict Arnold late in May to be the American commander in Philadelphia. When the British evacuated the city, Arnold moved into General Howe's house and proceeded to use his new authority to try to make a fortune.

TWENTY-FIVE

MONMOUTH TO MIDDLEBROOK

1778–1779

WHILE ESPIONAGE IS an ancient practice, Washington was the first military commander to have an extensive intelligence organization in his operational command. His apparatus embraced security, counterintelligence and positive intelligence, penetration of the enemy's operations, and placement of false information with enemy agents. Most of the system operated from Washington's own cocked hat. This prevented trouble when counterintelligence agents picked up his spies going into the enemy lines. After they were brought to his office for severe "questioning," Washington arranged for their escape to the enemy, carrying bitter tales of their mistreatment.

As the war progressed, Washington's network included an array of bright young college graduates, respectable businessmen, state governors, tavern-keepers, semiliterate farmers, barmaids, dear old ladies in Quaker bonnets who carried vegetables to the enemy, young boys who could wriggle past the enemy lines, the American lady who owned the waxworks museum in London, several of Sir Henry Clinton's trusted agents, Lord Cornwallis' valet, and one of Lord North's diplomatic emissaries. Washington's operations were kept secret even after the war. The identities of several agents were not discovered until the twentieth century. Many are still known only by initials or numbers.

In the campaigns around New York every move of the British fleet and army was watched. Washington had spies at Trenton, before he attacked, and his agents gave him information on all the roads in the area. After the second battle of Trenton, their intelligence enabled him to elude Lord Cornwallis with ease. Long before the British occupied Philadelphia, Washington had his agents planted there. They reported to Major John Clark, Jr., and to Captain Allan McLane. They tipped off Washington that the British would try to draw him into a general engagement at Whitemarsh. They also warned Lafayette just in time that the British would try to capture him.

Washington particularly liked having his fearless young cavalrymen as intelligence officers. These included Captain McLane, Benjamin Tallmadge, and Henry Lee. His aides, Robert Hanson Harrison, John Laurens, and Alexander Hamilton, also became adept in the work. By the summer of 1778 Washington had designated Tallmadge to head his network; he occupied this post for five years. In his deliberately restrained memoirs Tallmadge referred only to the "private correspondence" he had undertaken for the general. Congress scraped together five hundred guineas in gold for this service and subsequently added another two thousand guineas.

It is remarkable that a Virginia farmer was able to outwit the more sophisticated British in this deadly game. They had experience and unlimited secret service funds in solid specie, but their operations, though aided by many Tories, were far more clumsy. From the time Washington left Manhattan in October 1776 until his return there at the end of 1783, it appears that only one American agent was caught and sent to the gallows, while Washington hanged at least ten enemy spies, including the head of British intelligence.

PLANS

Washington cried out frequently in his letters to spare no expense in getting information. Indian raids on the frontier, stimulated by British agents, caused him much concern. He reluctantly dispatched two Pennsylvania and Virginia regiments to Fort Pitt in May for frontier protection. In the same month he informed his war council that approximately three thousand of his men were ill, some from disease, many from inoculation for smallpox. In weighing reports of the projected British evacuation of Philadelphia, he had to take into account his own natural inclination to attack and the need to protect his sick and his military supplies. His councils were divided and the advice he received from his senior generals was too often deficient.

On June 8 Gates, stationed in Peekskill, wrote Washington that he was sure the British would attack up the Hudson and then move into New England.

Washington replied in an appraisal, which turned out to be correct, that he thought they would try only coastal raids in the area. On June 12 Charles Lee informed Washington, whose intelligence had made it almost certain that Clinton would cross New Jersey, that the British would not go to New York. Instead they would either move westward in Pennsylvania in order to connect with the Indians or try to get hold of a large tract of land somewhere else. He added: "I have particular reasons to think that they have cast their eyes on the lower counties of the Delaware, and some of the Maryland counties on the eastern shore." Lee had sent them a plan, while a prisoner, for ending the war by taking possession of that area.

Washington made early preparations to counter British moves across New Jersey. He ordered Brigadier William Maxwell into the state with 1,200 continentals and asked Major General Philemon Dickinson to alert the state's militia. His general officers in the state were requested to get intelligence, to destroy all bridges the enemy might use, and to block the roads with felled trees. Washington's great worry was that the British, moving directly across the Delaware while he was proceeding from Valley Forge to that river, would gain a day's march on him. As nearly as he could calculate in June, he had about 12,000 troops fit for duty in Pennsylvania and somewhat under 1,000 militia. According to the reliable figures of Joseph Galloway, the British had around 29,000 men of all ranks in the military and naval forces in Philadelphia. Although Washington could not know this accurately, Clinton planned to march around 16,500 of these to New York, the remainder going by sea.[*]

---

[*] In general, histories of the revolution give wildly varying numbers of troops present at battles. The discrepancies appear to have risen from the differing forms of returns: (a) total effectives of all ranks; (b) effectives, excluding officers; (c) rank and file, omitting sergeants, drummers, and fifers, and those "on command," that is, on detached duty; and (d) rank and file present and fit for duty. This last figure leaves out those who were sick, wounded, or on furlough.

Washington's troop returns for August 1776 ranged from 17,200 under (a) down to 10,500 under (d). Total British forces in the United States, just before Monmouth, vary in the same categories from 42,000 to 27,000.

Clinton always preferred to underrepresent his troop strength while exaggerating Washington's. Lord George Germain, who could also count, protested, with much asperity, against Clinton's practice of minimizing the strength of the troops sent at such expense from Great Britain. Clinton's memoirs state that there were 18,000 continentals facing him in New Jersey and these had increased to 20,000 by the time he got to New York.

Using Clinton's numbering, Washington had around 9,800 rank and file present and fit for duty at Monmouth to oppose Clinton's 14,700. Even if the militia are added to Washington's total, the British outnumbered the Americans by a third. The difference remains approximately the same if category (b) is used to describe the opposing forces.

Washington estimated to his war council that Clinton had 10,000 rank and file present and fit for duty. There is reason to suppose, in view of the timidity of his general officers, that he understated the enemy in order to give them more courage in their decisions.

Washington's May war council had concluded that he should remain on the defensive. A further meeting was held on June 17 to consider alternative plans if the British moved, including attacking their flanks or bringing them to a general engagement. Only two of the fifteen general officers present voted for the latter policy.

At 11:30 the next morning Washington received word that Clinton had abandoned Philadelphia and was on his way across New Jersey. Within three hours, twelve of his regiments were marching to the Delaware. The rest of the army was on its way early the following morning. From then on, each Washington letter cried out for every scrap of information from his generals in New Jersey as well as from the state's governor.

On June 21, at what is now New Hope, Washington again crossed the Delaware, this time in suffocating heat. Heavy and repeated thunderstorms added to the humidity and discomfort and made the primitive roads a morass. They delayed his march but equally hindered the enemy, who were burdened by a baggage train of fifteen hundred wagons, guarded by five or six thousand rank and file. They also had to move trees and other obstacles and repair the bridges that the Americans had destroyed. In a week they had covered only 40 miles. This gave Washington his much-desired chance to march directly east across New Jersey and intercept Clinton, moving northeast from Mount Holly to Allentown, New Jersey.

VICTORY AT MONMOUTH

From this point on Washington put the exact time of writing on requests for intelligence and asked his reporting officers to do the same, stressing that even a half hour would make a difference in his operations.

On June 24 he called a council of his general officers. Present were Lee, Greene, Stirling, Lafayette, Steuben, Knox, Poor, Wayne, Woodford, Paterson, Scott, and Du Portail. Alexander Hamilton was secretary.

The psychologically acute Lafayette, like nearly everyone, had taken his measure of Lee after his arrival from the British lines: "His visage was ugly, his spirit sarcastic, his heart ambitious and mean, his character inconsistent; on the whole a queer fellow." Lee spoke, almost too symbolically, during a full eclipse of the sun. He argued against an attack. The Americans, if necessary, he said, should build a bridge of gold to help the British to cross New Jersey, for they could never beat the better-trained British army. Lee was persuasive and a number of generals supported his view. The meeting finally advised Washington only to go so far as to detach fifteen hundred men to harass the British flanks.

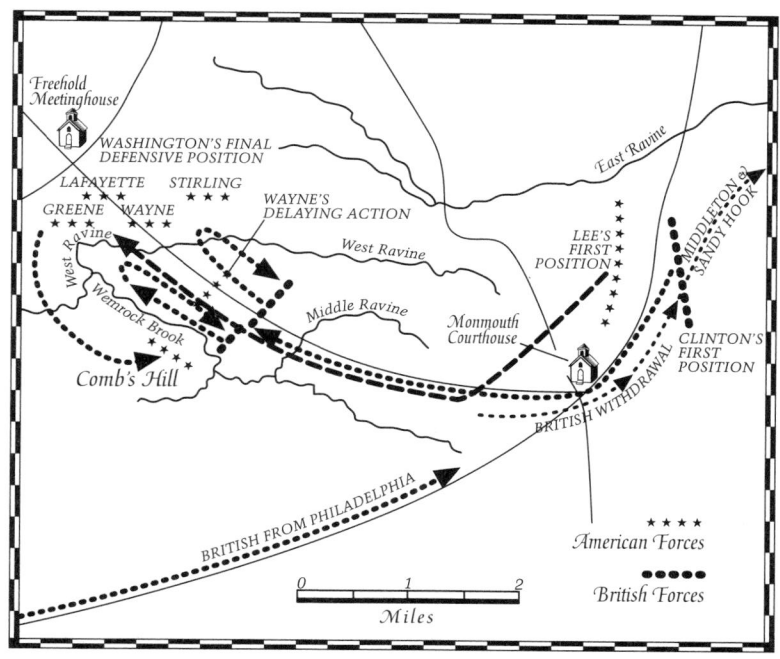

Freehold
Meetinghouse

WASHINGTON'S FINAL
DEFENSIVE POSITION

East Ravine

LAFAYETTE   STIRLING
GREENE   WAYNE

WAYNE'S
DELAYING ACTION

West Ravine

LEE'S
FIRST
POSITION

MIDDLETON &
SANDY HOOK

West Ravine

Wemrock Brook

Middle Ravine

Monmouth
Courthouse

CLINTON'S
FIRST
POSITION

Comb's Hill

BRITISH WITHDRAWAL

BRITISH FROM PHILADELPHIA

★ ★ ★ ★
American Forces

●●●●●
British Forces

0   1   2
Miles

Battle of Monmouth, June 28, 1778

Hamilton subsequently described the meeting in a letter to Elias Boudinot: "The General unluckily called a council of war, the result of which would have done honour to the most honourable society of midwives, and to them only. The purport was, that we should keep at a comfortable distance from the enemy, and keep up a vain parade of annoying them in detachment... General Lee was the *primum mobile* of this sage plan. The General, on mature reconsideration of what had been resolved on, determined to pursue a different line of conduct at all hazards." In this he was joined by Greene, Lafayette, and Wayne, who pleaded with him to do more. Greene wrote Washington: "I am not for hazarding a general action unnecessarily, but I am clearly of opinion for making a serious impression with the light troops and for having the army in supporting distance... If we suffer the enemy to pass through the Jerseys without attacking, I think we shall ever regret it... People expect something from us and our strength demands it. I am by no means for rash measures but we must preserve our reputations and I think we can make a very serious impression without any great risk and if it should amount to a general action I think the chance is greatly in our favour."

After the meeting Washington dispatched Morgan to the enemy's right flank, Maxwell to the left, and Scott to the left and rear. Washington wrote Scott:

> *You are immediately to march with the detachment, under your command, towards Allen Town, in order to fall in with the enemy's left flank and rear, and give them all the annoyance in your power. You will carefully collect intelligence as you advance and govern your motions accordingly; and you will take every precaution for the security of your detachment consistent with the objects it is intended to promote. You will co-operate, as far as may be proper, with the other troops in the neighbourhood of the enemy. You will keep me continually and punctually advised of every occurrence that happens, either with respect to the Enemy or yourself. Lt. Colo. White is ordered to join you with the detachment of Cavalry under his command.*

Washington next day selected a delighted Lafayette to march with approximately fifteen hundred troops to join Scott, to take over the command and, in Washington's words, "if a proper opening shd. be given, by operating against them with the whole force of your command." Washington added that if Lafayette attacked in force he would be "supported or covered, as circumstances should require, by the whole army." Washington consulted Lee about his command because of the latter's seniority. He initially agreed but then, hearing that Lafayette would have an additional body of troops, numbering five thousand or more, and that other generals thought his absence would

One of at least seven portraits of Washington painted by Charles Wilson Peale. *(The Bettmann Archive)*

Alexander Hamilton, a valued
and trusted aide of Washington's during the Revolution.
(The Bettmann Archive)

LAFAYETTE.

The Marquis de
Lafayette, who
sailed to America
at his own expense
to assist Americans
in the war for
independence.
He was wounded
at the Battle of
Brandywine and
stood by
Washington at
Valley Forge
during the terrible
winter of 1777-
1778. *(The
Bettmann Archive)*

Benedict Arnold, the most infamous man in American history. Arnold helped the Americans win important victories at Ft. Ticonderoga and at the Battle of Saratoga before committing treason. *(The Bettmann Archive)*

General "Mad" Anthony Wayne also endured the harsh conditions at Valley Forge. Later he fought in the great victory at Monmouth, led an audacious attack on Stony Point, N.Y., and participated in the siege of Cornwallis at Yorktown, Va. *(The Bettmann Archive)*

GENERAL WAYNE.

Daniel Morgan, one of Washington's fiercest officers. Morgan crushed the British at the Battle of the Cowpens on Jan. 17, 1781. *(The Bettmann Archive)*

"Light Horse Harry" Lee, one of Washington's finest cavalry leaders. In July, 1779, he accomplished one of the most daring raids of the war, surprising the British post at Paulus Hook, New Jersey, and capturing 160 prisoners. *(The Bettmann Archive)*

The Compte de Rochambeau, selected by King Louis XVI because of his *savoir-faire* to command the French troops assisting Washington. In mid-August, 1781, he and Washington began marching their troops from New York towards Virginia's peninsula, where they trapped the British under Lord Cornwallis (portrait by Raynaud). *(The Bettmann Archive)*

Admiral Lord Charles Cornwallis became Washington's central military foe. On Oct. 19, 1781 he surrendered his forces at Yorktown, thus effectively ending the American Revolutionary War. *(The Bettmann Archive)*

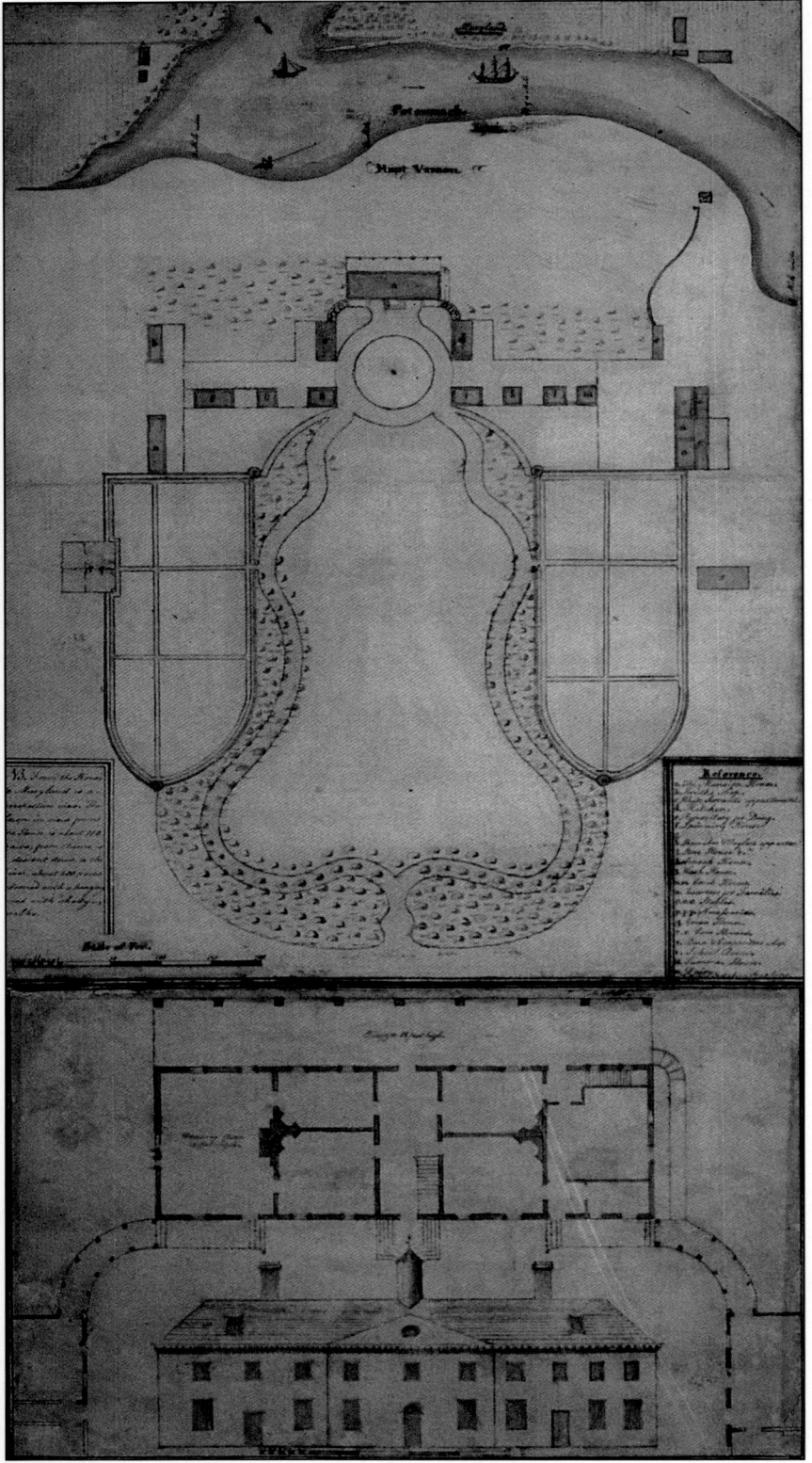

Map of the
Mount Vernon
mansion and its
grounds (by
Samuel Vaughan,
1787). *(The
Mount Vernon
Ladies' Association
of the Union)*

Martha Washington by Archibald
Robertson (1782). *(The Bettmann Archive)*

Bust of George
Washington by Houdon.
(The Bettmann Archive)

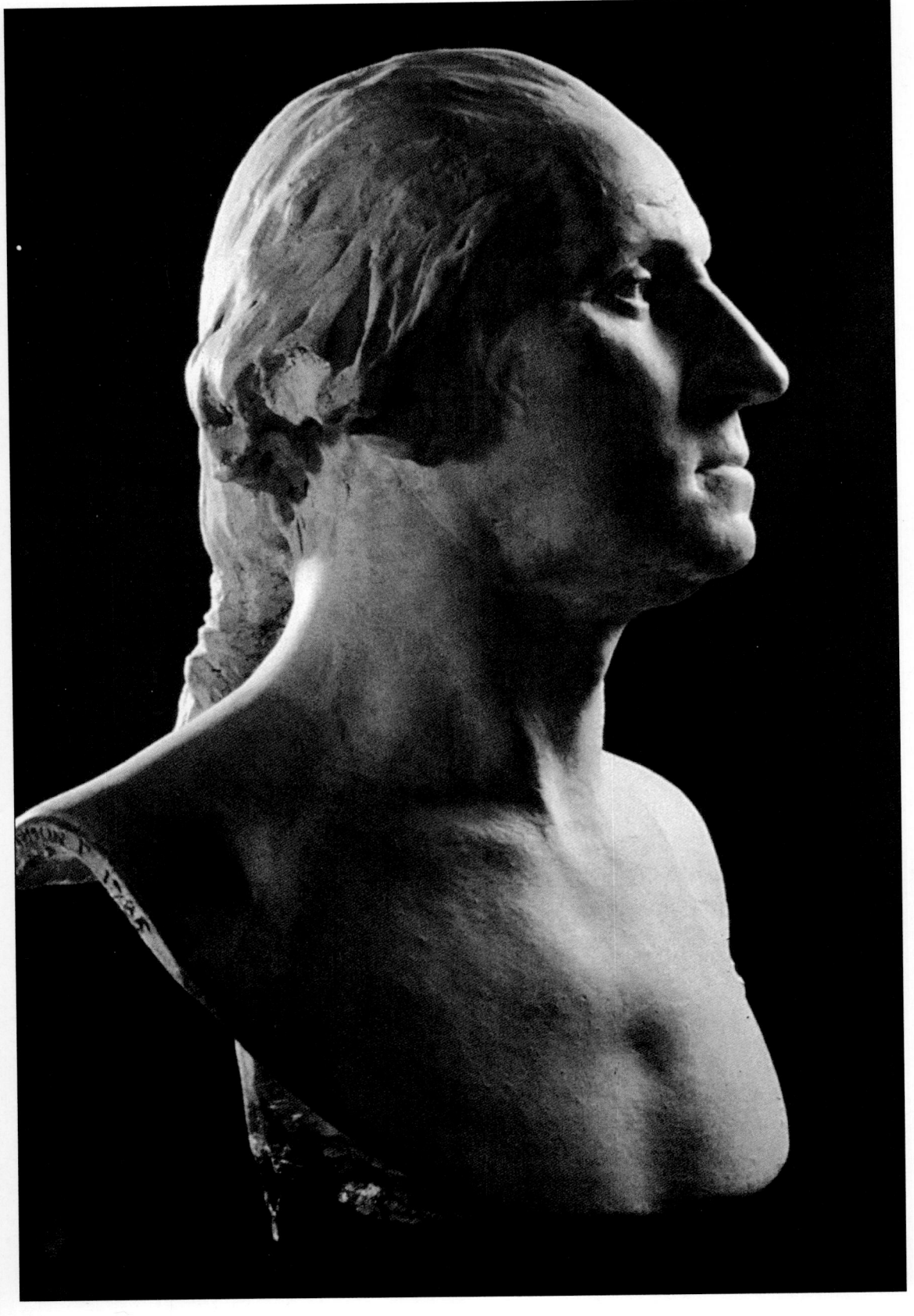

Another Houdon bust of Washington (1785). *(The Mount Vernon Ladies' Association of the Union)*

look peculiar, he protested that he should have it after all. Hamilton afterwards commented that Lee's conduct "was very childish." He told Lafayette that his "fortune and honor" were at stake. The French general said that, if it were a matter of his honor, he would cheerfully acquiesce in any decision by Washington. This put the commander in chief in a dilemma. Lee had told him that he would be "disgraced" while Washington did not want to offend Lafayette. He reached an unfortunate compromise decision, which he relayed to Lee on June 26:

> *Your uneasiness, on account of the command of yesterday's detachment, fills me with concern, as it is not in my power fully to remove it, without wounding the feelings of the Marquis de la Fayette. I have thought of an expedient which though not quite equal to either of your views, may in some measure answer both; and that is to make another detachment for this Army for the purpose of aiding and supporting the several detachments now under the command of the Marquis and giving you the command of the whole, under certain restrictions; which, circumstances arising from your own conduct yesterday, render almost unavoidable. The expedient which I would propose is for you to march towards the Marquis with Scott's and Varnum's brigades. Give him notice that you are advancing to support him, that you are to have command of the whole advanced body; but as he may have formed some enterprise... which will not admit of delay or alteration, you will desire him to proceed as if no change had happened, and you will give him every assistance and countenance in you power.*

He wrote Lafayette the same day, ending on a much more affectionate note: "General Lee's uneasiness on account of Yesterday's transaction rather increasing than abating, and your politeness in wishing to ease him of it, has induced me to detach him from this Army, with a part of it, to reinforce, or at least cover, the several detachments under your command, at present. At the same time I felt for General Lee's distress of mind, I have had an eye to your wishes, and the delicacy of your situation; and have, therefore, obtained a promise from him, that when he gives you notice of his approach and command, he will request you to prosecute any plan you have already concerted for the purpose of attacking or otherwise annoying the Enemy. This is the only expedient I could think of to answer both your views... I wish it may prove agreeable to you, as I am with the warmest wishes for your honour and glory, and with the sincerest esteem and affection."

On June 25 Lee was dispatched to Englishtown with two additional regiments, making the American vanguard more than five thousand men stationed five miles from the enemy. He ordered Lafayette not to move too fast and exhaust his men in the excessive heat. That night a heavy rainstorm added to the discomfort. Ferocious New Jersey mosquitoes indiscriminately attacked British and American troops.

From the twenty-fifth to the twenty-eighth Hamilton was everywhere, acting as the eyes and ears of Lafayette and Washington. His written intelligence reports were models, giving necessary information without an unnecessary word. Late on the night of the twenty-sixth, the prescient Lafayette wrote Washington: "I do not believe General Lee intends to make any attack tomorrow, for then I would have been directed to fall immediately upon them without making eleven miles entirely out of the way. I am here as near as I will be at Englishtown."

On the twenty-seventh Lee took command of the advance forces. That day he was called to Washington's headquarters and given orders to attack the enemy. Washington promised to bring up the main body of troops to his support. He was told to post a patrol to give instant warning if Sir Henry Clinton decided to move during the night. General Dickinson and his militia were assigned this duty. At a conference with the officers under his immediate command Lee gave no indication as to his plans for the morning.

On June 27 the British were encamped around the Monmouth County Courthouse at Freehold. Lee and Lafayette were just beyond Englishtown, while the main army under Washington was about five miles to the rear. Late that night Lee informed Washington he thought the British would attack him, though there is no evidence that they had anything in mind but heading away to the heights at Middletown. At four in the morning the van of the British army began to move off towards the coast. Washington had this information from Dickinson by 5 A.M. He sent a hurried order to Lee to attack, adding that he was bringing forward the rest of the army. Washington had around sixty-seven hundred men, with Stirling in command on the left and Greene on the right. Morgan and his riflemen were far off on the enemy's left flank, too far as it turned out, to do any good that day. That Sunday, June 28, soon became unbearably hot with the temperature going to ninety-six degrees. The British nonetheless moved off rapidly.

Lee reacted very slowly to Washington's orders and to information of the British movement. Not until seven did he march with the main part of his troops. From this point on Lee had no plans and no control. He hesitated, waiting at one point a half hour, during which he told Dickinson he had provided false intelligence. The various bodies of troops moved without command; where Lee did give orders, they were confused and contradictory. Wayne, Lafayette, and Scott endeavored to come up with the enemy but other troops remained behind. When British cavalry and infantry appeared, Lee began to move back with some of his troops, leaving the forward parties to fend for themselves. They were forced to rejoin him though without orders to do so; suddenly the whole advance force was retreating, after having fired almost no shots.

This was an unexpected bonus for Sir Henry Clinton, whose only objective to that point had been to leave Monmouth as rapidly as possible. Clinton had his best troops nearby including such famous regiments as the Black Watch, Guards, and Grenadiers. He ordered Lord Cornwallis to attack and sent word to General Grant, with Knyphausen's advance troops, to join with his forces. Clinton complained many years later that Grant refused to obey "under most frivolous pretenses."

Washington's aides whom he had sent forward found disorder, Lee twice telling Richard Meade, "They are all in confusion." Another aide, Harrison, asked Lee's aide the reason for the confusion. He was told that British foot and horse were coming along. Harrison replied that the American army was there to meet them. Washington in the rear was puzzled by the absence of battle sounds. He spurred forward and, on encountering Lee, demanded an explanation for the disorder and his failure to obey. Lee missed the question and Washington repeated it. Lee said that there had been confusing intelligence and contradictory orders, people had interfered, and he could not fight the British under such conditions. He added that in any case he had consistently opposed an attack. Washington told him that he was expected to obey orders and that he should not have undertaken the advance unless he intended to go through with it. It is unclear whether Lee went to the rear or stayed at the scene, but thereafter he played no important role in the battle. Washington himself took over the command.

By this time the American van had retreated more than two miles with the British in hot pursuit. Wayne had fought a delaying action and Washington ordered two additional regiments to stand with Wayne. He then hurried back to get his remaining troops, throwing Greene's division to the right, Stirling's to the left, and Lafayette to the rear of center. Knox and Du Portail directed the highly effective artillery. Officers and men responded with a disciplined enthusiasm previously unknown in the American army. Washington's report to Congress of July 1 gave the essentials of the subsequent battle:

> *After marching about five miles, to my great surprise and mortification, I met the whole advanced Corps retreating, and, as I was told, by General Lee's orders, without having made any opposition, except one fire given by a party under the command of Colo. Butler, on their being charged by the Enemy's Cavalry, who were repulsed. I proceeded immediately to the Rear of the corps, which I found closely*

pressed by the Enemy, and gave directions for forming part of the retreating troops, who, by the brave and spirited conduct of the Officers, and aided by some pieces of well served Artillery, checked the Enemy's Advance, and gave time to make a disposition of the left wing and second line of the Army upon an eminence, and in a wood a little in the Rear covered by a morass in front. On this were placed some Batteries of Cannon by Lord Stirling who commanded the left Wing, which played upon the Enemy with great effect, and seconded by parties of Infantry detached to oppose them, effectually put a stop to their advance.

…The command of the Right Wing… was given to General Greene. For the expedition of the march, and to counteract any attempt to turn our Right, I had ordered him to file off by the new church, two miles from English Town, and fall into the Monmouth Road, a small distance in the Rear of the Court House, while the rest of the Column moved directly on towards the Court House. On intelligence of the Retreat, he marched up and took a very advantageous position on the Right.

The enemy by this time, finding themselves very warmly opposed in front made an attempt to turn our left flank; but they were bravely repulsed and driven back by detached parties of Infantry. They also made a movement to our Right, with as little success, General Greene having advanced a Body of Troops with Artillery to a commanding piece of Ground, which not only disappointed their design of turning our Right, but severely infiladed those in front of the Left Wing. In addition to this, General Wayne advanced with a Body of Troops and kept up so severe and well directed a fire that the Enemy were soon compelled to retire behind the defile where the first stand in the beginning of the Action had been made.

In this situation, the Enemy had both their flanks secured by thick Woods and Morasses, while their front could only be approached thro' a narrow pass. I resolved nevertheless to attack them, and for that purpose ordered General Poor with his own and the Carolina Brigade, to move round upon their Right, and General Woodford upon their left, and the Artillery to gall them in front, but the impediments in their way prevented their getting within reach before it was dark. They remained upon the Ground they had been directed to occupy, during the Night, with intention to begin the attack early the next morning, and the Army continued lying upon their Arms in the field of Action, to be in readiness to support them… About 12 OClock the Enemy marched away…

Were I to conclude my account of this day's transactions without expressing my obligations to the Officers of the Army in general, I should do injustice to their merit, and violence to my own feelings. They seemed to vie with each other in manifesting their Zeal and Bravery. The Catalogue of those who distinguished themselves is too long to admit of particularising individuals; I cannot however forbear mentioning Brigadier General Wayne whose good conduct and bravery thro' the whole action deserves particular commendation.

The Behaviour of the troops in general, after they recovered from the first surprise occasioned by the Retreat of the advanced Corps, was such as could not be surpassed.

In general orders after the battle Washington expressed his particular thanks to Dickinson and the Jersey militia, and to Knox, who invariably at every battle received special encomia from the commander in chief. Wayne, who was honored by a mention in the dispatch to Congress, expressed his opinion of the battle in more earthy prose than Washington's: "Tell the Phil'a ladies, that the heavenly, sweet, pretty red coats—the accomplished gentlemen of the Guards and Grenadiers have humbled themselves on the plains of Monmouth."

London had repeatedly urged its commanders in America to bring Washington to a general engagement and to defeat him. The king and cabinet correctly believed that this was the only way to suppress the rebellion and to reestablish British rule. The opportunity was at hand. The British army, though badly mauled, was larger than Washington's and included many of the crack regiments of Great Britain. Washington was there and prepared to fight a general action the next day. Sir Henry Clinton declined. Shortly after midnight the British picked up and ran. They had been moving across New Jersey at six miles a day. By midmorning they were thirteen miles away, after one of the most rapid retreats in history. Thereafter, in the north, the British army largely confined its operations to war on civilians.

Washington did not learn for several days the extent of his victory. During the following week his army and the local inhabitants buried around 300 enemy dead. The number of wounded generally ran in a ratio of three or four to one killed. Prisoners taken on the battlefield and by desertion numbered about 800. Washington's estimate that the enemy suffered 2,000 casualties is probably accurate and may even have been conservative. American losses were around 350, some being from heatstroke rather than enemy action.

Washington praised everyone except Lee and himself for the day's action against superior forces and the largest British army Washington was ever to fight. Those who were closest to him that day gave their opinion. Hamilton wrote to Elias Boudinot: "I never saw the General to so much advantage. His coolness and firmness were admirable. He instantly took measures for checking the enemy's advance, and giving time to the army, which was very near, to form and make a proper disposition... on a very advantageous piece of ground... America owes a great deal to General Washington for this day's work. A general rout, dismay, and disgrace would have attended the whole army in any other hands than his. By his own good sense and fortitude, he turned the fate of the day. Other officers have great merit in performing their parts well, but he directed the whole with the skill of a master workman... Our troops, after the first impulse from mismanagement, behaved with more spirit and moved with greater order than the British troops." John Laurens wrote his father: "The merits of restoring the day, is due to the general; and his conduct was such throughout the affair as has greatly increased my love and esteem for him." James McHenry noted that Washington had "unfolded surprising abilities which produced uncommon effects." Lafayette wrote at a much later date: "Never was General Washington greater in war than in this action. His presence stopped the retreat. His dispositions fixed the victory. His fine appearance on horseback, his calm courage roused by the animation produced by the vexation of the morning, gave him the air best calculated to arouse enthusiasm."

Elias Boudinot replied to Hamilton: "The general I always revered and loved ever since I know him, but in this instance he rose superior to himself. Every lip dwells on his praise, for even his pretended friends (for none dare to acknowledge themselves his enemies) are obliged to croak it forth."

The cruel winter at Valley Forge and the Conway cabal made Washington commander in fact of the armies. The great victory at Monmouth made him, by acclamation, father of the nation.

TWO LETTERS

On July 10 Washington received the unanimous thanks of Congress for his "distinguished exertions in forming the line of battle; and for his great good conduct in leading on the attack and gaining the important victory at Monmouth over the British grand army." Henry Laurens, president of Congress, wrote: "Love and respect for your excellency are impressed on the heart of every grateful American, and your name will be revered by posterity." There were further thanks by Congress to the "gallant officers and men under this command." This latter resolution Washington published. Four days later Washington received a letter from Admiral the comte d'Estaing, who had arrived off the American coast with twelve ships of the line and six frigates:

I have the honor to inform your Excellency of the arrival of the King's fleet, charged by his Majesty with the glorious task of giving his allies, the United States of America, the most striking proofs of his affection... The talents and great actions of

General Georges Washington have secured to him, in the eyes of all Europe, the truly sublime title of Liberator of America. Accept, Sir, the homage that every man, that every military man, owes you; and be pleased that I solicit with military and naval frankness from the first moment so flattering a friendship as yours; I will try to render myself worthy of it by my respectful devotion to your country; It is prescribed by my orders and inspires my heart.

For Washington and Lafayette this direct military assistance by France and the first effort to implement the alliance were cheering, but they introduced new problems that were to test Washington's developing diplomatic skills to the utmost. After handling the turbulent congressmen and sensitive generals who were his countrymen, Washington often found it easier to deal with the courtly and usually more tactful French.

IDYLLIC DAYS

The American army rested for two days not far from the battlefield and then made a long, hot, and nearly waterless march of twenty miles to Brunswick, where Washington kept headquarters for nearly a week. On July 4 the army paraded to celebrate the second anniversary of American independence. Thirteen cannon were discharged and three cheers were given for the United States. Washington again invited his principal officers to dine with him and that night they held a ball. From Brunswick they moved on through the then-beautiful New Jersey countryside to Paramus. James McHenry, a physician who had recently been appointed aide to the commander in chief, left a record of their stop at Passaic Falls and of their subsequent movements:

After viewing these falls we seated ourselves round the General under a large spreading oak within view of the spray and in hearing of the noise. A fine cool spring bubbled out most charmingly from the bottom of the tree. The travelling canteens were immediately emptied and a modest repast spread before us, of cold ham, tongue, and some biscuit. With the assistance of a little spirit we composed some excellent grog. Then we chatted away a very cheerful half hour and then took our leave of the friendly oak—its refreshing spring—and the meek falls of Passaic—less boisterous than those of Niagara, or the more gentle Cohoes or the waters of the Mohawk.

From hence we passed thro' a fertile country to a place called Paramus. We stopped at a Mrs. Watkins whose house was marked for headquarters. But the General receiving a note of invitation from a Mrs. Provost [later Mrs. Aaron Burr] to make

*her Hermitage, as it was called, the seat of his stay while at Paramus, we only
dined with Mrs. Watkins and her two charming daughters, who sang us several
pretty songs in a very agreeable manner.*

*At Mrs. Provost we found some fair refugees from New York who were on a visit to
the lady of the Hermitage; with them we talked—and walked—and laughed—and
danced and gallanted away the leisure hours of four days and four nights and
would have gallanted—and danced and laughed and talked and walked with
them till now had not the General given orders for our departure. We left them...
without much sighing.*

McHenry and Alexander Hamilton, who were later in Washington's cabinet,
were highly competitive in pursuit of women, on the rare occasions the
general let them have free time. At Doylestown McHenry found a pretty
Quaker girl and wrote: "Hamilton thou shalt not tread on this ground." Three
days later he described with pleasure the "charming girls" on the Jersey side,
adding that one of the general's guards was more favored than Hamilton.

THE FRENCH FLEET

Bad luck and quite a lot of bad manners on the part of some Americans and
French soured the first months of the alliance between the ancient French
kingdom and the two-year-old United States.

The French dispatched their fleet to America with great promptness before
Britain could organize for a French war. They had chosen a soldier, General
d'Estaing, for the command and commissioned him vice admiral. This paper
act did not make him a skilled sea lord and it annoyed other admirals. The fleet
encountered bad weather on its way to America and the trip took nearly three
months. The French had no idea that the British had abandoned Philadelphia,
and they went first to the Delaware and then north to Sandy Hook, which they
reached on July 11. Had they arrived eleven days earlier they might have cut off
Clinton at the Hook, isolating most of the British army on a land spit.

Washington had heard of the fleet's arrival before he received d'Estaing's
letter and wrote him a warm letter of welcome. D'Estaing, in saluting
Washington, also sent a note introducing the marquis de Chouin, a relative of
the French naval minister, who would concert French plans with him.
Washington responded to d'Estaing on July 17:

The arrival of a fleet, belonging to his most Christian majesty, on our coast, is an

*event that makes me truly happy and permit me to observe that the pleasure I feel
on the occasion is greatly increased by the command being placed in a Gentleman of
such distinguished talents, experience and reputation as the Count d'Estaing. I am
fully persuaded that every possible exertion will be made by you to accomplish the
important purposes of your destination…*

*I esteem myself highly honored by the desire you express, with a frankness which
must always be pleasing, of possessing a place in my friendship; at the same time
allow me to assure you that I shall consider myself peculiarly happy if I can but
improve the prepossessions you are pleased to entertain in my favour, into a cordial
and lasting amity.*

*Major de Chouin, who arrived this day at my Quarters, has given me a very full
and satisfactory explanation of your situation and views and in return I have
freely communicated to him my ideas of every matter interesting to our mutual
operations.*

Washington had already sent his French-speaking aide, John Laurens, of
Huguenot descent, to see d'Estaing. He now added Hamilton and the marquis de fleury. Washington found two experienced pilots and four merchant
marine captains to aid d'Estaing in the coastal waters. He appealed to the state
governors to order their privateers and frigates to cooperate with the French.
As a hospitable Virginian, he also dispatched two hundred sheep, fifty head of
cattle, and a quantity of poultry for the French navy. He sent his commissary
to help procure further supplies. He asked Sullivan, who commanded in
Rhode Island, to call up five thousand New England militia, in case d'Estaing
decided to attack the British in Newport rather than New York.

By July 21 Washington had his main army at White Plains, about fifteen
miles from Manhattan. There he reported to his war council that the
Continental Army numbered 16,700 rank and file, the highest figure of the
war. However, around 4,700 were on duty in New England, western New York,
and the Hudson Highlands. His immediate command had slightly under
12,000 rank and file. His council advised against attacking New York, where
at this time Clinton, in addition to his 3,600 troops in Rhode Island, had over
28,000 rank and file who were under siege by an enemy of less than half its
numbers. On August 20 Washington wrote to Thomas Nelson of Virginia:

*It is not a little pleasing, nor less wonderful to contemplate, that after two years'
Maneuvering and undergoing the strangest vicissitudes that perhaps ever attended
any one contest since the creation, both Armies are brought back to the very point*

they set out from, and that that which was the offending party in the beginning, is now reduced to the use of the spade and pick axe for defence. The hand of Providence has been so conspicuous in all this that he must be worse than an infidel that lacks faith, and more than wicked that has not gratitude to acknowledge his obligations, but it will be time enough for me to turn preacher when my present appointment ceases.

For a brief period the French operated outside Sandy Hook, with Washington on tenterhooks hoping the French fleet could attack Lord Howe's ships. The British peace commission felt humiliated. They had arrived in Philadelphia without knowledge that the British army would retreat. That army had suffered a severe defeat. Their overtures to Congress had been rejected with contempt. As a last straw, a French fleet, which they had not even been warned about, was off the coast of New York and obviously eager for battle. By July 22 Carlisle was writing George Selwyn: "We are blocked up by a French fleet. We are kept in prison, as we dare not ride beyond our posts towards the country ... If certain events, which are not improbable, should take place, we shall be inevitably starved."

The French-American land and naval siege was brief. French warships drew around five feet more water than their British counterparts. Though several French sailors lost their lives, and d'Estaing and Laurens were nearly drowned in looking for channels, the admiral had to conclude that his ships could not pass the bar at New York harbor. With American encouragement d'Estaing turned to Newport, the only other point in the United States that the British occupied.

The tempestuous Sullivan, who, Washington had once written, complained more than any other general officer, was in command in Rhode Island. Washington dispatched two brigades to him under Lafayette, who was more than anxious to fight alongside French forces. Washington subsequently sent General Greene, a native Rhode Islander, to the state. Lafayette had to divide his expected command with Greene. Washington tactfully appealed to him to consent. Lafayette replied in his usual graceful way: "I willingly part with the half my detachment... Any thing, my dear General, which you will order or even wish, shall always be infinitely agreeable to me."

Greene had considered himself hurt when Washington mildly rebuked him for not coming to headquarters when ordered to do so. He wrote Washington on July 21: "Your Excellency has made me very unhappy. I can submit very patiently to deserved censure; but it wounds my feelings exceedingly to meet with a rebuke, for doing what I conceived to be a proper part of my duty." He offered his resignation. The commander in chief replied to him the same day:

"I cannot at this time (having many People round me, and Letters by the Southern Post to read) go fully into the contents of your letter of this date, but with the same truth I have ever done, I still assure you, that you retain the same hold of my affections... With equal truth I can, and do assure you, that I have ever been happy in your friendship, and have no scruples in declaring, that I think myself indebted to your Abilities, honour and candour, to your attachment to me, and your faithful Services to the Public, in every capacity you have served it since we have been together in the Army. But my dear Sir, these must not debar me the privileges of a friend (for it was the voice of friendship that spoke to you) when I complained of Neglect; I was four or five days without seeing a single person in your department, and at a time when I wished for you in two capacities, having business of the utmost importance to settle with the Count de Estaing... But let me beseech you my dear Sir not to harbor any distrusts of my friendship, or conceive that I mean to wound the feelings of a Person whom I greatly esteem and regard." Greene, fully mollified, went off to his command.

In informing Sullivan of his orders on July 27, Washington told him that he assumed d'Estaing would send some of his troops ashore to join the attack on the British. D'Estaing's wishes as to who should command should govern Sullivan completely. He added: "Harmony and the best understanding between us should be a Capital and first object. The Count himself is a Land Officer and of the high rank of Lt. General in the French Army."

D'Estaing wrote Washington of his many problems and difficulties, his shortages of supplies and water, and his ignorance of the American coast. On August 8 Washington took time to express his appreciation to the admiral: "I most sincerely sympathize with you in the regret you feel at the obstacles and difficulties you have heretofore encountered. Your case has certainly been a case of peculiar hardship, but you justly have the consolation which arises from a reflection that no exertions possible have been wanting in you to insure success... The disappointments you have experienced proceed from circumstances which no human foresight or activity can control." He added that he had written to the governor of Connecticut to send water as soon as possible "to relieve the sufferings of the brave officers and men under your command."

Washington exerted every effort to get intelligence of British fleet movements that might endanger d'Estaing. On August 8 he sent information that Lord Howe was on the way to Rhode Island with part of his naval force. To his agent, Caleb Brewster, who operated a whaleboat between Connecticut and enemy-held Long Island, he wrote: "Let me entreat that you will continue to use every possible means to obtain intelligence of the Enemys motions, not only those which are Marching Eastward, upon Long Island, but others...

Have a strict watch kept upon the Enemy's Ships of War, and give me the earliest notice of their sailing from the hook... Let an eye also be had on the Transports, whether they are preparing for the reception of Troops... Know what number of Men are upon Long Island; whether they are moving or stationary; what is become of their draft Horses; whether they appear to be collecting of them for a move. How they are supplied with Provisions; what arrivals; whether with Men, or Provisions. And whether any troops have Imbarked for Rhode Island or Elsewhere."

Sullivan sent back highly optimistic reports that he would take the British garrison at Newport. When d'Estaing arrived off Narragansett Bay, the British burned several of their own frigates. Sullivan was so wound up with excitement that he ordered d'Estaing, a more experienced officer, to do things with his fleet and troops that were not practical. There was early friction between the allies. The Americans were slow in their preparations and the French tended to look down on them. De Chouin reported to d'Estaing that the American militia looked like "Tartar hordes," while John Hancock, who had shown up as a militia general, was "old, gouty and infirm." Hancock's gout was famous, but he was eight years younger than d'Estaing.

After many discussions the French and Americans agreed on a combined land and sea assault for August 9 but Sullivan, to d'Estaing's annoyance, moved a day in advance. Just as the French got under way, Lord Howe and his fleet showed up. The French abandoned their plans in order to chase the British. Sullivan's chance for glory was gone and he was furious, particularly as most of his militia then went home.

At this point, after the French fleet had outmaneuvered the British, the famous gales of Narragansett Bay, usually coming later, rose and badly damaged both fleets. D'Estaing lost the masts and rudder of his flagship. Howe took his damaged fleet to New York, while d'Estaing briefly put into Narragansett Bay to inform Sullivan that he would go to Boston for repairs. This was in accordance with orders from the French naval minister, but Sullivan and his officers reacted vehemently against the proposal.

Sullivan induced all of his generals except Lafayette to protest to d'Estaing that his actions were derogatory to French honor and injurious to the alliance. Lafayette was furious and threatened to draw his sword on Sullivan but the other officers apologized to him. Nonetheless Lafayette wrote Washington that he felt himself more an enemy in the American camp than he might have in the British, and he wrote in anguish to d'Estaing. Sullivan did not stop there but informed his troops in general orders that their allies had refused to help. At this point Greene intervened and Sullivan issued a halfhearted apology the next day.

In the meantime Sullivan fought a pitched battle with the British on Rhode Island. The Americans somewhat bested the enemy, and Sullivan then brought his troops to the mainland. He got off just in time to avoid Sir Henry Clinton, who arrived in the bay with four thousand troops. When d'Estaing reached Boston, the city blamed him for the failure of the Newport expedition. American sailors fought the French. A French officer was killed in the riot. The first fruits of the alliance were bitter for each side. The whole affair was immediately dumped onto Washington as everyone, including Congress, turned to him. With infinite tact he saw to it that the enemy gained no advantage from the disputes. To General William Heath, in command at Boston, he wrote on August 28:

The unfortunate circumstance of the French fleet having left Rhode Island at so critical a moment, I am apprehensive, if not prudently managed, will have many injurious consequences, besides merely the loss of the advantages we should have reaped from succeeding in the Expedition. It will not only tend to discourage the people, and weaken their confidence in the new alliance, but may possibly produce prejudices and resentments, which may operate against giving the fleet such effectual assistance in its present distress, as the exigence of our affairs and our true interests demand. It will certainly be sound policy to combat these effects, and whatever private opinion may be entertained, to give the most favorable construction of what has happened to the public, and at the same time to put the French fleet, as soon as possible, in condition to defend itself and be useful to us. The departure of the fleet from Rhode Island is not yet publicly announced here, but when it is, I intend to ascribe it to necessity, from the damage suffered in the late storm. This, it appears to me, is the Idea which ought to be generally propagated. As I doubt not the force of these Reasons will strike you equally with myself, I would recommend to you to use your utmost influence to palliate and soften matters, and induce those, whose business it is to provide succours of every kind for the fleet, to employ the utmost zeal and activity in doing it. It is our duty to make the best of our misfortunes, and not to suffer passions to interfere with our interest and the public good.

To Sullivan he wrote two letters. The first, on August 28, said: "Should the expedition fail, thro' the abandonment of the French fleet, the Officers concerned will be apt to complain loudly. But prudence dictates that we should put the best face upon the matter... The Reasons are too obvious... that our British and internal enemies would be glad to improve the least matter of complaint and disgust against and between us and our new allies into a serious rupture." He followed this with another letter on September 1: "The disagreement between the army under your command and the fleet has given me very singular uneasiness... first impressions, you know, are generally longest remembered, and will serve to fix in a great degree our national character among the French. In our conduct towards them we should remember that they are a people old in war, very strict in military etiquette and apt to take fire where others scarcely seem warmed. Permit me to recommend in the most particular manner, the cultivation of harmony and good agreement, and your endeavors to destroy that ill humour which may have got into the officers. It is of the greatest importance, also, that the... soldiers and the people should know nothing of the misunderstanding... I have one thing more... to say. I make no doubt but you will do all in your power to forward the repairs of the French fleet."

To Greene he wrote: "I depend much upon your temper and influence to conciliate that animosity which I plainly perceive by a letter from the Marquis, subsists between the American officers and the French in our service. This you may depend will extend itself to the Count and the officers and men to his whole fleet, should they return to Rhode Island, except upon their arrival, they find a reconciliation has taken place. The Marquis speaks kindly of a letter from you to him upon this subject. He will therefore take any advice coming from you in a friendly light, and if he can be pacified, the other French Gentlemen will of course be satisfied as they look up to him as their Head... I beg you will take every measure to keep the protest... from being made public... I fully depend upon your exerting yourself to heal all private animosities."

To Lafayette, who told Washington that his heart had been wounded "by that very people I came from so far to love and support," he wrote on September 1: "I feel every thing that hurts the Sensibility of a Gentleman; and consequently, upon the present occasion, feel for you and for our good and great Allys the French. I feel myself hurt also at every illiberal and unthinking reflection which may have been cast upon Count D'Estaing or the conduct of the fleet under his command; and lastly I feel for my Country. Let me entreat you my dear Marquis to take no exception at unmeaning expressions, uttered perhaps without Consideration, and in the first transport of disappointed hope. Everybody, Sir, who reasons, will acknowledge the advantages which we have derived from the French fleet, and the Zeal of the Commander of it, but in a free and republican Government, you cannot restrain the voice of the multitude; every man will speak as he thinks, or more properly without thinking, consequently will adjudge of Effects without attending to the Causes. The censures which have been levelled at the French fleet would more than probably have fallen in a much higher degree on our own (if we had one) in the same situation... Let me beseech you therefore my good Sir to afford a healing hand to the wound... I, your friend, have no doubt but that you will use your utmost endeavors to restore harmony, that the honour, glory and mutual Interest of the two Nations may be promoted and cemented in the firmest manner." Finally, Washington sat down and wrote a lengthy letter to d'Estaing:

> *If the deepest regret that the best concerted enterprise and bravest exertions should have been rendered fruitless by a disaster which human prudence is incapable of foreseeing or preventing can alleviate disappointment, you may be assured that the whole Continent sympathizes with you; it will be a consolation to you to reflect that the thinking part of Mankind do not form their judgement from events; and that their equity will ever attach equal glory to those actions which deserve success, as to those which have been crowned with it. It is in the trying circumstances to which your Excellency has been exposed that the virtues of a great Mind are displayed in their brightest lustre; and that the General's Character is better known than in the moment of Victory; it was yours, by every title which can give it...*
>
> *I exceedingly lament that in addition to our misfortunes, there has been the least suspension of harmony and good understanding between the Generals of allied Nations, whose views, like their interests must be the same. On the first intimation of it I employed my influence in restoring what I regarded as essential to the permanence of a Union founded on mutual inclination and the strongest ties of reciprocal advantage.*

Thanks to Washington everything quieted down. General Heath, in command at Boston, gave the fullest assistance in repairing the French fleet and in suppressing anti-French talk and action. The Massachusetts council called on d'Estaing to offer all the help the state could provide. Congress sent a resolution to d'Estaing praising him "as a brave and wise officer" who had rendered every benefit to the United States that circumstances permitted. Sullivan informed Washington that, having subdued his "passion," he had sent an apology to d'Estaing and dispatched Lafayette to Boston to help get the French fleet repaired. John Hancock and General Greene also went to Boston to aid d'Estaing. Bostonians gave it out that it was British prisoners who had attacked the French.

By September 16 Greene was writing Washington: "All the French officers are extravagantly fond of your Excellency but the Admiral more so than the rest." D'Estaing, fully appeased, sent Washington a message that might serve more than two hundred years later, when French-American friendship runs into storms:

If during the coming centuries, we of America and France are to live in amity and confidence, we must banish recriminations and prevent complaints. I trust the two nations will not be forced to depart from moderation in their conduct but that they will reflect in all their public affairs that firmness and consideration for public interests necessary to unity between the two great nations.

John Hancock presented a copy of a Peale portrait of Washington to Admiral d'Estaing. Lafayette wrote enthusiastically to Washington that Hancock had also promised him one. He mentioned that he had never seen a man so glad to have a picture "as the Admiral was to receive yours." Those who dined aboard the *Languedoc*, the flagship commanded by naval Captain and army General Louis de Bougainville (after whom the plant was named), noticed it hung in a conspicuous place, its frame decorated with laurels. In early November, d'Estaing sailed with all his ships and troops, and Washington's picture, for the West Indies, leaving the British in control of the seas off North America.

On September 23 Washington expressed his disappointment to his brother John: "Had the British garrison at Newport been captured," he said, it would "have hastened the departure of the Troops in New York as fast as their Canvas wings could convey them."

LAFAYETTE CHALLENGES CARLISLE

With the alliance repaired, Lafayette turned back to fighting the British. The commissioners of Albion called France a land of "perfidy." Lafayette immediately wrote to d'Estaing to tell him he would send Lord Carlisle a billet-doux challenging him to a duel. "I have nothing to do here that is very interesting and, while killing Lord Carlisle, I can at the same time transact more interesting business at White Plains." Washington was immediately dragged into this affair. Lafayette had requested Washington's "advice," by which he meant approval, but the latter replied on October 4:

The generous Spirit of Chivalry, exploded by the rest of the World, finds a refuge, My dear friend, in the sensibility of your Nation only. But it is in vain to cherish it, unless you can find Antagonists to support it... In our days it is to be feared that your opponent, sheltering himself behind Modern opinion, and under this present public Character of Commissioner, would turn a virtue of such ancient date, into ridicule... Besides, experience has proved, that chance is as often as much concerned in deciding these matters as bravery... I would not therefore have your life, by the remotest possibility, exposed, when it may be reserved for so many greater occasions. His excellency the Admiral, I flatter myself, will be in Sentiment with me.

D'Estaing and Carlisle reacted precisely as Washington predicted. The fatherly admiral was horrified and asked Washington to intervene to stop the duel. This he had already done and he replied to d'Estaing on October 24:

The coincidence between Your Excellency's sentiments... and those which I expressed to him on the same subject, are peculiarly flattering to me. I am happy to find that my disapprobation of the measure was founded on the same arguments...

I omitted neither serious reasoning nor pleasantry to divert him from a Scheme in which he could be so easily foiled... He intimated that Your Excellency did not discountenance it, and that he had pledged himself to the principal Officers of the French squadron... The charms of vindicating the honor of his country were irresistible... Though his ardour was an overmatch for my advice and influence, I console myself with the reflexion that his lordship will not accept the challenge... [He] has probably answered it in a strain of pleasantry.

Lord Carlisle, after considerable discussion at British headquarters, decided that he need not accept. He wrote rather ironically to Lafayette that he could not take the proposed duel very seriously, for he had spoken only as the king's commissioner, and Admirals Byron and d'Estaing were better fitted to decide national disputes. Lafayette had, however, made his point about French honor. The younger French and American officers thought highly of his action.

BRITISH TROUBLES

When Lord Cornwallis returned to America with the British commissioners and looked at the situation and the orders to retreat, he offered his resignation to London. This was refused on the ground that he was next in line to succeed Sir Henry Clinton.

There was not much for the commissioners to do in New York, especially as Congress ignored their communications. They occasionally lectured Americans, pointing out that America belonged not to them but to the British empire. A member of the commission, George Johnstone, probably acting on his own, wrote letters to Robert Morris and Joseph Reed, implying that they were men of great integrity but if they restored America to Great Britain, suitable rewards would be forthcoming for them, as well as for Washington and

Henry Laurens if they also helped. Washington correctly described these approaches as of a pulse-feeling cast but Congress decided to make the most of them. They published Johnstone's letters with a stern warning that they would have nothing further to do with a man who had made such "Daring and atrocious attempts to corrupt [our] integrity."

Johnstone in a great huff denied the allegations. Washington commented in a letter of September 12 to Henry Laurens: "He tries to convince you that he is not at all hurt by, or offended at, the interdiction of Congress. That he is not in a passion, while he exhibits a striking proof of his being cut to the quick, and actually biting his fingers in an agony of passion."

Carlisle was not at all pleased with this development, nor was William Eden who noted that Americans lacked "those principles of implied honour and confidence under which it is usual to transact business in Europe," that is, they complained out loud when offered bribes. Johnstone resigned from the commission and sailed back to England to tell the king that Congress should be destroyed.

On July 27 Sir Henry Clinton wrote to London to say that Washington's armies now numbered nearly 28,000 troops, and further additions to his forces could be expected after the harvests. (Washington, in fact, had the previously mentioned 16,700 men stretching from Boston and Rhode Island to New Jersey.) Clinton complained that he himself had only 26,000 rank and file who were fit for duty. He therefore did not know what his future plans might be. According to orders he had received from London, he was to dispatch 8,000 to the West Indies and Florida, plus troops to Canada which, he said, would make his command very small. Lord George Germain replied that, according to his own calculations, even after sending them, Clinton would still have more than 22,000 rank and file.

Sir Henry's projected attack on Newport, which was intended to capture the American forces there, totally failed when Sullivan evacuated Rhode Island. In frustration, Sir Henry sent General Charles Grey, later Earl Grey, to burn the towns of New Bedford and Fairhaven and to steal sheep from the farmers of Martha's Vineyard. Grey's activities were slightly repaid that spring when John Paul Jones raided Whitehaven, England, and also seized HMS *Drake* and several other prizes in English waters. On August 9 Lord Sandwich reported to the king that a French fleet under d'Orvilliers had fought a British fleet under Keppel and "the damage sustained [by the English] is very great indeed."

Lord Howe, after an abortive attempt to blockade d'Estaing at Boston, returned to New York and turned his command over to Admiral Byron. Howe sailed for England, having earlier asked for his recall.

The two remaining peace commissioners, Carlisle and Eden, decided that they too had had enough and they resigned. Carlisle had been pessimistic almost from the day he landed. On July 21 he informed his wife that "the common people hate us in their hearts, notwithstanding all that is said of their secret attachment to the mother country." By October he was writing his friend, George Selwyn: "Everything is upon a great scale on this continent. The rivers are immense; the climate violent in heat and cold; the prospects magnificent; the thunder and lightening tremendous.... We have nothing on so great a scale with us but our blunders, our misconduct, our ruin, our losses, our disgraces and misfortunes."

Though he wrote such private letters, Carlisle knew on which side his bread was sugared and he took care not to tell the same story to the king and ministers. He informed Germain in October: "The spirit of revolt is much abated... The French connection is generally disliked." On returning home the commissioners reported that there was a great upsurge in American loyalty to the king, which would further increase as soon as British strength was shown. Sir Henry Clinton commented in his memoirs that they painted a false picture of sentiment in America.

Before they left the United States, the peace commissioners issued a manifesto to the "British colonies," ordering them to break their alliance with the wicked French; otherwise Great Britain would be forced to lay the country waste to make it useless to France. By this time Americans were benumbed by threats and reacted only mildly. The severest castigations came from Englishmen of the character of Lord Rockingham who called it an "accursed proclamation." Washington commented to d'Estaing on October 27: "The British Commissioners, I believe, will not trouble us with any more of their harangues. They authorize us to consider the last as a farewell speech, preparatory to their final exit. They will not need our aid to accelerate their political death." On October 4 he had written to Gouverneur Morris: "God grant [the enemy] may embrace the opportunity of bidding an eternal adieu to our, once quit of them, happy land."

Lord Cornwallis took advantage of the serious illness of his wife to sail home with the commissioners. He did not expect to return to America. Generals Grey and Pigot and a General Jones also asked London for permission to return to England. On October 8 Sir Henry Clinton sent in his resignation to Lord George Germain, the second British commander in chief to do so within a year. Clinton said that, in accordance with his instructions, he had despatched troops to Bermuda, Halifax, Georgia, and the West Indies, and the forces remaining to him were too few to mount an offensive.

This scurrying to quit was a shock to the British cabinet. A long red and blue line of heroes had come up against the modest and humorous George Washington: Gage, the two Howes, Burgoyne, von Heister, Pigot, Cornwallis, St. Leger, Percy, Riedesel, Phillips, Fraser, Grey, Grant, Clinton, and Jones. By the end of 1778 only Clinton and Pigot were left in America, along with Phillips and Riedesel, who were prisoners. Pigot departed in 1779. George III was running out of generals. He and Germain placated Clinton with long flattering letters and sinecure appointments. Like Lord North, he was doomed to stay to the end. In November Lord North again beseeched the king to let his servant depart. The king replied on November 14 with more firmness than syntax:

> *If Lord North can see with the same degree of enthusiasm I do, the beauty, excellence, and perfection of the British Constitution as by Law Established, and consider that if any one branch of the Empire is allowed to cast off its dependency, that the others will infallibly follow the Example, that consequently though an arduous struggle that is worth going through any difficulty to preserve to the latest Posterity what the Wisdom of our Ancestors have carefully transmitted to us; he will not allow despondency to fill a place in his breast, but resolve not merely out of Duty to fill his post, but will resolve with Vigour to meet every obstacle that may arise he shall meet with most cordial Support from me; but the times require Vigour or the State will be ruined.*

Lord North answered that he would serve his master with all the firmness and resolution he could muster but that "his spirits, strength, memory, judgement and abilities [are] sensibly and considerably impaired."

THE FRONTIERS AND CANADA

The king's troops, aided by Tories and Indians, were also active on the frontiers of Pennsylvania and New York. In July they raided Wyoming Valley near the present Wilkes-Barre, destroying a thousand houses, scalping 227 Americans, and torturing many to death. The town of German flats in the Mohawk Valley was levelled to the ground and all the cattle and provisions of the inhabitants were taken. In November the houses in Cherry Valley went to the flames and more than thirty women and children, as well as many soldiers, were massacred.

This needless brutality put Washington in the difficult position intended. He had far fewer troops than the British, and these were stretched over a wide area. In July he detached a Pennsylvania and a New York regiment and part of

Morgan's corps to meet the attacks. By September he was writing the governor of New York that he was willing to send another regiment though he could ill spare it. In October he assigned General Hand to command all troops engaged in protecting the frontiers. The Indian and British ravages persuaded him that in the next campaign he should send troops against the Indians in order to break their power as an ally of Great Britain.

Congress gave him another problem when that body decided that the troops who had surrendered at Saratoga should be moved from Massachusetts to Charlottesville, Virginia. He had to arrange this difficult task primarily with the help of state militia. Sir Henry Clinton, knowing Washington had dispatched forces against the Indians, attempted to move up the Hudson to rescue the convention troops, but he arrived well after they had crossed the river. On December 12 Washington wrote Joseph Reed:

> *Sir Harry's late extra Maneuvre up the North River kept me upon the March and countermarch from the 5th until yesterday… What did, or could prompt the Knight to this expedition I am at a loss to discover… [I cannot conceive] that he could be so much out in point of intelligence to mistime matters so egregiously… I could not help being uneasy lest disaster might happen and posted back from Elizabeth Town at 4 O'clock on the Morning of the 5th and got within 12 or 15 Miles of King's Ferry, when I was met by an Express informing me that the Enemy had landed at that place, burn'd two or three small logged cabins with 9 Barrels of spoilt Herrings, and had reimbarked… for New York… Thus ended this notable expedition which was conducted… with so much secrecy that all the flag boats to and from the City were stopped and not a mouse permitted to move within their lines.*

Congress now returned to its old dream of taking Canada. This time Washington decided that Congress should make no more disastrous moves in that direction without carefully weighing every factor involved. Busy as he was, he worked much of the summer in appraising the situation, since Canada was the principal supply point for the Six Nations, who were attacking on the frontiers. In September he asked General Jacob Bayley, stationed in northern New York, to make an intelligence assessment of the Canadian garrison and defense system, the attitude of the people and clergy, the disposition of the Indians, the system of government, the size of the crops, and whether Canadians would welcome Americans as liberators. He also asked Generals Gates and Bayley to formulate a plan for a military invasion. In sending this first appraisal to Congress he suggested that, so long as the British were in the United States, "we shall find employment enough in defending ourselves, without meditating conquests."

On November 4 Washington received a resolution and plan from Congress for a full-scale invasion of Canada to be undertaken in cooperation with the French. This plan provided for attacks on Quebec and Montreal and invasions from Detroit and Niagara. During the following week Washington wrote a critique that was one of his most admirable state pieces. With political clairvoyance he wrote that someday France might no longer be an ally and could be a greater threat to American independence than Great Britain. Washington outlined his letter, then drafted and redrafted it before forwarding it on November 11. Congress had requested that he send a copy of his reply to Lafayette as a means of getting French help for the invasion. Washington suggested that this was unwise because he had to discuss the many weaknesses and wants in the army and these should be known only to Americans. He then indicated he thought the Canadian plan was unsound:

> *I consider it as my duty and what Congress expects from me, to give my reasons for this opinion, with that frankness and candour which the importance of the subject demands...*

> *It seems to me impolitic to enter into engagements with the Court of France for carrying on a combined operation of any kind, without a moral certainty of being able to fulfill our part...*

> *So far from being a moral certainty of our complying with our engagements, it may, in my opinion, be very safely pronounced that if the enemy keep possession of their present posts at New York and Rhode Island, it will be impracticable either to furnish the men or the necessary supplies...*

> *If I rightly understand the plan in consideration, it requires for its execution 12,600 Men, rank and file. Besides these, to open a passage through a Wilderness for the march of the several bodies of Troops, to provide the means of... transportation by land and Water, to establish posts... to build and man Vessels... these and many other purposes... will demand a much larger proportion of Artificers and persons to be employed in manual and laborous Offices, than are usual in the Ordinary course of military operations. When we add the whole together, the aggregate number of men requisite... will be little less than double the number heretofore in the field...*

> *The State of our Supplies for transporting and subsisting the troops will stand upon a footing equally bad... We have encountered extreme difficulties in these respects... in the Heart of the country... In Canada we should be carrying on the*

War at an immense distance, in a country... incapable of affording any aid, and the great part of it hostile...

...All the reasons which induce France and the United States to wish to wrest Canada and Halifax from the dominion of England, operate with her, perhaps more forcibly to use every possible effort for their defence. To hope to find them in a defenceless state, must be founded in a supposition of the total incapacity of Britain... We may run into a dangerous error by estimating her power so low...

A strong garrison has been lately sent to Halifax... The English are not greatly superior to the French by Sea in America...

...If the French troops should arrive before Quebec, I think their success against that strong place, fortified by every advantage of nature and of art would be extremely doubtful... [an attack] on Detroit... if well conducted, should [succeed] without very great difficulty. The case is very different with respect to Niagara. This I am informed is one of the strongest fortresses in America; and can only be reduced by regular approaches or by famine. (In accomplishing this last war and a conquest as far as Montreal... General Amherst exhausted two campaigns, with all the advantages he derived from the United Efforts of Britain and America... with plenty of Seamen... and money...)

The body of Troops to penetrate by way of the River St. Francis must meet with great obstacles... We may find ourselves in the bosom of an enemy's Country, obliged to combat their whole force with one inferior and reduced by a tedious and wasting march...

The plan proposed appears to me not only too extensive... but too complex. To succeed, it requires such a fortunate coincidence of circumstances as could hardly be hoped and cannot be relied on.

One draft of this letter contains typical Washington phraseology: "Your Number of Eaters will be little, if any, under 20,000... This Provision... is to be transported in wagons or by Pack horses some hundreds of miles the great part of which thro' an uninhabited Country." But he gave it a more dignified turn in the final polish. Washington added a political critique of the plan in a private letter to Henry Laurens, president of Congress:

I have one objection, untouched in my public letter, which is in my estimation, insurmountable, and alarms all my feelings for the true and permanent interests of my country. This is the introduction of a large body of French troops into Canada, and putting them in possession of the capital of that Province, attached to them by all the ties of blood, habits, manners, religion and former connexions of government... Let us realize for a moment the striking advantages France would derive from the possession of Canada; the acquisition of an extensive territory... the opening of a vast... commerce with the Indian nations... the having ports of her own on this continent... the facility of awing and controuling these states, the natural and most formidable rival of every maritime power in Europe.

France acknowledged for some time past the most powerful monarchy in Europe, able now to dispute the empire of the sea with Great Britain... possessed of New Orleans on our right, Canada on our left and seconded by the numerous tribes of Indians on our Rear... a people... whom she knows so well how to conciliate; would, it is much to be apprehended have it in her power to give law to these states... I am heartily disposed to entertain the most favourable sentiments of our new ally... but it is a maxim founded on the universal experience of mankind, that no nation is to be trusted farther than it is bound by interest; and no prudent statesman or politician will venture to depart from it.

Laurens replied that his military arguments against the attack on Canada were sufficiently persuasive that there was no need to bring up political objections in Congress. Thereafter Canada was left alone.

THE FALL OF CHARLES LEE

On December 22, 1778, Washington announced the results of the courts-martial of Generals Arthur St. Clair, Philip Schuyler, and Charles Lee. In a fit of vindictiveness over the loss of Ticonderoga in the summer of 1777, Congress had ordered St. Clair tried for treachery and cowardice and Schuyler for negligence. The fort had fallen to overwhelming British forces and the only negligence had been that of General Gates. St. Clair and Schuyler were acquitted unanimously and "with the highest honor." The trial of Lee was held at his request. Following the battle of Monmouth he wrote to Washington on June 30:

From the knowledge I have of your Excellency's character, I must conclude that nothing but the misinformation of some very stupid, or misrepresentation of some very wicked person, could have occasioned your making use of such very singular expressions as you did on my coming up to the ground where you had taken post. They implied that I was guilty either of disobedience of orders, or want of conduct, or want of courage. Your Excellency will therefore infinitely oblige me by letting me

know on which of these three articles you ground your charge, that I may prepare
for my justification which I have the happiness to be confident that I can do to the
army, to the Congress, to America, and to the world in general... I ever had, and
I hope I ever shall have the greatest respect and veneration for General
Washington; I think him endowed with many great and good qualities, but in this
instance, I must pronounce that he has been guilty of an act of cruel injustice... I
have a right to demand some reparation for the injury committed and unless I can
obtain it I must... retire from the service... In justice to you, I must repeat that I
from my soul believe, that it was not a motion of your own breast, but instigated
by some of those dirty earwigs who will for ever insinuate themselves near persons
in high office.

Washington issued orders that day for the arrest and court-martial of Lee. He wrote him: "I received your Letter (dated thro' mistake the 1st. of July) expressed as I conceive, in terms highly improper. I am not conscious of having made use of any very singular expression at the time of my meeting you, as you intimate. What I recollect to have said was dictated by duty and warranted by the occasion. As soon as circumstances will permit, you shall have an opportunity, either of justifying yourself to the army, to Congress, to America, and to the world in General; or of convincing them that you were guilty of a breach of orders and of misbehaviour before the enemy of the 28th. Inst. in not attacking them as you had been directed and in making an unnecessary, disorderly, and shameful retreat."

Lee's court-martial was held under considerable difficulties since the army was in movement from New Jersey to White Plains. The court reached its verdict about August 12. It found Lee guilty of disobedience of orders, misbehaviour, and disrespect to the commander in chief. He was sentenced to suspension from the army for a year.

St. Clair was tried subsequently to Lee, and Schuyler after St. Clair. Congress did not act on the results until December when all three verdicts were confirmed. Before his year of suspension was up, Lee wrote a sarcastic letter to Congress, and that body dismissed him from the army.

Lee had very little to do until his death in 1782, and he spent much of the time denouncing Washington. He suggested on one occasion, in a letter published July 6, 1779, in the *Maryland Journal* that Joseph Reed certainly knew the truth about the commander in chief. Reed, however, had become very nimble in shifting with the prevailing winds. He informed Washington that all he had ever said to Lee was: "With a thousand good and great qualities, there is a want of decision to complete the perfect military character." Reed denounced Lee's "malevolence" and his attempts to make Reed a "false witness." He congratulated Washington on the "public affection" enjoyed by him. John Laurens, Washington's aide, challenged Lee to a duel and shot him in the side. Lee's mind deteriorated; late in 1779 he described Washington to Gates as "dark, designing sordid ambitious vain proud arrogant and vindictive," adding that he was planning Lee's assassination.

After Lee's death, Washington wrote his sister in England on April 30, 1783, expressing "condolence of the loss of so near a relation; who was possessed of many great qualities." For his epitaph Washington, consciously or not, selected a phrase from Lee's letter to him of June 30, 1778.

PHILADELPHIA

Washington established his headquarters at Middlebrook, New Jersey, on December 11 and put his army in winter quarters there. This village was in a much more fertile area than Valley Forge. The army was better housed and fed than in the preceding winter and, thanks to French supplies, more warmly clothed. The winter was a remarkably mild one with relatively little frost or snow after the middle of January. To Joseph Reed, who had been elected head of the executive council of Pennsylvania, Washington wrote on December 12:

> Were I to give into private conveniency and amusement, I should not be able to resist the invitation of my friends to make Phila. (instead of a squeezed up room or two) my quarters for the Winter; but the affairs of the army require my constant attention and presence, and circumstanced as matters are at this time, calls for some degree of care and address to keep it from crumbling. As Peace and retirement are my ultimate aim, and the most pleasing and flattering hope of my Soul, every thing advancive of this end, contributes to my satisfaction… and will reconcile any place and all circumstances to my feelings whilst I continue in Service.

Congress, however, summoned Washington to Philadelphia for consultation on the 1779 campaign. He slipped quietly into the city on December 22. His wife was already there from Mount Vernon. The couple stayed with Henry Laurens who, having resigned his post as president of Congress, was replaced by John Jay, also of Huguenot descent. To assist in discussions with Congress, Washington had with him General Greene as well as his aides Laurens, Tilghman, and Hamilton. All five army men were shocked by Philadelphia. Under the influence of war, the British occupation and the greatly depreciated currency, the once-sober Quaker capital had become dissipated, with gambling, theatres, and all night balls and routs interfering with the work of

Congress. Joseph Reed's party to celebrate his election cost two thousand pounds; nearly a hundred glasses were broken. General Benedict Arnold, the city's military commander, was living in high style and courting the Tory Elizabeth Shippen. Washington was revolted. He wrote his stepson, Jack Custis, on January 2: "You say I shall be surprised at the slow progress made by [the Virginia] assembly in the passage of the bills through both houses. I really am not, nor shall I, I believe, be surprised at anything; for it appears to me that idleness and dissipation seem to have taken such fast hold of every body, that I shall not be at all surprised if there should be a general wreck of everything." To Benjamin Harrison in Virginia he wrote eight days after his arrival:

Our Affairs are in a more distressed, ruinous, and deplorable condition than they have been in Since the commencement of the War. By a faithful labourer then in the cause. By a Man who is daily injuring his private Estate without even the smallest earthly advantage not common to all in case of a favourable Issue to the dispute. By one who wishes the prosperity of America most devoutly and sees or thinks he sees it, on the brink of ruin, you are beseeched most earnestly, my dear Colo. Harrison, to exert yourself in endeavouring to rescue your Country, by... sending your best Men to Congress; these characters must not slumber, nor sleep at home, in such times of pressing danger... While the common interests of America are mouldering and sinking into irretrievable (if a remedy is not soon applied) ruin... If I was called upon to draw a picture of the times, and of Men; from what I have seen, heard, and in part know, I should in one word say that idleness, dissipation and extravagance seem to have laid fast hold of most of them... An insatiable thirst for riches seems to have got the better of every other consideration... That party disputes and personal quarrels are the great business of the day whilst the momentous concerns of an empire, a great and accumulated debt; ruined finances, depreciated money, and want of credit (which in their consequences is the want of every thing) are but secondary considerations and postponed from day to day, from week to week as if our affairs wore the most promising aspect; after drawing this picture, which from my Soul I believe to be a true one I need to repeat to you that I am alarmed and wish to see my Country men aroused. I have no resentments, nor do I mean to point out any particular character; this I can declare upon my honour for I have every attention paid me by Congress that I can reasonably expect and have reason to think that I stand well in their estimation... Your Money is now sinking 5 pr. Ct. a Day in this city... And yet an assembly, a concert, a Dinner, or Supper (that will cost three or four hundred pounds) will not only take Men off from acting but even from thinking of this business while a great part of the Officers of your Army from absolute necessity are quitting the Service and the more virtuous few rather than do this are sinking by sure degrees into beggary and want.

On December 28 Washington attended a Masonic festival in honor of St. John the Evangelist as well as services at Christ Church. There Dr. William Smith, later rector of the college at Chestertown, Maryland, renamed for Washington, referred to him as the "American Cincinnatus." He had also been called, most inappropriately, the "American Fabius Maximus," in praise and in sarcasm, but the "masterly inactivity" of Fabius, "the delayer," was totally foreign to his nature and desire. Nonetheless he had to conclude that with a weak Congress, inadequate public backing for the army's needs, and no credit, he could only continue a defensive war. He made clear that under these circumstances the Canada conquest was a mirage and Congress acquiesced. He proposed instead an expedition to end the Indian attacks on the frontier, and Congress approved this plan. For the rest the army could act only to contain Clinton in his two northern ports. Congress at this time gave Washington full authority to direct all military operations in all parts of the country, the most comprehensive power he had received.

Before he left Philadelphia, Washington learned that some of the British troops sent south from New York had taken Savannah in December and had moved on to Augusta. Much of Georgia came under their control. This was of no great military significance, but it added a new dimension to Washington's problems. He did not yet know that the king and Germain had decided that the war could be won more easily in the south than in the north.

On January 6 the Washingtons attended a dance at the house of Mrs. Samuel Powel, whose husband had been mayor of Philadelphia. Benjamin Franklin's daughter, Sarah Bache, was there and she wrote her father in Paris a few days later: "I have lately been several times invited abroad with the General and Mrs. Washington. He always inquires after you in the most affectionate manner, and speaks of you highly. We danced at Mrs. Powel's your birthday [old style] or night I should say, in company together, and he told me it was the anniversary of his marriage; it was just twenty years that night."

Washington's officers bore the gaiety of Philadelphia with disapproval. Tench Tilghman wrote to his fellow aide, James McHenry, at Middlebrook: "I suppose you think we must be by this time so wedded to sweet Philadelphia that it will break our hearts to leave it. Far from it... we anxiously await the moment that gives us liberty to return to humble Middlebrook. Philadelphia may answer very well for a man with his pockets well lined, whose pursuit is idleness and dissipation. But to us, it is intolerable... By the body of my father, as honest Sancho used to swear, we have advanced as far in luxury in the 3d year of our independency as... Greece and Rome did in twice as many hundred." General Greene summed it up to General McDougall in February: "I spent a month in the most agreeable and disagreeable manner I ever did a month in my life. We had the most splendid entertainment imaginable; large assemblies, evening balls, etc. It was hard service to go through the duties of the day. I was obliged to rise early and go to bed late... Our great Fabius Maximus was the glory and admiration of the city. Every exertion was made to show him respect and make his time agreeable; but the exhibition was such a scene of luxury and profusion they gave him more pain than pleasure."

On January 29, after posing for a portrait by Charles Peale at the request of Pennsylvania, Washington urgently asked Congress to let him return to the army. He and Martha went off a few days later, arriving at Middlebrook on February 5.

About the end of the year a Pennsylvania German almanac was published for 1779. On its cover was a laureled head labelled "Waschington." Above it was an angel trumpeting the words "Des Landes Vater," the first known use of this term.

MIDDLEBROOK

Washington, no *cunctator*, at once set to work to organize all possible intelligence for the frontier campaign. His knowledge of the Indian tribes and of much of the territory involved was clearly revealed in his letters. He sent out a heavy correspondence, with detailed questions to his officers and agents, westward to Detroit and north to New Hampshire. He also appealed to Pennsylvania to collect all state maps and surveys of the areas around the Allegheny and Susquehanna Rivers.

To General McIntosh at Pittsburgh he had addressed lengthy instructions before leaving Philadelphia: "I would wish you to have the Country well explored between Pittsburgh and Detroit... also the water conveyances to that post (Detroit) by the Scioto and other waters, leading out of the Ohio towards Lake Erie, and the distance of portage between the heads of those Rivers and the Waters of the lake... I would also have you make yourself perfectly informed of the water and land communications between Pittsburgh and Presquile; what kind of Craft can pass up French Creek (or River la Beuf) and whether such Craft can be transported across from French Creek to the Lake... When the Northern Indians go to War with the Southern, they fall into the Allegheny River and come down from thence to Fort Pitt... whether they make use of any water Carriage is a matter worth enquiring into... Let it also be inquired how far this route is wide of the falls of Niagara and Lake Erie."

Other letters went to his officers: "Let me know... how far Rochester is from Mahcomac? and how far is it from Middle Brook to Mahcomac, what kind of road, and which is the best Route? I wish to be informed of the distances from Chemung and Ononaquaga to Niagara? Which is the easiest and best route to the principal settlements of the Six Nations... How far it is from Cannedessago to Chessie a capital Seneca Village?"

By March he sent more standardized questionnaires to all general and field officers having knowledge of the Indian country. They were sweeping in detail and covered road and water routes, distances, limits of navigation, when grass would grow for forage, the best types of batteaux and canoes to use, and the strength and fortifications of all Indian villages.

To his quartermaster General Greene he sent orders to provide 150 batteaux, 1,500 axes, 1,000 spades and shovels, 2,000 knapsacks, 3,000 canteens, 6,000 horse shoes, 1,000 horse bells and a great miscellany of saws, files, quill pens, orderly books, ink stands, paper, and candlesticks.

With some reluctance Washington chose Gates to head the army going west but Gates refused, in a letter the commander in chief thought rather brusque. He therefore selected Sullivan, whose tactlessness would matter little in the West. By early summer he and his army were ready to move.

CAMP LIFE

Though Washington's officers had complained of the constant gaiety at Philadelphia, life at camp was not entirely ascetic. On the first anniversary of the French alliance Washington gave a dinner followed by fireworks and a ball. According to General Knox, the dance was attended by seventy or more ladies and four to five times as many officers. Washington opened the dance with Mrs. Knox, perhaps the fattest woman there. A few days later General Greene and his wife gave a ball at which Washington and Mrs. Greene danced for three hours without sitting down.

On February 25 Dr. James Thacher, a surgeon attached to the army, attended a headquarters dinner where George and Martha Washington presided. He wrote in his journal the next day: "It is natural to view with keen attention the countenance of an illustrious man, with a secret hope of discovering in his features some peculiar trace of excellence, which distinguishes him from and elevates him above his fellow mortals. These expectations are realized in a peculiar manner, in viewing the person of George Washington.

His tall and noble stature and just proportions, his fine, cheerful open countenance, simple and modest deportment, are all calculated to interest every
beholder in his favour, and to command veneration and respect... In conversation his Excellency's expressive countenance is peculiarly pleasing and
interesting; a placid smile is frequently observed on his lips... He is polite and
attentive to each individual... Mrs. Washington combines in an uncommon
degree, great dignity of manner with the most pleasing affability, but possesses
no striking marks of beauty."

On May 2 the United States army paraded for the first time for distinguished foreign visitors, Conrad Gérard, the French minister, and Don Juan
de Miralles of Spain. Spain was displaying little enthusiasm for revolution in
the western hemisphere. Miralles had been sent as an unaccredited agent to
Philadelphia. Dr. Thacher recorded the event:

> The whole of our army in this quarter was paraded... in a spacious field... At the
> signal of thirteen cannon, the great and splendid cavalcade approached... A very
> beautiful troop of light horse, commanded by major Lee, a Virginian, marched in
> front, then followed His Excellency the Commander in Chief and his aids... next
> the foreign ministers... and the general officers... [They] passed in front of the line
> of the army, from right to left in review, and received the military honours due their
> rank; after which the gentlemen dismounted and retired to the stage, and took seats
> with Mrs. Washington, Mrs. Greene, Mrs. Knox and a number of other ladies...
> The army then performed the field maneuvers and evolutions, with firing of
> cannon and musketry.

Thacher noted that Washington looked "incomparably more majestic" than
the foreigners. Gérard and Miralles politely praised everything. Later Miralles
sent the Washingtons some Cuban products, chocolate, sugar, guava jelly, and
crystal flasks.

The main purpose of the meeting was to enable Gérard and Washington to
discuss overall strategy in the event d'Estaing could return with his fleet from
the West Indies. Washington was cautious, in view of what had happened at
Newport, his limited supplies and troops, and his planned expedition to the
West. Gérard talked of attacks on Nova Scotia and Newfoundland, but these
points were too far removed. Washington wanted a second joint operation
against Newport, provided that this time the French had superiority of sea
power, but Gérard could not assure this. The conversations ended with an
agreement that a Franco-American attack on Savannah, now held by the
British, offered the most feasible immediate operation. If this were successful,
further joint operations in the North could be reviewed. Gérard clearly found

Washington a relief after dealing with Congress, about which he often complained to Versailles. He wrote from Middlebrook to the French foreign minister: "I have had many conversations with General Washington, some of which have continued for three hours... I will now say only that I have formed as high an opinion of the powers of his mind, his moderation, his patriotism, and his virtues, as I had before from common report conceived of his military talents and of the incalculable services he has rendered to his country." Washington quickly turned from the French to another group of allies, the Delaware Indian chiefs. He made them a simple and humorous speech on May 12:

Brothers: I am happy to see you here... I am glad also you have left all our friends of the Delaware Nation well.

Brothers: I have read your paper. The things you have said are weighty things, and I have considered them well... I rejoice in the new assurances you give of your friendship...

Brothers: I am a Warrior. My words are few and plain; but I will make good what I say. 'Tis my business to destroy the enemies of these states and to protect their friends. You have seen how we have withstood the English for four years; and how their great Armies have dwindled away and come to very little; and how what remains of them... are glad to stay upon Two or three little Islands... The English, Brothers, are a boasting people. They talk of doing a great deal; but they do very little. They fly away on their Ships from one part of our Country to another; but as soon as our Warriors get together they leave it and go to some other part. They took Boston and Philadelphia... but when they saw our Warriors... they were forced to leave them.

Brothers: We have till lately fought the English all alone. Now the Great King of France... has taken up the Hatchet with us, and we have sworn never to bury it, till we have punished the English and made them sorry for All the wicked things they had in their Hearts to do against these States...

Brothers: I am glad you have brought three of the children of your principal Chiefs to be educated with us. I am sure Congress will open the Arms of love to them... This is a great mark of your confidence... You do well to wish to learn our arts and ways of life, and above all, the religion of Jesus Christ. This will make you a greater and happier people...

Brothers: When you have seen all you wish to see, I will then wish you a good

journey to Philadelphia. I hope you may find there every thing your hearts can wish,
that when you return home you may be able to tell your Nation good things of us.

Two days later Washington held another army parade for the Indian chiefs. Dr. Thacher commented: "His Excellency, with his usual dignity, followed by his mulatto servant, riding a beautiful grey steed, passed in front of the line and received the salute. He was accompanied by a singular group of savages, whose appearance was beyond description ludicrous, their personal decorations equally farcical having their faces painted of various colors, jewels suspended from their ears and nose... tufts of hair on the crown... and dirty blankets." Martha Washington nearly collapsed with laughter. She described the sight of her husband surrounded by Indians as "funny" and "ridiculous." She mentioned that some of them "were fairly fine-looking but most of them appeared worse than Falstaff's gang... The General says it was done to keep the Indians friendly towards us." The general also extracted every ounce of intelligence he could from them.

Martha Washington was bundled off in a hurry to Mount Vernon at the beginning of June with a lot of good stories to tell. Sir Henry Clinton, prodded urgently by London to beat Washington, had moved up the Hudson to Stony Point.

TWENTY-SIX

MIDDLEBROOK
TO WEST POINT

1779–1780

W HEN THE CAMPAIGN of 1778 closed, Lafayette asked permission to return to France to offer his services to Louis XVI. On October 6 Washington endorsed his request to Congress for a furlough, adding that he was reluctant to part with an officer "who unites to all the military fire of youth, an uncommon maturity of judgment." In praising his "bravery and conduct," he suggested that Congress give Lafayette a suitable testimonial.

Congress voted him leave and their hearty thanks for his "services... courage and abilities on many signal occasions." They ordered Benjamin Franklin to procure an "elegant sword... to be presented in the name of the United States" to the young general. In addition the president wrote "To our Great, Faithful, and Beloved Friend and Ally, Louis the Sixteenth," praising Lafayette for his wisdom, gallantry, and patience under the hardships of war.

Washington also sent a note to Franklin describing Lafayette's many brave exploits and his own "particular friendship for him." He forwarded it to Lafayette on December 29 with a letter:

I am persuaded, My dear Marquis, there is no need of fresh proofs to convince you either of my affection for you personally or of the high opinion I entertain of your military talents and merit. Yet as you are on the point of returning to your country, I cannot forbear indulging my friendship by adding to the many honourable testimonies you have received from Congress, the inclosed letter [to Franklin.] I have there endeavoured to give him an idea of the value this country sets upon you; and the interest I take in your happiness cannot but make me desire you may be equally dear to your own.

Adieu, my Dear Marquis. My best wishes will ever attend you.

From Boston Lafayette wrote a farewell note: "To hear from you, my most respected friend, will be the greatest happiness I can feel... I hope you will quietly enjoy the pleasure of being with Mrs. Washington, without any disturbance from the enemy, till I join you again... Farewell, my most beloved general... The sails are just going to be hoisted... I hope your french friend will ever be dear to you... With what emotion I now leave the coast you inhabit, and with what affection and respect I'll for ever be, my dear General, your respectful and sincere friend."

Lafayette had violated the king's orders when he went to the United States. Louis XVI had to place him under technical arrest on his arrival in Paris. In a graceful gesture he was confined for one week in the great Hotel de Noailles. He was then released to call on the king and to receive wild popular acclaim. Louis XVI promoted him from captain to colonel of the king's dragoons and assigned him to the army that was assembling to invade England. The failure of the Spanish and French fleets to cooperate led to the abandonment of the plan. Lafayette looked around for other ways to help Americans.

Lafayette asked Franklin whether the French cabinet was doing all it could for him and whether America needed anything more. Franklin replied that the ministers were splendid, that America did need more money and supplies, but he knew that France had heavy war expenditures and he did not want to ask. Lafayette did the asking; as he later told Franklin, he could be much more demanding than the American minister. He requested ships, troops, supplies of every sort, and money loans and grants. The cabinet, particularly Vergennes, had not planned to send an army to America or to bankrupt France but Lafayette eventually won many points. He was so importunate that the prime minister, the comte de Maurepas, grumbled that he wanted everything but the furniture at Versailles for "his dear Americans. The king can deny him nothing."

Washington had noted Lafayette's maturity of judgement. With all his romantic nature and desire to place the French flag on the soil of "insolent" England, he was down to earth in detailing the kind of officers needed for

America. He said the French would find the Americans rather difficult people; tough officers should be selected who could live on little, be tactful to the natives, endure boredom, and get on without any of the pleasures of France. His romanticism came out when he asked to head the troops but the king could not nominate a captain, just raised to colonel, over all his generals.

Washington's letters to Lafayette did not reach him before he left Boston. They did not hear from each other for months, although each bombarded the other with letters. Lafayette wrote in June that he was afflicted at being so far from his dearest friend, particularly with the campaign opening. He added, "I have a wife, my dear General, who is in love with you... She begs you will receive her compliments and make them acceptable to Mrs. Washington." He also asked Washington to tell Congress not to go on "loudly disputing together," for it was making a poor impression in Europe. Soon he was hinting to Washington that troops might be on their way and that Madame de Lafayette was expecting a child.

He expressed to Congress the "unbounded affection and admiration which I shall ever feel for them... To the letter congress was pleased to write on my account, I owe the many favours the king has conferred upon me; there was no time lost in appointing me to the command of his own regiment of dragoons, and everything he could have done, everything I could have wished, I have received on account of your recommendation."

Washington did not get Lafayette's July letter until the end of September, but he expressed his pleasure at receiving it, in two inordinately long letters, one of which, he said, reached nearly from West Point to Paris. He was delighted by the reception Lafayette had received and said how pleased he would be to have him return, either as "head of a corps of gallant French or as a Major Genl. commanding a division of the American Army." He hoped he would bring his wife. "I love every body that is dear to you." He congratulated Lafayette and his wife on their expected child, "this fresh pledge she is about to give you of her love." He made a complete summary of all the operations to October 1779, concluding his letter of the twentieth: "It only remains for me now to beg the favour of you to present my respectful compliments to *your* (but have I not a right, as you say she had made a tender of her love to *me*, to call her *my*) amiable and lovely Marchioness." On December 24 a son was born to the marquise and christened George Washington de Lafayette, names that were to be regarded with horror by the reactionary regimes of Napoleon and the Bourbons.

Partly because of a delay in receiving it, and perhaps from some modesty on his part, Lafayette did not show his letter from Washington to Franklin until he was in France nearly a year. On March 5, 1780, Franklin wrote

Washington that he had only lately received it but he had formed the same regard and esteem for Lafayette that Washington held for him. He continued:

> *Should peace arrive after another campaign or two, and afford us a little leisure, I should be happy to see your Excellency in Europe and to accompany you, if my age and strength would permit, in visiting some of its ancient and most famous kingdoms. You would, on this side of the sea, enjoy the great reputation you have acquired, pure and free from those little shades that the jealousy and envy of a man's countrymen... are ever endeavouring to cast over living merit. Here you would know, and enjoy, what posterity will say of Washington. For a thousand leagues have nearly the same effect with a thousand years... At present I enjoy that pleasure for you; as I frequently hear the old generals of this martial country, who study the maps of America, speak with sincere approbation and great applause of your conduct; and join in giving you the character of one of the greatest captains of the age.*

Washington's generalship—even more than Franklin's diplomatic skills, which could not operate in a vacuum—produced the final financial, naval, and military support of the court of France. Another factor favored the Americans. France was largely fighting a naval war and the army had found little chance for glory. The younger officers in particular were more than anxious to do as Lafayette in America and their attitude influenced the court.

Franklin forwarded to Lafayette the congressional sword inscribed with an account of his battles together with a letter: "By the help of the exquisite artists France affords, I find it easy to express everything but the sense we have of your worth and our obligations to you." Lafayette replied that the "goodness of the United States... far surpasses any idea I could have conceived... In some of the devices I cannot help finding too honourable a reward for those slight services, which, in concert with my fellow soldiers, and under the godlike American Hero's orders, I had the good luck to render. The sight of these actions, where I was a witness of American bravery and patriotic spirit, I shall ever enjoy with that pleasure, which becomes a heart, glowing with love for the nation and the most ardent zeal for their glory and happiness."

Franklin had complained to Congress that they were wasting some of the money lent by France, for he found orders from Philadelphia for tea, gewgaws, and frivolities. (His own daughter did not escape censure when she asked him for feathers from France and he answered: "*Feathers*... feathers, my dear girl, may be had in America from every cock's tail.") When France made a grant of six million livres early in 1780, Franklin was told it was to be spent only by Washington since it might be wasted by the various committees of

Congress. Franklin protested, but very mildly, and forwarded the information to Congress with a note that the giver had the right to make the terms. Congress was outraged at this rather justifiable slap, but, at Washington's insistence, the French minister found a qualifying clause that enabled the legislature to regain control.

In the autumn of 1779 the king tapped Lieutenant General the Comte de Rochambeau to head the French army in America. He had been a soldier since he entered military academy when Washington was eight. Like Washington, he was a colonel at twenty-two. He had served under Saxe, once a famous French marshal; fought at Klostercamp; and became inspector general of the French infantry. He was short and stocky, solid and cool, and a disciplinarian intensely knowledgeable in his profession. He was carefully selected as a man who would be tactful with Americans while maintaining an army of high discipline in a foreign country.

ENGLAND'S TROUBLES

A well-known characteristic of George III and his war ministers was their quite human preference for hearing what they wanted to hear and believing what they wanted to believe. They expected flattery, servility, and reports that cheered. The American Tories, British officers, and courtiers were more than willing to supply these. They contributed to the king's determination to proceed with the war at all costs. His papers are full of reports that the great majority of Americans were loyal to him, the Congress and the French alliance were hated, and the American army was small and starving. All that had to be done was to beat Washington, to destroy the coastal towns, and to get the Indians to provide "a diminution of the number of Americans." Some of the reports were quite accurate—that Washington had been reduced to 3,300 men at the end of 1776, to 6,000 at Morristown, and to 4,000 at Valley Forge. George III may have wondered what the more than 75,000 soldiers, sailors, and marines he had sent to America had been doing and why there were contradictory reports from Sir Henry Clinton claiming that Washington had moved from Valley Forge to Monmouth with an army of 18,000, which grew to 20,000 a month later.

The court might be euphoric and the king in constant expectation that Americans were about to "sue for pardon," but many of his subjects were far more realistic. The growth of royal power and corruption, the prolonged war with its constant increase in loans and taxes, the casualty lists with nothing to show for them, and the sympathy of the best English for the Americans resulted in a continuous growth of opposition that came close to revolution in England.

The defeat in July 1778 of Keppel's fleet by the French, in which, as Sandwich reported to the king, their fleet was badly damaged, shocked British naval pride. A Tory vice admiral, Hugh Palliser, brought charges against Keppel, a Whig, and the affair became a heated political dispute. Keppel had the ardent support of the great Whig lords, two of the king's brothers, and Burke and Fox. When he was acquitted on February 11, 1779, there was a great outburst of popular enthusiasm for the Whigs and a harrying of the Tories. Mobs broke loose and burned Palliser's house to the ground. An attack was made on the houses of North and Germain. The mob then surged over to the admiralty and, as Walpole reported, forced the very frightened Lord Sandwich to flee with his mistress, Martha Ray. A few weeks later, Miss Ray was murdered by a disappointed lover, and the kindly king sent his condolences to the first lord of the admiralty.

From London William Eden wrote Sir Henry Clinton that he had better take every action possible, including the bribing of American leaders, before the mischief makers succeeded in stopping the war. Germain also suggested to Clinton the extensive use of bribes, adding that he would "cheerfully" approve such expenditures.

Resolutions in Parliament denouncing Sandwich for sending Keppel out against a larger French fleet were beaten, but other attacks were made on the Germain ministry. General Grey, who had served with Howe and Clinton, said that the idea of conquering America was impractical, and Lord North told the king that his statement had caused a great stir. Further resolutions petitioning the king to stop the "unnatural war" with America and to withdraw all his forces in order to fight France failed. The king told North on June 11 that there was "but one Sensible, one great line to follow, the being ever ready to make Peace when to be obtained without submitting to terms that in their consequence must annihilate this Empire."

On June 15 North wrote the king that his "faculties of mind & body are daily diminishing, & he is sorry to say, that the difficulties of this country are increasing," and he ought to resign. The king answered that "the times are certainly hazardous, but that ought to rouze the Spirit of Every Englishman to support me." Two days later he received the Spanish declaration of war on England.

In the autumn two cabinet members quit in protest. North continued to be depressed about the war, the dissensions in the cabinet, and the fact that others were permitted to resign. On November 3 he wrote the king that he could not come around to the palace that day "having been detained... by a most material and perplexing public distress arising from the great quantity of bills drawn at New York and Quebec... the greater part of which will become due before Christmas... and there has not yet occurd any method of paying them." The following day Charles Jenkinson reported to the king that the attorney general, after threatening to resign, had decided not to, but he would have nothing to do with Lord North thereafter.

The king told North that he had not treated his fellow cabinet members well and that was why they were quitting. North replied that he had been unhappy in his post for ten years, he had been "criminal" in keeping it, and now he felt miserable and guilty when no one, including the king, approved of his conduct.

A fresh wind in British politics appeared in Yorkshire, where voters overwhelmingly passed a petition to Parliament stating that the great sums voted in the budgets had been squandered and used too often for corrupt purposes. The increase in the power of the Crown was endangering the liberties of the country and it should be curtailed. The Yorkshire Resolves inflamed England. Soon twenty-six English counties endorsed them. Committees of association and correspondence were established in counties, towns, and cities, which voted to send delegates to a general convention. So great was the voice of the country that Parliament could not brush aside the petitions as it had those from Philadelphia.

After a bitter struggle, Parliament, by a majority of eighteen votes, passed the famous resolve of John Dunning: "It is necessary to declare that the influence of the Crown has increased, is increasing, and ought to be diminished." North, in reporting this to the king, said he ought now to quit and that he had been warning him for four years this would occur. The king assured North the resolutions "can by no means be looked on as personal to him; I wish I did not feel at whom they are *personally levelled.*" Four days later the king felt more assured and told North: "It is attachment to my Country that alone actuates my purposes and Lord North shall see that at least there is one person willing to preserve unspoiled the most beautiful Combination that was ever formed." The king soon regained control and the Dunning resolution for the moment was the high point of opposition to the Crown.

THE HUDSON

Lord George Germain had informed Sir Henry Clinton in January that the members of the Carlisle commission had given the cabinet "a perfect knowledge of the real state of affairs in America." In consequence Clinton should bring Washington to "a general and decisive action" but in any case drive him back to the Highlands of New York or to New Jersey, whereupon, as the commissioners had reported, the inhabitants would freely return to allegiance to their king. In addition Clinton should continue burning the coastal towns of New England and Virginia and bring renewed Indian raids on the frontier farms. He promised Clinton nearly seven thousand reinforcements in 1779.

On May 5 Clinton sent an expedition to Virginia to ravage the tidewater region. When this force returned, Sir Henry moved up the Hudson on May 30 with six thousand troops and easily took the poorly defended American works at Verplanck's and Stony Points. The British set to work to improve the fortifications. This greatly inconvenienced the American army, whose connection with New England now had to be maintained by a route farther up the Hudson. The move also threatened West Point, which Washington considered the key defense post in America. Washington moved his army to Smith's Clove in Orange County, some fourteen miles west of the West Point area, to meet any attempt Clinton might make on the fort. Not long afterwards he changed his headquarters to New Windsor, near Newburgh, and then to the Moore house, a mile north of West Point.

Clinton left around eleven hundred men at the two forts with orders to make Stony Point a strong fortress. He then moved back to New York and sent a pillaging expedition into Connecticut. Its commanders were William Tryon, former royal governor of New York, and Sir George Collier, a naval commodore who had taken part in the raids on Virginia. They landed near New Haven where, after doing much damage, they were driven off by the militia. They then proceeded to burn down the towns of Fairfield, Norwalk, and Horse Neck (now more elegantly called Greenwich). As a result of their activities, the New England societies for preserving antiquities have had less work to do.

At Washington's request General Parsons made a survey of the damage. He reported that the British at Fairfield had burned 97 houses, 67 barns, 3 churches, 2 schoolhouses, and numerous shops. At Norwalk they destroyed 130 houses, 87 barns, and 2 churches, as well as numerous other buildings. On September 12 Washington wrote Lafayette of the destruction by "the intrepid and magnanimous Tryon who, in defiance of all the opposition... by the Women and Children... of these towns, performed this notable exploit with 2000 brave and generous Britons, adding thereby fresh lustre to their Arms and dignity to their King."

Washington, with no naval force of consequence, could not prevent such raids but the burning of the towns made him anxious to retaliate. He had picked General Wayne to command at Fort Montgomery, five miles north of Stony Point, and urged him to get every intelligence on the work being done there, adding that he had an attack on the fort "much at heart." Wayne selected Captain Allan McLane to go into the fort, under a flag of truce, where he made a rapid assessment of the situation. Wayne, McLane, and Light Horse Harry Lee subsequently held the fort under continual observation. On July 6 Washington himself came over to look at the works. He and Wayne went over all possible means of attack, Washington writing these out in detail. After receiving reports of the destruction in Connecticut, he told Wayne it was "infinitely desirable" that the attack be made in the near future.

Captain McLane's diary report of the July 15 engagement was brief: "At ten o'clock rode with Majors Posey and Lee to reconnoitre the enemy's lines. Genl. Waine moved down from the forest... At 8 o'clock at night moved my company close to the enemy's sentrys... At 30 minutes past 12 o'clock the light infantry began the attack on the lines, Genl. Waine at their head. They rushed on with fixed bayonets and carried the lines in 25 minutes—killed one capt., 21 privates, wounded 4 subalterns, 66 privates, took one colonel, 4 captains, 15 subalterns, 468 men."

At 2 A.M. Wayne sent a dispatch to Washington: "Dear Genl. This fort & Garrison with Coln. Johnson are our's. Our Officers & Men behaved like men who are determined to be free." American casualties were about ninety.

Sir Henry Clinton, greatly shocked, recalled his troops who were planning further raids on Connecticut. The American Tories in New York and London bitterly attacked Clinton for the defeat, while the English Whigs raised horrified hands at his destruction of defenseless towns.

On July 21 Washington sent Wayne's report to Congress with a lengthy letter. He said: "to the encomiums he has deservedly bestowed on the officers and men under his command, it gives me pleasure to add that his own conduct throughout the whole of this arduous enterprise, merits the warmest approbation of Congress. He improved upon the plan recommended by me and executed it in a manner that does signal honour to his judgment and to his bravery. In a critical moment of the assault he received a flesh wound in the head with a musket-ball; but continued leading on his men with unshaken firmness." Washington explained to Congress that he and his engineers had gone over the fortifications after the battle and had decided that Stony Point would need far more troops and materials than he could spare. It would have to be fortified against both land and river and this was too expensive. He had therefore ordered the British guns and supplies removed and the fortifications destroyed.

Washington followed with another blow at the British that was less complete. Light Horse Harry Lee itched to emulate Mad Anthony Wayne. Washington and Lee together planned the attack on Paulus (or Powle's) Hook on the point near the present Jersey City. Several plans that Lee proposed were rejected by Washington as risking too many troops, but they finally agreed on an expedition of four hundred men. It was an impudent plan, to be carried out under the nose of the British garrison at New York and the Royal Navy in the Hudson. The attack was set for shortly after midnight on August 18. A part of the attacking force got lost on the way and the remainder arrived much later than the plan anticipated. Lee pushed through nevertheless, carried the fort by surprise, largely because of British negligence, and took off 158 officers and men.

Congress passed resolutions of high praise for Washington, Wayne, and Lee, awarding the latter two gold medals. According to his usual habit, Washington published to his troops everything but congressional praise of the commander in chief.

CLINTON AND WASHINGTON

The blow at Paulus Hook, only a short distance by water from the great British fortifications on Manhattan, quite unnerved Clinton. Both the army and the Tories blamed him for two humiliating episodes. From Clinton's headquarters Colonel Charles Stuart reported to his father, Lord Bute, that Clinton was "tremendously depressed... His temper from these two unlucky blows... became much soured."

Two days after Lee's raid, Sir Henry Clinton again offered his resignation to Lord George Germain, suggesting that Lord Cornwallis was much more suitable for the command. Cornwallis had departed with the peace commissioners to see his ill wife and had not intended to return. When she died, he found England gloomy and he again offered his services to the king. He returned to America in July and this gave Clinton his chance. Again London refused, saying how badly he was needed in America. With the political troubles at home and the wide criticism of the American war, the government could not afford further resignations by its commanders. Washington was in a much more cheerful mood than Clinton. On August 16 he wrote from West Point to John Cochran, one of his army physicians:

I have asked Mrs. Cockran and Mrs. Livingston to dine with me to morrow; but ought I not to apprize them of their fare?...

It is needless to premise that my table is large enough to hold the ladies... To say how it is usually covered is rather more essential... Since our arrival at this happy spot, we have had a Ham (sometimes a shoulder) of Bacon, to grace the head of the table; a piece of roast Beef adorns the foot; and a small dish of Greens or Beans (almost imperceptible) decorates the center.

When the Cook has a mind to cut a figure (and this I presume he will attempt to do to morrow) we have two Beefsteak Pyes, or dishes of Crabs, in addition one on each side the center dish, dividing the distance between dish and dish to about Six feet, which without them, would be near twelve a part. Of late, he has had the surprizing luck to discover that apples make pyes; and it's a question if amidst the violence of his efforts, we do not get one of apples instead of having both of Beef.

If the ladies can put up with such entertainment and will submit to partake of it on plates, once tin but now Iron; (not become so by the labour of scowering) I shall be happy to see them.

INTELLIGENCE

Washington, aided by his small special congressional fund, continued to develop his intelligence apparatus. He informed Congress that he often had to use "ambiguous characters," and to let them carry goods in to the enemy, as "cover to their mission." However some of them had been picked up for violating state laws against trading with the enemy; he had then to intervene to save them from prosecution but he thereby lost their services. He developed an unexpected talent in writing crude dialogue to be used by his double agents:

Where is Mr. Washington and what number of men has he with him?

Cant tell the number exactly. Some says eight thousand and very knowing has ten thousand. I dont think he has 8000 with himself, besides the Jersey Brigade, another brigade at which I hear is at Paramus…

Whether there is any discontent among the soldiers.

I cant say theres much discontent among the sodgers, tho' their Money is so bad. They get plenty of provisions and have got better cloes now than ever they had. They are very well off only for hatts. They give them a good deal of rum and whiskey, and this I suppose helps with the lies their officers are always telling them…

PS dont send your next letter by the same hand, for I have reason to be suspitious. I would not send this by him. When he left me he went strait to Washingtons head quarters.

He instructed "Samuel Culper, Sr." (Abraham Woodhull), through Benjamin Tallmadge, to try to get his messages out through New Jersey instead of the slower Long Island-Connecticut route, to note the numbers of each British regiment moving, whether they were being recruited, and what they were doing with their wagons and horses. He had observers on the Jersey coast to watch all enemy ship movements. He heard that Lord Cornwallis was back in New York within two days of his arrival.

To one of his double agents, operating within Clinton's command, Washington wrote on August 12 requesting that he report to Clinton that Washington had about 18,000 men present and fit for duty, plus another 2,000 levies on the way. He had arranged for more who could be assembled at any time. He had sufficient boats on hand to transport 5,000 of these troops. Washington had, in reality, about 9,500 rank and file on hand, fit for duty. It is not clear whether Sir Henry Clinton's greatly exaggerated reports to London of Washington's strength were in consequence of these false reports, or whether Clinton enlarged them in order to draw reinforcements from England.

"Samuel Culper, Jr." (Robert Townsend) was particularly asked not to change his employment but to be "under cover of his usual business." This was the merchant firm of Oakman and Townsend, which supplied British ships. Both "Culpers" were provided with a secret ink developed by Sir James Jay that could be brought to light only by use of another chemical. They were instructed by Washington to use good paper and to write ordinary business and family letters "in the Tory stile," and to use almanacs and ledger books with blank space for the secret ink. Washington referred to Culper, Jr., whom he did not know, as "the old gentleman," though Townsend was only twenty-five. Washington frequently praised the reports of these two most trusted agents who reported for years from enemy-held territory.

Philadelphia was the one place from which Washington could get little information. On August 1, 1779, he wrote to Edmund Randolph, a member of Congress from Virginia, to say: "I shall be happy in such communications as your leizure... will permit you to transmit me, for I am as totally unacquainted with the political state of things, and what is going forward in the great National Council, as if I was an alien; when a competent knowledge of the temper and designs of our Allies... and the complexion of Affairs in Europe might, as they ought to do, have a considerable influence on the operations of our Army, and would, in many cases, determine the propriety of measures which, under a cloud of darkness, can only be groped at."

GENERAL ARNOLD

Benedict Arnold had been in trouble with his accounts and handling of government property almost since he had entered the service. As soon as he became military commander of Philadelphia, he made an agreement with the army's clothier general, James Mease, about whose incompetence Washington had long complained. This agreement provided that a portion of the goods bought with public funds for the army's account would be sold in what was essentially a grey market. The public would be reimbursed the original purchase price and Arnold and his confrere would pocket the difference. There were also opportunities for trading with the British, who paid for supplies in good money at New York. It is probable that Arnold also used wagons, requisitioned from the state by his authority, for transporting his goods. He gave a pass to a Miss Hannah Levy, who was trading with the enemy, to proceed to New York; she had been associated with David Franks, who had been arrested for passing intelligence to the British.

Arnold was considered by many in Philadelphia to be too close to the Tories there. He married Elizabeth Shippen, a friend of Captain John André, aide to Sir Henry Clinton. Amidst all this smoke, the Pennsylvania council, headed by Joseph Reed, brought charges in Congress against Arnold for giving Miss Levy a pass, using requisitioned wagons for his purposes, and other misdemeanors. As usual any problem was dumped onto Washington and he, at the insistence of Congress, had to order Arnold court-martialed. This he did a few days after Arnold's marriage. Because of rapid army movements the court could not sit until the end of the year.

Exactly when Arnold decided that the British paid better is not known. Carl Van Doren, in his classic *Secret History of the American Revolution*, believes it may have been late in 1778 but that his first overtures to the British took place not long after Washington issued his court-martial order. Sir Henry Clinton handed the assignment of dealing with Arnold to Captain André, who headed British intelligence. André had done the millinery and costumes for the Meschianza ball in Philadelphia and while there got to know Peggy Arnold quite well. Working with André was another intelligence officer, Captain George Beckwith, aide to the German General Knyphausen in New York. In corresponding with André and Beckwith, Arnold first called himself "Monk," after the general who turned from the Puritans to the Cavaliers and thereby earned a dukedom. He later used "Gustavus" after the Swedish king who freed his country from the Danes.

Arnold offered to supply André with intelligence but information meant fighting Washington and this was not what the British craved. André made this clear very early in the correspondence. He wanted Arnold to surrender an army with an important post, offering to pay two guineas per American head. This was a very cheap method of winning. To this point, each American killed, wounded, or captured had cost the British treasury over three thousand guineas. From the beginning, Arnold insisted on a proper reward if he succeeded and on ten thousand pounds if he failed. There was much haggling over this latter point for more than a year. In the meantime Arnold continued to transmit valuable information as an evidence of good faith.

When Sir Henry Clinton went with André to South Carolina in December 1778, the negotiations temporarily broke off but resumed the following year. That same month Arnold had his court-martial. One of the charges preferred by Pennsylvania was that he had been too friendly to Tories. Since Reed was the prime mover, Arnold replied in court: "I can with boldness say to my persecutors... and to the chief of them... that in the hour of danger, when the affairs of America wore a gloomy aspect, when our illustrious General was retreating through New Jersey with a handful of men, I did not propose to my associates basely to quit the General, and sacrifice the cause of my country, by going over to the enemy... I can say I never basked in the sunshine of my General's favour, and courted him to his face, when I was at the same time treating him with the greatest disrespect and villifying his character when absent."

Though he put in an energetic defense, Arnold was convicted on two charges and ordered reprimanded by the commander in chief. Not until April 1780 did all the papers go through the court to Washington, then to Congress, and back to Washington. In public orders Washington noted that he would have preferred to commend Arnold, but he now had to declare that his conduct had been imprudent and improper. With this light sentence, Arnold was free to take a command, but he did not request one until summer.

SULLIVAN AND THE INDIANS

Sullivan had been a rather tempestuous and none too lucky general, and there were protests when he was selected to head the campaign against the Indians. Washington answered that he had to work with the material available and with due respect to seniority. He would have preferred Schuyler but neither he nor Gates wanted the job.

Sullivan, after taking command on March 6, complained of everything, including his lack of intelligence, troops, supplies, boats, roads, maps, boots, uniforms, and money. He was, in fact, handed a difficult assignment: to march from eastern Pennsylvania through the wilderness to the Finger Lakes of New York, and to coordinate with New York forces moving west and troops marching from Fort Pitt northward. He complained so much that Congress, the Pennsylvania council, and, finally, Washington, found him exasperating. Some of Sullivan's complaints to Congress were forwarded to Washington, who had worked with great energy on plans, intelligence, and supplies for the expedition. On August 15 and 21 Washington sent long replies to Congress, with copies of much of his extensive correspondence preparing for the expedition. He said: "I am sorry to find… Genl. Sullivan… has mistated several particulars of importance, and that in providing for his own justification in case of misfortune, he had left the matter upon such a footing as to place me in a delicate situation." He quoted Sullivan as saying: "The plan for carrying on the expedition was not agreeable to his mind, nor were the number of men for it sufficient." Washington noted that he wanted "to have two bodies, each superior to the whole force of the enemy" and this was not practical. Sullivan said he had finally gotten supplies for General James Clinton's army in the north, but in fact Washington had ordered these months before. He also complained that his men were bare; Washington quoted his orders or authorizations for 10,000 pairs of shoes, 3,500 shirts, and large supplies of overalls. Though a complainer, Sullivan drove through the final expedition with dispatch. On October 17 Washington issued general orders to his troops:

> *The Commander in Chief has now the pleasure to congratulate the Army on the complete and full success of General Sullivan… against the Senecas and other tribes of the six Nations… Their whole country has been overrun and laid waste and they themselves compelled to place their own security in a precipitate flight to the British fortress at Niagara… The whole of this has been done with a loss of less than 40 men on our part, including the killed, wounded and captured and those that died natural deaths.*

CABAL

Sullivan resigned from the army in December, for reasons of health and because his criticisms of Congress and the board of war had made him many enemies. In his farewell letter to Washington, he referred to a speech made by Colonel William Tudor in Boston in March 1779. Tudor had been John Adams' law clerk. Presumably owing to Adams' influence he was made judge advocate of the army in 1775, wherein he acted as Adams' eyes and ears. The pair thereafter exchanged gossipy letters on the faults of the army and its generals.

Tudor's speech raised the danger signal that a popular general, at the head of a victorious army, might be even more threatening to America than the British tyrant. Others had already cried that Washington was not only too popular but also too virtuous and good, which made him even more danger-ous. Sullivan wrote to Washington on December 1: "Permit me to inform your Excellency, that the faction raised against you in 1777, into which General Conway was unfortunately and imprudently drawn, is not yet destroyed. The members are waiting to collect strength and seize some favorable moment to appear in force. I speak not from conjecture but from certain knowledge. Their plan is to take every method of proving the danger arising from a com-mander who enjoys the full and intimate confidence of his army... They will endeavor to convert your virtue into arrows with which they will seek to wound you... If you will take the trouble to read Mr. Tudors oration... you will find every line calculated to answer this purpose: The words are Tudor's but the thoughts are borrowed... The next step is to persuade congress that the military power of America should be placed in three or four different hands, each having a separate quarter of the continent assigned him, each comman-der to answer to congress only for his conduct. This, they say, will prevent one aspiring commander from enslaving his country and put it in the power of congress, with the assistance of the commanders, to punish the attempt... The present time is unfavorable to their designs, they well know that the voice of citizens and soldiers would be almost unanimously against them... I am well convinced that they cannot succeed, yet I thought it my duty, in the moment of my departure, to give your Excellency this notice... Could you have believed four years since that those adulators, those persons so tenderly and so friendly used as were General Gates, Mifflin, Reed, and Tudor, would become your secret and bitter, though unprovoked enemies." Washington replied to Sullivan on December 1:

I assure you, my Dear Sir, I am sensibly touched by so striking an instance of your friendship...

I am particularly indebted to you for the interesting information you give me of the views of a certain party. Against intrigues of this kind, incident to every man in a public station, his best support will be a faithful discharge of his duty, and he must rely on the justice of his country for the event.

I flatter myself it is unnecessary for me to repeat to you how high a place you hold in my esteem. The confidence you have experienced, and the manner in which you have been employed on several important occasions, testify the value I set upon your military qualifications and the regret I must feel that circumstances have deprived the army of your services.

The French also picked up stories similar to Sullivan's. The marquis de Fleury, who had been commended by Washington and Wayne and given a medal by Congress for bravery at Stony Point, reported to France that New England and Pennsylvania were again pushing Gates as a rival to Washington. He added that Congress was "eternally barking" that Washington had too godlike a virtue.

On April 16, 1780, the new French minister, the chevalier de La Luzerne, informed his foreign minister that members of Congress, in expressing fear of Washington's influence, spoke of "his virtues as an additional reason for taking alarm." By June the opposition in Congress was strong enough to place Gates in command in the South, without consulting the commander in chief.

WASHINGTON ON THE 1779 CAMPAIGN

Washington continued to send long, chatty letters to his friends about the campaign and future prospects. On October 25 he wrote from West Point to Benjamin Harrison in Virginia:

The Pennsylvania Gazettes… will have conveyed official accts. to the public of all occurrances of any importance… It may not be amiss to observe that, except the plundering expedition to Virginia and the burning one in Connecticut, the enemy have wasted another campaign… in their ship-bound Islands and strong-holds, without doing a single thing advancive of the end in view, unless by delays and placing their whole dependance in the depreciation of our money, and the wretched management of our finances, they expect to accomplish it.

In the meanwhile they have suffered, I do not know what other term to give it, a third part of the Continental Troops which altogether were inferior to theirs, to be employed in the total destruction of all the Country inhabited by the hostile tribes of the Six Nations, their good and faithful Allies! While the other two thirds… confined them within very circumscribed bounds, at the same time bestowing an immensity of labour on this Post, more important to us, considered in all its consequences, than any other in America.

There is something so truly unaccountable in all this that I do not know how to reconcile it with their own views, or to any principle of common sense… The latter end of May… Genl. Clinton moved up to Kings-ferry in force, and possessed himself of Stony and Verplanks Points... since which these Posts have changed Masters frequently, and after employing the enemy a whole campaign, costing them near a thousand men... and infinite labour, is at length in Status-quo...

It is now 30 days since Congress gave me official notice of Count D'Estaing's intended co-operation, and no authentic acct. of him is since come to hand. The probability therefore is that we shall have hot work in a cold season.

D'ESTAING AWAITED

When Washington heard that a French fleet was on its way north from the West Indies, he redoubled his efforts to get information from New York and Clinton's headquarters. He also had observers on the coastal points looking hopefully for the fleet. He drew up intelligence and operating plans and had French officers and Alexander Hamilton ready to dash to sea with them. D'Estaing, however, got no farther north than Georgia.

In the meantime, the governor of Jamaica, expecting d'Estaing to attack him, had sent an urgent appeal to Clinton to send relief troops. Clinton dispatched Lord Cornwallis south with four thousand men but they got very quick word that d'Estaing was heading for the American coast. The British fleet returned to New York. Clinton decided to gather all his forces into New York for a stout defense. He abandoned his outposts on the Hudson. He also pulled his ships and nearly four thousand men from Newport to New York, a move that opened the harbor to its later use by the French fleet.

Gates was in command at Rhode Island and was, as usual, slow in transmitting this major development to Washington. In his restrained way Washington sent Gates a note, with very veiled sarcasm, that he had word of the British evacuation but "not hearing from you I have concluded that your express had met with some accident." Later he received a report from Gates, but the officer messenger had not come by his headquarters, explaining that he had to take this important intelligence to Congress. In acknowledging Gates' letter, Washington said he regretted not having been able to ask the officer for details. He added another quiet prod: "Altho' your letter is silent upon the subject, I cannot doubt that you are on the march before this for Hartford... Indeed I hoped the instant the Enemy had embarked that you would have pushed the Troops on." On November 1 Washington wrote to Edmund Pendleton, another Virginia friend:

I will, while my eyes are turning Southwardly (impatiently looking for or expecting to hear something decisively of Count d'Estaing) make my acknowledgements for [your letter]...

Stony Point which has been a bone of contention the whole campaign... is totally evacuated. Rhode Island is also abandoned and the enemys whole force is drawn to a point at New York...

...Another Campaign having been wasted; having had their Arms disgraced, and all their projects blasted, it may be conceiv'd that the enemy, like an enraged Monster summoning his whole strength, will make some violent effort, if they should be relieved from their present apprehension of the French fleet. If they do not detach for the West Indies (and I do not see how this is practical while they remain inferior at Sea) they must from the disagreeableness of their situation, feel themselves under a kind of necessity of attempting some bold, enterprizing stroke, to give, in some degree, eclat to their Arms, spirits to the Tories, and hope to the Ministry.

Washington's prediction turned out to be accurate. The wounded British lion from this point on showed unexpected ferocity. The next eighteen months were the most bitter of all the war years for America. The British came close to cutting off the South and New England both by sea and by the Hudson. Had these operations succeeded, a new British invasion was scheduled from Canada into western New York and Pennsylvania. Further attacks were planned on Baltimore and Philadelphia.

D'ESTAING IS BEATEN

The French regarded the West Indies as more important than the United States and this was a major defect in the alliance. Whenever the French could spare ships for American waters, they did so for very brief periods only, as when d'Estaing first appeared off New England and then sailed for the Indies. It happened again at Savannah. It was also to happen at Yorktown when the French fleet just barely gave Washington time to effect a successful siege.

Congress had dispatched General Benjamin Lincoln to Charleston to command its defense. He arrived there with reserve troops in time to break a British attack on the city in May 1779. Savannah, however, and much of Georgia, remained in British hands. The South Carolinians appealed to d'Estaing in the West Indies to aid a combined land and sea assault on the port. D'Estaing agreed, provided that he had American supporting troops. He arrived off Savannah on September 8 with 22 ships of the line, 11 frigates, and 100 transports with some 5,000 troops. Lincoln marched from Charleston with around 1,600 continentals, to which were added Casimir Pulaski's cavalry of 500. Other American militia came in during the attack. Defending the city were 2,500 of the enemy, to which were added about 800 rushed from nearby Beaufort.

D'Estaing began the regulation eighteenth-century siege, which could be calculated with precision but which also gave time to the Savannah garrison to strengthen its defenses. Although it got under way a little more than two weeks after d'Estaing's arrival, it was not fully ready to operate until October 3. D'Estaing, with an anxious eye on possible storms or hurricanes and on British activity in the Caribbean, decided on October 9 to abandon the siege and make a direct assault on the town. The attackers were beaten back with a loss of more than eight hundred in killed and wounded. On October 20 the French departed for the West Indies. Washington termed it a "disaster."

General Lincoln sent John Laurens north with a full account and pleas for help. Laurens, Washington's former aide, had volunteered for duty in South Carolina when his own state was threatened. Washington ordered his Virginia and North Carolina troops to march the long distance from West Point to Charleston. He told Lincoln they could be "ill spared" but he would do what he could. At the same time he ordered the New England and New York militia, whom he had summoned in hope that D'Estaing would proceed north, to return home.

Sir Henry Clinton called the British victory "the greatest event that has happened the whole war." He began preparations for what was most unusual for the British, a large-scale winter campaign in the South.

WINTER AT MORRISTOWN

Washington established his quarters in the Jacob Ford house in Morristown on December 1. Those weather experts, the oldest inhabitants, had complained that the summer of 1778 was the hottest on record. Now they were to have new tales, for the winter of 1779–1780 was the severest of the eighteenth century and perhaps in the history of the United States. Valley Forge is the most famous of the war winters but Morristown was even crueler.

The winter began early. In January it was sixteen below zero in New York. The New Jersey rivers were ice three feet thick. The Hudson River and New York Bay were so solidly frozen that cavalry and cannon crossed from Manhattan to New Jersey and Staten Island. Undrifted snow was four feet deep in New Jersey. Dr. Thacher's January journal noted: "The weather for several days has been remarkably cold and stormy. On the 3d... we experienced one of the most tremendous snow-storms ever remembered; no man could endure its violence many minutes without danger of his life. Several marquees were torn asunder and blown down over the officers' heads in the night, and some of the soldiers were actually covered in their tents and buried like sheep under the snow."

To add to the misery of weather, which prevented supplies from reaching the troops, there had been a severe drought that summer. The water mills for grinding flour had dried up and there were few reserves. Washington reported to Congress on January 5 that "the late violent storm has so blocked up the Roads that it will be some days before the scanty supplies in this quarter can be brought to camp. The Troops, both Officers and Men have borne their distress with a patience scarcely to be conceived. Many of the latter have been without meat entirely and short of bread and none but on very scanty supplies." Washington had to order the horses' corn fodder served to his troops, preferring to let the animals starve.

In desperation, Washington appealed to the civil authorities in every county of New Jersey to ask the inhabitants to help feed his starving men. He told his officers that he would, if necessary, requisition the food, but he would avoid this until the last possible minutes. The inhabitants, many of them poor and with very little themselves, gave everything asked. Washington wrote General Schuyler on January 30:

> *We have had the virtue and patience of the army put to the severest trial... I hardly thought it possible that we should be able to keep it together, nor could it have been done but for the exertions of the Magistrates in the several counties of this state, on whom I was obliged to call, [and] expose our situation... I allotted to each county a certain proportion of flour or grain and a certain number of cattle... and for the honour of the Magistrates and good disposition of the people I must add that my requisitions were punctually complied with and in many Counties exceeded... At one time the Soldiers ate every kind of horse food but Hay.*

Washington was so distressed that he became waspish, and Greene, his quartermaster general, suffered. Martha Washington reached Morristown just after Christmas, in time for the great blizzards. A few days later Mrs. Greene, pregnant, came to camp with her small son, George Washington. Greene constructed a kitchen for his wife but had not, after repeated requests, built one for Washington's wife and staff. Washington fired a note to Greene on January 22:

> *I have been at my prest. Quarters since the 1st. Of Decr. and have not a Kitchen to*

*Cook a Dinner in, altho' the Logs have been put together some considerable time by
my own Guard... Eighteen belonging to my family and all Mrs. Fords are crowded
together in her Kitchen and scarce one of them able to speak for the colds they have
caught.*

*I have repeatedly taken notice of this inconveniency... and have been told that
boards were not to be had. I acquiesced... To share a common lot and participate
[in] the inconveniencies which the Army... are obliged to undergo has, with me,
been a fundamental principle; and while I conceived this to be the case universally,
I was perfectly content; that it is not so, I [appeal] to your own observation...*

*Equally opposed is it to my wishes that you should be troubled in matters respecting
my accomodations, further than to give the necessary orders and furnish materials,
without which orders are nugatory; from what you said I am fully satisfied that the
persons to whom you entrusted the business are alone to blame; for certain I am
they might, by attention, have obtained (equally with others) as many boards as
would have answered my purposes long 'ere this.*

Greene in February, having asked Washington for money for supplies, was
told there was not a dollar in the military chest. At this time Greene wrote to
Joseph Reed, head of the Pennsylvania council, to say that "a southern gentleman" was severely criticizing his state for not supplying food to save the
army. He asked Reed not to mention the source from which he had this information. "I have difficulties enough without adding to them."

The weather was still bitter in March. On the eighteenth Washington wrote
Lafayette that he had sent North Carolina and Virginia troops to Charleston,
"but the extreme cold, the deep Snows and other impediments have retarded
the progress of the march. The oldest people now living in this country do no
remember so hard a Winter... The severity of the frost exceeded anything of
the kind that had ever been experienced in this climate before."

That winter Congress practically ceased to function as a legislature. Its currency and credit were nearly worthless. Thereafter, Congress merely issued
requests, which Washington described as timid, to the various states for
troops and supplies. On March 26 he bluntly told Congress that the supplies
requested were far below the minimum needs of the army and that there was
no power to enforce the requisitions. On the following day Washington estimated his total northern army strength at 10,400 rank and file but the terms
of service of around 2,500 were about to expire. In spite of this, he decided
on April 4 to send his Maryland and Delaware lines south to aid in the defense
of Charleston.

The French minister reported to Versailles that, in his judgement, not only were American finances disordered, but the supply services were so swollen that they employed "nine thousand men... receiving enormous salaries who devour the army's substance while it is suffering from famine."

FALL OF CHARLESTON

On Boxing Day 1779, just before the harbor froze, Sir Henry Clinton and Lord Cornwallis left New York with more than a hundred ships and transports, five thousand seamen, and eight thousand rank and file. The ill winds that were blowing so bitterly at Morristown also blew at sea. Many of the ships and transports foundered, including one carrying Clinton's artillery. Clinton also lost most of his cavalry and transport horses on the way. Not until February 11 did the first of the ships put into the Savannah River. Clinton stripped the navy of many of its guns and ordered replacements of supplies, horses, and powder from the Bahamas, Saint Augustine, and Jamaica.

After learning that Lincoln intended a serious defense of Charleston, Clinton called for Lord Rawdon to bring more troops from New York. After providing a jolly St. Patrick's Day dinner—where the volunteers of Ireland sang that, like the good saint, they would drive the rebellious vermin from the land—Rawdon sailed for Charleston with three thousand reinforcements. By the time Clinton was ready to move, he had an army of more than ten thousand rank and file, in addition to the navy.

Lincoln, in command at Charleston, was moderately experienced but not very able. After learning on January 23, from a captured British transport, that Clinton was coming south with ninety sail, he wrote Washington: "It is, my dear Sir, among my first misfortunes that I am not near enough to your Excellency to have the advantage of your advice and direction. I feel my own insufficiency and want of experience. I can promise you nothing but a disposition to serve my country."

Lincoln had only a small naval force. His continentals were few, at first no more than twelve hundred but reinforcements, slowly drifting in from the north brought them to more than two thousand. South and North Carolina provided militia but when their enlistment period ended, they went home. Lincoln had trouble getting powder and arms from the state government, which insisted on orders from Congress.

By March 15 John Laurens was writing Washington a lengthy and accurate appraisal of the situation, referring in his letter to a map of Charleston that he knew the general had. He pointed out that it was going to be nearly impossible to stop the enemy navy from passing the bar at the harbor and that the fortifications to the north at Charleston Neck were incomplete. He appealed to Washington to come in person to save the situation. On April 26 Washington replied: "The impracticability of defending the bar, I fear amounts to the loss of the town and garrison... The propriety of defending the town depended on the probability of defending the bar, and when this ceased, the attempt ought to have been relinquished."

After explaining that the disorders in the northern army were such that he could not leave nor could he propose such a move to Congress, he added: "Be assured my dear Laurens that I am extremely sensible to the expressions of your attachment and that I feel all for you in your present situation which the warmest friendship can dictate. I am confident you will do your duty and in doing it you must run great hazards. May success attend you, and restore you with fresh laurels to your friends, to your Country, and to me. With every sentiment of regard and Affection."

By March 29 Clinton was a mile from the forts on the neck. On April 8 Admiral Arbuthnot's fleet moved across the bar into the harbor. A strangling network was drawn around the city, cutting its food supplies. On April 14 American cavalry guarding an escape route in the north were beaten by Colonel Banastre Tarleton's dragoons. On May 12, after long negotiations, Lincoln and his army surrendered. Clinton counted as prisoners some 5,500 men, but he did this by including all males of military age in the town. The Continental Army prisoners, including the sick, were somewhat over 2,000, with perhaps another 2,000 militia. Each side lost under 300 in killed and wounded. It was the most classic and best conducted British victory and the worst American defeat of the war.

The British military forces, on taking the city, engaged in wholesale official and private looting. The division of spoils between the Royal Army and Navy was still being disputed in London while Washington was serving his second term as president.

With most of the southern American army captured, Clinton easily established posts across the interior of South Carolina, to add to those in Georgia. A detachment of the Virginia line under Colonel Abraham Buford, which had made the weary march from West Point through the bitter winter and snows encountered Tarleton's cavalry at Waxhaws near the South Carolina border. They were quickly beaten and surrendered. More than half the men were killed immediately or so badly wounded they died within a few days. Thereafter Tarleton was known as the Butcher. South Carolina was now under the king's peace.

LONDON

No news could have been more timely for London or well received than the fall of Charleston. Lord George Germain wrote Clinton on the fourth anniversary of American independence that the victory was "glorious" and had given "his Majesty the highest satisfaction."

The king needed cheering. The British lower classes, not represented at all in Parliament, had parodied the polite petitioning rebellion of the upper classes by erupting in mob action in June. Technically the cause was a protest against parliamentary bills to relieve the disabilities of Roman Catholics. As Trevelyan noted, the gathering mobs had fewer and fewer good Protestants and more and more bad citizens. The lower classes had long been harassed by harsh penal laws, press gangs, rising prices, and higher taxes. Many of the imposts added by North each year fell on such necessities of the poor as candles, salt, sugar, and beer.

The London mobs, stimulated by Lord George Gordon, grew in size and then in venom. They surged to Whitehall and attacked the House of Lords. Many lords, including two members of the king's cabinet and the archbishop of York, were roughed up and two peers nearly killed. Lord Mansfield's house and those of three London judges were burned to the ground. The prime minister's house and the Bank of England were attacked. Huge fires burned for several nights. Nearly three hundred persons were killed and many more wounded. The riot was finally suppressed by the king and army. Twenty-three of those involved were hanged. Gordon was clapped in the tower, where he was joined in October by Henry Laurens, who had been captured by the British. Charleston and the Gordon riots combined temporarily to strengthen the king's hands in domestic and foreign policy. He now could persuade many that the war was proceeding with success in America and that domestic opposition was a form of revolution. In addition, following the fall of Charleston, he received a peace feeler from the French prime minister.

On August 3 Germain wrote Clinton: "The reduction of the whole Province [of South Carolina] and the concurrence of all our accounts from the provinces in rebellion of the distress of the inhabitants and their anxious desire to return to the King's obedience, together with the reduced state of Mr. Washington's force, the decay of the power of Congress, and the total failure of their paper money, open a flattering prospect of a speedy and happy termination of the American war. Your able and vigorous conduct in your respective commands [warring general and peace commissioner] leaves no room to apprehend anything will be wanting to accelerate this happy event."

WASHINGTON, I AM HERE

Here I am, my dear general, and, in the midst of the joy I feel in finding myself again one of your loving soldiers, I take but the time of telling you that I came from France on board a fregatt which the king gave me for my passage. I have affairs of the utmost importance I should at first comunicate to you alone... Tomorrow we go up to the town, and the day after I'll set off in my usual way to join my beloved and respected friend and General... Adieu...

Lafayette.

Writing this in Boston Harbor on April 27, he thus informed the surprised Washington of his return. Boston, too, had not known he was coming but the word passed fast. When Lafayette got off the ship, nearly the whole town was out cheering. The church bells rang, the cannon boomed, and he was hauled in a coach through immense crowds to John Hancock's house on Boston Common. By May 10 he was at Morristown with a full report of the French military and naval reinforcements on their way. After their conference Washington sent Lafayette directly to Congress to arrange American cooperation with the French forces.

The army's distresses increased the nearer Rochambeau approached the coast. On May 26 Washington wrote that the army was meatless and for the first time troops had mutinied. The Connecticut line decided to go home to eat. He informed Governor Trumbull that his state's troops were finally persuaded to stay but he did not know how long he could keep starving men in camp. He wrote Congress that in addition to having no food, they had not been paid for five months and could not even attempt to buy rations.

To Joseph Jones, a member of Congress, Washington wrote on May 31: "I see one head gradually changing into thirteen; I see one Army branching into thirteen; and instead of looking up to Congress as the supreme controuling power of the United States are considering themselves as dependent on their respective States... I see the powers of Congress declining too fast for the consequence and respect which is due them as the grand representative body of America, and I am fearful of the consequences of it."

By June 20 Washington was writing anguished but polite letters to Congress saying the French would expect plans for cooperation and attack, but he had heard nothing of the supplies and troops he could expect from the states. He could make no plans, therefore, though American "honor and reputation" were at stake as well as "the justice and gratitude due our allies." He added an especially distressed note that his men were without shirts or overalls. He found "mortifying" and "distressing" the prospect of marching an American army as naked as savages before the elegant French. On June 30 he pleaded with the governors of all states north of Maryland to forward their recruits since he had only a handful of men in his army. On July 4 Washington wrote to the head of New Hampshire that, six weeks after the states had been called upon for recruits, only thirty had shown up.

THE SUMMER

If anything, Lord George Germain had underestimated the troubles facing Washington in 1780. Although Clinton reported to London in July that Washington had an army of twelve thousand, the American commander had only thirty-two hundred men fit for duty.

Sir Henry Clinton returned to New York on June 18, covered with laurels. There he was informed that General von Knyphausen, upon hearing of Washington's general plight and of the mutiny, had sent five thousand men to Springfield, New Jersey, eight miles from the main American base at Morristown. The militia were able to drive them back to Connecticut Farms (now Union, New Jersey), where the British and German forces burned a church, a parsonage, and a number of houses. Knyphausen was then forced back to the coast.

Clinton, while in Charleston, had been planning just such an attack, to be undertaken on his return, but the British high command in America had now begun to disintegrate. The frigate, bringing Clinton's plans, was mistaken for an enemy ship and driven from New York by the Royal Navy. Many transports carrying troops ran aground in a fog near New York. Clinton, on his arrival, found that, instead of his planned all-out war against Washington, he had to rescue Knyphausen. In this situation he received a message from Benedict Arnold that French troops and naval forces were on their way to America. Clinton, perturbed by this news, felt no part of New Jersey could be held. He ordered a diversionary move up the Hudson to Verplanck's Point, but finding that Admiral Arbuthnot had given his fleet entirely different sailing orders, he abandoned the plan.

In the meantime Washington, alarmed for the safety of West Point and Morristown, moved with part of his troops to Pompton, which would bring him within fairly quick marching distance to the Hudson. Knyphausen made one last effort at attack, again reaching Springfield, where he was routed by Greene and his continentals, together with the local militia. He retreated to Staten Island. Sir Henry was furious when he found that the whole futile business had cost the British more losses than they had suffered in taking Charleston.

On July 10, Rochambeau, his fifty-one hundred troops, and eight ships of the line under Admiral the Chevalier de Ternay, arrived off Newport and began their disembarkation. They were rather coldly received by the town, which had been occupied by Americans and then British and again by Americans, but General Heath in command at Boston soon appeared to see that they were warmly welcomed. He wrote Washington that he was "charmed" by the French officers.

Before they landed, Washington had one more diplomatic problem. On May 24 he had ordered Dr. James Craik, his personal physician and head of the army's hospital services, to set up a medical service for the French in Providence. He asked the governor of Rhode Island to help, assuring him that the French would reimburse the state in hard money for any expenses. The French commissary, Louis Ethis De Corny, went with Craik to help organize the hospital. The state government, because of Washington's interest, assigned the French the Rhode Island College building, now Brown's University Hall. This caused a great uproar and no end of trouble for De Corny. The college president, the Reverend James Manning, excitedly warned that Providence would soon be infected with French diseases. Two members of the Brown family, Nicholas and Joseph, declared that the citizens of the town ought to blow up the hospital. They threatened the carpenters who were at work with loss of employment and suits for damages. De Corny had to pacify the workers with bonds of indemnification. He complained to Washington, who apologized for the "reprehensible" conduct of the persons connected with the college.

Washington's foresight had been fortunate, since more than twenty-three hundred French soldiers and sailors, most of whom had been on board ship for ninety days, were hospitalized with scurvy. Till they could recover the French forces were much weakened.

On July 13 Rear Admiral Thomas Graves, who had been dispatched in a hurry by Lord Sandwich to intercept the French fleet, arrived off New York with six ships of the line, having crossed much more quickly than the French. Vice Admiral Marriot Arbuthnot thus acquired heavy naval superiority over de Ternay's fleet.

By this time Washington's intelligence service had become more effective than Sir Henry Clinton's. The British service under Captains André and Beckwith was, at this point, more interested in playing Benedict Arnold on its line than in arranging to fight. Washington learned on July 15 of the arrival of Graves' ships, but Clinton did not hear until July 18 that the French had landed eight days earlier in Newport. This gave the allies much needed time to begin their fortifications before Clinton could start to make plans. Fortunate for them also was the bad blood existing between Clinton and Arbuthnot, which made their cooperation minimal at a critical period. With their superior fleet the British by July 21 had established an effective blockade of Newport, but they had not coordinated their plans with Clinton.

Washington had expected large French supplies of arms and powder but he heard on July 22 that these had not arrived with the fleet. That day he begged the state of Connecticut to lend him arms. He also wrote Lafayette: "Another thing that gives me concern is the non-arrival of our arms and powder... With every effort we can make we shall fall short by at least four or five thousand arms, and two hundred tons of powder. We must, of necessity, my Dear Marquis, however painful it is to abuse the generosity of our friends, know of the French, whether they can assist us with a loan of that quantity." On July 24 Washington learned that Clinton had embarked on an expedition against Rochambeau. By July 27 he was marching his troops from New Jersey to the east bank of the Hudson. Washington planned to move south as rapidly as possible to King's Bridge in order to strike at New York if Clinton moved a major portion of his forces to Newport. When Clinton got into a dispute with Admiral Arbuthnot and returned to New York, Washington recrossed the Hudson.

GREENE RESIGNS

General Greene, who had been an effective quartermaster general, but now was without money or credit, had complained to Congress. After the representatives recommended changes in his organization, he resigned. His letter was abrupt enough for Congress to be incensed, and many members wanted to throw him out of the army. Washington's trusted friend in Congress, Joseph Jones, so informed Washington, who answered on August 13:

> *In your letter... an idea is held up as if the acceptance of General Greene's resignation of the Qr. Mrs. department was not all that Congress meant to do with him. If by this is in contemplation to suspend him from command in the line (of which he made an express reservation at the time of entering on the other duty) and it is not already enacted, let me beseech you to consider _well_ what you are about before your resolve.*
>
> *I shall neither condemn, or acquit Genl. Greenes conduct for the act of resignation, because all the antecedents are necessary to form a right judgment of the matter,*

and possibly, if the affair is ever brought before the public, you may find him treading on better ground than you seem to imagine; but this is by the by. My sole aim at present is to advise you of what I think would be the consequences of suspending him from his command in the line... without a proper trial. A procedure of this kind must touch the feelings of every Officer; it will shew in a conspicuous point of view the uncertain tenure by which they hold their commissions. In a word it will exhibit such a specimen of power that I question much if there is an Officer in the whole line that will hold a Commission beyond the end of the Campaign if they do till then. Such an act in the most Despotic Government would be attended at least with loud complaints.

...The suspension of Genls. Schuyler and St. Clair, tho it was preceded by the loss of Ticonderoga... was by no means viewed with a satisfactory eye by many discerning Men... Suffer not my Friend, if it is within the compass of your abilities to prevent it, so disagreeable an event to take place... I fear... I feel it must lead to very disagreeable and injurious consequences. Genl. Greene has his numerous Friends out of the Army as well as in it, and from his Character and consideration in the world, he might not, when he felt himself wounded in so summary a way, withhold from a discussion that could not at best promote the public cause. As a Military Officer he stands very fair and deservedly so, in the opinion of all his acquaintances.

These sentiments are the result of my own reflections on the matter... I do not know that Genl. Greene has ever heard of the matter and I hope he never may.

Greene presumably never knew of Washington's impassioned plea on his behalf. By the time Washington's letter got to Jones, Congress had cooled down. Arrangements were made with Greene that he temporarily continue as quartermaster general, on his own terms, until a new appointee, Colonel Timothy Pickering, could take over.

BATTLE OF CAMDEN

On August 16 General Gates suffered a disastrous defeat at Camden, South Carolina. Washington had pleaded with him on July 18 to keep him fully informed of his operations in the South. On August 12 he repeated his request, assuring Gates that he would send him all intelligence of value. Gates did not write, and, as he had done before, informed Congress of the battle on August 20 but did not report it to Washington for another ten days.

Much has been written about the battle, but the facts, particularly in relation to American losses, are obscure. Lord Cornwallis with 2,200 troops, most of them regulars, unexpectedly encountered Gates with approximately 3,000 troops, two-thirds untrained militia. With Cornwallis were Lord Rawdon and his tough Irish volunteers and Tarleton and his even rougher legion. When battle began, the Virginia militia on the American left broke and ran and the North Carolina militia quickly followed. Only the 1,100 continentals under General Kalb stood up and in fact drove back the British until they were overwhelmed by numbers. Kalb was killed after fighting bravely. The American army was pursued from the field and scattered in every direction. Gates himself that night reached Charlotte sixty miles away. Three days later he was at Hillsborough, 180 miles from Camden. The British suffered around 325 casualties, while the Americans lost about 1,000 killed, wounded, and captured. One hundred and fifty of these were later retaken by Colonel Francis Marion. More than two-thirds of the continentals who had done most of the fighting showed up later to fight again. When Gates did not write Washington two weeks after the battle, he sent a straightforward manly letter:

My public letter to Congress has been surely submitted to your Excellency… The militia broke so early in the day… that very few have fallen into the hands of the enemy.

By the firmness and bravery of the Continental troops the victory is far from bloodless on the part of the foe, they having upwards of 500 men, with officers in proportion, killed and wounded. I do not think Lord Cornwallis will be able to reap any advantages of consequence from his victory as this State seems animated to reinstate and support the army. Virginia, I am confident, will not be less patriotic. By the joint exertions of these two states, there is good reason to hope that, should the events of the campaign be prosperous to your Excellency, South Carolina might be again recovered. Lord Cornwallis remained with his army at Camden… I am cantoning ours at Salisbury, Guilford, Hillsborough and Cross Creek. This is absolutely necessary as we have no magazine of provisions and are only supplied from hand to mouth. Four days after the action of the 16th, fortune seemed determined to distress us; for Colonel Sumter… halted with the wagons and prisoners he had taken on the 15th; by some indiscretion the men were surprised, cut off from their arms, the whole routed and prisoners retaken.

What encouragement the numerous disaffected in this State may give Lord Cornwallis to advance further into the country I cannot yet say. Colonel Sumter… has reinstated and increased his corps to upwards of 1,000 men. I have directed him to continue to harass the enemy on that side. Lord Cornwallis will therefore be cautious how he makes any considerable movement to the eastward... The main body is cantoned in his front. Anxious for the public good I shall continue my unwearied endeavours to stop the progress of the enemy, to reinstate our affairs, to recommence an offensive war and recover all our losses in the southern States. But if being unfortunate is the sole reason for removing me from command, I shall most cheerfully submit to the orders of Congress and resign an office few generals would be anxious to possess, and where the utmost skill and fortitude are subject to be baffled by the difficulties which must for a time surround the chief in command here.

Five days later Gates followed with another letter to Washington: "If I can yet render good service to the United States, it will be necessary it should be seen that I have the support of Congress and your Excellency; otherwise some men may think they please my superiors by blaming me, and thus recommend themselves to favour. But you, sir, will be too generous to lend an ear to such men, if such there be, and will show your greatness of soul rather by protecting than slighting an unfortunate. If, on the contrary, I am not supported and countenance is given to everyone who will speak disrespectfully of me it will be better for Congress to remove me at once... This, sir, I submit to your candour and honour, and shall cheerfully await the decisions of my superiors."

Washington had too much experience with militia, and with the conditions under which Gates had fought, to criticize. On the contrary, as soon as he had studied Gates' reports, he wrote Congress at length, strongly attacking the militia system of the South, noting that they would always break in battle as they had done at Camden. He recommended a permanent southern Continental Army of at least six thousand men, plus cavalry and artillery, together with sufficient supplies of food and forage. To Gates, Washington wrote on October 8, apologizing for the delay occasioned by his conference with the French:

The behaviour of the Continental Troops does them infinite honour. The accounts, which the Enemy give of the action, shew that their Victory was dearly bought. Under present circumstances, the system which you are pursuing seems infinitely proper. It would answer no good purpose to take a position near the enemy, while you are so far inferior in force. If they can be kept in check, by the irregular troops under Colo. Sumter and other active Officers, they will gain nothing by the time which must be necessarily spent by you, in collecting the new Army, forming Magazines and replacing the Stores which were lost in the Action...

It was owing to the fatal policy of temporary enlistments, that the enemy were enabled to gain the footing which they hold in the southern States, and it is much to be feared that the same Cause will be attended with an increase of disagreeable effects...

Preparations have been sometime making for an embarkation from New York. The destination is publickly said to be to the southward, and I think probability is in favour of that report. Should a further extension of their conquests in that quarter be their object, I am in hopes that the force collecting by the exertions of North Carolina, Virginia and Maryland, will keep them confined to the limits of South Carolina at least.

Gates and his reorganized, if small, force were sufficient to prevent Cornwallis (who was burdened by his sick and wounded and a shortage of supplies) from moving into North Carolina for three weeks after his victory. One of the enemy armies was soon knocked out completely while Gates was still in command. Cornwallis was forced to retreat to South Carolina, precisely as Washington hoped.

Congress was neither as understanding nor as generous as Washington was to Gates. On the day the successful battle of King's Mountain took place, the delegates instructed the commander in chief to recall Gates, to hold a court of inquiry on his conduct, and to nominate another general to head the southern department. Other people were even harsher. On September 11, Benedict Arnold took time off from his correspondence with British intelligence to tell General Greene: "It is an unfortunate piece of business to that hero and may possibly blot his escutcheon with indelible infamy." Alexander Hamilton, without Washington's knowledge, wrote on September 6 to James Duane, a New York congressman: "What think you of the conduct of this great man? I am his enemy personally for unjust and unprovoked attacks on my character... Did ever any one hear of such a flight? His best troops placed on the side strongest by nature, his worst, on the weakest... 'Tis impossible to give a more complete picture of military absurdity... Was there ever an instance of a General running away, as Gates has done, from his whole army? And was there ever so precipitous a flight? One hundred and eighty miles in three days and a half. It does admirable credit to the activity of a man at his time of life. But it disgraces the General and the Soldier... Will he be changed or not. If he is changed, for God's sake overcome prejudice, and send Greene."

This was total insubordination on Hamilton's part. His letters tended to be considered by their recipients as conveying the views of the commander in chief. The attempt to get Congress to dismiss Gates was an infringement of the legislative prerogative, which Washington himself never attempted.

THE ARMY TAKES A FEW COWS

By the middle of August the troops again faced starvation, since the states had been backward in sending supplies. To his agonized distress, Washington had to send out forage parties to take, by requisition, the little the inhabitants of Bergen County had. In his urgent appeal to the governors of New England and the middle states, he explained his actions and needs:

> *I am under the disagreeable necessity of informing you that the Army is again reduced to an extremity of distress... The greater part [was] without Meat from the 21st to the 26th. To endeavour to obtain some relief, I moved down to this place [Englewood], with a view to stripping the lower parts of the County of the remainder of its Cattle, which after a most rigorous exaction was found to afford two and three days supply only, and those, consisting of Milch Cows and Calves of one or two years old. When this scanty pittance is consumed, I know not what will be our next resource... Military coercion is no longer of any avail, as nothing further can possibly be collected from the Country in which we are obliged to take a position, without depriving the inhabitants of the last morsel...*

> *It has been no inconsiderable support of our cause to have had it in our power to contrast the conduct of our Army with that of the enemy, and to convince the inhabitants that while their rights were wantonly violated by the British Troops, by ours they were respected. This distinction must now unhappily cease, and we must assume the odious character of the plunderer instead of the protectors of the people... We have not yet been absolutely without flour, but we have <u>this</u> day but <u>one</u> days supply...*

> *...Altho' the troops have upon every occasion hitherto borne their wants with unparalleled patience, it will be dangerous to trust too often to a repetition of the causes of discontent.*

On August 30 he wrote his brother Samuel: "The flattering prospect which seemed to be opening to our view in the Month of May is vanishing like the Morning Dew. The States, instead of sending the full number of men required of them by the first of July [and] the consequent supplies, have not furnished one half of them yet... At best, the Troops we have, are only fed from hand to Mouth and for the last four or five days have been without Meat. In short, the limits of a letter would convey very inadequate ideas of our disagreeable situation; and the wretched manner in which our business is conducted. I shall not attempt it, therefore, but leave it to some future Pen, and a more favourable period for truths to shine."

CONFERENCE WITH ROCHAMBEAU

Lafayette had been acting as American liaison with Lieutenant General Rochambeau. While he might be major general in the American army, to the French commander he was a twenty-two-year-old French captain who had recently received the rather honorary rank of colonel. Washington wanted to plan a joint French-American attack on New York but this was difficult with the French blockaded. In addition, Rochambeau expected a second French division, with additional naval forces, and he did not intend to move until they arrived.

Washington's instructions to Lafayette of August 3 were clear: "I would not wish to press the French General and Admiral to any thing to which they show a disinclination... Only inform them what we can do, what we are willing to undertake, and let them intirely consult their own inclination for the rest. Our prospects are not so flattering as to justify our being very pressing to engage them in our views. I shall however go on with all our preparations and hope circumstances will ultimately favour us."

Nonetheless, Lafayette pushed Rochambeau hard to do something, telling him that the French could always beat the British. Rochambeau chided him firmly but with great politeness. He said that he had had forty years' experience, French troops could be beaten even by the British, he had seen too many Savannahs, and he did not intend to take chances with the lives of his men. He made it clear that he would make all arrangements directly with Washington and wanted to confer with him. This was a difficult meeting to plan since Washington had to be on the alert against any move by Clinton into the Highlands or New Jersey, and Rochambeau equally so for attacks on Newport.

On August 25, while his army was rounding up cattle, Washington received dispatches from Rochambeau, saying that the long-awaited second division of French troops and its supporting fleet had been blocked up in Brest and no one knew when they might get out. Thus both sections of the French forces were paralyzed and with them any offensive plans Washington might want to undertake.

On September 14 Admiral Sir George Rodney, with ten ships of the line, arrived in New York from the West Indies, an unexpected bonus for Sir Henry Clinton. This gave him overwhelming naval as well as military superiority. Rodney was an unscrupulous fellow and so greedy that Lord Sandwich had to assure the king that the admiralty commissioners in the West Indies had enough control of supplies there to prevent Rodney from taking too much for his own pocket. Nonetheless he was a fighting admiral and more than welcome to Clinton, who was fed to the teeth with Arbuthnot. Clinton took him immediately into his confidence on his plan to purchase West Point from Benedict Arnold. Rodney agreed to make his naval forces available for any "attack."

On September 20 Washington held his meeting with Comte de Rochambeau in Hartford. Since each was prepared to like the other, the conference was successful so far as human relations went, but in planning nothing was accomplished. The French could only say that they had been in touch with Count de Guichen, in command of the French fleet in the West Indies, but they did not know whether he would come to their aid. Claude Blanchard, the French commissary, recorded in his diary that the French officers had "returned enchanted" by Washington.

On October 4 Washington summarized the meeting to James Duane: "The interview at Hartford produced nothing conclusive, because neither side knew with certainty what was to be expected. We would only combine possible plans on the supposition of the possible events; and engage mutually to do every thing in our powers against the next campaign."

On September 23 Washington left Hartford for West Point, where he intended to go over the defense system with Benedict Arnold. Not long after he set out, three American militiamen captured a prisoner near Tarrytown who identified himself as a British officer but who was carrying extensive documentation of West Point's fortifications.

TWENTY-SEVEN

WEST POINT

1780

W HEN EVERYTHING LOOKED bleakest for Washington, the British made two capital blunders. In the North, their intelligence handled a major operation so ineptly that its chief was hanged on October 2. Three days later a new breed of southern mountaineers destroyed a British army at King's Mountain. As enemy power disintegrated with increasing momentum, Washington made ready to strike and kill.

CAPTAIN ANDRÉ

John André, aide to Major General Charles Grey, had been the chief designer of the 1778 ball at Philadelphia to honor Sir William Howe. André was enraptured by his own costume. He wore, he said, a "hat of white satin... enlivened by red, white and black plumes." His "hair tied with contrasted colors of the dress, hung in flowing curls." He had a coat "of white satin... the sleeves made very full, but of pink, confined with a row of straps of white satin laced with silver upon a black edging." He also wore "a large pink scarf... with a white bow... and a pink and white sword belt and pink bows... Fastened to the knees."

André had been quartered with General Grey in Franklin's house in Philadelphia. Had Franklin ever learned of the costume André designed there, he could have written one of his merriest pieces. When the British army retreated, André took many books and pieces of china belonging to Franklin. He also removed, presumably on General Grey's orders, a portrait by Benjamin Wilson. This was presented to the White House many years afterwards by one of Grey's descendants.

André was thirty in 1780. He was an excellent linguist, a fair artist, and a mediocre poet. Above all he had a gift of the tongue and high ambition. In three years he moved from subaltern to Clinton's intelligence and administrative chief. Before Grey left America, he recommended André to Clinton, who made him his aide and gave him the intelligence assignment. In 1779 when Clinton's adjutant general and deputy adjutant both resigned, André was made deputy adjutant. Clinton asked London to give him a majority, but Lord Amherst ruled that he was too far down the captain's list to be promoted. André continued to call himself a major, presumably as an acting or local rank. André's intelligence assignment was of utmost importance to the British, but William Smith, Tory chief justice of New York, observed in his diary that André spent more time performing on the stage than getting information about Washington's army.

André's 1779 negotiations with Arnold, in which he urged him to take an important command that he could surrender, were broken off when Clinton and André went to Charleston. During their absence, Captain George Beckwith took over British intelligence in New York. He formulated a plan to kidnap Washington but nothing came of it. He sent urgent inquiries to one of his spies for information on Washington's forces, supplies, recruiting, militia, and cavalry. The agent, who was in the American service, forwarded them to Washington. On March 7 Washington himself carefully wrote out misleading answers to "Beekwith's letter." When Beckwith received reports of the May 30 mutiny of the Connecticut line, he sent three spies to the American lines. They were caught and later hanged on Washington's orders the following month.

Benedict Arnold resumed negotiations with British intelligence in May 1780. In correspondence with Arnold, Beckwith used the names of "G. B. Ring" and "M. De l'Anneau," symbolic of an identical pair of rings, one of which he sent to Arnold for identification. On June 4 Washington asked Arnold to undertake, very secretly, the printing in Philadelphia of a proclamation in French to the inhabitants of Canada declaring that the French were coming to rescue them. Washington and Lafayette had devised this as a ruse to fool the British. Arnold immediately forwarded a copy to British intelligence, which perhaps took it more seriously than if it had come from a less reliable channel.

When Arnold resumed his correspondence, he moved to meet André's demand that he take command of a major post. He asked General Schuyler to intercede with Washington to get him West Point. As he was frequently to do, he pleaded that his war wounds prevented him from taking a field command. On June 12 he was at Morristown on his way to Connecticut. He hinted his desire for West Point to Washington. The commander in chief seems to have told Arnold that he would think it over. Arnold informed Beckwith, nevertheless, that he was certain to have it. The day after his interview with Washington, Arnold inspected the West Point fortifications and sent a full report on them to British intelligence. At the same time Arnold let them know that six French ships of the line and six thousand troops would soon arrive in America. To make sure of his West Point appointment, he subsequently asked Robert Livingston, New York's chancellor, to put in a good word for him with Washington. This Livingston did at the end of June.

When Arnold returned from his Connecticut trip, he again talked with Washington and thought he was assured of the command. On July 7 he so informed André, who had resumed his post as head of British intelligence. Sir Henry Clinton was so elated that he told William Smith that he thought the rebellion would soon end in a crash. André had offered Arnold two guineas per American head in 1779. The blood bargaining resumed in earnest in early July of 1780. Arnold again insisted that he get ten thousand pounds whether he succeeded or failed, but André balked at this. He proposed they meet under a flag of truce to discuss it. Arnold said he wanted £20,000 for West Point. André, in turn, suggested he could give £20,000 provided the British captured at least three thousand troops. Thus the price per man was upped from about two guineas to a little more than six guineas, but this was still a bargain. At the same time André informed Arnold he would have to break off the negotiations temporarily, since Sir Henry Clinton was going to make some attempt against the French at Newport.

During the summer the agents of General Robert Howe, who had the West Point command, picked up a New York rumor that an American general was about to sell out. Howe informed both Washington and Greene but nothing further seems to have been done about it. At about the same period, Arnold told André that some of his trusted agents were, in fact, working for Howe.

Around July 21 Arnold left for Washington's camp; his wife, Peggy, remained in Philadelphia as an intermediary, forwarding letters between her husband and British intelligence. On July 31 the commander in chief told Arnold he was being given command of the army's left wing. Washington later recalled that Arnold remained completely silent when told this. Peggy Arnold, informed of it a few days later at Robert Morris' house, fell into a state of hysterics. Those present interpreted this as concern for her husband, which in fact it was. Subsequently Arnold told Washington's aides that his wound still prevented him from the hard riding of a campaign. Because of this the commander in chief announced on August 3 that Arnold would command the Hudson River area, including West Point.

Earlier, on July 15, Washington had written to the board of war, approving the promotion of Major John Jameson, following the resignation of a lieutenant colonel in Sheldon's dragoons who formed an important part of his intelligence operations. On August 4 he further announced that he had appointed Lieutenant Colonel James Livingston to command the forts at Stony and Verplanck's Points.

Arnold continued to send messages to the British through Philadelphia but this was a slow process, sometimes taking as much as three-and-a-half weeks to reach them. In turn, Arnold did not receive André's offer of £20,000 for West Point and three thousand troops until August 24. On August 30, however, Arnold contrived to send a note to New York by an Irish-born member of the Connecticut legislature, William Heron, who had offered, through William Smith in New York, to spy for the British. Heron appears to have opened Arnold's letter and to have noted that it was written in commercial form, disguising his acceptance as a business deal. It was signed "Gustavus," Arnold's code name, and addressed to "John Anderson," André's feigned name. Heron decided that Arnold was conducting a speculation in New York. To ingratiate himself with the American army, he handed the letter to General Samuel Parsons, who filed it.

On September 3 Arnold found means to transmit another letter to André by a flag boat bringing a woman from Quebec into New York. He suggested a meeting between them, with André posing as an American secret agent, at the headquarters of Colonel Elisha Sheldon of the second dragoons. That same day Major Jean-Louis Villefranche, the West Point engineer, sent Arnold plans of three of the redoubts and promised to forward the remaining drawings as soon as possible. Arnold in turn wrote to Colonel Livingston to say that he was sending him sixty flatboats. If the enemy attacked the fort, Livingston was to embark all his troops and cannon from the east bank of the Hudson and "come with them to West Point." The next day, in response to his earlier order, Arnold received from Major Sebastian Bauman, head of artillery, lists of ordnance and the alarm guns and signals to be used in case of an enemy assault.

In a clumsy move on September 7, the British intelligence chief sent a letter to Sheldon, suggesting that he see Mr. G. at Dobbs Ferry on September 11. This was signed "John Anderson." Sheldon, puzzled by it and odd references to Anderson entering the lines by stealth, forwarded the letter to Arnold the next day asking its meaning. He added that he had never heard of Mr. G. or of Anderson. In any case he was not in good health and he could not ride to Dobbs Ferry.

Arnold had apparently forgotten to inform Sheldon of the name of his supposed agent and of the proposal for a meeting. On September 10 Arnold wrote to André not to trust Sheldon with any further communication. It is hardly possible that the next move, the sudden arrest of Colonel Sheldon, could have been coincidental. Somewhere between September 10 and 12, a Dr. Darius Stoddard preferred charges that led to Sheldon's being relieved of his command and ordered court-martialed. John Jameson, just promoted to lieutenant colonel, became acting commander of the second dragoons at this critical point. Sheldon was subsequently acquitted with honor and Stoddard was severely reprimanded by the court for bringing false and malicious accusations.

Washington had reports from New York, as early as September 2, that the enemy might be preparing to move up the Hudson. He informed Arnold that he was ordering two Connecticut regiments to join Sheldon's dragoons at North Castle. On September 10, Washington had further reports that the British were drawing in troops from Long Island.

On September 6 Peggy Arnold left Philadelphia to join her husband at West Point. André soon became more and more open in his actions and desires to talk to Arnold. On September 11 he and Colonel Beverley Robinson, the New York Tory who owned the house that Arnold used for headquarters, went to Dobbs Ferry. Arnold came down by barge late in the evening, but André had made no arrangements for his reception and a British gunboat fired on him. He was forced away and André returned to New York.

On September 13, Colonel Livingston, in command on the Hudson's east bank, wrote to Arnold that Robinson had been seen around Tarrytown in a boat, pretending to establish a flag contact but Livingston was sure he had espionage in mind. He asked Arnold if he should not try to give him "a check." Arnold cautioned him against this. The same day Arnold wrote to Benjamin Tallmadge that if "Anderson" reached his lines, he was to send him to Arnold with a cavalry escort.

By September 14 Rodney and his ten ships were in New York. This addition to the British forces made André even more eager and impetuous to establish early contact with Arnold. That same day Washington informed Arnold that he would be at Peekskill on September 18, on his way to see Rochambeau, and to keep his trip very secret. Arnold encoded the message and sent it to André. On the eighteenth, Washington wrote General Greene, who was to take command in his absence, that he was much worried about Rodney's arrival, particularly as Colonel Jameson had told him that Clinton had seventy troop transports ready to move "at a moment's warning." There might be an early attack on West Point and Greene should move his troops towards Tappan.

On September 16, time being of the essence for the British and Arnold having proposed a meeting on the twentieth, André sent Colonel Robinson up the Hudson on a British war sloop, appropriately named *Vulture*. The ship anchored off Tellers Point, only five miles below Verplanck's Point, which was under the command of the suspicious Colonel Livingston. That same day Clinton and Rodney met to discuss plans for taking either West Point or Newport. The following day Clinton wrote Rodney he hoped that they would agree on the former post. At the same time Robinson sent a letter to Arnold, under a flag of truce, enclosing another letter ostensibly addressed to General Putnam. Robinson hinted that he wanted to discuss his private affairs, including the house used by Arnold, which had been taken by the New York state government. These arrived so openly at his quarters that he spoke of them to his aides, as well as to Colonel Lamb, who commanded at West Point. They all heartily damned Robinson and suggested that Arnold show the letters to General Washington. Arnold escorted Washington across on the ferry, from which all could see the spy ship anchored below. Arnold showed Robinson's letters to Washington, who said that letters on civilian affairs should go to the governor of New York.

On the following day Arnold sent Robinson a "public" reply, indicating that he could not discuss any civil business of this kind, but he enclosed private letters saying that he would meet the British emissaries on the twentieth. He enclosed a copy of an earlier letter to André, pointing out that he had twenty-five hundred troops towards the needed three thousand and he would be able to get more. The original had already gotten to Beckwith in New York, who had forwarded it to André. On its receipt André started for Dobbs Ferry. He arrived there on the twentieth and proceeded by sloop to the *Vulture* to be in time for the meeting.

In the meantime Arnold had engaged the services of a Joshua Smith, who lived in a farmhouse down the river from West Point. He was the brother of William Smith, Clinton's chief justice. Because of this he seems to have leaned over backward to show his loyalty to the patriots by an extra willingness to help Arnold. When the latter requested his assistance in getting an intelligence agent from New York, he agreed. Smith was also to recruit two brothers, tenant farmers, who lived on his property on the Hudson's west bank. They were to be engaged to row to and from the *Vulture* as needed. On the night André waited on his ship, one of the brothers decided he was just too tired to row out and pick him up. Having waited all night in vain, André wrote worriedly to Clinton that this was the second meeting that had failed, Robinson had been seen with him before, and people might begin to ask questions. He said that he would wait another day, pretending to be too sick to return to New York. Arnold, too, was much annoyed at this miscarriage.

On September 21 there was a skirmish between the *Vulture's* gunboat and Livingston's troops. The British were driven off. American and enemy versions differ as to the cause. The British claimed the shore battery had waved a flag of truce. Livingston insisted the British had attempted to come ashore "to steal sheep." Using this as an excuse for correspondence, the captain of the *Vulture* sent a protest to Arnold at a violation of flags. It was in André's hand-writing and signed for the *Vulture's* captain by John Anderson, secretary. Enclosed was a letter from Robinson saying that they would expect Mr. Smith that evening.

That night, September 21, Arnold again had to deal with Smith's very inde-pendent tenant farmers, Joseph and Samuel Cahoon. Samuel allowed to Arnold as how it was risky to row about at night with American patrols on the river. He asked Arnold why he didn't do it in the daytime like everyone else, and, in any case, his wife did not want him to go. Joseph later testified in New England tones: "I... told him I did not choose to go. He then said there was no hurt in going, at all; and if anything should come against me, he would defend me... I told him he could not clear me if there was any bad in it." Finally both brothers told Arnold they "had no mind to go."

The fate of the British empire was at stake. Fortune and titles were waiting for Arnold. The whole British high command and Admiral Rodney were "a tiptoe" but everything had to wait while he argued with two pigheaded American farmers. Arnold, in desperation, said they were unpatriotic, the country needed their services, and if they refused to go he would arrest them immediately. They consented with bad grace but they were even more intractable in the morning.

About midnight the Cahoons rowed Smith to the *Vulture* to pick up "John Anderson," who wore a cloak over his red coat. Arnold took two horses and rode downriver from Smith's house to meet them at a point below Haverstraw. For four days thereafter, no one on the *Vulture* had any word of André.

Arnold and André conferred all night while Smith and the boatmen waited. Near dawn Smith mentioned to Arnold that it would soon be light. He asked the Cahoons to take André back to his ship but they said they were too tired. Smith and the Cahoons rowed back to the Smith farm, while André and Arnold proceeded there by horseback.

On the opposite side of the Hudson Colonel Livingston had also been busy. Late the preceding afternoon Arnold had complained to him about the firing on the *Vulture's* boat. Livingston expressed his annoyance at having the ship there, with Robinson aboard, and he asked Arnold for heavy guns to drive the *Vulture* away. Arnold brushed him aside. Livingston hauled a light four pounder that night from Verplanck's Point to Tellers Point. At daybreak, just as Arnold and André turned into Smith's house, they saw firing from the opposite side. Livingston kept up his attack on the *Vulture* for two hours, accurately hitting the rigging, hull, sails, and boats. He stopped only when his magazine exploded. André saw the *Vulture* pull off down the Hudson.

In the morning, after delivering all the West Point documents to André, Arnold returned to Robinson's house across the Hudson, while Robinson himself floated downstream. Smith was nearly as thick about everything as his tenants. He knew that André wore a British officer's uniform, but Arnold had assured him that he was only a merchant and wore it for vanity. That night Smith told him to take it off and gave him civilian clothes. André was informed he was to be delivered across the Hudson and go back by land. He did not care much for this change and protested but Smith seems to have told him he would have no trouble. André slipped Arnold's documents into his boots.

Smith and André proceeded to King's Ferry and crossed to Verplanck's Point. Smith had a jolly conversation with Colonel Livingston, who invited him in for a drink, but Smith said he had a friend with him and they had to go on.

On September 19, the day that André received Arnold's note inviting him to a meeting the following day, an American militiaman, John Paulding, escaped from a British prison in New York and made for Westchester. This was the second time he had been captured and had suffered brutal treatment. His good coat had been taken by the British, who gave him a ragged one of a kind worn by Tories and called a "refugee coat." He rejoined his militia unit in Westchester.

Not long after leaving Livingston, Smith and André were stopped and questioned by an American patrol. Their pass from Arnold was sufficient but they were warned not to proceed because of the large number of Tory partisans on the road. They spent the night in a small farmhouse. The next morning they were up early. At Pine's Bridge, Smith said goodbye to André and returned to Peekskill, feeling he had done good service for General Arnold.

André rode on with the West Point papers in his boots, his plans completed, and glory near. Just north of Tarrytown, John Paulding in his refugee coat stepped out of the bushes and levelled his gun. With him were two other young militiamen, Isaac Van Wart and David Williams. André noticed Paulding's coat and asked him if he were of the "lower Party." Paulding said yes and André said good, for he was a British officer on urgent business. When they announced they were Americans, he produced Arnold's pass but they would have none of it. The three men took him into the woods, searched him, and found the hidden documents. André offered every kind of bribe in golden guineas but the three "simple peasants," as Alexander Hamilton was to term them, hauled him off to Colonel Jameson at North Castle.

Much of what happened thereafter, in the period from September 23 to 25, during which Arnold was permitted to escape, is a still an unresolved riddle. It is known that Jameson took actions that were subsequently described by Washington as "the egregious folly, or the bewildered conception of Lieut. Colo. Jameson who seemed lost in astonishment and not to have known what he was doing."

As nearly as can be determined, André, an accomplished actor, attempted, with some success, to bluff. He claimed to be acting on urgent business for Jameson's commanding officer, General Arnold, and demanded to be taken to him at once, so the matter could be cleared up. It is nearly certain that Jameson knew that Arnold was, in fact, expecting such a man. It was apparent at the same time that there were flaws in the story. André was going in the wrong direction, and he did have highly secret papers on American defenses. Jameson devised a compromise to protect himself against any possible charges by Arnold. He decided to send André to Arnold, while forwarding the papers to General Washington. In so doing Jameson informed Arnold that he had caught "a certain John Anderson going into New York. He had a pass signed with your name. He had a parcel of papers... which I think of a very dangerous tendency." At the same time he wrote Washington:

> *Inclos'd you'll receive a parcel of Papers taken from a certain John Anderson who has a pass signed by General Arnold as may be seen. The Papers were found under the feet of his Stockings he offer'd the Men that took him one hundred Guineas and as many goods as they wou'd please to ask. I have sent the Prisoner to General Arnold he is very desirous of the Papers and every thing being sent with him. But as I think they are of a very dangerous tendency I thought it more proper your Excellency should see them.*

Washington was en route back from his Hartford conference. The messenger, thinking he was returning by the more southern route, headed for Danbury. It is unclear at this point why Jameson, after thinking it over, decided it might be wrong to dispatch André to Arnold. He sent a further rider out to ask the escorting party to deliver the prisoner to lower Salem, to be held in tight security. Nonetheless the messenger was to proceed to Arnold with the Jameson note.

Sometime during the afternoon of September 24, the day after he was caught, André confessed to the chief of his guard. He also wrote a letter to General Washington, identifying himself as Major André, adjutant general of the British army, who was involuntarily out of uniform. There was still a chance to catch Arnold and, as it turned out, more than ample time. The Robinson house was little over three hours' ride from lower Salem but the messenger, with the note from Jameson to Arnold, took eighteen or more hours to cover the distance. Jameson's subsequent excuse to Washington was that he had expected Arnold to come to his camp where he would have been seized. It never occurred to him, he said, that a British warship, the *Vulture*, was in the Hudson.

Sometime that day, after André's confession, the messenger with the papers for Washington reappeared, saying he had not been able to find him. Jameson added André's confession to the documents and directed the messenger to try to find him on the northern route from Hartford. Meanwhile, Washington, on his way to Fishkill, had planned to spend that night at the Robinson house with Arnold. On his way south from Fishkill, he met the French minister, the chevalier de Luzerne, who was overjoyed and begged General Washington to have the goodness to dine with him and spend the night, so he could hear all about the conference with Rochambeau. Washington politely agreed to his request. On the night of September 24, Washington, Lafayette, and Luzerne dined and slept in Fishkill. Mr. and Mrs. Arnold were in the Robinson house seven miles to the south. André was a prisoner sixteen miles to the southeast of Arnold. Robinson was on the *Vulture*, near Ossining, writing a worried letter to Sir Henry Clinton.

ARNOLD FLEES

Washington got up early in the morning of September 25 and rode for Arnold's headquarters. He sent two of his aides ahead to say he was on his way. Near the house, about half past nine, he and Lafayette turned off to examine two redoubts. While they were doing so, a messenger rode to the house and delivered the note from Colonel Jameson. With Washington expected at any moment, Arnold dashed upstairs to tell his wife that the conspiracy was broken and he was leaving immediately. He came down and informed his aides that he had an urgent summons to West Point and he would return within the hour. As he was mounting his horse, he met four of Washington's dragoons, who told him that his excellency was nearby. Arnold asked them to stable their horses and then rode rapidly down the hill to his waiting barge. He ordered the men to pull off, saying he had a matter of great importance and they were to row him to the *Vulture*. When he got aboard, he gave Beverley Robinson the first news of André for which they had been waiting since Thursday evening.

Robinson at once adopted what was to be the official British line. He wrote Washington that André had come ashore under Arnold's flag and pass and under his direction. "Under these circumstances Major André cannot be detained by you... I must desire you will order him to be set at liberty." Arnold also wrote Washington a letter in which the handwriting shook and the ink blotted noticeably at two points: first, when he proclaimed that his wife was "innocent," and again when he expressed a hope that Washington would protect her against American "fury." He concluded "With great regard and esteem." The *Vulture* then pushed off for New York.

When Washington got to Arnold's quarters, he was informed that Arnold was at West Point. He crossed the river to meet him there. Colonel Lamb, the puzzled commandant, apologized profusely for not knowing that Washington was coming and said that he had not seen Arnold for two days. On looking over the fortifications Washington found signs of neglect and disrepair everywhere. He recrossed the river about two hours later. At around four in the afternoon, Jameson's long-delayed letter reached him.

Washington sent Hamilton racing down the river to see if he could find any way of stopping Arnold but it was too late. At Verplanck's Point he was handed the letters that had been sent ashore from the *Vulture* by Arnold and Robinson. Hamilton immediately sent an urgent note to Greene outlining what had happened and asking him to send additional troops to West Point.

When he returned with the news, Washington talked to Arnold's two aides, Major David S. Franks and Lieutenant Colonel Richard Varick, telling them he was sure they were not involved but for their protection he would have to place them under temporary arrest and examine their and Arnold's papers. They informed him of the frequent exchanges of visits between Arnold and Joshua Smith. Upstairs Mrs. Arnold was having hysterics, and Varick said she had had them earlier in the day when Washington was across the river. When the commander in chief went to see her to help calm her, she said he was going to kill her baby. She went on this way for some time, her acting aided by a natural tendency to emotion.

Washington ordered Jameson to send André to headquarters "under the care of such a party and so many officers as to preclude him from escaping... General Arnold... went off to day to the enemy. André must not escape." Washington turned at once to organizing the defenses on both banks of the Hudson against a British attack which, he wrote, might even come that night. He called in everyone, including Colonels Lamb and Livingston, who were in command at the nearby forts. He sent urgent messages putting the whole army on the alert.

Washington ordered Wayne's division to come at top speed from Haverstraw to West Point. They set off at two in the morning, scrambled through sixteen miles of dark and rutted roads in four hours, showing up just as dawn broke. Wayne wrote six days later to H. A. Sheel: "When our approach was announced to the General he thought it fabulous, but when convinced of the reality he received us like a god, and retiring to take a short repose exclaimed, 'All is safe. I again am happy.' May he long, very long continue so!"

Not long after the arrival of Wayne, Tallmadge and a hundred dragoons arrived with André in tow. At about the same time Joshua Smith was brought as a captive to headquarters.

PAULDING, VAN WART, AND WILLIAMS

John Paulding was sent by Colonel Jameson to Washington, shortly after André was brought to camp, to explain the circumstances of the capture and to enable Washington to express his gratitude. On October 7 he wrote Congress: "I have now the pleasure to communicate the names of the Three persons who captured Major André, and who refused to release him notwithstanding the most earnest importunities and assurances of a liberal reward on his part. Their conduct merits our warmest esteem and, I beg leave to add, that I think the public will do well to make them a handsome gratuity. They have prevented in all probability our suffering one of the severest strokes of the war that could have been meditated against us. Their names are John Paulding, David Williams and Isaac Van Wart." On November 3 Congress awarded each of them silver medals and lifetime annual pensions of two hundred dollars.

SIR HENRY CLINTON

Arnold's arrival in New York on September 26 was a severe shock to Clinton, whose great dream of bringing the rebellion to an abrupt end lay crushed. He reacted with increasing hysteria over the next two weeks.

William Smith, his chief justice, noted in his diary: "The *Vulture* has been ten days up the river with Major André and Colonel Robinson... The Secret is now out, for... General Arnold came... this day to town. The people exult much, but it is not known yet that André was catched with his papers... Some great error has been committed by André or Sir H. Clinton... I fancy that Sir H. Clinton has intrigued with Arnold for some time, and that his reliance upon its success is the cause of his neglecting Rhode Island." Two days later Clinton told Smith that the war would have been over, and Washington and Rochambeau his prisoners, had all gone well. Now, as Smith correctly surmised, he had wasted a whole summer depending on Arnold, and he was nowhere.

Not until the following day was Clinton certain that André was to be treated as a common spy. On September 26 he had written Washington: "The King's Adjutant General in America has been stopt under Major General Arnold's Passports, and is detained a Prisoner... A flag of Truce was sent to receive Major André." He therefore expected him to be released. On September 30 Washington forwarded to Clinton the court-martial verdict, adding that André had come ashore to execute measures "very foreign to a flag to truce" and André himself had said it was impossible to suppose he had come ashore under such protection.

Clinton was utterly shaken. Not only had the plot failed but a British officer and gentleman who was his most trusted adviser was to be hanged. He hastily called a council of his generals and legal officers to draw up a memorandum proving André was not a spy. The conference was not entirely happy. Two lawyers, William Franklin, former governor of New Jersey, and John Kempe, attorney general of New York, raised questions that indicated they thought André had been properly convicted. Clinton, however, was so distressed about this discussion that they all finally voted that André was not guilty. Clinton ordered his New York governor, General James Robertson, his lieutenant governor, Andrew Elliot, and his chief justice to call on Washington and explain why André was not a spy. At Dobbs Ferry only Robertson, as a military officer, was allowed ashore. He held an extended conversation with General Greene that got nowhere. Robertson proposed that Washington check with Rochambeau and Knyphausen on the European laws concerning spies but this suggestion did not go over well. Greene may have hinted that André would be released in exchange for Arnold. After the conference adjourned, Robertson informed Clinton that he was sure "André will not be hurt." Clinton was writing to Washington and the British ship was still anchored at Dobbs Ferry, awaiting favorable news, when André's effects were delivered to the British.

Both Clinton and Washington thought that André had not been very clever when he met John Paulding. Clinton said: "I wish our poor friend André had not been a little too much off his guard when the militia questioned him." Washington wrote: "An unaccountable deprivation of presence of Mind in a man of the first abilities and the virtuous conduct of three Militia men, threw the Adjutant General of the British forces in America... into our hands." Unlike some on Washington's staff, General Greene had instantly perceived the truth about André. In announcing to the army the defection of Arnold and the capture of the adjutant general, he wrote: "Our Enemies despairing of carrying their point by force are practicing every base art to effect by bribery and Corruption what they cannot accomplish in a manly way."

ANDRÉ HANGED

A board of fourteen general officers, headed by Greene, tried André for espionage and on September 29 sentenced him to death. The head of British intelligence was hanged at noon on October 2. The purchase price he had offered per American head worked out at a little under thirty silver dollars.

No more unlikely candidate for canonization could have been chosen than André, who had masterminded the West Point plot and bumbled it into ruin. During his captivity he displayed vanity, great gifts of speech and charm, and an absence of all guilt feelings. Throughout André maintained that he was there because of bad luck only. He said nothing of his offers to Arnold to come into the American lines by stealth, to meet him under a false flag, nor did he ever admit to a lengthy correspondence with Arnold, nor to urging him to seek a post for betrayal that he would buy. He maintained to the last that he was a gentleman of honor. With charm and good manners, he persuaded many Americans to believe this, including Hamilton and Major Tallmadge, America's own intelligence chief, whose memoir of the events following the capture of his opposite number is highly suspect. Washington, who never saw André, seems to have been persuaded by them that he was "more unfortunable then criminal." André was helped in his pose because the whole army exploded in fury at Arnold, and the pleasant actor seemed to be a victim rather than the author of the plot.

When Tallmadge took André down the Hudson to his trial at Tappan, the prisoner pointed to the plateau where he was to land with British troops and gallantly attack the fort that he had arranged with Arnold to surrender. For this act, he told Tallmadge, he expected to be made a brigadier. He boasted a great deal about his importance to Sir Henry Clinton. He so impressed Tallmadge that the latter wrote on September 30 to Colonel Samuel Webb: "He is a young fellow of the greatest accomplishment, and was the prime minister of Sir Harry on all occasions... Unfortunate Man! He will undoubtedly suffer death tomorrow and tho' he knows his fate, seems to be as cheerful as if he was going to an Assembly... Had he been tried by a Court of Ladies, he is so *genteel, handsome, polite* a young Gentleman, that I am confident they would have acquitted him."

THE ROLE OF HAMILTON

Alexander Hamilton was more moved by Peggy Arnold and John André than anyone else. His biographer and editor, Henry Cabot Lodge, ascribed this to "the tenderness of his nature." His feeling for Mrs. Arnold is the more understandable since female conspirators were hardly thought possible in America. Hamilton wrote to his fiancée, Elizabeth Schuyler, daughter of the general, on September 25:

> *Arnold, hearing of it being detected, immediately fled to the enemy. I went in pursuit... On my return, I saw an amiable woman frantic with distress for the loss of a husband she tenderly loved... It was the most affecting scene I ever was witness to. She for a considerable time intirely lost her senses. The General went up to see her, and she upbraided him being in a plot to murder her child: One moment she raved; another she melted into tears... All the sweetness of beauty, all the loveliness of innocence, all the tenderness of a wife and all the fondness of a mother showed in her appearance and conduct...*
>
> *This morning she is more composed... She received us in bed, with every circumstance that could interest our sympathy. Her sufferings were so eloquent that I wished myself her brother, to have a right to become her defender. As it is, I have entreated her to enable me to give her proofs of my friendship.*

Hamilton frequently visited André and was completely charmed by him. André did not want to be hanged but to die in front of a firing squad as became a soldier. They talked it over and Hamilton agreed to take a letter from André to Washington:

> *Buoyed above the terror of death by the consciousness of a life devoted to honourable pursuits, and stained with no action that can give me remorse, I trust that the request I make to your Excellency... will not be rejected. Sympathy towards a soldier will surely induce your Excellency and a military tribunal to adopt the mode of my death to the feelings of a man of honour. Let me hope, Sir, that... if aught in my misfortunes marks me as the victim of policy and not of resentment, I shall experience the operations of these feelings in your breast, by being informed I am not to die on a gibbet.*

Washington ignored the letter. Hamilton was bitter about this intransigence. On October 2 he wrote his fiancée: "I must inform you that I urged a compliance with André's request to be shot and I do not think it would have had an ill effect; but some people are only sensible to motives of policy, and sometimes from a narrow disposition mistake it. When André's tale comes to be told, and present resentment is over, the refusing him the privilege of choosing the manner of death will be branded with too much obduracy."

After the execution Hamilton praised André in an October 11 letter to John Laurens: "There was something singularly interesting in... André. To an excellent understanding well improved by education and travel, he united a peculiar elegance of mind and manners, and the advantage of a pleasing person. 'Tis said he possessed a pretty taste for the fine arts... His sentiments were elevated, and inspired esteem; they had a softness that conciliated affection. His elocution was handsome; his address easy, polite and insinuating."

THE COW CHASE

That summer André, whose father was in trade, had begun a lengthy satirical poem in the style of the ballad of Chevy Chase, mocking a raid by Anthony Wayne on a British outpost at Bull's Ferry on July 21. The raid was not successful though Wayne succeeded in driving off some cattle. The poem expressed André's contempt for Americans as a lesser breed. He called Wayne a tanner by trade and rhymed that "steers shall know / And tauntingly deride / And call to mind in ev'ry low / The tanning of his hide." He mocked at Hamilton who "Rode like a soldier big," at Henry Lee, a "drover," adding an unkind comment about Parson Caldwell, whose wife had been killed, and two of whose churches had been burned by the British. André included schoolboy references to emetics and nature's needs. He spoke of Irvine's troops joining Wayne like two sewers flowing into a drain: "So meet these dung-born tribes in one." The last canto was published on the day that André was caught. It concluded:

> And now I've closed my epic strain,
> I tremble as I show it
> Lest this same warrior-drover, Wayne
> Should ever catch the poet.

Wayne's troops were guards at André's execution. After it was over, an anonymous American added a verse:

When the epic strain was sung
The Poet by the neck was hung
And to this cost he finds too late
The <u>dung born tribe</u> decides his fate.

EFFECT ON GENERAL CLINTON

Sir Henry Clinton reacted to André's execution with fury at Washington, the intended victim. He wrote his family in England a letter, amounting to four printed pages, that is often quite incoherent. In its self-pity, guilt, hatred, and fear, it contrasts sharply with Washington's letters of the period:

> *[October 4]…The Circumstances of poor André's capture throws a damp upon all, upon me greater than I can describe. Should he suffer you will easily believe it will be impossible for me to continue to serve… Respecting the coup manquee I do not feel it… Washington seems a moderate man all my friends say… he will not dare execute the sentence… I wish I may obtain leave to resign this command… Good God what a coup manquee… I am of course in very bad spirits… If I can return to my country without any more shocks I may live to enjoy a good old age…*

> *[October 9] The horrid deed is done. Washington has committed premeditated murder… I feel beyond words to describe… He is become a murderer and a Jesuit.*

Clinton's next problem was to inform the British government of the fiasco for which he was responsible as commander in chief. His government had encouraged him to use bribery, treachery, and corruption as the means to victory, but did not care for failure. Sir Henry therefore had to lie. He sent back only such documents, dating from the last days of the negotiation, as might support his case that André had been invited by Arnold to accept the surrender of West Point. He summarized the earlier negotiations in a mass of disingenuous phrases and falsehoods.

The British government reacted angrily against what appeared to be an unjust murder of a gallant soldier. The case presented to the British public caused a great outcry against Washington. A friend of André, Ann Seward, "the Swan of Lichfield," produced a rather dreadful "monody," indicting Washington, whose "Nero-thirst of guiltless blood" had made him "a cool, determined murderer of the brave." She hoped he would be hanged and have "eternal mildew on the ruthless head." From all this André received an unjustified immortal glory. The king gave him a posthumous baronetcy. Many years later he was reburied in Westminster Abbey. Altogether he got more recognition than Sir Henry ever did.

The ignominious end of the André-Arnold plot paralyzed Clinton's will to fight. Years later he wrote in his memoirs: "The unfortunate discovery of my design put an end, of course, to the proposed move up the Hudson River." There was no military reason to add "of course." The British military and naval forces in New York were far superior to anything Washington could mobilize for West Point's defense. Rodney wrote privately to Lord George Germain on December 22: "The Highlands up Hudson's River... cut off all communication between the northern and southern provinces... This is the post Arnold was to have betrayed, and which he assured me, as he did [Clinton] he would answer with his head should be taken in ten days. But, to my infinite surprize, cold water was immediately thrown upon it, notwithstanding it had but a few days before the arrival of Arnold been told me that it was of infinite consequence, and if taken would ruin the rebels."

The following summer Arnold again proposed an attack on West Point, to which Clinton replied that he was willing to consider it, "provided Washington was at a safe distance." Nothing developed even after the American commander headed for Virginia.

From the time of André's capture, Clinton made no important move against Washington until his abortive sortie from New York on the day that Cornwallis surrendered. His memoirs after October 1780 are concerned almost exclusively with Cornwallis' southern operations, which he heartily criticized. However wrong Cornwallis might have been in strategy and tactics, he fought in this period, and the British forgave him but not Clinton.

THE BATTLE OF KING'S MOUNTAIN

Clinton's later memoirs described the effects of King's Mountain, the battle fought three days after André was hanged, as "an event which was immediately productive of the worst consequences to the King's affairs in South Carolina, and unhappily proved the first link in a chain of evils that followed each other in regular succession until they at last ended in the total loss of America."

Cornwallis in moving north had split his forces in three. Far to the left was Major Patrick Ferguson with twelve hundred men who moved towards King's Mountain just inside the South Carolina line. Lord Rawdon later reported that "a numerous army now appeared on the frontiers, drawn from Nolachucky and other settlements beyond the mountains whose very names had been unknown to us." These attacked from Augusta north. Some who went after Ferguson came from what is now Tennessee, though most were North Carolinians. Ferguson retreated onto King's Mountain. Nine lines of Americans surrounded the hill and moved up, inexorably, shooting from behind the trees. Ferguson was killed, and every member of the enemy force of one thousand (two hundred being absent foraging) were killed, wounded, or captured. Fourteen thousand small arms were taken. American casualties were under one hundred.

Lord Cornwallis rapidly retreated into South Carolina from Charlotte. According to Clinton, this American victory "overset in a moment all the happy effects of Charleston... and... Camden and so encouraged that spirit of rebellion in both Carolinas that it could never be afterwards humbled. For no sooner had the news of it spread than multitudes of disaffected flew to arms from all parts, and menaced every British post on both frontiers, 'carrying terror even to the gates of Charleston'... Lord Cornwallis must have experienced extreme mortification from... the return of an army which he had, three months before, as he thought, so completely annihilated that not even a guard of six men could be collected to cover its General's flight to Hillsboro."

MR. AND MRS. ARNOLD

Two days after her husband's defection, Washington sent Peggy Arnold to Philadelphia with an escort and a pass. The latter expressed Washington's faith in her innocence and requested his countrymen to treat her with "delicacy and tenderness." She was not unaware, as she travelled, and while she stayed in Philadelphia, of a universal outburst of gratitude to God, which culminated in Congress setting aside a day of thanksgiving for preserving "the person of our commander in chief."

Peggy Arnold knew, too, that effigies of her husband were being burned throughout the nation. What was harder to take when she got to the house of her father, Edward Shippen, was her family's detestation of her husband. They denounced him as base and treacherous, while warmly sympathizing with her misfortune. This was rather hard on a participant in the plot.

The Pennsylvania council had searched Arnold's house and found evidence of his peculations and a letter from André to Peggy. While it referred to millinery and feminine things, it was in fact a greeting to a fellow conspirator. The Pennsylvania press suggested she might have had other correspondence. The council, in spite of her family's protests, exiled her. Her father took her to the British lines at New York.

Sir Henry Clinton gave the king's commission as colonel to the "trusty and well beloved Benedict Arnold," with temporary rank of brigadier in America. He also gave him an immediate cash settlement of £6,315 as an addition to a small earlier payment made by André. It was not long before the Americans intercepted a London banker's letter that said that he had bought for Arnold £7,000 worth of British 4 percent consols at a discount of 30 percent. This was a last service to Arnold by Washington, whose resistance had sent British bonds to new lows.

Carl van Doren listed all of Arnold's rewards. In addition to cash, he had half-pay for life, while his wife and children received pensions or king's commissions. The Arnolds and their children drew nearly £50,000 from the British government over the next sixty-seven years. This was a high return for Arnold's fifteen months of active service subsequent to his treason.

Arnold was faithful neither to Clinton nor to his wife. It was not long before Clinton discovered that Arnold was intriguing with Germain against him. Eventually he tried to get Clinton's high post. Five years later he took a mistress by whom he had an illegitimate child.

Four months after he received his British commission, Arnold, on an independent command in Virginia, got into an unseemly quarrel with the Royal Navy over a division of loot. He wrote to Commodore Thomas Symonds on February 5, 1781, objecting to a letter by him which failed, so Arnold complained, to live up to a verbal agreement on the spoils: "How far these sentiments can be reconciled with the strict honour which ought to govern among gentlemen, the world will judge... I shall bring the matter to the attention of the Commander in Chief."

TWENTY-EIGHT

WEST POINT TO WESTCHESTER

1780

W ASHINGTON HAD FOUGHT a holding operation for five-and-a-half years against forces superior by sea and by land. Large doses of French sea power had been vitally needed from the first days of the alliance but except for d'Estaing's disappointing appearances, they had never come. Rochambeau and his French troops were tied to Newport; they had been of little help to Washington and drained America's limited food supplies. On September 12, 1780, Washington appealed to Admiral the Comte de Guichen for naval support from the West Indies. He pointed out the great efforts that America had made in hope of French sea support:

The Chevalier de Ternay has informed you of his being blocked in the port of Rhode Island, by a superior British fleet; and the French troops are of course under a necessity of remaining there for the security of the fleet... Nor indeed could they be more useful to us in any other position, a naval superiority being essential to every enterprise in these States.

In consequence of the expected [naval] aid, great exertions have been made on our part for offensive operations; an additional expense (immense to this country in its present exhausted state) has been incurred; great expectations have been excited among the people...

The situation of America at this time is critical; the Government without finances; its paper credit sunk... the resources of the country much diminished by a five Years war, in which it has made efforts beyond its ability. Clinton... In possession of one of our capital towns, and a large part of the State to which it belongs; the savages desolating the other frontier; [with] a fleet superior to that of our allies, not only to protect him against any attempts of ours, but to facilitate those he may project against us. Lord Cornwallis... in complete possession of two States, Georgia and South Carolina; a third, North Carolina, at his mercy...

...General Gates... [has] met with a total defeat near Camden, in which many of his troops have been cut off, and the remainder dispersed...

The enemy are said to be now making a detachment from New York for a southern destination; if they push their successes in that quarter, there is no saying where their career may end. The opposition will be feeble, unless we can give succour from hence, which, from a variety of causes, must depend on a naval superiority.

...Any succour you could send in consequence of this letter, must arrive too late for an enterprise against New York; but an unequivocal naval superiority would I hope enable us to act decisively in the Southern extremity.

Convinced as I am that the independence of America is the primary object of war, with your Court, it is unnecessary to offer any other motives to engage your exertions in our favor. I might otherwise remark that the destruction of the enemy here would greatly facilitate the reduction of their [the British West Indian] Islands...

I am happy in this opportunity of congratulating you on the advantages you have reaped in your different combats... My happiness would be complete if the coasts of this Continent should add to your laurels.

Guichen returned to France, and this request never reached him. Instead, Washington had to face the arrival of Admiral Rodney and new British reinforcements. Soon thereafter the British moved southward, in a climax of violence, for a final attempt to break America's will to resist. At the same time, the comte de Vergennes was negotiating with other European powers to get France out of an expensive war, even at the price of leaving the United States dismembered. Repeated American appeals for naval assistance were ignored until the summer of 1781. Then, in an overwhelming gesture, the French threw their entire West Indian naval garrison to Washington's support, leaving their Caribbean posts nearly defenseless.

A DIFFERENCE OF OPINION

When he returned to the West Indies, Rodney wrote Lord George Germain on December 22, 1780:

> *Believe me, my dear Lord, you must not expect an end of the American war till you can find a general of active spirit, and who hates the Americans from principle. Such a man with the sword of war and justice on his side will do wonders, for in this war I am convinced the sword should cut deep. Nothing but making the Americans feel every calamity their perfidy deserves can bring them to their senses.*

Rodney noted that Arnold was "greatly beloved" by American troops and that Washington's soldiers would desert if they were promised land and their pay arrears. Washington, he added, could be "bought" with a peerage. Rodney thought the sword of justice had not cut deeply enough but Americans differed. John Rutledge, governor of South Carolina, had written two weeks before to his state's delegates in Congress:

> *It is really melancholy to see the desolate condition of Mr. Hill's plantation... all his fine iron-works, mills, dwelling houses... reduced to ashes... I was shocked to see the ragged, shabby condition of our brave and virtuous men, who would not remain in the power of the enemy but have taken to arms.*

> *This, however, is but a faint description of the sufferings of our country, for it is beyond a doubt the enemy have hanged many of our people... Tarleton has... hung one Johnson, a magistrate of respectable character. They have also burnt a prodigious number of houses, and turned a vast many women... with their children, almost naked into the woods.*

> *In short, the enemy seem determined, if they can, to break every man's spirit, if they cannot ruin him. Engagements of capitulations and proclamations are no security against their oppressions and cruelties.*

GREENE TO THE SOUTH

Having previously selected three generals—Robert Howe, Lincoln, and Gates, who had been defeated—Congress now directed Washington to choose the new southern commander. He had no hesitation; on October 14, the day after receiving the order, Washington informed Greene:

As Congress have been pleased to leave the Officer to command on this occasion to my choice, it is my wish to appoint You; and from the pressing situation of affairs in that quarter, of which You are not unapprised, that You should arrive there, as soon as circumstances will possibly admit. Besides my own inclination to this choice I have the satisfaction to inform You, that from a <u>Letter</u> I have received, it concurs with the wishes of the Delegates of the three Southern States most immediately interested in the present operations of the Enemy; and I have no doubt it will be perfectly agreeable to the sentiments of the Whole.

To John Matthews, who had written Washington on behalf of Georgia and North and South Carolina, he replied on October 23: "You have your wish in the officer appointed to the Southern command; I think I am giving you a General; but what can a General do, without men, without arms, without clothing, without stores, without provisions?" He added that he was also sending south a partisan corps under Henry Lee, an officer, he said, who had "great resources of genius." Shortly afterward Washington informed Congress that he had also decided to send General von Steuben there, since the new army had to be organized and trained. Steuben was competent not only to do this but was well-suited for a field command. These moves were typical of Washington, who sent officers he could ill spare.

Washington wrote many letters of introduction for Greene to his southern friends. Greene noted that the commander in chief's name was far more potent in opening all doors than his own reputation. He took command of an infinitesimal army on December 3, with fewer than 1,500 men fit for duty and only half of these regulars. The enemy under Lord Cornwallis had altogether about 13,300 effectives in the southern states, though many were on garrison duty.

Gates, whose only son had just died, retired from the war to await the holding of a court-martial that never assembled. Greene, with some of his commander's magnanimity, wrote Washington that many officers thought well of Gates and that he would be able to acquit himself honorably. The Virginia Assembly passed a resolution expressing their "high regard and esteem" for Gates, which made his retirement in that state easier. On January 9, 1781, a little more than a month after taking over, Greene wrote Joseph Reed, describing the usual difficulties the American army had faced for so many years:

Measures are taking in Virginia which promise us some aid though very trifling... I overtook the army at Charlotte... The appearance of the troops was wretched beyond description... The wants of this army are so numerous and various that the shortest way of telling you is to inform you that we have nothing... We are living upon charity... An army naked and subsisted in this manner, and not more than one-third equal to the enemy will make but a poor fight, especially as one has been accustomed to victory and the other to flight... General Morgan is upon Broad River with a little flying army, and Colonel Washington since his arrival there has defeated a party of Tories.

BATTLE OF COWPENS

Eight days later, General Daniel Morgan won the most brilliant single victory of the Revolutionary War. Military historians have gone back to Hannibal's victory over the Romans at Cannae in 216 B.C. to find its counterpart. The Dupuys' *Compact History of the Revolutionary War* considers it "probably the closest approach to tactical perfection ever seen on the American continent—a complete double envelopment, the dream of every professional soldier." Morgan's force, according to his own account, consisted of 800 men, of whom 300 or so were continentals. Others credit him with as many as 1,040 but Sir Henry Clinton wrote that Morgan's "number and species of troops were greatly inferior to Tarleton, who had 1,100 men, including 300 cavalry."

The American militia had been accustomed to breaking and running at the first sign of battle. The British came to depend on this, expecting then to move on to victory. This time Morgan devised a planned militia retreat, which would bring Tarleton's forces forward to meet experienced continentals. Placing expert southern riflemen on his front, he stationed the militia under Colonel Andrew Pickens directly behind them. The riflemen were instructed to hold their fire, then to pick off British officers and sergeants, and to retreat in orderly fashion, continuing to shoot. As Tarleton's troops moved forward, riflemen and militia fired, bringing down more than one hundred British. The militia then moved rapidly to the rear. Sir Henry Clinton, in describing the battle's next stage, failed to guess what happened. He wrote that American "militia were driven back and everything seemed to promise victory... It was suddenly wrested from [Tarleton] by an unexpected fire from the Continental troops while the King's troops were... charging in loose, flimsy order." Colonel William Washington, a cavalryman, had yelled to Morgan: "They are coming on like a mob. Give them one fire and I'll charge them."

Although there was the usual confusion of battle among the Americans, the ensuing moves were perfect. The withdrawing militia, led by Pickens, went around the American rear to come in the left, while Colonel Washington's cavalry moved in to the British right. The whole enemy force was encircled.

Tarleton, with a few dragoons, escaped and was pursued for nearly twenty-five miles by Washington's horsemen.

It was an astonishing victory. More than 900 of Tarleton's 1,140 men were killed, wounded, or captured. American casualties were 73. Morgan took an immense baggage train, more than 100 horses and 800 muskets. In sending his much-admired guerrilla general to the South, Washington had calculated well. As a result, Cowpens was the second notable victory, after King's Mountain, on the road to Yorktown.

THE GENERAL AND THE CHEVALIER

One of the most attractive of the Frenchmen who came to America was Major General the Chevalier (and later Marquis) de Chastellux. While he was chief of staff to Rochambeau and an experienced soldier, he was also a man of letters, interested in poetry, music, philosophy, and even economics; a member of the French Academy; and a friend of Voltaire and Franklin. Of all the French who came, he left the most extensive and interesting diary account: *Travels in North America*. He was not always quite tactful, for he described Mrs. Washington as "fat," and looking "like a German princess" and Mrs. Schuyler as a "big Dutchwoman."

George Washington took to him at once. Chastellux in turn greatly admired the general and has given posterity admirable accounts of his battles. His description of his visit to Washington's camp in 1780 has often been mined by biographers:

November 23... After riding two miles beyond the right flank of the army, and after passing through thick woods on the right, I found myself in a little plain, where I saw a rather handsome farm: a small camp which seemed to cover it, a large tent pitched in the yard, and several wagons round it convinced me that this was the headquarters of "his Excellency"... M. De La Fayette was conversing in the yard with a tall man, six feet two inches high, of a noble and mild appearance. It was the general himself. I soon dismounted and approached him. The greetings were brief; the feelings which animated me and his kindly disposition towards me were not feigned. He conducted me into his house, where I found the company still at table, although the dinner had long been over. He presented me to Generals Knox, Wayne, Howe, etc., and his "family," then composed of Colonels Hamilton and Tilghman... A fresh dinner was prepared for me... A few glasses of claret and Madeira accelerated the acquaintances I had to make, and I soon felt myself at ease near the greatest and best of men. The goodness and benevolence which characterize him are evident in all that surrounds him; but the confidence he calls forth is never familiar, for the sentiment he inspires has the same origin in every individual, a profound esteem for his virtues and a high opinion of his talents...

November 24... We availed ourselves of the opportunity of following [Washington] to [Lafayette's] camp. We found all his troops in order of battle... himself at their head, expressing by his bearing and countenance that he was happier in receiving me here than at his estate in Auvergne. The confidence and attachment of the troops are to him invaluable possessions, well-acquired riches, which nobody can take from him; but what, in my opinion, is still more flattering for a young man of his age, is the influence, the consideration he has acquired in the political, as well as in the military order. I do not fear contradiction when I say that private letters from him have frequently produced more effect on some states than the strongest exhortations from congress...

November 26... I got on horseback, after breakfasting with the General. He thoughtfully gave me the horse he had been riding two days earlier and which I had greatly commended. I found the horse as good as he was handsome, but above all, perfectly well broken and well trained, having a good mouth, easy in hand, and stopping short in gallop without bearing the bit. I mention these minute particulars, because it is the general himself who breaks in all his own horses, and because he is a very excellent and bold horseman, leaping the highest fences and going extremely quick, without standing upon his stirrups, bearing on the bridle, or letting his horse run wild...

...General Knox... took us back to headquarters... He is a man of thirty-five, very fat, but very active and of a gay and amiable character... On our return to headquarters... I had an opportunity of conversing more particularly with General Wayne... He is sensible and his conversation is agreeable and animated...

Here would be the proper place to give the portrait of General Washington, but what can my testimony add to the idea already formed of him? The continent of North America, from Boston to Charleston, is a great book, every page of which presents his praise... The strongest characteristic of this respectable man is the perfect harmony which reigns between the physical and moral qualities which compose his personality. One trait alone enables you to judge of all the rest. If you are shown medals of Caesar, or Trajan or Alexander, you will still, upon examining their faces, ask what was their stature and the form of their bodies; but if you discover, in a heap of ruins, the head or the limb of an antique Apollo, be not curious about the other parts, but rest assured that all belong to a god... It is not my intention to exaggerate. I wish only to express the impression General Washington has left on my mind, the idea of a perfect whole... This is the seventh year that he has commanded the army, and that he has obeyed Congress; more need not be said, especially in America, where they know how to appreciate all the merits contained in this simple fact... If anything can be more marvelous than such a character, it is the unanimity of the public suffrage in his favor. Soldier, Magistrate, People, all love and admire him; all speak of him only in terms of affection and admiration...

In speaking of this perfect whole... I have not excluded exterior form. His stature is noble and lofty, he is well built, and exactly proportioned; his physiognomy mild and agreeable, but such as to render it impossible to speak particularly of any one of his features, so that on leaving him, you have only the recollection of a fine face... His smile is always the smile of benevolence.

But it is interesting, above all, to see him in the midst of the general officers of his army. General in a republic, he has not the imposing pomp of a <u>Marechal de France</u> who gives <u>the</u> <u>order</u>; a hero in a republic, he excites another sort of respect, which seems to spring from the sole idea that the safety of each individual is attached to his person... When one sees the battalion of the General's guards encamped within the precincts of the house; nine wagons, destined to carry his baggage, ranged in his yard; a great number of grooms holding very fine horses belonging to the general officers and their aids-de-camp; when one observes the perfect order that reigns... one is tempted to apply to the Americans what Pyrrhus said of the Romans: "Truly these people have nothing barbarous in their discipline!"*

DISTRESSES

Washington, with his customary courtesy, effectively concealed from Chastellux the worries that gnawed at him.

On November 12, 1780, Sullivan had written to suggest that he urge the French to move to the Hudson. Such a move would introduce a new threat to Sir Henry Clinton, and thus keep the British from sending further reinforcements southward. On November 28 Gouverneur Morris proposed that the General attack New York for the same reason. Washington replied to Sullivan,

---

* Washington did not see this comment on him by Chastellux until the summer of 1786. With his usual humor he wrote him on August 18: "Colonel Humphreys has put into my hands the translation of that part in which you say such, and so many handsome things of me; that (altho' no sceptic on ordinary occasions) I may perhaps be allowed to doubt whether your friendship and partiality have not, In this one instance, acquired an ascendancy over your cooler judgment."

who understood his problems, and to Morris, who did not. He informed Sullivan that he had strongly urged Rochambeau to move to the New York area but Rochambeau declared that he was tied completely to the blockaded French fleet. Washington further noted that, as usual, the army lacked clothing. "We are *feelingly* reminded of it... Congress will deceive themselves if they imagine that the Army... can rub through a second campaign as the last. It would be as unreasonable as to suppose that because a man had rolled a Snowball 'till it had acquired the size of a horse that he might do so till it was as large as a House." He detailed to Morris his deficiencies and inferiorities and noted that it "was with difficulty I could remove the army to its places of Cantonment where it would be well for the Troops, if like Chameleons, they could live upon Air, or like the Bear, suck their paws for sustenance during the rigor of the approaching season."

On January 1 General Stark wrote Washington pleading for money since he had not received a penny of pay for two years. Washington replied two days later that the army did not have a farthing in the military chest and it had been three months since he himself had been able to draw even for his own food. Chastellux had no hint of any of these problems.

Martha Washington made her usual long winter trip from Mount Vernon to the Hudson. She arrived at Washington's winter headquarters at New Windsor in time for Christmas and for the first major mutiny in the American army.

THE MUTINIES

Washington had frequently predicted that American troops could not be pushed around much more or he would have no army. On December 16 General Wayne described to President Reed of Pennsylvania the miserable conditions of his state's troops—their dry bread and beef; their worn coats and tattered linen; their threadbare blankets, each of which had to be shared among three soldiers; their lack of pay for a year; and "their more than Roman virtue."

On January 1, 1781, the Pennsylvania line mutinied. In the calmer atmosphere of April 18, Washington could write to Greene that it had arisen "more from the effect of an over charge of spirits on the first of January than of premeditated design." Before he reached the stage where he could appraise it with some humor, he had to live with it, as it spread to the troops of other states.

Late on the night of January 1, rockets and guns went off in the Pennsylvania camp at Mount Kemble. When the officers found it was a mutiny, they tried to quell it, and two of them were shot. General Wayne appeared, but the mutineers said their quarrel was not with him but with Congress and Pennsylvania. After great disorder half the camp set out for Philadelphia, "being much agitated with liquor when they went off." The amount of alcohol each man had that day was only half a pint but it had been downed on almost empty stomachs.

Word quickly reached the British. Sir Henry Clinton rushed troops across Staten Island to a point near Amboy. He also sent out proclamations offering the Pennsylvanians pardons and all their back pay, but this was a patriotic revolt, and the men repeatedly said that if the enemy appeared they would turn around and fight. The Pennsylvanians halted at Princeton, where two British spies caught up with them. They were held by the revolters and later turned over to the army, which hanged them.

President Reed of Pennsylvania, acting under the authority of his state and of Congress, moved to address the grievances of the men. As he put it so handsomely, he had only one life and his country deserved it. In anxiety to please, he agreed to meet all their complaints, real or imaginary. They were to be given their back pay and some clothing, which were reasonable adjustments, but then Reed listened to the plea that some men were being held beyond their enlistment dates. He agreed that if they signed a paper stating when they had enlisted and under what terms, and this showed that they had finished their service, they would be released. This was too easy a way out, and more than thirteen hundred men claimed their discharges. The remainder, about eleven hundred men, were given a two-month furlough. With one swoop, Reed knocked out about 20 percent of Washington's army.

Washington made various comments. His January 22 letter to New York and the New England states said that "an accommodation took place, which will not only subvert the Pennsylvania Line, but have a pernicious influence on the whole army." On January 27 he wrote the New Jersey commissioners: "In transacting terms of enlistments with the Pennsylvanians, for want of proper care, the greatest part of the line has been dismissed, though only a small proportion was intitled to a dismissal. Authentic and unequivocal proofs have been since found that a majority of the discharged men were fairly and explicitly enlisted for the war. The evil arose from admitting the oaths of individuals before the vouchers could be assembled." On February 3 he wrote to General St. Clair to say that perjury did not relieve the soldiers from their engagement to serve and they should be rounded up. St. Clair replied there were so many this would be difficult. In any case it might be considered a governmental "breach of faith."

After the Pennsylvanians revolted, Washington appealed to the states to produce more clothing and pay. His letter to New Jersey succeeded in part, for their troops received extra cash, which they promptly spent on liquor. With a whoop and a holler, on the evening of January 20, the New Jersey troops at Pompton set off for Trenton to seek redress of their grievances. This time Washington took the strongest possible steps to keep civilians out and to suppress the mutiny himself. He sent an urgent message to the congressional committee at Trenton not to talk to them. He asked the governor of New Jersey for militia help and requested that he make no "compromise with the mutineers." He selected General Howe to march with a large detachment for Ringwood with orders of January 22, "to compel the mutineers to unconditional submission... I am to desire you will grant no terms while they are with arms in their hands or in a state of resistance... If you succeed in compelling the revolted troops to a surrender you will instantly execute a few of the most active and most incendiary leaders."

Heavy snows blocked the roads but Washington got through to Ringwood by sleigh. One problem he had was outlined in his January 25 letter to his quartermaster general, Timothy Pickering: "My horses, I am told, have not had a mouthful of long or short forage for three days. They have eaten up their mangers and are now (though wanted for immediate use) scarcely able to stand. I should be glad to know if there is any prospect of relief for them."

Howe's troops, as Washington wrote in their praise on January 30, marched from West Point to Ringwood "through rough and mountainous roads rendered almost impassable by snow." As it turned out, the New Jersey mutiny was small scale, with only two hundred or so men involved. When Washington got to Ringwood on January 27, Howe marched to the scene and surrounded the huts of the mutineers with heavy guns. There were no negotiations. They were ordered out in five minutes. They came out without arms. Fifteen ringleaders were selected, tried by court-martial, and sentenced to death. Twelve of the fifteen were then chosen to shoot the other three. After the first two were shot, the third was pardoned. The revolt was over. Washington then wrote to the New Jersey commission that "having punished guilt and supported authority, it now becomes proper to do justice." He urged the commissioners to give the fullest hearing to all complaints.

VIEWS ON NATIONAL UNITY

Washington had earlier received a letter of January 8 from Robert R. Livingston, chancellor of New York and a member of Congress. He hoped Washington would not mind his saying that the economic distresses of the state were great. The inhabitants, poor as they were, were so heavily taxed that they were sending many complaints and petitions to the state Assembly. Since New York's government was weak and subject to popular pressure, it would be impossible to raise any more money, at least until they could see that other states bore an equal burden.

Washington during the war often expressed the country's need for union and a strong central government, the more so as the authority of Congress grew weaker and weaker. The previous October 22 he had told William Fitzhugh that "instead of one head and director, we have, or soon shall have, thirteen, which is as much a monster in politicks as it would be in the human form." After apologizing to Livingston on January 31 for a delay in answering, because of the mutinies of troops without pay, clothing, and provisions, Washington continued:

> *To learn from so good authority as your information that the distresses of the Citizens of this State are maturing into complaints which are likely to produce serious consequences, is a circumstance as necessary to be known, as it is unpleasing to hear...*

> *To trace these evils to their sources is by no means difficult; and errors once discovered are more than half corrected. This, I hope, is our case at present; but there can be no radical cure till Congress is vested by the several States with full and ample Powers to enact Laws for general purposes, and till the executive business is placed in the hands of able Men and responsible characters. Requisitions, then, will be supported by Law. Jealousies, and this ill timed compliances arising from distrust, and the fear of doing more than a Sister State, will cease. Business will be properly arranged; System and order will take place, and economy must follow; but not till we have corrected the fundamental errors enumerated above.*

> *It would be no difficult matter to prove that less than half the present expenditures... is more than sufficient if we had money, and these alterations in our political movements were adopted, to answer all our purposes. Taxes of course would be lessened, the burthen would be equal and light, and men sharing a common lot would neither murmur nor despond.*

COLONEL HAMILTON MUTINIES

Amidst Washington's unceasing major troubles, Alexander Hamilton, his aide, engaged in a unilateral quarrel with the commander in chief.

Hamilton's longtime feeling that he was doing mere clerical work and finding no chance for glory boiled over when Washington failed to heed his pleas for Captain André. Not long after André met his death, Hamilton began to pull wires to obtain a staff assignment or field command. He asked Greene and Lafayette to recommend that he be made adjutant general. Washington politely pointed out to both generals that he could not appoint a lieutenant colonel to the post. The adjutant was second in command to the inspector general. His staff colonels would find it "disagreeable" to report to him. Lafayette informed Hamilton that the general's "friendship and gratitude" to him were extensive. "When he thinks he can do it," he would give him a suitable post. In December, Hamilton married Betsy Schuyler, the well-connected daughter of General Schuyler.

Hamilton did not lack for friends. When Congress asked John Laurens if he would accept appointment as special minister to France, to request further aid, he suggested Hamilton as more suitable. The members said they did not know him very well; they preferred Laurens. On January 29, General John Sullivan, now sitting in Congress for New Hampshire, wrote Washington that Congress had decided to have ministers of war, foreign affairs, marine, and finance. He wondered what Washington would think of "Colo. Hamilton as a Financier." The general replied that he had never discussed this field with him but he thought "that there are few men to be found, of his age, who has a more general knowledge than he possesses... or who exceeds him in probity and Sterling virtue."

On February 16, the twenty-six-year-old Hamilton contrived a dispute with Washington. He subsequently wrote a version that tells only part of the story and this not necessarily accurately. The missing portion, which involved a letter misplaced by Hamilton, can be deduced from Washington's correspondence. On January 25 Washington sent to the British fleet commander in New York a formal complaint that American prisoners were "suffering all the extremities of distress from a too crowded and in all respects disagreeable and unwholesome situation on board the prison-ships, and from the want of food and other necessities." A Captain George Dawson of the Royal Navy, replying on February 2, rejected the charges. He listed the Americans' rations, thereby unwittingly disclosing that they had a diet below that of British prisoners in American hands. Washington sent the correspondence to Congress on February 13 indicating that he was studying what action to take.

On February 16 Washington and Hamilton worked out a lengthy letter to Abraham Skinner, American commissary of prisoners, on proposals for an exchange of General Burgoyne and other British prisoners. When Washington asked Hamilton to get Dawson's letter, he could not find it. The exact circumstances are unimportant but Washington was annoyed, and Hamilton, according to camp reports, said he would not be talked to like a menial. On February 18 Hamilton wrote to General Schuyler: "Two days ago, The General and I passed each other on the stairs. He told me he wanted to speak to me. I answered that I would wait upon him immediately. I went below, and delivered Mr. Tilghman a letter to be sent to The Commissary, containing an order of a pressing and interesting nature. Returning to The General I was stopped in the way by the Marquis De La Fayette, and we conversed together about a minute on a matter of business. He can testify how impatient I was to get back, and that I left him in a manner which, but for our intimacy, would have been more than abrupt. Instead of finding the General as usual in his room, I met him at the head of the stairs, where, accosting me in a very angry tone, 'Colonel Hamilton' (said he,) 'you have kept me waiting at the head of the stairs these ten minutes. I must tell you Sir you treat me with disrespect.' I replied without petulancy, but with decision: 'I am not conscious of it Sir, but since you have thought it necessary to tell me so we part.'"

Hamilton then said that, within the hour, Tench Tilghman came with a verbal message from Washington expressing praise of Hamilton's abilities and integrity and a hope that he would come around and talk to him so that the breach could be healed. Hamilton reported to Schuyler that he had rejected the proposal but agreed to stay on Washington's staff until two absent aides returned to camp. He continued:

> I always disliked the office of an Aide de camp as having in it a kind of personal dependence... Infected however with the enthusiasm of the times, an idea of the General's character, which experience taught me to be unfounded, overcame my scruples, and induced me to accept his invitation to enter into his family. I believe you know the place I held in The General's confidence and councils which will make it the more extraordinary to you to learn that for three years past I have felt no friendship for him and have professed none. The truth is our own dispositions are the opposites of each other & the pride of my temper would not suffer me to profess what I did not feel. Indeed when advances of this kind have been made to me on his part, they were received in a manner that showed at least I had no inclination to court them... You are too good a judge of human nature not to be sensible how this conduct in me must have operated on a man to whom all the world is offering incense. With this key you will easily unlock the present mystery.
>
> ...The General is a very honest man. His competitors have slender abilities, and less integrity. His popularity has often been essential to the safety of America, and is still of great importance to it...

I wish what I have said to make no other impression than to satisfy you I have not been in the wrong.

It is probable that Hamilton preferred that only his own version circulate. Two days later, the missing letter from Dawson was found. Washington then dictated a letter to Hamilton ordering Abraham Skinner to give British prisoners the same diet as American prisoners in New York. Hamilton, as the only French-speaking aide, stayed through the subsequent conferences with Rochambeau. Thereafter he found other work and no little glory at Yorktown.

LAURENS TO PARIS

John Laurens had studied in Geneva and spoke French well enough for his mission as a special American minister to Versailles. He had been wounded three times and exchanged as a prisoner of war. For these reasons, and because his father had been its president, he was better known to Congress than Hamilton. Henry Laurens had been appointed minister to Holland, but the British picked him up at sea. The first American president to visit England, he was clapped in the Tower of London and rigorously treated. In sending John Laurens to France, Congress gave him a chance to institute negotiations for his father's release by offering Burgoyne in exchange.

Rochambeau had sent his own son from Newport to the French court to plead for more money for his troops, for the additional division of five thousand men that had been promised America, and for naval support. Rochambeau, though writing of American needs, concentrated on his own irksome position. Laurens was sent to explain that the American army had nearly reached the end of its rope. Before he left, he held lengthy conversations with Washington on the presentation to be made at Versailles. Lafayette, still only twenty-three, sent Vergennes a sharp and brilliant summary of the American position on January 20:

With a naval inferiority, it is impossible to make war in America. It is that which prevents us from attacking any point that might be carried with two or three thousand men. It is that which reduces us to defensive operations, as dangerous as they are humiliating. The English are conscious of this truth, and all their movements prove how much they desire to retain the empire of the sea. The harbours, the country, and all the resources it offers appear to invite us to send thither a naval force. If we had possessed but a maritime superiority this spring, much might have been achieved with the army that M. De Rochambeau brought with him, and it would not have been necessary to have awaited the division he announced to us. If M. De Guichen had stopped at Rhode Island on his way to France, Arbuthnot would have been ruined, and not all Rodney's efforts could have prevented our gaining victories.

Since the hour of the arrival of the French, their inferiority has never for one moment ceased, and the English and the Tories have dared to say that France wished to kindle, without extinguishing, the flame. This calumny becomes more dangerous at a period when English detachments are wasting the South; when under the protection of some frigates, corps of fifteen hundred men are repairing to Virginia without our being able to get to them...

The result, sir, of all this is that... it becomes, from a political and military point of view, necessary to give us... a decided naval superiority for the next campaign; and also, sir, to give us money enough to place the regular army and ten thousand... militia in this part of the country; a Southern army... formed by the five southern states... Immense sums of money could not transport resources of equal value from Europe to America, but these, without a succour of money, although established on the very theatre of war, will become useless... All that credit, persuasion and force could achieve has been done—but that can hold out no longer.

...The Continental troops have as much courage and real discipline as those that are opposed to them. They are more inured to privation, more patient than Europeans... The recruits whom we are expecting... have seen more gunshots than three-fourths of the European soldiers... The militia... are not deficient in ardour and in discipline but would be most useful in the labours of a siege.

It had not occurred to Lafayette, the soul of honor, that French policy towards the United States was deliberately machiavellian. France's aim was to separate the country from Great Britain, while keeping America sufficiently weak to make it a French satellite. There is a long-standing myth that the American war was responsible for France's subsequent bankruptcy and revolution. France's financial aid to the United States was small and grudging. From 1775 to 1780 grants totalled only $600,000, of which a portion disappeared in internal French bribes. France advanced a further $1.6 million in loans at ungenerous terms.

Before Laurens' departure, Congress forwarded to Franklin a copy of his instructions to ask for a loan of $5 million. Franklin discussed the request with Vergennes who dismissed it but agreed to a grant of $1.1 million, equivalent to twenty months' pocket money for Marie Antoinette. Vergennes' subsidy was carefully calculated to barely keep the American army in being. Laurens reached Paris with a shopping list far in excess of the grant. He asked the ministers to reconsider and advance the larger sum in repayable loans. Franklin complained that he was too brusque with the government but this made no difference in French policy. Vergennes did say he would guarantee a loan in the Netherlands to the amount of $2 million. Since he knew the money could not then be raised, the offer was entirely *pro forma*.

The French court decided to send a fleet under the comte de Grasse to the West Indies, to cooperate with the Spanish against the British in the Caribbean. De Grasse was given an option to go to American waters, if circumstances permitted. Laurens returned to America just in time to join Washington and Rochambeau on their way to Virginia.

UTI POSSIDETIS

The European powers played war as a form of musical chairs. When they tired of fighting, the belligerents kept whatever real estate they occupied at the time the music stopped, though they might thereafter swap countries and islands.

While John Laurens was in France begging for help, Vergennes was engaged in arranging for other courts to "mediate" the war. Maurepas, the prime minister, had sent peace feelers to England as early as 1780. Necker, the finance minister, had also proposed peace with Great Britain, suggesting that partial independence be allowed a few American states. George III concluded that France was in financial difficulties and he should therefore hold out for complete American submission.

At this point the British held most of Georgia and South Carolina, a large part of North Carolina, much of Virginia and New York, and a naval base in Maine. In addition they controlled substantial areas of the Northwest Territory. Under Vergennes' mediation, America would have been left with the ports of Boston and Philadelphia and not much else on the sea, with the British and Spanish across the mountains. Washington was aware of the danger. He wrote Thomas Jefferson on June 8: "The progress which the enemy are making in Virginia is very alarming not only to the State immediately invaded but to all the rest, as I strongly suspect from the most recent European intelligences, that they are endeavouring to make as large seeming conquests as possible, that they may urge the plea of uti possidetis in the proposed mediation."

JOHN ADAMS

Fortunately John Adams, who had been a headache for Washington and Franklin, was in Europe, fully ready to take on the French foreign ministry.

Franklin had won all hearts in Paris but this had not deflected, to the slightest degree, French government policy based on its own self-interest. What the United States needed was a man to stick up for his country, and this Adams did to a degree that alarmed Franklin and Vergennes. Adams' touch of paranoia was often misdirected but in this case it gave him dazzling insight.

Adams' vanity was attractive because he could be humorous about it. He had no humor about his country. Arriving in France as minister, with full powers to make a treaty of peace and commerce with Great Britain, he aroused Vergennes' suspicions, while Adams was won over, at first, by Vergennes' charming insincerity. With time on his hands, he busied himself addressing the comte de Vergennes as a representative of a fully equal power: "The state of things in America has really become alarming, and this merely for want of a few French men-of-war on the coast... The flourishing state of France's maritime and commerce, and the decisive influence of her councils... all the world will allow to be owing in great measure... to her new connections with the United States... The United States of America are a great and powerful people, whatever European statesmen may think of them."

By the following year, while Vergennes was busy with his scheme to dismember the United States, Adams was writing him: "The dignity of North America does not consist in diplomatic ceremonials or any of the subtleties of etiquette; it consists solely in reason, justice, truth, the rights of mankind and the interests of the nations of Europe... The United States have assumed their equal station among the nations. They have assumed a sovereignty which they acknowledge to hold only from God and their own swords."

Vergennes' reactions were direct and simple. He ordered Luzerne, his minister at Philadelphia, to instruct Congress, which eagerly desired their crumbs of gold from France, to clip the wings of John Adams. In June 1781 Congress directed Adams to place himself under the authority of Vergennes and to do nothing without his knowledge and concurrence. In addition Congress appointed three other ministers coequal with him in peace negotiations. Adams received these revised instructions as he was on his way to the Netherlands. He conveyed his suspicions to his diary: "Keep us poor. Depress us. Keep us weak. Make us feel our obligations. Impress our minds with a sense of gratitude. Let Europe see our dependence. Make Europe believe we are in great distress and danger... Propagate bad news, to discourage the merchants and bankers from lending us money. Is there anything in these jealousies and insinuations?"

LONDON

On December 17, 1780, Lord North complained to the king that Britain's declaration of war on Holland would cause him great trouble in raising more loans. He again said his mind and body were going and he ought to resign. On January 14, North wrote the king that Britain would have to raise an extra £3 million for the army in America, which he had not anticipated. The expenses, he said, "are increased to an amazing degree." Lord Stormont, a few days later, suggested to the king he might try to bribe Russia to enter the war by offering her Minorca.

In the newly elected Parliament, a young man named William Pitt was returned from Appleby, Westmorland, where Washington's father, uncle, and two half brothers had gone to school. By June Horace Walpole was writing that Pitt, with all his father's oratory, had "answered Lord North and tore him limb from limb." As Greene and Cornwallis fought throughout the South, Pitt described Cornwallis' efforts as "a series of ineffective victories or severe defeats—victories only celebrated with temporary triumph over our brethren whom we would trample down, or defeats which fill the land with mourning for the loss of dear and valuable relations, slain in the impious cause of enforcing unconditional submission." Lord North continued to command heavy majorities for continuing the war but he was hammered at from all sides, and his heart had long gone out of the business.

WAR IN VIRGINIA

In December Sir Henry Clinton sent Benedict Arnold to Virginia with orders to take a post at Portsmouth, to move up the James River destroying supplies, and, if possible, to block any attempt by Washington, Congress, or Governor Jefferson to relieve Greene's army in the Carolinas. Clinton was not entirely sure of Arnold's trustworthiness or judgement. He assigned to his staff Lieutenant Colonels Thomas Dundas and John Simcoe; Arnold was ordered to consult with them on all operations.

Arnold arrived in Virginia on December 30 and proceeded rapidly up the James to Westover and Richmond. Jefferson heard by December 31 that a British fleet had arrived but he took little action and, when he did act, it was too late. By January 3, Arnold had driven Jefferson out of the capital at Richmond. He destroyed arms, ammunition, government records, and the state's most important foundry. Arnold then returned to Portsmouth, where he remained until spring. Steuben, in command of the handful of Continental troops in the state, wrote of his disgust, for the northern governors had done far better when invasion came than the southern governors had.

Washington advised Jefferson in early February that, despite sporadic raids of this kind, he should not neglect to send all possible aid and reinforcements to Greene, who was fighting the main British army in the South; the longer it was kept out of Virginia the better. At almost the same time Washington wrote Jefferson that a chance had come to send aid south since a severe storm had damaged the British fleet blockading Rhode Island. For a glorious moment it looked as though relief could go by sea and Arnold could be captured and hanged.

THE FRENCH ENVOY INTERFERES

The chevalier de La Luzerne had, once before, accidentally prevented Washington from capturing Arnold when, on his way to Rhode Island, he persuaded Washington to spend a night at Fishkill rather than West Point. The next morning Arnold went off to the enemy. Luzerne again managed to foul up a daring plan to close in on Arnold. The French minister at Philadelphia was engaged in diplomatic pool, which looked to Spanish and French interests rather than American. He had two objectives: to prevent the Northwest Territory, the future middle west of the United States, from becoming American at the peace, and to keep the navigation of the Mississippi in Spanish hands.

In his operations, conflicting private and public interests were at work. The private Illinois-Wabash Company owned or claimed large parts of the Northwest Territory that Virginia considered hers by original charter. The company's stockholders included a number of prominent Marylanders, as well as the former French minister, Conrad Gérard, brother of Joseph Gérard de Rayneval, French undersecretary of foreign affairs; and the French consul at Philadelphia, John Holker.

The Articles of Confederation, supposed to form a more perfect union of the states, had never been ratified. Maryland refused to sign unless Virginia and other states surrendered their claims to western lands. Luzerne was anxious to accomplish this in order to facilitate France's operations at the peace table. In addition, he wanted the Articles approved, since under the new constitution four states, rather than the previous six, could block foreign treaties.

This would make it easier for pro-French factions to control American foreign policy. While the minister was pushing the states to ratify, he proposed to Vergennes that future French financial aid be directed to individual states rather than to Congress. Thus he hoped further to divide and conquer the new weak nation.

It was not difficult to get Jefferson's Virginia to surrender the western lands. This left Maryland as a holdout. With the British raiding the Chesapeake, Luzerne had only to hint that future French aid was contingent on the Articles being passed. Ratification came quickly in February 1781. Without consulting Washington, Luzerne then requested Rochambeau and Destouches to send a small naval force to the Chesapeake.

Washington received word on February 7 of the storm that had broken the British blockade of Newport on January 29. He immediately forwarded to Rochambeau his latest information of Arnold's movements, suggesting that Destouches and his fleet ought to proceed to the Chesapeake. By February 15, having had further Virginia intelligence, Washington sent a rather hurried letter, clumsily drafted by Hamilton, proposing to Rochambeau an immediate plan to capture Arnold. Washington would detach Lafayette and twelve hundred continentals to move as rapidly as possible by land to Virginia. He hoped, in turn, that Rochambeau would cooperate by sending the whole of the French fleet southward, together with a thousand troops and as much siege artillery as he could spare. He noted that "the capture of Arnold and his detachment will be an event particularly agreeable to the Country; a great relief to the Southern states and of important utility in our future operations." On February 20, Lafayette, with his continental detachment, headed rapidly south, the young general marching his troops thirty or more miles a day.

On February 20 Rochambeau replied that Luzerne had only asked for some frigates and one ship of the line and had not mentioned any troops. He had sent these to Virginia under Captain Armand de Tilly. Arnold, who had been a merchant mariner and had fought naval battles on Lake Champlain, was too clever to be caught by de Tilly, who had no ground forces. He moved his small boats up the Elizabeth River. The French expedition was not totally unsuccessful, for the fleet caught a British warship and several merchantmen. The French returned to Newport fifteen days after leaving port.

On February 27 Washington received word from Rochambeau and Destouches that, following their initial failure, they had decided to proceed with his plan. He wrote immediately to Lafayette to wait at Head of Elk for word of French naval movements. He informed Destouches that he had received the news "with peculiar pleasure" and he would proceed, as soon as possible, to Newport, to discuss the plans. By March 5 Lafayette was at Head of Elk.

THE NEWPORT MEETING

Washington left New Windsor on March 2, riding at his best speed to Newport. He was met at Jamestown, Rhode Island, on March 6 by the French admiral's barge, which carried him to the flagship, the *Duc de Bourgogne*. His one anxiety was to see everything start. He was informed the next day that the French fleet, loaded with troops and provisions, was ready to sail. Several days elapsed before they were under way.

Rochambeau had often expressed the wish of the French army to see "their general." This was Washington's first chance to review allied troops. The French formed an honor guard stretching from the wharf to Rochambeau's house, where Washington stayed. The next night Newport was illuminated, the town council having voted funds so that every house could have candles. The French held a ball in his honor, which he opened by dancing with Margaret Champlin; French officers took the instruments for the appropriate opening tune: "A Successful Campaign."

Washington greatly impressed the French. Claude Blanchard, their commissary, noted that he was "handsome, noble and gracious... I mark, as a fortunate day, that in which I have been able to behold a man so truly great." Another officer wrote to an American about "the arrival of the celebrated Washington, the Atlas of your country... We had not eyes enough to see him with. Man is born with a tendency to pride and the further he progresses in his career in an elevated rank the more his self love nourishes this vice in him but, so far from this, Washington, although born with every superior quality, adds to them an imposing modesty, which will always cause him to be admired by those who have the good fortune to see him; as for esteem he has already drawn to himself that of all Europe."

Washington stayed a week with the French then headed back to his camp. At Bristol, the principal people of the town rode out on horseback to greet him. The entire population was out to cheer and to drop flowers and evergreens in his way through the town. At Providence everyone again turned out. Count Dumas noted in his memoirs that the children, carrying torches, crowded so thickly around "their father," that no one could move. Washington pointed to them and told Dumas: "We may be beaten by the English but there is an army they can never beat." By March 17 he was back at New Windsor, anxious for every letter from the south.

WASHINGTON APOLOGIZES

The second French naval expedition returned to Newport in nearly as fast time as the first eighteen days. The British fleet had been allowed six weeks for repairs after the storm. A superior British force chased the French to the Chesapeake. An indecisive battle was fought in which two French and three British ships were damaged. Destouches quickly retired to Newport, leaving Arbuthnot in command of the Chesapeake. Sir Henry Clinton at once dispatched Major General William Phillips and twenty-five hundred troops to Virginia, where they arrived on March 26. Clinton mentioned in his memoirs that the French expedition could not have failed had it got under way earlier, but a seven weeks' delay can be long in war.

Washington heard on March 30 that the whole enterprise had fallen through, making it the fourth time the French navy had failed to cooperate effectively with American plans. Nonetheless he wrote the French minister on March 31 that he was sure there would be "universal admiration of the good conduct and bravery of the French forces." He sent similar letters to Rochambeau and Destouches.

Two days before writing the French, Washington had sent a note to Lund Washington, his Mount Vernon manager, mainly about his farm and personal affairs but he added: "It was unfortunate, but this I mention in confidence, that the French fleet and detachment did not undertake the enterprize they are now upon, when I first proposed it to them; the destruction of Arnolds Corps would then have been inevitable before the British fleet could have been in a condition to put to Sea... The small squadron... could not, as I foretold, do anything without a land force." The letter was a highly restrained comment on a disaster that put the southern states in an even more critical situation. The British captured the letter and printed it in *Rivington's Gazette*.

It is difficult to see why American historians have chided Washington for the remarks. Douglas Southall Freeman was perhaps the most critical, for he has a whole chapter called "Washington's Pen Runs Away with Him," and he terms the letter "imprudent," "unrestrained," and "offensive," adding that it was humiliating for Washington and insulting to the allies.

Rochambeau wrote Washington a dignified complaint, saying that the proposal had not reached him until ten days after the first French squadron sailed. He said nothing about the failure of the French to consult the commander in chief about their operations. On April 30 Washington offered Rochambeau a straightforward regret that he had unintentionally given pain to the French, but he deftly placed a thorn amidst the roses: "I have lately learnt (though not officially) that the cause of the delay I have alluded to was a want of Supplies for the fleet. Impressed with a real esteem for, and confidence in the Chevalier Des Touches, I heard this circumstance with satisfaction."

With spring, Washington could not help thinking that he had not seen Mount Vernon for nearly six years. He wrote General John Armstrong on March 25:

Our affairs are brought to an awful crisis, that the hand of Providence, I trust, may be more conspicuous in our deliverance.

The many remarkable interpositions of the divine government in the hours of our deepest distress and darkness, have been too luminous to suffer me to doubt the happy issue of the present conflict; but the period for its accomplishment may be too far distant for a person of my years, whose Morning and Evening hours, and every moment (unoccupied by business), pants for retirement; and for those domestic and rural enjoyments which in my estimation far surpasses the highest pagentry of the world.

In his letter to Lund Washington criticizing the slow tactics of the French, he had asked: "How many Lambs have you had this Spring? How many Colts are you like to have? Is your covered way done? What are you going about next? Have you any prospects of getting paint and Oyl?... Have you made good the decayed trees... Have you made any attempts to reclaim more Land for Meadow?... An acct. Of these things would be satisfactory to me, and infinitely amusing... as I have these kind of improvements very much at heart."

On April 18 Lund Washington wrote him that a British vessel had anchored off Mount Vernon, stolen some slaves, and destroyed a boat. Lund said he had taken refreshments on board the ship in an endeavor to regain the negroes. On April 30 Washington sent a sharp reply: "I am very sorry to hear of your loss. I am a little sorry to hear of my own; but that which gives me most concern is that you should go on board the enemy's vessels, and furnish them with refreshments. It would have been a less painful circumstance for me to have heard that, in consequence of your non-compliance with their request, they had burnt my House and laid the Plantation in ruins. You ought to have considered yourself as my representative, and should have reflected on the bad example of communication with the enemy." Washington added that he knew Lund was trying to protect his property but the whole thing was "ill-Judged." He added that so long as the British controlled the seas, there was no way to stop the raids, and he expected his house to be burned. He suggested that Lund move out the most valuable and least bulky objects.

WAR IN THE SOUTH

According to his published notes on the state, Thomas Jefferson, as governor of Virginia, was commander in chief of its fifty thousand militia. When Steuben asked for two thousand men to march south to reinforce Greene against the main enemy, Cornwallis, Jefferson rejected the request, although this strategy had been strongly urged on him by Washington. Steuben then asked him to move against the British at Portsmouth but the governor again disapproved.

Lafayette reconnoitered the Chesapeake after learning that a fleet had been sighted to the south. To his distress he found the ships to be British. Moving to Annapolis, he was temporarily blockaded there. On his own credit, he provided his men with $9,000 worth of clothing. When the joint forces of Phillips and Arnold moved to Petersburg, he marched rapidly south to save Richmond at the end of April, even though his forces were only a quarter of the enemy's. On May 10 the Virginia Assembly resolved to meet thereafter in Charlottesville. Shortly afterwards, on May 24, Lafayette wrote to Washington from Richmond, describing his situation:

> *I ardently wish my conduct may meet with your approbation. Had I followed the first impulsion of my temper, I would have risked some things more. But I have been guarding against my own warmth, and this consideration that a general defeat... would involve this State and our affairs in ruin, had rendered me extremely cautious in my movements. Indeed, I am... more crippled in my projects than we have been in the Northern States.*

> *...Public stores and private property being removed from Richmond, this place is a less important object. I don't believe it would be prudent to expose the troops for the sake of a few houses... Was I to fight a battle, I'll be cut to pieces, the militia dispersed, and the arms lost. Was I to decline fighting, the country would think herself given up. I am therefore determined to skirmish, but not to engage too far...*

> *Was I any ways equal to the enemy, I would be extremely happy in my present command. But I am not strong enough even to get beaten. Government in this state has no energy.*

On June 5, Tarleton and 250 dragoons rode swiftly to Charlottesville to capture the governor and legislature. Virginia's commander in chief, warned just in time, fled to the West. Tarleton seized one congressman and eight members of the Virginia Assembly. Thus Thomas Jefferson, who had pledged his fellow Signers' lives, fortunes, and sacred honor, ignominiously ended his governorship. He was replaced by a militia general, Thomas Nelson, Jr.

From this point on, thanks in large part to Washington's foresight, Lafayette's position began to improve. Steuben had spent the winter drilling a continental battalion, intended to aid Greene in North and South Carolina. When Jefferson, to Greene's anger, intervened to forbid this part of the Virginia line from leaving the state, they were added to Lafayette's forces in June. Wayne had also spent much time that winter and spring in rebuilding the Pennsylvania line, which had been decimated by Reed. He marched south with his new troops that same month, bringing Lafayette's total to twenty-five hundred regulars. To these were soon added nearly eight hundred North Carolina riflemen. The new governor of Virginia restored energy to the state government, especially its defenses. Before long Lafayette had an additional twenty-two hundred militia, making his force opposed to Cornwallis much more formidable than it had been. While he was not strong enough for a general engagement, he was sufficiently so to stop further raids and to harry the enemy onto the peninsula between the James and the York Rivers. That summer of 1781 the entire success of the allied operations and the future of the United States of America was to depend on Lafayette's skill in keeping Cornwallis bottled up.

On May 2, 1781, Lord George Germain sent peremptory orders to Sir Henry Clinton: "I am commanded by His Majesty to acquaint you that the recovery of the southern provinces and the prosecution of our conquests from south to north is to be considered as the chief and principal employment of all the forces which can be spared... until it is accomplished." It was the American army, however, that was to carry out Germain's plan almost to the letter.

Presumably Germain viewed the three southernmost states as safely under British control. With their rear secure, the British could then move on to Virginia and then up into Maryland. Whatever Germain may have believed, the southern states were in fact anything but secure.

Lord Cornwallis had received Clinton's instructions that Charleston was to be kept at all costs, and South Carolina be made perfectly secure, before he moved north for further operations. In the March 15 battle of Guilford Court House, North Carolina, Cornwallis had beaten Greene, but he thereby lost a quarter of his forces. He thereupon retreated to Wilmington, the state's principal seaport, from which he moved north to Virginia. Greene almost immediately determined to push straight into South Carolina. There he was defeated by Lord Rawdon at Hobkirk's Hill on April 25, but, as he put it in words that became famous, "We fight, get beat, rise and fight again."

This battle's effect was outweighed by a general uprising in South Carolina and Georgia, encouraged by the presence of an American army. Partisans under Henry Lee, Andrew Pickens, Thomas Sumter, and Francis Marion attacked throughout the area. Within six weeks almost every interior post in the two states had fallen to the Americans. By July Lee was almost at the gates of Charleston. Before Washington set foot in Virginia, the British were effectively confined to three ports in the three southernmost states.

WETHERSFIELD CONFERENCE

When Rochambeau's son returned from France discouraged because few of his father's requests had been granted, the French general asked for a further conference with Washington to plan the 1781 campaign.

As Washington was getting ready, he received news of a signal honor. In early 1776, before independence was declared, Harvard had given him its honorary degree. Less-giddy Yale waited five years. In May 1781, he was awarded the college's doctorate, with a letter from President Ezra Stiles: "We cannot add to the accumulation of glory which shines around the name of Washington, and which none but himself thinks unmerited." Stiles also had the grace to recognize and compliment Washington's "literary merits."

On May 1 Washington resumed the diary he had broken off in June 1775. It contains interesting points that are not always covered in letters, such as verbal instructions to intelligence agents and where he stayed while travelling. Washington reached Wethersfield, Connecticut, in time for extensive conversations with the state's governor, before Rochambeau and Chastellux arrived on May 21. He attended church with Connecticut's chief executive. The minister's text: "Blessed are the poor in spirit, for theirs is the kingdom of heaven," was painfully apt in view of the deficiencies of supplies, men, and money that Washington listed in his diary.

Admiral the Comte de Barras, who had arrived from France to take command from the Chevalier Destouches, intended to attend the conference but the British admiral, Arbuthnot, showed up off Newport and de Barras stayed put.

The French found Wethersfield as picturesque as it is, in large degree, today. Baron Cromot du Bourg thought the town charming. "It would be impossible to find prettier houses and a more beautiful view." From the steeple of the church where Washington, in Congregational fashion, had worshipped all day, du Bourg noted the rich country he could see for fifty miles around.

Washington informed Rochambeau at their conferences of May 22 and 23 that he had brought along intercepted dispatches from Germain to Clinton, in which Lord George said that he expected the southern states to be conquered and thereafter every effort should be made to bring Maryland and Pennsylvania back to "obedience." Neither Washington nor Rochambeau knew at this time that Cornwallis had reached Virginia. Rochambeau told Washington, in turn, that none of the additional troops he had asked for from France would be forthcoming. Indeed his government had even cancelled the second division, which they had promised the Americans in the spring of 1780.

Washington and Rochambeau agreed that, in spite of the distances and difficulties, the main objective in a combined operation would probably be the southern states. It was necessary to make every effort to deceive the enemy. A plan for this purpose was devised, which was described by Washington in a letter of July 31, 1788, to Noah Webster. The American general, by letter and otherwise, was to make it clear that New York was to be the sole objective. The plan was the easier to carry out because de Barras did not have sufficient transports to move Rochambeau's army from Newport to Virginia, and therefore the French would march by land, joining the American army on the Hudson. The deception was so skillfully carried out that it not only fooled Sir Henry Clinton but also a remarkable number of later biographers and historians, who believed that Rochambeau forced the march to Yorktown on a reluctant Washington.

LETTERS TO JOHN HANCOCK

Washington had promised Rochambeau that he would make every effort to fill his continental battalions, to raise supplies and ammunition from the states, and to provide militia from Massachusetts and Rhode Island to guard the French guns at Providence.

Washington began at Wethersfield, and continued in the spring and summer from other points, an extensive unilateral correspondence with John Hancock, governor of Massachusetts. By July 8 he was writing Hancock: "I have not been honored with an answer to my several letters of the 24th and 25th of May, of the 2nd, 4th, 15th, and 25th of last Month, and am of course unable to form any estimate of what may be expected in consequence of my requisitions. This puts me in rather an awkward situation, as I cannot give His Excellency Count Rochambeau, who has formed a junction with me, that official assurance of support which I had promised upon the faith of the States." Washington wrote further letters on July 14, July 30, and August 4. On August 24 Washington apologized to the governor of Rhode Island for "the neglect or Inattention of your Sister State, who have been repeatedly requested to send on their Quota."

Washington had also asked Hancock to send Massachusetts militia into the Albany region in order to release continental troops for his army. When he ordered his Albany continentals to join the main forces, the inhabitants there protested that there were no militia and they would be without protection. Washington ordered one New York regiment to remain there temporarily, which delayed their march for Yorktown.

In a confused reply of August 15 Hancock acknowledged receipt of "several" letters. He seemed surprised about everything: the militia requests for Newport and Albany, and Washington's requisitions of powder. Some of these he said he had forgotten about or he thought maybe he had taken care of them. By the time Washington received this letter he was on his way to Virginia.

As soon he returned to New Windsor, Washington learned that Thomas Jefferson's government in Virginia had collapsed. His diary for June 7 noted that he had received a letter from Pennsylvania's Joseph Reed which "afforded little hope of provision or other things from that State and was more productive of what they had done than what they meant to do." Slightly offsetting his lack of aid from the states were letters from Greene, who reported that Lord Rawdon had abandoned Camden; Orangeburg, Fort Motte, and Granby were recaptured; and the American army was investing Ninety Six and Augusta.

BRITISH INTELLIGENCE AND THE PILOTS

On June 10 Rochambeau informed Washington that de Grasse would definitely appear in American waters that summer. Washington replied on June 13 that, while they had decided New York was the only possible point of attack under existing circumstances, if de Grasse brought naval superiority or, even better, his whole fleet, other areas of operation might be "more practicable." Both officers knew this meant Virginia.

The British intercepted messengers carrying Rochambeau's accounts of Wethersfield to Luzerne and Washington's to Lafayette. These outlined the plans for attacking New York, but Sir Henry failed to detect that they were to be flexible and contingent upon circumstances. Clinton quite correctly noted in his memoirs that Washington had been much alarmed by the British invasion in the South, but Washington's supposed plans to attack him equally alarmed Clinton. He wrote Cornwallis that, in view of Lafayette's feeble forces of continentals in Virginia and Washington's proposal to besiege New York with as many as twenty thousand men, he was to return a part of his forces as soon as possible.

On June 23 Clinton received intelligence from Newport that the French frigate *Concorde* was taking ten American pilots to the West Indies. He did not know that Rochambeau's letters were also aboard; these pleaded with de

Grasse to bring with him all the ships, troops, and money that he could scrape together. On June 28 Clinton forwarded the intelligence about the pilots to Rodney in the West Indies, not then realizing that de Barras had, in fact, sent thirty pilots, allowing one for each ship that de Grasse might be in a position to bring.

About July 12 Captain George Beckwith received corrective and more accurate information from Newport, which noted that, in addition to the ten pilots from Rhode Island, the *Concorde* had previously taken on fourteen at Boston. "Their destination is for the West Indies, to pilot the Count de Grasse's squadron upon the Coast, who certainly comes with a powerful body of troops and ships. I conceive their design is to give Mr. Rodney the slip, and their object at present is certainly New York; if that is thought impracticable, Virginia." This was perhaps the most important single report received by British intelligence during the war, but there is no indication that it made the slightest difference to Sir Henry Clinton's planning.

This was the year when the British military and naval high commands were seized with idiocy. In the spring Germain informed Clinton's aide in London that he considered the war as practically finished, with Washington's small army reduced to starvation, the French cooped up in Newport, and the South nearly reconquered. He wrote Clinton that he was sending him four thousand additional troops and, with these, he should surely have enough men to end the rebellion. He assured him that, while de Grasse had gone to the Indies, Rodney would be watching him so carefully that Clinton had nothing to worry about from that source.

Clinton did not fret about de Grasse until it was too late. He spent his time writing Germain that he did not have enough troops to end the war. He said that Washington and the French together had thirty thousand men, in the North and South, plus many thousand militia and what could he do? (In fact, Clinton with his reinforcements had nearly thirty-seven thousand effectives, whereas the continentals and the French numbered around sixteen thousand.) Cornwallis marched back and forth in Virginia with no warning whatsoever of what was impending, before settling down on a peninsula, where the Royal Navy would assure his security.

Rodney in the West Indies, although he heard of the arrival of thirty American pilots before he returned to England, took no hint from this. He had already ordered fourteen British ships of the line to go north under Sir Samuel Hood and saw no reason to change his plans. He informed the British admiral at New York, eight days after de Grasse had sailed for the Chesapeake with twenty-eight ships, that he thought de Grasse would take "at least 12" ships north. Sir Samuel Hood, as he proceeded with a fleet half the size of de

Grasse's, informed Sir Henry Clinton, on August 25, that he was bringing enough force "fully to defeat any designs of the enemy, let de Grasse bring or send what ships he may in aid of those under de Barras."

THE FRENCH AND AMERICANS JOIN

The French were more than glad to get away from the small island and town they had occupied since the preceding summer. But they did not leave with undue haste. Washington at one point asked Rochambeau if he could hurry a bit in order to put pressure on Clinton to remove troops from the South.

The French marching routes were planned and drawn by Alexandre Berthier, later chief of staff to Napoleon. Rochambeau left Wethersfield on May 23, but his army did not quit Newport until June 10. By June 17 the French were no farther than Providence. Thereafter they moved at about half the speed of Lafayette on his way to Virginia. The troops were well disciplined and behaved, and this made a lasting and pleasant impression on the Americans. The officers were delighted with the acacia trees in bloom and found the Connecticut town of Windham and its girls charming. They did not reach Westchester and their Phillipsburg encampment until July 6. On July 15 Washington noted that the British sloop of war, the *Savage*, which had been the American *General Washington*, and several other vessels went easily up the Hudson past his defenses.

While waiting for the French, Washington had moved his headquarters to Dobbs Ferry, to be nearer Manhattan. On July 9 he noted in his diary: "Received a Letter from the Marqs. De la Fayette [dated June 28] informing me of Cornwallis' retreat to Williamsburg—that he had pushed his Rear and had obtained advantages—having killed 60 and wounded an hundred with small loss. Southern accts. Though not official speak of the reduction of Augusta and Ninety Six by the Arms of Major Genl. Greene."

Cornwallis' move towards Yorktown had been, in part, occasioned by Clinton's capture of the Wethersfield documents and his immediate call on Cornwallis for more troops. There began a series of misunderstandings between Cornwallis and Clinton, resulting in squabbles that lasted for years and that Clinton rehashed till his death. Clinton suggested that Cornwallis move against Philadelphia and Baltimore, that he return troops to protect New York, and that he establish bases in Virginia, which would have access to Britain's sea power. For his part, Cornwallis established only one base, which proved inadequate for its purpose. Furthermore, not only did he refuse to return troops to New York, he suggested instead that Clinton move all his troops to Virginia. Amidst this squabbling, Clinton neglected to warn Cornwallis that a heavy French sea and land force might be going to Virginia.

On July 20 Washington wrote in his diary: "Count de Rochambeau having called upon me... for a definitive plan of campaign [for de Grasse]... I could not but acknowledge that the uncertainties under which we labour—the few Men who have joined [as continentals or militia] and the ignorance in which I am kept by some of the States on whom I mostly depended—especially Massachusetts from whose Governor I have not received a line... rendered it impracticable for me to do more than prepare, first, for the enterprise against New York, and secondly for the relief of the Southern States, if after all my efforts and earnest applications to these States, it should be found at the arrival of Count de Grasse, that I had neither Men nor means adequate to the first object." Washington noted the same day that he had ordered General Knox to "suspend the Transport of the heavy Cannon and Stores from Philadelphia lest we should have to carry them back."

Though Washington thus gave a clear indication that everything pointed to the South, sound tactics indicated that he continue all preparations for a siege of New York. If more continentals were sent by the states and de Grasse arrived with sufficient troops and naval support, the operation might still be carried out. If not, the preparations would worry and harass Sir Henry Clinton and put pressure on him to recall troops from Virginia. In addition, some portion of the efforts would be useful either way. Washington, for example, ordered the building of a hundred new boats and the repair of all existing vessels on the Hudson. These could be used for ferrying southbound troops across the river or for waterborne attacks on Staten or Manhattan Island.

On July 20 Lafayette had written Washington that he wanted to rejoin the main army for its operations. On July 30, using indirection for fear the enemy would capture the letter, Washington told Lafayette to stay in Virginia "until matters are reduced to a greater degree of certainty than they are at present, especially when I tell you that, from the change of circumstances with which a removal of part of the Enemy's force from Virginia to New York will be attended, it is more than probable that we shall also entirely change our plan of operations." He noted that the proposed change would be difficult, not because they lacked sufficient force to move south but because of transport problems by land. "I should not however hesitate in encountering these difficulties great as they are, had we prospects of transporting ourselves in a manner, safe easy and expeditious. Your penetration will point out my meaning"; that is the march south would be foreshortened by 175 miles if de Grasse could move the troops by sea from the head of the Chesapeake. He noted that he had asked de Barras to proceed to Virginia to aid Lafayette, but he preferred to sit in Newport to await "greater plans."

On August 1 Washington asked Knox to estimate all the ordnance and stores that would be available south of the Hudson. He also requested Robert Morris, who had been made superintendent of finance in the government, to look into the amount of shipping that could be made ready quickly at Philadelphia and in the Chesapeake Bay, in order "to carry a Body of Men suddenly round by Water."

The time around New York was not wasted, for the Americans and French got to know each other during numerous reconnaissance and skirmishing parties. On July 3 a first attempt by Washington at a landing from the Jersey shore, above Spuyten Duyvel, failed when the duke de Lauzun's cavalry, who had a long ride through excessive heat, did not arrive in time to support General Lincoln. On July 18 Washington, with Rochambeau and Duportail, crossed the Hudson to reconnoiter the enemy's Manhattan defenses. Although he had left the island more than five years previously, Washington remembered and noted in his diary many details of the fortifications and the ensuing changes. In particular he remarked that the island's trees had all been cut down (for firewood) and a new growth of waist-high bushes had taken their place. On July 21 the French and American commanders, with a large part of both armies to screen them, reconnoitered the Bronx from King's Bridge, Clinton's only connection with the mainland, to Frog's Neck. Washington noted that the British defenses at Forts Knyphausen (once Washington), Tryon, and Laurel Hill were "formidable." By the end of July he had about abandoned all hope of an attack on New York as too strong for his few troops. During the operations, the French were assessing their American commander. They also studied his campaigns, leaving around maps of Princeton and Trenton in compliment to him. The French at their first meeting with Washington in 1780 had been, as Blanchard reported, "enchanted." They were now all curious to see him in action. Luckily many were diarists and letter writers. Baron Cromot du Bourg wrote: "Washington is a very fine looking man, but this did not surprise me as much as I expected from the descriptions I had heard of him. His physiognomy is noble in the highest degree, and his manners are those of one perfectly accustomed to society, quite a rare thing certainly in America." After their reconnaissance at Morrisania, du Bourg added: "I need not mention the sang froid of General Washington, it is well-known; but this great man is a thousand times more noble and splendid at the head of his army than at any other time."

Comte Louis-Philippe de Ségur, son of the French war minister, wrote: "When I looked at Washington I found a perfect accord between the impression made by his appearance and the idea I had formed of him... His figure was noble and tall; the expression in his face was pleasant and kind; his smile was gentle, his manners simple without being familiar. He did not flaunt the magnificence displayed by generals under our monarchies; he was the embodiment of the republican hero. He inspired rather than commanded respect and, in the eyes of all the men around him, one could read their real affection and whole-hearted confidence in a chief, upon whom they seemed to rely entirely for their security."

Ségur had heard of the hordes of ill-dressed peasants who had swarmed around Gage at Boston, and he noted that he expected the American troops to be a rabble in unkempt camps. "One may imagine how surprised I was when I saw a well-disciplined army, presenting in every detail, the very image of order, reason, training and experience." Other officers noted their relief at finding that the American troops, though they had inadequate clothing and few resources, were disciplined and well-trained.

The French were particularly pleased to observe Washington at close quarters at the dinner table where, after the meal, he relaxed in long conversations over glasses of wine. Claude Blanchard, the French quartermaster general, noted that he had a "most gracious and amiable smile. He is affable and converses with his officers familiarly and gaily." The comte de Dumas commented that he enlivened all the after-dinner conversations with his "unaffected cheerfulness."

The doughty little padre of the Soissonais regiment, Abbé Claude Robin, went with the French army on horseback from Providence to Yorktown. He wrote that he found the trip very hard, with the marches beginning at two in the morning, and the long, hot days going by without food or drink. He commented that he felt embarrassed because the young nobles of the army, who had every luxury in France, bore it all so cheerfully. On August 4 he achieved his desire to see the commander in chief: "I saw Washington... I gazed at him eagerly to find... the marks of genius... He has a tall, noble, and well-proportioned figure, and an open, kind and calm expression... Throughout all [this country] he appears like a benevolent God; old men, women, children all flock eagerly to catch a glimpse of him; people follow him through the towns with torches, his arrival is marked by public illuminations... The Americans, a cold people... are inflamed by the very mention of his name."

TWENTY-NINE

WESTCHESTER TO YORKTOWN

1781

ALTHOUGH IN RETROSPECT the Yorktown operations appear remarkably smooth and speedy, the odds against their success were great. De Grasse had promised the fullest aid but Washington's past experience of French assurances had not been good. Hurricanes or the Royal Navy might have delayed or stopped de Grasse. The strength of the British fleet in American and Caribbean waters, with expected reinforcements under Admiral Digby, was near that of the French. The British were the more experienced seamen, and their copper-bottomed ships were faster. Had they used any skill de Grasse might never have been master of the Chesapeake. Even so the French fleet, when it achieved clear superiority, came close to ruining the operation.

In his first proposal de Grasse gave Washington no more than sixty-two days to achieve his objective. Possibly the time was even less, for de Grasse said he had to be back in the Caribbean by October 15. The French army had taken six weeks to march from Newport to Westchester. Washington now had to move far larger forces three times this distance, in the heat of the summer, with immense ferrying problems over seven major intervening rivers. Upon reaching Virginia he had to conduct a siege. Sir Henry Clinton had required sixty-six days to effect the conquest of Charleston, with British forces welded together in years of warfare. The French and American armies had been together for the first time and for only a few weeks. The French officers were knowledgeable in engineering and siege warfare, but only the oldest had ever been in battle, and that was twenty years before. Rochambeau's last previous siege had been in 1756; his troops were green and untested. Nevertheless Washington took all the risks on his shoulders. Four days after hearing that de Grasse was on his way, the combined armies with their artillery and stores were crossing the Hudson.[*]

AUGUST 14–16

Washington had received the dispatch from de Barras on August 14, informing him that de Grasse would leave Cap François on August 3 with twenty-five to twenty-nine ships of the line and thirty-two hundred troops. De Grasse hoped that everything would be in perfect readiness to begin operations at once, since he could spare only a few weeks. At the same time de Barras informed Washington that he himself had decided to go off on an expedition to Newfoundland. As he explained to Rochambeau, de Grasse had once served under him as a cadet but was now his superior in rank. Rochambeau wrote to de Barras to protest, with Washington adding a footnote that he had heard a reinforcement was coming under Admiral Digby. This might endanger de Grasse's fleet if de Barras did not stay. De Barras then agreed to abandon his northern expedition, but he did not get under way from Newport until two weeks after his receipt of the message announcing de Grasse's departure from Cap François.

On August 15 Washington wrote to Lafayette, ordering his express horsemen to "ride Night and Day" with the letter. He informed Lafayette that de Grasse would soon be off the Virginia coast, and he was to take every possible step to prevent Cornwallis from escaping to North Carolina. At this point Washington did not know of Cornwallis' plans, but the next day he recorded heartening intelligence.

Letters from the Marqs. de la Fayette and others inform that Lord Cornwallis with the Troops from Hampton Road, had proceeded up York River and landed at York and Gloucester Towns where they were throwing up Works on the 6th. Inst.

---

[*] The distance from Dobbs Ferry to York varied from about 440 miles by land and to 550 miles by sea. The latter was longer because ships had to round the lower peninsula to reach the York river.

On August 15 Cornwallis reported to Clinton that he had seventy-five hundred army rank and file, plus around fifteen hundred Tories, marines, and sailors for his defenses. The following day he wrote that he was working on the Gloucester fort but that he had not yet removed all of his forces from Portsmouth.

In the meantime, the twenty-eight French ships of the line under de Grasse were moving north between the Bahamas and the Florida coast, a channel not usually used and therefore away from prying British eyes. De Barras, with his eight ships, was moving reluctantly and slowly to join but taking care to bring with him the heavy French siege guns from Rhode Island.

The Royal Navy, for its part, was everywhere. Admiral Graves, who had been on sea patrol, returned to New York on August 16 with his seven ships of the line. Clinton thought he and Graves should prepare an attack on de Barras at Newport, but Graves said two of his vessels had to be repaired. Hood was approaching the American coast with fourteen ships. Somewhere in the North Atlantic were Admiral Digby and three ships that Lord Sandwich had persuaded the cabinet to send to America as reinforcements. Rodney, claiming illness, though probably his main objective was to take home loot from his capture of St. Eustatius, sailed for England on August 1 on his flagship. He also detached two other ships for eastward convoy duty home, thus neatly neutralizing the westward-moving Digby. Rodney left six other ships under the charge of Admiral Sir Peter Parker in the Caribbean. Parker kept one; three he sent to England on convoy. He dispatched two more to America, but too late to be of help. Thus, while two French admirals were moving to join thirty-six French ships, five British admirals were scattering thirty-three of theirs over the wide Atlantic.

On August 17 Clinton received intelligence that de Grasse was on his way north with twenty-eight ships and seven thousand troops. Clinton informed Graves that he did not credit the report. Graves replied that it seemed to be someone's "heated imagination."

AUGUST 18–31

As Washington put it in his diary, the Jersey troops and the Canadian regiment were quickly "thrown over at Dobbs Ferry." They were marched down to Chatham and Springfield, opposite Staten Island, as if they were the vanguard of an attacking force. The French proceeded to build a bakery there, indicating it was to be a permanent encampment. For security reasons the remainder of the troops were sent north to cross at Kings Ferry. By August 21 all American troops were west of the Hudson. The French were slow in getting under way. Washington commented in his diary that their horses were in bad condition and they needed "better management" of them.

The French, in moving north, crossed Pine's Bridge, near which Joshua Smith had left André almost eleven months before. Claude Blanchard, sent on with a message from Rochambeau apologizing for the slowness of his troops, found Washington quietly taking tea in the Smith house, where André had spent the day after meeting Arnold. The French, more encumbered with baggage and stores than the Americans and having the larger number of troops, took five days to cross the river. While waiting for them, Washington took Rochambeau on a tour of West Point. He also, according to his diary, mounted "30 flat Boats (able to carry about 40 Men each) upon carriages, as well with a design to deceive the enemy as to our real movement, as to be useful to me in Virginia when I get there." Clinton quickly received intelligence warnings that they might be used for an attack on Staten Island.

The American army was full of rumors on their destination, but Washington kept his confidence from all but a trusted few. He had long given up calling formal councils of war; instead, where necessary, he asked his officers for written opinions. That way, he said, he could make the decision and keep it secret instead of sharing it with a dozen others. His new military secretary, Jonathan Trumbull, Jr., who had taken the place of Robert Hanson Harrison, noted on August 21 that the many "conjectures" were "curious [and] indeed laughable." Dr. James Thacher also recorded his impressions that day and the next:

> Our destination has been for some time a matter of perplexing doubt and uncertainty; bets have run high on one side that we were to occupy the ground marked out on the Jersey shore… and on the other, that we… are actually destined to Virginia…

> We crossed at King's Ferry, 21st instant, and encamped at Haverstraw. A number of batteaux, mounted on carriages, have followed in our train, supposed for the purpose of conveying troops over to Staten Island.

> Resumed our line of march, passing rapidly through Paramus, Acquackanack, Springfield and Princeton. We have now passed all the enemy's posts and are pursuing our route with increasing rapidity towards Philadelphia; wagons have been prepared to carry the soldiers' packs, that they may press forward with greater facility. Our destination can no longer be a secret. The British army under Lord Cornwallis is unquestionably the object.

Washington's burdens became greater when his quartermaster general,

Timothy Pickering, went off for a holiday visit to his family. The commander in chief had to assume that job as well as his own. Washington's letters flowed out in streams from Dobbs Ferry, Kings Ferry, Chatham, New Brunswick, and Trenton. He asked his intelligence officers to get every scrap of information from New York on Sir Henry Clinton's movements and reactions to his march. He sent his geographer, Simeon De Witt, to make surveys and sketches of the roads from New Brunswick to Elkton (to use their modern names). He asked the governors of Connecticut and Rhode Island to rush provisions to de Barras at Newport, which he could carry to Virginia. He wrote Lafayette requesting information on horses and wagons that would be available for use in Virginia. He also requested him to send as many boats as possible to Head of Elk, adding that he depended on Lafayette's "Military Genius and Judgment" to keep Cornwallis from escaping. He gave Rochambeau detailed marching instructions for his troops and where boats might be available for speedier transport than by land. He dispatched expresses to Trenton to assemble all vessels to ferry the armies across the Delaware. He wrote Robert Morris, superintendent of finance, that there was great discontent in the American forces at not having been paid for so long. He asked him to scrape some specie together. "I make no doubt that a little douceur of hard money would put them in proper temper."

Washington ordered Brigadier Louis Du Portail, his able French chief of engineers, to proceed at full speed south with letters to Lafayette and de Grasse. Du Portail was later to be Louis XVI's war minister, while General Knox held a similar position in Washington's cabinet. While the armies were crossing New Jersey in good fashion, Washington went on to Philadelphia with Rochambeau and Chastellux. He noted in his diary for August 30:

> *I set out myself for Philadelphia to arrange matters there, provide Vessels and hasten the transportation of the Ordnance, Stores, &ca., directing, before I set out, the second York regiment [which had been delayed because of John Hancock's negligence] to follow with the Boats, Intrenching Tools &ca. the French Rear to Trenton.*

About one in the afternoon Washington and his French colleagues were escorted into the city by the Philadelphia Light Horse Troop amid, as Robert Morris noted in his diary, the "universal acclamations of the citizens." That afternoon the president of Congress gave a dinner where toasts were drunk to the United States, France, Spain, and the Netherlands. The local press next day reported: "In the evening the city was illuminated, and his Excellency walked through some of the principal streets, attended by a numerous concourse of people, eagerly pressing to see their beloved General."

Washington found too few ships at Philadelphia to move both stores and troops south, and he and Rochambeau agreed to march the armies to Head of Elk. As Washington was entering Philadelphia, Admiral de Grasse was moving into Chesapeake Bay with his twenty-eight warships and accompanying frigates and transports. Intelligence reports had been reaching Sir Henry Clinton which indicated that Washington's army appeared to be moving towards Baltimore and that de Grasse was coming with a large fleet. Clinton wrote to Cornwallis on August 27:

> I cannot well ascertain Mr. Washington's real intentions by this move of the army. But it is possible he means for the present to suspend his offensive operations against this post and to take a defensive stand at the old post of Morristown, from whence he may detach to the southward... This move of the enemy may be only a feint and they may return to their former position, which they certainly will do if de Grasse arrives.

Clinton, in conjunction with Admiral Graves, had been making preparations for an attack on de Barras at Newport and was paying relatively little attention to Washington. The French admiral, who had been so slow the preceding winter, was now equally dilatory in getting under way from Newport but not as slow as the British. He sailed south on August 25. Fortunately for de Barras, the two British ships were slow in being repaired. By the time Graves was ready to move, de Barras had gone. On August 25 Hood reached New York with fourteen ships; the two admirals decided to drop the Newport plan and go south.

On September 2 Clinton reported to Cornwallis that the newly arrived HMS *Pegasus* had sighted forty French sail. "However," Clinton continued, "as Rear Admiral Graves (after being joined by Sir Samuel Hood) sailed from hence on the 31st. *ultimo* with a fleet of nineteen sail besides some fifty-gun ships, I flatter myself Your Lordship will have little to apprehend from that of the French."

SEPTEMBER 1–15

On the day that Clinton wrote this letter, de Grasse began landing the Marquis Claude-Anne de Saint-Simon's army division. Lafayette did his best to tidy up the ragged continentals but he did not have much to work with. When they met, although Saint-Simon was a major general in the French army and Lafayette only a colonel, the former graciously agreed to go under his command. On the same day, Du Portail reached de Grasse's flagship, the *Ville de*

Paris, of 110 guns, the largest warship then afloat. He gave him Washington's letters and an account of the march that was being made to Yorktown. Immediately thereafter de Grasse dispatched a letter by a fast cutter to Baltimore to let Washington know of his arrival.

De Grasse was almost as tall as Washington though much fatter. He was notable for his short temper, a quality possessed by most admirals, and for his nervousness, a quality not always associated with the sea. In his conferences with Lafayette and Du Portail, de Grasse seemed chagrined that Washington and his armies were not already at Yorktown and ready to start. He mentioned the approaching hurricane season and his need to leave in six weeks. He suggested that Lafayette and Saint-Simon, together with some marines that de Grasse offered to send ashore, proceed to demolish Cornwallis. This was a remarkable request since de Grasse had been present with d'Estaing at Savannah where, in his great hurry, d'Estaing changed a siege into an assault and was badly beaten. Lafayette and Du Portail advised against this. At the same time they assured him that Washington would shortly be at Head of Elk, ready to move troops down the Chesapeake Bay by water. He would need the help of de Grasse's frigates and transports.

On September 5 Graves and Hood, with their nineteen ships of the line and a few frigates, appeared off Chesapeake Bay looking for de Barras' fleet which, they expected, might be reinforced by de Grasse. The British scouting ship reported fourteen French ships of the line present in the bay. A curious feature of the ensuing battle is that the British admirals never guessed that de Barras was not part of the large fleet they fought.

De Grasse had been rather negligent in his watches. When Graves moved in, two thousand of his men were ashore and four of his ships were too far away to do any good. De Grasse signalled his fleet to move without the missing men; they hoisted sail in disorderly fashion. The British were amazed to count twenty-four ships of the line straggling out of the bay.

Not much can be said for the seamanship of either European power in the ensuing battle, which has many names, including the battle of the Chesapeake. De Grasse had the advantage of about three hundred more guns, but he failed to used them decisively. De Barras showed up while both fleets were off the coast but, claiming that he could not distinguish French ships from English, he did not join the battle. In the early stages, five ships of the French van separated from their main body. They should have been tempting targets for the British, but Graves was more concerned with maneuvering his fleet on a parallel with the French. This gave the French time to improve their formation. In moving towards the French, Graves deployed his ships in such fashion that Hood, who had led the British van, was left straggling in the rear.

In turn, the rear of the French fleet failed to hold their line and drifted south. The British admiral gave confused and conflicting signals. In the end, only fifteen of the French ships engaged twelve of the British. Seven British and three French ships were severely damaged and three others of Graves' fleet suffered minor damage. Later, four French ships became detached and were very ineffectively attacked by the enemy van. The engagement ended at dusk. British casualties were 336 and French 220. One English ship, later found to be leaking, was blown up on Graves' order.

Although de Grasse was the technical victor, he did not care to re-engage; indeed, he avoided it and eventually moved to join de Barras. The two French fleets were united by September 13; there were now thirty-six warships forming the sea defenses of Yorktown. The British admirals decided "to proceed with all despatch for New York," where their ships were put in repair.

During his five Philadelphia days, Washington was busier than ever giving orders, holding conferences, and sending out letters. He directed General Lincoln to send all heavy ordnance and baggage by water and lighter pieces by land. He added: "You will please to use every Exertion for dispatch in your Movement, as not a Moments Time is to be lost." He directed part of his troops to move by water from Jersey to Delaware. He forwarded to Lafayette intelligence of the movement of the British fleet to the Chesapeake. He dispatched an officer to Christiana, Delaware, to direct the unloading of ordnance and troops at the head of the creek there, and to repair the road to Elkton. He sent an engineering officer to Williamsburg by way of Baltimore, Georgetown, and Fredericksburg to survey the roads and to request all government officials and militia to get them into quick repair. He wrote the governors of Maryland, Delaware, and New Jersey to beg for supplies and clothing. He provided Rochambeau with routes and distances for the French wagons that were going overland. He wrote General Greene a lengthy letter giving intelligence of all his moves. He noted that he had no word of de Grasse and that a British fleet had apparently gone to the Chesapeake. "You will readily conceive that the present Time is as interesting and anxious a Moment as I have ever experienced." He sent General Heath, in command on the Hudson, an urgent request to send down one hundred head of cattle each week for his army.

On September 2 he wrote to Lafayette who, although four days short of his twenty-fourth birthday, was the kingpin of the whole operation, to say that he calculated that the troops to be assembled at Yorktown would be sufficient for a siege. What chiefly worried him was being able to move enough heavy cannon, stores, and ammunition to prosecute "a Siege with rapidity, energy and success." He reported that Knox was making every exertion possible. He also

The Approach to Yorktown and the Battle of Chesapeake,
August–September, 1781

noted the problem of feeding, clothing, and getting medicines for the troops. He concluded:

> *But my dear Marquis, I am distressed beyond expression, to know what is become of the Count de Grasse, and for fear that the English fleet, by occupying the Chesapeake (towards which my last accounts said they were steering) should frustrate all our flattering prospects in that quarter. I am also not a little solicitous for the Count de Barras, who was to have sailed from Rhode Island on the 23d Ulto. and from whom I have heard nothing since that time. Of many contingencies we will hope for the most propitious events.*

> *Should the retreat of Lord Cornwallis by water, be cut off by the arrival of either of the French fleets, I am persuaded you will do all in your power to prevent his escape by land. May that great felicity be reserved for you!*

> *You See how critically important the present Moment is: for my own part I am determined still to persist with unremitting ardour in my present Plan, unless some inevitable and insuperable obstacles are thrown in our way.*

> *Adieu my dear Marquis! If you get any thing New from any quarter, send it, I pray you, on the Spur of Speed, for I am almost all impatience and anxiety.*

On September 5 all the American troops being south of Philadelphia and the French rearguard having reached it, Washington left at high speed for Head of Elk, the principal point for shipments by water or land to Williamsburg. Rochambeau decided to go by riverboat from Philadelphia to Chester in order to examine the fortifications along the Delaware. When Washington was a few miles south of Chester, an express from Baltimore met him with de Grasse's letter, announcing that he had arrived safely and that he had debarked troops to join Lafayette. The French officers said that they had never seen a man so moved with joy. On the instant, he whirled around to gallop back to Chester to await Rochambeau. As his boat moved in, the rather serious Rochambeau was astonished to see Washington jumping up and down, waving his hat and handkerchief in sheer exuberance, as he shouted the news. According to Cromot du Bourg, Washington gave Rochambeau the Gallic embrace when he landed.

Washington moved on to Christiana to inspect the landing places there and to give instructions for unloading supplies sent by ship. He then rode across the Delaware peninsula to Head of Elk. There he found far less shipping available than he had hoped but enough to transport two thousand Americans and French to Williamsburg. He sent expresses to Baltimore to find out how much additional shipping could be provided at that port. He added urgent letters to everyone he knew on Maryland's eastern shore, asking them to send to Baltimore all available "craft and vessels." He wrote Comte de Grasse to congratulate him on his arrival and to let him know that the van of the French and American armies was now going aboard transports and would shortly be on their way. He told Lafayette how prudently he had acted and that they would meet in a few days. He sent detailed instructions to General Lincoln on the embarkation of troops and supplies, even covering such points as baking bread and providing salt provisions. He acknowledged Du Portail's letter, telling him that de Grasse would stay only a few weeks. Washington added: "Our measures must be forced, and every intermediate moment employed to the greatest advantage." It was a great misfortune, he added, that they did not have enough sea transport and that he would have to march a large part of the army to Baltimore. He wrote to the governors of Maryland and Virginia to raise all the forage they could for the teams that were on their way. He directed the payment to the army of a month's salary, which Robert Morris had forwarded from Philadelphia. He asked his quartermaster general, Timothy Pickering, to report for duty from his vacation.

Now more anxious than ever to get to Williamsburg and Yorktown, Washington started out with Rochambeau and Chastellux for Mount Vernon. With tact (and possibly also because Washington was riding too fast for them), the French officers persuaded him to go on ahead so that he would have a day at Mount Vernon with his wife before they appeared. As he rode through Baltimore, the city was illuminated in his honor. The citizens, as usual, fired salutes and gave him a speech. Early on September 9, 1781, Washington and three aides set out to ride the sixty miles from Baltimore to Mount Vernon. That evening he was home for the first time since May 4, 1775.

The moment Washington arrived he wrote to the Fairfax County Lieutenant, Peter Waggoner, to hold all the country militia that had been assembled to go to Yorktown. Instead, Waggoner was ordered, "with out a moment's loss of time," to repair the roads from the Georgetown ferry landing to the Occoquan ford. He added to Waggoner that French and American army wagons and their cavalry and cattle would be travelling the roads in a very few days. He also instructed General Weedon to repair all the roads further down, from the Rappahannock to Caroline Court House, and to provide carriages and fresh horses for Rochambeau and Chastellux.

The following day Washington wrote to his deputy quartermaster at Alexandria to inform him that he had heard the landings at Georgetown were in disrepair. He was ordered to look to them at once and also to make ready proper ferry service from Georgetown to Virginia. General Weedon was further directed, if he did not have enough shipping at Baltimore for all his troops, to start them marching south. "The time is fast slipping away; the most expeditious Mode should be taken to collect our whole Force at the Point of Operation." That same day he wrote Lafayette:

> We are thus far, My Dear Marquis, on our way to you. The Count de Rochambeau has just arrived, General Chastellux will [soon] be here, and we propose (after resting tomorrow) to be at Fredericksburg on the night of the 12th; the 13th we shall reach the New Castle and the next day we expect the pleasure of seeing you at your Encampment.
>
> Should there be any danger as we approach you, I shall be obliged if you will send a party of Horse towards New Kent Court House to meet us...
>
> P.S. I hope you will keep Lord Cornwallis safe, without Provisions or Forage until we arrive.

On September 14 an anxious Washington reached Williamsburg. Colonel St. George Tucker described the scene in a letter to his wife next day:

> I wrote you yesterday that General Washington had not yet arrived. About four o'clock in the afternoon his approach was announced. He had passed our camp... before we had time to parade the militia. The French line had just time to form. The Continentals had more leisure. He approached without any pomp or parade, attended only by a few horsemen and his own servants. The Count de Rochambeau and Gen. Hand, with one or two more officers, were with him. I met him as I was endeavoring to get to camp from town in order to parade the brigade; but he had already passed it. To my great surprise he recognized my features and spoke to me immediately by name. Gen. Nelson, the Marquis, etc., rode up immediately after. Never was more joy painted in any countenances than theirs. The Marquis rode up with precipitation, clasped the General in his arms and embraced him with an arder not easily described.
>
> The whole army and all the town were presently in motion. The General—at the request of the Marquis de St. Simon—rode through the French lines. The troops were paraded for the purpose and cut a most splendid figure. He then visited the Continental line. As he entered the camp the cannon from the park of artillery and from every brigade announced the happy event. His train by this time was much increased; and men, women and children seemed to vie with each other in demonstrations of joy and eagerness to see their beloved countryman.

Within hours Washington received word from de Grasse that he was back in

Chesapeake Bay, with de Barras, and that he had captured two British frigates on the way in. Washington immediately gave orders to start all troops moving down the Chesapeake. He sent a letter of congratulation to de Grasse for driving off the British fleet. This, he said, will "give us happiest Presages of the most complete Success in our combined Operations on this Bay." He asked de Grasse to send a cutter to pick up Rochambeau and him for an early conference with the admiral. He expressed his thanks that French transports were moving his troops to the Yorktown peninsula.

General Thomas Nelson, Jr., Virginia's governor, was of double assistance to Washington. As commander of the state militia, he had seen to it that almost 30 percent of Washington's American forces present were state troops. As chief executive of the commonwealth, he stretched his powers to the fullest to requisition food, fodder, teams, and entrenching tools. Maryland's governor, Thomas Sim Lee, also worked industriously to forward provisions and tools for the troops.

In New York, Sir Henry Clinton continued in a state of euphoria and inaction, while American and French troops moved across Pennsylvania and Maryland. Benedict Arnold, who had been recalled from Virginia, pleaded with him to be allowed to attack West Point, Philadelphia, or elsewhere. Clinton finally allowed him an expedition to New London, a few miles from his birthplace at Norwich. Arnold burned the town, destroying some 65 houses and numerous other buildings. He took two small forts, bayoneting more than 75 men after they surrendered. This was the last effective action Clinton was able to take against the Americans.

Two days later the last major battle of the revolution, south of Virginia, was fought at Eutaw Springs. There Greene, Marion, Henry Lee, Otho Williams, Andrew Pickens, and William Washington fought so savagely that the British forces suffered a loss of 40 percent. The survivors retreated hurriedly to Charleston, their only remaining post in South Carolina. The British now held only five fortified points in America, but these were on the sea, and the French commanded the sea.

SEPTEMBER 16–30

Once word came from Washington, the immense machinery was again in motion. French and American transports moved south from Annapolis, Baltimore, and Head of Elk. The duc de Lauzun and his cavalry galloped across the Virginia countryside. Wagons, with flour, guns, and ammunition, moved creakily down bad roads and across ferries over the Potomac,

Pamunkey, Rappahannock, and York Rivers. De Barras unloaded the French siege guns. American vessels, which had accompanied him from Newport, sent ashore the supplies Washington had ordered from Connecticut and Rhode Island. Horses and teams were impressed everywhere to move the guns and food. Bakeries were set up and roads repaired.

The great nagging question for Washington was whether all forces and supplies could be assembled and the siege effected before de Grasse had to take off for the West Indies. On September 17 Washington, Rochambeau, Chastellux, Knox, and Du Portail boarded the captured *Queen Charlotte*, which had been His Majesty's ship, named for His Majesty's wife. They arrived next day at the *Ville de Paris*, where they were given full military honors. Washington opened the conference with praise of France and de Grasse:

> *The noble and generous Support which is given to this Country by His Most Christian Majesty does, as it ought, fill the breast of every American with gratitude and Love: The zeal and alacrity with which His Officers strive to carry his Royal intentions into execution, merit our highest admiration and applause.*

Washington then came to his main point. The operation he was engaged in was difficult because he had to bring troops from such a distance. Peace for Europe and independence for the United States hung on success at Yorktown. It was impossible to determine how long the siege would take. It could be done slowly but surely. The alternative, if French fleet support were to be withdrawn, would have to be an assault without "regard to the lives of men." This would be "bloody and precarious." He begged de Grasse to let him know how long he would stay. De Grasse answered that he had planned to leave by October 15, but he could now assure Washington that he would stay till the end of the month, and he would not take Saint-Simon's troops before then. De Grasse was less satisfactory in his reply to other questions. He said he was prepared to lend marines only for an assault (a coup de main) and he would have to think over Washington's request for ships to be stationed above the British fortifications on the York River.

Violent storms faced the American and French officers when they attempted to go ashore. They did not reach Williamsburg for four days while Washington fumed with impatience. He found that everything had been going smoothly in his absence and almost all the troops from Head of Elk had landed. Three days later most of the remaining troops from Annapolis and Baltimore were debarking.

In New York Clinton had received firsthand accounts from Graves that he had fought twenty-four French ships of the line and that he was sure de Barras' ships had been part of the squadron. Two British ships in New York, which had not sailed with Graves, had completed their repairs, bringing total British naval forces to a possible twenty-one. With the expected arrival of Digby's three ships and two from Jamaica, Clinton figured the British and French fleet would be about equal. Not until September 23, while Washington was rolling on the seas, did Clinton hear from Cornwallis that de Barras' squadron had indeed joined with de Grasse's. There was still hope, though, and Clinton prepared to move with five thousand troops to the relief of Cornwallis. He informed him that he expected to be ready by October 5.

On September 11 Digby reached New York; aboard his flagship was the sixteen-year-old Prince (later King) William. He wrote his father that he had been greeted by "an immense concourse of people who appeared very loyal, continually crying out, 'God bless King George!'... They appear in general very well affected to our Government, but particularly the Dissenters and Quakers... [one of whom said] 'God bless thy father. It is not for want of respect I do not take my hat off, but because my religion requires it.'" William Smith, the Tory chief justice, who had long held a dim view of Clinton and of the British war efforts, noted that the population, after learning of the Chesapeake defeat, had raved at the navy. He wrote with irony that the prince's presence "may supply our deficiency."

Washington received quick word that Digby had reached New York with reinforcements but the number of his ships was variously reported as three to ten. He did not take the news too seriously since the French still had a wide margin of superiority. He wrote to General David Forman, who was watching enemy movements at New York, that Digby's arrival "cannot... have any influence on our projects, or in the least retard our operations, while there are 36 French ships of the line in the bay. Every thing has hitherto succeeded to our wishes... In a very few days, I hope the Enemy at York will be completely invested. And although Lord Cornwallis has endeavored to strengthen himself as much as possible, and has a considerable Army with him, yet the prospects of his reduction, from the superiority of the Naval and land force, are as favorable as possibly could have been expected."

The following day, Rochambeau's aide, Baron von Closen, handed Washington an unpleasant shock in the form of a letter written by de Grasse only five days after their conference. Washington had sent the intelligence of Digby to de Grasse by the baron, who reported that "the news of Digby's arrival and of the approaching departure of Hood's fleet from New York alarmed and disquieted these excitable gentlemen of the navy." De Grasse informed Washington he was leaving as soon as he could hoist sail. He did not dare risk having his fleet trapped in the bay. He might go outside the capes, or to New

York, or perhaps be forced to return to Martinique. Rochambeau and Washington, greatly alarmed, sent urgent pleas to de Grasse to stay. Washington said, "I cannot conceal... the painful anxiety under which I have laboured since the receipt of your letter." He emphasized that the reduction of Cornwallis was certain and would go a long way towards terminating the war. He noted the "uncommon exertions and fatigues" undergone by both armies and the disgrace that would ensue. He flattered and praised the admiral, saying he was sure he could stop any British attempt to force the bay. His ships were vitally needed to transport food and artillery for the army. He added that de Grasse was superior to any force the British could bring. Fortunately the Admiral received word from the French naval minister that only three ships had been sent out with Digby, and he replied to Washington that he would stay.

As the army got ready to move, Washington took care of one minor item. He wrote to Robert Morris in Philadelphia: "It is of such essential consequence, in my opinion, that the Army should be regularly supplied with rum during the present operation, that I cannot forbear interesting myself on the subject. When we take into consideration how precious the lives of our men are, how much their Health depends upon a liberal use of spirits, in the judgment of the most Skillful Physicians, who are best acquainted with the climate; how meritorious their Services have been, and what severe and incessant duties are expected from them, we cannot hesitate to determine that the Public ought to incur a small expense, to answer the most valuable purposes." He asked him to ship fifty hogsheads as soon as possible. He also marked "warmly endorsed" a request to the board of war for blankets for the "poor fellows" in the hospitals. On September 27 the commander in chief issued general orders at Williamsburg: "The whole Army will March by the right in one Column at 5 o'clock tomorrow Morning precisely."

By nightfall the French and Americans had reached the outskirts of York. The following day Cornwallis, to save his men and ammunition, and in expectation of relief from Clinton, abandoned his outer works and holed in for the siege. Washington noted in his diary: "Immediately upon which we possessed them, and made those on our left (with a little alteration) very serviceable to us."

OCTOBER 1–17

The total land forces under Lord Cornwallis' command numbered approximately eighty-five hundred British, Hessian, and Anspach infantry, artillery, and cavalry. There were also around fifteen hundred naval rank and file on about twenty-six transports and frigates and many small vessels.

The Siege of Yorktown, September–October, 1781

Americans and French continued to straggle into the peninsula by foot, ship, boat, wagon, and horse until the day of Cornwallis' surrender. At their peak the combined armies under Washington numbered close to twenty thousand, the largest force he had ever commanded.

On the extreme left (all figures being rank and file rather than totals) were the Marquis de Saint-Simon's West Indian regiments—Gatinois, Touraine, and Agenois—numbering 3,000. Next were Rochambeau's regiments—Saintonge, Soissonois, Royal Deux-Ponts, and Bourbonnois—3,600 men under Baron Antoine de Viomenil. The American continental line—around 5,700—was in three divisions under Steuben, Lincoln, and Lafayette. In addition there were 3,200 Virginia militia and state troops. Half of these were placed under the governor of Virginia on the extreme right, behind a rather large creek, where they would be secure but also act as a reserve.

Across the York River, facing Dundas' infantry and Tarleton's cavalry, were the duc de Lauzun's 600 cavalry, half the Virginia militia, and a battalion of 800 French marines, added by the comte de Grasse, and placed under the command of the marquis de Choisy. From Washington's point of view, his most important officers were Du Portail, head of the engineers, who was to erect the parallels; and Knox, chief of artillery, who had to smash the British fortifications before an infantry attack could take place.

From October 1 to 6, as Washington wrote in his diary, "nothing occurred of Importance. Much diligence was used in debarking and transporting the Stores, Cannon, &ca. from Trebells Landing (distant 6 miles) on James River to Camp; which for want of Teams went on heavily, and in preparing Fascines, Gabions, &ca. for the Siege, as also in reconnoitering the Enemies defenses, and their situation as perfectly as possible, to form our parallels and mode of attack. The Teams which were sent around [by land] from the head of Elk, having arrived by this time, we were enabled to bring forward our heavy artillery and Stores with more convenience and dispatch and everything being prepared for opening Trenches, 1500 Fatigue men [working parties] and 2800 to cover them, were ordered for service."

The one weakness, in Washington's view, was that the whole of the York River above Gloucester and York remained unguarded. At his conference with de Grasse, he asked that ships be stationed there, though they would have to pass the English batteries. On October 1 he repeated to de Grasse his fear that Cornwallis, with most of his force, might escape up the river and head for New York. With a touch of humor he reported that his own experience with shore batteries had been that they were not very effective against ships. In again asking for naval support, he added reassuring intelligence from New York as to the number of British vessels laid up for repairs. De Grasse continued to raise objections, saying that he would have to send naval observers ashore and that he did not have proper pilots or protection against fireships. De Grasse and Washington were still discussing this when Cornwallis made a final attempt to escape by that route sixteen days later.

The trenches were dug by the working parties operating under fifty-five detailed instructions prepared by Washington and completed by the morning of October 6. Washington commented that the work had been done with such "secrecy and dispatch" that the enemy was unaware it was going on. "The next two days were employed in completing our parallel, finishing the redoubts in them and establishing Batteries." By this time the allied forces were 600–800 yards from Cornwallis. The French under Saint-Simon opened fire on October 9; later Washington himself fired the first American shot. He recorded in his diary:

> *About 3 o'clock P.M. the French opened a battery on our extreme left of 4 Sixteen pounders, and Six Morters and Howitzers and at 5 o'clock an American battery of Six 18s and 24s; four Morters and 2 Howitzers began to play from the extremity of our right. Both with good effect as they compelled the Enemy to withdraw from their ambrazures the Pieces which had previously kept up a constant firing.*

In the next two days the French and Americans opened up with thirty more guns. On the tenth the French destroyed a British frigate and three smaller craft. On the same day Cornwallis sent a desperate message to Clinton at New York: "Nothing but a direct move to York River—which includes a successful naval action—can save me... On the evening of the 9th the enemy's batteries opened and have since continued firing without intermission... We have lost about seventy men, and many of our works are considerably damaged. With such works on disadvantageous ground, against so powerful an attack we cannot hope to make a long resistance." By October 12, Washington was running his parallels within three hundred yards of the enemy's lines. On October 14 the batteries were moved up to the second parallel.

At Clinton's headquarters in New York there was a panic atmosphere as the Royal Navy and Army screamed at each other to do something quickly. Graves worked day and night to get his fleet ready to move Clinton's relief troops. Press gangs were at work to obtain sailors. The richer Tories aided in any way they could. Admiral Hood wrote to London on October 14 that the repairs on the ships "have gone on unaccountably tedious, which has filled me with apprehension that we shall be too late to give relief to Lord Cornwallis... I think very meanly of the ability of the present commanding officer [Graves.]"

Two strong British redoubts on the right still kept the allied armies from extending their full parallel. These had to be taken by assault, but they were first subjected to heavy bombardment. Redoubt nine was given to the French and ten to the Americans. Count William Deux-Ponts (also known as Zweibrucken) led the French attack. Alexander Hamilton, who had finally won the field command about which he had raised so much fuss, successfully appealed to lead the assault on the other redoubt. Accompanying him was John Laurens, back from France, and once more Washington's aide. Hamilton, with 400 men, stormed the redoubt, which had 45 men, and captured it quickly. The other was occupied by 120 British. The French had much more trouble but it too was carried. The second parallel was complete and new batteries were hauled up.

On October 16 the enemy made a sortie but this accomplished little except to knock out a few guns temporarily. That night Cornwallis made a last attempt to move his men across to Gloucester, hoping that he could break through de Choisy and move north. He got some troops across but a rain, referred to by Tarleton as a "squall" and by Cornwallis as "a most violent storm," made him abandon his plan.

October 17 was the anniversary of Burgoyne's surrender, and the American officers who had been at Saratoga were planning a celebration dinner. Soon after the allied batteries opened fire, a drummer beat a "parley" and a British officer waved a white flag. All firing ceased. The officer was led into the American lines where he handed over a letter for delivery to Washington:

Sir

I propose a cessation of hostilities for twenty four hours, and that two officers may be appointed by each side, to meet at Mr. Moore's house, to settle terms for the surrender of the posts of York and Gloucester. I have the honour to be

> *Sir*
> *Your most obedient & most humble servant*
> *Cornwallis*
> *His Excellency*
> *General Washington*

It had taken but sixty-four days from the receipt of de Barras' letter at Dobbs Ferry for Washington to have in his hand this offer to surrender the posts at Gloucester and York (later Yorktown). The rest of the story is well-known. Washington gave him two hours to forward his proposals in writing. Cornwallis attempted to get the terms that had been given Burgoyne.

Washington rejected these and outlined what he was prepared to grant. The following day the British commissioners, Lieutenant Colonel Thomas Dundas and Major Alexander Ross, Cornwallis' aide, met with Vicomte Louis-Marie de Noailles, representing the French, and Colonel John Laurens, Washington's aide, of Huguenot descent, for the Americans. For Laurens this was a particularly noteworthy day, inasmuch as Lord Cornwallis was titular governor of the Tower of London, where his father was imprisoned.

The British haggled and procrastinated all day, possibly in a forlorn hope that Clinton might arrive. A main problem was the treatment of American Tories who were serving with Cornwallis. Washington considered them governed by the civil laws of their states rather than military law. A tacit agreement seems to have been made that a number were allowed to go to New York as paroled prisoners, and thus be saved from possible death, but the principle was maintained. The draft treaty was ready late that night between "His Excellency General Washington Commander in Chief of the combined Armies of America & France... His Excellency the Count de Rochambeau Lieutenant General of the Armies of the King of France... His Excellency the Count de Grasse Lieutenant General of the Naval Armies of His Most Christian Majesty... And the Right Honourable Earl Cornwallis Lieut. General of his Majesty's Forces... and... Thomas Symonds Esq. Commanding His Britannick Majesty's Naval Forces."

On October 19 Washington wrote in his diary: "In the Morning early I had them copied and sent word to Lord Cornwallis that I expected to have them signed at 11 o'clock and that the Garrison would March out at two o'clock, both of which were accordingly done." Dr. James Thacher left a more extensive portrait of the surrender:

This is to us a most glorious day... Preparations are now making to receive as captives that vindictive, haughty commander and that victorious army, who by their robberies and murders, have so long been a scourge...

At about twelve o'clock, the combined army was arranged and drawn up in two lines extending more than a mile in length. The Americans were drawn up... on the right, and the French occupied the left. At the head of the former, the great American commander... took his station, attended by his aides. At the head of the latter was posted the excellent Count Rochambeau and his suite. The French troops, in complete uniform, displayed a martial and noble appearance, their band of music... is a delightful novelty and produced while marching to the grounds, a most enchanting effect... Every countenance beamed with satisfaction and joy. The Concourse of spectators from the country was prodigious...

It was about two o'clock when the captive army advanced… Every eye was prepared to gaze on Lord Cornwallis… but he disappointed our anxious expectations; pretending indisposition, he made General O'Hara his substitute as the leader of his army… Having arrived at the head of the Line, General O'Hara, elegantly mounted, advanced to his excellency the commander-in-chief… With his usual dignity and politeness, his excellency pointed to Major General Lincoln for directions, by whom the British army was conducted into a spacious field, where it was intended they should ground their arms.

The tradition is that the British band played "The World Turned Upside Down," with its appropriate lines "Goody Bull and her daughter together fell out. Both squabbled, and wrangled, and made a damned rout." However, this is unsupported by tangible evidence.

Aside from having conducted one of the great concentrations of military history and its speediest large-scale siege, Washington had achieved victory with remarkably little loss of life. He had written to Robert Morris "how precious the lives of our men are," and all his movements at the siege were destined to preserve rather than squander lives. Winston Churchill has said: "Battles are won by slaughter and maneuver. The greater the general, the more he contributes in maneuver, the less he demands in slaughter." The battle of Blenheim, where the great grandfather of Martha Washington's first husband was Marlborough's aide, cost the duke 12,000 men in killed and wounded. The battle of Yorktown, of far greater significance than Blenheim, resulted in around 350 casualties among the French and Americans.

The British lost a force close to 10,000 and numerous ships and small vessels which had been sunk. Twenty-four transports were captured, along with more than 200 cannon and 7,300 small arms. Numerous horses and wagons were also taken, many of which had been seized from Virginians. A great grandnephew of Marlborough, Lord Chewton, was among the prisoners.

On the day of the surrender, Graves and Clinton sailed from Sandy Hook to rescue Cornwallis.

THE VICTORY DISPATCHES

Unofficial news went north in one of de Grasse's ships sailing to Annapolis. When Governor Lee of Maryland got the word on October 20, he ordered an express to "ride night and day" for Philadelphia. Lee's messenger roused the president of Congress at two in the morning of October 22.

The carrying of a victory dispatch was considered the highest honor a general could bestow on a member of his staff. Washington chose Lieutenant Colonel Tench Tilghman, his aide of longest service, about whom he had written on May 11 to Congress:

> *This Gentn. came out a Captn. of one the light Infy. Companies of Philadelphia, served in the flying Camp in 1776. In August of the same Year he joined my family and has been in every action where the Main Army was concerned. He has been a zealous Servant and slave to the Public, and a faithful assistant to me for near five years, a great part of which time he refused to receive pay. Honor and gratitude interests me in his favour, and makes me solicitous to obtain his commission.*

While Congress and the capital anxiously waited for official word, Tilghman ran into bad luck on his way north. He wrote Washington that the stupidity of his boatman had cost him a night's run, while, because of a calm, he had taken a day to cross the bay from Annapolis. He did not reach Philadelphia till early in the morning of October 24.

Jacky Custis had been present at the siege. He was taken ill and it is not certain whether he witnessed the surrender. When his great great grandfather handed Marlborough's dispatch to Queen Anne, she rewarded him with a thousand guineas, a diamond-studded miniature of herself and, later, a governorship. On Tilghman's arrival, the members of Congress each contributed one dollar to cover his expenses. They later voted him a horse and sword. Philadelphia was ordered illuminated from six to nine that night. All citizens were warned to behave and give "a general discountenance to the least appearance of riot," which did not prevent the breaking of windows in Quaker houses.

On October 29 Congress ordered "that two stands of colours taken from the British army under the capitulation of York, be presented to His Excellency General Washington in the name of the United States." The duke of Marlborough was awarded Blenheim palace.

The news of Yorktown spread rapidly. On October 23 Tories in New York heard cannon fire from New Jersey and rightly guessed that Americans were celebrating a dreaded event. The next day Sir Henry Clinton picked up refugees at sea who informed him that Cornwallis had offered to capitulate on the seventeenth and no firing had been heard thereafter. That same day an American schooner reached Newport with the news. Riders carried it into Massachusetts and Connecticut. General Greene and his army in South Carolina celebrated it when they had the news a few days later. De Grasse dispatched two of his fastest frigates across the Atlantic, one carrying the comte des Deux-Ponts, the other the duc de Lauzun, with duplicate reports, as well as letters from Washington to Franklin and Adams. They were so fast that Paris newspapers with the account of Yorktown reached London the day Germain received Clinton's melancholy report. Maurepas, the French prime minister, heard of the victory from Lauzun before his death on November 21.

THE SNATCHES

During the move to Virginia and the subsequent siege, Washington's intelligence network worked at top form. Its members operating from Philadelphia, New York, and elsewhere accomplished two of the great feats of intelligence history.

Richard Peters, secretary to the board of war, had opened communication with a member of the staff of James Rivington, publisher of the violently Tory *New York Gazette*. Rivington was also the king's printer, entrusted with confidential official documents. When Admiral Graves gave him his secret naval signals to print, Peters' spy smuggled a copy to Philadelphia by another trusted agent. Peters took the signals to the French minister for immediate transmission to de Grasse. When additional signals were developed for Graves and Clinton to use on their expedition to the Chesapeake, these were forwarded to Peters. In sending them to Washington, Peters asked him what other intelligence he might like from Rivington's shop.

De Grasse, after copying the second set, returned them to Washington who, in turn, on October 29 transmitted them to the French minister for the use of the whole French fleet, adding: "I... hope they may be of signal Advantage to the Commanders of his Most Christian Majesty's Naval Armies."

Another success was recorded at Philadelphia when congressional operators discovered that Cornwallis was getting some of his letters out from Yorktown to New York by way of Tangier Island. Among the letters seized was one written in Clinton's secret code. James Lovell, a member of Congress, cracked the code and forwarded the cipher, as well as vital intelligence on Cornwallis' troops and supplies, to Washington. He replied to Lovell on October 6:

I am much obliged by the Communication you have been pleased to make me in your Favr. of 21st ulto.

My Secretary has taken a Copy of the Cyphers, and by help of one of the Alphabets has been able to decypher one paragraph of a Letter lately intercepted going from Ld Cornwallis to Sir Hy Clinton.

THE WAR CONTINUES

Generals Clinton and Washington reached identical conclusions as to what would happen if de Grasse remained in American waters. On October 20 Washington wrote de Grasse:

Charles Town, the principal Maritime port of the British in the southern parts of the Continent, the Grand Deposit and point of Support for the present Theatre of the War, is open to a combined attack, and might be carried with as much certainty, as the place which has just surrendered.

The capture would destroy the last hope which induces the Enemy to continue the war.

It will depend upon Yr. Excellcy. therefore to terminate the War, and enable the allies to dictate the Law in a Treaty. A Campaign so glorious and so fertile in consequences could be reserved only for the Count de Grasse.

It rarely happens, that such a combination of means as are in our hands at present, can be seasonably obtained by the most strenuous of human exertions.

A decisively superior fleet, the Fortune and talent of whose Commander overawe all the naval force that the most incredible efforts of the enemy have been able to collect. An army flushed with success and demanding only to be conducted to new attacks, and the very session which is proper for operating against the points in question.

Washington further appraised the situation to Lafayette, indicating that if de Grasse agreed to stay an additional sixty days, the three remaining British armies at Wilmington, Charleston, and Savannah would be captured. While still at sea, Sir Henry Clinton wrote to Germain on October 29 in much the same terms: "I beg leave to prophesy... that every station we hold in America is in peril, if the enemy can retain a naval superiority in these seas only for a few weeks."

Throughout the siege of Yorktown, Washington thought constantly about the valiant Greene who had driven the enemy to Charleston and who needed only the help of de Grasse, and part of the northern army, to win final glory. Washington kept him fully apprised of the situation at York but told him he was pessimistic about de Grasse. He praised highly the action at Eutaw Springs: "How happy am I, my dear Sir, in at length having it in my power to congratulate you upon a victory as splendid as I hope it will prove important. Fortune must have been coy indeed had she not yielded at last to so persevering a pursuer as you have been; I hope now she is yours, she will change her appelation of fickle to constant." He sent Colonel Robert Morris to Greene with instructions to tell him that Washington wished "from principles of generosity and justice to see him crowned with those Laurels which from his unparalleled exertions, he so richly deserves." Morris was told to emphasize that, if Washington went south, it was not to take glory from Greene, but because only he could command French troops.

Although Washington went aboard de Grasse's flagship to ask for further aid, the admiral rejected his request. Washington then asked him if he could at least land troops near Wilmington, North Carolina. De Grasse at first agreed, and Washington made arrangements; he then refused to do even this. By October 28 Washington was reduced to begging the admiral to remain a few more days in order to protect his movements of troops, stores, and sick and wounded in the Chesapeake area. De Grasse agreed after Graves' fleet, with Clinton aboard, returned to New York.

A commander who stretches his instructions is praised rather than condemned if he wins. De Grasse, in the face of an opportunity for certain victories that would have been of inestimable value to France as well as America, sailed away in early November. In February he captured the flyspeck island of Saint Kitts. In April he was disastrously defeated by Rodney and carried prisoner to England.

DEATH OF JACKY CUSTIS

In the days before de Grasse left, Washington's time was spent in getting his troops ready to return to the Hudson and in preparing Wayne's and Gist's brigades for their march south. Washington's diary of November 5 noted that they "began their March and were to be joined by all the Cavalry that could be equipped of the first, third and fourth Regimts. at"—the diary thus abruptly broke off, apparently when Washington heard that Jacky Custis was dying at nearby Eltham of typhus, which he had contracted at Yorktown. Washington arrived at the house a few hours before Custis died in the presence of his stepfather, mother, wife, and daughter. It was a crushing blow for Martha Washington, who had borne so much for more than six years, to lose her last living child. Washington's aides had ridden with him and waited at a nearby tavern. The kindly Washington, with all his troubles, thought of them and sent a note over to Jonathan Trumbull, Jr.:

My dear Sir: I came here in time to see Mr. Custis breathe his last. About Eight o'clock yesterday Evening he expired. The deep and solemn distress of the Mother, and affliction of the Wife of this amiable young Man, requires every comfort in my power to afford them; the last rites of the deceased I must also see performed; these will take me three or four days; when I shall proceed with Mrs. Washington and Mrs. Custis to Mount Vernon.

As the dirty tavern you are now at cannot be very comfortable; and in spite of Mr. Sterne's observation, the House of Mourning is not very agreeable.* It is my wish, that all of the Gentn. of my family, except yourself, who I beg may come here and remain with me, may proceed on at their leizure to Mount Vernon and wait there for me. Colo. Cobb will join you on the road at the Tavern we breakfasted at (this side Ruffens.) My best wishes attend the Gentn. and with much sincerity and affection.

On November 13 Washington reached Mount Vernon with the grieving ladies.

VERGENNES AND THE AMERICANS

Horace Walpole recorded a rumor, circulating in London, that the dying French prime minister, having been told of the British defeat at Yorktown, quoted from Racine: "Mes derniers regards ont vu fuir les Romains."

On November 26 Franklin in Passy, and Adams in Amsterdam, sent each other similar letters. Franklin said: "Most heartily do I congratulate you on the glorious news!" Adams wrote: "With unfeigned joy I congratulate your Excellency on the glorious news."

The United States had been instrumental in giving France what turned out to be her only decisive victory of the war. Her reward was a sneer from Vergennes to the French minister at Philadelphia that perhaps now the Americans would snap out of their lethargy. He instructed his minister to inform Congress that the United States would receive no further monetary help from France. Congress had already written Franklin to ask for more aid. On December 31 Vergennes returned a brusque reply to Franklin, referring to the "successive variations and augmentations of your demands on me for funds." After going into the status of the current loan, he continued: "There will be nothing more supplied than the million [$185,000] above mentioned; and, if the drafts which you have already accepted, exceed that sum, it must be for you to contrive the means of meeting them." Having thus refused

---

* It is difficult to choose precisely the quotation Washington had in mind in his reference to *Tristram Shandy*. Possibly it was Laurence Sterne's observation: "Labour, sorrow, grief, sickness, want, and woe, are the sauces of life."

further help to a country, an ally, which had borne nearly seven years of war, Vergennes concluded that he could now control the coming peace. John Adams, at Vergennes' request, had been ordered by Congress to subordinate his activities to the wishes of the French foreign—and now prime—minister. With Yorktown in his pocket, John Adams proceeded to push for the total independence of the United States. Against the disapproval of Vergennes and the undercover intrigues of the French ambassador at The Hague, Adams determined to win the Netherlands' recognition of the United States. He worked on the old Dutch spirit of republicanism and liberty as well as that country's mistrust of France and Britain. At the end of February, the province of Friesland instructed its delegates to vote for recognition. Other provinces and cities fell into line. On April 19, 1782, the seventh anniversary of Lexington, the States General formally recognized the United States of America. By August subscriptions were pouring into the Dutch bankers for the first private American foreign loan raised abroad. Adams was able to raise nearly $700,000 on the same terms as Dutch loans to France. In October he set out for the peace table.

APPENDIX A

BIBLIOGRAPHICAL NOTE

EDITING

This biography was developed as a primary work on George Washington. Its objective was to make his story as autobiographical as possible, with added comments by Washington's contemporaries in their own words.

Editing of quoted manuscripts has been confined to changes that clarify the texts. Punctuation has been added or deleted; obscure abbreviations have been spelled out; slips of the pen and other errors have been corrected; and a few modern terms have been substituted for obsolete words. Material inserted within a quote is bracketed.

In numerous cases several copies exist of original documents, while various recipients got much the same letter. There are progressive drafts, a copy for the Washington files, later transcripts, and the final document. In some cases only a file copy is available. In a few others, all originals have disappeared and only a printed version exists. In all quoted manuscripts, the closest available approach to the final paper has been chosen.

The Fitzpatrick transcripts of the diaries and writings were extensively used, and corrections were made when needed according to the new Virginia edition. The original manuscripts were employed (a) for the presidency and (b) where there was doubt as to the transcription.

Although the existing manuscripts are extensive, a considerable part is missing. Tampering with and careless handling of the papers began almost at the moment of Washington's death. Martha Washington is presumed to have burned all but two letters from her husband. Martha and Bushrod Washington and Nelly Lewis gave away letters as souvenirs. Other papers, stored by John Marshall, were subject to the indignity of being eaten by rats. Various papers were simply stolen. Surviving correspondence of Washington's parents, brothers, and sisters is scarce. In some periods, such as the campaign of 1758, various letters have disappeared, making reconstruction of some events difficult.

MANUSCRIPTS AND OTHER PRIMARY SOURCES

George Washington

The principal collection of Washington's writings is the 64,786 documents in *The Papers of President Washington* at the Library of Congress. There is a 295 page index to the original documents that are in its collection. The Manuscript Division has numerous copies of papers in other libraries, thanks to the indefatigable work of John C. Fitzpatrick.

In 1788 David Humphreys, who had been a wartime aide to General Washington, came to stay at Mount Vernon. He started a draft biography of the man, and Washington himself made some interesting comments and additions, which showed his vivid memory of events. In 1991 the University of Georgia Press published an edited version of Humphreys' work, which was put together from three archival sources. Unfortunately the result is disappointing because Humphreys seems to have lacked the curiosity to ask about aspects of Washington's life that modern biographers would love to know.

The biography by John Marshall, the first writer to have unlimited access to Washington's papers, is of special interest. He lived through and participated in many events of the period, and some of his writings have a ring of authenticity which no later biographer can hope to capture. The judicious manner in which he treated Washington's presidency and final years maddened his distant cousin, Thomas Jefferson. The value of Mason Weem's biography is noted in the text and in Appendix C.

The main published source of pre-1775 letters to Washington has been the five-volume work of Stanislaus Murray Hamilton, which appeared in 1901. It is also valuable for transcripts of various Washington family wills. Jared Spark's

1853 edition of letters to Washington and his 1834–1837 *Writings* are less trustworthy for, being a Harvard man, he thought he could improve Washington's prose.

Washington's Contemporaries

In using the writings of those around Washington, efforts were made to secure the most authentic texts available. In numerous cases, these were at the Library of Congress. For the years 1789–1797, in particular, letters and memoranda to Washington, in the presidential papers, were employed. The major printed sources of original documents that supplemented these are well known.

Collected Writings

The Adams Papers, ed. L. H. Butterfield (Harvard, 1961).

The Papers of Alexander Hamilton, ed. Harold C. Syrett (Columbia, 1961–1976).

The Works of Alexander Hamilton, ed. Henry C. Lodge (Putnam's, 1904).

The Papers of Thomas Jefferson, ed. Julian P. Boyd (Putnam's, 1950).

The Works of Thomas Jefferson, ed. Paul L. Ford (Princeton, 1904).

The Correspondence of King George III, ed. Sir John Fortescue (Macmillan, 1927–1928).

The American Rebellion: Sir Henry Clinton's Story, ed. William B. Willcox (Yale, 1954).

Anthony Wayne: Correspondence 1792–6, ed. Richard C. Knopf (Pittsburgh, 1960).

The Correspondence of John Jay, ed. Henry P. Johnson (Putnam's, 1891).

Letters of Benjamin Rush, ed. L. H. Butterfield (Princeton, 1951).

The Correspondence of William Shirley, ed. Charles R. King (Putnam's, 1894).

The Life and Correspondence of Rufus King, ed. Charles R. King (Putnam's, 1894).

The Life and Correspondence of James McHenry, ed. Bernard C. Steiner (Burrows, 1907).

The Papers of George Washington, (University Press of Virginia, 1976–).

Benjamin Franklin: Writings, ed. J. A. Leo Lemay (Library of America, 1987).

George Washington: A Collection, ed. W. B. Allen (Liberty Classics, 1988).

Diaries, Journals, and Memoirs

Christopher Gist (Kennikat reprint, 1964).

Claude Blanchard (Albany, 1876).

Ambrose Serle (Huntington Library, 1940).

James Thacher (Cottons and Barnard, 1823).

Benjamin Tallmadge (Giliss, 1904).

Jacob Hiltzheimer (Philadelphia, 1893).

Albigence Waldo (*Pennsylvania Magazine*, 1897).

François-Jean de Chastellux, ed. Howard C. Rice, Jr. (North Carolina, 1963).

Josiah Quincy, Jr. (Wilson, 1874).

Claude Robin (Paris, 1782).

Cromot du Bourg (*Magazine of American History*, 1880–1881).

William Byrd, Vol. II (Dietz, 1942); Vol. III (Oxford, 1958).

Ludwig von Closen (North Carolina, 1958).

Ewald, Johann. *Diary of the American War: A Hessian Journal*, (Yale, 1979).

Philadelphia Merchant: The Diary of Thomas P. Cope, ed. Eliza Cope Harrison (Gateway, 1978).

Others

The U. S. Geological Survey Maps, Fredericksburg and Wakefield Quadrangels, and the U. S. Coast and Geodetic Survey Chart of the Rappahannock were of particular value in attempting to locate early Washington farms.

Statutes at Large (Richmond, Virginia [Henning], 1810–1823).

Hoppin, Charles A., "The House in Which George Washington Was Born," Tyler's Quarterly (Vol. VIII, October, 1925: The Washington Ancestry, 1931).

Private Affairs of George Washington, Stephen Decatur, Jr. (using Tobias Lear's presidential account for his first term, Houghton Mifflin, 1933).

Commager, H. S. and R. B. Morris, *The Spirit of Seventy-Six* (Bobb-Merrill, 1958).

Songs and Ballads of the American Revolution (Kennikat reprint, 1964).

Letters from America, by German officers, ed. Ray W. Pettengill (Kennikat reprint, 1964).

Baker, W. S., *Itinerary of George Washington, 1775–1783* (Lippincott, 1892).

D. A. R., *Patriot Index*, (1966) has dates of birth and death, and names of wives, not always available elsewhere.

Hinchcliffe, E., "The Washingtons at Whitehaven and Appleby," *Transactions of the Cumberland and Westmorland Antiquarian Society* (vol. LXXI, 1971).

Campaigns of the American Revolution: An Atlas of Manuscript Maps, eds. Douglas W. Marshall and Howard H. Peckham (Michigan, 1976).

The American Campaigns of Rochambeau's Army, 1780, 1781, 1782, 1783, eds. Howard C. Rice, Jr. and Anne S. K. Brown (Princeton, Brown 1972).

Notes on Debates in the Federal Convention of 1787, reported by James Madison, introduction by Adrienne Koch (Ohio, 1966).

Leonard Baker, John Marshall: A Life in Law (Macmillan, 1974).

George Washington Atlas (George Washington Bicentennial Commission, 1932).

Peter Oliver's Origin and Progress of the American Rebellion: A Tory View, eds. Douglass Adair and John A. Schutz (Stanford, 1961).

Thomas, Peter G. D. *Lord North* (St. Martin's Press, 1976). No mention is made of General Washington.

Currey, Cecil B. *Code Number 72 Ben Franklin: Patriot or Spy* (Prentice Hall, 1972).

The West Point Atlas of American Wars, Brigadier General Vincent J. Esposito (USA edit., Praeger, 1959).

The Statistical History of the United States: Colonial Times to the Present, prepared by the Census Bureau (Basic Books, 1976).

Pellew, George, *John Jay* (Chelsea House Reprint, 1980).

Brighton, Ray. *The Checkered Career of Tobias Lear* (Portsmouth (PH) Marien Society, 1985).

Randall, Willard Sterne. *Benedict Arnold Patriot and Traitor* (Morrow, 1990).

Leckie, Robert. *George Washington's War* (Harper Perennial, 1992).

Higginbotham, Dan. *War and Society in Revolutionary America* (South Carolina, 1988).

George Washington's Beautiful Nelly, ed. Particia Brady (South Carolina, 1991).

Minutes of the Vestry, Truio Parish, Virginia 1932–1785 (Gateway Reprint, 1995).

THE CHIEF JUSTICE
AND THE ANGLICAN PRIEST

I N 1800, AS the eighteenth century was ending, two Virginians worked on biographies of George Washington. The first was John Marshall, Chief Justice of the United States, who had access to all Washington's papers through Associate Justice Bushrod Washington, who had inherited them. Marshall began describing Washington's life with the "Birth of Mr. Washington," unintentionally suggesting that Washington, like Athena, had arrived fully grown and armed. He summed up Washington's ancestry, birth, and upbringing in four paragraphs, mentioning however that Washington's mother had instilled in him "principles of religion and virtue."

The Reverend Mason Locke Weems, who had been ordained in England, wanted to emphasize Washington's virtues in private life as a model for young Americans. Possibly he was influenced by Light Horse Lee's funeral oration, from which, when quoted, an important part is omitted: "First in war, first in peace, first in the hearts of his countrymen, he was second to none in the humble and endearing scenes of private life."

Weems wrote: "Of those private deeds of Washington very little has been said. In most of the elegant orations pronounced to his praise, you see nothing of Washington beneath *the clouds*—nothing of Washington the *dutiful son*—the affectionate brother—the cheerful schoolboy—the diligent surveyor—the neat draftsman—the laborious farmer—the widow's husband—

the orphan's father—the poor man's friend. No! This is not the Washington you see; 'tis only Washington the HERO, and the Demigod...."

Weems had the advantage of being able to interview many relatives and friends of Washington who had known him from early childhood and who remembered his father. Weems' wife was a niece by marriage of Dr. James Craik, Washington's intimate friend for almost half a century. It was James Craik, Jr., who introduced Weems to Washington at Mount Vernon. Later he occasionally preached in Washington's Phick Episcopal Church.

Without Weems far less would be known about Washington's earliest years. It was a kinswoman of Washington who recalled that, at his Potomac farm, Washington's father, a giant of a man, worked to instill the proper virtues in George, particularly to be truthful at all times. So the story of the hatchet and the cherry tree, related by this lady to Weems, has its own ring of truth. The recollection of Washington's cousin, Lewis Willis, that he was the only boy strong enough to throw a stone across the Rappahannock River is perhaps more endearing. Weems wrote with verve, rollicking humor, and rolling and occasionally Homeric prose, all intermingled with bad dialogue. He made a lasting impression on one reader.

On his way to Washington in 1861, Abraham Lincoln, the fifteenth successor to the first president, addressed the New Jersey State Senate: "I cannot but remember the part that New Jersey holds in our early history.... May I be pardoned if upon this occasion, I mention that away back in my childhood... I got hold of a small book, such as one as few of the younger members have ever seen, 'Weems' Life of Washington'.... I recollect thinking then, boy even though I was, that there must have been something more than common that these men struggled for.... something that held out great promise to all the people of the world to all time to come."

GEORGE WASHINGTON: SPURIOUS AND DUBIOUS DOCUMENTATION

"I would have the National character of America be pure and immaculate."
— Washington to George William Fairfax, July 10, 1783.

The well-known myths and legends surrounding Washington were not troublesome in writing his biography. What was disconcerting was to find that numerous documents, many prepared by his own countrymen, were questionable or false. This addendum to the biography reviews a fair sampling of them, including many that were uncritically used by various Washington biographers.

The first fabrication appeared in 1754 when the August issue of *The London Magazine* was published, along with a June 4th letter from Williamsburg purportedly written by "Major General" Washington on May 31 to an unidentified brother. The report was based primarily on Washington's May 29 dispatches to Lieutenant Governor Dinwiddie. His brothers lived on the Northern Neck, quite far from Williamsburg. The distances involved would have made it virtually impossible for a genuine letter to have reached London, by this indirect route, in time for an August publication. The letter is also suspect because of its uncharacteristic phraseology, which subjected Washington to some ridicule in England. He was made to say that expected reinforcements "will enable us to exert our noble courage with spirit. P. S. I fortunately escaped without any wound... I heard the bullets whistle, and, believe me, there is something charming in the sound." Washington was a soldier and an experienced shot; the last sentence was a silly attribution. George II put it very well when he was quoted as saying: "He would not say so, if he had heard many."[1] In 1756 the French government published *Mémoire*, which included a partial distortion, for propaganda purposes, of the Washington journal notes which they had captured shortly after the battle.[2] Thomas Paine drew on this for a portion of his 1796 attack on the president.[3] In 1777 the London government produced a series of forged letters from General Washington to his wife, stepson, and Mount Vernon manager, which even the English press viewed with skepticism.[4] They were republished in 1796 by Benjamin Bache, in an attempt to discredit Washington. During the revolution, the British produced other crude fabrications, such as additions to genuine captured letters and an "account" of the trial of Thomas Hickey at New York in 1776. Many were intended to portray the dissolute behavior of the American commander-in-chief.[5]

After Washington's death, not much attention was paid to the minutiae of his early life. John Marshall's five volumes devoted less than two pages to his ancestry, birth, education, and growth to manhood. Mason Locke Weems, however, who had interviewed old friends and relatives, referred to his birth at Pope's Creek, his subsequent removal, as a small boy, to a house across from

---

[1] John C. Fitzpatrick, ed., *The Writings of George Washington*, Washington, D.C., 1931–1944, Vol. 1, pp. 63–66 and 70–71, and *The London Magazine*, August, 1754, pp. 370–371. In quoting George II, Horace Walpole referred to Washington's "rodomontade."

[2] Fitzpatrick, *Writings*, Vol. 1, pp. 84–89 and Douglas Southall Freeman, *George Washington*, New York, 1948–1957, Vol. 1, pp. 540–545.

[3] Freeman, Vol. 7, Prepared by J. A. Carroll and M. W. Ashworth, p, 428.

[4] Worthington C. Ford, ed., *The Writings of George Washington*, New York, 1889, Vol. IV, pp. 132 et seq. has the text of the letters. On March 3, 1797, the President, in an official letter to the Secretary of State, dismissed them as forgeries. Fitzpatrick, Writings, Vol. 35, pp. 414–416.

[5] This anti-American propaganda, circulated by the British in 1775-1778, would be too trivial to mention but for the fact that some of the tales were revived in 1970 by a New York scribbler for the same purpose.

Rupert Hughes, *George Washington*, Vol. 2, pp. 290–291 and 402–405, included them as forgeries. According to Hughes, the *Gentleman's Magazine* also published a doctored version of a genuine Washington letter.

Fredericksburg, and his return to Pope's Creek to attend school, at age 11, while living with his half brother, Augustine Washington, Jr.[6]

In 1815, George Washington Parke Custis placed a monument at a spot near Pope's Creek, as the supposed birthplace of Washington. Eighty-one years later the United States government erected a more permanent shaft near the place chosen by Custis. With the approach of the 1932 bicentennial, the federal government, in cooperation with private groups, made efforts to locate the places where Washington had lived until he settled permanently at Mount Vernon in 1754. While the available documentation turned out to be scanty, this did not prevent the government from making categorical declarations about his youthful years; many of these appear to be wrong or unproven.

When Augustine Washington, George's father, came of age he inherited 1,100 acres of land in Westmoreland County. Some of the land was on Mattox Creek and, presumably, the rest was mostly in Washington's parish, which included Bridge's Creek and may have been bordered to the east by Pope's Creek. After 1717 Augustine extended his holdings on the peninsula. By the time he died in 1743, he was able to leave seven hundred acres west of

---

[6] Mason Locke Weems, *The Life of Washington*, Harvard, 1962, pp. 7, 8 and 19-20. In a remarkable piece of research, Edgar Hinchcliffe, Librarian of Appleby School, Cumbria, England, in "The Washingtons at Whitehaven and Appleby," *Transactions of the Cumberland & Westmoreland Antiquarian & Archaeological Society*, Vol. LWWI, 1971, pp. 151-198, indicated that Lawrence and Augustine Washington, Jr., had been ushers (assistant masters) on the teaching staff of the Appleby Grammar School, a notable public school. They were well qualified therefore to be George's tutors.

Weems did introduce into his "Life" several tales which some thought dubious but a couple of these, including the cherry tree, came from an elderly kinswoman of the general. A great deal of what Weems reported has been verified in other sources, much as the research of Mr. Hinchcliffe has confirmed the statement that George went to live with Augustine, Jr., after their father's death. One of Weems's principal informants was Dr. James Craik, whose wife was aunt to Mrs. Weems, and whose son, Dr. James Craik, Jr., introduced the clergyman to Washington at Mount Vernon. Craik was an intimate friend of Washington from the French and Indian War days until the general's death. As a result, Weems has some remarkable details not available elsewhere. He noted, for example, that while the young Washington was in Frederick County, "he boarded in the house of the widow Stevenson, generally pronounced *Stinson*. This lady had seven sons—William and Valentine Crawford, by her first husband; and John, Hugh, Dick, Jim and Mark Stinson, by her last husband. These seven young men, in Herculean size and strength, were equal, perhaps, to any seven sons of any one mother in Christendom." The widowed Mrs. Honora Stephenson and all seven of her sons are mentioned, some of them frequently, in Washington's diaries and correspondence. His letter to Tobias Lear, November 30, 1786, confirms the pronunciation, by noting that Col. John Stephenson, whom Lear was to see, was "commonly called Stinson." Weems also reported that Hugh Stevenson would say that, in their younger days, when wrestling, "He and his brother John had often laid the conqueror of England on his back."

It is curious that Weems is endlessly attacked by those who have never read him. Essentially his life of Washington is one written for Americans. He is recommended reading.

Bridge's Creek to his son, John, and much, perhaps most of the area from Bridge's Creek to Pope's Creek, to another son, Augustine, Jr.7

Around 1723–1724 Augustine engaged a carpenter to build what he called "my house."[8] While the phrase has been interpreted to mean what it would currently imply, his residence, this is by no means a certain rendering. The various Washington deeds and wills of the period contain such phrases as "all houses, edifices, buildings, tobacco houses, etc.," indicating there were numerous structures through the wide area inherited or acquired by Augustine Washington. A trust deed of February 23, 1726–7 indicates that he was then living on the Abingdon tract, between Pope's and Bridge's Creeks.[9] This statement can be taken to refer only to the day on which it was written. It is possible to infer that, four years later, he brought his second wife to live in the same house, but there is no supporting evidence for or against it. Furthermore, no description of the 1724 house exists other than an implication it was frame and of modest size. The current elegant "Birthplace," erected for the Washington bicentennial, probably bears little relation to the early house, while the term "Wakefield" was applied to the farm well after George Washington's departure.

Augustine Washington was elected in 1735 to the vestry of Truro Parish, where the future Mount Vernon farm was located. The vestry met rarely, twice in 1735, once in 1736, and three times in 1737. Augustine Washington missed one meeting in 1736 and in 1737. To some this seemed to indicate that young George at three, and for two years afterwards, was roaming his future estate. Too much was read into this. The area around Little Hunting Creek was still largely unsettled wilderness. Mrs. Augustine Washington was pregnant in 1735 and 1736, the year her husband departed for England. It is highly unlikely that he moved his family from their many relatives and accustomed life in Westmoreland to a pioneer venture while he was absent from Virginia.[10]

The Bicentennial Commission also appears to have been responsible for the misnomer "Epsewasson" being applied to the farm that was to be Mount Vernon. In 1674 Nicholas Spencer and John Washington received a patent

---

7 Wills of Lawrence and Augustine Washington, Stanislaus Murray Hamilton, ed., *Letters to Washington*, New York, 1901, Vol. III, pp. 392–402. See also Westmoreland Co. Deeds, No. 9, Agreement between Augustine and John Washington, Deed of Exchange, March 29, 1743, with a plat of Augustine Washington's holdings. Copy supplied by Virginia Historical Society. For consistency, Pope's and Bridge's Creeks have been spelled in current fashion but, historically, the apostrophe was often dropped and sometimes the possessive as well.

8 Freeman, Vol. 1, pp. 536–536.

9 Westmoreland Co. Vol. 8–1, p. 226. Copy supplied by George Washington Birthplace.

10 Truro Parish records, photostat, Library of Congress. Family members told Weems that Augustine Washington and children moved directly from Pope's Creek to the Rappahannock.

from Lord Culpepper for an estimated 5,000 acres located between Little Hunting and Epsewasson Creeks, the latter apparently an early name for Dogue Run. In 1690 the tract was divided between the Spencer and Washington heirs. If Epsewasson was ever used descriptively, it applied only to the Spencer half. The Washington wills call their land Little Hunting or Hunting Creek.[11]

In 1932 the United States government introduced what was to be a troublesome document for future biographers. This was a map purporting to be of a farm on the Rappahannock River, where the Washingtons supposedly moved when George was six or seven. The drawing made by Lawrence Martin, chief of the map division of the Library of Congress, employed Washington's own handwriting along the plat prepared for the government. This was taken from the hasty survey notes Washington made on September 13, 1771 "of the Fields where my Mother lives."[12] The absurdity of the Martin claim was that he placed it on a U.S. topographic map at a place where neither his mother nor George had ever lived. Indeed the farm where she was living in 1771 was considerably up the river and west of the Rappahannock Falls and Falmouth. She had moved there about 1747 when her brother, Joseph Ball, wrote her a letter marked "nigh the falls." George Washington's notes indicate that her farm was north of the Fitzhugh lands and bordered on the property of James Hunter, Jr., who ran the ferry next to Mrs. Washington's property.

It is clear that the farm where Washington's mother lived was west of Falmouth because the road to Stafford Court House (now Stafford) running more or less northeast would have gone there directly. The 1932 map, placing the farm well below Falmouth, so located the Stafford Road that it would lead down to King George County. Where the Washingtons lived on the Rappahannock until Augustine Washington's death has never been accurately determined. It is not of much importance. From the evidence suggested by Weems it may have been located in parkland about Catham.

There is a tendency for centennial observances to bring out bad history. In July, 1876, an American novelist, Constance Cary Harrison, announced to the world in *Scribner's* magazine that Sarah Cary Fairfax, her great great grandaunt, had been the "object of George Washington's early and passionate love." On March 30 of the following year, *The New York Herald* published a purported letter by Washington to Mrs. Fairfax, dated Fort Cumberland,

---

[11] The patent by Lord Culpepper is quoted in the 1972 *Annual Report*, Mount Vernon Ladies Association of the Union, p. 38. Mr. Morse's research indicated that Epsewasson may have been first applied as a name to a 19th century farm on Dogue Run.

[12] *George Washington Atlas*, Washington, 1932, Plate 9, and Washington's Survey notes, September 13, 1771.

September 12, 1758.[13] This letter then subsurfaced for many years; it was given to Harvard's Houghton Library in 1958. A second letter in a similar vein, dated September 20, 1758, was sold at auction in New York in 1969. The author, convinced that most of the text of the letters did not sound like anything Washington ever wrote, undertook an investigation into their authenticity. In this he had the aid of Mount Vernon and the Manuscript Division of the Library of Congress. He alone is responsible for the conclusions.[14] The historical discrepancies are too great for them to have been written by George Washington. They have, nonetheless, fooled many biographers, the media, such great corporations as GM and NBC, and the *Smithsonian* magazine at least twice. The letters sound as if they were written by a Victorian lady novelist; it seems hardly a coincidence that the letters were discovered by such a novelist. It is hard to believe that anyone could suppose their purple prose emanated from the crisp, direct pen of Colonel Washington. Nor is it possible that the colonel, in writing to George Fairfax about the reconstruction of Mount Vernon in preparation for his new bride, would enclose a love letter to his friend's wife.

A comparison was made between the September 12 letter and two notes sent by Washington to Mrs. Fairfax in February of the same year.[15] The formal and restrained terminology of the latter is quite different but very typical of his prose. The elongated G. and W. of his signature, in contrast with the later letter, correspond to his handwriting of the period. There are other discrepancies. Washington was made to refer to "the unseasonable haste" of

---

[13] Fitzpatrick, *Writings*, Vol. 2, pp. 287–289.

[14] The *Smithsonian*, November, 1973, reproduced the Sally letters as if genuine and also an extract of the "letter" from Lord Fairfax to Mrs. Mary Washington, which was composed about 1903 by S. Weir Mitchell for *The Young George Washington*, New York, 1904, p. 76. The noted Washington scholar, John C. Fitzpatrick, rightly pronounced it spurious, though it was "naively printed in various places," in *George Washington Himself*, Indianapolis, 1933, p. 518.

When Henry Cabot Lodge and Woodrow Wilson undertook their lives of Washington in the 1890s, they were well aware of the Sally letters. Wilson ignored them, while Lodge made only an oblique reference to them. Rupert Hughes, writing for the sesquicentennial year, 1926, devoted page after page to Mrs. Fairfax. When Washington was supposed to have written: "'Tis true, I profess myself a votary of love,'" Hughes added: "this is George Washington writing! And he professes himself a votary of love!" The repellence of the phrase ought to have served as a warning.

[15] The Historical Society of Pennsylvania and the Boston Public Library supplied copies of George Washington's letters to Mrs. Fairfax, the first written about February 11 and the second dated February 13, 1758. The former was incorrectly listed in Fitzpatrick, *Writings*, Vol. 1, pp. 476–477, as written in 1756. Internal evidence in the first letter (its reference to "the President" who was John Blair, acting governor) together with Blair's letter of February 5 to GW (Hamilton, *Letters to GW*, Vol. II, pp./ 262–264) make it reasonably probable that the "Saturday morning" of the letter was February 11.

his express rider who left the Fairfax house September 1, not reaching Fort Cumberland until September 11. By contrast the extant historical letter from George Fairfax to Washington, at the Library of Congress, indicates that the return rider left the fort on September 12, arriving at Belvoir two days later.[16] Washington was made to write that Mrs. Spotswood had "already become a reigning Toast in this Camp."[17] Wilson Miles Cary subsequently identified her as Mrs. John Spotswood, widowed in 1757. However, there is an existing letter at the Library of Congress, from Captain Charles Smith to Washington, September 7, 1758, referring to Col. John Spotswood's death "about seven days ago."[18] In any case this was a frontier post in a savage war, and Washington was a disciplinarian who did not tolerate highjinks in his camp. Finally Washington was supposed to have written that his hours were "melancholy dull." In fact, this able and energetic commander had received orders, a few days previously, to be prepared to move all his effective troops to Ray's Town (Bedford, Pennsylvania) en route to Fort Duquesne, the moment he received the orders of his commanding general, John Forbes. He was instructed to bring all his ammunition, many tons of food supplies, 50 head of cattle, and 200 horses.[19]

The second Sally letter also contains discrepancies in relation to historical fact. A copy in the Hamilton auction catalogue is dated September 19th at Ray's Town. However, General Forbes wrote that Washington left there for Fort Cumberland on September 18, probably reaching there on the 19th. He was there on September 20th, not at Ray's Town, and thus he was nearly two days' march from General Forbes' headquarters. Late in the evening of the 20th Forbes received a preliminary report of a military disaster. Yet, in his letter, Washington provided Mrs. Fairfax with details of the battle, which he could not have had for another three days. He also acknowledged receipt of a letter from her that day, although the mail from Belvoir did not reach him until the 21st. On the 25th Washington prepared an urgent summary of the battle for Virginia's governor.[20]

---

[16] George William Fairfax to GW, September 15, 1758, Hamilton, Vol. III, p. 100.

[17] W. M. Cary, *Saily Cary: A Long Hidden Romance of Washington's Life*, New York, 1916.

[18] A. Hamilton, *Letters to GW*, Vol. III, p. 87.

[19] Henry Bouquet to GW, September 4, 1758, *ibid*, pp. 82–85.

[20] Fitzpatrick, *Writings*, Vol. 37, pp. 482–3. Copy of original supplied by Mount Vernon. The addressee was George William Fairfax, not John Augustine Washington as stated by Fitzpatrick.

INDEX